Structure Definitions

arpcom	80	mrt		
arphdr	682	mrtctl		
		msghdr		
bpf_d	1033			
bpf_hdr	1029	osockaddr		
bpf_if	1029			
		pdevinit	78	
cmsghdr	482	protosw	188	
domain	187	radix_mask	578	
		radix_node	575	
ether_arp	682	radix_node_head	574	
ether_header	102	rawcb	647	
ether_multi	342	route	220	
		route_cb	625	
icmp	308	rt_addrinfo	623	
ifaddr	73	rtentry	579	
ifa_msghdr	622	rt_metrics	580	
ifconf	117	rt_msghdr	622	
if_msghdr	622			
ifnet	67	selinfo	531	
ifqueue	71	sl_softc	83	
ifreq	117	sockaddr	75	
igmp	384	sockaddr_dl	87	
in_addr	160	sockaddr_in	160	
in_aliasreq	174	sockaddr_inarp	701	
in_ifaddr	161	sockbuf	476	
in_multi	345	socket	438	
inpcb	716	socket_args	444	
iovec	481	sockproto	626	
ip	211	sysent	443	
ipasfrag	287			
ip_moptions	347	tcpcb	804	
ip_mreq	356	tcp_debug	916	
ipoption	265	tcphdr	801	
ipovly	760	tcpiphdr	803	
ipq	286	timeval	106	
ip_srcrt	258			
ip_timestamp	262	udphdr	759	
		udpiphdr	759	
le_softc	80	uio	485	
lgrplctl	411			
linger	542	vif	406	
llinfo_arp	682	vifctl	407	
mbuf	38	walkarg	632	

Praise for
TCP/IP Illustrated, Volume 1: The Protocols

"*TCP/IP Illustrated* has already become my most-likely-to-have-the-answer reference book, the first resource I turn to with a networking question. The book is, all publisher hype aside, an instant classic, and I, for one, am thrilled that something like this is now available."

> **— Vern Paxson, ;*login*:, March/April 1994**

"This is sure to be the bible for TCP/IP developers and users."

> **— Robert A. Ciampa, Network Engineer, Synernetics, division of 3COM**

"... the difference is that Stevens wants to show as well as tell about the protocols. His principal teaching tools are straight-forward explanations, exercises at the ends of chapters, byte-by-byte diagrams of headers and the like, and listings of actual traffic as examples."

> **— Walter Zintz, *Unix World*, December 1993**

"*TCP/IP Illustrated, Volume 1* is based on practical examples that reinforce the theory — distinguishing this book from others on the subject, and making it both readable and informative."

> **— Peter M. Haverlock, Consultant, IBM TCP/IP Development**

"While all of Stevens' books are excellent, this new opus is awesome. Although many books describe the TCP/IP protocols, the author provides a level of depth and real-world detail lacking from the competition."

> **— Steven Baker, *Unix Review*, March 1994**

"*TCP/IP Illustrated, Volume 1* is an excellent reference for developers, network administrators or anyone who needs to understand TCP/IP technology."

> **— Bob Williams, V.P. Marketing, NetManage, Inc.**

"W. Richard Stevens has produced a fine text and reference work."

> **— Scott Bradner, Consultant, Harvard University OIT/NSD**

"Even marketing weenies (of a technical bent) will appreciate this book, as it is clearly written, and uses lots of diagrams. I especially like the author's thoughtful use of asides—set in smaller type and indented—to explain this or that concept. "

> **— Ron Jeffries, *ATM USER*, January 1994**

"Stevens takes a subject that has been written about rather prolifically, TCP/IP, and does something fresh and useful with it."

> **— Jason Levitt, *Open Systems Today*, March 7, 1994**

More Praise for
TCP/IP Illustrated, Volume 1: The Protocols

"This book is a stone jewel. ... Written by W. Richard Stevens, this book probably provides the most comprehensive view of TCP/IP available today in print."

 — *Boardwatch*, **April/May 1994**

"...you can't get a better understanding of the workings of TCP/IP anywhere."

 — **Tom Nolle,** *Netwatcher*, **January 1994**

"The book covers all the basic TCP/IP applications, including Telnet, NFS (Network File System), FTP (file transfer protocol) and TFTP (trivial FTP)."

 — *Data Communications*, **January 21, 1994**

"The diagrams he uses are excellent and his writing style is clear and readable. Please read it and keep it on your bookshelf."

 — **Elizabeth Zinkann,** *Sys Admin*, **November 1993**

"Stevens' Unix-oriented investigations will be invaluable to the network programmer or specialist who wishes to really understand how the TCP/IP stack is put together."

 — **Joel Snyder,** *Internet World*, **March/April 1994 issue**

"All aspects of the transmission control protocol/Internet protocol (TCP/IP) are covered here, from link layer and static/dynamic routing implementations to applications such as SNMP and Telnet."

 — *Telecommunications*, **March 1994**

"The author of *TCP/IP Illustrated* has succeeded in creating another indispensable tome of networking knowledge. This is the most comprehensible and complete book I have read on TCP/IP. It takes a different slant than other books, by presenting not only details of TCP, IP, ARP, ICMP, routing, etc., but actually shows these protocols (and common Internet tools) in action."

 — **Eli Charne,** *ConneXions*, **July 1994**

"The word 'illustrated' distinguishes this book from its many rivals."

 — **Stan Kelly-Bootle,** *Unix Review*, **December 1993**

TCP/IP Illustrated, Volume 2

Addison-Wesley Professional Computing Series

Brian W. Kernighan, Consulting Editor

Please see our web site (http://www.awl.com/cseng/series/professionalcomputing) for more information on these titles.

TCP/IP Illustrated, Volume 2
The Implementation

Gary R. Wright
W. Richard Stevens

ADDISON–WESLEY

Boston • San Francisco • New York • Toronto • Montreal
London • Munich • Paris • Madrid
Capetown • Sydney • Tokyo • Singapore • Mexico City

The publisher offers discounts on this book when ordered in quantity for special sales. For more information please contact:

Pearson Education Corporate Sales Division
201 W. 103rd Street
Indianapolis, IN 46290
(800) 428-5331
corpsales@pearsoned.com

Visit AW on the Web: www.awl.com/cseng/

Library of Congress Cataloging-in-Publication Data
(Revised for vol. 2)

Stevens, W. Richard.
    TCP/IP illustrated.

    (Addison-Wesley professional computing series)
    Vol. 2 by Gary R. Wright, W. Richard Stevens.
    Includes bibliographical references and indexes.
    Contents: v. 1. The protocols – v.2. The
implementation
    1. TCP/IP (Computer network protocol) I Wright,
Gary R..,   II. Title.   III. Series.
TK5105.55.S74   1994   004.6'2   93–40000
ISBN 0-201-63346-9 (v.1)
ISBN 0-201-63354-X (v.2)

The BSD Daemon used on the cover of this book is reproduced with the permission of Marshall Kirk McKusick.

Text printed on recycled and acid-free paper.
ISBN 020163354X
13 1415161718 CRW 04 03 02 01

13th Printing   July 2001

To my parents and my sister,
for their love and support.
—G.R.W.

To my parents,
for the gift of an education,
and the example of a work ethic.
—W.R.S.

Contents

Preface

Introduction

This book describes and presents the source code for the common reference implementation of TCP/IP: the implementation from the Computer Systems Research Group (CSRG) at the University of California at Berkeley. Historically this has been distributed with the 4.x BSD system (Berkeley Software Distribution). This implementation was first released in 1982 and has survived many significant changes, much fine tuning, and numerous ports to other Unix and non-Unix systems. This is not a toy implementation, but the foundation for TCP/IP implementations that are run daily on hundreds of thousands of systems worldwide. This implementation also provides router functionality, letting us show the differences between a host implementation of TCP/IP and a router.

We describe the implementation and present the entire source code for the kernel implementation of TCP/IP, approximately 15,000 lines of C code. The version of the Berkeley code described in this text is the 4.4BSD-Lite release. This code was made publicly available in April 1994, and it contains numerous networking enhancements that were added to the 4.3BSD Tahoe release in 1988, the 4.3BSD Reno release in 1990, and the 4.4BSD release in 1993. (Appendix B describes how to obtain this source code.) The 4.4BSD release provides the latest TCP/IP features, such as multicasting and long fat pipe support (for high-bandwidth, long-delay paths). Figure 1.1 (p. 4) provides additional details of the various releases of the Berkeley networking code.

This book is intended for anyone wishing to understand how the TCP/IP protocols are implemented: programmers writing network applications, system administrators responsible for maintaining computer systems and networks utilizing TCP/IP, and any programmer interested in understanding how a large body of nontrivial code fits into a real operating system.

Organization of the Book

The following figure shows the various protocols and subsystems that are covered. The italic numbers by each box indicate the chapters in which that topic is described.

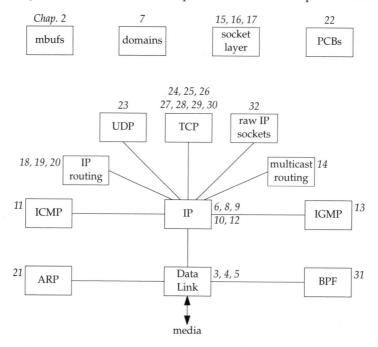

We take a bottom-up approach to the TCP/IP protocol suite, starting at the data-link layer, then the network layer (IP, ICMP, IGMP, IP routing, and multicast routing), followed by the socket layer, and finishing with the transport layer (UDP, TCP, and raw IP).

Intended Audience

This book assumes a basic understanding of how the TCP/IP protocols work. Readers unfamiliar with TCP/IP should consult the first volume in this series, [Stevens 1994], for a thorough description of the TCP/IP protocol suite. This earlier volume is referred to throughout the current text as *Volume 1*. The current text also assumes a basic understanding of operating system principles.

We describe the implementation of the protocols using a data-structures approach. That is, in addition to the source code presentation, each chapter contains pictures and descriptions of the data structures used and maintained by the source code. We show how these data structures fit into the other data structures used by TCP/IP and the kernel. Heavy use is made of diagrams throughout the text—there are over 250 diagrams.

This data-structures approach allows readers to use the book in various ways. Those interested in all the implementation details can read the entire text from start to finish, following through all the source code. Others might want to understand how the protocols are implemented by understanding all the data structures and reading all the text, but not following through all the source code.

We anticipate that many readers are interested in specific portions of the book and will want to go directly to those chapters. Therefore many forward and backward references are provided throughout the text, along with a thorough index, to allow individual chapters to be studied by themselves. The inside back covers contain an alphabetical cross-reference of all the functions and macros described in the book and the starting page number of the description. Exercises are provided at the end of the chapters; most solutions are in Appendix A to maximize the usefulness of the text as a self-study reference.

Source Code Copyright

All of the source code presented in this book, other than Figures 1.2 and 8.27, is from the 4.4BSD-Lite distribution. This software is publicly available through many sources (Appendix B).

All of this source code contains the following copyright notice.

```
/*
 * Copyright (c) 1982, 1986, 1988, 1990, 1993, 1994
 *      The Regents of the University of California.  All rights reserved.
 *
 * Redistribution and use in source and binary forms, with or without
 * modification, are permitted provided that the following conditions
 * are met:
 * 1. Redistributions of source code must retain the above copyright
 *    notice, this list of conditions and the following disclaimer.
 * 2. Redistributions in binary form must reproduce the above copyright
 *    notice, this list of conditions and the following disclaimer in the
 *    documentation and/or other materials provided with the distribution.
 * 3. All advertising materials mentioning features or use of this software
 *    must display the following acknowledgement:
 *       This product includes software developed by the University of
 *       California, Berkeley and its contributors.
 * 4. Neither the name of the University nor the names of its contributors
 *    may be used to endorse or promote products derived from this software
 *    without specific prior written permission.
 *
 * THIS SOFTWARE IS PROVIDED BY THE REGENTS AND CONTRIBUTORS ``AS IS'' AND
 * ANY EXPRESS OR IMPLIED WARRANTIES, INCLUDING, BUT NOT LIMITED TO, THE
 * IMPLIED WARRANTIES OF MERCHANTABILITY AND FITNESS FOR A PARTICULAR PURPOSE
 * ARE DISCLAIMED.  IN NO EVENT SHALL THE REGENTS OR CONTRIBUTORS BE LIABLE
 * FOR ANY DIRECT, INDIRECT, INCIDENTAL, SPECIAL, EXEMPLARY, OR CONSEQUENTIAL
 * DAMAGES (INCLUDING, BUT NOT LIMITED TO, PROCUREMENT OF SUBSTITUTE GOODS
 * OR SERVICES; LOSS OF USE, DATA, OR PROFITS; OR BUSINESS INTERRUPTION)
 * HOWEVER CAUSED AND ON ANY THEORY OF LIABILITY, WHETHER IN CONTRACT, STRICT
 * LIABILITY, OR TORT (INCLUDING NEGLIGENCE OR OTHERWISE) ARISING IN ANY WAY
 * OUT OF THE USE OF THIS SOFTWARE, EVEN IF ADVISED OF THE POSSIBILITY OF
 * SUCH DAMAGE.
 */
```

Acknowledgments

We thank the technical reviewers who read the manuscript and provided important feedback on a tight timetable: Ragnvald Blindheim, Jon Crowcroft, Sally Floyd, Glen Glater, John Gulbenkian, Don Hering, Mukesh Kacker, Berry Kercheval, Brian W. Kernighan, Ulf Kieber, Mark Laubach, Steven McCanne, Craig Partridge, Vern Paxson, Steve Rago, Chakravardhi Ravi, Peter Salus, Doug Schmidt, Keith Sklower, Ian Lance Taylor, and G. N. Ananda Vardhana. A special thanks to the consulting editor, Brian Kernighan, for his rapid, thorough, and helpful reviews throughout the course of the project, and for his continued encouragement and support.

Our thanks (again) to the National Optical Astronomy Observatories (NOAO), especially Sidney Wolff, Richard Wolff, and Steve Grandi, for providing access to their networks and hosts. Our thanks also to the U.C. Berkeley CSRG: Keith Bostic and Kirk McKusick provided access to the latest 4.4BSD system, and Keith Sklower provided the modifications to the 4.4BSD-Lite software to run under BSD/386 V1.1.

G.R.W. wishes to thank John Wait, for several years of gentle prodding; Dave Schaller, for his encouragement; and Jim Hogue, for his support during the writing and production of this book.

W.R.S. thanks his family, once again, for enduring another "small" book project. Thank you Sally, Bill, Ellen, and David.

The hardwork, professionalism, and support of the team at Addison-Wesley has made the authors' job that much easier. In particular, we wish to thank John Wait for his guidance and Kim Dawley for her creative ideas.

Camera-ready copy of the book was produced by the authors. It is only fitting that a book describing an industrial-strength software system be produced with an industrial-strength text processing system. Therefore one of the authors chose to use the Groff package written by James Clark, and the other author agreed begrudgingly.

We welcome electronic mail from any readers with comments, suggestions, or bug fixes: `tcpipiv2-book@aw.com`. Each author will gladly blame the other for any remaining errors.

Gary R. Wright   W. Richard Stevens
http://www.connix.com/~gwright   http://www.kohala.com/~rstevens
Middletown, Connecticut   *Tucson, Arizona*

November 1994

1

Introduction

1.1   Introduction

This chapter provides an introduction to the Berkeley networking code. We start with a description of the source code presentation and the various typographical conventions used throughout the text. A quick history of the various releases of the code then lets us see where the source code shown in this book fits in. This is followed by a description of the two predominant programming interfaces used under both Unix and non-Unix systems to write programs that use the TCP/IP protocols.

We then show a simple user program that sends a UDP datagram to the daytime server on another host on the local area network, causing the server to return a UDP datagram with the current time and date on the server as a string of ASCII text. We follow the datagram sent by the process all the way down the protocol stack to the device driver, and then follow the reply received from server all the way up the protocol stack to the process. This trivial example lets us introduce many of the kernel data structures and concepts that are described in detail in later chapters.

The chapter finishes with a look at the organization of the source code that is presented in the book and a review of where the networking code fits in the overall organization.

1.2   Source Code Presentation

Presenting 15,000 lines of source code, regardless of the topic, is a challenge in itself. The following format is used for all the source code in the text:

1

—— *tcp_subr.c*

```
381 void
382 tcp_quench(inp, errno)
383 struct inpcb *inp;
384 int      errno;
385 {
386     struct tcpcb *tp = intotcpcb(inp);

387     if (tp)
388         tp->snd_cwnd = tp->t_maxseg;
389 }
```
—— *tcp_subr.c*

Set congestion window to one segment

387–388　　This is the `tcp_quench` function from the file `tcp_subr.c`. These source filenames refer to files in the 4.4BSD-Lite distribution, which we describe in Section 1.13.
Each nonblank line is numbered. The text describing portions of the code begins with
the starting and ending line numbers in the left margin, as shown with this paragraph.
Sometimes the paragraph is preceded by a short descriptive heading, providing a summary statement of the code being described.

　　The source code has been left as is from the 4.4BSD-Lite distribution, including
occasional bugs, which we note and discuss when encountered, and occasional editorial
comments from the original authors. The code has been run through the GNU Indent
program to provide consistency in appearance. The tab stops have been set to four-
column boundaries to allow the lines to fit on a page. Some `#ifdef` statements and
their corresponding `#endif` have been removed when the constant is always defined
(e.g., GATEWAY and MROUTING, since we assume the system is operating as a router and
as a multicast router). All `register` specifiers have been removed. Sometimes a comment has been added and typographical errors in the comments have been fixed, but
otherwise the code has been left alone.

　　The functions vary in size from a few lines (`tcp_quench` shown earlier) to
`tcp_input`, which is the biggest at 1100 lines. Functions that exceed about 40 lines are
normally broken into pieces, which are shown one after the other. Every attempt is
made to place the code and its accompanying description on the same page or on facing
pages, but this isn't always possible without wasting a large amount of paper.

　　Many cross-references are provided to other functions that are described in the text.
To avoid appending both a figure number and a page number to each reference, the
inside back covers contain an alphabetical cross-reference of all the functions and
macros described in the book, and the starting page number of the description. Since
the source code in the book is taken from the publicly available 4.4BSD-Lite release, you
can easily obtain a copy: Appendix B details various ways. Sometimes it helps to have
an on-line copy to search through [e.g., with the Unix `grep`(1) program] as you follow
the text.

　　Each chapter that describes a source code module normally begins with a listing of
the source files being described, followed by the global variables, the relevant statistics
maintained by the code, some sample statistics from an actual system, and finally the
SNMP variables related to the protocol being described. The global variables are often

defined across various source files and headers, so we collect them in one table for easy reference. Showing all the statistics at this point simplifies the later discussion of the code when the statistics are updated. Chapter 25 of Volume 1 provides all the details on SNMP. Our interest in this text is in the information maintained by the TCP/IP routines in the kernel to support an SNMP agent running on the system.

Typographical Conventions

In the figures throughout the text we use a constant-width font for variable names and the names of structure members (m_next), a slanted constant-width font for names that are defined constants (*NULL*) or constant values (*512*), and a bold constant-width font with braces for structure names (**mbuf{}**). Here is an example:

mbuf{}	
m_next	*NULL*
m_len	*512*

In tables we use a constant-width font for variable names and the names of structure members, and the slanted constant-width font for the names of defined constants. Here is an example:

m_flags	Description
M_BCAST	sent/received as link-level broadcast

We normally show all #define symbols this way. We show the value of the symbol if necessary (the value of M_BCAST is irrelevant) and sort the symbols alphabetically, unless some other ordering makes sense.

> Throughout the text we'll use indented, parenthetical notes such as this to describe historical points or implementation minutae.

We refer to Unix commands using the name of the command followed by a number in parentheses, as in grep(1). The number in parentheses is the section number in the 4.4BSD manual of the "manual page" for the command, where additional information can be located.

1.3   History

This book describes the common reference implementation of TCP/IP from the Computer Systems Research Group at the University of California at Berkeley. Historically this has been distributed with the 4.x BSD system (Berkeley Software Distribution) and with the "BSD Networking Releases." This source code has been the starting point for many other implementations, both for Unix and non-Unix operating systems.

Figure 1.1 shows a chronology of the various BSD releases, indicating the important TCP/IP features. The releases shown on the left side are publicly available source code releases containing all of the networking code: the protocols themselves, the kernel

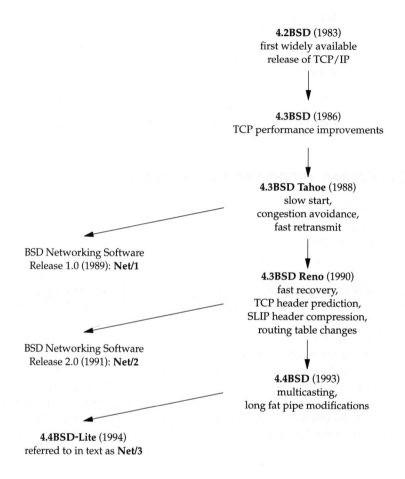

Figure 1.1   Various BSD releases with important TCP/IP features.

routines for the networking interface, and many of the applications and utilities (such as Telnet and FTP).

Although the official name of the software described in this text is the *4.4BSD-Lite* distribution, we'll refer to it simply as *Net/3*.

While the source code is distributed by U. C. Berkeley and is called the *Berkeley Software Distribution*, the TCP/IP code is really the merger and consolidation of the works of various researchers, both at Berkeley and at other locations.

Throughout the text we'll use the term *Berkeley-derived implementation* to refer to vendor implementations such as SunOS 4.x, System V Release 4 (SVR4), and AIX 3.2, whose TCP/IP code was originally developed from the Berkeley sources. These implementations have much in common, often including the same bugs!

> Not shown in Figure 1.1 is that the first release with the Berkeley networking code was actually 4.1cBSD in 1982. 4.2BSD, however, was the widely released version in 1983.

BSD releases prior to 4.1cBSD used a TCP/IP implementation developed at Bolt Beranek and Newman (BBN) by Rob Gurwitz and Jack Haverty. Chapter 18 of [Salus 1994] provides additional details on the incorporation of the BBN code into 4.2BSD. Another influence on the Berkeley TCP/IP code was the TCP/IP implementation done by Mike Muuss at the Ballistics Research Lab for the PDP-11.

Limited documentation exists on the changes in the networking code from one release to the next. [Karels and McKusick 1986] describe the changes from 4.2BSD to 4.3BSD, and [Jacobson 1990d] describes the changes from 4.3BSD Tahoe to 4.3BSD Reno.

1.4   Application Programming Interfaces

Two popular *application programming interfaces* (APIs) for writing programs to use the Internet protocols are *sockets* and *TLI* (Transport Layer Interface). The former is sometimes called *Berkeley sockets*, since it was widely released with the 4.2BSD system (Figure 1.1). It has, however, been ported to many non-BSD Unix systems and many non-Unix systems. The latter, originally developed by AT&T, is sometimes called *XTI* (X/Open Transport Interface) in recognition of the work done by X/Open, an international group of computer vendors who produce their own set of standards. XTI is effectively a superset of TLI.

This is not a programming text, but we describe the sockets interface since sockets are used by applications to access TCP/IP in Net/3 (and in all other BSD releases). The sockets interface has also been implemented on a wide variety of non-Unix systems. The programming details for both sockets and TLI are available in [Stevens 1990].

System V Release 4 (SVR4) also provides a sockets API for applications to use, although the implementation differs from what we present in this text. Sockets in SVR4 are based on the "streams" subsystem that is described in [Rago 1993].

1.5   Example Program

We'll use the simple C program shown in Figure 1.2 to introduce many features of the BSD networking implementation in this chapter.

```
 1 /*
 2  * Send a UDP datagram to the daytime server on some other host,
 3  * read the reply, and print the time and date on the server.
 4  */

 5 #include     <sys/types.h>
 6 #include     <sys/socket.h>
 7 #include     <netinet/in.h>
 8 #include     <arpa/inet.h>
 9 #include     <stdio.h>
10 #include     <stdlib.h>
11 #include     <string.h>

12 #define BUFFSIZE    150             /* arbitrary size */
```

```
13 int
14 main()
15 {
16      struct sockaddr_in serv;
17      char     buff[BUFFSIZE];
18      int      sockfd, n;

19      if ((sockfd = socket(PF_INET, SOCK_DGRAM, 0)) < 0)
20          err_sys("socket error");

21      bzero((char *) &serv, sizeof(serv));
22      serv.sin_family = AF_INET;
23      serv.sin_addr.s_addr = inet_addr("140.252.1.32");
24      serv.sin_port = htons(13);

25      if (sendto(sockfd, buff, BUFFSIZE, 0,
26                  (struct sockaddr *) &serv, sizeof(serv)) != BUFFSIZE)
27          err_sys("sendto error");

28      if ((n = recvfrom(sockfd, buff, BUFFSIZE, 0,
29                  (struct sockaddr *) NULL, (int *) NULL)) < 2)
30          err_sys("recvfrom error");
31      buff[n - 2] = 0;                    /* null terminate */
32      printf("%s\n", buff);

33      exit(0);
34 }
```

Figure 1.2   Example program: send a datagram to the UDP daytime server and read a response.

Create a datagram socket

19–20   `socket` creates a UDP socket and returns a descriptor to the process, which is stored in the variable `sockfd`. The error-handling function `err_sys` is shown in Appendix B.2 of [Stevens 1992]. It accepts any number of arguments, formats them using `vsprintf`, prints the Unix error message corresponding to the `errno` value from the system call, and then terminates the process.

> We've now used the term *socket* in three different ways. (1) The API developed for 4.2BSD to allow programs to access the networking protocols is normally called the *sockets API* or just the *sockets interface*. (2) socket is the name of a function in the sockets API. (3) We refer to the end point created by the call to socket as a socket, as in the comment "create a datagram socket."
>
> Unfortunately, there are still more uses of the term *socket*. (4) The return value from the socket function is called a *socket descriptor* or just a *socket*. (5) The Berkeley implementation of the networking protocols within the kernel is called the *sockets implementation*, compared to the System V streams implementation, for example. (6) The combination of an IP address and a port number is often called a socket, and a pair of IP addresses and port numbers is called a *socket pair*. Fortunately, it is usually obvious from the discussion what the term *socket* refers to.

Fill in `sockaddr_in` structure with server's address

21–24   An Internet socket address structure (`sockaddr_in`) is filled in with the IP address (140.252.1.32) and port number (13) of the daytime server. Port number 13 is the standard Internet daytime server, provided by most TCP/IP implementations [Stevens 1994,

Fig. 1.9]. Our choice of the server host is arbitrary—we just picked a local host (Figure 1.17) that provides the service.

The function `inet_addr` takes an ASCII character string representing a *dotted-decimal* IP address and converts it into a 32-bit binary integer in the network byte order. (The network byte order for the Internet protocol suite is big endian. [Stevens 1990, Chap. 4] discusses host and network byte order, and little versus big endian.) The function `htons` takes a short integer in the host byte order (which could be little endian or big endian) and converts it into the network byte order (big endian). On a system such as a Sparc, which uses big endian format for integers, `htons` is typically a macro that does nothing. In BSD/386, however, on the little endian 80386, `htons` can be either a macro or a function that swaps the 2 bytes in a 16-bit integer.

Send datagram to server

25–27   The program then calls `sendto`, which sends a 150-byte datagram to the server. The contents of the 150-byte buffer are indeterminate since it is an uninitialized array allocated on the run-time stack, but that's OK for this example because the server never looks at the contents of the datagram that it receives. When the server receives a datagram it sends a reply to the client. The reply contains the current time and date on the server in a human-readable format.

Our choice of 150 bytes for the client's datagram is arbitrary. We purposely pick a value greater than 100 and less than 208 to show the use of an mbuf chain later in this chapter. We also want a value less than 1472 to avoid fragmentation on an Ethernet.

Read datagram returned by server

28–32   The program reads the datagram that the server sends back by calling `recvfrom`. Unix servers typically send back a 26-byte string of the form

```
Sat Dec 11 11:28:05 1993\r\n
```

where `\r` is an ASCII carriage return and `\n` is an ASCII linefeed. Our program overwrites the carriage return with a null byte and calls `printf` to output the result.

We go into lots of detail about various parts of this example in this and later chapters as we examine the implementation of the functions `socket`, `sendto`, and `recvfrom`.

1.6   System Calls and Library Functions

All operating systems provide service points through which programs request services from the kernel. All variants of Unix provide a well-defined, limited number of kernel entry points known as *system calls*. We cannot change the system calls unless we have the kernel source code. Unix Version 7 provided about 50 system calls, 4.4BSD provides about 135, and SVR4 has around 120.

The system call interface is documented in Section 2 of the *Unix Programmer's Manual*. Its definition is in the C language, regardless of how system calls are invoked on any given system.

The Unix technique is for each system call to have a function of the same name in the standard C library. An application calls this function, using the standard C calling sequence. This function then invokes the appropriate kernel service, using whatever technique is required on the system. For example, the function may put one or more of the C arguments into general registers and then execute some machine instruction that generates a software interrupt into the kernel. For our purposes, we can consider the system calls to be C functions.

Section 3 of the *Unix Programmer's Manual* defines the general purpose functions available to programmers. These functions are not entry points into the kernel, although they may invoke one or more of the kernel's system calls. For example, the `printf` function may invoke the `write` system call to perform the output, but the functions `strcpy` (copy a string) and `atoi` (convert ASCII to integer) don't involve the operating system at all.

From an implementor's point of view, the distinction between a system call and a library function is fundamental. From a user's perspective, however, the difference is not as critical. For example, if we run Figure 1.2 under 4.4BSD, when the program calls the three functions `socket`, `sendto`, and `recvfrom`, each ends up calling a function of the same name within the kernel. We show the BSD kernel implementation of these three system calls later in the text.

If we run the program under SVR4, where the socket functions are in a user library that calls the "streams" subsystem, the interaction of these three functions with the kernel is completely different. Under SVR4 the call to `socket` ends up invoking the kernel's `open` system call for the file `/dev/udp` and then pushes the streams module `sockmod` onto the resulting stream. The call to `sendto` results in a `putmsg` system call, and the call to `recvfrom` results in a `getmsg` system call. These SVR4 details are not critical in this text. We want to point out only that the implementation can be totally different while providing the same API to the application.

This difference in implementation technique also accounts for the manual page for the `socket` function appearing in Section 2 of the 4.4BSD manual but in Section 3n (the letter *n* stands for the networking subsection of Section 3) of the SVR4 manuals.

Finally, the implementation technique can change from one release to the next. For example, in Net/1 `send` and `sendto` were implemented as separate system calls within the kernel. In Net/3, however, `send` is a library function that calls `sendto`, which is a system call:

```
send(int s, char *msg, int len, int flags)
{
    return(sendto(s, msg, len, flags, (struct sockaddr *) NULL, 0));
}
```

The advantage in implementing `send` as a library function that just calls `sendto` is a reduction in the number of system calls and in the amount of code within the kernel. The disadvantage is the additional overhead of one more function call for the process that calls `send`.

Since this text describes the Berkeley implementation of TCP/IP, most of the functions called by the process (`socket`, `bind`, `connect`, etc.) are implemented directly in the kernel as system calls.

1.7 Network Implementation Overview

Net/3 provides a general purpose infrastructure capable of simultaneously supporting multiple communication protocols. Indeed, 4.4BSD supports four distinct communication protocol families:

1. TCP/IP (the Internet protocol suite), the topic of this book.

2. XNS (Xerox Network Systems), a protocol suite that is similar to TCP/IP; it was popular in the mid-1980s for connecting Xerox hardware (such as printers and file servers), often using an Ethernet. Although the code is still distributed with Net/3, few people use this protocol suite today, and many vendors who use the Berkeley TCP/IP code remove the XNS code (so they don't have to support it).

3. The OSI protocols [Rose 1990; Piscitello and Chapin 1993]. These protocols were designed during the 1980s as the ultimate in open-systems technology, to replace all other communication protocols. Their appeal waned during the early 1990s, and as of this writing their use in real networks is minimal. Their place in history is still to be determined.

4. The Unix domain protocols. These do not form a true protocol suite in the sense of communication protocols used to exchange information between different systems, but are provided as a form of *interprocess communication* (IPC).

   The advantage in using the Unix domain protocols for IPC between two processes on the same host, versus other forms of IPC such as System V message queues [Stevens 1990], is that the Unix domain protocols are accessed using the same API (sockets) as are the other three communication protocols. Message queues, on the other hand, and most other forms of IPC, have an API that is completely different from both sockets and TLI. Having IPC between two processes on the same host use the networking API makes it easy to migrate a client–server application from one host to many hosts. Two different protocols are provided in the Unix domain—a reliable, connection-oriented, byte-stream protocol that looks like TCP, and an unreliable, connectionless, datagram protocol that looks like UDP.

   > Although the Unix domain protocols can be used as a form of IPC between two processes on the same host, these processes could also use TCP/IP to communicate with each other. There is no requirement that processes communicating using the Internet protocols reside on different hosts.

The networking code in the kernel is organized into three layers, as shown in Figure 1.3. On the right side of this figure we note where the seven layers of the OSI reference model [Piscitello and Chapin 1993] fit in the BSD organization.

1. The *socket layer* is a protocol-independent interface to the protocol-dependent layer below. All system calls start at the protocol-independent socket layer. For example, the protocol-independent code in the socket layer for the bind system call comprises a few dozen lines of code: these verify that the first argument is a

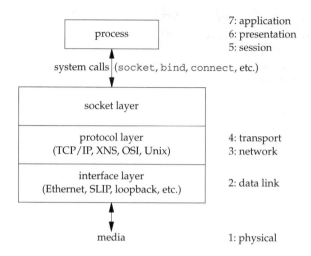

Figure 1.3   The general organization of networking code in Net/3.

valid socket descriptor and that the second argument is a valid pointer in the process. The protocol-dependent code in the layer below is then called, which might comprise hundreds of lines of code.

2. The *protocol layer* contains the implementation of the four protocol families that we mentioned earlier (TCP/IP, XNS, OSI, and Unix domain). Each protocol suite may have its own internal structure, which we don't show in Figure 1.3. For example, in the Internet protocol suite, IP is the lowest layer (the network layer) with the two transport layers (TCP and UDP) above IP.

3. The *interface layer* contains the device drivers that communicate with the network devices.

1.8   Descriptors

Figure 1.2 begins with a call to socket, specifying the type of socket desired. The combination of the Internet protocol family (PF_INET) and a datagram socket (SOCK_DGRAM) gives a socket whose protocol is UDP.

The return value from socket is a descriptor that shares all the properties of other Unix descriptors: read and write can be called for the descriptor, you can dup it, it is shared by the parent and child after a call to fork, its properties can be modified by calling fcntl, it can be closed by calling close, and so on. We see in our example that the socket descriptor is the first argument to both the sendto and recvfrom functions. When our program terminates (by calling exit), all open descriptors including the socket descriptor are closed by the kernel.

We now introduce the data structures that are created by the kernel when the process calls `socket`. We describe these data structures in more detail in later chapters.

Everything starts with the process table entry for the process. One of these exists for each process during its lifetime.

A descriptor is an index into an array within the process table entry for the process. This array entry points to an open file table structure, which in turn points to an i-node or v-node structure that describes the file. Figure 1.4 summarizes this relationship.

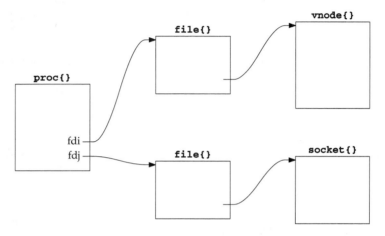

Figure 1.4   Fundamental relationship between kernel data structures starting with a descriptor.

In this figure we also show a descriptor that refers to a socket, which is the focus of this text. We place the notation `proc{}` above the process table entry, since its definition in C is

```
struct proc {
    ...
}
```

and we use this notation for structures in our figures throughout the text.

[Stevens 1992, Sec. 3.10] shows how the relationships between the descriptor, file table structure, and i-node or v-node change as the process calls `dup` and `fork`. The relationships between these three data structures exists in all versions of Unix, although the details change with different implementations. Our interest in this text is with the `socket` structure and the Internet-specific data structures that it points to. But we need to understand how a descriptor leads to a `socket` structure, since the socket system calls start with a descriptor.

Figure 1.5 shows more details of the Net/3 data structures for our example program, if the program is executed as

```
a.out
```

without redirecting standard input (descriptor 0), standard output (descriptor 1), or standard error (descriptor 2). In this example, descriptors 0, 1, and 2 are connected to our terminal, and the lowest-numbered unused descriptor is 3 when `socket` is called.

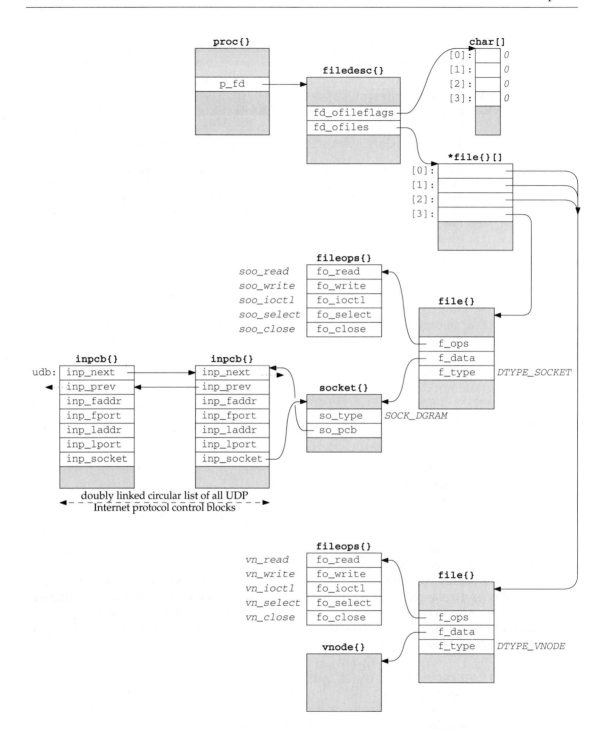

Figure 1.5   Kernel data structures after call to socket in example program.

When a process executes a system call such as socket, the kernel has access to the process table structure. The entry p_fd in this structure points to the filedesc structure for the process. There are two members of this structure that interest us now: fd_ofileflags is a pointer to an array of characters (the per-descriptor flags for each descriptor), and fd_ofiles is a pointer to an array of pointers to file table structures. The per-descriptor flags are 8 bits wide since only 2 bits can be set for any descriptor: the close-on-exec flag and the mapped-from-device flag. We show all these flags as 0.

> We purposely call this section "Descriptors" and not "File Descriptors" since Unix descriptors can refer to lots of things other than files: sockets, pipes, directories, devices, and so on. Nevertheless, much of Unix literature uses the adjective *file* when talking about descriptors, which is an unnecessary qualification. Here the kernel data structure is called filedesc{} even though we're about to describe socket descriptors. We'll use the unqualified term *descriptor* whenever possible.

The data structure pointed to by the fd_ofiles entry is shown as *file{}[] since it is an array of pointers to file structures. The index into this array and the array of descriptor flags is the nonnegative descriptor itself: 0, 1, 2, and so on. In Figure 1.5 we show the entries for descriptors 0, 1, and 2 pointing to the same file structure at the bottom of the figure (since all three descriptors refer to our terminal). The entry for descriptor 3 points to a different file structure for our socket descriptor.

The f_type member of the file structure specifies the descriptor type as either DTYPE_SOCKET or DTYPE_VNODE. V-nodes are a general mechanism that allows the kernel to support different types of filesystems—a disk filesystem, a network filesystem (such as NFS), a filesystem on a CD-ROM, a memory-based filesystem, and so on. Our interest in this text is not with v-nodes, since TCP/IP sockets always have a type of DTYPE_SOCKET.

The f_data member of the file structure points to either a socket structure or a vnode structure, depending on the type of descriptor. The f_ops member points to a vector of five function pointers. These function pointers are used by the read, readv, write, writev, ioctl, select, and close system calls, since these system calls work with either a socket descriptor or a nonsocket descriptor. Rather than look at the f_type value each time one of these system calls is invoked and then jump accordingly, the implementors chose always to jump indirectly through the corresponding entry in the fileops structure instead.

Notationally we use a fixed-width font (fo_read) to show the name of a structure member and a slanted fixed-width font (*soo_read*) to show the contents of a structure member. Also note that sometimes we show the pointer to a structure arriving at the top left corner (e.g., the filedesc structure) and sometimes at the top right corner (e.g., both file structures and both fileops structures). This is to simplify the figures.

Next we come to the socket structure that is pointed to by the file structure when the descriptor type is DTYPE_SOCKET. In our example, the socket type (SOCK_DGRAM for a datagram socket) is stored in the so_type member. An Internet protocol control block (PCB) is also allocated: an inpcb structure. The so_pcb member of the socket structure points to the inpcb, and the inp_socket member of the inpcb structure points to the socket structure. Each points to the other because the activity for a given socket can occur from two directions: "above" or "below."

1. When the process executes a system call, such as sendto, the kernel starts with the descriptor value and uses fd_ofiles to index into the vector of file structure pointers, ending up with the file structure for the descriptor. The file structure points to the socket structure, which points to the inpcb structure.

2. When a UDP datagram arrives on a network interface, the kernel searches through all the UDP protocol control blocks to find the appropriate one, minimally based on the destination UDP port number and perhaps the destination IP address, source IP address, and source port numbers too. Once the inpcb structure is located, the kernel finds the corresponding socket structure through the inp_socket pointer.

The members inp_faddr and inp_laddr contain the foreign and local IP addresses, and the members inp_fport and inp_lport contain the foreign and local port numbers. The combination of the local IP address and the local port number is often called a *socket*, as is the combination of the foreign IP address and the foreign port number.

We show another inpcb structure with the name udb on the left in Figure 1.5. This is a global structure that is the head of a linked list of all UDP PCBs. We show the two members inp_next and inp_prev that form a doubly linked circular list of all UDP PCBs. For notational simplicity in the figure, we show two parallel horizontal arrows for the two links instead of trying to have the heads of the arrows going to the top corners of the PCBs. The inp_prev member of the inpcb structure on the right points to the udb structure, not the inp_prev member of that structure. The dotted arrows from udb.inp_prev and the inp_next member of the other PCB indicate that there may be other PCBs on the doubly linked list that we don't show.

We've looked at many kernel data structures in this section, most of which are described further in later chapters. The key points to understand now are:

1. The call to socket by our process ends up allocating the lowest unused descriptor (3 in our example). This descriptor is used by the process in all subsequent system calls that refer to this socket.

2. The following kernel structures are allocated and linked together: a file structure of type DTYPE_SOCKET, a socket structure, and an inpcb structure. Lots of initialization is performed on these structures that we don't show: the file structure is marked for read and write (since the call to socket always returns a descriptor that can be read or written), the default sizes of the input and output buffers are set in the socket structure, and so on.

3. We showed nonsocket descriptors for our standard input, output, and error to show that *all* descriptors end up at a file structure, and it is from that point on that differences appear between socket descriptors and other descriptors.

1.9   Mbufs (Memory Buffers) and Output Processing

A fundamental concept in the design of the Berkeley networking code is the memory buffer, called an *mbuf*, used throughout the networking code to hold various pieces of information. Our simple example (Figure 1.2) lets us examine some typical uses of mbufs. In Chapter 2 we describe mbufs in more detail.

Mbuf Containing Socket Address Structure

In the call to `sendto`, the fifth argument points to an Internet socket address structure (named `serv`) and the sixth argument specifies its length (which we'll see later is 16 bytes). One of the first things done by the socket layer for this system call is to verify that these arguments are valid (i.e., the pointer points to a piece of memory in the address space of the process) and then copy the socket address structure into an mbuf. Figure 1.6 shows the resulting mbuf.

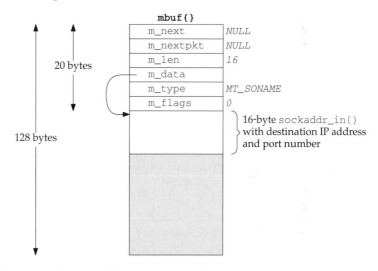

Figure 1.6   Mbuf containing destination address for `sendto`.

The first 20 bytes of the mbuf is a header containing information about the mbuf. This 20-byte header contains four 4-byte fields and two 2-byte fields. The total size of the mbuf is 128 bytes.

Mbufs can be linked together using the `m_next` and `m_nextpkt` members, as we'll see shortly. Both are null pointers in this example, which is a stand-alone mbuf.

The `m_data` member points to the data in the mbuf and the `m_len` member specifies its length. For this example, `m_data` points to the first byte of data in the mbuf (the byte immediately following the mbuf header). The final 92 bytes of the mbuf data area (108 − 16) are unused (the shaded portion of Figure 1.6).

The `m_type` member specifies the type of data contained in the mbuf, which for this example is `MT_SONAME` (socket name). The final member in the header, `m_flags`, is zero in this example.

Mbuf Containing Data

Continuing our example, the socket layer copies the data buffer specified in the call to
sendto into one or more mbufs. The second argument to sendto specifies the start of
the data buffer (buff), and the third argument is its size in bytes (150). Figure 1.7
shows how two mbufs hold the 150 bytes of data.

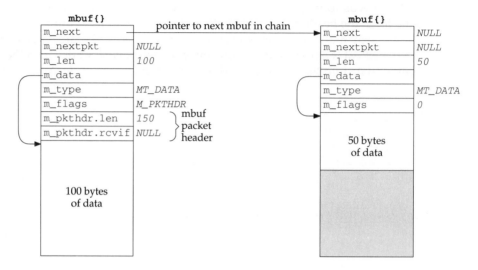

Figure 1.7   Two mbufs holding 150 bytes of data.

This arrangement is called an *mbuf chain*. The m_next member in each mbuf links
together all the mbufs in a chain.

The next change we see is the addition of two members, m_pkthdr.len and
m_pkthdr.rcvif, to the mbuf header in the first mbuf of the chain. These two members comprise the *packet header* and are used only in the first mbuf of a chain. The
m_flags member contains the value M_PKTHDR to indicate that this mbuf contains a
packet header. The len member of the packet header structure contains the total length
of the mbuf chain (150 in this example), and the next member, rcvif, we'll see later
contains a pointer to the received interface structure for received packets.

Since mbufs are *always* 128 bytes, providing 100 bytes of data storage in the first
mbuf on the chain and 108 bytes of storage in all subsequent mbufs on the chain, two
mbufs are needed to store 150 bytes of data. We'll see later that when the amount of
data exceeds 208 bytes, instead of using three or more mbufs, a different technique is
used—a larger buffer, typically 1024 or 2048 bytes, called a *cluster* is used.

One reason for maintaining a packet header with the total length in the first mbuf
on the chain is to avoid having to go through all the mbufs on the chain to sum their
m_len members when the total length is needed.

Prepending IP and UDP Headers

After the socket layer copies the destination socket address structure into an mbuf (Figure 1.6) and the data into an mbuf chain (Figure 1.7), the protocol layer corresponding to the socket descriptor (a UDP socket) is called. Specifically, the UDP output routine is called and pointers to the mbufs that we've examined are passed as arguments. This routine needs to prepend an IP header and a UDP header in front of the 150 bytes of data, fill in the headers, and pass the mbufs to the IP output routine.

The way that data is prepended to the mbuf chain in Figure 1.7 is to allocate another mbuf, make it the front of the chain, and copy the packet header from the mbuf with 100 bytes of data into the new mbuf. This gives us the three mbufs shown in Figure 1.8.

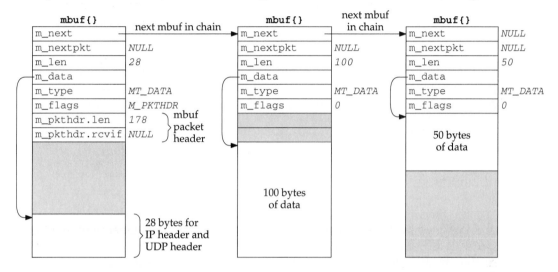

Figure 1.8   Mbuf chain from Figure 1.7 with another mbuf for IP and UDP headers prepended.

The IP header and UDP header are stored at the end of the new mbuf that becomes the head of the chain. This allows for any lower-layer protocols (e.g., the interface layer) to prepend its headers in front of the IP header if necessary, without having to copy the IP and UDP headers. The m_data pointer in the first mbuf points to the start of these two headers, and m_len is 28. Future headers that fit in the 72 bytes of unused space between the packet header and the IP header can be prepended before the IP header by adjusting the m_data pointer and the m_len accordingly. Shortly we'll see that the Ethernet header is built here in this fashion.

Notice that the packet header has been moved from the mbuf with 100 bytes of data into the new mbuf. The packet header must always be in the first mbuf on the chain. To accommodate this movement of the packet header, the M_PKTHDR flag is set in the first mbuf and cleared in the second mbuf. The space previously occupied by the packet header in the second mbuf is now unused. Finally, the length member in the packet header is incremented by 28 bytes to become 178.

The UDP output routine then fills in the UDP header and as much of the IP header as it can. For example, the destination address in the IP header can be set, but the IP checksum will be left for the IP output routine to calculate and store.

The UDP checksum is calculated and stored in the UDP header. Notice that this requires a complete pass of the 150 bytes of data stored in the mbuf chain. So far the kernel has made two complete passes of the 150 bytes of user data: once to copy the data from the user's buffer into the kernel's mbufs, and now to calculate the UDP checksum. Extra passes over the data can degrade the protocol's performance, and in later chapters we describe alternative implementation techniques that avoid unnecessary passes.

At this point the UDP output routine calls the IP output routine, passing a pointer to the mbuf chain for IP to output.

IP Output

The IP output routine fills in the remaining fields in the IP header including the IP checksum, determines the outgoing interface to which the datagram should be given (this is the IP routing function), fragments the IP datagram if necessary, and calls the interface output function.

Assuming the outgoing interface is an Ethernet, a general-purpose Ethernet output function is called, again with a pointer to the mbuf chain as an argument.

Ethernet Output

The first function of the Ethernet output function is to convert the 32-bit IP address into its corresponding 48-bit Ethernet address. This is done using ARP (Address Resolution Protocol) and may involve sending an ARP request on the Ethernet and waiting for an ARP reply. While this takes place, the mbuf chain to be output is held, waiting for the reply.

The Ethernet output routine then prepends a 14-byte Ethernet header to the first mbuf in the chain, immediately before the IP header (Figure 1.8). This contains the 6-byte Ethernet destination address, 6-byte Ethernet source address, and 2-byte Ethernet frame type.

The mbuf chain is then added to the end of the output queue for the interface. If the interface is not currently busy, the interface's "start output" routine is called directly. If the interface is busy, its output routine will process the new mbuf on its queue when it is finished with the buffers already on its output queue.

When the interface processes an mbuf that's on its output queue, it copies the data to its transmit buffer and initiates the output. In our example, 192 bytes are copied to the transmit buffer: the 14-byte Ethernet header, 20-byte IP header, 8-byte UDP header, and 150 bytes of user data. This is the third complete pass of the data by the kernel. Once the data is copied from the mbuf chain into the device's transmit buffer, the mbuf chain is released by the Ethernet device driver. The three mbufs are put back into the kernel's pool of free mbufs.

Summary of UDP Output

In Figure 1.9 we give an overview of the processing that takes place when a process calls `sendto` to transmit a single UDP datagram. The relationship of the processing that we've described to the three layers of kernel code (Figure 1.3) is also shown.

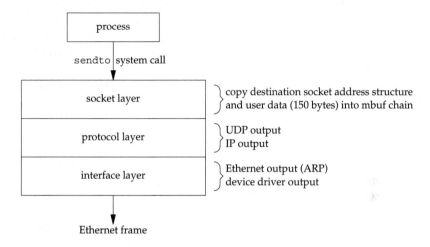

Figure 1.9   Processing performed by the three layers for simple UDP output.

Function calls pass control from the socket layer to the UDP output routine, to the IP output routine, and then to the Ethernet output routine. Each function call passes a pointer to the mbuf chain to be output. At the lowest layer, the device driver, the mbuf chain is placed on the device's output queue and the device is started, if necessary. The function calls return in reverse order of their call, and eventually the system call returns to the process. Notice that there is no queueing of the UDP data until it arrives at the device driver. The higher layers just prepend their header and pass the mbuf to the next lower layer.

At this point our program calls `recvfrom` to read the server's reply. Since the input queue for the specified socket is empty (assuming the reply has not been received yet), the process is put to sleep.

1.10   Input Processing

Input processing is different from the output processing just described because the input is *asynchronous*. That is, the reception of an input packet is triggered by a receive-complete interrupt to the Ethernet device driver, not by a system call issued by the process. The kernel handles this device interrupt and schedules the device driver to run.

Ethernet Input

The Ethernet device driver processes the interrupt and, assuming it signifies a normal receive-complete condition, the data bytes are read from the device into an mbuf chain. In our example, 54 bytes of data are received and copied into a single mbuf: the 20-byte IP header, 8-byte UDP header, and 26 bytes of data (the time and date on the server). Figure 1.10 shows the format of this mbuf.

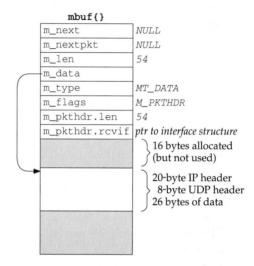

Figure 1.10   Single mbuf to hold input Ethernet data.

This mbuf is a packet header (the `M_PKTHDR` flag is set in `m_flags`) since it is the first mbuf of a data record. The `len` member in the packet header contains the total length of data and the `rcvif` member contains a pointer to the interface structure corresponding to the received interface (Chapter 3). We see that the `rcvif` member is used for received packets but not for output packets (Figures 1.7 and 1.8).

The first 16 bytes of the data portion of the mbuf are allocated for an interface layer header, but are not used. Since the amount of data (54 bytes) fits in the remaining 84 bytes of the mbuf, the data is stored in the mbuf itself.

The device driver passes the mbuf to a general Ethernet input routine which looks at the type field in the Ethernet frame to determine which protocol layer should receive the packet. In this example, the type field will specify an IP datagram, causing the mbuf to be added to the IP input queue. Additionally, a software interrupt is scheduled to cause the IP input process routine to be executed. The device's interrupt handling is then complete.

IP Input

IP input is asynchronous and is scheduled to run by a software interrupt. The software interrupt is set by the interface layer when it receives an IP datagram on one of the system's interfaces. When the IP input routine executes it loops, processing each IP datagram on its input queue and returning when the entire queue has been processed.

The IP input routine processes each IP datagram that it receives. It verifies the IP header checksum, processes any IP options, verifies that the datagram was delivered to the right host (by comparing the destination IP address of the datagram with the host's IP addresses), and forwards the datagram if the system was configured as a router and the datagram is destined for some other IP address. If the IP datagram has reached its final destination, the protocol field in the IP header specifies which protocol's input routine is called: ICMP, IGMP, TCP, or UDP. In our example, the UDP input routine is called to process the UDP datagram.

UDP Input

The UDP input routine verifies the fields in the UDP header (the length and optional checksum) and then determines whether or not a process should receive the datagram. In Chapter 23 we discuss exactly how this test is made. A process can receive all datagrams destined to a specified UDP port, or the process can tell the kernel to restrict the datagrams it receives based on the source and destination IP addresses and source and destination port numbers.

In our example, the UDP input routine starts at the global variable udb (Figure 1.5) and goes through the linked list of UDP protocol control blocks, looking for one with a local port number (inp_lport) that matches the destination port number of the received UDP datagram. This will be the PCB created by our call to socket, and the inp_socket member of this PCB points to the corresponding socket structure, allowing the received data to be queued for the correct socket.

> In our example program we never specify the local port number for our application. We'll see in Exercise 23.3 that a side effect of writing the first UDP datagram to a socket that has not yet bound a local port number is the automatic assignment by the kernel of a local port number (termed an *ephemeral port*) to that socket. That's how the inp_lport member of the PCB for our socket gets set to some nonzero value.

Since this UDP datagram is to be delivered to our process, the sender's IP address and UDP port number are placed into an mbuf, and this mbuf and the data (26 bytes in our example) are appended to the receive queue for the socket. Figure 1.11 shows the two mbufs that are appended to the socket's receive queue.

Comparing the second mbuf on this chain (the one of type MT_DATA) with the mbuf in Figure 1.10, the m_len and m_pkthdr.len members have both been decremented by 28 (20 bytes for the IP header and 8 for the UDP header) and the m_data pointer has been incremented by 28. This effectively removes the IP and UDP headers, leaving only the 26 bytes of data to be appended to the socket's receive queue.

The first mbuf in the chain contains a 16-byte Internet socket address structure with the sender's IP address and UDP port number. Its type is MT_SONAME, similar to the mbuf in Figure 1.6. This mbuf is created by the socket layer to return this information to the calling process through the recvfrom or recvmsg system calls. Even though there is room (16 bytes) in the second mbuf on this chain for this socket address structure, it must be stored in its own mbuf since it has a different type (MT_SONAME versus MT_DATA).

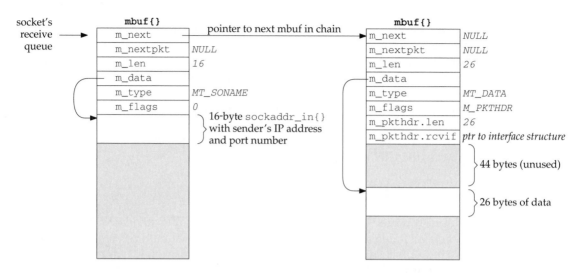

Figure 1.11   Sender's address and data.

The receiving process is then awakened. If the process is asleep waiting for data to arrive (which is the scenario in our example), the process is marked as run-able for the kernel to schedule. A process can also be notified of the arrival of data on a socket by the `select` system call or with the `SIGIO` signal.

Process Input

Our process has been asleep in the kernel, blocked in its call to `recvfrom`, and the process now wakes up. The 26 bytes of data appended to the socket's receive queue by the UDP layer (the received datagram) are copied by the kernel from the mbuf into our program's buffer.

Notice that our program sets the fifth and sixth arguments to `recvfrom` to null pointers, telling the system call that we're not interested in receiving the sender's IP address and UDP port number. This causes the `recvfrom` system call to skip the first mbuf in the chain (Figure 1.11), returning only the 26 bytes of data in the second mbuf. The kernel's `recvfrom` code then releases the two mbufs in Figure 1.11 and returns them to its pool of free mbufs.

1.11   Network Implementation Overview Revisited

Figure 1.12 summarizes the communication that takes place between the layers for both network output and network input. It repeats Figure 1.3 considering only the Internet protocols and emphasizing the communications between the layers.

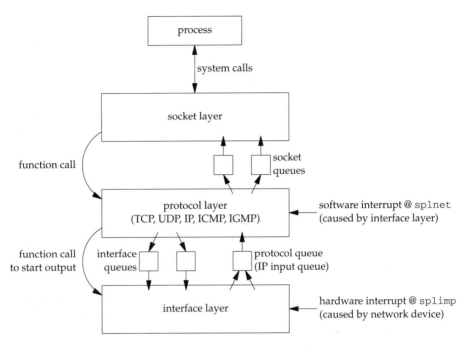

Figure 1.12   Communication between the layers for network input and output.

The notations splnet and splimp are discussed in the next section.

We use the plural terms *socket queues* and *interface queues* since there is one queue per socket and one queue per interface (Ethernet, loopback, SLIP, PPP, etc.), but we use the singular term *protocol queue* because there is a single IP input queue. If we considered other protocol layers, we would have one input queue for the XNS protocols and one for the OSI protocols.

1.12   Interrupt Levels and Concurrency

We saw in Section 1.10 that the processing of input packets by the networking code is asynchronous and interrupt driven. First, a device interrupt causes the interface layer code to execute, which posts a software interrupt that later causes the protocol layer code to execute. When the kernel is finished with these interrupt levels the socket code will execute.

There is a priority level assigned to each hardware and software interrupt. Figure 1.13 shows the normal ordering of the eight priority levels, from the lowest (no interrupts blocked) to the highest (all interrupts blocked).

Function	Description
spl0	normal operating mode, nothing blocked (lowest priority)
splsoftclock	low-priority clock processing
splnet	network protocol processing
spltty	terminal I/O
splbio	disk and tape I/O
splimp	network device I/O
splclock	high-priority clock processing
splhigh	all interrupts blocked (highest priority)
splx(s)	(see text)

Figure 1.13   Kernel functions that block selected interrupts.

Table 4.5 of [Leffler et al. 1989] shows the priority levels used in the VAX implementation. The Net/3 implementation for the 386 uses the eight functions shown in Figure 1.13, but splsoftclock and splnet are at the same level, and splclock and splhigh are also at the same level.

The name *imp* that is used for the network interface level comes from the acronym IMP (Interface Message Processor), which was the original type of router used on the ARPANET.

The ordering of the different priority levels means that a higher-priority interrupt can preempt a lower-priority interrupt. Consider the sequence of events depicted in Figure 1.14.

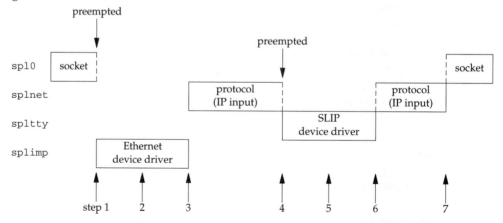

Figure 1.14   Example of priority levels and kernel processing.

1.   While the socket layer is executing at spl0, an Ethernet device driver interrupt occurs, causing the interface layer to execute at splimp. This interrupt preempts the socket layer code. This is the asynchronous execution of the interface input routine.

2.   While the Ethernet device driver is running, it places a received packet onto the IP input queue and schedules a software interrupt to occur at splnet. The

software interrupt won't take effect immediately since the kernel is currently running at a higher priority level (`splimp`).

3. When the Ethernet device driver completes, the protocol layer executes at `splnet`. This is the asynchronous execution of the IP input routine.

4. A terminal device interrupt occurs (say the completion of a SLIP packet) and it is handled immediately, preempting the protocol layer, since terminal I/O (`spltty`) is a higher priority than the protocol layer (`splnet`) in Figure 1.13. This is the asynchronous execution of the interface input routine.

5. The SLIP driver places the received packet onto the IP input queue and schedules another software interrupt for the protocol layer.

6. When the SLIP driver completes, the preempted protocol layer continues at `splnet`, finishes processing the packet received from the Ethernet device driver, and then processes the packet received from the SLIP driver. Only when there are no more input packets to process will it return control to whatever it preempted (the socket layer in this example).

7. The socket layer continues from where it was preempted.

One concern with these different priority levels is how to handle data structures shared between the different levels. Examples of shared data structures are the three we show between the different levels in Figure 1.12—the socket, interface, and protocol queues. For example, while the IP input routine is taking a received packet off its input queue, a device interrupt can occur, preempting the protocol layer, and that device driver can add another packet to the IP input queue. These shared data structures (the IP input queue in this example, which is shared between the protocol layer and the interface layer) can be corrupted if nothing is done to coordinate the shared access.

The Net/3 code is sprinkled with calls to the functions `splimp` and `splnet`. These two calls are always paired with a call to `splx` to return the processor to the previous level. For example, here is the code executed by the IP input function at the protocol layer to check if there is another packet on its input queue to process:

```
struct mbuf    *m;
int   s;

s = splimp();
IF_DEQUEUE(&ipintrq, m);
splx(s);

if (m == 0)
    return;
```

The call to `splimp` raises the CPU priority to the level used by the network device drivers, preventing any network device driver interrupt from occurring. The previous priority level is returned as the value of the function and stored in the variable s. Then the macro `IF_DEQUEUE` is executed to remove the next packet at the head of the IP input queue (`ipintrq`), placing the pointer to this mbuf chain in the variable m. Finally the CPU priority is returned to whatever it was when `splimp` was called, by calling `splx` with an argument of s (the saved value from the earlier call to `splimp`).

Since all network device driver interrupts are disabled between the calls to `splimp` and `splx`, the amount of code between these calls should be minimal. If interrupts are disabled for an extended period of time, additional device interrupts could be ignored, and data might be lost. For this reason the test of the variable m (to see if there is another packet to process) is performed after the call to `splx`, and not before the call.

The Ethernet output routine needs these `spl` calls when it places an outgoing packet onto an interface's queue, tests whether the interface is currently busy, and starts the interface if it was not busy.

```
struct mbuf   *m;
int   s;

s = splimp();
/*
 * Queue message on interface, and start output if interface not active.
 */
if (IF_QFULL(&ifp->if_snd)) {
    IF_DROP(&ifp->if_snd);      /* queue is full, drop packet */
    splx(s);
    error = ENOBUFS;
    goto bad;
}

IF_ENQUEUE(&ifp->if_snd, m);   /* add the packet to interface queue */

if ((ifp->if_flags & IFF_OACTIVE) == 0)
    (*ifp->if_start)(ifp);      /* start interface */

splx(s);
```

The reason device interrupts are disabled in this example is to prevent the device driver from taking the next packet off its send queue while the protocol layer is adding a packet to that queue. The driver's send queue is a data structure shared between the protocol layer and the interface layer.

We'll see calls to the `spl` functions throughout the source code.

1.13 Source Code Organization

Figure 1.15 shows the organization of the Net/3 networking source tree, assuming it is located in the `/usr/src/sys` directory.

This text focuses on the `netinet` directory, which contains all the TCP/IP source code. We also look at some files in the `kern` and `net` directories. The former contains the protocol-independent socket code, and the latter contains some general networking functions used by the TCP/IP routines, such as the routing code.

Briefly, the files contained in each directory are as follows:

- `i386`: the Intel 80x86-specific directories. For example, the directory `i386/isa` contains the device drivers specific to the ISA bus. The directory `i386/stand` contains the stand-alone bootstrap code.

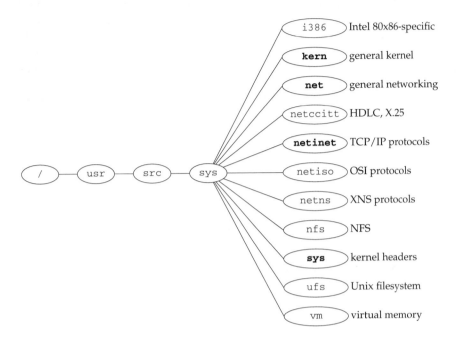

Figure 1.15   Net/3 source code organization.

- kern: general kernel files that don't belong in one of the other directories. For example, the kernel files to handle the fork and exec system calls are in this directory. We look at only a few files in this directory—the ones for the socket system calls (the socket layer in Figure 1.3).

- net: general networking files, for example, general network interface functions, the BPF (BSD Packet Filter) code, the SLIP driver, the loopback driver, and the routing code. We look at some of the files in this directory.

- netccitt: interface code for the OSI protocols, including the HDLC (high-level data-link control) and X.25 drivers.

- netinet: the code for the Internet protocols: IP, ICMP, IGMP, TCP, and UDP. This text focuses on the files in this directory.

- netiso: the OSI protocols.

- netns: the Xerox XNS protocols.

- nfs: code for Sun's Network File System.

- sys: system headers. We look at several headers in this directory. The files in this directory also appear in the directory /usr/include/sys.

- ufs: code for the Unix filesystem, sometimes called the *Berkeley fast filesystem*. This is the normal disk-based filesystem.

- vm: code for the virtual memory system.

Figure 1.16 gives another view of the source code organization, this time mapped to our three kernel layers. We ignore directories such as `netimp` and `nfs` that we don't consider in this text.

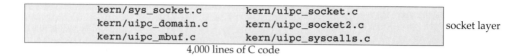

net/ (routing)	netinet/ (TCP/IP)	netns/ (XNS)	netiso/ (OSI)	kern/ (Unix domain)	protocol layer
2,100	13,000	6,000	26,000	750	

net/ (Ethernet, ARP)	net/if_sl* (SLIP)	net/if_loop* (loopback)	net/bpf* (BPF)	Ethernet device driver	interface layer
500	1,750	250	2,000	1,000 per driver	

Figure 1.16 Net/3 source code organization mapped to three kernel layers.

The numbers below each box are the approximate number of lines of C code for that feature, which includes all comments in the source files.

We don't look at all the source code shown in this figure. The `netns` and `netiso` directories are shown for comparison against the Internet protocols. We only consider the shaded boxes.

1.14 Test Network

Figure 1.17 shows the test network that is used for all the examples in the text. Other than the host `vangogh` at the top of the figure, all the IP addresses belong to the class B network ID 140.252, and all the hostnames belong to the `.tuc.noao.edu` domain. (`noao` stands for "National Optical Astronomy Observatories" and `tuc` stands for Tucson.) For example, the system in the lower right has a complete hostname of `svr4.tuc.noao.edu` and an IP address of 140.252.13.34. The notation at the top of each box is the operating system running on that system.

The host at the top has a complete name of `vangogh.cs.berkeley.edu` and is reachable from the other hosts across the Internet.

This figure is nearly identical to the test network used in Volume 1, although some of the operating systems have been upgraded and the dialup link between `sun` and `netb` now uses PPP instead of SLIP. Additionally, we have replaced the Net/2 networking code provided with BSD/386 V1.1 with the Net/3 networking code.

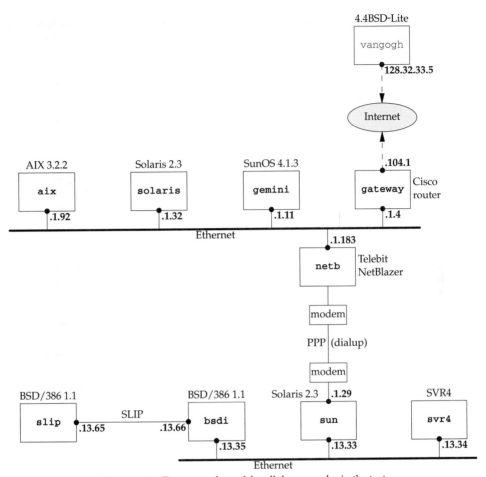

Figure 1.17   Test network used for all the examples in the text.

1.15 Summary

This chapter provided an overview of the Net/3 networking code. Using a simple program (Figure 1.2) that sends a UDP datagram to a daytime server and receives a reply, we've followed the resulting output and input through the kernel. Mbufs hold the information being output and the received IP datagrams. The next chapter examines mbufs in more detail.

UDP output occurs when the process executes the sendto system call, while IP input is asynchronous. When an IP datagram is received by a device driver, the datagram is placed onto IP's input queue and a software interrupt is scheduled to cause the IP input function to execute. We reviewed the different interrupt levels used by the networking code within the kernel. Since many of the networking data structures are shared by different layers that can execute at different interrupt priorities, the code must be careful when accessing or modifying these shared structures. We'll encounter calls to the spl functions in almost every function that we look at.

The chapter finishes with a look at the overall organization of the source code in Net/3, focusing on the code that this text examines.

Exercises

1.1 Type in the example program (Figure 1.2) and run it on your system. If your system has a system call tracing capability, such as trace (SunOS 4.x), truss (SVR4), or ktrace (4.4BSD), use it to determine the system calls invoked by this example.

1.2 In our example that calls IF_DEQUEUE in Section 1.12, we noted that the call to splimp blocks network device drivers from interrupting. While Ethernet drivers execute at this level, what happens to SLIP drivers?

2

Mbufs: Memory Buffers

2.1 Introduction

Networking protocols place many demands on the memory management facilities of the kernel. These demands include easily manipulating buffers of varying sizes, prepending and appending data to the buffers as the lower layers encapsulate data from higher layers, removing data from buffers (as headers are removed as data packets are passed up the protocol stack), and minimizing the amount of data copied for all these operations. The performance of the networking protocols is directly related to the memory management scheme used within the kernel.

In Chapter 1 we introduced the memory buffer used throughout the Net/3 kernel: the *mbuf*, which is an abbreviation for "memory buffer." In this chapter we look in more detail at mbufs and at the functions within the kernel that are used to manipulate them, as we will encounter mbufs on almost every page of the text. Understanding mbufs is essential for understanding the rest of the text.

The main use of mbufs is to hold the user data that travels from the process to the network interface, and vice versa. But mbufs are also used to contain a variety of other miscellaneous data: source and destination addresses, socket options, and so on.

Figure 2.1 shows the four different kinds of mbufs that we'll encounter, depending on the `M_PKTHDR` and `M_EXT` flags in the `m_flags` member. The differences between the four mbufs in Figure 2.1, from left to right, are as follows:

1. If `m_flags` equals 0, the mbuf contains only data. There is room in the mbuf for up to 108 bytes of data (the `m_dat` array). The `m_data` pointer points somewhere in this 108-byte buffer. We show it pointing to the start of the buffer, but it can point anywhere in the buffer. The `m_len` member specifies the number of bytes of data, starting at `m_data`. Figure 1.6 was an example of this type of mbuf.

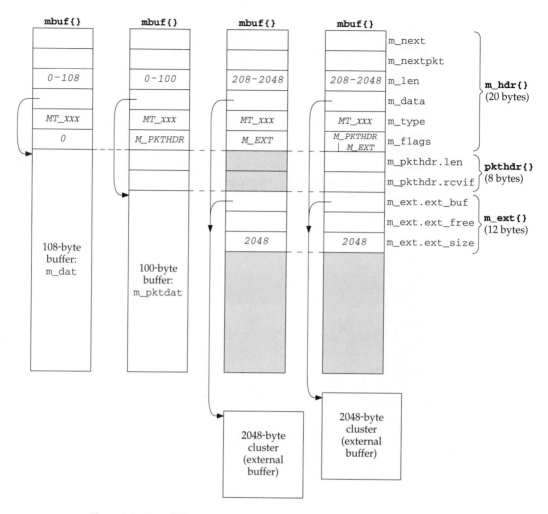

Figure 2.1   Four different types of mbufs, depending on the m_flags value.

In Figure 2.1 there are six members in the m_hdr structure, and its total size is 20 bytes. When we look at the C definition of this structure (Figure 2.8) we'll see that the first four members occupy 4 bytes each and the last two occupy 2 bytes each. We don't try to differentiate between the 4-byte members and the 2-byte members in Figure 2.1.

2. The second type of mbuf has an m_flags value of M_PKTHDR, specifying a *packet header*, that is, the first mbuf describing a packet of data. The data is still contained within the mbuf itself, but because of the 8 bytes taken by the packet header, only 100 bytes of data fit within this mbuf (in the m_pktdat array). Figure 1.10 was an example of this type of mbuf.

The m_pkthdr.len value is the total length of all the data in the mbuf chain for this packet: the sum of the m_len values for all the mbufs linked through the m_next pointer, as shown in Figure 1.8. The m_pkthdr.rcvif member is not used for output packets, but for received packets it contains a pointer to the received interface's ifnet structure (Figure 3.6).

3. The next type of mbuf does not contain a packet header (M_PKTHDR is not set) but contains more than 208 bytes of data, so an external buffer called a *cluster* is used (M_EXT is set). Room is still allocated in the mbuf itself for the packet header structure, but it is unused—we show it shaded in Figure 2.1. Instead of using multiple mbufs to contain the data (the first with 100 bytes of data, and all the rest with 108 bytes of data each), Net/3 allocates a cluster of size 1024 or 2048 bytes. The m_data pointer in the mbuf points somewhere inside this cluster.

    The Net/3 release supports seven different architectures. Four define the size of a cluster as 1024 bytes (the traditional value) and three define it as 2048. The reason 1024 has been used historically is to save memory: if the cluster size is 2048, about one-quarter of each cluster is unused for Ethernet packets (1500 bytes maximum). We'll see in Section 27.5 that the Net/3 TCP never sends more than the cluster size per TCP segment, so with a cluster size of 1024, almost one-third of each 1500-byte Ethernet frame is unused. But [Mogul 1993, Figure 15.15] shows that a sizable performance improvement occurs on an Ethernet when maximum-sized frames are sent instead of 1024-byte frames. This is a performance-versus-memory tradeoff. Older systems used 1024-byte clusters to save memory while newer systems with cheaper memory use 2048 to increase performance. Throughout this text we assume a cluster size of 2048.

    > Unfortunately different names have been used for what we call *clusters*. The constant MCLBYTES is the size of these buffers (1024 or 2048) and the names of the macros to manipulate these buffers are MCLGET, MCLALLOC, and MCLFREE. This is why we call them *clusters*. But we also see that the mbuf flag is M_EXT, which stands for "external" buffer. Finally, [Leffler et al. 1989] calls them *mapped pages*. This latter name refers to their implementation, and we'll see in Section 2.9 that clusters can be shared when a copy is required.

    > We would expect the minimum value of m_len to be 209 for this type of mbuf, not 208 as we indicate in the figure. That is, a record with 208 bytes of data can be stored in two mbufs, with 100 bytes in the first and 108 in the second. The source code, however, has a bug and allocates a cluster if the size is greater than or equal to 208.

4. The final type of mbuf contains a packet header and contains more than 208 bytes of data. Both M_PKTHDR and M_EXT are set.

There are numerous additional points we need to make about Figure 2.1:

*   The size of the mbuf structure is always 128 bytes. This means the amount of unused space following the m_ext structure in the two mbufs on the right in Figure 2.1 is 88 bytes $(128 - 20 - 8 - 12)$.

*   A data buffer with an m_len of 0 bytes is OK since some protocols (e.g., UDP) allow 0-length records.

- In each of the mbufs we show the m_data member pointing to the beginning of the corresponding buffer (either the mbuf buffer itself or a cluster). This pointer can point anywhere in the corresponding buffer, not necessarily the front.

- Mbufs with a cluster always contain the starting address of the buffer (m_ext.ext_buf) and its size (m_ext.ext_size). We assume a size of 2048 throughout this text. The m_data and m_ext.ext_buf members are not the same (as we show) unless m_data also points to the first byte of the buffer. The third member of the m_ext structure, ext_free, is not currently used by Net/3.

- The m_next pointer links together the mbufs forming a single packet (record) into an *mbuf chain*, as in Figure 1.8.

- The m_nextpkt pointer links multiple packets (records) together to form a *queue of mbufs*. Each packet on the queue can be a single mbuf or an mbuf chain. The first mbuf of each packet contains a packet header. If multiple mbufs define a packet, the m_nextpkt member of the first mbuf is the only one used—the m_nextpkt member of the remaining mbufs on the chain are all null pointers.

Figure 2.2 shows an example of two packets on a queue. It is a modification of Figure 1.8. We have placed the UDP datagram onto the interface output queue (showing that the 14-byte Ethernet header has been prepended to the IP header in the first mbuf on the chain) and have added a second packet to the queue: a TCP segment containing 1460 bytes of user data. The TCP data is contained in a cluster and an mbuf has been prepended to contain its Ethernet, IP, and TCP headers. With the cluster we show that the data pointer into the cluster (m_data) need not point to the front of the cluster. We show that the queue has a head pointer and a tail pointer. This is how the interface output queues are handled in Net/3. We have also added the m_ext structure to the mbuf with the M_EXT flag set and have shaded in the unused pkthdr structure of this mbuf.

> The first mbuf with the packet header for the UDP datagram has a type of MT_DATA, but the first mbuf with the packet header for the TCP segment has a type of MT_HEADER. This is a side effect of the different way UDP and TCP prepend the headers to their data, and makes no difference. Mbufs of these two types are essentially the same. It is the m_flags value of M_PKTHDR in the first mbuf on the chain that indicates a packet header.

> Careful readers may note a difference between our picture of an mbuf (the Net/3 mbuf, Figure 2.1) and the picture in [Leffler et al. 1989, p. 290], a Net/1 mbuf. The changes were made in Net/2: adding the m_flags member, renaming the m_act pointer to be m_nextpkt, and moving this pointer to the front of the mbuf.

> The difference in the placement of the protocol headers in the first mbuf for the UDP and TCP examples is caused by UDP calling M_PREPEND (Figure 23.15 and Exercise 23.1) while TCP calls MGETHDR (Figure 26.25).

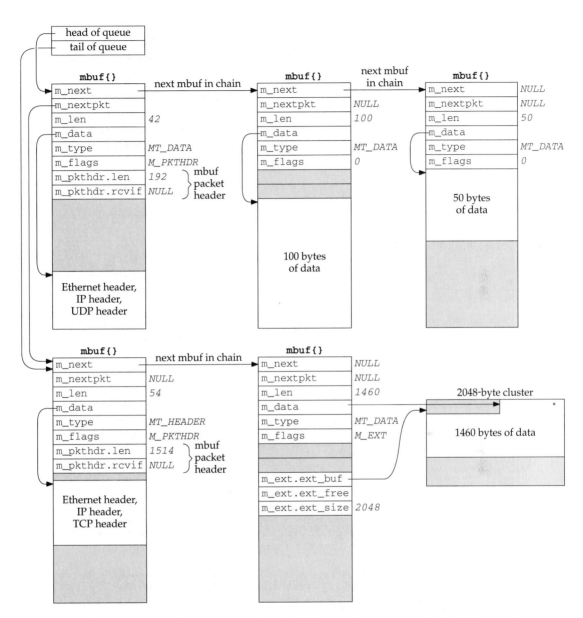

Figure 2.2 Two packets on a queue: first with 192 bytes of data and second with 1514 bytes of data.

2.2   Code Introduction

The mbuf functions are in a single C file and the mbuf macros and various mbuf definitions are in a single header, as shown in Figure 2.3.

File	Description
`sys/mbuf.h`	mbuf structure, mbuf macros and definitions
`kern/uipc_mbuf.c`	mbuf functions

Figure 2.3   Files discussed in this chapter.

Global Variables

One global variable is introduced in this chapter, shown in Figure 2.4.

Variable	Datatype	Description
`mbstat`	`struct mbstat`	mbuf statistics (Figure 2.5)

Figure 2.4   Global variables introduced in this chapter.

Statistics

Various statistics are maintained in the global structure `mbstat`, described in Figure 2.5.

mbstat member	Description
`m_clfree`	#free clusters
`m_clusters`	#clusters obtained from page pool
`m_drain`	#times protocol's drain functions called to reclaim space
`m_drops`	#times failed to find space (not used)
`m_mbufs`	#mbufs obtained from page pool (not used)
`m_mtypes[256]`	counter of current mbuf allocations: MT_*xxx* index
`m_spare`	spare field (not used)
`m_wait`	#times waited for space (not used)

Figure 2.5   Mbuf statistics maintained in the `mbstat` structure.

This structure can be examined with the `netstat -m` command; Figure 2.6 shows some
sample output. The two values printed for the number of mapped pages in use are
m_clusters (34) minus m_clfree (32), giving the number of clusters currently in use
(2), and m_clusters (34).

   The number of Kbytes of memory allocated to the network is the mbuf memory
(99×128 bytes) plus the cluster memory (34×2048 bytes) divided by 1024. The percentage in use is the mbuf memory (99×128 bytes) plus the cluster memory in use (2×2048
bytes) divided by the total network memory (80 Kbytes), times 100.

netstat -m output	mbstat member
99 mbufs in use:	
1 mbufs allocated to data	m_mtypes[MT_DATA]
43 mbufs allocated to packet headers	m_mtypes[MT_HEADER]
17 mbufs allocated to protocol control blocks	m_mtypes[MT_PCB]
20 mbufs allocated to socket names and addresses	m_mtypes[MT_SONAME]
18 mbufs allocated to socket options	m_mtypes[MT_SOOPTS]
2/34 mapped pages in use	(see text)
80 Kbytes allocated to network (20% in use)	(see text)
0 requests for memory denied	m_drops
0 requests for memory delayed	m_wait
0 calls to protocol drain routines	m_drain

Figure 2.6   Sample mbuf statistics.

Kernel Statistics

The mbuf statistics show a common technique that we see throughout the Net/3 sources. The kernel keeps track of certain statistics in a global variable (the mbstat structure in this example). A process (in this case the netstat program) examines the statistics while the kernel is running.

    Rather than provide system calls to fetch the statistics maintained by the kernel, the process obtains the address within the kernel of the data structure in which it is interested by reading the information saved by the link editor when the kernel was built. The process then calls the kvm(3) functions to read the corresponding location in the kernel's memory by using the special file /dev/mem. If the kernel's data structure changes from one release to the next, any program that reads that structure must also change.

2.3   Mbuf Definitions

There are a few constants that we encounter repeatedly when dealing with mbufs. Their values are shown in Figure 2.7. All are defined in mbuf.h except MCLBYTES, which is defined in /usr/include/machine/param.h.

Constant	Value (#bytes)	Description
MCLBYTES	2048	size of an mbuf cluster (external buffer)
MHLEN	100	max amount of data in mbuf with packet header
MINCLSIZE	208	smallest amount of data to put into cluster
MLEN	108	max amount of data in normal mbuf
MSIZE	128	size of each mbuf

Figure 2.7   Mbuf constants from mbuf.h.

2.4 `mbuf` Structure

Figure 2.8 shows the definition of the `mbuf` structure.

——————————————————————————————————— mbuf.h

```
60 /* header at beginning of each mbuf: */
61 struct m_hdr {
62     struct mbuf *mh_next;        /* next buffer in chain */
63     struct mbuf *mh_nextpkt;     /* next chain in queue/record */
64     int     mh_len;              /* amount of data in this mbuf */
65     caddr_t mh_data;             /* pointer to data */
66     short   mh_type;             /* type of data (Figure 2.10) */
67     short   mh_flags;            /* flags (Figure 2.9) */
68 };

69 /* record/packet header in first mbuf of chain; valid if M_PKTHDR set */
70 struct pkthdr {
71     int     len;                 /* total packet length */
72     struct ifnet *rcvif;         /* receive interface */
73 };

74 /* description of external storage mapped into mbuf, valid if M_EXT set */
75 struct m_ext {
76     caddr_t ext_buf;             /* start of buffer */
77     void    (*ext_free) ();      /* free routine if not the usual */
78     u_int   ext_size;            /* size of buffer, for ext_free */
79 };

80 struct mbuf {
81     struct m_hdr m_hdr;
82     union {
83         struct {
84             struct pkthdr MH_pkthdr;    /* M_PKTHDR set */
85             union {
86                 struct m_ext MH_ext;    /* M_EXT set */
87                 char    MH_databuf[MHLEN];
88             } MH_dat;
89         } MH;
90         char    M_databuf[MLEN];        /* !M_PKTHDR, !M_EXT */
91     } M_dat;
92 };

93 #define m_next      m_hdr.mh_next
94 #define m_len       m_hdr.mh_len
95 #define m_data      m_hdr.mh_data
96 #define m_type      m_hdr.mh_type
97 #define m_flags     m_hdr.mh_flags
98 #define m_nextpkt   m_hdr.mh_nextpkt
99 #define m_act       m_nextpkt
100 #define m_pkthdr    M_dat.MH.MH_pkthdr
101 #define m_ext       M_dat.MH.MH_dat.MH_ext
102 #define m_pktdat    M_dat.MH.MH_dat.MH_databuf
103 #define m_dat       M_dat.M_databuf
```

——————————————————————————————————— mbuf.h

Figure 2.8 Mbuf structures.

The mbuf structure is defined as an m_hdr structure, followed by a union. As the comments indicate, the contents of the union depend on the flags M_PKTHDR and M_EXT.

93–103   These 11 #define statements simplify access to the members of the structures and unions within the mbuf structure. We will see this technique used throughout the Net/3 sources whenever we encounter a structure containing other structures or unions.

We previously described the purpose of the first two members in the mbuf structure: the m_next pointer links mbufs together into an mbuf chain and the m_nextpkt pointer links mbuf chains together into a *queue of mbufs*.

Figure 1.8 differentiated between the m_len member of each mbuf and the m_pkthdr.len member in the packet header. The latter is the sum of all the m_len members of all the mbufs on the chain.

There are five independent values for the m_flags member, shown in Figure 2.9.

m_flags	Description
M_BCAST	sent/received as link-level broadcast
M_EOR	end of record
M_EXT	cluster (external buffer) associated with this mbuf
M_MCAST	sent/received as link-level multicast
M_PKTHDR	first mbuf that forms a packet (record)
M_COPYFLAGS	M_PKTHDR | M_EOR | M_BCAST | M_MCAST

Figure 2.9   m_flags values.

We have already described the M_EXT and M_PKTHDR flags. M_EOR is set in an mbuf containing the end of a record. The Internet protocols (e.g., TCP) never set this flag, since TCP provides a byte-stream service without any record boundaries. The OSI and XNS transport layers, however, do use this flag. We will encounter this flag in the socket layer, since this layer is protocol independent and handles data to and from all the transport layers.

The next two flags, M_BCAST and M_MCAST, are set in an mbuf when the packet will be sent to or was received from a link-layer broadcast address or multicast address. These two constants are flags between the protocol layer and the interface layer (Figure 1.3).

The final value, M_COPYFLAGS, specifies the flags that are copied when an mbuf containing a packet header is copied.

Figure 2.10 shows the MT_*xxx* constants used in the m_type member to identify the type of data stored in the mbuf. Although we tend to think of an mbuf as containing user data that is sent or received, mbufs can contain a variety of different data structures. Recall in Figure 1.6 that an mbuf was used to hold a socket address structure with the destination address for the sendto system call. Its m_type member was set to MT_SONAME.

Not all of the mbuf type values in Figure 2.10 are used in Net/3. Some are historical (MT_HTABLE), and others are not used in the TCP/IP code but are used elsewhere in the

Mbuf m_type	Used in Net/3 TCP/IP code	Description	Memory type
MT_CONTROL	•	extra-data protocol message	M_MBUF
MT_DATA	•	dynamic data allocation	M_MBUF
MT_FREE		should be on free list	M_FREE
MT_FTABLE	•	fragment reassembly header	M_FTABLE
MT_HEADER	•	packet header	M_MBUF
MT_HTABLE		IMP host tables	M_HTABLE
MT_IFADDR		interface address	M_IFADDR
MT_OOBDATA		expedited (out-of-band) data	M_MBUF
MT_PCB		protocol control block	M_PCB
MT_RIGHTS		access rights	M_MBUF
MT_RTABLE		routing tables	M_RTABLE
MT_SONAME	•	socket name	M_MBUF
MT_SOOPTS	•	socket options	M_SOOPTS
MT_SOCKET		socket structure	M_SOCKET

Figure 2.10   Values for m_type member.

kernel. For example, MT_OOBDATA is used by the OSI and XNS protocols, but TCP handles out-of-band data differently (as we describe in Section 29.7). We describe the use of other mbuf types when we encounter them later in the text.

The final column of this figure shows the M_*xxx* values associated with the piece of memory allocated by the kernel for the different types of mbufs. There are about 60 possible M_*xxx* values assigned to the different types of memory allocated by the kernel's malloc function and MALLOC macro. Figure 2.6 showed the mbuf allocation statistics from the netstat -m command including the counters for each MT_*xxx* type. The vmstat -m command shows the kernel's memory allocation statistics including the counters for each M_*xxx* type.

Since mbufs have a fixed size (128 bytes) there is a limit for what an mbuf can be used for—the data contents cannot exceed 108 bytes. Net/2 used an mbuf to hold a TCP protocol control block (which we cover in Chapter 24), using the mbuf type of MT_PCB. But 4.4BSD increased the size of this structure from 108 bytes to 140 bytes, forcing the use of a different type of kernel memory allocation for the structure.

Observant readers may have noticed that in Figure 2.10 we say that mbufs of type MT_PCB are not used, yet Figure 2.6 shows a nonzero counter for this type. The Unix domain protocols use this type of mbuf, and it is important to remember that the statistics are for mbuf usage across all protocol suites, not just the Internet protocols.

2.5   Simple Mbuf Macros and Functions

There are more than two dozen macros and functions that deal with mbufs (allocate an mbuf, free an mbuf, etc.). We look at the source code for only a few of the macros and functions, to show how they're implemented.

Some operations are provided as both a macro and function. The macro version has an uppercase name that begins with M, and the function has a lowercase name that begins with m_. The difference in the two is the standard time-versus-space tradeoff. The macro version is expanded inline by the C preprocessor each time it is used (requiring more code space), but it executes faster since it doesn't require a function call (which can be expensive on some architectures). The function version, on the other hand, becomes a few instructions each time it is invoked (push the arguments onto the stack, call the function, etc.), taking less code space but more execution time.

m_get Function

We'll look first at the function that allocates an mbuf: m_get, shown in Figure 2.11. This function merely expands the macro MGET.

—— uipc_mbuf.c
```
134 struct mbuf *
135 m_get(nowait, type)
136 int      nowait, type;
137 {
138     struct mbuf *m;

139     MGET(m, nowait, type);
140     return (m);
141 }
```
—— uipc_mbuf.c

Figure 2.11   m_get function: allocate an mbuf.

> Notice that the Net/3 code does not use ANSI C argument declarations. All the Net/3 system headers, however, *do* provide ANSI C function prototypes for all kernel functions, if an ANSI C compiler is being used. For example, the <sys/mbuf.h> header includes the line
>
> >   struct mbuf *m_get(int, int);
>
> These function prototypes provide compile-time checking of the arguments and return values whenever a kernel function is called.

The caller specifies the nowait argument as either M_WAIT or M_DONTWAIT, depending whether it wants to wait if the memory is not available. As an example of the difference, when the socket layer asks for an mbuf to store the destination address of the sendto system call (Figure 1.6) it specifies M_WAIT, since blocking at this point is OK. But when the Ethernet device driver asks for an mbuf to store a received frame (Figure 1.10) it specifies M_DONTWAIT, since it is executing as a device interrupt handler and cannot be put to sleep waiting for an mbuf. In this case it is better for the device driver to discard the Ethernet frame if the memory is not available.

MGET Macro

Figure 2.12 shows the MGET macro. A call to MGET to allocate the mbuf to hold the destination address for the sendto system call (Figure 1.6) might look like

```
    MGET(m, M_WAIT, MT_SONAME);
    if (m == NULL)
        return(ENOBUFS);
```

Even though the caller specifies M_WAIT, the return value must still be checked, since, as we'll see in Figure 2.13, waiting for an mbuf does not guarantee that one will be available.

mbuf.h

```
154 #define MGET(m, how, type) { \
155     MALLOC((m), struct mbuf *, MSIZE, mbtypes[type], (how)); \
156     if (m) { \
157         (m)->m_type = (type); \
158         MBUFLOCK(mbstat.m_mtypes[type]++;) \
159         (m)->m_next = (struct mbuf *)NULL; \
160         (m)->m_nextpkt = (struct mbuf *)NULL; \
161         (m)->m_data = (m)->m_dat; \
162         (m)->m_flags = 0; \
163     } else \
164         (m) = m_retry((how), (type)); \
165 }
```

mbuf.h

Figure 2.12   MGET macro.

154–157   MGET first calls the kernel's MALLOC macro, which is the general-purpose kernel memory allocator. The array mbtypes converts the mbuf MT_*xxx* value into the corresponding M_*xxx* value (Figure 2.10). If the memory can be allocated, the m_type member is set to the argument's value.

158   The kernel structure that keeps mbuf statistics for each type of mbuf is incremented (mbstat). The macro MBUFLOCK changes the processor priority (Figure 1.13) while executing the statement specified as its argument, and then resets the priority to its previous value. This prevents network device interrupts from occurring while the statement mbstat.m_mtypes[type]++; is executing, because mbufs can be allocated at various layers within the kernel. Consider a system that implements the ++ operator in C using three steps: (1) load the current value into a register, (2) increment the register, and (3) store the register into memory. Assume the counter's value is 77 and MGET is executing at the socket layer. Assume steps 1 and 2 are executed (the register's value is 78) and a device interrupt occurs. If the device driver also executes MGET for the same type of mbuf, the value in memory is fetched (77), incremented (78), and stored back into memory. When step 3 of the interrupted execution of MGET resumes, it stores its register (78) into memory. But the counter should be 79, not 78, so the counter has been corrupted.

159–160   The two mbuf pointers, m_next and m_nextpkt, are set to null pointers. It is the caller's responsibility to add the mbuf to a chain or queue, if necessary.

161–162   Finally the data pointer is set to point to the beginning of the 108-byte mbuf buffer and the flags are set to 0.

163–164   If the call to the kernel's memory allocator fails, m_retry is called (Figure 2.13). The first argument is either M_WAIT or M_DONTWAIT.

m_retry Function

Figure 2.13 shows the m_retry function.

```
                                                                    uipc_mbuf.c
92 struct mbuf *
93 m_retry(i, t)
94 int      i, t;
95 {
96     struct mbuf *m;

97     m_reclaim();
98 #define m_retry(i, t)    (struct mbuf *)0
99     MGET(m, i, t);
100 #undef m_retry
101    return (m);
102 }
                                                                    uipc_mbuf.c
```

Figure 2.13 m_retry function.

92–97   The first function called by m_retry is m_reclaim. We'll see in Section 7.4 that each protocol can define a "drain" function to be called by m_reclaim when the system gets low on available memory. We'll also see in Figure 10.32 that when IP's drain function is called, all IP fragments waiting to be reassembled into IP datagrams are discarded. TCP's drain function does nothing and UDP doesn't even define a drain function.

98–102   Since there's a chance that more memory *might* be available after the call to m_reclaim, the MGET macro is called again, to try to obtain the mbuf. Before expanding the MGET macro (Figure 2.12), m_retry is defined to be a null pointer. This prevents an infinite loop if the memory still isn't available: the expansion of MGET will set m to this null pointer instead of calling the m_retry function. After the expansion of MGET, this temporary definition of m_retry is undefined, in case there is another reference to MGET later in the source file.

Mbuf Locking

In the functions and macros that we've looked at in this section, other than the call to MBUFLOCK in Figure 2.12, there are no calls to the spl functions to protect these functions and macros from being interrupted. What we haven't shown, however, is that the macro MALLOC contains an splimp at the beginning and an splx at the end. The macro MFREE contains the same protection. Mbufs are allocated and released at all layers within the kernel, so the kernel must protect the data structures that it uses for memory allocation.

Additionally, the macros MCLALLOC and MCLFREE, which allocate and release an mbuf cluster, are surrounded by an splimp and an splx, since they modify a linked list of available clusters.

Since the memory allocation and release macros along with the cluster allocation and release macros are protected from interrupts, we normally do not encounter calls to the spl functions around macros and functions such as MGET and m_get.

2.6   `m_devget` and `m_pullup` Functions

We encounter the `m_pullup` function when we show the code for IP, ICMP, IGMP, UDP, and TCP. It is called to guarantee that the specified number of bytes (the size of the corresponding protocol header) are contiguous in the first mbuf of a chain; otherwise the specified number of bytes are copied to a new mbuf and made contiguous. To understand the usage of `m_pullup` we must describe its implementation and its interaction with both the `m_devget` function and the `mtod` and `dtom` macros. This description also provides additional insight into the usage of mbufs in Net/3.

`m_devget` Function

When an Ethernet frame is received, the device driver calls the function `m_devget` to create an mbuf chain and copy the frame from the device into the chain. Depending on the length of the received frame (excluding the Ethernet header), there are four different possibilities for the resulting mbuf chain. The first two possibilities are shown in Figure 2.14.

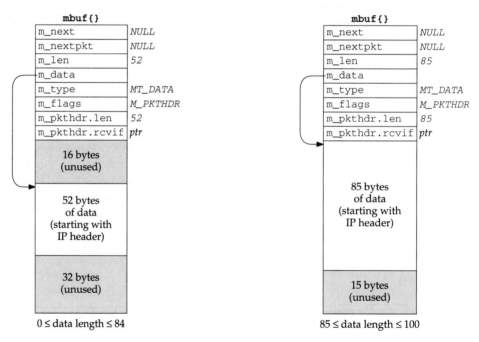

Figure 2.14   First two types of mbufs created by `m_devget`.

1.   The left mbuf in Figure 2.14 is used when the amount of data is between 0 and 84 bytes. In this figure we assume there are 52 bytes of data: a 20-byte IP header and a 32-byte TCP header (the standard 20-byte TCP header plus 12 bytes of TCP options)

but no TCP data. Since the data in the mbuf returned by m_devget starts with the IP header, the realistic minimum value for m_len is 28: 20 bytes for an IP header, 8 bytes for a UDP header, and a 0-length UDP datagram.

m_devget leaves 16 bytes unused at the beginning of the mbuf. Although the 14-byte Ethernet header is not stored here, room is allocated for a 14-byte Ethernet header on output, should the same mbuf be used for output. We'll encounter two functions that generate a response by using the received mbuf as the outgoing mbuf: icmp_reflect and tcp_respond. In both cases the size of the received datagram is normally less than 84 bytes, so it costs nothing to leave room for 16 bytes at the front, which saves time when building the outgoing datagram. The reason 16 bytes are allocated, and not 14, is to have the IP header longword aligned in the mbuf.

2. If the amount of data is between 85 and 100 bytes, the data still fits in a packet header mbuf, but there is no room for the 16 bytes at the beginning. The data starts at the beginning of the m_pktdat array and any unused space is at the end of this array. The mbuf on the right in Figure 2.14 shows this example, assuming 85 bytes of data.

3. Figure 2.15 shows the third type of mbuf created by m_devget. Two mbufs are required when the amount of data is between 101 and 207 bytes. The first 100 bytes are stored in the first mbuf (the one with the packet header), and the remainder are stored in the second mbuf. In this example we show a 104-byte datagram. No attempt is made to leave 16 bytes at the beginning of the first mbuf.

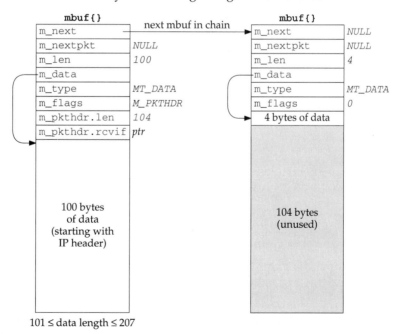

Figure 2.15   Third type of mbuf created by m_devget.

4. Figure 2.16 shows the fourth type of mbuf created by `m_devget`. If the amount of data is greater than or equal to 208 (`MINCLBYTES`), one or more clusters are used. The example in the figure assumes a 1500-byte Ethernet frame with 2048-byte clusters. If 1024-byte clusters are in use, this example would require two mbufs, each with the `M_EXT` flag set, and each pointing to a cluster.

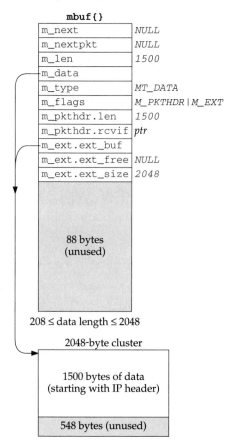

Figure 2.16   Fourth type of mbuf created by `m_devget`.

`mtod` and `dtom` Macros

The two macros `mtod` and `dtom` are also defined in `mbuf.h`. They simplify complex mbuf structure expressions.

```
#define   mtod(m,t)   ((t)((m)->m_data))
#define   dtom(x)     ((struct mbuf *)((int)(x) & ~(MSIZE-1)))
```

`mtod` ("mbuf-to-data") returns a pointer to the data associated with an mbuf, and casts the pointer to a specified type. For example, the code

```
struct mbuf *m;
struct ip *ip;

ip = mtod(m, struct ip *);
ip->ip_v = IPVERSION;
```

stores in ip the data pointer of the mbuf (m_data). The type cast is required by the C compiler and the code then references the IP header using the pointer ip. We see this macro used when a C structure (often a protocol header) is stored in an mbuf. This macro works if the data is stored in the mbuf itself (Figures 2.14 and 2.15) or if the data is stored in a cluster (Figure 2.16).

The macro dtom ("data-to-mbuf") takes a pointer to data anywhere within the data portion of the mbuf and returns a pointer to the mbuf structure itself. For example, if we know that ip points within the data area of an mbuf, the sequence

```
struct mbuf *m;
struct ip *ip;

m = dtom(ip);
```

stores the pointer to the beginning of the mbuf in m. By knowing that MSIZE (128) is a power of 2, and that mbufs are always aligned by the kernel's memory allocator on MSIZE byte blocks of memory, dtom just clears the appropriate low-order bits in its argument pointer to find the beginning of the mbuf.

There is a problem with dtom: it doesn't work if its argument points to a cluster, or within a cluster, as in Figure 2.16. Since there is no pointer from the cluster back to the mbuf structure, dtom cannot be used. This leads to the next function, m_pullup.

m_pullup Function and Contiguous Protocol Headers

The m_pullup function has two purposes. The first is when one of the protocols (IP, ICMP, IGMP, UDP, or TCP) finds that the amount of data in the first mbuf (m_len) is less than the size of the minimum protocol header (e.g., 20 for IP, 8 for UDP, 20 for TCP). m_pullup is called on the assumption that the remaining part of the header is in the next mbuf on the chain. m_pullup rearranges the mbuf chain so that the first N bytes of data are contiguous in the first mbuf on the chain. N is an argument to the function that must be less than or equal to 100 (MHLEN). If the first N bytes are contiguous in the first mbuf, then both of the macros mtod and dtom will work.

For example, we'll encounter the following code in the IP input routine:

```
if (m->m_len < sizeof(struct ip) &&
    (m = m_pullup(m, sizeof(struct ip))) == 0) {
        ipstat.ips_toosmall++;
        goto next;
}
ip = mtod(m, struct ip *);
```

If the amount of data in the first mbuf is less than 20 (the size of the standard IP header), m_pullup is called. m_pullup can fail for two reasons: (1) if it needs another mbuf

and its call to MGET fails, or (2) if the total amount of data in the mbuf chain is less than
the requested number of contiguous bytes (what we called *N*, which in this case is 20).
The second reason is the most common cause of failure. In this example, if m_pullup
fails, an IP counter is incremented and the IP datagram is discarded. Notice that this
code assumes the reason for failure is that the amount of data in the mbuf chain is less
than 20 bytes.

In actuality, m_pullup is rarely called in this scenario (notice that C's && operator
only calls it when the mbuf length is smaller than expected) and when it is called, it normally fails. The reason can be seen by looking at Figure 2.14 through Figure 2.16: there
is room in the first mbuf, or in the cluster, for at least 100 contiguous bytes, starting with
the IP header. This allows for the maximum IP header of 60 bytes followed by 40 bytes
of TCP header. (The other protocols—ICMP, IGMP, and UDP—have headers smaller
than 40 bytes.) If the data bytes are available in the mbuf chain (the packet is not
smaller than the minimum required by the protocol), then the required number of bytes
should always be contiguous in the first mbuf. But if the received packet is too short
(m_len is less than the expected minimum), then m_pullup is called and it returns an
error, since the required amount of data is not available in the mbuf chain.

> Berkeley-derived kernels maintain a variable named MPFail that is incremented each time
> m_pullup fails. On a Net/3 system that had received over 27 million IP datagrams, MPFail
> was 9. The counter ipstat.ips_toosmall was also 9 and all the other protocol counters
> (i.e., ICMP, IGMP, UDP, and TCP) following a failure of m_pullup were 0. This confirms our
> statement that most failures of m_pullup are because the received IP datagram was too small.

m_pullup and IP Fragmentation and Reassembly

The second use of m_pullup concerns IP reassembly and TCP reassembly. Assume IP
receives a packet of length 296, which is a fragment of a larger IP datagram. The mbuf
passed from the device driver to IP input looks like the one we showed in Figure 2.16:
the 296 bytes of data are stored in a cluster. We show this in Figure 2.17.

The problem is that the IP fragmentation algorithm keeps the individual fragments
on a doubly linked list, using the source and destination IP address fields in the IP
header to hold the forward and backward list pointers. (These two IP addresses are
saved, of course, in the head of the list, since they must be put back into the reassembled datagram. We describe this in Chapter 10.) But if the IP header is in a cluster, as
shown in Figure 2.17, these linked list pointers would be in the cluster, and when the list
is traversed at some later time, the pointer to the IP header (i.e., the pointer to the beginning of the cluster) could not be converted into the pointer to the mbuf. This is the
problem we mentioned earlier in this section: the dtom macro cannot be used if m_data
points into a cluster, because there is no back pointer from the cluster to the mbuf. IP
fragmentation cannot store the links in the cluster as shown in Figure 2.17.

To solve this problem the IP fragmentation routine *always* calls m_pullup when a
fragment is received, if the fragment is contained in a cluster. This forces the 20-byte IP
header into its own mbuf. The code looks like

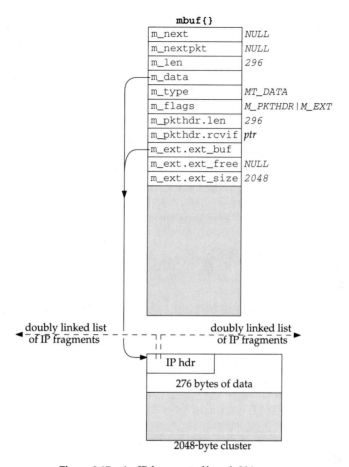

Figure 2.17   An IP fragment of length 296.

```
if (m->m_flags & M_EXT) {
    if ((m = m_pullup(m, sizeof(struct ip))) == 0) {
        ipstat.ips_toosmall++;
        goto next;
    }
    ip = mtod(m, struct ip *);
}
```

Figure 2.18 shows the resulting mbuf chain, after m_pullup is called. m_pullup allocates a new mbuf, prepends it to the chain, and moves the first 40 bytes of data from the cluster into the new mbuf. The reason it moves 40 bytes, and not just the requested 20, is to try to save an additional call at a later time when IP passes the datagram to a higher-layer protocol (e.g., ICMP, IGMP, UDP, or TCP). The magic number 40 (max_protohdr in Figure 7.17) is because the largest protocol header normally encountered is the combination of a 20-byte IP header and a 20-byte TCP header. (This

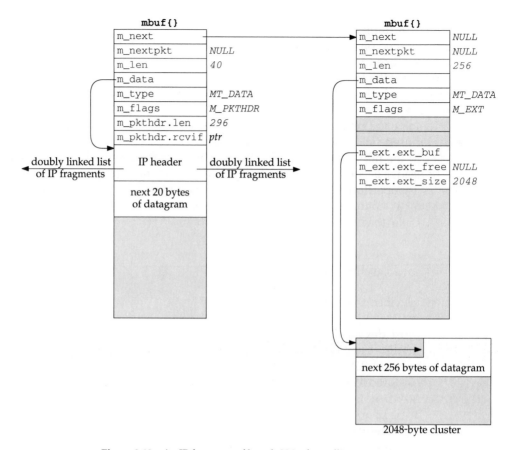

Figure 2.18 An IP fragment of length 296, after calling m_pullup.

assumes that other protocol suites, such as the OSI protocols, are not compiled into the kernel.)

In Figure 2.18 the IP fragmentation algorithm can save a pointer to the IP header contained in the mbuf on the left, and this pointer can be converted into a pointer to the mbuf itself using dtom at a later time.

Avoidance of m_pullup by TCP Reassembly

The reassembly of TCP segments uses a different technique to avoid calling m_pullup. This is because m_pullup is expensive: memory is allocated and data is copied from a cluster to an mbuf. TCP tries to avoid data copying whenever possible.

Chapter 19 of Volume 1 mentions that about one-half of TCP data is bulk data (often 512 or more bytes of data per segment) and the other half is interactive data (of which about 90% of the segments contain less than 10 bytes of data). Hence, when TCP receives segments from IP they are usually in the format shown on the left of Figure 2.14 (a small amount of interactive data, stored in the mbuf itself) or in the format shown in

Figure 2.16 (bulk data, stored in a cluster). When TCP segments arrive out of order, they are stored on a doubly linked list by TCP. As with IP fragmentation, fields in the IP header are used to hold the list pointers, which is OK since these fields are no longer needed once the IP datagram is accepted by TCP. But the same problem arises with the conversion of a list pointer into the corresponding mbuf pointer, when the IP header is stored in a cluster (Figure 2.17).

To solve the problem, we'll see in Section 27.9 that TCP stores the mbuf pointer in some unused fields in the TCP header, providing a back pointer of its own from the cluster to the mbuf, just to avoid calling `m_pullup` for every out-of-order segment. If the IP header is contained in the data portion of the mbuf (Figure 2.18), then this back pointer is superfluous, since the `dtom` macro would work on the list pointer. But if the IP header is contained in a cluster, this back pointer is required. We'll examine the source code that implements this technique when we describe `tcp_reass` in Section 27.9.

Summary of `m_pullup` Usage

We've described three main points about `m_pullup`.

- Most device drivers do not split the first portion of an IP datagram between mbufs. Therefore the possible calls to `m_pullup` that we'll encounter in every protocol (IP, ICMP, IGMP, UDP, and TCP), just to assure that the protocol header is stored contiguously, rarely take place. When these calls to `m_pullup` do occur, it is normally because the IP datagram is too small, in which case `m_pullup` returns an error, the datagram is discarded, and an error counter is incremented.

- `m_pullup` is called for every received IP fragment, when the IP fragment is stored in a cluster. This means that `m_pullup` is called for almost every received fragment, since the length of most fragments is greater than 208 bytes.

- As long as TCP segments are not fragmented by IP, the receipt of a TCP segment, whether it be in order or out of order, should not invoke `m_pullup`. This is one reason to avoid IP fragmentation with TCP.

2.7   Summary of Mbuf Macros and Functions

Figure 2.19 lists the macros and Figure 2.20 lists the functions that we'll encounter in the code that operates on mbufs. The macros in Figure 2.19 are shown as function prototypes, not as `#define` statements, to show the data types of the arguments. We will not go through the source code implementation of these routines since they are concerned primarily with manipulating the mbuf data structures and involve no networking issues. Also, there are additional mbuf macros and functions used elsewhere in the Net/3 sources that we don't show in these two figures since we won't encounter them in the text.

In all the prototypes the argument *nowait* is either M_WAIT or M_DONTWAIT, and the argument *type* is one of the MT_*xxx* constants shown in Figure 2.10.

Macro	Description
MCLGET	Get a cluster (an external buffer) and set the data pointer (m_data) of the existing mbuf pointed to by *m* to point to the cluster. If memory for a cluster is not available, the M_EXT flag in the mbuf is not set on return. void **MCLGET**(struct mbuf *m, int *nowait*);
MFREE	Free the single mbuf pointed to by *m*. If *m* points to a cluster (M_EXT is set), the cluster's reference count is decremented but the cluster is not released until its reference count reaches 0 (as discussed in Section 2.9). On return, the pointer to *m*'s successor (pointed to by m->m_next, which can be null) is stored in *n*. void **MFREE**(struct mbuf *m, struct mbuf *n);
MGETHDR	Allocate an mbuf and initialize it as a packet header. This macro is similar to MGET (Figure 2.12) except the M_PKTHDR flag is set and the data pointer (m_data) points to the 100-byte buffer just beyond the packet header. void **MGETHDR**(struct mbuf *m, int *nowait*, int *type*);
MH_ALIGN	Set the m_data pointer of an mbuf containing a packet header to provide room for an object of size *len* bytes at the end of the mbuf's data area. The data pointer is also longword aligned. void **MH_ALIGN**(struct mbuf *m, int *len*);
M_PREPEND	Prepend *len* bytes of data in front of the data in the mbuf pointed to by *m*. If room exists in the mbuf, just decrement the pointer (m_data) and increment the length (m_len) by *len* bytes. If there is not enough room, a new mbuf is allocated, its m_next pointer is set to *m*, a pointer to the new mbuf is stored in *m*, and the data pointer of the new mbuf is set so that the *len* bytes of data go at the end of the mbuf (i.e., MH_ALIGN is called). Also, if a new mbuf is allocated and the existing mbuf had its packet header flag set, the packet header is moved from the existing mbuf to the new one. void **M_PREPEND**(struct mbuf *m, int *len*, int *nowait*);
dtom	Convert the pointer *x*, which must point somewhere within the data area of an mbuf, into a pointer to the beginning of the mbuf. struct mbuf ***dtom**(void *x);
mtod	Type cast the pointer to the data area of the mbuf pointed to by *m* to *type*. *type* **mtod**(struct mbuf *m, *type*);

Figure 2.19   Mbuf macros that we'll encounter in the text.

As an example of M_PREPEND, this macro was called when the IP and UDP headers were prepended to the user's data in the transition from Figure 1.7 to Figure 1.8, causing another mbuf to be allocated. But when this macro was called again (in the transition from Figure 1.8 to Figure 2.2) to prepend the Ethernet header, room already existed in the mbuf for the headers.

> The data type of the last argument for m_copydata is caddr_t, which stands for "core address." This data type is normally defined in <sys/types.h> to be a char *. It was originally used internally by the kernel, but got externalized when used by certain system calls. For example, the mmap system call, in both 4.4BSD and SVR4, uses caddr_t as the type of the first argument and as the return value type.

Function	Description
m_adj	Remove *len* bytes of data from the mbuf chain pointed to by *m*. If *len* is positive, that number of bytes is trimmed from the start of the data in the mbuf chain, otherwise the absolute value of *len* bytes is trimmed from the end of the data in the mbuf chain. void **m_adj**(struct mbuf *m, int *len*);
m_cat	Concatenate the mbuf chain pointed to by *n* to the end of the mbuf chain pointed to by *m*. We encounter this function when we describe IP reassembly (Chapter 10). void **m_cat**(struct mbuf *m, struct mbuf *n);
m_copy	A three-argument version of m_copym that implies a fourth argument of M_DONTWAIT. struct mbuf ***m_copy**(struct mbuf *m, int *offset*, int *len*);
m_copydata	Copy *len* bytes of data from the mbuf chain pointed to by *m* into the buffer pointed to by *cp*. The copying starts from the specified byte *offset* from the beginning of the data in the mbuf chain. void **m_copydata**(struct mbuf *m, int *offset*, int *len*, caddr_t *cp*);
m_copyback	Copy *len* bytes of data from the buffer pointed to by cp into the mbuf chain pointed to by *m*. The data is stored starting at the specified byte *offset* in the mbuf chain. The mbuf chain is extended with additional mbufs if necessary. void **m_copyback**(struct mbuf *m, int *offset*, int *len*, caddr_t *cp*);
m_copym	Create a new mbuf chain and copy *len* bytes of data starting at *offset* from the mbuf chain pointed to by *m*. A pointer to the new mbuf chain is returned as the value of the function. If *len* equals the constant M_COPYALL, the remainder of the mbuf chain starting at *offset* is copied. We say more about this function in Section 2.9. struct mbuf ***m_copym**(struct mbuf *m, int *offset*, int *len*, int *nowait*);
m_devget	Create a new mbuf chain with a packet header and return the pointer to the chain. The len and rcvif fields in the packet header are set to *len* and *ifp*. The function *copy* is called to copy the data from the device interface (pointed to by *buf*) into the mbuf. If *copy* is a null pointer, the function bcopy is called. *off* is 0 since trailer protocols are no longer supported. We described this function in Section 2.6. struct mbuf ***m_devget**(char *buf*, int *len*, int *off*, struct ifnet *ifp*, void (**copy*)(const void *, void *, u_int));
m_free	A function version of the macro MFREE. struct mbuf ***m_free**(struct mbuf *m);
m_freem	Free all the mbufs in the chain pointed to by *m*. void **m_freem**(struct mbuf *m);
m_get	A function version of the MGET macro. We showed this function in Figure 2.12. struct mbuf ***m_get**(int *nowait*, int *type*);
m_getclr	This function calls the MGET macro to get an mbuf and then zeros the 108-byte buffer. struct mbuf ***m_getclr**(int *nowait*, int *type*);
m_gethdr	A function version of the MGETHDR macro. struct mbuf ***m_gethdr**(int *nowait*, int *type*);
m_pullup	Rearrange the existing data in the mbuf chain pointed to by *m* so that the first *len* bytes of data are stored contiguously in the first mbuf in the chain. If this function succeeds, then the mtod macro returns a pointer that correctly references a structure of size *len*. We described this function in Section 2.6. struct mbuf ***m_pullup**(struct mbuf *m, int *len*);

Figure 2.20 Mbuf functions that we'll encounter in the text.

2.8   Summary of Net/3 Networking Data Structures

This section summarizes the types of data structures we'll encounter in the Net/3 networking code. Other data structures are used in the Net/3 kernel (interested readers should examine the <sys/queue.h> header), but the following are the ones we'll encounter in this text.

1. An mbuf chain: a list of mbufs, linked through the m_next pointer. We've seen numerous examples of these already.

2. A linked list of mbuf chains with a head pointer only. The mbuf chains are linked using the m_nextpkt pointer in the first mbuf of each chain.

    Figure 2.21 shows this type of list. Examples of this data structure are a socket's send buffer and receive buffer.

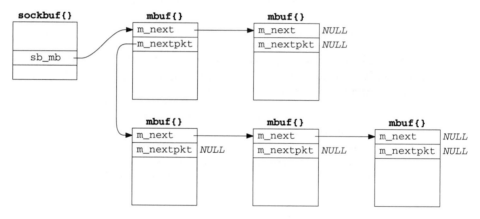

Figure 2.21   Linked list of mbuf chains with head pointer only.

The top two mbufs form the first record on the queue, and the three mbufs on the bottom form the second record on the queue. For a record-based protocol, such as UDP, we can encounter multiple records per queue, but for a protocol such as TCP that has no record boundaries, we'll find only a single record (one mbuf chain possibly consisting of multiple mbufs) per queue.

To append an mbuf to the first record on the queue requires going through all the mbufs comprising the first record, until the one with a null m_next pointer is encountered. To append an mbuf chain comprising a new record to the queue requires going through all the records until the one with a null m_nextpkt pointer is encountered.

3. A linked list of mbuf chains with head and tail pointers.

    Figure 2.22 shows this type of list. We encounter this with the interface queues (Figure 3.13), and showed an earlier example in Figure 2.2.

    The only change in this figure from Figure 2.21 is the addition of a tail pointer, to simplify the addition of new records.

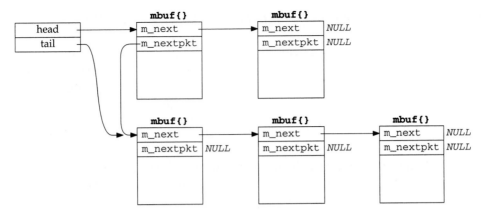

Figure 2.22   Linked list with head and tail pointers.

4.   A doubly linked, circular list.

Figure 2.23 shows this type of list, which we encounter with IP fragmentation and reassembly (Chapter 10), protocol control blocks (Chapter 22), and TCP's out-of-order segment queue (Section 27.9).

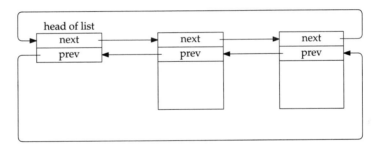

Figure 2.23   Doubly linked, circular list.

The elements in the list are not mbufs—they are structures of some type that are defined with two consecutive pointers: a next pointer followed by a previous pointer. Both pointers must appear at the beginning of the structure. If the list is empty, both the next and previous pointers of the head entry point to the head entry.

For simplicity in the figure we show the back pointers pointing at another back pointer. Obviously all the pointers contain the address of the structure pointed to, that is the address of a forward pointer (since the forward and backward pointer are always at the beginning of the structure).

This type of data structure allows easy traversal either forward or backward, and allows easy insertion or deletion at any point in the list.

The functions insque and remque (Figure 10.20) are called to insert and delete elements in the list.

2.9   `m_copy` and Cluster Reference Counts

One obvious advantage with clusters is being able to reduce the number of mbufs required to contain large amounts of data. For example, if clusters were not used, it would require 10 mbufs to contain 1024 bytes of data: the first one with 100 bytes of data, the next eight with 108 bytes of data each, and the final one with 60 bytes of data. There is more overhead involved in allocating and linking 10 mbufs, than there is in allocating a single mbuf containing the 1024 bytes in a cluster. A disadvantage with clusters is the potential for wasted space. In our example it takes 2176 bytes using a cluster ($2048 + 128$), versus 1280 bytes without a cluster (10×128).

An additional advantage with clusters is being able to share a cluster between multiple mbufs. We encounter this with TCP output and the `m_copy` function, but describe it in more detail now.

As an example, assume the application performs a `write` of 4096 bytes to a TCP socket. Assuming the socket's send buffer was previously empty, and that the receiver's window is at least 4096, the following operations take place. One cluster is filled with the first 2048 bytes by the socket layer and the protocol's send routine is called. The TCP send routine appends the mbuf to its send buffer, as shown in Figure 2.24, and calls `tcp_output`.

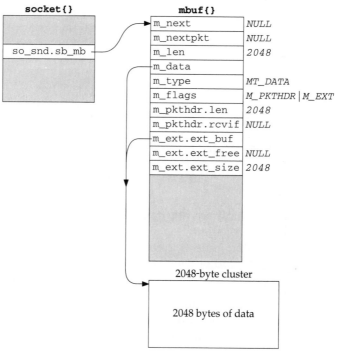

Figure 2.24   TCP socket send buffer containing 2048 bytes of data.

The `socket` structure contains the `sockbuf` structure, which holds the head of the list of mbufs in the send buffer: `so_snd.sb_mb`.

Assuming a TCP maximum segment size (MSS) of 1460 for this connection (typical for an Ethernet), `tcp_output` builds a segment to send containing the first 1460 bytes of data. It also builds an mbuf containing the IP and TCP headers, leaves room for a link-layer header (16 bytes), and passes this mbuf chain to IP output. The mbuf chain ends up on the interface's output queue, which we show in Figure 2.25.

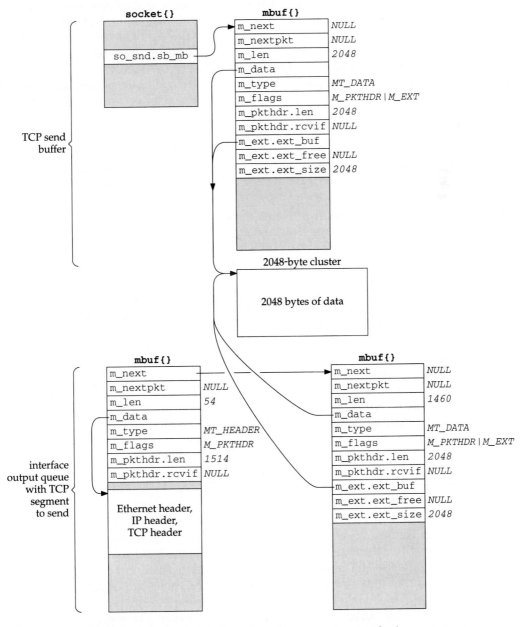

Figure 2.25 TCP socket send buffer and resulting segment on interface's output queue.

In our UDP example in Section 1.9, UDP took the mbuf chain containing the datagram, prepended an mbuf for the protocol headers, and passed the chain to IP output. UDP did not keep the mbuf in its send buffer. TCP cannot do this since TCP is a reliable protocol and it must maintain a *copy* of the data that it sends, until the data is acknowledged by the other end.

In this example tcp_output calls the function m_copy, requesting a copy be made of 1460 bytes, starting at offset 0 from the start of its send buffer. But since the data is in a cluster, m_copy creates an mbuf (the one on the lower right of Figure 2.25) and initializes it to point to the correct place in the existing cluster (the beginning of the cluster in this example). The length of this mbuf is 1460, even though an additional 588 bytes of data are in the cluster. We show the length of the mbuf chain as 1514, accounting for the Ethernet, IP, and TCP headers.

> We also show this mbuf on the lower right of Figure 2.25 containing a packet header, yet this isn't the first mbuf in the chain. When m_copy makes a copy of an mbuf that contains a packet header and the copy starts from offset 0 in the original mbuf, the packet header is also copied verbatim. Since this mbuf is not the first mbuf in the chain, this extraneous packet header is just ignored. The m_pkthdr.len value of 2048 in this extraneous packet header is also ignored.

This sharing of clusters prevents the kernel from copying the data from one mbuf into another—a big savings. It is implemented by providing a reference count for each cluster that is incremented each time another mbuf points to the cluster, and decremented each time a cluster is released. Only when the reference count reaches 0 is the memory used by the cluster available for some other use. (See Exercise 2.4.)

For example, when the bottom mbuf chain in Figure 2.25 reaches the Ethernet device driver and its contents have been copied to the device, the driver calls m_freem. This function releases the first mbuf with the protocol headers and then notices that the second mbuf in the chain points to a cluster. The cluster reference count is decremented, but since its value becomes 1, it is left alone. It cannot be released since it is still in the TCP send buffer.

Continuing our example, tcp_output returns after passing the 1460-byte segment to IP, since the remaining 588 bytes in the send buffer don't comprise a full-sized segment. (In Chapter 26 we describe in detail the conditions under which tcp_output sends data.) The socket layer continues processing the data from the application: the remaining 2048 bytes are placed into an mbuf with a cluster, TCP's send routine is called again, and this new mbuf is appended to the socket's send buffer. Since a full-sized segment can be sent, tcp_output builds another mbuf chain with the protocol headers and the next 1460 bytes of data. The arguments to m_copy specify a starting offset of 1460 bytes from the start of the send buffer and a length of 1460 bytes. This is shown in Figure 2.26, assuming the mbuf chain is again on the interface output queue (so the length of the first mbuf in the chain reflects the Ethernet, IP, and TCP headers).

This time the 1460 bytes of data come from two clusters: the first 588 bytes are from the first cluster in the send buffer and the next 872 bytes are from the second cluster in the send buffer. It takes two mbufs to describe these 1460 bytes, but again m_copy does not copy the 1460 bytes of data—it references the existing clusters.

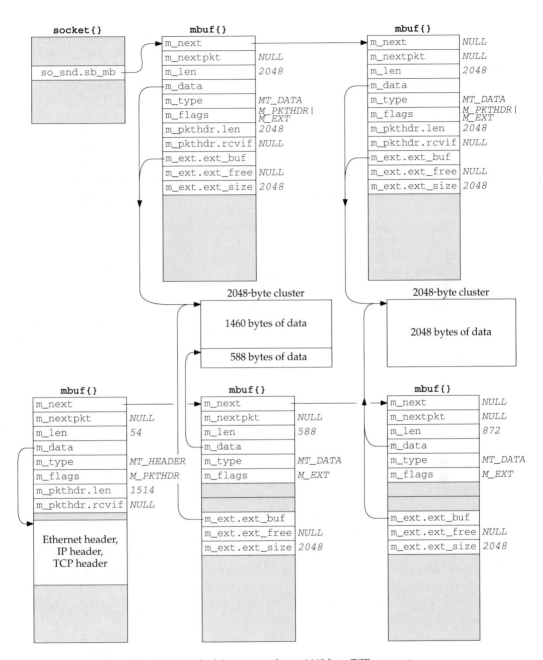

Figure 2.26 Mbuf chain to send next 1460-byte TCP segment.

This time we do not show a packet header with either of the mbufs on the bottom right of Figure 2.26. The reason is that the starting offset in the call to m_copy is nonzero. Also, we show the second mbuf in the socket send buffer containing a packet header, even though it is not the first mbuf in the chain. This is a property of the sosend function, and this extraneous packet header is just ignored.

We encounter the m_copy function about a dozen times throughout the text. Although the name implies that a physical copy is made of the data, if the data is contained in a cluster, an additional reference is made to the cluster instead.

2.10   Alternatives

Mbufs are far from perfect and they are berated regularly. Nevertheless, they form the basis for all the Berkeley-derived networking code in use today.

A research implementation of the Internet protocols by Van Jacobson [Partridge 1993] has done away with the complex mbuf data structures in favor of large contiguous buffers. [Jacobson 1993] claims a speed improvement of one to two orders of magnitude, although many other changes were made besides getting rid of mbufs.

The complexity of mbufs is a tradeoff that avoids allocating large fixed buffers that are rarely filled to capacity. At the time mbufs were being designed, a VAX-11/780 with 4 megabytes of memory was a big system, and memory was an expensive resource that needed to be carefully allocated. Today memory is inexpensive, and the focus has shifted toward higher performance and simplicity of code.

The performance of mbufs is also dependent on the amount of data stored in the mbuf. [Hutchinson and Peterson 1991] show that the amount of time required for mbuf processing is nonlinear with respect to the amount of data.

2.11   Summary

We'll encounter mbufs in almost every function in the text. Their main purpose is to hold the user data that travels from the process to the network interface, and vice versa, but mbufs are also used to contain a variety of other miscellaneous data: source and destination addresses, socket options, and so on.

There are four types of mbufs, depending whether the M_PKTHDR and M_EXT flags are on or off:

- no packet header, with 0 to 108 bytes of data in mbuf itself,
- packet header, with 0 to 100 bytes of data in mbuf itself,
- no packet header, with data in cluster (external buffer), and
- packet header, with data in cluster (external buffer).

We looked at the source code for a few of the mbuf macros and functions, but did not present the source code for all the mbuf routines. Figures 2.19 and 2.20 provide the function prototypes and descriptions of all the mbuf routines that we encounter in the text.

We looked at the operation of two functions that we'll encounter: m_devget, which is called by many network device drivers to store a received frame; and m_pullup, which is called by all the input routines to place the required protocol headers into contiguous storage in an mbuf.

The clusters (external buffers) pointed to by an mbuf can be shared by m_copy. This is used, for example, by TCP output, because a copy of the data being transmitted must be maintained by the sender until that data is acknowledged by the other end. Sharing clusters through reference counts is a performance improvement over making a physical copy of the data.

Exercises

2.1   In Figure 2.9 the M_COPYFLAGS value was defined. Why was the M_EXT flag not copied?

2.2   In Section 2.6 we listed two reasons that m_pullup can fail. There are really three reasons. Obtain the source code for this function (Appendix B) and discover the additional reason.

2.3   To avoid the problems we described in Section 2.6 with the dtom macro when the data is in a cluster, why not just add a back pointer to the mbuf for each cluster?

2.4   Since the size of an mbuf cluster is a power of 2 (typically 1024 or 2048), space cannot be taken within the cluster for the reference count. Obtain the Net/3 sources (Appendix B) and determine where these reference counts are stored.

2.5   In Figure 2.5 we noted that the two counters m_drops and m_wait are not currently implemented. Modify the mbuf routines to increment these counters when appropriate.

3

Interface Layer

3.1 Introduction

This chapter starts our discussion of Net/3 at the bottom of the protocol stack with the interface layer, which includes the hardware and software that sends and receives packets on locally attached networks.

We use the term *device driver* to refer to the software that communicates with the hardware and *network interface* (or just *interface*) for the hardware and device driver for a particular network.

The Net/3 interface layer attempts to provide a hardware-independent programming interface between the network protocols and the drivers for the network devices connected to a system. The interface layer provides for all devices:

- a well-defined set of interface functions,
- a standard set of statistics and control flags,
- a device-independent method of storing protocol addresses, and
- a standard queueing method for outgoing packets.

There is no requirement that the interface layer provide reliable delivery of packets, only a best-effort service is required. Higher protocol layers must compensate for this lack of reliability. This chapter describes the generic data structures maintained for all network interfaces. To illustrate the relevant data structures and algorithms, we refer to three particular network interfaces from Net/3:

1. An AMD 7990 LANCE Ethernet interface: an example of a broadcast-capable local area network.

2. A Serial Line IP (SLIP) interface: an example of a point-to-point network running over asynchronous serial lines.

3. A loopback interface: a logical network that returns all outgoing packets as input packets.

3.2   Code Introduction

The generic interface structures and initialization code are found in three headers and two C files. The device-specific initialization code described in this chapter is found in three different C files. All eight files are listed in Figure 3.1.

File	Description
`sys/socket.h`	address structure definitions
`net/if.h`	interface structure definitions
`net/if_dl.h`	link-level structure definitions
`kern/init_main.c`	system and interface initialization
`net/if.c`	generic interface code
`net/if_loop.c`	loopback device driver
`net/if_sl.c`	SLIP device driver
`hp300/dev/if_le.c`	LANCE Ethernet device driver

Figure 3.1   Files discussed in this chapter.

Global Variables

The global variables introduced in this chapter are described in Figure 3.2.

Variable	Data type	Description
pdevinit	struct pdevinit []	array of initialization parameters for pseudo-devices such as SLIP and loopback interfaces
ifnet	struct ifnet *	head of list of ifnet structures
ifnet_addrs	struct ifaddr **	array of pointers to link-level interface addresses
if_indexlim	int	size of ifnet_addrs array
if_index	int	index of the last configured interface
ifqmaxlen	int	maximum size of interface output queues
hz	int	the clock-tick frequency for this system (ticks/second)

Figure 3.2   Global variables introduced in this chapter.

SNMP Variables

The Net/3 kernel collects a wide variety of networking statistics. In most chapters we summarize the statistics and show how they relate to the standard TCP/IP information and statistics defined in the Simple Network Management Protocol Management Information Base (SNMP MIB-II). RFC 1213 [McCloghrie and Rose 1991] describe SNMP MIB-II, which is organized into 10 distinct information groups shown in Figure 3.3.

SNMP Group	Description
System	general information about the system
Interfaces	network interface information
Address Translation	network-address-to-hardware-address- translation tables (deprecated)
IP	IP protocol information
ICMP	ICMP protocol information
TCP	TCP protocol information
UDP	UDP protocol information
EGP	EGP protocol information
Transmission	media-specific information
SNMP	SNMP protocol information

Figure 3.3   SNMP groups in MIB-II.

Net/3 does not include an SNMP agent. Instead, an SNMP agent for Net/3 is implemented as a process that accesses the kernel statistics in response to SNMP queries through the mechanism described in Section 2.2.

While most of the MIB-II variables are collected by Net/3 and may be accessed directly by an SNMP agent, others must be derived indirectly. MIB-II variables fall into three categories: (1) simple variables such as an integer value, a timestamp, or a byte string; (2) lists of simple variables such as an individual routing entry or an interface description entry; and (3) lists of lists such as the entire routing table and the list of all interface entries.

> The ISODE package includes a sample SNMP agent for Net/3. See Appendix B for information about ISODE.

Figure 3.4 shows the one simple variable maintained for the SNMP interface group. We describe the SNMP interface table later in Figure 4.7.

SNMP variable	Net/3 variable	Description
ifNumber	if_index + 1	if_index is the index of the last interface in the system and starts at 0; 1 is added to get ifNumber, the number of interfaces in the system.

Figure 3.4   Simple SNMP variable in the interface group.

3.3   ifnet Structure

The ifnet structure contains information common to all interfaces. During system initialization, a separate ifnet structure is allocated for each network device. Every ifnet structure has a list of one or more protocol addresses associated with it. Figure 3.5 illustrates the relationship between an interface and its addresses.

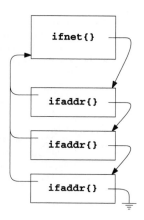

Figure 3.5   Each ifnet structure has a list of associated ifaddr structures.

The interface in Figure 3.5 is shown with three protocol addresses stored in ifaddr structures. Although some network interfaces, such as SLIP, support only a single protocol, others, such as Ethernet, support multiple protocols and need multiple addresses. For example, a system may use a single Ethernet interface for both Internet and OSI protocols. A type field identifies the contents of each Ethernet frame, and since the Internet and OSI protocols employ different addressing schemes, the Ethernet interface must have an Internet address and an OSI address. All the addresses are connected by a linked list (the arrows on the right of Figure 3.5), and each contains a back pointer to the related ifnet structure (the arrows on the left of Figure 3.5).

It is also possible for a single network interface to support multiple addresses within a single protocol. For example, two Internet addresses may be assigned to a single Ethernet interface in Net/3.

> This feature first appeared in Net/2. Having two IP addresses for an interface is useful when renumbering a network. During a transition period, the interface can accept packets addressed to the old and new addresses.

The ifnet structure is large so we describe it in five sections:

- implementation information,
- hardware information,
- interface statistics,
- function pointers, and
- the output queue.

Figure 3.6 shows the implementation information contained in the ifnet structure.

80–82   if_next joins the ifnet structures for all the interfaces into a linked list. The if_attach function constructs the list during system initialization. if_addrlist points to the list of ifaddr structures for the interface (Figure 3.16). Each ifaddr structure holds addressing information for a protocol that expects to communicate through the interface.

```
                                                                                   ── if.h
80 struct ifnet {
81     struct ifnet *if_next;        /* all struct ifnets are chained */
82     struct ifaddr *if_addrlist;   /* linked list of addresses per if */
83     char    *if_name;             /* name, e.g. 'le' or 'lo' */
84     short   if_unit;              /* sub-unit for lower level driver */
85     u_short if_index;             /* numeric abbreviation for this if  */
86     short   if_flags;             /* Figure 3.7 */
87     short   if_timer;             /* time 'til if_watchdog called */
88     int     if_pcount;            /* number of promiscuous listeners */
89     caddr_t if_bpf;               /* packet filter structure */
                                                                                   ── if.h
```

Figure 3.6   ifnet structure: implementation information.

Common interface information

83–86   if_name is a short string that identifies the interface type, and if_unit identifies
multiple instances of the same type. For example, if a system had two SLIP interfaces,
both would have an if_name consisting of the 2 bytes "sl" and an if_unit of 0 for
the first interface and 1 for the second. if_index uniquely identifies the interface
within the kernel and is used by the sysctl system call (Section 19.14) as well as in the
routing domain.

> Sometimes an interface is not uniquely identified by a protocol address. For example, several
> SLIP connections can have the same local IP address. In these cases, if_index specifies the
> interface explicitly.

if_flags specifies the operational state and properties of the interface. A process
can examine all the flags but cannot change the flags marked in the "Kernel only" column in Figure 3.7. The flags are accessed with the SIOCGIFFLAGS and SIOCSIFFLAGS
commands described in Section 4.4.

if_flags	Kernel only	Description
IFF_BROADCAST	•	the interface is for a broadcast network
IFF_MULTICAST	•	the interface supports multicasting
IFF_POINTOPOINT	•	the interface is for a point-to-point network
IFF_LOOPBACK		the interface is for a loopback network
IFF_OACTIVE	•	a transmission is in progress
IFF_RUNNING	•	resources are allocated for this interface
IFF_SIMPLEX	•	the interface cannot receive its own transmissions
IFF_LINK0	see text	defined by device driver
IFF_LINK1	see text	defined by device driver
IFF_LINK2	see text	defined by device driver
IFF_ALLMULTI		the interface is receiving all multicast packets
IFF_DEBUG		debugging is enabled for the interface
IFF_NOARP		don't use ARP on this interface
IFF_NOTRAILERS		avoid using trailer encapsulation
IFF_PROMISC		the interface receives all network packets
IFF_UP		the interface is operating

Figure 3.7   if_flags values.

The IFF_BROADCAST and IFF_POINTOPOINT flags are mutually exclusive.

The macro IFF_CANTCHANGE is a bitwise OR of all the flags in the "Kernel only" column.

The device-specific flags (IFF_LINK*x*) may or may not be modifiable by a process depending on the device. For example, Figure 3.29 shows how these flags are defined by the SLIP driver.

Interface timer

87   if_timer is the time in seconds until the kernel calls the if_watchdog function for the interface. This function may be used by the device driver to collect interface statistics at regular intervals or to reset hardware that isn't operating correctly.

BSD Packet Filter

88–89   The next two members, if_pcount and if_bpf, support the *BSD Packet Filter* (BPF). Through BPF, a process can receive copies of packets transmitted or received by an interface. As we discuss the device drivers, we also describe how packets are passed to BPF. BPF itself is described in Chapter 31.

The next section of the ifnet structure, shown in Figure 3.8, describes the hardware characteristics of the interface.

```
                                                                           ── if.h
90     struct if_data {
91 /* generic interface information */
92          u_char  ifi_type;       /* Figure 3.9 */
93          u_char  ifi_addrlen;    /* media address length */
94          u_char  ifi_hdrlen;     /* media header length */
95          u_long  ifi_mtu;        /* maximum transmission unit */
96          u_long  ifi_metric;     /* routing metric (external only) */
97          u_long  ifi_baudrate;   /* linespeed */

                          /* other ifnet members */

138 #define if_mtu      if_data.ifi_mtu
139 #define if_type     if_data.ifi_type
140 #define if_addrlen  if_data.ifi_addrlen
141 #define if_hdrlen   if_data.ifi_hdrlen
142 #define if_metric   if_data.ifi_metric
143 #define if_baudrate if_data.ifi_baudrate
                                                                           ── if.h
```

Figure 3.8   ifnet structure: interface characteristics.

Net/3 and this text use the short names provided by the #define statements on lines 138 through 143 to specify the ifnet members.

Interface characteristics

90–92   if_type specifies the hardware address type supported by the interface. Figure 3.9 lists several common values from net/if_types.h.

if_type	Description
IFT_OTHER	unspecified
IFT_ETHER	Ethernet
IFT_ISO88023	IEEE 802.3 Ethernet (CMSA/CD)
IFT_ISO88025	IEEE 802.5 token ring
IFT_FDDI	Fiber Distributed Data Interface
IFT_LOOP	loopback interface
IFT_SLIP	serial line IP

Figure 3.9   if_type: data-link types.

93–94   if_addrlen is the length of the datalink address and if_hdrlen is the length of
the header attached to any outgoing packet by the hardware. An Ethernet network, for
example, has an address length of 6 bytes and a header length of 14 bytes (Figure 4.8).

95   if_mtu is the maximum transmission unit of the interface: the size in bytes of the
largest unit of data that the interface can transmit in a single output operation. This is
an important parameter that controls the size of packets created by the network and
transport protocols. For Ethernet, the value is 1500.

96–97   if_metric is usually 0; a higher value makes routes through the interface less
favorable. if_baudrate specifies the transmission speed of the interface. It is set only
by the SLIP interface.

Interface statistics are collected by the next group of members in the ifnet structure shown in Figure 3.10.

Interface statistics

98–111   Most of these statistics are self-explanatory. if_collisions is incremented when
packet transmission is interrupted by another transmission on shared media such as
Ethernet. if_noproto counts the number of packets that can't be processed because
the protocol is not supported by the system or the interface (e.g., an OSI packet that
arrives at a system that supports only IP). The SLIP interface increments if_noproto
if a non-IP packet is placed on its output queue.

> These statistics were not part of the ifnet structure in Net/1. They were added to support
> the standard SNMP MIB-II variables for interfaces.
>
> if_iqdrops is accessed only by the SLIP device driver. SLIP and the other network drivers
> increment if_snd.ifq_drops (Figure 3.13) when IF_DROP is called. ifq_drops was
> already in the BSD software when the SNMP statistics were added. The ISODE SNMP agent
> ignores if_iqdrops and uses ifsnd.ifq_drops.

Change timestamp

112–113   if_lastchange records the last time any of the statistics were changed.

—— *if.h*
```
 98  /* volatile statistics */
 99         u_long  ifi_ipackets;   /* #packets received on interface */
100         u_long  ifi_ierrors;    /* #input errors on interface */
101         u_long  ifi_opackets;   /* #packets sent on interface */
102         u_long  ifi_oerrors;    /* #output errors on interface */
103         u_long  ifi_collisions; /* #collisions on csma interfaces */
104         u_long  ifi_ibytes;     /* #bytes received */
105         u_long  ifi_obytes;     /* #bytes sent */
106         u_long  ifi_imcasts;    /* #packets received via multicast */
107         u_long  ifi_omcasts;    /* #packets sent via multicast */
108         u_long  ifi_iqdrops;    /* #packets dropped on input, for this
109                                     interface */
110         u_long  ifi_noproto;    /* #packets destined for unsupported
111                                     protocol */
112         struct timeval ifi_lastchange;  /* last updated */
113     } if_data;
```
```

                            /* other ifnet members */

```
```
144  #define if_ipackets if_data.ifi_ipackets
145  #define if_ierrors  if_data.ifi_ierrors
146  #define if_opackets if_data.ifi_opackets
147  #define if_oerrors  if_data.ifi_oerrors
148  #define if_collisions   if_data.ifi_collisions
149  #define if_ibytes   if_data.ifi_ibytes
150  #define if_obytes   if_data.ifi_obytes
151  #define if_imcasts  if_data.ifi_imcasts
152  #define if_omcasts  if_data.ifi_omcasts
153  #define if_iqdrops  if_data.ifi_iqdrops
154  #define if_noproto  if_data.ifi_noproto
155  #define if_lastchange   if_data.ifi_lastchange
```
—— *if.h*

Figure 3.10   ifnet structure: interface statistics.

Once again, Net/3 and this text use the short names provided by the #define statements on lines 144 through 155 to specify the ifnet members.

The next section of the ifnet structure, shown in Figure 3.11, contains pointers to the standard interface-layer functions, which isolate device-specific details from the network layer. Each network interface implements these functions as appropriate for the particular device.

Interface functions

114–129   Each device driver initializes its own ifnet structure, including the seven function pointers, at system initialization time. Figure 3.12 describes the generic functions.

We will see the comment /* XXX */ throughout Net/3. It is a warning to the reader that the code is obscure, contains nonobvious side effects, or is a quick solution to a more difficult problem. In this case, it indicates that if_done is not used in Net/3.

if.h

```
114 /* procedure handles */
115     int     (*if_init)          /* init routine */
116             (int);
117     int     (*if_output)        /* output routine (enqueue) */
118             (struct ifnet *, struct mbuf *, struct sockaddr *,
119              struct rtentry *);
120     int     (*if_start)         /* initiate output routine */
121             (struct ifnet *);
122     int     (*if_done)          /* output complete routine */
123             (struct ifnet *);   /* (XXX not used; fake prototype) */
124     int     (*if_ioctl)         /* ioctl routine */
125             (struct ifnet *, int, caddr_t);
126     int     (*if_reset)
127             (int);              /* new autoconfig will permit removal */
128     int     (*if_watchdog)      /* timer routine */
129             (int);
```

if.h

Figure 3.11   ifnet structure: interface procedures.

Function	Description
if_init	initialize the interface
if_output	queue outgoing packets for transmission
if_start	initiate transmission of packets
if_done	cleanup after transmission completes (not used)
if_ioctl	process I/O control commands
if_reset	reset the interface device
if_watchdog	periodic interface routine

Figure 3.12   ifnet structure: function pointers.

In Chapter 4 we look at the device-specific functions for the Ethernet, SLIP, and loopback interfaces, which the kernel calls indirectly through the pointers in the ifnet structure. For example, if ifp points to an ifnet structure,

```
(*ifp->if_start)(ifp)
```

calls the if_start function of the device driver associated with the interface.

The remaining member of the ifnet structure is the output queue for the interface and is shown in Figure 3.13.

if.h

```
130     struct ifqueue {
131         struct mbuf *ifq_head;
132         struct mbuf *ifq_tail;
133         int     ifq_len;        /* current length of queue */
134         int     ifq_maxlen;     /* maximum length of queue */
135         int     ifq_drops;      /* packets dropped because of full queue */
136     } if_snd;                   /* output queue */
137 };
```

if.h

Figure 3.13   ifnet structure: the output queue.

130–137   if_snd is the queue of outgoing packets for the interface. Each interface has its own ifnet structure and therefore its own output queue. ifq_head points to the first packet on the queue (the next one to be output), ifq_tail points to the last packet on the queue, if_len is the number of packets currently on the queue, and ifq_maxlen is the maximum number of buffers allowed on the queue. This maximum is set to 50 (from the global integer ifqmaxlen, which is initialized at compile time from IFQ_MAXLEN) unless the driver changes it. The queue is implemented as a linked list of mbuf chains. ifq_drops counts the number of packets discarded because the queue was full. Figure 3.14 lists the macros and functions that access a queue.

Function	Description
IF_QFULL	Is *ifq* full? int **IF_QFULL**(struct ifqueue **ifq*);
IF_DROP	IF_DROP only increments the ifq_drops counter associated with *ifq*. The name is misleading; the *caller* drops the packet. void **IF_DROP**(struct ifqueue **ifq*);
IF_ENQUEUE	Add the packet *m* to the end of the *ifq* queue. Packets are linked together by m_nextpkt in the mbuf header. void **IF_ENQUEUE**(struct ifqueue **ifq*, struct mbuf **m*);
IF_PREPEND	Insert the packet *m* at the front of the *ifq* queue. void **IF_PREPEND**(struct ifqueue **ifq*, struct mbuf **m*);
IF_DEQUEUE	Take the first packet off the *ifq* queue. *m* points to the dequeued packet or is null if the queue was empty. void **IF_DEQUEUE**(struct ifqueue **ifq*, struct mbuf **m*);
if_qflush	Discard all packets on the queue *ifq*, for example, when an interface is shut down. void **if_qflush**(struct ifqueue **ifq*);

Figure 3.14   ifqueue routines.

The first five routines are macros defined in net/if.h and the last routine, if_qflush, is a function defined in net/if.c. The macros often appear in sequences such as:

```
s = splimp();
if (IF_QFULL(inq)) {
    IF_DROP(inq);        /* queue is full, drop new packet */
    m_freem(m);
} else
    IF_ENQUEUE(inq, m);  /* there is room, add to end of queue */
splx(s);
```

This code fragment attempts to add a packet to the queue. If the queue is full, IF_DROP increments ifq_drops and the packet is discarded. Reliable protocols such as TCP

will retransmit discarded packets. Applications using an unreliable protocol such as
UDP must detect and handle the retransmission on their own.

Access to the queue is bracketed by splimp and splx to block network interrupts
and to prevent the network interrupt service routines from accessing the queue while it
is in an indeterminate state.

> m_freem is called before splx because the mbuf code has a critical section that runs at
> splimp. It would be wasted effort to call splx before m_freem only to enter another critical
> section during m_freem (Section 2.5).

3.4   ifaddr Structure

The next structure we look at is the interface address structure, ifaddr, shown in Figure 3.15. Each interface maintains a linked list of ifaddr structures because some data
links, such as Ethernet, support more than one protocol. A separate ifaddr structure
describes each address assigned to the interface, usually one address per protocol.
Another reason to support multiple addresses is that many protocols, including TCP/IP,
support multiple addresses assigned to a single physical interface. Although Net/3
supports this feature, many implementations of TCP/IP do not.

```
                                                                                   if.h
217 struct ifaddr {
218         struct  ifaddr *ifa_next;      /* next address for interface */
219         struct  ifnet *ifa_ifp;        /* back-pointer to interface */
220         struct  sockaddr *ifa_addr;    /* address of interface */
221         struct  sockaddr *ifa_dstaddr; /* other end of p-to-p link */
222 #define ifa_broadaddr   ifa_dstaddr    /* broadcast address interface */
223         struct  sockaddr *ifa_netmask; /* used to determine subnet */
224         void    (*ifa_rtrequest)();    /* check or clean routes */
225         u_short ifa_flags;             /* mostly rt_flags for cloning */
226         short   ifa_refcnt;            /* references to this structure */
227         int     ifa_metric;            /* cost for this interface */
228 };
                                                                                   if.h
```

Figure 3.15   ifaddr structure.

217–219   The ifaddr structure links all addresses assigned to an interface together by
ifa_next and contains a pointer, ifa_ifp, back to the interface's ifnet structure.
Figure 3.16 shows the relationship between the ifnet structures and the ifaddr structures.

220   ifa_addr points to a protocol address for the interface and ifa_netmask points
to a bit mask that selects the network portion of ifa_addr. Bits that represent the network portion of the address are set to 1 in the mask, and the host portion of the address
is set to all 0 bits. Both addresses are stored as sockaddr structures (Section 3.5). Figure 3.38 shows an address and its related mask structure. For IP addresses, the mask
selects the network and subnet portions of the IP address.

221–223   ifa_dstaddr (or its alias ifa_broadaddr) points to the protocol address of the
interface at the other end of a point-to-point link or to the broadcast address assigned to

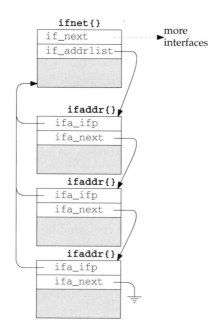

Figure 3.16   ifnet and ifaddr structures.

the interface on a broadcast network such as Ethernet. The mutually exclusive flags
IFF_BROADCAST and IFF_POINTOPOINT (Figure 3.7) in the interface's ifnet structure specify the applicable name.

224–228   ifa_rtrequest, ifa_flags, and ifa_metric support routing lookups for the
interface.

ifa_refcnt counts references to the ifaddr structure. The macro IFAFREE only
releases the structure when the reference count drops to 0, such as when addresses are
deleted with the SIOCDIFADDR ioctl command. The ifaddr structures are refer-
ence-counted because they are shared by the interface and routing data structures.

> IFAFREE decrements the counter and returns if there are other references. This is the common
> case and avoids a function call overhead for all but the last reference. If this is the last refer-
> ence, IFAFREE calls the function ifafree, which releases the structure.

3.5   sockaddr **Structure**

Addressing information for an interface consists of more than a single host address.
Net/3 maintains host, broadcast, and network masks in structures derived from a
generic sockaddr structure. By using a generic structure, hardware and protocol-
specific addressing details are hidden from the interface layer.

Figure 3.17 shows the current definition of the structure as well as the definition
from earlier BSD releases—an osockaddr structure.

```
                                                                      socket.h
120 struct sockaddr {
121     u_char  sa_len;              /* total length */
122     u_char  sa_family;          /* address family (Figure 3.19) */
123     char    sa_data[14];        /* actually longer; address value */
124 };

271 struct osockaddr {
272     u_short sa_family;          /* address family (Figure 3.19) */
273     char    sa_data[14];        /* up to 14 bytes of direct address */
274 };
                                                                      socket.h
```

Figure 3.17   sockaddr and osockaddr structures.

Figure 3.18 illustrates the organization of these structures.

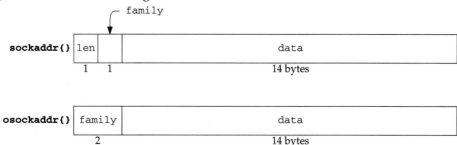

Figure 3.18   sockaddr and osockaddr structures (sa_ prefix dropped).

In many figures, we omit the common prefix in member names. In this case, we've dropped the sa_ prefix.

sockaddr structure

120–124 Every protocol has its own address format. Net/3 handles generic addresses in a sockaddr structure. sa_len specifies the length of the address (OSI and Unix domain protocols have variable-length addresses) and sa_family specifies the type of address. Figure 3.19 lists the *address family* constants that we encounter.

sa_family	Protocol
AF_INET	Internet
AF_ISO, AF_OSI	OSI
AF_UNIX	Unix
AF_ROUTE	routing table
AF_LINK	data link
AF_UNSPEC	(see text)

Figure 3.19   sa_family constants.

The contents of a sockaddr when AF_UNSPEC is specified depends on the context. In most cases, it contains an Ethernet hardware address.

The sa_len and sa_family members allow protocol-independent code to manipulate variable-length sockaddr structures from multiple protocol families. The remaining member, sa_data, contains the address in a protocol-dependent format. sa_data is defined to be an array of 14 bytes, but when the sockaddr structure overlays a larger area of memory sa_data may be up to 253 bytes long. sa_len is only a single byte, so the size of the entire address including sa_len and sa_family must be less than 256 bytes.

> This is a common C technique that allows the programmer to consider the last member in a structure to have a variable length.

Each protocol defines a specialized sockaddr structure that duplicates the sa_len and sa_family members but defines the sa_data member as required for that protocol. The address stored in sa_data is a transport address; it contains enough information to identify multiple communication end points on the same host. In Chapter 6 we look at the Internet address structure sockaddr_in, which consists of an IP address and a port number.

osockaddr structure

271–274   The osockaddr structure is the definition of a sockaddr before the 4.3BSD Reno release. Since the length of an address was not explicitly available in this definition, it was not possible to write protocol-independent code to handle variable-length addresses. The desire to include the OSI protocols, which utilize variable-length addresses, motivated the change in the sockaddr definition seen in Net/3. The osockaddr structure is supported for binary compatibility with previously compiled programs.

> We have omitted the binary compatibility code from this text.

3.6   ifnet and ifaddr Specialization

The ifnet and ifaddr structures contain general information applicable to all network interfaces and protocol addresses. To accommodate additional device and protocol-specific information, each driver defines and each protocol allocates a specialized version of the ifnet and ifaddr structures. These specialized structures always contain an ifnet or ifaddr structure as their first member so that the common information can be accessed without consideration for the additional specialized information.

Most device drivers handle multiple interfaces of the same type by allocating an array of its specialized ifnet structures, but others (such as the loopback driver) handle only one interface. Figure 3.20 shows the arrangement of specialized ifnet structures for our sample interfaces.

Notice that each device's structure begins with an ifnet structure, followed by all the device-dependent data. The loopback interface declares only an ifnet structure, since it doesn't require any device-dependent data. We show the Ethernet and SLIP driver's softc structures with the array index of 0 in Figure 3.20 since both drivers

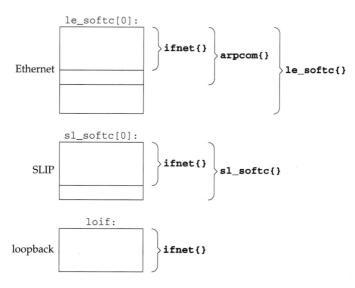

Figure 3.20   Arrangement of ifnet structures within device-dependent structures.

support multiple interfaces. The maximum number of interfaces of any given type is limited by a configuration parameter when the kernel is built.

The arpcom structure (Figure 3.26) is common to all Ethernet drivers and contains information for the Address Resolution Protocol (ARP) and Ethernet multicasting. The le_softc structure (Figure 3.25) contains additional information unique to the LANCE Ethernet device driver.

Each protocol stores addressing information for each interface in a list of specialized ifaddr structures. The Internet protocols use an in_ifaddr structure (Section 6.5) and the OSI protocols an iso_ifaddr structure. In addition to protocol addresses, the kernel assigns each interface a *link-level address* when the interface is initialized, which identifies the interface within the kernel.

The kernel constructs the link-level address by allocating memory for an ifaddr structure and two sockaddr_dl structures—one for the link-level address itself and one for the link-level address mask. The sockaddr_dl structures are accessed by OSI, ARP, and the routing algorithms. Figure 3.21 shows an Ethernet interface with a link-level address, an Internet address, and an OSI address. The construction and initialization of the link-level address (the ifaddr and the two sockaddr_dl structures) is described in Section 3.11.

3.7   Network Initialization Overview

All the structures we have described are allocated and attached to each other during kernel initialization. In this section we give a broad overview of the initialization steps. In later sections we describe the specific device- and protocol-initialization steps.

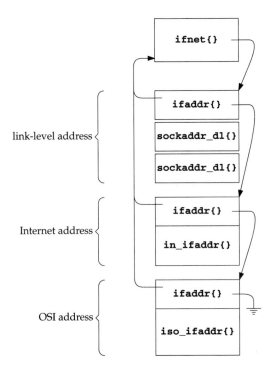

Figure 3.21   An interface address list containing link-level, Internet, and OSI addresses.

Some devices, such as the SLIP and loopback interfaces, are implemented entirely in software. These *pseudo-devices* are represented by a pdevinit structure (Figure 3.22) stored in the global pdevinit array. The array is constructed during kernel configuration. For example:

```
struct pdevinit pdevinit[] = {
    { slattach, 1 },
    { loopattach, 1 },
    { 0, 0 }
};
```

─── device.h
```
120 struct pdevinit {
121     void    (*pdev_attach) (int);    /* attach function */
122     int     pdev_count;              /* number of devices */
123 };
```
─── device.h

Figure 3.22   pdevinit structure.

120–123   In the pdevinit structures for the SLIP and the loopback interface, pdev_attach is set to slattach and loopattach respectively. When the attach function is called, pdev_count is passed as the only argument and specifies the number of devices to create. Only one loopback device is created but multiple SLIP devices may be created if the administrator configures the SLIP entry accordingly.

The network initialization functions from `main` are shown in Figure 3.23.

```
                                                                        ─── init_main.c
70 main(framep)
71 void    *framep;
72 {

                          /* nonnetwork code */

96      cpu_startup();                    /* locate and initialize devices */

                          /* nonnetwork code */

172     /* Attach pseudo-devices. (e.g., SLIP and loopback interfaces) */
173     for (pdev = pdevinit; pdev->pdev_attach != NULL; pdev++)
174         (*pdev->pdev_attach) (pdev->pdev_count);
175     /*
176      * Initialize protocols.  Block reception of incoming packets
177      * until everything is ready.
178      */
179     s = splimp();
180     ifinit();                        /* initialize network interfaces */
181     domaininit();                    /* initialize protocol domains */
182     splx(s);

                          /* nonnetwork code */

231     /* The scheduler is an infinite loop. */
232     scheduler();
233     /* NOTREACHED */
234 }
                                                                        ─── init_main.c
```

Figure 3.23   main function: network initialization.

70–96   `cpu_startup` locates and initializes all the hardware devices connected to the system, including any network interfaces.

97–174   After the kernel initializes the hardware devices, it calls each of the `pdev_attach` functions contained within the `pdevinit` array.

175–234   `ifinit` and `domaininit` finish the initialization of the network interfaces and protocols and `scheduler` begins the kernel process scheduler. `ifinit` and `domaininit` are described in Chapter 7.

In the following sections we describe the initialization of the Ethernet, SLIP, and loopback interfaces.

3.8   Ethernet Initialization

As part of `cpu_startup`, the kernel locates any attached network devices. The details of this process are beyond the scope of this text. Once a device is identified, a device-specific initialization function is called. Figure 3.24 shows the initialization functions for our three sample interfaces.

Device	Initialization Function
LANCE Ethernet	`leattach`
SLIP	`slattach`
loopback	`loopattach`

Figure 3.24   Network interface initialization functions.

Each device driver for a network interface initializes a specialized `ifnet` structure and calls `if_attach` to insert the structure into the linked list of interfaces. The `le_softc` structure shown in Figure 3.25 is the specialized `ifnet` structure for our sample Ethernet driver (Figure 3.20).

```
                                                                      ─── if_le.c
69 struct le_softc {
70     struct arpcom sc_ac;        /* common Ethernet structures */
71 #define sc_if    sc_ac.ac_if     /* network-visible interface */
72 #define sc_addr sc_ac.ac_enaddr /* hardware Ethernet address */



                              /* device-specific members */



95 } le_softc[NLE];
                                                                      ─── if_le.c
```

Figure 3.25   `le_softc` structure.

`le_softc` structure

69-95   An array of `le_softc` structures (with NLE elements) is declared in `if_le.c`. Each structure starts with `sc_ac`, an `arpcom` structure common to all Ethernet interfaces, followed by device-specific members. The `sc_if` and `sc_addr` macros simplify access to the `ifnet` structure and Ethernet address within the `arpcom` structure, `sc_ac`, shown in Figure 3.26.

```
                                                                      ─── if_ether.h
95 struct arpcom {
96     struct ifnet ac_if;         /* network-visible interface */
97     u_char  ac_enaddr[6];       /* ethernet hardware address */
98     struct in_addr ac_ipaddr;   /* copy of ip address - XXX   */
99     struct ether_multi *ac_multiaddrs;  /* list of ether multicast addrs */
100    int     ac_multicnt;        /* length of ac_multiaddrs list */
101 };
                                                                      ─── if_ether.h
```

Figure 3.26   `arpcom` structure.

arpcom **structure**

95–101   The first member of the arpcom structure, ac_if, is an ifnet structure as shown in Figure 3.20. ac_enaddr is the Ethernet hardware address copied by the LANCE device driver from the hardware when the kernel locates the device during cpu_startup. For our sample driver, this occurs in the leattach function (Figure 3.27). ac_ipaddr is the *last* IP address assigned to the device. We discuss address assignment in Section 6.6, where we'll see that an interface can have several IP addresses. See also Exercise 6.3. ac_multiaddrs is a list of Ethernet multicast addresses represented by ether_multi structures. ac_multicnt counts the entries in the list. The multicast list is discussed in Chapter 12.

Figure 3.27 shows the initialization code for the LANCE Ethernet driver.
106–115   The kernel calls leattach once for each LANCE card it finds in the system.

> The single argument points to an hp_device structure, which contains HP-specific information since this driver is written for an HP workstation.

le points to the specialized ifnet structure for the card (Figure 3.20) and ifp points to the first member of that structure, sc_if, a generic ifnet structure. The device-specific initializations are not included in Figure 3.27 and are not discussed in this text.

Copy the hardware address from the device

126–137   For the LANCE device, the Ethernet address assigned by the manufacturer is copied from the device to sc_addr (which is sc_ac.ac_enaddr—see Figure 3.26) one nibble (4 bits) at a time in this for loop.

> lestd is a device-specific table of offsets to locate information relative to hp_addr, which points to LANCE-specific information.

The complete address is output to the console by the printf statement to indicate that the device exists and is is operational.

Initialize the ifnet structure

150–157   leattach copies the device unit number from the hp_device structure into if_unit to identify multiple interfaces of the same type. if_name is "le" for this device; if_mtu is 1500 bytes (ETHERMTU), the maximum transmission unit for Ethernet; if_init, if_reset, if_ioctl, if_output, and if_start all point to device-specific implementations of the generic functions that control the network interface. Section 4.1 describes these functions.

158   All Ethernet devices support IFF_BROADCAST. The LANCE device does not receive its own transmissions, so IFF_SIMPLEX is set. The driver and hardware supports multicasting so IFF_MULTICAST is also set.

159–162   bpfattach registers the interface with BPF and is described with Figure 31.8. The if_attach function inserts the initialized ifnet structure into the linked list of interfaces (Section 3.11).

if_le.c

```
106 leattach(hd)
107 struct hp_device *hd;
108 {
109     struct lereg0 *ler0;
110     struct lereg2 *ler2;
111     struct lereg2 *lemem = 0;
112     struct le_softc *le = &le_softc[hd->hp_unit];
113     struct ifnet *ifp = &le->sc_if;
114     char    *cp;
115     int     i;
```

```
                        /* device-specific code */
```

```
126     /*
127      * Read the ethernet address off the board, one nibble at a time.
128      */
129     cp = (char *) (lestd[3] + (int) hd->hp_addr);
130     for (i = 0; i < sizeof(le->sc_addr); i++) {
131         le->sc_addr[i] = (*++cp & 0xF) << 4;
132         cp++;
133         le->sc_addr[i] |= *++cp & 0xF;
134         cp++;
135     }
136     printf("le%d: hardware address %s\n", hd->hp_unit,
137             ether_sprintf(le->sc_addr));
```

```
                        /* device-specific code */
```

```
150     ifp->if_unit = hd->hp_unit;
151     ifp->if_name = "le";
152     ifp->if_mtu = ETHERMTU;
153     ifp->if_init = leinit;
154     ifp->if_reset = lereset;
155     ifp->if_ioctl = leioctl;
156     ifp->if_output = ether_output;
157     ifp->if_start = lestart;
158     ifp->if_flags = IFF_BROADCAST | IFF_SIMPLEX | IFF_MULTICAST;
159     bpfattach(&ifp->if_bpf, ifp, DLT_EN10MB, sizeof(struct ether_header));
160     if_attach(ifp);
161     return (1);
162 }
```

if_le.c

Figure 3.27   `leattach` function.

3.9   SLIP Initialization

The SLIP interface relies on a standard asynchronous serial device initialized within the call to `cpu_startup`. The SLIP pseudo-device is initialized when `main` calls `slattach` indirectly through the `pdev_attach` pointer in SLIP's `pdevinit` structure.

Each SLIP interface is described by an `sl_softc` structure shown in Figure 3.28.

—— *if_slvar.h*
```
43 struct sl_softc {
44     struct ifnet sc_if;              /* network-visible interface */
45     struct ifqueue sc_fastq;         /* interactive output queue */
46     struct tty *sc_ttyp;             /* pointer to tty structure */
47     u_char *sc_mp;                   /* pointer to next available buf char */
48     u_char *sc_ep;                   /* pointer to last available buf char */
49     u_char *sc_buf;                  /* input buffer */
50     u_int    sc_flags;               /* Figure 3.29 */
51     u_int    sc_escape;              /* =1 if last char input was FRAME_ESCAPE */
52     struct slcompress sc_comp;       /* tcp compression data */
53     caddr_t sc_bpf;                  /* BPF data */
54 };
```
—— *if_slvar.h*

Figure 3.28   `sl_softc` structure.

43–54   As with all interface structures, `sl_softc` starts with an `ifnet` structure followed by device-specific information.

In addition to the output queue found in the `ifnet` structure, a SLIP device maintains a separate queue, `sc_fastq`, for packets requesting low-delay service—typically generated by interactive applications.

`sc_ttyp` points to the associated terminal device. The two pointers `sc_buf` and `sc_ep` point to the first and last bytes of the buffer for an incoming SLIP packet. `sc_mp` points to the location for the next incoming byte and is advanced as additional bytes arrive.

The four flags defined by the SLIP driver are shown in Figure 3.29.

Constant	sc_softc member	Description
SC_COMPRESS	sc_if.if_flags	IFF_LINK0; compress TCP traffic
SC_NOICMP	sc_if.if_flags	IFF_LINK1; suppress ICMP traffic
SC_AUTOCOMP	sc_if.if_flags	IFF_LINK2; auto-enable TCP compression
SC_ERROR	sc_flags	error detected; discard incoming frame

Figure 3.29   SLIP `if_flags` and `sc_flags` values.

SLIP defines the three interface flags reserved for the device driver in the `ifnet` structure and one additional flag defined in the `sl_softc` structure.

`sc_escape` is used by the IP encapsulation mechanism for serial lines (Section 5.3), while TCP header compression (Section 29.13) information is kept in `sc_comp`.

The BPF information for the SLIP device is pointed to by `sc_bpf`.

The `sl_softc` structure is initialized by `slattach`, shown in Figure 3.30.

135–152   Unlike `leattach`, which initializes only one interface at a time, the kernel calls `slattach` once and `slattach` initializes all the SLIP interfaces. Hardware devices are initialized as they are discovered by the kernel during `cpu_startup`, while pseudo-devices are initialized all at once when `main` calls the `pdev_attach` function for the device. `if_mtu` for a SLIP device is 296 bytes (`SLMTU`). This accommodates the

—— *if_sl.c*
```
135 void
136 slattach()
137 {
138     struct sl_softc *sc;
139     int     i = 0;

140     for (sc = sl_softc; i < NSL; sc++) {
141         sc->sc_if.if_name = "sl";
142         sc->sc_if.if_next = NULL;
143         sc->sc_if.if_unit = i++;
144         sc->sc_if.if_mtu = SLMTU;
145         sc->sc_if.if_flags =
146             IFF_POINTOPOINT | SC_AUTOCOMP | IFF_MULTICAST;
147         sc->sc_if.if_type = IFT_SLIP;
148         sc->sc_if.if_ioctl = slioctl;
149         sc->sc_if.if_output = sloutput;
150         sc->sc_if.if_snd.ifq_maxlen = 50;
151         sc->sc_fastq.ifq_maxlen = 32;
152         if_attach(&sc->sc_if);
153         bpfattach(&sc->sc_bpf, &sc->sc_if, DLT_SLIP, SLIP_HDRLEN);
154     }
155 }
```
—— *if_sl.c*

Figure 3.30 slattach function.

standard 20-byte IP header, the standard 20-byte TCP header, and 256 bytes of user data
(Section 5.3).

A SLIP network consists of two interfaces at each end of a serial communication
line. slattach turns on IFF_POINTOPOINT, SC_AUTOCOMP, and IFF_MULTICAST in
if_flags.

The SLIP interface limits the length of its output packet queue, if_snd, to 50 and
its own internal queue, sc_fastq, to 32. Figure 3.42 shows that the length of the
if_snd queue defaults to 50 (ifqmaxlen) if the driver does not select a length, so the
initialization here is redundant.

> The Ethernet driver doesn't set its output queue length explicitly and relies on ifinit (Fig-
> ure 3.42) to set it to the system default.

if_attach expects a pointer to an ifnet structure so slattach passes the
address of sc_if, an ifnet structure and the first member of the sl_softc structure.

A special program, slattach, is run (from the /etc/netstart initialization file)
after the kernel has been initialized and joins the SLIP interface and an asynchronous
serial device by opening the serial device and issuing ioctl commands (Section 5.3).

153–155   For each SLIP device, slattach calls bpfattach to register the interface with
BPF.

3.10 Loopback Initialization

Finally, we show the initialization for the single loopback interface. The loopback interface places any outgoing packets back on an appropriate input queue. There is no hardware device associated with the interface. The loopback pseudo-device is initialized
when main calls loopattach indirectly through the pdev_attach pointer in the
loopback's pdevinit structure. Figure 3.31 shows the loopattach function.

―― if_loop.c
```
41 void
42 loopattach(n)
43 int     n;
44 {
45      struct ifnet *ifp = &loif;

46      ifp->if_name = "lo";
47      ifp->if_mtu = LOMTU;
48      ifp->if_flags = IFF_LOOPBACK | IFF_MULTICAST;
49      ifp->if_ioctl = loioctl;
50      ifp->if_output = looutput;
51      ifp->if_type = IFT_LOOP;
52      ifp->if_hdrlen = 0;
53      ifp->if_addrlen = 0;
54      if_attach(ifp);
55      bpfattach(&ifp->if_bpf, ifp, DLT_NULL, sizeof(u_int));
56 }
```
―― if_loop.c

Figure 3.31 Loopback interface initialization.

41–56   The loopback if_mtu is set to 1536 bytes (LOMTU). In if_flags, IFF_LOOPBACK
and IFF_MULTICAST are set. A loopback interface has no link header or hardware
address, so if_hdrlen and if_addrlen are set to 0. if_attach finishes the initialization of the ifnet structure and bpfattach registers the loopback interface with
BPF.

> The loopback MTU should be at least 1576 ($40 + 3 \times 512$) to leave room for a standard TCP/IP
> header. Solaris 2.3, for example, sets the loopback MTU to 8232 ($40 + 8 \times 1024$). These calcula-
> tions are biased toward the Internet protocols; other protocols may have default headers larger
> than 40 bytes.

3.11 if_attach Function

The three interface initialization functions shown earlier each call if_attach to complete initialization of the interface's ifnet structure and to insert the structure on the
list of previously configured interfaces. Also, in if_attach, the kernel initializes and
assigns each interface a link-level address. Figure 3.32 illustrates the data structures
constructed by if_attach.

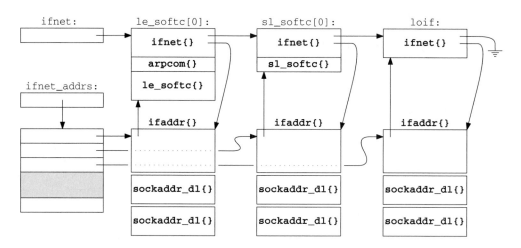

Figure 3.32   `ifnet` list.

In Figure 3.32, `if_attach` has been called three times: from `leattach` with an `le_softc` structure, from `slattach` with an `sl_softc` structure, and from `loopattach` with a generic `ifnet` structure. Each time it is called it adds another `ifnet` structure to the `ifnet` list, creates a link-level `ifaddr` structure for the interface (which contains two `sockaddr_dl` structures, Figure 3.33), and initializes an entry in the `ifnet_addrs` array.

> The structures contained within `le_softc[0]` and `sl_softc[0]` are nested as shown in Figure 3.20.

After this initialization, the interfaces are configured only with link-level addresses. IP addresses, for example, are not configured until much later by the `ifconfig` program (Section 6.6).

The link-level address contains a logical address for the interface and a hardware address if supported by the network (e.g., a 48-bit Ethernet address for `le0`). The hardware address is used by ARP and the OSI protocols, while the logical address within a `sockaddr_dl` contains a name and numeric index for the interface within the kernel, which supports a table lookup for converting between an interface index and the associated `ifaddr` structure (`ifa_ifwithnet`, Figure 6.32).

The `sockaddr_dl` structure is shown in Figure 3.33.

55–57   Recall from Figure 3.18 that `sdl_len` specifies the length of the entire address and `sdl_family` specifies the address family, in this case `AF_LINK`.

58   `sdl_index` identifies the interface within the kernel. In Figure 3.32 the Ethernet interface would have an index of 1, the SLIP interface an index of 2, and the loopback interface an index of 3. The global integer `if_index` contains the last index assigned by the kernel.

60   `sdl_type` is initialized from the `if_type` member of the `ifnet` structure associated with this datalink address.

```
                                                                              if_dl.h
55 struct sockaddr_dl {
56     u_char  sdl_len;          /* Total length of sockaddr */
57     u_char  sdl_family;       /* AF_LINK */
58     u_short sdl_index;        /* if != 0, system given index for
59                                  interface */
60     u_char  sdl_type;         /* interface type (Figure 3.9) */
61     u_char  sdl_nlen;         /* interface name length, no trailing 0
62                                  reqd. */
63     u_char  sdl_alen;         /* link level address length */
64     u_char  sdl_slen;         /* link layer selector length */
65     char    sdl_data[12];     /* minimum work area, can be larger;
66                                  contains both if name and ll address */
67 };

68 #define LLADDR(s) ((caddr_t)((s)->sdl_data + (s)->sdl_nlen))
                                                                              if_dl.h
```

Figure 3.33 sockaddr_dl structure.

61–68   In addition to a numeric index, each interface has a text name formed from the if_name and if_unit members of the ifnet structure. For example, the first SLIP interface is called "sl0" and the second is called "sl1". The text name is stored at the front of the sdl_data array, and sdl_nlen is the length of this name in bytes (3 in our SLIP example).

The datalink address is also stored in the structure. The macro LLADDR converts a pointer to a sockaddr_dl structure into a pointer to the first byte beyond the text name. sdl_alen is the length of the hardware address. For an Ethernet device, the 48-bit hardware address appears in the sockaddr_dl structure beyond the text name. Figure 3.38 shows an initialized sockaddr_dl structure.

Net/3 does not use sdl_slen.

if_attach updates two global variables. The first, if_index, holds the index of the last interface in the system and the second, ifnet_addrs, points to an array of ifaddr pointers. Each entry in the array points to the link-level address of an interface. The array provides quick access to the link-level address for every interface in the system.

The if_attach function is long and consists of several tricky assignment statements. We describe it in four parts, starting with Figure 3.34.

59–74   if_attach has a single argument, ifp, a pointer to the ifnet structure that has been initialized by a network device driver. Net/3 keeps all the ifnet structures on a linked list headed by the global pointer ifnet. The while loop locates the end of the list and saves the address of the null pointer at the end of the list in p. After the loop, the new ifnet structure is attached to the end of the ifnet list, if_index is incremented, and the new index is assigned to ifp->if_index.

Resize ifnet_addrs array if necessary

75–85   The first time through if_attach, the ifnet_addrs array doesn't exist so space for 16 entries $(16 = 8 \ll 1)$ is allocated. When the array becomes full, a new array of twice the size is allocated and the entries from the old array are copied to the new array.

```
                                                                            —— if.c
59 void
60 if_attach(ifp)
61 struct ifnet *ifp;
62 {
63     unsigned socksize, ifasize;
64     int     namelen, unitlen, masklen, ether_output();
65     char    workbuf[12], *unitname;
66     struct ifnet **p = &ifnet;  /* head of interface list */
67     struct sockaddr_dl *sdl;
68     struct ifaddr *ifa;
69     static int if_indexlim = 8; /* size of ifnet_addrs array */
70     extern void link_rtrequest();

71     while (*p)                      /* find end of interface list */
72         p = &((*p)->if_next);
73     *p = ifp;
74     ifp->if_index = ++if_index; /* assign next index */

75     /* resize ifnet_addrs array if necessary */
76     if (ifnet_addrs == 0 || if_index >= if_indexlim) {
77         unsigned n = (if_indexlim <<= 1) * sizeof(ifa);
78         struct ifaddr **q = (struct ifaddr **)
79                     malloc(n, M_IFADDR, M_WAITOK);

80         if (ifnet_addrs) {
81             bcopy((caddr_t) ifnet_addrs, (caddr_t) q, n / 2);
82             free((caddr_t) ifnet_addrs, M_IFADDR);
83         }
84         ifnet_addrs = q;
85     }
                                                                            —— if.c
```

Figure 3.34 if_attach function: assign interface index.

> if_indexlim is a static variable private to if_attach. if_indexlim is updated by the <<= operator.

The malloc and free functions in Figure 3.34 are *not* the standard C library functions of the same name. The second argument in the kernel versions specifies a type, which is used by optional diagnostic code in the kernel to detect programming errors. If the third argument to malloc is M_WAITOK, the function blocks the calling process if it needs to wait for free memory to become available. If the third argument is M_DONTWAIT, the function does not block and returns a null pointer when no memory is available.

The next section of if_attach, shown in Figure 3.35, prepares a text name for the interface and computes the size of the link-level address.

Create link-level name and compute size of link-level address

86–99   if_attach constructs the name of the interface from if_unit and if_name. The function sprint_d converts the numeric value of if_unit to a string stored in workbuf. masklen is the number of bytes occupied by the information before sdl_data in the sockaddr_dl array plus the size of the text name for the interface

---
——— if.c

```
86      /* create a Link Level name for this device */
87      unitname = sprint_d((u_int) ifp->if_unit, workbuf, sizeof(workbuf));
88      namelen = strlen(ifp->if_name);
89      unitlen = strlen(unitname);

90      /* compute size of sockaddr_dl structure for this device */
91 #define _offsetof(t, m) ((int)((caddr_t)&((t *)0)->m))
92      masklen = _offsetof(struct sockaddr_dl, sdl_data[0]) +
93              unitlen + namelen;
94      socksize = masklen + ifp->if_addrlen;
95 #define ROUNDUP(a) (1 + (((a) - 1) | (sizeof(long) - 1)))
96      socksize = ROUNDUP(socksize);
97      if (socksize < sizeof(*sdl))
98          socksize = sizeof(*sdl);
99      ifasize = sizeof(*ifa) + 2 * socksize;
```
——— if.c

Figure 3.35   if_attach function: compute size of link-level address.

(namelen + unitlen). The function rounds socksize, which is masklen plus the
hardware address length (if_addrlen), up to the boundary of a long integer
(ROUNDUP). If this is less than the size of a sockaddr_dl structure, the standard
sockaddr_dl structure is used. ifasize is the size of an ifaddr structure plus two
times socksize, so it can hold the sockaddr_dl structures.

In the next section, if_attach allocates and links the structures together, as shown
in Figure 3.36.

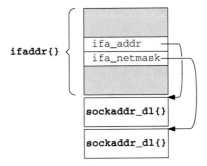

Figure 3.36   The link-level address and mask assigned during if_attach.

In Figure 3.36 there is a gap between the ifaddr structure and the two sockaddr_dl structures to illustrate that they are allocated in a contiguous area of memory but that they are not
defined by a single C structure.

The organization shown in Figure 3.36 is repeated in the in_ifaddr structure; the
pointers in the generic ifaddr portion of the structure point to specialized sockaddr
structures allocated in the device-specific portion of the structure, in this case,
sockaddr_dl structures. Figure 3.37 shows the initialization of these structures.

```
                                                                            if.c
100     if (ifa = (struct ifaddr *) malloc(ifasize, M_IFADDR, M_WAITOK)) {
101         bzero((caddr_t) ifa, ifasize);

102         /* First: initialize the sockaddr_dl address */
103         sdl = (struct sockaddr_dl *) (ifa + 1);
104         sdl->sdl_len = socksize;
105         sdl->sdl_family = AF_LINK;
106         bcopy(ifp->if_name, sdl->sdl_data, namelen);
107         bcopy(unitname, namelen + (caddr_t) sdl->sdl_data, unitlen);
108         sdl->sdl_nlen = (namelen += unitlen);
109         sdl->sdl_index = ifp->if_index;
110         sdl->sdl_type = ifp->if_type;
111         ifnet_addrs[if_index - 1] = ifa;
112         ifa->ifa_ifp = ifp;
113         ifa->ifa_next = ifp->if_addrlist;
114         ifa->ifa_rtrequest = link_rtrequest;
115         ifp->if_addrlist = ifa;
116         ifa->ifa_addr = (struct sockaddr *) sdl;

117         /* Second: initialize the sockaddr_dl mask */
118         sdl = (struct sockaddr_dl *) (socksize + (caddr_t) sdl);
119         ifa->ifa_netmask = (struct sockaddr *) sdl;
120         sdl->sdl_len = masklen;
121         while (namelen != 0)
122             sdl->sdl_data[--namelen] = 0xff;
123     }
                                                                            if.c
```

Figure 3.37 if_attach function: allocate and initialize link-level address.

The address

100–116   If enough memory is available, bzero fills the new structure with 0s and sdl points to the first sockaddr_dl just after the ifaddr structure. If no memory is available, the code is skipped.

sdl_len is set to the length of the sockaddr_dl structure, and sdl_family is set to AF_LINK. A text name is constructed within sdl_data from if_name and unitname, and the length is saved in sdl_nlen. The interface's index is copied into sdl_index as well as the interface type into sdl_type. The allocated structure is inserted into the ifnet_addrs array and linked to the ifnet structure by ifa_ifp and if_addrlist. Finally, the sockaddr_dl structure is connected to the ifnet structure with ifa_addr. Ethernet interfaces replace the default function, link_rtrequest with arp_rtrequest. The loopback interface installs loop_rtrequest. We describe ifa_rtrequest and arp_rtrequest in Chapters 19 and 21. link_rtrequest and loop_rtrequest are left for readers to investigate on their own. This completes the initialization of the first sockaddr_dl structure.

The mask

117–123   The second sockaddr_dl structure is a bit mask that selects the text name that appears in the first structure. ifa_netmask from the ifaddr structure points to the mask structure (which in this case selects the interface text name and not a network mask). The while loop turns on the bits in the bytes corresponding to the name.

Figure 3.38 shows the two initialized `sockaddr_dl` structures for our example
Ethernet interface, where `if_name` is "le", `if_unit` is 0, and `if_index` is 1.

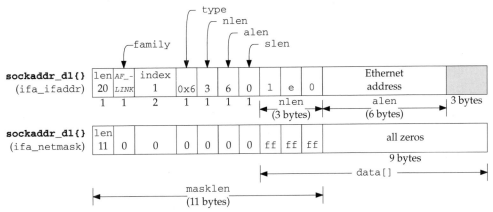

Figure 3.38   The initialized Ethernet `sockaddr_dl` structures (`sdl_` prefix omitted).

In Figure 3.38, the address is shown after `ether_ifattach` has done additional
initialization of the structure (Figure 3.41).

Figure 3.39 shows the structures after the first interface has been attached by
`if_attach`.

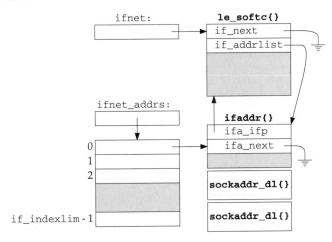

Figure 3.39   The `ifaddr` and `sockaddr_dl` structures after `if_attach` is called for the first time.

At the end of `if_attach`, the `ether_ifattach` function is called for Ethernet
devices, as shown in Figure 3.40.

124–127   `ether_ifattach` isn't called earlier (from `leattach`, for example) because it
copies the Ethernet hardware address into the `sockaddr_dl` allocated by `if_attach`.

> The XXX comment indicates that the author found it easier to insert the code here once than to
> modify all the Ethernet drivers.

```
                                                                                  if.c
124      /* XXX -- Temporary fix before changing 10 ethernet drivers */
125      if (ifp->if_output == ether_output)
126          ether_ifattach(ifp);
127 }
                                                                                  if.c
```

Figure 3.40   `if_attach` function: Ethernet initialization.

`ether_ifattach` **function**

The `ether_ifattach` function performs the `ifnet` structure initialization common to all Ethernet devices.

```
                                                                       if_ethersubr.c
338 void
339 ether_ifattach(ifp)
340 struct ifnet *ifp;
341 {
342     struct ifaddr *ifa;
343     struct sockaddr_dl *sdl;

344     ifp->if_type = IFT_ETHER;
345     ifp->if_addrlen = 6;
346     ifp->if_hdrlen = 14;
347     ifp->if_mtu = ETHERMTU;
348     for (ifa = ifp->if_addrlist; ifa; ifa = ifa->ifa_next)
349         if ((sdl = (struct sockaddr_dl *) ifa->ifa_addr) &&
350             sdl->sdl_family == AF_LINK) {
351             sdl->sdl_type = IFT_ETHER;
352             sdl->sdl_alen = ifp->if_addrlen;
353             bcopy((caddr_t) ((struct arpcom *) ifp)->ac_enaddr,
354                 LLADDR(sdl), ifp->if_addrlen);
355             break;
356         }
357 }
                                                                       if_ethersubr.c
```

Figure 3.41   `ether_ifattach` function.

338–357   For an Ethernet device, `if_type` is `IFT_ETHER`, the hardware address is 6 bytes long, the entire Ethernet header is 14 bytes in length, and the Ethernet MTU is 1500 (`ETHERMTU`).

> The MTU was already assigned by `leattach`, but other Ethernet device drivers may not have performed this initialization.

Section 4.3 discusses the Ethernet frame organization in more detail. The `for` loop locates the link-level address for the interface and then initializes the Ethernet hardware address information in the `sockaddr_dl` structure. The Ethernet address that was copied into the `arpcom` structure during system initialization is now copied into the link-level address.

3.12 ifinit Function

After the interface structures are initialized and linked together, main (Figure 3.23) calls
ifinit, shown in Figure 3.42.

```
                                                                                  if.c
43 void
44 ifinit()
45 {
46      struct ifnet *ifp;

47      for (ifp = ifnet; ifp; ifp = ifp->if_next)
48          if (ifp->if_snd.ifq_maxlen == 0)
49              ifp->if_snd.ifq_maxlen = ifqmaxlen;      /* set default length */
50      if_slowtimo(0);
51 }
                                                                                  if.c
```

Figure 3.42 ifinit function.

43–51   The for loop traverses the interface list and sets the maximum size of each interface
output queue to 50 (ifqmaxlen) if it hasn't already been set by the interface's attach
function.

> An important consideration for the size of the output queue is the number of packets required
> to send a maximum-sized datagram. For Ethernet, if a process calls sendto with 65,507 bytes
> of data, it is fragmented into 45 fragments and each fragment is put onto the interface output
> queue. If the queue were much smaller, the process could never send that large a datagram, as
> the queue wouldn't have room.

if_slowtimo starts the interface watchdog timers. When an interface timer
expires, the kernel calls the watchdog function for the interface. An interface can reset
the timer periodically to prevent the watchdog function from being called, or set
if_timer to 0 if the watchdog function is not needed. Figure 3.43 shows the
if_slowtimo function.

```
                                                                                  if.c
338 void
339 if_slowtimo(arg)
340 void    *arg;
341 {
342     struct ifnet *ifp;
343     int     s = splimp();

344     for (ifp = ifnet; ifp; ifp = ifp->if_next) {
345         if (ifp->if_timer == 0 || --ifp->if_timer)
346             continue;
347         if (ifp->if_watchdog)
348             (*ifp->if_watchdog) (ifp->if_unit);
349     }
350     splx(s);
351     timeout(if_slowtimo, (void *) 0, hz / IFNET_SLOWHZ);
352 }
                                                                                  if.c
```

Figure 3.43 if_slowtimo function.

338–343   The single argument, arg, is not used but is required by the prototype for the slow
            timeout functions (Section 7.4).

344–352   if_slowtimo ignores interfaces with if_timer equal to 0; if if_timer does not
            equal 0, if_slowtimo decrements if_timer and calls the if_watchdog function
            associated with the interface when the timer reaches 0. Packet processing is blocked by
            splimp during if_slowtimo. Before returning, ip_slowtimo calls timeout to
            schedule a call to itself in hz/IFNET_SLOWHZ clock ticks. hz is the number of clock
            ticks that occur in 1 second (often 100). It is set at system initialization and remains con-
            stant thereafter. Since IFNET_SLOWHZ is defined to be 1, the kernel calls if_slowtimo
            once every hz clock ticks, which is once per second.

>   The functions scheduled by the timeout function are called back by the kernel's callout
>   function. See [Leffler et al. 1989] for additional details.

3.13   Summary

In this chapter we have examined the ifnet and ifaddr structures that are allocated
for each network interface found at system initialization time. The ifnet structures are
linked into the ifnet list. The link-level address for each interface is initialized,
attached to the ifnet structure's address list, and entered into the if_addrs array.

We discussed the generic sockaddr structure and its sa_family, and sa_len
members, which specify the type and length of every address. We also looked at the initialization of the sockaddr_dl structure for a link-level address.

In this chapter, we introduced the three example network interfaces that we use
throughout the book.

Exercises

3.1   The netstat program on many Unix systems lists network interfaces and their configura-
        tion. Try netstat -i on a system you have access to. What are the names (if_name) and
        maximum transmission units (if_mtu) of the network interfaces?

3.2   In if_slowtimo (Figure 3.43) the splimp and splx calls appear outside the loop. What
        are the advantages and disadvantages of this arrangement compared with placing the calls
        within the loop?

3.3   Why is SLIP's interactive queue shorter than SLIP's standard output queue?

3.4   Why aren't if_hdrlen and if_addrlen initialized in slattach?

3.5   Draw a picture similar to Figure 3.38 for the SLIP and loopback devices.

4

Interfaces: Ethernet

4.1 Introduction

In Chapter 3 we discussed the data structures used by all interfaces and the initialization of those data structures. In this chapter we show how the Ethernet device driver operates once it has been initialized and is receiving and transmitting frames. The second half of this chapter covers the generic ioctl commands for configuring network devices. Chapter 5 covers the SLIP and loopback drivers.

We won't go through the entire source code for the Ethernet driver, since it is around 1,000 lines of C code (half of which is concerned with the hardware details of one particular interface card), but we do look at the device-independent Ethernet code and how the driver interfaces with the rest of the kernel.

If the reader is interested in going through the source code for a driver, the Net/3 release contains the source code for many different interfaces. Access to the interface's technical specifications is required to understand the device-specific commands. Figure 4.1 shows the various drivers provided with Net/3, including the LANCE driver, which we discuss in this text.

Network device drivers are accessed through the seven function pointers in the ifnet structure (Figure 3.11). Figure 4.2 lists the entry points to our three example drivers.

Input functions are not included in Figure 4.2 as they are interrupt-driven for network devices. The configuration of interrupt service routines is hardware-dependent and beyond the scope of this book. We'll identify the functions that handle device interrupts, but not the mechanism by which these functions are invoked.

Device	File
DEC DEUNA Interface	`vax/if/if_de.c`
3Com Ethernet Interface	`vax/if/if_ec.c`
Excelan EXOS 204 Interface	`vax/if/if_ex.c`
Interlan Ethernet Communications Controller	`vax/if/if_il.c`
Interlan NP100 Ethernet Communications Controller	`vax/if/if_ix.c`
Digital Q-BUS to NI Adapter	`vax/if/if_qe.c`
CMC ENP-20 Ethernet Controller	`tahoe/if/if_enp.c`
Excelan EXOS 202(VME) & 203(QBUS)	`tahoe/if/if_ex.c`
ACC VERSAbus Ethernet Controller	`tahoe/if/if_ace.c`
AMD 7990 LANCE Interface	**`hp300/dev/if_le.c`**
NE2000 Ethernet	`i386/isa/if_ne.c`
Western Digital 8003 Ethernet Adapter	`i386/isa/if_we.c`

Figure 4.1   Ethernet drivers available in Net/3.

`ifnet`	Ethernet	SLIP	Loopback	Description
`if_init`	`leinit`			hardware initialization
`if_output`	`ether_output`	`sloutput`	`looutput`	accept and queue frame for transmission
`if_start`	`lestart`			begin transmission of frame
`if_done`				output complete (unused)
`if_ioctl`	`leioctl`	`slioctl`	`loioctl`	handle `ioctl` commands from a process
`if_reset`	`lereset`			reset the device to a known state
`if_watchdog`				watch the device for failures or collect statistics

Figure 4.2   Interface functions for the example drivers.

Only the `if_output` and `if_ioctl` functions are called with any consistency. `if_init`, `if_done`, and `if_reset` are never called or only called from device-specific code (e.g., `leinit` is called directly by `leioctl`). `if_start` is called only by the `ether_output` function.

4.2   Code Introduction

The code for the Ethernet device driver and the generic interface `ioctl`s resides in two headers and three C files, which are listed in Figure 4.3.

File	Description
`netinet/if_ether.h`	Ethernet structures
`net/if.h`	`ioctl` command definitions
`net/if_ethersubr.c`	generic Ethernet functions
`hp300/dev/if_le.c`	LANCE Ethernet driver
`net/if.c`	`ioctl` processing

Figure 4.3   Files discussed in this chapter.

Global Variables

The global variables shown in Figure 4.4 include the protocol input queues, the LANCE interface structure, and the Ethernet broadcast address.

Variable	Datatype	Description
arpintrq clnlintrq ipintrq	struct ifqueue struct ifqueue struct ifqueue	ARP input queue CLNP input queue IP input queue
le_softc	struct le_softc []	LANCE Ethernet interface
etherbroadcastaddr	u_char []	Ethernet broadcast address

Figure 4.4   Global variables introduced in this chapter.

le_softc is an array, since there can be several Ethernet interfaces.

Statistics

The statistics collected in the ifnet structure for each interface are described in Figure 4.5.

ifnet member	Description	Used by SNMP
if_collisions	#collisions on CSMA interfaces	
if_ibytes	total #bytes received	•
if_ierrors	#packets received with input errors	•
if_imcasts	#packets received as multicasts or broadcasts	•
if_ipackets	#packets received on interface	•
if_iqdrops	#packets dropped on input, by this interface	•
if_lastchange	time of last change to statistics	•
if_noproto	#packets destined for unsupported protocol	•
if_obytes	total #bytes sent	•
if_oerrors	#output errors on interface	•
if_omcasts	#packets sent as multicasts	•
if_opackets	#packets sent on interface	•
if_snd.ifq_drops	#packets dropped during output	•
if_snd.ifq_len	#packets in output queue	

Figure 4.5   Statistics maintained in the ifnet structure.

Figure 4.6 shows some sample output from the netstat command, which includes statistics from the ifnet structure.

The first column contains if_name and if_unit displayed as a string. If the interface is shut down (IFF_UP is not set), an asterisk appears next to the name. In Figure 4.6, sl0, sl2, and sl3 are shut down.

The second column shows if_mtu. The output under the "Network" and "Address" headings depends on the type of address. For link-level addresses, the contents of sdl_data from the sockaddr_dl structure are displayed. For IP addresses,

netstat -i output								
Name	Mtu	Network	Address	Ipkts	Ierrs	Opkts	Oerrs	Coll
le0	1500	<Link>8.0.9.13.d.33		28680519	814	29234729	12	942798
le0	1500	128.32.33	128.32.33.5	28680519	814	29234729	12	942798
sl0*	296	<Link>		54036	0	45402	0	0
sl0*	296	128.32.33	128.32.33.5	54036	0	45402	0	0
sl1	296	<Link>		40397	0	33544	0	0
sl1	296	128.32.33	128.32.33.5	40397	0	33544	0	0
sl2*	296	<Link>		0	0	0	0	0
sl3*	296	<Link>		0	0	0	0	0
lo0	1536	<Link>		493599	0	493599	0	0
lo0	1536	127	127.0.0.1	493599	0	493599	0	0

Figure 4.6 Sample interface statistics.

the subnet and unicast addresses are displayed. The remaining columns are
if_ipackets, if_ierrors, if_opackets, if_oerrors, and if_collisions.

- Approximately 3% of the packets collide on output ($942,798/29,234,729 = 3\%$).
- The SLIP output queues are never full on this machine since there are no output errors for the SLIP interfaces.
- The 12 Ethernet output errors are problems detected by the LANCE hardware during transmission. Some of these errors may also be counted as collisions.
- The 814 Ethernet input errors are also problems detected by the hardware, such as packets that are too short or that have invalid checksums.

SNMP Variables

Figure 4.7 shows a single interface entry object (ifEntry) from the SNMP interface table (ifTable), which is constructed from the ifnet structures for each interface.

The ISODE SNMP agent derives ifSpeed from if_type and maintains an internal variable for ifAdminStatus. The agent reports ifLastChange based on if_lastchange in the ifnet structure but relative to the agent's boot time, not the boot time of the system. The agent returns a null variable for ifSpecific.

4.3   Ethernet Interface

Net/3 Ethernet device drivers all follow the same general design. This is common for most Unix device drivers because the writer of a driver for a new interface card often starts with a working driver for another card and modifies it. In this section we'll provide a brief overview of the Ethernet standard and outline the design of an Ethernet driver. We'll refer to the LANCE driver to illustrate the design.

Figure 4.8 illustrates Ethernet encapsulation of an IP packet.

Interface table, index = < *ifIndex* >		
SNMP variable	`ifnet` member	Description

`ifIndex`
`ifDescr`
`ifType`
`ifMtu`
`ifSpeed`
	`if_index`
	`if_name`
	`if_type`
	`if_mtu`
	(see text)
		uniquely identifies the interface
		text name of interface
		type of interface (e.g., Ethernet, SLIP, etc.)
		MTU of the interface in bytes
		nominal speed of the interface in bits per
		    second

`ifPhysAddress`
`ifAdminStatus`
`ifOperStatus`
 	
`ifLastChange`
`ifInOctets`
	`ac_enaddr`
	(see text)
	`if_flags`
	
	(see text)
	`if_ibytes`
		media address (from arpcom structure)
		desired state of the interface (`IFF_UP` flag)
		operational state of the interface (`IFF_UP`
		    flag)
		last time the statistics changed
		total #input bytes

`ifInUcastPkts`	`if_ipackets -` `if_imcasts`	#input unicast packets

`ifInNUcastPkts`
`ifInDiscards`
 	
`ifInErrors`
`ifInUnknownProtos`
`ifOutOctets`
	`if_imcasts`
	`if_iqdrops`
	
	`if_ierrors`
	`if_noproto`
	`if_obytes`
		#input broadcast or multicast packets
		#packets discarded because of
		    implementation limits
		#packets with errors
		#packets destined to an unknown protocol
		#output bytes

`ifOutUcastPkts`	`if_opackets -` `if_omcasts`	#output unicast packets

`ifOutNUcastPkts`
`ifOutDiscards`
 	
`ifOutErrors`
`ifOutQLen`
`ifSpecific`
	`if_omcasts`
	`if_snd.ifq_drops`
	
	`if_oerrors`
	`if_snd.ifq_len`
	n/a
		#output broadcast or multicast packets
		#output packets dropped because of
		    implementation limits
		#output packets dropped because of errors
		output queue length
		SNMP object ID for media-specific
		    information (not implemented)

Figure 4.7   Variables in interface table: `ifTable`.

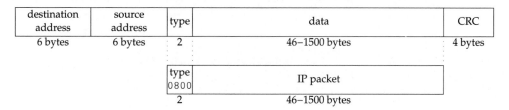

Figure 4.8   Ethernet encapsulation of an IP packet.

Ethernet frames consist of 48-bit destination and source addresses followed by a 16-bit type field that identifies the format of the data carried by the frame. For IP packets, the type is `0x0800` (2048). The frame is terminated with a 32-bit CRC (cyclic redundancy check), which detects errors in the frame.

We are describing the original Ethernet framing standard published in 1982 by Digital Equipment Corp., Intel Corp., and Xerox Corp., as it is the most common form used today in TCP/IP networks. An alternative form is specified by the IEEE (Institute of Electrical and Electronics Engineers) 802.2 and 802.3 standards. Section 2.2 in Volume 1 describes the differences between the two forms. See [Stallings 1987] for more information on the IEEE standards.

Encapsulation of IP packets for Ethernet is specified by RFC 894 [Hornig 1984] and for 802.3 networks by RFC 1042 [Postel and Reynolds 1988].

We will refer to the 48-bit Ethernet addresses as *hardware addresses*. The translation from IP to hardware addresses is done by the ARP protocol described in Chapter 21 (RFC 826 [Plummer 1982]) and from hardware to IP addresses by the RARP protocol (RFC 903 [Finlayson et al. 1984]). Ethernet addresses come in two types, *unicast* and *multicast*. A unicast address specifies a single Ethernet interface, and a multicast address specifies a group of Ethernet interfaces. An Ethernet *broadcast* is a multicast received by all interfaces. Ethernet unicast addresses are assigned by the device's manufacturer, although some devices allow the address to be changed by software.

Some DECNET protocols require the hardware addresses of a multihomed host to be identical, so DECNET must be able to change the Ethernet unicast address of a device.

Figure 4.9 illustrates the data structures and functions that are part of the Ethernet interface.

In figures, a function is identified by an ellipse (leintr), data structures by a box (le_softc[0]), and a group of functions by a rounded box (ARP protocol).

In the top left corner of Figure 4.9 we show the input queues for the OSI Connectionless Network Layer (clnl) protocol, IP, and ARP. We won't say anything more about clnlintrq, but include it to emphasize that ether_input demultiplexes Ethernet frames into multiple protocol queues.

Technically, OSI uses the term Connectionless Network *Protocol* (CLNP versus CLNL) but we show the terminology used by the Net/3 code. The official standard for CLNP is ISO 8473. [Stallings 1993] summarizes the standard.

The le_softc interface structure is in the center of Figure 4.9. We are interested only in the ifnet and arpcom portions of the structure. The remaining portions are specific to the LANCE hardware. We showed the ifnet structure in Figure 3.6 and the arpcom structure in Figure 3.26.

leintr Function

We start with the reception of Ethernet frames. For now, we assume that the hardware has been initialized and the system has been configured so that leintr is called when the interface generates an interrupt. In normal operation, an Ethernet interface receives frames destined for its unicast hardware address and for the Ethernet broadcast address. When a complete frame is available, the interface generates an interrupt and the kernel calls leintr.

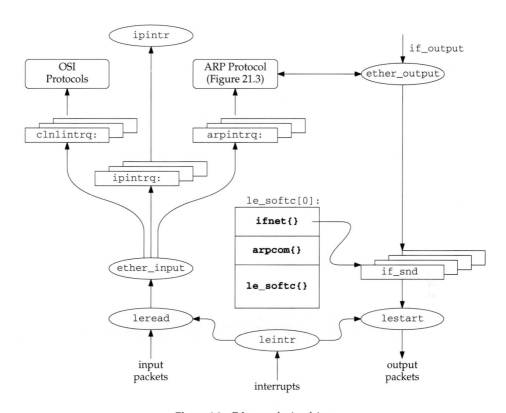

Figure 4.9 Ethernet device driver.

In Chapter 12, we'll see that many Ethernet interfaces may be configured to receive Ethernet multicast frames (other than broadcasts).

Some interfaces can be configured to run in *promiscuous mode* in which the interface receives all frames that appear on the network. The tcpdump program described in Volume 1 can take advantage of this feature using BPF.

leintr examines the hardware and, if a frame has arrived, calls leread to transfer the frame from the interface to a chain of mbufs (with m_devget). If the hardware reports that a frame transmission has completed or an error has been detected (such as a bad checksum), leintr updates the appropriate interface statistics, resets the hardware, and calls lestart, which attempts to transmit another frame.

All Ethernet device drivers deliver their received frames to ether_input for further processing. The mbuf chain constructed by the device driver does not include the Ethernet header, so it is passed as a separate argument to ether_input. The ether_header structure is shown in Figure 4.10.

38–42   The Ethernet CRC is not generally available. It is computed and checked by the interface hardware, which discards frames that arrive with an invalid CRC. The Ethernet device driver is responsible for converting ether_type between network and host byte order. Outside of the driver, it is always in host byte order.

```
                                                                  ── if_ether.h
38 struct ether_header {
39     u_char  ether_dhost[6];    /* Ethernet destination address */
40     u_char  ether_shost[6];    /* Ethernet source address */
41     u_short ether_type;        /* Ethernet frame type */
42 };
                                                                  ── if_ether.h
```

Figure 4.10   The `ether_header` structure.

`leread` Function

The `leread` function (Figure 4.11) starts with a contiguous buffer of memory passed to
it by `leintr` and constructs an `ether_header` structure and a chain of mbufs. The
chain contains the data from the Ethernet frame. `leread` also passes the incoming
frame to BPF.

```
                                                                  ── if_le.c
528 leread(unit, buf, len)
529 int      unit;
530 char     *buf;
531 int      len;
532 {
533     struct le_softc *le = &le_softc[unit];
534     struct ether_header *et;
535     struct mbuf *m;
536     int     off, resid, flags;

537     le->sc_if.if_ipackets++;
538     et = (struct ether_header *) buf;
539     et->ether_type = ntohs((u_short) et->ether_type);
540     /* adjust input length to account for header and CRC */
541     len = len - sizeof(struct ether_header) - 4;
542     off = 0;

543     if (len <= 0) {
544         if (ledebug)
545             log(LOG_WARNING,
546                 "le%d: ierror(runt packet): from %s: len=%d\n",
547                 unit, ether_sprintf(et->ether_shost), len);
548         le->sc_runt++;
549         le->sc_if.if_ierrors++;
550         return;
551     }
552     flags = 0;
553     if (bcmp((caddr_t) etherbroadcastaddr,
554             (caddr_t) et->ether_dhost, sizeof(etherbroadcastaddr)) == 0)
555         flags |= M_BCAST;
556     if (et->ether_dhost[0] & 1)
557         flags |= M_MCAST;

558     /*
559      * Check if there's a bpf filter listening on this interface.
560      * If so, hand off the raw packet to enet.
561      */
```

```
562      if (le->sc_if.if_bpf) {
563          bpf_tap(le->sc_if.if_bpf, buf, len + sizeof(struct ether_header));

564          /*
565           * Keep the packet if it's a broadcast or has our
566           * physical ethernet address (or if we support
567           * multicast and it's one).
568           */

569          if ((flags & (M_BCAST | M_MCAST)) == 0 &&
570              bcmp(et->ether_dhost, le->sc_addr,
571                  sizeof(et->ether_dhost)) != 0)
572              return;
573      }
574      /*
575       * Pull packet off interface.  Off is nonzero if packet
576       * has trailing header; m_devget will then force this header
577       * information to be at the front, but we still have to drop
578       * the type and length which are at the front of any trailer data.
579       */
580      m = m_devget((char *) (et + 1), len, off, &le->sc_if, 0);
581      if (m == 0)
582          return;
583      m->m_flags |= flags;
584      ether_input(&le->sc_if, et, m);
585 }
```
——— *if_le.c*

Figure 4.11   leread function.

528–539   The leintr function passes three arguments to leread: unit, which identifies the particular interface card that received a frame; buf, which points to the received frame; and len, the number of bytes in the frame (including the header and the CRC).

The function constructs the ether_header structure by pointing et to the front of the buffer and converting the Ethernet type value to host byte order.

540–551   The number of data bytes is computed by subtracting the sizes of the Ethernet header and the CRC from len. *Runt packets*, which are too short to be a valid Ethernet frame, are logged, counted, and discarded.

552–557   Next, the destination address is examined to determine if it is the Ethernet broadcast or an Ethernet multicast address. The Ethernet broadcast address is a special case of an Ethernet multicast address; it has every bit set. etherbroadcastaddr is an array defined as

```
u_char  etherbroadcastaddr[6] = { 0xff, 0xff, 0xff, 0xff, 0xff, 0xff };
```

> This is a convenient way to define a 48-bit value in C. This technique works only if we assume that characters are 8-bit values—something that isn't guaranteed by ANSI C.

If bcmp reports that etherbroadcastaddr and ether_dhost are the same, the M_BCAST flag is set.

An Ethernet multicast addresses is identified by the low-order bit of the most significant byte of the address. Figure 4.12 illustrates this.

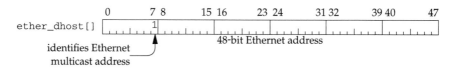

Figure 4.12   Testing for an Ethernet multicast address.

In Chapter 12 we'll see that not all Ethernet multicast frames are IP multicast datagrams and that IP must examine the packet further.

If the multicast bit is on in the address, M_MCAST is set in the flags variable. The order of the tests is important: first ether_input compares the entire 48-bit address to the Ethernet broadcast address, and if they are different it checks the low-order bit of the most significant byte to identify an Ethernet multicast address (Exercise 4.1).

558–573   If the interface is tapped by BPF, the frame is passed directly to BPF by calling bpf_tap. We'll see that for SLIP and the loopback interfaces, a special BPF frame is constructed since those networks do not have a link-level header (unlike Ethernet).

When an interface is tapped by BPF, it can be configured to run in promiscuous mode and receive all Ethernet frames that appear on the network instead of the subset of frames normally received by the hardware. The packet is discarded by leread if it was sent to a unicast address that does not match the interface's address.

574–585   m_devget (Section 2.6) copies the data from the buffer passed to leread to an mbuf chain it allocates. The first argument to m_devget points to the first byte after the Ethernet header, which is the first data byte in the frame. If m_devget runs out of memory, leread returns immediately. Otherwise the broadcast and multicast flags are set in the first mbuf in the chain, and ether_input processes the packet.

ether_input Function

ether_input, shown in Figure 4.13, examines the ether_header structure to determine the type of data that has been received and then queues the received packet for processing.

————————————————————————————————— if_ethersubr.c
```
196 void
197 ether_input(ifp, eh, m)
198 struct ifnet *ifp;
199 struct ether_header *eh;
200 struct mbuf *m;
201 {
202     struct ifqueue *inq;
203     struct llc *l;
204     struct arpcom *ac = (struct arpcom *) ifp;
205     int      s;

206     if ((ifp->if_flags & IFF_UP) == 0) {
207         m_freem(m);
208         return;
209     }
210     ifp->if_lastchange = time;
```

```
211     ifp->if_ibytes += m->m_pkthdr.len + sizeof(*eh);
212     if (bcmp((caddr_t) etherbroadcastaddr, (caddr_t) eh->ether_dhost,
213            sizeof(etherbroadcastaddr)) == 0)
214        m->m_flags |= M_BCAST;
215     else if (eh->ether_dhost[0] & 1)
216        m->m_flags |= M_MCAST;
217     if (m->m_flags & (M_BCAST | M_MCAST))
218        ifp->if_imcasts++;

219     switch (eh->ether_type) {
220     case ETHERTYPE_IP:
221        schednetisr(NETISR_IP);
222        inq = &ipintrq;
223        break;

224     case ETHERTYPE_ARP:
225        schednetisr(NETISR_ARP);
226        inq = &arpintrq;
227        break;

228     default:
229        if (eh->ether_type > ETHERMTU) {
230           m_freem(m);
231           return;
232        }
```

```
                                        /* OSI code */
```

```
307     }

308     s = splimp();
309     if (IF_QFULL(inq)) {
310        IF_DROP(inq);
311        m_freem(m);
312     } else
313        IF_ENQUEUE(inq, m);
314     splx(s);
315  }
```
                                                                  —— *if_ethersubr.c*

Figure 4.13   ether_input function.

Broadcast and multicast recognition

196–209   The arguments to ether_input are ifp, a pointer to the receiving interface's ifnet structure; eh, a pointer to the Ethernet header of the received packet; and m, a pointer to the received packet (excluding the Ethernet header).

Any packets that arrive on an inoperative interface are silently discarded. The interface may not have been configured with a protocol address, or may have been disabled by an explicit request from the ifconfig(8) program (Section 6.6).

210–218   The variable time is a global timeval structure that the kernel maintains with the current time and date, as the number of seconds and microseconds past the Unix Epoch (00:00:00 January 1, 1970, Coordinated Universal Time [UTC]). A brief discussion of

UTC can be found in [Itano and Ramsey 1993]. We'll encounter the `timeval` structure throughout the Net/3 sources:

```
struct timeval {
    long  tv_sec;       /* seconds */
    long  tv_usec;      /* and microseconds */
};
```

`ether_input` updates `if_lastchange` with the current time and increments `if_ibytes` by the size of the incoming packet (the packet length plus the 14-byte Ethernet header).

Next, `ether_input` repeats the tests done by `leread` to determine if the packet is a broadcast or multicast packet.

> Some kernels may not have been compiled with the BPF code, so the test must also be done in `ether_input`.

Link-level demultiplexing

219–227   `ether_input` jumps according to the Ethernet type field. For an IP packet, `schednetisr` schedules an IP software interrupt and the IP input queue, `ipintrq`, is selected. For an ARP packet, the ARP software interrupt is scheduled and `arpintrq` is selected.

> An *isr* is an interrupt service routine.
>
> In previous BSD releases, ARP packets were processed immediately while at the network interrupt level by calling `arpinput` directly. By queueing the packets, they can be processed at the software interrupt level.
>
> If other Ethernet types are to be handled, a kernel programmer would add additional cases here. Alternately, a process can receive other Ethernet types using BPF. For example, RARP servers are normally implemented using BPF under Net/3.

228–307   The `default` case processes unrecognized Ethernet types or packets that are encapsulated according to the 802.3 standard (such as the OSI connectionless transport). The Ethernet *type* field and the 802.3 *length* field occupy the same position in an Ethernet frame. The two encapsulations can be distinguished because the range of types in an Ethernet encapsulation is distinct from the range of lengths in the 802.3 encapsulation (Figure 4.14). We have omitted the OSI code. [Stallings 1993] contains a description of the OSI link-level protocols.

Range	Description
0 — 1500	IEEE 802.3 *length* field
1501 — 65535	Ethernet *type* field:
2048	IP packet
2054	ARP packet

Figure 4.14   Ethernet *type* and 802.3 *length* fields.

There are many additional Ethernet type values that are assigned to various protocols; we don't show them in Figure 4.14. RFC 1700 [Reynolds and Postel 1994] contains a list of the more common types.

Queue the packet

308–315   Finally, `ether_input` places the packet on the selected queue or discards the packet if the queue is full. We'll see in Figures 7.23 and 21.16 that the default limit for the IP and ARP input queues is 50 (`ipqmaxlen`) packets each.

When `ether_input` returns, the device driver tells the hardware that it is ready to receive the next packet, which may already be present in the device. The packet input queues are processed when the software interrupt scheduled by `schednetisr` occurs (Section 1.12). Specifically, `ipintr` is called to process the packets on the IP input queue, and `arpintr` is called to process the packets on the ARP input queue.

`ether_output` Function

We now examine the output of Ethernet frames, which starts when a network-level protocol such as IP calls the `if_output` function, specified in the interface's `ifnet` structure. The `if_output` function for all Ethernet devices is `ether_output` (Figure 4.2). `ether_output` takes the data portion of an Ethernet frame, encapsulates it with the 14-byte Ethernet header, and places it on the interface's send queue. This is a large function so we describe it in four parts:

- verification,
- protocol-specific processing,
- frame construction, and
- interface queueing.

Figure 4.15 includes the first part of the function.

49–64   The arguments to `ether_output` are `ifp`, which points to the outgoing interface's `ifnet` structure; `m0`, the packet to send; `dst`, the destination address of the packet; and `rt0`, routing information.

65–67   The macro `senderr` is called throughout `ether_output`.

```
#define senderr(e) { error = (e); goto bad;}
```

`senderr` saves the error code and jumps to `bad` at the end of the function, where the packet is discarded and `ether_output` returns `error`.

If the interface is up and running, `ether_output` updates the last change time for the interface. Otherwise, it returns `ENETDOWN`.

Host route

68–74   `rt0` points to the routing entry located by `ip_output` and passed to `ether_output`. If `ether_output` is called from BPF, `rt0` can be null, in which case control passes to the code in Figure 4.16. Otherwise, the route is verified. If the route is not valid, the routing tables are consulted and `EHOSTUNREACH` is returned if a route cannot be located. At this point, `rt0` and `rt` point to a valid route for the next-hop destination.

—————————————————————————— if_ethersubr.c

```
49 int
50 ether_output(ifp, m0, dst, rt0)
51 struct ifnet *ifp;
52 struct mbuf *m0;
53 struct sockaddr *dst;
54 struct rtentry *rt0;
55 {
56     short   type;
57     int     s, error = 0;
58     u_char  edst[6];
59     struct mbuf *m = m0;
60     struct rtentry *rt;
61     struct mbuf *mcopy = (struct mbuf *) 0;
62     struct ether_header *eh;
63     int     off, len = m->m_pkthdr.len;
64     struct arpcom *ac = (struct arpcom *) ifp;

65     if ((ifp->if_flags & (IFF_UP | IFF_RUNNING)) != (IFF_UP | IFF_RUNNING))
66         senderr(ENETDOWN);
67     ifp->if_lastchange = time;
68     if (rt = rt0) {
69         if ((rt->rt_flags & RTF_UP) == 0) {
70             if (rt0 = rt = rtalloc1(dst, 1))
71                 rt->rt_refcnt--;
72             else
73                 senderr(EHOSTUNREACH);
74         }
75         if (rt->rt_flags & RTF_GATEWAY) {
76             if (rt->rt_gwroute == 0)
77                 goto lookup;
78             if (((rt = rt->rt_gwroute)->rt_flags & RTF_UP) == 0) {
79                 rtfree(rt);
80                 rt = rt0;
81 lookup:         rt->rt_gwroute = rtalloc1(rt->rt_gateway, 1);

82                 if ((rt = rt->rt_gwroute) == 0)
83                     senderr(EHOSTUNREACH);
84             }
85         }
86         if (rt->rt_flags & RTF_REJECT)
87             if (rt->rt_rmx.rmx_expire == 0 ||
88                 time.tv_sec < rt->rt_rmx.rmx_expire)
89                 senderr(rt == rt0 ? EHOSTDOWN : EHOSTUNREACH);
90     }
```

—————————————————————————— if_ethersubr.c

Figure 4.15 ether_output function: verification.

Gateway route

75–85   If the next hop for the packet is a gateway (versus a final destination), a route to the gateway is located and pointed to by rt. If a gateway route cannot be found, EHOSTUNREACH is returned. At this point, rt points to the route for the next-hop destination. The next hop may be a gateway or the final destination.

Avoid ARP flooding

86–90   The RTF_REJECT flag is enabled by the ARP code to discard packets to the destination when the destination is not responding to ARP requests. This is described with Figure 21.24.

ether_output processing continues according to the destination address of the packet. Since Ethernet devices respond only to Ethernet addresses, to send a packet, ether_output must find the Ethernet address that corresponds to the IP address of the next-hop destination. The ARP protocol (Chapter 21) implements this translation. Figure 4.16 shows how the driver accesses the ARP protocol.

```
                                                               ── if_ethersubr.c
 91     switch (dst->sa_family) {

 92     case AF_INET:
 93         if (!arpresolve(ac, rt, m, dst, edst))
 94             return (0);         /* if not yet resolved */
 95         /* If broadcasting on a simplex interface, loopback a copy */
 96         if ((m->m_flags & M_BCAST) && (ifp->if_flags & IFF_SIMPLEX))
 97             mcopy = m_copy(m, 0, (int) M_COPYALL);
 98         off = m->m_pkthdr.len - m->m_len;
 99         type = ETHERTYPE_IP;
100         break;
101     case AF_ISO:


                            /* OSI code */


142     case AF_UNSPEC:
143         eh = (struct ether_header *) dst->sa_data;
144         bcopy((caddr_t) eh->ether_dhost, (caddr_t) edst, sizeof(edst));
145         type = eh->ether_type;
146         break;

147     default:
148         printf("%s%d: can't handle af%d\n", ifp->if_name, ifp->if_unit,
149                 dst->sa_family);
150         senderr(EAFNOSUPPORT);
151     }
                                                               ── if_ethersubr.c
```

Figure 4.16   ether_output function: network protocol processing.

IP output

91–101   ether_output jumps according to sa_family in the destination address. We show only the AF_INET, AF_ISO, and AF_UNSPEC cases in Figure 4.16 and have omitted the code for AF_ISO.

The AF_INET case calls arpresolve to determine the Ethernet address corresponding to the destination IP address. If the Ethernet address is already in the ARP cache, arpresolve returns 1 and ether_output proceeds. Otherwise this IP packet is held by ARP, and when ARP determines the address, it calls ether_output from the function in_arpinput.

Assuming the ARP cache contains the hardware address, `ether_output` checks if the packet is going to be broadcast and if the interface is simplex (i.e., it can't receive its own transmissions). If both tests are true, `m_copy` makes a copy of the packet. After the `switch`, the copy is queued as if it had arrived on the Ethernet interface. This is required by the definition of broadcasting; the sending host must receive a copy of the packet.

> We'll see in Chapter 12 that multicast packets may also be looped back to be received on the output interface.

Explicit Ethernet output

142–146   Some protocols, such as ARP, need to specify the Ethernet destination and type explicitly. The address family constant `AF_UNSPEC` indicates that `dst` points to an Ethernet header. `bcopy` duplicates the destination address in `edst` and assigns the Ethernet type to `type`. It isn't necessary to call `arpresolve` (as for `AF_INET`) because the Ethernet destination address has been provided explicitly by the caller.

Unrecognized address families

147–151   Unrecognized address families generate a console message and `ether_output` returns `EAFNOSUPPORT`.

In the next section of `ether_output`, shown in Figure 4.17, the Ethernet frame is constructed.

―――――――――――――――――――――――――――――――――――― *if_ethersubr.c*
```
152        if (mcopy)
153            (void) looutput(ifp, mcopy, dst, rt);
154        /*
155         * Add local net header.  If no space in first mbuf,
156         * allocate another.
157         */
158        M_PREPEND(m, sizeof(struct ether_header), M_DONTWAIT);
159        if (m == 0)
160            senderr(ENOBUFS);
161        eh = mtod(m, struct ether_header *);
162        type = htons((u_short) type);
163        bcopy((caddr_t) &type, (caddr_t) &eh->ether_type,
164            sizeof(eh->ether_type));
165        bcopy((caddr_t)edst, (caddr_t)eh->ether_dhost, sizeof (edst));
166        bcopy((caddr_t)ac->ac_enaddr, (caddr_t)eh->ether_shost,
167            sizeof(eh->ether_shost));
```
―――――――――――――――――――――――――――――――――――― *if_ethersubr.c*

Figure 4.17   `ether_output` function: Ethernet frame construction.

Ethernet header

152–167   If the code in the `switch` made a copy of the packet, the copy is processed as if it had been received on the output interface by calling `looutput`. The loopback interface and `looutput` are described in Section 5.4.

M_PREPEND ensures that there is room for 14 bytes at the front of the packet.

> Most protocols arrange to leave room at the front of the mbuf chain so that M_PREPEND needs only to adjust some pointers (e.g., sosend for UDP output in Section 16.7 and igmp_sendreport in Section 13.6).

ether_output forms the Ethernet header from type, edst, and ac_enaddr (Figure 3.26). ac_enaddr is the unicast Ethernet address associated with the output interface and is the source Ethernet address for all frames transmitted on the interface. ether_output overwrites the source address the caller may have specified in the ether_header structure with ac_enaddr. This makes it more difficult to forge the source address of an Ethernet frame.

At this point, the mbuf contains a complete Ethernet frame except for the 32-bit CRC, which is computed by the Ethernet hardware during transmission. The code shown in Figure 4.18 queues the frame for transmission by the device.

```
                                                                  ── if_ethersubr.c
168     s = splimp();
169     /*
170      * Queue message on interface, and start output if interface
171      * not yet active.
172      */
173     if (IF_QFULL(&ifp->if_snd)) {
174         IF_DROP(&ifp->if_snd);
175         splx(s);
176         senderr(ENOBUFS);
177     }
178     IF_ENQUEUE(&ifp->if_snd, m);
179     if ((ifp->if_flags & IFF_OACTIVE) == 0)
180         (*ifp->if_start)(ifp);
181     splx(s);
182     ifp->if_obytes += len + sizeof(struct ether_header);
183     if (m->m_flags & M_MCAST)
184         ifp->if_omcasts++;
185     return (error);

186 bad:
187     if (m)
188         m_freem(m);
189     return (error);
190 }
                                                                  ── if_ethersubr.c
```

Figure 4.18   ether_output function: output queueing.

168–185   If the output queue is full, ether_output discards the frame and returns ENOBUFS. If the output queue is not full, the frame is placed on the interface's send queue, and the interface's if_start function transmits the next frame if the interface is not already active.

186–190   The senderr macro jumps to bad where the frame is discarded and an error code is returned.

`lestart` Function

The `lestart` function dequeues frames from the interface output queue and arranges for them to be transmitted by the LANCE Ethernet card. If the device is idle, the function is called to begin transmitting frames. An example appears at the end of `ether_output` (Figure 4.18), where `lestart` is called indirectly through the interface's `if_start` function.

If the device is busy, it generates an interrupt when it completes transmission of the current frame. The driver calls `lestart` to dequeue and transmit the next frame. Once started, the protocol layer can queue frames without calling `lestart` since the driver dequeues and transmits frames until the queue is empty.

Figure 4.19 shows the `lestart` function. `lestart` assumes `splimp` has been called to block any device interrupts.

Interface must be initialized

325–333   If the interface is not initialized, `lestart` returns immediately.

Dequeue frame from output queue

335–342   If the interface is initialized, the next frame is removed from the queue. If the interface output queue is empty, `lestart` returns.

Transmit frame and pass to BPF

343–350   `leput` copies the frame in `m` to the hardware buffer pointed to by the first argument to `leput`. If the interface is tapped by BPF, the frame is passed to `bpf_tap`. We have omitted the device-specific code that initiates the transmission of the frame from the hardware buffer.

Repeat if device is ready for more frames

359   `lestart` stops passing frames to the device when `le->sc_txcnt` equals `LETBUF`. Some Ethernet interfaces can queue more than one outgoing Ethernet frame. For the LANCE driver, `LETBUF` is the number of hardware transmit buffers available to the driver, and `le->sc_txcnt` keeps track of how many of the buffers are in use.

Mark device as busy

360–362   Finally, `lestart` turns on `IFF_OACTIVE` in the `ifnet` structure to indicate the device is busy transmitting frames.

> There is an unfortunate side effect to queueing multiple frames in the device for transmission. According to [Jacobson 1988a], the LANCE chip is able to transmit queued frames with very little delay between frames. Unfortunately, some [broken] Ethernet devices drop the frames because they can't process the incoming data fast enough.

> This interacts badly with an application such as NFS that sends large UDP datagrams (often greater than 8192 bytes) that are fragmented by IP and queued in the LANCE device as multiple Ethernet frames. Fragments are lost on the receiving side, resulting in many incomplete datagrams and high delays as NFS retransmits the entire UDP datagram.

> Jacobson noted that Sun's LANCE driver only queued one frame at a time, perhaps to avoid this problem.

――――――――――――――――――――――――――――――――――― *if_le.c*

```
325 lestart(ifp)
326 struct ifnet *ifp;
327 {
328     struct le_softc *le = &le_softc[ifp->if_unit];
329     struct letmd *tmd;
330     struct mbuf *m;
331     int     len;

332     if ((le->sc_if.if_flags & IFF_RUNNING) == 0)
333         return (0);
```

                                 /* device-specific code */

```
335     do {
```

                                 /* device-specific code */

```
340         IF_DEQUEUE(&le->sc_if.if_snd, m);
341         if (m == 0)
342             return (0);
343         len = leput(le->sc_r2->ler2_tbuf[le->sc_tmd], m);
344         /*
345          * If bpf is listening on this interface, let it
346          * see the packet before we commit it to the wire.
347          */
348         if (ifp->if_bpf)
349             bpf_tap(ifp->if_bpf, le->sc_r2->ler2_tbuf[le->sc_tmd],
350                     len);
```

                                 /* device-specific code */

```
359     } while (++le->sc_txcnt < LETBUF);
360     le->sc_if.if_flags |= IFF_OACTIVE;
361     return (0);
362 }
```

――――――――――――――――――――――――――――――――――― *if_le.c*

Figure 4.19 lestart function.

4.4   `ioctl` System Call

The `ioctl` system call supports a generic command interface used by a process to access features of a device that aren't supported by the standard system calls. The prototype for `ioctl` is:

```
int ioctl(int fd, unsigned long com, ...);
```

fd is a descriptor, usually a device or network connection. Each type of descriptor supports its own set of `ioctl` commands specified by the second argument, *com*. A third argument is shown as "..." in the prototype, since it is a pointer of some type that depends on the `ioctl` command being invoked. If the command is retrieving information, the third argument must point to a buffer large enough to hold the data. In this text, we discuss only the `ioctl` commands applicable to socket descriptors.

> The prototype we show for system calls is the one used by a process to issue the system call. We'll see in Chapter 15 that the function within the kernel that implements a system call has a different prototype.

We describe the implementation of the `ioctl` system call in Chapter 17 but we discuss the implementation of individual `ioctl` commands throughout the text.

The first `ioctl` commands we discuss provide access to the network interface structures that we have described. Throughout the text we summarize `ioctl` commands as shown in Figure 4.20.

Command	Third argument	Function	Description
SIOCGIFCONF	struct ifconf *	ifconf	retrieve list of interface configuration
SIOCGIFFLAGS	struct ifreq *	ifioctl	get interface flags
SIOCGIFMETRIC	struct ifreq *	ifioctl	get interface metric
SIOCSIFFLAGS	struct ifreq *	ifioctl	set interface flags
SIOCSIFMETRIC	struct ifreq *	ifioctl	set interface metric

Figure 4.20   Interface `ioctl` commands.

The first column shows the symbolic constant that identifies the `ioctl` command (the second argument, *com*). The second column shows the type of the third argument passed to the `ioctl` system call for the command shown in the first column. The third column names the function that implements the command.

Figure 4.21 shows the organization of the various functions that process `ioctl` commands. The shaded functions are the ones we describe in this chapter. The remaining functions are described in other chapters.

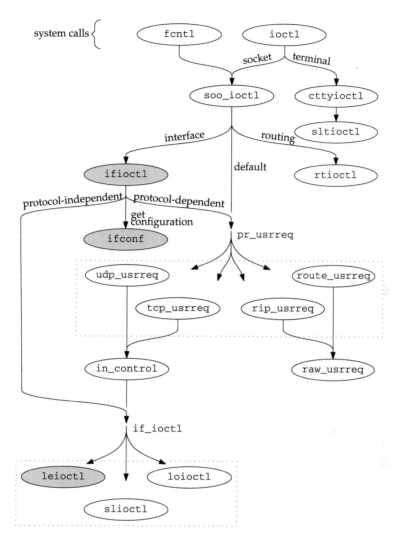

Figure 4.21 ioctl functions described in this chapter.

`ifioctl` **Function**

The `ioctl` system call routes the five commands shown in Figure 4.20 to the `ifioctl`
function shown in Figure 4.22.

```
                                                                        ─ if.c
394 int
395 ifioctl(so, cmd, data, p)
396 struct socket *so;
397 int     cmd;
398 caddr_t data;
399 struct proc *p;
400 {
401     struct ifnet *ifp;
402     struct ifreq *ifr;
403     int     error;

404     if (cmd == SIOCGIFCONF)
405         return (ifconf(cmd, data));

406     ifr = (struct ifreq *) data;
407     ifp = ifunit(ifr->ifr_name);
408     if (ifp == 0)
409         return (ENXIO);
410     switch (cmd) {
```

```
              /* other interface ioctl commands (Figures 4.29 and 12.11) */
```

```
447     default:
448         if (so->so_proto == 0)
449             return (EOPNOTSUPP);
450         return ((*so->so_proto->pr_usrreq) (so, PRU_CONTROL,
451                                         cmd, data, ifp));
452     }
453     return (0);
454 }
                                                                        ─ if.c
```

Figure 4.22 `ifioctl` function: overview and `SIOCGIFCONF`.

394–405   For the `SIOCGIFCONF` command, `ifioctl` calls `ifconf` to construct a table of
variable-length `ifreq` structures.

406–410   For the remaining `ioctl` commands, the data argument is a pointer to an `ifreq`
structure. `ifunit` searches the `ifnet` list for an interface with the text name provided
by the process in `ifr->ifr_name` (e.g., "sl0", "le1", or "lo0"). If there is no matching interface, `ifioctl` returns `ENXIO`. The remaining code depends on `cmd` and is
described with Figure 4.29.

447–454   If the interface `ioctl` command is not recognized, `ifioctl` forwards the command to the user-request function of the protocol associated with the socket on which
the request was made. For IP, these commands are issued on a UDP socket and
`udp_usrreq` is called. The commands that fall into this category are described in Figure 6.10. Section 23.10 describes the `udp_usrreq` function in detail.

If control falls out of the `switch`, 0 is returned.

ifconf **Function**

ifconf provides a standard way for a process to discover the interfaces present and the addresses configured on a system. Interface information is represented by ifreq and ifconf structures shown in Figures 4.23 and 4.24.

```
                                                                                   if.h
262 struct  ifreq {
263 #define IFNAMSIZ     16
264     char    ifr_name[IFNAMSIZ];                     /* if name, e.g. "en0" */
265     union {
266         struct  sockaddr ifru_addr;
267         struct  sockaddr ifru_dstaddr;
268         struct  sockaddr ifru_broadaddr;
269         short   ifru_flags;
270         int ifru_metric;
271         caddr_t ifru_data;
272     } ifr_ifru;
273 #define ifr_addr     ifr_ifru.ifru_addr          /* address */
274 #define ifr_dstaddr ifr_ifru.ifru_dstaddr        /* other end of p-to-p link */
275 #define ifr_broadaddr   ifr_ifru.ifru_broadaddr /* broadcast address */
276 #define ifr_flags    ifr_ifru.ifru_flags         /* flags */
277 #define ifr_metric   ifr_ifru.ifru_metric        /* metric */
278 #define ifr_data     ifr_ifru.ifru_data          /* for use by interface */
279 };
                                                                                   if.h
```

Figure 4.23 ifreq structure.

262–279   An ifreq structure contains the name of an interface in ifr_name. The remaining members in the union are accessed by the various ioctl commands. As usual, macros simplify the syntax required to access the members of the union.

```
                                                                                   if.h
292 struct  ifconf {
293     int ifc_len;                          /* size of associated buffer */
294     union {
295         caddr_t ifcu_buf;
296         struct  ifreq *ifcu_req;
297     } ifc_ifcu;
298 #define ifc_buf ifc_ifcu.ifcu_buf    /* buffer address */
299 #define ifc_req ifc_ifcu.ifcu_req    /* array of structures returned */
300 };
                                                                                   if.h
```

Figure 4.24 ifconf structure.

292–300   In the ifconf structure, ifc_len is the size in bytes of the buffer pointed to by ifc_buf. The buffer is allocated by a process but filled in by ifconf with an array of variable-length ifreq structures. For the ifconf function, ifr_addr is the relevant member of the union in the ifreq structure. Each ifreq structure has a variable length because the length of ifr_addr (a sockaddr structure) varies according to the type of address. The sa_len member from the sockaddr structure must be used to

locate the end of each entry. Figure 4.25 illustrates the data structures manipulated by
ifconf.

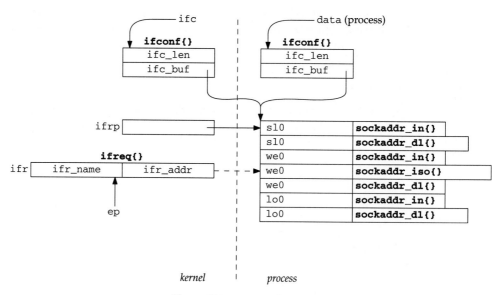

Figure 4.25 ifconf data structures.

In Figure 4.25, the data on the left is in the kernel and the data on the right is in a
process. We'll refer to this figure as we discuss the ifconf function listed in Figure 4.26.

462–474   The two arguments to ifconf are: cmd, which is ignored; and data, which points
to a copy of the ifconf structure specified by the process.

ifc is data cast to a ifconf structure pointer. ifp traverses the interface list
starting at ifnet (the head of the list), and ifa traverses the address list for each interface. cp and ep control the construction of the text interface name within ifr, which is
the ifreq structure that holds an interface name and address before they are copied to
the process's buffer. ifrp points to this buffer and is advanced after each address is
copied. space is the number of bytes remaining in the process's buffer, cp is used to
search for the end of the name, and ep marks the last possible location for the numeric
portion of the interface name.

                                                                                    ────── *if.c*
```
462 int
463 ifconf(cmd, data)
464 int     cmd;
465 caddr_t data;
466 {
467     struct ifconf *ifc = (struct ifconf *) data;
468     struct ifnet *ifp = ifnet;
469     struct ifaddr *ifa;
470     char    *cp, *ep;
471     struct ifreq ifr, *ifrp;
472     int     space = ifc->ifc_len, error = 0;
```

```
473    ifrp = ifc->ifc_req;
474    ep = ifr.ifr_name + sizeof(ifr.ifr_name) - 2;

475    for (; space > sizeof(ifr) && ifp; ifp = ifp->if_next) {
476        strncpy(ifr.ifr_name, ifp->if_name, sizeof(ifr.ifr_name) - 2);
477        for (cp = ifr.ifr_name; cp < ep && *cp; cp++)
478            continue;
479        *cp++ = '0' + ifp->if_unit;
480        *cp = '\0';
481        if ((ifa = ifp->if_addrlist) == 0) {
482            bzero((caddr_t) & ifr.ifr_addr, sizeof(ifr.ifr_addr));
483            error = copyout((caddr_t) & ifr, (caddr_t) ifrp,
484                            sizeof(ifr));
485            if (error)
486                break;
487            space -= sizeof(ifr), ifrp++;
488        } else
489            for (; space > sizeof(ifr) && ifa; ifa = ifa->ifa_next) {
490                struct sockaddr *sa = ifa->ifa_addr;
491                if (sa->sa_len <= sizeof(*sa)) {
492                    ifr.ifr_addr = *sa;
493                    error = copyout((caddr_t) & ifr, (caddr_t) ifrp,
494                                    sizeof(ifr));
495                    ifrp++;
496                } else {
497                    space -= sa->sa_len - sizeof(*sa);
498                    if (space < sizeof(ifr))
499                        break;
500                    error = copyout((caddr_t) & ifr, (caddr_t) ifrp,
501                                    sizeof(ifr.ifr_name));
502                    if (error == 0)
503                        error = copyout((caddr_t) sa,
504                                    (caddr_t) & ifrp->ifr_addr, sa->sa_len);
505                    ifrp = (struct ifreq *)
506                        (sa->sa_len + (caddr_t) & ifrp->ifr_addr);
507                }
508                if (error)
509                    break;
510                space -= sizeof(ifr);
511            }
512    }
513    ifc->ifc_len -= space;
514    return (error);
515 }
```
                                                                        —— *if.c*

Figure 4.26 ifconf function.

475–488   The for loop traverses the list of interfaces. For each interface, the text name is
copied to ifr_name followed by the text representation of the if_unit number. If no
addresses have been assigned to the interface, an address of all 0s is constructed, the
resulting ifreq structure is copied to the process, space is decreased, and ifrp is
advanced.

489–515   If the interface has one or more addresses, the for loop processes each one. The address is added to the interface name in `ifr` and then `ifr` is copied to the process. Addresses longer than a standard `sockaddr` structure don't fit in `ifr` and are copied directly out to the process. After each address, `space` and `ifrp` are adjusted. After all the interfaces are processed, the length of the buffer is updated (`ifc->ifc_len`) and `ifconf` returns. The `ioctl` system call takes care of copying the new contents of the `ifconf` structure back to the `ifconf` structure in the process.

Example

Figure 4.27 shows the configuration of the interface structures after the Ethernet, SLIP, and loopback interfaces have been initialized.

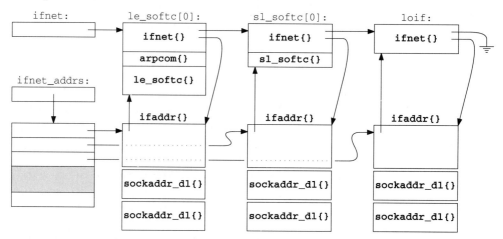

Figure 4.27   Interface and address data structures.

Figure 4.28 shows the contents of `ifc` and `buffer` after the following code is executed.

```
struct ifconf ifc;     /* SIOCGIFCONF adjusts this */
char buffer[144];      /* contains interface addresses when ioctl returns */
int s;                 /* any socket */

ifc.ifc_len = 144;
ifc.ifc_buf = buffer;
if (ioctl(s, SIOCGIFCONF, &ifc) < 0 ) {
    perror("ioctl failed");
    exit(1);
}
```

There are no restrictions on the type of socket specified with the `SIOCGIFCONF` command, which, as we have seen, returns the addresses for all protocol families.

In Figure 4.28, `ifc_len` has been changed from 144 to 108 by `ioctl` since the three addresses returned in the buffer only occupy 108 (3×36) bytes. Three `sockaddr_dl` addresses are returned and the last 36 bytes of the buffer are unused. The first 16 bytes of each entry contain the text name of the interface. In this case only 3 of the 16 bytes are used.

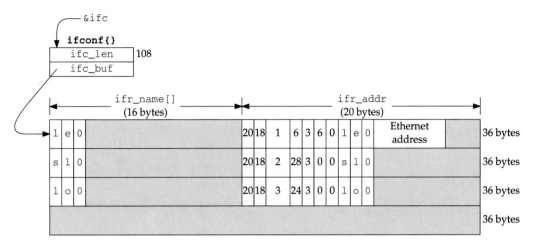

Figure 4.28 Data returned by the SIOCGIFCONF command.

ifr_addr has the form of a sockaddr structure, so the first value is the length (20 bytes) and the second value is the type of address (18, AF_LINK). The next value is sdl_index, which is different for each interface as is sdl_type (6, 28, and 24 correspond to IFT_ETHER, IFT_SLIP, and IFT_LOOP).

The next three values are sa_nlen (the length of the text name), sa_alen (the length of the hardware address), and sa_slen (unused). sa_nlen is 3 for all three entries. sa_alen is 6 for the Ethernet address and 0 for both the SLIP and loopback interfaces. sa_slen is always 0.

Finally, the text interface name appears, followed by the hardware address (Ethernet only). Neither the SLIP nor the loopback interface store a hardware-level address in the sockaddr_dl structure.

In the example, only sockaddr_dl addresses are returned (because no other address types were configured in Figure 4.27), so each entry in the buffer is the same size. If other addresses (e.g., IP or OSI addresses) were configured for an interface, they would be returned along with the sockaddr_dl addresses, and the size of each entry would vary according to the type of address returned.

Generic Interface ioctl commands

The four remaining interface commands from Figure 4.20 (SIOCGIFFLAGS, SIOCGIFMETRIC, SIOCSIFFLAGS, and SIOCSIFMETRIC) are handled by the ifioctl function. Figure 4.29 shows the case statements for these commands.

SIOCGIFFLAGS and SIOCGIFMETRIC

410–416   For the two SIOCGxxx commands, ifioctl copies the if_flags or if_metric value for the interface into the ifreq structure. For the flags, the ifr_flags member of the union is used and for the metric, the ifr_metric member is used (Figure 4.23).

---

if.c
```
410        switch (cmd) {
411        case SIOCGIFFLAGS:
412            ifr->ifr_flags = ifp->if_flags;
413            break;

414        case SIOCGIFMETRIC:
415            ifr->ifr_metric = ifp->if_metric;
416            break;

417        case SIOCSIFFLAGS:
418            if (error = suser(p->p_ucred, &p->p_acflag))
419                return (error);
420            if (ifp->if_flags & IFF_UP && (ifr->ifr_flags & IFF_UP) == 0) {
421                int    s = splimp();
422                if_down(ifp);
423                splx(s);
424            }
425            if (ifr->ifr_flags & IFF_UP && (ifp->if_flags & IFF_UP) == 0) {
426                int    s = splimp();
427                if_up(ifp);
428                splx(s);
429            }
430            ifp->if_flags = (ifp->if_flags & IFF_CANTCHANGE) |
431                (ifr->ifr_flags & ~IFF_CANTCHANGE);
432            if (ifp->if_ioctl)
433                (void) (*ifp->if_ioctl) (ifp, cmd, data);
434            break;

435        case SIOCSIFMETRIC:
436            if (error = suser(p->p_ucred, &p->p_acflag))
437                return (error);
438            ifp->if_metric = ifr->ifr_metric;
439            break;
```
if.c

Figure 4.29 ifioctl function: flags and metrics.

SIOCSIFFLAGS

417–429   To change the interface flags, the calling process must have superuser privileges. If the process is shutting down a running interface or bringing up an interface that isn't running, if_down or if_up are called respectively.

Ignore IFF_CANTCHANGE flags

430–434   Recall from Figure 3.7 that some interface flags cannot be changed by a process. The expression (ifp->if_flags & IFF_CANTCHANGE) clears the interface flags that *can* be changed by the process, and the expression (ifr->ifr_flags & ~IFF_CANTCHANGE) clears the flags in the *request* that may *not* be changed by the process. The two expressions are ORed together and saved as the new value for ifp->if_flags. Before returning, the request is passed to the if_ioctl function associated with the device (e.g., leioctl for the LANCE driver—Figure 4.31).

SIOCSIFMETRIC

435–439   Changing the interface metric is easier; as long as the process has superuser privileges, ifioctl copies the new metric into if_metric for the interface.

if_down and if_up Functions

With the ifconfig program, an administrator can enable and disable an interface by setting or clearing the IFF_UP flag through the SIOCSIFFLAGS command. Figure 4.30 shows the code for the if_down and if_up functions.

```
                                                                                ─ if.c
292 void
293 if_down(ifp)
294 struct ifnet *ifp;
295 {
296     struct ifaddr *ifa;

297     ifp->if_flags &= ~IFF_UP;
298     for (ifa = ifp->if_addrlist; ifa; ifa = ifa->ifa_next)
299         pfctlinput(PRC_IFDOWN, ifa->ifa_addr);
300     if_qflush(&ifp->if_snd);
301     rt_ifmsg(ifp);
302 }

308 void
309 if_up(ifp)
310 struct ifnet *ifp;
311 {
312     struct ifaddr *ifa;

313     ifp->if_flags |= IFF_UP;
314     rt_ifmsg(ifp);
315 }
                                                                                ─ if.c
```

Figure 4.30   if_down and if_up functions.

292–302   When an interface is shut down, the IFF_UP flag is cleared and the PRC_IFDOWN command is issued by pfctlinput (Section 7.7) for each address associated with the interface. This gives each protocol an opportunity to respond to the interface being shut down. Some protocols, such as OSI, terminate connections using the interface. IP attempts to reroute connections through other interfaces if possible. TCP and UDP ignore failing interfaces and rely on the routing protocols to find alternate paths for the packets.

if_qflush discards any packets queued for the interface. The routing system is notified of the change by rt_ifmsg. TCP retransmits the lost packets automatically; UDP applications must explicitly detect and respond to this condition on their own.

308–315   When an interface is enabled, the IFF_UP flag is set and rt_ifmsg notifies the routing system that the interface status has changed.

Ethernet, SLIP, and Loopback

We saw in Figure 4.29 that for the SIOCSIFFLAGS command, ifioctl calls the
if_ioctl function for the interface. In our three sample interfaces, the slioctl and
loioctl functions return EINVAL for this command, which is ignored by ifioctl.
Figure 4.31 shows the leioctl function and SIOCSIFFLAGS processing of the LANCE
Ethernet driver.

```
                                                                      ─── if_le.c
614 leioctl(ifp, cmd, data)
615 struct ifnet *ifp;
616 int     cmd;
617 caddr_t data;
618 {
619     struct ifaddr *ifa = (struct ifaddr *) data;
620     struct le_softc *le = &le_softc[ifp->if_unit];
621     struct lereg1 *ler1 = le->sc_r1;
622     int     s = splimp(), error = 0;

623     switch (cmd) {
```

```
                    /* SIOCSIFADDR code (Figure 6.28) */
```

```
638     case SIOCSIFFLAGS:
639         if ((ifp->if_flags & IFF_UP) == 0 &&
640             ifp->if_flags & IFF_RUNNING) {
641             LERDWR(le->sc_r0, LE_STOP, ler1->ler1_rdp);
642             ifp->if_flags &= ~IFF_RUNNING;
643         } else if (ifp->if_flags & IFF_UP &&
644                 (ifp->if_flags & IFF_RUNNING) == 0)
645             leinit(ifp->if_unit);
646         /*
647          * If the state of the promiscuous bit changes, the interface
648          * must be reset to effect the change.
649          */
650         if (((ifp->if_flags ^ le->sc_iflags) & IFF_PROMISC) &&
651             (ifp->if_flags & IFF_RUNNING)) {
652             le->sc_iflags = ifp->if_flags;
653             lereset(ifp->if_unit);
654             lestart(ifp);
655         }
656         break;
```

```
            /* SIOCADDMULTI and SIOCDELMULTI code (Figure 12.31) */
```

```
672     default:
673         error = EINVAL;
674     }
675     splx(s);
676     return (error);
677 }
```
```
                                                                      ─── if_le.c
```

Figure 4.31 leioctl function: SIOCSIFFLAGS.

614–623   `leioctl` casts the third argument, `data`, to an `ifaddr` structure pointer and saves the value in `ifa`. The `le` pointer references the `le_softc` structure indexed by `ifp->if_unit`. The `switch` statement, based on `cmd`, makes up the main body of the function.

638–656   Only the `SIOCSIFFLAGS` case is shown in Figure 4.31. By the time `ifioctl` calls `leioctl`, the interface flags have been changed. The code shown here forces the physical interface into a state that matches the configuration of the flags. If the interface is going down (`IFF_UP` is not set), but the interface is operating, the interface is shut down. If the interface is going up but is not operating, the interface is initialized and restarted.

If the promiscuous bit has been changed, the interface is shut down, reset, and restarted to implement the change.

> The expression including the exclusive OR and `IFF_PROMISC` is true only if the request changes the `IFF_PROMISC` bit.

672–677   The `default` case for unrecognized commands posts `EINVAL`, which is returned at the end of the function.

4.5   Summary

In this chapter we described the implementation of the LANCE Ethernet device driver, which we refer to throughout the text. We saw how the Ethernet driver detects broadcast and multicast addresses on input, how the Ethernet and 802.3 encapsulations are detected, and how incoming frames are demultiplexed to the appropriate protocol queue. In Chapter 21 we'll see how IP addresses (unicast, broadcast, and multicast) are converted into the correct Ethernet addresses on output.

Finally, we discussed the protocol-specific `ioctl` commands that access the interface-layer data structures.

Exercises

4.1   In `leread`, the `M_MCAST` flag (in addition to `M_BCAST`) is always set when a broadcast packet is received. Compare this behavior to the code in `ether_input`. Why are the flags set in `leread` and `ether_input`? Does it matter? Which is correct?

4.2   In `ether_input` (Figure 4.13), what would happen if the test for the broadcast address and the test for a multicast address were swapped? What would happen if the `if` on the test for a multicast address were not preceded by an `else`?

5

Interfaces: SLIP and Loopback

5.1 Introduction

In Chapter 4 we looked at the Ethernet interface. In this chapter we describe the SLIP and loopback interfaces, as well as the `ioctl` commands used to configure all network interfaces. The TCP compression algorithm used by the SLIP driver is described in Section 29.13. The loopback driver is straightforward and we discuss it here in its entirety.

Figure 5.1, which also appeared as Figure 4.2, lists the entry points to our three example drivers.

ifnet	Ethernet	SLIP	Loopback	Description
if_init	leinit			initialize hardware
if_output	ether_output	sloutput	looutput	accept and queue packet for transmission
if_start	lestart			begin transmission of frame
if_done				output complete (unused)
if_ioctl	leioctl	slioctl	loioctl	handle `ioctl` commands from a process
if_reset	lereset			reset the device to a known state
if_watchdog				watch the device for failures or collect statistics

Figure 5.1 Interface functions for the example drivers.

5.2 Code Introduction

The files containing code for SLIP and loopback drivers are listed in Figure 5.2.

File	Description
net/if_slvar.h	SLIP definitions
net/if_sl.c	SLIP driver functions
net/if_loop.c	loopback driver

Figure 5.2   Files discussed in this chapter.

Global Variables

The SLIP and loopback interface structures are described in this chapter.

Variable	Datatype	Description
sl_softc	struct sl_softc []	SLIP interface
loif	struct ifnet	loopback interface

Figure 5.3   Global variables introduced in this chapter.

sl_softc is an array, since there can be many SLIP interfaces. loif is not an array, since there can be only one loopback interface.

Statistics

The statistics from the ifnet structure described in Chapter 4 are also updated by the SLIP and loopback drivers. One other variable (which is not in the ifnet structure) collects statistics; it is shown in Figure 5.4.

Variable	Description	Used by SNMP
tk_nin	#bytes received by any serial interface (updated by SLIP driver)	

Figure 5.4   tk_nin variable.

5.3   SLIP Interface

A SLIP interface communicates with a remote system across a standard asynchronous serial line. As with Ethernet, SLIP defines a standard way to frame IP packets as they are transmitted on the serial line. Figure 5.5 shows the encapsulation of an IP packet into a SLIP frame when the IP packet contains SLIP's reserved characters.

Packets are separated by the SLIP END character 0xc0. If the END character appears in the IP packet, it is prefixed with the SLIP ESC character 0xdb and transmitted as 0xdc instead. When the ESC character appears in the IP packet, it is prefixed with the ESC character 0xdb and transmitted as 0xdd.

Since there is no type field in SLIP frames (as there is with Ethernet), SLIP is suitable only for carrying IP packets.

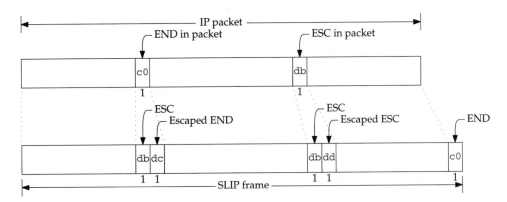

Figure 5.5   SLIP encapsulation of an IP packet.

SLIP is described in RFC 1055 [Romkey 1988], where its many weaknesses and nonstandard status are also stated. Volume 1 contains a more detailed description of SLIP encapsulation.

The Point-to-Point Protocol (PPP) was designed to address SLIP's problems and to provide a standard method for transmitting frames across a serial link. PPP is defined in RFC 1332 [McGregor 1992] and RFC 1548 [Simpson 1993]. Net/3 does not contain an implementation of PPP, so we do not discuss it in this text. See Section 2.6 of Volume 1 for more information regarding PPP. Appendix B describes where to obtain a reference implementation of PPP.

The SLIP Line Discipline: `SLIPDISC`

In Net/3 the SLIP interface relies on an asynchronous serial device driver to send and receive the data. Traditionally these device drivers have been called TTYs (teletypes). The Net/3 TTY subsystem includes the notion of a *line discipline* that acts as a filter between the physical device and I/O system calls such as `read` and `write`. A line discipline implements features such as line editing, newline and carriage-return processing, tab expansion, and more. The SLIP interface appears as a line discipline to the TTY subsystem, but it does not pass incoming data to a process reading from the device and does not accept outgoing data from a process writing to the device. Instead, the SLIP interface passes incoming packets to the IP input queue and accepts outgoing packets through the `if_output` function in SLIP's `ifnet` structure. The kernel identifies line disciplines by an integer constant, which for SLIP is `SLIPDISC`.

Figure 5.6 shows a traditional line discipline on the left and the SLIP discipline on the right. We show the process on the right as `slattach` since it is the program that initializes a SLIP interface. The details of the TTY subsystem and line disciplines are outside the scope of this text. We present only the information required to understand the workings of the SLIP code. For more information about the TTY subsystem see [Leffler et al. 1989]. Figure 5.7 lists the functions that implement the SLIP driver. The middle columns indicate whether the function implements line discipline features, network interface features, or both.

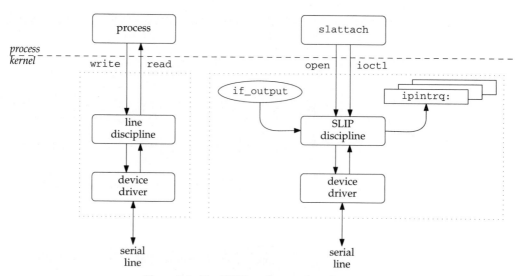

Figure 5.6 The SLIP interface as a line discipline.

Function	Network Interface	Line Discipline	Description
slattach	•		initialize and attach sl_softc structures to ifnet list
slinit	•		initialize the SLIP data structures
sloutput	•		queue outgoing packets for transmission on associated TTY device
slioctl	•		process socket ioctl requests
sl_btom	•		convert a device buffer to an mbuf chain
slopen		•	attach sl_softc structure to TTY device and initialize driver
slclose		•	detach sl_softc structure from TTY device, mark interface as down, and release memory
sltioctl		•	process TTY ioctl commands
slstart	•	•	dequeue packet and begin transmitting data on TTY device
slinput	•	•	process incoming byte from TTY device, queue incoming packet if an entire frame has been received

Figure 5.7 The functions in the SLIP device driver.

The SLIP driver in Net/3 supports compression of TCP packet headers for better throughput. We discuss header compression in Section 29.13, so Figure 5.7 omits the functions that implement this feature.

> The Net/3 SLIP interface also supports an escape sequence. When detected by the receiver, the sequence shuts down SLIP processing and returns the device to the standard line discipline. We omit this processing from our discussion.

Figure 5.8 shows the complex relationship between SLIP as a line discipline and SLIP as a network interface.

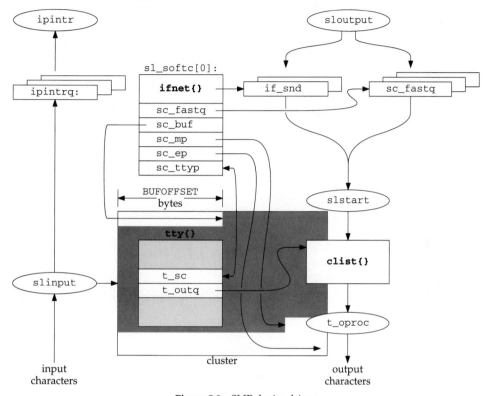

Figure 5.8   SLIP device driver.

In Net/3 sc_ttyp and t_sc point to the tty structure and the sl_softc[0] structure respectively. Instead of cluttering the figure with two arrows, we use a double-ended arrow positioned at each pointer to illustrated the two links between the structures.

Figure 5.8 contains a lot of information:

- The network interface is represented by the sl_softc structure and the TTY device by the tty structure.

- Incoming bytes are stored in the cluster (shown behind the tty structure). When a complete SLIP frame is received, the enclosed IP packet is put on the ipintrq by slinput.

- Outgoing packets are dequeued from if_snd or sc_fastq, converted to SLIP frames, and passed to the TTY device by slstart. The TTY buffers outgoing bytes in the clist structure. The t_oproc function drains and transmits the bytes held in the clist structure.

SLIP Initialization: `slopen` and `slinit`

We discussed in Section 3.7 how `slattach` initializes the `sl_softc` structures. The interface remains initialized but inoperative until a program (usually `slattach`) opens a TTY device (e.g., `/dev/tty01`) and issues an `ioctl` command to replace the standard line discipline with the SLIP discipline. At this point the TTY subsystem calls the line discipline's open function (in this case `slopen`), which establishes the association between a particular TTY device and a particular SLIP interface. `slopen` is shown in Figure 5.9.

```
                                                                    ── if_sl.c
181 int
182 slopen(dev, tp)
183 dev_t    dev;
184 struct tty *tp;
185 {
186     struct proc *p = curproc;    /* XXX */
187     struct sl_softc *sc;
188     int     nsl;
189     int     error;

190     if (error = suser(p->p_ucred, &p->p_acflag))
191         return (error);

192     if (tp->t_line == SLIPDISC)
193         return (0);

194     for (nsl = NSL, sc = sl_softc; --nsl >= 0; sc++)
195         if (sc->sc_ttyp == NULL) {
196             if (slinit(sc) == 0)
197                 return (ENOBUFS);
198             tp->t_sc = (caddr_t) sc;
199             sc->sc_ttyp = tp;
200             sc->sc_if.if_baudrate = tp->t_ospeed;
201             ttyflush(tp, FREAD | FWRITE);
202             return (0);
203         }
204     return (ENXIO);
205 }
                                                                    ── if_sl.c
```

Figure 5.9 The `slopen` function.

181–193   Two arguments are passed to `slopen`: dev, a kernel device identifier that `slopen` does not use; and tp, a pointer to the `tty` structure associated with the TTY device. First some precautions: if the process does not have superuser privileges, or if the TTY's line discipline is set to `SLIPDISC` already, `slopen` returns immediately.

194–205   The `for` loop searches the array of `sl_softc` structures for the first unused entry, calls `slinit` (Figure 5.10), joins the `tty` and `sl_softc` structures by `t_sc` and `sc_ttyp`, and copies the TTY output speed (`t_ospeed`) into the SLIP interface. `ttyflush` discards any pending input or output data in the TTY queues. `slopen` returns `ENXIO` if a SLIP interface structure is not available, or 0 if it was successful.

Notice that the first available sl_softc structure is associated with the TTY device. There need not be a fixed mapping between TTY devices and SLIP interfaces if the system has more than one SLIP line. In fact, the mapping depends on the order in which slattach opens and closes the TTY devices.

The slinit function shown in Figure 5.10 initializes the sl_softc structure.

```
                                                                            ── if_sl.c
156 static int
157 slinit(sc)
158 struct sl_softc *sc;
159 {
160     caddr_t p;

161     if (sc->sc_ep == (u_char *) 0) {
162         MCLALLOC(p, M_WAIT);
163         if (p)
164             sc->sc_ep = (u_char *) p + SLBUFSIZE;
165         else {
166             printf("sl%d: can't allocate buffer\n", sc - sl_softc);
167             sc->sc_if.if_flags &= ~IFF_UP;
168             return (0);
169         }
170     }
171     sc->sc_buf = sc->sc_ep - SLMAX;
172     sc->sc_mp = sc->sc_buf;
173     sl_compress_init(&sc->sc_comp);
174     return (1);
175 }
                                                                            ── if_sl.c
```

Figure 5.10 The slinit function.

156–175   The slinit function allocates an mbuf cluster and attaches it to the sl_softc structure with three pointers. Incoming bytes are stored in the cluster until an entire SLIP frame has been received. sc_buf always points to the start of the packet in the cluster, sc_mp points to the location of the next byte to be received, and sc_ep points to the end of the cluster. sl_compress_init initializes the TCP header compression state for this link (Section 29.13).

In Figure 5.8 we see that sc_buf does not point to the first byte in the cluster. slinit leaves room for 148 bytes (BUFOFFSET), as the incoming packet may have a compressed header that will expand to fill this space. The bytes that have already been received are shaded in the cluster. We see that sc_mp points to the byte just after the last byte received and sc_ep points to the end of the cluster. Figure 5.11 shows the relationships between several SLIP constants.

All that remains to make the interface operational is to assign it an IP address. As with the Ethernet driver, we postpone the discussion of address assignment until Section 6.6.

Constant	Value	Description
MCLBYTES	2048	size of an mbuf cluster
SLBUFSIZE	2048	maximum size of an uncompressed SLIP packet—including a BPF header
SLIP_HDRLEN	16	size of SLIP BPF header
BUFOFFSET	148	maximum size of an expanded TCP/IP header plus room for a BPF header
SLMAX	1900	maximum size of a compressed SLIP packet stored in a cluster
SLMTU	296	optimal size of SLIP packet; results in minimal delay with good bulk throughput
SLIP_HIWAT	100	maximum number of bytes to queue in TTY output queue
BUFOFFSET + SLMAX = SLBUFSIZE = MCLBYTES		

Figure 5.11   SLIP constants.

SLIP Input Processing: `slinput`

The TTY device driver delivers incoming characters to the SLIP line discipline one at a time by calling `slinput`. Figure 5.12 shows the `slinput` function but omits the end-of-frame processing, which is discussed separately.

———————————————————————————————— if_sl.c
```
527 void
528 slinput(c, tp)
529 int     c;
530 struct tty *tp;
531 {
532     struct sl_softc *sc;
533     struct mbuf *m;
534     int     len;
535     int     s;
536     u_char  chdr[CHDR_LEN];

537     tk_nin++;
538     sc = (struct sl_softc *) tp->t_sc;
539     if (sc == NULL)
540         return;
541     if (c & TTY_ERRORMASK || ((tp->t_state & TS_CARR_ON) == 0 &&
542                               (tp->t_cflag & CLOCAL) == 0)) {
543         sc->sc_flags |= SC_ERROR;
544         return;
545     }
546     c &= TTY_CHARMASK;

547     ++sc->sc_if.if_ibytes;

548     switch (c) {

549     case TRANS_FRAME_ESCAPE:
550         if (sc->sc_escape)
551             c = FRAME_ESCAPE;
552         break;
```

```
553     case TRANS_FRAME_END:
554         if (sc->sc_escape)
555             c = FRAME_END;
556         break;

557     case FRAME_ESCAPE:
558         sc->sc_escape = 1;
559         return;

560     case FRAME_END:
```

```
                        /* FRAME_END code (Figure 5.13) */
```

```
636     }
637     if (sc->sc_mp < sc->sc_ep) {
638         *sc->sc_mp++ = c;
639         sc->sc_escape = 0;
640         return;
641     }
642     /* can't put lower; would miss an extra frame */
643     sc->sc_flags |= SC_ERROR;

644 error:
645     sc->sc_if.if_ierrors++;
646 newpack:
647     sc->sc_mp = sc->sc_buf = sc->sc_ep - SLMAX;
648     sc->sc_escape = 0;
649 }
```
———————————————————————————————— if_sl.c

Figure 5.12   slinput function.

527–545   The arguments to slinput are c, the next input character; and tp, a pointer to the device's tty structure. The global integer tk_nin counts the incoming characters for all TTY devices. slinput converts tp->t_sc to sc, a pointer to an sl_softc structure. If there is no interface associated with the TTY device, slinput returns immediately.

The first argument to slinput is an integer. In addition to the received character, c contains control information sent from the TTY device driver in the high-order bits. If an error is indicated in c or the modem-control lines are not enabled and should not be ignored, SC_ERROR is set and slinput returns. Later, when slinput processes the END character, the frame is discarded. The CLOCAL flag indicates that the system should treat the line as a local line (i.e., not a dialup line) and should not expect to see modem-control signals.

546–636   slinput discards the control bits in c by masking it with TTY_CHARMASK, updates the count of bytes received on the interface, and jumps based on the received character:

- If c is an escaped ESC character and the *previous* character was an ESC, slinput replaces c with an ESC character.

- If c is an escaped END character and the *previous* character was an ESC, slinput replaces c with an END character.

- If c is the SLIP ESC character, sc_escape is set and slinput returns immediately (i.e., the ESC character is discarded).

- If c is the SLIP END character, the packet is put on the IP input queue. The processing for the SLIP frame end character is shown in Figure 5.13.

The common flow of control through this switch statement is to fall through (there is no default case). Most bytes are data and don't match any of the four cases. Control also falls through the switch in the first two cases.

637–649   If control falls through the switch, the received character is part of the IP packet. The character is stored in the cluster (if there is room), the pointer is advanced, sc_escape is cleared, and slinput returns.

If the cluster is full, the character is discarded and slinput sets SC_ERROR. Control reaches error when the cluster is full or when an error is detected in the end-of-frame processing. At newpack the cluster pointers are reset for a new packet, sc_escape is cleared, and slinput returns.

Figure 5.13 shows the FRAME_END code omitted from Figure 5.12.

─── *if_sl.c*

```
560    case FRAME_END:
561        if (sc->sc_flags & SC_ERROR) {
562            sc->sc_flags &= ~SC_ERROR;
563            goto newpack;
564        }
565        len = sc->sc_mp - sc->sc_buf;
566        if (len < 3)
567            /* less than min length packet - ignore */
568            goto newpack;

569        if (sc->sc_bpf) {
570            /*
571             * Save the compressed header, so we
572             * can tack it on later.  Note that we
573             * will end up copying garbage in some
574             * cases but this is okay.  We remember
575             * where the buffer started so we can
576             * compute the new header length.
577             */
578            bcopy(sc->sc_buf, chdr, CHDR_LEN);
579        }
580        if ((c = (*sc->sc_buf & 0xf0)) != (IPVERSION << 4)) {
581            if (c & 0x80)
582                c = TYPE_COMPRESSED_TCP;
583            else if (c == TYPE_UNCOMPRESSED_TCP)
584                *sc->sc_buf &= 0x4f;     /* XXX */
585            /*
586             * We've got something that's not an IP packet.
587             * If compression is enabled, try to decompress it.
588             * Otherwise, if auto-enable compression is on and
589             * it's a reasonable packet, decompress it and then
590             * enable compression.  Otherwise, drop it.
591             */
```

```
592              if (sc->sc_if.if_flags & SC_COMPRESS) {
593                  len = sl_uncompress_tcp(&sc->sc_buf, len,
594                                      (u_int) c, &sc->sc_comp);
595                  if (len <= 0)
596                      goto error;
597              } else if ((sc->sc_if.if_flags & SC_AUTOCOMP) &&
598                          c == TYPE_UNCOMPRESSED_TCP && len >= 40) {
599                  len = sl_uncompress_tcp(&sc->sc_buf, len,
600                                      (u_int) c, &sc->sc_comp);
601                  if (len <= 0)
602                      goto error;
603                  sc->sc_if.if_flags |= SC_COMPRESS;
604              } else
605                  goto error;
606          }
607      if (sc->sc_bpf) {
608          /*
609           * Put the SLIP pseudo-"link header" in place.
610           * We couldn't do this any earlier since
611           * decompression probably moved the buffer
612           * pointer.  Then, invoke BPF.
613           */
614          u_char *hp = sc->sc_buf - SLIP_HDRLEN;

615          hp[SLX_DIR] = SLIPDIR_IN;
616          bcopy(chdr, &hp[SLX_CHDR], CHDR_LEN);
617          bpf_tap(sc->sc_bpf, hp, len + SLIP_HDRLEN);
618      }
619      m = sl_btom(sc, len);
620      if (m == NULL)
621          goto error;

622      sc->sc_if.if_ipackets++;
623      sc->sc_if.if_lastchange = time;
624      s = splimp();
625      if (IF_QFULL(&ipintrq)) {
626          IF_DROP(&ipintrq);
627          sc->sc_if.if_ierrors++;
628          sc->sc_if.if_iqdrops++;
629          m_freem(m);
630      } else {
631          IF_ENQUEUE(&ipintrq, m);
632          schednetisr(NETISR_IP);
633      }
634      splx(s);
635      goto newpack;
```
——— *if_sl.c*

Figure 5.13 slinput function: end-of-frame processing.

560–579   slinput discards an incoming SLIP packet immediately if SC_ERROR was set while the packet was being received or if the packet is less than 3 bytes in length (remember that the packet may be compressed).

If the SLIP interface is tapped by BPF, slinput saves a copy of the (possibly compressed) header in the chdr array.

580–606   By examining the first byte of the packet, slinput determines if it is an uncompressed IP packet, a compressed TCP segment, or an uncompressed TCP segment. The type is saved in c and the type information is removed from the first byte of data (Section 29.13). If the packet appears to be compressed and compression is enabled, sl_uncompress_tcp attempts to uncompress the packet. If compression is not enabled, auto-enable compression is on, and if the packet is large enough sl_uncompress_tcp is also called. If it is a compressed TCP packet, the compression flag is set.

slinput discards packets it does not recognize by jumping to error. Section 29.13 discusses the header compression techniques in more detail. The cluster now contains a complete uncompressed packet.

607–618   After SLIP has decompressed the packet, the header and data are passed to BPF. Figure 5.14 shows the layout of the buffer constructed by slinput.

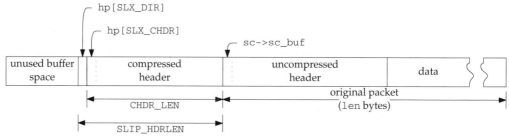

Figure 5.14   SLIP packet in BPF format.

The first byte of the BPF header encodes the direction of the packet, in this case incoming (SLIPDIR_IN). The next 15 bytes contain the compressed header. The entire packet is passed to bpf_tap.

619–635   sl_btom converts the cluster to an mbuf chain. If the packet is small enough to fit in a single mbuf, sl_btom copies the packet from the cluster to a newly allocated mbuf packet header; otherwise sl_btom attaches the cluster to an mbuf and allocates a new cluster for the interface. This is faster than copying from one cluster to another. We do not show sl_btom in this text.

Since only IP packets are transmitted on a SLIP interface, slinput does not have to select a protocol queue (as it does in the Ethernet driver). The packet is queued on ipintrq, an IP software interrupt is scheduled, and slinput jumps to newpack, where it updates the cluster packet pointers and clears sc_escape.

> While the SLIP driver increments if_ierrors if the packet cannot be queued on ipintrq, neither the Ethernet nor loopback drivers increment this statistic in the same situation.

Access to the IP input queue must be protected by splimp even though slinput is called at spltty. Recall from Figure 1.14 that an splimp interrupt can preempt spltty processing.

SLIP Output Processing: `sloutput`

As with all network interfaces, output processing begins when a network-level protocol calls the interface's `if_output` function. For the Ethernet driver, the function is `ether_output`. For SLIP, the function is `sloutput` (Figure 5.15).

```
                                                                  ─────── if_sl.c
259 int
260 sloutput(ifp, m, dst, rtp)
261 struct ifnet *ifp;
262 struct mbuf *m;
263 struct sockaddr *dst;
264 struct rtentry *rtp;
265 {
266     struct sl_softc *sc = &sl_softc[ifp->if_unit];
267     struct ip *ip;
268     struct ifqueue *ifq;
269     int     s;

270     /*
271      * Cannot happen (see slioctl).  Someday we will extend
272      * the line protocol to support other address families.
273      */
274     if (dst->sa_family != AF_INET) {
275         printf("sl%d: af%d not supported\n", sc->sc_if.if_unit,
276                 dst->sa_family);
277         m_freem(m);
278         sc->sc_if.if_noproto++;
279         return (EAFNOSUPPORT);
280     }
281     if (sc->sc_ttyp == NULL) {
282         m_freem(m);
283         return (ENETDOWN);        /* sort of */
284     }
285     if ((sc->sc_ttyp->t_state & TS_CARR_ON) == 0 &&
286         (sc->sc_ttyp->t_cflag & CLOCAL) == 0) {
287         m_freem(m);
288         return (EHOSTUNREACH);
289     }
290     ifq = &sc->sc_if.if_snd;
291     ip = mtod(m, struct ip *);
292     if (sc->sc_if.if_flags & SC_NOICMP && ip->ip_p == IPPROTO_ICMP) {
293         m_freem(m);
294         return (ENETRESET);      /* XXX ? */
295     }
296     if (ip->ip_tos & IPTOS_LOWDELAY)
297         ifq = &sc->sc_fastq;
298     s = splimp();
299     if (IF_QFULL(ifq)) {
300         IF_DROP(ifq);
301         m_freem(m);
302         splx(s);
303         sc->sc_if.if_oerrors++;
304         return (ENOBUFS);
305     }
```

```
306        IF_ENQUEUE(ifq, m);
307        sc->sc_if.if_lastchange = time;
308        if (sc->sc_ttyp->t_outq.c_cc == 0)
309            slstart(sc->sc_ttyp);
310        splx(s);
311        return (0);
312 }
```
――― *if_sl.c*

Figure 5.15 `sloutput` function.

259–289   The four arguments to `sloutput` are: `ifp`, a pointer to the SLIP `ifnet` structure (in this case an `sl_softc` structure); `m`, a pointer to the packet to be queued for output; `dst`, the next-hop destination for the packet; and `rtp`, a pointer to a route entry. The fourth argument is not used by `sloutput`, but it is required since `sloutput` must match the prototype for the `if_output` function in the `ifnet` structure.

`sloutput` ensures that `dst` is an IP address, that the interface is connected to a TTY device, and that the TTY device is operating (i.e., the carrier is on or should be ignored). An error is returned immediately if any of these tests fail.

290–291   The SLIP interface maintains two queues of outgoing packets. The standard queue, `if_snd`, is selected by default.

292–295   If the outgoing packet contains an ICMP message and `SC_NOICMP` is set for the interface, the packet is discarded. This prevents a SLIP link from being overwhelmed by extraneous ICMP packets (e.g., ECHO packets) sent by a malicious user (Chapter 11).

The error code `ENETRESET` indicates that the packet was discarded because of a policy decision (versus a network failure). We'll see in Chapter 11 that the error is silently discarded unless the ICMP message was generated locally, in which case an error is returned to the process that tried to send the message.

> Net/2 returned a 0 in this case. To a diagnostic tool such as `ping` or `traceroute` it would appear as if the packet disappeared since the output operation would report a successful completion.

> In general, ICMP messages can be discarded. They are not required for correct operation, but discarding them makes troubleshooting more difficult and may lead to less than optimal routing decisions, poorer performance, and wasted network resources.

296–297   If the TOS field in the outgoing packet specifies low-delay service (`IPTOS_LOWDELAY`), the output queue is changed to `sc_fastq`.

> RFC 1700 and RFC 1349 [Almquist 1992] specify the TOS settings for the standard protocols. Low-delay service is specified for Telnet, Rlogin, FTP (control), TFTP, SMTP (command phase), and DNS (UDP query). See Section 3.2 of Volume 1 for more details.

> In previous BSD releases, the `ip_tos` was not set correctly by applications. The SLIP driver implemented TOS queueing by examining the transport headers contained within the IP packet. If it found TCP packets for the FTP (command), Telnet, or Rlogin ports, the packet was queued as if `IPTOS_LOWDELAY` was specified. Many routers continue this practice, since many implementations of these interactive services still do not set `ip_tos`.

298–312   The packet is now placed on the selected queue, the interface statistics are updated, and (if the TTY output queue is empty) `sloutput` calls `slstart` to initiate transmission of the packet.

> SLIP increments `if_oerrors` if the interface queue is full; `ether_output` does not.

Unlike the Ethernet output function (`ether_output`), `sloutput` does not construct a data-link header for the outgoing packet. Since the only other system on a SLIP network is at the other end of the serial link, there is no need for hardware addresses or a protocol, such as ARP, to convert between IP addresses and hardware addresses. Protocol identifiers (such as the Ethernet *type* field) are also superfluous, since a SLIP link carries only IP packets.

`slstart` Function

In addition to the call by `sloutput`, the TTY device driver calls `slstart` when it drains its output queue and needs more bytes to transmit. The TTY subsystem manages its queues through a `clist` structure. In Figure 5.8 the output clist `t_outq` is shown below `slstart` and above the device's `t_oproc` function. `slstart` adds bytes to the queue, while `t_oproc` drains the queue and transmits the bytes.

The `slstart` function is shown in Figure 5.16.

318–358   When `slstart` is called, `tp` points to the device's `tty` structure. The body of `slstart` consists of a single `for` loop. If the output queue `t_outq` is not empty, `slstart` calls the output function for the device, `t_oproc`, which transmits as many bytes as the device will accept. If more than 100 bytes (`SLIP_HIWAT`) remain in the TTY output queue, `slstart` returns instead of adding another packet's worth of bytes to the queue. The output device generates an interrupt when it has transmitted all the bytes, and the TTY subsystem calls `slstart` when the output list is empty.

If the TTY output queue is empty, a packet is dequeued from `sc_fastq` or, if `sc_fastq` is empty, from the `if_snd` queue, thus transmitting all interactive packets before any other packets.

> There are no standard SNMP variables to count packets queued according to the TOS fields. The XXX comment in line 353 indicates that the SLIP driver is counting low-delay packets in `if_omcasts`, *not* multicast packets.

359–383   If the SLIP interface is tapped by BPF, `slstart` makes a copy of the output packet before any header compression occurs. The copy is saved on the stack in the `bpfbuf` array .

384–388   If compression is enabled and the packet contains a TCP segment, `sloutput` calls `sl_compress_tcp`, which attempts to compress the packet. The resulting packet type is returned and logically ORed with the first byte in IP header (Section 29.13).

389–398   The compressed header is now copied into the BPF header, and the direction recorded as `SLIPDIR_OUT`. The completed BPF packet is passed to `bpf_tap`.

483–484   `slstart` returns if the `for` loop terminates.

```
318 void
319 slstart(tp)
320 struct tty *tp;
321 {
322     struct sl_softc *sc = (struct sl_softc *) tp->t_sc;
323     struct mbuf *m;
324     u_char *cp;
325     struct ip *ip;
326     int     s;
327     struct mbuf *m2;
328     u_char  bpfbuf[SLMTU + SLIP_HDRLEN];
329     int     len;
330     extern int cfreecount;
331     for (;;) {
332         /*
333          * If there is more in the output queue, just send it now.
334          * We are being called in lieu of ttstart and must do what
335          * it would.
336          */
337         if (tp->t_outq.c_cc != 0) {
338             (*tp->t_oproc) (tp);
339             if (tp->t_outq.c_cc > SLIP_HIWAT)
340                 return;
341         }
342         /*
343          * This happens briefly when the line shuts down.
344          */
345         if (sc == NULL)
346             return;

347         /*
348          * Get a packet and send it to the interface.
349          */
350         s = splimp();
351         IF_DEQUEUE(&sc->sc_fastq, m);
352         if (m)
353             sc->sc_if.if_omcasts++;     /* XXX */
354         else
355             IF_DEQUEUE(&sc->sc_if.if_snd, m);
356         splx(s);
357         if (m == NULL)
358             return;

359         /*
360          * We do the header compression here rather than in sloutput
361          * because the packets will be out of order if we are using TOS
362          * queueing, and the connection id compression will get
363          * munged when this happens.
364          */
365         if (sc->sc_bpf) {
366             /*
367              * We need to save the TCP/IP header before it's
368              * compressed.  To avoid complicated code, we just
369              * copy the entire packet into a stack buffer (since
```

```
370                          * this is a serial line, packets should be short
371                          * and/or the copy should be negligible cost compared
372                          * to the packet transmission time).
373                          */
374                         struct mbuf *m1 = m;
375                         u_char *cp = bpfbuf + SLIP_HDRLEN;

376                         len = 0;
377                         do {
378                             int     mlen = m1->m_len;

379                             bcopy(mtod(m1, caddr_t), cp, mlen);
380                             cp += mlen;
381                             len += mlen;
382                         } while (m1 = m1->m_next);
383                     }
384                 if ((ip = mtod(m, struct ip *))->ip_p == IPPROTO_TCP) {
385                     if (sc->sc_if.if_flags & SC_COMPRESS)
386                         *mtod(m, u_char *) |= sl_compress_tcp(m, ip,
387                                                         &sc->sc_comp, 1);
388                 }
389                 if (sc->sc_bpf) {
390                     /*
391                      * Put the SLIP pseudo-"link header" in place.   The
392                      * compressed header is now at the beginning of the
393                      * mbuf.
394                      */
395                     bpfbuf[SLX_DIR] = SLIPDIR_OUT;
396                     bcopy(mtod(m, caddr_t), &bpfbuf[SLX_CHDR], CHDR_LEN);
397                     bpf_tap(sc->sc_bpf, bpfbuf, len + SLIP_HDRLEN);
398                 }


                                    /* packet output code */


483         }
484 }
```

—— *if_sl.c*

Figure 5.16   `slstart` function: packet dequeueing.

The next section of `slstart` (Figure 5.17) discards packets if the system is low on memory, and implements a simple technique for discarding data generated by noise on the serial line. This is the code omitted from Figure 5.16.

399–409   If the system is low on clist structures, the packet is discarded and counted as a collision. By continuing the loop instead of returning, `slstart` quickly discards all remaining packets queued for output. Each iteration discards a packet, since the device still has too many bytes queued for output. Higher-level protocols must detect the lost packets and retransmit them.

410–418   If the TTY output queue is empty, the communication line may have been idle for a period of time and the receiver at the other end may have received extraneous data created by line noise. `slstart` places an extra SLIP END character in the output queue. A 0-length frame or a frame created by noise on the line should be discarded by the SLIP interface or IP protocol at the receiver.

```
                                                                    ──── if_sl.c
399            sc->sc_if.if_lastchange = time;
400            /*
401             * If system is getting low on clists, just flush our
402             * output queue (if the stuff was important, it'll get
403             * retransmitted).
404             */
405            if (cfreecount < CLISTRESERVE + SLMTU) {
406                m_freem(m);
407                sc->sc_if.if_collisions++;
408                continue;
409            }
410            /*
411             * The extra FRAME_END will start up a new packet, and thus
412             * will flush any accumulated garbage.  We do this whenever
413             * the line may have been idle for some time.
414             */
415            if (tp->t_outq.c_cc == 0) {
416                ++sc->sc_if.if_obytes;
417                (void) putc(FRAME_END, &tp->t_outq);
418            }
                                                                    ──── if_sl.c
```

Figure 5.17   `slstart` function: resource shortages and line noise.

Figure 5.18 illustrates this technique for discarding line noise and is attributed to Phil Karn in RFC 1055. In Figure 5.18, the second end-of-frame (END) is transmitted because the line was idle for a period of time. The invalid frame created by the noise and the END byte is discarded by the receiving system.

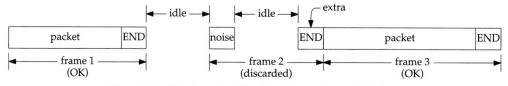

Figure 5.18   Karn's method for discarding noise on a SLIP line.

In Figure 5.19 there is no noise on the line and the 0-length frame is discarded by the receiving system.

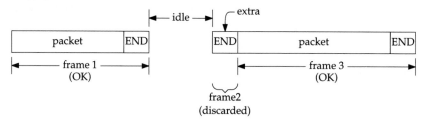

Figure 5.19   Karn's method with no noise.

The next section of `slstart` (Figure 5.20) transfers the data from an mbuf to the output queue for the TTY device.

```
                                                                  ── if_sl.c
419          while (m) {
420              u_char *ep;

421              cp = mtod(m, u_char *);
422              ep = cp + m->m_len;
423              while (cp < ep) {
424                  /*
425                   * Find out how many bytes in the string we can
426                   * handle without doing something special.
427                   */
428                  u_char *bp = cp;

429                  while (cp < ep) {
430                      switch (*cp++) {
431                      case FRAME_ESCAPE:
432                      case FRAME_END:
433                          --cp;
434                          goto out;
435                      }
436                  }
437              out:
438                  if (cp > bp) {
439                      /*
440                       * Put n characters at once
441                       * into the tty output queue.
442                       */
443                      if (b_to_q((char *) bp, cp - bp,
444                              &tp->t_outq))
445                          break;
446                      sc->sc_if.if_obytes += cp - bp;
447                  }
448                  /*
449                   * If there are characters left in the mbuf,
450                   * the first one must be special..
451                   * Put it out in a different form.
452                   */
453                  if (cp < ep) {
454                      if (putc(FRAME_ESCAPE, &tp->t_outq))
455                          break;
456                      if (putc(*cp++ == FRAME_ESCAPE ?
457                              TRANS_FRAME_ESCAPE : TRANS_FRAME_END,
458                              &tp->t_outq)) {
459                          (void) unputc(&tp->t_outq);
460                          break;
461                      }
462                      sc->sc_if.if_obytes += 2;
463                  }
464              }
465              MFREE(m, m2);
466              m = m2;
467          }
                                                                  ── if_sl.c
```

Figure 5.20   slstart function: packet transmission.

419–467   The outer `while` loop in this section is executed once for each mbuf in the chain. The middle `while` loop transfers the data from each mbuf to the output device. The inner `while` loop advances `cp` until it finds an END or ESC character. `b_to_q` transfers the bytes between `bp` and `cp`. END and ESC characters are escaped and queued with two calls to `putc`. This middle loop is repeated until all the bytes in the mbuf are passed to the TTY device's output queue. Figure 5.21 illustrates this process with an mbuf containing a SLIP END character and a SLIP ESC character.

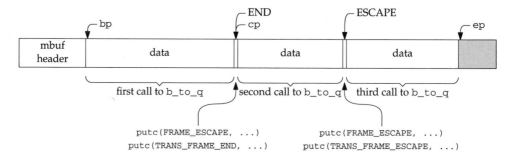

Figure 5.21   SLIP transmission of a single mbuf.

bp marks the beginning of the first section of the mbuf to transfer with `b_to_q`, and `cp` marks the end of the first section. `ep` marks the end of the data in the mbuf.

If `b_to_q` or `putc` fail (i.e., data cannot be queued on the TTY device), the `break` causes `slstart` to fall out of the middle `while` loop. The failure indicates that the kernel has run out of clist resources. After each mbuf is copied to the TTY device, or when an error occurs, the mbuf is released, m is advanced to the next mbuf in the chain, and the outer `while` loop continues until all the mbufs in the chain have been processed.

Figure 5.22 shows the processing done by `slstart` to complete the outgoing frame.

```
                                                                      ── if_sl.c
468        if (putc(FRAME_END, &tp->t_outq)) {
469            /*
470             * Not enough room.  Remove a char to make room
471             * and end the packet normally.
472             * If you get many collisions (more than one or two
473             * a day) you probably do not have enough clists
474             * and you should increase "nclist" in param.c.
475             */
476            (void) unputc(&tp->t_outq);
477            (void) putc(FRAME_END, &tp->t_outq);
478            sc->sc_if.if_collisions++;
479        } else {
480            ++sc->sc_if.if_obytes;
481            sc->sc_if.if_opackets++;
482        }
                                                                      ── if_sl.c
```

Figure 5.22   `slstart` function: end-of-frame processing.

468–482   Control reaches this code when the outer `while` loop has finished queueing the bytes on the output queue. The driver sends a SLIP END character, which terminates the frame.

If an error occurred while queueing the bytes, the outgoing frame is invalid and is detected by the receiving system because of an invalid checksum or length.

Whether or not the frame is terminated because of an error, if the END character does not fit on the output queue, the *last* character on the queue is discarded and `slstart` ends the frame. This guarantees that an END character is transmitted. The invalid frame is discarded at the destination.

SLIP Packet Loss

The SLIP interface provides a good example of a best-effort service. SLIP discards packets if the TTY is overloaded; it truncates packets if resources are unavailable after the packet transmission has started, and it inserts extraneous null packets to detect and discard line noise. In each of these cases, no error message is generated. SLIP depends on IP and the transport layers to detect damaged and missing packets.

On a router forwarding packets from a fast interface such as Ethernet to a low-speed SLIP line, a large percentage of packets are discarded if the sender does not recognize the bottleneck and respond by throttling back the data rate. In Section 25.11 we'll see how TCP detects and responds to this condition. Applications using a protocol without flow control, such as UDP, must recognize and respond to this condition on their own (Exercise 5.8).

SLIP Performance Considerations

The MTU of a SLIP frame (`SLMTU`), the clist high-water mark (`SLIP_HIWAT`), and SLIP's TOS queueing strategies are all designed to minimize the delay inherent in a slow serial link for interactive traffic.

1. A small MTU improves the delay for interactive data (such as keystrokes and echoes), but hurts the throughput for bulk data transfer. A large MTU improves bulk data throughput, but increases interactive delays. Another problem with SLIP links is that a single typed character is burdened with 40 bytes of TCP and IP header information, which increases the communication delay.

   The solution is to pick an MTU large enough to provide good interactive response time and decent bulk data throughput, and to compress TCP/IP headers to reduce the per-packet overhead. RFC 1144 [Jacobson 1990a] describes a compression scheme and the timing calculations that result in selecting an MTU of 296 for a typical 9600 bits/sec asynchronous SLIP link. We describe Compressed SLIP (CSLIP) in Section 29.13. Sections 2.10 and 7.2 of Volume 1 summarize the timing considerations and illustrate the delay on SLIP links.

2. If too many bytes are buffered in the clist (because `SLIP_HIWAT` is set too high), the TOS queueing will be thwarted as new interactive traffic waits behind the large amount of buffered data. If SLIP passes 1 byte at a time to the TTY driver

(because SLIP_HIWAT is set too low), the device calls slstart for each byte and the line is idle for a brief period of time after each byte is transferred. Setting SLIP_HIWAT to 100 minimizes the amount of data queued at the device and reduces the frequency at which the TTY subsystem must call slstart to approximately once every 100 characters.

3. As described, the SLIP driver provides TOS queueing by transmitting interactive traffic from the sc_fastq queue before other traffic on the standard interface queue, if_snd.

slclose Function

For completeness, we show the slclose function, which is called when the slattach program closes SLIP's TTY device and terminates the connection to the remote system.

```
                                                                    ─ if_sl.c
210 void
211 slclose(tp)
212 struct tty *tp;
213 {
214     struct sl_softc *sc;
215     int     s;

216     ttywflush(tp);
217     s = splimp();                    /* actually, max(spltty, splnet) */
218     tp->t_line = 0;
219     sc = (struct sl_softc *) tp->t_sc;
220     if (sc != NULL) {
221         if_down(&sc->sc_if);
222         sc->sc_ttyp = NULL;
223         tp->t_sc = NULL;
224         MCLFREE((caddr_t) (sc->sc_ep - SLBUFSIZE));
225         sc->sc_ep = 0;
226         sc->sc_mp = 0;
227         sc->sc_buf = 0;
228     }
229     splx(s);
230 }
                                                                    ─ if_sl.c
```

Figure 5.23   slclose function.

210–230   tp points to the TTY device to be closed. slclose flushes any remaining data out to the serial device, blocks TTY and network processing, and resets the TTY to the default line discipline. If the TTY device is attached to a SLIP interface, the interface is shut down, the links between the two structures are severed, the mbuf cluster associated with the interface is released, and the pointers into the now-discarded cluster are reset. Finally, splx reenables the TTY and network interrupts.

`sltioctl` **Function**

Recall that a SLIP interface has two roles to play in the kernel:

- as a network interface, and
- as a TTY line discipline.

Figure 5.7 indicated that `slioctl` processes `ioctl` commands issued for a SLIP interface through a socket descriptor. In Section 4.4 we showed how `ifioctl` calls `slioctl`. We'll see a similar pattern for `ioctl` commands that we cover in later chapters.

Figure 5.7 also indicated that `sltioctl` processes `ioctl` commands issued for the TTY device associated with a SLIP network interface. The one command recognized by `sltioctl` is shown in Figure 5.24.

Command	Argument	Function	Description
SLIOCGUNIT	int *	sltioctl	return interface unit associated with the TTY device

Figure 5.24   `sltioctl` commands.

The `sltioctl` function is shown in Figure 5.25.

―― *if_sl.c*
```
236 int
237 sltioctl(tp, cmd, data, flag)
238 struct tty *tp;
239 int     cmd;
240 caddr_t data;
241 int     flag;
242 {
243     struct sl_softc *sc = (struct sl_softc *) tp->t_sc;

244     switch (cmd) {
245     case SLIOCGUNIT:
246         *(int *) data = sc->sc_if.if_unit;
247         break;

248     default:
249         return (-1);
250     }
251     return (0);
252 }
```
―― *if_sl.c*

Figure 5.25   `sltioctl` function.

236–252   The `t_sc` pointer in the `tty` structure points to the associated `sl_softc` structure. The unit number of the SLIP interface is copied from `if_unit` to `*data`, which is eventually returned to the process (Section 17.5).

`if_unit` is initialized by `slattach` when the system is initialized, and `t_sc` is initialized by `slopen` when the `slattach` program selects the SLIP line discipline for the TTY device. Since the mapping between a TTY device and a SLIP `sl_softc` structure is established at run time, a process can discover the interface structure selected by the SLIOCGUNIT command.

5.4   Loopback Interface

Any packets sent to the loopback interface (Figure 5.26) are immediately queued for input. The interface is implemented entirely in software.

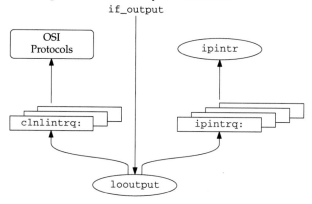

Figure 5.26   Loopback device driver.

looutput, the if_output function for the loopback interface, places outgoing packets on the input queue for the protocol specified by the packet's destination address.

We already saw that ether_output may call looutput to queue a copy of an outgoing broadcast packet when the device has set IFF_SIMPLEX. In Chapter 12, we'll see that multicast packets may be also be looped back in this way. looutput is shown in Figure 5.27.

———————————————————————— if_loop.c
```
57 int
58 looutput(ifp, m, dst, rt)
59 struct ifnet *ifp;
60 struct mbuf *m;
61 struct sockaddr *dst;
62 struct rtentry *rt;
63 {
64     int      s, isr;
65     struct ifqueue *ifq = 0;

66     if ((m->m_flags & M_PKTHDR) == 0)
67         panic("looutput no HDR");
68     ifp->if_lastchange = time;
69     if (loif.if_bpf) {
70         /*
71          * We need to prepend the address family as
72          * a four byte field.  Cons up a dummy header
```

```
 73              * to pacify bpf.  This is safe because bpf
 74              * will only read from the mbuf (i.e., it won't
 75              * try to free it or keep a pointer to it).
 76              */
 77             struct mbuf m0;
 78             u_int   af = dst->sa_family;

 79             m0.m_next = m;
 80             m0.m_len = 4;
 81             m0.m_data = (char *) &af;

 82             bpf_mtap(loif.if_bpf, &m0);
 83         }
 84     m->m_pkthdr.rcvif = ifp;

 85     if (rt && rt->rt_flags & (RTF_REJECT | RTF_BLACKHOLE)) {
 86         m_freem(m);
 87         return (rt->rt_flags & RTF_BLACKHOLE ? 0 :
 88                 rt->rt_flags & RTF_HOST ? EHOSTUNREACH : ENETUNREACH);
 89     }
 90     ifp->if_opackets++;
 91     ifp->if_obytes += m->m_pkthdr.len;
 92     switch (dst->sa_family) {
 93     case AF_INET:
 94         ifq = &ipintrq;
 95         isr = NETISR_IP;
 96         break;

 97     case AF_ISO:
 98         ifq = &clnlintrq;
 99         isr = NETISR_ISO;
100         break;

101     default:
102         printf("lo%d: can't handle af%d\n", ifp->if_unit,
103                 dst->sa_family);
104         m_freem(m);
105         return (EAFNOSUPPORT);
106     }
107     s = splimp();
108     if (IF_QFULL(ifq)) {
109         IF_DROP(ifq);
110         m_freem(m);
111         splx(s);
112         return (ENOBUFS);
113     }
114     IF_ENQUEUE(ifq, m);
115     schednetisr(isr);
116     ifp->if_ipackets++;
117     ifp->if_ibytes += m->m_pkthdr.len;
118     splx(s);
119     return (0);
120 }
```
—— *if_loop.c*

Figure 5.27 The `looutput` function.

57–68   The arguments to `looutput` are the same as those to `ether_output` since both are called indirectly through the `if_output` pointer in their `ifnet` structures: `ifp`, a pointer to the outgoing interface's `ifnet` structure; `m`, the packet to send; `dst`, the destination address of the packet; and `rt`, routing information. If the first mbuf on the chain does not contain a packet, `looutput` calls `panic`.

Figure 5.28 shows the logical layout for a BPF loopback packet.

Figure 5.28   BPF loopback packet: logical format.

69–83   The driver constructs the BPF loopback packet header in `m0` on the stack and connects `m0` to the mbuf chain containing the original packet. Note the unusual declaration of `m0`. It is an *mbuf*, not a pointer to an mbuf. `m_data` in `m0` points to `af`, which is also allocated on the stack. Figure 5.29 shows this arrangement.

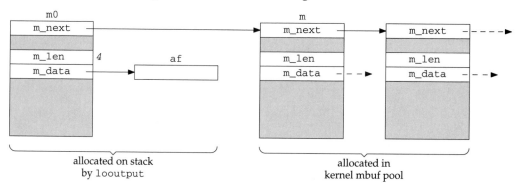

Figure 5.29   BPF loopback packet: mbuf format.

`looutput` copies the destination's address family into `af` and passes the new mbuf chain to `bpf_mtap`, which processes the packet. Contrast this to `bpf_tap`, which accepts the packet in a single contiguous buffer not in an mbuf chain. As the comment indicates, BPF never releases mbufs in a chain, so it is safe to pass `m0` (which points to an mbuf on the stack) to `bpf_mtap`.

84–89   The remainder of `looutput` contains *input* processing for the packet. Even though this is an output function, the packet is being looped back to appear as input. First, `m->m_pkthdr.rcvif` is set to point to the receiving interface. If the caller provided a routing entry, `looutput` checks to see if it indicates that the packet should be rejected (`RTF_REJECT`) or silently discarded (`RTF_BLACKHOLE`). A black hole is implemented by discarding the mbuf and returning 0. It appears to the caller as if the packet has been transmitted. To reject a packet, `looutput` returns `EHOSTUNREACH` if the route is for a host and `ENETUNREACH` if the route is for a network.

The various RTF_*xxx* flags are described in Figure 18.25.

90–120   `looutput` then selects the appropriate protocol input queue and software interrupt by examining `sa_family` in the packet's destination address. It then queues recognized packets and schedules a software interrupt with `schednetisr`.

5.5   Summary

We described the two remaining interfaces to which we refer throughout the text: `sl0`, a SLIP interface, and `lo0`, the standard loopback interface.

We showed the relationship between the SLIP interface and the SLIP line discipline, described the SLIP encapsulation method, and discussed TOS processing for interactive traffic and other performance considerations for the SLIP driver.

We showed how the loopback interface demultiplexes outgoing packets based on their destination address family and places the packet on the appropriate input queue.

Exercises

5.1   Why does the loopback interface not have an input function?

5.2   Why do you think mo is allocated on the stack in Figure 5.27?

5.3   Perform an analysis of SLIP characteristics for a 19,200 bps serial line. Should the SLIP MTU be changed for this line?

5.4   Derive a formula to select a SLIP MTU based on the speed of the serial line.

5.5   What happens if a packet is too large to fit in SLIP's input buffer?

5.6   An earlier version of `slinput` did not set `SC_ERROR` when a packet overflowed the input buffer. How would the error be detected in this case?

5.7   In Figure 4.31 `le` is initialized by indexing the `le_softc` array with `ifp->if_unit`. Can you think of another method for initializing `le`?

5.8   How can a UDP application recognize when its packets are being discarded because of a bottleneck in the network?

6

IP Addressing

6.1 Introduction

This chapter describes how Net/3 manages IP addressing information. We start with the in_ifaddr and sockaddr_in structures, which are based on the generic ifaddr and sockaddr structures.

The remainder of the chapter covers IP address assignment and several utility functions that search the interface data structures and manipulate IP addresses.

IP Addresses

Although we assume that readers are familiar with the basic Internet addressing system, several issues are worth pointing out.

In the IP model, it is the network interfaces on a system (a host or a router) that are assigned addresses, not the system itself. In the case of a system with multiple interfaces, the system is *multihomed* and has more than one IP address. A router is, by definition, multihomed. As we'll see, this architectural feature has several subtle ramifications.

Five classes of IP addresses are defined. Class A, B, and C addresses support *unicast* communication. Class D addresses support IP *multicasting*. In a multicast communication, a single source sends a datagram to multiple destinations. Class D addresses and multicasting protocols are described in Chapter 12. Class E addresses are experimental. Packets received with class E addresses are discarded by hosts that aren't participating in the experiment.

It is important that we emphasize the difference between *IP multicasting* and *hardware multicasting*. Hardware multicasting is a feature of the data-link hardware used to transmit packets to multiple hardware interfaces. Some network hardware, such as Ethernet, supports data-link multicasting. Other hardware may not.

IP multicasting is a software feature implemented in IP systems to transmit packets to multiple IP addresses that may be located throughout the internet.

We assume that the reader is familiar with subnetting of IP networks (RFC 950 [Mogul and Postel 1985] and Chapter 3 of Volume 1). We'll see that each network interface has an associated subnet mask, which is critical in determining if a packet has reached its final destination or if it needs to be forwarded. In general, when we refer to the network portion of an IP address we are including any subnet that may defined. When we need to differentiate between the network and the subnet, we do so explicitly.

The loopback network, 127.0.0.0, is a special class A network. Addresses of this form must never appear outside of a host. Packets sent to this network are looped back and received by the host.

> RFC 1122 requires that all addresses within the loopback network be handled correctly. Since the loopback interface must be assigned an address, many systems select 127.0.0.1 as the loopback address. If the system is not configured correctly, addresses such as 127.0.0.2 may not be routed to the loopback interface but instead may be transmitted on an attached network, which is prohibited. Some systems may correctly route the packet to the loopback interface where it is dropped since the destination address does not match the configured address: 127.0.0.1.
>
> Figure 18.2 shows a Net/3 system configured to reject packets sent to a loopback address other than 127.0.0.1.

Typographical Conventions for IP Addresses

We usually display IP addresses in *dotted-decimal* notation. Figure 6.1 lists the range of IP address for each address class.

Class	Range	Type
A	0.0.0.0 to 127.255.255.255	
B	128.0.0.0 to 191.255.255.255	unicast
C	192.0.0.0 to 223.255.255.255	
D	224.0.0.0 to 239.255.255.255	multicast
E	240.0.0.0 to 247.255.255.255	experimental

Figure 6.1   Ranges for different classes of IP addresses.

For some of our examples, the subnet field is not aligned with a byte boundary (i.e., a network/subnet/host division of 16/11/5 in a class B network). It can be difficult to identify the portions of such address from the dotted-decimal notation so we'll also use block diagrams to illustrate the contents of IP addresses. We'll show each address with three parts: network, subnet, and host. The shading of each part indicates its contents. Figure 6.2 illustrates both the block notation and the dotted-decimal notation using the Ethernet interface of the host sun from our sample network (Section 1.14).

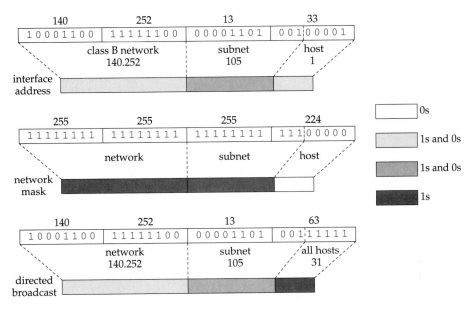

Figure 6.2   Alternate IP address notations.

When a portion of the address is not all 0s or all 1s, we use the two intermediate shades. We have two types of intermediate shades so we can distinguish network and subnet portions or to show combinations of address as in Figure 6.31.

Hosts and Routers

Systems on an internet can generally be divided into two types: *hosts* and *routers*. A host usually has a single network interface and is either the source or destination for an IP packet. A router has multiple network interfaces and forwards packets from one network to the next as the packet moves toward its destination. To perform this function, routers exchange information about the network topology using a variety of specialized routing protocols. IP routing issues are complex, and they are discussed starting in Chapter 18.

A system with multiple network interfaces is still called a *host* if it does not route packets between its network interfaces. A system may be both a host and a router. This is often the case when a router provides transport-level services such as Telnet access for configuration, or SNMP for network management. When the distinction between a host and router is unimportant, we use the term *system*.

Careless configuration of a router can disrupt the normal operation of a network, so RFC 1122 states that a system must default to operate as a host and must be explicitly configured by an administrator to operate as a router. This purposely discourages administrators from operating general-purpose host computers as routers without careful consideration. In Net/3, a system acts as a router if the global integer `ipforwarding` is nonzero and as a host if `ipforwarding` is 0 (the default).

A router is often called a *gateway* in Net/3, although the term *gateway* is now more often associated with a system that provides application-level routing, such as an electronic mail gateway, and not one that forwards IP packets. We use the term *router* and assume that `ipforwarding` is nonzero in this book. We have also included all code conditionally included when `GATEWAY` is defined during compilation of the Net/3 kernel, which defines `ipforwarding` to be 1.

6.2   Code Introduction

The two headers and two C files listed in Figure 6.3 contain the structure definitions and utility functions described in this chapter.

File	Description
`netinet/in.h`	Internet address definitions
`netinet/in_var.h`	Internet interface definitions
`netinet/in.c`	Internet initialization and utility functions
`netinet/if.c`	Internet interface utility functions

Figure 6.3   Files discussed in this chapter.

Global Variables

The two global variables introduced in this chapter are listed in Figure 6.4.

Variable	Datatype	Description
`in_ifaddr`	`struct in_ifaddr *`	head of `in_ifaddr` structure list
`in_interfaces`	`int`	number of IP capable interfaces

Figure 6.4   Global variables introduced in this chapter.

6.3   Interface and Address Summary

A sample configuration of all the interface and address structures described in this chapter is illustrated in Figure 6.5.

Figure 6.5 shows our three example interfaces: the Ethernet interface, the SLIP interface, and the loopback interface. All have a link-level address as the first node in their address list. The Ethernet interface is shown with two IP addresses, the SLIP interface with one IP address, and the loopback interface has an IP address and an OSI address.

Note that all the IP addresses are linked into the `in_ifaddr` list and all the link-level addresses can be accessed from the `ifnet_addrs` array.

The `ifa_ifp` pointers within each `ifaddr` structure have been omitted from Figure 6.5 for clarity. The pointers refer back to the `ifnet` structure that heads the list containing the `ifaddr` structure.

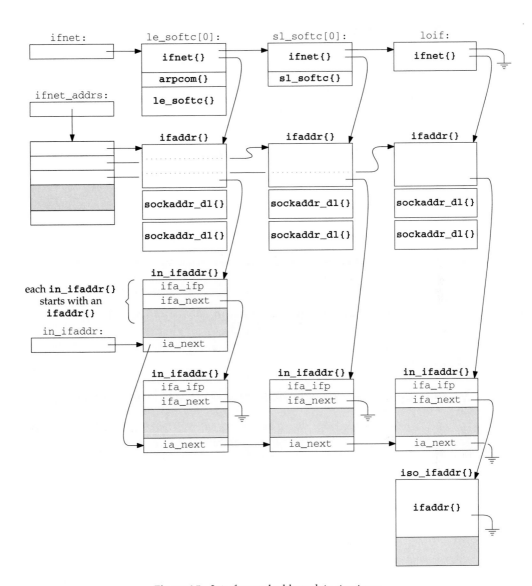

Figure 6.5   Interface and address data structures.

The following sections describe the data structures contained in Figure 6.5 and the IP-specific `ioctl` commands that examine and modify the structures.

6.4   `sockaddr_in` Structure

We discussed the generic `sockaddr` and `ifaddr` structures in Chapter 3. Now we show the structures specialized for IP: `sockaddr_in` and `in_ifaddr`. Addresses in the Internet domain are held in a `sockaddr_in` structure:

```
                                                                        — in.h
68 struct in_addr {
69      u_long  s_addr;              /* 32-bit IP address, net byte order */
70 };

106 struct sockaddr_in {
107     u_char  sin_len;             /* sizeof (struct sockaddr_in) = 16 */
108     u_char  sin_family;          /* AF_INET */
109     u_short sin_port;            /* 16-bit port number, net byte order */
110     struct in_addr sin_addr;
111     char    sin_zero[8];         /* unused */
112 };
                                                                        — in.h
```

Figure 6.6   `sockaddr_in` structure.

68–70   Net/3 stores 32-bit Internet addresses in network byte order in an `in_addr` structure for historical reasons. The structure has a single member, s_addr, which contains the address. That organization is kept in Net/3 even though it is superfluous and clutters the code.

106–112   `sin_len` is always 16 (the size of the `sockaddr_in` structure) and `sin_family` is AF_INET. `sin_port` is a 16-bit value in network (not host) byte order used to demultiplex transport-level messages. `sin_addr` specifies a 32-bit Internet address.

Figure 6.6 shows that the `sin_port`, `sin_addr`, and `sin_zero` members of `sockaddr_in` overlay the `sa_data` member of `sockaddr`. `sin_zero` is unused in the Internet domain but must consist of all 0 bytes (Section 22.7). It pads the `sockaddr_in` structure to the length of a `sockaddr` structure.

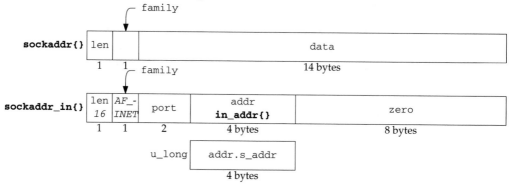

Figure 6.7   The organization of a `sockaddr_in` structure (`sin_` omitted).

Usually, when an Internet addresses is stored in a `u_long` it is in host byte order to facilitate comparisons and bit operations on the address. s_addr within the `in_addr` structure (Figure 6.7) is a notable exception.

6.5   `in_ifaddr` Structure

Figure 6.8 shows the interface address structure defined for the Internet protocols. For each IP address assigned to an interface, an `in_ifaddr` structure is allocated and added to the interface address list and to the global list of IP addresses (Figure 6.5).

```
                                                                        — in_var.h
41 struct in_ifaddr {
42          struct  ifaddr ia_ifa;            /* protocol-independent info    */
43 #define ia_ifp          ia_ifa.ifa_ifp
44 #define ia_flags        ia_ifa.ifa_flags
45          struct  in_ifaddr *ia_next;       /* next internet addresses list */
46          u_long  ia_net;                   /* network number of interface  */
47          u_long  ia_netmask;               /* mask of net part             */
48          u_long  ia_subnet;                /* subnet number, including net */
49          u_long  ia_subnetmask;            /* mask of subnet part          */
50          struct  in_addr ia_netbroadcast;  /* to recognize net broadcasts  */
51          struct  sockaddr_in ia_addr;      /* space for interface name     */
52          struct  sockaddr_in ia_dstaddr;   /* space for broadcast addr     */
53 #define ia_broadaddr     ia_dstaddr
54          struct  sockaddr_in ia_sockmask;  /* space for general netmask    */
55          struct  in_multi *ia_multiaddrs;  /* list of multicast addresses  */
56 };
                                                                        — in_var.h
```

Figure 6.8   The `in_ifaddr` structure.

41–45   `in_ifaddr` starts with the generic interface address structure, `ia_ifa`, followed by the IP-specific members. The `ifaddr` structure was shown in Figure 3.15. The two macros, `ia_ifp` and `ia_flags`, simplify access to the interface pointer and interface address flags stored in the generic `ifaddr` structure. `ia_next` maintains a linked list of all Internet addresses that have been assigned to any interface. This list is independent of the list of link-level `ifaddr` structures associated with each interface and is accessed through the global list `in_ifaddr`.

46–54   The remaining members (other than `ia_multiaddrs`) are included in Figure 6.9, which shows the values for the three interfaces on `sun` from our example class B network. The addresses stored as `u_long` variables are kept in host byte order; the `in_addr` and `sockaddr_in` variables are in network byte order. `sun` has a PPP interface, but the information shown in this table is the same for a PPP interface or for a SLIP interface.

55–56   The last member of the `in_ifaddr` structure points to a list of `in_multi` structures (Section 12.6), each of which contains an IP multicast address associated with the interface.

6.6   Address Assignment

In Chapter 4 we showed the initialization of the interface structures when they are recognized at system initialization time. Before the Internet protocols can communicate through the interfaces, they must be assigned an IP address. Once the Net/3 kernel is

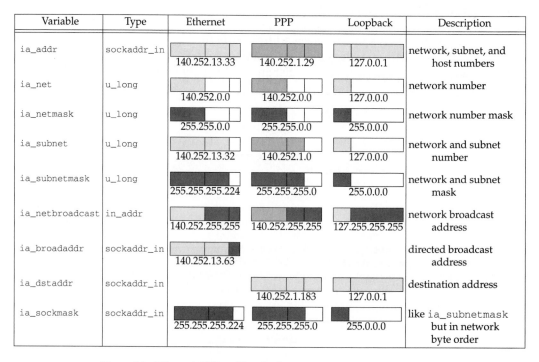

Variable	Type	Ethernet	PPP	Loopback	Description
ia_addr	sockaddr_in	140.252.13.33	140.252.1.29	127.0.0.1	network, subnet, and host numbers
ia_net	u_long	140.252.0.0	140.252.0.0	127.0.0.0	network number
ia_netmask	u_long	255.255.0.0	255.255.0.0	255.0.0.0	network number mask
ia_subnet	u_long	140.252.13.32	140.252.1.0	127.0.0.0	network and subnet number
ia_subnetmask	u_long	255.255.255.224	255.255.255.0	255.0.0.0	network and subnet mask
ia_netbroadcast	in_addr	140.252.255.255	140.252.255.255	127.255.255.255	network broadcast address
ia_broadaddr	sockaddr_in	140.252.13.63			directed broadcast address
ia_dstaddr	sockaddr_in		140.252.1.183	127.0.0.1	destination address
ia_sockmask	sockaddr_in	255.255.255.224	255.255.255.0	255.0.0.0	like ia_subnetmask but in network byte order

Figure 6.9   Ethernet, PPP, and loopback in_ifaddr structures on sun.

running, the interfaces are configured by the ifconfig program, which issues configuration commands through the ioctl system call on a socket. This is normally done by the /etc/netstart shell script, which is executed when the system is bootstrapped.

Figure 6.10 shows the ioctl commands discussed in this chapter. The addresses associated with the commands must be from the same address family supported by the socket on which the commands are issued (i.e., you can't configure an OSI address through a UDP socket). For IP addresses, the ioctl commands are issued on a UDP socket.

Command	Argument	Function	Description
SIOCGIFADDR	struct ifreq *	in_control	get interface address
SIOCGIFNETMASK	struct ifreq *	in_control	get interface netmask
SIOCGIFDSTADDR	struct ifreq *	in_control	get interface destination address
SIOCGIFBRDADDR	struct ifreq *	in_control	get interface broadcast address
SIOCSIFADDR	struct ifreq *	in_control	set interface address
SIOCSIFNETMASK	struct ifreq *	in_control	set interface netmask
SIOCSIFDSTADDR	struct ifreq *	in_control	set interface destination address
SIOCSIFBRDADDR	struct ifreq *	in_control	set interface broadcast address
SIOCDIFADDR	struct ifreq *	in_control	delete interface address
SIOCAIFADDR	struct in_aliasreq *	in_control	add interface address

Figure 6.10   Interface ioctl commands.

The commands that get address information start with SIOCG, and the commands that set address information start with SIOCS. SIOC stands for *socket ioctl*, the G for *get*, and the S for *set*.

In Chapter 4 we looked at five *protocol-independent* ioctl commands. The commands in Figure 6.10 modify the addressing information associated with an interface. Since addresses are protocol-specific, the command processing is *protocol-dependent*. Figure 6.11 highlights the ioctl-related functions associated with these commands.

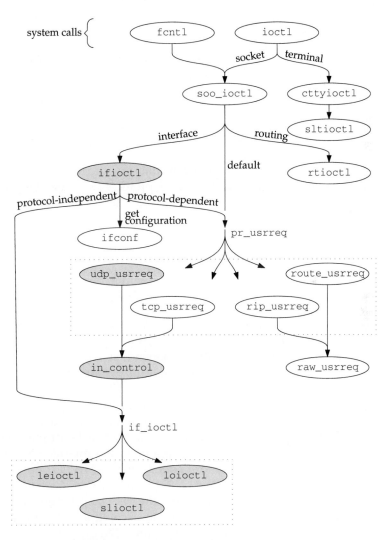

Figure 6.11   ioctl functions described in this chapter.

`ifioctl` Function

As shown in Figure 6.11, `ifioctl` passes protocol-dependent `ioctl` commands to the `pr_usrreq` function of the protocol associated with the socket. Control is passed to `udp_usrreq` and immediately to `in_control` where most of the processing occurs. If the same commands are issued on a TCP socket, control would also end up at `in_control`. Figure 6.12 repeats the `default` code from `ifioctl`, first shown in Figure 4.22.

─── *if.c*
```
447     default:
448         if (so->so_proto == 0)
449             return (EOPNOTSUPP);
450         return ((*so->so_proto->pr_usrreq) (so, PRU_CONTROL,
451                                             cmd, data, ifp));
452     }
453     return (0);
454 }
```
─── *if.c*

Figure 6.12 `ifioctl` function: protocol-specific commands.

447–454   The function passes all the relevant data for the `ioctl` commands listed in Figure 6.10 to the user-request function of the protocol associated with the socket on which the request was made. For a UDP socket, `udp_usrreq` is called. Section 23.10 describes the `udp_usrreq` function in detail. For now, we need to look only at the `PRU_CONTROL` code from `udp_usrreq`:

```
if (req == PRU_CONTROL)
    return (in_control(so, (int)m, (caddr_t)addr, (struct ifnet *)control));
```

`in_control` Function

Figure 6.11 shows that control can reach `in_control` through the `default` case in `soo_ioctl` or through the protocol-dependent case in `ifioctl`. In both cases, `udp_usrreq` calls `in_control` and returns whatever `in_control` returns. Figure 6.13 shows `in_control`.

132–145   `so` points to the socket on which the `ioctl` (specified by the second argument, `cmd`) was issued. The third argument, `data`, points to the data (second column of Figure 6.10) to be used or returned by the command. The last argument, `ifp`, is null (non-interface `ioctl` from `soo_ioctl`) or points to the interface named in the `ifreq` or `in_aliasreq` structures (interface `ioctl` from `ifioctl`). `in_control` initializes `ifa` and `ifra` to access `data` as an `ifreq` or as an `in_aliasreq` structure.

146–152   If `ifp` points to an `ifnet` structure, the `for` loop locates the *first* address on the Internet address list associated with the interface. If an address is found, `ia` points to its `in_ifaddr` structure, otherwise, `ia` is null.

If `ifp` is null, `cmd` will not match any of the cases in the first `switch` or any of the nondefault cases in the second `switch`. The `default` case in the second `switch` returns `EOPNOTSUPP` when `ifp` is null.

── *in.c*
```
132 in_control(so, cmd, data, ifp)
133 struct socket *so;
134 int      cmd;
135 caddr_t data;
136 struct ifnet *ifp;
137 {
138     struct ifreq *ifr = (struct ifreq *) data;
139     struct in_ifaddr *ia = 0;
140     struct ifaddr *ifa;
141     struct in_ifaddr *oia;
142     struct in_aliasreq *ifra = (struct in_aliasreq *) data;
143     struct sockaddr_in oldaddr;
144     int      error, hostIsNew, maskIsNew;
145     u_long  i;

146     /*
147      * Find address for this interface, if it exists.
148      */
149     if (ifp)
150         for (ia = in_ifaddr; ia; ia = ia->ia_next)
151             if (ia->ia_ifp == ifp)
152                 break;

153     switch (cmd) {
```

                        /* establish preconditions for commands */

```
218     }
219     switch (cmd) {
```

                        /* perform the commands */

```
326     default:
327         if (ifp == 0 || ifp->if_ioctl == 0)
328             return (EOPNOTSUPP);
329         return ((*ifp->if_ioctl) (ifp, cmd, data));
330     }
331     return (0);
332 }
```
── *in.c*

Figure 6.13   in_control function.

153–330   The first switch in in_control makes sure all the preconditions for each command are met before the second switch processes the command. The individual cases are described in the following sections.

If the default case is executed in the second switch, ifp points to an interface structure, and the interface has an if_ioctl function, then in_control passes the ioctl command to the interface for device-specific processing.

Net/3 does not define any interface commands that would be processed by the default case. But the driver for a particular device might define its own interface ioctl commands and they would be processed by this case.

331–332   We'll see that many of the cases within the switch statements return directly. If control falls through both switch statements, in_control returns 0. Several of the cases do break out of the second switch.

We look at the interface ioctl commands in the following order:

- assigning an address, network mask, or destination address;
- assigning a broadcast address;
- retrieving an address, network mask, destination address, or broadcast address;
- assigning multiple addresses to an interface; or
- deleting an address.

For each group of commands, we describe the precondition processing done in the first switch statement and then the command processing done in the second switch statement.

Preconditions: SIOCSIFADDR, SIOCSIFNETMASK, and SIOCSIFDSTADDR

Figure 6.14 shows the precondition testing for SIOCSIFADDR, SIOCSIFNETMASK, and SIOCSIFDSTADDR.

Superuser only

166–172   If the socket was not created by a superuser process, these commands are prohibited and in_control returns EPERM. If no interface is associated with the request, the kernel panics. The panic should never happen since ifioctl returns if it can't locate an interface (Figure 4.22).

The SS_PRIV flag is set by socreate (Figure 15.16) when a superuser process creates a socket. Because the test here is against the flag and not the effective user ID of the process, a set-user-ID root process can create a socket, and give up its superuser privileges, but still issue privileged ioctl commands.

Allocate structure

173–191   If ia is null, the command is requesting a new address. in_control allocates an in_ifaddr structure, clears it with bzero, and links it into the in_ifaddr list for the system and into the if_addrlist list for the interface.

Initialize structure

192–201   The next portion of code initializes the in_ifaddr structure. First the generic pointers in the ifaddr portion of the structure are initialized to point to the sockaddr_in structures in the in_ifaddr structure. The function also initializes the ia_sockmask and ia_broadaddr structures as necessary. Figure 6.15 illustrates the in_ifaddr structure after this initialization.

202–206   Finally, in_control establishes the back pointer from the in_ifaddr to the interface's ifnet structure.

Net/3 counts only nonloopback interfaces in in_interfaces.

―― *in.c*
```
166      case SIOCSIFADDR:
167      case SIOCSIFNETMASK:
168      case SIOCSIFDSTADDR:
169          if ((so->so_state & SS_PRIV) == 0)
170              return (EPERM);

171          if (ifp == 0)
172              panic("in_control");
173          if (ia == (struct in_ifaddr *) 0) {
174              oia = (struct in_ifaddr *)
175                  malloc(sizeof *oia, M_IFADDR, M_WAITOK);
176              if (oia == (struct in_ifaddr *) NULL)
177                  return (ENOBUFS);
178              bzero((caddr_t) oia, sizeof *oia);
179              if (ia = in_ifaddr) {
180                  for (; ia->ia_next; ia = ia->ia_next)
181                      continue;
182                  ia->ia_next = oia;
183              } else
184                  in_ifaddr = oia;
185              ia = oia;
186              if (ifa = ifp->if_addrlist) {
187                  for (; ifa->ifa_next; ifa = ifa->ifa_next)
188                      continue;
189                  ifa->ifa_next = (struct ifaddr *) ia;
190              } else
191                  ifp->if_addrlist = (struct ifaddr *) ia;

192              ia->ia_ifa.ifa_addr = (struct sockaddr *) &ia->ia_addr;
193              ia->ia_ifa.ifa_dstaddr
194                  = (struct sockaddr *) &ia->ia_dstaddr;
195              ia->ia_ifa.ifa_netmask
196                  = (struct sockaddr *) &ia->ia_sockmask;
197              ia->ia_sockmask.sin_len = 8;
198              if (ifp->if_flags & IFF_BROADCAST) {
199                  ia->ia_broadaddr.sin_len = sizeof(ia->ia_addr);
200                  ia->ia_broadaddr.sin_family = AF_INET;
201              }
202              ia->ia_ifp = ifp;
203              if (ifp != &loif)
204                  in_interfaces++;
205          }
206          break;
```
―― *in.c*

Figure 6.14   in_control function: address assignment.

Address Assignment: SIOCSIFADDR

The precondition code has ensured that ia points to an in_ifaddr structure to be modified by the SIOCSIFADDR command. Figure 6.16 shows the code executed by in_control in the second switch for this command.

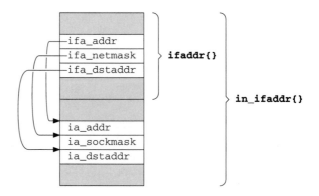

Figure 6.15   An in_ifaddr structure after initialization by in_control.

```
                                                                    in.c
259      case SIOCSIFADDR:
260          return (in_ifinit(ifp, ia,
261                        (struct sockaddr_in *) &ifr->ifr_addr, 1));
                                                                    in.c
```

Figure 6.16   in_control function: address assignment.

259–261   in_ifinit does all the work. The IP address included within the ifreq structure (ifr_addr) is passed to in_ifinit.

in_ifinit Function

The major steps in in_ifinit are:

- copy the address into the structure and inform the hardware of the change,
- discard any routes configured with the previous address,
- establish a subnet mask for the address,
- establish a default route to the attached network (or host), and
- join the all-hosts group on the interface.

The code is described in three parts, starting with Figure 6.17.

353–359   The four arguments to in_ifinit are: ifp, a pointer to the interface structure; ia, a pointer to the in_ifaddr structure to be changed; sin, a pointer to the requested IP address; and scrub, which indicates if existing routes for this interface should be discarded. i holds the IP address in host byte order.

Assign address and notify hardware

360–374   in_ifinit saves the previous address in oldaddr in case it must be restored when an error occurs. If the interface has an if_ioctl function defined, in_control calls it. The three functions leioctl, slioctl, and loioctl for the sample interfaces are described in the next section. The previous address is restored and in_control returns if an error occurs.

```
                                                                        in.c
353 in_ifinit(ifp, ia, sin, scrub)
354 struct ifnet *ifp;
355 struct in_ifaddr *ia;
356 struct sockaddr_in *sin;
357 int      scrub;
358 {
359     u_long  i = ntohl(sin->sin_addr.s_addr);
360     struct sockaddr_in oldaddr;
361     int     s = splimp(), flags = RTF_UP, error, ether_output();

362     oldaddr = ia->ia_addr;
363     ia->ia_addr = *sin;
364     /*
365      * Give the interface a chance to initialize
366      * if this is its first address,
367      * and to validate the address if necessary.
368      */
369     if (ifp->if_ioctl &&
370         (error = (*ifp->if_ioctl) (ifp, SIOCSIFADDR, (caddr_t) ia))) {
371         splx(s);
372         ia->ia_addr = oldaddr;
373         return (error);
374     }
375     if (ifp->if_output == ether_output) {    /* XXX: Another Kludge */
376         ia->ia_ifa.ifa_rtrequest = arp_rtrequest;
377         ia->ia_ifa.ifa_flags |= RTF_CLONING;
378     }
379     splx(s);
380     if (scrub) {
381         ia->ia_ifa.ifa_addr = (struct sockaddr *) &oldaddr;
382         in_ifscrub(ifp, ia);
383         ia->ia_ifa.ifa_addr = (struct sockaddr *) &ia->ia_addr;
384     }
                                                                        in.c
```

Figure 6.17 in_ifinit function: address assignment and route initialization.

Ethernet configuration

375–378   For Ethernet devices, arp_rtrequest is selected as the link-level routing function and the RTF_CLONING flag is set. arp_rtrequest is described in Section 21.13 and RTF_CLONING is described at the end of Section 19.4. As the XXX comment suggests, putting the code here avoids changing all the Ethernet drivers.

Discard previous routes

379–384   If the caller requests that existing routes be scrubbed, the previous address is reattached to ifa_addr while in_ifscrub locates and invalidates any routes based on the old address. After in_ifscrub returns, the new address is restored.

The section of in_ifinit shown in Figure 6.18 constructs the network and subnet masks.

─── *in.c*

```
385        if (IN_CLASSA(i))
386            ia->ia_netmask = IN_CLASSA_NET;
387        else if (IN_CLASSB(i))
388            ia->ia_netmask = IN_CLASSB_NET;
389        else
390            ia->ia_netmask = IN_CLASSC_NET;
391        /*
392         * The subnet mask usually includes at least the standard network part,
393         * but may be smaller in the case of supernetting.
394         * If it is set, we believe it.
395         */
396        if (ia->ia_subnetmask == 0) {
397            ia->ia_subnetmask = ia->ia_netmask;
398            ia->ia_sockmask.sin_addr.s_addr = htonl(ia->ia_subnetmask);
399        } else
400            ia->ia_netmask &= ia->ia_subnetmask;
401        ia->ia_net = i & ia->ia_netmask;
402        ia->ia_subnet = i & ia->ia_subnetmask;
403        in_socktrim(&ia->ia_sockmask);
```
─── *in.c*

Figure 6.18 in_ifinit function: network and subnet masks.

Construct network mask and default subnetmask

385–400   A tentative network mask is constructed in ia_netmask based on whether the address is a class A, class B, or class C address. If no subnetwork mask is associated with the address yet, ia_subnetmask and ia_sockmask are initialized to the tentative mask in ia_netmask.

 If a subnet has been specified, in_ifinit logically ANDs the tentative netmask and the existing submask together to get a new network mask. This operation may clear some of the 1 bits in the tentative netmask (it can never set the 0 bits, since 0 logically ANDed with anything is 0). In this case, the network mask has fewer 1 bits than would be expected by considering the class of the address.

> This is called *supernetting* and is described in RFC 1519 [Fuller et al. 1993]. A supernet is a grouping of several class A, class B, or class C networks. Supernetting is also discussed in Section 10.8 of Volume 1.

 An interface is configured by default *without subnetting* (i.e., the network and subnetwork masks are the same). An explicit request (with SIOCSIFNETMASK or SIOCAIFADDR) is required to enable subnetting (or supernetting).

Construct network and subnetwork numbers

401–403   The network and subnetwork numbers are extracted from the new address by the network and subnet masks. The function in_socktrim sets the length of in_sockmask (which is a sockaddr_in structure) by locating the last byte that contains a 1 bit in the mask.

 Figure 6.19 shows the last section of in_ifinit, which adds a route for the interface and joins the all-hosts multicast group.

```
                                                                            ── in.c
404      /*
405       * Add route for the network.
406       */
407      ia->ia_ifa.ifa_metric = ifp->if_metric;
408      if (ifp->if_flags & IFF_BROADCAST) {
409          ia->ia_broadaddr.sin_addr.s_addr =
410              htonl(ia->ia_subnet | ~ia->ia_subnetmask);
411          ia->ia_netbroadcast.s_addr =
412              htonl(ia->ia_net | ~ia->ia_netmask);
413      } else if (ifp->if_flags & IFF_LOOPBACK) {
414          ia->ia_ifa.ifa_dstaddr = ia->ia_ifa.ifa_addr;
415          flags |= RTF_HOST;
416      } else if (ifp->if_flags & IFF_POINTOPOINT) {
417          if (ia->ia_dstaddr.sin_family != AF_INET)
418              return (0);
419          flags |= RTF_HOST;
420      }
421      if ((error = rtinit(&(ia->ia_ifa), (int) RTM_ADD, flags)) == 0)
422          ia->ia_flags |= IFA_ROUTE;
423      /*
424       * If the interface supports multicast, join the "all hosts"
425       * multicast group on that interface.
426       */
427      if (ifp->if_flags & IFF_MULTICAST) {
428          struct in_addr addr;

429          addr.s_addr = htonl(INADDR_ALLHOSTS_GROUP);
430          in_addmulti(&addr, ifp);
431      }
432      return (error);
433  }
                                                                            ── in.c
```

Figure 6.19 in_ifinit function: routing and multicast groups.

Establish route for host or network

404–422   The next step is to create a route for the network specified by the new address. in_ifinit copies the routing metric from the interface to the in_ifaddr structure, constructs the broadcast addresses if the interface supports broadcasts, and forces the destination address to be the same as the assigned address for loopback interfaces. If a point-to-point interface does not yet have an IP address assigned to the other end of the link, in_ifinit returns before trying to establish a route for the invalid address.

in_ifinit initializes flags to RTF_UP and logically ORs in RTF_HOST for loopback and point-to-point interfaces. rtinit installs a route to the network (RTF_HOST not set) or host (RTF_HOST set) for the interface. If rtinit succeeds, the IFA_ROUTE flag in ia_flags is set to indicate that a route is installed for this address.

Join all-hosts group

423–433   Finally, a multicast capable interface must join the all-hosts multicast group when it is initialized. in_addmulti does the work and is described in Section 12.11.

Network Mask Assignment: `SIOCSIFNETMASK`

Figure 6.20 shows the processing for the network mask command.

```
                                                                    ── in.c
262    case SIOCSIFNETMASK:
263        i = ifra->ifra_addr.sin_addr.s_addr;
264        ia->ia_subnetmask = ntohl(ia->ia_sockmask.sin_addr.s_addr = i);
265        break;
                                                                    ── in.c
```

Figure 6.20   `in_control` function: network mask assignment.

262–265   `in_control` extracts the requested netmask from the `ifreq` structure and stores it in `ia_sockmask` in network byte order and in `ia_subnetmask` in host byte order.

Destination Address Assignment: `SIOCSIFDSTADDR`

For point-to-point interfaces, the address of the system on the other end of the link is specified by the `SIOCSIFDSTADDR` command. Figure 6.14 showed the precondition processing for the code shown in Figure 6.21.

```
                                                                    ── in.c
236    case SIOCSIFDSTADDR:
237        if ((ifp->if_flags & IFF_POINTOPOINT) == 0)
238            return (EINVAL);
239        oldaddr = ia->ia_dstaddr;
240        ia->ia_dstaddr = *(struct sockaddr_in *) &ifr->ifr_dstaddr;
241        if (ifp->if_ioctl && (error = (*ifp->if_ioctl)
242                              (ifp, SIOCSIFDSTADDR, (caddr_t) ia))) {
243            ia->ia_dstaddr = oldaddr;
244            return (error);
245        }
246        if (ia->ia_flags & IFA_ROUTE) {
247            ia->ia_ifa.ifa_dstaddr = (struct sockaddr *) &oldaddr;
248            rtinit(&(ia->ia_ifa), (int) RTM_DELETE, RTF_HOST);
249            ia->ia_ifa.ifa_dstaddr =
250                (struct sockaddr *) &ia->ia_dstaddr;
251            rtinit(&(ia->ia_ifa), (int) RTM_ADD, RTF_HOST | RTF_UP);
252        }
253        break;
                                                                    ── in.c
```

Figure 6.21   `in_control` function: destination address assignment.

236–245   Only point-to-point networks have destination addresses, so `in_control` returns `EINVAL` for other networks. After saving the current destination address in `oldaddr`, the code sets the new address and informs the interface through the `if_ioctl` function. If an error occurs, the old address is restored.

246–253   If the address has a route previously associated with it, that route is deleted by the first call to `rtinit` and a new route to the new destination is installed by the second call to `rtinit`.

Retrieving Interface Information

Figure 6.22 shows the precondition processing for the SIOCSIFBRDADDR command as well as the ioctl commands that return interface information to the calling process.

```
                                                                        in.c
207      case SIOCSIFBRDADDR:
208          if ((so->so_state & SS_PRIV) == 0)
209              return (EPERM);
210          /* FALLTHROUGH */

211      case SIOCGIFADDR:
212      case SIOCGIFNETMASK:
213      case SIOCGIFDSTADDR:
214      case SIOCGIFBRDADDR:
215          if (ia == (struct in_ifaddr *) 0)
216              return (EADDRNOTAVAIL);
217          break;
                                                                        in.c
```

Figure 6.22   in_control function: preconditions.

207–217   The broadcast address may only be set through a socket created by a superuser process. The SIOCSIFBRDADDR command and the four SIOCG*xxx* commands work only when an address is already defined for the interface, in which case ia won't be null (ia was set by in_control, Figure 6.13). If ia is null, EADDRNOTAVAIL is returned.

The processing of these five commands (four *get* commands and one *set* command) is shown in Figure 6.23.

```
                                                                        in.c
220      case SIOCGIFADDR:
221          *((struct sockaddr_in *) &ifr->ifr_addr) = ia->ia_addr;
222          break;

223      case SIOCGIFBRDADDR:
224          if ((ifp->if_flags & IFF_BROADCAST) == 0)
225              return (EINVAL);
226          *((struct sockaddr_in *) &ifr->ifr_dstaddr) = ia->ia_broadaddr;
227          break;

228      case SIOCGIFDSTADDR:
229          if ((ifp->if_flags & IFF_POINTOPOINT) == 0)
230              return (EINVAL);
231          *((struct sockaddr_in *) &ifr->ifr_dstaddr) = ia->ia_dstaddr;
232          break;

233      case SIOCGIFNETMASK:
234          *((struct sockaddr_in *) &ifr->ifr_addr) = ia->ia_sockmask;
235          break;


                 /* processing for SIOCSIFDSTADDR command (Figure 6.21) */
```

```
254        case SIOCSIFBRDADDR:
255            if ((ifp->if_flags & IFF_BROADCAST) == 0)
256                return (EINVAL);
257            ia->ia_broadaddr = *(struct sockaddr_in *) &ifr->ifr_broadaddr;
258            break;
```
―― *in.c*

Figure 6.23 in_control function: processing.

220–235   The unicast address, broadcast address, destination address, or netmask are copied
into the ifreq structure. A broadcast address is available only from a network interface that supports broadcasts, and a destination address is available only from a point-
to-point interface.

254–258   The broadcast address is copied from the ifreq structure only when the interface
supports broadcasts.

Multiple IP Addresses per Interface

The SIOCG*xxx* and SIOCS*xxx* commands operate only on the first IP address associated
with an interface—the first address located by the loop at the start of in_control (Figure 6.25). To support multiple IP addresses per interface, the additional addresses must
be assigned and configured with the SIOCAIFADDR command. In fact, SIOCAIFADDR
can do everything the SIOCG*xxx* and SIOCS*xxx* commands do. The ifconfig program uses SIOCAIFADDR to configure all of the address information for an interface.

As noted earlier, having multiple addresses per interface can ease the transition
when hosts or networks are renumbered. A fault-tolerant software system might use
this feature to allow a backup system to assume the IP address of a failed system.

The -alias option to Net/3's ifconfig program passes information about the
additional addresses to the kernel in an in_aliasreq structure, shown in Figure 6.24.

―― *in_var.h*
```
59 struct in_aliasreq {
60     char    ifra_name[IFNAMSIZ];     /* interface name, e.g. "en0" */
61     struct sockaddr_in ifra_addr;
62     struct sockaddr_in ifra_broadaddr;
63 #define ifra_dstaddr ifra_broadaddr
64     struct sockaddr_in ifra_mask;
65 };
```
―― *in_var.h*

Figure 6.24 in_aliasreq structure.

59–65   Notice that unlike the ifreq structure, there is no union defined within the
in_aliasreq structure. With SIOCAIFADDR, the address, broadcast address, and
mask can be specified in a single ioctl call.

SIOCAIFADDR adds a new address or changes the information associated with an
existing address. SIOCDIFADDR deletes the in_ifaddr structure for the matching IP
address. Figure 6.25 shows the precondition processing for the SIOCAIFADDR and
SIOCDIFADDR commands, which assumes that the loop at the start of in_control
(Figure 6.13) has set ia to point to the *first* IP address associated with the interface specified in ifra_name (if it exists).

```
                                                                      ─── in.c
154        case SIOCAIFADDR:
155        case SIOCDIFADDR:
156            if (ifra->ifra_addr.sin_family == AF_INET)
157                for (oia = ia; ia; ia = ia->ia_next) {
158                    if (ia->ia_ifp == ifp &&
159                        ia->ia_addr.sin_addr.s_addr ==
160                        ifra->ifra_addr.sin_addr.s_addr)
161                        break;
162                }
163            if (cmd == SIOCDIFADDR && ia == 0)
164                return (EADDRNOTAVAIL);
165            /* FALLTHROUGH to Figure 6.14 */
                                                                      ─── in.c
```

Figure 6.25 in_control function: adding and deleting addresses.

154–165   Because the SIOCDIFADDR code looks only at the first two members of *ifra, the code shown in Figure 6.25 works for SIOCAIFADDR (when ifra points to an in_aliasreq structure) and for SIOCDIFADDR (when ifra points to an ifreq structure). The first two members of the in_aliasreq and ifreq structures are identical.

For both commands, the for loop continues the search started by the loop at the start of in_control by looking for the in_ifaddr structure with the same IP address specified by ifra->ifra_addr. For the delete command, EADDRNOTAVAIL is returned if the address isn't found.

After the loop and the test for the delete command, control falls through to the code we described in Figure 6.14. For the add command, the code in Figure 6.14 allocates a new in_ifaddr structure if one was not found that matched the address in the in_aliasreq structure.

Additional IP Addresses: SIOCAIFADDR

At this point ia points to a new in_ifaddr structure or to an old in_ifaddr structure with an IP address that matched the address in the request. The SIOCAIFADDR processing is shown in Figure 6.26.

266–277   Since SIOCAIFADDR can create a new address or change the information associated with an existing address, the maskIsNew and hostIsNew flags keep track of what has changed so that routes can be updated if necessary at the end of the function.

By default, the code assumes that a new IP address is being assigned to the interface (hostIsNew starts at 1). If the length of the new address is 0, in_control copies the current address into the request and changes hostIsNew to 0. If the length is not 0 and the new address matches the old address, this request does not contain a new address and hostIsNew is set to 0.

278–284   If a netmask is specified in the request, any routes using the current address are discarded and in_control installs the new mask.

285–290   If the interface is a point-to-point interface and the request includes a new destination address, in_scrub discards any routes using the address, the new destination address is installed, and maskIsNew is set to 1 to force the call to in_ifinit, which reconfigures the interface.

in.c

```
266     case SIOCAIFADDR:
267         maskIsNew = 0;
268         hostIsNew = 1;
269         error = 0;
270         if (ia->ia_addr.sin_family == AF_INET) {
271             if (ifra->ifra_addr.sin_len == 0) {
272                 ifra->ifra_addr = ia->ia_addr;
273                 hostIsNew = 0;
274             } else if (ifra->ifra_addr.sin_addr.s_addr ==
275                     ia->ia_addr.sin_addr.s_addr)
276                 hostIsNew = 0;
277         }
278         if (ifra->ifra_mask.sin_len) {
279             in_ifscrub(ifp, ia);
280             ia->ia_sockmask = ifra->ifra_mask;
281             ia->ia_subnetmask =
282                 ntohl(ia->ia_sockmask.sin_addr.s_addr);
283             maskIsNew = 1;
284         }
285         if ((ifp->if_flags & IFF_POINTOPOINT) &&
286             (ifra->ifra_dstaddr.sin_family == AF_INET)) {
287             in_ifscrub(ifp, ia);
288             ia->ia_dstaddr = ifra->ifra_dstaddr;
289             maskIsNew = 1;        /* We lie; but the effect's the same */
290         }
291         if (ifra->ifra_addr.sin_family == AF_INET &&
292             (hostIsNew || maskIsNew))
293             error = in_ifinit(ifp, ia, &ifra->ifra_addr, 0);
294         if ((ifp->if_flags & IFF_BROADCAST) &&
295             (ifra->ifra_broadaddr.sin_family == AF_INET))
296             ia->ia_broadaddr = ifra->ifra_broadaddr;
297         return (error);
```

in.c

Figure 6.26 in_control function: SIOCAIFADDR processing.

291–297   If a new address has been configured or a new mask has been assigned, in_ifinit makes all the appropriate changes to support the new configuration (Figure 6.17). Note that the last argument to in_ifinit is 0. This indicates that it isn't necessary to scrub any routes since that has already been taken care of. Finally, the broadcast address is copied from the in_aliasreq structure if the interface supports broadcasts.

Deleting IP Addresses: SIOCDIFADDR

The SIOCDIFADDR command, which deletes IP addresses from an interface, is shown in Figure 6.27. Remember that ia points to the in_ifaddr structure to be deleted (i.e., the one that matched the request).

298–323   The precondition code arranged for ia to point to the address to be deleted. in_ifscrub deletes any routes associated with the address. The first if deletes the

```
                                                                       ── in.c
298        case SIOCDIFADDR:
299            in_ifscrub(ifp, ia);
300            if ((ifa = ifp->if_addrlist) == (struct ifaddr *) ia)
301                /* ia is the first address in the list */
302                ifp->if_addrlist = ifa->ifa_next;
303            else {
304                /* ia is *not* the first address in the list */
305                while (ifa->ifa_next &&
306                        (ifa->ifa_next != (struct ifaddr *) ia))
307                    ifa = ifa->ifa_next;
308                if (ifa->ifa_next)
309                    ifa->ifa_next = ((struct ifaddr *) ia)->ifa_next;
310                else
311                    printf("Couldn't unlink inifaddr from ifp\n");
312            }
313            oia = ia;
314            if (oia == (ia = in_ifaddr))
315                in_ifaddr = ia->ia_next;
316            else {
317                while (ia->ia_next && (ia->ia_next != oia))
318                    ia = ia->ia_next;
319                if (ia->ia_next)
320                    ia->ia_next = oia->ia_next;
321                else
322                    printf("Didn't unlink inifadr from list\n");
323            }
324            IFAFREE((&oia->ia_ifa));
325            break;
                                                                       ── in.c
```

Figure 6.27 in_control function: deleting addresses.

structure for the interface address list. The second if deletes the structure from the Internet address list (in_ifaddr).

324–325   IFAFREE only releases the structure when the reference count drops to 0.

> The additional references would be from entries in the routing table.

6.7 Interface ioctl Processing

We now look at the specific ioctl processing done by each of our sample interfaces in the leioctl, slioctl, and loioctl functions when an address is assigned to the interface.

in_ifinit is called by the SIOCSIFADDR code in Figure 6.16 and by the SIOCAIFADDR code in Figure 6.26. in_ifinit always issues the SIOCSIFADDR command through the interface's if_ioctl function (Figure 6.17).

`leioctl` Function

Figure 4.31 showed SIOCSIFFLAGS command processing of the LANCE driver. Figure 6.28 shows the SIOCSIFADDR command processing.

if_le.c

```
614 leioctl(ifp, cmd, data)
615 struct ifnet *ifp;
616 int       cmd;
617 caddr_t data;
618 {
619     struct ifaddr *ifa = (struct ifaddr *) data;
620     struct le_softc *le = &le_softc[ifp->if_unit];
621     struct lereg1 *ler1 = le->sc_r1;
622     int       s = splimp(), error = 0;

623     switch (cmd) {
624     case SIOCSIFADDR:
625         ifp->if_flags |= IFF_UP;
626         switch (ifa->ifa_addr->sa_family) {
627         case AF_INET:
628             leinit(ifp->if_unit);    /* before arpwhohas */
629             ((struct arpcom *) ifp)->ac_ipaddr =
630                 IA_SIN(ifa)->sin_addr;
631             arpwhohas((struct arpcom *) ifp, &IA_SIN(ifa)->sin_addr);
632             break;
633         default:
634             leinit(ifp->if_unit);
635             break;
636         }
637         break;
```
```
                  /* SIOCSIFFLAGS command (Figure 4.31) */
         /* SIOCADDMULTI and SIOCDELMULTI commands (Figure 12.31) */
```
```
672     default:
673         error = EINVAL;
674     }
675     splx(s);
676     return (error);
677 }
```

if_le.c

Figure 6.28   `leioctl` function.

614–637   Before processing the command, data is converted to an ifaddr structure pointer and ifp->if_unit selects the appropriate le_softc structure for this request.

The interface is marked as up and the hardware is initialized by leinit. For Internet addresses, the IP address is stored in the arpcom structure and a *gratuitous ARP* for the address is issued. Gratuitous ARP is discussed in Section 21.5 and in Section 4.7 of Volume 1.

Unrecognized commands

672–677   EINVAL is returned for unrecognized commands.

slioctl **Function**

The slioctl function (Figure 6.29) processes the SIOCSIFADDR and SIOCSIFDSTADDR command for the SLIP device driver.

——— if_sl.c
```
653 int
654 slioctl(ifp, cmd, data)
655 struct ifnet *ifp;
656 int     cmd;
657 caddr_t data;
658 {
659     struct ifaddr *ifa = (struct ifaddr *) data;
660     struct ifreq *ifr;
661     int    s = splimp(), error = 0;

662     switch (cmd) {
663     case SIOCSIFADDR:
664         if (ifa->ifa_addr->sa_family == AF_INET)
665             ifp->if_flags |= IFF_UP;
666         else
667             error = EAFNOSUPPORT;
668         break;

669     case SIOCSIFDSTADDR:
670         if (ifa->ifa_addr->sa_family != AF_INET)
671             error = EAFNOSUPPORT;
672         break;
```

```
                  /* SIOCADDMULTI and SIOCDELMULTI commands (Figure 12.29)*/
```

```
688     default:
689         error = EINVAL;
690     }
691     splx(s);
692     return (error);
693 }
```
——— if_sl.c

Figure 6.29   slioctl function: SIOCSIFADDR and SIOCSIFDSTADDR commands.

663–672   For both commands, EAFNOSUPPORT is returned if the address is not an IP address. The SIOCSIFADDR command enables IFF_UP.

Unrecognized commands

688–693   EINVAL is returned for unrecognized commands.

`loioctl` **Function**

The `loioctl` function and its implementation of the `SIOCSIFADDR` command is shown in Figure 6.30.

```
                                                                    ─ if_loop.c
135 int
136 loioctl(ifp, cmd, data)
137 struct ifnet *ifp;
138 int     cmd;
139 caddr_t data;
140 {
141     struct ifaddr *ifa;
142     struct ifreq *ifr;
143     int     error = 0;

144     switch (cmd) {
145     case SIOCSIFADDR:
146         ifp->if_flags |= IFF_UP;
147         ifa = (struct ifaddr *) data;
148         /*
149          * Everything else is done at a higher level.
150          */
151         break;
```

```
            /* SIOCADDMULTI and SIOCDELMULTI commands (Figure 12.30) */
```

```
167     default:
168         error = EINVAL;
169     }
170     return (error);
171 }
                                                                    ─ if_loop.c
```

Figure 6.30   `loioctl` function: `SIOCSIFADDR` command.

135–151   For Internet addresses, `loioctl` sets `IFF_UP` and returns immediately.

Unrecognized commands

167–171   `EINVAL` is returned for unrecognized commands.

Notice that for all three example drivers, assigning an address causes the interface to be marked as up (`IFF_UP`).

6.8   Internet Utility Functions

Figure 6.31 lists several functions that manipulate Internet addresses or that rely on the
ifnet structures shown in Figure 6.5, usually to discover subnetting information that
cannot be obtained from the 32-bit IP address alone. The implementation of these functions consists primarily of traversing data structures and manipulating bit masks. The
reader can find these functions in netinet/in.c.

Function	Description
in_netof	Returns network and subnet portions of *in*. The host bits are set to 0. For class D addresses, returns the class D prefix bits and 0 bits for the multicast group. u_long **in_netof**(struct in_addr *in*);
in_canforward	Returns true if an IP packet addressed to *in* is eligible for forwarding. Class D and E addresses, loopback network addresses, and addresses with a network number of 0 must not be forwarded. int **in_canforward**(struct in_addr *in*);
in_localaddr	Returns true if the host *in* is located on a directly connected network. If the global variable subnetsarelocal is nonzero, then subnets of all directly connected networks are also considered local. int **in_localaddr**(struct in_addr *in*);
in_broadcast	Return true if *in* is a broadcast address associated with the interface pointed to by *ifp*. int **in_broadcast**(struct in_addr *in*, struct ifnet **ifp*);

Figure 6.31   Internet address functions.

Net/2 had a bug in in_canforward that permitted loopback addresses to be forwarded.
Since most Net/2 systems are configured to recognize only a single loopback address, such as
127.0.0.1, Net/2 systems often forward other addresses in the loopback network (e.g., 127.0.0.2)
along the default route.

A telnet to 127.0.0.2 may not do what you expect! (Exercise 6.6)

6.9   `ifnet` Utility Functions

Several functions search the data structures shown in Figure 6.5. The functions listed in
Figure 6.32 accept addresses for any protocol family, since their argument is a pointer to
a `sockaddr` structure, which contains the address family. Contrast this to the functions
in Figure 6.31, each of which takes a 32-bit IP address as an argument. These functions
are defined in `net/if.c`.

Function	Description
`ifa_ifwithaddr`	Search the `ifnet` list for an interface with a unicast or broadcast address of *addr*. Return a pointer to the matching `ifaddr` structure or a null pointer if no match is found. `struct ifaddr * `**`ifa_ifwithaddr`**`(struct sockaddr *addr);`
`ifa_ifwithdstaddr`	Search the `ifnet` list for the interface with a destination address of *addr*. Return a pointer to the matching `ifaddr` structure or a null pointer if no match is found. `struct ifaddr * `**`ifa_ifwithdstaddr`**`(struct sockaddr *addr);`
`ifa_ifwithnet`	Search the `ifnet` list for the address on the same network as *addr*. Return a pointer to the most specific matching `ifaddr` structure or a null pointer if no match is found. `struct ifaddr * `**`ifa_ifwithnet`**`(struct sockaddr *addr);`
`ifa_ifwithaf`	Search the `ifnet` list for the first address in the same address family as *addr*. Return a pointer to the matching `ifaddr` structure or a null pointer if no match is found. `struct ifaddr * `**`ifa_ifwithaf`**`(struct sockaddr *addr);`

`ifaof_ifpforaddr`	Search the address list of *ifp* for the address that matches *addr*. The order of preference is for an exact match, the destination address on a point-to-point link, an address on the same network, and finally an address in the same address family. Return a pointer to the matching `ifaddr` structure or a null pointer if no match is found.
	
	`struct ifaddr * `**`ifaof_ifpforaddr`**`(struct sockaddr *addr,`
	`                  struct ifnet *ifp);`

`ifa_ifwithroute`	Returns a pointer to the `ifaddr` structure for the appropriate local interface for the destination (`dst`), and gateway (`gateway`) specified.
	
	`struct ifaddr * `**`ifa_ifwithroute`**`(int flags,`
	`                  struct sockaddr *dst, struct sockaddr *gateway)`

`ifunit`	Return a pointer to the `ifnet` structure associated with *name*. `struct ifnet * `**`ifunit`**`(char *name);`

Figure 6.32   `ifnet` utility functions.

6.10 Summary

In this chapter we presented an overview of the IP addressing mechanisms and
described interface address structures and protocol address structures that are specialized for IP: the in_ifaddr and sockaddr_in structures.

  We described how interfaces are configured with IP-specific information through
the ifconfig program and the ioctl interface commands.

  Finally, we summarized several utility functions that manipulate IP addresses and
search the interface data structures.

Exercises

6.1   Why do you think sin_addr in the sockaddr_in structure was originally defined as a
       structure?

6.2   ifunit("sl0") returns a pointer to which structure in Figure 6.5?

6.3   Why is the IP address duplicated in ac_ipaddr when it is already contained in an ifaddr
       structure on the interface's address list?

6.4   Why do you think IP interface addresses are accessed through a UDP socket and not a raw
       IP socket?

6.5   Why does in_socktrim change sin_len to match the length of the mask instead of using
       the standard length of a sockaddr_in structure?

6.6   What happens when the connection request segment from a telnet 127.0.0.2 command
       is erroneously forwarded by a Net/2 system and is eventually recognized and accepted by
       a system along the default route?

7

Domains and Protocols

7.1 Introduction

In this chapter we describe the Net/3 data structures that support the concurrent operation of multiple network protocols. We'll use the Internet protocols to illustrate the construction and initialization of these data structures at system initialization time. This chapter presents the necessary background material for our discussion of the IP protocol processing layer, which begins in Chapter 8.

Net/3 groups related protocols into a *domain,* and identifies each domain with a *protocol family* constant. Net/3 also groups protocols by the addressing method they employ. Recall from Figure 3.19 that address families also have identifying constants. Currently every protocol within a domain uses the same type of address and every address type is used by a single domain. As a result, a domain can be uniquely identified by its protocol family or address family constant. Figure 7.1 lists the protocols and constants that we discuss.

Protocol family	Address family	Protocol
PF_INET	AF_INET	Internet
PF_OSI, PF_ISO	AF_OSI, AF_ISO	OSI
PF_LOCAL, PF_UNIX	AF_LOCAL, AF_UNIX	local IPC (Unix)
PF_ROUTE	AF_ROUTE	routing tables
n/a	AF_LINK	link-level (e.g., Ethernet)

Figure 7.1 Common protocol and address family constants.

PF_LOCAL and AF_LOCAL are the primary identifiers for protocols that support communication between processes on the same host and are part of the POSIX.12 standard. Before Net/3, PF_UNIX and AF_UNIX identified these protocols. The UNIX constants remain for backward compatibility and are used by Net/3 and in this text.

The PF_UNIX domain supports interprocess communication on a single Unix host. See [Stevens 1990] for details. The PF_ROUTE domain supports communication between a process and the routing facilities in the kernel (Chapter 18). We reference the PF_OSI protocols occasionally, as some features of Net/3 exist only to support the OSI protocols, but do not discuss them in any detail. Most of our discussions are about the PF_INET protocols.

7.2   Code Introduction

Two headers and two C files are covered in this chapter. Figure 7.2 describes the four files.

File	Description
`netinet/domain.h` `netinet/protosw.h`	`domain` structure definition `protosw` structure definition
`netinet/in_proto.c` `kern/uipc_domain.c`	IP `domain` and `protosw` structures initialization and search functions

Figure 7.2   Files discussed in this chapter.

Global Variables

Figure 7.3 describes several important global data structures and system parameters that are described in this chapter and referenced throughout Net/3.

Variable	Datatype	Description

`domains`
`inetdomain`
`inetsw`
	`struct domain *`
	`struct domain`
	`struct protosw[]`
		linked list of domains
		`domain` structure for the Internet protocols
		array of `protosw` structures for the Internet protocols

`max_linkhdr`
`max_protohdr`
`max_hdr`
`max_datalen`
	`int`
	`int`
	`int`
	`int`
		see Figure 7.17
		see Figure 7.17
		see Figure 7.17
		see Figure 7.17

Figure 7.3   Global variables introduced in this chapter.

Statistics

No statistics are collected by the code described in this chapter, but Figure 7.4 shows the statistics table allocated and initialized by the `ip_init` function. The only way to look at this table is with a kernel debugger.

Variable	Datatype	Description
`ip_ifmatrix`	`int[][]`	two-dimensional array to count packets routed between any two interfaces

Figure 7.4   Statistics collected in this chapter.

7.3 `domain` Structure

A protocol domain is represented by a `domain` structure shown in Figure 7.5.

```
                                                                      ── domain.h
42 struct domain {
43      int      dom_family;           /* AF_xxx */
44      char     *dom_name;
45      void     (*dom_init)           /* initialize domain data structures */
46               (void);
47      int      (*dom_externalize)    /* externalize access rights */
48               (struct mbuf *);
49      int      (*dom_dispose)        /* dispose of internalized rights */
50               (struct mbuf *);
51      struct protosw *dom_protosw, *dom_protoswNPROTOSW;
52      struct domain *dom_next;
53      int      (*dom_rtattach)       /* initialize routing table */
54               (void **, int);
55      int      dom_rtoffset;         /* an arg to rtattach, in bits */
56      int      dom_maxrtkey;         /* for routing layer */
57 };
                                                                      ── domain.h
```

Figure 7.5 The `domain` structure definition.

42–57   `dom_family` is one of the address family constants (e.g., `AF_INET`) and specifies the addressing employed by the protocols in the domain. `dom_name` is a text name for the domain (e.g., `"internet"`).

> The `dom_name` member is not accessed by any part of the Net/3 kernel, but the `fstat(1)` program uses `dom_name` when it formats socket information.

`dom_init` points to the function that initializes the domain. `dom_externalize` and `dom_dispose` point to functions that manage access rights sent across a communication path within the domain. The Unix domain implements this feature to pass file descriptors between processes. The Internet domain does not implement access rights.

`dom_protosw` and `dom_protoswNPROTOSW` point to the start and end of an array of `protosw` structures. `dom_next` points to the next domain in a linked list of domains supported by the kernel. The linked list of all domains is accessed through the global pointer `domains`.

The next three members, `dom_rtattach`, `dom_rtoffset`, and `dom_maxrtkey`, hold routing information for the domain. They are described in Chapter 18.

Figure 7.6 shows an example `domains` list.

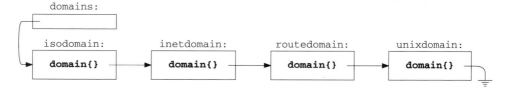

Figure 7.6 `domains` list.

7.4   `protosw` Structure

At compile time, Net/3 allocates and initializes a `protosw` structure for each protocol in the kernel and groups the structures for all protocols within a single domain into an array. Each `domain` structure references the appropriate array of `protosw` structures. A kernel may provide multiple interfaces to the same protocol by providing multiple `protosw` entries. For example, in Section 7.5 we describe three different entries for the IP protocol.

```
                                                                            protosw.h
57 struct protosw {
58      short   pr_type;                /* see (Figure 7.8) */
59      struct domain *pr_domain;       /* domain protocol a member of */
60      short   pr_protocol;            /* protocol number */
61      short   pr_flags;               /* see Figure 7.9 */
62 /* protocol-protocol hooks */
63      void    (*pr_input) ();         /* input to protocol (from below) */
64      int     (*pr_output) ();        /* output to protocol (from above) */
65      void    (*pr_ctlinput) ();      /* control input (from below) */
66      int     (*pr_ctloutput) ();     /* control output (from above) */
67 /* user-protocol hook */
68      int     (*pr_usrreq) ();        /* user request from process */
69 /* utility hooks */
70      void    (*pr_init) ();          /* initialization hook */
71      void    (*pr_fasttimo) ();      /* fast timeout (200ms) */
72      void    (*pr_slowtimo) ();      /* slow timeout (500ms) */
73      void    (*pr_drain) ();         /* flush any excess space possible */
74      int     (*pr_sysctl) ();        /* sysctl for protocol */
75 };
                                                                            protosw.h
```

Figure 7.7   The `protosw` structure definition.

57–61   The first four members in the structure identify and characterize the protocol. `pr_type` specifies the communication semantics of the protocol. Figure 7.8 lists the possible values for `pr_type` and the corresponding Internet protocols.

pr_type	Protocol semantics	Internet protocols
SOCK_STREAM	reliable bidirectional byte-stream service	TCP
SOCK_DGRAM	best-effort transport-level datagram service	UDP
SOCK_RAW	best-effort network-level datagram service	ICMP, IGMP, raw IP
SOCK_RDM	reliable datagram service (not implemented)	n/a
SOCK_SEQPACKET	reliable bidirectional record stream service	n/a

Figure 7.8   `pr_type` specifies the protocol's semantics.

`pr_domain` points to the associated `domain` structure, `pr_protocol` numbers the protocol within the domain, and `pr_flags` specifies additional characteristics of the protocol. Figure 7.9 lists the possible values for `pr_flags`.

pr_flags	Description
PR_ATOMIC	each process request maps to a single protocol request
PR_ADDR	protocol passes addresses with each datagram
PR_CONNREQUIRED	protocol is connection oriented
PR_WANTRCVD	notify protocol when a process receives data
PR_RIGHTS	protocol supports access rights

Figure 7.9 pr_flags values.

If PR_ADDR is supported by a protocol, PR_ATOMIC must also be supported. PR_ADDR and PR_CONNREQUIRED are mutually exclusive.

When PR_WANTRCVD is set, the socket layer notifies the protocol layer when it has passed data from the socket receive buffer to a process (i.e., when more space becomes available in the receive buffer).

PR_RIGHTS indicates that access right control messages can be passed across the connection. Access rights require additional support within the kernel to ensure proper cleanup if the receiving process does not consume the messages. Only the Unix domain supports access rights, where they are used to pass descriptors between processes.

Figure 7.10 shows the relationship between the protocol type, the protocol flags, and the protocol semantics.

pr_type	PR_			Record boundaries?	Reliable?	Example	
	ADDR	ATOMIC	CONNREQUIRED			Internet	Other
SOCK_STREAM			•	none	•	TCP	SPP
SOCK_SEQPACKET			•	explicit	•		TP4
	•	•	•	implicit	•		SPP
SOCK_RDM		•	•	implicit	see text		RDP
SOCK_DGRAM	•	•		implicit		UDP	
SOCK_RAW	•	•		implicit		ICMP	

Figure 7.10 Protocol characteristics and examples.

Figure 7.10 does not include the PR_WANTRCVD or PR_RIGHTS flags. PR_WANTRCVD is always set for reliable connection-oriented protocols.

To understand communication semantics of a protosw entry in Net/3, we must consider the PR_*xxx* flags and pr_type together. In Figure 7.10 we have included two columns ("Record boundaries?" and "Reliable?") to describe the additional semantics that are implicitly specified by pr_type. Figure 7.10 shows three types of reliable protocols:

- Connection-oriented byte stream protocols such as TCP and SPP (from the XNS protocol family). These protocols are identified by SOCK_STREAM.

- Connection-oriented stream protocols with record boundaries are specified by SOCK_SEQPACKET. Within this type of protocol, PR_ATOMIC indicates whether records are implicitly specified by each output request or are explicitly specified by setting the MSG_EOR flag on output. TP4 from the OSI protocol family requires explicit record boundaries, and SPP assumes implicit record boundaries.

  SPP supports both SOCK_STREAM and SOCK_SEQPACKET semantics.

- The third type of reliable protocol provides a connection-oriented service with implicit record boundaries and is specified by SOCK_RDM. RDP does not guarantee that records are received in the order that they are sent. RDP is described in [Partridge 1987] and specified by RFC 1151 [Partridge and Hinden 1990].

Two types of unreliable protocols are shown in Figure 7.10:

- A transport-level datagram protocol, such as UDP, which includes multiplexing and checksums, is specified by SOCK_DGRAM.

- A network-level datagram protocol, such as ICMP, which is specified by SOCK_RAW. In Net/3, only superuser processes may create a SOCK_RAW socket (Figure 15.18).

62–68   The next five members are function pointers providing access to the protocol from other protocols. pr_input handles incoming data from a lower-level protocol, pr_output handles outgoing data from a higher-level protocol, pr_ctlinput handles control information from below, and pr_ctloutput handles control information from above. pr_usrreq handles all communication requests from a process.

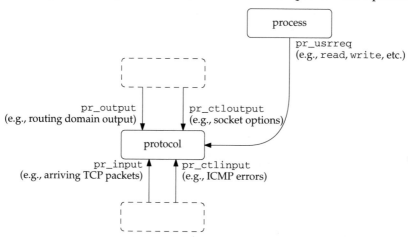

Figure 7.11   The five main entry points to a protocol.

69–75   The remaining five members are utility functions for the protocol. pr_init handles initialization. pr_fasttimo and pr_slowtimo are called every 200 ms and 500 ms respectively to perform periodic protocol functions, such as updating retransmission timers. `pr_drain` is called by `m_reclaim` when memory is in short supply (Figure 2.13). It is a request that the protocol release as much memory as possible. `pr_sysctl` provides an interface for the `sysctl(8)` command, a way to modify system-wide parameters, such as enabling packet forwarding or UDP checksum calculations.

7.5 IP domain and protosw Structures

The `domain` and `protosw` structures for all protocols are declared and initialized statically. For the Internet protocols, the `inetsw` array contains the `protosw` structures. Figure 7.12 summarizes the protocol information in the `inetsw` array. Figure 7.13 shows the definition of the array and the definition of the `domain` structure for the Internet protocols.

inetsw[]	pr_protocol	pr_type	Description	Acronym
0	0	0	Internet Protocol	IP
1	IPPROTO_UDP	SOCK_DGRAM	User Datagram Protocol	UDP
2	IPPROTO_TCP	SOCK_STREAM	Transmission Control Protocol	TCP
3	IPPROTO_RAW	SOCK_RAW	Internet Protocol (raw)	IP (raw)
4	IPPROTO_ICMP	SOCK_RAW	Internet Control Message Protocol	ICMP
5	IPPROTO_IGMP	SOCK_RAW	Internet Group Management Protocol	IGMP
6	0	SOCK_RAW	Internet Protocol (raw, default)	IP (raw)

Figure 7.12   Internet domain protocols.

39–77   Three `protosw` structures in the `inetsw` array provide access to IP. The first, `inetsw[0]`, specifies administrative functions for IP and is accessed only by the kernel. The other two entries, `inetsw[3]` and `inetsw[6]`, are identical except for their `pr_protocol` values and provide a *raw* interface to IP. `inetsw[3]` processes any packets that are received for unrecognized protocols. `inetsw[6]` is the default raw protocol, which the `pffindproto` function (Section 7.6) returns when no other match is found.

> In releases before Net/3, packets transmitted through `inetsw[3]` did not have an IP header prepended. It was the responsibility of the process to construct the correct header. Packets transmitted through `inetsw[6]` had an IP header prepended by the kernel. 4.3BSD Reno introduced the `IP_HDRINCL` socket option (Section 32.8), so the distinction between `inetsw[3]` and `inetsw[6]` is no longer relevant.

The raw interface allows a process to send and receive IP packets without an intervening transport protocol. One use of the raw interface is to implement a transport protocol outside the kernel. Once the protocol has stablized, it can be moved into the kernel to improve its performance and availability to other processes. Another use is for diagnostic tools such as `traceroute`, which uses the raw IP interface to access IP directly. Chapter 32 discusses the raw IP interface. Figure 7.14 summarizes the IP `protosw` structures.

```
                                                                  in_proto.c
39 struct protosw inetsw[] =
40 {
41      {0, &inetdomain, 0, 0,
42       0, ip_output, 0, 0,
43       0,
44       ip_init, 0, ip_slowtimo, ip_drain, ip_sysctl
45      },
46      {SOCK_DGRAM, &inetdomain, IPPROTO_UDP, PR_ATOMIC | PR_ADDR,
47       udp_input, 0, udp_ctlinput, ip_ctloutput,
48       udp_usrreq,
49       udp_init, 0, 0, 0, udp_sysctl
50      },
51      {SOCK_STREAM, &inetdomain, IPPROTO_TCP, PR_CONNREQUIRED | PR_WANTRCVD,
52       tcp_input, 0, tcp_ctlinput, tcp_ctloutput,
53       tcp_usrreq,
54       tcp_init, tcp_fasttimo, tcp_slowtimo, tcp_drain,
55      },
56      {SOCK_RAW, &inetdomain, IPPROTO_RAW, PR_ATOMIC | PR_ADDR,
57       rip_input, rip_output, 0, rip_ctloutput,
58       rip_usrreq,
59       0, 0, 0, 0,
60      },
61      {SOCK_RAW, &inetdomain, IPPROTO_ICMP, PR_ATOMIC | PR_ADDR,
62       icmp_input, rip_output, 0, rip_ctloutput,
63       rip_usrreq,
64       0, 0, 0, 0, icmp_sysctl
65      },
66      {SOCK_RAW, &inetdomain, IPPROTO_IGMP, PR_ATOMIC | PR_ADDR,
67       igmp_input, rip_output, 0, rip_ctloutput,
68       rip_usrreq,
69       igmp_init, igmp_fasttimo, 0, 0,
70      },
71      /* raw wildcard */
72      {SOCK_RAW, &inetdomain, 0, PR_ATOMIC | PR_ADDR,
73       rip_input, rip_output, 0, rip_ctloutput,
74       rip_usrreq,
75       rip_init, 0, 0, 0,
76      },
77 };

78 struct domain inetdomain =
79 {AF_INET, "internet", 0, 0, 0,
80  inetsw, &inetsw[sizeof(inetsw) / sizeof(inetsw[0])], 0,
81  rn_inithead, 32, sizeof(struct sockaddr_in)};
                                                                  in_proto.c
```

Figure 7.13 The Internet domain and protosw structures.

78–81   The domain structure for the Internet protocols is shown at the end of Figure 7.13.
The Internet domain uses AF_INET style addressing, has a text name of "internet",
has no initialization or control-message functions, and has its protosw structures in the
inetsw array.

The routing initialization function for the Internet protocols is rn_inithead. The

protosw	inetsw[0]	inetsw[3 and 6]	Description
pr_type	0	SOCK_RAW	IP provides raw packet services
pr_domain	&inetdomain	&inetdomain	both protocols are part of the Internet domain
pr_protocol	0	IPPROTO_RAW or 0	both IPPROTO_RAW (255) and 0 are reserved (RFC 1700) and should never appear in an IP datagram
pr_flags	0	PR_ATOMIC|PR_ADDR	socket layer flags, not used by IP
pr_input	null	rip_input	receive unrecognized datagrams from IP, ICMP, or IGMP
pr_output	ip_output	rip_output	prepare and send datagrams to the IP and hardware layers respectively
pr_ctlinput	null	null	not used by IP
pr_ctloutput	null	rip_ctloutput	respond to configuration requests from a process
pr_usrreq	null	rip_usrreq	respond to protocol requests from a process
pr_init	ip_init	null or rip_init	ip_init does all initialization
pr_fasttimo	null	null	not used by IP
pr_slowtimo	ip_slowtimo	null	slow timeout is used by IP reassembly algorithm
pr_drain	ip_drain	null	release memory if possible
pr_sysctl	ip_sysctl	null	modify systemwide parameters

Figure 7.14   The IP inetsw entries.

The only difference between inetsw[3] and inetsw[6] is in their pr_protocol numbers and the initialization function rip_init, which is defined only in inetsw[6] so that it is called only once during initialization.

offset of an IP address from the beginning of a sockaddr_in structure is 32 bits and the size of the structure is 16 bytes (Figure 18.27).

domaininit Function

At system initialization time (Figure 3.23), the kernel calls domaininit to link the domain and protosw structures. domaininit is shown in Figure 7.15.

37–42   The ADDDOMAIN macro declares and links a single domain structure. For example, ADDDOMAIN(unix) expands to

```
extern struct domain unixdomain;
unixdomain.dom_next = domains;
domains = &unixdomain;
```

> The __CONCAT macro is defined in sys/defs.h and concatenates two symbols. For example, __CONCAT(unix,domain) produces unixdomain.

43–54   domaininit constructs the list of domains by calling ADDDOMAIN for each supported domain.

—————————————————————— uipc_domain.c

```
37 /* simplifies code in domaininit */

38 #define ADDDOMAIN(x)      { \
39     extern struct domain __CONCAT(x,domain); \
40     __CONCAT(x,domain.dom_next) = domains; \
41     domains = &__CONCAT(x,domain); \
42 }

43 domaininit()
44 {
45     struct domain *dp;
46     struct protosw *pr;
47     /* The C compiler usually defines unix. We don't want to get
48      * confused with the unix argument to ADDDOMAIN
49      */

50 #undef unix
51     ADDDOMAIN(unix);
52     ADDDOMAIN(route);
53     ADDDOMAIN(inet);
54     ADDDOMAIN(iso);

55     for (dp = domains; dp; dp = dp->dom_next) {
56         if (dp->dom_init)
57             (*dp->dom_init) ();
58         for (pr = dp->dom_protosw; pr < dp->dom_protoswNPROTOSW; pr++)
59             if (pr->pr_init)
60                 (*pr->pr_init) ();
61     }

62     if (max_linkhdr < 16)          /* XXX */
63         max_linkhdr = 16;
64     max_hdr = max_linkhdr + max_protohdr;
65     max_datalen = MHLEN - max_hdr;
66     timeout(pffasttimo, (void *) 0, 1);
67     timeout(pfslowtimo, (void *) 0, 1);
68 }
```

—————————————————————— uipc_domain.c

Figure 7.15 domaininit function.

Since the symbol unix is often predefined by the C preprocessor, Net/3 explicitly undefines it here so ADDDOMAIN works correctly.

Figure 7.16 shows the linked domain and protosw structures in a kernel configured to support the Internet, Unix, and OSI protocol families.

55–61   The two nested for loops locate every domain and protocol in the kernel and call the initialization functions dom_init and pr_init if they are defined. For the Internet protocols, the following functions are called (Figure 7.13): ip_init, udp_init, tcp_init, igmp_init, and rip_init.

62–65   The parameters computed in domaininit control the layout of packets in the mbufs to avoid extraneous copying of data. max_linkhdr and max_protohdr are set during protocol initialization. domaininit enforces a lower bound of 16 for max_linkhdr. The value of 16 leaves room for a 14-byte Ethernet header ending on a 4-byte boundary. Figures 7.17 and 7.18 list the parameters and typical values.

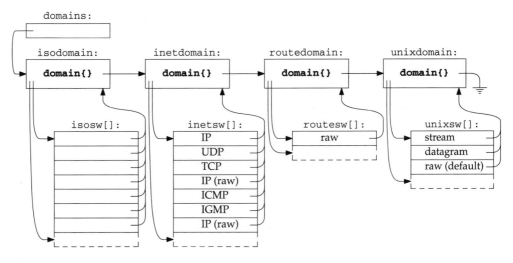

Figure 7.16   The domain list and protosw arrays after initialization.

Variable	Value	Description
max_linkhdr	16	maximum number of bytes added by link layer
max_protohdr	40	maximum number of bytes added by network and transport layers
max_hdr	56	max_linkhdr + max_protohdr
max_datalen	44	number of data bytes available in packet header mbuf after accounting for the link and protocol headers

Figure 7.17   Parameters used to minimize copying of protocol data.

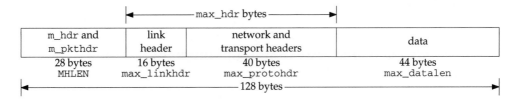

Figure 7.18   Mbuf and associated maximum header lengths.

max_protohdr is a soft limit that measures the expected protocol header size. In the Internet domain, the IP and TCP headers are usually 20 bytes in length but both can be up to 60 bytes. The penalty for exceeding max_protohdr is the time required to push back the data to make room for the larger than expected protocol header.

66–68   domaininit initiates pfslowtimo and pffasttimo by calling timeout. The third argument specifies when the kernel should call the functions, in this case in 1 clock tick. Both functions are shown in Figure 7.19.

```
153 void
154 pfslowtimo(arg)
155 void    *arg;
156 {
157     struct domain *dp;
158     struct protosw *pr;

159     for (dp = domains; dp; dp = dp->dom_next)
160         for (pr = dp->dom_protosw; pr < dp->dom_protoswNPROTOSW; pr++)
161             if (pr->pr_slowtimo)
162                 (*pr->pr_slowtimo) ();
163     timeout(pfslowtimo, (void *) 0, hz / 2);
164 }

165 void
166 pffasttimo(arg)
167 void    *arg;
168 {
169     struct domain *dp;
170     struct protosw *pr;

171     for (dp = domains; dp; dp = dp->dom_next)
172         for (pr = dp->dom_protosw; pr < dp->dom_protoswNPROTOSW; pr++)
173             if (pr->pr_fasttimo)
174                 (*pr->pr_fasttimo) ();
175     timeout(pffasttimo, (void *) 0, hz / 5);
176 }
```
uipc_domain.c

Figure 7.19 pfslowtimo and pffasttimo functions.

153–176   These nearly identical functions use two for loops to call the pr_slowtimo or pr_fasttimo function for each protocol, if they are defined. The functions schedule themselves to be called 500 and 200 ms later by calling timeout, which we described with Figure 3.43.

7.6   pffindproto and pffindtype Functions

The pffindproto and pffindtype functions look up a protocol by number (e.g., IPPROTO_TCP) or by type (e.g., SOCK_STREAM). As we'll see in Chapter 15, these functions are called to locate the appropriate protosw entry when a process creates a socket.

69–84   pffindtype performs a linear search of domains for the specified family and then searches the protocols within the domain for the first one of the specified type.

85–107   pffindproto searches domains exactly as pffindtype does but looks for the family, type, and protocol specified by the caller. If pffindproto does not find a (protocol, type) match within the specified protocol family, and type is SOCK_RAW, and the domain has a default raw protocol (pr_protocol equals 0), then pffindproto selects the default raw protocol instead of failing completely. For example, a call such as

—————————————————————————— uipc_domain.c

```
69 struct protosw *
70 pffindtype(family, type)
71 int      family, type;
72 {
73     struct domain *dp;
74     struct protosw *pr;

75     for (dp = domains; dp; dp = dp->dom_next)
76         if (dp->dom_family == family)
77             goto found;
78     return (0);
79   found:
80     for (pr = dp->dom_protosw; pr < dp->dom_protoswNPROTOSW; pr++)
81         if (pr->pr_type && pr->pr_type == type)
82             return (pr);
83     return (0);
84 }

85 struct protosw *
86 pffindproto(family, protocol, type)
87 int      family, protocol, type;
88 {
89     struct domain *dp;
90     struct protosw *pr;
91     struct protosw *maybe = 0;

92     if (family == 0)
93         return (0);
94     for (dp = domains; dp; dp = dp->dom_next)
95         if (dp->dom_family == family)
96             goto found;
97     return (0);
98   found:
99     for (pr = dp->dom_protosw; pr < dp->dom_protoswNPROTOSW; pr++) {
100         if ((pr->pr_protocol == protocol) && (pr->pr_type == type))
101             return (pr);

102         if (type == SOCK_RAW && pr->pr_type == SOCK_RAW &&
103             pr->pr_protocol == 0 && maybe == (struct protosw *) 0)
104             maybe = pr;
105     }
106     return (maybe);
107 }
```

—————————————————————————— uipc_domain.c

Figure 7.20   pffindproto and pffindtype functions.

```
    pffindproto(PF_INET, 27, SOCK_RAW);
```

returns a pointer to inetsw[6], the default raw IP protocol, since Net/3 does not include support for protocol 27. With access to raw IP, a process could implement protocol 27 services on its own using the kernel to manage the sending and receiving of the IP packets.

Protocol 27 is reserved for the Reliable Datagram Protocol (RFC 1151).

Both functions return a pointer to the `protosw` structure for the selected protocol, or a null pointer if they don't find a match.

Example

We'll see in Section 15.6 that when an application calls

```
socket(PF_INET, SOCK_STREAM, 0);      /* TCP socket */
```

`pffindtype` gets called as

```
pffindtype(PF_INET, SOCK_STREAM);
```

Figure 7.12 shows that `pffindtype` will return a pointer to `inetsw[2]`, since TCP is the first SOCK_STREAM protocol in the array. Similarly,

```
socket(PF_INET, SOCK_DGRAM, 0);      /* UDP socket */
```

leads to

```
pffindtype(PF_INET, SOCK_DGRAM);
```

which returns a pointer to UDP in `inetsw[1]`.

7.7   `pfctlinput` Function

The `pfctlinput` function issues a control request to every protocol in every domain. It is used when an event that may affect every protocol occurs, such as an interface shutdown or routing table change. ICMP calls `pfctlinput` when an ICMP redirect message arrives (Figure 11.14), since the redirect can affect all the Internet protocols (e.g., UDP and TCP).

```
                                                                      uipc_domain.c
142 pfctlinput(cmd, sa)
143 int     cmd;
144 struct sockaddr *sa;
145 {
146     struct domain *dp;
147     struct protosw *pr;

148     for (dp = domains; dp; dp = dp->dom_next)
149         for (pr = dp->dom_protosw; pr < dp->dom_protoswNPROTOSW; pr++)
150             if (pr->pr_ctlinput)
151                 (*pr->pr_ctlinput) (cmd, sa, (caddr_t) 0);
152 }
                                                                      uipc_domain.c
```

Figure 7.21   `pfctlinput` function.

142–152   The two nested `for` loops locate every protocol in every domain. `pfctlinput` issues the protocol control command specified by `cmd` by calling each protocol's `pr_ctlinput` function. For UDP, `udp_ctlinput` is called and for TCP, `tcp_ctlinput` is called.

7.8   IP Initialization

As shown in Figure 7.13, the Internet domain does not have an initialization function but the individual Internet protocols do. For now, we look only at `ip_init`, the IP initialization function. In Chapters 23 and 24 we discuss the UDP and TCP initialization functions. Before we can discuss the code, we need to describe the `ip_protox` array.

Internet Transport Demultiplexing

A network-level protocol like IP must demultiplex incoming datagrams and deliver them to the appropriate transport-level protocols. To do this, the appropriate `protosw` structure must be derived from a protocol number present in the datagram. For the Internet protocols, this is done by the `ip_protox` array.

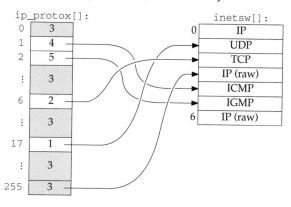

Figure 7.22   The `ip_protox` array maps the protocol number to an entry in the `inetsw` array.

The index into the `ip_protox` array is the protocol value from the IP header (`ip_p`, Figure 8.8). The entry selected is the index of the protocol in the `inetsw` array that processes the datagram. For example, a datagram with a protocol number of 6 is processed by `inetsw[2]`, the TCP protocol. The kernel constructs `ip_protox` during protocol initialization, described in Figure 7.23.

`ip_init` Function

The `ip_init` function is called by `domaininit` (Figure 7.15) at system initialization time.

71–78   `pffindproto` returns a pointer to the raw protocol (`inetsw[3]`, Figure 7.14). Net/3 panics if the raw protocol cannot be located, since it is a required part of the kernel. If it is missing, the kernel has been misconfigured. IP delivers packets that arrive for an unknown transport protocol to this protocol where they may be handled by a process outside the kernel.

79–85   The next two loops initialize the `ip_protox` array. The first loop sets each entry in the array to `pr`, the index of the default protocol (3 from Figure 7.22). The second loop examines each protocol in `inetsw` (other than the entries with protocol numbers of 0 or

—— *ip_input.c*

```
71 void
72 ip_init()
73 {
74     struct protosw *pr;
75     int     i;

76     pr = pffindproto(PF_INET, IPPROTO_RAW, SOCK_RAW);
77     if (pr == 0)
78         panic("ip_init");
79     for (i = 0; i < IPPROTO_MAX; i++)
80         ip_protox[i] = pr - inetsw;
81     for (pr = inetdomain.dom_protosw;
82          pr < inetdomain.dom_protoswNPROTOSW; pr++)
83         if (pr->pr_domain->dom_family == PF_INET &&
84             pr->pr_protocol && pr->pr_protocol != IPPROTO_RAW)
85             ip_protox[pr->pr_protocol] = pr - inetsw;
86     ipq.next = ipq.prev = &ipq;
87     ip_id = time.tv_sec & 0xffff;
88     ipintrq.ifq_maxlen = ipqmaxlen;
89     i = (if_index + 1) * (if_index + 1) * sizeof(u_long);
90     ip_ifmatrix = (u_long *) malloc(i, M_RTABLE, M_WAITOK);
91     bzero((char *) ip_ifmatrix, i);
92 }
```

—— *ip_input.c*

Figure 7.23   `ip_init` function.

`IPPROTO_RAW`) and sets the matching entry in `ip_protox` to refer to the appropriate `inetsw` entry. Therefore, `pr_protocol` in each `protosw` structure must be the protocol number expected to appear in the incoming datagram.

86–92   `ip_init` initializes the IP reassembly queue, `ipq` (Section 10.6), seeds `ip_id` from the system clock, and sets the maximum size of the IP input queue (`ipintrq`) to 50 (`ipqmaxlen`). `ip_id` is set from the system clock to provide a random starting point for datagram identifiers (Section 10.6). Finally, `ip_init` allocates a two-dimensional array, `ip_ifmatrix`, to count packets routed between the interfaces in the system.

> There are many variables within Net/3 that may be modified by a system administrator. To allow these variables to be changed at run time and without recompiling the kernel, the default value represented by a constant (`IFQ_MAXLEN` in this case) is assigned to a variable (`ipqmaxlen`) at compile time. A system administrator can use a kernel debugger such as adb to change `ipqmaxlen` and reboot the kernel with the new value. If Figure 7.23 used `IFQ_MAXLEN` directly, it would require a recompile of the kernel to change the limit.

7.9   `sysctl` **System Call**

The `sysctl` system call accesses and modifies Net/3 systemwide parameters. The system administrator can modify the parameters through the `sysctl(8)` program. Each parameter is identified by a hierarchical list of integers and has an associated type. The prototype for the system call is:

```
int sysctl(int *name, u_int namelen, void *old, size_t *oldlenp, void *new,
           size_t newlen);
```

name points to an array containing *namelen* integers. The old value is returned in the area pointed to by *oldp,* and the new value is passed in the area pointed to by *newp.*
Figure 7.24 summarizes the organization of the names related to networking.

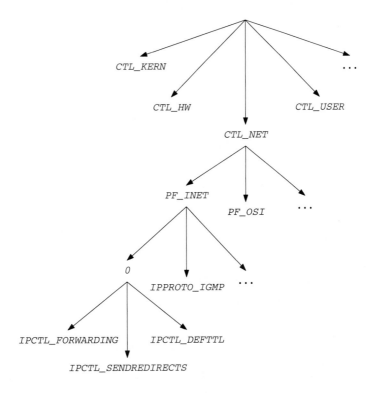

Figure 7.24   `sysctl` names.

In Figure 7.24, the full name for the IP forwarding flag would be

```
CTL_NET, PF_INET, 0, IPCTL_FORWARDING
```

with the four integers stored in an array.

net_sysctl **Function**

Each level of the sysctl naming scheme is handled by a different function. Figure 7.25 shows the functions that handle the Internet parameters.

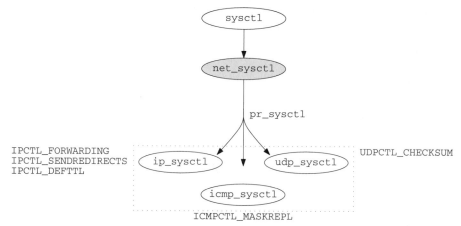

Figure 7.25 sysctl functions for Internet parameters.

The top-level names are processed by sysctl. The network-level names are processed by net_sysctl, which dispatches control based on the family and protocol to the pr_sysctl function specified in the protocol's protosw entry.

> sysctl is implemented in the kernel by the __sysctl function, which we do not discuss in this text. It contains code to move the sysctl arguments to and from the kernel and a switch statement to select the appropriate function to process the arguments, in this case net_sysctl.

Figure 7.26 shows the net_sysctl function.

108–119   The arguments to net_sysctl are the same as those to the sysctl system call with the addition of p, which points to the current process structure.

120–134   The next two integers in the name are taken to be the protocol family and protocol numbers as specified in the domain and protosw structures. If no family is specified, 0 is returned. If a family is specified, the for loop searches the domain list for a matching family. ENOPROTOOPT is returned if a match is not found.

135–141   Within a matching domain, the second for loop locates the first matching protocol that has the pr_sysctl function defined. When a match is found, the request is passed to the pr_sysctl function for the protocol. Notice that name is advanced to pass the remaining integers down to the next level. If no matching protocol is found, ENOPROTOOPT is returned.

Figure 7.27 shows the pr_sysctl functions defined for the Internet protocols.

—————————————————————————————— *uipc_domain.c*
```
108 net_sysctl(name, namelen, oldp, oldlenp, newp, newlen, p)
109 int     *name;
110 u_int    namelen;
111 void    *oldp;
112 size_t *oldlenp;
113 void    *newp;
114 size_t  newlen;
115 struct proc *p;
116 {
117     struct domain *dp;
118     struct protosw *pr;
119     int     family, protocol;

120     /*
121      * All sysctl names at this level are nonterminal;
122      * next two components are protocol family and protocol number,
123      * then at least one additional component.
124      */
125     if (namelen < 3)
126         return (EISDIR);          /* overloaded */
127     family = name[0];
128     protocol = name[1];

129     if (family == 0)
130         return (0);
131     for (dp = domains; dp; dp = dp->dom_next)
132         if (dp->dom_family == family)
133             goto found;
134     return (ENOPROTOOPT);
135   found:
136     for (pr = dp->dom_protosw; pr < dp->dom_protoswNPROTOSW; pr++)
137         if (pr->pr_protocol == protocol && pr->pr_sysctl)
138             return ((*pr->pr_sysctl) (name + 2, namelen - 2,
139                                     oldp, oldlenp, newp, newlen));
140     return (ENOPROTOOPT);
141 }
```
—————————————————————————————— *uipc_domain.c*

Figure 7.26 net_sysctl function.

pr_protocol	inetsw[]	pr_sysctl	Description	Reference
0	0	*ip_sysctl*	IP	Section 8.9
IPPROTO_UDP	1	*udp_sysctl*	UDP	Section 23.11
IPPROTO_ICMP	4	*icmp_sysctl*	ICMP	Section 11.14

Figure 7.27 pr_sysctl functions for the Internet protocol family.

In the routing domain, pr_sysctl points to the sysctl_rtable function, which is described in Chapter 19.

7.10 Summary

We started this chapter by describing the `domain` and `protosw` structures that describe and group protocols within the Net/3 kernel. We saw that all the `protosw` structures for a domain are allocated in an array at compile time and that `inetdomain` and the `inetsw` array describe the Internet protocols. We took a closer look at the three `inetsw` entries that describe the IP protocol: one for the kernel's use and the other two for access to IP by a process.

At system initialization time `domaininit` links the domains into the `domains` list, calls the domain and protocol initialization functions, and calls the fast and slow time-out functions.

The two functions `pffindproto` and `pffindtype` search the domain and protocol lists by protocol number or type. `pfctlinput` sends a control command to every protocol.

Finally we described the IP initialization procedure including transport demultiplexing by the `ip_protox` array.

Exercises

7.1   What call to the `pffindproto` returns a pointer to `inetsw[6]`?

8

IP: Internet Protocol

8.1 Introduction

In this chapter we describe the structure of an IP packet and the basic IP processing including input, forwarding, and output. We assume that the reader is familiar with the basic operation of the IP protocol. For more background on IP, see Chapters 3, 9 and 12 of Volume 1. RFC 791 [Postel 1981a] is the official specification for IP. RFC 1122 [Braden 1989a] contains clarifications of RFC 791.

In Chapter 9 we discuss option processing and in Chapter 10 we discuss fragmentation and reassembly. Figure 8.1 illustrates the general organization of the IP layer.

We saw in Chapter 4 how network interfaces place incoming IP packets on the IP input queue, ipintrq, and how they schedule a software interrupt. Since hardware interrupts have a higher priority than software interrupts, several packets may be placed on the queue before a software interrupt occurs. During software interrupt processing, the ipintr function removes and processes packets from ipintrq until the queue is empty. At the final destination, IP reassembles packets into datagrams and passes the datagrams directly to the appropriate transport-level protocol by a function call. If the packets haven't reached their final destination, IP passes them to ip_forward if the host is configured to act as a router. The transport protocols and ip_forward pass outgoing packets to ip_output, which completes the IP header, selects an output interface, and fragments the outgoing packet if necessary. The resulting packets are passed to the appropriate network interface output function.

When an error occurs, IP discards the packet and under certain conditions may send an error message to the source of the original packet. These messages are part of ICMP (Chapter 11). Net/3 sends ICMP error messages by calling icmp_error, which accepts an mbuf containing the erroneous packet, the type of error found, and an option

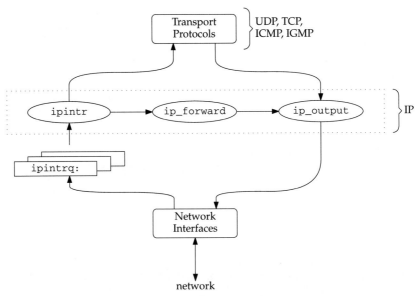

Figure 8.1   IP layer processing.

code that provides additional information depending on the type of error. In this chapter, we describe why and when IP sends ICMP messages, but we postpone a detailed discussion of ICMP itself until Chapter 11.

8.2   Code Introduction

Two headers and three C files are discussed in this chapter.

File	Description
net/route.h	route entries
netinet/ip.h	IP header structure
netinet/ip_input.c	IP input processing
netinet/ip_output.c	IP output processing
netinet/in_cksum.c	Internet checksum algorithm

Figure 8.2   Files discussed in this chapter.

Global Variables

Several global variables appear in the IP processing code. They are described in Figure 8.3.

Variable	Datatype	Description
`in_ifaddr`	`struct in_ifaddr *`	IP address list
`ip_defttl`	`int`	default TTL for IP packets
`ip_id`	`int`	last ID assigned to an outgoing IP packet
`ip_protox`	`int[]`	demultiplexing array for IP packets
`ipforwarding`	`int`	should the system forward IP packets?
`ipforward_rt`	`struct route`	cache of most recent forwarded route
`ipintrq`	`struct ifqueue`	IP input queue
`ipqmaxlen`	`int`	maximum length of IP input queue
`ipsendredirects`	`int`	should the system send ICMP redirects?
`ipstat`	`struct ipstat`	IP statistics

Figure 8.3   Global variables introduced in this chapter.

Statistics

All the statistics collected by IP are found in the `ipstat` structure described by Figure 8.4. Figure 8.5 shows some sample output of these statistics, from the `netstat -s` command. These statistics were collected after the host had been up for 30 days.

`ipstat` member	Description	Used by SNMP
`ips_badhlen`	#packets with invalid IP header length	•
`ips_badlen`	#packets with inconsistent IP header and IP data lengths	•
`ips_badoptions`	#packets discovered with errors in option processing	•
`ips_badsum`	#packets with bad checksum	•
`ips_badvers`	#packets with an IP version other than 4	•
`ips_cantforward`	#packets received for unreachable destination	•
`ips_delivered`	#datagrams delivered to upper level	•
`ips_forward`	#packets forwarded	•
`ips_fragdropped`	#fragments dropped (duplicates or out of space)	•
`ips_fragments`	#fragments received	•
`ips_fragtimeout`	#fragments timed out	•
`ips_noproto`	#packets with an unknown or unsupported protocol	•
`ips_reassembled`	#datagrams reassembled	•
`ips_tooshort`	#packets with invalid data length	•
`ips_toosmall`	#packets too small to contain IP packet	•
`ips_total`	total #packets received	•
`ips_cantfrag`	#packets discarded because of the don't fragment bit	•
`ips_fragmented`	#datagrams successfully fragmented	•
`ips_localout`	#datagrams generated at system (i.e., not forwarded)	•
`ips_noroute`	#packets discarded—no route to destination	•
`ips_odropped`	#packets dropped because of resource shortages	•
`ips_ofragments`	#fragments created for output	•
`ips_rawout`	total #raw ip packets generated	
`ips_redirectsent`	#redirect messages sent	

Figure 8.4   Statistics collected in this chapter.

netstat -s output	ipstat members
27,881,978 total packets received	ips_total
6 bad header checksums	ips_badsum
9 with size smaller than minimum	ips_tooshort
14 with data size < data length	ips_toosmall
0 with header length < data size	ips_badhlen
0 with data length < header length	ips_badlen
0 with bad options	ips_badoptions
0 with incorrect version number	ips_badvers
72,786 fragments received	ips_fragments
0 fragments dropped (dup or out of space)	ips_fragdropped
349 fragments dropped after timeout	ips_fragtimeout
16,557 packets reassembled ok	ips_reassembled
27,390,665 packets for this host	ips_delivered
330,882 packets for unknown/unsupported protocol	ips_noproto
97,939 packets forwarded	ips_forward
6,228 packets not forwardable	ips_cantforward
0 redirects sent	ips_redirectsent
29,447,726 packets sent from this host	ips_localout
769 packets sent with fabricated ip header	ips_rawout
0 output packets dropped due to no bufs, etc.	ips_odropped
0 output packets discarded due to no route	ips_noroute
260,484 output datagrams fragmented	ips_fragmented
796,084 fragments created	ips_ofragments
0 datagrams that can't be fragmented	ips_cantfrag

Figure 8.5 Sample IP statistics.

The value for ips_noproto is high because it can count ICMP host unreachable messages when there is no process ready to receive the messages. See Section 32.5 for more details.

SNMP Variables

Figure 8.6 shows the relationship between the SNMP variables in the IP group and the statistics collected by Net/3.

SNMP variable	ipstat member	Description
ipDefaultTTL	ip_defttl	default TTL for datagrams (64 "hops")
ipForwarding	ipforwarding	is system acting as a router?
ipReasmTimeout	IPFRAGTTL	reassembly timeout for fragments (30 seconds)
ipInReceives	ips_total	total #IP packets received

ipInHdrErrors	ips_badsum +
	    ips_tooshort +
	    ips_toosmall +
	    ips_badhlen +
	    ips_badlen +
	    ips_badoptions +
	    ips_badvers
		#packets with errors in IP header

ipInAddrErrors	ips_cantforward	#IP packets discarded because of misdelivery (ip_output failure also)
ipForwDatagrams	ips_forward	#IP packets forwarded
ipReasmReqds	ips_fragments	#fragments received
ipReasmFails	ips_fragdropped + ips_fragtimeout	#fragments dropped
ipReasmOKs	ips_reassembled	#datagrams successfully reassembled
ipInDiscards	(not implemented)	#datagrams discarded because of resource limitations
ipInUnknownProtos	ips_noproto	#datagrams with an unknown or unsupported protocol
ipInDelivers	ips_delivered	#datagrams delivered to transport layer
ipOutRequests	ips_localout	#datagrams generated by transport layers
ipFragOKs	ips_fragmented	#datagrams successfully fragmented
ipFragFails	ips_cantfrag	#IP packets discarded because of don't fragment bit
ipFragCreates	ips_ofragments	#fragments created for output
ipOutDiscards	ips_odropped	#IP packets dropped because of resource shortages
ipOutNoRoutes	ips_noroute	#IP packets discarded because of no route

Figure 8.6 Simple SNMP variables in IP group.

8.3   IP Packets

To be accurate while discussing Internet protocol processing, we must define a few
terms. Figure 8.7 illustrates the terms that describe data as it passes through the various
Internet layers.

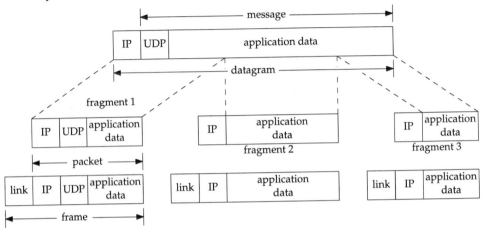

Figure 8.7   Frames, packets, fragments, datagrams, and messages.

We call the data passed to IP by a transport protocol a *message*. A message typically
contains a transport header and application data. UDP is the transport protocol illustrated in Figure 8.7. IP prepends its own header to the message to form a *datagram*. If
the datagram is too large for transmission on the selected network, IP splits the datagram into several *fragments*, each of which contains its own IP header and a portion of
the original datagram. Figure 8.7 shows a datagram split into three fragments.

An IP fragment or an IP datagram small enough to not require fragmentation are
called *packets* when presented to the data-link layer for transmission. The data-link
layer prepends its own header and transmits the resulting *frame*.

IP concerns itself only with the IP header and does not examine or modify the message itself (other than to perform fragmentation). Figure 8.8 shows the structure of the
IP header.

Figure 8.8 includes the member names of the `ip` structure (shown in Figure 8.9)
through which Net/3 accesses the IP header.

47–67   Since the physical order of bit fields in memory is machine and compiler dependent, the `#if`s ensure that the compiler lays out the structure members in the order
specified by the IP standard. In this way, when Net/3 overlays an `ip` structure on an IP
packet in memory, the structure members access the correct bits in the packet.

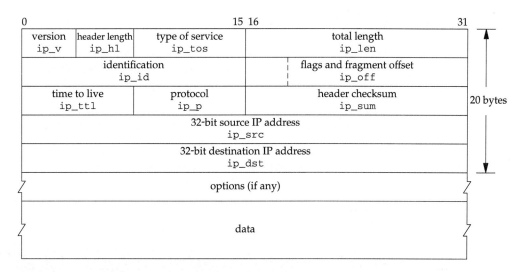

Figure 8.8   IP datagram, including the `ip` structure names.

ip.h

```
40 /*
41  * Structure of an internet header, naked of options.
42  *
43  * We declare ip_len and ip_off to be short, rather than u_short
44  * pragmatically since otherwise unsigned comparisons can result
45  * against negative integers quite easily, and fail in subtle ways.
46  */
47 struct ip {
48 #if BYTE_ORDER == LITTLE_ENDIAN
49     u_char  ip_hl:4,             /* header length */
50             ip_v:4;              /* version */
51 #endif
52 #if BYTE_ORDER == BIG_ENDIAN
53     u_char  ip_v:4,              /* version */
54             ip_hl:4;             /* header length */
55 #endif
56     u_char  ip_tos;              /* type of service */
57     short   ip_len;              /* total length */
58     u_short ip_id;               /* identification */
59     short   ip_off;              /* fragment offset field */
60 #define IP_DF 0x4000             /* dont fragment flag */
61 #define IP_MF 0x2000             /* more fragments flag */
62 #define IP_OFFMASK 0x1fff        /* mask for fragmenting bits */
63     u_char  ip_ttl;              /* time to live */
64     u_char  ip_p;                /* protocol */
65     u_short ip_sum;              /* checksum */
66     struct in_addr ip_src, ip_dst;  /* source and dest address */
67 };
```

ip.h

Figure 8.9   `ip` structure.

The IP header contains the format of the IP packet and its contents along with addressing, routing, and fragmentation information.

The format of an IP packet is specified by `ip_v`, the version, which is always 4; `ip_hl`, the header length measured in 4-byte units; `ip_len`, the packet length measured in bytes; `ip_p`, the transport protocol that created the data within the packet; and `ip_sum`, the checksum that detects changes to the header while in transit.

A standard IP header is 20 bytes long, so `ip_hl` must be greater than or equal to 5. A value greater than 5 indicates that IP options appear just after the standard header. The maximum value of `ip_hl` is 15 ($2^4 - 1$), which allows for up to 40 bytes of options ($20 + 40 = 60$). The maximum length of an IP datagram is 65535 ($2^{16} - 1$) bytes since `ip_len` is a 16-bit field. Figure 8.10 illustrates this organization.

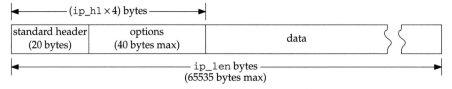

Figure 8.10   Organization of an IP packet with options.

Because `ip_hl` is measured in 4-byte units, IP options must always be padded to a 4-byte boundary.

8.4   Input Processing: `ipintr` Function

In Chapters 3, 4, and 5 we described how our example network interfaces queue incoming datagrams for protocol processing:

1. The Ethernet interface demultiplexes incoming frames with the type field found in the Ethernet header (Section 4.3).

2. The SLIP interface handles only IP packets, so demultiplexing is unnecessary (Section 5.3).

3. The loopback interface combines output and input processing in the function `looutput` and demultiplexes datagrams with the `sa_family` member of the destination address (Section 5.4).

In each case, after the interface queues the packet on `ipintrq`, it schedules a software interrupt through `schednetisr`. When the software interrupt occurs, the kernel calls `ipintr` if IP processing has been scheduled by `schednetisr`. Before the call to `ipintr`, the CPU priority is changed to `splnet`.

`ipintr` Overview

`ipintr` is a large function that we discuss in four parts: (1) verification of incoming packets, (2) option processing and forwarding, (3) packet reassembly, and (4) demultiplexing. Packet reassembly occurs in `ipintr`, but it is complex enough that we discuss it separately in Chapter 10. Figure 8.11 shows the overall organization of `ipintr`.

── ip_input.c
```
100 void
101 ipintr()
102 {
103     struct ip *ip;
104     struct mbuf *m;
105     struct ipq *fp;
106     struct in_ifaddr *ia;
107     int     hlen, s;

108  next:
109      /*
110       * Get next datagram off input queue and get IP header
111       * in first mbuf.
112       */
113      s = splimp();
114      IF_DEQUEUE(&ipintrq, m);
115      splx(s);
116      if (m == 0)
117          return;
```

```
                        /* input packet processing */
           /* Figures 8.12, 8.13, 8.15, 10.11, and 12.40 */
```

```
332      goto next;
333  bad:
334      m_freem(m);
335      goto next;
336 }
```
── ip_input.c

Figure 8.11 `ipintr` function.

100–117   The label `next` marks the start of the main packet processing loop. `ipintr` removes packets from `ipintrq` and processes them until the queue is empty. If control falls through to the end of the function, the `goto` passes control back to the top of the function at `next`. `ipintr` blocks incoming packets with `splimp` so that the network interrupt routines (such as `slinput` and `ether_input`) don't run while it accesses the queue.

332–336   The label `bad` marks the code that silently discards packets by freeing the associated mbuf and returning to the top of the processing loop at `next`. Throughout `ipintr`, errors are handled by jumping to `bad`.

Verification

We start with Figure 8.12: dequeueing packets from `ipintrq` and verifying their contents. Damaged or erroneous packets are silently discarded.

```
118    /*
119     * If no IP addresses have been set yet but the interfaces
120     * are receiving, can't do anything with incoming packets yet.
121     */
122    if (in_ifaddr == NULL)
123        goto bad;
124    ipstat.ips_total++;
125    if (m->m_len < sizeof(struct ip) &&
126                (m = m_pullup(m, sizeof(struct ip))) == 0) {
127        ipstat.ips_toosmall++;
128        goto next;
129    }
130    ip = mtod(m, struct ip *);
131    if (ip->ip_v != IPVERSION) {
132        ipstat.ips_badvers++;
133        goto bad;
134    }
135    hlen = ip->ip_hl << 2;
136    if (hlen < sizeof(struct ip)) {        /* minimum header length */
137        ipstat.ips_badhlen++;
138        goto bad;
139    }
140    if (hlen > m->m_len) {
141        if ((m = m_pullup(m, hlen)) == 0) {
142            ipstat.ips_badhlen++;
143            goto next;
144        }
145        ip = mtod(m, struct ip *);
146    }
147    if (ip->ip_sum = in_cksum(m, hlen)) {
148        ipstat.ips_badsum++;
149        goto bad;
150    }
151    /*
152     * Convert fields to host representation.
153     */
154    NTOHS(ip->ip_len);
155    if (ip->ip_len < hlen) {
156        ipstat.ips_badlen++;
157        goto bad;
158    }
159    NTOHS(ip->ip_id);
160    NTOHS(ip->ip_off);
161    /*
162     * Check that the amount of data in the buffers
163     * is as at least much as the IP header would have us expect.
164     * Trim mbufs if longer than we expect.
165     * Drop packet if shorter than we expect.
166     */
167    if (m->m_pkthdr.len < ip->ip_len) {
168        ipstat.ips_tooshort++;
169        goto bad;
170    }
```

```
171        if (m->m_pkthdr.len > ip->ip_len) {
172            if (m->m_len == m->m_pkthdr.len) {
173                m->m_len = ip->ip_len;
174                m->m_pkthdr.len = ip->ip_len;
175            } else
176                m_adj(m, ip->ip_len - m->m_pkthdr.len);
177        }
```
——— *ip_input.c*

Figure 8.12 `ipintr` function.

IP version

118–134   If the `in_ifaddr` list (Section 6.5) is empty, no IP addresses have been assigned to
the network interfaces, and `ipintr` must discard all IP packets; without addresses,
`ipintr` can't determine whether the packet is addressed to the system. Normally this
is a transient condition occurring during system initialization when the interfaces are
operating but have not yet been configured. We described address assignment in Section 6.6.

Before `ipintr` accesses any IP header fields, it must verify that `ip_v` is 4
(`IPVERSION`). RFC 1122 requires an implementation to silently discard packets with
unrecognized version numbers.

> Net/2 didn't check `ip_v`. Most IP implementations in use today, including Net/2, were cre-
> ated after IP version 4 was standardized and have never needed to distinguish between pack-
> ets from different IP versions. Since revisions to IP are now in progress, implementations in
> the near future will have to check `ip_v`.

> IEN 119 [Forgie 1979] and RFC 1190 [Topolcic 1990] describe experimental protocols using IP
> versions 5 and 6. Version 6 has also been selected as the version for the next revision to the
> official IP standard (IPv6). Versions 0 and 15 are reserved, and the remaining versions are
> unassigned.

In C, the easiest way to process data located in an untyped area of memory is to
overlay a structure on the area of memory and process the structure members instead of
the raw bytes. As described in Chapter 2, an mbuf chain stores a logical sequence of
bytes, such as an IP packet, into many physical mbufs connected to each other on a
linked list. Before the overlay technique can be applied to the IP packet headers, the
header must reside in a contiguous area of memory (i.e., it isn't split between two
mbufs).

135–146   The following steps ensure that the IP header (including options) is in a contiguous
area of memory:

- If the data within the first mbuf is smaller than a standard IP header (20 bytes),
  `m_pullup` relocates the standard header into a contiguous area of memory.

  > It is improbable that the link layer would split even the largest (60 bytes) IP header into
  > two mbufs necessitating the use of `m_pullup` as described.

- `ip_hl` is multiplied by 4 to get the header length in bytes, which is saved in
  `hlen`.

- If hlen, the length of the IP packet header in bytes, is less than the length of a standard header (20 bytes), it is invalid and the packet is discarded.

- If the entire header is still not in the first mbuf (i.e., the packet contains IP options), m_pullup finishes the job.

> Again, this should not be necessary.

Checksum processing is an important part of all the Internet protocols. Each protocol uses the same algorithm (implemented by the function in_cksum) but on different parts of the packet. For IP, the checksum protects only the IP header (and options if present). For transport protocols, such as UDP or TCP, the checksum covers the data portion of the packet and the transport header.

IP checksum

147–150   ipintr stores the checksum computed by in_cksum in the ip_sum field of the header. An undamaged header should have a checksum of 0.

> As we'll see in Section 8.7, ip_sum must be cleared before the checksum on an outgoing packet is computed. By storing the result from in_cksum in ip_sum, the packet is prepared for forwarding (although the TTL has not been decremented yet). The ip_output function does not depend on this behavior; it recomputes the checksum for the forwarded packet.

If the result is nonzero the packet is silently discarded. We discuss in_cksum in more detail in Section 8.7.

Byte ordering

151–160   The Internet standards are careful to specify the byte ordering of multibyte integer values in protocol headers. NTOHS converts all the 16-bit values in the IP header from from network byte order to host byte order: the packet length (ip_len), the datagram identifier (ip_id), and the fragment offset (ip_off). NTOHS is a null macro if the two formats are the same. Conversion to host byte order here obviates the need to perform a conversion every time Net/3 examines the fields.

Packet length

161–177   If the logical size of the packet (ip_len) is greater than the amount of data stored in the mbuf chain (m_pkthdr.len), some bytes are missing and the packet is dropped. If the mbuf chain is larger than the packet, the extra bytes are trimmed.

> A common cause for lost bytes is data arriving on a serial device with little or no buffering, such as on many personal computers. The incoming bytes are discarded by the device and IP discards the resulting packet.

> These extra bytes may arise, for example, on an Ethernet device when an IP packet is smaller than the minimum size required by Ethernet. The frame is transmitted with extra bytes that are discarded here. This is one reason why the length of the IP packet is stored in the header; IP allows the link layer to pad packets.

At this point, the complete IP header is available, the logical size and the physical size of the packet are the same, and the checksum indicates that the header arrived undamaged.

To Forward or Not To Forward?

The next section of ipintr, shown in Figure 8.13, calls ip_dooptions (Chapter 9) to process IP options and then determines whether or not the packet has reached its final destination. If it hasn't reached its final destination, Net/3 may attempt to forward the packet (if the system is configured as a router). If it has reached its final destination, it is passed to the appropriate transport-level protocol.

```
                                                                  ─── ip_input.c
178     /*
179      * Process options and, if not destined for us,
180      * ship it on.  ip_dooptions returns 1 when an
181      * error was detected (causing an icmp message
182      * to be sent and the original packet to be freed).
183      */
184     ip_nhops = 0;                   /* for source routed packets */
185     if (hlen > sizeof(struct ip) && ip_dooptions(m))
186                 goto next;

187     /*
188      * Check our list of addresses, to see if the packet is for us.
189      */
190     for (ia = in_ifaddr; ia; ia = ia->ia_next) {
191 #define satosin(sa) ((struct sockaddr_in *)(sa))

192         if (IA_SIN(ia)->sin_addr.s_addr == ip->ip_dst.s_addr)
193             goto ours;

194         /* Only examine broadcast addresses for the receiving interface */
195         if (ia->ia_ifp == m->m_pkthdr.rcvif &&
196             (ia->ia_ifp->if_flags & IFF_BROADCAST)) {
197             u_long  t;

198             if (satosin(&ia->ia_broadaddr)->sin_addr.s_addr ==
199                 ip->ip_dst.s_addr)
200                 goto ours;
201             if (ip->ip_dst.s_addr == ia->ia_netbroadcast.s_addr)
202                 goto ours;
203             /*
204              * Look for all-0's host part (old broadcast addr),
205              * either for subnet or net.
206              */
207             t = ntohl(ip->ip_dst.s_addr);
208             if (t == ia->ia_subnet)
209                 goto ours;
210             if (t == ia->ia_net)
211                 goto ours;
212         }
213     }

                /* multicast code (Figure 12.39) */
```

```
258      if (ip->ip_dst.s_addr == (u_long) INADDR_BROADCAST)
259          goto ours;
260      if (ip->ip_dst.s_addr == INADDR_ANY)
261          goto ours;

262      /*
263       * Not for us; forward if possible and desirable.
264       */
265      if (ipforwarding == 0) {
266          ipstat.ips_cantforward++;
267          m_freem(m);
268      } else
269          ip_forward(m, 0);
270      goto next;

271  ours:
```
——— *ip_input.c*

Figure 8.13   `ipintr` continued.

Option processing

178–186   The source route from the previous packet is discarded by clearing `ip_nhops` (Section 9.6). If the packet header is larger than a default header, it must include options that are processed by `ip_dooptions`. If `ip_dooptions` returns 0, `ipintr` should continue processing the packet; otherwise `ip_dooptions` has completed processing of the packet by forwarding or discarding it, and `ipintr` can process the next packet on the input queue. We postpone further discussion of option processing until Chapter 9.

After option processing, `ipintr` decides whether the packet has reached its final destination by comparing `ip_dst` in the IP header with the IP addresses configured for all the local interfaces. `ipintr` must consider several broadcast addresses, one or more unicast addresses, and any multicast addresses that are associated with the interface.

Final destination?

187–261   `ipintr` starts by traversing `in_ifaddr` (Figure 6.5), the list of configured Internet addresses, to see if there is a match with the destination address of the packet. A series of comparisons are made for each `in_ifaddr` structure found in the list. There are four general cases to consider:

- an exact match with one of the interface addresses (first row of Figure 8.14),

- a match with the one of the broadcast addresses associated with the *receiving* interface (middle four rows of Figure 8.14),

- a match with one of the multicast groups associated with the *receiving* interface (Figure 12.39), or

- a match with one of the two limited broadcast addresses (last row of Figure 8.14).

Figure 8.14 illustrates the addresses that would be tested for a packet arriving on the Ethernet interface of the host `sun` in our sample network, excluding multicast addresses, which we discuss in Chapter 12.

Variable	Ethernet	SLIP	Loopback	Lines (Figure 8.13)
`ia_addr`	140.252.13.33	140.252.1.29	127.0.0.1	192–193
`ia_broadaddr`	140.252.13.63			198–200
`ia_netbroadcast`	140.252.255.255			201–202
`ia_subnet`	140.252.13.32			207–209
`ia_net`	140.252.0.0			210–211
`INADDR_BROADCAST`		255.255.255.255		258–259
`INADDR_ANY`		0.0.0.0		260–261

Figure 8.14 Comparisons to determine whether or not a packet has reached its final destination.

The tests with `ia_subnet`, `ia_net`, and `INADDR_ANY` are not required as they represent obsolete broadcast addresses used by 4.2BSD. Unfortunately, many TCP/IP implementations have been derived from 4.2BSD, so it may be important to recognize these old broadcast addresses on some networks.

Forwarding

262–271   If `ip_dst` does not match any of the addresses, the packet has not reached its final destination. If `ipforwarding` is not set, the packet is discarded. Otherwise, `ip_forward` attempts to route the packet toward its final destination.

> A host may discard packets that arrive on an interface other than the one specified by the destination address of the packet. In this case, Net/3 would not search the entire `in_ifaddr` list; only addresses assigned to the receiving interface would be considered. RFC 1122 calls this a *strong end system* model.

> For a multihomed host, it is uncommon for a packet to arrive at an interface that does not correspond to the packet's destination address, unless specific host routes have been configured. The host routes force neighboring routers to consider the multihomed host as the next-hop router for the packets. The *weak end system* model requires that the host accept these packets. An implementor is free to choose either model. Net/3 implements the weak end system model.

Reassembly and Demultiplexing

Finally, we look at the last section of `ipintr` (Figure 8.15) where reassembly and demultiplexing occur. We have omitted the reassembly code and postpone its discussion until Chapter 10. The omitted code sets the pointer `ip` to null if it could not reassemble a complete datagram. Otherwise, `ip` points to a complete datagram that has reached its final destination.

─── *ip_input.c*

```
                        /* reassembly (Figure 10.11) */

325     /*
326      * If control reaches here, ip points to a complete datagram.
327      * Otherwise, the reassembly code jumps back to next (Figure 8.11)
328      * Switch out to protocol's input routine.
329      */
330     ipstat.ips_delivered++;
331     (*inetsw[ip_protox[ip->ip_p]].pr_input) (m, hlen);
332     goto next;
```
─── *ip_input.c*

Figure 8.15 `ipintr` continued.

Transport demultiplexing

325–332   The protocol specified in the datagram (`ip_p`) is mapped with the `ip_protox` array (Figure 7.22) to an index into the `inetsw` array. `ipintr` calls the `pr_input` function from the selected `protosw` structure to process the transport message contained within the datagram. When `pr_input` returns, `ipintr` proceeds with the next packet on `ipintrq`.

It is important to notice that transport-level processing for each packet occurs within the processing loop of `ipintr`. There is no queueing of incoming packets between IP and the transport protocols, unlike the queueing in SVR4 streams implementations of TCP/IP.

8.5 Forwarding: `ip_forward` Function

A packet arriving at a system other than its final destination needs to be forwarded. `ipintr` calls the function `ip_forward`, which implements the forwarding algorithm, only when `ipforwarding` is nonzero (Section 6.1) or when the packet includes a source route (Section 9.6). When the packet includes a source route, `ip_dooptions` calls `ip_forward` with the second argument, `srcrt`, set to 1.

`ip_forward` interfaces with the routing tables through a `route` structure shown in Figure 8.16

─── *route.h*

```
46 struct route {
47     struct rtentry *ro_rt;      /* pointer to struct with information */
48     struct sockaddr ro_dst;     /* destination of this route */
49 };
```
─── *route.h*

Figure 8.16 `route` structure.

46–49   There are only two members in a `route` structure: `ro_rt`, a pointer to an `rtentry` structure; and `ro_dst`, a `sockaddr` structure, which specifies the destination associated with the route entry pointed to by `ro_rt`. The destination is the key used to find route information in the kernel's routing tables. Chapter 18 has a detailed description of the `rtentry` structure and the routing tables.

We show `ip_forward` in two parts. The first part makes sure the system is permitted to forward the packet, updates the IP header, and selects a route for the packet. The second part handles ICMP redirect messages and passes the packet to `ip_output` for transmission.

Is packet eligible for forwarding?

867–871   The first argument to `ip_forward` is a pointer to an mbuf chain containing the packet to be forwarded. If the second argument, `srcrt`, is nonzero, the packet is being forwarded because of a source route option (Section 9.6).

879–884   The `if` statement identifies and discards the following packets:

- link-level broadcasts

  Any network interface driver that supports broadcasts must set the `M_BCAST` flag for a packet received as a broadcast. `ether_input` (Figure 4.13) sets `M_BCAST` if the packet was addressed to the Ethernet broadcast address. Link-level broadcast packets are never forwarded.

  > Packets addressed to a unicast IP address but sent as a link-level broadcast are prohibited by RFC 1122 and are discarded here.

- loopback packets

  `in_canforward` returns 0 for packets addressed to the loopback network. These packets may have been passed to `ip_forward` by `ipintr` because the loopback interface was not configured correctly.

- network 0 and class E addresses

  `in_canforward` returns 0 for these packets. These destination addresses are invalid and packets addressed to them should not be circulating in the network since no host will accept them.

- class D addresses

  Packets addressed to a class D address should be processed by the multicast forwarding function, `ip_mforward`, not by `ip_forward`. `in_canforward` rejects class D (multicast) addresses.

RFC 791 specifies that every system that processes a packet must decrement the time-to-live (TTL) field by at least 1 even though TTL is measured in seconds. Because of this requirement, TTL is usually considered a bound on the number of hops an IP packet may traverse before being discarded. Technically, a router that held a packet for more than 1 second could decrement `ip_ttl` by more than 1.

```
                                                                      ip_input.c
867  void
868  ip_forward(m, srcrt)
869  struct mbuf *m;
870  int      srcrt;
871  {
872       struct ip *ip = mtod(m, struct ip *);
873       struct sockaddr_in *sin;
874       struct rtentry *rt;
875       int      error, type = 0, code;
876       struct mbuf *mcopy;
877       n_long  dest;
878       struct ifnet *destifp;
879       dest = 0;
880       if (m->m_flags & M_BCAST || in_canforward(ip->ip_dst) == 0) {
881            ipstat.ips_cantforward++;
882            m_freem(m);
883            return;
884       }
885       HTONS(ip->ip_id);
886       if (ip->ip_ttl <= IPTTLDEC) {
887            icmp_error(m, ICMP_TIMXCEED, ICMP_TIMXCEED_INTRANS, dest, 0);
888            return;
889       }
890       ip->ip_ttl -= IPTTLDEC;
891       sin = (struct sockaddr_in *) &ipforward_rt.ro_dst;
892       if ((rt = ipforward_rt.ro_rt) == 0 ||
893            ip->ip_dst.s_addr != sin->sin_addr.s_addr) {
894            if (ipforward_rt.ro_rt) {
895                 RTFREE(ipforward_rt.ro_rt);
896                 ipforward_rt.ro_rt = 0;
897            }
898            sin->sin_family = AF_INET;
899            sin->sin_len = sizeof(*sin);
900            sin->sin_addr = ip->ip_dst;
901            rtalloc(&ipforward_rt);
902            if (ipforward_rt.ro_rt == 0) {
903                 icmp_error(m, ICMP_UNREACH, ICMP_UNREACH_HOST, dest, 0);
904                 return;
905            }
906            rt = ipforward_rt.ro_rt;
907       }
908       /*
909        * Save at most 64 bytes of the packet in case
910        * we need to generate an ICMP message to the src.
911        */
912       mcopy = m_copy(m, 0, imin((int) ip->ip_len, 64));
913       ip_ifmatrix[rt->rt_ifp->if_index +
914                 if_index * m->m_pkthdr.rcvif->if_index]++;
                                                                      ip_input.c
```

Figure 8.17   ip_forward function: route selection.

The question arises: How long is the longest path in the Internet? This metric is called the *diameter* of a network. There is no way to discover the diameter other than through empirical methods. A 37-hop path was posted in [Olivier 1994].

Decrement TTL

885–890   The packet identifier is converted back to network byte order since it isn't needed for forwarding and it should be in the correct order if `ip_forward` sends an ICMP error message, which includes the invalid IP header.

> Net/3 neglects to convert `ip_len`, which `ipintr` converted to host byte order. The authors noted that on big endian machines this does not cause a problem since the bytes are never swapped. On little endian machines, such as a 386, this bug allows the byte-swapped value to be returned in the IP header within the ICMP error. This bug was observed in ICMP packets returned from SVR4 (probably Net/1 code) running on a 386 and from AIX 3.2 (4.3BSD Reno code).

If `ip_ttl` has reached 1 (IPTTLDEC), an ICMP time exceeded message is returned to the sender and the packet is discarded. Otherwise, `ip_forward` decrements `ip_ttl` by IPTTLDEC.

A system should never receive an IP datagram with a TTL of 0, but Net/3 generates the correct ICMP error if this happens since `ip_ttl` is examined after the packet is considered for local delivery and before it is forwarded.

Locate next hop

891–907   The IP forwarding algorithm caches the most recent route, in the global `route` structure `ipforward_rt`, and applies it to the current packet if possible. Research has shown that consecutive packets tend to have the same destination address ([Jain and Routhier 1986] and [Mogul 1991]), so this *one-behind* cache minimizes the number of routing lookups. If the cache (`ipforward_rt`) is empty or the current packet is to a different destination than the route entry in `ipforward_rt`, the previous route is discarded, `ro_dst` is initialized to the new destination, and `rtalloc` finds a route to the current packet's destination. If no route can be found for the destination, an ICMP host unreachable error is returned and the packed discarded.

908–914   Since `ip_output` discards the packet when an error occurs, `m_copy` makes a copy of the first 64 bytes in case `ip_forward` sends an ICMP error message. `ip_forward` does not abort if the call to `m_copy` fails. In this case, the error message is not sent. `ip_ifmatrix` records the number of packets routed between interfaces. The counter with the indexes of the receiving and sending interfaces is incremented.

Redirect Messages

A first-hop router returns an ICMP redirect message to the source host when the host incorrectly selects the router as the packet's first-hop destination. The IP networking model assumes that hosts are relatively ignorant of the overall internet topology and assigns the responsibility of maintaining correct routing tables to routers. A redirect message from a router informs a host that it has selected an incorrect route for a packet. We use Figure 8.18 to illustrate redirect messages.

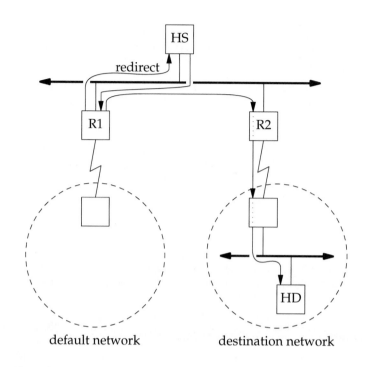

Figure 8.18   Router R1 is redirecting host HS to use router R2 to reach HD.

Generally, an administrator configures a host to send packets for remote networks to a default router. In Figure 8.18, host HS has R1 configured as its default router. When it first attempts to send a packet to HD it sends the packet to R1, not knowing that R2 is the appropriate choice. R1 recognizes the mistake, forwards the packet to R2, and sends a redirect message back to HS. After receiving the redirect, HS updates its routing tables so that the next packet to HD is sent directly to R2.

RFC 1122 recommends that only routers send redirect messages and that hosts must update their routing tables when receiving ICMP redirect messages (Section 11.8). Since Net/3 calls `ip_forward` only when the system is configured as a router, Net/3 follows RFC 1122's recommendations.

In Figure 8.19, `ip_forward` determines whether or not it should send a redirect message.

Leaving on receiving interface?

915–929   The rules by which a router recognizes redirect situations are complicated. First, redirects are applicable only when a packet is received and resent on the same interface (`rt_ifp` and `rcvif`). Next, the selected route must not have been itself created or modified by an ICMP redirect message (`RTF_DYNAMIC | RTF_MODIFIED`), nor can the route be to the default destination (0.0.0.0). This ensures that the system does not propagate routing information for which it is not an authoritative source, and that it does not share its default route with other systems.

ip_input.c

```
915     /*
916      * If forwarding packet is using same interface that it came in on,
917      * perhaps should send a redirect to sender to shortcut a hop.
918      * Only send redirect if source is sending directly to us,
919      * and if packet was not source routed (or has any options).
920      * Also, don't send redirect if forwarding using a default route
921      * or a route modified by a redirect.
922      */
923 #define satosin(sa) ((struct sockaddr_in *)(sa))
924     if (rt->rt_ifp == m->m_pkthdr.rcvif &&
925         (rt->rt_flags & (RTF_DYNAMIC | RTF_MODIFIED)) == 0 &&
926         satosin(rt_key(rt))->sin_addr.s_addr != 0 &&
927         ipsendredirects && !srcrt) {
928 #define RTA(rt) ((struct in_ifaddr *)(rt->rt_ifa))
929         u_long  src = ntohl(ip->ip_src.s_addr);

930         if (RTA(rt) &&
931             (src & RTA(rt)->ia_subnetmask) == RTA(rt)->ia_subnet) {
932             if (rt->rt_flags & RTF_GATEWAY)
933                 dest = satosin(rt->rt_gateway)->sin_addr.s_addr;
934             else
935                 dest = ip->ip_dst.s_addr;
936             /* Router requirements says to only send host redirects */
937             type = ICMP_REDIRECT;
938             code = ICMP_REDIRECT_HOST;
939         }
940     }
```

ip_input.c

Figure 8.19   `ip_forward` continued.

Generally, routing protocols use the special destination 0.0.0.0 to locate a default route. When a specific route to a destination is not available, the route associated with destination 0.0.0.0 directs the packet toward a default router.

Chapter 18 has more information about default routes.

The global integer `ipsendredirects` specifies whether the system has administrative authority to send redirects (Section 8.9). By default, `ipsendredirects` is 1. Redirects are suppressed when the system is source routing a packet as indicated by the `srcrt` argument passed to `ip_forward`, since presumably the source host wanted to override the decisions of the intermediate routers.

Send redirect?

930–931   This test determines if the packet originated on the local subnet. If the subnet mask bits of the source address and the outgoing interface's address are the same, the addresses are on the same IP network. If the source and the outgoing interface are on the same network, then this system should not have received the packet, since the source could have sent the packet directly to the correct first-hop router. The ICMP redirect message informs the host of the correct first-hop destination. If the packet originated on some other subnet, then the previous system was a router and this system does not send a redirect; the mistake will be corrected by a routing protocol.

In any case, routers are required to ignore redirect messages. Despite the requirement, Net/3 does not discard redirect messages when `ipforwarding` is set (i.e., when it is configured to be a router).

Select appropriate router

932–940   The ICMP redirect message contains the address of the correct next system, which is a router's address if the destination host is not on the directly connected network or the host address if the destination host is on the directly connected network.

RFC 792 describes four types of redirect messages: (1) network, (2) host, (3) TOS and network, and (4) TOS and host. RFC 1009 recommends against sending network redirects at any time because of the impossibility of guaranteeing that the host receiving the redirect can determine the appropriate subnet mask for the destination network. RFC 1122 recommends that hosts treat network redirects as host redirects to avoid this ambiguity. Net/3 sends only host redirects and ignores any TOS considerations. In Figure 8.20, `ipintr` passes the packet and any ICMP messages to the link layer.

> The redirect messages were standardized before subnetting. In a nonsubnetted internet, network redirects are useful but in a subnetted internet they are ambiguous since they do not include a subnet mask.

Forward packet

941–954   At this point, `ip_forward` has a route for the packet and has determined if an ICMP redirect is warranted. `ip_output` sends the packet to the next hop as specified in the route `ipforward_rt`. The `IP_ALLOWBROADCAST` flag allows the packet being forwarded to be a directed broadcast to a local network. If `ip_output` succeeds and no redirect message needs to be sent, the copy of the first 64 bytes of the packet is discarded and `ip_forward` returns.

Send ICMP error?

955–983   `ip_forward` may need to send an ICMP message because `ip_output` failed or a redirect is pending. If there is no copy of the original packet (there might have been a buffer shortage at the time the copy was attempted), the message can't be sent and `ip_forward` returns. If a redirect is pending, `type` and `code` have been previously set, but if `ip_output` failed, the `switch` statement sets up the new ICMP type and code values based on the return value from `ip_output`. `icmp_error` sends the message. The ICMP message from a failed `ip_output` overrides any pending redirect message.

It is important to recognize the significance of the `switch` statement that handles errors from `ip_output`. It translates local system errors into the appropriate ICMP error message, which is returned to the packet's source. Figure 8.21 summarizes the errors. Chapter 11 describes the ICMP messages in more detail.

> Net/3 always generates the ICMP source quench when `ip_output` returns ENOBUFS. The Router Requirements RFC [Almquist and Kastenholz 1994] deprecate the source quench and state that a router should not generate them.

ip_input.c

```
941         error = ip_output(m, (struct mbuf *) 0, &ipforward_rt,
942                         IP_FORWARDING | IP_ALLOWBROADCAST, 0);
943         if (error)
944             ipstat.ips_cantforward++;
945         else {
946             ipstat.ips_forward++;
947             if (type)
948                 ipstat.ips_redirectsent++;
949             else {
950                 if (mcopy)
951                     m_freem(mcopy);
952                 return;
953             }
954         }
955         if (mcopy == NULL)
956             return;
957         destifp = NULL;

958         switch (error) {

959         case 0:                         /* forwarded, but need redirect */
960             /* type, code set above */
961             break;

962         case ENETUNREACH:               /* shouldn't happen, checked above */
963         case EHOSTUNREACH:
964         case ENETDOWN:
965         case EHOSTDOWN:
966         default:
967             type = ICMP_UNREACH;
968             code = ICMP_UNREACH_HOST;
969             break;

970         case EMSGSIZE:
971             type = ICMP_UNREACH;
972             code = ICMP_UNREACH_NEEDFRAG;
973             if (ipforward_rt.ro_rt)
974                 destifp = ipforward_rt.ro_rt->rt_ifp;
975             ipstat.ips_cantfrag++;
976             break;

977         case ENOBUFS:
978             type = ICMP_SOURCEQUENCH;
979             code = 0;
980             break;
981         }
982         icmp_error(mcopy, type, code, dest, destifp);
983 }
```

ip_input.c

Figure 8.20 `ip_forward` continued.

Error code from ip_output	ICMP message generated	Description
EMSGSIZE	ICMP_UNREACH_NEEDFRAG	The outgoing packet was too large for the selected interface and fragmentation was prohibited (Chapter 10).
ENOBUFS	ICMP_SOURCEQUENCH	The interface queue is full or the kernel is running short of free memory. This message is an indication to the source host to lower the data rate.
EHOSTUNREACH ENETDOWN EHOSTDOWN default	ICMP_UNREACH_HOST	A route to the host could not be found. The outgoing interface specified by the route is not operating. The interface could not send the packet to the selected host. Any unrecognized error is reported as an ICMP_UNREACH_HOST error.

Figure 8.21   Errors from ip_output.

8.6   Output Processing: `ip_output` Function

The IP output code receives packets from two sources: `ip_forward` and the transport protocols (Figure 8.1). It would seem reasonable to expect IP output operations to be accessed by `inetsw[0].pr_output`, but this is not the case. The standard Internet transport protocols (ICMP, IGMP, UDP, and TCP) call `ip_output` directly instead of going through the `inetsw` table. For the standard Internet transport protocols, the generality of the `protosw` structure is not necessary, since the calling functions are not accessing IP in a protocol-independent context. In Chapter 20 we'll see that the protocol-independent routing sockets call `pr_output` to access IP.

We describe `ip_output` in three sections:

- header initialization,
- route selection, and
- source address selection and fragmentation.

Header Initialization

The first section of `ip_output`, shown in Figure 8.22, merges options into the outgoing packet and completes the IP header for packets that are passed from the transport protocols (not those from `ip_forward`).

44–59   The arguments to `ip_output` are: m0, the packet to send; opt, the IP options to include; ro, a cached route to the destination; flags, described in Figure 8.23; and imo, a pointer to multicast options described in Chapter 12.

IP_FORWARDING is set by `ip_forward` and `ip_mforward` (multicast packet forwarding) and prevents `ip_output` from resetting any of the IP header fields.

ip_output.c

```
44 int
45 ip_output(m0, opt, ro, flags, imo)
46 struct mbuf *m0;
47 struct mbuf *opt;
48 struct route *ro;
49 int      flags;
50 struct ip_moptions *imo;
51 {
52     struct ip *ip, *mhip;
53     struct ifnet *ifp;
54     struct mbuf *m = m0;
55     int      hlen = sizeof(struct ip);
56     int      len, off, error = 0;
57     struct route iproute;
58     struct sockaddr_in *dst;
59     struct in_ifaddr *ia;

60     if (opt) {
61         m = ip_insertoptions(m, opt, &len);
62         hlen = len;
63     }
64     ip = mtod(m, struct ip *);
65     /*
66      * Fill in IP header.
67      */
68     if ((flags & (IP_FORWARDING | IP_RAWOUTPUT)) == 0) {
69         ip->ip_v = IPVERSION;
70         ip->ip_off &= IP_DF;
71         ip->ip_id = htons(ip_id++);
72         ip->ip_hl = hlen >> 2;
73         ipstat.ips_localout++;
74     } else {
75         hlen = ip->ip_hl << 2;
76     }
```

ip_output.c

Figure 8.22 ip_output function.

Flag	Description
IP_FORWARDING	This is a forwarded packet.
IP_ROUTETOIF	Ignore routing tables and route directly to interface.
IP_ALLOWBROADCAST	Allow broadcast packets to be sent.
IP_RAWOUTPUT	Packet contains a preconstructed IP header.

Figure 8.23 ip_output: flags values.

The MSG_DONTROUTE flag to send, sendto, and sendmsg enables IP_ROUTETOIF for a single write (Section 16.4) while the SO_DONTROUTE socket option enables IP_ROUTETOIF for *all* writes on a particular socket (Section 8.8). The flag is passed by each of the transport protocols to ip_output.

The IP_ALLOWBROADCAST flag can be set by the SO_BROADCAST socket option (Section 8.8) but is passed only by UDP. The raw IP protocol sets IP_ALLOWBROADCAST by default. TCP does not support broadcasts, so IP_ALLOWBROADCAST is not passed by TCP to ip_output. There is no per-request flag for broadcasting.

Construct IP header

60–73   If the caller provides any IP options they are merged with the packet by ip_insertoptions (Section 9.8), which returns the new header length.

We'll see in Section 8.8 that a process can set the IP_OPTIONS socket option to specify the IP options for a socket. The transport layer for the socket (TCP or UDP) always passes these options to ip_output.

The IP header of a forwarded packet (IP_FORWARDING) or a packet with a preconstructed header (IP_RAWOUTPUT) should not be modified by ip_output. Any other packet (e.g., a UDP or TCP packet that originates at this host) needs to have several IP header fields initialized. ip_output sets ip_v to 4 (IPVERSION), clears ip_off except for the DF bit, which is left as provided by the caller (Chapter 10), and assigns a unique identifier to ip->ip_id from the global integer ip_id, which is immediately incremented. Remember that ip_id was seeded from the system clock during protocol initialization (Section 7.8). ip_hl is set to the header length measured in 32-bit words.

Most of the remaining fields in the IP header—length, offset, TTL, protocol, TOS, and the destination address—have already been initialized by the transport protocol. The source address may not be set, in which case it is selected after a route to the destination has been located (Figure 8.25).

Packet already includes header

74–76   For a forwarded packet (or a raw IP packet with a header), the header length (in bytes) is saved in hlen for use by the fragmentation algorithm.

Route Selection

After completing the IP header, the next task for ip_output is to locate a route to the destination. This is shown in Figure 8.24.

── *ip_output.c*
```
77      /*
78       * Route packet.
79       */
80      if (ro == 0) {
81          ro = &iproute;
82          bzero((caddr_t) ro, sizeof(*ro));
83      }
84      dst = (struct sockaddr_in *) &ro->ro_dst;
85      /*
86       * If there is a cached route,
87       * check that it is to the same destination
88       * and is still up.  If not, free it and try again.
89       */
```

```
 90     if (ro->ro_rt && ((ro->ro_rt->rt_flags & RTF_UP) == 0 ||
 91                    dst->sin_addr.s_addr != ip->ip_dst.s_addr)) {
 92         RTFREE(ro->ro_rt);
 93         ro->ro_rt = (struct rtentry *) 0;
 94     }
 95     if (ro->ro_rt == 0) {
 96         dst->sin_family = AF_INET;
 97         dst->sin_len = sizeof(*dst);
 98         dst->sin_addr = ip->ip_dst;
 99     }
100     /*
101      * If routing to interface only,
102      * short circuit routing lookup.
103      */
104 #define ifatoia(ifa)    ((struct in_ifaddr *)(ifa))
105 #define sintosa(sin)    ((struct sockaddr *)(sin))
106     if (flags & IP_ROUTETOIF) {
107         if ((ia = ifatoia(ifa_ifwithdstaddr(sintosa(dst)))) == 0 &&
108             (ia = ifatoia(ifa_ifwithnet(sintosa(dst)))) == 0) {
109             ipstat.ips_noroute++;
110             error = ENETUNREACH;
111             goto bad;
112         }
113         ifp = ia->ia_ifp;
114         ip->ip_ttl = 1;
115     } else {
116         if (ro->ro_rt == 0)
117             rtalloc(ro);
118         if (ro->ro_rt == 0) {
119             ipstat.ips_noroute++;
120             error = EHOSTUNREACH;
121             goto bad;
122         }
123         ia = ifatoia(ro->ro_rt->rt_ifa);
124         ifp = ro->ro_rt->rt_ifp;
125         ro->ro_rt->rt_use++;
126         if (ro->ro_rt->rt_flags & RTF_GATEWAY)
127             dst = (struct sockaddr_in *) ro->ro_rt->rt_gateway;
128     }
```

```
                    /* multicast destination (Figure 12.40) */
```

―― *ip_output.c*

Figure 8.24 `ip_output` continued.

Verify cached route

77–99   A cached route may be provided to `ip_output` as the `ro` argument. In Chapter 24 we'll see that UDP and TCP maintain a route cache associated with each socket. If a route has not been provided, `ip_output` sets `ro` to point to the temporary `route` structure `iproute`.

If the cached destination is not to the current packet's destination, the route is discarded and the new destination address placed in dst.

Bypass routing

100–114   A caller can prevent packet routing by setting the IP_ROUTETOIF flag (Section 8.8). If this flag is set, ip_output must locate an interface directly connected to the destination network specified in the packet. ifa_ifwithdstaddr searches point-to-point interfaces, while in_ifwithnet searches all the others. If neither function finds an interface connected to the destination network, ENETUNREACH is returned; otherwise, ifp points to the selected interface.

> This option allows routing protocols to bypass the local routing tables and force the packets to exit the system by a particular interface. In this way, routing information can be exchanged with other routers even when the local routing tables are incorrect.

Locate route

115–122   If the packet is being routed (IP_ROUTETOIF is off) and there is no cached route, rtalloc locates a route to the address specified by dst. ip_output returns EHOSTUNREACH if rtalloc fails to find a route. If ip_forward called ip_output, EHOSTUNREACH is converted to an ICMP error. If a transport protocol called ip_output, the error is passed back to the process (Figure 8.21).

123–128   ia is set to point to an address (the ifaddr structure) of the selected interface and ifp points to the interface's ifnet structure. If the next hop is not the packet's final destination, dst is changed to point to the next-hop router instead of the packet's final destination. The destination address within the IP header remains unchanged, but the interface layer must deliver the packet to dst, the next-hop router.

Source Address Selection and Fragmentation

The final section of ip_output, shown in Figure 8.25, ensures that the IP header has a valid source address and then passes the packet to the interface associated with the route. If the packet is larger than the interface's MTU, it must be fragmented and transmitted in pieces. As we did with the reassembly code, we omit the fragmentation code here and postpone discussion of it until Chapter 10.

—— ip_output.c

```
212     /*
213      * If source address not specified yet, use address
214      * of outgoing interface.
215      */
216     if (ip->ip_src.s_addr == INADDR_ANY)
217         ip->ip_src = IA_SIN(ia)->sin_addr;
218     /*
219      * Look for broadcast address and
220      * verify user is allowed to send
221      * such a packet.
222      */
```

```
223     if (in_broadcast(dst->sin_addr, ifp)) {
224         if ((ifp->if_flags & IFF_BROADCAST) == 0) {        /* interface check */
225             error = EADDRNOTAVAIL;
226             goto bad;
227         }
228         if ((flags & IP_ALLOWBROADCAST) == 0) {        /* application check */
229             error = EACCES;
230             goto bad;
231         }
232         /* don't allow broadcast messages to be fragmented */
233         if ((u_short) ip->ip_len > ifp->if_mtu) {
234             error = EMSGSIZE;
235             goto bad;
236         }
237         m->m_flags |= M_BCAST;
238     } else
239         m->m_flags &= ~M_BCAST;

240 sendit:
241     /*
242      * If small enough for interface, can just send directly.
243      */
244     if ((u_short) ip->ip_len <= ifp->if_mtu) {
245         ip->ip_len = htons((u_short) ip->ip_len);
246         ip->ip_off = htons((u_short) ip->ip_off);
247         ip->ip_sum = 0;
248         ip->ip_sum = in_cksum(m, hlen);
249         error = (*ifp->if_output) (ifp, m,
250                                 (struct sockaddr *) dst, ro->ro_rt);
251         goto done;
252     }

                        /* fragmentation (Section 10.3) */

339 done:
340     if (ro == &iproute && (flags & IP_ROUTETOIF) == 0 && ro->ro_rt)
341         RTFREE(ro->ro_rt);
342     return (error);
343 bad:
344     m_freem(m0);
345     goto done;
346 }
```
                                                                    —— *ip_output.c*

Figure 8.25 ip_output continued.

Select source address

212–239   If ip_src has not been specified, then ip_output selects ia, the IP address of the outgoing interface, as the source address. This couldn't be done earlier when the other IP header fields were filled in because a route hadn't been selected yet. Forwarded packets always have a source address, but packets that originate at the local host may not if the sending process has not explicitly selected one.

If the destination IP address is a broadcast address, the interface must support broadcasting (IFF_BROADCAST, Figure 3.7), the caller must explicitly enable broadcasting (IP_ALLOWBROADCAST, Figure 8.23), and the packet must be small enough to be sent without fragmentation.

> This last test is a policy decision. Nothing in the IP protocol specification explicitly prohibits the fragmentation of broadcast packets. By requiring the packet to fit within the MTU of the interface, however, there is an increased chance that the broadcast packet will be received at every interface, because there is a better chance of receiving one undamaged packet than of receiving two or more undamaged packets.

If any of these conditions are not met, the packet is dropped and EADDRNOTAVAIL, EACCES, or EMSGSIZE is returned to the caller. Otherwise, M_BCAST is set on the outgoing packet, which tells the interface output function to send the packet as a link-level broadcast. In Section 21.10 we'll see that arpresolve translates the IP broadcast address to the Ethernet broadcast address.

If the destination address is not a broadcast address, ip_output clears M_BCAST.

> If M_BCAST were not cleared, the reply to a request packet that arrived as a broadcast might be accidentally returned as a broadcast. We'll see in Chapter 11 that ICMP replies are constructed within the request packet in this way as are TCP RST packets (Section 26.9).

Send packet

240–252   If the packet is small enough for the selected interface, ip_len and ip_off are converted to network byte order, the IP checksum is computed with in_cksum (Section 8.7), and the packet is passed to the if_output function of the selected interface.

Fragment packet

253–338   Larger packets must be fragmented before they can be sent. We have omitted that code here and describe it in Chapter 10 instead.

Cleanup

339–346   A reference count is maintained for the route entries. Recall that ip_output may use a temporary route structure (iproute) if the argument ro is null. If necessary, RTFREE releases the route entry within iproute and decrements the reference count. The code at bad discards the current packet before returning.

> Reference counting is a memory management technique. The programmer must count the number of external references to a data structure; when the count returns to 0, the memory can be safely returned to the free pool. Reference counting requires some discipline by the programmer, who must explicitly increase and decrease the reference count when appropriate.

8.7   Internet Checksum: in_cksum Function

Two operations dominate the time required to process packets: copying the data and computing checksums ([Kay and Pasquale 1993]). The flexible nature of the mbuf data structure is the primary method of reducing copy operations in Net/3. Efficient computing of checksums is harder since it is very hardware dependent. Net/3 contains several implementations of in_cksum.

Version	Source file
portable C	`sys/netinet/in_cksum.c`
SPARC	`net3/sparc/sparc/in_cksum.c`
68k	`net3/luna68k/luna68k/in_cksum.c`
VAX	`sys/vax/vax/in_cksum.c`
Tahoe	`sys/tahoe/tahoe/in_cksum.c`
HP 3000	`sys/hp300/hp300/in_cksum.c`
Intel 80386	`sys/i386/i386/in_cksum.c`

Figure 8.26 `in_cksum` versions in Net/3.

Even the portable C implementation has been optimized considerably. RFC 1071 [Braden, Borman, and Partridge 1988] and RFC 1141 [Mallory and Kullberg 1990] discuss the design and implementation of the Internet checksum function. RFC 1141 has been updated by RFC 1624 [Rijsinghani 1994]. From RFC 1071:

1. Adjacent bytes to be checksummed are paired to form 16-bit integers, and the one's complement sum of these 16-bit integers is formed.

2. To generate a checksum, the checksum field itself is cleared, the 16-bit one's complement sum is computed over the bytes concerned, and the one's complement of this sum is placed in the checksum field.

3. To verify a checksum, the one's complement sum is computed over the same set of bytes, including the checksum field. If the result is all 1 bits (–0 in one's complement arithmetic, as explained below), the check succeeds.

Briefly, when addition is performed on integers in one's complement representation, the result is obtained by summing the two integers and adding any carry bit to the result to obtain the final sum. In one's complement arithmetic the negative of a number is formed by complementing each bit. There are two representations of 0 in one's complement arithmetic: all 0 bits, and all 1 bits. A more detailed discussion of one's complement representations and arithmetic can be found in [Mano 1993].

The checksum algorithm computes the value to place in the checksum field of the IP header before sending the packet. To compute this value, the checksum field in the header is set to 0 and the one's complement sum on the entire header (including options) is computed. The header is processed as an array of 16-bit integers. Let's call the result of this computation a. Since the checksum field is explicitly set to 0, a is also the sum of all the IP header fields except the checksum. The one's complement of a, denoted $-a$, is placed in the checksum field and the packet is sent.

If no bits are altered in transit, the computed checksum at the destination should be the complement of $(a + -a)$. The sum $(a + -a)$ in one's complement arithmetic is –0 (all 1 bits) and its complement is 0 (all 0 bits). So the computed checksum of an undamaged packet at the destination should always be 0. This is what we saw in Figure 8.12. The following C code (which is not part of Net/3) is a naive implementation of this algorithm:

```
 1 unsigned short
 2 cksum(struct ip *ip, int len)
 3 {
 4     long    sum = 0;              /* assume 32 bit long, 16 bit short */

 5     while (len > 1) {
 6         sum += *((unsigned short *) ip)++;
 7         if (sum & 0x80000000)    /* if high-order bit set, fold */
 8             sum = (sum & 0xFFFF) + (sum >> 16);
 9         len -= 2;
10     }

11     if (len)                     /* take care of left over byte */
12         sum += (unsigned short) *(unsigned char *) ip;

13     while (sum >> 16)
14         sum = (sum & 0xFFFF) + (sum >> 16);

15     return ~sum;
16 }
```

Figure 8.27   A naive implementation of the IP checksum calculation.

1–16   The only performance enhancement here is to accumulate the carry bits in the high-order 16 bits of sum. The accumulated carries are added to the low-order 16 bits when the loop terminates, until no more carries occur. RFC 1071 calls this *deferred carries*. This technique is useful on machines that don't have an add-with-carry instruction or when detecting a carry is expensive.

Now we show the portable C version from Net/3. It utilizes the deferred carry technique and works with packets stored in an mbuf chain.

42–140   Our naive checksum implementation assumed that all the bytes to be checksummed were in a contiguous buffer instead of in mbuf chains. This version of the checksum calculation handles the mbufs correctly using the same underlying algorithm: 16-bit words are summed in a 32-bit integer with the carries deferred. For mbufs with an odd number of bytes, the extra byte is saved and paired with the first byte of the next mbuf. Since unaligned access to 16-bit words is invalid or incurs a severe performance penalty on most architectures, a misaligned byte is saved and in_cksum continues adding with the next aligned word. in_cksum is careful to byte swap the sum when this occurs to ensure that even-numbered and odd-numbered data bytes are collected in separate sum bytes as required by the checksum algorithm.

Loop unrolling

93–115   The three while loops in the function add 16 words, 4 words, and 1 word to the sum during each iteration. The unrolled loops reduce the loop overhead and can be considerably faster than a straightforward loop on some architectures. The price is increased code size and complexity.

```
                                                                    ———————————— in_cksum.c
42 #define ADDCARRY(x)   (x > 65535 ? x -= 65535 : x)
43 #define REDUCE {l_util.l = sum; sum = l_util.s[0] + l_util.s[1]; ADDCARRY(sum);}

44 int
45 in_cksum(m, len)
46 struct mbuf *m;
47 int     len;
48 {
49     u_short *w;
50     int     sum = 0;
51     int     mlen = 0;
52     int     byte_swapped = 0;

53     union {
54         char    c[2];
55         u_short s;
56     } s_util;
57     union {
58         u_short s[2];
59         long    l;
60     } l_util;

61     for (; m && len; m = m->m_next) {
62         if (m->m_len == 0)
63             continue;
64         w = mtod(m, u_short *);
65         if (mlen == -1) {
66             /*
67              * The first byte of this mbuf is the continuation of a
68              * word spanning between this mbuf and the last mbuf.
69              *
70              * s_util.c[0] is already saved when scanning previous mbuf.
71              */
72             s_util.c[1] = *(char *) w;
73             sum += s_util.s;
74             w = (u_short *) ((char *) w + 1);
75             mlen = m->m_len - 1;
76             len--;
77         } else
78             mlen = m->m_len;
79         if (len < mlen)
80             mlen = len;
81         len -= mlen;
82         /*
83          * Force to even boundary.
84          */
85         if ((1 & (int) w) && (mlen > 0)) {
86             REDUCE;
87             sum <<= 8;
88             s_util.c[0] = *(u_char *) w;
89             w = (u_short *) ((char *) w + 1);
90             mlen--;
91             byte_swapped = 1;
92         }
```

```
 93          /*
 94           * Unroll the loop to make overhead from
 95           * branches &c small.
 96           */
 97          while ((mlen -= 32) >= 0) {
 98              sum += w[0]; sum += w[1]; sum += w[2]; sum += w[3];
 99              sum += w[4]; sum += w[5]; sum += w[6]; sum += w[7];
100              sum += w[8]; sum += w[9]; sum += w[10]; sum += w[11];
101              sum += w[12]; sum += w[13]; sum += w[14]; sum += w[15];

102              w += 16;
103          }
104          mlen += 32;
105          while ((mlen -= 8) >= 0) {
106              sum += w[0]; sum += w[1]; sum += w[2]; sum += w[3];

107              w += 4;
108          }
109          mlen += 8;
110          if (mlen == 0 && byte_swapped == 0)
111              continue;
112          REDUCE;
113          while ((mlen -= 2) >= 0) {
114              sum += *w++;
115          }
116          if (byte_swapped) {
117              REDUCE;
118              sum <<= 8;
119              byte_swapped = 0;
120              if (mlen == -1) {
121                  s_util.c[1] = *(char *) w;
122                  sum += s_util.s;
123                  mlen = 0;
124              } else
125                  mlen = -1;
126          } else if (mlen == -1)
127              s_util.c[0] = *(char *) w;
128      }
129      if (len)
130          printf("cksum: out of data\n");
131      if (mlen == -1) {
132          /* The last mbuf has odd # of bytes. Follow the standard (the odd
133             byte may be shifted left by 8 bits or not as determined by
134             endian-ness of the machine) */
135          s_util.c[1] = 0;
136          sum += s_util.s;
137      }
138      REDUCE;
139      return (~sum & 0xffff);
140 }
```
                                                                                    in_cksum.c

Figure 8.28   An optimized portable C implementation of the IP checksum calculation.

More Optimizations

RFC 1071 mentions two optimizations that don't appear in Net/3: a combined copy-with-checksum operation and incremental checksum updates. Merging the copy and checksum operations is not as important for the IP header checksum as it is for the TCP and UDP checksums, which cover many more bytes. This merged operation is discussed in Section 23.12. [Partridge and Pink 1993] report that an inline version of the IP header checksum is faster than calling the more general in_cksum function and can be done in six to eight assembler instructions (for the standard 20-byte IP header).

The design of the checksum algorithm allows a packet to be changed and the checksum updated without reexamining all the bytes. RFC 1071 contains a brief discussion of this topic. RFCs 1141 and 1624 contain more detailed discussions. A typical use of this technique occurs during packet forwarding. In the common case, when a packet has no options, only the TTL field changes during forwarding. The checksum in this case can be recomputed by a single addition with an end-around carry.

In addition to being more efficient, an incremental checksum can help detect headers corrupted by buggy software. A corrupted header is detected by the next system if the checksum is computed incrementally, but if it is recomputed from scratch, the checksum incorporates the erroneous bytes and the corrupted header is not detected by the next system. The end-to-end checksum used by UDP or TCP detects the error at the final destination. We'll see in Chapters 23 and 25 that the UDP and TCP checksums incorporate several parts of the IP header.

For an example of the checksum function that utilizes hardware add-with-carry instructions to compute the checksum 32 bits at a time, see the VAX implementation of in_cksum in the file sys/vax/in_cksum.c.

8.8   setsockopt and getsockopt System Calls

Net/3 provides access to several networking features through the setsockopt and getsockopt system calls. These system calls support a generic interface used by a process to access features of a networking protocol that aren't supported by the standard system calls. The prototypes for these two calls are:

```
int setsockopt(int s, int level, int optname, const void *optval, int optlen);

int getsockopt(int s, int level, int optname, void *optval, int *optlen);
```

Most socket options affect only the socket on which they are issued. Compare this to sysctl parameters, which affect the entire system. The socket options associated with multicasting are a notable exception and are described in Chapter 12.

setsockopt and getsockopt set and get options at all levels of the communication stack. Net/3 processes options according to the protocol associated with s and the identifier specified by *level*. Figure 8.29 lists possible values for *level* within the protocols that we discuss.

We describe the implementation of the setsockopt and getsockopt system calls in Chapter 17, but we discuss the implementation of individual options within the

Domain	Protocol	*level*	Function	Reference
any	any	SOL_SOCKET	sosetopt and sogetopt	Figures 17.5 and 17.11
IP	UDP	IPPROTO_IP	ip_ctloutput	Figure 8.31
	TCP	IPPROTO_TCP IPPROTO_IP	tcp_ctloutput ip_ctloutput	Section 30.6 Figure 8.31
	raw IP ICMP IGMP	IPPROTO_IP	rip_ctloutput and ip_ctloutput	Section 32.8

Figure 8.29   setsockopt and getsockopt arguments.

optname	*optval* type	Function	Description
IP_OPTIONS	void *	in_pcbopts	set or get IP options to be included in outgoing datagrams
IP_TOS	int	ip_ctloutput	set or get IP TOS for outgoing datagrams
IP_TTL	int	ip_ctloutput	set or get IP TTL for outgoing datagrams
IP_RECVDSTADDR	int	ip_ctloutput	enable or disable queueing of IP destination address (UDP only)
IP_RECVOPTS	int	ip_ctloutput	enable or disable queueing of incoming IP options as control information (UDP only, not implemented)
IP_RECVRETOPTS	int	ip_ctloutput	enable or disable queueing of reversed source route associated with incoming datagram (UDP only, not implemented)

Figure 8.30   Socket options: IPPROTO_IP level for SOCK_RAW, SOCK_DGRAM, or SOCK_STREAM sockets.

appropriate chapters. In this chapter, we cover the options that provide access to IP features.

Throughout the text we summarize socket options as shown in Figure 8.30. This figure shows the options for the IPPROTO_IP level. The option appears in the first column, the data type of the variable pointed to by *optval* appears in the second column, and the third column shows the function that processes the option.

Figure 8.31 shows the overall organization of the ip_ctloutput function, which handles most of the IPPROTO_IP options. In Section 32.8 we show the additional IPPROTO_IP options that work with SOCK_RAW sockets.

431–447   ip_ctloutput's first argument, op, is either PRCO_SETOPT or PRCO_GETOPT. The second argument, so, points to the socket on which the request was issued. level must be IPPROTO_IP. optname is the option to change or to retrieve, and mp points indirectly to an mbuf that contains the related data for the option. m is initialized to point to the mbuf referenced by *mp.

448–500   If an unrecognized option is specified in the call to setsockopt (and therefore to the PRCO_SETOPT case of the switch), ip_ctloutput releases any mbuf passed by the caller and returns EINVAL.

```
                                                                   ip_output.c
431 int
432 ip_ctloutput(op, so, level, optname, mp)
433 int       op;
434 struct socket *so;
435 int       level, optname;
436 struct mbuf **mp;
437 {
438     struct inpcb *inp = sotoinpcb(so);
439     struct mbuf *m = *mp;
440     int      optval;
441     int      error = 0;

442     if (level != IPPROTO_IP) {
443         error = EINVAL;
444         if (op == PRCO_SETOPT && *mp)
445             (void) m_free(*mp);
446     } else
447         switch (op) {

448         case PRCO_SETOPT:
449             switch (optname) {


                    /* PRCO_SETOPT processing (Figures 8.32 and 12.17) */


493             freeit:
494             default:
495                 error = EINVAL;
496                 break;
497             }
498             if (m)
499                 (void) m_free(m);
500             break;

501         case PRCO_GETOPT:
502             switch (optname) {


                    /* PRCO_GETOPT processing (Figures 8.33 and 12.17) */


546             default:
547                 error = ENOPROTOOPT;
548                 break;
549             }
550             break;
551         }
552     return (error);
553 }
                                                                   ip_output.c
```

Figure 8.31 ip_ctloutput function: overview.

501-553   Unrecognized options passed to getsockopt result in ip_ctloutput returning
ENOPROTOOPT. In this case, the caller releases the mbuf.

PRCO_SETOPT Processing

The processing for PRCO_SETOPT is shown in Figure 8.32.

—— *ip_output.c*
```
450              case IP_OPTIONS:
451                  return (ip_pcbopts(&inp->inp_options, m));
452           case IP_TOS:
453           case IP_TTL:
454           case IP_RECVOPTS:
455           case IP_RECVRETOPTS:
456           case IP_RECVDSTADDR:
457               if (m->m_len != sizeof(int))
458                      error = EINVAL;
459           else {
460                   optval = *mtod(m, int *);
461                   switch (optname) {
462                   case IP_TOS:
463                       inp->inp_ip.ip_tos = optval;
464                       break;
465                   case IP_TTL:
466                       inp->inp_ip.ip_ttl = optval;
467                       break;
468 #define OPTSET(bit) \
469     if (optval) \
470         inp->inp_flags |= bit; \
471     else \
472         inp->inp_flags &= ~bit;
473                   case IP_RECVOPTS:
474                       OPTSET(INP_RECVOPTS);
475                       break;
476                   case IP_RECVRETOPTS:
477                       OPTSET(INP_RECVRETOPTS);
478                       break;
479                   case IP_RECVDSTADDR:
480                       OPTSET(INP_RECVDSTADDR);
481                       break;
482                   }
483               }
484           break;
```
—— *ip_output.c*

Figure 8.32 ip_ctloutput function: PRCO_SETOPT processing.

450–451   IP_OPTIONS is processed by ip_pcbopts (Figure 9.32).

452–484   The IP_TOS, IP_TTL, IP_RECVOPTS, IP_RECVRETOPTS, and IP_RECVDSTADDR options all expect an integer to be available in the mbuf pointed to by m. The integer is stored in optval and then used to change the ip_tos or ip_ttl values associated with the socket or to set or clear the INP_RECVOPTS, INP_RECVRETOPTS, or INP_RECVDSTADDR flags associated with the socket. The macro OPTSET sets (or clears) the specified bit if optval is nonzero (or 0).

Figure 8.30 showed that IP_RECVOPTS and IP_RECVRETOPTS were not implemented. In Chapter 23, we'll see that the settings of these options are ignored by UDP.

PRCO_GETOPT Processing

Figure 8.33 shows the code that retrieves the IP options when PRCO_GETOPT is specified.

```
                                                               ip_output.c
503            case IP_OPTIONS:
504                *mp = m = m_get(M_WAIT, MT_SOOPTS);
505                if (inp->inp_options) {
506                    m->m_len = inp->inp_options->m_len;
507                    bcopy(mtod(inp->inp_options, caddr_t),
508                          mtod(m, caddr_t), (unsigned) m->m_len);
509                } else
510                    m->m_len = 0;
511                break;

512            case IP_TOS:
513            case IP_TTL:
514            case IP_RECVOPTS:
515            case IP_RECVRETOPTS:
516            case IP_RECVDSTADDR:
517                *mp = m = m_get(M_WAIT, MT_SOOPTS);
518                m->m_len = sizeof(int);
519                switch (optname) {

520                case IP_TOS:
521                    optval = inp->inp_ip.ip_tos;
522                    break;

523                case IP_TTL:
524                    optval = inp->inp_ip.ip_ttl;
525                    break;

526 #define OPTBIT(bit)  (inp->inp_flags & bit ? 1 : 0)

527                case IP_RECVOPTS:
528                    optval = OPTBIT(INP_RECVOPTS);
529                    break;

530                case IP_RECVRETOPTS:
531                    optval = OPTBIT(INP_RECVRETOPTS);
532                    break;

533                case IP_RECVDSTADDR:
534                    optval = OPTBIT(INP_RECVDSTADDR);
535                    break;
536                }
537                *mtod(m, int *) = optval;
538                break;
                                                               ip_output.c
```

Figure 8.33 ip_ctloutput function: PRCO_GETOPT processing.

503–538   For IP_OPTIONS, ip_ctloutput returns an mbuf containing a copy of the options associated with the socket. For the remaining options, ip_ctloutput returns the value of `ip_tos`, `ip_ttl`, or the state of the flag associated with the option. The value is returned in the mbuf pointed to by `m`. The macro `OPTBIT` returns 1 (or 0) if `bit` is on (or off) in `inp_flags`.

Notice that the IP options are stored in the protocol control block (`inp`, Chapter 22) associated with the socket.

8.9   `ip_sysctl` Function

Figure 7.27 showed that the `ip_sysctl` function is called when the protocol and family identifiers are 0 in a call to `sysctl`. Figure 8.34 shows the three parameters supported by `ip_sysctl`.

`sysctl` constant	Net/3 variable	Description
`IPCTL_FORWARDING`	`ipforwarding`	Should the system forward IP packets?
`IPCTL_SENDREDIRECTS`	`ipsendredirects`	Should the system send ICMP redirects?
`IPCTL_DEFTTL`	`ip_defttl`	Default TTL for IP packets.

Figure 8.34 `ip_sysctl` parameters.

Figure 8.35 shows the `ip_sysctl` function.

```
                                                                         ── ip_input.c
984 int
985 ip_sysctl(name, namelen, oldp, oldlenp, newp, newlen)
986 int     *name;
987 u_int   namelen;
988 void    *oldp;
989 size_t  *oldlenp;
990 void    *newp;
991 size_t  newlen;
992 {
993     /* All sysctl names at this level are terminal. */
994     if (namelen != 1)
995         return (ENOTDIR);

996     switch (name[0]) {
997     case IPCTL_FORWARDING:
998         return (sysctl_int(oldp, oldlenp, newp, newlen, &ipforwarding));
999     case IPCTL_SENDREDIRECTS:
1000        return (sysctl_int(oldp, oldlenp, newp, newlen,
1001                        &ipsendredirects));
1002    case IPCTL_DEFTTL:
1003        return (sysctl_int(oldp, oldlenp, newp, newlen, &ip_defttl));
1004    default:
1005        return (EOPNOTSUPP);
1006    }
1007    /* NOTREACHED */
1008 }
                                                                         ── ip_input.c
```

Figure 8.35 `ip_sysctl` function.

984–995   Since `ip_sysctl` does not forward `sysctl` requests to any other functions, there can be only one remaining component in `name`. If not, `ENOTDIR` is returned.

996–1008   The `switch` statement selects the appropriate call to `sysctl_int`, which accesses or modifies `ipforwarding`, `ipsendredirects`, or `ip_defttl`. `EOPNOTSUPP` is returned for unrecognized options.

8.10   Summary

IP is a best-effort datagram service that provides the delivery mechanism for all other Internet protocols. The standard IP header is 20 bytes long, but may be followed by up to 40 bytes of options. IP can split large datagrams into fragments to be transmitted and reassembles the fragments at the final destination. Option processing is discussed in Chapter 9, and fragmentation and reassembly is discussed in Chapter 10.

   `ipintr` ensures that IP headers have arrived undamaged and determines if they have arrived at their final destination by comparing the destination address to the IP addresses of the system's interfaces and to several broadcast addresses. `ipintr` passes datagrams that have reached their final destination to the transport protocol specified within the packet. If the system is configured as a router, datagrams that have not reached their final destination are sent to `ip_forward` for routing toward their final destination. Packets have a limited lifetime. If the TTL field drops to 0, the packet is dropped by `ip_forward`.

   The Internet checksum function is used by many of the Internet protocols and implemented by `in_cksum` in Net/3. The IP checksum covers only the header (and options), not the data, which must be protected by checksums at the transport protocol level. As one of the most time-consuming operations in IP, the checksum function is often optimized for each platform.

Exercises

8.1   Should IP accept broadcast packets when there are no IP addresses assigned to any interfaces?

8.2   Modify `ip_forward` and `ip_output` to do an incremental update of the IP checksum when a packet without options is being forwarded.

8.3   Why is it necessary to check for a link-level broadcast (`M_BCAST` flag in an mbuf) and for an IP-level broadcast (`in_canforward`) when rejecting packets for forwarding? When would a packet arrive as a link-level broadcast but with an IP unicast destination?

8.4   Why isn't an error message returned to the sender when an IP packet arrives with checksum errors?

8.5   Assume that a process on a multihomed host has selected an explicit source address for its outgoing packets. Furthermore, assume that the packet's destination is reached through an interface other than the one selected as the packet's source address. What happens when the first-hop router discovers that the packets should be going through a different router? Is a redirect message sent to the host?

8.6   A new host is attached to a subnetted network and is configured to perform routing (`ipforwarding` equals 1) but its network interface has not been assigned a subnet mask. What happens when this host receives a subnet broadcast packet?

8.7   Why is it necessary to decrement `ip_ttl` after testing it (versus before) in Figure 8.17?

8.8   What would happen if two routers each considered the other the best next-hop destination for a packet?

8.9   Which addresses would not be checked in Figure 8.14 for a packet arriving at the SLIP interface? Would any additional addresses be checked that aren't listed in Figure 8.14?

8.10   `ip_forward` converts the fragment id from host byte order to network byte order before calling `icmp_error`. Why does it not also convert the fragment offset?

9

IP Option Processing

9.1 Introduction

Recall from Chapter 8 that the IP input function (`ipintr`) processes options after it verifies the packet's format (checksum, length, etc.) and before it determines whether the packet has reached its final destination. This implies that a packet's options are processed by every router it encounters and by the final destination host.

RFCs 791 and 1122 specify the IP options and processing rules. This chapter describes the format and processing of most IP options. We'll also show how a transport protocol can specify the IP options to be included in an IP datagram.

An IP packet can include optional fields that are processed before the packet is forwarded or accepted by a system. An IP implementation can handle options in any order; for Net/3, it is the order in which the options appear in the packet. Figure 9.1 shows that up to 40 bytes of options may follow the standard IP header.

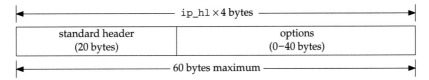

Figure 9.1 An IP header may contain 0 to 40 bytes of IP options.

9.2 Code Introduction

Two headers describe the data structures for IP options. Option processing code is found in two C files. Figure 9.2 lists the relevant files.

File	Description
`netinet/ip.h`	`ip_timestamp` structure
`netinet/ip_var.h`	`ipoption` structure
`netinet/ip_input.c`	option processing
`netinet/ip_output.c`	`ip_insertoptions` function

Figure 9.2   Files discussed in this chapter.

Global Variables

The two global variables described in Figure 9.3 support the reversal of source routes.

Variable	Datatype	Description
`ip_nhops`	`int`	hop count for previous source route
`ip_srcrt`	`struct ip_srcrt`	previous source route

Figure 9.3   Global variables introduced in this chapter.

Statistics

The only statistic updated by the options processing code is `ips_badoptions` from the `ipstat` structure, which Figure 8.4 described.

9.3   Option Format

The IP option field may contain 0 or more individual options. The two types of options, single-byte and multibyte, are illustrated in Figure 9.4.

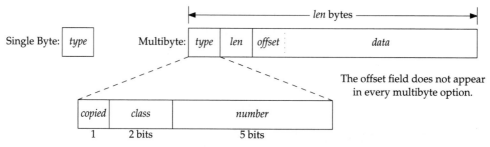

Figure 9.4   The organization of single-byte and multibyte IP options.

All options start with a 1-byte *type* field. In multibyte options, the *type* field is followed immediately by a *len* field, and the remaining bytes are the *data*. The first byte of the *data* field for many options is a 1-byte *offset* field, which points to a byte within the *data* field. The *len* byte covers the *type*, *len*, and *data* fields in its count. The *type* is further divided into three internal fields: a 1-bit *copied* flag, a 2-bit *class* field, and a 5-bit *number* field. Figure 9.5 lists the currently defined IP options. The first two options are single-byte options; the remainder are multibyte options.

Constant	Type		Length (bytes)	Net/3	Description
	Decimal	Binary			
IPOPT_EOL	0–0–0 0	0–00–00000	1	•	end of option list (EOL)
IPOPT_NOP	0–0–1 1	0–00–00001	1	•	no operation (NOP)
IPOPT_RR	0–0–7 7	0–00–00111	varies	•	record route
IPOPT_TS	0–2–4 68	0–10–00100	varies	•	timestamp
IPOPT_SECURITY	1–0–2 130	1–00–00010	11		basic security
IPOPT_LSRR	1–0–3 131	1–00–00011	varies	•	loose source and record route (LSRR)
	1–0–5 133	1–00–00101	varies		extended security
IPOPT_SATID	1–0–8 136	1–00–01000	4		stream identifier
IPOPT_SSRR	1–0–9 137	1–00–01001	varies	•	strict source and record route (SSRR)

Figure 9.5 IP options defined by RFC 791.

The first column shows the Net/3 constant for the option, followed by the decimal and binary values of the type in columns 2 and 3, and the expected length of the option in column 4. The Net/3 column shows those options that are implemented in Net/3 by ip_dooptions. IP must silently ignore any option it does not understand. We don't describe the options that are not implemented in Net/3: security and stream ID. The stream ID option is obsolete and the security options are used primarily by the U.S. military. See RFC 791 for more information.

Net/3 examines the *copied* flag when it fragments a packet with options (Section 10.4). The flag indicates whether the individual option should be copied into the IP header of the fragments. The *class* field groups related options as described in Figure 9.6. All the options in Figure 9.5 have a *class* of 0 except for the timestamp option, which has a *class* of 2.

class	Description
0	control
1	reserved
2	debugging and measurement
3	reserved

Figure 9.6 The *class* field within an IP option.

9.4   ip_dooptions Function

In Figure 8.13 we saw that ipintr calls ip_dooptions just before it checks the destination address of the packet. ip_dooptions is passed a pointer, m, to a packet and processes the options it knows about. If ip_dooptions forwards the packet, as can happen with the LSRR and SSRR options, or discards the packet because of an error, it returns 1. If it doesn't forward the packet, ip_dooptions returns 0 and ipintr continues processing the packet.

ip_dooptions is a long function, so we show it in parts. The first part initializes a for loop to process each option in the header.

When processing an individual option, cp points to the first byte of the option. Figure 9.7 illustrates how the *type*, *length*, and, when applicable, the *offset* fields are accessed with constant offsets from cp.

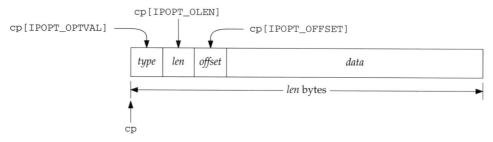

Figure 9.7   Access to IP option fields is by constant offsets.

The RFCs refer to the *offset* field as a *pointer*, which is slightly more descriptive than the term *offset*. The value of *offset* is the index (starting with *type* at index 1) of a byte within the option, and not a 0-based offset from *type*. The minimum value for *offset* is 4 (IPOPT_MINOFF), which points to the first byte of the *data* field in a multibyte option.

Figure 9.8 shows the overall organization of the ip_dooptions function.

553–566   ip_dooptions initializes the ICMP error type, type, to ICMP_PARAMPROB, which is a generic value for any error that does not have a specific error type of its own. For ICMP_PARAMPROB, code is the offset within the packet of the erroneous byte. This is the default ICMP error message; some options change these values.

> ip points to an ip structure with a size of 20 bytes, so ip + 1 points to the next ip structure following the IP header. Since ip_dooptions wants the address of the *byte* after the IP header, the cast converts the resulting pointer to a pointer to an unsigned byte (u_char). Therefore cp points to the first byte beyond the standard IP header, which is the first byte of the IP options.

EOL and NOP processing

567–582   The for loop processes each option in the order it appears in the packet. An EOL option terminates the loop, as does an invalid option length (i.e., the option length indicates that the option data extends beyond the IP header). A NOP option is skipped when it appears. The default case for the switch statement implements the requirement that a system ignore unknown options.

The following sections describe each of the options handled within the switch statement. If ip_dooptions processes all the options in the packet without finding an error, control falls through to the code after the switch.

Source route forwarding

719–724   If the packet needs to be forwarded, forward is set by the SSRR or LSRR option processing code. The packet is passed to ip_forward with a 1 as the second argument to specify that the packet is source routed.

ip_input.c

```
553 int
554 ip_dooptions(m)
555 struct mbuf *m;
556 {
557     struct ip *ip = mtod(m, struct ip *);
558     u_char *cp;
559     struct ip_timestamp *ipt;
560     struct in_ifaddr *ia;
561     int     opt, optlen, cnt, off, code, type = ICMP_PARAMPROB, forward = 0;
562     struct in_addr *sin, dst;
563     n_time  ntime;

564     dst = ip->ip_dst;
565     cp = (u_char *) (ip + 1);
566     cnt = (ip->ip_hl << 2) - sizeof(struct ip);
567     for (; cnt > 0; cnt -= optlen, cp += optlen) {
568         opt = cp[IPOPT_OPTVAL];
569         if (opt == IPOPT_EOL)
570             break;
571         if (opt == IPOPT_NOP)
572             optlen = 1;
573         else {
574             optlen = cp[IPOPT_OLEN];
575             if (optlen <= 0 || optlen > cnt) {
576                 code = &cp[IPOPT_OLEN] - (u_char *) ip;
577                 goto bad;
578             }
579         }
580         switch (opt) {

581         default:
582             break;
```

```
                        /* option processing */
```

```
719     }
720     if (forward) {
721         ip_forward(m, 1);
722         return (1);
723     }
724     return (0);

725 bad:
726     ip->ip_len -= ip->ip_hl << 2;   /* XXX icmp_error adds in hdr length */
727     icmp_error(m, type, code, 0, 0);
728     ipstat.ips_badoptions++;
729     return (1);
730 }
```

ip_input.c

Figure 9.8 ip_dooptions function.

Recall from Section 8.5 that ICMP redirects are not generated for source-routed packets—this is the reason for the second argument to `ip_forward`.

`ip_dooptions` returns 1 if the packet has been forwarded. If the packet does not include a source route, 0 is returned to `ipintr` to indicate that the datagram needs further processing. Note that source route forwarding occurs whether the system is configured as a router (`ipforwarding` equals 1) or not.

This is a somewhat controversial policy, but is mandated by RFC 1122. RFC 1127 [Braden 1989c] describes this as an open issue.

Error handling

725–730   If an error occurs within the `switch`, `ip_dooptions` jumps to `bad`. The IP header length is subtracted from the packet length since `icmp_error` assumes the header length is not included in the packet length. `icmp_error` sends the appropriate error message, and `ip_dooptions` returns 1 to prevent `ipintr` from processing the discarded packet.

The following sections describe each of the options that are processed by Net/3.

9.5   Record Route Option

The record route option causes the route taken by a packet to be recorded within the packet as it traverses an internet. The size of the option is fixed by the source host when it constructs the option and must be large enough to hold all the expected addresses. Recall that only 40 bytes of options may appear in an IP packet. The record route option has 3 bytes of overhead followed by a list of addresses (4 bytes each). If it is the only option, up to 9 ($3 + 4 \times 9 = 39$) addresses may appear. Once the allocated space in the option has been filled, the packet is forwarded as usual but no more addresses are recorded by the intermediate systems.

Figure 9.9 illustrates the format of a record route option and Figure 9.10 shows the source code.

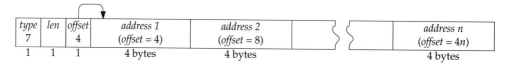

Figure 9.9   The record route option. n must be ≤ 9.

647–657   If the option offset is too small, `ip_dooptions` sends an ICMP parameter problem error. The variable `code` is set to the byte offset of the invalid option offset within the packet, and the ICMP parameter problem error has this `code` value when the error is generated at the label `bad` (Figure 9.8). If there is no space in the option for additional addresses, the option is ignored and processing continues with the next option.

Record address

658–673   If `ip_dst` is one of the systems addresses (the packet has arrived at its destination), the address of the receiving interface is recorded in the option; otherwise the address of

```
                                                              ─── ip_input.c
647        case IPOPT_RR:
648            if ((off = cp[IPOPT_OFFSET]) < IPOPT_MINOFF) {
649                code = &cp[IPOPT_OFFSET] - (u_char *) ip;
650                goto bad;
651            }
652            /*
653             * If no space remains, ignore.
654             */
655            off--;                    /* 0 origin */
656            if (off > optlen - sizeof(struct in_addr))
657                    break;
658            bcopy((caddr_t) (&ip->ip_dst), (caddr_t) & ipaddr.sin_addr,
659                    sizeof(ipaddr.sin_addr));
660            /*
661             * locate outgoing interface; if we're the destination,
662             * use the incoming interface (should be same).
663             */
664            if ((ia = (INA) ifa_ifwithaddr((SA) & ipaddr)) == 0 &&
665                (ia = ip_rtaddr(ipaddr.sin_addr)) == 0) {
666                type = ICMP_UNREACH;
667                code = ICMP_UNREACH_HOST;
668                goto bad;
669            }
670            bcopy((caddr_t) & (IA_SIN(ia)->sin_addr),
671                    (caddr_t) (cp + off), sizeof(struct in_addr));
672            cp[IPOPT_OFFSET] += sizeof(struct in_addr);
673            break;
                                                              ─── ip_input.c
```

Figure 9.10 ip_dooptions function: record route option processing.

the outgoing interface as provided by ip_rtaddr is recorded. (The INA and SA macros
are defined in Figure 9.15.) The offset is updated to point to the next available address
position in the option. If ip_rtaddr can't find a route to the destination, an ICMP host
unreachable error is sent.

   Section 7.3 of Volume 1 contains examples of the record route option.

ip_rtaddr Function

   The ip_rtaddr function consults a route cache and, if necessary, the complete routing
tables to locate a route to a given IP address. It returns a pointer to the in_ifaddr
structure associated with the outgoing interface for the route. The function is shown in
Figure 9.11.

Check IP forwarding cache

735–741   If the route cache is empty, or if dest, the only argument to ip_rtaddr, does not
match the destination in the route cache, the routing tables must be consulted to select
an outgoing interface.

```
                                                                    ─────── ip_input.c
735 struct in_ifaddr *
736 ip_rtaddr(dst)
737 struct in_addr dst;
738 {
739     struct sockaddr_in *sin;

740     sin = (struct sockaddr_in *) &ipforward_rt.ro_dst;

741     if (ipforward_rt.ro_rt == 0 || dst.s_addr != sin->sin_addr.s_addr) {
742         if (ipforward_rt.ro_rt) {
743             RTFREE(ipforward_rt.ro_rt);
744             ipforward_rt.ro_rt = 0;
745         }
746         sin->sin_family = AF_INET;
747         sin->sin_len = sizeof(*sin);
748         sin->sin_addr = dst;

749         rtalloc(&ipforward_rt);
750     }
751     if (ipforward_rt.ro_rt == 0)
752         return ((struct in_ifaddr *) 0);
753     return ((struct in_ifaddr *) ipforward_rt.ro_rt->rt_ifa);
754 }
                                                                    ─────── ip_input.c
```

Figure 9.11   ip_rtaddr function: locate outgoing interface.

Locate route

742–750   The old route (if any) is discarded and the new destination address is stored in
*sin (which is the ro_dst member of the forwarding cache). rtalloc searches the
routing tables for a route to the destination.

Return route information

751–754   If no route is available, a null pointer is returned. Otherwise, a pointer to the interface address structure associated with the selected route is returned.

9.6   Source and Record Route Options

Normally a packet is forwarded along a path chosen by the intermediate routers. The
source and record route options allow the source host to specify an explicit path to the
destination that overrides routing decisions of the intermediate routers. Furthermore,
the route is recorded as the packet travels toward its destination.

A *strict* route includes the address of every intermediate router between the source
and destination; a *loose* route specifies only some of the intermediate routers. Routers
are free to choose any path between two systems listed in a loose route, whereas no
intermediate routers are allowed between the systems listed in a strict route. We'll use
Figure 9.12 to illustrate source route processing.

A, B, and C are routers and HS and HD are the source and destination hosts. Since
each interface has its own IP address, we see that router A has three addresses: A_1, A_2,

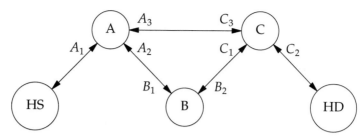

Figure 9.12 Source route example.

and A_3. Similarly, routers B and C have multiple addresses. Figure 9.13 shows the format of the source and record route options.

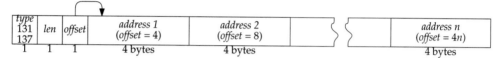

Figure 9.13 The loose and strict source routing options.

The source and destination addresses in the IP header and the offset and address list in the option specify the route and the packet's current location within the route. Figure 9.14 shows how this information changes as the packet follows the loose source route from HS to A to B to C to HD. The loose source route specified by the process are the four IP addresses: A_3, B_1, C_1, and HD. Each row represents the state of the packet when *sent* by the system shown in the first column. The last line shows the packet as received by HD. Figure 9.15 shows the relevant code.

System	IP Header		Source Route Option	
	`ip_src`	`ip_dst`	*offset*	addresses
HS	HS	A_3	4	• B_1 C_1 HD
A	HS	B_1	8	A_2 • C_1 HD
B	HS	C_1	12	A_2 B_2 • HD
C	HS	HD	16	A_2 B_2 C_2 •
HD	HS	HD	16	A_2 B_2 C_2 •

Figure 9.14 The source route option is modified as a packet traverses the route.

The • marks the position of *offset* relative to the addresses within the route. Notice that the address of the outgoing interface is placed in the option by each system. In particular, the original route specified A_3 as the first-hop destination but the output interface, A_2, was recorded in the route. In this way, the route taken by the packet is recorded in the option. This recorded route should be reversed by the destination system and attached to any reply packets so that they follow the same path as the initial packet but in the reverse direction.

Except for UDP, Net/3 reverses a received source route when responding.

```
583                 /*
584                  * Source routing with record.
585                  * Find interface with current destination address.
586                  * If none on this machine then drop if strictly routed,
587                  * or do nothing if loosely routed.
588                  * Record interface address and bring up next address
589                  * component.  If strictly routed make sure next
590                  * address is on directly accessible net.
591                  */
592             case IPOPT_LSRR:
593             case IPOPT_SSRR:
594                 if ((off = cp[IPOPT_OFFSET]) < IPOPT_MINOFF) {
595                     code = &cp[IPOPT_OFFSET] - (u_char *) ip;
596                     goto bad;
597                 }
598                 ipaddr.sin_addr = ip->ip_dst;
599                 ia = (struct in_ifaddr *)
600                     ifa_ifwithaddr((struct sockaddr *) &ipaddr);
601                 if (ia == 0) {
602                     if (opt == IPOPT_SSRR) {
603                         type = ICMP_UNREACH;
604                         code = ICMP_UNREACH_SRCFAIL;
605                         goto bad;
606                     }
607                     /*
608                      * Loose routing, and not at next destination
609                      * yet; nothing to do except forward.
610                      */
611                     break;
612                 }
613                 off--;                  /* 0 origin */
614                 if (off > optlen - sizeof(struct in_addr)) {
615                     /*
616                      * End of source route.  Should be for us.
617                      */
618                     save_rte(cp, ip->ip_src);
619                     break;
620                 }
621                 /*
622                  * locate outgoing interface
623                  */
624                 bcopy((caddr_t) (cp + off), (caddr_t) & ipaddr.sin_addr,
625                     sizeof(ipaddr.sin_addr));
626                 if (opt == IPOPT_SSRR) {
627 #define INA struct in_ifaddr *
628 #define SA  struct sockaddr *
629                     if ((ia = (INA) ifa_ifwithdstaddr((SA) & ipaddr)) == 0)
630                         ia = (INA) ifa_ifwithnet((SA) & ipaddr);
631                 } else
632                     ia = ip_rtaddr(ipaddr.sin_addr);
633                 if (ia == 0) {
634                     type = ICMP_UNREACH;
635                     code = ICMP_UNREACH_SRCFAIL;
```

```
636                        goto bad;
637                    }
638                    ip->ip_dst = ipaddr.sin_addr;
639                    bcopy((caddr_t) & (IA_SIN(ia)->sin_addr),
640                          (caddr_t) (cp + off), sizeof(struct in_addr));
641                    cp[IPOPT_OFFSET] += sizeof(struct in_addr);
642                    /*
643                     * Let ip_intr's mcast routing check handle mcast pkts
644                     */
645                    forward = !IN_MULTICAST(ntohl(ip->ip_dst.s_addr));
646                    break;
```
—— *ip_input.c*

Figure 9.15   ip_dooptions function: LSRR and SSRR option processing.

583–612   Net/3 sends an ICMP parameter problem error with the appropriate value of code
if the option offset is smaller than 4 (IPOPT_MINOFF). If the destination address of the
packet does not match one of the local addresses and the option is a strict source route
(IPOPT_SSRR), an ICMP source route failure error is sent. If a local address isn't listed
in the route, the previous system sent the packet to the wrong host. This isn't an error
for a loose source route (IPOPT_LSRR); it means IP must forward the packet toward the
destination.

End of source route

613–620   Decrementing off converts it to a byte offset from the start of the option. If
ip_dst in the IP header is one of the local addresses and off points beyond the end of
the source route, there are no more addresses in the source route and the packet has
reached its final destination. save_rte makes a copy of the route in the static structure
ip_srcrt and saves the number of addresses in the route in the global ip_nhops (Figure 9.18).

> ip_srcrt is declared as an external static structure since it is only accessed by the functions
> declared in ip_input.c.

Update packet for next hop

621–637   If ip_dst is one of the local addresses and offset points to an address within the
option, this system is an intermediate system specified in the source route and the
packet has not reached its final destination. During strict routing, the next system must
be on a directly connected network. ifa_ifwithdst and ifa_ifwithnet locate a
route to the next system by searching the configured interfaces for a matching destination address (a point-to-point interface) or a matching network address (a broadcast
interface). During loose routing, ip_rtaddr (Figure 9.11) locates the route to the next
system by querying the routing tables. If no interface or route is found for the next system, an ICMP source route failure error is sent.

638–644   If an interface or a route is located, ip_dooptions sets ip_dst to the IP address
pointed to by off. Within the source route option, the intermediate address is replaced
with the address of the outgoing interface, and the offset is incremented to point to the
next address in the route.

Multicast destinations

645–646   If the new destination address is not a multicast address, setting forward to 1 indicates that the packet should be forwarded after ip_dooptions processes all the
options instead of returning the packet to ipintr.

Multicast addresses within a source route enable two multicast routers to communicate through intermediate routers that don't support multicasting. Chapter 14 describes
this technique in more detail.

Section 8.5 of Volume 1 contains more examples of the source route options.

save_rte Function

RFC 1122 requires that the route recorded in a packet be made available to the transport
protocol at the final destination. The transport protocols must reverse the route and
attach it to any reply packets. The function save_rte, shown in Figure 9.18, saves
source routes in an ip_srcrt structure, shown in Figure 9.16

```
                                                                ─── ip_input.c
57 int       ip_nhops = 0;
58 static struct ip_srcrt {
59     struct in_addr dst;           /* final destination */
60     char    nop;                  /* one NOP to align */
61     char    srcopt[IPOPT_OFFSET + 1];    /* OPTVAL, OLEN and OFFSET */
62     struct in_addr route[MAX_IPOPTLEN / sizeof(struct in_addr)];
63 } ip_srcrt;
                                                                ─── ip_input.c
```

Figure 9.16 ip_srcrt structure.

The declaration of route is incorrect, though the error is benign. It should be

struct in_addr route[(MAX_IPOPTLEN - 3)/ sizeof(struct in_addr)];

The discussion with Figures 9.26 and 9.27 covers this in more detail.

57–63   This code defines the ip_srcrt structure and declares the static variable
ip_srcrt. Only two functions access ip_srcrt: save_rte, which copies the source
route from an incoming packet into ip_srcrt; and ip_srcroute, which creates a
reversed source route from ip_srcrt. Figure 9.17 illustrates source route processing.

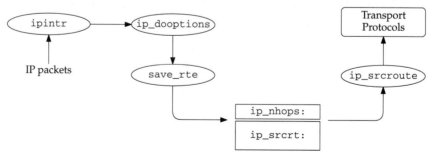

Figure 9.17 Processing of reversed source routes.

```
                                                                    ip_input.c
759 void
760 save_rte(option, dst)
761 u_char *option;
762 struct in_addr dst;
763 {
764     unsigned olen;

765     olen = option[IPOPT_OLEN];
766     if (olen > sizeof(ip_srcrt) - (1 + sizeof(dst)))
767         return;
768     bcopy((caddr_t) option, (caddr_t) ip_srcrt.srcopt, olen);
769     ip_nhops = (olen - IPOPT_OFFSET - 1) / sizeof(struct in_addr);
770     ip_srcrt.dst = dst;
771 }
                                                                    ip_input.c
```

Figure 9.18 save_rte function.

759–771   ip_dooptions calls save_rte when a source routed packet has reached its final destination. option is a pointer to a packet's source route option, and dst is ip_src from the packet's header (i.e., the destination of the return route, HS from Figure 9.12). If the option length is larger than the ip_srcrt structure, save_rte returns immediately.

> This would never happen, as the ip_srcrt structure is larger than the largest option length (40 bytes).

save_rte copies the option into ip_srcrt, computes and saves the number of hops in the source route in ip_nhops, and saves the destination of the return route in dst.

ip_srcroute Function

When responding to a packet, ICMP and the standard transport protocols must reverse any source route that the packet carried. The reversed source route is constructed from the saved route by ip_srcroute, which is shown in Figure 9.19.

777–783   ip_srcroute reverses the route saved in the ip_srcrt structure and returns the result formatted as an ipoption structure (Figure 9.26). If ip_nhops is 0, there is no saved route, so ip_srcroute returns a null pointer.

> Recall that in Figure 8.13, ipintr cleared ip_nhops when a valid packet arrives. The transport protocols must call ip_srcroute and save the reversed route themselves before the next packet arrives. As noted earlier, this is OK since the transport layer (TCP or UDP) is called by ipintr for each packet, before the next packet on IP's input queue is processed.

Allocate mbuf for source route

784–790   If ip_nhops is nonzero, ip_srcroute allocates an mbuf and sets m_len large enough to include the first-hop destination, the option header information (OPTSIZ), and the reversed route. If the allocation fails, a null pointer is returned as if there were no source route available.

```
                                                                      ——— ip_input.c
777 struct mbuf *
778 ip_srcroute()
779 {
780     struct in_addr *p, *q;
781     struct mbuf *m;

782     if (ip_nhops == 0)
783         return ((struct mbuf *) 0);
784     m = m_get(M_DONTWAIT, MT_SOOPTS);
785     if (m == 0)
786         return ((struct mbuf *) 0);

787 #define OPTSIZ  (sizeof(ip_srcrt.nop) + sizeof(ip_srcrt.srcopt))

788     /* length is (nhops+1)*sizeof(addr) + sizeof(nop + srcrt header) */
789     m->m_len = ip_nhops * sizeof(struct in_addr) + sizeof(struct in_addr) +
790             OPTSIZ;

791     /*
792      * First save first hop for return route
793      */
794     p = &ip_srcrt.route[ip_nhops - 1];
795     *(mtod(m, struct in_addr *)) = *p--;

796     /*
797      * Copy option fields and padding (nop) to mbuf.
798      */
799     ip_srcrt.nop = IPOPT_NOP;
800     ip_srcrt.srcopt[IPOPT_OFFSET] = IPOPT_MINOFF;
801     bcopy((caddr_t) & ip_srcrt.nop,
802             mtod(m, caddr_t) + sizeof(struct in_addr), OPTSIZ);
803     q = (struct in_addr *) (mtod(m, caddr_t) +
804                             sizeof(struct in_addr) + OPTSIZ);
805 #undef OPTSIZ
806     /*
807      * Record return path as an IP source route,
808      * reversing the path (pointers are now aligned).
809      */
810     while (p >= ip_srcrt.route) {
811         *q++ = *p--;
812     }
813     /*
814      * Last hop goes to final destination.
815      */
816     *q = ip_srcrt.dst;
817     return (m);
818 }
                                                                      ——— ip_input.c
```

Figure 9.19   ip_srcroute function.

791–804   p is initialized to point to the end of the incoming route, and ip_srcroute copies
the last recorded address to the front of the mbuf where it becomes the outgoing first-
hop destination for the reversed route. Then the function copies a NOP option (Exercise 9.4) and the source route information into the mbuf.

805–818   The `while` loop copies the remaining IP addresses from the source route into the mbuf in reverse order. The last address in the route is set to the source address from the incoming packet, which `save_rte` placed in `ip_srcrt.dst`. A pointer to the mbuf is returned. Figure 9.20 illustrates the construction of the reversed route with the route from Figure 9.12.

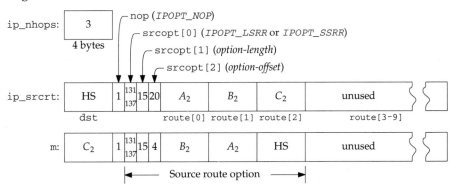

Figure 9.20   `ip_srcroute` reverses the route in `ip_srcrt`.

9.7   Timestamp Option

The timestamp option causes each system to record its notion of the current time within the option as the packet traverses an internet. The time is expected to be in milliseconds since midnight UTC, and is recorded in a 32-bit field.

If the system does not keep accurate UTC (within a few minutes) or the time is not updated at least 15 times per second, it is not considered a standard time. A nonstandard time must have the high-order bit of the timestamp field set.

There are three types of timestamp options, which Net/3 accesses through the `ip_timestamp` structure shown in Figure 9.22.

114–133   As in the `ip` structure (Figure 8.10), `#if`s ensure that the bit fields access the correct bits in the option. Figure 9.21 lists the three types of timestamp options specified by `ipt_flg`.

ipt_flg	Value	Description
IPOPT_TS_TSONLY	0	record timestamps
IPOPT_TS_TSANDADDR	1	record addresses and timestamps
	2	reserved
IPOPT_TS_PRESPEC	3	record timestamps only at the prespecified systems
	4–15	reserved

Figure 9.21   Possible values for `ipt_flg`.

The originating host must construct the timestamp option with a data area large enough to hold all expected timestamps and addresses. For a timestamp option with an

—— *ip.h*

```
114 struct ip_timestamp {
115      u_char  ipt_code;          /* IPOPT_TS */
116      u_char  ipt_len;           /* size of structure (variable) */
117      u_char  ipt_ptr;           /* index of current entry */
118 #if BYTE_ORDER == LITTLE_ENDIAN
119      u_char  ipt_flg:4,         /* flags, see below */
120              ipt_oflw:4;        /* overflow counter */
121 #endif
122 #if BYTE_ORDER == BIG_ENDIAN
123      u_char  ipt_oflw:4,        /* overflow counter */
124              ipt_flg:4;         /* flags, see below */
125 #endif
126      union ipt_timestamp {
127          n_long  ipt_time[1];
128          struct ipt_ta {
129              struct in_addr ipt_addr;
130              n_long  ipt_time;
131          } ipt_ta[1];
132      } ipt_timestamp;
133 };
```

—— *ip.h*

Figure 9.22   `ip_timestamp` structure and constants.

`ipt_flg` of 3, the originating host fills in the addresses of the systems at which a time-stamp should be recorded when it constructs the option. Figure 9.23 shows the organization of the three timestamp options.

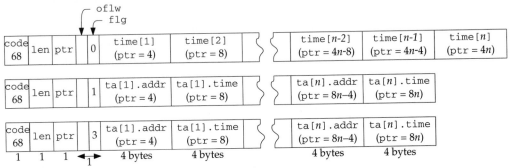

Figure 9.23   The three timestamp options (`ipt_` omitted).

Because only 40 bytes are available for IP options, the timestamp options are limited to nine timestamps (`ipt_flg` equals 0) or four pairs of addresses and timestamps (`ipt_flg` equals 1 or 3). Figure 9.24 shows the processing for the three different timestamp option types.

674–684   `ip_dooptions` sends an ICMP parameter problem error if the option length is less than 5 bytes (the minimum size of a timestamp option). The `oflw` field counts the number of systems unable to register timestamps because the data area of the option was full. `oflw` is incremented if the data area is full, and when it itself overflows at 16 (it is a 4-bit field), an ICMP parameter problem error is sent.

ip_input.c

```
674          case IPOPT_TS:
675              code = cp - (u_char *) ip;
676              ipt = (struct ip_timestamp *) cp;
677              if (ipt->ipt_len < 5)
678                  goto bad;
679              if (ipt->ipt_ptr > ipt->ipt_len - sizeof(long)) {
680                  if (++ipt->ipt_oflw == 0)
681                      goto bad;
682                  break;
683              }
684              sin = (struct in_addr *) (cp + ipt->ipt_ptr - 1);
685              switch (ipt->ipt_flg) {

686              case IPOPT_TS_TSONLY:
687                  break;

688              case IPOPT_TS_TSANDADDR:
689                  if (ipt->ipt_ptr + sizeof(n_time) +
690                      sizeof(struct in_addr) > ipt->ipt_len)
691                          goto bad;
692                  ipaddr.sin_addr = dst;
693                  ia = (INA) ifaof_ifpforaddr((SA) & ipaddr,
694                                              m->m_pkthdr.rcvif);
695                  if (ia == 0)
696                      continue;
697                  bcopy((caddr_t) & IA_SIN(ia)->sin_addr,
698                      (caddr_t) sin, sizeof(struct in_addr));
699                  ipt->ipt_ptr += sizeof(struct in_addr);
700                  break;

701              case IPOPT_TS_PRESPEC:
702                  if (ipt->ipt_ptr + sizeof(n_time) +
703                      sizeof(struct in_addr) > ipt->ipt_len)
704                          goto bad;
705                  bcopy((caddr_t) sin, (caddr_t) & ipaddr.sin_addr,
706                      sizeof(struct in_addr));
707                  if (ifa_ifwithaddr((SA) & ipaddr) == 0)
708                      continue;
709                  ipt->ipt_ptr += sizeof(struct in_addr);
710                  break;

711              default:
712                  goto bad;
713              }
714              ntime = iptime();
715              bcopy((caddr_t) & ntime, (caddr_t) cp + ipt->ipt_ptr - 1,
716                  sizeof(n_time));
717              ipt->ipt_ptr += sizeof(n_time);
718          }
719      }
```

ip_input.c

Figure 9.24 `ip_dooptions` function: timestamp option processing.

Timestamp only

685–687   For a timestamp option with an `ipt_flg` of 0 (`IPOPT_TS_TSONLY`), all the work is done after the `switch`.

Timestamp and address

688–700   For a timestamp option with an `ipt_flg` of 1 (`IPOPT_TS_TSANDADDR`), the address of the receiving interface is recorded (if room remains in the data area), and the option pointer is advanced. Because Net/3 supports multiple IP addresses on a single interface, `ip_dooptions` calls `ifaof_ifpforaddr` to select the address that best matches the original destination address of the packet (i.e., the destination before any source routing has occurred). If there is no match, the timestamp option is skipped. (`INA` and `SA` were defined in Figure 9.15.)

Timestamp at prespecified addresses

701–710   If `ipt_flg` is 3 (`IPOPT_TS_PRESPEC`), `ifa_ifwithaddr` determines if the next address specified in the option matches one of the system's addresses. If not, this option requires no processing at this system; the `continue` forces `ip_dooptions` to proceed to the next option. If the next address matches one of the system's addresses, the option pointer is advanced to the next position and control continues after the `switch`.

Insert timestamp

711–713   Invalid `ipt_flg` values are caught at `default` where control jumps to `bad`.

714–719   The timestamps are placed in the option by the code that follows the `switch` statement. `iptime` returns the number of milliseconds since midnight UTC. `ip_dooptions` records the timestamp and increments the option offset to the next position.

`iptime` Function

Figure 9.25 shows the implementation of `iptime`.

```
                                                                    ── ip_icmp.c
458 n_time
459 iptime()
460 {
461     struct timeval atv;
462     u_long  t;

463     microtime(&atv);
464     t = (atv.tv_sec % (24 * 60 * 60)) * 1000 + atv.tv_usec / 1000;
465     return (htonl(t));
466 }
                                                                    ── ip_icmp.c
```

Figure 9.25 `iptime` function.

458–466   `microtime` returns the time since midnight January 1, 1970, UTC, in a `timeval` structure. The number of milliseconds since midnight is computed using `atv` and returned in network byte order.

Section 7.4 of Volume 1 provides several timestamp option examples.

9.8   **ip_insertoptions** Function

We saw in Section 8.6 that the ip_output function accepts a packet and options. When
the function is called from ip_forward, the options are already part of the packet so
ip_forward always passes a null option pointer to ip_output. The transport protocols, however, may pass options to ip_output where they are merged with the packet
by ip_insertoptions (called by ip_output in Figure 8.22).

ip_insertoptions expects the options to be formatted in an ipoption structure, shown in Figure 9.26.

─── *ip_var.h*

```
92 struct ipoption {
93     struct in_addr ipopt_dst;    /* first-hop dst if source routed */
94     char    ipopt_list[MAX_IPOPTLEN];   /* options proper */
95 };
```

─── *ip_var.h*

Figure 9.26   ipoption structure.

92–95   The structure has only two members: ipopt_dst, which contains the first-hop destination if the option list contains a source route, and ipopt_list, which is an array of
at most 40 (MAX_IPOPTLEN) bytes of options formatted as we have described in this
chapter. If the option list does not include a source route, ipopt_dst is all 0s.

Note that the ip_srcrt structure (Figure 9.16) and the mbuf returned by
ip_srcroute (Figure 9.19) both conform to the format specified by the ipoption
structure. Figure 9.27 compares the ip_srcrt and ipoption structures.

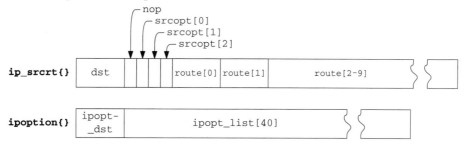

Figure 9.27   The ip_srcrt and ipoption structures.

The ip_srcrt structure is 4 bytes larger than the ipoption structure. The last entry in the
route array (route[9]) is never filled because it would make the source route option 44 bytes
long, larger than the IP header can accommodate (Figure 9.16).

The ip_insertoptions function is shown in Figure 9.28.

352–364   ip_insertoptions has three arguments: m, the outgoing packet; opt, the options
formatted in an ipoption structure; and phlen, a pointer to an integer where the new
header length (after options are inserted) is returned. If the size of packet with the
options exceeds the maximum packet size of 65,535 (IP_MAXPACKET) bytes, the options
are silently discarded. ip_output does not expect ip_insertoptions ever to fail, so
there is no way to report the error. Fortunately, few applications attempt to send a maximally sized datagram, let alone one with options.

---
ip_output.c

```
352 static struct mbuf *
353 ip_insertoptions(m, opt, phlen)
354 struct mbuf *m;
355 struct mbuf *opt;
356 int     *phlen;
357 {
358     struct ipoption *p = mtod(opt, struct ipoption *);
359     struct mbuf *n;
360     struct ip *ip = mtod(m, struct ip *);
361     unsigned optlen;

362     optlen = opt->m_len - sizeof(p->ipopt_dst);
363     if (optlen + (u_short) ip->ip_len > IP_MAXPACKET)
364         return (m);                 /* XXX should fail */
365     if (p->ipopt_dst.s_addr)
366         ip->ip_dst = p->ipopt_dst;
367     if (m->m_flags & M_EXT || m->m_data - optlen < m->m_pktdat) {
368         MGETHDR(n, M_DONTWAIT, MT_HEADER);
369         if (n == 0)
370             return (m);
371         n->m_pkthdr.len = m->m_pkthdr.len + optlen;
372         m->m_len -= sizeof(struct ip);
373         m->m_data += sizeof(struct ip);
374         n->m_next = m;
375         m = n;
376         m->m_len = optlen + sizeof(struct ip);
377         m->m_data += max_linkhdr;
378         bcopy((caddr_t) ip, mtod(m, caddr_t), sizeof(struct ip));
379     } else {
380         m->m_data -= optlen;
381         m->m_len += optlen;
382         m->m_pkthdr.len += optlen;
383         ovbcopy((caddr_t) ip, mtod(m, caddr_t), sizeof(struct ip));
384     }
385     ip = mtod(m, struct ip *);
386     bcopy((caddr_t) p->ipopt_list, (caddr_t) (ip + 1), (unsigned) optlen);
387     *phlen = sizeof(struct ip) + optlen;
388     ip->ip_len += optlen;
389     return (m);
390 }
```

ip_output.c

Figure 9.28 ip_insertoptions function.

365–366   If ipopt_dst.s_addr specifies a nonzero address, then the options include a
source route and ip_dst in the packet's header is replaced with the first-hop destination from the source route.

In Section 26.2 we'll see that TCP calls MGETHDR to allocate a separate mbuf for the
IP and TCP headers. Figure 9.29 shows the mbuf organization for a TCP segment
before the code in lines 367 to 378 is executed.

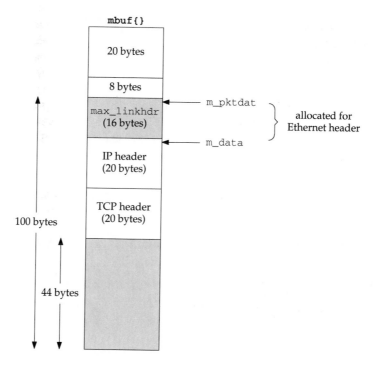

Figure 9.29 ip_insertoptions function: TCP segment.

If the options to be inserted occupy more than 16 bytes, the test on line 367 is true and MGETHDR is called to allocate an additional mbuf. Figure 9.30 shows the organization of the mbufs after the options have been copied into the new mbuf.

367–378   If the packet header is stored in a cluster, or the first mbuf does not have room for the options, ip_insertoptions allocates a new packet header mbuf, initializes its length, trims the IP header from the old mbuf, and moves the header from the old mbuf to the new mbuf.

As described in Section 23.6, UDP uses M_PREPEND to place the UDP and IP headers at the end of an mbuf, separate from the data. This is illustrated in Figure 9.31.

Because the headers are located at the end of the mbuf, there is always room for IP options in the mbuf and the condition on line 367 is always false for UDP.

379–384   If the packet has room at the beginning of the mbuf's data area for the options, m_data and m_len are adjusted to contain optlen more bytes, and the current IP header is moved by ovbcopy (which can handle overlapping source and destinations) to leave room for the options.

385–390   ip_insertoptions can now copy the ipopt_list member of the ipoption structure directly into the mbuf just after the IP header. ip_insertoptions stores the new header length in *phlen, adjusts the datagram length (ip_len), and returns a pointer to the packet header mbuf.

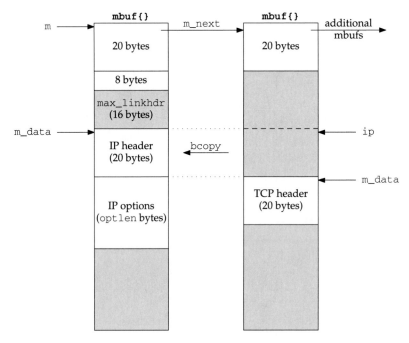

Figure 9.30   `ip_insertoptions` function: TCP segment, after options have been copied.

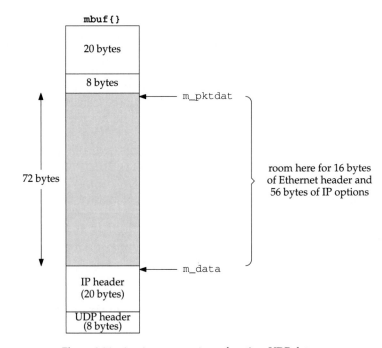

Figure 9.31   `ip_insertoptions` function: UDP datagram.

9.9 `ip_pcbopts` Function

The `ip_pcbopts` function converts the list of IP options provided with the
`IP_OPTIONS` socket option into the form expected by `ip_output`: an `ipoption`
structure.

――― ip_output.c

```
559 int
560 ip_pcbopts(pcbopt, m)
561 struct mbuf **pcbopt;
562 struct mbuf *m;
563 {
564     int cnt, optlen;
565     u_char *cp;
566     u_char  opt;

567     /* turn off any old options */
568     if (*pcbopt)
569         (void) m_free(*pcbopt);
570     *pcbopt = 0;
571     if (m == (struct mbuf *) 0 || m->m_len == 0) {
572         /*
573          * Only turning off any previous options.
574          */
575         if (m)
576             (void) m_free(m);
577         return (0);
578     }
579     if (m->m_len % sizeof(long))
580             goto bad;
581     /*
582      * IP first-hop destination address will be stored before
583      * actual options; move other options back
584      * and clear it when none present.
585      */
586     if (m->m_data + m->m_len + sizeof(struct in_addr) >= &m->m_dat[MLEN])
587             goto bad;
588     cnt = m->m_len;
589     m->m_len += sizeof(struct in_addr);
590     cp = mtod(m, u_char *) + sizeof(struct in_addr);
591     ovbcopy(mtod(m, caddr_t), (caddr_t) cp, (unsigned) cnt);
592     bzero(mtod(m, caddr_t), sizeof(struct in_addr));

593     for (; cnt > 0; cnt -= optlen, cp += optlen) {
594         opt = cp[IPOPT_OPTVAL];
595         if (opt == IPOPT_EOL)
596             break;
597         if (opt == IPOPT_NOP)
598             optlen = 1;
599         else {
600             optlen = cp[IPOPT_OLEN];
601             if (optlen <= IPOPT_OLEN || optlen > cnt)
602                 goto bad;
603         }
```

```
604              switch (opt) {
605              default:
606                  break;
607              case IPOPT_LSRR:
608              case IPOPT_SSRR:
609                  /*
610                   * user process specifies route as:
611                   *   ->A->B->C->D
612                   * D must be our final destination (but we can't
613                   * check that since we may not have connected yet).
614                   * A is first hop destination, which doesn't appear in
615                   * actual IP option, but is stored before the options.
616                   */
617                  if (optlen < IPOPT_MINOFF - 1 + sizeof(struct in_addr))
618                          goto bad;
619                  m->m_len -= sizeof(struct in_addr);
620                  cnt -= sizeof(struct in_addr);
621                  optlen -= sizeof(struct in_addr);
622                  cp[IPOPT_OLEN] = optlen;
623                  /*
624                   * Move first hop before start of options.
625                   */
626                  bcopy((caddr_t) & cp[IPOPT_OFFSET + 1], mtod(m, caddr_t),
627                          sizeof(struct in_addr));
628                  /*
629                   * Then copy rest of options back
630                   * to close up the deleted entry.
631                   */
632                  ovbcopy((caddr_t) (&cp[IPOPT_OFFSET + 1] +
633                              sizeof(struct in_addr)),
634                          (caddr_t) & cp[IPOPT_OFFSET + 1],
635                          (unsigned) cnt + sizeof(struct in_addr));
636                  break;
637              }
638          }
639          if (m->m_len > MAX_IPOPTLEN + sizeof(struct in_addr))
640                  goto bad;
641          *pcbopt = m;
642          return (0);
643      bad:
644          (void) m_free(m);
645          return (EINVAL);
646      }
```

─── *ip_output.c*

Figure 9.32 ip_pcbopts function.

559–562   The first argument, pcbopt, references the pointer to the current list of options.
The function replaces this pointer with a pointer to the new list of options constructed
from options specified in the mbuf chain pointed to by the second argument, m. The
option list prepared by the process to be included with the IP_OPTIONS socket option
looks like a standard list of IP options except for the format of the LSRR and SSRR
options. For these options, the first-hop destination is included as the first address in

the route. Figure 9.14 shows that the first-hop destination appears as the destination address in the outgoing packet, not as the first address in the route.

Discard previous options

563–580   Any previous options are discarded by `m_free` and `*pcbopt` is cleared. If the process passed an empty mbuf or didn't pass an mbuf at all, the function returns immediately without installing any new options.

If the new list of options is not padded to a 4-byte boundary, `ip_pcbopts` jumps to `bad`, discards the list and returns `EINVAL`.

The remainder of the function rearranges the list to look like an `ipoption` structure. Figure 9.33 illustrates this process.

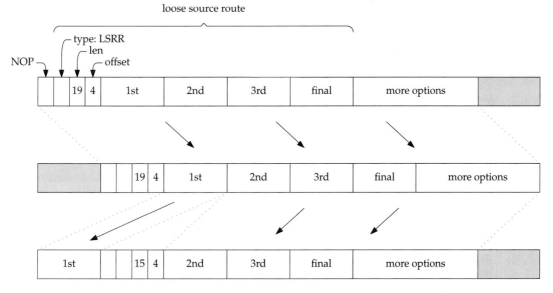

Figure 9.33   `ip_pcbopts` option list processing.

Make room for first-hop destination

581–592   If there is room in the mbuf, all the data is shifted by 4 bytes (the size of an `in_addr` structure) toward the end of the mbuf. `ovbcopy` performs the copy. `bzero` clears the 4 bytes at the start of the mbuf.

Scan option list

593–606   The `for` loop scans the option list looking for LSRR and SSRR options. For multi-byte options, the loop also verifies that the length of the option is reasonable.

Rearrange LSRR or SSRR option

607–638   When the loop locates a LSRR or SSRR option, it decrements the mbuf size, the loop index, and the option length by 4, since the first address in the option will be removed and shifted to the front of the mbuf.

`bcopy` moves the first address and `ovbcopy` shifts the remainder of the options by 4 bytes to fill the gap left by the first address.

Cleanup

639–646   After the loop, the size of the option list (including the first-hop address) must be no more than 44 (MAX_IPOPTLEN + 4) bytes. A larger list does not fit in the IP packet header. The list is saved in *pcbopt and the function returns.

9.10 Limitations

Options are rarely present in IP datagrams other than those created by administrative and diagnostic tools. Volume 1 discusses two of the more common tools, `ping` and `traceroute`. It is difficult to write applications that utilize IP options. The programming interfaces are poorly documented and not well standardized. Most vendor supplied applications, such as Telnet and FTP, do not provide a way for a user to specify options such as a source route.

The usefulness of the record route, timestamp, and source route options in a large internet is limited by the maximum size of an IP header. Most routes contain more hops than can be represented in the 40 option bytes. When multiple options appear in the same packet, the available space is almost useless. IPv6 addresses this problem with a more flexible option header design.

During fragmentation, IP copies only some options into the noninitial fragments, since the options in noninitial fragments are discarded during reassembly. Only options from the initial fragment are made available to the transport protocol at the destination (Section 10.6). But some, such as source route, must be copied to each fragment, even if they are discarded in noninitial fragments at the destination.

9.11 Summary

In this chapter we showed the format and processing of IP options. We didn't cover the security and stream ID options since they are not implemented in Net/3.

We saw that the size of multibyte options is fixed by the source host when it constructs the option. The usefulness of IP options is severely limited by the small maximum option header size of 40 bytes.

The source route options require the most support. Incoming source routes are saved by `save_rte` and reversed by `ip_srcroute`. A host that does not normally forward packets may forward source routed packets, but RFC 1122 requires this capability to be disabled by default. Net/3 does not have a switch for this feature and always forwards source routed packets.

Finally, we saw how options are merged into an outgoing packet by `ip_insertoptions`.

Exercises

9.1   What would happen if a packet contained two different source route options?

9.2   Some commercial routers can be configured to discard packets based on their IP destination address. In this way, a machine or group of machines can be isolated from the larger internet beyond the router. Describe how source routed packets can bypass this mechanism. Assume that there is at least one host within the network that the router is not blocking, and that it forwards source routed datagrams.

9.3   Some hosts may not be configured with a default route. In general, this prevents communication with the host since the host can't route to destinations outside its directly connected networks. Describe how a source route can enable communication with this type of host.

9.4   Why is a NOP used in the `ip_srcrt` structure in Figure 9.16?

9.5   Can a nonstandard time value be confused with a standard time value in the timestamp options?

9.6   `ip_dooptions` saves the destination address of the packet in `dest` before processing any options (Figure 9.8). Why?

10

IP Fragmentation and Reassembly

10.1 Introduction

In this chapter we describe the IP fragmentation and reassembly processing that we postponed in Chapter 8.

IP has an important capability of being able to fragment a packet when it is too large to be transmitted by the selected hardware interface. The oversized packet is split into two or more IP fragments, each of which is small enough to be transmitted on the selected network. Fragments may be further split by routers farther along the path to the final destination. Thus, at the destination host, an IP datagram can be contained in a single IP packet or, if it was fragmented in transit, it can arrive in multiple IP packets. Because individual fragments may take different paths to the destination host, only the destination host has a chance to see all the fragments. Thus only the destination host can reassemble the fragments into a complete datagram to be delivered to the appropriate transport protocol.

Figure 8.5 shows that 0.3% (72,786/27,881,978) of the packets received were fragments and 0.12% (260,484/(29,447,726 − 796,084)) of the datagrams sent were fragmented. On `world.std.com`, 9.5% of the packets received were fragments. `world` has more NFS activity, which is a common source of IP fragmentation.

Three fields in the IP header implement fragmentation and reassembly: the identification field (`ip_id`), the flags field (the 3 high-order bits of `ip_off`), and the offset field (the 13 low-order bits of `ip_off`). The flags field is composed of three 1-bit flags. Bit 0 is reserved and must be 0, bit 1 is the "don't fragment" (DF) flag, and bit 2 is the "more fragments" (MF) flag. In Net/3, the flag and offset fields are combined and accessed by `ip_off`, as shown in Figure 10.1.

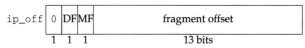

Figure 10.1   `ip_off` controls fragmentation of an IP packet.

Net/3 accesses the DF and MF bits by masking `ip_off` with `IP_DF` and `IP_MF` respectively. An IP implementation must allow an application to request that the DF bit be set in an outgoing datagram.

> Net/3 does not provide *application-level* control over the DF bit when using UDP or TCP.

> A process may construct and send its own IP headers with the raw IP interface (Chapter 32). The DF bit may be set by the transport layers directly such as when TCP performs *path MTU discovery*.

The remaining 13 bits of `ip_off` specify the fragment's position within the original datagram, measured in 8-byte units. Accordingly, every fragment except the last must contain a multiple of 8 bytes of data so that the following fragment starts on an 8-byte boundary. Figure 10.2 illustrates the relationship between the byte offset within the original datagram and the fragment offset (low-order 13 bits of `ip_off`) in the fragment's IP header.

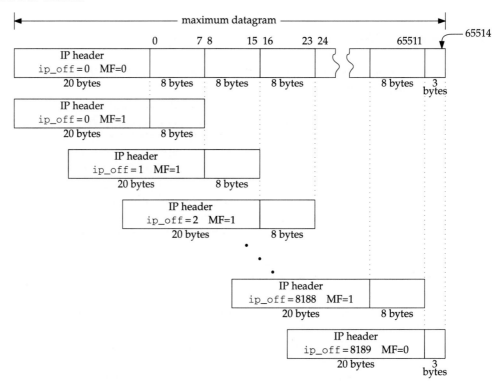

Figure 10.2   Fragmentation of a 65535-byte datagram.

Figure 10.2 shows a maximally sized IP datagram divided into 8190 fragments. Each fragment contains 8 bytes except the last, which contains only 3 bytes. We also show the MF bit set in all the fragments except the last. This is an unrealistic example, but it illustrates several implementation issues.

The numbers above the original datagram are the byte offsets for the *data* portion of the datagram. The fragment offset (ip_off) is computed from the start of the data portion of the datagram. It is impossible for a fragment to include a byte beyond offset 65514 since the reassembled datagram would be larger than 65535 bytes—the maximum value of the ip_len field. This restricts the maximum value of ip_off to 8189 ($8189 \times 8 = 65512$), which leaves room for 3 bytes in the last fragment. If IP options are present, the offset must be smaller still.

Because an IP internet is connectionless, fragments from one datagram may be interleaved with those from another at the destination. ip_id uniquely identifies the fragments of a particular datagram. The source system sets ip_id in each datagram to a unique value for all datagrams using the same source (ip_src), destination (ip_dst), and protocol (ip_p) values for the lifetime of the datagram on the internet.

To summarize, ip_id identifies the fragments of a particular datagram, ip_off positions the fragment within the original datagram, and the MF bit marks every fragment except the last.

10.2 Code Introduction

The reassembly data structures appear in a single header. Reassembly and fragmentation processing is found in two C files. The three files are listed in Figure 10.3.

File	Description
netinet/ip_var.h	reassembly data structures
netinet/ip_output.c netinet/ip_input.c	fragmentation code reassembly code

Figure 10.3   Files discussed in this chapter.

Global Variables

Only one global variable, ipq, is described in this chapter.

Variable	Type	Description
ipq	struct ipq *	reassembly list

Figure 10.4   Global variable introduced in this chapter.

Statistics

The statistics modified by the fragmentation and reassembly code are shown in Figure 10.5. They are a subset of the statistics included in the `ipstat` structure described by Figure 8.4.

ipstat member	Description
ips_cantfrag	#datagrams not sent because fragmentation was required but was prohibited by the DF bit
ips_odropped	#output packets dropped because of a memory shortage
ips_ofragments	#fragments transmitted
ips_fragmented	#packets fragmented for output

Figure 10.5   Statistics collected in this chapter.

10.3   Fragmentation

We now return to `ip_output` and describe the fragmentation code. Recall from Figure 8.25 that if a packet fits within the MTU of the selected outgoing interface, it is transmitted in a single link-level frame. Otherwise the packet must be fragmented and transmitted in multiple frames. A packet may be a complete datagram or it may itself be a fragment that was created by a previous system. We describe the fragmentation code in three parts:

- determine fragment size (Figure 10.6),
- construct fragment list (Figure 10.7), and
- construct initial fragment and send fragments (Figure 10.8).

ip_output.c

```
253      /*
254       * Too large for interface; fragment if possible.
255       * Must be able to put at least 8 bytes per fragment.
256       */
257      if (ip->ip_off & IP_DF) {
258          error = EMSGSIZE;
259          ipstat.ips_cantfrag++;
260          goto bad;
261      }
262      len = (ifp->if_mtu - hlen) & ~7;
263      if (len < 8) {
264          error = EMSGSIZE;
265          goto bad;
266      }
```

ip_output.c

Figure 10.6   `ip_output` function: determine fragment size.

253–261   The fragmentation algorithm is straightforward, but the implementation is complicated by the manipulation of the mbuf structures and chains. If fragmentation is

prohibited by the DF bit, `ip_output` discards the packet and returns `EMSGSIZE`. If the
datagram was generated on this host, a transport protocol passes the error back to the
process, but if the datagram is being forwarded, `ip_forward` generates an ICMP destination unreachable error with an indication that the packet could not be forwarded
without fragmentation (Figure 8.21).

Net/3 does not implement the path MTU discovery algorithms used to probe the
path to a destination and discover the largest transmission unit supported by all the
intervening networks. Sections 11.8 and 24.2 of Volume 1 describe path MTU discovery
for UDP and TCP.

262–266   `len`, the number of data bytes in each fragment, is computed as the MTU of the
interface less the size of the packet's header and then rounded down to an 8-byte
boundary by clearing the low-order 3 bits (`& ~7`). If the MTU is so small that each fragment contains less than 8 bytes, `ip_output` returns `EMSGSIZE`.

Each new fragment contains an IP header, some of the options from the original
packet, and at most `len` data bytes.

The code in Figure 10.7, which is the start of a C compound statement, constructs
the list of fragments starting with the second fragment. The original packet is converted
into the initial fragment after the list is created (Figure 10.8).

267–269   The extra block allows `mhlen`, `firstlen`, and `mnext` to be declared closer to their
use in the function. These variables are in scope until the end of the block and hide any
similarly named variables outside the block.

270–276   Since the original mbuf chain becomes the first fragment, the `for` loop starts with
the offset of the second fragment: `hlen + len`. For each fragment `ip_output` takes the
following actions:

277–284   • Allocate a new packet mbuf and adjust its `m_data` pointer to leave room for a
16-byte link-layer header (`max_linkhdr`). If `ip_output` didn't do this, the
network interface driver would have to allocate an additional mbuf to hold the
link header or move the data. Both are time-consuming tasks that are easily
avoided here.

285–290   • Copy the IP header and IP options from the original packet into the new packet.
The former is copied with a structure assignment. `ip_optcopy` copies only
those options that get copied into each fragment (Section 10.4).

291–297   • Set the offset field (`ip_off`) for the fragment including the MF bit. If MF is set
in the original packet, then MF is set in all the fragments. If MF is not set in the
original packet, then MF is set for every fragment except the last.

298   • Set the length of this fragment accounting for a shorter header (`ip_optcopy`
may not have copied all the options) and a shorter data area for the last fragment. The length is stored in network byte order.

299–305   • Copy the data from the original packet into this fragment. `m_copy` allocates
additional mbufs if necessary. If `m_copy` fails, `ENOBUFS` is posted. Any mbufs
already allocated are discarded at `sendorfree`.

```
                                                                   ip_output.c
267     {

268         int     mhlen, firstlen = len;
269         struct mbuf **mnext = &m->m_nextpkt;

270         /*
271          * Loop through length of segment after first fragment,
272          * make new header and copy data of each part and link onto chain.
273          */
274         m0 = m;
275         mhlen = sizeof(struct ip);
276         for (off = hlen + len; off < (u_short) ip->ip_len; off += len) {
277             MGETHDR(m, M_DONTWAIT, MT_HEADER);
278             if (m == 0) {
279                 error = ENOBUFS;
280                 ipstat.ips_odropped++;
281                 goto sendorfree;
282             }
283             m->m_data += max_linkhdr;
284             mhip = mtod(m, struct ip *);
285             *mhip = *ip;
286             if (hlen > sizeof(struct ip)) {
287                 mhlen = ip_optcopy(ip, mhip) + sizeof(struct ip);
288                 mhip->ip_hl = mhlen >> 2;
289             }
290             m->m_len = mhlen;
291             mhip->ip_off = ((off - hlen) >> 3) + (ip->ip_off & ~IP_MF);
292             if (ip->ip_off & IP_MF)
293                 mhip->ip_off |= IP_MF;
294             if (off + len >= (u_short) ip->ip_len)
295                 len = (u_short) ip->ip_len - off;
296             else
297                 mhip->ip_off |= IP_MF;
298             mhip->ip_len = htons((u_short) (len + mhlen));
299             m->m_next = m_copy(m0, off, len);
300             if (m->m_next == 0) {
301                 (void) m_free(m);
302                 error = ENOBUFS;     /* ??? */
303                 ipstat.ips_odropped++;
304                 goto sendorfree;
305             }
306             m->m_pkthdr.len = mhlen + len;
307             m->m_pkthdr.rcvif = (struct ifnet *) 0;
308             mhip->ip_off = htons((u_short) mhip->ip_off);
309             mhip->ip_sum = 0;
310             mhip->ip_sum = in_cksum(m, mhlen);
311             *mnext = m;
312             mnext = &m->m_nextpkt;
313             ipstat.ips_ofragments++;
314         }
                                                                   ip_output.c
```

Figure 10.7 ip_output function: construct fragment list.

306–314   • Adjust the mbuf packet header of the newly created fragment to have the correct
                total length, clear the new fragment's interface pointer, convert `ip_off` to net-
                work byte order, compute the checksum for the new fragment, and link the frag-
                ment to the previous fragment through `m_nextpkt`.

            In Figure 10.8, `ip_output` constructs the initial fragment and then passes each
            fragment to the interface layer.

—— *ip_output.c*
```
315          /*
316           * Update first fragment by trimming what's been copied out
317           * and updating header, then send each fragment (in order).
318           */
319          m = m0;
320          m_adj(m, hlen + firstlen - (u_short) ip->ip_len);
321          m->m_pkthdr.len = hlen + firstlen;
322          ip->ip_len = htons((u_short) m->m_pkthdr.len);
323          ip->ip_off = htons((u_short) (ip->ip_off | IP_MF));
324          ip->ip_sum = 0;
325          ip->ip_sum = in_cksum(m, hlen);
326      sendorfree:
327          for (m = m0; m; m = m0) {
328              m0 = m->m_nextpkt;
329              m->m_nextpkt = 0;
330              if (error == 0)
331                  error = (*ifp->if_output) (ifp, m,
332                                      (struct sockaddr *) dst, ro->ro_rt);
333              else
334                  m_freem(m);
335          }

336          if (error == 0)
337              ipstat.ips_fragmented++;
338      }
```
—— *ip_output.c*

Figure 10.8   `ip_output` function: send fragments.

315–325   The original packet is converted into the first fragment by trimming the extra data
            from its end, setting the MF bit, converting `ip_len` and `ip_off` to network byte order,
            and computing the new checksum. All the IP options are retained in this fragment. At
            the destination host, only the IP options from the first fragment of a datagram are
            retained when the datagram is reassembled (Figure 10.28). Some options, such as
            source routing, must be copied into each fragment even though the option is discarded
            during reassembly.
326–338   At this point, `ip_output` has either a complete list of fragments or an error has
            occurred and the partial list of fragments must be discarded. The `for` loop traverses
            the list either sending or discarding fragments according to `error`. Any error encoun-
            tered while sending fragments causes the remaining fragments to be discarded.

10.4 `ip_optcopy` Function

During fragmentation, `ip_optcopy` (Figure 10.9) copies the options from the incoming packet (if the packet is being forwarded) or from the original datagram (if the datagram is locally generated) into the outgoing fragments.

ip_output.c

```
395 int
396 ip_optcopy(ip, jp)
397 struct ip *ip, *jp;
398 {
399     u_char *cp, *dp;
400     int     opt, optlen, cnt;

401     cp = (u_char *) (ip + 1);
402     dp = (u_char *) (jp + 1);
403     cnt = (ip->ip_hl << 2) - sizeof(struct ip);
404     for (; cnt > 0; cnt -= optlen, cp += optlen) {
405         opt = cp[0];
406         if (opt == IPOPT_EOL)
407             break;
408         if (opt == IPOPT_NOP) {
409             /* Preserve for IP mcast tunnel's LSRR alignment. */
410             *dp++ = IPOPT_NOP;
411             optlen = 1;
412             continue;
413         } else
414             optlen = cp[IPOPT_OLEN];
415         /* bogus lengths should have been caught by ip_dooptions */
416         if (optlen > cnt)
417             optlen = cnt;
418         if (IPOPT_COPIED(opt)) {
419             bcopy((caddr_t) cp, (caddr_t) dp, (unsigned) optlen);
420             dp += optlen;
421         }
422     }
423     for (optlen = dp - (u_char *) (jp + 1); optlen & 0x3; optlen++)
424         *dp++ = IPOPT_EOL;
425     return (optlen);
426 }
```

ip_output.c

Figure 10.9 `ip_optcopy` function.

395–422   The arguments to `ip_optcopy` are: `ip`, a pointer to the IP header of the outgoing packet; and `jp`, a pointer to the IP header of the newly created fragment. `ip_optcopy` initializes `cp` and `dp` to point to the first option byte in each packet and advances `cp` and `dp` as it processes each option. The first `for` loop copies a single option during each iteration stopping when it encounters an EOL option or when it has examined all the options. NOP options are copied to preserve any alignment constraints in the subsequent options.

The Net/2 release discarded NOP options.

If `IPOPT_COPIED` indicates that the *copied* bit is on, `ip_optcopy` copies the option to the new fragment. Figure 9.5 shows which options have the *copied* bit set. If an option length is too large, it is truncated; `ip_dooptions` should have already discovered this type of error.

423–426   The second `for` loop pads the option list out to a 4-byte boundary. This is required, since the packet's header length (`ip_hlen`) is measured in 4-byte units. It also ensures that the transport header that follows is aligned on a 4-byte boundary. This improves performance since many transport protocols are designed so that 32-bit header fields are aligned on 32-bit boundaries if the transport header starts on a 32-bit boundary. This arrangement increases performance on CPUs that have difficulty accessing unaligned 32-bit words.

Figure 10.10 illustrates the operation of `ip_optcopy`.

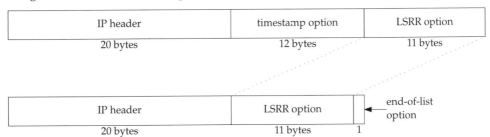

Figure 10.10   Not all options are copied during fragmentation.

In Figure 10.10 we see that `ip_optcopy` does not copy the timestamp option (its *copied* bit is 0) but does copy the LSRR option (its *copied* bit is 1). `ip_optcopy` has also added a single EOL option to pad the new options to a 4-byte boundary.

10.5 Reassembly

Now that we have described the fragmentation of a datagram (or of a fragment), we return to `ipintr` and the reassembly process. In Figure 8.15 we omitted the reassembly code from `ipintr` and postponed its discussion. `ipintr` can pass only entire datagrams up to the transport layer for processing. Fragments that are received by `ipintr` are passed to `ip_reass`, which attempts to reassemble fragments into complete datagrams. The code from `ipintr` is shown in Figure 10.11.

271–279   Recall that `ip_off` contains the DF bit, the MF bit, and the fragment offset. The DF bit is masked out and if either the MF bit or fragment offset is nonzero, the packet is a fragment that must be reassembled. If both are zero, the packet is a complete datagram, the reassembly code is skipped and the `else` clause at the end of Figure 10.11 is executed, which excludes the header length from the total datagram length.

280–286   `m_pullup` moves data in an external cluster into the data area of the mbuf. Recall that the SLIP interface (Section 5.3) may return an entire IP packet in an external cluster if it does not fit in a single mbuf. Also `m_devget` can return the entire packet in a cluster (Section 2.6). Before the `dtom` macro will work (Section 2.6), `m_pullup` must move the IP header from the cluster into the data area of an mbuf.

ip_input.c

```
271    ours:
272        /*
273         * If offset or IP_MF are set, must reassemble.
274         * Otherwise, nothing need be done.
275         * (We could look in the reassembly queue to see
276         * if the packet was previously fragmented,
277         * but it's not worth the time; just let them time out.)
278         */
279        if (ip->ip_off & ~IP_DF) {
280            if (m->m_flags & M_EXT) {    /* XXX */
281                if ((m = m_pullup(m, sizeof(struct ip))) == 0) {
282                    ipstat.ips_toosmall++;
283                    goto next;
284                }
285                ip = mtod(m, struct ip *);
286            }
287            /*
288             * Look for queue of fragments
289             * of this datagram.
290             */
291            for (fp = ipq.next; fp != &ipq; fp = fp->next)
292                if (ip->ip_id == fp->ipq_id &&
293                    ip->ip_src.s_addr == fp->ipq_src.s_addr &&
294                    ip->ip_dst.s_addr == fp->ipq_dst.s_addr &&
295                    ip->ip_p == fp->ipq_p)
296                    goto found;
297            fp = 0;
298        found:

299            /*
300             * Adjust ip_len to not reflect header,
301             * set ip_mff if more fragments are expected,
302             * convert offset of this to bytes.
303             */
304            ip->ip_len -= hlen;
305            ((struct ipasfrag *) ip)->ipf_mff &= ~1;
306            if (ip->ip_off & IP_MF)
307                ((struct ipasfrag *) ip)->ipf_mff |= 1;
308            ip->ip_off <<= 3;

309            /*
310             * If datagram marked as having more fragments
311             * or if this is not the first fragment,
312             * attempt reassembly; if it succeeds, proceed.
313             */
314            if (((struct ipasfrag *) ip)->ipf_mff & 1 || ip->ip_off) {
315                ipstat.ips_fragments++;
316                ip = ip_reass((struct ipasfrag *) ip, fp);
317                if (ip == 0)
318                    goto next;
319                ipstat.ips_reassembled++;
320                m = dtom(ip);
321            } else if (fp)
322                ip_freef(fp);
```

```
323        } else
324            ip->ip_len -= hlen;
```
                                                                                    ———— *ip_input.c*

Figure 10.11   `ipintr` function: fragment processing.

287–297   Net/3 keeps incomplete datagrams on the global doubly linked list, `ipq`. The name is somewhat confusing since the data structure isn't a queue. That is, insertions and deletions can occur anywhere in the list, not just at the ends. We'll use the term *list* to emphasize this fact.

  `ipintr` performs a linear search of the list to locate the appropriate datagram for the current fragment. Remember that fragments are uniquely identified by the 4-tuple: {`ip_id`, `ip_src`, `ip_dst`, `ip_p`}. Each entry in `ipq` is a list of fragments and `fp` points to the appropriate list if `ipintr` finds a match.

> Net/3 uses linear searches to access many of its data structures. While simple, this method can become a bottleneck in hosts supporting large numbers of network connections.

298–303   At `found`, the packet is modified by `ipintr` to facilitate reassembly:

304   • `ipintr` changes `ip_len` to exclude the standard IP header and any options. We must keep this in mind to avoid confusion with the standard interpretation of `ip_len`, which includes the standard header, options, and data. `ip_len` is also changed if the reassembly code is skipped because this is not a fragment.

305–307   • `ipintr` copies the MF flag into the low-order bit of `ipf_mff`, which overlays `ip_tos` (`&= ~1` clears the low-order bit only). Notice that `ip` must be cast to a pointer to an `ipasfrag` structure before `ipf_mff` is a valid member. Section 10.6 and Figure 10.14 describe the `ipasfrag` structure.

> Although RFC 1122 requires the IP layer to provide a mechanism that enables the transport layer to set `ip_tos` for every outgoing datagram, it only recommends that the IP layer pass `ip_tos` values to the transport layer at the destination host. Since the low-order bit of the TOS field must always be 0, it is available to hold the MF bit while `ip_off` (where the MF bit is normally found) is used by the reassembly algorithm.

  `ip_off` can now be accessed as a 16-bit offset instead of 3 flag bits and a 13-bit offset.

308   • `ip_off` is multiplied by 8 to convert from 8-byte to 1-byte units.

  `ipf_mff` and `ip_off` determine if `ipintr` should attempt reassembly. Figure 10.12 describes the different cases and the corresponding actions. Remember that `fp` points to the list of fragments the system has previously received for the datagram. Most of the work is done by `ip_reass`.

309–322   If `ip_reass` is able to assemble a complete datagram by combining the current fragment with previously received fragments, it returns a pointer to the reassembled datagram. If reassembly is not possible, `ip_reass` saves the fragment and `ipintr` jumps to `next` to process the next packet (Figure 8.12).

323–324   This `else` branch is taken when a complete datagram arrives and `ip_hlen` is modified as described earlier. This is the normal flow, since most received datagrams are not fragments.

ip_off	ipf_mff	fp	Description	Action
0	false	null	complete datagram	no assembly required
0	false	nonnull	complete datagram	discard the previous fragments
any	true	null	fragment of new datagram	initialize new fragment list with this fragment
any	true	nonnull	fragment of incomplete datagram	insert into existing fragment list, attempt reassembly
nonzero	false	null	tail fragment of new datagram	initialize new fragment list
nonzero	false	nonnull	tail fragment of incomplete datagram	insert into existing fragment list, attempt reassembly

Figure 10.12   IP fragment processing in `ipintr` and `ip_reass`.

If a complete datagram is available after reassembly processing, it is passed up to the appropriate transport protocol by `ipintr` (Figure 8.15):

```
(*inetsw[ip_protox[ip->ip_p]].pr_input)(m, hlen);
```

10.6   `ip_reass` Function

`ipintr` passes `ip_reass` a fragment to be processed, and a pointer to the matching reassembly header from `ipq`. `ip_reass` attempts to assemble and return a complete datagram or links the fragment into the datagram's reassembly list for reassembly when the remaining fragments arrive. The head of each reassembly list is an `ipq` structure, show in Figure 10.13.

```
                                                                      ─── ip_var.h
52 struct ipq {
53     struct ipq *next, *prev;    /* to other reass headers */
54     u_char  ipq_ttl;            /* time for reass q to live */
55     u_char  ipq_p;              /* protocol of this fragment */
56     u_short ipq_id;             /* sequence id for reassembly */
57     struct ipasfrag *ipq_next, *ipq_prev;
58     /* to ip headers of fragments */
59     struct in_addr ipq_src, ipq_dst;
60 };
                                                                      ─── ip_var.h
```

Figure 10.13   `ipq` structure.

52–60   The four fields required to identify a datagram's fragments, `ip_id`, `ip_p`, `ip_src`, and `ip_dst`, are kept in the `ipq` structure at the head of each reassembly list. Net/3 constructs the list of datagrams with `next` and `prev` and the list of fragments with `ipq_next` and `ipq_prev`.

The IP header of incoming IP packets is converted to an `ipasfrag` structure (Figure 10.14) before it is placed on a reassembly list.

```
                                                               ───────── ip_var.h
66 struct  ipasfrag {
67 #if BYTE_ORDER == LITTLE_ENDIAN
68     u_char  ip_hl:4,
69           ip_v:4;
70 #endif
71 #if BYTE_ORDER == BIG_ENDIAN
72     u_char  ip_v:4,
73           ip_hl:4;
74 #endif
75     u_char  ipf_mff;         /* XXX overlays ip_tos: use low bit
76                              * to avoid destroying tos;
77                              * copied from (ip_off&IP_MF) */
78     short   ip_len;
79     u_short ip_id;
80     short   ip_off;
81     u_char  ip_ttl;
82     u_char  ip_p;
83     u_short ip_sum;
84     struct  ipasfrag *ipf_next; /* next fragment */
85     struct  ipasfrag *ipf_prev; /* previous fragment */
86 };
                                                               ───────── ip_var.h
```

Figure 10.14 ipasfrag structure.

66–86   ip_reass collects fragments for a particular datagram on a circular doubly linked list joined by the ipf_next and ipf_prev members. These pointers overlay the source and destination addresses in the IP header. The ipf_mff member overlays ip_tos from the ip structure. The other members are the same.

Figure 10.15 illustrates the relationship between the fragment header list (ipq) and the fragments (ipasfrag).

Down the left side of Figure 10.15 is the list of reassembly headers. The first node in the list is the global ipq structure, ipq. It never has a fragment list associated with it. The ipq list is a doubly linked list used to support fast insertions and deletions. The next and prev pointers reference the next or previous ipq structure, which we have shown by terminating the arrows at the corners of the structures.

Each ipq structure is the head node of a circular doubly linked list of ipasfrag structures. Incoming fragments are placed on these fragment lists ordered by their fragment offset. We've highlighted the pointers for these lists in Figure 10.15.

Figure 10.15 still does not show all the complexity of the reassembly structures. The reassembly code is difficult to follow because it relies so heavily on casting pointers to three different structures on the underlying mbuf. We've seen this technique already, for example, when an ip structure overlays the data portion of an mbuf.

Figure 10.16 illustrates the relationship between an mbuf, an ipq structure, an ipasfrag structure, and an ip structure.

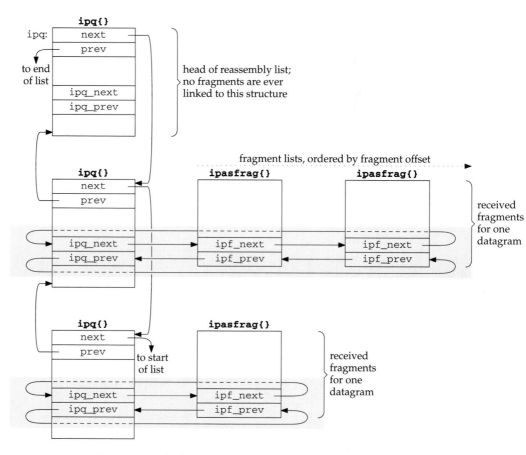

Figure 10.15 The fragment header list, ipq, and fragments.

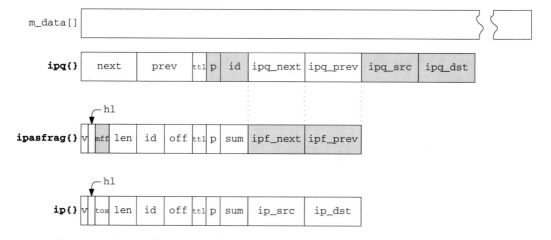

Figure 10.16 An area of memory can be accessed through multiple structures.

A lot of information is contained within Figure 10.16:

- All the structures are located within the data area of an mbuf.
- The ipq list consists of ipq structures joined by next and prev. Within the structure, the four fields that uniquely identify an IP datagram are saved (shaded in Figure 10.16).
- Each ipq structure is treated as an ipasfrag structure when accessed as the head of a linked list of fragments. The fragments are joined by ipf_next and ipf_prev, which overlay the ipq structures' ipq_next and ipq_prev members.
- Each ipasfrag structure overlays the ip structure from the incoming fragment. The data that arrived with the fragment follows the structure in the mbuf. The members that have a different meaning in the ipasfrag structure than they do in the ip structure are shaded.

Figure 10.15 showed the physical connections between the reassembly structures and Figure 10.16 illustrated the overlay technique used by ip_reass. In Figure 10.17 we show the reassembly structures from a logical point of view: this figure shows the reassembly of three datagrams and the relationship between the ipq list and the ipasfrag structures.

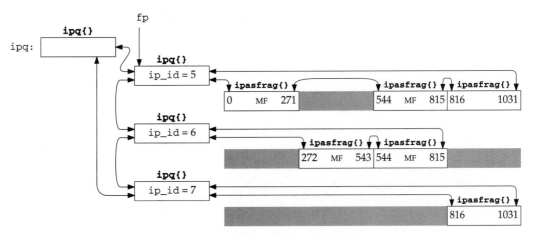

Figure 10.17   Reassembly of three IP datagrams.

The head of each reassembly list contains the id, protocol, source, and destination address of the original datagram. Only the ip_id field is shown in the figure. Each fragment list is ordered by the offset field, the fragment is labeled with MF if the MF bit is set, and missing fragments appear as shaded boxes. The numbers within each fragment show the starting and ending byte offset for the fragment relative to the *data portion* of the original datagram, not to the IP header of the original datagram.

The example is constructed to show three UDP datagrams with no IP options and 1024 bytes of data each. The total length of each datagram is 1052 (20 + 8 + 1024) bytes, which is well within the 1500-byte MTU of an Ethernet. The datagrams encounter a SLIP link on the way to the destination, and the router at that link fragments the datagrams to fit within a typical 296-byte SLIP MTU. Each datagram arrives as four fragments. The first fragment contain a standard 20-byte IP header, the 8-byte UDP header, and 264 bytes of data. The second and third fragments contain a 20-byte IP header and 272 bytes of data. The last fragment has a 20-byte header and 216 bytes of data ($1032 = 272 \times 3 + 216$).

In Figure 10.17, datagram 5 is missing a single fragment containing bytes 272 through 543. Datagram 6 is missing the first fragment, bytes 0 through 271, and the end of the datagram starting at offset 816. Datagram 7 is missing the first three fragments, bytes 0 through 815.

Figure 10.18 lists `ip_reass`. Remember that `ipintr` calls `ip_reass` when an IP fragment has arrived for this host, and after any options have been processed.

```
                                                                ─── ip_input.c
337 /*
338  * Take incoming datagram fragment and try to
339  * reassemble it into whole datagram.  If a chain for
340  * reassembly of this datagram already exists, then it
341  * is given as fp; otherwise have to make a chain.
342  */
343 struct ip *
344 ip_reass(ip, fp)
345 struct ipasfrag *ip;
346 struct ipq *fp;
347 {
348     struct mbuf *m = dtom(ip);
349     struct ipasfrag *q;
350     struct mbuf *t;
351     int     hlen = ip->ip_hl << 2;
352     int     i, next;

353     /*
354      * Presence of header sizes in mbufs
355      * would confuse code below.
356      */
357     m->m_data += hlen;
358     m->m_len -= hlen;
```

```
                            /* reassembly code */
```

```
465     dropfrag:
466     ipstat.ips_fragdropped++;
467     m_freem(m);
468     return (0);
469 }
                                                                ─── ip_input.c
```

Figure 10.18   `ip_reass` function: datagram reassembly.

343–358   When `ip_reass` is called, `ip` points to the fragment and `fp` either points to the matching `ipq` structure or is null.

Since reassembly involves only the data portion of each fragment, ip_reass adjusts m_data and m_len from the mbuf containing the fragment to exclude the IP header in each fragment.

465–469   When an error occurs during reassembly, the function jumps to dropfrag, which increments ips_fragdropped, discards the fragment, and returns a null pointer.

Dropping fragments usually incurs a serious performance penalty at the transport layer since the entire datagram must be retransmitted. TCP is careful to avoid fragmentation, but a UDP application must take steps to avoid fragmentation on its own. [Kent and Mogul 1987] explain why fragmentation should be avoided.

All IP implementations must to be able to reassemble a datagram of up to 576 bytes. There is no general way to determine the size of the largest datagram that can be reassembled by a remote host. We'll see in Section 27.5 that TCP has a mechanism to determine the size of the maximum datagram that can be processed by the remote host. UDP has no such mechanism, so many UDP-based protocols (e.g., RIP, TFTP, BOOTP, SNMP, and DNS) are designed around the 576-byte limit.

We'll show the reassembly code in seven parts, starting with Figure 10.19.

```
                                                            ─────────── ip_input.c
359      /*
360       * If first fragment to arrive, create a reassembly queue.
361       */
362      if (fp == 0) {
363          if ((t = m_get(M_DONTWAIT, MT_FTABLE)) == NULL)
364              goto dropfrag;
365          fp = mtod(t, struct ipq *);
366          insque(fp, &ipq);
367          fp->ipq_ttl = IPFRAGTTL;
368          fp->ipq_p = ip->ip_p;
369          fp->ipq_id = ip->ip_id;
370          fp->ipq_next = fp->ipq_prev = (struct ipasfrag *) fp;
371          fp->ipq_src = ((struct ip *) ip)->ip_src;
372          fp->ipq_dst = ((struct ip *) ip)->ip_dst;
373          q = (struct ipasfrag *) fp;
374          goto insert;
375      }
                                                            ─────────── ip_input.c
```

Figure 10.19 ip_reass function: create reassembly list.

Create reassembly list

359–366   When fp is null, ip_reass creates a reassembly list with the first fragment of the new datagram. It allocates an mbuf to hold the head of the new list (an ipq structure), and calls insque to insert the structure in the list of reassembly lists.

Figure 10.20 lists the functions that manipulate the datagram and fragment lists.

> The functions insque and remque are defined in machdep.c for the 386 version of Net/3. Each machine has its own machdep.c file in which customized versions of kernel functions are defined, typically to improve performance. This file also contains architecture-dependent functions such as the interrupt handler support, cpu and device configuration, and memory management functions.

Function	Description
insque	Insert *node* just after *prev*. void **insque**(void *node, void *prev);
remque	Remove *node* from list. void **remque**(void *node);
ip_enq	Insert fragment *p* just after fragment *prev*. void **ip_enq**(struct ipasfrag *p, struct ipasfrag *prev);
ip_deq	Remove fragment *p*. void **ip_deq**(struct ipasfrag *p);

Figure 10.20   Queueing functions used by ip_reass.

insque and remque exist primarily to maintain the kernel's run queue. Net/3 can use them for the datagram reassembly list because both lists have next and previous pointers as the first two members of their respective node structures. These functions work for any similarly structured list, although the compiler may issue some warnings. This is yet another example of accessing memory through two different structures.

In all the kernel structures the next pointer always precedes the previous pointer (Figure 10.14, for example). This is because the insque and remque functions were first implemented on the VAX using the insque and remque hardware instructions, which require this ordering of the forward and backward pointers.

The fragment lists are not joined with the first two members of the ipasfrag structures (Figure 10.14) so Net/3 calls ip_enq and ip_deq instead of insque and remque.

Reassembly timeout

367   The time-to-live field (ipq_ttl) is required by RFC 1122 and limits the time Net/3 waits for fragments to complete a datagram. It is different from the TTL field in the IP header, which limits the amount of time a packet circulates in the internet. The IP header TTL field is reused as the reassembly timeout since the header TTL is not needed once the fragment arrives at its final destination.

In Net/3, the initial value of the reassembly timeout is 60 (IPFRAGTTL). Since ipq_ttl is decremented every time the kernel calls ip_slowtimo and the kernel calls ip_slowtimo every 500 ms, the system discards an IP reassembly list if it hasn't assembled a complete IP datagram within 30 seconds of receiving any one of the datagram's fragments. The reassembly timer starts ticking on the first call to ip_slowtimo after the list is created.

RFC 1122 recommends that the reassembly time be between 60 and 120 seconds and that an ICMP time exceeded error be sent to the source host if the timer expires and the first fragment of the datagram has been received. The header and options of the other fragments are always discarded during reassembly and an ICMP error must contain the first 64 bits of the erroneous datagram (or less if the datagram was shorter than 8 bytes). So, if the kernel hasn't received fragment 0, it can't send an ICMP message.

Net/3's timer is a bit too short and Net/3 neglects to send the ICMP message when a fragment is discarded. The requirement to return the first 64 bits of the datagram ensures that the first portion of the transport header is included, which allows the error message to be returned to the application that generated it. Note that TCP and UDP purposely put their port numbers in the first 8 bytes of their headers for this reason.

Datagram identifiers

368–375   ip_reass saves ip_p, ip_id, ip_src, and ip_dst in the ipq structure allocated for this datagram, points the ipq_next and ipq_prev pointers to the ipq structure (i.e., it constructs a circular list with one node), points q at this structure, and jumps to insert (Figure 10.25) where it inserts the first fragment, ip, into the new reassembly list.

The next part of ip_reass, shown in Figure 10.21, is executed when fp is not null and locates the correct position in the existing list for the new fragment.

```
                                                                                    ─ ip_input.c
376      /*
377       * Find a fragment which begins after this one does.
378       */
379      for (q = fp->ipq_next; q != (struct ipasfrag *) fp; q = q->ipf_next)
380          if (q->ip_off > ip->ip_off)
381              break;
                                                                                    ─ ip_input.c
```

Figure 10.21 ip_reass function: find position in reassembly list.

376–381   Since fp is not null, the for loop searches the datagram's fragment list to locate a fragment with an offset greater than ip_off.

The byte ranges contained within fragments may overlap at the destination. This can happen when a transport-layer protocol retransmits a datagram that gets sent along a route different from the one followed by the original datagram. The fragmentation pattern may also be different resulting in overlaps at the destination. The transport protocol must be able to force IP to use the original ID field in order for the datagram to be recognized as a retransmission at the destination.

Net/3 does not provide a mechanism for a transport protocol to ensure that IP ID fields are reused on a retransmitted datagram. ip_output always assigns a new value by incrementing the global integer ip_id when preparing a new datagram (Figure 8.22). Nevertheless, a Net/3 system could receive overlapping fragments from a system that lets the transport layer retransmit IP datagrams with the same ID field.

Figure 10.22 illustrates the different ways in which the fragment may overlap with existing fragments. The fragments are numbered according to the order in which they *arrive* at the destination host. The reassembled fragment is shown at the bottom of Figure 10.22 The shaded areas of the fragments are the duplicate bytes that are discarded.

In the following discussion, an *earlier* fragment is a fragment that previously arrived at the host.

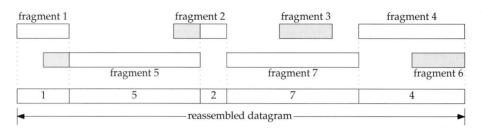

Figure 10.22   The byte range of fragments may overlap at the destination.

The code in Figure 10.23 trims or discards incoming fragments.

382–396   `ip_reass` discards bytes that overlap the end of an earlier fragment by trimming the new fragment (the front of fragment 5 in Figure 10.22) or discarding the new fragment (fragment 6) if all its bytes arrived in an earlier fragment (fragment 4).

The code in Figure 10.24 trims or discards existing fragments.

397–412   If the current fragment partially overlaps the front of an earlier fragment, the duplicate data is trimmed from the earlier fragment (the front of fragment 2 in Figure 10.22). Any earlier fragments that are completely overlapped by the arriving fragment are discarded (fragment 3).

In Figure 10.25, the incoming fragment is inserted into the reassembly list.

413–426   After trimming, `ip_enq` inserts the fragment into the list and the list is scanned to determine if all the fragments have arrived. If any fragment is missing, or the last fragment in the list has `ipf_mff` set, `ip_reass` returns 0 and waits for more fragments.

When the current fragment completes a datagram, the entire list is converted to an mbuf chain by the code shown in Figure 10.26.

427–440   If all the fragments for the datagram have been received, the `while` loop reconstructs the datagram from the fragments with `m_cat`.

Figure 10.27 shows the relationships between mbufs and the `ipq` structure for a datagram composed of three fragments.

The darkest areas in the figure mark the data portions of a packet and the lighter shaded areas mark the unused portions of the mbufs. We show three fragments each contained in a chain of two mbufs; a packet header, and a cluster. The `m_data` pointer in the first mbuf of each fragment points to the packet data, not the packet header. Therefore, the mbuf chain constructed by `m_cat` includes only the data portion of the fragments.

This is the typical scenario when a fragment contains more than 208 bytes of data (Section 2.6). The "frag" portion of the mbufs is the IP header from the fragment. The `m_data` pointer of the first mbuf in each chain points beyond "opts" because of the code in Figure 10.18.

Figure 10.28 shows the reassembled datagram using the mbufs from all the fragments. Notice that the IP header and options from fragments 2 and 3 are not included in the reassembled datagram.

```
                                                      ──────────── ip_input.c
382       /*
383        * If there is a preceding fragment, it may provide some of
384        * our data already.  If so, drop the data from the incoming
385        * fragment.  If it provides all of our data, drop us.
386        */
387       if (q->ipf_prev != (struct ipasfrag *) fp) {
388           i = q->ipf_prev->ip_off + q->ipf_prev->ip_len - ip->ip_off;
389           if (i > 0) {
390               if (i >= ip->ip_len)
391                   goto dropfrag;
392               m_adj(dtom(ip), i);
393               ip->ip_off += i;
394               ip->ip_len -= i;
395           }
396       }
                                                      ──────────── ip_input.c
```

Figure 10.23   ip_reass function: trim incoming packet.

```
                                                      ──────────── ip_input.c
397       /*
398        * While we overlap succeeding fragments trim them or,
399        * if they are completely covered, dequeue them.
400        */
401       while (q != (struct ipasfrag *) fp && ip->ip_off + ip->ip_len > q->ip_off) {
402           i = (ip->ip_off + ip->ip_len) - q->ip_off;
403           if (i < q->ip_len) {
404               q->ip_len -= i;
405               q->ip_off += i;
406               m_adj(dtom(q), i);
407               break;
408           }
409           q = q->ipf_next;
410           m_freem(dtom(q->ipf_prev));
411           ip_deq(q->ipf_prev);
412       }
                                                      ──────────── ip_input.c
```

Figure 10.24   ip_reass function: trim existing packets.

```
                                                      ──────────── ip_input.c
413   insert:
414       /*
415        * Stick new fragment in its place;
416        * check for complete reassembly.
417        */
418       ip_enq(ip, q->ipf_prev);
419       next = 0;
420       for (q = fp->ipq_next; q != (struct ipasfrag *) fp; q = q->ipf_next) {
421           if (q->ip_off != next)
422               return (0);
423           next += q->ip_len;
424       }
425       if (q->ipf_prev->ipf_mff & 1)
426           return (0);
                                                      ──────────── ip_input.c
```

Figure 10.25   ip_reass function: insert packet.

—————————————————————————— ip_input.c

```
427    /*
428     * Reassembly is complete; concatenate fragments.
429     */
430    q = fp->ipq_next;
431    m = dtom(q);
432    t = m->m_next;
433    m->m_next = 0;
434    m_cat(m, t);
435    q = q->ipf_next;
436    while (q != (struct ipasfrag *) fp) {
437        t = dtom(q);
438        q = q->ipf_next;
439        m_cat(m, t);
440    }
```

—————————————————————————— ip_input.c

Figure 10.26   ip_reass function: reassemble datagram.

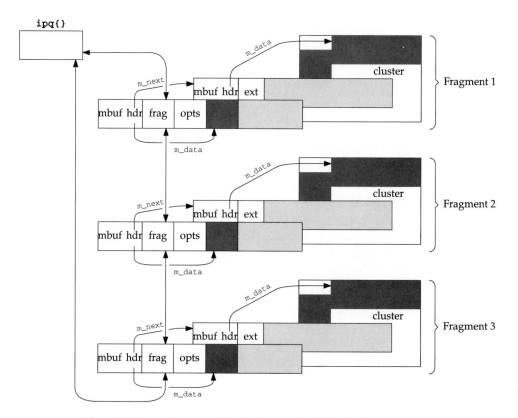

Figure 10.27   m_cat reassembles the fragments within mbufs.

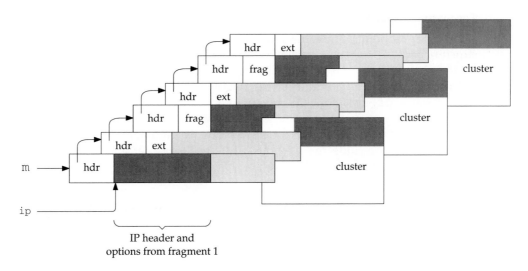

Figure 10.28   The reassembled datagram.

The header of the first fragment is still being used as an `ipasfrag` structure. It is restored to a valid IP datagram header by the code shown in Figure 10.29.

ip_input.c
```
441     /*
442      * Create header for new ip packet by
443      * modifying header of first packet;
444      * dequeue and discard fragment reassembly header.
445      * Make header visible.
446      */
447     ip = fp->ipq_next;
448     ip->ip_len = next;
449     ip->ipf_mff &= ~1;
450     ((struct ip *) ip)->ip_src = fp->ipq_src;
451     ((struct ip *) ip)->ip_dst = fp->ipq_dst;
452     remque(fp);
453     (void) m_free(dtom(fp));
454     m = dtom(ip);
455     m->m_len += (ip->ip_hl << 2);
456     m->m_data -= (ip->ip_hl << 2);
457     /* some debugging cruft by sklower, below, will go away soon */
458     if (m->m_flags & M_PKTHDR) {    /* XXX this should be done elsewhere */
459         int     plen = 0;
460         for (t = m; m; m = m->m_next)
461             plen += m->m_len;
462         t->m_pkthdr.len = plen;
463     }
464     return ((struct ip *) ip);
```
ip_input.c

Figure 10.29   `ip_reass` function: datagram reassembly.

Reconstruct datagram header

441–456   ip_reass points ip to the first fragment in the list and changes the ipasfrag structure back to an ip structure by restoring the length of the datagram to ip_len, the source address to ip_src, the destination address to ip_dst; and by clearing the low-order bit in ipf_mff. (Recall from Figure 10.14 that ipf_mff in the ipasfrag structure overlays ipf_tos in the ip structure.)

ip_reass removes the entire packet from the reassembly list with remque, discards the ipq structure that was the head of the list, and adjusts m_len and m_data in the first mbuf to include the previously hidden IP header and options from the first fragment.

Compute packet length

457–464   The code here is always executed, since the first mbuf for the datagram is always a packet header. The for loop computes the number of data bytes in the mbuf chain and saves the value in m_pkthdr.len.

The purpose of the *copied* bit in the option type field should be clear now. Since the only options retained at the destination are those that appear in the first fragment, only options that control processing of the packet as it travels toward its destination are copied. Options that collect information while in transit are not copied, since the information collected is discarded at the destination when the packet is reassembled.

10.7   ip_slowtimo Function

As shown in Section 7.4, each protocol in Net/3 may specify a function to be called every 500 ms. For IP, that function is ip_slowtimo, shown in Figure 10.30, which times out the fragments on the reassembly list.

515–534   ip_slowtimo traverses the list of partial datagrams and decrements the reassembly TTL field. ip_freef is called if the field drops to 0 to discard the fragments associated with the datagram. ip_slowtimo runs at splnet to prevent the lists from being modified by incoming packets.

ip_freef is shown in Figure 10.31.

470–486   ip_freef removes and releases every fragment on the list pointed to by fp and then releases the list itself.

ip_drain Function

In Figure 7.14 we showed that IP defines ip_drain as the function to be called when the kernel needs additional memory. This usually occurs during mbuf allocation, which we described with Figure 2.13. ip_drain is shown in Figure 10.32.

538–545   The simplest way for IP to release memory is to discard all the IP fragments on the reassembly list. For IP fragments that belong to a TCP segment, TCP eventually retransmits the data. IP fragments that belong to a UDP datagram are lost and UDP-based protocols must handle this at the application layer.

```
515 void                                                              ip_input.c
516 ip_slowtimo(void)
517 {
518     struct ipq *fp;
519     int     s = splnet();

520     fp = ipq.next;
521     if (fp == 0) {
522         splx(s);
523         return;
524     }
525     while (fp != &ipq) {
526         --fp->ipq_ttl;
527         fp = fp->next;
528         if (fp->prev->ipq_ttl == 0) {
529             ipstat.ips_fragtimeout++;
530             ip_freef(fp->prev);
531         }
532     }
533     splx(s);
534 }
```
                                                                      ip_input.c

Figure 10.30 ip_slowtimo function.

```
474 void                                                              ip_input.c
475 ip_freef(fp)
476 struct ipq *fp;
477 {
478     struct ipasfrag *q, *p;

479     for (q = fp->ipq_next; q != (struct ipasfrag *) fp; q = p) {
480         p = q->ipf_next;
481         ip_deq(q);
482         m_freem(dtom(q));
483     }
484     remque(fp);
485     (void) m_free(dtom(fp));
486 }
```
                                                                      ip_input.c

Figure 10.31 ip_freef function.

```
538 void                                                              ip_input.c
539 ip_drain()
540 {
541     while (ipq.next != &ipq) {
542         ipstat.ips_fragdropped++;
543         ip_freef(ipq.next);
544     }
545 }
```
                                                                      ip_input.c

Figure 10.32 ip_drain function.

10.8 Summary

In this chapter we showed how `ip_output` splits an outgoing datagram into fragments
if it is too large to be transmitted on the selected network. Since fragments may themselves be fragmented as they travel toward their final destination and may take multiple
paths, only the destination host can reassemble the original datagram.

`ip_reass` accepts incoming fragments and attempts to reassemble datagrams. If it
is successful, the datagram is passed back to `ipintr` and then to the appropriate transport protocol. Every IP implementation must reassemble datagrams of up to 576 bytes.
The only limit for Net/3 is the number of mbufs that are available. `ip_slowtimo` discards incomplete datagrams when all their fragments haven't been received within a
reasonable amount of time.

Exercises

10.1   Modify `ip_slowtimo` to send an ICMP time exceeded message when it discards an
incomplete datagram (Figure 11.1).

10.2   The recorded route in a fragmented datagram may be different in each fragment. When a
datagram is reassembled at the destination host, which return route is available to the
transport protocols?

10.3   Draw a picture showing the mbufs involved in the `ipq` structure and its associated fragment list for the fragment with an ID of 7 in Figure 10.17.

10.4   [Auerbach 1994] suggests that after fragmenting a datagram, the last fragment should be
sent first. If the receiving system gets that last fragment first, it can use the offset to allocate an appropriately sized reassembly buffer for the datagram. Modify `ip_output` to
send the last fragment first.

> [Auerbach 1994] notes that some commercial TCP/IP implementations have been known to
> crash if they receive the last fragment first.

10.5   Use the statistics in Figure 8.5 to answer the following questions. What is the average
number of fragments per reassembled datagram? What is the average number of fragments created when an outgoing datagram is fragmented?

10.6   What happens to a packet when the reserved bit in `ip_off` is set?

11

ICMP: Internet Control Message Protocol

11.1 Introduction

ICMP communicates error and administrative messages between IP systems and is an integral and required part of any IP implementation. The specification for ICMP appears in RFC 792 [Postel 1981b]. RFC 950 [Mogul and Postel 1985] and RFC 1256 [Deering 1991a] define additional ICMP message types. RFC 1122 [Braden 1989a] also provides important details on ICMP.

ICMP has its own transport protocol number (1) allowing ICMP messages to be carried within an IP datagram. Application programs can send and receive ICMP messages directly through the raw IP interface discussed in Chapter 32.

We can divide the ICMP messages into two classes: errors and queries. Query messages are defined in pairs: a request and its reply. ICMP error messages always include the IP header (and options) along with at least the first 8 bytes of the data from the initial fragment of the IP datagram that caused the error. The standard assumes that the 8 bytes includes any demultiplexing information from the transport protocol header of the original packet, which allows a transport protocol to deliver an ICMP error to the correct process.

TCP and UDP port numbers appear within the first 8 bytes of their respective headers.

Figure 11.1 shows all the currently defined ICMP messages. The messages above the double line are ICMP requests and replies; those below the double line are ICMP errors.

type and code	Description	PRC_
ICMP_ECHO	echo request	
ICMP_ECHOREPLY	echo reply	
ICMP_TSTAMP	timestamp request	
ICMP_TSTAMPREPLY	timestamp reply	
ICMP_MASKREQ	address mask request	
ICMP_MASKREPLY	address mask reply	
ICMP_IREQ	information request (obsolete)	
ICMP_IREQREPLY	information reply (obsolete)	
ICMP_ROUTERADVERT	router advertisement	
ICMP_ROUTERSOLICIT	router solicitation	
ICMP_REDIRECT	better route available	
ICMP_REDIRECT_NET	better route available for network	PRC_REDIRECT_HOST
ICMP_REDIRECT_HOST	better route available for host	PRC_REDIRECT_HOST
ICMP_REDIRECT_TOSNET	better route available for TOS and network	PRC_REDIRECT_HOST
ICMP_REDIRECT_TOSHOST	better route available for TOS and host	PRC_REDIRECT_HOST
other	unrecognized code	
ICMP_UNREACH	destination unreachable	
ICMP_UNREACH_NET	network unreachable	PRC_UNREACH_NET
ICMP_UNREACH_HOST	host unreachable	PRC_UNREACH_HOST
ICMP_UNREACH_PROTOCOL	protocol unavailable at destination	PRC_UNREACH_PROTOCOL
ICMP_UNREACH_PORT	port inactive at destination	PRC_UNREACH_PORT
ICMP_UNREACH_SRCFAIL	source route failed	PRC_UNREACH_SRCFAIL
ICMP_UNREACH_NEEDFRAG	fragmentation needed and DF bit set	PRC_MSGSIZE
ICMP_UNREACH_NET_UNKNOWN	destination network unknown	PRC_UNREACH_NET
ICMP_UNREACH_HOST_UNKNOWN	destination host unknown	PRC_UNREACH_HOST
ICMP_UNREACH_ISOLATED	source host isolated	PRC_UNREACH_HOST
ICMP_UNREACH_NET_PROHIB	communication with destination network administratively prohibited	PRC_UNREACH_NET
ICMP_UNREACH_HOST_PROHIB	communication with destination host administratively prohibited	PRC_UNREACH_HOST
ICMP_UNREACH_TOSNET	network unreachable for type of service	PRC_UNREACH_NET
ICMP_UNREACH_TOSHOST	host unreachable for type of service	PRC_UNREACH_HOST
13	communication administratively prohibited by filtering	
14	host precedence violation	
15	precedence cutoff in effect	
other	unrecognized code	
ICMP_TIMXCEED	time exceeded	
ICMP_TIMXCEED_INTRANS	IP time-to-live expired in transit	PRC_TIMXCEED_INTRANS
ICMP_TIMXCEED_REASS	reassembly time-to-live expired	PRC_TIMXCEED_REASS
other	unrecognized code	
ICMP_PARAMPROB	problem with IP header	
0	unspecified header error	PRC_PARAMPROB
ICMP_PARAMPROB_OPTABSENT	required option missing	PRC_PARAMPROB
other	byte offset of invalid byte	
ICMP_SOURCEQUENCH	request to slow transmission	PRC_QUENCH
other	unrecognized type	

Figure 11.1 ICMP message types and codes.

type **and** code	icmp_input	UDP	TCP	errno
ICMP_ECHO *ICMP_ECHOREPLY*	icmp_reflect rip_input			
ICMP_TSTAMP *ICMP_TSTAMPREPLY*	icmp_reflect rip_input			
ICMP_MASKREQ *ICMP_MASKREPLY*	icmp_reflect rip_input			
ICMP_IREQ *ICMP_IREQREPLY*	rip_input rip_input			
ICMP_ROUTERADVERT *ICMP_ROUTERSOLICIT*	rip_input rip_input			

ICMP_REDIRECT
    ICMP_REDIRECT_NET
    ICMP_REDIRECT_HOST
    ICMP_REDIRECT_TOSNET
    ICMP_REDIRECT_TOSHOST
    other
	
	 pfctlinput
	 pfctlinput
	 pfctlinput
	 pfctlinput
	 rip_input
		
		 in_rtchange
		 in_rtchange
		 in_rtchange
		 in_rtchange
			
			 in_rtchange
			 in_rtchange
			 in_rtchange
			 in_rtchange	

ICMP_UNREACH
    ICMP_UNREACH_NET
    ICMP_UNREACH_HOST
    ICMP_UNREACH_PROTOCOL
    ICMP_UNREACH_PORT
    ICMP_UNREACH_SRCFAIL
    ICMP_UNREACH_NEEDFRAG
    ICMP_UNREACH_NET_UNKNOWN
    ICMP_UNREACH_HOST_UNKNOWN
    ICMP_UNREACH_ISOLATED
    ICMP_UNREACH_NET_PROHIB
 	
    ICMP_UNREACH_HOST_PROHIB
 	
    ICMP_UNREACH_TOSNET
    ICMP_UNREACH_TOSHOST
    13
 	
    14
    15
    other
	
	 pr_ctlinput
	 pr_ctlinput
	 pr_ctlinput
	 pr_ctlinput
	 pr_ctlinput
	 pr_ctlinput
	 pr_ctlinput
	 pr_ctlinput
	 pr_ctlinput
	 pr_ctlinput
	
	 pr_ctlinput
	
	 pr_ctlinput
	 pr_ctlinput
	 rip_input
	
	 rip_input
	 rip_input
	 rip_input
		
		 udp_notify
		 udp_notify
		 udp_notify
		 udp_notify
		 udp_notify
		 udp_notify
		 udp_notify
		 udp_notify
		 udp_notify
		 udp_notify
		
		 udp_notify
		
		 udp_notify
		 udp_notify
			
			 tcp_notify
			 tcp_notify
			 tcp_notify
			 tcp_notify
			 tcp_notify
			 tcp_notify
			 tcp_notify
			 tcp_notify
			 tcp_notify
			 tcp_notify
			
			 tcp_notify
			
			 tcp_notify
			 tcp_notify
				
				 EHOSTUNREACH
				 EHOSTUNREACH
				 ECONNREFUSED
				 ECONNREFUSED
				 EHOSTUNREACH
				 EMSGSIZE
				 EHOSTUNREACH
				 EHOSTUNREACH
				 EHOSTUNREACH
				 EHOSTUNREACH
				
				 EHOSTUNREACH
				
				 EHOSTUNREACH
				 EHOSTUNREACH

ICMP_TIMXCEED
    ICMP_TIMXCEED_INTRANS
    ICMP_TIMXCEED_REASS
    other
	
	 pr_ctlinput
	 pr_ctlinput
	 rip_input
		
		 udp_notify
		 udp_notify
			
			 tcp_notify
			 tcp_notify	

ICMP_PARAMPROB
    0
    ICMP_PARAMPROB_OPTABSENT
    other
	
	 pr_ctlinput
	 pr_ctlinput
	 rip_input
		
		 udp_notify
		 udp_notify
			
			 tcp_notify
			 tcp_notify
				
				 ENOPROTOOPT
				 ENOPROTOOPT

ICMP_SOURCEQUENCH	pr_ctlinput	udp_notify	tcp_quench	
other	rip_input			

Figure 11.2 ICMP message types and codes (continued).

Figures 11.1 and 11.2 contain a lot of information:

- The `PRC_` column shows the mapping between the ICMP messages and the protocol-independent error codes processed by Net/3 (Section 11.6). This column is blank for requests and replies, since no error is generated in that case. If this column is blank for an ICMP error, the code is not recognized by Net/3 and the error message is silently discarded.

- Figure 11.3 shows where we discuss each of the functions listed in Figure 11.2.

Function	Description	Reference
icmp_reflect	generate reply to ICMP request	Section 11.12
in_rtchange	update IP routing tables	Figure 22.34
pfctlinput	report error to all protocols	Section 7.7
pr_ctlinput	report error to the protocol associated with the socket	Section 7.4
rip_input	process unrecognized ICMP messages	Section 32.5
tcp_notify	ignore or report error to process	Figure 27.12
tcp_quench	slow down the output	Figure 27.13
udp_notify	report error to process	Figure 23.31

Figure 11.3   Functions called during ICMP input processing.

- The `icmp_input` column shows the function called by `icmp_input` for each ICMP message.

- The UDP column shows the functions that process ICMP messages for UDP sockets.

- The TCP column shows the functions that process ICMP messages for TCP sockets. Note that ICMP source quench errors are handled by `tcp_quench`, not `tcp_notify`.

- If the `errno` column is blank, the kernel does not report the ICMP message to the process.

- The last line in the tables shows that unrecognized ICMP messages are delivered to the raw IP protocol where they may be received by processes that have arranged to receive ICMP messages.

In Net/3, ICMP is implemented as a transport-layer protocol above IP and does not generate errors or requests; it formats and sends these messages on behalf of the other protocols. ICMP passes incoming errors and replies to the appropriate transport protocol or to processes that are waiting for ICMP messages. On the other hand, ICMP responds to most incoming ICMP requests with an appropriate ICMP reply. Figure 11.4 summarizes this information.

ICMP message type	Incoming	Outgoing
request	kernel responds with reply	generated by a process
reply	passed to raw IP	generated by kernel
error	passed to transport protocols and raw IP	generated by IP or transport protocols
unknown	passed to raw IP	generated by a process

Figure 11.4   ICMP message processing.

11.2 Code Introduction

The two files listed in Figure 11.5 contain the ICMP data structures, statistics, and processing code described in this chapter.

File	Description
netinet/ip_icmp.h	ICMP structure definitions
netinet/ip_icmp.c	ICMP processing

Figure 11.5   Files discussed in this chapter.

Global Variables

The global variables shown in Figure 11.6 are introduced in this chapter.

Variable	Type	Description
icmpmaskrepl	int	enables the return of ICMP address mask replies
icmpstat	struct icmpstat	ICMP statistics (Figure 11.7)

Figure 11.6   Global variables introduced in this chapter.

Statistics

Statistics are collected by the members of the `icmpstat` structure shown in Figure 11.7.

`icmpstat` member	Description	Used by SNMP
`icps_oldicmp` `icps_oldshort`	#errors discarded because datagram was an ICMP message #errors discarded because IP datagram was too short	• •

`icps_badcode`
`icps_badlen`
`icps_checksum`
`icps_tooshort`
	#ICMP messages discarded because of an invalid code
	#ICMP messages discarded because of an invalid ICMP body
	#ICMP messages discarded because of a bad ICMP checksum
	#ICMP messages discarded because of a short ICMP header
		•
		•
		•
		•

`icps_outhist[]` `icps_inhist[]`	array of output counters; one for each ICMP type array of input counters; one for each ICMP type	• •
`icps_error` `icps_reflect`	#of calls to `icmp_error` (excluding redirects) #ICMP messages reflected by the kernel	

Figure 11.7   Statistics collected in this chapter.

We'll see where these counters are incremented as we proceed through the code.

Figure 11.8 shows some sample output of these statistics, from the `netstat -s` command.

`netstat -s` output	`icmpstat` member
84124 calls to icmp_error	`icps_error`
0 errors not generated 'cuz old message was icmp	`icps_oldicmp`
Output histogram:	`icps_outhist[]`
echo reply: 11770	`ICMP_ECHOREPLY`
destination unreachable: 84118	`ICMP_UNREACH`
time exceeded: 6	`ICMP_TIMXCEED`
6 messages with bad code fields	`icps_badcode`
0 messages < minimum length	`icps_badlen`
0 bad checksums	`icps_checksum`
143 messages with bad length	`icps_tooshort`
Input histogram:	`icps_inhist[]`
echo reply: 793	`ICMP_ECHOREPLY`
destination unreachable: 305869	`ICMP_UNREACH`
source quench: 621	`ICMP_SOURCEQUENCH`
routing redirect: 103	`ICMP_REDIRECT`
echo: 11770	`ICMP_ECHO`
time exceeded: 25296	`ICMP_TIMXCEED`
11770 message responses generated	`icps_reflect`

Figure 11.8   Sample ICMP statistics.

SNMP Variables

Figure 11.9 shows the relationship between the variables in the SNMP ICMP group and the statistics collected by Net/3.

SNMP variable	`icmpstat` member	Description
`icmpInMsgs`	see text	#ICMP messages received

`icmpInErrors`	`icps_badcode +`
	`icps_badlen +`
	`icps_checksum +`
	`icps_tooshort`
		#ICMP messages discarded because of an error

`icmpInDestUnreachs`
`icmpInTimeExcds`
`icmpInParmProbs`
`icmpInSrcQuenchs`
`icmpInRedirects`
`icmpInEchos`
`icmpInEchoReps`
`icmpInTimestamps`
`icmpInTimestampReps`
`icmpInAddrMasks`
`icmpInAddrMaskReps`
	`icps_inhist[]` counter	#ICMP messages received for each type

`icmpOutMsgs`
`icmpOutErrors`
	see text
	`icps_oldicmp +`
	`icps_oldshort`
		#ICMP messages sent
		#ICMP errors not sent because of an error

`icmpOutDestUnreachs`
`icmpOutTimeExcds`
`icmpOutParmProbs`
`icmpOutSrcQuenchs`
`icmpOutRedirects`
`icmpOutEchos`
`icmpOutEchoReps`
`icmpOutTimestamps`
`icmpOutTimestampReps`
`icmpOutAddrMasks`
`icmpOutAddrMaskReps`
	`icps_outhist[]` counter	#ICMP messages sent for each type

Figure 11.9   Simple SNMP variables in ICMP group.

`icmpInMsgs` is the sum of the counts in the `icps_inhist` array and `icmpInErrors`, and `icmpOutMsgs` is the sum of the counts in the `icps_outhist` array and `icmpOutErrors`.

11.3 `icmp` Structure

Net/3 accesses an ICMP message through the `icmp` structure shown in Figure 11.10.

ip_icmp.h

```
42 struct icmp {
43     u_char  icmp_type;              /* type of message, see below */
44     u_char  icmp_code;             /* type sub code */
45     u_short icmp_cksum;            /* ones complement cksum of struct */
46     union {
47         u_char  ih_pptr;            /* ICMP_PARAMPROB */
48         struct in_addr ih_gwaddr;    /* ICMP_REDIRECT */
49         struct ih_idseq {
50             n_short icd_id;
51             n_short icd_seq;
52         } ih_idseq;
53         int     ih_void;

54         /* ICMP_UNREACH_NEEDFRAG -- Path MTU Discovery (RFC1191) */
55         struct ih_pmtu {
56             n_short ipm_void;
57             n_short ipm_nextmtu;
58         } ih_pmtu;
59     } icmp_hun;
60 #define icmp_pptr    icmp_hun.ih_pptr
61 #define icmp_gwaddr  icmp_hun.ih_gwaddr
62 #define icmp_id      icmp_hun.ih_idseq.icd_id
63 #define icmp_seq     icmp_hun.ih_idseq.icd_seq
64 #define icmp_void    icmp_hun.ih_void
65 #define icmp_pmvoid  icmp_hun.ih_pmtu.ipm_void
66 #define icmp_nextmtu    icmp_hun.ih_pmtu.ipm_nextmtu
67     union {
68         struct id_ts {
69             n_time  its_otime;
70             n_time  its_rtime;
71             n_time  its_ttime;
72         } id_ts;
73         struct id_ip {
74             struct ip idi_ip;
75             /* options and then 64 bits of data */
76         } id_ip;
77         u_long  id_mask;
78         char    id_data[1];
79     } icmp_dun;
80 #define icmp_otime   icmp_dun.id_ts.its_otime
81 #define icmp_rtime   icmp_dun.id_ts.its_rtime
82 #define icmp_ttime   icmp_dun.id_ts.its_ttime
83 #define icmp_ip      icmp_dun.id_ip.idi_ip
84 #define icmp_mask    icmp_dun.id_mask
85 #define icmp_data    icmp_dun.id_data
86 };
```

ip_icmp.h

Figure 11.10 `icmp` structure.

42–45   icmp_type identifies the particular message, and icmp_code further specifies the message (the first column of Figure 11.1). icmp_cksum is computed with the same algorithm as the IP header checksum and protects the entire ICMP message (not just the header as with IP).

46–79   The unions icmp_hun (header union) and icmp_dun (data union) access the various ICMP messages according to icmp_type and icmp_code. Every ICMP message uses icmp_hun; only some utilize icmp_dun. Unused fields must be set to 0.

80–86   As we have seen with other nested structures (e.g., mbuf, le_softc, and ether_arp) the #define macros simplify access to structure members.

Figure 11.11 shows the overall structure of an ICMP message and reiterates that an ICMP message is encapsulated within an IP datagram. We show the specific structure of each message when we encounter it in the code.

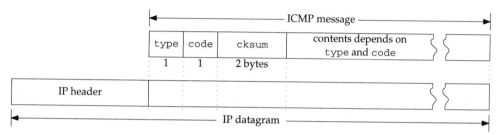

Figure 11.11   An ICMP message (icmp_ omitted).

11.4 ICMP protosw Structure

The protosw structure in inetsw[4] (Figure 7.13) describes ICMP and supports both kernel and process access to the protocol. We show this structure in Figure 11.12. Within the kernel, incoming ICMP messages are processed by icmp_input. Outgoing ICMP messages generated by processes are handled by rip_output. The three functions beginning with rip_ are described in Chapter 32.

Member	inetsw[4]	Description
pr_type	SOCK_RAW	ICMP provides raw packet services
pr_domain	&inetdomain	ICMP is part of the Internet domain
pr_protocol	IPPROTO_ICMP (1)	appears in the ip_p field of the IP header
pr_flags	PR_ATOMIC|PR_ADDR	socket layer flags, not used by ICMP
pr_input	icmp_input	receives ICMP messages from the IP layer
pr_output	rip_output	sends ICMP messages to the IP layer
pr_ctlinput	0	not used by ICMP
pr_ctloutput	rip_ctloutput	respond to administrative requests from a process
pr_usrreq	rip_usrreq	respond to communication requests from a process
pr_init	0	not used by ICMP
pr_fasttimo	0	not used by ICMP
pr_slowtimo	0	not used by ICMP
pr_drain	0	not used by ICMP
pr_sysctl	icmp_sysctl	modify ICMP parameters

Figure 11.12   ICMP inetsw entry.

11.5 Input Processing: `icmp_input` Function

Recall that `ipintr` demultiplexes datagrams based on the transport protocol number, `ip_p`, in the IP header. For ICMP messages, `ip_p` is 1, and through `ip_protox`, it selects `inetsw[4]`.

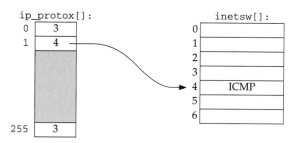

Figure 11.13   An `ip_p` value of 1 selects `inetsw[4]`.

The IP layer calls `icmp_input` indirectly through the `pr_input` function of `inetsw[4]` when an ICMP message arrives (Figure 8.15).

  We'll see in `icmp_input` that each ICMP message may be processed up to three times: by `icmp_input`, by the transport protocol associated with the IP packet within an ICMP error message, and by a process that registers interest in receiving ICMP messages. Figure 11.14 shows the overall organization of ICMP input processing.

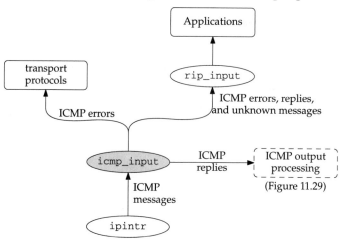

Figure 11.14   ICMP input processing.

  We discuss `icmp_input` in five sections: (1) verification of the received message, (2) ICMP error messages, (3) ICMP requests messages, (4) ICMP redirect messages, (5) ICMP reply messages. Figure 11.15 shows the first portion of the `icmp_input` function.

ip_icmp.c

```
131 static struct sockaddr_in icmpsrc = { sizeof (struct sockaddr_in), AF_INET };
132 static struct sockaddr_in icmpdst = { sizeof (struct sockaddr_in), AF_INET };
133 static struct sockaddr_in icmpgw = { sizeof (struct sockaddr_in), AF_INET };
134 struct sockaddr_in icmpmask = { 8, 0 };

135 void
136 icmp_input(m, hlen)
137 struct mbuf *m;
138 int     hlen;
139 {
140     struct icmp *icp;
141     struct ip *ip = mtod(m, struct ip *);
142     int     icmplen = ip->ip_len;
143     int     i;
144     struct in_ifaddr *ia;
145     void    (*ctlfunc) (int, struct sockaddr *, struct ip *);
146     int     code;
147     extern u_char ip_protox[];

148     /*
149      * Locate icmp structure in mbuf, and check
150      * that not corrupted and of at least minimum length.
151      */
152     if (icmplen < ICMP_MINLEN) {
153         icmpstat.icps_tooshort++;
154         goto freeit;
155     }
156     i = hlen + min(icmplen, ICMP_ADVLENMIN);
157     if (m->m_len < i && (m = m_pullup(m, i)) == 0) {
158         icmpstat.icps_tooshort++;
159         return;
160     }
161     ip = mtod(m, struct ip *);
162     m->m_len -= hlen;
163     m->m_data += hlen;
164     icp = mtod(m, struct icmp *);
165     if (in_cksum(m, icmplen)) {
166         icmpstat.icps_checksum++;
167         goto freeit;
168     }
169     m->m_len += hlen;
170     m->m_data -= hlen;

171     if (icp->icmp_type > ICMP_MAXTYPE)
172         goto raw;
173     icmpstat.icps_inhist[icp->icmp_type]++;
174     code = icp->icmp_code;
175     switch (icp->icmp_type) {
```

```
                        /* ICMP message processing */
```

```
317    default:
318        break;
319    }
320  raw:
321    rip_input(m);
322    return;

323  freeit:
324    m_freem(m);
325 }
```
—— *ip_icmp.c*

Figure 11.15 icmp_input function.

Static structures

131–134   These four structures are statically allocated to avoid the delays of dynamic allocation every time icmp_input is called and to minimize the size of the stack since
icmp_input is called at interrupt time when the stack size is limited. icmp_input
uses these structures as temporary variables.

> The naming of icmpsrc is misleading since icmp_input uses it as a temporary
> sockaddr_in variable and it never contains a source address. In the Net/2 version of
> icmp_input, the source address of the message was copied to icmpsrc at the end of the
> function before the message was delivered to the raw IP mechanism by the raw_input func-
> tion. Net/3 calls rip_input, which expects only a pointer to the packet, instead of
> raw_input. Despite this change, icmpsrc retains its name from Net/2.

Validate message

135–139   icmp_input expects a pointer to the datagram containing the received ICMP message (m) and the length of the datagram's IP header in bytes (hlen). Figure 11.16 lists
several constants and a macro that simplify the detection of invalid ICMP messages in
icmp_input.

Constant/Macro	Value	Description
ICMP_MINLEN	8	minimum size of an ICMP message
ICMP_TSLEN	20	size of ICMP timestamp messages
ICMP_MASKLEN	12	size of ICMP address mask messages
ICMP_ADVLENMIN	36	minimum size of an ICMP error (advise) message
		$(IP + ICMP + BADIP = 20 + 8 + 8 = 36)$
ICMP_ADVLEN(p)	36 + *optsize*	size of an ICMP error message including *optsize* bytes of IP
		options from the invalid packet p.

Figure 11.16 Constants and a macro referenced by ICMP to validate messages.

140–160   icmp_input pulls the size of the ICMP message from ip_len and stores it in
icmplen. Remember from Chapter 8 that ipintr excludes the length of the header
from ip_len. If the message is too short to be a valid ICMP message, icps_tooshort
is incremented and the message discarded. If the ICMP header and the IP header are
not contiguous in the first mbuf, m_pullup ensures that the ICMP header and the IP
header of any enclosed IP packet are in a single mbuf.

Verify checksum

161–170   `icmp_input` hides the IP header in the mbuf and verifies the ICMP checksum with `in_cksum`. If the message is damaged, `icps_checksum` is incremented and the message discarded.

Verify type

171–175   If the message type (`icmp_type`) is out of the recognized range, `icmp_input` jumps around the `switch` to `raw` (Section 11.9). If it is in the recognized range, `icmp_input` duplicates `icmp_code` and the `switch` processes the message according to `icmp_type`.

After the processing within the ICMP `switch` statement, `icmp_input` sends ICMP messages to `rip_input` where they are distributed to processes that are prepared to receive ICMP messages. The only messages that are not passed to `rip_input` are damaged messages (length or checksum errors) and ICMP request messages, which are handled exclusively by the kernel. In both cases, `icmp_input` returns immediately, skipping the code at `raw`.

Raw ICMP input

317–325   `icmp_input` passes the incoming message to `rip_input`, which distributes it to listening processes based on the protocol and the source and destination addresses within the message (Chapter 32).

The raw IP mechanism allows a process to send and to receive ICMP messages directly, which is desirable for several reasons:

- New ICMP messages can be handled by a process without having to modify the kernel (e.g., router advertisement, Figure 11.28).

- Utilities for sending ICMP requests and processing the replies can be implemented as a process instead of as a kernel module (`ping` and `traceroute`).

- A process can augment the kernel processing of a message. This is common with the ICMP redirect messages that are passed to a routing daemon after the kernel has updated its routing tables.

11.6 Error Processing

We first consider the ICMP error messages. A host receives these messages when a datagram that it sent cannot successfully be delivered to its destination. The intended destination host or an intermediate router generates the error message and returns it to the originating system. Figure 11.17 illustrates the format of the various ICMP error messages.

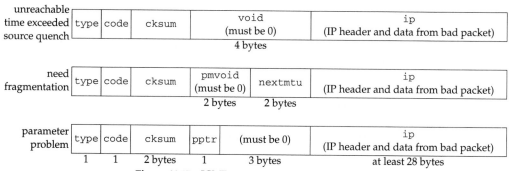

Figure 11.17   ICMP error messages (icmp_ omitted).

The code in Figure 11.18 is from the switch shown in Figure 11.15.

```
                                                                          ip_icmp.c
176    case ICMP_UNREACH:
177        switch (code) {
178        case ICMP_UNREACH_NET:
179        case ICMP_UNREACH_HOST:
180        case ICMP_UNREACH_PROTOCOL:
181        case ICMP_UNREACH_PORT:
182        case ICMP_UNREACH_SRCFAIL:
183            code += PRC_UNREACH_NET;
184            break;

185        case ICMP_UNREACH_NEEDFRAG:
186            code = PRC_MSGSIZE;
187            break;

188        case ICMP_UNREACH_NET_UNKNOWN:
189        case ICMP_UNREACH_NET_PROHIB:
190        case ICMP_UNREACH_TOSNET:
191            code = PRC_UNREACH_NET;
192            break;

193        case ICMP_UNREACH_HOST_UNKNOWN:
194        case ICMP_UNREACH_ISOLATED:
195        case ICMP_UNREACH_HOST_PROHIB:
196        case ICMP_UNREACH_TOSHOST:
197            code = PRC_UNREACH_HOST;
198            break;

199        default:
200            goto badcode;
201        }
202        goto deliver;

203    case ICMP_TIMXCEED:
204        if (code > 1)
205            goto badcode;
206        code += PRC_TIMXCEED_INTRANS;
207        goto deliver;
```

```
208        case ICMP_PARAMPROB:
209            if (code > 1)
210                goto badcode;
211            code = PRC_PARAMPROB;
212            goto deliver;

213        case ICMP_SOURCEQUENCH:
214            if (code)
215                goto badcode;
216            code = PRC_QUENCH;

217     deliver:
218        /*
219         * Problem with datagram; advise higher level routines.
220         */
221        if (icmplen < ICMP_ADVLENMIN || icmplen < ICMP_ADVLEN(icp) ||
222            icp->icmp_ip.ip_hl < (sizeof(struct ip) >> 2)) {
223            icmpstat.icps_badlen++;
224            goto freeit;
225        }
226        NTOHS(icp->icmp_ip.ip_len);
227        icmpsrc.sin_addr = icp->icmp_ip.ip_dst;
228        if (ctlfunc = inetsw[ip_protox[icp->icmp_ip.ip_p]].pr_ctlinput)
229            (*ctlfunc) (code, (struct sockaddr *) &icmpsrc,
230                            &icp->icmp_ip);
231        break;

232     badcode:
233        icmpstat.icps_badcode++;
234        break;
```
                                                                    ── *ip_icmp.c*

Figure 11.18   `icmp_input` function: error messages.

176–216   The processing of ICMP errors is minimal since responsibility for responding to ICMP errors lies primarily with the transport protocols. `icmp_input` maps `icmp_type` and `icmp_code` to a set of protocol-independent error codes represented by the PRC_ constants. There is an implied ordering of the PRC_ constants that matches the ICMP code values. This explains why `code` is incremented by a PRC_ constant.

If the type and code are recognized, `icmp_input` jumps to `deliver`. If the type and code are not recognized, `icmp_input` jumps to `badcode`.

217–225   If the message length is incorrect for the error being reported, `icps_badlen` is incremented and the message discarded. Net/3 always discards invalid ICMP messages, without generating an ICMP error about the invalid message. This prevent an infinite sequence of error messages from forming between two faulty implementations.

226–231   `icmp_input` calls the `pr_ctlinput` function of the transport protocol that created the *original* IP datagram by demultiplexing the incoming packets to the correct transport protocol based on `ip_p` from the original datagram. `pr_ctlinput` (if it is defined for the protocol) is passed the error code (`code`), the destination of the original IP datagram (`icmpsrc`), and a pointer to the invalid datagram (`icmp_ip`). We discuss these errors with Figures 23.31 and 27.12.

232–234   `icps_badcode` is incremented and control breaks out of the `switch` statement.

Constant	Description
PRC_HOSTDEAD	host appears to be down
PRC_IFDOWN	network interface shut down
PRC_MSGSIZE	invalid message size
PRC_PARAMPROB	header incorrect
PRC_QUENCH	someone said to slow down
PRC_QUENCH2	congestion bit says slow down
PRC_REDIRECT_HOST	host routing redirect
PRC_REDIRECT_NET	network routing redirect
PRC_REDIRECT_TOSHOST	redirect for TOS and host
PRC_REDIRECT_TOSNET	redirect for TOS and network
PRC_ROUTEDEAD	select new route if possible
PRC_TIMXCEED_INTRANS	packet lifetime expired in transit
PRC_TIMXCEED_REASS	fragment lifetime expired during reassembly
PRC_UNREACH_HOST	no route available to host
PRC_UNREACH_NET	no route available to network
PRC_UNREACH_PORT	destination says port is not active
PRC_UNREACH_PROTOCOL	destination says protocol is not available
PRC_UNREACH_SRCFAIL	source route failed

Figure 11.19 The protocol-independent error codes.

While the PRC_ constants are ostensibly protocol independent, they are primarily based on the Internet protocols. This results in some loss of specificity when a protocol outside the Internet domain maps its errors to the PRC_ constants.

11.7 Request Processing

Net/3 responds to properly formatted ICMP request messages but passes invalid ICMP request messages to rip_input. We show in Chapter 32 how ICMP request messages may be generated by an application process.

Most ICMP request messages received by Net/3 generate a reply message, except the router advertisement message. To avoid allocation of a new mbuf for the reply, icmp_input converts the mbuf containing the incoming request to the reply and returns it to the sender. We discuss each request separately.

Echo Query: ICMP_ECHO and ICMP_ECHOREPLY

For all its simplicity, an ICMP echo request and reply is arguably the single most powerful diagnostic tool available to a network administrator. Sending an ICMP echo request is called *pinging* a host, a reference to the ping program that most systems provide for manually sending ICMP echo requests. Chapter 7 of Volume 1 discusses ping in detail.

> The program ping is named after sonar pings used to locate objects by listening for the echo generated as the ping is reflected by the other objects. Volume 1 incorrectly described the name as standing for Packet InterNet Groper.

Figure 11.20 shows the structure of an ICMP echo and reply message.

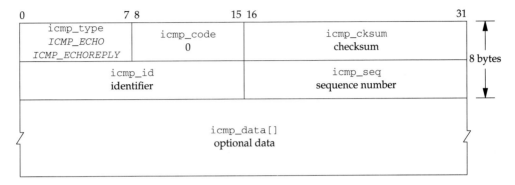

Figure 11.20   ICMP echo request and reply.

`icmp_code` is always 0. `icmp_id` and `icmp_seq` are set by the sender of the request and returned without modification in the reply. The source system can match requests and replies with these fields. Any data that arrives in `icmp_data` is also reflected. Figure 11.21 shows the ICMP echo processing and also the common code in `icmp_input` that implements the reflection of ICMP requests.

ip_icmp.c

```
235     case ICMP_ECHO:
236         icp->icmp_type = ICMP_ECHOREPLY;
237         goto reflect;



                        /* other ICMP request processing */


277     reflect:
278         ip->ip_len += hlen;      /* since ip_input deducts this */
279         icmpstat.icps_reflect++;
280         icmpstat.icps_outhist[icp->icmp_type]++;
281         icmp_reflect(m);
282         return;
```

ip_icmp.c

Figure 11.21   `icmp_input` function: echo request and reply.

235–237   `icmp_input` converts an echo request into an echo reply by changing `icmp_type` to `ICMP_ECHOREPLY` and jumping to `reflect` to send the reply.

277–282   After constructing the reply for each ICMP request, `icmp_input` executes the code at `reflect`. The correct datagram length is restored, the number of requests and the type of ICMP messages are counted in `icps_reflect` and `icps_outhist[]`, and `icmp_reflect` (Section 11.12) sends the reply back to the requestor.

Timestamp Query: `ICMP_TSTAMP` and `ICMP_TSTAMPREPLY`

The ICMP timestamp message is illustrated in Figure 11.22.

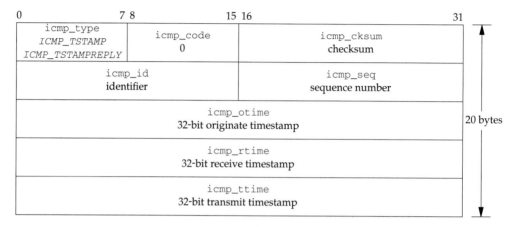

Figure 11.22   ICMP timestamp request and reply.

`icmp_code` is always 0. `icmp_id` and `icmp_seq` serve the same purpose as those in the ICMP echo messages. The sender of the request sets `icmp_otime` (the time the request originated); `icmp_rtime` (the time the request was received) and `icmp_ttime` (the time the reply was transmitted) are set by the sender of the reply. All times are in milliseconds since midnight UTC; the high-order bit is set if the time value is recorded in nonstandard units, as with the IP timestamp option.

Figure 11.23 shows the code that implements the timestamp messages.

```
238        case ICMP_TSTAMP:
239            if (icmplen < ICMP_TSLEN) {
240                icmpstat.icps_badlen++;
241                break;
242            }
243            icp->icmp_type = ICMP_TSTAMPREPLY;
244            icp->icmp_rtime = iptime();
245            icp->icmp_ttime = icp->icmp_rtime;   /* bogus, do later! */
246            goto reflect;
```
———————————————————————— ip_icmp.c

———————————————————————— ip_icmp.c

Figure 11.23   `icmp_input` function: timestamp request and reply.

238–246   `icmp_input` responds to an ICMP timestamp request by changing `icmp_type` to `ICMP_TSTAMPREPLY`, recording the current time in `icmp_rtime` and `icmp_ttime`, and jumping to `reflect` to send the reply.

It is difficult to set `icmp_rtime` and `icmp_ttime` accurately. When the system executes this code, the message may have already waited on the IP input queue to be processed and `icmp_rtime` is set too late. Likewise, the datagram still requires processing and may be delayed in the transmit queue of the network interface so icmp_ttime is set too early here. To set the timestamps closer to the true receive and transmit times would require modifying the interface drivers for every network to understand ICMP messages (Exercise 11.8).

Address Mask Query: `ICMP_MASKREQ` and `ICMP_MASKREPLY`

The ICMP address mask request and reply are illustrated in Figure 11.24.

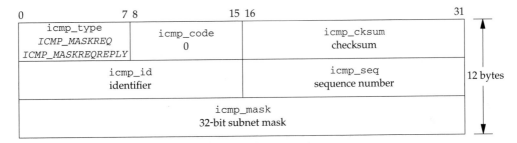

Figure 11.24   ICMP address mask request and reply.

RFC 950 [Mogul and Postel 1985] added the address mask messages to the original ICMP specification. They enable a system to discover the subnet mask in use on a network.

RFC 1122 forbids sending mask replies unless a system has been explicitly configured as an authoritative agent for address masks. This prevents a system from sharing an incorrect address mask with every system that sends a request. Without administrative authority to respond, a system should ignore address mask requests.

If the global integer icmpmaskrepl is nonzero, Net/3 responds to address mask requests. The default value is 0 and can be changed by icmp_sysctl through the sysctl(8) program (Section 11.14).

> In Net/2 systems there was no mechanism to control the reply to address mask requests. As a result, it is very important to configure Net/2 interfaces with the correct address mask; the information is shared with any system on the network that sends an address mask request.

The address mask message processing is shown in Figure 11.25.

247–256   If the system is not configured to respond to mask requests, or if the request is too short, this code breaks out of the switch and passes the message to rip_input (Figure 11.15).

> Net/3 fails to increment icps_badlen here. It does increment icps_badlen for all other ICMP length errors.

Select subnet mask

257–267   If the request was sent to 0.0.0.0 or 255.255.255.255, the source address is saved in icmpdst where it is used by ifaof_ifpforaddr to locate the in_ifaddr structure

```
                                                                              ——————— ip_icmp.c
247     case ICMP_MASKREQ:
248 #define satosin(sa) ((struct sockaddr_in *)(sa))
249         if (icmpmaskrepl == 0)
250             break;
251         /*
252          * We are not able to respond with all ones broadcast
253          * unless we receive it over a point-to-point interface.
254          */
255         if (icmplen < ICMP_MASKLEN)
256             break;
257         switch (ip->ip_dst.s_addr) {

258         case INADDR_BROADCAST:
259         case INADDR_ANY:
260             icmpdst.sin_addr = ip->ip_src;
261             break;

262         default:
263             icmpdst.sin_addr = ip->ip_dst;
264         }
265         ia = (struct in_ifaddr *) ifaof_ifpforaddr(
266                         (struct sockaddr *) &icmpdst, m->m_pkthdr.rcvif);
267         if (ia == 0)
268             break;
269         icp->icmp_type = ICMP_MASKREPLY;
270         icp->icmp_mask = ia->ia_sockmask.sin_addr.s_addr;
271         if (ip->ip_src.s_addr == 0) {
272             if (ia->ia_ifp->if_flags & IFF_BROADCAST)
273                 ip->ip_src = satosin(&ia->ia_broadaddr)->sin_addr;
274             else if (ia->ia_ifp->if_flags & IFF_POINTOPOINT)
275                 ip->ip_src = satosin(&ia->ia_dstaddr)->sin_addr;
276         }
                                                                              ——————— ip_icmp.c
```

Figure 11.25 icmp_input function: address mask request and reply.

on the same network as the source address. If the source address is 0.0.0.0 or 255.255.255.255, ifaof_ifpforaddr returns a pointer to the first IP address associated with the receiving interface.

The default case (for unicast or directed broadcasts) saves the destination address for ifaof_ifpforaddr.

Convert to reply

269–270   The request is converted into a reply by changing icmp_type and by copying the selected subnet mask, ia_sockmask, into icmp_mask.

Select destination address

271–276   If the source address of the request is all 0s ("this host on this net," which can be used only as a source address during bootstrap, RFC 1122), then the source does not know its own address and Net/3 must broadcast the reply so the source system can receive the message. In this case, the destination for the reply is ia_broadaddr or ia_dstaddr if the receiving interface is on a broadcast or point-to-point network, respectively. `icmp_input` puts the destination address for the reply in `ip_src` since the code at `reflect` (Figure 11.21) calls `icmp_reflect`, which reverses the source and destination addresses. The addresses of a unicast request remain unchanged.

Information Query: `ICMP_IREQ` and `ICMP_IREQREPLY`

The ICMP information messages are obsolete. They were intended to allow a host to discover the number of an attached IP network by broadcasting a request with 0s in the network portion of the source and destination address fields. A host responding to the request would return a message with the appropriate network numbers filled in. Some other method was required for a host to discover the host portion of the address.

RFC 1122 recommends that a host not implement the ICMP information messages because RARP (RFC 903 [Finlayson et al. 1984]), and BOOTP (RFC 951 [Croft and Gilmore 1985]) are better suited for discovering addresses. A new protocol, the Dynamic Host Configuration Protocol (DHCP), described in RFC 1541 [Droms 1993], will probably replace and augment the capabilities of BOOTP. It is currently a proposed standard.

> Net/2 did respond to ICMP information request messages, but Net/3 passes them on to `rip_input`.

Router Discovery: `ICMP_ROUTERADVERT` and `ICMP_ROUTERSOLICIT`

RFC 1256 defines the ICMP router discovery messages. The Net/3 kernel does not process these messages directly but instead passes them, by `rip_input`, to a user-level daemon, which sends and responds to the messages.

Section 9.6 of Volume 1 discusses the design and operation of these messages.

11.8 Redirect Processing

Figure 11.26 shows the format of ICMP redirect messages.

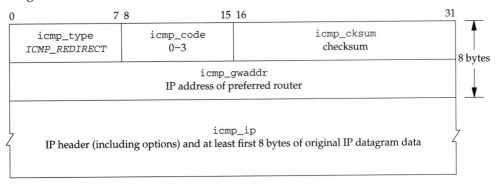

Figure 11.26   ICMP redirect message.

The last `case` to discuss in `icmp_input` is `ICMP_REDIRECT`. As discussed in Section 8.5, a redirect message arrives when a packet is sent to the wrong router. The router forwards the packet to the correct router and sends back a ICMP redirect message, which the system incorporates into its routing tables.

Figure 11.27 shows the code executed by `icmp_input` to process redirect messages.

```
                                                                    ─ ip_icmp.c
283        case ICMP_REDIRECT:
284            if (code > 3)
285                goto badcode;
286            if (icmplen < ICMP_ADVLENMIN || icmplen < ICMP_ADVLEN(icp) ||
287                icp->icmp_ip.ip_hl < (sizeof(struct ip) >> 2)) {
288                icmpstat.icps_badlen++;
289                break;
290            }
291            /*
292             * Short circuit routing redirects to force
293             * immediate change in the kernel's routing
294             * tables.  The message is also handed to anyone
295             * listening on a raw socket (e.g. the routing
296             * daemon for use in updating its tables).
297             */
298            icmpgw.sin_addr = ip->ip_src;
299            icmpdst.sin_addr = icp->icmp_gwaddr;
300            icmpsrc.sin_addr = icp->icmp_ip.ip_dst;
301            rtredirect((struct sockaddr *) &icmpsrc,
302                       (struct sockaddr *) &icmpdst,
303                       (struct sockaddr *) 0, RTF_GATEWAY | RTF_HOST,
304                       (struct sockaddr *) &icmpgw, (struct rtentry **) 0);
305            pfctlinput(PRC_REDIRECT_HOST, (struct sockaddr *) &icmpsrc);
306            break;
                                                                    ─ ip_icmp.c
```

Figure 11.27 `icmp_input` function: redirect messages.

Validate

283–290   `icmp_input` jumps to `badcode` (Figure 11.18, line 232) if the redirect message includes an unrecognized ICMP code, and drops out of the switch if the message has an invalid length or if the enclosed IP packet has an invalid header length. Figure 11.16 showed that 36 (`ICMP_ADVLENMIN`) is the minimum size of an ICMP error message, and `ICMP_ADVLEN(icp)` is the minimum size of an ICMP error message including any IP options that may be in the packet pointed to by `icp`.

291–300   `icmp_input` assigns to the static structures `icmpgw`, `icmpdst`, and `icmpsrc`, the source address of the redirect message (the gateway that sent the message), the recommended router for the original packet (the first-hop destination), and the final destination of the original packet.

> Here, `icmpsrc` does not contain a source address—it is a convenient location for holding the destination address instead of declaring another `sockaddr` structure.

Update routes

301–306   Net/3 follows RFC 1122 recommendations and treats a network redirect and a host redirect identically. The redirect information is passed to `rtredirect`, which updates the routing tables. The redirected destination (saved in `icmpsrc`) is passed to `pfctlinput`, which informs all the protocol domains about the redirect (Section 7.7). This gives the protocols an opportunity to invalidate any route caches to the destination.

> According to RFC 1122, network redirects should be treated as host redirects since they may provide incorrect routing information when the destination network is subnetted. In fact, RFC 1009 requires routers *not* to send network redirects when the network is subnetted. Unfortunately, many routers violate this requirement. Net/3 never sends network redirects.

ICMP redirect messages are a fundamental part of the IP routing architecture. While classified as an error message, redirect messages appear during normal operations on any network with more than a single router. Chapter 18 covers IP routing issues in more detail.

11.9 Reply Processing

The kernel does not process any of the ICMP reply messages. ICMP requests are generated by processes, never by the kernel, so the kernel passes any replies that it receives to processes waiting for ICMP messages. In addition, the ICMP router discovery messages are passed to `rip_input`.

―― *ip_icmp.c*
```
307          /*
308           * No kernel processing for the following;
309           * just fall through to send to raw listener.
310           */
311      case ICMP_ECHOREPLY:
312      case ICMP_ROUTERADVERT:
313      case ICMP_ROUTERSOLICIT:
314      case ICMP_TSTAMPREPLY:
315      case ICMP_IREQREPLY:
316      case ICMP_MASKREPLY:
317      default:
318          break;
319      }
320  raw:
321      rip_input(m);
322      return;
```
―― *ip_icmp.c*

Figure 11.28 `icmp_input` function: reply messages.

307–322   No actions are required by the kernel for ICMP reply messages, so execution continues after the `switch` statement at `raw`. Note that the `default` case for the `switch` statement (unrecognized ICMP messages) also passes control to the code at `raw`.

11.10 Output Processing

Outgoing ICMP messages are generated in several ways. We saw in Chapter 8 that IP calls `icmp_error` to generate and send ICMP error messages. ICMP reply messages are sent by `icmp_reflect`, and it is possible for a process to generate ICMP messages through the raw ICMP protocol. Figure 11.29 shows how these functions relate to ICMP output processing.

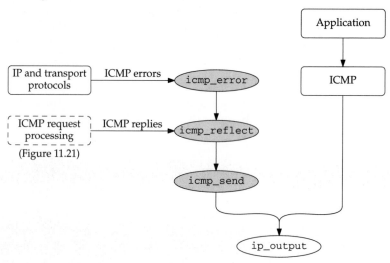

Figure 11.29 ICMP output processing.

11.11 `icmp_error` Function

The `icmp_error` function constructs an ICMP error message at the request of IP or the transport protocols and passes it to `icmp_reflect`, where it is returned to the source of the invalid datagram. The function is shown in three parts:

- validate the message (Figure 11.30),
- construct the header (Figure 11.32), and
- include the original datagram (Figure 11.33).

46–57   The arguments are: n, a pointer to an mbuf chain containing the invalid datagram; `type` and `code`, the ICMP error type and code values; `dest`, the next-hop router address included in ICMP redirect messages; and `destifp`, a pointer to the outgoing interface for the original IP packet. `mtod` converts the mbuf pointer n to `oip`, a pointer to the `ip` structure in the mbuf. The length in bytes of the original IP header is kept in `oiplen`.

58–75   All ICMP errors except redirect messages are counted in `icps_error`. Net/3 does not consider redirect messages as errors and `icps_error` is not an SNMP variable.

```
                                                                              ip_icmp.c
46 void
47 icmp_error(n, type, code, dest, destifp)
48 struct mbuf *n;
49 int      type, code;
50 n_long   dest;
51 struct ifnet *destifp;
52 {
53     struct ip *oip = mtod(n, struct ip *), *nip;
54     unsigned oiplen = oip->ip_hl << 2;
55     struct icmp *icp;
56     struct mbuf *m;
57     unsigned icmplen;

58     if (type != ICMP_REDIRECT)
59         icmpstat.icps_error++;
60     /*
61      * Don't send error if not the first fragment of message.
62      * Don't error if the old packet protocol was ICMP
63      * error message, only known informational types.
64      */
65     if (oip->ip_off & ~(IP_MF | IP_DF))
66         goto freeit;
67     if (oip->ip_p == IPPROTO_ICMP && type != ICMP_REDIRECT &&
68         n->m_len >= oiplen + ICMP_MINLEN &&
69         !ICMP_INFOTYPE(((struct icmp *) ((caddr_t) oip + oiplen))->icmp_type)) {
70         icmpstat.icps_oldicmp++;
71         goto freeit;
72     }
73     /* Don't send error in response to a multicast or broadcast packet */
74     if (n->m_flags & (M_BCAST | M_MCAST))
75         goto freeit;
                                                                              ip_icmp.c
```

Figure 11.30   `icmp_error` function: validation.

`icmp_error` discards the invalid datagram, `oip`, and does not send an error message if:

- some bits of `ip_off`, except those represented by `IP_MF` and `IP_DF`, are nonzero (Exercise 11.10). This indicates that `oip` is not the first fragment of a datagram and that ICMP must not generate error messages for trailing fragments of a datagram.

- the invalid datagram is itself an ICMP error message. `ICMP_INFOTYPE` returns true if `icmp_type` is an ICMP request or response type and false if it is an error type. This rule avoids creating an infinite sequence of errors about errors.

  Net/3 does not consider ICMP redirect messages errors, although RFC 1122 does.

- the datagram arrived as a link-layer broadcast or multicast (indicated by the `M_BCAST` and `M_MCAST` flags).

ICMP error messages must not be sent in two other circumstances:

- The datagram was sent to an IP broadcast or IP multicast address.
- The datagram's source address is not a unicast IP address (i.e., the source address is a 0 address, a loopback address, a broadcast address, a multicast address, or a class E address)

Net/3 fails to check for the first case. The second case is addressed by the `icmp_reflect` function (Section 11.12).

> Interestingly, the Deering multicast extensions to Net/2 do discard datagrams of the first type. Since the Net/3 multicast code was derived from the Deering multicast extensions, it appears the test was removed.

These restrictions attempt to prevent a single broadcast datagram with an error from triggering ICMP error messages from every host on the network. These *broadcast storms* can disrupt communication on a network for an extended period of time as all the hosts attempt to send an error message simultaneously.

These rules apply to ICMP error messages but not to ICMP replies. As RFCs 1122 and 1127 discuss, responding to broadcast requests is allowed but neither recommended nor discouraged. Net/3 responds only to broadcast requests with a unicast source address, since `ip_output` will drop ICMP messages returned to a broadcast address (Figure 11.39).

Figure 11.31 illustrates the construction of an ICMP error message.

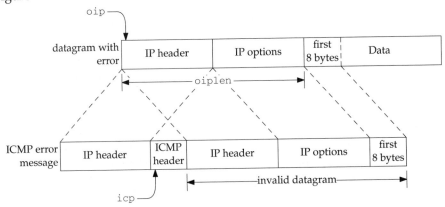

Figure 11.31   The construction of an ICMP error message.

The code in Figure 11.32 builds the error message.

76–106   `icmp_error` constructs the ICMP message header in the following way:

- `m_gethdr` allocates a new packet header mbuf. `MH_ALIGN` positions the mbuf's data pointer so that the ICMP header, the IP header (and options) of the invalid datagram, and up to 8 bytes of the invalid datagram's data are located at the end of the mbuf.

```
                                                                      ip_icmp.c
 76      /*
 77       * First, formulate icmp message
 78       */
 79      m = m_gethdr(M_DONTWAIT, MT_HEADER);
 80      if (m == NULL)
 81          goto freeit;
 82      icmplen = oiplen + min(8, oip->ip_len);
 83      m->m_len = icmplen + ICMP_MINLEN;
 84      MH_ALIGN(m, m->m_len);
 85      icp = mtod(m, struct icmp *);
 86      if ((u_int) type > ICMP_MAXTYPE)
 87          panic("icmp_error");
 88      icmpstat.icps_outhist[type]++;
 89      icp->icmp_type = type;
 90      if (type == ICMP_REDIRECT)
 91          icp->icmp_gwaddr.s_addr = dest;
 92      else {
 93          icp->icmp_void = 0;
 94          /*
 95           * The following assignments assume an overlay with the
 96           * zeroed icmp_void field.
 97           */
 98          if (type == ICMP_PARAMPROB) {
 99              icp->icmp_pptr = code;
100              code = 0;
101          } else if (type == ICMP_UNREACH &&
102                  code == ICMP_UNREACH_NEEDFRAG && destifp) {
103              icp->icmp_nextmtu = htons(destifp->if_mtu);
104          }
105      }
106      icp->icmp_code = code;
                                                                      ip_icmp.c
```

Figure 11.32 icmp_error function: message header construction.

- icmp_type, icmp_code, icmp_gwaddr (for redirects), icmp_pptr (for parameter problems), and icmp_nextmtu (for the fragmentation required message) are initialized. The icmp_nextmtu field implements the extension to the fragmentation required message described in RFC 1191. Section 24.2 of Volume 1 describes the *path MTU discovery* algorithm, which relies on this message.

Once the ICMP header has been constructed, a portion of the original datagram must be attached to the header, as shown in Figure 11.33.

107–125   The IP header, options, and data (a total of icmplen bytes) are copied from the invalid datagram into the ICMP error message. Also, the header length is added back into the invalid datagram's ip_len.

> In udp_usrreq, UDP also adds the header length back into the invalid datagram's ip_len. The result is an ICMP message with an incorrect datagram length in the IP header of the invalid packet. The authors found that many systems based on Net/2 code have this bug. Net/1 systems do not have this problem.

```
                                                                      ip_icmp.c
107        bcopy((caddr_t) oip, (caddr_t) & icp->icmp_ip, icmplen);
108        nip = &icp->icmp_ip;
109        nip->ip_len = htons((u_short) (nip->ip_len + oiplen));

110        /*
111         * Now, copy old ip header (without options)
112         * in front of icmp message.
113         */
114        if (m->m_data - sizeof(struct ip) < m->m_pktdat)
115                    panic("icmp len");
116        m->m_data -= sizeof(struct ip);
117        m->m_len += sizeof(struct ip);
118        m->m_pkthdr.len = m->m_len;
119        m->m_pkthdr.rcvif = n->m_pkthdr.rcvif;
120        nip = mtod(m, struct ip *);
121        bcopy((caddr_t) oip, (caddr_t) nip, sizeof(struct ip));
122        nip->ip_len = m->m_len;
123        nip->ip_hl = sizeof(struct ip) >> 2;
124        nip->ip_p = IPPROTO_ICMP;
125        nip->ip_tos = 0;
126        icmp_reflect(m);

127    freeit:
128        m_freem(n);
129 }
                                                                      ip_icmp.c
```

Figure 11.33   `icmp_error` function: including the original datagram.

Since `MH_ALIGN` located the ICMP message at the end of the mbuf, there should be enough room to prepend an IP header at the front. The IP header (excluding options) is copied from the invalid datagram to the front of the ICMP message.

> The Net/2 release included a bug in this portion of the code: the last `bcopy` in the function moved `oiplen` bytes, which includes the options from the invalid datagram. Only the standard header without options should be copied.

The IP header is completed by restoring the correct datagram length (`ip_len`), header length (`ip_hl`), and protocol (`ip_p`), and clearing the TOS field (`ip_tos`).

> RFCs 792 and 1122 recommend that the TOS field be set to 0 for ICMP messages.

126–129   The completed message is passed to `icmp_reflect`, where it is sent back to the source host. The invalid datagram is discarded.

11.12 `icmp_reflect` Function

`icmp_reflect` sends ICMP replies and errors back to the source of the request or back to the source of the invalid datagram. It is important to remember that `icmp_reflect` reverses the source and destination addresses in the datagram before sending it. The rules regarding source and destination addresses of ICMP messages are complex. Figure 11.34 summarizes the actions of several functions in this area.

Function	Summary
icmp_input	Replace an all-0s source address in address mask requests with the broadcast or destination address of the receiving interface.
icmp_error	Discard error messages caused by datagrams sent as link-level broadcasts or multicasts. Should discard (but does not) messages caused by datagrams sent to IP broadcast or multicast addresses.
icmp_reflect	Discard messages instead of returning them to a multicast or experimental address. Convert nonunicast destinations to the address of the receiving interface, which makes the destination address a valid source address for the return message. Swap the source and destination addresses.
ip_output	Discards outgoing broadcasts at the request of ICMP (i.e., discards errors generated by packets sent to a broadcast address)

Figure 11.34 ICMP discard and address summary.

We describe the icmp_reflect function in three parts: source and destination address selection, option construction, and assembly and transmission. Figure 11.35 shows the first part of the function.

Set destination address

329–345   icmp_reflect starts by making a copy of ip_dst and moving ip_src, the source of the request or error datagram, to ip_dst. icmp_error and icmp_reflect ensure that ip_src is a valid destination address for the error message. ip_output discards any packets sent to a broadcast address.

Select source address

346–371   icmp_reflect selects a source address for the message by searching in_ifaddr for the interface with a unicast or broadcast address matching the destination address of the original datagram. On a multihomed host, the matching interface may not be the interface on which the datagram was received. If there is no match, the in_ifaddr structure of the receiving interface is selected or, failing that (the interface may not be configured for IP), the first address in in_ifaddr. The function sets ip_src to the selected address and changes ip_ttl to 255 (MAXTTL) because the error is a new datagram.

> RFC 1700 recommends that the TTL field of all IP packets be set to 64. Many systems, however, set the TTL of ICMP messages to 255 nowadays.

> There is a tradeoff associated with TTL values. A small TTL prevents a packet from circulating in a routing loop but may not allow a packet to reach a site far (many hops) away. A large TTL allows packets to reach distant hosts but lets packets circulate in routing loops for a longer period of time.

```
                                                                    ip_icmp.c
329  void
330  icmp_reflect(m)
331  struct mbuf *m;
332  {
333      struct ip *ip = mtod(m, struct ip *);
334      struct in_ifaddr *ia;
335      struct in_addr t;
336      struct mbuf *opts = 0, *ip_srcroute();
337      int     optlen = (ip->ip_hl << 2) - sizeof(struct ip);

338      if (!in_canforward(ip->ip_src) &&
339          ((ntohl(ip->ip_src.s_addr) & IN_CLASSA_NET) !=
340          (IN_LOOPBACKNET << IN_CLASSA_NSHIFT))) {
341          m_freem(m);              /* Bad return address */
342          goto done;               /* Ip_output() will check for broadcast */
343      }
344      t = ip->ip_dst;
345      ip->ip_dst = ip->ip_src;
346      /*
347       * If the incoming packet was addressed directly to us,
348       * use dst as the src for the reply.  Otherwise (broadcast
349       * or anonymous), use the address which corresponds
350       * to the incoming interface.
351       */
352      for (ia = in_ifaddr; ia; ia = ia->ia_next) {
353          if (t.s_addr == IA_SIN(ia)->sin_addr.s_addr)
354              break;
355          if ((ia->ia_ifp->if_flags & IFF_BROADCAST) &&
356              t.s_addr == satosin(&ia->ia_broadaddr)->sin_addr.s_addr)
357              break;
358      }
359      icmpdst.sin_addr = t;
360      if (ia == (struct in_ifaddr *) 0)
361          ia = (struct in_ifaddr *) ifaof_ifpforaddr(
362                          (struct sockaddr *) &icmpdst, m->m_pkthdr.rcvif);
363      /*
364       * The following happens if the packet was not addressed to us,
365       * and was received on an interface with no IP address.
366       */
367      if (ia == (struct in_ifaddr *) 0)
368          ia = in_ifaddr;
369      t = IA_SIN(ia)->sin_addr;
370      ip->ip_src = t;
371      ip->ip_ttl = MAXTTL;
                                                                    ip_icmp.c
```

Figure 11.35 icmp_reflect function: address selection.

RFC 1122 *requires* that source route options, and *recommends* that record route and timestamp options, from an incoming echo request or timestamp request, be attached to a reply. The source route must be reversed in the process. RFC 1122 is silent on how these options should be handled on other types of ICMP replies. Net/3 applies these rules to the address mask request, since it calls `icmp_reflect` (Figure 11.21) after constructing the address mask reply.

The next section of code (Figure 11.36) constructs the options for the ICMP message.

```
                                                                    ─── ip_icmp.c
372     if (optlen > 0) {
373         u_char *cp;
374         int     opt, cnt;
375         u_int   len;

376         /*
377          * Retrieve any source routing from the incoming packet;
378          * add on any record-route or timestamp options.
379          */
380         cp = (u_char *) (ip + 1);
381         if ((opts = ip_srcroute()) == 0 &&
382             (opts = m_gethdr(M_DONTWAIT, MT_HEADER))) {
383             opts->m_len = sizeof(struct in_addr);
384             mtod(opts, struct in_addr *)->s_addr = 0;
385         }
386         if (opts) {
387             for (cnt = optlen; cnt > 0; cnt -= len, cp += len) {
388                 opt = cp[IPOPT_OPTVAL];
389                 if (opt == IPOPT_EOL)
390                     break;
391                 if (opt == IPOPT_NOP)
392                     len = 1;
393                 else {
394                     len = cp[IPOPT_OLEN];
395                     if (len <= 0 || len > cnt)
396                         break;
397                 }
398                 /*
399                  * Should check for overflow, but it "can't happen"
400                  */
401                 if (opt == IPOPT_RR || opt == IPOPT_TS ||
402                     opt == IPOPT_SECURITY) {
403                     bcopy((caddr_t) cp,
404                         mtod(opts, caddr_t) + opts->m_len, len);
405                     opts->m_len += len;
406                 }
407             }
408             /* Terminate & pad, if necessary */
409             if (cnt = opts->m_len % 4) {
410                 for (; cnt < 4; cnt++) {
411                     *(mtod(opts, caddr_t) + opts->m_len) =
412                         IPOPT_EOL;
413                     opts->m_len++;
414                 }
415             }
416         }
                                                                    ─── ip_icmp.c
```

Figure 11.36 `icmp_reflect` function: option construction.

Get reversed source route

372–385   If the incoming datagram did not contain options, control passes to line 430 (Figure 11.37). The error messages that `icmp_error` sends to `icmp_reflect` never have IP options, and so the following code applies only to ICMP requests that are converted to replies and passed directly to `icmp_reflect`.

cp points to the start of the options for the *reply*. `ip_srcroute` reverses and returns any source route option saved when `ipintr` processed the datagram. If `ip_srcroute` returns 0, the request did not contain a source route option so `icmp_reflect` allocates and initializes an mbuf to serve as an empty `ipoption` structure.

Add record route and timestamp options

386–416   If `opts` points to an mbuf, the `for` loop searches the options from the *original* IP header and appends the record route and timestamp options to the source route returned by `ip_srcroute`.

The options in the original header must be removed before the ICMP message can be sent. This is done by the code shown in Figure 11.37.

```
                                                             ──────────── ip_icmp.c
417              /*
418               * Now strip out original options by copying rest of first
419               * mbuf's data back, and adjust the IP length.
420               */
421              ip->ip_len -= optlen;
422              ip->ip_hl = sizeof(struct ip) >> 2;
423              m->m_len -= optlen;
424              if (m->m_flags & M_PKTHDR)
425                  m->m_pkthdr.len -= optlen;
426              optlen += sizeof(struct ip);
427              bcopy((caddr_t) ip + optlen, (caddr_t) (ip + 1),
428                      (unsigned) (m->m_len - sizeof(struct ip)));
429          }
430      m->m_flags &= ~(M_BCAST | M_MCAST);
431      icmp_send(m, opts);
432  done:
433      if (opts)
434          (void) m_free(opts);
435  }
                                                             ──────────── ip_icmp.c
```

Figure 11.37   `icmp_reflect` function: final assembly.

Remove original options

417–429   `icmp_reflect` removes the options from the original request by moving the ICMP message up to the end of the IP header. This is shown in Figure 11.38). The new options, which are in the mbuf pointed to by `opts`, are reinserted by `ip_output`.

Send message and cleanup

430–435   The broadcast and multicast flags are explicitly cleared before passing the message and options to `icmp_send`, after which the mbuf containing the options is released.

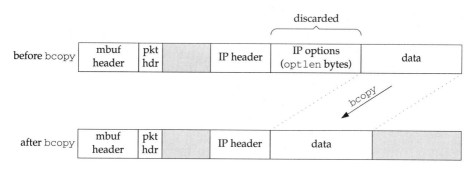

Figure 11.38 icmp_reflect: removal of options.

11.13 `icmp_send` Function

`icmp_send` (Figure 11.39) processes all outgoing ICMP messages and computes the
ICMP checksum before passing them to the IP layer.

```
                                                                        ip_icmp.c
440 void
441 icmp_send(m, opts)
442 struct mbuf *m;
443 struct mbuf *opts;
444 {
445     struct ip *ip = mtod(m, struct ip *);
446     int     hlen;
447     struct icmp *icp;

448     hlen = ip->ip_hl << 2;
449     m->m_data += hlen;
450     m->m_len -= hlen;
451     icp = mtod(m, struct icmp *);
452     icp->icmp_cksum = 0;
453     icp->icmp_cksum = in_cksum(m, ip->ip_len - hlen);
454     m->m_data -= hlen;
455     m->m_len += hlen;
456     (void) ip_output(m, opts, NULL, 0, NULL);
457 }
                                                                        ip_icmp.c
```

Figure 11.39 icmp_send function.

440–457   As it does when checking the ICMP checksum in `icmp_input`, Net/3 adjusts the
mbuf data pointer and length to hide the IP header and lets `in_cksum` look only at the
ICMP message. The computed checksum is placed in the header at `icmp_cksum` and
the datagram and any options are passed to `ip_output`. The ICMP layer does not
maintain a route cache, so `icmp_send` passes a null pointer to `ip_output` instead of a
route entry as the third argument. `icmp_send` also does not pass any control flags to
`ip_output` (the fourth argument). In particular, `IP_ALLOWBROADCAST` isn't passed,
so `ip_output` discards any ICMP messages with a broadcast destination address (i.e.,
the original datagram arrived with an invalid source address).

11.14 `icmp_sysctl` Function

The `icmp_sysctl` function for IP supports the single option listed in Figure 11.40. The system administrator can modify the option through the `sysctl`(8) program.

`sysctl` constant	Net/3 variable	Description
`ICMPCTL_MASKREPL`	`icmpmaskrepl`	Should system respond to ICMP address mask requests?

Figure 11.40   `icmp_sysctl` parameters.

Figure 11.41 shows the `icmp_sysctl` function.

——— *ip_icmp.c*
```
467 int
468 icmp_sysctl(name, namelen, oldp, oldlenp, newp, newlen)
469 int    *name;
470 u_int   namelen;
471 void   *oldp;
472 size_t *oldlenp;
473 void   *newp;
474 size_t  newlen;
475 {
476     /* All sysctl names at this level are terminal. */
477     if (namelen != 1)
478         return (ENOTDIR);

479     switch (name[0]) {
480     case ICMPCTL_MASKREPL:
481         return (sysctl_int(oldp, oldlenp, newp, newlen, &icmpmaskrepl));
482     default:
483         return (ENOPROTOOPT);
484     }
485     /* NOTREACHED */
486 }
```
——— *ip_icmp.c*
Figure 11.41   `icmp_sysctl` function.

467–478   ENOTDIR is returned if the required ICMP `sysctl` name is missing.

479–486   There are no options below the ICMP level, so this function calls `sysctl_int` to modify `icmpmaskrepl` or returns ENOPROTOOPT if the option is not recognized.

11.15 Summary

The ICMP protocol is implemented as a transport layer above IP, but it is tightly integrated with the IP layer. We've seen that the kernel responds directly to ICMP request messages but passes errors and replies to the appropriate transport protocol or application program for processing. The kernel makes immediate changes to the routing tables when an ICMP redirect message arrives but also passes redirects to any waiting processes, typically a routing daemon.

In Sections 23.9 and 27.6 we'll see how the UDP and TCP protocols respond to ICMP error messages, and in Chapter 32 we'll see how a process can generate ICMP requests.

Exercises

11.1 What is the source address of an ICMP address mask reply message generated by a request with a destination address of 0.0.0.0?

11.2 Describe how a link-level broadcast of a packet with a forged unicast source address can interfere with the operation of another host on the network.

11.3 RFC 1122 suggests that a host should discard an ICMP redirect message if the new first-hop router is on a different subnet from the old first-hop router or if the message came from a router other than the current first-hop router for the final destination included in the message. Why should this advice be followed?

11.4 If the ICMP information request is obsolete, why does `icmp_input` pass it to `rip_input` instead of discarding it?

11.5 We pointed out that Net/3 does not convert the offset and length field of an IP packet to network byte order before including the packet in an ICMP error message. Why is this inconsequential in the case of the IP offset field?

11.6 Describe a situation in which `ifaof_ifpforaddr` from Figure 11.25 returns a null pointer.

11.7 What happens to data included after the timestamps in a timestamp query?

11.8 Implement the following changes to improve the ICMP timestamp code:

Add a timestamp field to the mbuf packet header. Have the device drivers record the exact time a packet is received in this field and have the ICMP timestamp code copy the value into the `icmp_rtime` field.

On output, have the ICMP timestamp code store the byte offset of where in the packet to store the current time in the timestamp field. Modify a device driver to insert the timestamp right before sending the packet.

11.9 Modify `icmp_error` to return up to 64 bytes (as does Solaris 2.x) of the original datagram in ICMP error messages.

11.10 In Figure 11.30, what happens to a packet that has the high-order bit of `ip_off` set?

11.11 Why is the return value from `ip_output` discarded in Figure 11.39?

12

IP Multicasting

12.1 Introduction

Recall from Chapter 8 that class D IP addresses (224.0.0.0 to 239.255.255.255) do not identify individual interfaces in an internet but instead identify groups of interfaces. For this reason, class D addresses are called *multicast groups*. A datagram with a class D destination address is delivered to every interface in an internet that has *joined* the corresponding multicast group.

Experimental applications on the Internet that take advantage of multicasting include audio and video conferencing applications, resource discovery tools, and shared whiteboards.

Group membership is determined dynamically as interfaces join and leave groups based on requests from processes running on each system. Since group membership is relative to an interface, it is possible for a multihomed host to have different group membership lists for each interface. We'll refer to group membership on a particular interface as an {interface, group} pair.

Group membership on a single network is communicated between systems by the IGMP protocol (Chapter 13). Multicast routers propagate group membership information using multicast routing protocols (Chapter 14), such as DVMRP (Distance Vector Multicast Routing Protocol). A standard IP router may support multicast routing, or multicast routing may be handled by a router dedicated to that purpose.

Networks such as Ethernet, token ring, and FDDI directly support hardware multicasting. In Net/3, if an interface supports multicasting, the IFF_MULTICAST bit is on in if_flags in the interface's ifnet structure (Figure 3.7). We'll use Ethernet to illustrate hardware-supported IP multicasting, since Ethernet is in widespread use and Net/3 includes sample Ethernet drivers. Multicast services are trivially implemented on point-to-point networks such as SLIP and the loopback interface.

IP multicasting services may not be available on a particular interface if the local network does not support hardware-level multicast. RFC 1122 does not prevent the interface layer from providing a software-level multicast service as long as it is transparent to IP.

RFC 1112 [Deering 1989] describes the host requirements for IP multicasting. There are three levels of conformance:

Level 0   The host cannot send or receive IP multicasts.

Such a host should silently discard any packets it receives with a class D destination address.

Level 1   The host can send but cannot receive IP multicasts.

A host is not required to join an IP multicast group before sending a datagram to the group. A multicast datagram is sent in the same way as a unicast datagram except the destination address is the IP multicast group. The network drivers must recognize this and multicast the datagram on the local network.

Level 2   The host can send and receive IP multicasts.

To receive IP multicasts, the host must be able to join and leave multicast groups and must support IGMP for exchanging group membership information on at least one interface. A multihomed host may support multicasting on a subset of its interfaces.

Net/3 meets the level 2 host requirements and can additionally act as a multicast router. As with unicast IP routing, we assume that the system we are describing is a multicast router and we include the Net/3 multicast routing code in our presentation.

Well-Known IP Multicast Groups

As with UDP and TCP port numbers, the *Internet Assigned Numbers Authority* (IANA) maintains a list of registered IP multicast groups. The current list can be found in RFC 1700. For more information about the IANA, see RFC 1700. Figure 12.1 shows only some of the well-known groups.

Group	Description	Net/3 constant
224.0.0.0	reserved	`INADDR_UNSPEC_GROUP`
224.0.0.1	all systems on this subnet	`INADDR_ALLHOSTS_GROUP`
224.0.0.2	all routers on this subnet	
224.0.0.3	unassigned	
224.0.0.4	DVMRP routers	
224.0.0.255	unassigned	`INADDR_MAX_LOCAL_GROUP`
224.0.1.1	NTP Network Time Protocol	
224.0.1.2	SGI-Dogfight	

Figure 12.1   Some registered IP multicast groups.

The first 256 groups (224.0.0.0 to 224.0.0.255) are reserved for protocols that implement IP unicast and multicast routing mechanisms. Datagrams sent to any of these groups are not forwarded beyond the local network by multicast routers, regardless of the TTL value in the IP header.

> RFC 1075 places this requirement only on the 224.0.0.0 and 224.0.0.1 groups but mrouted, the most common multicast routing implementation, restricts the remaining groups as described here. Group 224.0.0.0 (INADDR_UNSPEC_GROUP) is reserved and group 224.0.0.255 (INADDR_MAX_LOCAL_GROUP) marks the last local multicast group.

Every level-2 conforming system is required to join the 224.0.0.1 (INADDR_ALLHOSTS_GROUP) group on all multicast interfaces at system initialization time (Figure 6.19) and remain a member of the group until the system is shut down. There is no multicast group that corresponds to every interface on an internet.

> Imagine if your voice-mail system had the option of sending a message to every voice mailbox in your company. Maybe you have such an option. Do you find it useful? Does it scale to larger companies? Can anyone send to the "all-mailbox" group, or is it restricted?

Unicast and multicast routers may join group 224.0.0.2 to communicate with each other. The ICMP router solicitation message and router advertisement messages may be sent to 224.0.0.2 (the all-routers group) and 224.0.0.1 (the all-hosts group), respectively, instead of to the limited broadcast address (255.255.255.255).

The 224.0.0.4 group supports communication between multicast routers that implement DVMRP. Other groups within the local multicast group range are similarly assigned for other routing protocols.

Beyond the first 256 groups, the remaining groups (224.0.1.0–239.255.255.255) are assigned to various multicast application protocols or remain unassigned. Figure 12.1 lists two examples, the Network Time Protocol (224.0.1.1), and SGI-Dogfight (224.0.1.2).

Throughout this chapter, we note that multicast packets are sent and received by the transport layer on a host. While the multicasting code is not aware of the specific transport protocol that sends and receives multicast datagrams, the only Internet transport protocol that supports multicasting is UDP.

12.2 Code Introduction

The basic multicasting code discussed in this chapter is contained within the same files as the standard IP code. Figure 12.2 lists the files that we examine.

File	Description
netinet/if_ether.h	Ethernet multicasting structure and macro definitions
netinet/in.h	more Internet multicast structures
netinet/in_var.h	Internet multicast structure and macro definitions
netinet/ip_var.h	IP multicast structures
net/if_ethersubr.c	Ethernet multicast functions
netinet/in.c	group membership functions
netinet/ip_input.c	input multicast processing
netinet/ip_output.c	output multicast processing

Figure 12.2 Files discussed in this chapter.

Global Variables

Three new global variables are introduced in this chapter:

Variable	Datatype	Description
ether_ipmulticast_min	u_char []	minimum Ethernet multicast address reserved for IP
ether_ipmulticast_max	u_char []	maximum Ethernet multicast address reserved for IP
ip_mrouter	struct socket *	pointer to socket created by multicast routing daemon

Figure 12.3 Global variables introduced in this chapter.

Statistics

The code in this chapter updates a few of the counters maintained in the global ipstat structure.

ipstat member	Description
ips_forward	#packets forwarded by this system
ips_cantforward	#packets that cannot be forwarded—system is not a router
ips_noroute	#packets that cannot be forwarded because a route is not available

Figure 12.4 Multicast processing statistics.

Link-level multicast statistics are collected in the ifnet structure (Figure 4.5) and may include multicasting of protocols other than IP.

12.3   Ethernet Multicast Addresses

An efficient implementation of IP multicasting requires IP to take advantage of hard-ware-level multicasting, without which each IP datagram would have to be broadcast to the network and every host would have to examine each datagram and discard those not intended for the host. The hardware filters unwanted datagrams before they reach the IP layer.

For the hardware filter to work, the network interface must convert the IP multicast group destination to a link-layer multicast address recognized by the network hard-ware. On point-to-point networks, such as SLIP and the loopback interface, the mapping is implicit since there is only one possible destination. On other networks, such as Ethernet, an explicit mapping function is required. The standard mapping for Ethernet applies to any network that employs 802.3 addressing.

Figure 4.12 illustrated the difference between an Ethernet unicast and multicast address: if the low-order bit of the high-order byte of the Ethernet address is a 1, it is a multicast address; otherwise it is a unicast address. Unicast Ethernet addresses are assigned by the interface's manufacturer, but multicast addresses are assigned dynami-cally by network protocols.

IP to Ethernet Multicast Address Mapping

Because Ethernet supports multiple protocols, a method to allocate the multicast addresses and prevent conflicts is needed. Ethernet addresses allocation is adminis-tered by the IEEE. A block of Ethernet multicast addresses is assigned to the IANA by the IEEE to support IP multicasting. The addresses in the block all start with `01:00:5e`.

> The block of Ethernet unicast addresses starting with `00:00:5e` is also assigned to the IANA but remains reserved for future use.

Figure 12.5 illustrates the construction of an Ethernet multicast address from a class D IP address.

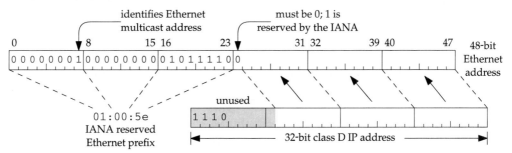

Figure 12.5   Mapping between IP and Ethernet addresses.

The mapping illustrated by Figure 12.5 is a many-to-one mapping. The high-order 9 bits of the class D IP address are not used when constructing the Ethernet address. 32 IP multicast groups map to a single Ethernet multicast address (Exercise 12.3). In

Section 12.14 we'll see how this affects input processing. Figure 12.6 shows the macro that implements this mapping in Net/3.

```
                                                                       —— if_ether.h
61 #define ETHER_MAP_IP_MULTICAST(ipaddr, enaddr) \
62      /* struct in_addr *ipaddr; */ \
63      /* u_char enaddr[6];      */ \
64 { \
65      (enaddr)[0] = 0x01; \
66      (enaddr)[1] = 0x00; \
67      (enaddr)[2] = 0x5e; \
68      (enaddr)[3] = ((u_char *)ipaddr)[1] & 0x7f; \
69      (enaddr)[4] = ((u_char *)ipaddr)[2]; \
70      (enaddr)[5] = ((u_char *)ipaddr)[3]; \
71 }
                                                                       —— if_ether.h
```

Figure 12.6   ETHER_MAP_IP_MULTICAST macro.

IP to Ethernet multicast mapping

61–71   ETHER_MAP_IP_MULTICAST implements the mapping shown in Figure 12.5. ipaddr points to the class D multicast address, and the matching Ethernet address is constructed in enaddr, an array of 6 bytes. The first 3 bytes of the Ethernet multicast address are 0x01, 0x00, and 0x5e followed by a 0 bit and then the low-order 23 bits of the class D IP address.

12.4   `ether_multi` Structure

For each Ethernet interface, Net/3 maintains a list of Ethernet multicast address ranges to be received by the hardware. This list defines the multicast filtering to be implemented by the device. Because most Ethernet devices are limited in the number of addresses they can selectively receive, the IP layer must be prepared to discard datagrams that pass through the hardware filter. Each address range is stored in an ether_multi structure:

```
                                                                       —— if_ether.h
147 struct ether_multi {
148     u_char  enm_addrlo[6];       /* low  or only address of range */
149     u_char  enm_addrhi[6];       /* high or only address of range */
150     struct arpcom *enm_ac;       /* back pointer to arpcom */
151     u_int   enm_refcount;        /* no. claims to this addr/range */
152     struct ether_multi *enm_next;   /* ptr to next ether_multi */
153 };
                                                                       —— if_ether.h
```

Figure 12.7   ether_multi structure.

Ethernet multicast addresses

147–153   enm_addrlo and enm_addrhi specify a range of Ethernet multicast addresses that should be received. A single Ethernet address is specified when enm_addrlo and enm_addrhi are the same. The entire list of ether_multi structures is attached to the `arpcom` structure of each Ethernet interface (Figure 3.26). Ethernet multicasting is independent of ARP—using the `arpcom` structure is a matter of convenience, since the structure is already included in every Ethernet interface structure.

> We'll see that the start and end of the ranges are always the same since there is no way in Net/3 for a process to specify an address range.

`enm_ac` points back to the `arpcom` structure of the associated interface and `enm_refcount` tracks the usage of the `ether_multi` structure. When the reference count drops to 0, the structure is released. `enm_next` joins the `ether_multi` structures for a single interface into a linked list. Figure 12.8 shows a list of three `ether_multi` structures attached to `le_softc[0]`, the `ifnet` structure for our sample Ethernet interface.

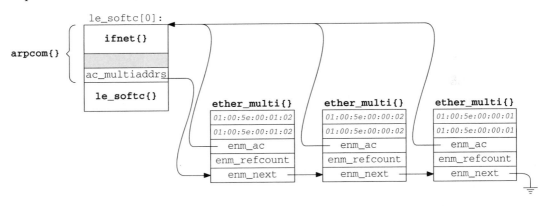

Figure 12.8   The LANCE interface with three `ether_multi` structures.

In Figure 12.8 we see that:

- The interface has joined three groups. Most likely they are: 224.0.0.1 (all-hosts), 224.0.0.2 (all-routers), and 224.0.1.2 (SGI-dogfight). Because the Ethernet to IP mapping is a one-to-many mapping, we cannot determine the exact IP multicast groups by examining the resulting Ethernet multicast addresses. The interface may have joined 225.0.0.1, 225.0.0.2, and 226.0.1.2, for example.
- The most recently joined group appears at the front of the list.
- The `enm_ac` back-pointer makes it easy to find the beginning of the list and to release an `ether_multi` structure, without having to implement a doubly linked list.
- The `ether_multi` structures apply to Ethernet devices only. Other multicast devices may have a different multicast implementation.

The `ETHER_LOOKUP_MULTI` macro, shown in Figure 12.9, searches an `ether_multi` list for a range of addresses.

—— *if_ether.h*
```
166 #define ETHER_LOOKUP_MULTI(addrlo, addrhi, ac, enm) \
167     /* u_char addrlo[6]; */ \
168     /* u_char addrhi[6]; */ \
169     /* struct arpcom *ac; */ \
170     /* struct ether_multi *enm; */ \
171 { \
172     for ((enm) = (ac)->ac_multiaddrs; \
173         (enm) != NULL && \
174         (bcmp((enm)->enm_addrlo, (addrlo), 6) != 0 || \
175          bcmp((enm)->enm_addrhi, (addrhi), 6) != 0); \
176         (enm) = (enm)->enm_next); \
177 }
```
—— *if_ether.h*

Figure 12.9 ETHER_LOOKUP_MULTI macro.

Ethernet multicast lookups

166–177   addrlo and addrhi specify the search range and ac points to the arpcom structure containing the list to search. The for loop performs a linear search, stopping at the end of the list or when enm_addrlo and enm_addrhi both match the supplied addrlo and addrhi addresses. When the loop terminates, enm is null or points to a matching ether_multi structure.

12.5 Ethernet Multicast Reception

After this section, this chapter discusses only IP multicasting, but it is possible in Net/3 to configure the system to receive any Ethernet multicast packet. Although not useful with the IP protocols, other protocol families within the kernel might be prepared to receive these multicasts. Explicit multicast configuration is done by issuing the ioctl commands shown in Figure 12.10.

Command	Argument	Function	Description
SIOCADDMULTI	struct ifreq *	ifioctl	add multicast address to reception list
SIOCDELMULTI	struct ifreq *	ifioctl	delete multicast address from reception list

Figure 12.10 Multicast ioctl commands.

These two commands are passed by ifioctl (Figure 12.11) directly to the device driver for the interface specified in the ifreq structure (Figure 6.12).

440–446   If the process does not have superuser privileges, or if the interface does not have an if_ioctl function, ifioctl returns an error; otherwise the request is passed directly to the device driver.

```
440     case SIOCADDMULTI:
441     case SIOCDELMULTI:
442         if (error = suser(p->p_ucred, &p->p_acflag))
443             return (error);
444         if (ifp->if_ioctl == NULL)
445             return (EOPNOTSUPP);
446         return ((*ifp->if_ioctl) (ifp, cmd, data));
```

Figure 12.11 ifioctl function: multicast commands.

12.6 in_multi Structure

The Ethernet multicast data structures described in Section 12.4 are not specific to IP; they must support multicast activity by any of the protocol families supported by the kernel. At the network level, IP maintains a list of IP multicast groups associated with each interface.

As a matter of implementation convenience, the IP multicast list is attached to the in_ifaddr structure associated with the interface. Recall from Section 6.5 that this structure contains the unicast address for the interface. There is no relationship between the unicast address and the attached multicast group list other than that they both are associated with the same interface.

> This is an artifact of the Net/3 implementation. It is possible for an implementation to support IP multicast groups on an interface that does not accept IP unicast packets.

Each IP multicast {interface, group} pair is described by an in_multi structure shown in Figure 12.12.

in_var.h

```
111 struct in_multi {
112     struct in_addr inm_addr;     /* IP multicast address */
113     struct ifnet *inm_ifp;       /* back pointer to ifnet */
114     struct in_ifaddr *inm_ia;    /* back pointer to in_ifaddr */
115     u_int   inm_refcount;        /* no. membership claims by sockets */
116     u_int   inm_timer;           /* IGMP membership report timer */
117     struct in_multi *inm_next;   /* ptr to next multicast address */
118 };
```
in_var.h

Figure 12.12 in_multi structure.

IP multicast addresses

111–118 inm_addr is a class D multicast address (e.g., 224.0.0.1, the all-hosts group). inm_ifp points back to the ifnet structure of the associated interface and inm_ia points back to the interface's in_ifaddr structure.

An in_multi structure exists only if at least one process on the system has notified the kernel that it wants to receive multicast datagrams for a particular {interface, group} pair. Since multiple processes may elect to receive datagrams sent to a particular pair, inm_refcount keeps track of the number of references to the pair. When no more processes are interested in the pair, inm_refcount drops to 0 and the structure is released. This action may cause an associated ether_multi structure to be released if its reference count also drops to 0.

inm_timer is part of the IGMP protocol implementation described in Chapter 13. Finally, inm_next points to the next in_multi structure in the list.

Figure 12.13 illustrates the relationship between an interface, its IP unicast address, and its IP multicast group list using the le_softc[0] sample interface.

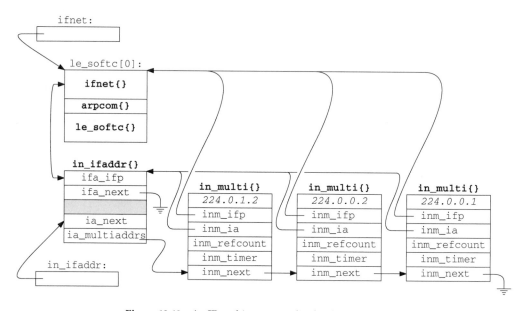

Figure 12.13   An IP multicast group list for the le interface.

We've omitted the corresponding ether_multi structures for clarity (but see Figure 12.34). If the system had two Ethernet cards, the second card would be managed through le_softc[1] and would have its own multicast group list attached to its arpcom structure. The macro IN_LOOKUP_MULTI (Figure 12.14) searches the IP multicast list for a particular multicast group.

IP multicast lookups

131–146   IN_LOOKUP_MULTI looks for the multicast group addr in the multicast group list associated with interface ifp. IFP_TO_IA searches the Internet address list, in_ifaddr, for the in_ifaddr structure associated with the interface identified by ifp. If IFP_TO_IA finds an interface, the for loop searches its IP multicast list. After the loop, inm is null or points to the matching in_multi structure.

in_var.h

```
131 #define IN_LOOKUP_MULTI(addr, ifp, inm) \
132     /* struct in_addr addr; */ \
133     /* struct ifnet *ifp; */ \
134     /* struct in_multi *inm; */ \
135 { \
136      struct in_ifaddr *ia; \
137 \
138     IFP_TO_IA((ifp), ia); \
139     if (ia == NULL) \
140         (inm) = NULL; \
141     else \
142         for ((inm) = ia->ia_multiaddrs; \
143             (inm) != NULL && (inm)->inm_addr.s_addr != (addr).s_addr; \
144             (inm) = inm->inm_next) \
145             continue; \
146 }
```

in_var.h

Figure 12.14   IN_LOOKUP_MULTI macro.

12.7 `ip_moptions` **Structure**

The `ip_moptions` structure contains the multicast options through which the transport layer controls multicast output processing. For example, the UDP call to `ip_output` is:

```
error = ip_output(m, inp->inp_options, &inp->inp_route,
                  inp->inp_socket->so_options & (SO_DONTROUTE|SO_BROADCAST),
                  inp->inp_moptions);
```

In Chapter 22 we'll see that `inp` points to an Internet protocol control block (PCB) and that UDP associates a PCB with each `socket` created by a process. Within the PCB, `inp_moptions` is a pointer to an `ip_moptions` structure. From this we see that a different `ip_moptions` structure may be passed to `ip_output` for each outgoing datagram. Figure 12.15 shows the definition of the `ip_moptions` structure.

ip_var.h

```
100 struct ip_moptions {
101     struct  ifnet *imo_multicast_ifp; /* ifp for outgoing multicasts */
102     u_char  imo_multicast_ttl;        /* TTL for outgoing multicasts */
103     u_char  imo_multicast_loop;       /* 1 => hear sends if a member */
104     u_short imo_num_memberships;      /* no. memberships this socket */
105     struct  in_multi *imo_membership[IP_MAX_MEMBERSHIPS];
106 };
```

ip_var.h

Figure 12.15   ip_moptions structure.

Multicast options

100–106   `ip_output` routes outgoing multicast datagrams through the interface pointed to by `imo_multicast_ifp` or, if `imo_multicast_ifp` is null, through the default interface for the destination multicast group (Chapter 14).

`imo_multicast_ttl` specifies the initial IP TTL value for outgoing multicasts. The default is 1, which causes multicast datagrams to remain on the local network.

If `imo_multicast_loop` is 0, the multicast datagram is not looped back and delivered to the transmitting interface even if the interface is a member of the multicast group. If `imo_multicast_loop` is 1, the multicast datagram is looped back to the transmitting interface if the interface is a member of the multicast group.

Finally, the integer `imo_num_memberships` and the array `imo_membership` maintain the list of {interface, group} pairs associated with the structure. Changes to the list are communicated to IP, which announces membership changes on the locally attached network. Each entry in the `imo_membership` array is a pointer to an `in_multi` structure attached to the `in_ifaddr` structure of the appropriate interface.

12.8 Multicast Socket Options

Several IP-level socket options, shown in Figure 12.10, provide process-level access to `ip_moptions` structures.

Command	Argument	Function	Description
`IP_MULTICAST_IF`	`struct in_addr`	`ip_ctloutput`	select default interface for outgoing multicasts
`IP_MULTICAST_TTL`	`u_char`	`ip_ctloutput`	select default TTL for outgoing multicasts
`IP_MULTICAST_LOOP`	`u_char`	`ip_ctloutput`	enable or disable loopback of outgoing multicasts
`IP_ADD_MEMBERSHIP`	`struct ip_mreq`	`ip_ctloutput`	join a multicast group
`IP_DROP_MEMBERSHIP`	`struct ip_mreq`	`ip_ctloutput`	leave a multicast group

Figure 12.16   Multicast socket options.

In Figure 8.31 we looked at the overall structure of the `ip_ctloutput` function. Figure 12.17 shows the cases relevant to changing and retrieving multicast options.

486–491   All the multicast options are handled through the `ip_setmoptions` and
539–549 `ip_getmoptions` functions. The `ip_moptions` structure passed by reference to `ip_getmoptions` or to `ip_setmoptions` is the one associated with the socket on which the `ioctl` command was issued.

> The error code returned when an option is not recognized is different for the get and set cases. ENOPROTOOPT is the more reasonable choice.

12.9 Multicast TTL Values

Multicast TTL values are difficult to understand because they have two purposes. The primary purpose of the TTL value, as with all IP packets, is to limit the lifetime of the packet within an internet and prevent it from circulating indefinitely. The second purpose is to contain packets within a region of the internet specified by administrative

```
                                                                    ip_output.c
448     case PRCO_SETOPT:
449         switch (optname) {

                            /* other set cases */

486         case IP_MULTICAST_IF:
487         case IP_MULTICAST_TTL:
488         case IP_MULTICAST_LOOP:
489         case IP_ADD_MEMBERSHIP:
490         case IP_DROP_MEMBERSHIP:
491             error = ip_setmoptions(optname, &inp->inp_moptions, m);
492             break;
493           freeit:
494         default:
495             error = EINVAL;
496             break;
497         }
498         if (m)
499             (void) m_free(m);
500         break;

501     case PRCO_GETOPT:
502         switch (optname) {

                            /* other get cases */

539         case IP_MULTICAST_IF:
540         case IP_MULTICAST_TTL:
541         case IP_MULTICAST_LOOP:
542         case IP_ADD_MEMBERSHIP:
543         case IP_DROP_MEMBERSHIP:
544             error = ip_getmoptions(optname, inp->inp_moptions, mp);
545             break;

546         default:
547             error = ENOPROTOOPT;
548             break;
549         }
                                                                    ip_output.c
```

Figure 12.17 ip_ctloutput function: multicast options.

boundaries. This administrative region is specified in subjective terms such as "this site," "this company," or "this state," and is relative to the starting point of the packet. The region associated with a multicast packet is called its *scope*.

The standard implementation of RFC 1112 multicasting merges the two concepts of lifetime and scope into the single TTL value in the IP header. In addition to discarding packets when the IP TTL drops to 0, *multicast* routers associate with each interface a TTL threshold that limits multicast transmission on that interface. A packet must have a

TTL greater than or equal to the interface's threshold value for it to be transmitted on the interface. Because of this, a multicast packet may be dropped even before its TTL value reaches 0.

Threshold values are assigned by an administrator when configuring a multicast router. These values define the scope of multicast packets. The significance of an initial TTL value for multicast datagrams is defined by the threshold policy used by the administrator and the distance between the source of the datagram and the multicast interfaces.

Figure 12.18 shows the recommended TTL values for various applications as well as recommended threshold values.

ip_ttl	Application	Scope
0		same interface
1		same subnet
31	local event video	
32		same site
63	local event audio	
64		same region
95	IETF channel 2 video	
127	IETF channel 1 video	
128		same continent
159	IETF channel 2 audio	
191	IETF channel 1 audio	
223	IETF channel 2 low-rate audio	
255	IETF channel 1 low-rate audio	
	unrestricted in scope	

Figure 12.18 TTL values for IP multicast datagrams.

The first column lists the starting value of ip_ttl in the IP header. The second column illustrates an application specific use of threshold values ([Casner 1993]). The third column lists the recommended scopes to associate with the TTL values.

For example, an interface that communicates to a network outside the local site would be configured with a multicast threshold of 32. The TTL field of any datagram that starts with a TTL of 32 (or less) is less than 32 when it reaches this interface (there is at least one hop between the source and the router) and is discarded before the router forwards it to the external network—even if the TTL is still greater than 0.

A multicast datagram that starts with a TTL of 128 would pass through site interfaces with a threshold of 32 (as long as it reached the interface within $128 - 32 = 96$ hops) but would be discarded by intercontinental interfaces with a threshold of 128.

The MBONE

A subset of routers on the Internet supports IP multicast routing. This multicast backbone is called the *MBONE*, which is described in [Casner 1993]. It exists to support experimentation with IP multicasting—in particular with audio and video data streams. In the MBONE, threshold values limit how far various data streams propagate. In Figure 12.18, we see that local event video packets always start with a TTL of

31. An interface with a threshold of 32 always blocks local event video. At the other end of the scale, IETF channel 1 low-rate audio is restricted only by the inherent IP TTL maximum of 255 hops. It propagates through the entire MBONE. An administrator of a multicast router within the MBONE can select a threshold value to accept or discard MBONE data streams selectively.

Expanding-Ring Search

Another use of the multicast TTL is to probe the internet for a resource by varying the initial TTL value of the probe datagram. This technique is called an *expanding-ring search* ([Boggs 1982]). A datagram with an initial TTL of 0 reaches only a resource on the local system associated with the outgoing interface. A TTL of 1 reaches the resource if it exists on the local subnet. A TTL of 2 reaches resources within two hops of the source. An application increases the TTL exponentially to probe a large internet quickly.

> RFC 1546 [Partridge, Mendez, and Milliken 1993] describes a related service called *anycasting*. As proposed, anycasting relies on a distinguished set of IP addresses to represent groups of hosts much like multicasting. Unlike multicast addresses, the network is expected to propagate an anycast packet until it is received by at least one host. This simplifies the implementation of an application, which no longer needs to perform expanding-ring searches.

12.10 `ip_setmoptions` Function

The bulk of the `ip_setmoptions` function consists of a `switch` statement to handle each option. Figure 12.19 shows the beginning and end of `ip_setmoptions`. The body of the `switch` is discussed in the following sections.

650–664   The first argument, `optname`, indicates which multicast option is being changed. The second argument, `imop`, references a pointer to an `ip_moptions` structure. If `*imop` is nonnull, `ip_setmoptions` modifies the structure it points to. Otherwise, `ip_setmoptions` allocates a new `ip_moptions` structure and saves its address in `*imop`. If no memory is available, `ip_setmoptions` returns `ENOBUFS` immediately. Any subsequent errors that occur are posted in `error`, which is returned to the caller at the end of the function. The third argument, `m`, points to an mbuf that contains the data for the option to be changed (second column of Figure 12.16).

Construct the defaults

665–679   When a new `ip_moptions` structure is allocated, `ip_setmoptions` initializes the default multicast interface pointer to null, initializes the default TTL to 1 (`IP_DEFAULT_MULTICAST_TTL`), enables the loopback of multicast datagrams, and clears the group membership list. With these defaults, `ip_output` selects an outgoing interface by consulting the routing tables, multicasts are kept on the local network, and the system receives its own multicast transmissions if the outgoing interface is a member of the destination group.

Process options

680–860   The body of `ip_setmoptions` consists of a `switch` statement with a case for each option. The `default` case (for unknown options) sets `error` to `EOPNOTSUPP`.

```
                                                                        ────── ip_output.c
650 int
651 ip_setmoptions(optname, imop, m)
652 int      optname;
653 struct ip_moptions **imop;
654 struct mbuf *m;
655 {
656     int     error = 0;
657     u_char  loop;
658     int     i;
659     struct in_addr addr;
660     struct ip_mreq *mreq;
661     struct ifnet *ifp;
662     struct ip_moptions *imo = *imop;
663     struct route ro;
664     struct sockaddr_in *dst;
665     if (imo == NULL) {
666         /*
667          * No multicast option buffer attached to the pcb;
668          * allocate one and initialize to default values.
669          */
670         imo = (struct ip_moptions *) malloc(sizeof(*imo), M_IPMOPTS,
671                                             M_WAITOK);
672         if (imo == NULL)
673             return (ENOBUFS);
674         *imop = imo;
675         imo->imo_multicast_ifp = NULL;
676         imo->imo_multicast_ttl = IP_DEFAULT_MULTICAST_TTL;
677         imo->imo_multicast_loop = IP_DEFAULT_MULTICAST_LOOP;
678         imo->imo_num_memberships = 0;
679     }
680     switch (optname) {

                            /* switch cases */

857     default:
858         error = EOPNOTSUPP;
859         break;
860     }
861     /*
862      * If all options have default values, no need to keep the structure.
863      */
864     if (imo->imo_multicast_ifp == NULL &&
865         imo->imo_multicast_ttl == IP_DEFAULT_MULTICAST_TTL &&
866         imo->imo_multicast_loop == IP_DEFAULT_MULTICAST_LOOP &&
867         imo->imo_num_memberships == 0) {
868         free(*imop, M_IPMOPTS);
869         *imop = NULL;
870     }
871     return (error);
872 }
                                                                        ────── ip_output.c
```

Figure 12.19   ip_setmoptions function.

Discard structure if defaults are OK

861–872   After the switch statement, ip_setmoptions examines the ip_moptions structure. If all the multicast options match their respective default values, the structure is
unnecessary and is released. ip_setmoptions returns 0 or the posted error code.

Selecting an Explicit Multicast Interface: IP_MULTICAST_IF

When optname is IP_MULTICAST_IF, the mbuf passed to ip_setmoptions contains
the unicast address of a multicast interface, which specifies the particular interface for
multicasts sent on this socket. Figure 12.20 shows the code for this option.

```
                                                                        —————————ip_output.c
681     case IP_MULTICAST_IF:
682         /*
683          * Select the interface for outgoing multicast packets.
684          */
685         if (m == NULL || m->m_len != sizeof(struct in_addr)) {
686             error = EINVAL;
687             break;
688         }
689         addr = *(mtod(m, struct in_addr *));
690         /*
691          * INADDR_ANY is used to remove a previous selection.
692          * When no interface is selected, a default one is
693          * chosen every time a multicast packet is sent.
694          */
695         if (addr.s_addr == INADDR_ANY) {
696             imo->imo_multicast_ifp = NULL;
697             break;
698         }
699         /*
700          * The selected interface is identified by its local
701          * IP address.  Find the interface and confirm that
702          * it supports multicasting.
703          */
704         INADDR_TO_IFP(addr, ifp);
705         if (ifp == NULL || (ifp->if_flags & IFF_MULTICAST) == 0) {
706             error = EADDRNOTAVAIL;
707             break;
708         }
709         imo->imo_multicast_ifp = ifp;
710         break;
                                                                        —————————ip_output.c
```

Figure 12.20 ip_setmoptions function: selecting a multicast output interface.

Validation

681–698   If no mbuf has been provided or the data within the mbuf is not the size of an
in_addr structure, ip_setmoptions posts an EINVAL error; otherwise the data is
copied into addr. If the interface address is INADDR_ANY, any previously selected
interface is discarded. Subsequent multicasts with this ip_moptions structure are

routed according to their destination group instead of through an explicitly named interface (Figure 12.40).

Select the default interface

699–710   If addr contains an address, INADDR_TO_IFP locates the matching interface. If a match can't be found or the interface does not support multicasting, EADDRNOTAVAIL is posted. Otherwise, ifp, the matching interface, becomes the multicast interface for output requests associated with this ip_moptions structure.

Selecting an Explicit Multicast TTL: IP_MULTICAST_TTL

When optname is IP_MULTICAST_TTL, the mbuf is expected to contain a single byte specifying the IP TTL for outgoing multicasts. This TTL is inserted by ip_output into every multicast datagram sent on the associated socket. Figure 12.21 shows the code for this option.

——————————————————————————————————— ip_output.c
```
711     case IP_MULTICAST_TTL:
712         /*
713          * Set the IP time-to-live for outgoing multicast packets.
714          */
715         if (m == NULL || m->m_len != 1) {
716             error = EINVAL;
717             break;
718         }
719         imo->imo_multicast_ttl = *(mtod(m, u_char *));
720         break;
```
——————————————————————————————————— ip_output.c

Figure 12.21 ip_setmoptions function: selecting an explicit multicast TTL.

Validate and select the default TTL

711–720   If the mbuf contains a single byte of data, it is copied into imo_multicast_ttl. Otherwise, EINVAL is posted.

Selecting Multicast Loopbacks: IP_MULTICAST_LOOP

In general, multicast applications come in two forms:

- An application with one sender per system and multiple remote receivers. In this configuration only one local process is sending datagrams to the group so there is no need to loopback outgoing multicasts. Examples include a multicast routing daemon and conferencing systems.

- An application with multiple senders and receivers on a system. Datagrams must be looped back so that each process receives the transmissions of the other senders on the system.

The IP_MULTICAST_LOOP option (Figure 12.22) selects the loopback policy associated with an ip_moptions structure.

```
                                                                              ip_output.c
721        case IP_MULTICAST_LOOP:
722            /*
723             * Set the loopback flag for outgoing multicast packets.
724             * Must be zero or one.
725             */
726            if (m == NULL || m->m_len != 1 ||
727                (loop = *(mtod(m, u_char *))) > 1) {
728                error = EINVAL;
729                break;
730            }
731            imo->imo_multicast_loop = loop;
732            break;
                                                                              ip_output.c
```

Figure 12.22 ip_setmoptions function: selecting multicast loopbacks.

Validate and select the loopback policy

721–732   If m is null, does not contain 1 byte of data, or the byte is not 0 or 1, EINVAL is posted. Otherwise, the byte is copied into imo_multicast_loop. A 0 indicates that datagrams should not be looped back, and a 1 enables the loopback mechanism.

Figure 12.23 shows the relationship between, the maximum scope of a multicast datagram, imo_multicast_ttl, and imo_multicast_loop.

imo_multicast-		Recipients			
		Outgoing	Local	Remote	Other
_loop	_ttl	Interface?	Network?	Networks?	Interfaces?
1	0	•			
1	1	•	•		
1	>1	•	•	•	see text

Figure 12.23 Loopback and TTL effects on multicast scope.

Figure 12.23 shows that the set of interfaces that may receive a multicast packet depends on what the loopback policy is for the transmission and what TTL value is specified in the packet. A packet may be received on an interface if the hardware receives its own transmissions, regardless of the loopback policy. A datagram may be routed through the network and arrive on another interface attached to the system (Exercise 12.6). If the sending system is itself a multicast router, outgoing packets may be forwarded to the other interfaces, but they will only be accepted for input processing on one interface (Chapter 14).

12.11 Joining an IP Multicast Group

Other than the IP all-hosts group, which the kernel automatically joins (Figure 6.19), membership in a group is driven by explicit requests from processes on the system. The process of joining (or leaving) a multicast group is more involved than the other multicast options. The in_multi list for an interface must be modified as well as any link-layer multicast structures such as the ether_multi list we described for Ethernet.

The data passed in the mbuf when optname is IP_ADD_MEMBERSHIP is an ip_mreq structure shown in Figure 12.24.

―― *in.h*
```
148 struct ip_mreq {
149     struct in_addr imr_multiaddr;   /* IP multicast address of group */
150     struct in_addr imr_interface;   /* local IP address of interface */
151 };
```
―― *in.h*

Figure 12.24 ip_mreq structure.

148-151   imr_multiaddr specifies the multicast group and imr_interface identifies the interface by its associated unicast IP address. The ip_mreq structure specifies the {interface, group} pair for membership changes.

Figure 12.25 illustrates the functions involved with joining and leaving a multicast group associated with our example Ethernet interface.

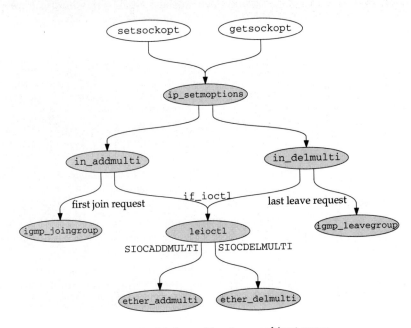

Figure 12.25 Joining and leaving a multicast group.

We start by describing the changes to the `ip_moptions` structure in the
`IP_ADD_MEMBERSHIP` case in `ip_setmoptions` (Figure 12.26). Then we follow the
request down through the IP layer, the Ethernet driver, and to the physical device—in
our case, the LANCE Ethernet card.

```
                                                                        ip_output.c
733     case IP_ADD_MEMBERSHIP:
734         /*
735          * Add a multicast group membership.
736          * Group must be a valid IP multicast address.
737          */
738         if (m == NULL || m->m_len != sizeof(struct ip_mreq)) {
739             error = EINVAL;
740             break;
741         }
742         mreq = mtod(m, struct ip_mreq *);
743         if (!IN_MULTICAST(ntohl(mreq->imr_multiaddr.s_addr))) {
744             error = EINVAL;
745             break;
746         }
747         /*
748          * If no interface address was provided, use the interface of
749          * the route to the given multicast address.
750          */
751         if (mreq->imr_interface.s_addr == INADDR_ANY) {
752             ro.ro_rt = NULL;
753             dst = (struct sockaddr_in *) &ro.ro_dst;
754             dst->sin_len = sizeof(*dst);
755             dst->sin_family = AF_INET;
756             dst->sin_addr = mreq->imr_multiaddr;
757             rtalloc(&ro);
758             if (ro.ro_rt == NULL) {
759                 error = EADDRNOTAVAIL;
760                 break;
761             }
762             ifp = ro.ro_rt->rt_ifp;
763             rtfree(ro.ro_rt);
764         } else {
765             INADDR_TO_IFP(mreq->imr_interface, ifp);
766         }
767         /*
768          * See if we found an interface, and confirm that it
769          * supports multicast.
770          */
771         if (ifp == NULL || (ifp->if_flags & IFF_MULTICAST) == 0) {
772             error = EADDRNOTAVAIL;
773             break;
774         }
```

```
775              /*
776               * See if the membership already exists or if all the
777               * membership slots are full.
778               */
779              for (i = 0; i < imo->imo_num_memberships; ++i) {
780                  if (imo->imo_membership[i]->inm_ifp == ifp &&
781                      imo->imo_membership[i]->inm_addr.s_addr
782                      == mreq->imr_multiaddr.s_addr)
783                      break;
784              }
785              if (i < imo->imo_num_memberships) {
786                  error = EADDRINUSE;
787                  break;
788              }
789              if (i == IP_MAX_MEMBERSHIPS) {
790                  error = ETOOMANYREFS;
791                  break;
792              }
793              /*
794               * Everything looks good; add a new record to the multicast
795               * address list for the given interface.
796               */
797              if ((imo->imo_membership[i] =
798                  in_addmulti(&mreq->imr_multiaddr, ifp)) == NULL) {
799                  error = ENOBUFS;
800                  break;
801              }
802              ++imo->imo_num_memberships;
803              break;
```
—— *ip_output.c*

Figure 12.26 ip_setmoptions function: joining a multicast group.

Validation

733–746   ip_setmoptions starts by validating the request. If no mbuf was passed, if it is not the correct size, or if the address (imr_multiaddr) within the structure is not a multicast group, then ip_setmoptions posts EINVAL. mreq points to the valid ip_mreq structure.

Locate the interface

747–774   If the unicast address of the interface (imr_interface) is INADDR_ANY, ip_setmoptions must locate the default interface for the specified group. A route structure is constructed with the group as the desired destination and passed to rtalloc, which locates a route for the group. If no route is available, the add request fails with the error EADDRNOTAVAIL. If a route is located, a pointer to the outgoing interface for the route is saved in ifp and the route entry, which is no longer needed, is released.

   If imr_interface is not INADDR_ANY, an explicit interface has been requested. The macro INADDR_TO_IFP searches for the interface with the requested unicast address. If an interface isn't found or if it does not support multicasting, the request fails with the error EADDRNOTAVAIL.

We described the `route` structure in Section 8.5. The function `rtalloc` is described in Section 19.2, and the use of the routing tables for selecting multicast interfaces is described in Chapter 14.

Already a member?

775-792   The last check performed on the request is to examine the `imo_membership` array to see if the selected interface is already a member of the requested group. If the `for` loop finds a match, or if the membership array is full, `EADDRINUSE` or `ETOOMANYREFS` is posted and processing of this option stops.

Join the group

793-803   At this point the request looks reasonable. `in_addmulti` arranges for IP to begin receiving multicast datagrams for the group. The pointer returned by `in_addmulti` points to a new or existing `in_multi` structure (Figure 12.12) in the interface's multicast group list. It is saved in the membership array and the size of the array is incremented.

`in_addmulti` **Function**

`in_addmulti` and its companion `in_delmulti` (Figures 12.27 and 12.36) maintain the list of multicast groups that an interface has joined. Join requests either add a new `in_multi` structure to the interface list or increase the reference count of an existing structure.

```
                                                                                ── in.c
469 struct in_multi *
470 in_addmulti(ap, ifp)
471 struct in_addr *ap;
472 struct ifnet *ifp;
473 {
474     struct in_multi *inm;
475     struct ifreq ifr;
476     struct in_ifaddr *ia;
477     int     s = splnet();

478     /*
479      * See if address already in list.
480      */
481     IN_LOOKUP_MULTI(*ap, ifp, inm);
482     if (inm != NULL) {
483         /*
484          * Found it; just increment the reference count.
485          */
486         ++inm->inm_refcount;
487     } else {
                                                                                ── in.c
```

Figure 12.27   `in_addmulti` function: first half.

Already a member

469-487   `ip_setmoptions` has already verified that `ap` points to a class D multicast address and that `ifp` points to a multicast-capable interface. `IN_LOOKUP_MULTI` (Figure 12.14)

determines if the interface is already a member of the group. If it is a member,
in_addmulti updates the reference count and returns.

If the interface is not yet a member of the group, the code in Figure 12.28 is executed.

─── *in.c*
```
487        } else {
488            /*
489             * New address; allocate a new multicast record
490             * and link it into the interface's multicast list.
491             */
492            inm = (struct in_multi *) malloc(sizeof(*inm),
493                                        M_IPMADDR, M_NOWAIT);
494            if (inm == NULL) {
495                splx(s);
496                return (NULL);
497            }
498            inm->inm_addr = *ap;
499            inm->inm_ifp = ifp;
500            inm->inm_refcount = 1;
501            IFP_TO_IA(ifp, ia);
502            if (ia == NULL) {
503                free(inm, M_IPMADDR);
504                splx(s);
505                return (NULL);
506            }
507            inm->inm_ia = ia;
508            inm->inm_next = ia->ia_multiaddrs;
509            ia->ia_multiaddrs = inm;
510            /*
511             * Ask the network driver to update its multicast reception
512             * filter appropriately for the new address.
513             */
514            ((struct sockaddr_in *) &ifr.ifr_addr)->sin_family = AF_INET;
515            ((struct sockaddr_in *) &ifr.ifr_addr)->sin_addr = *ap;
516            if ((ifp->if_ioctl == NULL) ||
517                (*ifp->if_ioctl) (ifp, SIOCADDMULTI, (caddr_t) & ifr) != 0) {
518                ia->ia_multiaddrs = inm->inm_next;
519                free(inm, M_IPMADDR);
520                splx(s);
521                return (NULL);
522            }
523            /*
524             * Let IGMP know that we have joined a new IP multicast group.
525             */
526            igmp_joingroup(inm);
527        }
528        splx(s);
529        return (inm);
530 }
```
─── *in.c*

Figure 12.28 in_addmulti function: second half.

Update the `in_multi` list

487–509   If the interface isn't a member yet, `in_addmulti` allocates, initializes, and inserts the new `in_multi` structure at the front of the `ia_multiaddrs` list in the interface's `in_ifaddr` structure (Figure 12.13).

Update the interface and announce the change

510–530   If the interface driver has defined an `if_ioctl` function, `in_addmulti` constructs an `ifreq` structure (Figure 4.23) containing the group address and passes the `SIOCADDMULTI` request to the interface. If the interface rejects the request, the `in_multi` structure is unlinked from the interface and released. Finally, `in_addmulti` calls `igmp_joingroup` to propagate the membership change to other hosts and routers.

   `in_addmulti` returns a pointer to the `in_multi` structure or null if an error occurred.

`slioctl` and `loioctl` Functions: `SIOCADDMULTI` and `SIOCDELMULTI`

Multicast group processing for the SLIP and loopback interfaces is trivial: there is nothing to do other than error checking. Figure 12.29 shows the SLIP processing.

```
                                                                    ──── if_sl.c
673     case SIOCADDMULTI:
674     case SIOCDELMULTI:
675         ifr = (struct ifreq *) data;
676         if (ifr == 0) {
677             error = EAFNOSUPPORT;    /* XXX */
678             break;
679         }
680         switch (ifr->ifr_addr.sa_family) {

681         case AF_INET:
682             break;

683         default:
684             error = EAFNOSUPPORT;
685             break;
686         }
687         break;
                                                                    ──── if_sl.c
```

Figure 12.29 `slioctl` function: multicast processing.

673–687   `EAFNOSUPPORT` is returned whether the request is empty or not for the `AF_INET` protocol family.

   Figure 12.30 shows the loopback processing.

152–166   The processing for the loopback interface is identical to the SLIP code in Figure 12.29. `EAFNOSUPPORT` is returned whether the request is empty or not for the `AF_INET` protocol family.

—— *if_loop.c*

```
152    case SIOCADDMULTI:
153    case SIOCDELMULTI:
154        ifr = (struct ifreq *) data;
155        if (ifr == 0) {
156            error = EAFNOSUPPORT;    /* XXX */
157            break;
158        }
159        switch (ifr->ifr_addr.sa_family) {

160        case AF_INET:
161            break;

162        default:
163            error = EAFNOSUPPORT;
164            break;
165        }
166        break;
```
—— *if_loop.c*

Figure 12.30 `loioctl` function: multicast processing.

`leioctl` Function: `SIOCADDMULTI` and `SIOCDELMULTI`

Recall from Figure 4.2 that `leioctl` is the `if_ioctl` function for the LANCE Ethernet driver. Figure 12.31 shows the code for the `SIOCADDMULTI` and `SIOCDELMULTI` options.

—— *if_le.c*

```
657    case SIOCADDMULTI:
658    case SIOCDELMULTI:
659        /* Update our multicast list  */
660        error = (cmd == SIOCADDMULTI) ?
661            ether_addmulti((struct ifreq *) data, &le->sc_ac) :
662            ether_delmulti((struct ifreq *) data, &le->sc_ac);

663        if (error == ENETRESET) {
664            /*
665             * Multicast list has changed; set the hardware
666             * filter accordingly.
667             */
668            lereset(ifp->if_unit);
669            error = 0;
670        }
671        break;
```
—— *if_le.c*

Figure 12.31 `leioctl` function: multicast processing.

657–671   `leioctl` passes add and delete requests directly to the `ether_addmulti` or `ether_delmulti` functions. Both functions return `ENETRESET` if the request changes the set of IP multicast addresses that must be received by the physical hardware. If this occurs, `leioctl` calls `lereset` to reinitialize the hardware with the new multicast reception list.

We don't show `lereset`, as it is specific to the LANCE Ethernet hardware. For multicasting, `lereset` arranges for the hardware to receive frames addressed to any of the Ethernet multicast addresses contained in the `ether_multi` list associated with the interface. The LANCE driver uses a hashing mechanism if each entry on the multicast list is a single address. The hash code allows the hardware to receive multicast packets selectively. If the driver finds an entry that describes a range of addresses, it abandons the hash strategy and configures the hardware to receive *all* multicast packets. If the driver must fall back to receiving all Ethernet multicast addresses, the `IFF_ALLMULTI` flag is on when `lereset` returns.

`ether_addmulti` Function

Every Ethernet driver calls `ether_addmulti` to process the `SIOCADDMULTI` request. This function maps the IP class D address to the appropriate Ethernet multicast address (Figure 12.5) and updates the `ether_multi` list. Figure 12.32 shows the first half of the `ether_addmulti` function.

Initialize address range

366–399   First, `ether_addmulti` initializes a range of multicast addresses in `addrlo` and `addrhi` (both are arrays of six unsigned characters). If the requested address is from the `AF_UNSPEC` family, `ether_addmulti` assumes the address is an explicit Ethernet multicast address and copies it into `addrlo` and `addrhi`. If the address is in the `AF_INET` family and is `INADDR_ANY` (0.0.0.0), `ether_addmulti` initializes `addrlo` to `ether_ipmulticast_min` and `addrhi` to `ether_ipmulticast_max`. These two constant Ethernet addresses are defined as:

```
u_char   ether_ipmulticast_min[6] = { 0x01, 0x00, 0x5e, 0x00, 0x00, 0x00 };
u_char   ether_ipmulticast_max[6] = { 0x01, 0x00, 0x5e, 0x7f, 0xff, 0xff };
```

> As with `etherbroadcastaddr` (Section 4.3), this is a convenient way to define a 48-bit constant.

IP multicast routers must listen for all IP multicasts. Specifying the group as `INADDR_ANY` is considered a request to join *every* IP multicast group. The Ethernet address range selected in this case spans the entire block of IP multicast addresses allocated to the IANA.

> The `mrouted(8)` daemon issues a `SIOCADDMULTI` request with `INADDR_ANY` when it begins routing packets for a multicast interface.

`ETHER_MAP_IP_MULTICAST` maps any other specific IP multicast group to the appropriate Ethernet multicast address. Requests for other address families are rejected with an `EAFNOSUPPORT` error.

While the Ethernet multicast list supports address ranges, there is no way for a process or the kernel to request a specific range, other than to enumerate the addresses, since `addrlo` and `addrhi` are always set to the same address.

The second half of `ether_addmulti`, shown in Figure 12.33, verifies the address range and adds it to the list if it is new.

```
                                                                        —— if_ethersubr.c
366 int
367 ether_addmulti(ifr, ac)
368 struct ifreq *ifr;
369 struct arpcom *ac;
370 {
371     struct ether_multi *enm;
372     struct sockaddr_in *sin;
373     u_char  addrlo[6];
374     u_char  addrhi[6];
375     int     s = splimp();

376     switch (ifr->ifr_addr.sa_family) {

377     case AF_UNSPEC:
378         bcopy(ifr->ifr_addr.sa_data, addrlo, 6);
379         bcopy(addrlo, addrhi, 6);
380         break;

381     case AF_INET:
382         sin = (struct sockaddr_in *) &(ifr->ifr_addr);
383         if (sin->sin_addr.s_addr == INADDR_ANY) {
384             /*
385              * An IP address of INADDR_ANY means listen to all
386              * of the Ethernet multicast addresses used for IP.
387              * (This is for the sake of IP multicast routers.)
388              */
389             bcopy(ether_ipmulticast_min, addrlo, 6);
390             bcopy(ether_ipmulticast_max, addrhi, 6);
391         } else {
392             ETHER_MAP_IP_MULTICAST(&sin->sin_addr, addrlo);
393             bcopy(addrlo, addrhi, 6);
394         }
395         break;

396     default:
397         splx(s);
398         return (EAFNOSUPPORT);
399     }
```
                                                                        —— if_ethersubr.c

Figure 12.32 ether_addmulti function: first half.

Already receiving

400–418   ether_addmulti checks the multicast bit (Figure 4.12) of the high and low addresses to ensure that they are indeed Ethernet multicast addresses. ETHER_LOOKUP_MULTI (Figure 12.9) determines if the hardware is already listening for the specified multicast addresses. If so, the reference count (enm_refcount) in the matching ether_multi structure is incremented and ether_addmulti returns 0.

Update ether_multi list

419–441   If this is a new address range, a new ether_multi structure is allocated, initialized, and linked to the ac_multiaddrs list in the interface's arpcom structure (Figure 12.8). If ENETRESET is returned by ether_addmulti, the device driver that called

```
                                                                    ———— if_ethersubr.c
400      /*
401       * Verify that we have valid Ethernet multicast addresses.
402       */
403      if ((addrlo[0] & 0x01) != 1 || (addrhi[0] & 0x01) != 1) {
404          splx(s);
405          return (EINVAL);
406      }
407      /*
408       * See if the address range is already in the list.
409       */
410      ETHER_LOOKUP_MULTI(addrlo, addrhi, ac, enm);
411      if (enm != NULL) {
412          /*
413           * Found it; just increment the reference count.
414           */
415          ++enm->enm_refcount;
416          splx(s);
417          return (0);
418      }
419      /*
420       * New address or range; malloc a new multicast record
421       * and link it into the interface's multicast list.
422       */
423      enm = (struct ether_multi *) malloc(sizeof(*enm), M_IFMADDR, M_NOWAIT);
424      if (enm == NULL) {
425          splx(s);
426          return (ENOBUFS);
427      }
428      bcopy(addrlo, enm->enm_addrlo, 6);
429      bcopy(addrhi, enm->enm_addrhi, 6);
430      enm->enm_ac = ac;
431      enm->enm_refcount = 1;
432      enm->enm_next = ac->ac_multiaddrs;
433      ac->ac_multiaddrs = enm;
434      ac->ac_multicnt++;
435      splx(s);
436      /*
437       * Return ENETRESET to inform the driver that the list has changed
438       * and its reception filter should be adjusted accordingly.
439       */
440      return (ENETRESET);
441  }
                                                                    ———— if_ethersubr.c
```

Figure 12.33   ether_addmulti function: second half.

the function knows that the multicast list has changed and the hardware reception filter
must be updated.

Figure 12.34 shows the relationships between the ip_moptions, in_multi, and
ether_multi structures after the LANCE Ethernet interface has joined the all-hosts
group.

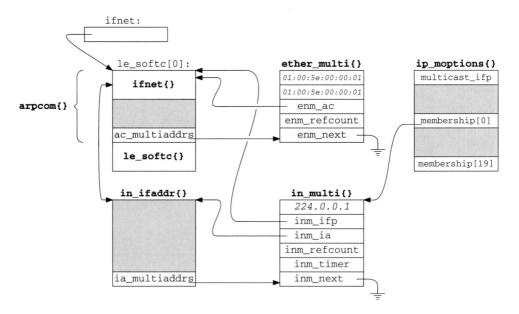

Figure 12.34   Overview of multicast data structures.

12.12 Leaving an IP Multicast Group

In general, the steps required to leave a group are the reverse of those required to join a group. The membership list in the `ip_moptions` structure is updated, the `in_multi` list for the IP interface is updated, and the `ether_multi` list for the device is updated. First, we return to `ip_setmoptions` and the `IP_DROP_MEMBERSHIP` case, which we show in Figure 12.35.

Validation

804–830   The mbuf must contain an `ip_mreq` structure, within the structure `imr_multiaddr` must be a multicast group, and there must be an interface associated with the unicast address `imr_interface`. If these conditions aren't met, `EINVAL` or `EADDRNOTAVAIL` is posted and processing continues at the end of the switch.

Delete membership references

831–856   The `for` loop searches the group membership list for an `in_multi` structure with the requested {interface, group} pair. If a match isn't found, `EADDRNOTAVAIL` is posted. Otherwise, `in_delmulti` updates the `in_multi` list and the second `for` loop removes the unused entry in the membership array by shifting subsequent entries to fill the gap. The size of the array is updated accordingly.

ip_output.c
```
804        case IP_DROP_MEMBERSHIP:
805            /*
806             * Drop a multicast group membership.
807             * Group must be a valid IP multicast address.
808             */
809            if (m == NULL || m->m_len != sizeof(struct ip_mreq)) {
810                error = EINVAL;
811                break;
812            }
813            mreq = mtod(m, struct ip_mreq *);
814            if (!IN_MULTICAST(ntohl(mreq->imr_multiaddr.s_addr))) {
815                error = EINVAL;
816                break;
817            }
818            /*
819             * If an interface address was specified, get a pointer
820             * to its ifnet structure.
821             */
822            if (mreq->imr_interface.s_addr == INADDR_ANY)
823                ifp = NULL;
824            else {
825                INADDR_TO_IFP(mreq->imr_interface, ifp);
826                if (ifp == NULL) {
827                    error = EADDRNOTAVAIL;
828                    break;
829                }
830            }
831            /*
832             * Find the membership in the membership array.
833             */
834            for (i = 0; i < imo->imo_num_memberships; ++i) {
835                if ((ifp == NULL ||
836                        imo->imo_membership[i]->inm_ifp == ifp) &&
837                    imo->imo_membership[i]->inm_addr.s_addr ==
838                    mreq->imr_multiaddr.s_addr)
839                    break;
840            }
841            if (i == imo->imo_num_memberships) {
842                error = EADDRNOTAVAIL;
843                break;
844            }
845            /*
846             * Give up the multicast address record to which the
847             * membership points.
848             */
849            in_delmulti(imo->imo_membership[i]);
850            /*
851             * Remove the gap in the membership array.
852             */
853            for (++i; i < imo->imo_num_memberships; ++i)
854                imo->imo_membership[i - 1] = imo->imo_membership[i];
855            --imo->imo_num_memberships;
856            break;
```
ip_output.c

Figure 12.35 ip_setmoptions function: leaving a multicast group.

`in_delmulti` Function

Since many processes may be receiving multicast datagrams, calling `in_delmulti` (Figure 12.36) results only in leaving the specified group when there are no more references to the `in_multi` structure.

in.c

```
534 int
535 in_delmulti(inm)
536 struct in_multi *inm;
537 {
538     struct in_multi **p;
539     struct ifreq ifr;
540     int     s = splnet();

541     if (--inm->inm_refcount == 0) {
542         /*
543          * No remaining claims to this record; let IGMP know that
544          * we are leaving the multicast group.
545          */
546         igmp_leavegroup(inm);
547         /*
548          * Unlink from list.
549          */
550         for (p = &inm->inm_ia->ia_multiaddrs;
551              *p != inm;
552              p = &(*p)->inm_next)
553             continue;
554         *p = (*p)->inm_next;
555         /*
556          * Notify the network driver to update its multicast reception
557          * filter.
558          */
559         ((struct sockaddr_in *) &(ifr.ifr_addr))->sin_family = AF_INET;
560         ((struct sockaddr_in *) &(ifr.ifr_addr))->sin_addr =
561             inm->inm_addr;
562         (*inm->inm_ifp->if_ioctl) (inm->inm_ifp, SIOCDELMULTI,
563                                     (caddr_t) & ifr);
564         free(inm, M_IPMADDR);
565     }
566     splx(s);
567 }
```

in.c

Figure 12.36   `in_delmulti` function.

Update `in_multi` structure

534–567   `in_delmulti` starts by decrementing the reference count of the `in_multi` structure and returning if the reference count is nonzero. If the reference count drops to 0, there are no longer any processes waiting for the multicast datagrams on the specified {interface, group} pair. `igmp_leavegroup` is called, but as we'll see in Section 13.8, the function does nothing.

The `for` loop traverses the linked list of `in_multi` structures until it locates the matching structure.

> The body of this `for` loop consists of the single `continue` statement. All the work is done by the expressions at the top of the loop. The `continue` is not required but stands out more clearly than a bare semicolon.

> The `ETHER_LOOKUP_MULTI` macro in Figure 12.9 does not use the `continue` and the bare semicolon is almost undetectable.

After the loop, the matching `in_multi` structure is unlinked and `in_delmulti` issues the `SIOCDELMULTI` request to the interface so that any device-specific data structures can be updated. For Ethernet interfaces, this means the `ether_multi` list is updated. Finally, the `in_multi` structure is released.

> The `SIOCDELMULTI` case for the LANCE driver was included in Figure 12.31 where we also discussed the `SIOCADDMULTI` case.

`ether_delmulti` **Function**

When IP releases an `in_multi` structure associated with an Ethernet device, the device may be able to release the matching `ether_multi` structure. We say *may* because IP may be unaware of other software listening for IP multicasts. When the reference count for the `ether_multi` structure drops to 0, it can be released. Figure 12.37 shows the `ether_delmulti` function.

445–479   `ether_delmulti` initializes the `addrlo` and `addrhi` arrays in the same way as `ether_addmulti` does.

Locate `ether_multi` **structure**

480–494   `ETHER_LOOKUP_MULTI` locates a matching `ether_multi` structure. If it isn't found, `ENXIO` is returned. If the matching structure is found, the reference count is decremented and if the result is nonzero, `ether_delmulti` returns immediately. In this case, the structure may not be released because another protocol has elected to receive the same multicast packets.

Delete `ether_multi` **structure**

495–511   The `for` loop searches the `ether_multi` list for the matching address range. The matching structure is unlinked from the list and released. Finally, the size of the list is updated and `ENETRESET` is returned so that the device driver can update its hardware reception filter.

```
445  int
446  ether_delmulti(ifr, ac)
447  struct ifreq *ifr;
448  struct arpcom *ac;
449  {
450      struct ether_multi *enm;
451      struct ether_multi **p;
452      struct sockaddr_in *sin;
453      u_char  addrlo[6];
454      u_char  addrhi[6];
455      int     s = splimp();

456      switch (ifr->ifr_addr.sa_family) {

457      case AF_UNSPEC:
458          bcopy(ifr->ifr_addr.sa_data, addrlo, 6);
459          bcopy(addrlo, addrhi, 6);
460          break;

461      case AF_INET:
462          sin = (struct sockaddr_in *) &(ifr->ifr_addr);
463          if (sin->sin_addr.s_addr == INADDR_ANY) {
464              /*
465               * An IP address of INADDR_ANY means stop listening
466               * to the range of Ethernet multicast addresses used
467               * for IP.
468               */
469              bcopy(ether_ipmulticast_min, addrlo, 6);
470              bcopy(ether_ipmulticast_max, addrhi, 6);
471          } else {
472              ETHER_MAP_IP_MULTICAST(&sin->sin_addr, addrlo);
473              bcopy(addrlo, addrhi, 6);
474          }
475          break;

476      default:
477          splx(s);
478          return (EAFNOSUPPORT);
479      }

480      /*
481       * Look up the address in our list.
482       */
483      ETHER_LOOKUP_MULTI(addrlo, addrhi, ac, enm);
484      if (enm == NULL) {
485          splx(s);
486          return (ENXIO);
487      }
488      if (--enm->enm_refcount != 0) {
489          /*
490           * Still some claims to this record.
491           */
492          splx(s);
493          return (0);
494      }
```

```
495     /*
496      * No remaining claims to this record; unlink and free it.
497      */
498     for (p = &enm->enm_ac->ac_multiaddrs;
499            *p != enm;
500            p = &(*p)->enm_next)
501         continue;
502     *p = (*p)->enm_next;
503     free(enm, M_IFMADDR);
504     ac->ac_multicnt--;
505     splx(s);
506     /*
507      * Return ENETRESET to inform the driver that the list has changed
508      * and its reception filter should be adjusted accordingly.
509      */
510     return (ENETRESET);
511 }
```
—— *if_ethersubr.c*

Figure 12.37 ether_delmulti function.

12.13 ip_getmoptions Function

Fetching the current option settings is considerably easier than setting them. All the
work is done by ip_getmoptions, shown in Figure 12.38.

Copy the option data and return

876–914   The three arguments to ip_getmoptions are: optname, the option to fetch; imo,
the ip_moptions structure; and mp, which points to a pointer to an mbuf. m_get allocates an mbuf to hold the option data. For each of the three options, a pointer (addr,
ttl, and loop, respectively) is initialized to the data area of the mbuf and the length of
the mbuf is set to the length of the option data.

For IP_MULTICAST_IF, the unicast address found by IFP_TO_IA is returned or
INADDR_ANY is returned if no explicit multicast interface has been selected.

For IP_MULTICAST_TTL, imo_multicast_ttl is returned or if an explicit multicast TTL has not been selected, 1 (IP_DEFAULT_MULTICAST_TTL) is returned.

For IP_MULTICAST_LOOP, imo_multicast_loop is returned or if an explicit
multicast loopback policy has not been selected, 1 (IP_DEFAULT_MULTICAST_LOOP) is
returned.

Finally, EOPNOTSUPP is returned if the option isn't recognized.

ip_output.c

```
876 int
877 ip_getmoptions(optname, imo, mp)
878 int     optname;
879 struct ip_moptions *imo;
880 struct mbuf **mp;
881 {
882     u_char *ttl;
883     u_char *loop;
884     struct in_addr *addr;
885     struct in_ifaddr *ia;

886     *mp = m_get(M_WAIT, MT_SOOPTS);

887     switch (optname) {

888     case IP_MULTICAST_IF:
889         addr = mtod(*mp, struct in_addr *);
890         (*mp)->m_len = sizeof(struct in_addr);
891         if (imo == NULL || imo->imo_multicast_ifp == NULL)
892             addr->s_addr = INADDR_ANY;
893         else {
894             IFP_TO_IA(imo->imo_multicast_ifp, ia);
895             addr->s_addr = (ia == NULL) ? INADDR_ANY
896                 : IA_SIN(ia)->sin_addr.s_addr;
897         }
898         return (0);

899     case IP_MULTICAST_TTL:
900         ttl = mtod(*mp, u_char *);
901         (*mp)->m_len = 1;
902         *ttl = (imo == NULL) ? IP_DEFAULT_MULTICAST_TTL
903             : imo->imo_multicast_ttl;
904         return (0);

905     case IP_MULTICAST_LOOP:
906         loop = mtod(*mp, u_char *);
907         (*mp)->m_len = 1;
908         *loop = (imo == NULL) ? IP_DEFAULT_MULTICAST_LOOP
909             : imo->imo_multicast_loop;
910         return (0);

911     default:
912         return (EOPNOTSUPP);
913     }
914 }
```

ip_output.c

Figure 12.38 ip_getmoptions function.

12.14 Multicast Input Processing: `ipintr` Function

Now that we have described multicast addressing, group memberships, and the various data structures associated with IP and Ethernet multicasting, we can move on to multicast datagram processing.

In Figure 4.13 we saw that an incoming Ethernet multicast packet is detected by `ether_input`, which sets the M_MCAST flag in the mbuf header before placing an IP packet on the IP input queue (`ipintrq`). The `ipintr` function processes each packet in turn. The multicast processing code we omitted from the discussion of `ipintr` appears in Figure 12.39.

The code is from the section of `ipintr` that determines if a packet is addressed to the local system or if it should be forwarded. At this point, the packet has been checked for errors and any options have been processed. `ip` points to the IP header within the packet.

Forward packets if configured as multicast router

214–245   This entire section of code is skipped if the destination address is not an IP multicast group. If the address is a multicast group and the system is configured as an IP multicast router (`ip_mrouter`), `ip_id` is converted to network byte order (the form that `ip_mforward` expects), and the packet is passed to `ip_mforward`. If `ip_mforward` returns a nonzero value, an error was detected or the packet arrived through a *multicast tunnel*. The packet is discarded and `ips_cantforward` incremented.

> We describe multicast tunnels in Chapter 14. They transport multicast packets between multicast routers separated by standard IP routers. Packets that arrive through a tunnel must be processed by `ip_mforward` and not `ipintr`.

If `ip_mforward` returns 0, `ip_id` is converted back to host byte order and `ipintr` may continue processing the packet.

If `ip` points to an IGMP packet, it is accepted and execution continues at `ours` (`ipintr`, Figure 10.11). A multicast router must accept all IGMP packets irrespective of their individual destination groups or of the group memberships of the incoming interface. The IGMP packets contain announcements of membership changes.

246–257   The remaining code in Figure 12.39 is executed whether or not the system is configured as a multicast router. IN_LOOKUP_MULTI searches the list of multicast groups that the interface has joined. If a match is not found, the packet is discarded. This occurs when the hardware filter accepts unwanted packets or when a group associated with the interface and the destination group of the packet map to the same Ethernet multicast address.

If the packet is accepted, execution continues at the label `ours` in `ipintr` (Figure 10.11).

```
214      if (IN_MULTICAST(ntohl(ip->ip_dst.s_addr))) {
215          struct in_multi *inm;
216          extern struct socket *ip_mrouter;

217          if (ip_mrouter) {
218              /*
219               * If we are acting as a multicast router, all
220               * incoming multicast packets are passed to the
221               * kernel-level multicast forwarding function.
222               * The packet is returned (relatively) intact; if
223               * ip_mforward() returns a non-zero value, the packet
224               * must be discarded, else it may be accepted below.
225               *
226               * (The IP ident field is put in the same byte order
227               * as expected when ip_mforward() is called from
228               * ip_output().)
229               */
230              ip->ip_id = htons(ip->ip_id);
231              if (ip_mforward(m, m->m_pkthdr.rcvif) != 0) {
232                  ipstat.ips_cantforward++;
233                  m_freem(m);
234                  goto next;
235              }
236              ip->ip_id = ntohs(ip->ip_id);

237              /*
238               * The process-level routing demon needs to receive
239               * all multicast IGMP packets, whether or not this
240               * host belongs to their destination groups.
241               */
242              if (ip->ip_p == IPPROTO_IGMP)
243                  goto ours;
244              ipstat.ips_forward++;
245          }
246          /*
247           * See if we belong to the destination multicast group on the
248           * arrival interface.
249           */
250          IN_LOOKUP_MULTI(ip->ip_dst, m->m_pkthdr.rcvif, inm);
251          if (inm == NULL) {
252              ipstat.ips_cantforward++;
253              m_freem(m);
254              goto next;
255          }
256          goto ours;
257      }
```

Figure 12.39 ipintr function: multicast input processing.

12.15 Multicast Output Processing: `ip_output` Function

When we discussed `ip_output` in Chapter 8, we postponed discussion of the `mp` argument to `ip_output` and the multicast processing code. In `ip_output`, if `mp` points to an `ip_moptions` structure, it overrides the default multicast output processing. The omitted code from `ip_output` appears in Figures 12.40 and 12.41. `ip` points to the outgoing packet, `m` points to the mbuf holding the packet, and `ifp` points to the interface selected by the routing tables for the destination group.

————————————————————— ip_output.c

```
129     if (IN_MULTICAST(ntohl(ip->ip_dst.s_addr))) {
130         struct in_multi *inm;
131         extern struct ifnet loif;

132         m->m_flags |= M_MCAST;
133         /*
134          * IP destination address is multicast.  Make sure "dst"
135          * still points to the address in "ro".  (It may have been
136          * changed to point to a gateway address, above.)
137          */
138         dst = (struct sockaddr_in *) &ro->ro_dst;
139         /*
140          * See if the caller provided any multicast options
141          */
142         if (imo != NULL) {
143             ip->ip_ttl = imo->imo_multicast_ttl;
144             if (imo->imo_multicast_ifp != NULL)
145                 ifp = imo->imo_multicast_ifp;
146         } else
147             ip->ip_ttl = IP_DEFAULT_MULTICAST_TTL;
148         /*
149          * Confirm that the outgoing interface supports multicast.
150          */
151         if ((ifp->if_flags & IFF_MULTICAST) == 0) {
152             ipstat.ips_noroute++;
153             error = ENETUNREACH;
154             goto bad;
155         }
156         /*
157          * If source address not specified yet, use address
158          * of outgoing interface.
159          */
160         if (ip->ip_src.s_addr == INADDR_ANY) {
161             struct in_ifaddr *ia;

162             for (ia = in_ifaddr; ia; ia = ia->ia_next)
163                 if (ia->ia_ifp == ifp) {
164                     ip->ip_src = IA_SIN(ia)->sin_addr;
165                     break;
166                 }
167         }
```

————————————————————— ip_output.c

Figure 12.40 `ip_output` function: defaults and source address.

Establish defaults

129–155   The code in Figure 12.40 is executed only if the packet is destined for a multicast group. If so, ip_output sets M_MCAST in the mbuf and dst is reset to the final destination as it may have been set to the next-hop router earlier in ip_output (Figure 8.24).

If an ip_moptions structure was passed, ip_ttl and ifp are changed accordingly. Otherwise, ip_ttl is set to 1 (IP_DEFAULT_MULTICAST_TTL), which prevents the multicast from escaping to a remote network. The interface selected by consulting the routing tables or the interface specified within the ip_moptions structure must support multicasting. If it does not, ip_output discards the packet and returns ENETUNREACH.

Select source address

156–167   If the source address is unspecified, the for loop finds the Internet unicast address associated with the outgoing interface and fills in ip_src in the IP header.

Unlike a unicast packet, an outgoing multicast packet may be transmitted on more than one interface if the system is configured as a multicast router. Even if the system is not a multicast router, the outgoing interface may be a member of the destination group and may need to receive the packet. Finally, we need to consider the multicast loopback policy and the loopback interface itself. Taking all this into account, there are three questions to consider:

- Should the packet be received on the outgoing interface?
- Should the packet be forwarded to other interfaces?
- Should the packet be transmitted on the outgoing interface?

Figure 12.41 shows the code from ip_output that answers these questions.

Loopback or not?

168–176   If IN_LOOKUP_MULTI determines that the outgoing interface is a member of the destination group and imo_multicast_loop is nonzero, the packet is queued for *input* on the output interface by ip_mloopback. In this case, the original packet is *not* considered for forwarding, since the copy is forwarded during input processing if necessary.

Forward or not?

178–197   If the packet is *not* looped back, but the system is configured as a multicast router and the packet is eligible for forwarding, ip_mforward distributes copies to other multicast interfaces. If ip_mforward does not return 0, ip_output discards the packet and does not attempt to transmit it. This indicates an error with the packet.

To prevent infinite recursion between ip_mforward and ip_output, ip_mforward always turns on IP_FORWARDING before calling ip_output. A datagram originating on the system is eligible for forwarding because the transport protocols do not turn on IP_FORWARDING.

ip_output.c

```
168          IN_LOOKUP_MULTI(ip->ip_dst, ifp, inm);
169          if (inm != NULL &&
170              (imo == NULL || imo->imo_multicast_loop)) {
171              /*
172               * If we belong to the destination multicast group
173               * on the outgoing interface, and the caller did not
174               * forbid loopback, loop back a copy.
175               */
176              ip_mloopback(ifp, m, dst);
177          } else {
178              /*
179               * If we are acting as a multicast router, perform
180               * multicast forwarding as if the packet had just
181               * arrived on the interface to which we are about
182               * to send.  The multicast forwarding function
183               * recursively calls this function, using the
184               * IP_FORWARDING flag to prevent infinite recursion.
185               *
186               * Multicasts that are looped back by ip_mloopback(),
187               * above, will be forwarded by the ip_input() routine,
188               * if necessary.
189               */
190              extern struct socket *ip_mrouter;
191              if (ip_mrouter && (flags & IP_FORWARDING) == 0) {
192                  if (ip_mforward(m, ifp) != 0) {
193                      m_freem(m);
194                      goto done;
195                  }
196              }
197          }
198          /*
199           * Multicasts with a time-to-live of zero may be looped-
200           * back, above, but must not be transmitted on a network.
201           * Also, multicasts addressed to the loopback interface
202           * are not sent -- the above call to ip_mloopback() will
203           * loop back a copy if this host actually belongs to the
204           * destination group on the loopback interface.
205           */
206          if (ip->ip_ttl == 0 || ifp == &loif) {
207              m_freem(m);
208              goto done;
209          }
210          goto sendit;
211      }
```

ip_output.c

Figure 12.41 `ip_output` function: loopback, forward, and send.

Transmit or not?

198–209   Packets with a TTL of 0 may be looped back, but they are never forwarded (`ip_mforward` discards them) and are never transmitted. If the TTL is 0 or if the output interface is the loopback interface, `ip_output` discards the packet since the TTL has expired or the packet has already been looped back by `ip_mloopback`.

Send packet

210–211   If the packet has made it this far, it is ready to be physically transmitted on the output interface. The code at `sendit` (`ip_output`, Figure 8.25) may fragment the datagram before passing it (or the resulting fragments) to the interface's `if_output` function. We'll see in Section 21.10 that the Ethernet output function, `ether_output`, calls `arpresolve`, which calls `ETHER_MAP_IP_MULTICAST` to construct an Ethernet multicast destination address based on the IP multicast destination address.

`ip_mloopback` Function

`ip_mloopback` relies on `looutput` (Figure 5.27) to do its job. Instead of passing a pointer to the loopback interface to `looutput`, `ip_mloopback` passes a pointer to the output multicast interface. The `ip_mloopback` function is shown in Figure 12.42.

```
                                                                        ─ ip_output.c
935 static void
936 ip_mloopback(ifp, m, dst)
937 struct ifnet *ifp;
938 struct mbuf *m;
939 struct sockaddr_in *dst;
940 {
941     struct ip *ip;
942     struct mbuf *copym;

943     copym = m_copy(m, 0, M_COPYALL);
944     if (copym != NULL) {
945         /*
946          * We don't bother to fragment if the IP length is greater
947          * than the interface's MTU.  Can this possibly matter?
948          */
949         ip = mtod(copym, struct ip *);
950         ip->ip_len = htons((u_short) ip->ip_len);
951         ip->ip_off = htons((u_short) ip->ip_off);
952         ip->ip_sum = 0;
953         ip->ip_sum = in_cksum(copym, ip->ip_hl << 2);
954         (void) looutput(ifp, copym, (struct sockaddr *) dst, NULL);
955     }
956 }
                                                                        ─ ip_output.c
```

Figure 12.42 `ip_mloopback` function.

Duplicate and queue packet

929–956   Copying the packet isn't enough; the packet must look as though it was received on the output interface, so `ip_mloopback` converts `ip_len` and `ip_off` to network byte order and computes the checksum for the packet. `looutput` takes care of putting the packet on the IP input queue.

12.16 Performance Considerations

The multicast implementation in Net/3 has several potential performance bottlenecks. Since many Ethernet cards do not support perfect filtering of multicast addresses, the operating system must be prepared to discard multicast packets that pass through the hardware filter. In the worst case, an Ethernet card may fall back to receiving all multicast packets, most of which must be discarded by `ipintr` when they are found not to contain a valid IP multicast group address.

IP uses a simple linear list and linear search to filter incoming IP datagrams. If the list grows to any appreciable length, a caching mechanism such as moving the most recently received address to the front of the list would help performance.

12.17 Summary

In this chapter we described how a single host processes IP multicast datagrams. We looked at the format of an IP class D address and an Ethernet multicast address and the mapping between the two.

We discussed the `in_multi` and `ether_multi` structures, and we saw that each IP multicast interface maintains its own group membership list and that each Ethernet interface maintains a list of Ethernet multicast addresses.

During input processing, IP multicasts are accepted only if they arrive on an interface that is a member of their destination group, although they may be forwarded to other interfaces if the system is configured as a multicast router.

Systems configured as multicast routers must accept all multicast packets on every interface. This can be done quickly by issuing the `SIOCADDMULTI` command for the `INADDR_ANY` address.

The `ip_moptions` structure is the cornerstone of multicast output processing. It controls the selection of an output interface, the TTL field of the multicast datagram, and the loopback policy. It also holds references to the `in_multi` structures, which determine when an interface joins or leaves an IP multicast group.

We also discussed the two concepts implemented by the multicast TTL value: packet lifetime and packet scope.

Exercises

12.1 What is the difference between sending an IP broadcast packet to 255.255.255.255 and sending an IP multicast to the all-hosts group 224.0.0.1?

12.2 Why are interfaces identified by their IP unicast addresses in the multicasting code? What must be changed so that an interface could send and receive multicast datagrams but not have a unicast IP address?

12.3 In Section 12.3 we said that 32 IP groups are mapped to a single Ethernet address. Since 9 bits of a 32-bit address are not included in the mapping, why didn't we say that 512 (2^9) IP groups mapped to a single Ethernet address?

12.4   Why do you think IP_MAX_MEMBERSHIPS is set to 20? Could it be set to a larger value? Hint: Consider the size of the ip_moptions structure (Figure 12.15).

12.5   What happens when a multicast datagram is looped back by IP and is also received by the hardware interface on which it is transmitted (i.e., a nonsimplex interface)?

12.6   Draw a picture of a network with a multihomed host so that a multicast packet sent on one interface may be received on the other interface even if the host is not acting as a multicast router.

12.7   Trace the membership add request through the SLIP and loopback interfaces instead of the Ethernet interface.

12.8   How could a process request that the kernel join more than IP_MAX_MEMBERSHIPS?

12.9   Computing the checksum on a looped back packet is superfluous. Design a method to avoid the checksum computation for loopback packets.

12.10   How many IP multicast groups could an interface join without reusing an Ethernet multicast address?

12.11   The careful reader might have noticed that in_delmulti assumes that the interface has defined an ioctl function when it issues the SIOCDELMULTI request. Why is this OK?

12.12   What happens to the mbuf allocated in ip_getmoptions if an unrecognized option is requested?

12.13   Why is the group membership mechanism separate from the binding mechanism used to receive unicast and broadcast datagrams?

13

IGMP: Internet Group Management Protocol

13.1 Introduction

IGMP conveys group membership information between hosts and routers on a local network. Routers periodically multicast IGMP queries to the all-hosts group. Hosts respond to the queries by multicasting IGMP report messages. The IGMP specification appears in RFC 1112. Chapter 13 of Volume 1 describes the specification of IGMP and provides some examples.

From an architecture perspective, IGMP is a transport protocol above IP. It has a protocol number (2) and its messages are carried in IP datagrams (as with ICMP). IGMP usually isn't accessed directly by a process but, as with ICMP, a process can send and receive IGMP messages through an IGMP socket. This feature enables multicast routing daemons to be implemented as user-level processes.

Figure 13.1 shows the overall organization of the IGMP protocol in Net/3.

The key to IGMP processing is the collection of `in_multi` structures shown in the center of Figure 13.1. An incoming IGMP query causes `igmp_input` to initialize a countdown timer for each `in_multi` structure. The timers are updated by `igmp_fasttimo`, which calls `igmp_sendreport` as each timer expires.

We saw in Chapter 12 that `ip_setmoptions` calls `igmp_joingroup` when a new `in_multi` structure is created. `igmp_joingroup` calls `igmp_sendreport` to announce the new group and enables the group's timer to schedule a second announcement a short time later. `igmp_sendreport` takes care of formatting an IGMP message and passing it to `ip_output`.

On the left and right of Figure 13.1 we see that a raw socket can send and receive IGMP messages directly.

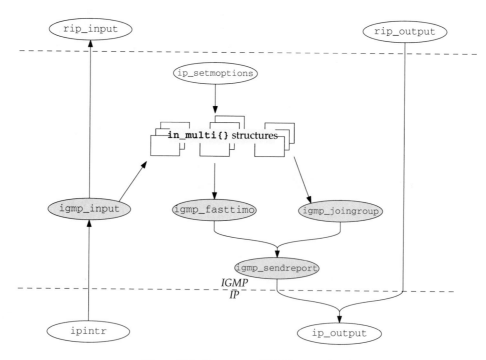

Figure 13.1   Summary of IGMP processing.

13.2   Code Introduction

The IGMP protocol is implemented in four files listed in Figure 13.2.

File	Description
netinet/igmp.h	IGMP protocol definitions
netinet/igmp_var.h	IGMP implementation definitions
netinet/in_var.h	IP multicast data structures
netinet/igmp.c	IGMP protocol implementation

Figure 13.2   Files discussed in this chapter.

Global Variables

Three new global variables, shown in Figure 13.3, are introduced in this chapter.

Statistics

IGMP statistics are maintained in the igmpstat variables shown in Figure 13.4.

Variable	Datatype	Description
`igmp_all_hosts_group`	`u_long`	all-hosts group address in network byte order
`igmp_timers_are_running`	`int`	true if any IGMP timer is active, false otherwise
`igmpstat`	`struct igmpstat`	IGMP statistics (Figure 13.4).

Figure 13.3   Global variables introduced in this chapter.

`igmpstat` **member**	Description
`igps_rcv_badqueries`	#messages received as invalid queries
`igps_rcv_badreports`	#messages received as invalid reports
`igps_rcv_badsum`	#messages received with bad checksum
`igps_rcv_ourreports`	#messages received as reports for local groups
`igps_rcv_queries`	#messages received as membership queries
`igps_rcv_reports`	#messages received as membership reports
`igps_rcv_tooshort`	#messages received with too few bytes
`igps_rcv_total`	total #IGMP messages received
`igps_snd_reports`	#messages sent as membership reports

Figure 13.4   IGMP statistics.

Figure 13.5 shows some sample output of these statistics, from the `netstat -p igmp` command on `vangogh.cs.berkeley.edu`.

`netstat -p igmp` **output**	`igmpstat` **member**
18774 messages received	`igps_rcv_total`
0 messages received with too few bytes	`igps_rcv_tooshort`
0 messages received with bad checksum	`igps_rcv_badsum`
18774 membership queries received	`igps_rcv_queries`
0 membership queries received with invalid field(s)	`igps_rcv_badqueries`
0 membership reports received	`igps_rcv_reports`
0 membership reports received with invalid field(s)	`igps_rcv_badreports`
0 membership reports received for groups to which we belong	`igps_rcv_ourreports`
0 membership reports sent	`igps_snd_reports`

Figure 13.5   Sample IGMP statistics.

From Figure 13.5 we can tell that `vangogh` is attached to a network where IGMP is being used, but that `vangogh` is not joining any multicast groups, since `igps_snd_reports` is 0.

SNMP Variables

There is no standard SNMP MIB for IGMP, but [McCloghrie and Farinacci 1994a] describes an experimental MIB for IGMP.

13.3   `igmp` Structure

An IGMP message is only 8 bytes long. Figure 13.6 shows the `igmp` structure used by Net/3.

—— igmp.h

```
43 struct igmp {
44     u_char  igmp_type;           /* version & type of IGMP message  */
45     u_char  igmp_code;           /* unused, should be zero          */
46     u_short igmp_cksum;          /* IP-style checksum               */
47     struct in_addr igmp_group;   /* group address being reported    */
48 };                               /* (zero for queries)              */
```

—— igmp.h

Figure 13.6   `igmp` structure.

43–44   A 4-bit version code and a 4-bit type code are contained within `igmp_type`. Figure 13.7 shows the standard values.

Version	Type	igmp_type	Description
1	1	0x11 (IGMP_HOST_MEMBERSHIP_QUERY)	membership query
1	2	0x12 (IGMP_HOST_MEMBERSHIP_REPORT)	membership report
1	3	0x13	DVMRP message (Chapter 14)

Figure 13.7   IGMP message types.

Only version 1 messages are used by Net/3. Multicast routers send type 1 (IGMP_HOST_MEMBERSHIP_QUERY) messages to solicit membership reports from hosts on the local network. The response to a type 1 IGMP message is a type 2 (IGMP_HOST_MEMBERSHIP_REPORT) message from the hosts reporting their multicast membership information. Type 3 messages transport multicast routing information between routers (Chapter 14). A host never processes type 3 messages. The remainder of this chapter discusses only type 1 and 2 messages.

45–46   `igmp_code` is unused in IGMP version 1, and `igmp_cksum` is the familiar IP checksum computed over all 8 bytes of the IGMP message.

47–48   `igmp_group` is 0 for queries. For replies, it contains the multicast group being reported.

Figure 13.8 shows the structure of an IGMP message relative to an IP datagram.

13.4   IGMP `protosw` Structure

Figure 13.9 describes the `protosw` structure for IGMP.

Although it is possible for a process to send raw IP packets through the IGMP `protosw` entry, in this chapter we are concerned only with how the kernel processes IGMP messages. Chapter 32 discusses how a process can access IGMP using a raw socket.

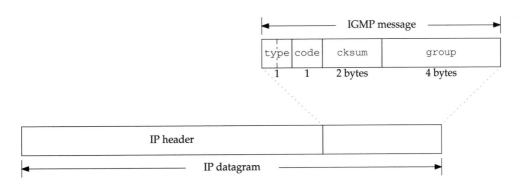

Figure 13.8   An IGMP message (igmp_ omitted).

Member	inetsw[5]	Description
pr_type	SOCK_RAW	IGMP provides raw packet services
pr_domain	&inetdomain	IGMP is part of the Internet domain
pr_protocol	IPPROTO_IGMP (2)	appears in the ip_p field of the IP header
pr_flags	PR_ATOMIC|PR_ADDR	socket layer flags, not used by protocol processing
pr_input	igmp_input	receives messages from IP layer
pr_output	rip_output	sends IGMP message to IP layer
pr_ctlinput	0	not used by IGMP
pr_ctloutput	rip_ctloutput	respond to administrative requests from a process
pr_usrreq	rip_usrreq	respond to communication requests from a process
pr_init	igmp_init	initialization for IGMP
pr_fasttimo	igmp_fasttimo	process pending membership reports
pr_slowtimo	0	not used by IGMP
pr_drain	0	not used by IGMP
pr_sysctl	0	not used by IGMP

Figure 13.9   The IGMP protosw structure.

There are three events that trigger IGMP processing:

- a local interface has joined a new multicast group (Section 13.5),
- an IGMP timer has expired (Section 13.6), and
- an IGMP query is received (Section 13.7).

There are also two events that trigger local IGMP processing but do not result in any messages being sent:

- an IGMP report is received (Section 13.7), and
- a local interface leaves a multicast group (Section 13.8).

These five events are discussed in the following sections.

13.5   Joining a Group: `igmp_joingroup` Function

We saw in Chapter 12 that `igmp_joingroup` is called by `in_addmulti` when a new `in_multi` structure is created. Subsequent requests to join the same group only increase the reference count in the `in_multi` structure; `igmp_joingroup` is not called. `igmp_joingroup` is shown in Figure 13.10

—— *igmp.c*

```
164 void
165 igmp_joingroup(inm)
166 struct in_multi *inm;
167 {
168     int      s = splnet();

169     if (inm->inm_addr.s_addr == igmp_all_hosts_group ||
170         inm->inm_ifp == &loif)
171         inm->inm_timer = 0;
172     else {
173         igmp_sendreport(inm);
174         inm->inm_timer = IGMP_RANDOM_DELAY(inm->inm_addr);
175         igmp_timers_are_running = 1;
176     }
177     splx(s);
178 }
```

—— *igmp.c*

Figure 13.10   `igmp_joingroup` function.

164–178   `inm` points to the new `in_multi` structure for the group. If the new group is the all-hosts group, or the membership request is for the loopback interface, `inm_timer` is disabled and `igmp_joingroup` returns. Membership in the all-hosts group is never reported, since every multicast host is assumed to be a member of the group. Sending a membership report to the loopback interface is unnecessary, since the local host is the only system on the loopback network and it already knows its membership status.

In the remaining cases, a report is sent immediately for the new group, and the group timer is set to a random value based on the group. The global flag `igmp_timers_are_running` is set to indicate that at least one timer is enabled. `igmp_fasttimo` (Section 13.6) examines this variable to avoid unnecessary processing.

When the timer for the new group expires, a second membership report is issued. The duplicate report is harmless, but it provides insurance in case the first report is lost or damaged. The report delay is computed by `IGMP_RANDOM_DELAY` (Figure 13.11).

59–73   According to RFC 1122, report timers should be set to a random time between 0 and 10 (`IGMP_MAX_HOST_REPORT_DELAY`) seconds. Since IGMP timers are decremented five (`PR_FASTHZ`) times per second, `IGMP_RANDOM_DELAY` must pick a random value between 1 and 50. If r is the random number computed by adding the total number of IP packets received, the host's primary IP address, and the multicast group, then

$$0 \le (r \bmod 50) \le 49$$

and

$$1 \le (r \bmod 50) + 1 \le 50$$

```
                                                                        ── igmp_var.h
59 /*
60  * Macro to compute a random timer value between 1 and (IGMP_MAX_REPORTING_
61  * DELAY * countdown frequency).  We generate a "random" number by adding
62  * the total number of IP packets received, our primary IP address, and the
63  * multicast address being timed-out.  The 4.3 random() routine really
64  * ought to be available in the kernel!
65  */
66 #define IGMP_RANDOM_DELAY(multiaddr) \
67      /* struct in_addr multiaddr; */ \
68      ( (ipstat.ips_total + \
69        ntohl(IA_SIN(in_ifaddr)->sin_addr.s_addr) + \
70        ntohl((multiaddr).s_addr) \
71        ) \
72        % (IGMP_MAX_HOST_REPORT_DELAY * PR_FASTHZ) + 1 \
73        )
                                                                        ── igmp_var.h
```

Figure 13.11   `IGMP_RANDOM_DELAY` function.

Zero is avoided because it would disable the timer and no report would be sent.

13.6 `igmp_fasttimo` Function

Before looking at `igmp_fasttimo`, we need to describe the mechanism used to traverse the `in_multi` structures.

To locate each `in_multi` structure, Net/3 must traverse the `in_multi` list for each interface. During a traversal, an `in_multistep` structure (shown in Figure 13.12) records the position.

```
                                                                        ── in_var.h
123 struct in_multistep {
124     struct in_ifaddr *i_ia;
125     struct in_multi  *i_inm;
126 };
                                                                        ── in_var.h
```

Figure 13.12   `in_multistep` function.

123–126   `i_ia` points to the *next* `in_ifaddr` interface structure and `i_inm` points to the *next* `in_multi` structure for the *current* interface.

The `IN_FIRST_MULTI` and `IN_NEXT_MULTI` macros (shown in Figure 13.13) traverse the lists.

154–169   If the `in_multi` list has more entries, `i_inm` is advanced to the next entry. When `IN_NEXT_MULTI` reaches the end of a multicast list, `i_ia` is advanced to the next interface and `i_inm` to the first `in_multi` structure associated with the interface. If the interface has no multicast structures, the `while` loop continues to advance through the interface list until all interfaces have been searched.

170–177   The `in_multistep` array is initialized to point to the first `in_ifaddr` structure in the `in_ifaddr` list and `i_inm` is set to null. `IN_NEXT_MULTI` finds the first `in_multi` structure.

```
                                                                        ──── in_var.h
147 /*
148  * Macro to step through all of the in_multi records, one at a time.
149  * The current position is remembered in "step", which the caller must
150  * provide.  IN_FIRST_MULTI(), below, must be called to initialize "step"
151  * and get the first record.  Both macros return a NULL "inm" when there
152  * are no remaining records.
153  */
154 #define IN_NEXT_MULTI(step, inm) \
155     /* struct in_multistep  step; */ \
156     /* struct in_multi *inm; */ \
157 { \
158     if (((inm) = (step).i_inm) != NULL) \
159         (step).i_inm = (inm)->inm_next; \
160     else \
161         while ((step).i_ia != NULL) { \
162             (inm) = (step).i_ia->ia_multiaddrs; \
163             (step).i_ia = (step).i_ia->ia_next; \
164             if ((inm) != NULL) { \
165                 (step).i_inm = (inm)->inm_next; \
166                 break; \
167             } \
168         } \
169 }

170 #define IN_FIRST_MULTI(step, inm) \
171     /* struct in_multistep step; */ \
172     /* struct in_multi *inm; */ \
173 { \
174     (step).i_ia = in_ifaddr; \
175     (step).i_inm = NULL; \
176     IN_NEXT_MULTI((step), (inm)); \
177 }
                                                                        ──── in_var.h
```

Figure 13.13   IN_FIRST_MULTI and IN_NEXT_MULTI structures.

We know from Figure 13.9 that igmp_fasttimo is the fast timeout function for
IGMP and is called five times per second. igmp_fasttimo (shown in Figure 13.14)
decrements multicast report timers and sends a report when the timer expires.

187–198   If igmp_timers_are_running is false, igmp_fasttimo returns immediately
instead of wasting time examining each timer.

199–213   igmp_fasttimo resets the running flag and then initializes step and inm with
IN_FIRST_MULTI. The igmp_fasttimo function locates each in_multi structure
with the while loop and the IN_NEXT_MULTI macro. For each structure:

- If the timer is 0, there is nothing to be done.
- If the timer is nonzero, it is decremented. If it reaches 0, an IGMP membership
  report is sent for the group.
- If the timer is still nonzero, then at least one timer is still running, so
  igmp_timers_are_running is set to 1.

igmp.c

```
187 void
188 igmp_fasttimo()
189 {
190     struct in_multi *inm;
191     int     s;
192     struct in_multistep step;

193     /*
194      * Quick check to see if any work needs to be done, in order
195      * to minimize the overhead of fasttimo processing.
196      */
197     if (!igmp_timers_are_running)
198         return;

199     s = splnet();
200     igmp_timers_are_running = 0;
201     IN_FIRST_MULTI(step, inm);
202     while (inm != NULL) {
203         if (inm->inm_timer == 0) {
204             /* do nothing */
205         } else if (--inm->inm_timer == 0) {
206             igmp_sendreport(inm);
207         } else {
208             igmp_timers_are_running = 1;
209         }
210         IN_NEXT_MULTI(step, inm);
211     }
212     splx(s);
213 }
```

igmp.c

Figure 13.14   igmp_fasttimo function.

igmp_sendreport Function

The igmp_sendreport function (shown in Figure 13.15) constructs and sends an IGMP report message for a single multicast group.

214–232   The single argument inm points to the in_multi structure for the group being reported. igmp_sendreport allocates a new mbuf and prepares it for an IGMP message. igmp_sendreport leaves room for a link-layer header and sets the length of the mbuf and packet to the length of an IGMP message.

233–245   The IP header and IGMP message is constructed one field at a time. The source address for the datagram is set to INADDR_ANY, and the destination address is the multicast group being reported. ip_output replaces INADDR_ANY with the unicast address of the outgoing interface. Every member of the group receives the report as does every multicast router (since multicast routers receive *all* IP multicasts).

246–260   Finally, igmp_sendreport constructs an ip_moptions structure to go along with the message sent to ip_output. The interface associated with the in_multi structure is selected as the outgoing interface; the TTL is set to 1 to keep the report on the local network; and, if the local system is configured as a router, multicast loopback is enabled for this request.

igmp.c

```
214 static void
215 igmp_sendreport(inm)
216 struct in_multi *inm;
217 {
218     struct mbuf *m;
219     struct igmp *igmp;
220     struct ip *ip;
221     struct ip_moptions *imo;
222     struct ip_moptions simo;

223     MGETHDR(m, M_DONTWAIT, MT_HEADER);
224     if (m == NULL)
225         return;
226     /*
227      * Assume max_linkhdr + sizeof(struct ip) + IGMP_MINLEN
228      * is smaller than mbuf size returned by MGETHDR.
229      */
230     m->m_data += max_linkhdr;
231     m->m_len = sizeof(struct ip) + IGMP_MINLEN;
232     m->m_pkthdr.len = sizeof(struct ip) + IGMP_MINLEN;

233     ip = mtod(m, struct ip *);
234     ip->ip_tos = 0;
235     ip->ip_len = sizeof(struct ip) + IGMP_MINLEN;
236     ip->ip_off = 0;
237     ip->ip_p = IPPROTO_IGMP;
238     ip->ip_src.s_addr = INADDR_ANY;
239     ip->ip_dst = inm->inm_addr;

240     igmp = (struct igmp *) (ip + 1);
241     igmp->igmp_type = IGMP_HOST_MEMBERSHIP_REPORT;
242     igmp->igmp_code = 0;
243     igmp->igmp_group = inm->inm_addr;
244     igmp->igmp_cksum = 0;
245     igmp->igmp_cksum = in_cksum(m, IGMP_MINLEN);

246     imo = &simo;
247     bzero((caddr_t) imo, sizeof(*imo));
248     imo->imo_multicast_ifp = inm->inm_ifp;
249     imo->imo_multicast_ttl = 1;

250     /*
251      * Request loopback of the report if we are acting as a multicast
252      * router, so that the process-level routing demon can hear it.
253      */
254     {
255         extern struct socket *ip_mrouter;
256         imo->imo_multicast_loop = (ip_mrouter != NULL);
257     }
258     ip_output(m, NULL, NULL, 0, imo);

259     ++igmpstat.igps_snd_reports;
260 }
```

igmp.c

Figure 13.15   `igmp_sendreport` function.

The process-level multicast router must hear the membership reports. In Section 12.14 we saw that IGMP datagrams are always accepted when the system is configured as a multicast router. Through the normal transport demultiplexing code, the messages are passed to igmp_input, the pr_input function for IGMP (Figure 13.9).

13.7 Input Processing: igmp_input Function

In Section 12.14 we described the multicast processing portion of ipintr. We saw that a multicast router accepts *any* IGMP message, but a multicast host accepts only IGMP messages that arrive on an interface that is a member of the destination multicast group (i.e., queries and membership reports for which the receiving interface is a member).

The accepted messages are passed to igmp_input by the standard protocol demultiplexing mechanism. The beginning and end of igmp_input are shown in Figure 13.16. The code for each IGMP message type is described in following sections.

Validate IGMP message

52-96   The function ipintr passes m, a pointer to the received packet (stored in an mbuf), and iphlen, the size of the IP header in the datagram.

The datagram must be large enough to contain an IGMP message (IGMP_MINLEN), must be contained within a standard mbuf header (m_pullup), and must have a correct IGMP checksum. If any errors are found, they are counted, the datagram is silently discarded, and igmp_input returns.

The body of igmp_input processes the validated messages based on the code in igmp_type. Remember from Figure 13.6 that igmp_type includes a version code and a type code. The switch statement is based on the combined value stored in igmp_type (Figure 13.7). Each case is described separately in the following sections.

Pass IGMP messages to raw IP

157-163   There is no default case for the switch statement. Any valid message (i.e., one that is properly formed) is passed to rip_input where it is delivered to any process listening for IGMP messages. IGMP messages with versions or types that are unrecognized by the kernel can be processed or discarded by the listening processes.

> The mrouted program depends on this call to rip_input so that it receives membership queries and reports.

Membership Query: IGMP_HOST_MEMBERSHIP_QUERY

RFC 1075 recommends that multicast routers issue an IGMP membership query at least once every 120 seconds. The query is sent to group 224.0.0.1 (the all-hosts group). Figure 13.17 shows how the message is processed by a host.

igmp.c

```
52 void
53 igmp_input(m, iphlen)
54 struct mbuf *m;
55 int     iphlen;
56 {
57     struct igmp *igmp;
58     struct ip *ip;
59     int      igmplen;
60     struct ifnet *ifp = m->m_pkthdr.rcvif;
61     int       minlen;
62     struct in_multi *inm;
63     struct in_ifaddr *ia;
64     struct in_multistep step;

65     ++igmpstat.igps_rcv_total;

66     ip = mtod(m, struct ip *);
67     igmplen = ip->ip_len;

68     /*
69      * Validate lengths
70      */
71     if (igmplen < IGMP_MINLEN) {
72         ++igmpstat.igps_rcv_tooshort;
73         m_freem(m);
74         return;
75     }
76     minlen = iphlen + IGMP_MINLEN;
77     if ((m->m_flags & M_EXT || m->m_len < minlen) &&
78         (m = m_pullup(m, minlen)) == 0) {
79         ++igmpstat.igps_rcv_tooshort;
80         return;
81     }
82     /*
83      * Validate checksum
84      */
85     m->m_data += iphlen;
86     m->m_len -= iphlen;
87     igmp = mtod(m, struct igmp *);
88     if (in_cksum(m, igmplen)) {
89         ++igmpstat.igps_rcv_badsum;
90         m_freem(m);
91         return;
92     }
93     m->m_data -= iphlen;
94     m->m_len += iphlen;
95     ip = mtod(m, struct ip *);

96     switch (igmp->igmp_type) {


                          /* switch cases */


157     }
```

```
158     /*
159      * Pass all valid IGMP packets up to any process(es) listening
160      * on a raw IGMP socket.
161      */
162     rip_input(m);
163 }
```
── *igmp.c*

Figure 13.16 `igmp_input` function.

── *igmp.c*
```
 97     case IGMP_HOST_MEMBERSHIP_QUERY:
 98         ++igmpstat.igps_rcv_queries;

 99         if (ifp == &loif)
100             break;

101         if (ip->ip_dst.s_addr != igmp_all_hosts_group) {
102             ++igmpstat.igps_rcv_badqueries;
103             m_freem(m);
104             return;
105         }
106         /*
107          * Start the timers in all of our membership records for
108          * the interface on which the query arrived, except those
109          * that are already running and those that belong to the
110          * "all-hosts" group.
111          */
112         IN_FIRST_MULTI(step, inm);
113         while (inm != NULL) {
114             if (inm->inm_ifp == ifp && inm->inm_timer == 0 &&
115                 inm->inm_addr.s_addr != igmp_all_hosts_group) {
116                 inm->inm_timer =
117                     IGMP_RANDOM_DELAY(inm->inm_addr);
118                 igmp_timers_are_running = 1;
119             }
120             IN_NEXT_MULTI(step, inm);
121         }

122         break;
```
── *igmp.c*

Figure 13.17   Input processing of the IGMP query message.

97–122   Queries that arrive on the loopback interface are silently discarded (Exercise 13.1). Queries by definition are sent to the all-hosts group. If a query arrives addressed to a different address, it is counted in `igps_rcv_badqueries` and discarded.

The receipt of a query message does not trigger an immediate flurry of IGMP membership reports. Instead, `igmp_input` resets the membership timers for each group associated with the interface on which the query was received to a random value with `IGMP_RANDOM_DELAY`. When the timer for a group expires, `igmp_fasttimo` sends a membership report. Meanwhile, the same activity is occurring on all the other hosts that received the IGMP query. As soon as the random timer for a particular group expires on one host, it is multicast to that group. This report cancels the timers on the other hosts so that only one report is multicast to the network. The routers, as well as any other members of the group, receive the report.

The one exception to this scenario is the all-hosts group. A timer is never set for this group and a report is never sent.

Membership Report: `IGMP_HOST_MEMBERSHIP_REPORT`

The receipt of an IGMP membership report is one of the two events we mentioned in Section 13.1 that does not result in an IGMP message. The effect of the message is local to the interface on which it was received. Figure 13.18 shows the message processing.

```
                                                                          igmp.c
123      case IGMP_HOST_MEMBERSHIP_REPORT:
124          ++igmpstat.igps_rcv_reports;

125          if (ifp == &loif)
126              break;

127          if (!IN_MULTICAST(ntohl(igmp->igmp_group.s_addr)) ||
128              igmp->igmp_group.s_addr != ip->ip_dst.s_addr) {
129              ++igmpstat.igps_rcv_badreports;
130              m_freem(m);
131              return;
132          }
133          /*
134           * KLUDGE: if the IP source address of the report has an
135           * unspecified (i.e., zero) subnet number, as is allowed for
136           * a booting host, replace it with the correct subnet number
137           * so that a process-level multicast routing demon can
138           * determine which subnet it arrived from.  This is necessary
139           * to compensate for the lack of any way for a process to
140           * determine the arrival interface of an incoming packet.
141           */
142          if ((ntohl(ip->ip_src.s_addr) & IN_CLASSA_NET) == 0) {
143              IFP_TO_IA(ifp, ia);
144              if (ia)
145                  ip->ip_src.s_addr = htonl(ia->ia_subnet);
146          }
147          /*
148           * If we belong to the group being reported, stop
149           * our timer for that group.
150           */
151          IN_LOOKUP_MULTI(igmp->igmp_group, ifp, inm);
152          if (inm != NULL) {
153              inm->inm_timer = 0;
154              ++igmpstat.igps_rcv_ourreports;
155          }
156          break;
                                                                          igmp.c
```

Figure 13.18   Input processing of the IGMP report message.

123–156   Reports sent to the loopback interface are discarded, as are membership reports sent
to the incorrect multicast group. That is, the message must be addressed to the group
identified within the message.

The source address of an incompletely initialized host might not include a network
or host number (or both). `igmp_report` looks at the class A network portion of the
address, which can only be 0 when the network and subnet portions of the address are
0. If this is the case, the source address is set to the subnet address, which includes the
network ID and subnet ID, of the receiving interface. The only reason for doing this is
to inform a process-level daemon of the receiving interface, which is identified by the
subnet number.

If the receiving interface belongs to the group being reported, the associated report
timer is reset to 0. In this way the first report sent to the group stops any other hosts
from issuing a report. It is only necessary for the router to know that at least one interface on the network is a member of the group. The router does not need to maintain an
explicit membership list or even a counter.

13.8 Leaving a Group: `igmp_leavegroup` Function

We saw in Chapter 12 that `in_delmulti` calls `igmp_leavegroup` when the last reference count in the associated `in_multi` structure drops to 0.

```
                                                                          igmp.c
179 void
180 igmp_leavegroup(inm)
181 struct in_multi *inm;
182 {
183     /*
184      * No action required on leaving a group.
185      */
186 }
                                                                          igmp.c
```

Figure 13.19 `igmp_leavegroup` function.

179–186   As we can see, IGMP takes no action when an interface leaves a group. No explicit
notification is sent—the next time a multicast router issues an IGMP query, the interface
does not generate an IGMP report for this group. If no report is generated for a group,
the multicast router assumes that all the interfaces have left the group and stops forwarding multicast packets for the group to the network.

If the interface leaves the group while a report is pending (i.e., the group's report
timer is running), the report is never sent, since the timer is discarded by `in_delmulti`
(Figure 12.36) along with the `in_multi` structure for the group when
`icmp_leavegroup` returns.

13.9 Summary

In this chapter we described IGMP, which communicates IP multicast membership information between hosts and routers on a single network. IGMP membership reports are generated when an interface joins a group, and on demand when multicast routers issue an IGMP report query message.

The design of IGMP minimizes the number of messages required to communicate membership information:

- Hosts announce their membership when they join a group.
- Response to membership queries are delayed for a random interval, and the first response suppresses any others.
- Hosts are silent when they leave a group.
- Membership queries are sent no more than once per minute.

Multicast routers share the IGMP information they collect with each other (Chapter 14) to route multicast datagrams toward remote members of the multicast destination group.

Exercises

13.1   Why isn't it necessary to respond to an IGMP query on the loopback interface?

13.2   Verify the assumption stated on lines 226 to 229 in Figure 13.15.

13.3   Is it necessary to set random delays for membership queries that arrive on a point-to-point network interface?

14

IP Multicast Routing

14.1 Introduction

The previous two chapters discussed multicasting on a single network. In this chapter we look at multicasting across an entire internet. We describe the operation of the `mrouted` program, which computes the multicast routing tables, and the kernel functions that forward multicast datagrams between networks.

> Technically, multicast *packets* are forwarded. In this chapter we assume that every multicast packet contains an entire datagram (i.e., there are no fragments), so we use the term *datagram* exclusively. Net/3 forwards IP fragments as well as IP datagrams.

Figure 14.1 shows several versions of `mrouted` and how they correspond to the BSD releases. The `mrouted` releases include both the user-level daemons and the kernel-level multicast code.

mrouted version	Description
1.2	modifies the 4.3BSD Tahoe release
2.0	included with 4.4BSD and Net/3
3.3	modifies SunOS 4.1.3

Figure 14.1 `mrouted` and IP multicasting releases.

IP multicast technology is an active area of research and development. This chapter discusses version 2.0 of the multicast software, which is included in Net/3 but is considered an obsolete implementation. Version 3.3 was released too late to be discussed fully in this text, but we will point out various 3.3 features along the way.

Because commercial multicast routers are not widely deployed, multicast networks are often constructed using multicast *tunnels*, which connect two multicast routers over a standard IP unicast internet. Multicast tunnels are supported by Net/3 and are constructed with the Loose Source Record Route (LSRR) option (Section 9.6). An improved tunneling technique encapsulates the IP multicast datagram within an IP unicast datagram and is supported by version 3.3 of the multicast code but is not supported by Net/3.

As in Chapter 12, we use the generic term *transport protocols* to refer to the protocols that send and receive multicast datagrams, but UDP is the only Internet protocol that supports multicasting.

14.2   Code Introduction

The three files listed in Figure 14.2 are discussed in this chapter.

File	Description
netinet/ip_mroute.h	multicast structure definitions
netinet/ip_mroute.c	multicast routing functions
netinet/raw_ip.c	multicast routing options

Figure 14.2   Files discussed in this chapter.

Global Variables

The global variables used by the multicast routing code are shown in Figure 14.3.

Variable	Datatype	Description
cached_mrt	struct mrt	one-behind cache for multicast routing
cached_origin	u_long	multicast group for one-behind cache
cached_originmask	u_long	mask for multicast group for one-behind cache
mrtstat	struct mrtstat	multicast routing statistics
mrttable	struct mrt *[]	hash table of pointers to multicast routes
numvifs	vifi_t	number of enabled multicast interfaces
viftable	struct vif[]	array of virtual multicast interfaces

Figure 14.3   Global variables introduced in this chapter.

Statistics

All the statistics collected by the multicast routing code are found in the mrtstat structure described by Figure 14.4. Figure 14.5 shows some sample output of these statistics, from the netstat -gs command.

`mrtstat` member	Description	Used by SNMP
mrts_mrt_lookups	#multicast route lookups	
mrts_mrt_misses	#multicast route cache misses	
mrts_grp_lookups	#group address lookups	
mrts_grp_misses	#group address cache misses	
mrts_no_route	#multicast route lookup failures	
mrts_bad_tunnel	#packets with malformed tunnel options	
mrts_cant_tunnel	#packets with no room for tunnel options	

Figure 14.4   Statistics collected in this chapter.

`netstat -gs` output	`mrtstat` members
multicast routing:	
329569328 multicast route lookups	mrts_mrt_lookups
9377023 multicast route cache misses	mrts_mrt_misses
242754062 group address lookups	mrts_grp_lookups
159317788 group address cache misses	mrts_grp_misses
65648 datagrams with no route for origin	mrts_no_route
0 datagrams with malformed tunnel options	mrts_bad_tunnel
0 datagrams with no room for tunnel options	mrts_cant_tunnel

Figure 14.5   Sample IP multicast routing statistics.

These statistics are from a system with two physical interfaces and one tunnel interface. These statistics show that the multicast route is found in the cache 98% of the time. The group address cache is less effective with only a 34% hit rate. The route cache is described with Figure 14.34 and the group address cache with Figure 14.21.

SNMP Variables

There is no standard SNMP MIB for multicast routing, but [McCloghrie and Farinacci 1994a] and [McCloghrie and Farinacci 1994b] describe some experimental MIBs for multicast routers.

14.3   Multicast Output Processing Revisited

In Section 12.15 we described how an interface is selected for an outgoing multicast datagram. We saw that `ip_output` is passed an explicit interface in the `ip_moptions` structure, or `ip_output` looks up the destination group in the routing tables and uses the interface returned in the route entry.

If, after selecting an outgoing interface, `ip_output` loops back the datagram, it is queued for input processing on the interface selected for *output* and is considered for forwarding when it is processed by `ipintr`. Figure 14.6 illustrates this process.

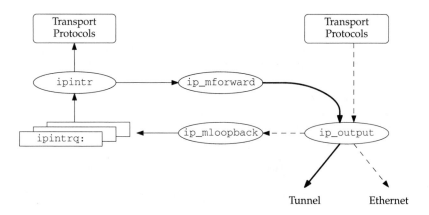

Figure 14.6   Multicast output processing with loopback.

In Figure 14.6 the dashed arrows represent the original outgoing datagram, which in this example is multicast on a local Ethernet. The copy created by `ip_mloopback` is represented by the thin arrows; this copy is passed to the transport protocols for input. The third copy is created when `ip_mforward` decides to forward the datagram through another interface on the system. The thickest arrows in Figure 14.6 represents the third copy, which in this example is sent on a multicast tunnel.

If the datagram is *not* looped back, `ip_output` passes it directly to `ip_mforward`, where it is duplicated and also processed as if it were received on the interface that `ip_output` selected. This process is shown in Figure 14.7.

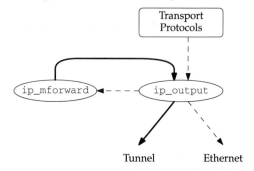

Figure 14.7   Multicast output processing with no loopback.

Whenever `ip_mforward` calls `ip_output` to send a multicast datagram, it sets the `IP_FORWARDING` flag so that `ip_output` does not pass the datagram back to `ip_mforward`, which would create an infinite loop.

`ip_mloopback` was described with Figure 12.42. `ip_mforward` is described in Section 14.8.

14.4 mrouted **Daemon**

Multicast routing is enabled and managed by a user-level process: the mrouted daemon. mrouted implements the router portion of the IGMP protocol and communicates
with other multicast routers to implement multicast routing between networks. The
routing algorithms are implemented in mrouted, but the multicast routing tables are
maintained in the kernel, which forwards the datagrams.

In this text we describe only the kernel data structures and functions that support
mrouted—we do not describe mrouted itself. We describe the Truncated Reverse Path
Broadcast (TRPB) algorithm [Deering and Cheriton 1990], used to select routes for
multicast datagrams, and the Distance Vector Multicast Routing Protocol (DVMRP),
used to convey information between multicast routers, in enough detail to make sense
of the kernel multicast code.

RFC 1075 [Waitzman, Partridge, and Deering 1988] describes an old version of
DVMRP. mrouted implements a newer version of DVMRP, which is not yet documented in an RFC. The best documentation for the current algorithm and protocol is
the source code release for mrouted. Appendix B describes where the source code can
be obtained.

The mrouted daemon communicates with the kernel by setting options on an
IGMP socket (Chapter 32). The options are summarized in Figure 14.8.

optname	optval type	Function	Description
DVMRP_INIT		ip_mrouter_init	mrouted is starting
DVMRP_DONE		ip_mrouter_done	mrouted is shutting down
DVMRP_ADD_VIF	struct vifctl	add_vif	add virtual interface
DVMRP_DEL_VIF	vifi_t	del_vif	delete virtual interface
DVMRP_ADD_LGRP	struct lgrplctl	add_lgrp	add multicast group entry for an interface
DVMRP_DEL_LGRP	struct lgrplctl	del_lgrp	delete multicast group entry for an interface
DVMRP_ADD_MRT	struct mrtctl	add_mrt	add multicast route
DVMRP_DEL_MRT	struct in_addr	del_mrt	delete multicast route

Figure 14.8 Multicast routing socket options.

The socket options shown in Figure 14.8 are passed to rip_ctloutput (Section 32.8)
by the setsockopt system call. Figure 14.9 shows the portion of rip_ctloutput
that handles the DVMRP_*xxx* options.

173–187   When setsockopt is called, op equals PRCO_SETOPT and all the options are
passed to the ip_mrouter_cmd function. For the getsockopt system call, op equals
PRCO_GETOPT and EINVAL is returned for all the options.

Figure 14.10 shows the ip_mrouter_cmd function.

> These "options" are more like commands, since they cause the kernel to update various data
> structures. We use the term *command* throughout the rest of this chapter to emphasize this fact.

── *raw_ip.c*

```
173    case DVMRP_INIT:
174    case DVMRP_DONE:
175    case DVMRP_ADD_VIF:
176    case DVMRP_DEL_VIF:
177    case DVMRP_ADD_LGRP:
178    case DVMRP_DEL_LGRP:
179    case DVMRP_ADD_MRT:
180    case DVMRP_DEL_MRT:
181        if (op == PRCO_SETOPT) {
182            error = ip_mrouter_cmd(optname, so, *m);
183            if (*m)
184                (void) m_free(*m);
185        } else
186            error = EINVAL;
187        return (error);
```

── *raw_ip.c*

Figure 14.9 `rip_ctloutput` function: DVMRP_*xxx* socket options.

── *ip_mroute.c*

```
84  int
85  ip_mrouter_cmd(cmd, so, m)
86  int      cmd;
87  struct socket *so;
88  struct mbuf *m;
89  {
90      int      error = 0;

91      if (cmd != DVMRP_INIT && so != ip_mrouter)
92          error = EACCES;
93      else
94          switch (cmd) {

95          case DVMRP_INIT:
96              error = ip_mrouter_init(so);
97              break;

98          case DVMRP_DONE:
99              error = ip_mrouter_done();
100             break;

101         case DVMRP_ADD_VIF:
102             if (m == NULL || m->m_len < sizeof(struct vifctl))
103                     error = EINVAL;
104             else
105                 error = add_vif(mtod(m, struct vifctl *));
106             break;

107         case DVMRP_DEL_VIF:
108             if (m == NULL || m->m_len < sizeof(short))
109                     error = EINVAL;
110             else
111                 error = del_vif(mtod(m, vifi_t *));
112             break;
```

```
113          case DVMRP_ADD_LGRP:
114              if (m == NULL || m->m_len < sizeof(struct lgrplctl))
115                      error = EINVAL;
116              else
117                  error = add_lgrp(mtod(m, struct lgrplctl *));
118              break;

119          case DVMRP_DEL_LGRP:
120              if (m == NULL || m->m_len < sizeof(struct lgrplctl))
121                      error = EINVAL;
122              else
123                  error = del_lgrp(mtod(m, struct lgrplctl *));
124              break;

125          case DVMRP_ADD_MRT:
126              if (m == NULL || m->m_len < sizeof(struct mrtctl))
127                      error = EINVAL;
128              else
129                  error = add_mrt(mtod(m, struct mrtctl *));
130              break;

131          case DVMRP_DEL_MRT:
132              if (m == NULL || m->m_len < sizeof(struct in_addr))
133                      error = EINVAL;
134              else
135                  error = del_mrt(mtod(m, struct in_addr *));
136              break;

137          default:
138              error = EOPNOTSUPP;
139              break;
140          }
141      return (error);
142 }
```
——— *ip_mroute.c*

Figure 14.10 ip_mrouter_cmd function.

84–92   The first command issued by mrouted must be DVMRP_INIT. Subsequent commands must come from the same socket as the DVMRP_INIT command. EACCES is returned when other commands are issued on a different socket.

94–142   Each case in the switch checks to see if the right amount of data was included with the command and then calls the matching function. If the command is not recognized, EOPNOTSUPP is returned. Any error returned from the matching function is posted in error and returned at the end of the function.

Figure 14.11 shows ip_mrouter_init, which is called when mrouted issues the DVMRP_INIT command during initialization.

146–157   If the command is issued on something other than a raw IGMP socket, or if DVMRP_INIT has already been set, EOPNOTSUPP or EADDRINUSE are returned respectively. A pointer to the socket on which the initialization command is issued is saved in the global ip_mrouter. Subsequent commands must be issued on this socket. This prevents the concurrent operation of more than one instance of mrouted.

――― *ip_mroute.c*
```
146 static int
147 ip_mrouter_init(so)
148 struct socket *so;
149 {
150     if (so->so_type != SOCK_RAW ||
151         so->so_proto->pr_protocol != IPPROTO_IGMP)
152         return (EOPNOTSUPP);

153     if (ip_mrouter != NULL)
154         return (EADDRINUSE);

155     ip_mrouter = so;

156     return (0);
157 }
```
――― *ip_mroute.c*

Figure 14.11   ip_mrouter_init function: DVMRP_INIT command.

The remainder of the DVMRP_*xxx* commands are described in the following sections.

14.5   Virtual Interfaces

When operating as a multicast router, Net/3 accepts incoming multicast datagrams, duplicates them and forwards the copies through one or more interfaces. In this way, the datagram is forwarded to other multicast routers on the internet.

An outgoing interface can be a physical interface or it can be a multicast *tunnel*. Each end of the multicast tunnel is associated with a physical interface on a multicast router. Multicast tunnels allow two multicast routers to exchange multicast datagrams even when they are separated by routers that cannot forward multicast datagrams. Figure 14.12 shows two multicast routers connected by a multicast tunnel.

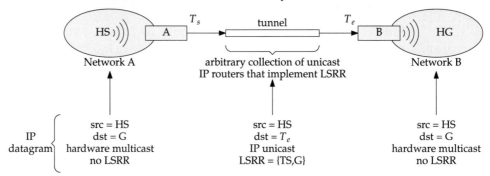

Figure 14.12   A multicast tunnel.

In Figure 14.12, the source host HS on network A is multicasting a datagram to group G. The only member of group G is on network B, which is connected to network A by a multicast tunnel. Router A receives the multicast (because multicast routers receive *all* multicasts), consults its multicast routing tables, and forwards the datagram through the multicast tunnel.

The tunnel starts on the *physical* interface on router A identified by the IP unicast address T_s. The tunnel ends on the *physical* interface on router B identified by the IP unicast address, T_e. The tunnel itself is an arbitrarily complex collection of networks connected by IP unicast routers that implement the LSRR option. Figure 14.13 shows how an IP LSRR option implements the multicast tunnel.

System	IP header		Source route option		Description
	ip_src	ip_dst	*offset*	addresses	
HS	HS	G			on network A
T_s	HS	T_e	8	T_s • G	on tunnel
T_e	HS	G	12	T_s see text •	after ip_dooptions on router B
T_e	HS	G			after ip_mforward on router B

Figure 14.13   LSRR multicast tunnel options.

The first line of Figure 14.13 shows the datagram sent by HS as a multicast on network A. Router A receives the datagram because multicast routers receive all multicasts on their locally attached networks.

To send the datagram through the tunnel, router A inserts an LSRR option in the IP header. The second line shows the datagram as it leaves A on the tunnel. The first address in the LSRR option is the source address of the tunnel and the second address is the destination group. The destination of the datagram is T_e—the other end of the tunnel. The LSRR offset points to the *destination group*.

The tunneled datagram is forwarded through the internet until it reaches the other end of the tunnel on router B.

The third line of the figure shows the datagram after it is processed by ip_dooptions on router B. Recall from Chapter 9 that ip_dooptions processes the LSRR option before the destination address of the datagram is examined by ipintr. Since the destination address of the datagram (T_e) matches one of the interfaces on router B, ip_dooptions copies the address identified by the option offset (G in this example) into the destination field of the IP header. In the option, G is replaced with the address returned by ip_rtaddr, which normally selects the outgoing interface for the datagram based on the IP destination address (G in this case). This address is irrelevant, since ip_mforward discards the entire option. Finally, ip_dooptions advances the option offset.

The fourth line in Figure 14.13 shows the datagram after ipintr calls ip_mforward, where the LSRR option is recognized and removed from the datagram header. The resulting datagram looks like the original multicast datagram and is processed by ip_mforward, which in our example forwards it onto network B as a multicast datagram where it is received by HG.

Multicast tunnels constructed with LSRR options are obsolete. Since the March 1993 release of mrouted, tunnels have been constructed by prepending another IP header to the IP multicast datagram. The protocol in the new IP header is set to 4 to indicate that the contents of the packet is another IP packet. This value is documented in RFC 1700 as the "IP in IP" protocol. LSRR tunnels are supported in newer versions of `mrouted` for backward compatibility.

Virtual Interface Table

For both physical interfaces and tunnel interfaces, the kernel maintains an entry in a *virtual interface* table, which contains information that is used only for multicasting. Each virtual interface is described by a `vif` structure (Figure 14.14). The global variable `viftable` is an array of these structures. An index to the table is stored in a `vifi_t` variable, which is an unsigned short integer.

```
                                                                    ip_mroute.h
105 struct vif {
106     u_char  v_flags;           /* VIFF_ flags */
107     u_char  v_threshold;       /* min ttl required to forward on vif */
108     struct in_addr v_lcl_addr; /* local interface address */
109     struct in_addr v_rmt_addr; /* remote address (tunnels only) */
110     struct ifnet *v_ifp;       /* pointer to interface */
111     struct in_addr *v_lcl_grps; /* list of local grps (phyints only) */
112     int     v_lcl_grps_max;    /* malloc'ed number of v_lcl_grps */
113     int     v_lcl_grps_n;      /* used number of v_lcl_grps */
114     u_long  v_cached_group;    /* last grp looked-up (phyints only) */
115     int     v_cached_result;   /* last look-up result (phyints only) */
116 };
                                                                    ip_mroute.h
```

Figure 14.14 `vif` structure.

105–110   The only flag defined for `v_flags` is `VIFF_TUNNEL`. When set, the interface is a tunnel to a remote multicast router. When not set, the interface is a physical interface on the local system. `v_threshold` is the multicast threshold, which we described in Section 12.9. `v_lcl_addr` is the unicast IP address of the local interface associated with this virtual interface. `v_rmt_addr` is the unicast IP address of the remote end of an IP multicast tunnel. Either `v_lcl_addr` or `v_rmt_addr` is nonzero, but never both. For physical interfaces, `v_ifp` is nonnull and points to the `ifnet` structure of the local interface. For tunnels, `v_ifp` is null.

111–116   The list of groups with members on the attached interface is kept as an array of IP multicast group addresses pointed to by `v_lcl_grps`, which is always null for tunnels. The size of the array is in `v_lcl_grps_max`, and the number of entries that are used is in `v_lcl_grps_n`. The array grows as needed to accommodate the group membership list. `v_cached_group` and `v_cached_result` implement a one-entry cache, which contain the group and result of the previous lookup.

Figure 14.15 illustrates the `viftable`, which has 32 (`MAXVIFS`) entries. `viftable[2]` is the last entry in use, so `numvifs` is 3. The size of the table is fixed when the kernel is compiled. Several members of the `vif` structure in the first entry of the table are shown. `v_ifp` points to an `ifnet` structure, `v_lcl_grps` points to an array of `in_addr` structures. The array has 32 (`v_lcl_grps_max`) entries, of which only 4 (`v_lcl_grps_n`) are in use.

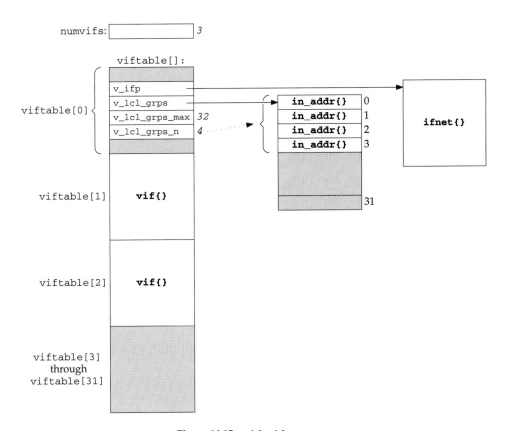

Figure 14.15 viftable array.

mrouted maintains viftable through the DVMRP_ADD_VIF and DVMRP_DEL_VIF commands. Normally all multicast-capable interfaces on the local system are added to the table when mrouted begins. Multicast tunnels are added when mrouted reads its configuration file, usually /etc/mrouted.conf. Commands in this file can also delete physical interfaces from the virtual interface table or change the multicast information associated with the interfaces.

A vifctl structure (Figure 14.16) is passed by mrouted to the kernel with the DVMRP_ADD_VIF command. It instructs the kernel to add an interface to the table of virtual interfaces.

――― *ip_mroute.h*
```
76 struct vifctl {
77     vifi_t  vifc_vifi;          /* the index of the vif to be added */
78     u_char  vifc_flags;         /* VIFF_ flags (Figure 14.14) */
79     u_char  vifc_threshold;     /* min ttl required to forward on vif */
80     struct in_addr vifc_lcl_addr;   /* local interface address */
81     struct in_addr vifc_rmt_addr;   /* remote address (tunnels only) */
82 };
```
――― *ip_mroute.h*

Figure 14.16 vifctl structure.

76–82   `vifc_vifi` identifies the index of the virtual interface within `viftable`. The remaining four members, `vifc_flags`, `vifc_threshold`, `vifc_lcl_addr`, and `vifc_rmt_addr`, are copied into the `vif` structure by the `add_vif` function.

add_vif **Function**

Figure 14.17 shows the `add_vif` function.

```
                                                                ─── ip_mroute.c
202 static int
203 add_vif(vifcp)
204 struct vifctl *vifcp;
205 {
206     struct vif *vifp = viftable + vifcp->vifc_vifi;
207     struct ifaddr *ifa;
208     struct ifnet *ifp;
209     struct ifreq ifr;
210     int     error, s;
211     static struct sockaddr_in sin =
212     {sizeof(sin), AF_INET};

213     if (vifcp->vifc_vifi >= MAXVIFS)
214         return (EINVAL);
215     if (vifp->v_lcl_addr.s_addr != 0)
216         return (EADDRINUSE);

217     /* Find the interface with an address in AF_INET family */
218     sin.sin_addr = vifcp->vifc_lcl_addr;
219     ifa = ifa_ifwithaddr((struct sockaddr *) &sin);
220     if (ifa == 0)
221         return (EADDRNOTAVAIL);

222     s = splnet();

223     if (vifcp->vifc_flags & VIFF_TUNNEL)
224         vifp->v_rmt_addr = vifcp->vifc_rmt_addr;
225     else {
226         /* Make sure the interface supports multicast */
227         ifp = ifa->ifa_ifp;
228         if ((ifp->if_flags & IFF_MULTICAST) == 0) {
229             splx(s);
230             return (EOPNOTSUPP);
231         }
232         /*
233          * Enable promiscuous reception of all IP multicasts
234          * from the interface.
235          */
236         satosin(&ifr.ifr_addr)->sin_family = AF_INET;
237         satosin(&ifr.ifr_addr)->sin_addr.s_addr = INADDR_ANY;
238         error = (*ifp->if_ioctl) (ifp, SIOCADDMULTI, (caddr_t) & ifr);
239         if (error) {
240             splx(s);
241             return (error);
242         }
243     }
```

```
244        vifp->v_flags = vifcp->vifc_flags;
245        vifp->v_threshold = vifcp->vifc_threshold;
246        vifp->v_lcl_addr = vifcp->vifc_lcl_addr;
247        vifp->v_ifp = ifa->ifa_ifp;

248        /* Adjust numvifs up if the vifi is higher than numvifs */
249        if (numvifs <= vifcp->vifc_vifi)
250            numvifs = vifcp->vifc_vifi + 1;

251        splx(s);
252        return (0);
253 }
```
── *ip_mroute.c*

Figure 14.17   add_vif function: DVMRP_ADD_VIF command.

Validate index

202–216   If the table index specified by mrouted in vifc_vifi is too large, or the table entry is already in use, EINVAL or EADDRINUSE is returned respectively.

Locate physical interface

217–221   ifa_ifwithaddr takes the unicast IP address in vifc_lcl_addr and returns a pointer to the associated ifnet structure. This identifies the physical interface to be used for this virtual interface. If there is no matching interface, EADDRNOTAVAIL is returned.

Configure tunnel interface

222–224   For a tunnel, the remote end of the tunnel is copied from the vifctl structure to the vif structure in the interface table.

Configure physical interface

225–243   For a physical interface, the link-level driver must support multicasting. The SIOCADDMULTI command used with INADDR_ANY configures the interface to begin receiving *all* IP multicast datagrams (Figure 12.32) because it is a multicast router. Incoming datagrams are forwarded when ipintr passes them to ip_mforward.

Save multicast information

244–253   The remaining interface information is copied from the vifctl structure to the vif structure. If necessary, numvifs is updated to record the number of virtual interfaces in use.

del_vif **Function**

The function del_vif, shown in Figure 14.18, deletes entries from the virtual interface table. It is called when mrouted sets the DVMRP_DEL_VIF command.

Validate index

257–268   If the index passed to del_vif is greater than the largest index in use or it references an entry that is not in use, EINVAL or EADDRNOTAVAIL is returned respectively.

```
                                                                    ip_mroute.c
257 static int
258 del_vif(vifip)
259 vifi_t *vifip;
260 {
261     struct vif *vifp = viftable + *vifip;
262     struct ifnet *ifp;
263     int     i, s;
264     struct ifreq ifr;

265     if (*vifip >= numvifs)
266         return (EINVAL);
267     if (vifp->v_lcl_addr.s_addr == 0)
268         return (EADDRNOTAVAIL);

269     s = splnet();

270     if (!(vifp->v_flags & VIFF_TUNNEL)) {
271         if (vifp->v_lcl_grps)
272             free(vifp->v_lcl_grps, M_MRTABLE);
273         satosin(&ifr.ifr_addr)->sin_family = AF_INET;
274         satosin(&ifr.ifr_addr)->sin_addr.s_addr = INADDR_ANY;
275         ifp = vifp->v_ifp;
276         (*ifp->if_ioctl) (ifp, SIOCDELMULTI, (caddr_t) & ifr);
277     }
278     bzero((caddr_t) vifp, sizeof(*vifp));

279     /* Adjust numvifs down */
280     for (i = numvifs - 1; i >= 0; i--)
281         if (viftable[i].v_lcl_addr.s_addr != 0)
282             break;
283     numvifs = i + 1;

284     splx(s);
285     return (0);
286 }
                                                                    ip_mroute.c
```

Figure 14.18   del_vif function: DVMRP_DEL_VIF command.

Delete interface

269–278   For a physical interface, the local group table is released, and the reception of all multicast datagrams is disabled by SIOCDELMULTI. The entry in viftable is cleared by bzero.

Adjust interface count

279–286   The for loop searches for the first active entry in the table starting at the largest previously active entry and working back toward the first entry. For unused entries, the s_addr member of v_lcl_addr (an in_addr structure) is 0. numvifs is updated accordingly and the function returns.

14.6   IGMP Revisited

Chapter 13 focused on the host part of the IGMP protocol. `mrouted` implements the
router portion of this protocol. For every physical interface, `mrouted` must keep track
of which multicast groups have members on the attached network. `mrouted` multicasts
an `IGMP_HOST_MEMBERSHIP_QUERY` datagram every 120 seconds and compiles the
resulting `IGMP_HOST_MEMBERSHIP_REPORT` datagrams into a membership array associated with each network. This array is *not* the same as the membership list we
described in Chapter 13.

From the information collected, `mrouted` constructs the multicast routing tables.
The list of groups is also used to suppress multicasts to areas of the multicast internet
that do not have members of the destination group.

The membership array is maintained only for physical interfaces. Tunnels are
point-to-point interfaces to another multicast router, so no group membership information is needed.

We saw in Figure 14.14 that `v_lcl_grps` points to an array of IP multicast groups.
`mrouted` maintains this list with the `DVMRP_ADD_LGRP` and `DVMRP_DEL_LGRP` commands. An `lgrplctl` (Figure 14.19) structure is passed with both commands.

```
                                                                    ── ip_mroute.h
87 struct lgrplctl {
88     vifi_t  lgc_vifi;
89     struct in_addr lgc_gaddr;
90 };
                                                                    ── ip_mroute.h
```

Figure 14.19 `lgrplctl` structure.

87–90   The {interface, group} pair is identified by `lgc_vifi` and `lgc_gaddr`. The interface index (`lgc_vifi`, an unsigned short) identifies a *virtual* interface, not a physical
interface.

When an `IGMP_HOST_MEMBERSHIP_REPORT` datagram is received, the functions
shown in Figure 14.20 are called.

`add_lgrp` **Function**

`mrouted` examines the source address of an incoming IGMP report to determine which
subnet and therefore which interface the report arrived on. Based on this information,
`mrouted` sets the `DVMRP_ADD_LGRP` command for the interface to update the membership table in the kernel. This information is also fed into the multicast routing algorithm to update the routing tables. Figure 14.21 shows the `add_lgrp` function.

Validate add request

291–301   If the request identifies an invalid interface, `EINVAL` is returned. If the interface is
not in use or is a tunnel, `EADDRNOTAVAIL` is returned.

If needed, expand group array

302–326   If the new group won't fit in the current group array, a new array is allocated. The
first time `add_lgrp` is called for an interface, an array is allocated to hold 32 groups.

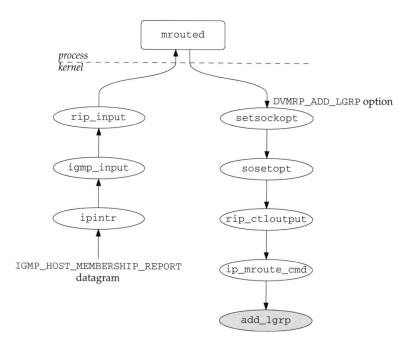

Figure 14.20   IGMP report processing.

Each time the array fills, add_lgrp allocates a new array of twice the previous size. The new array is allocated by malloc, cleared by bzero, and filled by copying the old array into the new one with bcopy. The maximum number of entries, v_lcl_grps_max, is updated, the old array (if any) is released, and the new array is attached to the vif entry with v_lcl_grps.

> The "paranoid" comment points out there is no guarantee that the memory allocated by malloc contains all 0s.

Add new group

327–332   The new group is copied into the next available entry and if the cache already contains the new group, the cache is marked as valid.

The lookup cache contains an address, v_cached_group, and a cached lookup result, v_cached_result. The grplst_member function always consults the cache before searching the membership array. If the given group matches v_cached_group, the cached result is returned; otherwise the membership array is searched.

del_lgrp Function

Group information is expired for each interface when no membership report has been received for the group within 270 seconds. mrouted maintains the appropriate timers and issues the DVMRP_DEL_LGRP command when the information expires. Figure 14.22 shows del_lgrp.

```
                                                                   ───── ip_mroute.c
291 static int
292 add_lgrp(gcp)
293 struct lgrplctl *gcp;
294 {
295     struct vif *vifp;
296     int     s;

297     if (gcp->lgc_vifi >= numvifs)
298         return (EINVAL);

299     vifp = viftable + gcp->lgc_vifi;
300     if (vifp->v_lcl_addr.s_addr == 0 || (vifp->v_flags & VIFF_TUNNEL))
301         return (EADDRNOTAVAIL);

302     /* If not enough space in existing list, allocate a larger one */
303     s = splnet();
304     if (vifp->v_lcl_grps_n + 1 >= vifp->v_lcl_grps_max) {
305         int     num;
306         struct in_addr *ip;

307         num = vifp->v_lcl_grps_max;
308         if (num <= 0)
309             num = 32;              /* initial number */
310         else
311             num += num;            /* double last number */
312         ip = (struct in_addr *) malloc(num * sizeof(*ip),
313                                 M_MRTABLE, M_NOWAIT);
314         if (ip == NULL) {
315             splx(s);
316             return (ENOBUFS);
317         }
318         bzero((caddr_t) ip, num * sizeof(*ip));     /* XXX paranoid */
319         bcopy((caddr_t) vifp->v_lcl_grps, (caddr_t) ip,
320             vifp->v_lcl_grps_n * sizeof(*ip));

321         vifp->v_lcl_grps_max = num;
322         if (vifp->v_lcl_grps)
323             free(vifp->v_lcl_grps, M_MRTABLE);
324         vifp->v_lcl_grps = ip;

325         splx(s);
326     }
327     vifp->v_lcl_grps[vifp->v_lcl_grps_n++] = gcp->lgc_gaddr;

328     if (gcp->lgc_gaddr.s_addr == vifp->v_cached_group)
329         vifp->v_cached_result = 1;

330     splx(s);
331     return (0);
332 }
                                                                   ───── ip_mroute.c
```

Figure 14.21   add_lgrp function: process DVMRP_ADD_LGRP command.

```
                                                                      ─── ip_mroute.c
337 static int
338 del_lgrp(gcp)
339 struct lgrplctl *gcp;
340 {
341     struct vif *vifp;
342     int     i, error, s;

343     if (gcp->lgc_vifi >= numvifs)
344         return (EINVAL);
345     vifp = viftable + gcp->lgc_vifi;
346     if (vifp->v_lcl_addr.s_addr == 0 || (vifp->v_flags & VIFF_TUNNEL))
347         return (EADDRNOTAVAIL);

348     s = splnet();

349     if (gcp->lgc_gaddr.s_addr == vifp->v_cached_group)
350         vifp->v_cached_result = 0;

351     error = EADDRNOTAVAIL;
352     for (i = 0; i < vifp->v_lcl_grps_n; ++i)
353         if (same(&gcp->lgc_gaddr, &vifp->v_lcl_grps[i])) {
354             error = 0;
355             vifp->v_lcl_grps_n--;
356             bcopy((caddr_t) & vifp->v_lcl_grps[i + 1],
357                   (caddr_t) & vifp->v_lcl_grps[i],
358                   (vifp->v_lcl_grps_n - i) * sizeof(struct in_addr));
359             error = 0;
360             break;
361         }
362     splx(s);
363     return (error);
364 }
                                                                      ─── ip_mroute.c
```

Figure 14.22   del_lgrp function: process DVMRP_DEL_LGRP command.

Validate interface index

337–347   If the request identifies an invalid interface, EINVAL is returned. If the interface is not in use or is a tunnel, EADDRNOTAVAIL is returned.

Update lookup cache

348–350   If the group to be deleted is in the cache, the lookup result is set to 0 (false).

Delete group

351–364   EADDRNOTAVAIL is posted in error in case the group is not found in the membership list. The for loop searches the membership array associated with the interface. If same (a macro that uses bcmp to compare the two addresses) is true, error is cleared and the group count is decremented. bcopy shifts the subsequent array entries down to delete the group and del_lgrp breaks out of the loop.

If the loop completes without finding a match, EADDRNOTAVAIL is returned; otherwise 0 is returned.

grplst_member Function

During multicast forwarding, the membership array is consulted to avoid sending data-grams on a network when no member of the destination group is present. grplst_member, shown in Figure 14.23, searches the list looking for the given group address.

```
368 static int                                                    ip_mroute.c
369 grplst_member(vifp, gaddr)
370 struct vif *vifp;
371 struct in_addr gaddr;
372 {
373     int     i, s;
374     u_long  addr;

375     mrtstat.mrts_grp_lookups++;

376     addr = gaddr.s_addr;
377     if (addr == vifp->v_cached_group)
378         return (vifp->v_cached_result);

379     mrtstat.mrts_grp_misses++;

380     for (i = 0; i < vifp->v_lcl_grps_n; ++i)
381         if (addr == vifp->v_lcl_grps[i].s_addr) {
382             s = splnet();
383             vifp->v_cached_group = addr;
384             vifp->v_cached_result = 1;
385             splx(s);
386             return (1);
387         }
388     s = splnet();
389     vifp->v_cached_group = addr;
390     vifp->v_cached_result = 0;
391     splx(s);
392     return (0);
393 }
                                                                  ip_mroute.c
```

Figure 14.23 grplst_member function.

Check the cache

368–379   If the requested group is located in the cache, the cached result is returned and the membership array is not searched.

Search the membership array

380–393   A linear search determines if the group is in the array. If it is found, the cache is updated to record the match and one is returned. If it is not found, the cache is updated to record the miss and 0 is returned.

14.7   Multicast Routing

As we mentioned at the start of this chapter, we will not be presenting the TRPB algorithm implemented by `mrouted`, but we do need to provide a general overview of the mechanism to describe the multicast routing table and the multicast routing functions in the kernel. Figure 14.24 shows the sample multicast network that we use to illustrate the algorithms.

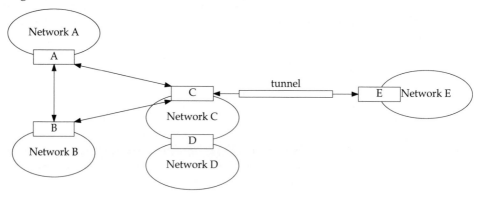

Figure 14.24   Sample multicast network.

In Figure 14.24, routers are shown as boxes and the ellipses are the multicast networks attached to the routers. For example, router D can multicast on network D and C. Router C can multicast to network C, to routers A and B through point-to-point interfaces, and to E through a multicast tunnel.

The simplest approach to multicast routing is to select a subset of the internet topology that forms a *spanning tree*. If each router forwards multicasts along the spanning tree, every router eventually receives the datagram. Figure 14.25 shows one spanning tree for our sample network, where host S on network A represents the source of a multicast datagram.

For a discussion of spanning trees, see [Tanenbaum 1989] or [Perlman 1992].

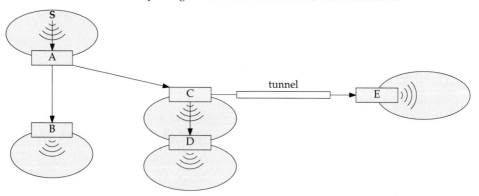

Figure 14.25   Spanning tree for network A.

We constructed the tree based on the shortest *reverse path* from every network back to the source in network A. In Figure 14.25, the link between routers B and C is omitted to form the spanning tree. The arrows between the source and router A, and between router C and D, emphasize that the multicast network is part of the spanning tree.

If the same spanning tree were used to forward a datagram from network C, the datagram would be forwarded along a longer path than needed to get to a recipient on network B. The algorithm described in RFC 1075 computes a separate spanning tree for each potential source network to avoid this problem. The routing tables contain a network number and subnet mask for each route, so that a single route applies to any host within the source subnet.

Because each spanning tree is constructed to provide the shortest reverse path to the source of the datagram, and every network receives every multicast datagram, this process is called *reverse path broadcasting* or RPB.

The RPB protocol has no knowledge of multicast group membership, so many datagrams are unnecessarily forwarded to networks that have no members in the destination group. If, in addition to computing the spanning trees, the routing algorithm records which networks are *leaves* and is aware of the group membership on each network, then routers attached to leaf networks can avoid forwarding datagrams onto the network when there there is no member of the destination group present. This is called *truncated reverse path broadcasting* (TRPB), and is implemented by version 2.0 of mrouted with the help of IGMP to keep track of membership in the leaf networks.

Figure 14.26 shows TRPB applied to a multicast sent from a source on network C and with a member of the destination group on network B.

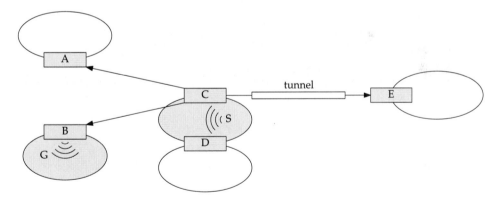

Figure 14.26   TRPB routing for network C.

We'll use Figure 14.26 to illustrate the terms used in the Net/3 multicast routing table. In this example, the shaded networks and routers receive a copy of the multicast datagram sent from the source on network C. The link between A and B is not part of the spanning tree and C does not have a link to D, since the multicast sent by the source is received directly by C and D.

In this figure, networks A, B, D, and E are leaf networks. Router C receives the multicast and forwards it through the interfaces attached to routers A, B, and E—even though sending it to A and E is wasted effort. This is a major weakness of the TRPB algorithm.

The interface associated with network C on router C is called the *parent* because it is the interface on which router C expects to receive multicasts originating from network C. The interfaces from router C to routers A, B, and E, are *child* interfaces. For router A, the point-to-point interface is the parent for the source packets from C and the interface for network A is a child. Interfaces are identified as a parent or as a child relative to the source of the datagram. Multicast datagrams are forwarded only to the associated child interfaces, and never to the parent interface.

Continuing with the example, networks A, D, and E are not shaded because they are leaf networks without members of the destination group, so the spanning tree is truncated at the routers and the datagram is not forwarded onto these networks. Router B forwards the datagram onto network B, since there is a member of the destination group on the network. To implement the truncation algorithm, each multicast router that receives the datagram consults the group table associated with every virtual interface in the router's `viftable`.

The final refinement to the multicast routing algorithm is called *reverse path multicasting* (RPM). The goal of RPM is to *prune* each spanning tree and avoid sending datagrams along branches of the tree that do not contain a member of the destination group. In Figure 14.26, RPM would prevent router C from sending a datagram to A and E, since there is no member of the destination group in those branches of the tree. Version 3.3 of `mrouted` implements RPM.

Figure 14.27 shows our example network, but this time only the routers and networks reached when the datagram is routed by RPM are shaded.

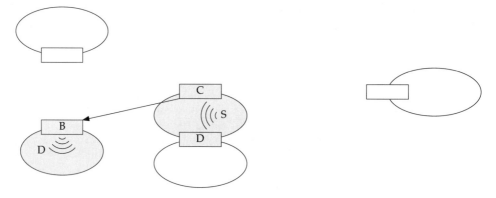

Figure 14.27   RPM routing for network C.

To compute the routing tables corresponding to the spanning trees we described, the multicast routers communicate with adjacent multicast routers to discover the multicast internet topology and the location of multicast group members. In Net/3, DVMRP is used for this communication. DVMRP messages are transmitted as IGMP datagrams and are sent to the multicast group 224.0.0.4, which is reserved for DVMRP communication (Figure 12.1).

In Figure 12.39, we saw that incoming IGMP packets are always accepted by a multicast router. They are passed to `igmp_input`, to `rip_input`, and then read by `mrouted` on a raw IGMP socket. `mrouted` sends DVMRP messages to other multicast routers on the same raw IGMP socket.

For more information about RPB, TRPB, RPM, and the DVMRP messages that are needed to implement these algorithms, see [Deering and Cheriton 1990] and the source code release of `mrouted`.

There are other multicast routing protocols in use on the Internet. Proteon routers implement the MOSPF protocol described in RFC 1584 [Moy 1994]. PIM (Protocol Independent Multicasting) is implemented by Cisco routers, starting with Release 10.2 of their operating software. PIM is described in [Deering et al. 1994].

Multicast Routing Table

We can now describe the implementation of the multicast routing tables in Net/3. The kernel's multicast routing table is maintained as a hash table with 64 entries (`MRTHASHSIZ`). The table is kept in the global array `mrttable`, and each entry points to a linked list of `mrt` structures, shown in Figure 14.28.

```
                                                                  ─── ip_mroute.h
120 struct mrt {
121     struct in_addr mrt_origin;    /* subnet origin of multicasts */
122     struct in_addr mrt_originmask;  /* subnet mask for origin */
123     vifi_t  mrt_parent;           /* incoming vif */
124     vifbitmap_t mrt_children;     /* outgoing children vifs */
125     vifbitmap_t mrt_leaves;       /* subset of outgoing children vifs */
126     struct mrt *mrt_next;         /* forward link */
127 };
                                                                  ─── ip_mroute.h
```

Figure 14.28 `mrt` structure.

120–127 `mrtc_origin` and `mrtc_originmask` identify an entry in the table. `mrtc_parent` is the index of the virtual interface on which all multicast datagrams from the origin are expected. The outgoing interfaces are identified within `mrtc_children`, which is a bitmap. Outgoing interfaces that are also leaves in the multicast routing tree are identified in `mrtc_leaves`, which is also a bitmap. The last member, `mrt_next`, implements a linked list in case multiple routes hash to the same array entry.

Figure 14.29 shows the organization of the multicast routing table. Each `mrt` structure is placed in the hash chain that corresponds to return value from the `nethash` function shown in Figure 14.31.

The multicast routing table maintained by the kernel is a subset of the routing table maintained within `mrouted` and contains enough information to support multicast forwarding within the kernel. Updates to the kernel table are sent with the `DVMRP_ADD_MRT` command, which includes the `mrtctl` structure shown in Figure 14.30.

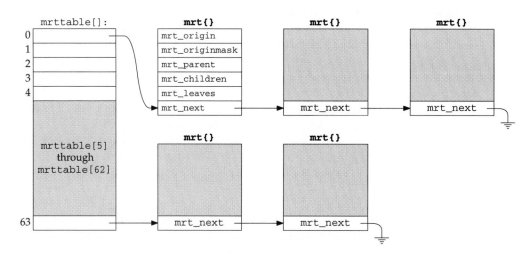

Figure 14.29   Multicast routing table.

```
                                                                    ─── ip_mroute.h
 95 struct mrtctl {
 96     struct in_addr mrtc_origin; /* subnet origin of multicasts */
 97     struct in_addr mrtc_originmask;    /* subnet mask for origin */
 98     vifi_t  mrtc_parent;        /* incoming vif */
 99     vifbitmap_t mrtc_children;  /* outgoing children vifs */
100     vifbitmap_t mrtc_leaves;    /* subset of outgoing children vifs */
101 };
                                                                    ─── ip_mroute.h
```

Figure 14.30   mrtctl structure.

95–101   The five members of the mrtctl structure carry the information we have already described (Figure 14.28) between mrouted and the kernel.

The multicast routing table is keyed by the source IP address of the multicast datagram. nethash (Figure 14.31) implements the hashing algorithm used for the table. It accepts the source IP address and returns a value between 0 and 63 (MRTHASHSIZ − 1).

```
                                                                    ─── ip_mroute.c
398 static  u_long
399 nethash(in)
400 struct in_addr in;
401 {
402     u_long  n;

403     n = in_netof(in);
404     while ((n & 0xff) == 0)
405         n >>= 8;
406     return (MRTHASHMOD(n));
407 }
                                                                    ─── ip_mroute.c
```

Figure 14.31   nethash function.

398–407   `in_netof` returns `in` with the host portion set to all 0s leaving only the class A, B, or C network of the sending host in `n`. The result is shifted to the right until the low-order 8 bits are nonzero. `MRTHASHMOD` is

```
#define MRTHASHMOD(h)    ((h) & (MRTHASHSIZ - 1))
```

The low-order 8 bits are logically ANDed with 63, leaving only the low-order 6 bits, which is an integer in the range 0 to 63.

> Doing two function calls (`nethash` and `in_netof`) to calculate a hash value is an expensive algorithm to compute a hash for a 32-bit address.

`del_mrt` Function

The `mrouted` daemon adds and deletes entries in the kernel's multicast routing table through the `DVMRP_ADD_MRT` and `DVMRP_DEL_MRT` commands. Figure 14.32 shows the `del_mrt` function.

```
                                                              ip_mroute.c
451 static int
452 del_mrt(origin)
453 struct in_addr *origin;
454 {
455     struct mrt *rt, *prev_rt;
456     u_long  hash = nethash(*origin);
457     int     s;

458     for (prev_rt = rt = mrttable[hash]; rt; prev_rt = rt, rt = rt->mrt_next)
459         if (origin->s_addr == rt->mrt_origin.s_addr)
460             break;
461     if (!rt)
462         return (ESRCH);

463     s = splnet();

464     if (rt == cached_mrt)
465         cached_mrt = NULL;

466     if (prev_rt == rt)
467         mrttable[hash] = rt->mrt_next;
468     else
469         prev_rt->mrt_next = rt->mrt_next;
470     free(rt, M_MRTABLE);

471     splx(s);
472     return (0);
473 }
                                                              ip_mroute.c
```

Figure 14.32   `del_mrt` function: process `DVMRP_DEL_MRT` command.

Find route entry

451–462   The `for` loop starts at the entry identified by `hash` (initialized in its declaration from `nethash`). If the entry is not located, `ESRCH` is returned.

Delete route entry

463–473   If the entry was stored in the cache, the cache is invalidated. The entry is unlinked from the hash chain and released. The `if` statement is needed to handle the special case when the matched entry is at the front of the list.

`add_mrt` **Function**

The `add_mrt` function is shown in Figure 14.33.

```
                                                                              ip_mroute.c
411 static int
412 add_mrt(mrtcp)
413 struct mrtctl *mrtcp;
414 {
415     struct mrt *rt;
416     u_long  hash;
417     int     s;

418     if (rt = mrtfind(mrtcp->mrtc_origin)) {
419         /* Just update the route */
420         s = splnet();
421         rt->mrt_parent = mrtcp->mrtc_parent;
422         VIFM_COPY(mrtcp->mrtc_children, rt->mrt_children);
423         VIFM_COPY(mrtcp->mrtc_leaves, rt->mrt_leaves);
424         splx(s);
425         return (0);
426     }
427     s = splnet();

428     rt = (struct mrt *) malloc(sizeof(*rt), M_MRTABLE, M_NOWAIT);
429     if (rt == NULL) {
430         splx(s);
431         return (ENOBUFS);
432     }
433     /*
434      * insert new entry at head of hash chain
435      */
436     rt->mrt_origin = mrtcp->mrtc_origin;
437     rt->mrt_originmask = mrtcp->mrtc_originmask;
438     rt->mrt_parent = mrtcp->mrtc_parent;
439     VIFM_COPY(mrtcp->mrtc_children, rt->mrt_children);
440     VIFM_COPY(mrtcp->mrtc_leaves, rt->mrt_leaves);
441     /* link into table */
442     hash = nethash(mrtcp->mrtc_origin);
443     rt->mrt_next = mrttable[hash];
444     mrttable[hash] = rt;

445     splx(s);
446     return (0);
447 }
                                                                              ip_mroute.c
```

Figure 14.33   add_mrt function: process DVMRP_ADD_MRT command.

Update existing route

411–427   If the requested route is already in the routing table, the new information is copied into the route and `add_mrt` returns.

Allocate new route

428–447   An `mrt` structure is constructed in a newly allocated mbuf with the information from `mrtctl` structure passed with the add request. The hash index is computed from `mrtc_origin`, and the new route is inserted as the first entry on the hash chain.

`mrtfind` Function

The multicast routing table is searched with the `mrtfind` function. The source of the datagram is passed to `mrtfind`, which returns a pointer to the matching `mrt` structure, or a null pointer if there is no match.

```
                                                                      ip_mroute.c
477 static struct mrt *
478 mrtfind(origin)
479 struct in_addr origin;
480 {
481     struct mrt *rt;
482     u_int   hash;
483     int     s;

484     mrtstat.mrts_mrt_lookups++;

485     if (cached_mrt != NULL &&
486         (origin.s_addr & cached_originmask) == cached_origin)
487         return (cached_mrt);

488     mrtstat.mrts_mrt_misses++;

489     hash = nethash(origin);
490     for (rt = mrttable[hash]; rt; rt = rt->mrt_next)
491         if ((origin.s_addr & rt->mrt_originmask.s_addr) ==
492             rt->mrt_origin.s_addr) {
493             s = splnet();
494             cached_mrt = rt;
495             cached_origin = rt->mrt_origin.s_addr;
496             cached_originmask = rt->mrt_originmask.s_addr;
497             splx(s);
498             return (rt);
499         }
500     return (NULL);
501 }
                                                                      ip_mroute.c
```

Figure 14.34   `mrtfind` function.

Check route lookup cache

477–488   The given source IP address (`origin`) is logically ANDed with the origin mask in the cache. If the result matches `cached_origin`, the cached entry is returned.

Check the hash table

489–501   `nethash` returns the hash index for the route entry. The `for` loop searches the hash chain for a matching route. When a match is found, the cache is updated and a pointer to the route is returned. If a match is not found, a null pointer is returned.

14.8   Multicast Forwarding: `ip_mforward` Function

Multicast forwarding is implemented entirely in the kernel. We saw in Figure 12.39 that `ipintr` passes incoming multicast datagrams to `ip_mforward` when `ip_mrouter` is nonnull, that is, when `mrouted` is running.

We also saw in Figure 12.40 that `ip_output` can pass multicast datagrams that originate on the local host to `ip_mforward` to be routed to interfaces other than the one interface selected by `ip_output`.

Unlike unicast forwarding, each time a multicast datagram is forwarded to an interface, a copy is made. For example, if the local host is acting as a multicast router and is connected to three different networks, multicast datagrams originating on the system are duplicated and queued for *output* on all three interfaces. Additionally, the datagram may be duplicated and queued for *input* if the multicast loopback flag was set by the application or if any of the outgoing interfaces receive their own transmissions.

Figure 14.35 shows a multicast datagram arriving on a physical interface.

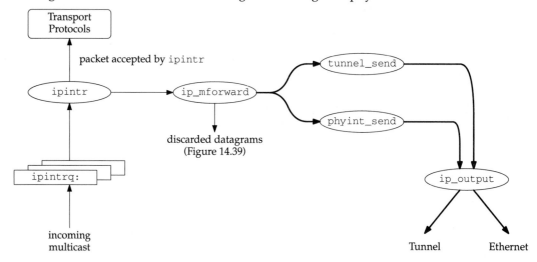

Figure 14.35   Multicast datagram arriving on physical interface.

In Figure 14.35, the interface on which the datagram arrived is a member of the destination group, so the datagram is passed to the transport protocols for input processing. The datagram is also passed to `ip_mforward`, where it is duplicated and forwarded to a physical interface and to a tunnel (the thick arrows), both of which must be different from the receiving interface.

Figure 14.36 shows a multicast datagram arriving on a tunnel.

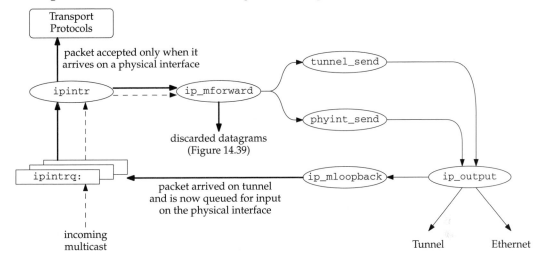

Figure 14.36   Multicast datagram arriving on a multicast tunnel.

In Figure 14.36, the datagram arriving on a physical interface associated with the local end of the tunnel is represented by the dashed arrows. It is passed to `ip_mforward`, which as we'll see in Figure 14.37 returns a nonzero value because the packet arrived on a tunnel. This causes `ipintr` to not pass the packet to the transport protocols.

`ip_mforward` strips the tunnel options from the packet, consults the multicast routing table, and, in this example, forwards the packet on another tunnel and on the same *physical* interface on which it arrived, as shown by the thin arrows. This is OK because the multicast routing tables are based on the *virtual* interfaces, not the physical interfaces.

In Figure 14.36 we assume that the physical interface is a member of the destination group, so `ip_output` passes the datagram to `ip_mloopback`, which queues it for processing by `ipintr` (the thick arrows). The packet is passed to `ip_mforward` again, where it is discarded (Exercise 14.4). `ip_mforward` returns 0 this time (because the packet arrived on a physical interface), so `ipintr` considers and accepts the datagram for input processing.

We show the multicast forwarding code in three parts:

- tunnel input processing (Figure 14.37),
- forwarding eligibility (Figure 14.39), and
- forward to outgoing interfaces (Figure 14.40).

ip_mroute.c

```
516  int
517  ip_mforward(m, ifp)
518  struct mbuf *m;
519  struct ifnet *ifp;
520  {
521      struct ip *ip = mtod(m, struct ip *);
522      struct mrt *rt;
523      struct vif *vifp;
524      int    vifi;
525      u_char *ipoptions;
526      u_long  tunnel_src;

527      if (ip->ip_hl < (IP_HDR_LEN + TUNNEL_LEN) >> 2 ||
528          (ipoptions = (u_char *) (ip + 1))[1] != IPOPT_LSRR) {
529          /* Packet arrived via a physical interface. */
530          tunnel_src = 0;
531      } else {
532          /*
533           * Packet arrived through a tunnel.
534           * A tunneled packet has a single NOP option and a
535           * two-element loose-source-and-record-route (LSRR)
536           * option immediately following the fixed-size part of
537           * the IP header.  At this point in processing, the IP
538           * header should contain the following IP addresses:
539           *
540           * original source        - in the source address field
541           * destination group      - in the destination address field
542           * remote tunnel end-point - in the first  element of LSRR
543           * one of this host's addrs - in the second element of LSRR
544           *
545           * NOTE: RFC-1075 would have the original source and
546           * remote tunnel end-point addresses swapped.  However,
547           * that could cause delivery of ICMP error messages to
548           * innocent applications on intermediate routing
549           * hosts!  Therefore, we hereby change the spec.
550           */
551          /* Verify that the tunnel options are well-formed.  */
552          if (ipoptions[0] != IPOPT_NOP ||
553              ipoptions[2] != 11 ||    /* LSRR option length  */
554              ipoptions[3] != 12 ||    /* LSRR address pointer */
555              (tunnel_src = *(u_long *) (&ipoptions[4])) == 0) {
556              mrtstat.mrts_bad_tunnel++;
557              return (1);
558          }
559          /* Delete the tunnel options from the packet. */
560          ovbcopy((caddr_t) (ipoptions + TUNNEL_LEN), (caddr_t) ipoptions,
561              (unsigned) (m->m_len - (IP_HDR_LEN + TUNNEL_LEN)));
562          m->m_len -= TUNNEL_LEN;
563          ip->ip_len -= TUNNEL_LEN;
564          ip->ip_hl -= TUNNEL_LEN >> 2;
565      }
```

ip_mroute.c

Figure 14.37 ip_mforward function: tunnel arrival.

516–526   The two arguments to `ip_mforward` are a pointer to the mbuf chain containing the
datagram; and a pointer to the `ifnet` structure of the receiving interface.

Arrival on physical interface

527–530   To distinguish between a multicast datagram arriving on a physical interface and a
tunneled datagram arriving on the same physical interface, the IP header is examined
for the characteristic LSRR option. If the header is too small to contain the option, or if
the options don't start with a NOP followed by an LSRR option, it is assumed that the
datagram arrived on a physical interface and `tunnel_src` is set to 0.

Arrival on a tunnel

531–558   If the datagram looks as though it arrived on a tunnel, the options are verified to
make sure they are well formed. If the options are not well formed for a multicast tunnel, `ip_mforward` returns 1 to indicate that the datagram should be discarded. Figure 14.38 shows the organization of the tunnel options.

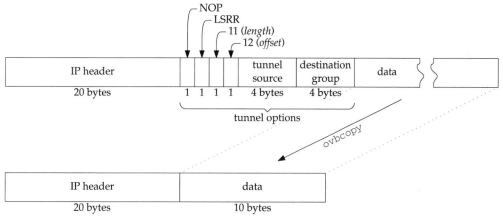

Figure 14.38   Multicast tunnel options.

In Figure 14.38 we assume there are no other options in the datagram, although that is not
required. Any other IP options will appear after the LSRR option, which is always inserted
before any other options by the multicast router at the start of the tunnel.

Delete tunnel options

559–565   If the options are OK, they are removed from the datagram by shifting the remaining options and data forward and adjusting `m_len` in the mbuf header and `ip_len` and
`ip_hl` in the IP header (Figure 14.38).

`ip_mforward` often uses `tunnel_source` as its return value, which is only
nonzero when the datagram arrives on a tunnel. When `ip_mforward` returns a
nonzero value, the caller discards the datagram. For `ipintr` this means that a datagram that arrives on a tunnel is passed to `ip_mforward` and discarded by `ipintr`.
The forwarding code strips out the tunnel information, duplicates the datagram, and
sends the datagrams with `ip_output`, which calls `ip_mloopback` if the interface is a
member of the destination group.

The next part of `ip_mforward`, shown in Figure 14.39, discards the datagram if it is ineligible for forwarding.

```
                                                                  ──────── ip_mroute.c
566     /*
567      * Don't forward a packet with time-to-live of zero or one,
568      * or a packet destined to a local-only group.
569      */
570     if (ip->ip_ttl <= 1 ||
571         ntohl(ip->ip_dst.s_addr) <= INADDR_MAX_LOCAL_GROUP)
572         return ((int) tunnel_src);

573     /*
574      * Don't forward if we don't have a route for the packet's origin.
575      */
576     if (!(rt = mrtfind(ip->ip_src))) {
577         mrtstat.mrts_no_route++;
578         return ((int) tunnel_src);
579     }
580     /*
581      * Don't forward if it didn't arrive from the parent vif for its origin.
582      */
583     vifi = rt->mrt_parent;
584     if (tunnel_src == 0) {
585         if ((viftable[vifi].v_flags & VIFF_TUNNEL) ||
586             viftable[vifi].v_ifp != ifp)
587             return ((int) tunnel_src);
588     } else {
589         if (!(viftable[vifi].v_flags & VIFF_TUNNEL) ||
590             viftable[vifi].v_rmt_addr.s_addr != tunnel_src)
591             return ((int) tunnel_src);
592     }
                                                                  ──────── ip_mroute.c
```

Figure 14.39 `ip_mforward` function: forwarding eligibility checks.

Expired TTL or local multicast

566–572   If `ip_ttl` is 0 or 1, the datagram has reached the end of its lifetime and is not forwarded. If the destination group is less than or equal to `INADDR_MAX_LOCAL_GROUP` (the 224.0.0.x groups, Figure 12.1), the datagram is not allowed beyond the local network and is not forwarded. In either case, `tunnel_src` is returned to the caller.

> Version 3.3 of `mrouted` supports administrative scoping of certain destination groups. An interface can be configured to discard datagrams addressed to these groups, similar to the automatic scoping of the 224.0.0.x groups.

No route available

573–579   If `mrtfind` cannot locate a route based on the *source* address of the datagram, the function returns. Without a route, the multicast router cannot determine to which interfaces the datagram should be forwarded. This might occur, for example, when the multicast datagrams arrive before the multicast routing table has been updated by `mrouted`.

Arrived on unexpected interface

580–592   If the datagram arrived on a physical interface but was expected to arrive on a tunnel or on a different physical interface, `ip_mforward` returns. If the datagram arrived on a tunnel but was expected to arrive on a physical interface or on a different tunnel, `ip_mforward` returns. A datagram may arrive on an unexpected interface when the routing tables are in transition because of changes in the group membership or in the physical topology of the network.

The final part of `ip_mforward` (Figure 14.40) sends the datagram on each of the outgoing interfaces specified in the multicast route entry.

```
                                                              ───────────────── ip_mroute.c
593      /*
594       * For each vif, decide if a copy of the packet should be forwarded.
595       * Forward if:
596       *         - the ttl exceeds the vif's threshold AND
597       *         - the vif is a child in the origin's route AND
598       *         - ( the vif is not a leaf in the origin's route OR
599       *             the destination group has members on the vif )
600       *
601       * (This might be speeded up with some sort of cache -- someday.)
602       */
603      for (vifp = viftable, vifi = 0; vifi < numvifs; vifp++, vifi++) {
604          if (ip->ip_ttl > vifp->v_threshold &&
605              VIFM_ISSET(vifi, rt->mrt_children) &&
606              (!VIFM_ISSET(vifi, rt->mrt_leaves) ||
607               grplst_member(vifp, ip->ip_dst))) {
608              if (vifp->v_flags & VIFF_TUNNEL)
609                  tunnel_send(m, vifp);
610              else
611                  phyint_send(m, vifp);
612          }
613      }
614      return ((int) tunnel_src);
615  }
                                                              ───────────────── ip_mroute.c
```

Figure 14.40   `ip_mforward` function: forwarding.

593–615   For each interface in `viftable`, a datagram is sent on the interface if

- the datagram's TTL is greater than the multicast threshold for the interface,
- the interface is a child interface for the route, and
- the interface is not connected to a leaf network.

If the interface is a leaf, the datagram is output only if there is a member of the destination group on the network (i.e., `grplst_member` returns a nonzero value).

`tunnel_send` forwards the datagram on tunnel interfaces; `phyint_send` is used for physical interfaces.

`phyint_send` Function

To send a multicast datagram on a physical interface, `phyint_send` (Figure 14.41) specifies the output interface explicitly in the `ip_moptions` structure it passes to `ip_output`.

```
                                                                   ip_mroute.c
616 static void
617 phyint_send(m, vifp)
618 struct mbuf *m;
619 struct vif *vifp;
620 {
621     struct ip *ip = mtod(m, struct ip *);
622     struct mbuf *mb_copy;
623     struct ip_moptions *imo;
624     int     error;
625     struct ip_moptions simo;

626     mb_copy = m_copy(m, 0, M_COPYALL);
627     if (mb_copy == NULL)
628         return;

629     imo = &simo;
630     imo->imo_multicast_ifp = vifp->v_ifp;
631     imo->imo_multicast_ttl = ip->ip_ttl - 1;
632     imo->imo_multicast_loop = 1;

633     error = ip_output(mb_copy, NULL, NULL, IP_FORWARDING, imo);
634 }
                                                                   ip_mroute.c
```

Figure 14.41   `phyint_send` function.

616–634   `m_copy` duplicates the outgoing datagram. The `ip_moptions` structure is set to force the datagram to be transmitted on the selected interface. The TTL value is decremented, and multicast loopback is enabled.

The datagram is passed to `ip_output`. The `IP_FORWARDING` flag avoids an infinite loop, where `ip_output` calls `ip_mforward` again.

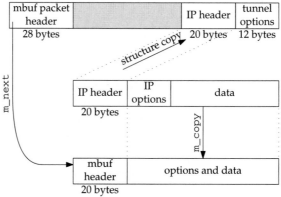

Figure 14.42   Inserting tunnel options.

tunnel_send Function

To send a datagram on a tunnel, tunnel_send (Figure 14.43) must construct the appropriate tunnel options and insert them in the header of the outgoing datagram. Figure 14.42 shows how tunnel_send prepares a packet for the tunnel.

```
                                                               ─────────────ip_mroute.c
635  static void
636  tunnel_send(m, vifp)
637  struct mbuf *m;
638  struct vif *vifp;
639  {
640      struct ip *ip = mtod(m, struct ip *);
641      struct mbuf *mb_copy, *mb_opts;
642      struct ip *ip_copy;
643      int      error;
644      u_char *cp;

645      /*
646       * Make sure that adding the tunnel options won't exceed the
647       * maximum allowed number of option bytes.
648       */
649      if (ip->ip_hl > (60 - TUNNEL_LEN) >> 2) {
650          mrtstat.mrts_cant_tunnel++;
651          return;
652      }
653      /*
654       * Get a private copy of the IP header so that changes to some
655       * of the IP fields don't damage the original header, which is
656       * examined later in ip_input.c.
657       */
658      mb_copy = m_copy(m, IP_HDR_LEN, M_COPYALL);
659      if (mb_copy == NULL)
660          return;
661      MGETHDR(mb_opts, M_DONTWAIT, MT_HEADER);
662      if (mb_opts == NULL) {
663          m_freem(mb_copy);
664          return;
665      }
666      /*
667       * Make mb_opts be the new head of the packet chain.
668       * Any options of the packet were left in the old packet chain head
669       */
670      mb_opts->m_next = mb_copy;
671      mb_opts->m_len = IP_HDR_LEN + TUNNEL_LEN;
672      mb_opts->m_data += MSIZE - mb_opts->m_len;
                                                               ─────────────ip_mroute.c
```

Figure 14.43 tunnel_send function: verify and allocate new header.

Will the tunnel options fit?

635–652   If there is no room in the IP header for the tunnel options, tunnel_send returns immediately and the datagram is not forwarded on the tunnel. It may be forwarded on other interfaces.

Duplicate the datagram and allocate mbuf for new header and tunnel options

653–672   In the call to m_copy, the starting offset for the copy is 20 (IP_HDR_LEN). The resulting mbuf chain contains the options and data for the datagram but not the IP header. mb_opts points to a new datagram header allocated by MGETHDR. The datagram header is prepended to mb_copy. Then m_len and m_data are adjusted to accommodate an IP header and the tunnel options.

The second half of tunnel_send, shown in Figure 14.44, modifies the headers of the outgoing packet and sends the packet.

```
                                                                    ip_mroute.c
673    ip_copy = mtod(mb_opts, struct ip *);
674    /*
675     * Copy the base ip header to the new head mbuf.
676     */
677    *ip_copy = *ip;
678    ip_copy->ip_ttl--;
679    ip_copy->ip_dst = vifp->v_rmt_addr;         /* remote tunnel end-point */
680    /*
681     * Adjust the ip header length to account for the tunnel options.
682     */
683    ip_copy->ip_hl += TUNNEL_LEN >> 2;
684    ip_copy->ip_len += TUNNEL_LEN;
685    /*
686     * Add the NOP and LSRR after the base ip header
687     */
688    cp = (u_char *) (ip_copy + 1);
689    *cp++ = IPOPT_NOP;
690    *cp++ = IPOPT_LSRR;
691    *cp++ = 11;                        /* LSRR option length */
692    *cp++ = 8;                         /* LSSR pointer to second element */
693    *(u_long *) cp = vifp->v_lcl_addr.s_addr;    /* local tunnel end-point */
694    cp += 4;
695    *(u_long *) cp = ip->ip_dst.s_addr;        /* destination group */

696    error = ip_output(mb_opts, NULL, NULL, IP_FORWARDING, NULL);
697  }
                                                                    ip_mroute.c
```

Figure 14.44   tunnel_send function: construct headers and send.

Modify IP header

673–679   The original IP header is copied from the original mbuf chain into the newly allocated mbuf header. The TTL in the header is decremented, and the destination is changed to be the other end of the tunnel.

Construct tunnel options

680–664   ip_hl and ip_len are adjusted to accommodate the tunnel options. The tunnel options are placed just after the IP header: a NOP, followed by the LSRR code, the length of the LSRR option (11 bytes), and a pointer to the *second* address in the option (8 bytes). The source route consists of the local tunnel end point followed by the destination group (Figure 14.13).

Send the tunneled datagram

665–697   ip_output sends the datagram, which now looks like a unicast datagram with an
LSRR option since the destination address is the unicast address of the other end of the
tunnel. When it reaches the other end of the tunnel, the tunnel options are stripped off
and the datagram is forwarded at that point, possibly through additional tunnels.

14.9 Cleanup: `ip_mrouter_done` Function

When mrouted shuts down, it issues the DVMRP_DONE command, which is handled by
the ip_mrouter_done function shown in Figure 14.45.

```
                                                                          ─ip_mroute.c
161 int
162 ip_mrouter_done()
163 {
164     vifi_t  vifi;
165     int     i;
166     struct ifnet *ifp;
167     int     s;
168     struct ifreq ifr;
169     s = splnet();
170     /*
171      * For each phyint in use, free its local group list and
172      * disable promiscuous reception of all IP multicasts.
173      */
174     for (vifi = 0; vifi < numvifs; vifi++) {
175         if (viftable[vifi].v_lcl_addr.s_addr != 0 &&
176             !(viftable[vifi].v_flags & VIFF_TUNNEL)) {
177             if (viftable[vifi].v_lcl_grps)
178                 free(viftable[vifi].v_lcl_grps, M_MRTABLE);
179             satosin(&ifr.ifr_addr)->sin_family = AF_INET;
180             satosin(&ifr.ifr_addr)->sin_addr.s_addr = INADDR_ANY;
181             ifp = viftable[vifi].v_ifp;
182             (*ifp->if_ioctl) (ifp, SIOCDELMULTI, (caddr_t) & ifr);
183         }
184     }
185     bzero((caddr_t) viftable, sizeof(viftable));
186     numvifs = 0;
187     /*
188      * Free any multicast route entries.
189      */
190     for (i = 0; i < MRTHASHSIZ; i++)
191         if (mrttable[i])
192             free(mrttable[i], M_MRTABLE);
193     bzero((caddr_t) mrttable, sizeof(mrttable));
194     cached_mrt = NULL;
195     ip_mrouter = NULL;
196     splx(s);
197     return (0);
198 }
                                                                          ─ip_mroute.c
```

Figure 14.45   ip_mrouter_done function: DVMRP_DONE command.

161–186   This function runs at `splnet` to avoid any interaction with the multicast forwarding code. For every physical multicast interface, the list of local groups is released and the `SIOCDELMULTI` command is issued to stop receiving multicast datagrams (Exercise 14.3). The entire `viftable` array is cleared by `bzero` and `numvifs` is set to 0.

187–198   Every active entry in the multicast routing table is released, the entire table is cleared with `bzero`, the cache is cleared, and `ip_mrouter` is reset.

> Each entry in the multicast routing table may be the first in a linked list of entries. This code introduces a memory leak by releasing only the first entry in the list.

14.10 Summary

In this chapter we described the general concept of internetwork multicasting and the specific functions within the Net/3 kernel that support it. We did not discuss the implementation of `mrouted`, but the source is readily available for the interested reader.

We described the virtual interface table and the differences between a physical interface and a tunnel, as well as the LSRR options used to implement tunnels in Net/3.

We illustrated the RPB, TRPB, and RPM algorithms and described the kernel tables used to forward multicast datagrams according to TRPB. The concept of parent and leaf networks was also discussed.

Exercises

14.1   In Figure 14.25, how many multicast routes are needed?

14.2   Why is the update to the group membership cache in Figure 14.23 protected by `splnet` and `splx`?

14.3   What happens when `SIOCDELMULTI` is issued for an interface that has explicitly joined a multicast group with the `IP_ADD_MEMBERSHIP` option?

14.4   When a datagram arrives on a tunnel and is accepted by `ip_mforward`, it may be looped back by `ip_output` when it is forwarded to a physical interface. Why does `ip_mforward` discard the looped-back packet when it arrives on the physical interface?

14.5   Redesign the group address cache to increase its effectiveness.

15

Socket Layer

15.1 Introduction

This chapter is the first of three that cover the socket-layer code in Net/3. The socket abstraction was introduced with the 4.2BSD release in 1983 to provide a uniform interface to network and interprocess communication protocols. The Net/3 release discussed here is based on the 4.3BSD Reno version of sockets, which is slightly different from the earlier 4.2 releases used by many Unix vendors.

As described in Section 1.7, the socket layer maps protocol-independent requests from a process to the protocol-specific implementation selected when the socket was created.

To allow standard Unix I/O system calls such as `read` and `write` to operate with network connections, the filesystem and networking facilities in BSD releases are integrated at the system call level. Network connections represented by sockets are accessed through a descriptor (a small integer) in the same way an open file is accessed through a descriptor. This allows the standard filesystem calls such as `read` and `write`, as well as network-specific system calls such as `sendmsg` and `recvmsg`, to work with a descriptor associated with a socket.

Our focus is on the implementation of sockets and the associated system calls and not on how a typical program might use the socket layer to implement network applications. For a detailed discussion of the process-level socket interface and how to program network applications see [Stevens 1990] and [Rago 1993].

Figure 15.1 shows the layering between the socket interface in a process and the protocol implementation in the kernel.

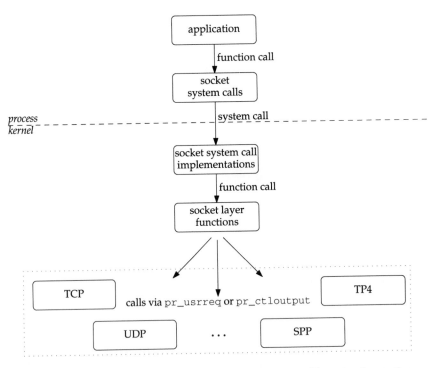

Figure 15.1   The socket layer converts generic requests to specific protocol operations.

`splnet` Processing

The socket layer contains many paired calls to `splnet` and `splx`. As discussed in Section 1.12, these calls protect code that accesses data structures shared between the socket layer and the protocol-processing layer. Without calls to `splnet`, a software interrupt that initiates protocol processing and changes the shared data structures will confuse the socket-layer code when it resumes.

We assume that readers understand these calls and we rarely point them out in our discussion.

15.2   Code Introduction

The three files listed in Figure 15.2 are described in this chapter.

Global Variables

The two global variable covered in this chapter are described in Figure 15.3.

File	Description
sys/socketvar.h	socket structure definitions
kern/uipc_syscalls.c kern/uipc_socket.c	system call implementation socket-layer functions

Figure 15.2   Files discussed in this chapter.

Variable	Datatype	Description
socketops	struct fileops	socket implementation of I/O system calls
sysent	struct sysent[]	array of system call entries

Figure 15.3   Global variable introduced in this chapter.

15.3   socket Structure

A socket represents one end of a communication link and holds or points to all the information associated with the link. This information includes the protocol to use, state information for the protocol (which includes source and destination addresses), queues of arriving connections, data buffers, and option flags. Figure 15.5 shows the definition of a socket and its associated buffers.

41–42   so_type is specified by the process creating a socket and identifies the communication semantics to be supported by the socket and the associated protocol. so_type shares the same values as pr_type shown in Figure 7.8. For UDP, so_type would be SOCK_DGRAM and for TCP it would be SOCK_STREAM.

43   so_options is a collection of flags that modify the behavior of a socket. Figure 15.4 describes the flags.

so_options	Kernel only	Description
SO_ACCEPTCONN	•	socket accepts incoming connections
SO_BROADCAST		socket can send broadcast messages
SO_DEBUG		socket records debugging information
SO_DONTROUTE		output operations bypass routing tables
SO_KEEPALIVE		socket probes idle connections
SO_OOBINLINE		socket keeps out-of-band data inline
SO_REUSEADDR		socket can reuse a local address
SO_REUSEPORT		socket can reuse a local address and port
SO_USELOOPBACK		routing domain sockets only; sending process receives its own routing requests

Figure 15.4   so_options values.

A process can modify all the socket options with the getsockopt and setsockopt system calls except SO_ACCEPTCONN, which is set by the kernel when the listen system call is issued on the socket.

```
                                                                    ── socketvar.h
41 struct socket {
42     short   so_type;           /* generic type, Figure 7.8 */
43     short   so_options;        /* from socket call, Figure 15.4 */
44     short   so_linger;         /* time to linger while closing */
45     short   so_state;          /* internal state flags, Figure 15.6 */
46     caddr_t so_pcb;            /* protocol control block */
47     struct protosw *so_proto;  /* protocol handle */
48 /*
49  * Variables for connection queueing.
50  * Socket where accepts occur is so_head in all subsidiary sockets.
51  * If so_head is 0, socket is not related to an accept.
52  * For head socket so_q0 queues partially completed connections,
53  * while so_q is a queue of connections ready to be accepted.
54  * If a connection is aborted and it has so_head set, then
55  * it has to be pulled out of either so_q0 or so_q.
56  * We allow connections to queue up based on current queue lengths
57  * and limit on number of queued connections for this socket.
58  */
59     struct socket *so_head;    /* back pointer to accept socket */
60     struct socket *so_q0;      /* queue of partial connections */
61     struct socket *so_q;       /* queue of incoming connections */
62     short   so_q0len;          /* partials on so_q0 */
63     short   so_qlen;           /* number of connections on so_q */
64     short   so_qlimit;         /* max number queued connections */
65     short   so_timeo;          /* connection timeout */
66     u_short so_error;          /* error affecting connection */
67     pid_t   so_pgid;           /* pgid for signals */
68     u_long  so_oobmark;        /* chars to oob mark */
69 /*
70  * Variables for socket buffering.
71  */
72     struct sockbuf {
73         u_long  sb_cc;         /* actual chars in buffer */
74         u_long  sb_hiwat;      /* max actual char count */
75         u_long  sb_mbcnt;      /* chars of mbufs used */
76         u_long  sb_mbmax;      /* max chars of mbufs to use */
77         long    sb_lowat;      /* low water mark */
78         struct mbuf *sb_mb;    /* the mbuf chain */
79         struct selinfo sb_sel; /* process selecting read/write */
80         short   sb_flags;      /* Figure 16.5 */
81         short   sb_timeo;      /* timeout for read/write */
82     } so_rcv, so_snd;
83     caddr_t so_tpcb;           /* Wisc. protocol control block XXX */
84     void    (*so_upcall) (struct socket * so, caddr_t arg, int waitf);
85     caddr_t so_upcallarg;      /* Arg for above */
86 };
                                                                    ── socketvar.h
```

Figure 15.5 struct socket definition.

44   so_linger is the time in clock ticks that a socket waits for data to drain while closing a connection (Section 15.15).

45   so_state represents the internal state and additional characteristics of the socket. Figure 15.6 lists the possible values for so_state.

so_state	Kernel only	Description
SS_ASYNC		socket should send asynchronous notification of I/O events
SS_NBIO		socket operations should not block the process
SS_CANTRCVMORE	•	socket cannot receive more data from peer
SS_CANTSENDMORE	•	socket cannot send more data to peer
SS_ISCONFIRMING	•	socket is negotiating a connection request
SS_ISCONNECTED	•	socket is connected to a foreign socket
SS_ISCONNECTING	•	socket is connecting to a foreign socket
SS_ISDISCONNECTING	•	socket is disconnecting from peer
SS_NOFDREF	•	socket is not associated with a descriptor
SS_PRIV	•	socket was created by a process with superuser privileges
SS_RCVATMARK	•	process has consumed all data received before the most recent out-of-band data was received

Figure 15.6   so_state values.

In Figure 15.6, the middle column shows that SS_ASYNC and SS_NBIO can be changed explicitly by a process by the fcntl and ioctl system calls. The other flags are implicitly changed by the process during the execution of system calls. For example, if the process calls connect, the SS_ISCONNECTED flag is set by the kernel when the connection is established.

SS_NBIO and SS_ASYNC Flags

By default, a process blocks waiting for resources when it makes an I/O request. For example, a read system call on a socket blocks if there is no data available from the network. When the data arrives, the process is unblocked and read returns. Similarly, when a process calls write, the kernel blocks the process until space is available in the kernel for the data. If SS_NBIO is set, the kernel does not block a process during I/O on the socket but instead returns the error code EWOULDBLOCK.

If SS_ASYNC is set, the kernel sends the SIGIO signal to the process or process group specified by so_pgid when the status of the socket changes for one of the following reasons:

- a connection request has completed,
- a disconnect request has been initiated,
- a disconnect request has been completed,
- half of a connection has been shut down,
- data has arrived on a socket,
- data has been sent from a socket (i.e., the output buffer has free space), or
- an asynchronous error has occurred on a UDP or TCP socket.

46   so_pcb points to a protocol control block that contains protocol-specific state information and parameters for the socket. Each protocol defines its own control block structure, so so_pcb is defined to be a generic pointer. Figure 15.7 lists the control block structures that we discuss.

so_pcb never points to a tcpcb structure directly; see Figure 22.1.

Protocol	Control block	Reference
UDP	struct inpcb	Section 22.3
TCP	struct inpcb	Section 22.3
	struct tcpcb	Section 24.5
ICMP, IGMP, raw IP	struct inpcb	Section 22.3
Route	struct rawcb	Section 20.3

Figure 15.7 Protocol control blocks.

47   so_proto points to the protosw structure of the protocol selected by the process during the socket system call (Section 7.4).

48–64   Sockets with SO_ACCEPTCONN set maintain two connection queues. Connections that are not yet established (e.g., the TCP three-way handshake is not yet complete) are placed on the queue so_q0. Connections that are established and are ready to be accepted (e.g., the TCP three-way handshake is complete) are placed on the queue so_q. The lengths of the queues are kept in so_q0len and so_qlen. Each queued connection is represented by its own socket. so_head in each queued socket points to the original socket with SO_ACCEPTCONN set.

The maximum number of queued connections for a particular socket is controlled by so_qlimit, which is specified by a process when it calls listen. The kernel silently enforces an upper limit of 5 (SOMAXCONN, Figure 15.24) and a lower limit of 0. A somewhat obscure formula shown with Figure 15.29 uses so_qlimit to control the number of queued connections.

Figure 15.8 illustrates a queue configuration in which three connections are ready to be accepted and one connection is being established.

65   so_timeo is a *wait channel* (Section 15.10) used during accept, connect, and close processing.

66   so_error holds an error code until it can be reported to a process during the next system call that references the socket.

67   If SS_ASYNC is set for a socket, the SIGIO signal is sent to the process (if so_pgid is greater than 0) or to the progress group (if so_pgid is less than 0). so_pgid can be changed or examined with the SIOCSPGRP and SIOCGPGRP ioctl commands. For more information about process groups see [Stevens 1992].

68   so_oobmark identifies the point in the input data stream at which out-of-band data was most recently received. Section 16.11 discusses socket support for out-of-band data and Section 29.7 discusses the semantics of out-of-band data in TCP.

69–82   Each socket contains two data buffers, so_rcv and so_snd, used to buffer incoming and outgoing data. These are structures contained within the socket structure, not

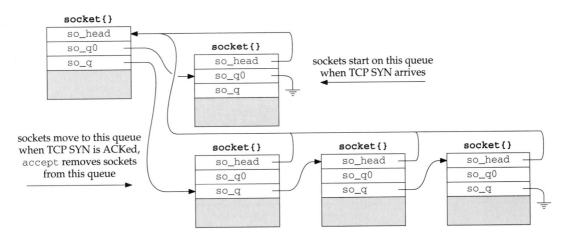

Figure 15.8   Socket connection queues.

pointers to structures. We describe the organization and use of the socket buffers in Chapter 16.

83–86   so_tpcb is not used by Net/3. so_upcall and so_upcallarg are used only by the NFS software in Net/3.

> NFS is unusual. In many ways it is a process-level application that has been moved into the kernel. The so_upcall mechanism triggers NFS input processing when data is added to a socket receive buffer. The tsleep and wakeup mechanism is inappropriate in this case, since the NFS protocol executes within the kernel, not as a process.

The files socketvar.h and uipc_socket2.c define several macros and functions that simplify the socket-layer code. Figure 15.9 summarizes them.

15.4 System Calls

A process interacts with the kernel through a collection of well-defined functions called *system calls*. Before showing the system calls that support networking, we discuss the system call mechanism itself.

The transfer of execution from a process to the protected environment of the kernel is machine- and implementation-dependent. In the discussion that follows, we use the 386 implementation of Net/3 to illustrate implementation specific operations.

In BSD kernels, each system call is numbered and the hardware is configured to transfer control to a single kernel function when the process executes a system call. The particular system call is identified as an integer argument to the function. In the 386 implementation, syscall is that function. Using the system call number, syscall indexes a table to locate the sysent structure for the requested system call. Each entry in the table is a sysent structure:

Name	Description
sosendallatonce	Does the protocol associated with *so* require each send system call to result in a single protocol request? int **sosendallatonce**(struct socket *so);
soisconnecting	Set the socket state to SS_ISCONNECTING. int **soisconnecting**(struct socket *so);
soisconnected	See Figure 15.30.
soreadable	Will a read on *so* return information without blocking? int **soreadable**(struct socket *so);
sowriteable	Will a write on *so* return without blocking? int **sowriteable**(struct socket *so);
socantsendmore	Set the SS_CANTSENDMORE flag. Wake up any processes sleeping on the send buffer. int **socantsendmore**(struct socket *so);
socantrcvmore	Set the SS_CANTRCVMORE flag. Wake up processes sleeping on the receive buffer. int **socantrcvmore**(struct socket *so);
sodisconnect	Issue the PRU_DISCONNECT request. int **sodisconnect**(struct socket *so);
soisdisconnecting	Clear the SS_ISCONNECTING flag. Set SS_ISDISCONNECTING, SS_CANTRCVMORE, and SS_CANTSENDMORE flags. Wake up any processes selecting on the socket. int **soisdisconnecting**(struct socket *so);
soisdisconnected	Clear the SS_ISCONNECTING, SS_ISCONNECTED, and SS_ISDISCONNECTING flags. Set the SS_CANTRCVMORE and SS_CANTSENDMORE flags. Wake up any processes selecting on the socket or waiting for close to complete. int **soisdisconnected**(struct socket *so);
soqinsque	Insert *so* on a queue associated with *head*. If *q* is 0, the socket is added to the end of so_q0, which holds incomplete connections. Otherwise, the socket is added to the end of so_q, which holds connections that are ready to be accepted. Net/1 incorrectly placed sockets at the front of the queue. int **soqinsque**(struct socket *head, struct socket *so, int q);
soqremque	Remove *so* from the queue identified by *q*. The socket queues are located by following *so->so_head*. int **soqremque**(struct socket *so, int q);

Figure 15.9   Socket macros and functions.

```
struct sysent {
    int sy_narg;          /* number of arguments */
    int (*sy_call) ();    /* implementing function */
};                        /* system call table entry */
```

Here are several entries from the `sysent` array, which is defined in `kern/init_sysent.c`.

```
struct sysent sysent[] = {
    /* ... */
    { 3, recvmsg },           /* 27 = recvmsg */
    { 3, sendmsg },           /* 28 = sendmsg */
    { 6, recvfrom },          /* 29 = recvfrom */
    { 3, accept },            /* 30 = accept */
    { 3, getpeername },       /* 31 = getpeername */
    { 3, getsockname },       /* 32 = getsockname */
    /* ... */
}
```

For example, the `recvmsg` system call is the 27th entry in the system call table, has three arguments, and is implemented by the `recvmsg` function in the kernel.

`syscall` copies the arguments from the calling process into the kernel and allocates an array to hold the results of the system call, which `syscall` returns to the process when the system call completes. `syscall` dispatches control to the kernel function associated with the system call. In the 386 implementation, this call looks like:

```
struct sysent *callp;
error = (*callp->sy_call)(p, args, rval);
```

where `callp` is a pointer to the relevant `sysent` structure, p is a pointer to the process table entry for the process that made the system call, `args` represents the arguments to the system call as an array of 32-bit words, and `rval` is an array of two 32-bit words to hold the return value of the system call. When we use the term *system call*, we mean the function within the kernel called by `syscall`, not the function within the process called by the application.

`syscall` expects the system call function (i.e., what `sy_call` points to) to return 0 if no errors occurred and a nonzero error code otherwise. If no error occurs, the kernel passes the values in `rval` back to the process as the return value of the system call (the one made by the application). If an error occurs, `syscall` ignores the values in `rval` and returns the error code to the process in a machine-dependent way so that the error is made available to the process in the external variable `errno`. The function called by the application returns –1 or a null pointer to indicate that `errno` should be examined.

The 386 implementation sets the carry bit to indicate that the value returned by `syscall` is an error code. The system call stub in the process stores the code in `errno` and returns –1 or a null pointer to the application. If the carry bit is not set, the value returned by `syscall` is returned by the stub.

To summarize, a function implementing a system call "returns" two values: one for the `syscall` function, and a second (found in `rval`) that `syscall` returns to the calling process when no error occurs.

Example

The prototype for the `socket` system call is:

```
int socket(int domain, int type, int protocol);
```

The prototype for the kernel function that implements the system call is

```
struct socket_args {
        int domain;
        int type;
        int protocol;
};
socket(struct proc *p, struct socket_args *uap, int *retval);
```

When an application calls `socket`, the process passes three separate integers to the kernel with the system call mechanism. `syscall` copies the arguments into an array of 32-bit values and passes a pointer to the array as the second argument to the kernel version of `socket`. The kernel version of `socket` treats the second argument as a pointer to an `socket_args` structure. Figure 15.10 illustrates this arrangement.

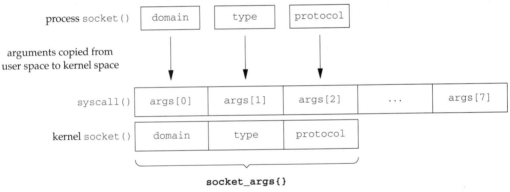

Figure 15.10   `socket` argument processing.

As illustrated by `socket`, each kernel function that implements a system call declares `args` not as a pointer to an array of 32-bit words, but as as a pointer to a structure specific to the system call.

> The implicit cast is legal only in traditional K&R C or in ANSI C when a prototype is not in effect. If a prototype is in effect, the compiler generates a warning.

`syscall` prepares the return value of 0 before executing the kernel system call function. If no error occurs, the system call function can return without clearing `*retval` and `syscall` returns 0 to the process.

System Call Summary

Figure 15.11 summarizes the system calls relevant to networking.

Category	Name	Function
setup	socket	create a new unnamed socket within a specified communication domain
	bind	assign a local address to a socket
server	listen	prepare a socket to accept incoming connections
	accept	wait for and accept connections
client	connect	establish a connection to a foreign socket
input	read	receive data into a single buffer
	readv	receive data into multiple buffers
	recv	receive data specifying options
	recvfrom	receive data and address of sender
	recvmsg	receive data into multiple buffers, control information, and receive the address of sender; specify receive options
output	write	send data from a single buffer
	writev	send data from multiple buffers
	send	send data specifying options
	sendto	send data to specified address
	sendmsg	send data from multiple buffers and control information to a specified address; specify send options
I/O	select	wait for I/O conditions
termination	shutdown	terminate connection in one or both directions
	close	terminate connection and release socket
administration	fcntl	modify I/O semantics
	ioctl	miscellaneous socket operations
	setsockopt	set socket or protocol options
	getsockopt	get socket or protocol options
	getsockname	get local address assigned to socket
	getpeername	get foreign address assigned to socket

Figure 15.11 Networking system calls in Net/3.

We present the setup, server, client, and termination calls in this chapter. The input and output system calls are discussed in Chapter 16 and the administrative calls in Chapter 17.

Figure 15.12 shows the sequence in which an application might use the calls. The I/O system calls in the large box can be called in any order. This is not a complete state diagram as some valid transitions are not included; just the most common ones are shown.

15.5 Processes, Descriptors, and Sockets

Before describing the socket system calls, we need to discuss the data structures that tie together processes, descriptors, and sockets. Figure 15.13 shows the structures and members relevant to our discussion. A more complete explanation of the file structures can be found in [Leffler et al. 1989].

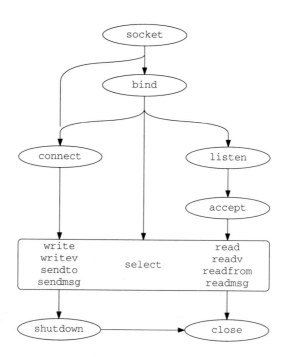

Figure 15.12   Network system call flowchart.

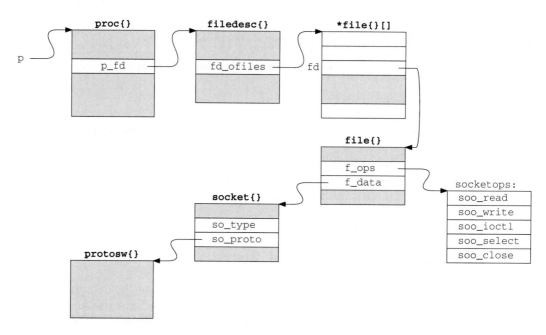

Figure 15.13   Process, file, and socket structures.

The first argument to a function implementing a system call is always p, a pointer to the proc structure of the calling process. The proc structure represents the kernel's notion of a process. Within the proc structure, p_fd points to a filedesc structure, which manages the descriptor table pointed to by fd_ofiles. The descriptor table is dynamically sized and consists of an array of pointers to file structures. Each file structure describes a single open file and can be shared between multiple processes.

Only a single file structure is shown in Figure 15.13. It is accessed by p->p_fd->fd_ofiles[fd]. Within the file structure, two members are of interest to us: f_ops and f_data. The implementation of I/O system calls such as read and write varies according to what type of I/O object is associated with a descriptor. f_ops points to a fileops structure containing a list of function pointers that implement the read, write, ioctl, select, and close system calls for the associated I/O object. Figure 15.13 shows f_ops pointing to a global fileops structure, socketops, which contains pointers to the functions for sockets.

f_data points to private data used by the associated I/O object. For sockets, f_data points to the socket structure associated with the descriptor. Finally, we see that so_proto in the socket structure points to the protosw structure for the protocol selected when the socket is created. Recall that each protosw structure is shared by all sockets associated with the protocol.

We now proceed to discuss the system calls.

15.6   socket **System Call**

The socket system call creates a new socket and associates it with a protocol as specified by the domain, type, and protocol arguments specified by the process. The function (shown in Figure 15.14) allocates a new descriptor, which identifies the socket in future system calls, and returns the descriptor to the process.

42–55   Before each system call a structure is defined to describe the arguments passed from the process to the kernel. In this case, the arguments are passed within a socket_args structure. All the socket-layer system calls have three arguments: p, a pointer to the proc structure for the calling process; uap, a pointer to a structure containing the arguments passed by the process to the system call; and retval, a value–result argument that points to the return value for the system call. Normally, we ignore the p and retval arguments and refer to the contents of the structure pointed to by uap as the arguments to the system call.

56–60   falloc allocates a new file structure and slot in the fd_ofiles array (Figure 15.13). fp points to the new structure and fd is the index of the structure in the fd_ofiles array. socket enables the file structure for read and write access and marks it as a socket. socketops, a global fileops structure shared by all sockets, is attached to the file structure by f_ops. The socketops variable is initialized at compile time as shown in Figure 15.15.

60–69   socreate allocates and initializes a socket structure. If socreate fails, the error code is posted in error, the file structure is released, and the descriptor slot cleared. If socreate succeeds, f_data is set to point to the socket structure and establishes

uipc_syscalls.c

```
42 struct socket_args {
43     int     domain;
44     int     type;
45     int     protocol;
46 };

47 socket(p, uap, retval)
48 struct proc *p;
49 struct socket_args *uap;
50 int    *retval;
51 {
52     struct filedesc *fdp = p->p_fd;
53     struct socket *so;
54     struct file *fp;
55     int     fd, error;

56     if (error = falloc(p, &fp, &fd))
57         return (error);
58     fp->f_flag = FREAD | FWRITE;
59     fp->f_type = DTYPE_SOCKET;
60     fp->f_ops = &socketops;
61     if (error = socreate(uap->domain, &so, uap->type, uap->protocol)) {
62         fdp->fd_ofiles[fd] = 0;
63         ffree(fp);
64     } else {
65         fp->f_data = (caddr_t) so;
66         *retval = fd;
67     }
68     return (error);
69 }
```

uipc_syscalls.c

Figure 15.14   socket system call.

Member	Value
fo_read	soo_read
fo_write	soo_write
fo_ioctl	soo_ioctl
fo_select	soo_select
fo_close	soo_close

Figure 15.15   socketops: the global fileops structure for sockets.

the association between the descriptor and the socket. fd is returned to the process through *retval. socket returns 0 or the error code returned by socreate.

socreate **Function**

Most socket system calls are divided into at least two functions, in the same way that socket and socreate are. The first function retrieves from the process all the data required, calls the second so*xxx* function to do the work, and then returns any results to the process. This split is so that the second function can be called directly by kernel-based network protocols, such as NFS. socreate is shown in Figure 15.16.

```
─────────────────────────────────────────────────────── uipc_socket.c
43 socreate(dom, aso, type, proto)
44 int     dom;
45 struct socket **aso;
46 int     type;
47 int     proto;
48 {
49     struct proc *p = curproc;    /* XXX */
50     struct protosw *prp;
51     struct socket *so;
52     int     error;

53     if (proto)
54         prp = pffindproto(dom, proto, type);
55     else
56         prp = pffindtype(dom, type);
57     if (prp == 0 || prp->pr_usrreq == 0)
58         return (EPROTONOSUPPORT);
59     if (prp->pr_type != type)
60         return (EPROTOTYPE);
61     MALLOC(so, struct socket *, sizeof(*so), M_SOCKET, M_WAIT);
62     bzero((caddr_t) so, sizeof(*so));
63     so->so_type = type;
64     if (p->p_ucred->cr_uid == 0)
65         so->so_state = SS_PRIV;
66     so->so_proto = prp;
67     error =
68         (*prp->pr_usrreq) (so, PRU_ATTACH,
69             (struct mbuf *) 0, (struct mbuf *) proto, (struct mbuf *) 0);
70     if (error) {
71         so->so_state |= SS_NOFDREF;
72         sofree(so);
73         return (error);
74     }
75     *aso = so;
76     return (0);
77 }
─────────────────────────────────────────────────────── uipc_socket.c
```

Figure 15.16   socreate function.

43–52   The four arguments to socreate are: dom, the requested protocol domain (e.g., PF_INET); aso, in which a pointer to a new socket structure is returned; type, the requested socket type (e.g., SOCK_STREAM); and proto, the requested protocol .

Find protocol switch table

53–60   If proto is nonzero, pffindproto looks for the specific protocol requested by the process. If proto is 0, pffindtype looks for a protocol within the specified domain with the semantics specified by type. Both functions return a pointer to a protosw structure of the matching protocol or a null pointer (Section 7.6).

Allocate and initialize `socket` structure

61–66   `socreate` allocates a new `socket` structure, fills it with 0s, records the `type`, and, if the calling process has superuser privileges, turns on `SS_PRIV` in the socket structure.

`PRU_ATTACH` request

67–69   The first example of the protocol-independent socket layer making a protocol-specific request appears in `socreate`. Recall from Section 7.4 and Figure 15.13 that `so->so_proto->pr_usrreq` is a pointer to the user-request function of the protocol associated with socket `so`. Every protocol provides this function in order to handle communication requests from the socket layer. The prototype for the function is:

```
int pr_usrreq(struct socket *so, int req, struct mbuf *m0, *m1, *m2);
```

The first argument, *so*, is a pointer to the relevant socket and *req* is a constant identifying the particular request. The next three arguments (*m0*, *m1*, and *m2*) are different for each request. They are always passed as pointers to `mbuf` structures, even if they have another type. Casts are used when necessary to avoid warnings from the compiler.

Figure 15.17 shows the requests available through the `pr_usrreq` function. The semantics of each request depend on the particular protocol servicing the request.

Request	Arguments			Description
	m0	*m1*	*m2*	
`PRU_ABORT`				abort any existing connection
`PRU_ACCEPT`		*address*		wait for and accept a connection
`PRU_ATTACH`		*protocol*		a new socket has been created
`PRU_BIND`		*address*		bind the address to the socket
`PRU_CONNECT`		*address*		establish association or connection to address
`PRU_CONNECT2`		*socket2*		connect two sockets together
`PRU_DETACH`				socket is being closed
`PRU_DISCONNECT`				break association between socket and foreign address
`PRU_LISTEN`				begin listening for connections
`PRU_PEERADDR`		*buffer*		return foreign address associated with socket
`PRU_RCVD`		*flags*		process has accepted some data
`PRU_RCVOOB`	*buffer*	*flags*		receive OOB data
`PRU_SEND`	*data*	*address*	*control*	send regular data
`PRU_SENDOOB`	*data*	*address*	*control*	send OOB data
`PRU_SHUTDOWN`				end communication with foreign address
`PRU_SOCKADDR`		*buffer*		return local address associated with socket

Figure 15.17   `pr_usrreq` requests.

PRU_CONNECT2 is supported only within the Unix domain, where it connects two local sockets to each other. Unix pipes are implemented in this way.

Cleanup and return

70–77   Returning to `socreate`, the function attaches the protocol switch table to the new socket and issues the `PRU_ATTACH` request to notify the protocol of the new end point. This request causes most protocols, including TCP and UDP, to allocate and initialize any structures required to support the new end point.

Superuser Privileges

Figure 15.18 summarizes the networking operations that require superuser access.

| Function | Superuser | | Description | Reference |
	Process	Socket		
in_control		•	interface address, netmask, and destination address assignment	Figure 6.14
in_control		•	broadcast address assignment	Figure 6.22
in_pcbbind	•		binding to an Internet port less than 1024	Figure 22.22
ifioctl	•		interface configuration changes	Figure 4.29
ifioctl	•		multicast address configuration (see text)	Figure 12.11
rip_usrreq	•		creating an ICMP, IGMP, or raw IP socket	Figure 32.10
slopen	•		associating a SLIP device with a tty device	Figure 5.9

Figure 15.18   Superuser privileges in Net/3.

The multicast ioctl commands (SIOCADDMULTI and SIOCDELMULTI) are accessible to non-superuser processes when they are invoked indirectly by the IP_ADD_MEMBERSHIP and IP_DROP_MEMBERSHIP socket options (Sections 12.11 and 12.12).

In Figure 15.18, the "Process" column identifies requests that must be made by a superuser process, and the "Socket" column identifies requests that must be issued on a socket *created* by a superuser process (i.e., the process does not need superuser privileges if it has access to the socket, Exercise 15.1). In Net/3, the suser function determines if the calling process has superuser privileges, and the SS_PRIV flag determines if the socket was created by a superuser process.

Since rip_usrreq tests SS_PRIV immediately after creating the socket with socreate, we show this function as accessible only from a superuser process.

15.7   getsock and sockargs Functions

These functions appear repeatedly in the implementation of the socket system calls. getsock maps a descriptor to a file table entry and sockargs copies arguments from the process to a newly allocated mbuf in the kernel. Both functions check for invalid arguments and return a nonzero error code accordingly.

Figure 15.19 shows the getsock function.

754–767   The function selects the file table entry specified by the descriptor fdes with fdp, a pointer to the filedesc structure. getsock returns a pointer to the open file structure in fpp or an error if the descriptor is out of the valid range, does not point to an open file, or does not have a socket associated with it.

Figure 15.20 shows the sockargs function.

768–783   The mechanism described in Section 15.4 copies pointer arguments for a system call from the process to the kernel but does not copy the data referenced by the pointers, since the semantics of each argument are known only by the specific system call and not

uipc_syscalls.c

```
754 getsock(fdp, fdes, fpp)
755 struct filedesc *fdp;
756 int     fdes;
757 struct file **fpp;
758 {
759     struct file *fp;

760     if ((unsigned) fdes >= fdp->fd_nfiles ||
761         (fp = fdp->fd_ofiles[fdes]) == NULL)
762         return (EBADF);
763     if (fp->f_type != DTYPE_SOCKET)
764         return (ENOTSOCK);
765     *fpp = fp;
766     return (0);
767 }
```

uipc_syscalls.c

Figure 15.19 getsock function.

uipc_syscalls.c

```
768 sockargs(mp, buf, buflen, type)
769 struct mbuf **mp;
770 caddr_t buf;
771 int     buflen, type;
772 {
773     struct sockaddr *sa;
774     struct mbuf *m;
775     int     error;

776     if ((u_int) buflen > MLEN) {
777         return (EINVAL);
778     }
779     m = m_get(M_WAIT, type);
780     if (m == NULL)
781         return (ENOBUFS);
782     m->m_len = buflen;
783     error = copyin(buf, mtod(m, caddr_t), (u_int) buflen);
784     if (error)
785         (void) m_free(m);
786     else {
787         *mp = m;
788         if (type == MT_SONAME) {
789             sa = mtod(m, struct sockaddr *);
790             sa->sa_len = buflen;
791         }
792     }
793     return (error);
794 }
```

uipc_syscalls.c

Figure 15.20 sockargs function.

by the generic system call mechanism. Several system calls use sockargs to follow the pointer arguments and copy the referenced data from the process into a newly allocated mbuf within the kernel. For example, sockargs copies the local socket address pointed to by bind's second argument from the process to an mbuf.

If the data does not fit in a single mbuf or an mbuf cannot be allocated, `sockargs` returns `EINVAL` or `ENOBUFS`. Note that a standard mbuf is used and not a packet header mbuf. `copyin` copies the data from the process into the mbuf. The most common error from `copyin` is `EACCES`, returned when the process provides an invalid address.

784–785   When an error occurs, the mbuf is discarded and the error code is returned. If there is no error, a pointer to the mbuf is returned in `mp`, and `sockargs` returns 0.

786–794   If `type` is `MT_SONAME`, the process is passing in a `sockaddr` structure. `sockargs` sets the internal length, `sa_len`, to the length of the argument just copied. This ensures that the size contained within the structure is correct even if the process did not initialize the structure correctly.

> Net/3 does include code to support applications compiled on a pre-4.3BSD Reno system, which did not have an `sa_len` member in the `sockaddr` structure, but that code is not shown in Figure 15.20.

15.8 `bind` System Call

The `bind` system call associates a local network transport address with a socket. A process acting as a client usually does not care what its local address is. In this case, it isn't necessary to call `bind` before the process attempts to communicate; the kernel selects and implicitly binds a local address to the socket as needed.

A server process almost always needs to bind to a specific well-known address. If so, the process must call `bind` before accepting connections (TCP) or receiving datagrams (UDP), because the clients establish connections or send datagrams to the well-known address.

A socket's foreign address is specified by `connect` or by one of the write calls that allow specification of foreign addresses (`sendto` or `sendmsg`).

Figure 15.21 shows `bind`.

70–82   The arguments to `bind` (passed within a `bind_args` structure) are: `s`, the socket descriptor; `name`, a pointer to a buffer containing the transport address (e.g., a `sockaddr_in` structure); and `namelen`, the size of the buffer.

83–90   `getsock` returns the `file` structure for the descriptor, and `sockargs` copies the local address from the process into an mbuf, `sobind` associates the address specified by the process with the socket. Before `bind` returns `sobind`'s result, the mbuf holding the address is released.

> Technically, a descriptor such as `s` identifies a `file` structure with an associated `socket` structure and is not itself a `socket` structure. We refer to such a descriptor as a socket to simplify our discussion.

We will see this pattern many times: arguments specified by the process are copied into an mbuf and processed as necessary, and then the mbuf is released before the system call returns. Although mbufs were designed explicitly to facilitate processing of network data packets, they are also effective as a general-purpose dynamic memory allocation mechanism.

uipc_syscalls.c

```
70 struct bind_args {
71     int     s;
72     caddr_t name;
73     int     namelen;
74 };

75 bind(p, uap, retval)
76 struct proc *p;
77 struct bind_args *uap;
78 int     *retval;
79 {
80     struct file *fp;
81     struct mbuf *nam;
82     int     error;

83     if (error = getsock(p->p_fd, uap->s, &fp))
84         return (error);
85     if (error = sockargs(&nam, uap->name, uap->namelen, MT_SONAME))
86         return (error);
87     error = sobind((struct socket *) fp->f_data, nam);
88     m_freem(nam);
89     return (error);
90 }
```

uipc_syscalls.c

Figure 15.21   bind function.

Another pattern illustrated by bind is that retval is unused in many system calls. In Section 15.4 we mentioned that retval is always initialized to 0 before syscall dispatches control to a system call. If 0 is the appropriate return value, the system calls do not need to change retval.

sobind **Function**

sobind, shown in Figure 15.22, is a wrapper that issues the PRU_BIND request to the protocol associated with the socket.

uipc_socket.c

```
78 sobind(so, nam)
79 struct socket *so;
80 struct mbuf *nam;
81 {
82     int     s = splnet();
83     int     error;

84     error =
85         (*so->so_proto->pr_usrreq) (so, PRU_BIND,
86                             (struct mbuf *) 0, nam, (struct mbuf *) 0);
87     splx(s);
88     return (error);
89 }
```

uipc_socket.c

Figure 15.22   sobind function.

78–89   sobind issues the PRU_BIND request. The local address, nam, is associated with the socket if the request succeeds; otherwise the error code is returned.

15.9 `listen` **System Call**

The listen system call, shown in Figure 15.23, notifies a protocol that the process is prepared to accept incoming connections on the socket. It also specifies a limit on the number of connections that can be queued on the socket, after which the socket layer refuses to queue additional connection requests. When this occurs, TCP ignores incoming connection requests. Queued connections are made available to the process when it calls accept (Section 15.11).

```
                                                           ——— uipc_syscalls.c
91 struct listen_args {
92     int     s;
93     int     backlog;
94 };

95 listen(p, uap, retval)
96 struct proc *p;
97 struct listen_args *uap;
98 int     *retval;
99 {
100     struct file *fp;
101     int     error;

102     if (error = getsock(p->p_fd, uap->s, &fp))
103         return (error);
104     return (solisten((struct socket *) fp->f_data, uap->backlog));
105 }
                                                           ——— uipc_syscalls.c
```

Figure 15.23 listen system call.

91–98   The two arguments passed to listen specify the socket descriptor and the connection queue limit.

99–105   getsock returns the file structure for the descriptor, s, and solisten passes the listen request to the protocol layer.

`solisten` **Function**

This function, shown in Figure 15.24, issues the PRU_LISTEN request and prepares the socket to receive connections.

90–109   After solisten issues the PRU_LISTEN request and pr_usrreq returns, the socket is marked as ready to accept connections. SS_ACCEPTCONN is not set if a connection is queued when pr_usrreq returns.

The maximum queue size for incoming connections is computed and saved in so_qlimit. Here Net/3 silently enforces a lower limit of 0 and an upper limit of 5 (SOMAXCONN) backlogged connections.

```
                                                                    ─── uipc_socket.c
90 solisten(so, backlog)
91 struct socket *so;
92 int      backlog;
93 {
94     int      s = splnet(), error;

95     error =
96         (*so->so_proto->pr_usrreq) (so, PRU_LISTEN,
97                     (struct mbuf *) 0, (struct mbuf *) 0, (struct mbuf *) 0);
98     if (error) {
99         splx(s);
100        return (error);
101    }
102    if (so->so_q == 0)
103        so->so_options |= SO_ACCEPTCONN;
104    if (backlog < 0)
105        backlog = 0;
106    so->so_qlimit = min(backlog, SOMAXCONN);
107    splx(s);
108    return (0);
109 }
                                                                    ─── uipc_socket.c
```

Figure 15.24 solisten function.

15.10 `tsleep` and `wakeup` Functions

When a process executing within the kernel cannot proceed because a kernel resource is unavailable, it waits for the resource by calling `tsleep`, which has the following proto-type:

```
int tsleep(caddr_t chan, int pri, char *mesg, int timeo);
```

The first argument to `tsleep`, *chan*, is called the *wait channel*. It identifies the particular resource or event such as an incoming network connection, for which the process is waiting. Many processes can be sleeping on a single wait channel. When the resource becomes available or when the event occurs, the kernel calls `wakeup` with the wait channel as the single argument. The prototype for `wakeup` is:

```
void wakeup(caddr_t chan);
```

All processes waiting for the channel are awakened and set to the run state. The kernel arranges for `tsleep` to return when each of the processes resumes execution.

The *pri* argument specifies the priority of the process when it is awakened, as well as several optional control flags for `tsleep`. By setting the PCATCH flag in *pri*, `tsleep` also returns when a signal arrives. *mesg* is a string identifying the call to `tsleep` and is included in debugging messages and in `ps` output. *timeo* sets an upper bound on the sleep period and is measured in clock ticks.

Figure 15.25 summarizes the return values from `tsleep`.

> A process never sees the ERESTART error because it is handled by the `syscall` function and never returned to a process.

tsleep()	Description
0	The process was awakened by a matching call to wakeup.
EWOULDBLOCK	The process was awakened after sleeping for *timeo* clock ticks and before the matching call to wakeup.
ERESTART	A signal was handled by the process during the sleep and the pending system call should be restarted.
EINTR	A signal was handled by the process during the sleep and the pending system call should fail.

Figure 15.25 tsleep return values.

Because all processes sleeping on a wait channel are awakened by wakeup, we always see a call to tsleep within a tight loop. Every process must determine if the resource is available before proceeding because another awakened process may have claimed the resource first. If the resource is not available, the process calls tsleep once again.

It is unusual for multiple processes to be sleeping on a single socket, so a call to wakeup usually causes only one process to be awakened by the kernel.

For a more detailed discussion of the sleep and wakeup mechanism see [Leffler et al. 1989].

Example

One use of multiple processes sleeping on the same wait channel is to have multiple server processes reading from a UDP socket. Each server calls recvfrom and, as long as no data is available, the calls block in tsleep. When a datagram arrives on the socket, the socket layer calls wakeup and each server is placed on the run queue. The first server to run receives the datagram while the others call tsleep again. In this way, incoming datagrams are distributed to multiple servers without the cost of starting a new process for each datagram. This technique can also be used to process incoming connection requests in TCP by having multiple processes call accept on the same socket. This technique is described in [Comer and Stevens 1993].

15.11 accept System Call

After calling listen, a process waits for incoming connections by calling accept, which returns a descriptor that references a new socket connected to a client. The original socket, s, remains unconnected and ready to receive additional connections. accept returns the address of the foreign system if name points to a valid buffer.

The connection-processing details are handled by the protocol associated with the socket. For TCP, the socket layer is notified when a connection has been established (i.e., when TCP's three-way handshake has completed). For other protocols, such as OSI's TP4, tsleep returns when a connection request has arrived. The connection is completed when explicitly confirmed by the process by reading or writing on the socket.

Figure 15.26 shows the implementation of `accept`.

———————————————————————————— uipc_syscalls.c
```
106 struct accept_args {
107     int     s;
108     caddr_t name;
109     int     *anamelen;
110 };

111 accept(p, uap, retval)
112 struct proc *p;
113 struct accept_args *uap;
114 int     *retval;
115 {
116     struct file *fp;
117     struct mbuf *nam;
118     int     namelen, error, s;
119     struct socket *so;

120     if (uap->name && (error = copyin((caddr_t) uap->anamelen,
121                                 (caddr_t) & namelen, sizeof(namelen))))
122         return (error);
123     if (error = getsock(p->p_fd, uap->s, &fp))
124         return (error);
125     s = splnet();
126     so = (struct socket *) fp->f_data;
127     if ((so->so_options & SO_ACCEPTCONN) == 0) {
128         splx(s);
129         return (EINVAL);
130     }
131     if ((so->so_state & SS_NBIO) && so->so_qlen == 0) {
132         splx(s);
133         return (EWOULDBLOCK);
134     }
135     while (so->so_qlen == 0 && so->so_error == 0) {
136         if (so->so_state & SS_CANTRCVMORE) {
137             so->so_error = ECONNABORTED;
138             break;
139         }
140         if (error = tsleep((caddr_t) & so->so_timeo, PSOCK | PCATCH,
141                         netcon, 0)) {
142             splx(s);
143             return (error);
144         }
145     }
146     if (so->so_error) {
147         error = so->so_error;
148         so->so_error = 0;
149         splx(s);
150         return (error);
151     }
152     if (error = falloc(p, &fp, retval)) {
153         splx(s);
154         return (error);
155     }
```

```
156     { struct socket *aso = so->so_q;
157       if (soqremque(aso, 1) == 0)
158         panic("accept");
159       so = aso;
160     }
161     fp->f_type = DTYPE_SOCKET;
162     fp->f_flag = FREAD | FWRITE;
163     fp->f_ops = &socketops;
164     fp->f_data = (caddr_t) so;
165     nam = m_get(M_WAIT, MT_SONAME);
166     (void) soaccept(so, nam);
167     if (uap->name) {
168       if (namelen > nam->m_len)
169         namelen = nam->m_len;
170       /* SHOULD COPY OUT A CHAIN HERE */
171       if ((error = copyout(mtod(nam, caddr_t), (caddr_t) uap->name,
172                       (u_int) namelen)) == 0)
173         error = copyout((caddr_t) & namelen,
174                     (caddr_t) uap->anamelen, sizeof(*uap->anamelen));
175     }
176     m_freem(nam);
177     splx(s);
178     return (error);
179 }
```
—— *uipc_syscalls.c*

Figure 15.26 accept system call.

106–114   The three arguments to accept (in the accept_args structure) are: s, the socket descriptor; name, a pointer to a buffer to be filled in by accept with the transport address of the foreign host; and anamelen, a pointer to the size of the buffer.

Validate arguments

116–134   accept copies the size of the buffer (*anamelen) into namelen, and getsock returns the file structure for the socket. If the socket is not ready to accept connections (i.e., listen has not been called) or nonblocking I/O has been requested and no connections are queued, EINVAL or EWOULDBLOCK are returned respectively.

Wait for a connection

135–145   The while loop continues until a connection is available, an error occurs, or the socket can no longer receive data. accept is not automatically restarted after a signal is caught (tsleep returns EINTR). The protocol layer wakes up the process when it inserts a new connection on the queue with sonewconn.
    Within the loop, the process waits in tsleep, which returns 0 when a connection is available. If tsleep is interrupted by a signal or the socket is set for nonblocking semantics, accept returns EINTR or EWOULDBLOCK (Figure 15.25).

Asynchronous errors

146–151   If an error occurred on the socket during the sleep, the error code is moved from the socket to the return value for accept, the socket error is cleared, and accept returns.

It is common for asynchronous events to change the state of a socket. The protocol processing layer notifies the socket layer of the change by setting so_error and waking any process waiting on the socket. Because of this, the socket layer must always examine so_error after waking to see if an error occurred while the process was sleeping.

Associate socket with descriptor

152–164   falloc allocates a descriptor for the new connection; the socket is removed from the accept queue by soqremque and attached to the file structure. Exercise 15.4 discusses the call to panic.

Protocol processing

167–179   accept allocates a new mbuf to hold the foreign address and calls soaccept to do protocol processing. The allocation and queueing of new sockets created during connection processing is described in Section 15.12. If the process provided a buffer to receive the foreign address, copyout copies the address from nam and the length from namelen to the process. If necessary, copyout silently truncates the name to fit in the process's buffer. Finally, the mbuf is released, protocol processing enabled, and accept returns.

Because only one mbuf is allocated for the foreign address, transport addresses must fit in one mbuf. Unix domain addresses, which are pathnames in the filesystem (up to 1023 bytes in length), may encounter this limit, but there is no problem with the 16-byte sockaddr_in structure for the Internet domain. The comment on line 170 indicates that this limitation could be removed by allocating and copying an mbuf chain.

soaccept Function

soaccept, shown in Figure 15.27, calls the protocol layer to retrieve the client's address for the new connection.

```
                                                                  ─── uipc_socket.c
184 soaccept(so, nam)
185 struct socket *so;
186 struct mbuf *nam;
187 {
188     int     s = splnet();
189     int     error;

190     if ((so->so_state & SS_NOFDREF) == 0)
191         panic("soaccept: !NOFDREF");
192     so->so_state &= ~SS_NOFDREF;
193     error = (*so->so_proto->pr_usrreq) (so, PRU_ACCEPT,
194                             (struct mbuf *) 0, nam, (struct mbuf *) 0);
195     splx(s);
196     return (error);
197 }
                                                                  ─── uipc_socket.c
```

Figure 15.27   soaccept function.

184–197   soaccept ensures that the socket is associated with a descriptor and issues the PRU_ACCEPT request to the protocol. After pr_usrreq returns, nam contains the name of the foreign socket.

15.12 sonewconn and soisconnected Functions

In Figure 15.26 we saw that accept waits for the protocol layer to process incoming connection requests and to make them available through so_q. Figure 15.28 uses TCP to illustrate this process.

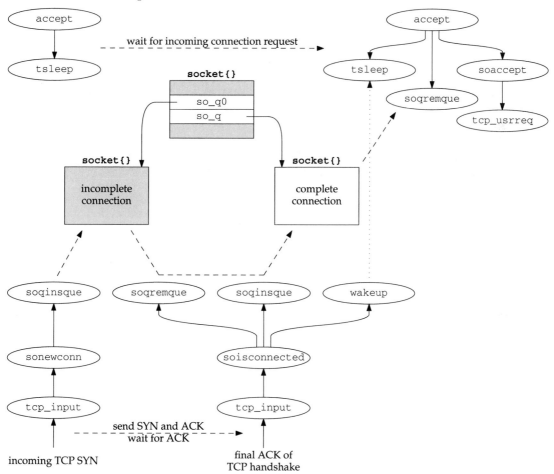

Figure 15.28   Incoming TCP connection processing.

In the upper left corner of Figure 15.28, accept calls tsleep to wait for incoming connections. In the lower left, tcp_input processes an incoming TCP SYN by calling sonewconn to create a socket for the new connection (Figure 28.7). sonewconn queues the socket on so_q0, since the three-way handshake is not yet complete.

When the final ACK of the TCP handshake arrives, `tcp_input` calls `soisconnected` (Figure 29.2), which updates the new socket, moves it from `so_q0` to `so_q`, and wakes up any processes that had called `accept` to wait for incoming connections.

The upper right corner of the figure shows the functions we described with Figure 15.26. When `tsleep` returns, `accept` takes the connection off `so_q` and issues the `PRU_ATTACH` request. The socket is associated with a new file descriptor and returned to the calling process.

Figure 15.29 shows the `sonewconn` function.

```
                                                                        ── uipc_socket2.c
123 struct socket *
124 sonewconn(head, connstatus)
125 struct socket *head;
126 int      connstatus;
127 {
128     struct socket *so;
129     int      soqueue = connstatus ? 1 : 0;

130     if (head->so_qlen + head->so_q0len > 3 * head->so_qlimit / 2)
131         return ((struct socket *) 0);
132     MALLOC(so, struct socket *, sizeof(*so), M_SOCKET, M_DONTWAIT);
133     if (so == NULL)
134         return ((struct socket *) 0);
135     bzero((caddr_t) so, sizeof(*so));
136     so->so_type = head->so_type;
137     so->so_options = head->so_options & ~SO_ACCEPTCONN;
138     so->so_linger = head->so_linger;
139     so->so_state = head->so_state | SS_NOFDREF;
140     so->so_proto = head->so_proto;
141     so->so_timeo = head->so_timeo;
142     so->so_pgid = head->so_pgid;
143     (void) soreserve(so, head->so_snd.sb_hiwat, head->so_rcv.sb_hiwat);
144     soqinsque(head, so, soqueue);
145     if ((*so->so_proto->pr_usrreq) (so, PRU_ATTACH,
146             (struct mbuf *) 0, (struct mbuf *) 0, (struct mbuf *) 0)) {
147         (void) soqremque(so, soqueue);
148         (void) free((caddr_t) so, M_SOCKET);
149         return ((struct socket *) 0);
150     }
151     if (connstatus) {
152         sorwakeup(head);
153         wakeup((caddr_t) & head->so_timeo);
154         so->so_state |= connstatus;
155     }
156     return (so);
157 }
                                                                        ── uipc_socket2.c
```

Figure 15.29   `sonewconn` function.

123–129   The protocol layer passes `head`, a pointer to the socket that is accepting the incoming connection, and `connstatus`, a flag to indicate the state of the new connection. For TCP, `connstatus` is always 0.

For TP4, connstatus is always SS_ISCONFIRMING. The connection is implicitly confirmed when a process begins reading from or writing to the socket.

Limit incoming connections

130–131   sonewconn prohibits additional connections when the following inequality is true:

$$so\_qlen + so\_q0len > \frac{3 \times so\_qlimit}{2}$$

This formula provides a fudge factor for connections that never complete and guarantees that listen(fd, 0) allows one connection. See Figure 18.23 in Volume 1 for an additional discussion of this formula.

Allocate new socket

132–143   A new socket structure is allocated and initialized. If the process calls setsockopt for the listening socket, the connected socket inherits several socket options because so_options, so_linger, so_pgid, and the sb_hiwat values are copied into the new socket structure.

Queue connection

144   soqueue was set from connstatus on line 129. The new socket is inserted onto so_q0 if soqueue is 0 (e.g., TCP connections) or onto so_q if connstatus is nonzero (e.g., TP4 connections).

Protocol processing

145–150   The PRU_ATTACH request is issued to perform protocol layer processing on the new connection. If this fails, the socket is dequeued and discarded, and sonewconn returns a null pointer.

Wakeup processes

151–157   If connstatus is nonzero, any processes sleeping in accept or selecting for readability on the socket are awakened. connstatus is logically ORed with so_state. This code is never executed for TCP connections, since connstatus is always 0 for TCP.

Protocols, such as TCP, that put incoming connections on so_q0 first, call soisconnected when the connection establishment phase completes. For TCP, this happens when the second SYN is ACKed on the connection.

Figure 15.30 shows soisconnected.

Queue incomplete connections

78–87   The socket state is changed to show that the connection has completed. When soisconnected is called for incoming connections, (i.e., when the local process is calling accept), head is nonnull.

If soqremque returns 1, the socket is queued on so_q and sorwakeup wakes up any processes using select to monitor the socket for connection arrival by testing for readability. If a process is blocked in accept waiting for the connection, wakeup causes the matching tsleep to return.

```
                                                                  ———— uipc_socket2.c
78 soisconnected(so)
79 struct socket *so;
80 {
81     struct socket *head = so->so_head;
82     so->so_state &= ~(SS_ISCONNECTING | SS_ISDISCONNECTING | SS_ISCONFIRMING);
83     so->so_state |= SS_ISCONNECTED;
84     if (head && soqremque(so, 0)) {
85         soqinsque(head, so, 1);
86         sorwakeup(head);
87         wakeup((caddr_t) & head->so_timeo);
88     } else {
89         wakeup((caddr_t) & so->so_timeo);
90         sorwakeup(so);
91         sowwakeup(so);
92     }
93 }
                                                                  ———— uipc_socket2.c
```

Figure 15.30   soisconnected function.

Wakeup processes waiting for new connection

88–93   If head is null, soqremque is not called since the process initiated the connection with the connect system call and the socket is not on a queue. If head is nonnull and soqremque returns 0, the socket is already on so_q. This happens with protocols such as TP4, which place connections on so_q before they are complete. wakeup awakens any process blocked in connect, and sorwakeup and sowwakeup take care of any processes that are using select to wait for the connection to complete.

15.13 connect System call

A server process calls the listen and accept system calls to wait for a remote process to initiate a connection. If the process wants to initiate a connection itself (i.e., a client), it calls connect.

For connection-oriented protocols such as TCP, connect establishes a connection to the specified foreign address. The kernel selects and implicitly binds an address to the local socket if the process has not already done so with bind.

For connectionless protocols such as UDP or ICMP, connect records the foreign address for use in sending future datagrams. Any previous foreign address is replaced with the new address.

Figure 15.31 shows the functions called when connect is used for UDP or TCP.

The left side of the figure shows connect processing for connectionless protocols, such as UDP. In this case the protocol layer calls soisconnected and the connect system call returns immediately.

The right side of the figure shows connect processing for connection-oriented protocols, such as TCP. In this case, the protocol layer begins the connection establishment and calls soisconnecting to indicate that the connection will complete some time in the future. Unless the socket is nonblocking, soconnect calls tsleep to wait for the

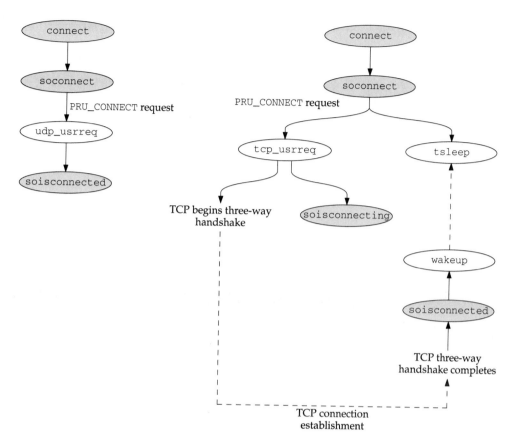

Figure 15.31   connect processing.

connection to complete. For TCP, when the three-way handshake is complete, the protocol layer calls soisconnected to mark the socket as connected and then calls wakeup to awaken the process and complete the connect system call.

Figure 15.32 shows the connect system call.

180–188   The three arguments to connect (in the connect_args structure) are: s, the socket descriptor; name, a pointer to a buffer containing the foreign address; and namelen, the length of the buffer.

189–200   getsock returns the socket as usual. A connection request may already be pending on a nonblocking socket, in which case EALREADY is returned. sockargs copies the foreign address from the process into the kernel.

Start connection processing

201–208   The connection attempt is started by calling soconnect. If soconnect reports an error, connect jumps to bad. If a connection has not completed by the time soconnect returns and nonblocking I/O is enabled, EINPROGRESS is returned immediately to avoid waiting for the connection to complete. Since connection establishment

uipc_syscalls.c

```
180 struct connect_args {
181     int     s;
182     caddr_t name;
183     int     namelen;
184 };

185 connect(p, uap, retval)
186 struct proc *p;
187 struct connect_args *uap;
188 int     *retval;
189 {
190     struct file *fp;
191     struct socket *so;
192     struct mbuf *nam;
193     int     error, s;

194     if (error = getsock(p->p_fd, uap->s, &fp))
195         return (error);
196     so = (struct socket *) fp->f_data;
197     if ((so->so_state & SS_NBIO) && (so->so_state & SS_ISCONNECTING))
198         return (EALREADY);
199     if (error = sockargs(&nam, uap->name, uap->namelen, MT_SONAME))
200         return (error);

201     error = soconnect(so, nam);
202     if (error)
203         goto bad;
204     if ((so->so_state & SS_NBIO) && (so->so_state & SS_ISCONNECTING)) {
205         m_freem(nam);
206         return (EINPROGRESS);
207     }
208     s = splnet();
209     while ((so->so_state & SS_ISCONNECTING) && so->so_error == 0)
210         if (error = tsleep((caddr_t) & so->so_timeo, PSOCK | PCATCH,
211                             netcon, 0))
212             break;
213     if (error == 0) {
214         error = so->so_error;
215         so->so_error = 0;
216     }
217     splx(s);
218 bad:
219     so->so_state &= ~SS_ISCONNECTING;
220     m_freem(nam);
221     if (error == ERESTART)
222         error = EINTR;
223     return (error);
224 }
```

uipc_syscalls.c

Figure 15.32   connect system call.

normally involves exchanging several packets with the remote system, it may take a while to complete. Further calls to connect return EALREADY until the connection completes. EISCONN is returned when the connection is complete.

Wait for connection establishment

208–217   The while loop continues until the connection is established or an error occurs. splnet prevents connect from missing a wakeup between testing the state of the socket and the call to tsleep. After the loop, error contains 0, the error code from tsleep, or the error from the socket.

218–224   The SS_ISCONNECTING flag is cleared since the connection has completed or the attempt has failed. The mbuf containing the foreign address is released and any error is returned.

soconnect **Function**

This function ensures that the socket is in a valid state for a connection request. If the socket is not connected or a connection is not pending, then the connection request is always valid. If the socket is already connected or a connection is pending, the new connection request is rejected for connection-oriented protocols such as TCP. For connectionless protocols such as UDP, multiple connection requests are OK but each new request replaces the previous foreign address.

Figure 15.33 shows the soconnect function.

```
                                                                     ─── uipc_socket.c
198 soconnect(so, nam)
199 struct socket *so;
200 struct mbuf *nam;
201 {
202     int     s;
203     int     error;

204     if (so->so_options & SO_ACCEPTCONN)
205         return (EOPNOTSUPP);
206     s = splnet();
207     /*
208      * If protocol is connection-based, can only connect once.
209      * Otherwise, if connected, try to disconnect first.
210      * This allows user to disconnect by connecting to, e.g.,
211      * a null address.
212      */
213     if (so->so_state & (SS_ISCONNECTED | SS_ISCONNECTING) &&
214         ((so->so_proto->pr_flags & PR_CONNREQUIRED) ||
215         (error = sodisconnect(so))))
216         error = EISCONN;
217     else
218         error = (*so->so_proto->pr_usrreq) (so, PRU_CONNECT,
219                             (struct mbuf *) 0, nam, (struct mbuf *) 0);
220     splx(s);
221     return (error);
222 }
                                                                     ─── uipc_socket.c
```

Figure 15.33   soconnect function.

198–222   soconnect returns EOPNOTSUPP if the socket is marked to accept connections, since a process cannot initiate connections if listen has already been called for the socket. EISCONN is returned if the protocol is connection oriented and a connection has already been initiated. For a connectionless protocol, any existing association with a foreign address is broken by sodisconnect.

The PRU_CONNECT request starts the appropriate protocol processing to establish the connection or the association.

Breaking a Connectionless Association

For connectionless protocols, the foreign address associated with a socket can be discarded by calling connect with an invalid name such as a pointer to a structure filled with 0s or a structure with an invalid size. sodisconnect removes a foreign address associated with the socket, and PRU_CONNECT returns an error such as EAFNOSUPPORT or EADDRNOTAVAIL, leaving the socket with no foreign address. This is a useful, although obscure, way of breaking the association between a connectionless socket and a foreign address without replacing it.

15.14 shutdown System Call

The shutdown system call, shown in Figure 15.34, closes the write-half, read-half, or both halves of a connection. For the read-half, shutdown discards any data the process hasn't yet read and any data that arrives after the call to shutdown. For the write-half, shutdown lets the protocol specify the semantics. For TCP, any remaining data will be sent followed by a FIN. This is TCP's half-close feature (Section 18.5 of Volume 1).

To destroy the socket and release the descriptor, close must be called. close can also be called directly without first calling shutdown. As with all descriptors, close is called by the kernel for sockets that have not been closed when a process terminates.

―――――――――――――――――――――――――――――――――――― *uipc_syscalls.c*
```
550 struct shutdown_args {
551     int     s;
552     int     how;
553 };

554 shutdown(p, uap, retval)
555 struct proc *p;
556 struct shutdown_args *uap;
557 int     *retval;
558 {
559     struct file *fp;
560     int     error;

561     if (error = getsock(p->p_fd, uap->s, &fp))
562         return (error);
563     return (soshutdown((struct socket *) fp->f_data, uap->how));
564 }
```
―――――――――――――――――――――――――――――――――――― *uipc_syscalls.c*

Figure 15.34   shutdown system call.

550–557   In the `shutdown_args` structure, s is the socket descriptor and how specifies which halves of the connection are to be closed. Figure 15.35 shows the expected values for how and how++ (which is used in Figure 15.36).

how	how++	Description
0	*FREAD*	shut down the read-half of the connection
1	*FWRITE*	shut down the write-half of the connection
2	*FREAD/FWRITE*	shut down both halves of the connection

Figure 15.35   shutdown system call options.

Notice that there is an implicit numerical relationship between how and the constants FREAD and FWRITE.

558–564   `shutdown` is a wrapper function for `soshutdown`. The socket associated with the descriptor is returned by `getsock`, `soshutdown` is called, and its value is returned.

soshutdown and sorflush Functions

The shut down of the read-half of a connection is handled in the socket layer by `sorflush`, and the shut down of the write-half of a connection is processed by the PRU_SHUTDOWN request in the protocol layer. The `soshutdown` function is shown in Figure 15.36.

```
                                                              ──────── uipc_socket.c
720 soshutdown(so, how)
721 struct socket *so;
722 int     how;
723 {
724     struct protosw *pr = so->so_proto;

725     how++;
726     if (how & FREAD)
727         sorflush(so);
728     if (how & FWRITE)
729         return ((*pr->pr_usrreq) (so, PRU_SHUTDOWN,
730             (struct mbuf *) 0, (struct mbuf *) 0, (struct mbuf *) 0));
731     return (0);
732 }
                                                              ──────── uipc_socket.c
```

Figure 15.36   soshutdown function.

720–732   If the read-half of the socket is being closed, `sorflush`, shown in Figure 15.37, discards the data in the socket's receive buffer and disables the read-half of the connection. If the write-half of the socket is being closed, the PRU_SHUTDOWN request is issued to the protocol.

733–747   The process waits for a lock on the receive buffer. Because of SB_NOINTR, sblock does not return when an interrupt occurs. splimp blocks network interrupts and protocol processing while the socket is modified, since the receive buffer may be accessed by the protocol layer as it processes incoming packets.

```
                                                                    ── uipc_socket.c
733 sorflush(so)
734 struct socket *so;
735 {
736     struct sockbuf *sb = &so->so_rcv;
737     struct protosw *pr = so->so_proto;
738     int     s;
739     struct sockbuf asb;

740     sb->sb_flags |= SB_NOINTR;
741     (void) sblock(sb, M_WAITOK);
742     s = splimp();
743     socantrcvmore(so);
744     sbunlock(sb);
745     asb = *sb;
746     bzero((caddr_t) sb, sizeof(*sb));
747     splx(s);

748     if (pr->pr_flags & PR_RIGHTS && pr->pr_domain->dom_dispose)
749         (*pr->pr_domain->dom_dispose) (asb.sb_mb);
750     sbrelease(&asb);
751 }
                                                                    ── uipc_socket.c
```

Figure 15.37   sorflush function.

socantrcvmore marks the socket to reject incoming packets. A copy of the
sockbuf structure is saved in asb to be used after interrupts are restored by splx.
The original sockbuf structure is cleared by bzero, so that the receive queue appears
to be empty.

Release control mbufs

748–751   Some kernel resources may be referenced by control information present in the
receive queue when shutdown was called. The mbuf chain is still available through
sb_mb in the copy of the sockbuf structure.

If the protocol supports access rights and has registered a dom_dispose function,
it is called here to release these resources.

> In the Unix domain it is possible to pass descriptors between processes with control messages.
> These messages contain pointers to reference counted data structures. The dom_dispose
> function takes care of discarding the references and the data structures if necessary to avoid
> creating an unreferenced structure and introducing a memory leak in the kernel. For more
> information on passing file descriptors within the Unix domain, see [Stevens 1990] and [Leffler
> et al. 1989].

Any input data pending when shutdown is called is discarded when sbrelease
releases any mbufs on the receive queue.

Notice that the shut down of the read-half of the connection is processed entirely by
the socket layer (Exercise 15.6) and the shut down of the write-half of the connection is
handled by the protocol through the PRU_SHUTDOWN request. TCP responds to the
PRU_SHUTDOWN by sending all queued data and then a FIN to close the write-half of the
TCP connection.

15.15 close System Call

The close system call works with any type of descriptor. When fd is the last descriptor that references the object, the object-specific close function is called:

    error = (*fp->f_ops->fo_close)(fp, p);

As shown in Figure 15.13, fp->f_ops->fo_close for a socket is the function soo_close.

soo_close Function

This function, shown in Figure 15.38, is a wrapper for the soclose function.

```
                                                                      ─── sys_socket.c
152 soo_close(fp, p)
153 struct file *fp;
154 struct proc *p;
155 {
156     int     error = 0;

157     if (fp->f_data)
158         error = soclose((struct socket *) fp->f_data);
159     fp->f_data = 0;
160     return (error);
161 }
                                                                      ─── sys_socket.c
```

Figure 15.38 soo_close function.

152–161   If a socket structure is associated with the file structure, soclose is called, f_data is cleared, and any posted error is returned.

soclose Function

This function aborts any connections that are pending on the socket (i.e., that have not yet been accepted by a process), waits for data to be transmitted to the foreign system, and releases the data structures that are no longer needed.
    soclose is shown in Figure 15.39.

Discard pending connections

129–141   If the socket was accepting connections, soclose traverses the two connection queues and calls soabort for each pending connection. If the protocol control block is null, the protocol has already been detached from the socket and soclose jumps to the cleanup code at discard.

> soabort issues the PRU_ABORT request to the socket's protocol and returns the result. soabort is not shown in this text. Figures 23.38 and 30.7 discuss how UDP and TCP handle this request.

———————————————————————————————— uipc_socket.c

```
129 soclose(so)
130 struct socket *so;
131 {
132     int     s = splnet();        /* conservative */
133     int     error = 0;

134     if (so->so_options & SO_ACCEPTCONN) {
135         while (so->so_q0)
136             (void) soabort(so->so_q0);
137         while (so->so_q)
138             (void) soabort(so->so_q);
139     }
140     if (so->so_pcb == 0)
141         goto discard;
142     if (so->so_state & SS_ISCONNECTED) {
143         if ((so->so_state & SS_ISDISCONNECTING) == 0) {
144             error = sodisconnect(so);
145             if (error)
146                 goto drop;
147         }
148         if (so->so_options & SO_LINGER) {
149             if ((so->so_state & SS_ISDISCONNECTING) &&
150                 (so->so_state & SS_NBIO))
151                 goto drop;
152             while (so->so_state & SS_ISCONNECTED)
153                 if (error = tsleep((caddr_t) & so->so_timeo,
154                             PSOCK | PCATCH, netcls, so->so_linger))
155                     break;
156         }
157     }
158 drop:
159     if (so->so_pcb) {
160         int     error2 =
161         (*so->so_proto->pr_usrreq) (so, PRU_DETACH,
162             (struct mbuf *) 0, (struct mbuf *) 0, (struct mbuf *) 0);
163         if (error == 0)
164             error = error2;
165     }
166 discard:
167     if (so->so_state & SS_NOFDREF)
168         panic("soclose: NOFDREF");
169     so->so_state |= SS_NOFDREF;
170     sofree(so);
171     splx(s);
172     return (error);
173 }
```

———————————————————————————————— uipc_socket.c

Figure 15.39   soclose function.

Break established connection or association

142–157   If the socket is not connected, execution continues at drop; otherwise the socket must be disconnected from its peer. If a disconnect is not in progress, sodisconnect starts the disconnection process. If the SO_LINGER socket option is set, soclose may need to wait for the disconnect to complete before returning. A nonblocking socket never waits for a disconnect to complete, so soclose jumps immediately to drop in that case. Otherwise, the connection termination is in progress and the SO_LINGER option indicates that soclose must wait some time for it to complete. The while loop continues until the disconnect completes, the linger time (so_linger) expires, or a signal is delivered to the process.

> If the linger time is set to 0, tsleep returns only when the disconnect completes (perhaps because of an error) or a signal is delivered.

Release data structures

158–173   If the socket still has an attached protocol, the PRU_DETACH request breaks the connection between this socket and the protocol. Finally the socket is marked as not having an associated file descriptor, which allows sofree to release the socket.

The sofree function is shown in Figure 15.40.

```
                                                             ──── uipc_socket.c
110 sofree(so)
111 struct socket *so;
112 {
113     if (so->so_pcb || (so->so_state & SS_NOFDREF) == 0)
114         return;
115     if (so->so_head) {
116         if (!soqremque(so, 0) && !soqremque(so, 1))
117             panic("sofree dq");
118         so->so_head = 0;
119     }
120     sbrelease(&so->so_snd);
121     sorflush(so);
122     FREE(so, M_SOCKET);
123 }
                                                             ──── uipc_socket.c
```

Figure 15.40   sofree function.

Return if socket still in use

110–114   If a protocol is still associated with the socket, or if the socket is still associated with a descriptor, sofree returns immediately.

Remove from connection queues

115–119   If the socket is on a connection queue (so_head is nonnull), soqremque is called to remove the socket. An attempt is made to remove the socket from the incomplete connection queue and if this fails, then from the completed connection queue. One of the removals must succeed or the kernel panics, since so_head was nonnull. so_head is cleared.

Discard send and receive queues

120–123   sbrelease discards any buffers in the send queue and sorflush discards any buffers in the receive queue. Finally, the socket itself is released.

15.16 Summary

In this chapter we looked at all the system calls related to network operations. The system call mechanism was described, and we traced the calls until they entered the protocol processing layer through the pr_usrreq function.

While looking at the socket layer, we avoided any discussion of address formats, protocol semantics, or protocol implementations. In the upcoming chapters we tie together the link-layer processing and socket-layer processing by looking in detail at the implementation of the Internet protocols in the protocol processing layer.

Exercises

15.1   How can a process *without* superuser privileges gain access to a socket created by a superuser process?

15.2   How can a process determine if the sockaddr buffer it provides to accept was too small to hold the foreign address returned by the call?

15.3   A feature proposed for IPv6 sockets is to have accept and recvfrom return a source route as an array of 128-bit IPv6 addresses instead of a single peer address. Since the array will not fit in a single mbuf, modify accept and recvfrom to handle an mbuf chain from the protocol layer instead of a single mbuf. Will the existing code work if the protocol layer returns the array in an mbuf cluster instead of a chain of mbufs?

15.4   Why is panic called when soqremque returns a null pointer in Figure 15.26?

15.5   Why does sorflush make a copy of the receive buffer?

15.6   What happens when additional data is received after sorflush has zeroed the socket's receive buffer? Read Chapter 16 before attempting this exercise.

16

Socket I/O

16.1 Introduction

In this chapter we discuss the system calls that read and write data on a network connection. The chapter is divided into three parts.

The first part covers the four system calls for sending data: `write`, `writev`, `sendto`, and `sendmsg`. The second part covers the four system calls for receiving data: `read`, `readv`, `recvfrom`, and `recvmsg`. The third part of the chapter covers the `select` system call, which provides a standard way to monitor the status of descriptors in general and sockets in particular.

The core of the socket layer is the `sosend` and `soreceive` functions. They handle all I/O between the socket layer and the protocol layer. As we'll see, the semantics of the various types of protocols overlap in these functions, making the functions long and complex.

16.2 Code Introduction

The three headers and four C files listed in Figure 16.1 are covered in this chapter.

Global Variables

The first two global variables shown in Figure 16.2 are used by the `select` system call. The third global variable controls the amount of memory allocated to a socket.

File	Description
sys/socket.h sys/socketvar.h sys/uio.h	structures and macro for sockets API socket structure and macros uio structure definition
kern/uipc_syscalls.c kern/uipc_socket.c kern/sys_generic.c kern/sys_socket.c	socket system calls socket layer processing select system call select processing for sockets

Figure 16.1   Files discussed in this chapter.

Variable	Datatype	Description
selwait	int	wait channel for select
nselcoll	int	flag used to avoid race conditions in select
sb_max	u_long	maximum number of bytes to allocate for a socket receive or send buffer

Figure 16.2   Global variables introduced in this chapter.

16.3   Socket Buffers

Section 15.3 showed that each socket has an associated send and receive buffer. The sockbuf structure definition from Figure 15.5 is repeated in Figure 16.3.

```
                                                              ─ socketvar.h
72      struct sockbuf {
73          u_long    sb_cc;         /* actual chars in buffer */
74          u_long    sb_hiwat;      /* max actual char count */
75          u_long    sb_mbcnt;      /* chars of mbufs used */
76          u_long    sb_mbmax;      /* max chars of mbufs to use */
77          long      sb_lowat;      /* low water mark */
78          struct mbuf *sb_mb;      /* the mbuf chain */
79          struct selinfo sb_sel;   /* process selecting read/write */
80          short     sb_flags;      /* Figure 16.5 */
81          short     sb_timeo;      /* timeout for read/write */
82      } so_rcv, so_snd;
                                                              ─ socketvar.h
```

Figure 16.3   sockbuf structure.

72–78   Each buffer contains control information as well as pointers to data stored in mbuf chains. sb_mb points to the first mbuf in the chain, and sb_cc is the total number of data bytes contained within the mbufs. sb_hiwat and sb_lowat regulate the socket flow control algorithms. sb_mbcnt is the total amount of memory allocated to the mbufs in the buffer.

Recall that each mbuf may store from 0 to 2048 bytes of data (if an external cluster is used). sb_mbmax is an upper bound on the amount of memory to be allocated as

mbufs for each socket buffer. Default limits are specified by each protocol when the
PRU_ATTACH request is issued by the socket system call. The high-water and low-
water marks may be modified by the process as long as the kernel-enforced hard limit
of 262,144 bytes per socket buffer (sb_max) is not exceeded. The buffering algorithms
are described in Sections 16.7 and 16.12. Figure 16.4 shows the default settings for the
Internet protocols.

Protocol	so_snd			so_rcv		
	sb_hiwat	sb_lowat	sb_mbmax	sb_hiwat	sb_lowat	sb_mbmax
UDP	9×1024	2048 (ignored)	$2 \times$ sb_hiwat	$40 \times (1024 + 16)$	1	$2 \times$ sb_hiwat
TCP	8×1024	2048	$2 \times$ sb_hiwat	8×1024	1	$2 \times$ sb_hiwat
raw IP ICMP IGMP	8×1024	2048 (ignored)	$2 \times$ sb_hiwat	8×1024	1	$2 \times$ sb_hiwat

Figure 16.4   Default socket buffer limits for the Internet protocols.

Since the source address of each incoming UDP datagram is queued with the data
(Section 23.8), the default UDP value for sb_hiwat is set to accommodate 40 1K datagrams and their associated sockaddr_in structures (16 bytes each).

79   sb_sel is a selinfo structure used to implement the select system call (Section 16.13).

80   Figure 16.5 lists the possible values for sb_flags.

sb_flags	Description
SB_LOCK	a process has locked the socket buffer
SB_WANT	a process is waiting to lock the buffer
SB_WAIT	a process is waiting for data (receive) or space (send) in this buffer
SB_SEL	one or more processes are selecting on this buffer
SB_ASYNC	generate asynchronous I/O signal for this buffer
SB_NOINTR	signals do not cancel a lock request
SB_NOTIFY	(SB_WAIT | SB_SEL | SB_ASYNC) a process is waiting for changes to the buffer and should be notified by wakeup when any changes occur

Figure 16.5   sb_flags values.

81–82   sb_timeo is measured in clock ticks and limits the time a process blocks during a
read or write call. The default value of 0 causes the process to wait indefinitely.
sb_timeo may be changed or retrieved by the SO_SNDTIMEO and SO_RCVTIMEO
socket options.

Socket Macros and Functions

There are many macros and functions that manipulate the send and receive buffers
associated with each socket. The macros and functions in Figure 16.6 handle buffer
locking and synchronization.

Name	Description
sblock	Acquires a lock for *sb*. If *wf* is M_WAITOK, the process sleeps waiting for the lock; otherwise EWOULDBLOCK is returned if the buffer cannot be locked immediately. EINTR or ERESTART is returned if the sleep is interrupted by a signal; 0 is returned otherwise. int **sblock**(struct sockbuf *sb, int *wf*);
sbunlock	Releases the lock on sb. Any other process waiting to lock *sb* is awakened. void **sbunlock**(struct sockbuf *sb);
sbwait	Calls tsleep to wait for protocol activity on *sb*. Returns result of tsleep. int **sbwait**(struct sockbuf *sb);
sowakeup	Notifies socket of protocol activity. Wakes up matching call to sbwait or to tsleep if any processes are selecting on *sb*. void **sowakeup**(struct socket *so, struct sockbuf *sb);
sorwakeup	Wakes up any process waiting for read events on *so* and sends the SIGIO signal if a process requested asynchronous notification of I/O. void **sorwakeup**(struct socket *so);
sowwakeup	Wakes up any process waiting for write events on *so* and sends the SIGIO signal if a process requested asynchronous notification of I/O. void **sowwakeup**(struct socket *so);

Figure 16.6   Macros and functions for socket buffer locking and synchronization.

Figure 16.7 includes the macros and functions used to set the resource limits for socket buffers and to append and delete data from the buffers. In the table, *m, m0, n,* and *control* are all pointers to mbuf chains. *sb* points to the send or receive buffer for a socket.

Name	Description
sbspace	The number of bytes that may be added to *sb* before it is considered full: min((sb_hiwat - sb_cc), (sb_mbmax - sb_mbcnt)). long **sbspace**(struct sockbuf *sb);
sballoc	*m* has been added to *sb*. Adjust sb_cc and sb_mbcnt in *sb* accordingly. void **sballoc**(struct sockbuf *sb, struct mbuf *m);
sbfree	m has been removed from sb. Adjust sb_cc and sb_mbcnt in sb accordingly. int **sbfree**(struct sockbuf *sb, struct mbuf *m);

Name	Description
sbappend	Append the mbufs in *m* to the end of the last record in *sb*. Call sbcompress. int **sbappend**(struct sockbuf *sb*, struct mbuf *m*);
sbappendrecord	Append the record in *m0* after the last record in *sb*. Call sbcompress. int **sbappendrecord**(struct sockbuf *sb*, struct mbuf *m0*);
sbappendaddr	Put address from *asa* in an mbuf. Concatenate address, *control*, and *m0*. Append the resulting mbuf chain after the last record in *sb*. int **sbappendaddr**(struct sockbuf *sb*, struct sockaddr *asa*, struct mbuf *m0*, struct mbuf *control*);
sbappendcontrol	Concatenate *control* and *m0*. Append the resulting mbuf chain after the last record in *sb*. int **sbappendcontrol**(struct sockbuf *sb*, struct mbuf *m0*, struct mbuf *control*);
sbinsertoob	Insert *m0* before first record in *sb* without out-of-band data. Call sbcompress. int **sbinsertoob**(struct sockbuf *sb*, struct mbuf *m0*);
sbcompress	Append *m* to *n* squeezing out any unused space. void **sbcompress**(struct sockbuf *sb*, struct mbuf *m*, struct mbuf *n*);
sbdrop	Discard *len* bytes from the front of *sb*. void **sbdrop**(struct sockbuf *sb*, int*len*);
sbdroprecord	Discard the first record in *sb*. Move the next record to the front. void **sbdroprecord**(struct sockbuf *sb*);
sbrelease	Call sbflush to release all mbufs in *sb*. Reset sb_hiwat and sb_mbmax values to 0. void **sbrelease**(struct sockbuf *sb*);
sbflush	Release all mbufs in *sb*. void **sbflush**(struct sockbuf *sb*);
soreserve	Set high-water and low-water marks. For the send buffer, call sbreserve with *sndcc*. For the receive buffer, call sbreserve with *rcvcc*. Initialize sb_lowat in both buffers to default values, Figure 16.4. ENOBUFS is returned if any limits are exceeded. int **soreserve**(struct socket *so*, int *sndcc*, int *rcvcc*);
sbreserve	Set high-water mark for *sb* to *cc*. Also drop low-water mark to *cc*. No memory is allocated by this function. int **sbreserve**(struct sockbuf *sb*, int *cc*);

Figure 16.7 Macros and functions for socket buffer allocation and manipulation.

16.4 `write`, `writev`, `sendto`, and `sendmsg` System Calls

These four system calls, which we refer to collectively as the *write system calls*, send data
on a network connection. The first three system calls are simpler interfaces to the most
general request, `sendmsg`.

All the write system calls, directly or indirectly, call `sosend`, which does the work
of copying data from the process to the kernel and passing data to the protocol associated with the socket. Figure 16.8 summarizes the flow of control.

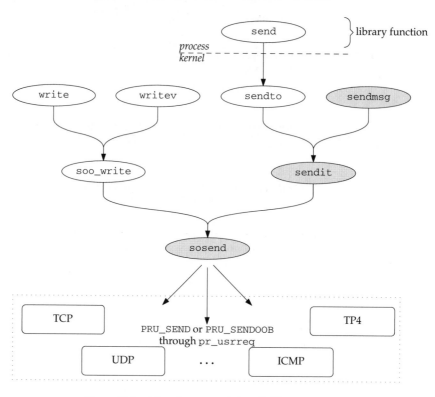

Figure 16.8 All socket output is handled by `sosend`.

In the following sections, we discuss the functions shaded in Figure 16.8. The other
four system calls and `soo_write` are left for readers to investigate on their own.

Figure 16.9 shows the features of these four system calls and a related library function (`send`).

> In Net/3, send is implemented as a library function that calls sendto. For binary compatibil-
> ity with previously compiled programs, the kernel maps the old send system call to the func-
> tion osend, which is not discussed in this text.

From the second column in Figure 16.9 we see that the `write` and `writev` system
calls are valid with any descriptor, but the remaining system calls are valid only with
socket descriptors.

Function	Type of descriptor	Number of buffers	Specify destination address?	Flags?	Control information?
write	any	1			
writev	any	[1..UIO_MAXIOV]			
send	socket only	1		•	
sendto	socket only	1	•	•	
sendmsg	socket only	[1..UIO_MAXIOV]	•	•	•

Figure 16.9 Write system calls.

The third column shows that `writev` and `sendmsg` accept data from multiple buffers. Writing from multiple buffers is called *gathering*. The analogous read operation is called *scattering*. In a gather operation the kernel accepts, in order, data from each buffer specified in an array of `iovec` structures. The array can have a maximum of `UIO_MAXIOV` elements. The structure is shown in Figure 16.10.

—— *uio.h*
```
41 struct iovec {
42     char   *iov_base;          /* Base address */
43     size_t  iov_len;           /* Length */
44 };
```
—— *uio.h*

Figure 16.10 `iovec` structure.

41–44   `iov_base` points to the start of a buffer of `iov_len` bytes.

Without this type of interface, a process would have to copy buffers into a single larger buffer or make multiple write system calls to send data from multiple buffers. Both alternatives are less efficient than passing an array of `iovec` structures to the kernel in a single call. With datagram protocols, the result of one `writev` is one datagram, which cannot be emulated with multiple writes.

Figure 16.11 illustrates the structures as they are used by `writev`, where `iovp` points to the first element of the array and `iovcnt` is the size of the array.

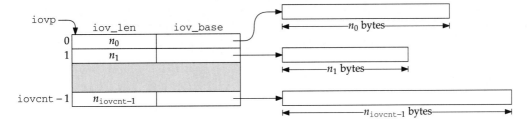

Figure 16.11 `iovec` arguments to `writev`.

Datagram protocols require a destination address to be associated with each write call. Since `write`, `writev`, and `send` do not accept an explicit destination, they may be called only after a destination has been associated with a connectionless socket by calling `connect`. A destination must be provided with `sendto` or `sendmsg`, or `connect` must have been previously called.

The fifth column in Figure 16.9 shows that the send*xxx* system calls accept optional control flags, which are described in Figure 16.12.

flags	Description	Reference
MSG_DONTROUTE	bypass routing tables for this message	Figure 16.23
MSG_DONTWAIT	do not wait for resources during this message	Figure 16.22
MSG_EOR	data marks the end of a logical record	Figure 16.25
MSG_OOB	send as out-of-band data	Figure 16.26

Figure 16.12   send*xxx* system calls: `flags` values.

As indicated in the last column of Figure 16.9, only the sendmsg system call supports control information. The control information and several other arguments to sendmsg are specified within a msghdr structure (Figure 16.13) instead of being passed separately.

```
                                                                ── socket.h
228 struct msghdr {
229     caddr_t msg_name;            /* optional address */
230     u_int   msg_namelen;         /* size of address */
231     struct iovec *msg_iov;       /* scatter/gather array */
232     u_int   msg_iovlen;          /* # elements in msg_iov */
233     caddr_t msg_control;         /* ancillary data, see below */
234     u_int   msg_controllen;      /* ancillary data buffer len */
235     int     msg_flags;           /* Figure 16.33 */
236 };
                                                                ── socket.h
```

Figure 16.13   msghdr structure.

msg_name should be declared as a pointer to a sockaddr structure, since it contains a network address.

228–236   The msghdr structure contains a destination address (msg_name and msg_namelen), a scatter/gather array (msg_iov and msg_iovlen), control information (msg_control and msg_controllen), and receive flags (msg_flags). The control information is formatted as a cmsghdr structure shown in Figure 16.14.

```
                                                                ── socket.h
251 struct cmsghdr {
252     u_int   cmsg_len;            /* data byte count, including hdr */
253     int     cmsg_level;          /* originating protocol */
254     int     cmsg_type;           /* protocol-specific type */
255 /* followed by  u_char  cmsg_data[]; */
256 };
                                                                ── socket.h
```

Figure 16.14   cmsghdr structure.

251–256   The control information is not interpreted by the socket layer, but the messages are typed (cmsg_type) and they have an explicit length (cmsg_len). Multiple control messages may appear in the control information mbuf.

Example

Figure 16.15 shows how a fully specified msghdr structure might look during a call to sendmsg.

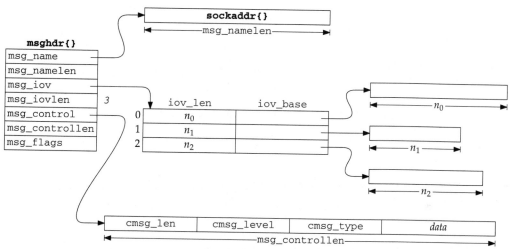

Figure 16.15   msghdr structure for sendmsg system call.

16.5   **sendmsg** System Call

Only the sendmsg system call provides access to all the features of the sockets API associated with output. The sendmsg and sendit functions prepare the data structures needed by sosend, which passes the message to the appropriate protocol. For SOCK_DGRAM protocols, a message is a datagram. For SOCK_STREAM protocols, a message is a sequence of bytes. For SOCK_SEQPACKET protocols, a message could be an entire record (implicit record boundaries) or part of a larger record (explicit record boundaries). A message is always an entire record (implicit record boundaries) for SOCK_RDM protocols.

> Even though the general sosend code handles SOCK_SEQPACKET and SOCK_RDM protocols, there are no such protocols in the Internet domain.

Figure 16.16 shows the sendmsg code.

307–321   There are three arguments to sendmsg: the socket descriptor; a pointer to a msghdr structure; and several control flags. The copyin function copies the msghdr structure from user space to the kernel.

Copy **iov** array

322–334   An iovec array with eight entries (UIO_SMALLIOV) is allocated automatically on the stack. If this is not large enough, sendmsg calls MALLOC to allocate a larger array. If

```
                                                             ———————— uipc_syscalls.c
307 struct sendmsg_args {
308     int     s;
309     caddr_t msg;
310     int     flags;
311 };

312 sendmsg(p, uap, retval)
313 struct proc *p;
314 struct sendmsg_args *uap;
315 int     *retval;
316 {
317     struct msghdr msg;
318     struct iovec aiov[UIO_SMALLIOV], *iov;
319     int     error;

320     if (error = copyin(uap->msg, (caddr_t) & msg, sizeof(msg)))
321         return (error);
322     if ((u_int) msg.msg_iovlen >= UIO_SMALLIOV) {
323         if ((u_int) msg.msg_iovlen >= UIO_MAXIOV)
324             return (EMSGSIZE);
325         MALLOC(iov, struct iovec *,
326                 sizeof(struct iovec) * (u_int) msg.msg_iovlen, M_IOV,
327                 M_WAITOK);
328     } else
329         iov = aiov;
330     if (msg.msg_iovlen &&
331         (error = copyin((caddr_t) msg.msg_iov, (caddr_t) iov,
332                     (unsigned) (msg.msg_iovlen * sizeof(struct iovec)))))
333             goto done;
334     msg.msg_iov = iov;
335     error = sendit(p, uap->s, &msg, uap->flags, retval);
336 done:
337     if (iov != aiov)
338         FREE(iov, M_IOV);
339     return (error);
340 }
```
                                                             ———————— uipc_syscalls.c

Figure 16.16   sendmsg system call.

the process specifies an array with more than 1024 (UIO_MAXIOV) entries, EMSGSIZE is
returned. copyin places a copy of the iovec array from user space into either the
array on the stack or the larger, dynamically allocated, array.

> This technique avoids the relatively expensive call to malloc in the most common case of
> eight or fewer entries.

sendit and cleanup

335–340   When sendit returns, the data has been delivered to the appropriate protocol or
an error has occurred. sendmsg releases the iovec array (if it was dynamically allocated) and returns sendit's result.

16.6 `sendit` Function

`sendit` is the common function called by `sendto` and `sendmsg`. `sendit` initializes a `uio` structure and copies control and address information from the process into the kernel. Before discussing `sosend`, we must explain the `uiomove` function and the `uio` structure.

`uiomove` Function

The prototype for this function is:

```
int uiomove(caddr_t cp, int n, struct uio *uio);
```

The `uiomove` function moves *n* bytes between a single buffer referenced by *cp* and the multiple buffers specified by an *iovec* array in *uio*. Figure 16.17 shows the definition of the `uio` structure, which controls and records the actions of the `uiomove` function.

```
                                                                  ─── uio.h
45 enum uio_rw {
46     UIO_READ, UIO_WRITE
47 };

48 enum uio_seg {                /* Segment flag values */
49     UIO_USERSPACE,            /* from user data space */
50     UIO_SYSSPACE,             /* from system space */
51     UIO_USERISPACE            /* from user instruction space */
52 };

53 struct uio {
54     struct iovec *uio_iov;    /* an array of iovec structures */
55     int     uio_iovcnt;       /* size of iovec array */
56     off_t   uio_offset;       /* starting position of transfer */
57     int     uio_resid;        /* remaining bytes to transfer */
58     enum uio_seg uio_segflg;  /* location of buffers */
59     enum uio_rw uio_rw;       /* direction of transfer */
60     struct proc *uio_procp;   /* the associated process */
61 };
                                                                  ─── uio.h
```

Figure 16.17 `uio` structure.

45–61   In the `uio` structure, `uio_iov` points to an array of `iovec` structures, `uio_offset` counts the number of bytes transferred by `uiomove`, and `uio_resid` counts the number of bytes remaining to be transferred. Each time `uiomove` is called, `uio_offset` increases by *n* and `uio_resid` decreases by *n*. `uiomove` adjusts the base pointers and buffer lengths in the `uio_iov` array to exclude any bytes that `uiomove` transfers each time it is called. Finally, `uio_iov` is advanced through each entry in the array as each buffer is transferred. `uio_segflg` indicates the location of the buffers specified by the base pointers in the `uio_iov` array and `uio_rw` indicates the direction of the transfer. The buffers may be located in the user data space, user instruction space, or kernel data space. Figure 16.18 summarizes the operation of `uiomove`. The descriptions use the argument names shown in the `uiomove` prototype.

uio_segflg	uio_rw	Description
UIO_USERSPACE	UIO_READ	scatter *n* bytes from a kernel buffer *cp* to process buffers
UIO_USERISPACE		
UIO_USERSPACE	UIO_WRITE	gather *n* bytes from process buffers into the kernel buffer *cp*
UIO_USERISPACE		
UIO_SYSSPACE	UIO_READ	scatter *n* bytes from the kernel buffer *cp* to multiple kernel buffers
	UIO_WRITE	gather *n* bytes from multiple kernel buffers into the kernel buffer *cp*

Figure 16.18   uiomove operation.

Example

Figure 16.19 shows a uio structure before uiomove is called.

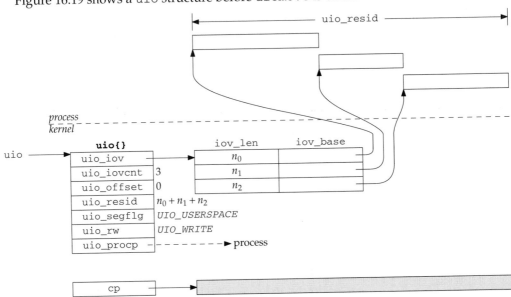

Figure 16.19   uiomove: before.

uio_iov points to the first entry in the iovec array. Each of the iov_base point-ers point to the start of their respective buffer in the address space of the process. uio_offset is 0, and uio_resid is the sum of size of the three buffers. cp points to a buffer within the kernel, typically the data area of an mbuf. Figure 16.20 shows the same data structures after

```
uiomove(cp, n, uio);
```

is executed where n includes all the bytes from the first buffer and only some of the bytes from the second buffer (i.e., $n_0 < n < n_0 + n_1$).

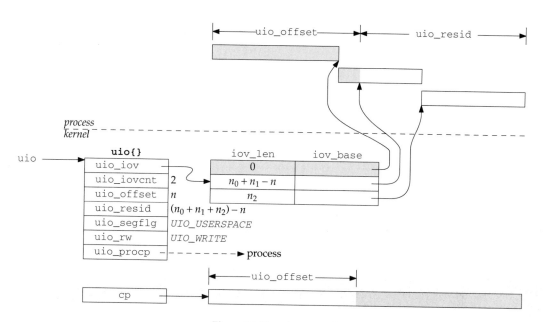

Figure 16.20 uiomove: after.

After uiomove, the first buffer has a length of 0 and its base pointer has been advanced to the end of the buffer. uio_iov now points to the second entry in the iovec array. The pointer in this entry has been advanced and the length decreased to reflect the transfer of some of the bytes in the buffer. uio_offset has been increased by n and uio_resid has been decreased by n. The data from the buffers in the process has been moved into the kernel's buffer because uio_rw was UIO_WRITE.

sendit Code

We can now discuss the sendit code shown in Figure 16.21.

Initialize auio

341–368   sendit calls getsock to get the file structure associated with the descriptor s and initializes the uio structure to gather the output buffers specified by the process into mbufs in the kernel. The length of the transfer is calculated by the for loop as the sum of the buffer lengths and saved in uio_resid. The first if within the loop ensures that the buffer length is nonnegative. The second if ensures that uio_resid does not overflow, since uio_resid is a signed integer and iov_len is guaranteed to be nonnegative.

Copy address and control information from the process

369–385   sockargs makes copies of the destination address and control information into mbufs if they are provided by the process.

```
341 sendit(p, s, mp, flags, retsize)
342 struct proc *p;
343 int     s;
344 struct msghdr *mp;
345 int     flags, *retsize;
346 {
347     struct file *fp;
348     struct uio auio;
349     struct iovec *iov;
350     int     i;
351     struct mbuf *to, *control;
352     int     len, error;

353     if (error = getsock(p->p_fd, s, &fp))
354         return (error);
355     auio.uio_iov = mp->msg_iov;
356     auio.uio_iovcnt = mp->msg_iovlen;
357     auio.uio_segflg = UIO_USERSPACE;
358     auio.uio_rw = UIO_WRITE;
359     auio.uio_procp = p;
360     auio.uio_offset = 0;           /* XXX */
361     auio.uio_resid = 0;
362     iov = mp->msg_iov;
363     for (i = 0; i < mp->msg_iovlen; i++, iov++) {
364         if (iov->iov_len < 0)
365             return (EINVAL);
366         if ((auio.uio_resid += iov->iov_len) < 0)
367             return (EINVAL);
368     }
369     if (mp->msg_name) {
370         if (error = sockargs(&to, mp->msg_name, mp->msg_namelen,
371                         MT_SONAME))
372             return (error);
373     } else
374         to = 0;
375     if (mp->msg_control) {
376         if (mp->msg_controllen < sizeof(struct cmsghdr)
377         ) {
378             error = EINVAL;
379             goto bad;
380         }
381         if (error = sockargs(&control, mp->msg_control,
382                         mp->msg_controllen, MT_CONTROL))
383             goto bad;
384     } else
385         control = 0;
386     len = auio.uio_resid;
387     if (error = sosend((struct socket *) fp->f_data, to, &auio,
388                     (struct mbuf *) 0, control, flags)) {
389         if (auio.uio_resid != len && (error == ERESTART ||
390                             error == EINTR || error == EWOULDBLOCK))
391             error = 0;
392         if (error == EPIPE)
393             psignal(p, SIGPIPE);
```

```
394        }
395        if (error == 0)
396            *retsize = len - auio.uio_resid;
397    bad:
398        if (to)
399            m_freem(to);
400        return (error);
401    }
```
—————————————————————————————————— uipc_syscalls.c

Figure 16.21 sendit function.

Send data and cleanup

386–401   uio_resid is saved in len so that the number of bytes transferred can be calculated if sosend does not accept all the data. The socket, destination address, uio structure, control information, and flags are all passed to sosend. When sosend returns,
sendit responds as follows:

- If sosend transfers some data and is interrupted by a signal or a blocking condition, the error is discarded and the partial transfer is reported.

- If sosend returns EPIPE, the SIGPIPE signal is sent to the process. error is
  not set to 0, so if a process catches the signal and the signal handler returns, or if
  the process ignores the signal, the write call returns EPIPE.

- If no error occurred (or it was discarded), the number of bytes transferred is calculated and saved in *retsize. Since sendit returns 0, syscall (Section 15.4) returns *retsize to the process instead of returning the error code.

- If any other error occurs, the error code is returned to the process.

Before returning, sendit releases the mbuf containing the destination address.
sosend is responsible for releasing the control mbuf.

16.7 sosend Function

sosend is one of the most complicated functions in the socket layer. Recall from Figure 16.8 that all five write calls eventually call sosend. It is sosend's responsibility to
pass the data and control information to the pr_usrreq function of the protocol associated with the socket according to the semantics supported by the protocol and the buffer limits specified by the socket. sosend never places data in the send buffer; it is the
protocol's responsibility to store and remove the data.

The interpretation of the send buffer's sb_hiwat and sb_lowat values by
sosend depends on whether the associated protocol implements reliable or unreliable
data transfer semantics.

Reliable Protocol Buffering

For reliable protocols, the send buffer holds both data that has not yet been transmitted and data that has been sent, but has not been acknowledged. sb_cc is the number of bytes of data that reside in the send buffer, and $0 \leq$ sb_cc $\leq$ sb_hiwat.

> sb_cc may temporarily exceed sb_hiwat when out-of-band data is sent.

It is sosend's responsibility to ensure that there is enough space in the send buffer before passing any data to the protocol layer through the pr_usrreq function. The protocol layer adds the data to the send buffer. sosend transfers data to the protocol in one of two ways:

- If PR_ATOMIC is set, sosend must preserve the message boundaries between the process and the protocol layer. In this case, sosend waits for enough space to become available to hold the entire message. When the space is available, an mbuf chain containing the entire message is constructed and passed to the protocol in a single call through the pr_usrreq function. RDP and SPP are examples of this type of protocol.

- If PR_ATOMIC is not set, sosend passes the message to the protocol one mbuf at a time and may pass a partial mbuf to avoid exceeding the high-water mark. This method is used with SOCK_STREAM protocols such as TCP and SOCK_SEQPACKET protocols such as TP4. With TP4, record boundaries are indicated explicitly with the MSG_EOR flag (Figure 16.12), so it is not necessary for the message boundaries to be preserved by sosend.

TCP applications have no control over the size of outgoing TCP segments. For example, a message of 4096 bytes sent on a TCP socket will be split by the socket layer into two mbufs with external clusters, containing 2048 bytes each, assuming there is enough space in the send buffer for 4096 bytes. Later, during protocol processing, TCP will segment the data according to the maximum segment size for the connection, which is normally less than 2048.

When a message is too large to fit in the available buffer space and the protocol allows messages to be split, sosend still does not pass data to the protocol until the free space in the buffer rises above sb_lowat. For TCP, sb_lowat defaults to 2048 (Figure 16.4), so this rule prevents the socket layer from bothering TCP with small chunks of data when the send buffer is nearly full.

Unreliable Protocol Buffering

With unreliable protocols (e.g., UDP), no data is ever stored in the send buffer and no acknowledgment is ever expected. Each message is passed immediately to the protocol where it is queued for transmission on the appropriate network device. In this case, sb_cc is always 0, and sb_hiwat specifies the maximum size of each write and indirectly the maximum size of a datagram.

Figure 16.4 shows that sb_hiwat defaults to 9216 (9×1024) for UDP. Unless the process changes sb_hiwat with the SO_SNDBUF socket option, an attempt to write a datagram larger than 9216 bytes returns with an error. Even then, other limitations of the protocol implementation may prevent a process from sending large datagrams. Section 11.10 of Volume 1 discusses these defaults and limits in other TCP/IP implementations.

> 9216 is large enough for a NFS write, which often defaults to 8192 bytes of data plus protocol headers.

sosend Code

Figure 16.22 shows an overview of the sosend function. We discuss the four shaded sections separately.

271–278   The arguments to sosend are: so, a pointer to the relevant socket; addr, a pointer to a destination address; uio, a pointer to a uio structure describing the I/O buffers in user space; top, an mbuf chain that holds data to be sent; control, an mbuf that holds control information to be sent; and flags, which contains options for this write call.

Normally, a process provides data to the socket layer through the uio mechanism and top is null. When the kernel itself is using the socket layer (such as with NFS), the data is passed to sosend as an mbuf chain pointed to by top, and uio is null.

279–304   The initialization code is described separately.

Lock send buffer

305–308   sosend's main processing loop starts at restart, where it obtains a lock on the send buffer with sblock before proceeding. The lock ensures orderly access to the socket buffer by multiple processes.

If MSG_DONTWAIT is set in flags, then SBLOCKWAIT returns M_NOWAIT, which tells sblock to return EWOULDBLOCK if the lock is not available immediately.

> MSG_DONTWAIT is used only by NFS in Net/3.

The main loop continues until sosend transfers all the data to the protocol (i.e., resid == 0).

Check for space

309–341   Before any data is passed to the protocol, various error conditions are checked and sosend implements the flow control and resource control algorithms described earlier. If sosend blocks waiting for more space to appear in the output buffer, it jumps back to restart before continuing.

Use data from top

342–350   Once space becomes available and sosend has obtained a lock on the send buffer, the data is prepared for delivery to the protocol layer. If uio is null (i.e., the data is in the mbuf chain pointed to by top), sosend checks MSG_EOR and sets M_EOR in the chain to mark the end of a logical record. The mbuf chain is ready for the protocol layer.

—————————————————————————————————————— *uipc_socket.c*
```
271 sosend(so, addr, uio, top, control, flags)
272 struct socket *so;
273 struct mbuf *addr;
274 struct uio *uio;
275 struct mbuf *top;
276 struct mbuf *control;
277 int     flags;
278 {
```

```
                        /* initialization (Figure 16.23) */
```

```
305   restart:
306     if (error = sblock(&so->so_snd, SBLOCKWAIT(flags)))
307         goto out;
308     do {                        /* main loop, until resid == 0 */
```

```
                /* wait for space in send buffer (Figure 16.24) */
```

```
342       do {
343           if (uio == NULL) {
344               /*
345                * Data is prepackaged in "top".
346                */
347               resid = 0;
348               if (flags & MSG_EOR)
349                   top->m_flags |= M_EOR;
350           } else
351               do {
```

```
            /* fill a single mbuf or an mbuf chain (Figure 16.25) */
```

```
396               } while (space > 0 && atomic);
```

```
                /* pass mbuf chain to protocol (Figure 16.26) */
```

```
412       } while (resid && space > 0);
413     } while (resid);
```

```
414   release:
415     sbunlock(&so->so_snd);
416   out:
417     if (top)
418         m_freem(top);
419     if (control)
420         m_freem(control);
421     return (error);
422 }
```
—————————————————————————————————————— *uipc_socket.c*

Figure 16.22   sosend function: overview.

Copy data from process

351–396   When uio is not null, sosend must transfer the data from the process. When PR_ATOMIC is set (e.g., UDP), this loop continues until all the data has been stored in a single mbuf chain. A break, which is not shown in Figure 16.22, causes the loop to terminate when all the data has been copied from the process, and sosend passes the entire chain to the protocol.

When PR_ATOMIC is not set (e.g., TCP), this loop is executed only once, filling a single mbuf with data from uio. In this case, the mbufs are passed one at a time to the protocol.

Pass data to the protocol

397–413   For PR_ATOMIC protocols, after the mbuf chain is passed to the protocol, resid is always 0 and control falls through the two loops to release. When PR_ATOMIC is not set, sosend continues filling individuals mbufs while there is more data to send and while there is still space in the buffer. If the buffer fills and there is still data to send, sosend loops back and waits for more space before filling the next mbuf. If all the data is sent, both loops terminate.

Cleanup

414–422   After all the data has been passed to the protocol, the socket buffer is unlocked, any remaining mbufs are discarded, and sosend returns.

The detailed description of sosend is shown in four parts:

- initialization (Figure 16.23),
- error and resource checking (Figure 16.24),
- data transfer (Figure 16.25), and
- protocol dispatch (Figure 16.26).

The first part of sosend shown in Figure 16.23 initializes various variables.

Compute transfer size and semantics

279–284   atomic is set if sosendallatonce is true (any protocol for which PR_ATOMIC is set) or the data has been passed to sosend as an mbuf chain in top. This flag controls whether data is passed to the protocol as a single mbuf chain or in separate mbufs.

285–297   resid is the number of bytes in the iovec buffers or the number of bytes in the top mbuf chain. Exercise 16.1 discusses why resid might be negative.

If requested, disable routing

298–303   dontroute is set when the routing tables should be bypassed for *this* message only. clen is the number of bytes in the optional control mbuf.

304   The macro snderr posts the error code, reenables protocol processing, and jumps to the cleanup code at out. This macro simplifies the error handling within the function.

Figure 16.24 shows the part of sosend that checks for error conditions and waits for space to appear in the send buffer.

```
                                                             ———— uipc_socket.c
279     struct proc *p = curproc;     /* XXX */
280     struct mbuf **mp;
281     struct mbuf *m;
282     long    space, len, resid;
283     int     clen = 0, error, s, dontroute, mlen;
284     int     atomic = sosendallatonce(so) || top;
285     if (uio)
286         resid = uio->uio_resid;
287     else
288         resid = top->m_pkthdr.len;
289     /*
290      * In theory resid should be unsigned.
291      * However, space must be signed, as it might be less than 0
292      * if we over-committed, and we must use a signed comparison
293      * of space and resid.  On the other hand, a negative resid
294      * causes us to loop sending 0-length segments to the protocol.
295      */
296     if (resid < 0)
297         return (EINVAL);
298     dontroute =
299         (flags & MSG_DONTROUTE) && (so->so_options & SO_DONTROUTE) == 0 &&
300         (so->so_proto->pr_flags & PR_ATOMIC);
301     p->p_stats->p_ru.ru_msgsnd++;
302     if (control)
303         clen = control->m_len;
304 #define snderr(errno)    { error = errno; splx(s); goto release; }
                                                             ———— uipc_socket.c
```

Figure 16.23   sosend function: initialization.

309   Protocol processing is suspended to prevent the buffer from changing while it is being examined. Before each transfer, sosend checks several conditions:

310–311   • If output from the socket is prohibited (e.g., the write-half of a TCP connection has been closed), EPIPE is returned.

312–313   • If the socket is in an error state (e.g., an ICMP port unreachable may have been generated by a previous datagram), so_error is returned. sendit discards the error if some data has been sent before the error occurs (Figure 16.21, line 389).

314–318   • If the protocol requires connections and a connection has not been established or a connection attempt has not been started, ENOTCONN is returned. sosend permits a write consisting of control information and no data even when a connection has not been established.

> The Internet protocols do not use this feature, but it is used by TP4 to send data with a connection request, to confirm a connection request, and to send data with a disconnect request.

319–321   • If a destination address is not specified for a connectionless protocol (e.g., the process calls send without establishing a destination with connect), EDESTADDREQ is returned.

```
                                                                  ─── uipc_socket.c
309         s = splnet();
310         if (so->so_state & SS_CANTSENDMORE)
311             snderr(EPIPE);
312         if (so->so_error)
313             snderr(so->so_error);
314         if ((so->so_state & SS_ISCONNECTED) == 0) {
315             if (so->so_proto->pr_flags & PR_CONNREQUIRED) {
316                 if ((so->so_state & SS_ISCONFIRMING) == 0 &&
317                     !(resid == 0 && clen != 0))
318                     snderr(ENOTCONN);
319             } else if (addr == 0)
320                 snderr(EDESTADDRREQ);
321         }
322         space = sbspace(&so->so_snd);
323         if (flags & MSG_OOB)
324             space += 1024;
325         if (atomic && resid > so->so_snd.sb_hiwat ||
326             clen > so->so_snd.sb_hiwat)
327             snderr(EMSGSIZE);
328         if (space < resid + clen && uio &&
329             (atomic || space < so->so_snd.sb_lowat || space < clen)) {
330             if (so->so_state & SS_NBIO)
331                 snderr(EWOULDBLOCK);
332             sbunlock(&so->so_snd);
333             error = sbwait(&so->so_snd);
334             splx(s);
335             if (error)
336                 goto out;
337             goto restart;
338         }
339         splx(s);
340         mp = &top;
341         space -= clen;
                                                                  ─── uipc_socket.c
```

Figure 16.24   sosend function: error and resource checking.

Compute available space

322–324   sbspace computes the amount of free space remaining in the send buffer. This is
an administrative limit based on the buffer's high-water mark, but is also limited by
sb_mbmax to prevent many small messages from consuming too many mbufs (Figure 16.6). sosend gives out-of-band data some priority by relaxing the limits on the
buffer size by 1024 bytes.

Enforce message size limit

325–327   If atomic is set and the message is larger than the high-water mark, EMSGSIZE is
returned; the message is too large to be accepted by the protocol—even if the buffer
were empty. If the control information is larger than the high-water mark, EMSGSIZE is
also returned. This is the test that limits the size of a datagram or record.

Wait for more space?

328–329   If there is not enough space in the send buffer, the data is from a process (versus from the kernel in `top`), and one of the following conditions is true, then `sosend` must wait for additional space before continuing:

- the message must be passed to protocol in a single request (`atomic` is set), or

- the message may be split, but the free space has dropped below the low-water mark, or

- the message may be split, but the control information does not fit in the available space.

When the data is passed to `sosend` in `top` (i.e., when `uio` is null), the data is already located in mbufs. Therefore `sosend` ignores the high- and low-water marks since no additional mbuf allocations are required to pass the data to the protocol.

If the send buffer low-water mark is not used in this test, an interesting interaction occurs between the socket layer and the transport layer that leads to performance degradation. [Crowcroft et al. 1992] provides details on this scenario.

Wait for space

330–338   If `sosend` must wait for space and the socket is nonblocking, `EWOULDBLOCK` is returned. Otherwise, the buffer lock is released and `sosend` waits with `sbwait` until the status of the buffer changes. When `sbwait` returns, `sosend` reenables protocol processing and jumps back to `restart` to obtain a lock on the buffer and to check the error and space conditions again before continuing.

By default, `sbwait` blocks until data can be sent. By changing `sb_timeo` in the buffer through the `SO_SNDTIMEO` socket option, the process selects an upper bound for the wait time. If the timer expires, `sbwait` returns `EWOULDBLOCK`. Recall from Figure 16.21 that this error is discarded by `sendit` if some data has already been transferred to the protocol. This timer does not limit the length of the entire call, just the inactivity time between filling mbufs.

339–341   At this point, `sosend` has determined that some data may be passed to the protocol. `splx` enables interrupts since they should not be blocked during the relatively long time it takes to copy data from the process to the kernel. `mp` holds a pointer used to construct the mbuf chain. The size of the control information (`clen`) is subtracted from the space available before `sosend` transfers any data from the process.

Figure 16.25 shows the section of `sosend` that moves data from the process to one or more mbufs in the kernel.

Allocate packet header or standard mbuf

351–360   When `atomic` is set, this code allocates a packet header during the first iteration of the loop and standard mbufs afterwards. When `atomic` is not set, this code always allocates a packet header since `top` is always cleared before entering the loop.

```
351                    do {                                              uipc_socket.c
352                        if (top == 0) {
353                            MGETHDR(m, M_WAIT, MT_DATA);
354                            mlen = MHLEN;
355                            m->m_pkthdr.len = 0;
356                            m->m_pkthdr.rcvif = (struct ifnet *) 0;
357                        } else {
358                            MGET(m, M_WAIT, MT_DATA);
359                            mlen = MLEN;
360                        }

361                        if (resid >= MINCLSIZE && space >= MCLBYTES) {
362                            MCLGET(m, M_WAIT);
363                            if ((m->m_flags & M_EXT) == 0)
364                                goto nopages;
365                            mlen = MCLBYTES;
366                            if (atomic && top == 0) {
367                                len = min(MCLBYTES - max_hdr, resid);
368                                m->m_data += max_hdr;
369                            } else
370                                len = min(MCLBYTES, resid);
371                            space -= MCLBYTES;
372                        } else {
373                        nopages:
374                            len = min(min(mlen, resid), space);
375                            space -= len;
376                            /*
377                             * For datagram protocols, leave room
378                             * for protocol headers in first mbuf.
379                             */
380                            if (atomic && top == 0 && len < mlen)
381                                MH_ALIGN(m, len);
382                        }

383                        error = uiomove(mtod(m, caddr_t), (int) len, uio);
384                        resid = uio->uio_resid;
385                        m->m_len = len;
386                        *mp = m;
387                        top->m_pkthdr.len += len;
388                        if (error)
389                            goto release;
390                        mp = &m->m_next;
391                        if (resid <= 0) {
392                            if (flags & MSG_EOR)
393                                top->m_flags |= M_EOR;
394                            break;
395                        }
396                    } while (space > 0 && atomic);
                                                                        uipc_socket.c
```

Figure 16.25 sosend function: data transfer.

If possible, use a cluster

361–371   If the message is large enough to make a cluster allocation worthwhile and space is greater than or equal to MCLBYTES, a cluster is attached to the mbuf by MCLGET. When space is less than MCLBYTES, the extra 2048 bytes will break the allocation limit for the buffer since the entire cluster is allocated even if resid is less than MCLBYTES.

If MCLGET fails, sosend jumps to nopages and uses a standard mbuf instead of an external cluster.

> The test against MINCLSIZE should use >, not >=, since a write of 208 (MINCLSIZE) bytes fits within two mbufs.

When atomic is set (e.g., UDP), the mbuf chain represents a datagram or record and max_hdr bytes are reserved at the front of the *first* cluster for protocol headers. Subsequent clusters are part of the same chain and do not need room for the headers.

If atomic is not set (e.g., TCP), no space is reserved since sosend does not know how the protocol will segment the outgoing data.

Notice that space is decremented by the size of the cluster (2048 bytes) and not by len, which is the number of data bytes to be placed in the cluster (Exercise 16.2).

Prepare the mbuf

372–382   If a cluster was not used, the number of bytes stored in the mbuf is limited by the smaller of: (1) the space in the mbuf, (2) the number of bytes in the message, or (3) the space in the buffer.

When atomic is set, MH_ALIGN locates the data at the end of the buffer for the first buffer in the chain. MH_ALIGN is skipped if the data completely fills the mbuf. This may or may not leave enough room for protocol headers, depending on how much data is placed in the mbuf. When atomic is not set, no space is set aside for the headers.

Get data from the process

383–395   uiomove copies len bytes of data from the process to the mbuf. After the transfer, the mbuf length is updated, the previous mbuf is linked to the new mbuf (or top points to the first mbuf), and the length of the mbuf chain is updated. If an error occurred during the transfer, sosend jumps to release.

When the last byte is transferred from the process, M_EOR is set in the packet if the process set MSG_EOR, and sosend breaks out of this loop.

> MSG_EOR applies only to protocols with explicit record boundaries such as TP4, from the OSI protocol suite. TCP does not support logical records and ignores the MSG_EOR flag.

Fill another buffer?

396   If atomic is set, sosend loops back and begins filling another mbuf.

> The test for space > 0 appears to be extraneous. space is irrelevant when atomic is not set since the mbufs are passed to the protocol one at a time. When atomic is set, this loop is entered only when there is enough space for the entire message. See also Exercise 16.2.

The last section of sosend, shown in Figure 16.26, passes the data and control mbufs to the protocol associated with the socket.

```
                                                                    uipc_socket.c
397              if (dontroute)
398                  so->so_options |= SO_DONTROUTE;
399              s = splnet();        /* XXX */
400              error = (*so->so_proto->pr_usrreq) (so,
401                              (flags & MSG_OOB) ? PRU_SENDOOB : PRU_SEND,
402                                              top, addr, control);
403              splx(s);
404              if (dontroute)
405                  so->so_options &= ~SO_DONTROUTE;
406              clen = 0;
407              control = 0;
408              top = 0;
409              mp = &top;
410              if (error)
411                  goto release;
412          } while (resid && space > 0);
413      } while (resid);
                                                                    uipc_socket.c
```

Figure 16.26   sosend function: protocol dispatch.

397–405   The socket's SO_DONTROUTE option is toggled if necessary before and after passing the data to the protocol layer to bypass the routing tables on this message. This is the only option that can be enabled for a single message and, as described with Figure 16.23, it is controlled by the MSG_DONTROUTE flag during a write.

pr_usrreq is bracketed with splnet and splx to block interrupts while the protocol is processing the message. This is a paranoid assumption since some protocols (such as UDP) may be able to do output processing without blocking interrupts, but this information is not available at the socket layer.

If the process tagged this message as out-of-band data, sosend issues the PRU_SENDOOB request; otherwise it issues the PRU_SEND request. Address and control mbufs are also passed to the protocol at this time.

406–413   clen, control, top, and mp are reset, since control information is passed to the protocol only once and a new mbuf chain is constructed for the next part of the message. resid is nonzero only when atomic is not set (e.g., TCP). In that case, if space remains in the buffer, sosend loops back to fill another mbuf. If there is no more space, sosend loops back to wait for more space (Figure 16.24).

We'll see in Chapter 23 that unreliable protocols, such as UDP, immediately queue the data for transmission on the network. Chapter 26 describes how reliable protocols, such as TCP, add the data to the socket's send buffer where it remains until it is sent to, and acknowledged by, the destination.

sosend Summary

sosend is a complex function. It is 142 lines long, contains three nested loops, one loop implemented with goto, two code paths based on whether PR_ATOMIC is set or not, and two concurrency locks. As with much software, some of the complexity has accumulated over the years. NFS added the MSG_DONTWAIT semantics and the possibility of receiving data from an mbuf chain instead of the buffers in a process. The SS_ISCONFIRMING state and MSG_EOR flag were introduced to handle the connection and record semantics of the OSI protocols.

A cleaner approach would be to implement a separate sosend function for each type of protocol and dispatch through a pr_send pointer in the protosw entry. This idea is suggested and implemented for UDP in [Partridge and Pink 1993].

Performance Considerations

As described in Figure 16.25, sosend, when possible, passes message in mbuf-sized chunks to the protocol layer. While this results in more calls to the protocol than building and passing an entire mbuf chain, [Jacobson 1988a] reports that it improves performance by increasing parallelism.

Transferring one mbuf at a time (up to 2048 bytes) allows the CPU to prepare a packet while the network hardware is transmitting. Contrast this to sending a large mbuf chain: while the chain is being constructed, the network and the receiving system are idle. On the system described in [Jacobson 1988a], this change resulted in a 20% increase in network throughput.

It is important to make sure the send buffer is always larger than the bandwidth-delay product of a connection (Section 20.7 of Volume 1). For example, if TCP discovers that the connection can hold 20 segments before an acknowledgment is received, the send buffer must be large enough to hold the 20 unacknowledged segments. If it is too small, TCP will run out of data to send before the first acknowledgment is returned and the connection will be idle for some period of time.

16.8 `read`, `readv`, `recvfrom`, and `recvmsg` System Calls

These four system calls, which we refer to collectively as *read system calls*, receive data from a network connection. The first three system calls are simpler interfaces to the most general read system call, recvmsg. Figure 16.27 summarizes the features of the four read system calls and one library function (recv).

Function	Type of descriptor	Number of buffers	Return sender's address?	Flags?	Return control information?
read	any	1			
readv	any	[1..UIO_MAXIOV]			
recv	sockets only	1		•	
recvfrom	sockets only	1	•	•	
recvmsg	sockets only	[1..UIO_MAXIOV]	•	•	•

Figure 16.27 Read system calls.

In Net/3, recv is implemented as a library function that calls recvfrom. For binary compatibility with previously compiled programs, the kernel maps the old recv system call to the function orecv. We discuss only the kernel implementation of recvfrom.

The `read` and `readv` system calls are valid with any descriptor, but the remaining calls are valid only with socket descriptors.

As with the write calls, multiple buffers are specified by an array of `iovec` structures. For datagram protocols, `recvfrom` and `recvmsg` return the source address associated with each incoming datagram. For connection-oriented protocols, `getpeername` returns the address associated with the other end of the connection. The flags associated with the receive calls are shown in Section 16.11.

As with the write calls, the receive calls utilize a common function, in this case `soreceive`, to do all the work. Figure 16.28 illustrates the flow of control for the read system calls.

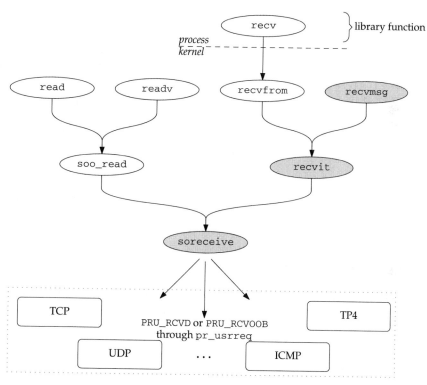

Figure 16.28   All socket input is processed by `soreceive`.

We discuss only the three shaded functions in Figure 16.28. The remaining functions are left for readers to investigate on their own.

16.9   `recvmsg` System Call

The `recvmsg` function is the most general read system call. Addresses, control information, and receive flags may be discarded without notification if a process uses one of the other read system calls while this information is pending. Figure 16.29 shows the `recvmsg` function.

```
                                                                              ── uipc_syscalls.c
433 struct recvmsg_args {
434     int    s;
435     struct msghdr *msg;
436     int    flags;
437 };

438 recvmsg(p, uap, retval)
439 struct proc *p;
440 struct recvmsg_args *uap;
441 int    *retval;
442 {
443     struct msghdr msg;
444     struct iovec aiov[UIO_SMALLIOV], *uiov, *iov;
445     int    error;

446     if (error = copyin((caddr_t) uap->msg, (caddr_t) & msg, sizeof(msg)))
447         return (error);
448     if ((u_int) msg.msg_iovlen >= UIO_SMALLIOV) {
449         if ((u_int) msg.msg_iovlen >= UIO_MAXIOV)
450             return (EMSGSIZE);
451         MALLOC(iov, struct iovec *,
452                 sizeof(struct iovec) * (u_int) msg.msg_iovlen, M_IOV,
453                 M_WAITOK);
454     } else
455         iov = aiov;
456     msg.msg_flags = uap->flags;
457     uiov = msg.msg_iov;
458     msg.msg_iov = iov;
459     if (error = copyin((caddr_t) uiov, (caddr_t) iov,
460                     (unsigned) (msg.msg_iovlen * sizeof(struct iovec))))
461             goto done;
462     if ((error = recvit(p, uap->s, &msg, (caddr_t) 0, retval)) == 0) {
463         msg.msg_iov = uiov;
464         error = copyout((caddr_t) & msg, (caddr_t) uap->msg, sizeof(msg));
465     }
466 done:
467     if (iov != aiov)
468         FREE(iov, M_IOV);
469     return (error);
470 }
                                                                              ── uipc_syscalls.c
```

Figure 16.29 recvmsg system call.

433–445   The three arguments to recvmsg are: the socket descriptor; a pointer to a msghdr structure; and several control flags.

Copy iov array

446–461   As with sendmsg, recvmsg copies the msghdr structure into the kernel, allocates a larger iovec array if the automatic array aiov is too small, and copies the array entries from the process into the kernel array pointed to by iov (Section 16.4). The flags provided as the third argument are copied into the msghdr structure.

recvit and cleanup

462–470   After recvit has received data, the msghdr structure is copied back into the process with the updated buffer lengths and flags. If a larger iovec structure was allocated, it is released before recvmsg returns.

16.10 recvit **Function**

The recvit function shown in Figures 16.30 and 16.31 is called from recv, recvfrom, and recvmsg. It prepares a uio structure for processing by soreceive based on the msghdr structure prepared by the recvxxx calls.

```
                                                                ─── uipc_syscalls.c
471 recvit(p, s, mp, namelenp, retsize)
472 struct proc *p;
473 int      s;
474 struct msghdr *mp;
475 caddr_t namelenp;
476 int     *retsize;
477 {
478     struct file *fp;
479     struct uio auio;
480     struct iovec *iov;
481     int      i;
482     int      len, error;
483     struct mbuf *from = 0, *control = 0;

484     if (error = getsock(p->p_fd, s, &fp))
485         return (error);
486     auio.uio_iov = mp->msg_iov;
487     auio.uio_iovcnt = mp->msg_iovlen;
488     auio.uio_segflg = UIO_USERSPACE;
489     auio.uio_rw = UIO_READ;
490     auio.uio_procp = p;
491     auio.uio_offset = 0;          /* XXX */
492     auio.uio_resid = 0;
493     iov = mp->msg_iov;
494     for (i = 0; i < mp->msg_iovlen; i++, iov++) {
495         if (iov->iov_len < 0)
496             return (EINVAL);
497         if ((auio.uio_resid += iov->iov_len) < 0)
498             return (EINVAL);
499     }
500     len = auio.uio_resid;
                                                                ─── uipc_syscalls.c
```

Figure 16.30   recvit function: initialize uio structure.

471–500   getsock returns the file structure for the descriptor s, and then recvit initializes the uio structure to describe a read transfer from the kernel to the process. The number of bytes to transfer is computed by summing the msg_iovlen members of the iovec array. The total is saved in uio_resid and in len.

The second half of recvit, shown in Figure 16.31, calls soreceive and copies the results back to the process.

—————————————————————————————————— uipc_syscalls.c

```
501     if (error = soreceive((struct socket *) fp->f_data, &from, &auio,
502         (struct mbuf **) 0, mp->msg_control ? &control : (struct mbuf **) 0,
503                         &mp->msg_flags)) {
504         if (auio.uio_resid != len && (error == ERESTART ||
505                             error == EINTR || error == EWOULDBLOCK))
506             error = 0;
507     }
508     if (error)
509         goto out;
510     *retsize = len - auio.uio_resid;
511     if (mp->msg_name) {
512         len = mp->msg_namelen;
513         if (len <= 0 || from == 0)
514             len = 0;
515         else {
516             if (len > from->m_len)
517                 len = from->m_len;
518             /* else if len < from->m_len ??? */
519             if (error = copyout(mtod(from, caddr_t),
520                             (caddr_t) mp->msg_name, (unsigned) len))
521                 goto out;
522         }
523         mp->msg_namelen = len;
524         if (namelenp &&
525             (error = copyout((caddr_t) & len, namelenp, sizeof(int)))) {
526             goto out;
527         }
528     }
529     if (mp->msg_control) {
530         len = mp->msg_controllen;
531         if (len <= 0 || control == 0)
532             len = 0;
533         else {
534             if (len >= control->m_len)
535                 len = control->m_len;
536             else
537                 mp->msg_flags |= MSG_CTRUNC;
538             error = copyout((caddr_t) mtod(control, caddr_t),
539                             (caddr_t) mp->msg_control, (unsigned) len);
540         }
541         mp->msg_controllen = len;
542     }
543 out:
544     if (from)
545         m_freem(from);
546     if (control)
547         m_freem(control);
548     return (error);
549 }
```

—————————————————————————————————— uipc_syscalls.c

Figure 16.31 recvit function: return results.

Call soreceive

501–510   soreceive implements the complex semantics of receiving data from the socket buffers. The number of bytes transferred is saved in *retsize and returned to the process. When an signal arrives or a blocking condition occurs after some data has been copied to the process (len is not equal to uio_resid), the error is discarded and the partial transfer is reported.

Copy address and control information to the process

511–542   If the process provided a buffer for an address or control information or both, the buffers are filled and their lengths adjusted according to what soreceive returned. An address may be truncated if the buffer is too small. This can be detected by the process if it saves the buffer length before the read call and compares it with the value returned by the kernel in the namelenp variable (or in the length field of the sockaddr structure). Truncation of control information is reported by setting MSG_CTRUNC in msg_flags. See also Exercise 16.7.

Cleanup

543–549   At out, the mbufs allocated for the source address and the control information are released.

16.11 soreceive **Function**

This function transfers data from the receive buffer of the socket to the buffers specified by the process. Some protocols provide an address specifying the sender of the data, and this can be returned along with additional control information that may be present. Before examining the code, we need to discuss the semantics of a receive operation, out-of-band data, and the organization of a socket's receive buffer.

Figure 16.32 lists the flags that are recognized by the kernel during soreceive.

flags	Description	Reference
MSG_DONTWAIT	do not wait for resources during this call	Figure 16.38
MSG_OOB	receive out-of-band data instead of regular data	Figure 16.39
MSG_PEEK	receive a copy of the data without consuming it	Figure 16.43
MSG_WAITALL	wait for data to fill buffers before returning	Figure 16.50

Figure 16.32   recv*xxx* system calls: flag values passed to kernel.

recvmsg is the only read system call that returns flags to the process. In the other calls, the information is discarded by the kernel before control returns to the process. Figure 16.33 lists the flags that recvmsg can set in the msghdr structure.

Out-of-Band Data

Out-of-band (OOB) data semantics vary widely among protocols. In general, protocols expedite OOB data along a previously established communication link. The OOB data might not remain in sequence with previously sent regular data. The socket layer

msg_flags	Description	Reference
MSG_CTRUNC	the control information received was larger than the buffer provided	Figure 16.31
MSG_EOR	the data received marks the end of a logical record	Figure 16.48
MSG_OOB	the buffer(s) contains out-of-band data	Figure 16.45
MSG_TRUNC	the message received was larger than the buffer(s) provided	Figure 16.51

Figure 16.33 recvmsg system call: msg_flag values returned by kernel.

supports two mechanisms to facilitate handling OOB data in a protocol-independent way: tagging and synchronization. In this chapter we describe the abstract OOB mechanisms implemented by the socket layer. UDP does not support OOB data. The relationship between TCP's urgent data mechanism and the socket OOB mechanism is described in the TCP chapters.

A sending process tags data as OOB data by setting the MSG_OOB flag in any of the send*xxx* calls. sosend passes this information to the socket's protocol, which provides any special services, such as expediting the data or using an alternate queueing strategy.

When a protocol receives OOB data, the data is set aside instead of placing it in the socket's receive buffer. A process receives the pending OOB data by setting the MSG_OOB flag in one of the recv*xxx* calls. Alternatively, the receiving process can ask the protocol to place OOB data inline with the regular data by setting the SO_OOBINLINE socket option (Section 17.3). When SO_OOBINLINE is set, the protocol places incoming OOB data in the receive buffer with the regular data. In this case, MSG_OOB is not used to receive the OOB data. Read calls return either all regular data or all OOB data. The two types are never mixed in the input buffers of a single input system call. A process that uses recvmsg to receive data can examine the MSG_OOB flag to determine if the returned data is regular data or OOB data that has been placed inline.

The socket layer supports synchronization of OOB and regular data by allowing the protocol layer to mark the point in the regular data stream at which OOB data was received. The receiver can determine when it has reached this mark by using the SIOCATMARK ioctl command after each read system call. When receiving regular data, the socket layer ensures that only the bytes preceding the mark are returned in a single message so that the receiver does not inadvertently pass the mark. If additional OOB data is received before the receiver reaches the mark, the mark is silently advanced.

Example

Figure 16.34 illustrates the two methods of receiving out-of-band data. In both examples, bytes A through I have been received as regular data, byte J as out-of-band data, and bytes K and L as regular data. The receiving process has accepted all data up to but not including byte A.

In the first example, the process can read bytes A through I or, if MSG_OOB is set, byte J. Even if the length of the read request is more than 9 bytes (A–I), the socket layer

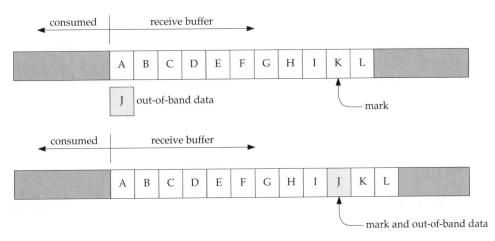

Figure 16.34 Receiving out-of-band data.

returns only 9 bytes to avoid passing the out-of-band synchronization mark. When byte I is consumed, `SIOCATMARK` is true; it is not necessary to consume byte J for the process to reach the out-of-band mark.

In the second example, the process can read only bytes A through I, at which point `SIOCATMARK` is true. A second call can read bytes J through L.

In Figure 16.34, byte J is *not* the byte identified by TCP's urgent pointer. The urgent pointer in this example would point to byte K. See Section 29.7 for details.

Other Receive Options

A process can set the `MSG_PEEK` flag to retrieve data without consuming it. The data remains on the receive queue until a read system call without `MSG_PEEK` is processed.

The `MSG_WAITALL` flag indicates that the call should not return until enough data can be returned to fulfill the entire request. Even if `soreceive` has some data that can be returned to the process, it waits until additional data has been received.

When `MSG_WAITALL` is set, `soreceive` can return without filling the buffer in the following cases:

- the read-half of the connection is closed,
- the socket's receive buffer is smaller than the size of the read,
- an error occurs while the process is waiting for additional data,
- out-of-band data becomes available, or
- the end of a logical record occurs before the read buffer is filled.

> NFS is the only software in Net/3 that uses the `MSG_WAITALL` and `MSG_DONTWAIT` flags. `MSG_DONTWAIT` can be set by a process to issue a nonblocking read system call without selecting nonblocking I/O with `ioctl` or `fcntl`.

Receive Buffer Organization: Message Boundaries

For protocols that support message boundaries, each message is stored in a single chain of mbufs. Multiple messages in the receive buffer are linked together by m_nextpkt to form a queue of mbufs (Figure 2.21). The protocol processing layer adds data to the receive queue and the socket layer removes data from the receive queue. The high-water mark for a receive buffer restricts the amount of data that can be stored in the buffer.

When PR_ATOMIC is not set, the protocol layer stores as much data in the buffer as possible and discards the portion of the incoming data that does not fit. For TCP, this means that any data that arrives and is outside the receive window is discarded. When PR_ATOMIC is set, the entire message must fit within the buffer. If the message does not fit, the protocol layer discards the entire message. For UDP, this means that incoming datagrams are discarded when the receive buffer is full, probably because the process is not reading datagrams fast enough.

Protocols with PR_ADDR set use sbappendaddr to construct an mbuf chain and add it to the receive queue. The chain contains an mbuf with the source address of the message, 0 or more control mbufs, followed by 0 or more mbufs containing the data.

For SOCK_SEQPACKET and SOCK_RDM protocols, the protocol builds an mbuf chain for each record and calls sbappendrecord to append the record to the end of the receive buffer if PR_ATOMIC is set. If PR_ATOMIC is not set (OSI's TP4), a new record is started with sbappendrecord. Additional data is added to the record with sbappend.

> It is not correct to assume that PR_ATOMIC indicates the buffer organization. For example, TP4 does not have PR_ATOMIC set, but supports record boundaries with the M_EOR flag.

Figure 16.35 illustrates the organization of a UDP receive buffer consisting of 3 mbuf chains (i.e., three datagrams). The m_type value for each mbuf is included.

In the figure, the third datagram has some control information associated with it. Three UDP socket options can cause control information to be placed in the receive buffer. See Figure 22.5 and Section 23.7 for details.

For PR_ATOMIC protocols, sb_lowat is ignored while data is being received. When PR_ATOMIC is not set, sb_lowat is the smallest number of bytes returned in a read system call. There are some exceptions to this rule, discussed with Figure 16.41.

Receive Buffer Organization: No Message Boundaries

When the protocol does not maintain message boundaries (i.e., SOCK_STREAM protocols such as TCP), incoming data is appended to the end of the last mbuf chain in the buffer with sbappend. Incoming data is trimmed to fit within the receive buffer, and sb_lowat puts a lower bound on the number of bytes returned by a read system call.

Figure 16.36 illustrates the organization of a TCP receive buffer, which contains only regular data.

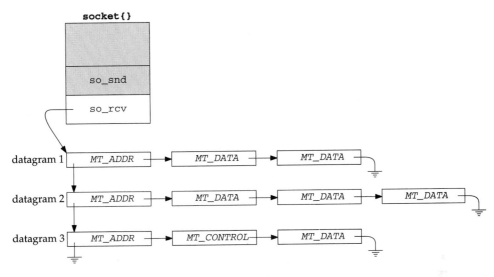

Figure 16.35   UDP receive buffer consisting of three datagrams.

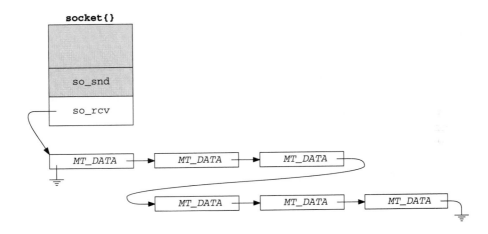

Figure 16.36   so_rcv buffer for TCP.

Control Information and Out-of-band Data

Unlike TCP, some stream protocols support control information and call sbappendcontrol to append the control information and the associated data as a new mbuf chain in the receive buffer. If the protocol supports inline OOB data, sbinsertoob inserts a new mbuf chain just after any mbuf chain that contains OOB data, but before any mbuf chain with regular data. This ensures that incoming OOB data is queued ahead of any regular data.

Figure 16.37 illustrates the organization of a receive buffer that contains control information and OOB data.

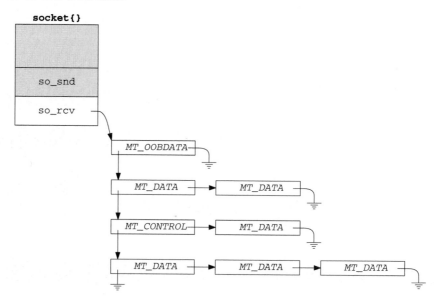

Figure 16.37 so_rcv buffer with control and OOB data.

The Unix domain stream protocol supports control information and the OSI TP4 protocol supports MT_OOBDATA mbufs. TCP does not support control data nor does it support the MT_OOBDATA form of out-of-band data. If the byte identified by TCP's urgent pointer is stored inline (SO_OOBINLINE is set), it appears as regular data, not OOB data. TCP's handling of the urgent pointer and the associated byte is described in Section 29.7.

16.12 soreceive Code

We now have enough background information to discuss soreceive in detail. While receiving data, soreceive must respect message boundaries, handle addresses and control information, and handle any special semantics identified by the read flags (Figure 16.32). The general rule is that soreceive processes one record per call and tries to return the number of bytes requested. Figure 16.38 shows an overview of the function.

439–446   soreceive has six arguments. so is a pointer to the socket. A pointer to an mbuf to receive address information is returned in *paddr. If mp0 points to an mbuf pointer, soreceive transfers the receive buffer data to an mbuf chain pointed to by *mp0. In this case, the uio structure is used only for the count in uio_resid. If mp0 is null, soreceive copies the data into buffers described by the uio structure. A pointer to the mbuf containing control information is returned in *controlp, and soreceive returns the flags described in Figure 16.33 in *flagsp.

447–453 `soreceive` starts by setting `pr` to point to the socket's protocol switch structure and saving `uio_resid` (the size of the receive request) in `orig_resid`. If control information or addressing information is copied from the kernel to the process, `orig_resid` is set to 0. If data is copied, `uio_resid` is updated. In either case, `orig_resid` will not equal `uio_resid`. This fact is used at the end of `soreceive` (Figure 16.51).

454–461 `*paddr` and `*controlp` are cleared. The flags passed to `soreceive` in `*flagsp` are saved in `flags` after the `MSG_EOR` flag is cleared (Exercise 16.8). `flagsp` is a value–result argument, but only the `recvmsg` system call can receive the result flags. If `flagsp` is null, `flags` is set to 0.

483–487 Before accessing the receive buffer, `sblock` locks the buffer. `soreceive` waits for the lock unless `MSG_DONTWAIT` is set in `flags`.

    This is another side effect of supporting calls to the socket layer from NFS within the kernel.

  Protocol processing is suspended, so `soreceive` is not interrupted while it examines the buffer. `m` is the first mbuf on the first chain in the receive buffer.

If necessary, wait for data

488–541 `soreceive` checks several conditions and if necessary waits for more data to arrive in the buffer before continuing. If `soreceive` sleeps in this code, it jumps back to `restart` when it wakes up to see if enough data has arrived. This continues until the request can be satisfied.

542–545 `soreceive` jumps to `dontblock` when it has enough data to satisfy the request. A pointer to the second chain in the receive buffer is saved in `nextrecord`.

Process address and control information

546–590 Address information and control information are processed before any other data is transferred from the receive buffer.

Setup data transfer

591–597 Since only OOB data or regular data is transferred in a single call to `soreceive`, this code remembers the type of data at the front of the queue so `soreceive` can stop the transfer when the type changes.

Mbuf data transfer loop

598–692 This loop continues as long as there are mbufs in the buffer (`m` is not null), the requested number of bytes has not been transferred (`uio_resid` > 0), and no error has occurred.

Cleanup

693–719 The remaining code updates various pointers, flags, and offsets; releases the socket buffer lock; enables protocol processing; and returns.

```
                                                                    — uipc_socket.c
439 soreceive(so, paddr, uio, mp0, controlp, flagsp)
440 struct socket *so;
441 struct mbuf **paddr;
442 struct uio *uio;
443 struct mbuf **mp0;
444 struct mbuf **controlp;
445 int     *flagsp;
446 {
447     struct mbuf *m, **mp;
448     int     flags, len, error, s, offset;
449     struct protosw *pr = so->so_proto;
450     struct mbuf *nextrecord;
451     int     moff, type;
452     int     orig_resid = uio->uio_resid;

453     mp = mp0;
454     if (paddr)
455         *paddr = 0;
456     if (controlp)
457         *controlp = 0;
458     if (flagsp)
459         flags = *flagsp & ~MSG_EOR;
460     else
461         flags = 0;
```

```
                        /* MSG_OOB processing and */
                  /* implicit connection confirmation */
```

```
483   restart:
484     if (error = sblock(&so->so_rcv, SBLOCKWAIT(flags)))
485         return (error);
486     s = splnet();
487     m = so->so_rcv.sb_mb;
```

```
                  /* if necessary, wait for data to arrive */
```

```
542   dontblock:
543     if (uio->uio_procp)
544         uio->uio_procp->p_stats->p_ru.ru_msgrcv++;
545     nextrecord = m->m_nextpkt;
```

```
                  /* process address and control information */
```

```
591     if (m) {
592         if ((flags & MSG_PEEK) == 0)
593             m->m_nextpkt = nextrecord;
594         type = m->m_type;
595         if (type == MT_OOBDATA)
596             flags |= MSG_OOB;
597     }
```

```
                              /* process data */


693      }                                         /* while more data and more space to fill */

                              /* cleanup */

715      release:
716          sbunlock(&so->so_rcv);
717          splx(s);
718          return (error);
719      }
```
———— uipc_socket.c

Figure 16.38 soreceive function: overview.

In Figure 16.39, soreceive handles requests for OOB data.

———— uipc_socket.c
```
462      if (flags & MSG_OOB) {
463          m = m_get(M_WAIT, MT_DATA);
464          error = (*pr->pr_usrreq)(so, PRU_RCVOOB,
465                  m, (struct mbuf *) (flags & MSG_PEEK), (struct mbuf *) 0);
466          if (error)
467              goto bad;
468          do {
469              error = uiomove(mtod(m, caddr_t),
470                          (int) min(uio->uio_resid, m->m_len), uio);
471              m = m_free(m);
472          } while (uio->uio_resid && error == 0 && m);
473      bad:
474          if (m)
475              m_freem(m);
476          return (error);
477      }
```
———— uipc_socket.c

Figure 16.39 soreceive function: out-of-band data.

Receive OOB data

462–477   Since OOB data is not stored in the receive buffer, soreceive allocates a standard mbuf and issues the PRU_RCVOOB request to the protocol. The while loop copies any data returned by the protocol to the buffers specified by uio. After the copy, soreceive returns 0 or the error code.

UDP always returns EOPNOTSUPP for the PRU_RCVOOB request. See Section 30.2 for details regarding TCP urgent processing. In Figure 16.40, soreceive handles connection confirmation.

——— *uipc_socket.c*
```
478        if (mp)
479            *mp = (struct mbuf *) 0;
480        if (so->so_state & SS_ISCONFIRMING && uio->uio_resid)
481            (*pr->pr_usrreq) (so, PRU_RCVD, (struct mbuf *) 0,
482                             (struct mbuf *) 0, (struct mbuf *) 0);
```
——— *uipc_socket.c*

Figure 16.40 `soreceive` function: connection confirmation.

Connection confirmation

478–482   If the data is to be returned in an mbuf chain, `*mp` is initialized to null. If the socket is in the `SO_ISCONFIRMING` state, the `PRU_RCVD` request notifies the protocol that the process is attempting to receive data.

> The `SO_ISCONFIRMING` state is used only by the OSI stream protocol, TP4. In TP4, a connection is not considered complete until a user-level process has confirmed the connection by attempting to send or receive data. The process can reject a connection by calling `shutdown` or `close`, perhaps after calling `getpeername` to determine where the connection came from.

Figure 16.38 showed that the receive buffer is locked before it is examined by the code in Figure 16.41. This part of `soreceive` determines if the read system call can be satisfied by the data that is already in the receive buffer.

——— *uipc_socket.c*
```
488        /*
489         * If we have less data than requested, block awaiting more
490         * (subject to any timeout) if:
491         *   1. the current count is less than the low water mark, or
492         *   2. MSG_WAITALL is set, and it is possible to do the entire
493         *   receive operation at once if we block (resid <= hiwat).
494         *   3. MSG_DONTWAIT is not set
495         *
496         * If MSG_WAITALL is set but resid is larger than the receive buffer,
497         * we have to do the receive in sections, and thus risk returning
498         * a short count if a timeout or signal occurs after we start.
499         */
500        if (m == 0 || ((flags & MSG_DONTWAIT) == 0 &&
501                       so->so_rcv.sb_cc < uio->uio_resid) &&
502            (so->so_rcv.sb_cc < so->so_rcv.sb_lowat ||
503            ((flags & MSG_WAITALL) && uio->uio_resid <= so->so_rcv.sb_hiwat)) &&
504            m->m_nextpkt == 0 && (pr->pr_flags & PR_ATOMIC) == 0) {
```
——— *uipc_socket.c*

Figure 16.41 `soreceive` function: enough data?

Can the call be satisfied now?

488–504   The general rule for `soreceive` is that it waits until enough data is in the receive buffer to satisfy the entire read. There are several conditions that cause an error or less data than was requested to be returned.

If any of the following conditions are true, the process is put to sleep to wait for more data to arrive so the call can be satisfied:

- There is no data in the receive buffer (m equals 0).

- There is not enough data to satisfy the entire read (sb_cc < uio_resid and MSG_DONTWAIT is not set), the minimum amount of data is *not* available (sb_cc < sb_lowat), and more data can be appended to this chain when it arrives (m_nextpkt is 0 and PR_ATOMIC is *not* set).

- There is not enough data to satisfy the entire read, a minimum amount of data *is* available, data can be added to this chain, but MSG_WAITALL indicates that soreceive should wait until the entire read can be satisfied.

If the conditions in the last case are met but the read is too large to be satisfied without blocking (uio_resid > sb_hiwat), soreceive continues without waiting for more data.

If there is some data in the buffer and MSG_DONTWAIT is set, soreceive does not wait for more data.

There are several reasons why waiting for more data may not be appropriate. In Figure 16.42, soreceive checks for these conditions and returns, or waits for more data to arrive.

Wait for more data?

505–534   At this point, soreceive has determined that it must wait for additional data to arrive before the read can be satisfied. Before waiting it checks for several additional conditions:

505–512 - If the socket is in an error state and *empty* (m is null), soreceive returns the error code. If there is an error and the receive buffer also contains data (m is nonnull), the data is returned and a subsequent read returns the error when there is no more data. If MSG_PEEK is set, the error is not cleared, since a read system call with MSG_PEEK set should not change the state of the socket.

513–518 - If the read-half of the connection has been closed and data remains in the receive buffer, sosend does not wait and returns the data to the process (at dontblock). If the receive buffer is empty, soreceive jumps to release and the read system call returns 0, which indicates that the read-half of the connection is closed.

519–523 - If the receive buffer contains out-of-band data or the end of a logical record, soreceive does not wait for additional data and jumps to dontblock.

524–528 - If the protocol requires a connection and it does not exist, ENOTCONN is posted and the function jumps to release.

529–534 - If the read is for 0 bytes or nonblocking semantics have been selected, the function jumps to release and returns 0 or EWOULDBLOCK, respectively.

Yes, wait for more data

535–541   soreceive has now determined that it must wait for more data, and that it is reasonable to do so (i.e., some data will arrive). The receive buffer is unlocked while the process sleeps in sbwait. If sbwait returns because of an error or a signal,

```
                                                              ———— uipc_socket.c
505        if (so->so_error) {
506            if (m)
507                goto dontblock;
508            error = so->so_error;
509            if ((flags & MSG_PEEK) == 0)
510                so->so_error = 0;
511            goto release;
512        }
513        if (so->so_state & SS_CANTRCVMORE) {
514            if (m)
515                goto dontblock;
516            else
517                goto release;
518        }
519        for (; m; m = m->m_next)
520            if (m->m_type == MT_OOBDATA || (m->m_flags & M_EOR)) {
521                m = so->so_rcv.sb_mb;
522                goto dontblock;
523            }
524        if ((so->so_state & (SS_ISCONNECTED | SS_ISCONNECTING)) == 0 &&
525            (so->so_proto->pr_flags & PR_CONNREQUIRED)) {
526            error = ENOTCONN;
527            goto release;
528        }
529        if (uio->uio_resid == 0)
530            goto release;
531        if ((so->so_state & SS_NBIO) || (flags & MSG_DONTWAIT)) {
532            error = EWOULDBLOCK;
533            goto release;
534        }
535        sbunlock(&so->so_rcv);
536        error = sbwait(&so->so_rcv);
537        splx(s);
538        if (error)
539            return (error);
540        goto restart;
541    }
                                                              ———— uipc_socket.c
```

Figure 16.42   soreceive function: wait for more data?

soreceive returns the error; otherwise the function jumps to restart to determine if the read can be satisfied now that more data has arrived.

As in sosend, a process can enable a receive timer for sbwait with the SO_RCVTIMEO socket option. If the timer expires before any data arrives, sbwait returns EWOULDBLOCK.

> The effect of this timer is not what one would expect. Since the timer gets reset every time there is activity on the socket buffer, the timer never expires if at least 1 byte arrives within the timeout interval. This can delay the return of the read system call for more than the value of the timer. sb_timeo is an inactivity timer and does not put an upper bound on the amount of time that may be required to satisfy the read system call.

At this point, soreceive is prepared to transfer some data from the receive buffer. Figure 16.43 shows the transfer of any address information.

uipc_socket.c

```
542    dontblock:
543       if (uio->uio_procp)
544           uio->uio_procp->p_stats->p_ru.ru_msgrcv++;
545       nextrecord = m->m_nextpkt;
546       if (pr->pr_flags & PR_ADDR) {
547           orig_resid = 0;
548           if (flags & MSG_PEEK) {
549               if (paddr)
550                   *paddr = m_copy(m, 0, m->m_len);
551               m = m->m_next;
552           } else {
553               sbfree(&so->so_rcv, m);
554               if (paddr) {
555                   *paddr = m;
556                   so->so_rcv.sb_mb = m->m_next;
557                   m->m_next = 0;
558                   m = so->so_rcv.sb_mb;
559               } else {
560                   MFREE(m, so->so_rcv.sb_mb);
561                   m = so->so_rcv.sb_mb;
562               }
563           }
564       }
```

uipc_socket.c

Figure 16.43   soreceive function: return address information.

dontblock

542–545   nextrecord maintains a reference to the next record that appears in the receive buffer. This is used at the end of soreceive to attach the remaining mbufs to the socket buffer after the first chain has been discarded.

Return address information

546–564   If the protocol provides addresses, such as UDP, the mbuf containing the address is removed from the mbuf chain and returned in *paddr. If paddr is null, the address is discarded.

Throughout soreceive, if MSG_PEEK is set, the data is not removed from the buffer.

The code in Figure 16.44 processes any control mbufs that are in the buffer.

Return control information

565–590   Each control mbuf is removed from the buffer (or copied if MSG_PEEK is set) and attached to *controlp. If controlp is null, the control information is discarded.

If the process is prepared to receive control information, the protocol has a dom_externalize function defined, and if the control mbuf contains a SCM_RIGHTS (access rights) message, the dom_externalize function is called. This function takes any kernel action associated with receiving the access rights. Only the Unix protocol

```
                                                                        — uipc_socket.c
565        while (m && m->m_type == MT_CONTROL && error == 0) {
566            if (flags & MSG_PEEK) {
567                if (controlp)
568                    *controlp = m_copy(m, 0, m->m_len);
569                m = m->m_next;
570            } else {
571                sbfree(&so->so_rcv, m);
572                if (controlp) {
573                    if (pr->pr_domain->dom_externalize &&
574                        mtod(m, struct cmsghdr *)->cmsg_type ==
575                        SCM_RIGHTS)
576                            error = (*pr->pr_domain->dom_externalize) (m);
577                    *controlp = m;
578                    so->so_rcv.sb_mb = m->m_next;
579                    m->m_next = 0;
580                    m = so->so_rcv.sb_mb;
581                } else {
582                    MFREE(m, so->so_rcv.sb_mb);
583                    m = so->so_rcv.sb_mb;
584                }
585            }
586            if (controlp) {
587                orig_resid = 0;
588                controlp = &(*controlp)->m_next;
589            }
590        }
```
                                                                        — uipc_socket.c

Figure 16.44   soreceive function: control information.

domain supports access rights, as discussed in Section 7.3. If the process is not prepared
to receive control information (controlp is null) the mbuf is discarded.

The loop continues while there are more mbufs with control information and no
error has occurred.

> For the Unix protocol domain, the dom_externalize function implements the semantics of
> passing file descriptors by modifying the file descriptor table of the receiving process.

After the control mbufs are processed, m points to the next mbuf on the chain. If the
chain does not contain any mbufs after the address, or after the control information, m is
null. This occurs, for example, when a 0-length UDP datagram is queued in the receive
buffer. In Figure 16.45 soreceive prepares to transfer the data from the mbuf chain.

Prepare to transfer data

591–597   After the control mbufs have been processed, the chain should contain regular, out-
of-band data mbufs or no mbufs at all. If m is null, soreceive is finished with this
chain and control drops to the bottom of the while loop. If m is not null, any remaining
chains (nextrecord) are reattached to m and the type of the next mbuf is saved in
type. If the next mbuf contains OOB data, MSG_OOB is set in flags, which is later

```
                                                              ─── uipc_socket.c
591    if (m) {
592        if ((flags & MSG_PEEK) == 0)
593            m->m_nextpkt = nextrecord;
594        type = m->m_type;
595        if (type == MT_OOBDATA)
596            flags |= MSG_OOB;
597    }
                                                              ─── uipc_socket.c
```

Figure 16.45 soreceive function: mbuf transfer setup.

returned to the process. Since TCP does not support the MT_OOBDATA form of out-of-band data, MSG_OOB will never be returned for reads on TCP sockets.

Figure 16.47 shows the first part of the mbuf transfer loop. Figure 16.46 lists the variables updated within the loop.

Variable	Description
moff	the offset of the next byte to transfer when MSG_PEEK is set
offset	the offset of the OOB mark when MSG_PEEK is set
uio_resid	the number of bytes remaining to be transferred
len	the number of bytes to be transferred from this mbuf; may be less than m_len if uio_resid is small, or if the OOB mark is near

Figure 16.46 soreceive function: loop variables.

598–600   During each iteration of the while loop, the data in a single mbuf is transferred to the output chain or to the uio buffers. The loop continues while there are more mbufs, the process's buffers are not full, and no error has occurred.

Check for transition between OOB and regular data

600–605   If, while processing the mbuf chain, the type of the mbuf changes, the transfer stops. This ensures that regular and out-of-band data are not both returned in the same message. This check does not apply to TCP.

Update OOB mark

606–611   The distance to the oobmark is computed and limits the size of the transfer, so the byte before the mark is the last byte transferred. The size of the transfer is also limited by the size of the mbuf. This code does apply to TCP.

612–625   If the data is being returned to the uio buffers, uiomove is called. If the data is being returned as an mbuf chain, uio_resid is adjusted to reflect the number of bytes moved.

To avoid suspending protocol processing for a long time, protocol processing is enabled during the call to uiomove. Additional data may appear in the receive buffer because of protocol processing while uiomove is running.

The code in Figure 16.48 adjusts all the pointers and offsets to prepare for the next mbuf.

```
                                                                  ————— uipc_socket.c
598    moff = 0;
599    offset = 0;
600    while (m && uio->uio_resid > 0 && error == 0) {
601        if (m->m_type == MT_OOBDATA) {
602            if (type != MT_OOBDATA)
603                break;
604        } else if (type == MT_OOBDATA)
605            break;
606        so->so_state &= ~SS_RCVATMARK;
607        len = uio->uio_resid;
608        if (so->so_oobmark && len > so->so_oobmark - offset)
609            len = so->so_oobmark - offset;
610        if (len > m->m_len - moff)
611            len = m->m_len - moff;
612        /*
613         * If mp is set, just pass back the mbufs.
614         * Otherwise copy them out via the uio, then free.
615         * Sockbuf must be consistent here (points to current mbuf,
616         * it points to next record) when we drop priority;
617         * we must note any additions to the sockbuf when we
618         * block interrupts again.
619         */
620        if (mp == 0) {
621            splx(s);
622            error = uiomove(mtod(m, caddr_t) + moff, (int) len, uio);
623            s = splnet();
624        } else
625            uio->uio_resid -= len;
                                                                  ————— uipc_socket.c
```

Figure 16.47   soreceive function: uiomove.

Finished with mbuf?

626–646   If all the bytes in the mbuf have been transferred, the mbuf must be discarded or the pointers advanced. If the mbuf contained the end of a logical record, MSG_EOR is set. If MSG_PEEK is set, soreceive skips to the next buffer. If MSG_PEEK is not set, the buffer is discarded if the data was copied by uiomove, or appended to mp if the data is being returned in an mbuf chain.

More data to process

647–657   There may be more data to process in the mbuf if the request didn't consume all the data, if so_oobmark cut the request short, or if additional data arrived during uiomove. If MSG_PEEK is set, moff is updated. If the data is to be returned on an mbuf chain, len bytes are copied and attached to the chain. The mbuf pointers and the receive buffer byte count are updated by the amount of data that was transferred.

Figure 16.49 contains the code that handles the OOB offset and the MSG_EOR processing.

```
626              if (len == m->m_len - moff) {
627                  if (m->m_flags & M_EOR)
628                      flags |= MSG_EOR;
629                  if (flags & MSG_PEEK) {
630                      m = m->m_next;
631                      moff = 0;
632                  } else {
633                      nextrecord = m->m_nextpkt;
634                      sbfree(&so->so_rcv, m);
635                      if (mp) {
636                          *mp = m;
637                          mp = &m->m_next;
638                          so->so_rcv.sb_mb = m = m->m_next;
639                          *mp = (struct mbuf *) 0;
640                      } else {
641                          MFREE(m, so->so_rcv.sb_mb);
642                          m = so->so_rcv.sb_mb;
643                      }
644                      if (m)
645                          m->m_nextpkt = nextrecord;
646                  }
647              } else {
648                  if (flags & MSG_PEEK)
649                      moff += len;
650                  else {
651                      if (mp)
652                          *mp = m_copym(m, 0, len, M_WAIT);
653                      m->m_data += len;
654                      m->m_len -= len;
655                      so->so_rcv.sb_cc -= len;
656                  }
657              }
```
uipc_socket.c

Figure 16.48 soreceive function: update buffer.

```
658          if (so->so_oobmark) {
659              if ((flags & MSG_PEEK) == 0) {
660                  so->so_oobmark -= len;
661                  if (so->so_oobmark == 0) {
662                      so->so_state |= SS_RCVATMARK;
663                      break;
664                  }
665              } else {
666                  offset += len;
667                  if (offset == so->so_oobmark)
668                      break;
669              }
670          }
671          if (flags & MSG_EOR)
672              break;
```
uipc_socket.c

Figure 16.49 soreceive function: out-of-band data mark.

Update OOB mark

658–670   If the out-of-band mark is nonzero, it is decremented by the number of bytes transferred. If the mark has been reached, SS_RCVATMARK is set and soreceive breaks out of the while loop. If MSG_PEEK is set, offset is updated instead of so_oobmark.

End of logical record

671–672   If the end of a logical record has been reached, soreceive breaks out of the mbuf processing loop so data from the next logical record is not returned with this message.

The loop in Figure 16.50 waits for more data to arrive when MSG_WAITALL is set and the request is not complete.

```
                                                                            uipc_socket.c
673              /*
674               * If the MSG_WAITALL flag is set (for non-atomic socket),
675               * we must not quit until "uio->uio_resid == 0" or an error
676               * termination.  If a signal/timeout occurs, return
677               * with a short count but without error.
678               * Keep sockbuf locked against other readers.
679               */
680              while (flags & MSG_WAITALL && m == 0 && uio->uio_resid > 0 &&
681                      !sosendallatonce(so) && !nextrecord) {
682                  if (so->so_error || so->so_state & SS_CANTRCVMORE)
683                      break;
684                  error = sbwait(&so->so_rcv);
685                  if (error) {
686                      sbunlock(&so->so_rcv);
687                      splx(s);
688                      return (0);
689                  }
690                  if (m = so->so_rcv.sb_mb)
691                      nextrecord = m->m_nextpkt;
692              }
693      }                                   /* while more data and more space to fill */
                                                                            uipc_socket.c
```

Figure 16.50   soreceive function: MSG_WAITALL processing.

MSG_WAITALL

673–681   If MSG_WAITALL is set, there is no more data in the receive buffer (m equals 0), the caller wants more data, sosendallatonce is false, and this is the last record in the receive buffer (nextrecord is null), then soreceive must wait for additional data.

Error or no more data will arrive

682–683   If an error is pending or the connection is closed, the loop is terminated.

Wait for data to arrive

684–689   sbwait returns when the receive buffer is changed by the protocol layer. If the wait was interrupted by a signal (error is nonzero), sosend returns immediately.

Synchronize m and nextrecord with receive buffer

690–692   m and nextrecord are updated, since the receive buffer has been modified by the protocol layer. If data arrived in the mbuf, m will be nonzero and the while loop terminates.

Process next mbuf

693   This is the end of the mbuf processing loop. Control returns to the loop starting on line 600 (Figure 16.47). As long as there is data in the receive buffer, more space to fill, and no error has occurred, the loop continues.

When soreceive stops copying data, the code in Figure 16.51 is executed.

```
                                                                   uipc_socket.c
694    if (m && pr->pr_flags & PR_ATOMIC) {
695        flags |= MSG_TRUNC;
696        if ((flags & MSG_PEEK) == 0)
697            (void) sbdroprecord(&so->so_rcv);
698    }
699    if ((flags & MSG_PEEK) == 0) {
700        if (m == 0)
701            so->so_rcv.sb_mb = nextrecord;
702        if (pr->pr_flags & PR_WANTRCVD && so->so_pcb)
703            (*pr->pr_usrreq) (so, PRU_RCVD, (struct mbuf *) 0,
704                             (struct mbuf *) flags, (struct mbuf *) 0,
705                             (struct mbuf *) 0);
706    }
707    if (orig_resid == uio->uio_resid && orig_resid &&
708        (flags & MSG_EOR) == 0 && (so->so_state & SS_CANTRCVMORE) == 0) {
709        sbunlock(&so->so_rcv);
710        splx(s);
711        goto restart;
712    }
713    if (flagsp)
714        *flagsp |= flags;
                                                                   uipc_socket.c
```

Figure 16.51 soreceive function: cleanup.

Truncated message

694–698   If the process received a partial message (a datagram or a record) because its receive buffer was too small, the process is notified by setting MSG_TRUNC and the remainder of the message is discarded. MSG_TRUNC (as with all receive flags) is available only to a process through the recvmsg system call, even though soreceive always sets the flags.

End of record processing

699–706   If MSG_PEEK is not set, the next mbuf chain is attached to the receive buffer and, if required, the protocol is notified that the receive operation has been completed by issuing the PRU_RCVD protocol request. TCP uses this feature to update the receive window for the connection.

Nothing transferred

707–712   If soreceive runs to completion, no data is transferred, the end of a record is not reached, and the read-half of the connection is still active, then the buffer is unlocked and soreceive jumps back to restart to continue waiting for data.

713–714   Any flags set during soreceive are returned in *flagsp, the buffer is unlocked, and soreceive returns.

Analysis

soreceive is a complex function. Much of the complication is because of the intricate manipulation of pointers and the multiple types of data (out-of-band, address, control, regular) and multiple destinations (process buffers, mbuf chain).

Similar to sosend, soreceive has collected features over the years. A specialized receive function for each protocol would blur the boundary between the socket layer and the protocol layer, but it would simplify the code considerably.

[Partridge and Pink 1993] describe the creation of a custom soreceive function for UDP to checksum datagrams while they are copied from the receive buffer to the process. They note that modifying the generic soreceive function to support this feature would "make the already complicated socket routines even more complex."

16.13 select System Call

In the following discussion we assume that the reader is familiar with the basic operation and semantics of select. For a detailed discussion of the application interface to select see [Stevens 1992].

Figure 16.52 shows the conditions detected by using select to monitor a socket.

Description	Detected by selecting for:		
	reading	writing	exceptions
data available for reading	•		
read-half of connection is closed	•		
listen socket has queued connection	•		
socket error is pending	•		
space available for writing and a connection exists or is not required		•	
write-half of connection is closed		•	
socket error is pending		•	
OOB synchronization mark is pending			•

Figure 16.52   select system call: socket events.

We start with the first half of the select system call, shown in Figure 16.53.

Validation and setup

390–410　Two arrays of three descriptor sets are allocated on the stack: `ibits` and `obits`. They are cleared by `bzero`. The first argument, `nd`, must be no larger than the maximum number of descriptors associated with the process. If `nd` is more than the number of descriptors currently allocated to the process, it is reduced to the current allocation. `ni` is set to the number of bytes needed to store a bit mask with `nd` bits (1 bit for each descriptor). For example, if the maximum number of descriptors is 256 (`FD_SETSIZE`), `fd_set` is represented as an array of 32-bit integers (`NFDBITS`), and `nd` is 65, then:

$$ni = \text{howmany}(65, 32) \times 4 = 3 \times 4 = 12$$

where `howmany(x,y)` returns the number of y-bit objects required to store x bits.

Copy file descriptor sets from process

411–418　The `getbits` macro uses `copyin` to transfer the file descriptor sets from the process to the three descriptor sets in `ibits`. If a descriptor set pointer is null, nothing is copied from the process.

Setup timeout value

419–438　If `tv` is null, `timo` is set to 0 and `select` will wait indefinitely. If `tv` is not null, the timeout value is copied into the kernel and rounded up to the resolution of the hardware clock by `itimerfix`. The current time is added to the timeout value by `timevaladd`. The number of clock ticks until the timeout is computed by `hzto` and saved in `timo`. If the resulting timeout is 0, `timo` is set to 1. This prevents `select` from blocking and implements the nonblocking semantics of an all-0s `timeval` structure.

The second half of `select`, shown in Figure 16.54, scans the file descriptors indicated by the process and returns when one or more become ready, or the timer expires, or a signal occurs.

Scan file descriptors

439–442　The loop that starts at `retry` continues until `select` can return. The current value of the global integer `nselcoll` is saved and the `P_SELECT` flag is set in the calling process's control block. If either of these change while `selscan` (Figure 16.55) is checking the file descriptors, it indicates that the status of a descriptor has changed because of interrupt processing and `select` must rescan the descriptors. `selscan` looks at every descriptor set in the three input descriptor sets and sets the matching descriptor in the output set if the descriptor is ready.

Error or some descriptors are ready

443–444　Return immediately if an error occurred or if a descriptor is ready.

Timeout expired?

445–451　If the process supplied a time limit and the current time has advanced beyond the timeout value, return immediately.

—— sys_generic.c

```
390 struct select_args {
391     u_int   nd;
392     fd_set  *in, *ou, *ex;
393     struct timeval *tv;
394 };
395 select(p, uap, retval)
396 struct proc *p;
397 struct select_args *uap;
398 int     *retval;
399 {
400     fd_set  ibits[3], obits[3];
401     struct timeval atv;
402     int     s, ncoll, error = 0, timo;
403     u_int   ni;
404     bzero((caddr_t) ibits, sizeof(ibits));
405     bzero((caddr_t) obits, sizeof(obits));
406     if (uap->nd > FD_SETSIZE)
407         return (EINVAL);
408     if (uap->nd > p->p_fd->fd_nfiles)
409         uap->nd = p->p_fd->fd_nfiles;   /* forgiving; slightly wrong */
410     ni = howmany(uap->nd, NFDBITS) * sizeof(fd_mask);
411 #define getbits(name, x) \
412     if (uap->name && \
413         (error = copyin((caddr_t)uap->name, (caddr_t)&ibits[x], ni))) \
414         goto done;
415     getbits(in, 0);
416     getbits(ou, 1);
417     getbits(ex, 2);
418 #undef  getbits
419     if (uap->tv) {
420         error = copyin((caddr_t) uap->tv, (caddr_t) & atv,
421                         sizeof(atv));
422         if (error)
423             goto done;
424         if (itimerfix(&atv)) {
425             error = EINVAL;
426             goto done;
427         }
428         s = splclock();
429         timevaladd(&atv, (struct timeval *) &time);
430         timo = hzto(&atv);
431         /*
432          * Avoid inadvertently sleeping forever.
433          */
434         if (timo == 0)
435             timo = 1;
436         splx(s);
437     } else
438         timo = 0;
```

—— sys_generic.c

Figure 16.53 select function: initialization.

———————————————————————————————————— sys_generic.c
```
439   retry:
440       ncoll = nselcoll;
441       p->p_flag |= P_SELECT;
442       error = selscan(p, ibits, obits, uap->nd, retval);
443       if (error || *retval)
444           goto done;
445       s = splhigh();
446       /* this should be timercmp(&time, &atv, >=) */
447       if (uap->tv && (time.tv_sec > atv.tv_sec ||
448               time.tv_sec == atv.tv_sec && time.tv_usec >= atv.tv_usec)) {
449           splx(s);
450           goto done;
451       }
452       if ((p->p_flag & P_SELECT) == 0 || nselcoll != ncoll) {
453           splx(s);
454           goto retry;
455       }
456       p->p_flag &= ~P_SELECT;
457       error = tsleep((caddr_t) & selwait, PSOCK | PCATCH, "select", timo);
458       splx(s);
459       if (error == 0)
460           goto retry;
461   done:
462       p->p_flag &= ~P_SELECT;
463       /* select is not restarted after signals... */
464       if (error == ERESTART)
465           error = EINTR;
466       if (error == EWOULDBLOCK)
467           error = 0;
468   #define putbits(name, x) \
469       if (uap->name && \
470           (error2 = copyout((caddr_t)&obits[x], (caddr_t)uap->name, ni))) \
471           error = error2;
472       if (error == 0) {
473           int     error2;

474           putbits(in, 0);
475           putbits(ou, 1);
476           putbits(ex, 2);
477   #undef putbits
478       }
479       return (error);
480   }
```
———————————————————————————————————— sys_generic.c

Figure 16.54   select function: second half.

Status changed during `selscan`

452–455   `selscan` can be interrupted by protocol processing. If the socket is modified during the interrupt, `P_SELECT` and `nselcoll` are changed and `select` must rescan the descriptors.

Wait for buffer changes

456–460   All processes calling `select` use `selwait` as the wait channel when they call `tsleep`. With Figure 16.60 we show that this causes some inefficiencies if more than one process is waiting for the same socket buffer. If `tsleep` returns without an error, `select` jumps to `retry` to rescan the descriptors.

Ready to return

461–480   At `done`, `P_SELECT` is cleared, `ERESTART` is changed to `EINTR`, and `EWOULDBLOCK` is changed to 0. These changes ensure that `EINTR` is returned when a signal occurs during `select` and 0 is returned when a timeout occurs.

The output descriptor sets are copied back to the process and `select` returns.

`selscan` Function

The heart of `select` is the `selscan` function shown in Figure 16.55. For every bit set in one of the three descriptor sets, `selscan` computes the descriptor associated with the bit and dispatches control to the `fo_select` function associated with the descriptor. For sockets, this is the `soo_select` function.

Locate descriptors to be monitored

481–496   The first `for` loop iterates through each of the three descriptor sets: read, write, and exception. The second `for` loop interates within each descriptor set. This loop is executed once for every 32 bits (`NFDBITS`) in the set.

The inner `while` loop checks all the descriptors identified by the 32-bit mask extracted from the current descriptor set and stored in `bits`. The function `ffs` returns the position within `bits` of the first 1 bit, starting at the low-order bit. For example, if `bits` is `1000` (with 28 leading 0s), `ffs(bits)` is 4.

Poll descriptor

497–500   From `i` and the return value of `ffs`, the descriptor associated with the bit is computed and stored in `fd`. The bit is cleared in `bits` (but not in the input descriptor set), the `file` structure associated with the descriptor is located, and `fo_select` is called.

The second argument to `fo_select` is one of the elements in the `flag` array. `msk` is the index of the outer `for` loop. So the first time through the loop, the second argument is `FREAD`, the second time it is `FWRITE`, and the third time it is 0. `EBADF` is returned if the descriptor is not valid.

Descriptor is ready

501–504   When a descriptor is found to be ready, the matching bit is set in the output descriptor set and `n` (the number of matches) is incremented.

505–510   The loops continue until all the descriptors are polled. The number of ready descriptors is returned in `*retval`.

sys_generic.c

```
481 selscan(p, ibits, obits, nfd, retval)
482 struct proc *p;
483 fd_set *ibits, *obits;
484 int     nfd, *retval;
485 {
486     struct filedesc *fdp = p->p_fd;
487     int     msk, i, j, fd;
488     fd_mask bits;
489     struct file *fp;
490     int     n = 0;
491     static int flag[3] =
492     {FREAD, FWRITE, 0};

493     for (msk = 0; msk < 3; msk++) {
494         for (i = 0; i < nfd; i += NFDBITS) {
495             bits = ibits[msk].fds_bits[i / NFDBITS];
496             while ((j = ffs(bits)) && (fd = i + --j) < nfd) {
497                 bits &= ~(1 << j);
498                 fp = fdp->fd_ofiles[fd];
499                 if (fp == NULL)
500                     return (EBADF);
501                 if ((*fp->f_ops->fo_select) (fp, flag[msk], p)) {
502                     FD_SET(fd, &obits[msk]);
503                     n++;
504                 }
505             }
506         }
507     }
508     *retval = n;
509     return (0);
510 }
```

sys_generic.c

Figure 16.55   selscan function.

soo_select Function

For every descriptor that selscan finds in the input descriptor sets, it calls the function referenced by the fo_select pointer in the fileops structure (Section 15.5) associated with the descriptor. In this text, we are interested only in socket descriptors and the soo_select function shown in Figure 16.56.

105–112   Each time soo_select is called, it checks the status of only one descriptor. If the descriptor is ready relative to the conditions specified in which, the function returns 1 immediately. If the descriptor is not ready, selrecord marks either the socket's receive or send buffer to indicate that a process is selecting on the buffer and then soo_select returns 0.

Figure 16.52 showed the read, write, and exceptional conditions for sockets. Here we see that the macros soreadable and sowriteable are consulted by soo_select. These macros are defined in sys/socketvar.h.

——— *sys_socket.c*

```
105 soo_select(fp, which, p)
106 struct file *fp;
107 int     which;
108 struct proc *p;
109 {
110     struct socket *so = (struct socket *) fp->f_data;
111     int     s = splnet();

112     switch (which) {

113     case FREAD:
114         if (soreadable(so)) {
115             splx(s);
116             return (1);
117         }
118         selrecord(p, &so->so_rcv.sb_sel);
119         so->so_rcv.sb_flags |= SB_SEL;
120         break;

121     case FWRITE:
122         if (sowriteable(so)) {
123             splx(s);
124             return (1);
125         }
126         selrecord(p, &so->so_snd.sb_sel);
127         so->so_snd.sb_flags |= SB_SEL;
128         break;

129     case 0:
130         if (so->so_oobmark || (so->so_state & SS_RCVATMARK)) {
131             splx(s);
132             return (1);
133         }
134         selrecord(p, &so->so_rcv.sb_sel);
135         so->so_rcv.sb_flags |= SB_SEL;
136         break;
137     }
138     splx(s);
139     return (0);
140 }
```

——— *sys_socket.c*

Figure 16.56   soo_select function.

Is socket readable?

113–120   The soreadable macro is:

```
#define soreadable(so) \
    ((so)->so_rcv.sb_cc >= (so)->so_rcv.sb_lowat || \
    ((so)->so_state & SS_CANTRCVMORE) || \
    (so)->so_qlen || (so)->so_error)
```

Since the receive low-water mark for UDP and TCP defaults to 1 (Figure 16.4), the
socket is readable if any data is in the receive buffer, if the read-half of the connection is
closed, if any connections are ready to be accepted, or if there is an error pending.

Is socket writeable?

121–128   The sowriteable macro is:

```
#define sowriteable(so) \
    (sbspace(&(so)->so_snd) >= (so)->so_snd.sb_lowat && \
    (((so)->so_state&SS_ISCONNECTED) || \
      ((so)->so_proto->pr_flags&PR_CONNREQUIRED)==0) || \
    ((so)->so_state & SS_CANTSENDMORE) || \
    (so)->so_error)
```

The default send low-water mark for UDP and TCP is 2048. For UDP, sowriteable is always true because sbspace is always equal to sb_hiwat, which is always greater than or equal to sb_lowat, and a connection is not required.

For TCP, the socket is not writeable when the free space in the send buffer is less than 2048 bytes. The other cases are described in Figure 16.52.

Are there any exceptional conditions pending?

129–140   For exceptions, so_oobmark and the SS_RCVATMARK flags are examined. An exceptional condition exists until the process has read past the synchronization mark in the data stream.

selrecord Function

Figure 16.57 shows the definition of the selinfo structure stored with each send and receive buffer (the sb_sel member from Figure 16.3).

```
                                                                    select.h
41 struct selinfo {
42     pid_t   si_pid;            /* process to be notified */
43     short   si_flags;          /* 0 or SI_COLL */
44 };
                                                                    select.h
```

Figure 16.57 selinfo structure.

41–44   When only one process has called select for a given socket buffer, si_pid is the process ID of the waiting process. When additional processes call select on the same buffer, SI_COLL is set in si_flags. This is called a *collision*. This is the only flag currently defined for si_flags.

The selrecord function shown in Figure 16.58 is called when soo_select finds a descriptor that is not ready. The function records enough information so that the process is awakened by the protocol processing layer when the buffer changes.

Already selecting on this descriptor

522–531   The first argument to selrecord points to the proc structure for the selecting process. The second argument points to the selinfo record to update (so_snd.sb_sel or so_rcv.sb_sel). If this process is already recorded in the selinfo record for this socket buffer, the function returns immediately. For example, the process called select with the read and exception bits set for the same descriptor.

```
                                                                          ── sys_generic.c
522  void
523  selrecord(selector, sip)
524  struct proc *selector;
525  struct selinfo *sip;
526  {
527      struct proc *p;
528      pid_t   mypid;

529      mypid = selector->p_pid;
530      if (sip->si_pid == mypid)
531          return;
532      if (sip->si_pid && (p = pfind(sip->si_pid)) &&
533          p->p_wchan == (caddr_t) & selwait)
534          sip->si_flags |= SI_COLL;
535      else
536          sip->si_pid = mypid;
537  }
                                                                          ── sys_generic.c
```

Figure 16.58   selrecord function.

Select collision with another process?

532–534   If another process is already selecting on this buffer, SI_COLL is set.

No collision

535–537   If there is no other process already selecting on this buffer, si_pid is 0 so the ID of
the current process is saved in si_pid.

selwakeup Function

When protocol processing changes the state of a socket buffer and only one process is
selecting on the buffer, Net/3 can immediately put that process on the run queue based
on the information it finds in the selinfo structure.

When the state changes and there is more than one process selecting on the buffer
(SI_COLL is set), Net/3 has no way of determining the set of processes interested in the
buffer. When we discussed the code in Figure 16.54, we pointed out that *every* process
that calls select uses selwait as the wait channel when calling tsleep. This means
the corresponding wakeup will schedule *all* the processes that are blocked in
select—even those that are not interested in activity on the buffer.

Figure 16.59 shows how selwakeup is called.

The protocol processing layer is responsible for notifying the socket layer by calling
one of the functions listed at the bottom of Figure 16.59 when an event occurs that
changes the state of a socket. The three functions shown at the bottom of Figure 16.59
cause selwakeup to be called and any process selecting on the socket to be scheduled
to run.

selwakeup is shown in Figure 16.60.

541–548   If si_pid is 0, there is no process selecting on the buffer and the function returns
immediately.

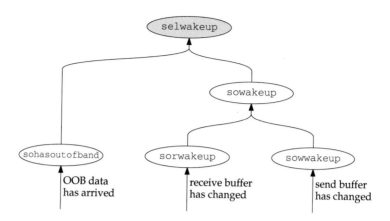

Figure 16.59 selwakeup processing.

```
541 void                                                                  ── sys_generic.c
542 selwakeup(sip)
543 struct selinfo *sip;
544 {
545     struct proc *p;
546     int     s;

547     if (sip->si_pid == 0)
548         return;
549     if (sip->si_flags & SI_COLL) {
550         nselcoll++;
551         sip->si_flags &= ~SI_COLL;
552         wakeup((caddr_t) & selwait);
553     }
554     p = pfind(sip->si_pid);
555     sip->si_pid = 0;
556     if (p != NULL) {
557         s = splhigh();
558         if (p->p_wchan == (caddr_t) & selwait) {
559             if (p->p_stat == SSLEEP)
560                 setrunnable(p);
561             else
562                 unsleep(p);
563         } else if (p->p_flag & P_SELECT)
564             p->p_flag &= ~P_SELECT;
565         splx(s);
566     }
567 }
```
── *sys_generic.c*

Figure 16.60 selwakeup function.

Wake all processes during a collision

549–553   If more than one process is selecting on the affected socket, nselcoll is incremented, the collision flag is cleared, and every process blocked in select is awakened. As mentioned with Figure 16.54, nselcoll forces select to rescan the descriptors if the buffers change before the process has blocked in tsleep (Exercise 16.9).

554–567   If the process identified by si_pid is waiting on selwait, it is scheduled to run. If the process is waiting on some other wait channel, the P_SELECT flag is cleared. The process can be waiting on some other wait channel if selrecord is called for a valid descriptor and then selscan finds a bad file descriptor in one of the descriptor sets. selscan returns EBADF, but the previously modified selinfo record is not reset. Later, when selwakeup runs, selwakeup may find the process identified by sel_pid is no longer waiting on the socket buffer so the selinfo information is ignored.

Only one process is awakened during selwakeup unless multiple processes are sharing the same descriptor (i.e., the same socket buffers), which is rare. On the machines to which the authors had access, nselcoll was always 0, which confirms the statement that select collisions are rare.

16.14 Summary

In this chapter we looked at the read, write, and select system calls for sockets.

We saw that sosend handles all output between the socket layer and the protocol processing layer and that soreceive handles all input.

The organization of the send buffer and receive buffers was described, as well as the default values and semantics of the high-water and low-water marks for the buffers.

The last part of the chapter discussed the implementation of select. We showed that when only one process is selecting on a descriptor, the protocol processing layer will awaken only the process identified in the selinfo structure. When there is a collision and more than one process is selecting on a descriptor, the protocol layer has no choice but to awaken every process that is selecting on *any* descriptor.

Exercises

16.1   What happens to resid in sosend when an unsigned integer larger than the maximum positive signed integer is passed in the write system call?

16.2   When sosend puts less than MCLBYTES of data in a cluster, space is reduced by the full MCLBYTES and may become negative, which terminates the loop that fills mbufs for atomic protocols. Is this a problem?

16.3   Datagram and stream protocols have very different semantics. Divide the sosend and soreceive functions each into two functions, one to handle messages, and one to handle streams. Other than making the code clearer, what are the advantages of making this change?

16.4   For PR_ATOMIC protocols, each write call specifies an implicit message boundary. The socket layer delivers the message as a single unit to the protocol. The MSG_EOR flag allows a process to specify explicit message boundaries. Why is the implicit technique insufficient?

16.5 What happens when sosend cannot immediately acquire a lock on the send buffer when the socket descriptor is marked as nonblocking and the process does not specify MSG_DONTWAIT?

16.6 Under what circumstances would sb_cc < sb_hiwat yet sbspace would report no free space? Why should a process be blocked in this case?

16.7 Why isn't the length of a control message copied back to the process by recvit as is the name length?

16.8 Why does soreceive clear MSG_EOR?

16.9 What might happen if the nselcoll code were removed from select and selwakeup?

16.10 Modify the select system call to return the time remaining in the timer when select returns.

17

Socket Options

17.1 Introduction

We complete our discussion of the socket layer in this chapter by discussing several system calls that modify the behavior of sockets.

The setsockopt and getsockopt system calls were introduced in Section 8.8, where we described the options that provide access to IP features. In this chapter we show the implementation of these two system calls and the socket-level options that are controlled through them.

The ioctl function was introduced in Section 4.4, where we described the protocol-independent ioctl commands for network interface configuration. In Section 6.7 we described the IP specific ioctl commands used to assign network masks as well as unicast, broadcast, and destination addresses. In this chapter we describe the implementation of ioctl and the related features of the fcntl function.

Finally, we describe the getsockname and getpeername system calls, which return address information for sockets and connections.

Figure 17.1 shows the functions that implement the socket option system calls. The shaded functions are described in this chapter.

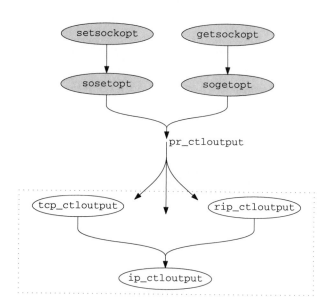

Figure 17.1   `setsockopt` and `getsockopt` system calls.

17.2   Code Introduction

The code in this chapter comes from the four files listed in Figure 17.2.

File	Description
`kern/kern_descrip.c`	`fcntl` system call
`kern/uipc_syscalls.c`	`setsockopt`, `getsockopt`, `getsockname`, and `getpeername` system calls
`kern/uipc_socket.c`	socket layer processing for `setsockopt` and `getsockopt`
`kern/sys_socket.c`	`ioctl` system call for sockets

Figure 17.2   Files discussed in this chapter.

Global Variables and Statistics

No new global variables are introduced and no statistics are collected by the system calls we describe in this chapter.

17.3 `setsockopt` System Call

Figure 8.29 listed the different protocol levels that can be accessed with this function (and with `getsockopt`). In this chapter we focus on the SOL_SOCKET level options, which are listed in Figure 17.3.

optname	*optval* type	Variable	Description
SO_SNDBUF	int	so_snd.sb_hiwat	send buffer high-water mark
SO_RCVBUF	int	so_rcv.sb_hiwat	receive buffer high-water mark
SO_SNDLOWAT	int	so_snd.sb_lowat	send buffer low-water mark
SO_RCVLOWAT	int	so_rcv.sb_lowat	receive buffer low-water mark
SO_SNDTIMEO	struct timeval	so_snd.sb_timeo	send timeout
SO_RCVTIMEO	struct timeval	so_rcv.sb_timeo	receive timeout
SO_DEBUG	int	so_options	record debugging information for this socket
SO_REUSEADDR	int	so_options	socket can reuse a local address
SO_REUSEPORT	int	so_options	socket can reuse a local port
SO_KEEPALIVE	int	so_options	protocol probes idle connections
SO_DONTROUTE	int	so_options	bypass routing tables
SO_BROADCAST	int	so_options	socket allows broadcast messages
SO_USELOOPBACK	int	so_options	routing domain sockets only; sending process receives its own routing messages
SO_OOBINLINE	int	so_options	protocol queues out-of-band data inline
SO_LINGER	struct linger	so_linger	socket lingers on close
SO_ERROR	int	so_error	get error status and clear; getsockopt only
SO_TYPE	int	so_type	get socket type; getsockopt only
other			ENOPROTOOPT returned

Figure 17.3 `setsockopt` and `getsockopt` options.

The prototype for `setsockopt` is

```
int setsockopt(int s, int level, int optname, void *optval, int optlen);
```

Figure 17.4 shows the code for this system call.

565–597   `getsock` locates the `file` structure for the socket descriptor. If `val` is nonnull, `valsize` bytes of data are copied from the process into an mbuf allocated by `m_get`. The data associated with an option can be no more than `MLEN` bytes in length, so if `valsize` is larger than `MLEN`, then `EINVAL` is returned. `sosetopt` is called and its value is returned.

```
                                                                              ─── uipc_syscalls.c
565 struct setsockopt_args {
566     int     s;
567     int     level;
568     int     name;
569     caddr_t val;
570     int     valsize;
571 };

572 setsockopt(p, uap, retval)
573 struct proc *p;
574 struct setsockopt_args *uap;
575 int     *retval;
576 {
577     struct file *fp;
578     struct mbuf *m = NULL;
579     int     error;

580     if (error = getsock(p->p_fd, uap->s, &fp))
581         return (error);
582     if (uap->valsize > MLEN)
583         return (EINVAL);
584     if (uap->val) {
585         m = m_get(M_WAIT, MT_SOOPTS);
586         if (m == NULL)
587             return (ENOBUFS);
588         if (error = copyin(uap->val, mtod(m, caddr_t),
589                         (u_int) uap->valsize)) {
590             (void) m_free(m);
591             return (error);
592         }
593         m->m_len = uap->valsize;
594     }
595     return (sosetopt((struct socket *) fp->f_data, uap->level,
596                 uap->name, m));
597 }
                                                                              ─── uipc_syscalls.c
```

Figure 17.4 setsockopt system call.

sosetopt Function

This function processes all the socket-level options and passes any other options to the pr_ctloutput function for the protocol associated with the socket. Figure 17.5 shows an overview of the function.

752–764   If the option is not for the socket level (SOL_SOCKET), the PRCO_SETOPT request is issued to the underlying protocol. Note that the protocol's pr_ctloutput function is being called and not its pr_usrreq function. Figure 17.6 shows which function is called for the Internet protocols.

765   The switch statement handles the socket-level options.

841–844   An unrecognized option causes ENOPROTOOPT to be returned after the mbuf holding the option is released.

—— uipc_socket.c

```
752 sosetopt(so, level, optname, m0)
753 struct socket *so;
754 int     level, optname;
755 struct mbuf *m0;
756 {
757     int     error = 0;
758     struct mbuf *m = m0;

759     if (level != SOL_SOCKET) {
760         if (so->so_proto && so->so_proto->pr_ctloutput)
761             return ((*so->so_proto->pr_ctloutput)
762                 (PRCO_SETOPT, so, level, optname, &m0));
763         error = ENOPROTOOPT;
764     } else {
765         switch (optname) {
```
```
                                      /* socket option processing */
```
```
841         default:
842             error = ENOPROTOOPT;
843             break;
844         }
845         if (error == 0 && so->so_proto && so->so_proto->pr_ctloutput) {
846             (void) ((*so->so_proto->pr_ctloutput)
847                 (PRCO_SETOPT, so, level, optname, &m0));
848             m = NULL;              /* freed by protocol */
849         }
850     }
851 bad:
852     if (m)
853         (void) m_free(m);
854     return (error);
855 }
```

—— uipc_socket.c

Figure 17.5 sosetopt function.

Protocol	pr_ctloutput Function	Reference
UDP	ip_ctloutput	Section 8.8
TCP	tcp_ctloutput	Section 30.6
ICMP IGMP raw IP	rip_ctloutput and ip_ctloutput	Section 8.8 and Section 32.8

Figure 17.6 pr_ctloutput functions.

845–855   Unless an error occurs, control always falls through the switch, where the option is passed to the associated protocol in case the protocol layer needs to respond to the request as well as the socket layer. None of the Internet protocols expect to process the socket-level options.

Notice that the return value from the call to the `pr_ctloutput` function is explicitly discarded in case the option is not expected by the protocol. `m` is set to null to avoid the call to `m_free`, since the protocol layer is responsible for releasing the mbuf.

Figure 17.7 shows the `linger` option and the options that set a single flag in the socket structure.

```
                                                                    ——— uipc_socket.c
766        case SO_LINGER:
767            if (m == NULL || m->m_len != sizeof(struct linger)) {
768                error = EINVAL;
769                goto bad;
770            }
771            so->so_linger = mtod(m, struct linger *)->l_linger;
772            /* fall thru... */

773        case SO_DEBUG:
774        case SO_KEEPALIVE:
775        case SO_DONTROUTE:
776        case SO_USELOOPBACK:
777        case SO_BROADCAST:
778        case SO_REUSEADDR:
779        case SO_REUSEPORT:
780        case SO_OOBINLINE:
781            if (m == NULL || m->m_len < sizeof(int)) {
782                error = EINVAL;
783                goto bad;
784            }
785            if (*mtod(m, int *))
786                so->so_options |= optname;
787            else
788                so->so_options &= ~optname;
789            break;
                                                                    ——— uipc_socket.c
```

Figure 17.7 `sosetopt` function: `linger` and flag options.

766–772   The linger option expects the process to pass a `linger` structure:

```
struct linger {
    int     l_onoff;     /* option on/off */
    int     l_linger;    /* linger time in seconds */
};
```

After making sure the process has passed data and it is the size of a `linger` structure, the `l_linger` member is copied into `so_linger`. The option is enabled or disabled after the next set of `case` statements. `so_linger` was described in Section 15.15 with the `close` system call.

773–789   These options are boolean flags set when the process passes a nonzero value and cleared when 0 is passed. The first check makes sure an integer-sized object (or larger) is present in the mbuf and then sets or clears the appropriate option.

Figure 17.8 shows the socket buffer options.

uipc_socket.c

```
790             case SO_SNDBUF:
791             case SO_RCVBUF:
792             case SO_SNDLOWAT:
793             case SO_RCVLOWAT:
794                 if (m == NULL || m->m_len < sizeof(int)) {
795                     error = EINVAL;
796                     goto bad;
797                 }
798                 switch (optname) {

799                 case SO_SNDBUF:
800                 case SO_RCVBUF:
801                     if (sbreserve(optname == SO_SNDBUF ?
802                                 &so->so_snd : &so->so_rcv,
803                                 (u_long) * mtod(m, int *)) == 0) {
804                         error = ENOBUFS;
805                         goto bad;
806                     }
807                     break;

808                 case SO_SNDLOWAT:
809                     so->so_snd.sb_lowat = *mtod(m, int *);
810                     break;
811                 case SO_RCVLOWAT:
812                     so->so_rcv.sb_lowat = *mtod(m, int *);
813                     break;
814                 }
815                 break;
```

uipc_socket.c

Figure 17.8 sosetopt function: socket buffer options.

790–815   This set of options changes the size of the send and receive buffers in a socket. The first test makes sure the required integer has been provided for all four options. For SO_SNDBUF and SO_RCVBUF, sbreserve adjusts the high-water mark but does no buffer allocation. For SO_SNDLOWAT and SO_RCVLOWAT, the low-water marks are adjusted.

Figure 17.9 shows the timeout options.

816–824   The timeout value for SO_SNDTIMEO and SO_RCVTIMEO is specified by the process in a timeval structure. If the right amount of data is not available, EINVAL is returned.

825–830   The time interval stored in the timeval structure must be small enough so that when it is represented as clock ticks, it fits within a short integer, since sb_timeo is a short integer.

The code on line 826 is incorrect. The time interval cannot be represented as a short integer if:

```
                                                                          ─── uipc_socket.c
816            case SO_SNDTIMEO:
817            case SO_RCVTIMEO:
818                {
819                    struct timeval *tv;
820                    short    val;

821                    if (m == NULL || m->m_len < sizeof(*tv)) {
822                        error = EINVAL;
823                        goto bad;
824                    }
825                    tv = mtod(m, struct timeval *);
826                    if (tv->tv_sec > SHRT_MAX / hz - hz) {
827                        error = EDOM;
828                        goto bad;
829                    }
830                    val = tv->tv_sec * hz + tv->tv_usec / tick;

831                    switch (optname) {

832                    case SO_SNDTIMEO:
833                        so->so_snd.sb_timeo = val;
834                        break;
835                    case SO_RCVTIMEO:
836                        so->so_rcv.sb_timeo = val;
837                        break;
838                    }
839                    break;
840                }
                                                                          ─── uipc_socket.c
```

Figure 17.9 sosetopt function: timeout options.

$$tv\_sec \times hz + \frac{tv\_usec}{tick} > SHRT\_MAX$$

where

$$tick = \frac{1,000,000}{hz} \quad \text{and } SHRT\_MAX = 32767$$

So EDOM should be returned if

$$tv\_sec > \frac{SHRT\_MAX}{hz} - \frac{tv\_usec}{tick \times hz} = \frac{SHRT\_MAX}{hz} - \frac{tv\_usec}{1,000,000}$$

The last term in this equation is not hz as specified in the code. The correct test is

```
    if (tv->tv_sec*hz + tv->tv_usec/tick > SHRT_MAX)
```

but see Exercise 17.3 for more discussion.

831–840   The converted time, val, is saved in the send or receive buffer as requested. sb_timeo limits the amount of time a process will wait for data in the receive buffer or space in the send buffer. See Sections 16.7 and 16.12 for details.

> The timeout values are passed as the last argument to tsleep, which expects an integer, so the process is limited to 65535 ticks. At 100 Hz, this less than 11 minutes.

17.4 `getsockopt` **System Call**

`getsockopt` returns socket and protocol options as requested. The prototype for this
system call is

```
int getsockopt(int s, int level, int name, caddr_t val, int *valsize);
```

The code is shown in Figure 17.10.

———————————————————————————————— *uipc_syscalls.c*
```
598 struct getsockopt_args {
599     int     s;
600     int     level;
601     int     name;
602     caddr_t val;
603     int     *avalsize;
604 };

605 getsockopt(p, uap, retval)
606 struct proc *p;
607 struct getsockopt_args *uap;
608 int     *retval;
609 {
610     struct file *fp;
611     struct mbuf *m = NULL;
612     int     valsize, error;

613     if (error = getsock(p->p_fd, uap->s, &fp))
614         return (error);
615     if (uap->val) {
616         if (error = copyin((caddr_t) uap->avalsize, (caddr_t) & valsize,
617                         sizeof(valsize)))
618             return (error);
619     } else
620         valsize = 0;
621     if ((error = sogetopt((struct socket *) fp->f_data, uap->level,
622                 uap->name, &m)) == 0 && uap->val && valsize && m != NULL) {
623         if (valsize > m->m_len)
624             valsize = m->m_len;
625         error = copyout(mtod(m, caddr_t), uap->val, (u_int) valsize);
626         if (error == 0)
627             error = copyout((caddr_t) & valsize,
628                         (caddr_t) uap->avalsize, sizeof(valsize));
629     }
630     if (m != NULL)
631         (void) m_free(m);
632     return (error);
633 }
```
———————————————————————————————— *uipc_syscalls.c*

Figure 17.10 `getsockopt` system call.

598–633   The code should look pretty familiar by now. `getsock` locates the socket, the size
of the option buffer is copied into the kernel, and `sogetopt` is called to get the value of
the requested option. The data returned by `sogetopt` is copied out to the buffer in the
process along with the possibly new length of the buffer. It is possible that the data will

be silently truncated if the process did not provide a large enough buffer. As usual, the mbuf holding the option data is released before the function returns.

`sogetopt` Function

As with `sosetopt`, the `sogetopt` function handles the socket-level options and passes any other options to the protocol associated with the socket. The beginning and end of the function are shown in Figure 17.11.

—————————————————————————————————— uipc_socket.c
```
856 sogetopt(so, level, optname, mp)
857 struct socket *so;
858 int     level, optname;
859 struct mbuf **mp;
860 {
861     struct mbuf *m;

862     if (level != SOL_SOCKET) {
863         if (so->so_proto && so->so_proto->pr_ctloutput) {
864             return ((*so->so_proto->pr_ctloutput)
865                     (PRCO_GETOPT, so, level, optname, mp));
866         } else
867             return (ENOPROTOOPT);
868     } else {
869         m = m_get(M_WAIT, MT_SOOPTS);
870         m->m_len = sizeof(int);

871         switch (optname) {
```

```
                                     /* socket option processing */
```

```
918         default:
919             (void) m_free(m);
920             return (ENOPROTOOPT);
921         }
922         *mp = m;
923         return (0);
924     }
925 }
```
—————————————————————————————————— uipc_socket.c

Figure 17.11   `sogetopt` function: overview.

856–871   As with `sosetopt`, options that do not pertain to the socket level are immediately passed to the protocol level through the `PRCO_GETOPT` protocol request. The protocol returns the requested option in the mbuf pointed to by `*mp`.

For socket-level options, a standard mbuf is allocated to hold the option value, which is normally an integer, so `m_len` is set to the size of an integer. The appropriate option is copied into the mbuf by the code in the `switch` statement.

918–925   If the `default` case is taken by the `switch`, the mbuf is released and `ENOPROTOOPT` returned. Otherwise, after the `switch` statement, the pointer to the mbuf is saved in *mp. When this function returns, getsockopt copies the option from the mbuf to the process and releases the mbuf.

In Figure 17.12 the linger option and the options that are implemented as boolean flags are processed.

─── *uipc_socket.c*
```
872        case SO_LINGER:
873             m->m_len = sizeof(struct linger);
874             mtod(m, struct linger *)->l_onoff =
875                   so->so_options & SO_LINGER;
876             mtod(m, struct linger *)->l_linger = so->so_linger;
877             break;

878        case SO_USELOOPBACK:
879        case SO_DONTROUTE:
880        case SO_DEBUG:
881        case SO_KEEPALIVE:
882        case SO_REUSEADDR:
883        case SO_REUSEPORT:
884        case SO_BROADCAST:
885        case SO_OOBINLINE:
886             *mtod(m, int *) = so->so_options & optname;
887             break;
```
─── *uipc_socket.c*

Figure 17.12   sogetopt function: SO_LINGER and boolean options.

872–877   The SO_LINGER option requires two copies, one for the flag into l_onoff and a second for the linger time into l_linger.

878–887   The remaining options are implemented as boolean flags. so_options is masked with optname, which results in a nonzero value if the option is on and 0 if the option is off. Notice that the return value is not necessarily 1 when the flag is on.

In the next part of sogetopt (Figure 17.13), the integer-valued options are copied into the mbuf.

─── *uipc_socket.c*
```
888        case SO_TYPE:
889             *mtod(m, int *) = so->so_type;
890             break;

891        case SO_ERROR:
892             *mtod(m, int *) = so->so_error;
893             so->so_error = 0;
894             break;

895        case SO_SNDBUF:
896             *mtod(m, int *) = so->so_snd.sb_hiwat;
897             break;

898        case SO_RCVBUF:
899             *mtod(m, int *) = so->so_rcv.sb_hiwat;
900             break;
```

```
901            case SO_SNDLOWAT:
902                *mtod(m, int *) = so->so_snd.sb_lowat;
903                break;

904            case SO_RCVLOWAT:
905                *mtod(m, int *) = so->so_rcv.sb_lowat;
906                break;
```
——— *uipc_socket.c*

Figure 17.13   sogetopt function: integer valued options.

888–906   Each option is copied as an integer into the mbuf. Notice that some of the options are stored as shorts in the kernel (e.g., the high-water and low-water marks) but returned as integers. Also, so_error is cleared once the value is copied into the mbuf. This is the only time that a call to getsockopt changes the state of the socket.

The fourth and last part of sogetopt is shown in Figure 17.14, where the SO_SNDTIMEO and SO_RCVTIMEO options are handled.

——— *uipc_socket.c*
```
907            case SO_SNDTIMEO:
908            case SO_RCVTIMEO:
909                {
910                    int     val = (optname == SO_SNDTIMEO ?
911                                   so->so_snd.sb_timeo : so->so_rcv.sb_timeo);

912                    m->m_len = sizeof(struct timeval);
913                    mtod(m, struct timeval *)->tv_sec = val / hz;
914                    mtod(m, struct timeval *)->tv_usec =
915                        (val % hz) / tick;
916                    break;
917                }
```
——— *uipc_socket.c*

Figure 17.14   sogetopt function: timeout options.

907–917   The sb_timeo value from the send or receive buffer is copied into val. A timeval structure is constructed in the mbuf based on the clock ticks in val.

> There is a bug in the calculation of tv_usec. The expression should be "(val % hz) * tick".

17.5 fcntl and ioctl System Calls

Due more to history than intent, several features of the sockets API can be accessed from either ioctl or fcntl. We have already discussed many of the ioctl commands and have mentioned fcntl several times.

Figure 17.15 highlights the functions described in this chapter.

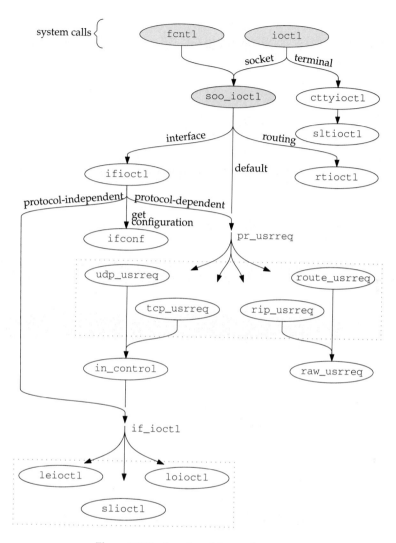

Figure 17.15   fcntl and ioctl functions.

The prototypes for ioctl and fcntl are:

```
int ioctl(int fd, unsigned long result, char *argp);

int fcntl(int fd, int cmd, ... /* int arg */);
```

Figure 17.16 summarizes the features of these two system calls as they relate to sockets. We show the traditional constants in Figure 17.16, since they appear in the code. For Posix compatibility, O_NONBLOCK can be used instead of FNONBLOCK, and O_ASYNC can be used instead of FASYNC.

Description	fcntl	ioctl
enable or disable nonblocking semantics by turning SS_NBIO on or off in so_state	FNONBLOCK file status flag	FIONBIO command
enable or disable asynchronous notification by turning SB_ASYNC on or off in sb_flags	FASYNC file status flag	FIOASYNC command
set or get so_pgid, which is the target process or process group for SIGIO and SIGURG signals	F_SETOWN or F_GETOWN	SIOCSPGRP or SIOCGPGRP commands
get number of bytes in receive buffer; return so_rcv.sb_cc		FIONREAD
return OOB synchronization mark; the SS_RCVATMARK flag in so_state		SIOCATMARK

Figure 17.16   fcntl and ioctl commands.

fcntl **Code**

Figure 17.17 shows an overview of the fcntl function.

—— kern_descrip.c

```
133 struct fcntl_args {
134     int     fd;
135     int     cmd;
136     int     arg;
137 };
138 /* ARGSUSED */
139 fcntl(p, uap, retval)
140 struct proc *p;
141 struct fcntl_args *uap;
142 int     *retval;
143 {
144     struct filedesc *fdp = p->p_fd;
145     struct file *fp;
146     struct vnode *vp;
147     int     i, tmp, error, flg = F_POSIX;
148     struct flock fl;
149     u_int   newmin;
150     if ((unsigned) uap->fd >= fdp->fd_nfiles ||
151         (fp = fdp->fd_ofiles[uap->fd]) == NULL)
152         return (EBADF);
153     switch (uap->cmd) {

                                /* command processing */

253     default:
254         return (EINVAL);
255     }
256     /* NOTREACHED */
257 }
```

—— kern_descrip.c

Figure 17.17   fcntl system call: overview.

133–153   After verifying that the descriptor refers to an open file, the switch statement processes the requested command.

253–257   If the command is not recognized, fcntl returns EINVAL.

Figure 17.18 shows only the cases from fcntl that are relevant to sockets.

―― *kern_descrip.c*
```
168     case F_GETFL:
169         *retval = OFLAGS(fp->f_flag);
170         return (0);

171     case F_SETFL:
172         fp->f_flag &= ~FCNTLFLAGS;
173         fp->f_flag |= FFLAGS(uap->arg) & FCNTLFLAGS;

174         tmp = fp->f_flag & FNONBLOCK;
175         error = (*fp->f_ops->fo_ioctl) (fp, FIONBIO, (caddr_t) & tmp, p);
176         if (error)
177             return (error);

178         tmp = fp->f_flag & FASYNC;
179         error = (*fp->f_ops->fo_ioctl) (fp, FIOASYNC, (caddr_t) & tmp, p);
180         if (!error)
181             return (0);

182         fp->f_flag &= ~FNONBLOCK;
183         tmp = 0;
184         (void) (*fp->f_ops->fo_ioctl) (fp, FIONBIO, (caddr_t) & tmp, p);
185         return (error);

186     case F_GETOWN:
187         if (fp->f_type == DTYPE_SOCKET) {
188             *retval = ((struct socket *) fp->f_data)->so_pgid;
189             return (0);
190         }
191         error = (*fp->f_ops->fo_ioctl)
192             (fp, (int) TIOCGPGRP, (caddr_t) retval, p);
193         *retval = -*retval;
194         return (error);

195     case F_SETOWN:
196         if (fp->f_type == DTYPE_SOCKET) {
197             ((struct socket *) fp->f_data)->so_pgid = uap->arg;
198             return (0);
199         }
200         if (uap->arg <= 0) {
201             uap->arg = -uap->arg;
202         } else {
203             struct proc *p1 = pfind(uap->arg);
204             if (p1 == 0)
205                 return (ESRCH);
206             uap->arg = p1->p_pgrp->pg_id;
207         }
208         return ((*fp->f_ops->fo_ioctl)
209             (fp, (int) TIOCSPGRP, (caddr_t) & uap->arg, p));
```
―― *kern_descrip.c*

Figure 17.18   fcntl system call: socket processing.

168–185   F_GETFL returns the current file status flags associated with the descriptor and F_SETFL sets the flags. The new settings for FNONBLOCK and FASYNC are passed to the associated socket by calling fo_ioctl, which for sockets is the soo_ioctl function described with Figure 17.20. The third call to fo_ioctl is made only if the second call fails. It clears the FNONBLOCK flag, but should instead restore the flag to its original setting.

186–209   F_GETOWN returns so_pgid, the process or process group associated with the socket. For a descriptor other than a socket, the TIOCGPGRP ioctl command is passed to the associated fo_ioctl function. F_SETOWN assigns a new value to so_pgid.

For a descriptor other than a socket, the process group is checked in this function, but for sockets, the value is checked just before a signal is sent in sohasoutofband and in sowakeup.

ioctl **Code**

We skip the ioctl system call itself and start with soo_ioctl in Figure 17.20, since most of the code in ioctl duplicates the code we described with Figure 17.17. We've already shown that this function sends routing commands to rtioctl, interface commands to ifioctl, and any remaining commands to the pr_usrreq function of the underlying protocol.

55–68   A few commands are handled by soo_ioctl directly. FIONBIO turns on nonblocking semantics if *data is nonzero, and turns them off otherwise. As we have seen, this flag affects the accept, connect, and close system calls as well as the various read and write system calls.

69–79   FIOASYNC enables or disables asynchronous I/O notification. Whenever there is activity on a socket, sowakeup gets called and if SS_ASYNC is set, the SIGIO signal is sent to the process or process group.

80–88   FIONREAD returns the number of bytes available in the receive buffer. SIOCSPGRP sets the process group associated with the socket, and SIOCGPGRP gets it. so_pgid is used as a target for the SIGIO signal as we just described and for the SIGURG signal when out-of-band data arrives for a socket. The signal is sent when the protocol layer calls the sohasoutofband function.

89–92   SIOCATMARK returns true if the socket is at the out-of-band synchronization mark, false otherwise.

ioctl commands, the FIO*xxx* and SIO*xxx* constants, have an internal structure illustrated in Figure 17.19.

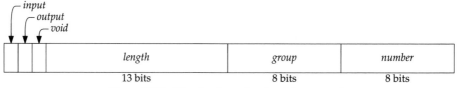

Figure 17.19   The structure of an ioctl command.

```
                                                                ─── sys_socket.c
55 soo_ioctl(fp, cmd, data, p)
56 struct file *fp;
57 int      cmd;
58 caddr_t data;
59 struct proc *p;
60 {
61      struct socket *so = (struct socket *) fp->f_data;
62      switch (cmd) {
63      case FIONBIO:
64          if (*(int *) data)
65              so->so_state |= SS_NBIO;
66          else
67              so->so_state &= ~SS_NBIO;
68          return (0);
69      case FIOASYNC:
70          if (*(int *) data) {
71              so->so_state |= SS_ASYNC;
72              so->so_rcv.sb_flags |= SB_ASYNC;
73              so->so_snd.sb_flags |= SB_ASYNC;
74          } else {
75              so->so_state &= ~SS_ASYNC;
76              so->so_rcv.sb_flags &= ~SB_ASYNC;
77              so->so_snd.sb_flags &= ~SB_ASYNC;
78          }
79          return (0);
80      case FIONREAD:
81          *(int *) data = so->so_rcv.sb_cc;
82          return (0);
83      case SIOCSPGRP:
84          so->so_pgid = *(int *) data;
85          return (0);
86      case SIOCGPGRP:
87          *(int *) data = so->so_pgid;
88          return (0);
89      case SIOCATMARK:
90          *(int *) data = (so->so_state & SS_RCVATMARK) != 0;
91          return (0);
92      }
93      /*
94       * Interface/routing/protocol specific ioctls:
95       * interface and routing ioctls should have a
96       * different entry since a socket's unnecessary
97       */
98      if (IOCGROUP(cmd) == 'i')
99          return (ifioctl(so, cmd, data, p));
100     if (IOCGROUP(cmd) == 'r')
101         return (rtioctl(cmd, data, p));
102     return ((*so->so_proto->pr_usrreq) (so, PRU_CONTROL,
103             (struct mbuf *) cmd, (struct mbuf *) data, (struct mbuf *) 0));
104 }
                                                                ─── sys_socket.c
```

Figure 17.20   soo_ioctl function.

If the third argument to `ioctl` is used as input, *input* is set. If the argument is used as output, *output* is set. If the argument is unused, *void* is set. *length* is the size of the argument in bytes. Related commands are in the same *group* but each command has its own *number* within the group. The macros in Figure 17.21 extract the components of an `ioctl` command.

Macro	Description
`IOCPARM_LEN(cmd)`	the *length* from *cmd*
`IOCBASECMD(cmd)`	the command with *length* set to 0
`IOCGROUP(cmd)`	the *group* from *cmd*

Figure 17.21   `ioctl` command macros.

93–104   The macro `IOCGROUP` extracts the 8-bit *group* from the command. Interface commands are handled by `ifioctl`. Routing commands are processed by `rtioctl`. All other commands are passed to the socket's protocol through the `PRU_CONTROL` request.

> As we describe in Chapter 19, Net/2 introduced a new interface to the routing tables in which messages are passed to the routing subsystem through a socket created in the `PF_ROUTE` domain. This method replaces the `ioctl` method shown here. `rtioctl` always returns `ENOTSUPP` in kernels that do not have compatibility code compiled in.

17.6   `getsockname` System Call

The prototype for this system call is:

```
int getsockname(int fd, caddr_t asa, int *alen);
```

`getsockname` retrieves the local address bound to the socket *fd* and places it in the buffer pointed to by *asa*. This is useful when the kernel has selected an address during an implicit bind or when the process specified a wildcard address (Section 22.5) during an explicit call to `bind`. The `getsockname` system call is shown in Figure 17.22.

682–715   `getsock` locates the `file` structure for the descriptor. The size of the buffer specified by the process is copied from the process into `len`. This is the first call to `m_getclr` that we've seen—it allocates a standard mbuf and clears it with `bzero`. The protocol processing layer is responsible for returning the local address in `m` when the `PRU_SOCKADDR` request is issued.

If the address is larger than the buffer specified by the process, it is silently truncated when it is copied out to the process. `*alen` is updated to the number of bytes copied out to the process. Finally, the mbuf is released and `getsockname` returns.

17.7   `getpeername` System Call

The prototype for this system call is:

```
int getpeername(int fd, caddr_t asa, int *alen);
```

```
                                                          ———————————— uipc_syscalls.c
682 struct getsockname_args {
683     int     fdes;
684     caddr_t asa;
685     int     *alen;
686 };

687 getsockname(p, uap, retval)
688 struct proc *p;
689 struct getsockname_args *uap;
690 int     *retval;
691 {
692     struct file *fp;
693     struct socket *so;
694     struct mbuf *m;
695     int     len, error;

696     if (error = getsock(p->p_fd, uap->fdes, &fp))
697         return (error);
698     if (error = copyin((caddr_t) uap->alen, (caddr_t) & len, sizeof(len)))
699         return (error);
700     so = (struct socket *) fp->f_data;
701     m = m_getclr(M_WAIT, MT_SONAME);
702     if (m == NULL)
703         return (ENOBUFS);
704     if (error = (*so->so_proto->pr_usrreq) (so, PRU_SOCKADDR, 0, m, 0))
705         goto bad;
706     if (len > m->m_len)
707         len = m->m_len;
708     error = copyout(mtod(m, caddr_t), (caddr_t) uap->asa, (u_int) len);
709     if (error == 0)
710         error = copyout((caddr_t) & len, (caddr_t) uap->alen,
711                         sizeof(len));
712 bad:
713     m_freem(m);
714     return (error);
715 }
                                                          ———————————— uipc_syscalls.c
```

Figure 17.22   getsockname system call.

The getpeername system call returns the address of the remote end of the connection associated with the specified socket. This function is often called when a server is invoked through a fork and exec by the process that calls accept (i.e., any server started by inetd). The server doesn't have access to the peer address returned by accept and must use getpeername. The returned address is often checked against an access list for the application, and the connection is closed if the address is not on the list.

Some protocols, such as TP4, utilize this function to determine if an incoming connection should be rejected or confirmed. In TP4, the connection associated with a socket returned by accept is not yet complete and must be confirmed before the connection completes. Based on the address returned by getpeername, the server can close the connection or implicitly confirm the connection by sending or receiving data. This

feature is irrelevant for TCP, since TCP doesn't make a connection available to `accept`
until the three-way handshake is complete. Figure 17.23 shows the `getpeername` function.

―――――――――――――――――――――――――――――――――――――― *uipc_syscalls.c*
```
719 struct getpeername_args {
720     int     fdes;
721     caddr_t asa;
722     int     *alen;
723 };

724 getpeername(p, uap, retval)
725 struct proc *p;
726 struct getpeername_args *uap;
727 int     *retval;
728 {
729     struct file *fp;
730     struct socket *so;
731     struct mbuf *m;
732     int     len, error;

733     if (error = getsock(p->p_fd, uap->fdes, &fp))
734         return (error);
735     so = (struct socket *) fp->f_data;
736     if ((so->so_state & (SS_ISCONNECTED | SS_ISCONFIRMING)) == 0)
737         return (ENOTCONN);
738     if (error = copyin((caddr_t) uap->alen, (caddr_t) & len, sizeof(len)))
739         return (error);
740     m = m_getclr(M_WAIT, MT_SONAME);
741     if (m == NULL)
742         return (ENOBUFS);
743     if (error = (*so->so_proto->pr_usrreq) (so, PRU_PEERADDR, 0, m, 0))
744         goto bad;
745     if (len > m->m_len)
746         len = m->m_len;
747     if (error = copyout(mtod(m, caddr_t), (caddr_t) uap->asa, (u_int) len))
748         goto bad;
749     error = copyout((caddr_t) & len, (caddr_t) uap->alen, sizeof(len));
750 bad:
751     m_freem(m);
752     return (error);
753 }
```
―――――――――――――――――――――――――――――――――――――― *uipc_syscalls.c*

Figure 17.23   `getpeername` system call.

719–753   The code here is almost identical to the `getsockname` code. `getsock` locates the
socket and `ENOTCONN` is returned if the socket is not yet connected to a peer or if the
connection is not in a confirmation state (e.g., TP4). If it is connected, the size of the
buffer is copied in from the process and an mbuf is allocated to hold the address. The
`PRU_PEERADDR` request is issued to get the remote address from the protocol layer. The
address and the length of the address are copied from the kernel mbuf to the buffer in
the process. The mbuf is released and the function returns.

17.8 Summary

In this chapter we discussed the six functions that modify the semantics of a socket. Socket options are processed by `setsockopt` and `getsockopt`. Additional options, some of which are not unique to sockets, are handled by `fcntl` and `ioctl`. Finally, connection information is available through `getsockname` and `getpeername`.

Exercises

17.1   Why do you think options are limited to the size of a standard mbuf (MHLEN, 128 bytes)?

17.2   Why does the code at the end of Figure 17.7 work for the SO_LINGER option?

17.3   There is a problem with the suggested code used to test the `timeval` structure in Figure 17.9 since `tv->tv_sec * hz` may cause an overflow. Suggest a change to the code to solve this problem.

18

Radix Tree Routing Tables

18.1 Introduction

The routing performed by IP, when it searches the routing table and decides which interface to send a packet out on, is a *routing mechanism*. This differs from a *routing policy*, which is a set of rules that decides which routes go into the routing table. The Net/3 kernel implements the routing mechanism while a routing daemon, typically `routed` or `gated`, implements the routing policy. The structure of the routing table must recognize that the packet forwarding occurs frequently—hundreds or thousands of times a second on a busy system—while routing policy changes are less frequent.

Routing is a detailed issue and we divide our discussion into three chapters.

- This chapter looks at the structure of the radix tree routing tables used by the Net/3 packet forwarding code. The tables are consulted by IP every time a packet is sent (since IP must determine which local interface receives the packet) and every time a packet is forwarded.

- Chapter 19 looks at the functions that interface between the kernel and the radix tree functions, and also at the routing messages that are exchanged between the kernel and routing processes—normally the routing daemons that implement the routing policy. These messages allow a process to modify the kernel's routing table (add a route, delete a route, etc.) and let the kernel notify the daemons when an asynchronous event occurs that might affect the routing policy (a redirect is received, an interface goes down, and so on).

- Chapter 20 presents the routing sockets that are used to exchange routing messages between the kernel and a process.

18.2 Routing Table Structure

Before looking at the internal structure of the Net/3 routing table, we need to understand the type of information contained in the table. Figure 18.1 is the bottom half of
Figure 1.17: the four systems on the author's Ethernet.

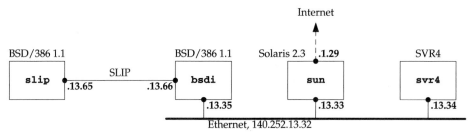

Figure 18.1   Subnet used for routing table example.

Figure 18.2 shows the routing table for `bsdi` in Figure 18.1.

```
bsdi $ netstat -rn
Routing tables

Internet:
Destination        Gateway          Flags      Refs      Use   Interface
default            140.252.13.33    UG S          0         3   le0
127                127.0.0.1        UG S   R      0         2   lo0
127.0.0.1          127.0.0.1        U  H          1        55   lo0
128.32.33.5        140.252.13.33    UGHS          2        16   le0
140.252.13.32      link#1           U     C       0         0   le0
140.252.13.33      8:0:20:3:f6:42   U  H  L       11    55146   le0
140.252.13.34      0:0:c0:c2:9b:26  U  H  L        0         3   le0
140.252.13.35      0:0:c0:6f:2d:40  U  H  L        1        12   lo0
140.252.13.65      140.252.13.66    U  H           0        41   sl0
224                link#1           U     C        0         0   le0
224.0.0.1          link#1           U  H  L        0         5   le0
```

Figure 18.2   Routing table on the host `bsdi`.

We have modified the "Flags" column from the normal `netstat` output, making it easier to see which flags are set for the various entries.

The routes in this table were entered as follows. Steps 1, 3, 5, 8, and 9 are performed
at system initialization when the `/etc/netstart` shell script is executed.

1. A default route is added by the `route` command to the host `sun`
    (140.252.13.33), which contains a PPP link to the Internet.

2. The entry for network 127 is typically created by a routing daemon such as
    `gated`, or it can be entered with the `route` command in the `/etc/netstart`
    file. This entry causes all packets sent to this network, other than references to
    the host 127.0.0.1 (which are covered by the more specific route entered in the
    next step), to be rejected by the loopback driver (Figure 5.27).

3. The entry for the loopback interface (127.0.0.1) is configured by `ifconfig`.

4. The entry for `vangogh.cs.berkeley.edu` (128.32.33.5) was created by hand using the `route` command. It specifies the same router as the default route (140.252.13.33), but having a host-specific route, instead of using the default route for this host, allows routing metrics to be stored in this entry. These metrics can optionally be set by the administrator, are used by TCP each time a connection is established to the destination host, and are updated by TCP when the connection is closed. We describe these metrics in more detail with Figure 27.3.

5. The interface `le0` is initialized using the `ifconfig` command. This causes the entry for network 140.252.13.32 to be entered into the routing table.

6. The entries for the other two hosts on the Ethernet, `sun` (140.252.13.33) and `svr4` (140.252.13.34), were created by ARP, as we describe in Chapter 21. These are temporary entries that are removed if they are not used for a certain period of time.

7. The entry for the local host, 140.252.13.35, is created the first time the host's own IP address is referenced. The interface is the loopback, meaning any IP datagrams sent to the host's own IP address are looped back internally. The automatic creation of this entry is new with 4.4BSD, as we describe in Section 21.13.

8. The entry for the host 140.252.13.65 is created when the SLIP interface is configured by `ifconfig`.

9. The `route` command adds the route to network 224 through the Ethernet interface.

10. The entry for the multicast group 224.0.0.1 (the all-hosts group) was created by running the Ping program, pinging the address 224.0.0.1. This is also a temporary entry that is removed if not used for a certain period of time.

The "Flags" column in Figure 18.2 needs a brief explanation. Figure 18.25 provides a list of all the possible flags.

U The route is up.

G The route is to a gateway (router). This is called an *indirect route*. If this flag is not set, the destination is directly connected; this is called a *direct route*.

H The route is to a host, that is, the destination is a complete host address. If this flag is *not* set, the route is to a network, and the destination is a network address: a network ID, or a combination of a network ID and a subnet ID. The `netstat` command doesn't show it, but each network route also contains a network mask. A host route has an implied mask of all one bits.

S The route is static. The three entries created by the `route` command in Figure 18.2 are static.

C   The route is cloned to create new routes. Two entries in this routing table have this flag set: (1) the route for the local Ethernet (140.252.13.32), which is cloned by ARP to create the host-specific routes of other hosts on the Ethernet, and (2) the route for multicast groups (224), which is cloned to create specific multicast group routes such as 224.0.0.1

L   The route contains a link-layer address. The host routes that ARP clones from the Ethernet network routes all have the link flag set. This applies to unicast and multicast addresses.

R   The loopback driver (the normal interface for routes with this flag) rejects all datagrams that use this route.

> The ability to enter a route with the "reject" flag was provided in Net/2. It provides a simple way of preventing datagrams destined to network 127 from appearing outside the host. See also Exercise 6.6.

Before 4.3BSD Reno, two distinct routing tables were maintained by the kernel for IP addresses: one for host routes and one for network routes. A given route was entered into one table or the other, based on the type of route. The default route was stored in the network routing table with a destination address of 0.0.0.0. There was an implied hierarchy: a search was made for a host route first, and if not found a search was made for a network route, and if still not found, a search was made for a default route. Only if all three searches failed was the destination unreachable. Section 11.5 of [Leffler et al. 1989] describes the hash table with linked lists used for the host and network routing tables in Net/1.

Major changes took place in the internal representation of the routing table with 4.3BSD Reno [Sklower 1991]. These changes allow the same routing table functions to access a routing table for other protocol suites, notably the OSI protocols, which use variable-length addresses, unlike the fixed-length 32-bit Internet addresses. The internal structure was also changed, to provide faster lookups.

The Net/3 routing table uses a Patricia tree structure [Sedgewick 1990] to represent both host addresses and network addresses. (Patricia stands for "Practical Algorithm to Retrieve Information Coded in Alphanumeric.") The address being searched for and the addresses in the tree are considered as sequences of bits. This allows the same functions to maintain and search one tree containing fixed-length 32-bit Internet addresses, another tree containing fixed-length 48-bit XNS addresses, and another tree containing variable-length OSI addresses.

> The idea of using Patricia trees for the routing table is attributed to Van Jacobson in [Sklower 1991]. These are actually binary radix tries with one-way branching removed.

An example is the easiest way to describe the algorithm. The goal of routing lookup is to find the most specific address that matches the given destination: the search key. The term *most specific* implies that a host address is preferred over a network address, which is preferred over a default address.

Each entry has an associated network mask, although no mask is stored with a host route; instead host routes have an implied mask of all one bits. An entry in the routing table matches a search key if the search key logically ANDed with the network mask of the entry equals the entry itself. A given search key might match multiple entries in the routing table, so with a single table for both network route and host routes, the table must be organized so that more-specific routes are considered before less-specific routes.

Consider the examples in Figure 18.3. The two search keys are 127.0.0.1 and 127.0.0.2, which we show in hexadecimal since the logical ANDing is easier to illustrate. The two routing table entries are the host entry for 127.0.0.1 (with an implied mask of 0xffffffff) and the network entry for 127.0.0.0 (with a mask of 0xff000000).

		search key = 127.0.0.1		search key = 127.0.0.2	
		host route	net route	host route	net route
1	search key	7f000001	7f000001	7f000002	7f000002
2	routing table key	7f000001	7f000000	7f000001	7f000000
3	routing table mask	ffffffff	ff000000	ffffffff	ff000000
4	logical AND of 1 and 3	7f000001	7f000000	7f000002	7f000000
	2 and 4 equal?	yes	yes	no	yes

Figure 18.3   Example routing table lookups for the two search keys 127.0.0.1 and 127.0.0.2.

Since the search key 127.0.0.1 matches both routing table entries, the routing table must be organized so that the more-specific entry (127.0.0.1) is tried first.

Figure 18.4 shows the internal representation of the Net/3 routing table corresponding to Figure 18.2. This table was built from the output of the netstat command with the -A flag, which dumps the tree structure of the routing tables.

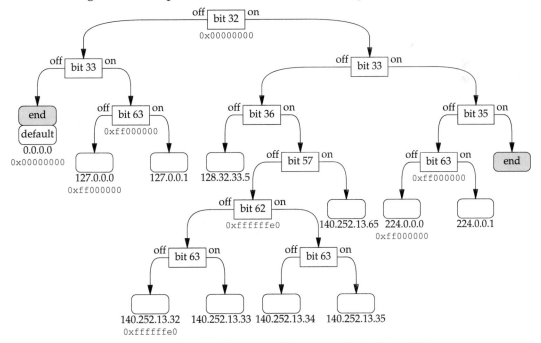

Figure 18.4   Net/3 routing table corresponding to Figure 18.2.

The two shaded boxes labeled "end" are leaves with special flags denoting the end of the tree. The left one has a key of all zero bits and the right one has a key of all one bits. The two boxes stacked together at the left, labeled "end" and "default," are a special representation used for duplicate keys, which we describe in Section 18.9.

The square-cornered boxes are called *internal nodes* or just *nodes*, and the boxes with rounded corners are called *leaves*. Each internal node corresponds to a bit to test in the search key, and a branch is made to the left or the right. Each leaf corresponds to either a host address or a network address. If there is a hexadecimal number beneath a leaf, that leaf is a network address and the number specifies the network mask for the leaf. The absence of a hexadecimal mask beneath a leaf node implies that the leaf is a host address with an implied mask of `0xffffffff`.

Some of the internal nodes also contain network masks, and we'll see how these are used in backtracking. Not shown in this figure is that every node also contains a pointer to its parent, to facilitate backtracking, deletion, and nonrecursive walks of the tree.

The bit comparisons are performed on socket address structures, so the bit positions given in Figure 18.4 are from the start of the socket address structure. Figure 18.5 shows the bit positions for a `sockaddr_in` structure.

Figure 18.5   Bit offsets in Internet socket address structure.

The highest-order bit of the IP address is at bit position 32 and the lowest-order bit is at bit position 63. We also show the length as 16 and the address family as 2 (`AF_INET`), as we'll encounter these two values throughout our examples.

To work through the examples we also need to show the bit representations of the various IP addresses in the tree. These are shown in Figure 18.6 along with some other IP addresses that are used in the examples that follow. The bit positions used in Figure 18.4 as branching points are shown in a bolder font.

We now provide some specific examples of how the routing table searches are performed.

Example—Host Match

Assume the host address 127.0.0.1 is the search key—the destination address being looked up. Bit 32 is off, so the left branch is made from the top of the tree. Bit 33 is on, so the right branch is made from the next node. Bit 63 is on, so the right branch is made from the next node. This next node is a leaf, so the search key (127.0.0.1) is compared to the address in the leaf (127.0.0.1). They match exactly so this routing table entry is returned by the lookup function.

	32-bit IP address (bits 32–63)							dotted-decimal
bit:	**3333** **2345**	**3333** **6789**	4444 0123	4444 4567	4455 8901	5555 2345	5555 6789	6666 0**123**	
	0000	1010	0000	0001	0000	0010	0000	0011	10.1.2.3
	0111	0000	0000	0000	0000	0000	0000	0001	112.0.0.1
	0111	1111	0000	0000	0000	0000	0000	0000	127.0.0.0
	0111	1111	0000	0000	0000	0000	0000	0001	127.0.0.1
	0111	1111	0000	0000	0000	0000	0000	0011	127.0.0.3
	1000	0000	0010	0000	0010	0001	0000	0101	128.32.33.5
	1000	0000	0010	0000	0010	0001	0000	0110	128.32.33.6
	1000	1100	1111	1100	0000	1101	0010	0000	140.252.13.32
	1000	1100	1111	1100	0000	1101	0010	0001	140.252.13.33
	1000	1100	1111	1100	0000	1101	0010	0010	140.252.13.34
	1000	1100	1111	1100	0000	1101	0010	0011	140.252.13.35
	1000	1100	1111	1100	0000	1101	0100	0001	140.252.13.65
	1110	0000	0000	0000	0000	0000	0000	0000	224.0.0.0
	1110	0000	0000	0000	0000	0000	0000	0001	224.0.0.1

Figure 18.6   Bit representations of the IP addresses in Figures 18.2 and 18.4.

Example—Host Match

Next assume the search key is the address 140.252.13.35. Bit 32 is on, so the right branch is made from the top of the tree. Bit 33 is off, bit 36 is on, bit 57 is off, bit 62 is on, and bit 63 is on, so the search ends at the leaf on the bottom labeled 140.252.13.35. The search key matches the routing table key exactly.

Example—Network Match

The search key is 127.0.0.2. Bit 32 is off, bit 33 is on, and bit 63 is off so the search ends up at the leaf labeled 127.0.0.0. The search key and the routing table key don't match exactly, so a network match is tried. The search key is logically ANDed with the network mask (0xff000000) and since the result equals the routing table key, this entry is considered a match.

Example—Default Match

The search key is 10.1.2.3. Bit 32 is off and bit 33 is off, so the search ends up at the leaf with the duplicate keys labeled "end" and "default." The routing table key that is duplicated in these two leaves is 0.0.0.0. The search key and the routing table key don't match exactly, so a network match is tried. This match is tried for all duplicate keys that have a network mask. The first key (the end marker) doesn't have a network mask, so it is skipped. The next key (the default entry) has a mask of 0x00000000. The search key is logically ANDed with this mask and since the result equals the routing table key (0), this entry is considered a match. The default route is used.

Example—Network Match with Backtracking

The search key is 127.0.0.3. Bit 32 is off, bit 33 is on, and bit 63 is on, so the search ends up at the leaf labeled 127.0.0.1. The search key and the routing table key don't match exactly. A network match cannot be attempted since this leaf does not have a network mask. Backtracking now takes place.

The backtracking algorithm is to move up the tree, one level at a time. If an internal node is encountered that contains a mask, the search key is logically ANDed with the mask and another search is made of the subtree starting at the node with the mask, looking for a match with the ANDed key. If a match isn't found, the backtrack keeps moving up the tree, until the top is reached.

In this example the search moves up one level to the node for bit 63 and this node contains a mask. The search key is logically ANDed with the mask (0xff000000), giving a new search key of 127.0.0.0. Another search is made starting at this node for 127.0.0.0. Bit 63 is off, so the left branch is taken to the leaf labeled 127.0.0.0. The new search key is compared to the routing table key and since they're equal, this leaf is the match.

Example—Backtracking Multiple Levels

The search key is 112.0.0.1. Bit 32 is off, bit 33 is on, and bit 63 is on, so the search ends up at the leaf labeled 127.0.0.1. The keys are not equal and the routing table entry does not have a network mask, so backtracking takes place.

The search moves up one level to the node for bit 63, which contains a mask. The search key is logically ANDed with the mask of 0xff000000 and another search is made starting at that node. Bit 63 is off in the new search key, so the left branch is made to the leaf labeled 127.0.0.0. A comparison is made but the ANDed search key (112.0.0.0) doesn't equal the search key in the table.

Backtracking continues up one level from the bit-63 node to the bit-33 node. But this node does not have a mask, so the backtracking continues upward. The next level is the top of the tree (bit 32) and it has a mask. The search key (112.0.0.1) is logically ANDed with the mask (0x00000000) and a new search started from that point. Bit 32 is off in the new search key, as is bit 33, so the search ends up at the leaf labeled "end" and "default." The list of duplicate keys is traversed and the default key matches the new search key, so the default route is used.

As we can see in this example, if a default route is present in the routing table, when the backtrack ends up at the top node in the tree, its mask is all zero bits, which causes the search to proceed to the leftmost leaf in the tree for a match with the default.

Example—Host Match with Backtracking and Cloning

The search key is 224.0.0.5. Bit 32 is on, bit 33 is on, bit 35 is off, and bit 63 is on, so the search ends up at the leaf labeled 224.0.0.1. This routing table key does not equal the search key, and the routing table entry does not contain a network mask, so backtracking takes place.

The backtrack moves one level up to the node that tests bit 63. This node contains the mask 0xff000000, so the search key ANDed with the mask yields a new search key of 224.0.0.0. Another search is made, starting at this node. Since bit 63 is off in the ANDed key, the left branch is taken to the leaf labeled 224.0.0.0. This routing table key matches the ANDed search key, so this entry is a match.

This route has the "clone" flag set (Figure 18.2), so a new leaf is created for the address 224.0.0.5. The new routing table entry is

```
Destination        Gateway               Flags      Refs       Use   Interface
224.0.0.5          link#1                UHL           0          0   le0
```

and Figure 18.7 shows the new arrangement of the right side of the routing table tree from Figure 18.4, starting with the node for bit 35. Notice that whenever a new leaf is added to the tree, two nodes are needed: one for the leaf and one for the internal node specifying the bit to test.

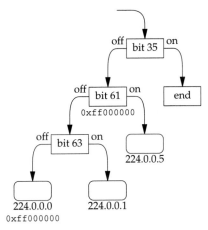

Figure 18.7   Modification of Figure 18.4 after inserting entry for 224.0.0.5.

This newly created entry is the one returned to the caller who was searching for 224.0.0.5.

The Big Picture

Figure 18.8 shows a bigger picture of all the data structures involved. The bottom portion of this figure is from Figure 3.32.

There are numerous points about this figure that we'll note now and describe in detail later in this chapter.

- rt_tables is an array of pointers to radix_node_head structures. There is one entry in the array for each address family. rt_tables[AF_INET] points to the top of the Internet routing table tree.

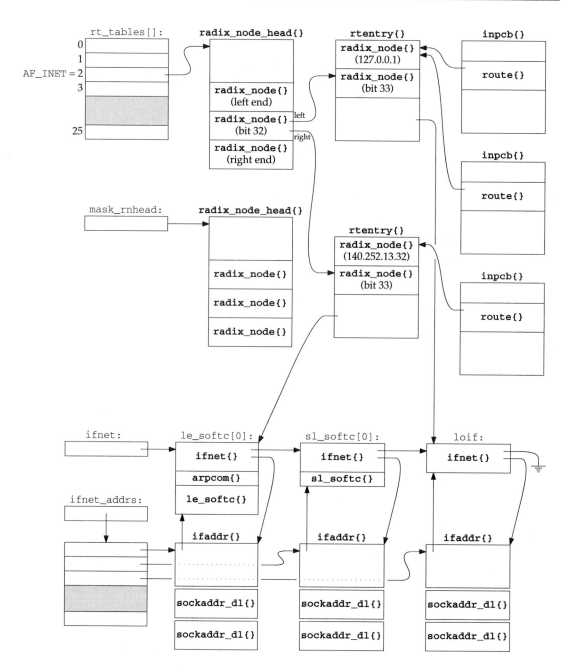

Figure 18.8   Data structures involved with routing tables.

- The `radix_node_head` structure contains three `radix_node` structures. These structures are built when the tree is initialized and the middle of the three is the top of the tree. This corresponds to the top box in Figure 18.4, labeled "bit 32." The first of the three `radix_node` structures is the leftmost leaf in Figure 18.4 (the shared duplicate with the default route) and the third of the three is the rightmost leaf. An empty routing table consists of just these three `radix_node` structures; we'll see how it is constructed by the `rn_inithead` function.

- The global `mask_rnhead` also points to a `radix_node_head` structure. This is the head of a separate tree of all the masks. Notice in Figure 18.4 that of the eight masks shown, one is duplicated four times and two are duplicated once. By keeping a separate tree for the masks, only one copy of each unique mask is maintained.

- The routing table tree is built from `rtentry` structures, and we show two of these in Figure 18.8. Each `rtentry` structure contains two `radix_node` structures, because each time a new entry is inserted into the tree, two nodes are required: an internal node corresponding to a bit to be tested, and a leaf node corresponding to a host route or a network route. In each `rtentry` structure we also show which bit test the internal node corresponds to and the address contained in the leaf node.

  The remainder of the `rtentry` structure is the focal point of information for this route. We show only a single pointer from this structure to the corresponding `ifnet` structure for the route, but this structure also contains a pointer to the `ifaddr` structure, the flags for the route, a pointer to another `rtentry` structure if this entry is an indirect route, the metrics for the route, and so on.

- Protocol control blocks (Chapter 22), of which one exists for each UDP and TCP socket (Figure 22.1), contain a `route` structure that points to an `rtentry` structure. The UDP and TCP output functions both pass a pointer to the `route` structure in a PCB as the third argument to `ip_output`, each time an IP datagram is sent. PCBs that use the same route point to the same routing table entry.

18.3 Routing Sockets

When the routing table changes were made with 4.3BSD Reno, the interaction of processes with the routing subsystem also changed—the concept of routing sockets was introduced. Prior to 4.3BSD Reno, fixed-length `ioctl`s were issued by a process (such as the `route` command) to modify the routing table. 4.3BSD Reno changed this to a more generalized message-passing scheme using the new PF_ROUTE domain. A process creates a raw socket in the PF_ROUTE domain and can send routing messages to the kernel, and receives routing messages from the kernel (e.g., redirects and other asynchronous notifications from the kernel).

Figure 18.9 shows the 12 different types of routing messages. The message type is the `rtm_type` field in the `rt_msghdr` structure, which we describe in Figure 19.16. Only five of the messages can be issued by a process (a write to a routing socket), but all 12 can be received by a process.

We'll defer our discussion of these routing messages until Chapter 19.

rtm_type	To kernel?	From kernel?	Description	Structure type
RTM_ADD	•	•	add route	rt_msghdr
RTM_CHANGE	•	•	change gateway, metrics, or flags	rt_msghdr
RTM_DELADDR		•	address being removed from interface	ifa_msghdr
RTM_DELETE	•	•	delete route	rt_msghdr
RTM_GET	•	•	report metrics and other route information	rt_msghdr
RTM_IFINFO		•	interface going up, down, etc.	if_msghdr
RTM_LOCK	•	•	lock specified metrics	rt_msghdr
RTM_LOSING		•	kernel suspects route is failing	rt_msghdr
RTM_MISS		•	lookup failed on this address	rt_msghdr
RTM_NEWADDR		•	address being added to interface	ifa_msghdr
RTM_REDIRECT		•	kernel told to use different route	rt_msghdr
RTM_RESOLVE		•	request to resolve destination to link-layer address	rt_msghdr

Figure 18.9   Types of messages exchanged across a routing socket.

18.4   Code Introduction

Three headers and five C files define the various structures and functions used for routing. These are summarized in Figure 18.10.

File	Description
net/radix.h	radix node definitions
net/raw_cb.h	routing control block definitions
net/route.h	routing structures
net/radix.c	radix node (Patricia tree) functions
net/raw_cb.c	routing control block functions
net/raw_usrreq.c	routing control block functions
net/route.c	routing functions
net/rtsock.c	routing socket functions

Figure 18.10   Files discussed in this chapter.

In general, the prefix rn_ denotes the radix node functions that search and manipulate the Patricia trees, the raw_ prefix denotes the routing control block functions, and the three prefixes route_, rt_, and rt denote the general routing functions.

> We use the term *routing control blocks* instead of *raw control blocks* in all the routing chapters, even though the files and functions begin with the prefix raw. This is to avoid confusion with the raw IP control blocks and functions, which we discuss in Chapter 32. Although the raw control blocks and their associated functions are used for more than just routing sockets in Net/3 (one of the raw OSI protocols uses these structures and functions), our use in this text is only with routing sockets in the PF_ROUTE domain.

Figure 18.11 shows the primary routing functions and their relationships. The shaded ellipses are the ones we cover in this chapter and the next two. We also show where each of the 12 routing message types are generated.

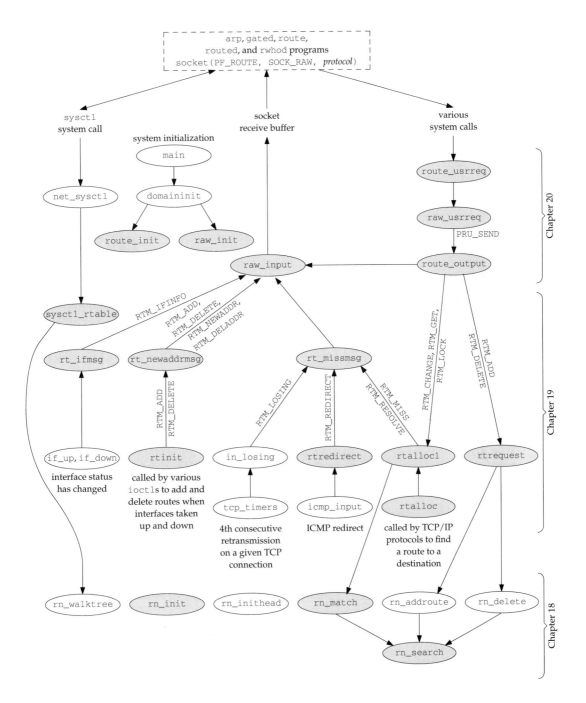

Figure 18.11   Relationships between the various routing functions.

rtalloc is the function called by the Internet protocols to look up routes to destinations. We've already encountered rtalloc in the ip_rtaddr, ip_forward, ip_output, and ip_setmoptions functions. We'll also encounter it later in the in_pcbconnect and tcp_mss functions.

We also show in Figure 18.11 that five programs typically create sockets in the routing domain:

- arp manipulates the ARP cache, which is stored in the IP routing table in Net/3 (Chapter 21),

- gated and routed are routing daemons that communicate with other routers and manipulate the kernel's routing table as the routing environment changes (routers and links go up or down),

- route is a program typically executed by start-up scripts or by the system administrator to add or delete routes, and

- rwhod issues a routing sysctl on start-up to determine the attached interfaces.

Naturally, any process (with superuser privilege) can open a routing socket to send and receive messages to and from the routing subsystem; we show only the common system programs in Figure 18.11.

Global Variables

The global variables introduced in the three routing chapters are shown in Figure 18.12.

Variable	Datatype	Description
rt_tables	struct radix_node_head * []	array of pointers to heads of routing tables
mask_rnhead	struct radix_node_head *	pointer to head of mask table
rn_mkfreelist	struct radix_mask *	head of linked list of available radix_mask structures
max_keylen	int	longest routing table key, in bytes
rn_zeros	char *	array of all zero bits, of length max_keylen
rn_ones	char *	array of all one bits, of length max_keylen
maskedKey	char *	array for masked search key, of length max_keylen
rtstat	struct rtstat	routing statistics (Figure 18.13)
rttrash	int	#routes not in table but not freed
rawcb	struct rawcb	head of doubly linked list of routing control blocks
raw_recvspace	u_long	default size of routing socket receive buffer, 8192 bytes
raw_sendspace	u_long	default size of routing socket send buffer, 8192 bytes
route_cb	struct route_cb	#routing socket listeners, per protocol, and total
route_dst	struct sockaddr	temporary for destination of routing message
route_src	struct sockaddr	temporary for source of routing message
route_proto	struct sockproto	temporary for protocol of routing message

Figure 18.12 Global variables in the three routing chapters.

Statistics

Some routing statistics are maintained in the global structure `rtstat`, described in Figure 18.13.

`rtstat` member	Description	Used by SNMP
rts_badredirect rts_dynamic rts_newgateway rts_unreach rts_wildcard	#invalid redirect calls #routes created by redirects #routes modified by redirects #lookups that failed #lookups matched by wildcard (never used)	

Figure 18.13   Routing statistics maintained in the `rtstat` structure.

We'll see where these counters are incremented as we proceed through the code. None are used by SNMP.

Figure 18.14 shows some sample output of these statistics from the `netstat -rs` command, which displays this structure.

`netstat -rs` output	`rtstat` member
1029 bad routing redirects 0 dynamically created routes 0 new gateways due to redirects 0 destinations found unreachable 0 uses of a wildcard route	rts_badredirect rts_dynamic rts_newgateway rts_unreach rts_wildcard

Figure 18.14   Sample routing statistics.

SNMP Variables

Figure 18.15 shows the IP routing table, named `ipRouteTable`, and the kernel variables that supply the corresponding value.

For `ipRouteType`, if the `RTF_GATEWAY` flag is set in `rt_flags`, the route is remote (4); otherwise the route is direct (3). For `ipRouteProto`, if either the `RTF_DYNAMIC` or `RTF_MODIFIED` flag is set, the route was created or modified by ICMP (4), otherwise the value is other (1). Finally, if the `rt_mask` pointer is null, the returned mask is all one bits (i.e., a host route).

18.5 Radix Node Data Structures

In Figure 18.8 we see that the head of each routing table is a `radix_node_head` and all the nodes in the routing tree, both the internal nodes and the leaves, are `radix_node` structures. The `radix_node_head` structure is shown in Figure 18.16.

IP routing table, index = < *ipRouteDest* >		
SNMP variable	Variable	Description
ipRouteDest	rt_key	Destination IP address. A value of 0.0.0.0 indicates a default entry.
ipRouteIfIndex	rt_ifp.if_index	Interface number: ifIndex.
ipRouteMetric1	−1	Primary routing metric. The meaning of the metric depends on the routing protocol (ipRouteProto). A value of −1 means it is not used.
ipRouteMetric2	−1	Alternative routing metric.
ipRouteMetric3	−1	Alternative routing metric.
ipRouteMetric4	−1	Alternative routing metric.
ipRouteNextHop	rt_gateway	IP address of next-hop router.
ipRouteType	(see text)	Route type: 1 = other, 2 = invalidated route, 3 = direct, 4 = indirect.
ipRouteProto	(see text)	Routing protocol: 1 = other, 4 = ICMP redirect, 8 = RIP, 13 = OSPF, 14 = BGP, and others.
ipRouteAge	(not implemented)	Number of seconds since route was last updated or determined to be correct.
ipRouteMask	rt_mask	Mask to be logically ANDed with destination IP address before being compared with ipRouteDest.
ipRouteMetric5	−1	Alternative routing metric.
ipRouteInfo	NULL	Reference to MIB definitions specific to this particular routing protocol.

Figure 18.15   IP routing table: ipRouteTable.

```
                                                                  ——— radix.h
 91 struct radix_node_head {
 92     struct radix_node *rnh_treetop;
 93     int     rnh_addrsize;        /* (not currently used) */
 94     int     rnh_pktsize;         /* (not currently used) */
 95     struct radix_node *(*rnh_addaddr)   /* add based on sockaddr */
 96             (void *v, void *mask,
 97              struct radix_node_head * head, struct radix_node nodes[]);
 98     struct radix_node *(*rnh_addpkt)    /* add based on packet hdr */
 99             (void *v, void *mask,
100              struct radix_node_head * head, struct radix_node nodes[]);
101     struct radix_node *(*rnh_deladdr)   /* remove based on sockaddr */
102             (void *v, void *mask, struct radix_node_head * head);
103     struct radix_node *(*rnh_delpkt)    /* remove based on packet hdr */
104             (void *v, void *mask, struct radix_node_head * head);
105     struct radix_node *(*rnh_matchaddr)    /* locate based on sockaddr */
106             (void *v, struct radix_node_head * head);
107     struct radix_node *(*rnh_matchpkt)  /* locate based on packet hdr */
108             (void *v, struct radix_node_head * head);
109     int     (*rnh_walktree)      /* traverse tree */
110             (struct radix_node_head * head, int (*f) (), void *w);

111     struct radix_node rnh_nodes[3];     /* top and end nodes */
112 };
                                                                  ——— radix.h
```

Figure 18.16   radix_node_head structure: the top of each routing tree.

92   `rnh_treetop` points to the top `radix_node` structure for the routing tree. Notice that three of these structures are allocated at the end of the `radix_node_head`, and the middle one of these is initialized as the top of the tree (Figure 18.8).

93–94   `rnh_addrsize` and `rnh_pktsize` are not currently used.

> `rnh_addrsize` is to facilitate porting the routing table code to systems that don't have a length byte in the socket address structure. `rnh_pktsize` is to allow using the radix node machinery to examine addresses in packet headers without having to copy the address into a socket address structure.

95–110   The seven function pointers, `rnh_addaddr` through `rnh_walktree`, point to functions that are called to operate on the tree. Only four of these pointers are initialized by `rn_inithead` and the other three are never used by Net/3, as shown in Figure 18.17.

Member	Initialized to (by `rn_inithead`)
`rnh_addaddr`	*rn_addroute*
`rnh_addpkt`	*NULL*
`rnh_deladdr`	*rn_delete*
`rnh_delpkt`	*NULL*
`rnh_matchaddr`	*rn_match*
`rnh_matchpkt`	*NULL*
`rnh_walktree`	*rn_walktree*

Figure 18.17 The seven function pointers in the `radix_node_head` structure.

111–112   Figure 18.18 shows the `radix_node` structure that forms the nodes of the tree. In Figure 18.8 we see that three of these are allocated in the `radix_node_head` and two are allocated in each `rtentry` structure.

—————————————————————————————————————— radix.h
```
40 struct radix_node {
41     struct radix_mask *rn_mklist;   /* list of masks contained in subtree */
42     struct radix_node *rn_p;     /* parent pointer */
43     short   rn_b;                /* bit offset; -1-index(netmask) */
44     char    rn_bmask;            /* node: mask for bit test */
45     u_char  rn_flags;            /* Figure 18.20 */
46     union {
47         struct {                 /* leaf only data: rn_b < 0 */
48             caddr_t rn_Key;      /* object of search */
49             caddr_t rn_Mask;     /* netmask, if present */
50             struct radix_node *rn_Dupedkey;
51         } rn_leaf;
52         struct {                 /* node only data: rn_b >= 0 */
53             int     rn_Off;      /* where to start compare */
54             struct radix_node *rn_L;    /* left pointer */
55             struct radix_node *rn_R;    /* right pointer */
56         } rn_node;
57     } rn_u;
58 };

59 #define rn_dupedkey rn_u.rn_leaf.rn_Dupedkey
60 #define rn_key      rn_u.rn_leaf.rn_Key
```

```
61 #define rn_mask      rn_u.rn_leaf.rn_Mask
62 #define rn_off       rn_u.rn_node.rn_Off
63 #define rn_l         rn_u.rn_node.rn_L
64 #define rn_r         rn_u.rn_node.rn_R
```
── *radix.h*

Figure 18.18   radix_node structure: the nodes of the routing tree.

41–45   The first five members are common to both internal nodes and leaves, followed by a
union defining three members if the node is a leaf, or a different three members if the
node is internal. As is common throughout the Net/3 code, a set of #define statements provide shorthand names for the members in the union.

41–42   rn_mklist is the head of a linked list of masks for this node. We describe this field
in Section 18.9. rn_p points to the parent node.

43   If rn_b is greater than or equal to 0, the node is an internal node, else the node is a
leaf. For the internal nodes, rn_b is the bit number to test: for example, its value is 32
in the top node of the tree in Figure 18.4. For leaves, rn_b is negative and its value is –1
minus the *index of the network mask*. This index is the first bit number where a 0 occurs.
Figure 18.19 shows the indexes of the masks from Figure 18.4.

	32-bit IP mask (bits 32–63)								index	rn_b
	3333	3333	4444	4444	4455	5555	5555	6666		
	2345	6789	0123	4567	8901	2345	6789	0123		
00000000:	0000	0000	0000	0000	0000	0000	0000	0000	0	–1
ff000000:	1111	1111	0000	0000	0000	0000	0000	0000	40	–41
ffffffe0:	1111	1111	1111	1111	1111	1111	1110	0000	59	–60

Figure 18.19   Example of mask indexes.

As we can see, the index of the all-zero mask is handled specially: its index is 0, not 32.

44   rn_bmask is a 1-byte mask used with the internal nodes to test whether the corresponding bit is on or off. Its value is 0 in leaves. We'll see how this member is used
with the rn_off member shortly.

45   Figure 18.20 shows the three values for the rn_flags member.

Constant	Description
RNF_ACTIVE	this node is alive (for rtfree)
RNF_NORMAL	leaf contains normal route (not currently used)
RNF_ROOT	node is in the radix_node_head structure

Figure 18.20   rn_flags values.

The RNF_ROOT flag is set only for the three radix nodes in the radix_node_head
structure: the top of the tree and the left and right end nodes. These three nodes can
never be deleted from the routing tree.

48–49   For a leaf, `rn_key` points to the socket address structure and `rn_mask` points to a socket address structure containing the mask. If `rn_mask` is null, the implied mask is all one bits (i.e., this route is to a host, not to a network).

Figure 18.21 shows an example corresponding to the leaf for 140.252.13.32 in Figure 18.4.

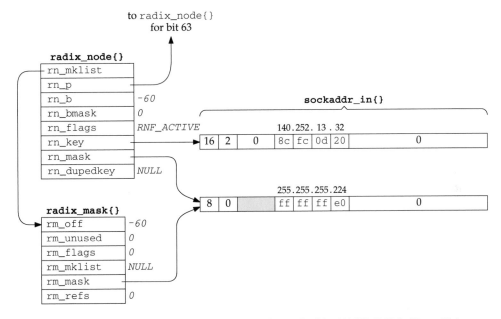

Figure 18.21   `radix_node` structure corresponding to leaf for 140.252.13.32 in Figure 18.4.

This example also shows a `radix_mask` structure, which we describe in Figure 18.22. We draw this latter structure with a smaller width, to help distinguish it as a different structure from the `radix_node`; we'll encounter both structures in many of the figures that follow. We describe the reason for the `radix_mask` structure in Section 18.9.

The `rn_b` of –60 corresponds to an index of 59. `rn_key` points to a `sockaddr_in`, with a length of 16 and an address family of 2 (`AF_INET`). The mask structure pointed to by `rn_mask` and `rm_mask` has a length of 8 and a family of 0 (this family is `AF_UNSPEC`, but it is never even looked at).

50–51   The `rn_dupedkey` pointer is used when there are multiple leaves with the same key. We describe these in Section 18.9.

52–58   We describe `rn_off` in Section 18.8. `rn_l` and `rn_r` are the left and right pointers for the internal node.

Figure 18.22 shows the `radix_mask` structure.

── radix.h
```
76 extern struct radix_mask {
77     short    rm_b;                 /* bit offset; -1-index(netmask) */
78     char     rm_unused;            /* cf. rn_bmask */
79     u_char   rm_flags;             /* cf. rn_flags */
80     struct radix_mask *rm_mklist;  /* more masks to try */
81     caddr_t rm_mask;               /* the mask */
82     int      rm_refs;              /* # of references to this struct */
83 }       *rn_mkfreelist;
```
── radix.h

Figure 18.22   radix_mask structure.

76–83   Each of these structures contains a pointer to a mask: rm_mask, which is really a pointer to a socket address structure containing the mask. Each radix_node structure points to a linked list of radix_mask structures, allowing multiple masks per node: rn_mklist points to the first, and then each rm_mklist points to the next. This structure definition also declares the global rn_mkfreelist, which is the head of a linked list of available structures.

18.6   Routing Structures

The focal points of access to the kernel's routing information are

1.   the rtalloc function, which searches for a route to a destination,

2.   the route structure that is filled in by this function, and

3.   the rtentry structure that is pointed to by the route structure.

Figure 18.8 showed that the protocol control blocks (PCBs) used by UDP and TCP (Chapter 22) contain a route structure, which we show in Figure 18.23.

── route.h
```
46 struct route {
47     struct rtentry *ro_rt;    /* pointer to struct with information */
48     struct sockaddr ro_dst;   /* destination of this route */
49 };
```
── route.h

Figure 18.23   route structure.

ro_dst is declared as a generic socket address structure, but for the Internet protocols it is a sockaddr_in. Notice that unlike most references to this type of structure, ro_dst is the structure itself, not a pointer to one.

At this point it is worth reviewing Figure 8.24, which shows the use of these routes every time an IP datagram is output.

• If the caller passes a pointer to a route structure, that structure is used. Otherwise a local route structure is used and it is set to 0, setting ro_rt to a null pointer. UDP and TCP pass a pointer to the route structure in their PCB to ip_output.

- If the `route` structure points to an `rtentry` structure (the `ro_rt` pointer is nonnull), and if the referenced interface is still up, and if the destination address in the `route` structure equals the destination address of the IP datagram, that route is used. Otherwise the socket address structure `ro_dst` is filled in with the destination IP address and `rtalloc` is called to locate a route to that destination. For a TCP connection the destination address of the datagram never changes from the destination address of the route, but a UDP application can send a datagram to a different destination with each `sendto`.

- If `rtalloc` returns a null pointer in `ro_rt`, a route was not found and `ip_output` returns an error.

- If the `RTF_GATEWAY` flag is set in the `rtentry` structure, the route is indirect (the G flag in Figure 18.2). The destination address (`dst`) for the interface output function becomes the IP address of the gateway, the `rt_gateway` member, not the destination address of the IP datagram.

Figure 18.24 shows the `rtentry` structure.

─── *route.h*
```
83 struct rtentry {
84     struct radix_node rt_nodes[2];   /* a leaf and an internal node */

85     struct sockaddr *rt_gateway;     /* value associated with rn_key */
86     short   rt_flags;               /* Figure 18.25 */
87     short   rt_refcnt;              /* #held references */
88     u_long  rt_use;                 /* raw #packets sent */
89     struct ifnet *rt_ifp;           /* interface to use */
90     struct ifaddr *rt_ifa;          /* interface address to use */
91     struct sockaddr *rt_genmask;     /* for generation of cloned routes */
92     caddr_t rt_llinfo;              /* pointer to link level info cache */
93     struct rt_metrics rt_rmx;       /* metrics: Figure 18.26 */
94     struct rtentry *rt_gwroute;     /* implied entry for gatewayed routes */
95 };

96 #define rt_key(r)    ((struct sockaddr *)((r)->rt_nodes->rn_key))
97 #define rt_mask(r)   ((struct sockaddr *)((r)->rt_nodes->rn_mask))
```
─── *route.h*

Figure 18.24   `rtentry` structure.

83–84   Two `radix_node` structures are contained within this structure. As we noted in the example with Figure 18.7, each time a new leaf is added to the routing tree a new internal node is also added. `rt_nodes[0]` contains the leaf entry and `rt_nodes[1]` contains the internal node. The two #define statements at the end of Figure 18.24 provide a shorthand access to the key and mask of this leaf node.

86   Figure 18.25 shows the various constants stored in `rt_flags` and the corresponding character output by `netstat` in the "Flags" column (Figure 18.2).

The `RTF_BLACKHOLE` flag is not output by `netstat` and the two with lowercase flag characters, `RTF_DONE` and `RTF_MASK`, are used in routing messages and not normally stored in the routing table entry.

85   If the `RTF_GATEWAY` flag is set, `rt_gateway` contains a pointer to a socket address structure containing the address (e.g., the IP address) of that gateway. Also,

Constant	netstat flag	Description
RTF_BLACKHOLE		discard packets without error (loopback driver: Figure 5.27)
RTF_CLONING	C	generate new routes on use (used by ARP)
RTF_DONE	d	kernel confirmation that message from process was completed
RTF_DYNAMIC	D	created dynamically (by redirect)
RTF_GATEWAY	G	destination is a gateway (indirect route)
RTF_HOST	H	host entry (else network entry)
RTF_LLINFO	L	set by ARP when rt_llinfo pointer valid
RTF_MASK	m	subnet mask present (not used)
RTF_MODIFIED	M	modified dynamically (by redirect)
RTF_PROTO1	1	protocol-specific routing flag
RTF_PROTO2	2	protocol-specific routing flag (ARP uses)
RTF_REJECT	R	discard packets with error (loopback driver: Figure 5.27)
RTF_STATIC	S	manually added entry (route program)
RTF_UP	U	route usable
RTF_XRESOLVE	X	external daemon resolves name (used with X.25)

Figure 18.25 rt_flags values.

rt_gwroute points to the rtentry for that gateway. This latter pointer was used in ether_output (Figure 4.15).

87   rt_refcnt counts the "held" references to this structure. We describe this counter at the end of Section 19.3. This counter is output as the "Refs" column in Figure 18.2.

88   rt_use is initialized to 0 when the structure is allocated; we saw it incremented in Figure 8.24 each time an IP datagram was output using the route. This counter is also the value printed in the "Use" column in Figure 18.2.

89–90 rt_ifp and rt_ifa point to the interface structure and the interface address structure, respectively. Recall from Figure 6.5 that a given interface can have multiple addresses, so minimally the rt_ifa is required.

92   The rt_llinfo pointer allows link-layer protocols to store pointers to their protocol-specific structures in the routing table entry. This pointer is normally used with the RTF_LLINFO flag. Figure 21.1 shows how ARP uses this pointer.

```
                                                                        route.h
54 struct rt_metrics {
55     u_long  rmx_locks;        /* bitmask for values kernel leaves alone */
56     u_long  rmx_mtu;          /* MTU for this path */
57     u_long  rmx_hopcount;     /* max hops expected */
58     u_long  rmx_expire;       /* lifetime for route, e.g. redirect */
59     u_long  rmx_recvpipe;     /* inbound delay-bandwith product */
60     u_long  rmx_sendpipe;     /* outbound delay-bandwith product */
61     u_long  rmx_ssthresh;     /* outbound gateway buffer limit */
62     u_long  rmx_rtt;          /* estimated round trip time */
63     u_long  rmx_rttvar;       /* estimated RTT variance */
64     u_long  rmx_pksent;       /* #packets sent using this route */
65 };
                                                                        route.h
```

Figure 18.26 rt_metrics structure.

93   Figure 18.26 shows the rt_metrics structure, which is contained within the rtentry structure. Figure 27.3 shows that TCP uses six members in this structure.

54–65   rmx_locks is a bitmask telling the kernel which of the eight metrics that follow must not be modified. The values for this bitmask are shown in Figure 20.13.

rmx_expire is used by ARP (Chapter 21) as a timer for each ARP entry. Contrary to the comment with rmx_expire, it is not used for redirects.

Figure 18.28 summarizes the structures that we've described, their relationships, and the various types of socket address structures they reference. The rtentry that we show is for the route to 128.32.33.5 in Figure 18.2. The other radix_node contained in the rtentry is for the bit 36 test right above this node in Figure 18.4. The two sockaddr_dl structures pointed to by the first ifaddr were shown in Figure 3.38. Also note from Figure 6.5 that the ifnet structure is contained within an le_softc structure, and the second ifaddr structure is contained within an in_ifaddr structure.

18.7 Initialization: route_init and rtable_init Functions

The initialization of the routing tables is somewhat obscure and takes us back to the domain structures in Chapter 7. Before outlining the function calls, Figure 18.27 shows the relevant fields from the domain structure (Figure 7.5) for various protocol families.

Member	OSI value	Internet value	Routing value	Unix value	XNS value	Comment
dom_family	AF_ISO	AF_INET	PF_ROUTE	AF_UNIX	AF_NS	
dom_init	0	0	route_init	0	0	
dom_rtattach	rn_inithead	rn_inithead	0	0	rn_inithead	
dom_rtoffset	48	32	0	0	16	in bits
dom_maxrtkey	32	16	0	0	16	in bytes

Figure 18.27   Members of domain structure relevant to routing.

The PF_ROUTE domain is the only one with an initialization function. Also, only the domains that require a routing table have a dom_rtattach function, and it is always rn_inithead. The routing domain and the Unix domain protocols do not require a routing table.

The dom_rtoffset member is the offset, in bits, (from the beginning of the domain's socket address structure) of the first bit to be examined for routing. The size of this structure in bytes is given by dom_maxrtkey. We saw earlier in this chapter that the offset of the IP address in the sockaddr_in structure is 32 bits. The dom_maxrtkey member is the size in bytes of the protocol's socket address structure: 16 for sockaddr_in.

Figure 18.29 outlines the steps involved in initializing the routing tables.

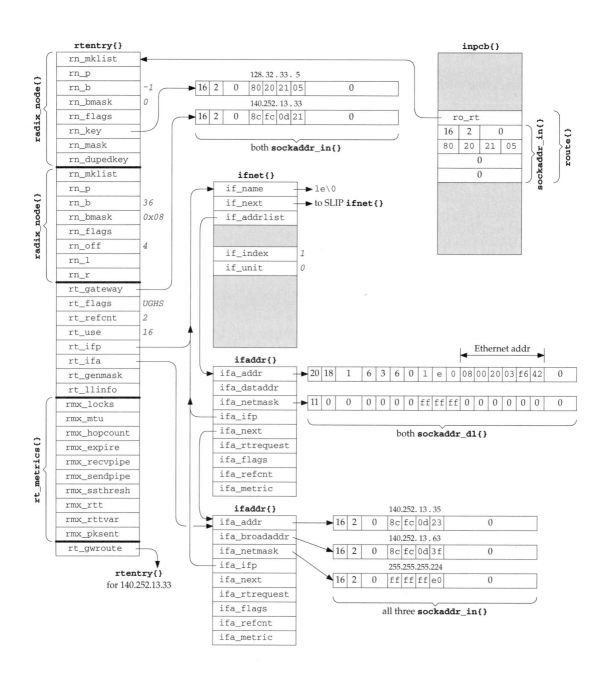

Figure 18.28 Summary of routing structures.

```
main()              /* kernel initialization */
{
    ...
    ifinit();
    domaininit();
    ...
}
domaininit()        /* Figure 7.15 */
{
    ...
    ADDDOMAIN(unix);
    ADDDOMAIN(route);
    ADDDOMAIN(inet);
    ADDDOMAIN(osi);
    ...
    for ( dp = all domains ) {
            (*dp->dom_init)();
            for ( pr = all protocols for this domain )
                    (*pr->pr_init)();
    }
}
raw_init()          /* pr_init() function for SOCK_RAW/PF_ROUTE protocol */
{
    initialize head of routing protocol control blocks;
}
route_init()        /* dom_init() function for PF_ROUTE domain */
{
    rn_init();
    rtable_init();
}
rn_init()
{
    for ( dp = all domains )
        if (dp->dom_maxrtkey > max_keylen)
            max_keylen = dp->dom_maxrtkey;
    allocate and initialize rn_zeros, rn_ones, masked_key;
    rn_inithead(&mask_rnhead);   /* allocate and init tree for masks */
}
rtable_init()
{
    for ( dp = all domains )
            (*dp->dom_rtattach)(&rt_tables[dp->dom_family]);
}
rn_inithead()       /* dom_rtattach() function for all protocol families */
{
    allocate and initialize one radix_node_head structure;
}
```

Figure 18.29   Steps involved in initialization of routing tables.

domaininit is called once by the kernel's main function when the system is initialized. The linked list of domain structures is built by the ADDDOMAIN macro and the linked list is traversed, calling each domain's dom_init function, if defined. As we saw in Figure 18.27, the only dom_init function is route_init, which is shown in Figure 18.30.

```
                                                                    route.c
49 void
50 route_init()
51 {
52     rn_init();   /* initialize all zeros, all ones, mask table */

53     rtable_init((void **) rt_tables);
54 }
                                                                    route.c
```

Figure 18.30   route_init function.

The function rn_init, shown in Figure 18.32, is called only once.

The function rtable_init, shown in Figure 18.31, is also called only once. It in turn calls all the dom_rtattach functions, which initialize a routing table tree for that domain.

```
                                                                    route.c
39 void
40 rtable_init(table)
41 void   **table;
42 {
43     struct domain *dom;
44     for (dom = domains; dom; dom = dom->dom_next)
45         if (dom->dom_rtattach)
46             dom->dom_rtattach(&table[dom->dom_family],
47                               dom->dom_rtoffset);
48 }
                                                                    route.c
```

Figure 18.31   rtable_init function: call each domain's dom_rtattach function.

We saw in Figure 18.27 that the only dom_rtattach function is rn_inithead, which we describe in the next section.

18.8   Initialization: `rn_init` and `rn_inithead` Functions

The function rn_init, shown in Figure 18.32, is called once by route_init to initialize some of the globals used by the radix functions.

```
                                                                    radix.c
750 void
751 rn_init()
752 {
753     char    *cp, *cplim;
754     struct domain *dom;
```

```
755        for (dom = domains; dom; dom = dom->dom_next)
756            if (dom->dom_maxrtkey > max_keylen)
757                max_keylen = dom->dom_maxrtkey;
758        if (max_keylen == 0) {
759            printf("rn_init: radix functions require max_keylen be set\n");
760            return;
761        }
762        R_Malloc(rn_zeros, char *, 3 * max_keylen);
763        if (rn_zeros == NULL)
764            panic("rn_init");
765        Bzero(rn_zeros, 3 * max_keylen);
766        rn_ones = cp = rn_zeros + max_keylen;
767        maskedKey = cplim = rn_ones + max_keylen;
768        while (cp < cplim)
769            *cp++ = -1;

770        if (rn_inithead((void **) &mask_rnhead, 0) == 0)
771            panic("rn_init 2");
772 }
```
—— *radix.c*

Figure 18.32 rn_init function.

Determine `max_keylen`

750–761   All the `domain` structures are examined and the global `max_keylen` is set to the largest value of `dom_maxrtkey`. In Figure 18.27 the largest value is 32 for `AF_ISO`, but in a typical system that excludes the OSI and XNS protocols, `max_keylen` is 16, the size of a `sockaddr_in` structure.

Allocate and initialize `rn_zeros`, `rn_ones`, and `maskedKey`

762–769   A buffer three times the size of `max_keylen` is allocated and the pointer stored in the global `rn_zeros`. `R_Malloc` is a macro that calls the kernel's `malloc` function, specifying a type of `M_RTABLE` and `M_DONTWAIT`. We'll also encounter the macros `Bcmp`, `Bcopy`, `Bzero`, and `Free`, which call kernel functions of similar names, with the arguments appropriately type cast.

This buffer is divided into three pieces, and each piece is initialized as shown in Figure 18.33.

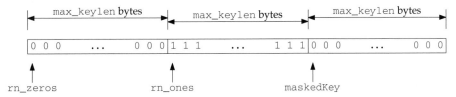

Figure 18.33 rn_zeros, rn_ones, and maskedKey arrays.

`rn_zeros` is an array of all zero bits, `rn_ones` is an array of all one bits, and `maskedKey` is an array used to hold a temporary copy of a search key that has been masked.

Initialize tree of masks

770–772   The function `rn_inithead` is called to initialize the head of the routing tree for the address masks; the `radix_node_head` structure pointed to by the global `mask_rnhead` in Figure 18.8.

From Figure 18.27 we see that `rn_inithead` is also the `dom_attach` function for all the protocols that require a routing table. Instead of showing the source code for this function, Figure 18.34 shows the `radix_node_head` structure that it builds for the Internet protocols.

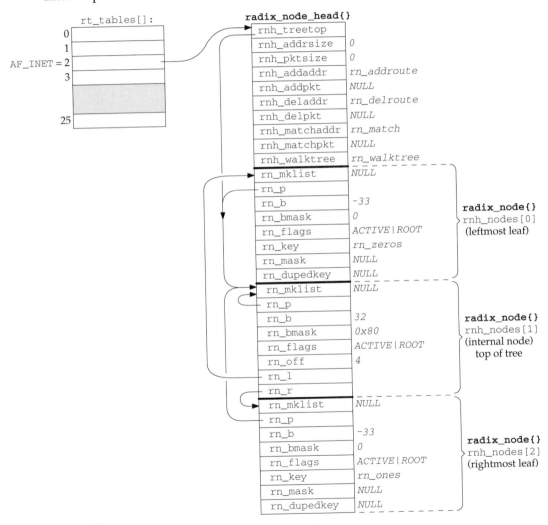

Figure 18.34   `radix_node_head` structure built by `rn_inithead` for Internet protocols.

The three `radix_node` structures form a tree: the middle of the three is the top (it is pointed to by `rnh_treetop`), the first of the three is the leftmost leaf of the tree, and the last of the three is the rightmost leaf of the tree. The parent pointer of all three nodes (`rn_p`) points to the middle node.

The value 32 for `rnh_nodes[1].rn_b` is the bit position to test. It is from the `dom_rtoffset` member of the Internet `domain` structure (Figure 18.27). Instead of performing shifts and masks during forwarding, the byte offset and corresponding byte mask are precomputed. The byte offset from the start of a socket address structure is in the `rn_off` member of the `radix_node` structure (4 in this case) and the byte mask is in the `rn_bmask` member (`0x80` in this case). These values are computed whenever a `radix_node` structure is added to the tree, to speed up the comparisons during forwarding. As additional examples, the offset and byte mask for the two nodes that test bit 33 in Figure 18.4 would be 4 and `0x40`, respectively. The offset and byte mask for the two nodes that test bit 63 would be 7 and `0x01`.

The value of –33 for the `rn_b` member of both leaves is negative one minus the index of the leaf.

The key of the leftmost node is all zero bits (`rn_zeros`) and the key of the rightmost node is all one bits (`rn_ones`).

All three nodes have the `RNF_ROOT` flag set. (We have omitted the `RNF_` prefix.) This indicates that the node is one of the three original nodes used to build the tree. These are the only nodes with this flag.

> One detail we have not mentioned is that the Network File System (NFS) also uses the routing table functions. For each mount point on the local host a `radix_node_head` structure is allocated, along with an array of pointers to these structures (indexed by the protocol family), similar to the `rt_tables` array. Each time this mount point is exported, the protocol address of the host that can mount this filesystem is added to the appropriate tree for the mount point.

18.9 Duplicate Keys and Mask Lists

Before looking at the source code that looks up entries in a routing table we need to understand two fields in the `radix_node` structure: `rn_dupedkey`, which forms a linked list of additional `radix_node` structures containing duplicate keys, and `rn_mklist`, which starts a linked list of `radix_mask` structures containing network masks.

We first return to Figure 18.4 and the two boxes on the far left of the tree labeled "end" and "default." These are duplicate keys. The leftmost node with the `RNF_ROOT` flag set (`rnh_nodes[0]` in Figure 18.34) has a key of all zero bits, but this is the same key as the default route. We would have the same problem with the rightmost end node in the tree, which has a key of all one bits, if an entry were created for 255.255.255.255, but this is the limited broadcast address, which doesn't appear in the routing table. In general, the radix node functions in Net/3 allow any key to be duplicated, if each occurrence has a unique mask.

Figure 18.35 shows the two nodes with a duplicate key of all zero bits. In this figure we have removed the `RNF_` prefix for the `rn_flags` and omit nonnull parent, left, and right pointers, which add nothing to the discussion.

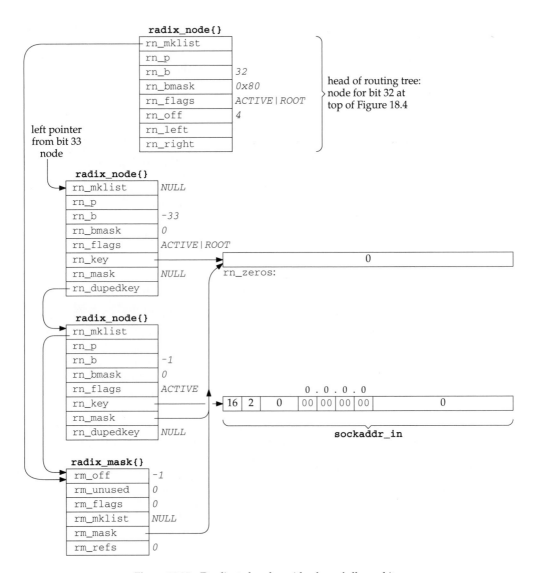

Figure 18.35 Duplicated nodes with a key of all zero bits.

The top node is the top of the routing tree—the node for bit 32 at the top of Figure 18.4. The next two nodes are leaves (their `rn_b` values are negative) with the `rn_dupedkey` member of the first pointing to the second. The first of these two leaves is the `rnh_nodes[0]` structure from Figure 18.34, which is the left end marker of the tree—its `RNF_ROOT` flag is set. Its key was explicitly set by `rn_inithead` to `rn_zeros`.

The second of these leaves is the entry for the default route. Its `rn_key` points to a `sockaddr_in` with the value 0.0.0.0, and it has a mask of all zero bits. Its `rn_mask` points to `rn_zeros`, since equivalent masks in the mask table are shared.

Normally keys are not shared, let alone shared with masks. The rn_key pointers of the two end markers (those with the RNF_ROOT flag) are special since they are built by rn_inithead (Figure 18.34). The key of the left end marker points to rn_zeros and the key of the right end marker points to rn_ones.

The final structure is a radix_mask structure and is pointed to by both the top node of the tree and the leaf for the default route. The list from the top node of the tree is used with the backtracking algorithm when the search is looking for a network mask. The list of radix_mask structures with an internal node specifies the masks that apply to subtrees starting at that node. In the case of duplicate keys, a mask list also appears with the leaves, as we'll see in the following example.

We now show a duplicate key that is added to the routing tree intentionally and the resulting mask list. In Figure 18.4 we have a host route for 127.0.0.1 and a network route for 127.0.0.0. The default mask for the class A network route is 0xff000000, as we show in the figure. If we divide the 24 bits following the class A network ID into a 16-bit subnet ID and an 8-bit host ID, we can add a route for the subnet 127.0.0 with a mask of 0xffffff00:

```
bsdi $ route add 127.0.0.0 -netmask 0xffffff00 140.252.13.33
```

Although it makes little practical sense to use network 127 in this fashion, our interest is in the resulting routing table structure. Although duplicate keys are not common with the Internet protocols (other than the previous example with the default route), duplicate keys are required to provide routes to subnet 0 of any network.

There is an implied priority in these three entries with a network ID of 127. If the search key is 127.0.0.1 it matches all three entries, but the host route is selected because it is the *most specific*: its mask (0xffffffff) has the most one bits. If the search key is 127.0.0.2 it matches both network routes, but the route for subnet 0, with a mask of 0xffffff00, is more specific than the route with a mask of 0xff000000. The search key 127.1.2.3 matches only the entry with a mask of 0xff000000.

Figure 18.36 shows the resulting tree structure, starting at the internal node for bit 33 from Figure 18.4. We show two boxes for the entry with the key of 127.0.0.0 since there are two leaves with this duplicate key.

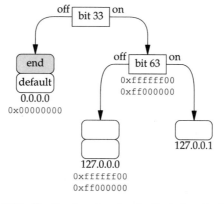

Figure 18.36   Routing tree showing duplicate keys for 127.0.0.0.

Figure 18.37 shows the resulting `radix_node` and `radix_mask` structures.

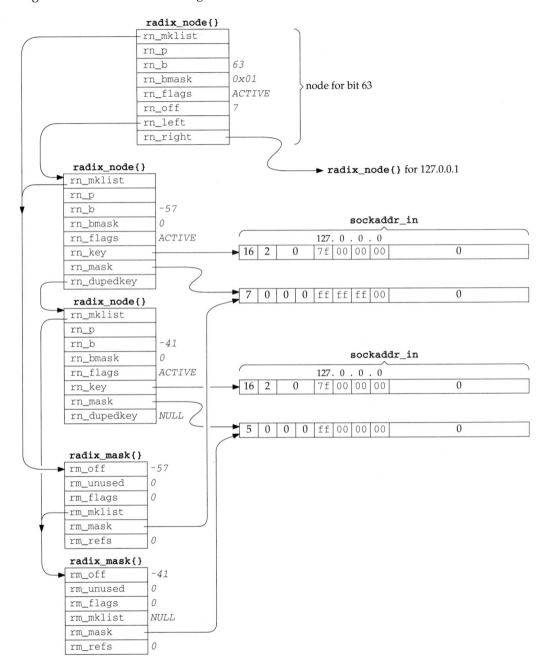

Figure 18.37   Example routing table structures for the duplicate keys for network 127.0.0.0.

First look at the linked list of radix_mask structures for each radix_node. The mask list for the top node (bit 63) consists of the entry for 0xffffff00 followed by 0xff000000. The more-specific mask comes first in the list so that it is tried first. The mask list for the second radix_node (the one with the rn_b of –57) is the same as that of the first. But the list for the third radix_node consists of only the entry with a mask of 0xff000000.

Notice that masks with the same value are shared but keys with the same value are not. This is because the masks are maintained in their own routing tree, explicitly to be shared, because equal masks are so common (e.g., every class C network route has the same mask of 0xffffff00), while equal keys are infrequent.

18.10 rn_match Function

We now show the rn_match function, which is called as the rnh_matchaddr function for the Internet protocols. We'll see that it is called by the rtalloc1 function, which is called by the rtalloc function. The algorithm is as follows:

1. Start at the top of the tree and go to the leaf corresponding to the bits in the search key. Check the leaf for an exact match (Figure 18.38).

2. Check the leaf for a network match (Figure 18.40).

3. Backtrack (Figure 18.43).

Figure 18.38 shows the first part of rn_match.

radix.c
```
135 struct radix_node *
136 rn_match(v_arg, head)
137 void    *v_arg;
138 struct radix_node_head *head;
139 {
140     caddr_t v = v_arg;
141     struct radix_node *t = head->rnh_treetop, *x;
142     caddr_t cp = v, cp2, cp3;
143     caddr_t cplim, mstart;
144     struct radix_node *saved_t, *top = t;
145     int     off = t->rn_off, vlen = *(u_char *) cp, matched_off;

146     /*
147      * Open code rn_search(v, top) to avoid overhead of extra
148      * subroutine call.
149      */
150     for (; t->rn_b >= 0;) {
151         if (t->rn_bmask & cp[t->rn_off])
152             t = t->rn_r;       /* right if bit on */
153         else
154             t = t->rn_l;       /* left if bit off */
155     }
```

```
156     /*
157      * See if we match exactly as a host destination
158      */
159     cp += off;
160     cp2 = t->rn_key + off;
161     cplim = v + vlen;
162     for (; cp < cplim; cp++, cp2++)
163         if (*cp != *cp2)
164             goto on1;
165     /*
166      * This extra grot is in case we are explicitly asked
167      * to look up the default.  Ugh!
168      */
169     if ((t->rn_flags & RNF_ROOT) && t->rn_dupedkey)
170         t = t->rn_dupedkey;
171     return t;
172 on1:
```
—————————————————————————————————— radix.c

Figure 18.38   rn_match function: go down tree, check for exact host match.

135–145   The first argument v_arg is a pointer to a socket address structure, and the second argument head is a pointer to the radix_node_head structure for the protocol. All protocols call this function (Figure 18.17) but each calls it with a different head argument.

In the assignment statements, off is the rn_off member of the top node of the tree (4 for Internet addresses, from Figure 18.34), and vlen is the length field from the socket address structure of the search key (16 for Internet addresses).

Go down the tree to the corresponding leaf

146–155   This loop starts at the top of the tree and moves down the left and right branches until a leaf is encountered (rn_b is less than 0). Each test of the appropriate bit is made using the precomputed byte mask in rn_bmask and the corresponding precomputed offset in rn_off. For Internet addresses, rn_off will be 4, 5, 6, or 7.

Check for exact match

156–164   When the leaf is encountered, a check is first made for an exact match. *All* bytes of the socket address structure, starting at the rn_off value for the protocol family, are compared. This is shown in Figure 18.39 for an Internet socket address structure.

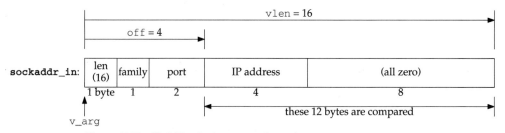

Figure 18.39   Variables during comparison of sockaddr_in structures.

As soon as a mismatch is found, a jump is made to on1.

Normally the final 8 bytes of the sockaddr_in are 0 but proxy ARP (Section 21.12) sets one of these bytes nonzero. This allows two routing table entries for a given IP address: one for the normal IP address (with the final 8 bytes of 0) and a proxy ARP entry for the same IP address (with one of the final 8 bytes nonzero).

The length byte in Figure 18.39 was assigned to vlen at the beginning of the function, and we'll see that rtalloc1 uses the family member to select the routing table to search. The port is never used by the routing functions.

Explicit check for default

165–172   Figure 18.35 showed that the default route is stored as a duplicate leaf with a key of 0. The first of the duplicate leaves has the RNF_ROOT flag set. Hence if the RNF_ROOT flag is set in the matching node and the leaf contains a duplicate key, the value of the pointer rn_dupedkey is returned (i.e., the pointer to the node containing the default route in Figure 18.35). If a default route has not been entered and the search matches the left end marker (a key of all zero bits), or if the search encounters the right end marker (a key of all one bits), the returned pointer t points to a node with the RNF_ROOT flag set. We'll see that rtalloc1 explicitly checks whether the matching node has this flag set, and considers such a match an error.

At this point in rn_match a leaf has been reached but it is not an exact match with the search key. The next part of the function, shown in Figure 18.40, checks whether the leaf is a network match.

```
                                                                    radix.c
173      matched_off = cp - v;
174      saved_t = t;
175      do {
176          if (t->rn_mask) {
177              /*
178               * Even if we don't match exactly as a host;
179               * we may match if the leaf we wound up at is
180               * a route to a net.
181               */
182              cp3 = matched_off + t->rn_mask;
183              cp2 = matched_off + t->rn_key;
184              for (; cp < cplim; cp++)
185                  if ((*cp2++ ^ *cp) & *cp3++)
186                      break;
187              if (cp == cplim)
188                  return t;
189              cp = matched_off + v;
190          }
191      } while (t = t->rn_dupedkey);
192      t = saved_t;
                                                                    radix.c
```

Figure 18.40   rn_match function: check for network match.

173–174   cp points to the unequal byte in the search key. matched_off is set to the offset of this byte from the start of the socket address structure.

175–183   The do while loop iterates through all duplicate leaves and each one with a network mask is compared. Let's work through the code with an example. Assume we're looking up the IP address 140.252.13.60 in the routing table in Figure 18.4. The search will end up at the node labeled 140.252.13.32 (bits 62 and 63 are both off), which contains a network mask. Figure 18.41 shows the structures when the `for` loop in Figure 18.40 starts executing.

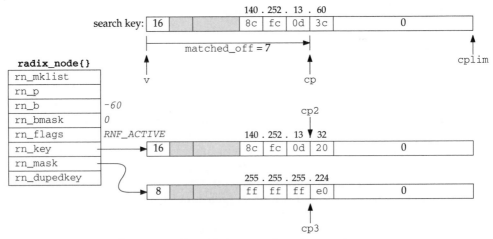

Figure 18.41   Example for network mask comparison.

The search key and the routing table key are both `sockaddr_in` structures, but the length of the mask is different. The mask length is the minimum number of bytes containing nonzero values. All the bytes past this point, up through `max_keylen`, are 0.

184–190   The search key is exclusive ORed with the routing table key, and the result logically ANDed with the network mask, one byte at a time. If the resulting byte is ever nonzero, the loop terminates because they don't match (Exercise 18.1). If the loop terminates normally, however, the search key ANDed with the network mask matches the routing table entry. The pointer to the routing table entry is returned.

Figure 18.42 shows how this example matches, and how the IP address 140.252.13.188 does not match, looking at just the fourth byte of the IP address. The search for both IP addresses ends up at this node since both addresses have bits 57, 62, and 63 off.

	search key = 140.252.13.60	search key = 140.252.13.188
search key byte (`*cp`):	0011 1100 = 3c	1011 1100 = bc
routing table key byte (`*cp2`):	0010 0000 = 20	0010 0000 = 20
exclusive OR:	0001 1100	1001 1100
network mask byte (`*cp3`):	1110 0000 = e0	1110 0000 = e0
logical AND:	0000 0000	1000 0000

Figure 18.42   Example of search key match using network mask.

The first example (140.252.13.60) matches since the result of the logical AND is 0 (and all the remaining bytes in the address, the key, and the mask are all 0). The other example does not match since the result of the logical AND is nonzero.

191   If the routing table entry has duplicate keys, the loop is repeated for each key.

The final portion of rn_match, shown in Figure 18.43, backtracks up the tree, looking for a network match or a match with the default.

── *radix.c*
```
193     /* start searching up the tree */
194     do {
195         struct radix_mask *m;
196         t = t->rn_p;
197         if (m = t->rn_mklist) {
198             /*
199              * After doing measurements here, it may
200              * turn out to be faster to open code
201              * rn_search_m here instead of always
202              * copying and masking.
203              */
204             off = min(t->rn_off, matched_off);
205             mstart = maskedKey + off;
206             do {
207                 cp2 = mstart;
208                 cp3 = m->rm_mask + off;
209                 for (cp = v + off; cp < cplim;)
210                     *cp2++ = *cp++ & *cp3++;
211                 x = rn_search(maskedKey, t);
212                 while (x && x->rn_mask != m->rm_mask)
213                     x = x->rn_dupedkey;
214                 if (x &&
215                     (Bcmp(mstart, x->rn_key + off,
216                         vlen - off) == 0))
217                     return x;
218             } while (m = m->rm_mklist);
219         }
220     } while (t != top);
221     return 0;
222 };
```
── *radix.c*

Figure 18.43 rn_match function: backtrack up the tree.

193–195   The do while loop continues up the tree, checking each level, until the top has been checked.

196   The pointer t is replaced with the pointer to the parent node, moving up one level. Having the parent pointer in each node simplifies backtracking.

197–210   Each level is checked only if the internal node has a nonnull list of masks. rn_mklist is a pointer to a linked list of radix_mask structures, each containing a mask that applies to the subtree starting at that node. The inner do while loop iterates through each radix_mask structure on the list.

Using the previous example, 140.252.13.188, Figure 18.44 shows the various data structures when the innermost for loop starts. This loop logically ANDs each byte of the search key with each byte of the mask, storing the result in the global maskedKey. The mask value is 0xfffffffe0 and the search would have backtracked from the leaf for 140.252.13.32 in Figure 18.4 two levels to the node that tests bit 62.

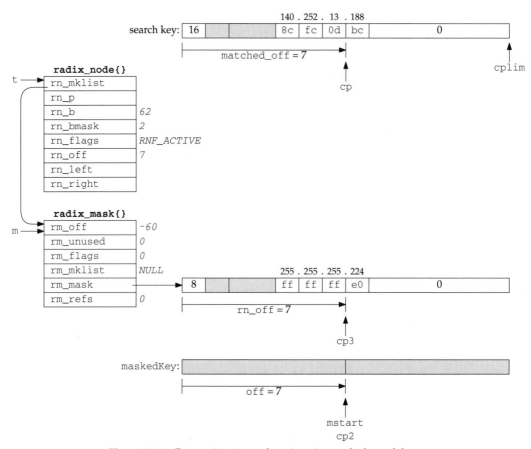

Figure 18.44   Preparation to search again using masked search key.

Once the `for` loop completes, the masking is complete, and `rn_search` (shown in Figure 18.48) is called with `maskedKey` as the search key and the pointer `t` as the top of the subtree to search. Figure 18.45 shows the value of `maskedKey` for our example.

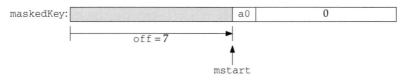

Figure 18.45   `maskedKey` when `rn_search` is called.

The byte `0xa0` is the logical AND of `0xbc` (188, the search key) and `0xe0` (the mask).

211   `rn_search` proceeds down the tree from its starting point, branching right or left depending on the key, until a leaf is reached. In this example the search key is the 9 bytes shown in Figure 18.45 and the leaf that's reached is the one labeled 140.252.13.32 in Figure 18.4, since bits 62 and 63 are off in the byte `0xa0`. Figure 18.46 shows the data structures when `Bcmp` is called to check if a match has been found.

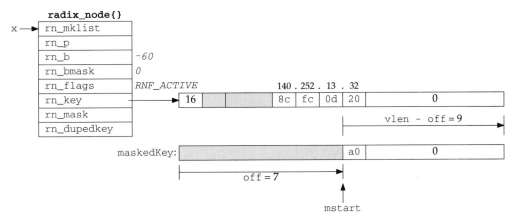

Figure 18.46 Comparison of maskedKey and new leaf.

Since the 9-byte strings are not the same, the comparison fails.

212–221   This while loop handles duplicate keys, each with a different mask. The only key of the duplicates that is compared is the one whose rn_mask pointer equals m->rm_mask. As an example, recall Figures 18.36 and 18.37. If the search starts at the node for bit 63, the first time through the inner do while loop m points to the radix_mask structure for 0xffffff00. When rn_search returns the pointer to the first of the duplicate leaves for 127.0.0.0, the rm_mask of this leaf equals m->rm_mask, so Bcmp is called. If the comparison fails, m is replaced with the pointer to the next radix_mask structure on the list (the one with a mask of 0xff000000) and the do while loop iterates around again with the new mask. rn_search again returns the pointer to the first of the duplicate leaves for 127.0.0.0, but its rn_mask does not equal m->rm_mask. The while steps to the next of the duplicate leaves and its rn_mask is the right one.

Returning to our example with the search key of 140.252.13.188, since the search from the node that tests bit 62 failed, the backtracking continues up the tree until the top is reached, which is the next node up the tree with a nonnull rn_mklist.

Figure 18.47 shows the data structures when the top node of the tree is reached. At this point maskedKey is computed (it is all zero bits) and rn_search starts at this node (the top of the tree) and continues down the two left branches to the leaf labeled "default" in Figure 18.4.

When rn_search returns, x points to the radix_node with an rn_b of −33, which is the first leaf encountered after the two left branches from the top of the tree. But x->rn_mask (which is null) does not equal m->rm_mask, so x is replaced with x->rn_dupedkey. The test of the while loop occurs again, but now x->rn_mask equals m->rm_mask, so the while loop terminates. Bcmp compares the 12 bytes of 0 starting at mstart with the 12 bytes of 0 stating at x->rn_key plus 4, and since they're equal, the function returns the pointer x, which points to the entry for the default route.

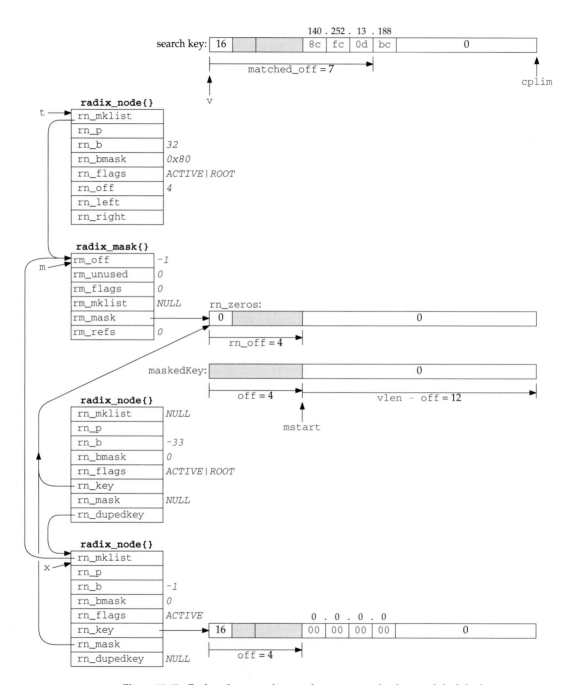

Figure 18.47   Backtrack to top of tree and `rn_search` that locates default leaf.

18.11 `rn_search` **Function**

`rn_search` was called in the previous section from `rn_match` to search a subtree of the routing table.

── *radix.c*
```
79 struct radix_node *
80 rn_search(v_arg, head)
81 void    *v_arg;
82 struct radix_node *head;
83 {
84     struct radix_node *x;
85     caddr_t v;

86     for (x = head, v = v_arg; x->rn_b >= 0;) {
87         if (x->rn_bmask & v[x->rn_off])
88             x = x->rn_r;        /* right if bit on */
89         else
90             x = x->rn_l;        /* left if bit off */
91     }
92     return (x);
93 };
```
── *radix.c*

Figure 18.48   `rn_search` function.

This loop is similar to the one in Figure 18.38. It compares one bit in the search key at each node, branching left if the bit is off or right if the bit is on, terminating when a leaf is encountered. The pointer to that leaf is returned.

18.12 Summary

Each routing table entry is identified by a key: the destination IP address in the case of the Internet protocols, which is either a host address or a network address with an associated network mask. Once the entry is located by searching for the key, additional information in the entry specifies the IP address of a router to which datagrams should be sent for the destination, a pointer to the interface to use, metrics, and so on.

The information maintained by the Internet protocols is the `route` structure, composed of just two elements: a pointer to a routing table entry and the destination address. We'll encounter one of these `route` structures in each of the Internet protocol control blocks used by UDP, TCP, and raw IP.

The Patricia tree data structure is well suited to routing tables. Routing table lookups occur much more frequently than adding or deleting routes, so from a performance standpoint using Patricia trees for the routing table makes sense. Patricia trees provide fast lookups at the expense of additional work in adding and deleting. Measurements in [Sklower 1991] comparing the radix tree approach to the Net/1 hash table show that the radix tree method is about two times faster in building a test tree and four times faster in searching.

Exercises

18.1   We said with Figure 18.3 that the general condition for matching a routing table entry is that the search key logically ANDed with the routing table mask equal the routing table key. But in Figure 18.40 a different test is used. Build a logic truth table showing that the two tests are the same.

18.2   Assume a Net/3 system needs a routing table with 20,000 entries (IP addresses). Approximately how much memory is required for this, ignoring the space required for the masks?

18.3   What is the limit imposed on the length of a routing table key by the `radix_node` structure?

19

Routing Requests and Routing Messages

19.1 Introduction

The various protocols within the kernel don't access the routing trees directly, using the functions from the previous chapter, but instead call a few functions that we describe in this chapter: `rtalloc` and `rtalloc1` are two that perform routing table lookups, `rtrequest` adds and deletes routing table entries, and `rtinit` is called by most interfaces when the interface goes up or down.

Routing messages communicate information in two directions. A process such as the `route` command or one of the routing daemons (`routed` or `gated`) writes routing messages to a routing socket, causing the kernel to add a new route, delete an existing route, or modify an existing route. The kernel also generates routing messages that can be read by any routing socket when events occur in which the processes might be interested: an interface has gone down, a redirect has been received, and so on. In this chapter we cover the formats of these routing messages and the information contained therein, and we save our discussion of routing sockets until the next chapter.

Another interface provided by the kernel to the routing tables is through the `sysctl` system call, which we describe at the end of this chapter. This system call allows a process to read the entire routing table or a list of all the configured interfaces and interface addresses.

19.2 `rtalloc` and `rtalloc1` Functions

`rtalloc` and `rtalloc1` are the functions normally called to look up an entry in the routing table. Figure 19.1 shows `rtalloc`.

route.c
```
58 void
59 rtalloc(ro)
60 struct route *ro;
61 {
62     if (ro->ro_rt && ro->ro_rt->rt_ifp && (ro->ro_rt->rt_flags & RTF_UP))
63         return;                      /* XXX */
64     ro->ro_rt = rtalloc1(&ro->ro_dst, 1);
65 }
```
route.c

Figure 19.1 `rtalloc` function.

58–65   The argument `ro` is often the pointer to a `route` structure contained in an Internet PCB (Chapter 22) which is used by UDP and TCP. If `ro` already points to an `rtentry` structure (`ro_rt` is nonnull), and that structure points to an interface structure, and the route is up, the function returns. Otherwise `rtalloc1` is called with a second argument of 1. We'll see the purpose of this argument shortly.

`rtalloc1`, shown in Figure 19.2, calls the `rnh_matchaddr` function, which is always `rn_match` (Figure 18.17) for Internet addresses.

66–76   The first argument is a pointer to a socket address structure containing the address to search for. The `sa_family` member selects the routing table to search.

Call `rn_match`

77–78   If the following three conditions are met, the search is successful.

1. A routing table exists for the protocol family,

2. `rn_match` returns a nonnull pointer, and

3. the matching `radix_node` does not have the `RNF_ROOT` flag set.

Remember that the two leaves that mark the end of the tree both have the `RNF_ROOT` flag set.

Search fails

94–101   If the search fails because any one of the three conditions is not met, the statistic `rts_unreach` is incremented and if the second argument to `rtalloc1` (`report`) is nonzero, a routing message is generated that can be read by any interested processes on a routing socket. The routing message has the type `RTM_MISS`, and the function returns a null pointer.

79   If all three of the conditions are met, the lookup succeeded and the pointer to the matching `radix_node` is stored in `rt` and `newrt`. Notice that in the definition of the `rtentry` structure (Figure 18.24) the two `radix_node` structures are at the beginning, and, as shown in Figure 18.8, the first of these two structures contains the leaf node. Therefore the pointer to a `radix_node` structure returned by `rn_match` is really a pointer to an `rtentry` structure, which is the matching leaf node.

```
                                                                      route.c
66 struct rtentry *
67 rtalloc1(dst, report)
68 struct sockaddr *dst;
69 int     report;
70 {
71     struct radix_node_head *rnh = rt_tables[dst->sa_family];
72     struct rtentry *rt;
73     struct radix_node *rn;
74     struct rtentry *newrt = 0;
75     struct rt_addrinfo info;
76     int     s = splnet(), err = 0, msgtype = RTM_MISS;

77     if (rnh && (rn = rnh->rnh_matchaddr((caddr_t) dst, rnh)) &&
78         ((rn->rn_flags & RNF_ROOT) == 0)) {
79         newrt = rt = (struct rtentry *) rn;
80         if (report && (rt->rt_flags & RTF_CLONING)) {
81             err = rtrequest(RTM_RESOLVE, dst, SA(0),
82                             SA(0), 0, &newrt);
83             if (err) {
84                 newrt = rt;
85                 rt->rt_refcnt++;
86                 goto miss;
87             }
88             if ((rt = newrt) && (rt->rt_flags & RTF_XRESOLVE)) {
89                 msgtype = RTM_RESOLVE;
90                 goto miss;
91             }
92         } else
93             rt->rt_refcnt++;
94     } else {
95         rtstat.rts_unreach++;
96       miss:if (report) {
97             bzero((caddr_t) & info, sizeof(info));
98             info.rti_info[RTAX_DST] = dst;
99             rt_missmsg(msgtype, &info, 0, err);
100        }
101    }
102    splx(s);
103    return (newrt);
104 }
                                                                      route.c
```

Figure 19.2 rtalloc1 function.

Create clone entries

80–82   If the caller specified a nonzero second argument, and if the RTF_CLONING flag is set, rtrequest is called with a command of RTM_RESOLVE to create a new rtentry structure that is a clone of the one that was located. This feature is used by ARP and for multicast addresses.

Clone creation fails

83–87   If `rtrequest` returns an error, `newrt` is set back to the entry returned by `rn_match` and its reference count is incremented. A jump is made to `miss` where an `RTM_MISS` message is generated.

Check for external resolution

88–91   If `rtrequest` succeeds but the newly cloned entry has the `RTF_XRESOLVE` flag set, a jump is made to `miss`, this time to generate an `RTM_RESOLVE` message. The intent of this message is to notify a user process when the route is created, and it could be used with the conversion of IP addresses to X.121 addresses.

Increment reference count for normal successful search

92–93   When the search succeeds but the `RTF_CLONING` flag is not set, this statement increments the entry's reference count. This is the normal flow through the function, which then returns the nonnull pointer.

For a small function, `rtalloc1` has many options in how it operates. There are seven different flows through the function, summarized in Figure 19.3.

	report argument	RTF_- CLONING flag	RTM_- RESOLVE return	RTF_- XRESOLVE flag	routing message generated	rt_refcnt	return value
entry not found	0						null
	1				RTM_MISS		null
entry found		0				++	ptr
	0					++	ptr
	1	1	OK	0		++	ptr
	1	1	OK	1	RTM_RESOLVE	++	ptr
	1	1	error		RTM_MISS	++	ptr

Figure 19.3 Summary of operation of `rtalloc1`.

We note that the first two rows (entry not found) are impossible if a default route exists. Also we show `rt_refcnt` being incremented in the fifth and sixth rows when the call to `rtrequest` with a command of `RTM_RESOLVE` is OK. The increment is done by `rtrequest`.

19.3 `RTFREE` Macro and `rtfree` Function

The `RTFREE` macro, shown in Figure 19.4, calls the `rtfree` function only if the reference count is less than or equal to 1, otherwise it just decrements the reference count.

209–213   The `rtfree` function, shown in Figure 19.5, releases an `rtentry` structure when there are no more references to it. We'll see in Figure 22.7, for example, that when a protocol control block is released, if it points to a routing entry, `rtfree` is called.

```
                                                                ─── route.h
209 #define RTFREE(rt) \
210     if ((rt)->rt_refcnt <= 1) \
211         rtfree(rt); \
212     else \
213         (rt)->rt_refcnt--;        /* no need for function call */
                                                                ─── route.h
```

Figure 19.4   RTFREE macro.

```
                                                                ─── route.c
105 void
106 rtfree(rt)
107 struct rtentry *rt;
108 {
109     struct ifaddr *ifa;

110     if (rt == 0)
111         panic("rtfree");
112     rt->rt_refcnt--;
113     if (rt->rt_refcnt <= 0 && (rt->rt_flags & RTF_UP) == 0) {
114         if (rt->rt_nodes->rn_flags & (RNF_ACTIVE | RNF_ROOT))
115             panic("rtfree 2");
116         rttrash--;
117         if (rt->rt_refcnt < 0) {
118             printf("rtfree: %x not freed (neg refs)\n", rt);
119             return;
120         }
121         ifa = rt->rt_ifa;
122         IFAFREE(ifa);
123         Free(rt_key(rt));
124         Free(rt);
125     }
126 }
                                                                ─── route.c
```

Figure 19.5   rtfree function: release an rtentry structure.

105–115   The entry's reference count is decremented and if it is less than or equal to 0 and the route is not usable, the entry can be released. If either of the flags RNF_ACTIVE or RNF_ROOT are set, this is an internal error. If RNF_ACTIVE is set, this structure is still part of the routing table tree. If RNF_ROOT is set, this structure is one of the end markers built by rn_inithead.

116   rttrash is a debugging counter of the number of routing entries not in the routing tree, but not released. It is incremented by rtrequest when it begins deleting a route, and then decremented here. Its value should normally be 0.

Release interface reference

117–122   A check is made that the reference count is not negative, and then IFAFREE decrements the reference count for the ifaddr structure and releases it by calling ifafree when it reaches 0.

Release routing memory

123–124   The memory occupied by the routing entry key and its gateway is released. We'll see in `rt_setgate` that the memory for both is allocated in one contiguous chunk, allowing both to be released with a single call to `Free`. Finally the `rtentry` structure itself is released.

Routing Table Reference Counts

The handling of the routing table reference count, `rt_refcnt`, differs from most other reference counts. We see in Figure 18.2 that most routes have a reference count of 0, yet the routing table entries without any references are not deleted. We just saw the reason in `rtfree`: an entry with a reference count of 0 is not deleted unless the entry's `RTF_UP` flag is not set. The only time this flag is cleared is by `rtrequest` when a route is deleted from the routing tree.

Most routes are used in the following fashion.

- If the route is created automatically as a route to an interface when the interface is configured (which is typical for Ethernet interfaces, for example), then `rtinit` calls `rtrequest` with a command of `RTM_ADD`, creating the new entry and setting the reference count to 1. `rtinit` then decrements the reference count to 0 before returning.

  A point-to-point interface follows a similar procedure, so the route starts with a reference count of 0.

  If the route is created manually by the `route` command or by a routing daemon, a similar procedure occurs, with `route_output` calling `rtrequest` with a command of `RTM_ADD`, setting the reference count to 1. This is then decremented by `route_output` to 0 before it returns.

  Therefore all newly created routes start with a reference count of 0.

- When an IP datagram is sent on a socket, be it TCP or UDP, we saw that `ip_output` calls `rtalloc`, which calls `rtalloc1`. In Figure 19.3 we saw that the reference count is incremented by `rtalloc1` if the route is found.

  The located route is called a *held route*, since a pointer to the routing table entry is being held by the protocol, normally in a `route` structure contained within a protocol control block. An `rtentry` structure that is being held by someone else cannot be deleted, which is why `rtfree` doesn't release the structure until its reference count reaches 0.

- A protocol releases a held route by calling `RTFREE` or `rtfree`. We saw this in Figure 8.24 when `ip_output` detects a change in the destination address. We'll encounter it in Chapter 22 when a protocol control block that holds a route is released.

Part of the confusion we'll encounter in the code that follows is that `rtalloc1` is often called to look up a route in order to verify that a route to the destination exists, but when the caller doesn't want to hold the route. Since rtalloc1 increments the counter, the caller immediately decrements it.

Consider a route being deleted by rtrequest. The RTF_UP flag is cleared, and if no one is holding the route (its reference count is 0), rtfree should be called. But rtfree considers it an error for the reference count to go below 0, so rtrequest checks whether its reference count is less than or equal to 0, and, if so, increments it and calls rtfree. Normally this sets the reference count to 1 and rtfree decrements it to 0 and deletes the route.

19.4   rtrequest Function

The rtrequest function is the focal point for adding and deleting routing table entries. Figure 19.6 shows some of the other functions that call it.

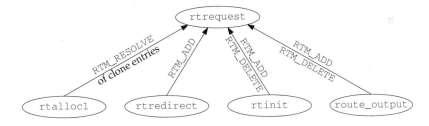

Figure 19.6   Summary of functions that call rtrequest.

rtrequest is a switch statement with one case per command: RTM_ADD, RTM_DELETE, and RTM_RESOLVE. Figure 19.7 shows the start of the function and the RTM_DELETE command.

—— *route.c*
```
290 int
291 rtrequest(req, dst, gateway, netmask, flags, ret_nrt)
292 int     req, flags;
293 struct sockaddr *dst, *gateway, *netmask;
294 struct rtentry **ret_nrt;
295 {
296     int     s = splnet();
297     int     error = 0;
298     struct rtentry *rt;
299     struct radix_node *rn;
300     struct radix_node_head *rnh;
301     struct ifaddr *ifa;
302     struct sockaddr *ndst;
303 #define senderr(x) { error = x ; goto bad; }

304     if ((rnh = rt_tables[dst->sa_family]) == 0)
305         senderr(ESRCH);
306     if (flags & RTF_HOST)
307         netmask = 0;
```

```
308        switch (req) {
309        case RTM_DELETE:
310            if ((rn = rnh->rnh_deladdr(dst, netmask, rnh)) == 0)
311                senderr(ESRCH);
312            if (rn->rn_flags & (RNF_ACTIVE | RNF_ROOT))
313                panic("rtrequest delete");
314            rt = (struct rtentry *) rn;
315            rt->rt_flags &= ~RTF_UP;
316            if (rt->rt_gwroute) {
317                rt = rt->rt_gwroute;
318                RTFREE(rt);
319                (rt = (struct rtentry *) rn)->rt_gwroute = 0;
320            }
321            if ((ifa = rt->rt_ifa) && ifa->ifa_rtrequest)
322                ifa->ifa_rtrequest(RTM_DELETE, rt, SA(0));
323            rttrash++;
324            if (ret_nrt)
325                *ret_nrt = rt;
326            else if (rt->rt_refcnt <= 0) {
327                rt->rt_refcnt++;
328                rtfree(rt);
329            }
330            break;
```
—— *route.c*

Figure 19.7   rtrequest function: RTM_DELETE command.

290–307   The second argument, dst, is a socket address structure specifying the key to be added or deleted from the routing table. The sa_family from this key selects the routing table. If the flags argument indicates a host route (instead of a route to a network), the netmask pointer is set to null, ignoring any value the caller may have passed.

Delete from routing tree

309–315   The rnh_deladdr function (rn_delete from Figure 18.17) deletes the entry from the routing table tree and returns a pointer to the corresponding rtentry structure. The RTF_UP flag is cleared.

Remove reference to gateway routing table entry

316–320   If the entry is an indirect route through a gateway, RTFREE decrements the rt_refcnt member of the gateway's entry and deletes it if the count reaches 0. The rt_gwroute pointer is set to null and rt is set back to point to the entry that was deleted.

Call interface request function

321–322   If an ifa_rtrequest function is defined for this entry, that function is called. This function is used by ARP, for example, in Chapter 21 to delete the corresponding ARP entry.

Return pointer or release reference

323–330   The rttrash global is incremented because the entry may not be released in the code that follows. If the caller wants the pointer to the rtentry structure that was deleted from the routing tree (if ret_nrt is nonnull), then that pointer is returned, but the entry cannot be released: it is the caller's responsibility to call rtfree when it is finished with the entry. If ret_nrt is null, the entry can be released: if the reference count is less than or equal to 0, it is incremented, and rtfree is called. The break causes the function to return.

Figure 19.8 shows the next part of the function, which handles the RTM_RESOLVE command. This function is called with this command only from rtalloc1, when a new entry is to be created from an entry with the RTF_CLONING flag set.

```
                                                                   ─── route.c
331     case RTM_RESOLVE:
332         if (ret_nrt == 0 || (rt = *ret_nrt) == 0)
333             senderr(EINVAL);
334         ifa = rt->rt_ifa;
335         flags = rt->rt_flags & ~RTF_CLONING;
336         gateway = rt->rt_gateway;
337         if ((netmask = rt->rt_genmask) == 0)
338             flags |= RTF_HOST;
339         goto makeroute;
                                                                   ─── route.c
```

Figure 19.8 rtrequest function: RTM_RESOLVE command.

331–339   The final argument, ret_nrt, is used differently for this command: it contains the pointer to the entry with the RTF_CLONING flag set (Figure 19.2). The new entry will have the same rt_ifa pointer, the same flags (with the RTF_CLONING flag cleared), and the same rt_gateway. If the entry being cloned has a null rt_genmask pointer, the new entry has its RTF_HOST flag set, because it is a host route; otherwise the new entry is a network route and the network mask of the new entry is copied from the rt_genmask value. We give an example of cloned routes with a network mask at the end of this section. This case continues at the label makeroute, which is in the next figure.

Figure 19.9 shows the RTM_ADD command.

Locate corresponding interface

340–342   The function ifa_ifwithroute finds the appropriate local interface for the destination (dst), returning a pointer to its ifaddr structure.

Allocate memory for routing table entry

343–348   An rtentry structure is allocated. Recall that this structure contains both the two radix_node structures for the routing tree and the other routing information. The structure is zeroed and the rt_flags are set from the caller's flags, including the RTF_UP flag.

Allocate and copy gateway address

349–352   The rt_setgate function (Figure 19.11) allocates memory for both the routing table key (dst) and its gateway. It then copies gateway into the new memory and sets the pointers rt_key, rt_gateway, and rt_gwroute.

route.c

```
340         case RTM_ADD:
341             if ((ifa = ifa_ifwithroute(flags, dst, gateway)) == 0)
342                 senderr(ENETUNREACH);

343        makeroute:
344            R_Malloc(rt, struct rtentry *, sizeof(*rt));
345            if (rt == 0)
346                senderr(ENOBUFS);
347            Bzero(rt, sizeof(*rt));
348            rt->rt_flags = RTF_UP | flags;
349            if (rt_setgate(rt, dst, gateway)) {
350                Free(rt);
351                senderr(ENOBUFS);
352            }
353            ndst = rt_key(rt);
354            if (netmask) {
355                rt_maskedcopy(dst, ndst, netmask);
356            } else
357                Bcopy(dst, ndst, dst->sa_len);

358            rn = rnh->rnh_addaddr((caddr_t) ndst, (caddr_t) netmask,
359                                  rnh, rt->rt_nodes);
360            if (rn == 0) {
361                if (rt->rt_gwroute)
362                    rtfree(rt->rt_gwroute);
363                Free(rt_key(rt));
364                Free(rt);
365                senderr(EEXIST);
366            }
367            ifa->ifa_refcnt++;
368            rt->rt_ifa = ifa;
369            rt->rt_ifp = ifa->ifa_ifp;
370            if (req == RTM_RESOLVE)
371                rt->rt_rmx = (*ret_nrt)->rt_rmx;      /* copy metrics */
372            if (ifa->ifa_rtrequest)
373                ifa->ifa_rtrequest(req, rt, SA(ret_nrt ? *ret_nrt : 0));
374            if (ret_nrt) {
375                *ret_nrt = rt;
376                rt->rt_refcnt++;
377            }
378            break;
379        }
380    bad:
381        splx(s);
382        return (error);
383 }
```

route.c

Figure 19.9 rtrequest function: RTM_ADD command.

Copy destination address

353–357   The destination address (the routing table key dst) must now be copied into the
memory pointed to by rn_key. If a network mask is supplied, rt_maskedcopy logically ANDs dst and netmask, forming the new key. Otherwise dst is copied into the

new key. The reason for logically ANDing dst and netmask is to guarantee that the key in the table has already been ANDed with its mask, so when a search key is compared against the key in the table only the search key needs to be ANDed. For example, the following command adds another IP address (an alias) to the Ethernet interface le0, with subnet 12 instead of 13:

```
bsdi $ ifconfig le0 inet 140.252.12.63 netmask 0xfffffffe0 alias
```

The problem is that we've incorrectly specified all one bits for the host ID. Nevertheless, when the key is stored in the routing table we can verify with netstat that the address is first logically ANDed with the mask:

```
Destination      Gateway         Flags     Refs     Use   Interface
140.252.12.32    link#1          U C         0        0   le0
```

Add entry to routing tree

358–366   The rnh_addaddr function (rn_addroute from Figure 18.17) adds this rtentry structure, with its destination and mask, to the routing table tree. If an error occurs, the structures are released and EEXIST returned (i.e., the entry is already in the routing table).

Store interface pointers

367–369   The ifaddr structure's reference count is incremented and the pointers to its ifaddr and ifnet structures are stored.

Copy metrics for newly cloned route

370–371   If the command was RTM_RESOLVE (not RTM_ADD), the entire metrics structure is copied from the cloned entry into the new entry. If the command was RTM_ADD, the caller can set the metrics after this function returns.

Call interface request function

372–373   If an ifa_rtrequest function is defined for this entry, that function is called. ARP uses this to perform additional processing for both the RTM_ADD and RTM_RESOLVE commands (Section 21.13).

Return pointer and increment reference count

374–378   If the caller wants a copy of the pointer to the new structure, it is returned through ret_nrt and the rt_refcnt reference count is incremented from 0 to 1.

Example: Cloned Routes with Network Masks

The only use of the rt_genmask value is with cloned routes created by the RTM_RESOLVE command in rtrequest. If an rt_genmask pointer is nonnull, then the socket address structure pointed to by this pointer becomes the network mask of the newly created route. In our routing table, Figure 18.2, the cloned routes are for the local Ethernet and for multicast addresses. The following example from [Sklower 1991] provides a different use of cloned routes. Another example is in Exercise 19.2.

Consider a class B network, say 128.1, that is behind a point-to-point link. The subnet mask is 0xffffff00, the typical value that uses 8 bits for the subnet ID and 8 bits for the host ID. We need a routing table entry for all possible 254 subnets, with a gateway value of a router that is directly connected to our host and that knows how to reach the link to which the 128.1 network is connected.

The easiest solution, assuming the gateway router isn't our default router, is a single entry with a destination of 128.1.0.0 and a mask of 0xffff0000. Assume, however, that the topology of the 128.1 network is such that each of the possible 254 subnets can have different operational characteristics: RTTs, MTUs, delays, and so on. If a separate routing table entry were used for each subnet, we would see that whenever a connection is closed, TCP would update the routing table entry with statistics about that route—its RTT, RTT variance, and so on (Figure 27.3). While we could create up to 254 entries by hand using the route command, one per subnet, a better solution is to use the cloning feature.

One entry is created by the system administrator with a destination of 128.1.0.0 and a network mask of 0xffff0000. Additionally, the RTF_CLONING flag is set and the genmask is set to 0xffffff00, which differs from the network mask. If the routing table is searched for 128.1.2.3, and an entry does not exist for the 128.1.2 subnet, the entry for 128.1 with the mask of 0xffff0000 is the best match. A new entry is created (since the RTF_CLONING flag is set) with a destination of 128.1.2 and a network mask of 0xffffff00 (the genmask value). The next time any host on this subnet is referenced, say 128.1.2.88, it will match this newly created entry.

19.5 `rt_setgate` **Function**

Each leaf in the routing tree has a key (rt_key, which is just the rn_key member of the radix_node structure contained at the beginning of the rtentry structure), and an associated gateway (rt_gateway). Both are socket address structures specified when the routing table entry is created. Memory is allocated for both structures by rt_setgate, as shown in Figure 19.10.

This example shows two of the entries from Figure 18.2, the ones with keys of 127.0.0.1 and 140.252.13.33. The former's gateway member points to an Internet socket address structure, while the latter's points to a data-link socket address structure that contains an Ethernet address. The former was entered into the routing table by the route system when the system was initialized, and the latter was created by ARP.

We purposely show the two structures pointed to by rt_key one right after the other, since they are allocated together by rt_setgate, which we show in Figure 19.11.

Set lengths from socket address structures

384–391   dlen is the length of the destination socket address structure, and glen is the length of the gateway socket address structure. The ROUNDUP macro rounds the value up to the next multiple of 4 bytes, but the size of most socket address structures is already a multiple of 4.

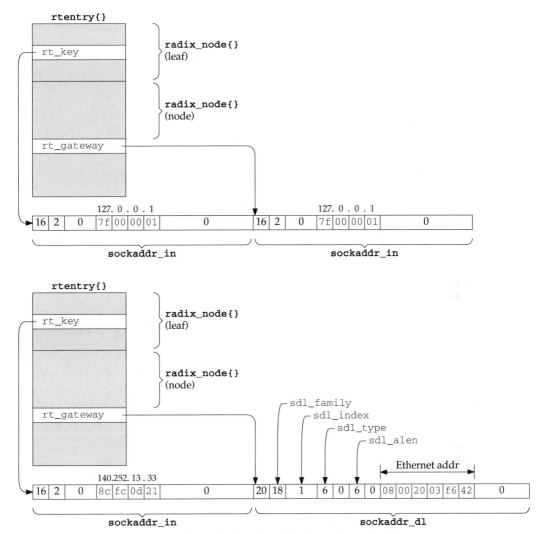

Figure 19.10   Example of routing table keys and associated gateways.

Allocate memory

392–397   If memory has not been allocated for this routing table key and gateway yet, or if glen is greater than the current size of the structure pointed to by rt_gateway, a new piece of memory is allocated and rn_key is set to point to the new memory.

Use memory already allocated for key and gateway

398–401   An adequately sized piece of memory is already allocated for the key and gateway, so new is set to point to this existing memory.

route.c

```
384 int
385 rt_setgate(rt0, dst, gate)
386 struct rtentry *rt0;
387 struct sockaddr *dst, *gate;
388 {
389     caddr_t new, old;
390     int     dlen = ROUNDUP(dst->sa_len), glen = ROUNDUP(gate->sa_len);
391     struct rtentry *rt = rt0;

392     if (rt->rt_gateway == 0 || glen > ROUNDUP(rt->rt_gateway->sa_len)) {
393         old = (caddr_t) rt_key(rt);
394         R_Malloc(new, caddr_t, dlen + glen);
395         if (new == 0)
396             return 1;
397         rt->rt_nodes->rn_key = new;
398     } else {
399         new = rt->rt_nodes->rn_key;
400         old = 0;
401     }
402     Bcopy(gate, (rt->rt_gateway = (struct sockaddr *) (new + dlen)), glen);
403     if (old) {
404         Bcopy(dst, new, dlen);
405         Free(old);
406     }
407     if (rt->rt_gwroute) {
408         rt = rt->rt_gwroute;
409         RTFREE(rt);
410         rt = rt0;
411         rt->rt_gwroute = 0;
412     }
413     if (rt->rt_flags & RTF_GATEWAY) {
414         rt->rt_gwroute = rtalloc1(gate, 1);
415     }
416     return 0;
417 }
```

route.c

Figure 19.11   rt_setgate function.

Copy new gateway

402   The new gateway structure is copied and rt_gateway is set to point to the socket
address structure.

Copy key from old memory to new memory

403–406   If a new piece of memory was allocated, the routing table key (dst) is copied right
before the gateway field that was just copied. The old piece of memory is released.

Release gateway routing pointer

407–412   If the routing table entry contains a nonnull rt_gwroute pointer, that structure is
released by RTFREE and the rt_gwroute pointer is set to null.

Locate and store new gateway routing pointer

413–415   If the routing table entry is an indirect route, rtalloc1 locates the entry for the new gateway, which is stored in rt_gwroute. If an invalid gateway is specified for an indirect route, an error is not returned by rt_setgate, but the rt_gwroute pointer will be null.

19.6   rtinit **Function**

There are four calls to rtinit from the Internet protocols to add or delete routes associated with interfaces.

- in_control calls rtinit twice when the destination address of a point-to-point interface is set (Figure 6.21). The first call specifies RTM_DELETE to delete any existing route to the destination; the second call specifies RTM_ADD to add the new route.
- in_ifinit calls rtinit to add a network route for a broadcast network or a host route for a point-to-point link (Figure 6.19). If the route is for an Ethernet interface, the RTF_CLONING flag is automatically set by in_ifinit.
- in_ifscrub calls rtinit to delete an existing route for an interface.

Figure 19.12 shows the first part of the rtinit function. The cmd argument is always RTM_ADD or RTM_DELETE.

Get destination address for route

452   If the route is to a host, the destination address is the other end of the point-to-point link. Otherwise we're dealing with a network route and the destination address is the unicast address of the interface (masked with ifa_netmask).

Mask network address with network mask

453–459   If a route is being deleted, the destination must be looked up in the routing table to locate its routing table entry. If the route being deleted is a network route and the interface has an associated network mask, an mbuf is allocated and the destination address is copied into the mbuf by rt_maskedcopy, logically ANDing the caller's address with the mask. dst is set to point to the masked copy in the mbuf, and that is the destination looked up in the next step.

Search for routing table entry

460–469   rtalloc1 searches the routing table for the destination address. If the entry is found, its reference count is decremented (since rtalloc1 incremented the reference count). If the pointer to the interface's ifaddr in the routing table does not equal the caller's argument, an error is returned.

Process request

470–473   rtrequest executes the command, either RTM_ADD or RTM_DELETE. When it returns, if an mbuf was allocated earlier, it is released.

```
                                                                          route.c
441  int
442  rtinit(ifa, cmd, flags)
443  struct ifaddr *ifa;
444  int     cmd, flags;
445  {
446      struct rtentry *rt;
447      struct sockaddr *dst;
448      struct sockaddr *deldst;
449      struct mbuf *m = 0;
450      struct rtentry *nrt = 0;
451      int     error;

452      dst = flags & RTF_HOST ? ifa->ifa_dstaddr : ifa->ifa_addr;
453      if (cmd == RTM_DELETE) {
454          if ((flags & RTF_HOST) == 0 && ifa->ifa_netmask) {
455              m = m_get(M_WAIT, MT_SONAME);
456              deldst = mtod(m, struct sockaddr *);
457              rt_maskedcopy(dst, deldst, ifa->ifa_netmask);
458              dst = deldst;
459          }
460          if (rt = rtalloc1(dst, 0)) {
461              rt->rt_refcnt--;
462              if (rt->rt_ifa != ifa) {
463                  if (m)
464                      (void) m_free(m);
465                  return (flags & RTF_HOST ? EHOSTUNREACH
466                          : ENETUNREACH);
467              }
468          }
469      }
470      error = rtrequest(cmd, dst, ifa->ifa_addr, ifa->ifa_netmask,
471                      flags | ifa->ifa_flags, &nrt);
472      if (m)
473          (void) m_free(m);
                                                                          route.c
```

Figure 19.12   rtinit function: call rtrequest to handle command.

Figure 19.13 shows the second half of rtinit.

Generate routing message on successful delete

474–480   If a route was deleted, and rtrequest returned 0 along with a pointer to the rtentry structure that was deleted (in nrt), a routing socket message is generated by rt_newaddrmsg. If the reference count is less than or equal to 0, it is incremented and the route is released by rtfree.

Successful add

481–482   If a route was added, and rtrequest returned 0 along with a pointer to the rtentry structure that was added (in nrt), the reference count is decremented (since rtrequest incremented it).

```
                                                                     ─── route.c
474    if (cmd == RTM_DELETE && error == 0 && (rt = nrt)) {
475        rt_newaddrmsg(cmd, ifa, error, nrt);
476        if (rt->rt_refcnt <= 0) {
477            rt->rt_refcnt++;
478            rtfree(rt);
479        }
480    }
481    if (cmd == RTM_ADD && error == 0 && (rt = nrt)) {
482        rt->rt_refcnt--;
483        if (rt->rt_ifa != ifa) {
484            printf("rtinit: wrong ifa (%x) was (%x)\n", ifa,
485                    rt->rt_ifa);
486            if (rt->rt_ifa->ifa_rtrequest)
487                rt->rt_ifa->ifa_rtrequest(RTM_DELETE, rt, SA(0));
488            IFAFREE(rt->rt_ifa);
489            rt->rt_ifa = ifa;
490            rt->rt_ifp = ifa->ifa_ifp;
491            ifa->ifa_refcnt++;
492            if (ifa->ifa_rtrequest)
493                ifa->ifa_rtrequest(RTM_ADD, rt, SA(0));
494        }
495        rt_newaddrmsg(cmd, ifa, error, nrt);
496    }
497    return (error);
498 }
                                                                     ─── route.c
```

Figure 19.13   rtinit function: second half.

Incorrect interface

483–494   If the pointer to the interface's ifaddr in the new routing table entry does not equal the caller's argument, an error occurred. Recall that rtrequest determines the ifa pointer that is stored in the new entry by calling ifa_ifwithroute (Figure 19.9). When this error occurs the following steps take place: an error message is output to the console, the ifa_rtrequest function is called (if defined) with a command of RTM_DELETE, the ifaddr structure is released, the rt_ifa pointer is set to the value specified by the caller, the interface reference count is incremented, and the new interface's ifa_rtrequest function (if defined) is called with a command of RTM_ADD.

Generate routing message

495   A routing socket message is generated by rt_newaddrmsg for the RTM_ADD command.

19.7 rtredirect Function

When an ICMP redirect is received, icmp_input calls rtredirect and then calls pfctlinput (Figure 11.27). This latter function calls udp_ctlinput and tcp_ctlinput, which go through all the UDP and TCP protocol control blocks. If the

PCB is connected to the foreign address that has been redirected, and if the PCB holds a route to that foreign address, the route is released by `rtfree`. The next time any of these control blocks is used to send an IP datagram to that foreign address, `rtalloc` will be called and the destination will be looked up in the routing table, possibly finding a new (redirected) route.

The purpose of `rtredirect`, the first half of which is shown in Figure 19.14, is to validate the information in the redirect, update the routing table immediately, and then generate a routing socket message.

```
                                                                          route.c
147 int
148 rtredirect(dst, gateway, netmask, flags, src, rtp)
149 struct sockaddr *dst, *gateway, *netmask, *src;
150 int      flags;
151 struct rtentry **rtp;
152 {
153     struct rtentry *rt;
154     int      error = 0;
155     short   *stat = 0;
156     struct rt_addrinfo info;
157     struct ifaddr *ifa;

158     /* verify the gateway is directly reachable */
159     if ((ifa = ifa_ifwithnet(gateway)) == 0) {
160         error = ENETUNREACH;
161         goto out;
162     }
163     rt = rtalloc1(dst, 0);
164     /*
165      * If the redirect isn't from our current router for this dst,
166      * it's either old or wrong.  If it redirects us to ourselves,
167      * we have a routing loop, perhaps as a result of an interface
168      * going down recently.
169      */
170 #define equal(a1, a2) (bcmp((caddr_t)(a1), (caddr_t)(a2), (a1)->sa_len) == 0)
171     if (!(flags & RTF_DONE) && rt &&
172         (!equal(src, rt->rt_gateway) || rt->rt_ifa != ifa))
173         error = EINVAL;
174     else if (ifa_ifwithaddr(gateway))
175         error = EHOSTUNREACH;
176     if (error)
177         goto done;
178     /*
179      * Create a new entry if we just got back a wildcard entry
180      * or if the lookup failed.  This is necessary for hosts
181      * which use routing redirects generated by smart gateways
182      * to dynamically build the routing tables.
183      */
184     if ((rt == 0) || (rt_mask(rt) && rt_mask(rt)->sa_len < 2))
185         goto create;
                                                                          route.c
```

Figure 19.14   `rtredirect` function: validate received redirect.

147–157   The arguments are `dst`, the destination IP address of the datagram that caused the redirect (HD in Figure 8.18); `gateway`, the IP address of the router to use as the new gateway field for the destination (R2 in Figure 8.18); `netmask`, which is a null pointer; `flags`, which is `RTF_GATEWAY` and `RTF_HOST`; `src`, the IP address of the router that sent the redirect (R1 in Figure 8.18); and `rtp`, which is a null pointer. We indicate that `netmask` and `rtp` are both null pointers when called by `icmp_input`, but these arguments might be nonnull when called from other protocols.

New gateway must be directly connected

158–162   The new gateway must be directly connected or the redirect is invalid.

Locate routing table entry for destination and validate redirect

163–177   `rtalloc1` searches the routing table for a route to the destination. The following conditions must all be true, or the redirect is invalid and an error is returned. Notice that `icmp_input` ignores any error return from `rtredirect`. ICMP does not generate an error in response to an invalid redirect—it just ignores it.

- the `RTF_DONE` flag must not be set;
- `rtalloc` must have located a routing table entry for `dst`;
- the address of the router that sent the redirect (`src`) must equal the current `rt_gateway` for the destination;
- the interface for the new gateway (the `ifa` returned by `ifa_ifwithnet`) must equal the current interface for the destination (`rt_ifa`), that is, the new gateway must be on the same network as the current gateway; and
- the new gateway cannot redirect this host to itself, that is, there cannot exist an attached interface with a unicast address or a broadcast address equal to `gateway`.

Must create a new route

178–185   If a route to the destination was not found, or if the routing table entry that was located is the default route, a new entry is created for the destination. As the comment indicates, a host with access to multiple routers can use this feature to learn of the correct router when the default is not correct. The test for finding the default route is whether the routing table entry has an associated mask and if the length field of the mask is less than 2, since the mask for the default route is `rn_zeros` (Figure 18.35).

Figure 19.15 shows the second half of this function.

Create new host route

186–195   If the current route to the destination is a network route and the redirect is a host redirect and not a network redirect, a new host route is created for the destination and the existing network route is left alone. We mentioned that the `flags` argument always specifies `RTF_HOST` since the Net/3 ICMP considers all received redirects as host redirects.

─── *route.c*

```
186      /*
187       * Don't listen to the redirect if it's
188       * for a route to an interface.
189       */
190      if (rt->rt_flags & RTF_GATEWAY) {
191          if (((rt->rt_flags & RTF_HOST) == 0) && (flags & RTF_HOST)) {
192              /*
193               * Changing from route to net => route to host.
194               * Create new route, rather than smashing route to net.
195               */
196            create:
197              flags |= RTF_GATEWAY | RTF_DYNAMIC;
198              error = rtrequest((int) RTM_ADD, dst, gateway,
199                                netmask, flags,
200                                (struct rtentry **) 0);
201              stat = &rtstat.rts_dynamic;
202          } else {
203              /*
204               * Smash the current notion of the gateway to
205               * this destination.  Should check about netmask!!!
206               */
207              rt->rt_flags |= RTF_MODIFIED;
208              flags |= RTF_MODIFIED;
209              stat = &rtstat.rts_newgateway;
210              rt_setgate(rt, rt_key(rt), gateway);
211          }
212      } else
213          error = EHOSTUNREACH;
214    done:
215      if (rt) {
216          if (rtp && !error)
217              *rtp = rt;
218          else
219              rtfree(rt);
220      }
221    out:
222      if (error)
223          rtstat.rts_badredirect++;
224      else if (stat != NULL)
225          (*stat)++;

226      bzero((caddr_t) & info, sizeof(info));
227      info.rti_info[RTAX_DST] = dst;
228      info.rti_info[RTAX_GATEWAY] = gateway;
229      info.rti_info[RTAX_NETMASK] = netmask;
230      info.rti_info[RTAX_AUTHOR] = src;
231      rt_missmsg(RTM_REDIRECT, &info, flags, error);
232  }
```

─── *route.c*

Figure 19.15 `rtredirect` function: second half.

Create route

196–201   `rtrequest` creates the new route, setting the `RTF_GATEWAY` and `RTF_DYNAMIC` flags. The `netmask` argument is a null pointer, since the new route is a host route with an implied mask of all one bits. `stat` points to a counter that is incremented later.

Modify existing host route

202–211   This code is executed when the current route to the destination is already a host route. A new entry is not created, but the existing entry is modified. The `RTF_MODIFIED` flag is set and `rt_setgate` changes the `rt_gateway` field of the routing table entry to the new gateway address.

Ignore if destination is directly connected

212–213   If the current route to the destination is a direct route (the `RTF_GATEWAY` flag is not set), it is a redirect for a destination that is already directly connected. `EHOSTUNREACH` is returned.

Return pointer and increment statistic

214–225   If a routing table entry was located, it is either returned (if `rtp` is nonnull and there were no errors) or released by `rtfree`. The appropriate statistic is incremented.

Generate routing message

226–232   An `rt_addrinfo` structure is cleared and a routing socket message is generated by `rt_missmsg`. This message is sent by `raw_input` to any processes interested in the redirect.

19.8 Routing Message Structures

Routing messages consist of a fixed-length header followed by up to eight socket address structures. The fixed-length header is one of the following three structures:

- `rt_msghdr`
- `if_msghdr`
- `ifa_msghdr`

Figure 18.11 provided an overview of which functions generated the different messages and Figure 18.9 showed which structure is used by each message type. The first three members of the three structures have the same data type and meaning: the message length, version, and type. This allows the receiver of the message to decode the message. Also, each structure has a member that encodes which of the eight potential socket address structures follow the structure (a bitmask): the `rtm_addrs`, `ifm_addrs`, and `ifam_addrs` members.

Figure 19.16 shows the most common of the structures, `rt_msghdr`. The `RTM_IFINFO` message uses an `if_msghdr` structure, shown in Figure 19.17. The `RTM_NEWADDR` and `RTM_DELADDR` messages use an `ifa_msghdr` structure, shown in Figure 19.18.

```
                                                                    ── route.h
139 struct rt_msghdr {
140     u_short rtm_msglen;         /* to skip over non-understood messages */
141     u_char  rtm_version;        /* future binary compatibility */
142     u_char  rtm_type;           /* message type */

143     u_short rtm_index;          /* index for associated ifp */
144     int     rtm_flags;          /* flags, incl. kern & message, e.g. DONE */
145     int     rtm_addrs;          /* bitmask identifying sockaddrs in msg */
146     pid_t   rtm_pid;            /* identify sender */
147     int     rtm_seq;            /* for sender to identify action */
148     int     rtm_errno;          /* why failed */
149     int     rtm_use;            /* from rtentry */
150     u_long  rtm_inits;          /* which metrics we are initializing */
151     struct rt_metrics rtm_rmx;  /* metrics themselves */
152 };
                                                                    ── route.h
```

Figure 19.16   rt_msghdr structure.

```
                                                                    ── if.h
235 struct if_msghdr {
236     u_short ifm_msglen;         /* to skip over non-understood messages */
237     u_char  ifm_version;        /* future binary compatability */
238     u_char  ifm_type;           /* message type */

239     int     ifm_addrs;          /* like rtm_addrs */
240     int     ifm_flags;          /* value of if_flags */
241     u_short ifm_index;          /* index for associated ifp */
242     struct if_data ifm_data;    /* statistics and other data about if */
243 };
                                                                    ── if.h
```

Figure 19.17   if_msghdr structure.

```
                                                                    ── if.h
248 struct ifa_msghdr {
249     u_short ifam_msglen;        /* to skip over non-understood messages */
250     u_char  ifam_version;       /* future binary compatability */
251     u_char  ifam_type;          /* message type */

252     int     ifam_addrs;         /* like rtm_addrs */
253     int     ifam_flags;         /* value of ifa_flags */
254     u_short ifam_index;         /* index for associated ifp */
255     int     ifam_metric;        /* value of ifa_metric */
256 };
                                                                    ── if.h
```

Figure 19.18   ifa_msghdr structure.

Note that the first three members across the three different structures have the same data types and meanings.

The three variables rtm_addrs, ifm_addrs, and ifam_addrs are bitmasks defining which socket address structures follow the header. Figure 19.19 shows the constants used with these bitmasks.

Bitmask		Array index		Name in rtsock.c	Description
Constant	Value	Constant	Value		
RTA_DST	0x01	RTAX_DST	0	dst	destination socket address structure
RTA_GATEWAY	0x02	RTAX_GATEWAY	1	gate	gateway socket address structure
RTA_NETMASK	0x04	RTAX_NETMASK	2	netmask	netmask socket address structure
RTA_GENMASK	0x08	RTAX_GENMASK	3	genmask	cloning mask socket address structure
RTA_IFP	0x10	RTAX_IFP	4	ifpaddr	interface name socket address structure
RTA_IFA	0x20	RTAX_IFA	5	ifaaddr	interface address socket address structure
RTA_AUTHOR	0x40	RTAX_AUTHOR	6		socket address structure for author of redirect
RTA_BRD	0x80	RTAX_BRD	7	brdaddr	broadcast or point-to-point destination address
		RTAX_MAX	8		#elements in an rti_info[] array

Figure 19.19   Constants used to refer to members of rti_info array.

The bitmask value is always the constant 1 left shifted by the number of bits specified by the array index. For example, 0x20 (RTA_IFA) is 1 left shifted by five bits (RTAX_IFA). We'll see this fact used in the code.

The socket address structures that are present always occur in order of increasing array index, one right after the other. For example, if the bitmask is 0x87, the first socket address structure contains the destination, followed by the gateway, followed by the network mask, followed by the broadcast address.

The array indexes in Figure 19.19 are used within the kernel to refer to its rt_addrinfo structure, shown in Figure 19.20. This structure holds the same bitmask that we described, indicating which addresses are present, and pointers to those socket address structures.

─── *route.h*
```
199 struct rt_addrinfo {
200     int     rti_addrs;           /* bitmask, same as rtm_addrs */
201     struct sockaddr *rti_info[RTAX_MAX];
202 };
```
─── *route.h*

Figure 19.20   rt_addrinfo structure: encode which addresses are present and pointers to them.

For example, if the RTA_GATEWAY bit is set in the rti_addrs member, then the member rti_info[RTAX_GATEWAY] is a pointer to a socket address structure containing the gateway's address. In the case of the Internet protocols, the socket address structure is a sockaddr_in containing the gateway's IP address.

The fifth column in Figure 19.19 shows the names used for the corresponding members of an rti_info array throughout the file rtsock.c. These definitions look like

        #define dst   info.rti_info[RTAX_DST]

We'll encounter these names in many of the source files later in this chapter. The RTAX_AUTHOR element is not assigned a name because it is never passed from a process to the kernel.

We've already encountered this rt_addrinfo structure twice: in rtalloc1 (Figure 19.2) and rtredirect (Figure 19.14). Figure 19.21 shows the format of this structure when built by `rtalloc1`, after a routing table lookup fails, when `rt_missmsg` is called.

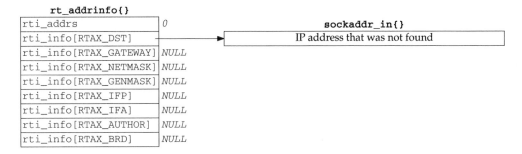

Figure 19.21 `rt_addrinfo` structure passed by `rtalloc1` to `rt_missmsg`.

All the unused pointers are null because the structure is set to 0 before it is used. Also note that the `rti_addrs` member is not initialized with the appropriate bitmask because when this structure is used within the kernel, a null pointer in the `rti_info` array indicates a nonexistent socket address structure. The bitmask is needed only for messages between a process and the kernel.

Figure 19.22 shows the format of the structure built by `rtredirect` when it calls `rt_missmsg`.

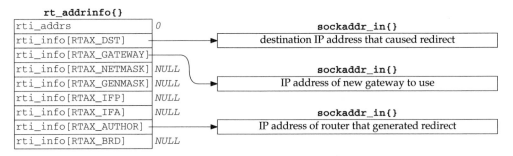

Figure 19.22 `rt_addrinfo` structure passed by `rtredirect` to `rt_missmsg`.

The following sections show how these structures are placed into the messages sent to a process.

Figure 19.23 shows the `route_cb` structure, which we'll encounter in the following sections. It contains four counters; one each for the IP, XNS, and OSI protocols, and an "any" counter. Each counter is the number of routing sockets currently in existence for that domain.

203–208   By keeping track of the number of routing socket listeners, the kernel avoids building a routing message and calling `raw_input` to send the message when there aren't any processes waiting for a message.

```
                                                           ─────── route.h
203 struct route_cb {
204     int     ip_count;            /* IP */
205     int     ns_count;            /* XNS */
206     int     iso_count;           /* ISO */
207     int     any_count;           /* sum of above three counters */
208 };
                                                           ─────── route.h
```

Figure 19.23   route_cb structure: counters of routing socket listeners.

19.9 `rt_missmsg` **Function**

The function `rt_missmsg`, shown in Figure 19.24, takes the structures shown in Figures 19.21 and 19.22, calls `rt_msg1` to build a corresponding variable-length message for a process in an mbuf chain, and then calls `raw_input` to pass the mbuf chain to all appropriate routing sockets.

```
                                                           ─────── rtsock.c
516 void
517 rt_missmsg(type, rtinfo, flags, error)
518 int     type, flags, error;
519 struct rt_addrinfo *rtinfo;
520 {
521     struct rt_msghdr *rtm;
522     struct mbuf *m;
523     struct sockaddr *sa = rtinfo->rti_info[RTAX_DST];

524     if (route_cb.any_count == 0)
525         return;

526     m = rt_msg1(type, rtinfo);
527     if (m == 0)
528         return;

529     rtm = mtod(m, struct rt_msghdr *);
530     rtm->rtm_flags = RTF_DONE | flags;
531     rtm->rtm_errno = error;
532     rtm->rtm_addrs = rtinfo->rti_addrs;

533     route_proto.sp_protocol = sa ? sa->sa_family : 0;
534     raw_input(m, &route_proto, &route_src, &route_dst);
535 }
                                                           ─────── rtsock.c
```

Figure 19.24   rt_missmsg function.

516–525   If there aren't any routing socket listeners, the function returns immediately.

Build message in mbuf chain

526–528   `rt_msg1` (Section 19.12) builds the appropriate message in an mbuf chain, and returns the pointer to the chain. Figure 19.25 shows an example of the resulting mbuf chain, using the `rt_addrinfo` structure from Figure 19.22. The information needs to be in an mbuf chain because `raw_input` calls `sbappendaddr` to append the mbuf chain to a socket's receive buffer.

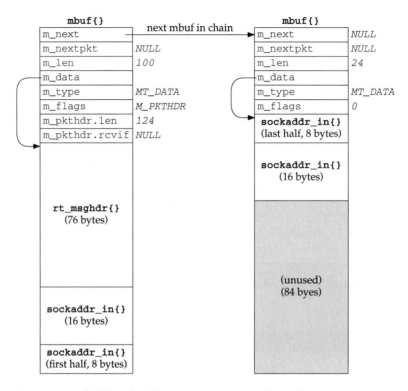

Figure 19.25   Mbuf chain built by rt_msg1 corresponding to Figure 19.22.

Finish building message

529–532   The two members rtm_flags and rtm_errno are set to the values passed by the caller. The rtm_addrs member is copied from the rti_addrs value. We showed this value as 0 in Figures 19.21 and 19.22, but rt_msg1 calculates and stores the appropriate bitmask, based on which pointers in the rti_info array are nonnull.

Set protocol of message, call raw_input

533–534   The final three arguments to raw_input specify the protocol, source, and destination of the routing message. These three structures are initialized as

```
struct  sockaddr  route_dst = { 2, PF_ROUTE, };
struct  sockaddr  route_src = { 2, PF_ROUTE, };
struct  sockproto route_proto = { PF_ROUTE, };
```

The first two structures are never modified by the kernel. The sockproto structure, shown in Figure 19.26, is one we haven't seen before.

—— *socket.h*
```
128 struct sockproto {
129     u_short sp_family;            /* address family */
130     u_short sp_protocol;          /* protocol */
131 };
```
—— *socket.h*

Figure 19.26   sockproto structure.

The family is never changed from its initial value of PF_ROUTE, but the protocol is set each time raw_input is called. When a process creates a routing socket by calling socket, the third argument (the protocol) specifies the protocol in which the process is interested. The caller of raw_input sets the sp_protocol member of the route_proto structure to the protocol of the routing message. In the case of rt_missmsg, it is set to the sa_family of the destination socket address structure (if specified by the caller), which in Figures 19.21 and 19.22 would be AF_INET.

19.10 rt_ifmsg Function

In Figure 4.30 we saw that if_up and if_down both call rt_ifmsg, shown in Figure 19.27, to generate a routing socket message when an interface goes up or down.

```
                                                                    ── rtsock.c
540 void
541 rt_ifmsg(ifp)
542 struct ifnet *ifp;
543 {
544     struct if_msghdr *ifm;
545     struct mbuf *m;
546     struct rt_addrinfo info;

547     if (route_cb.any_count == 0)
548         return;

549     bzero((caddr_t) & info, sizeof(info));
550     m = rt_msg1(RTM_IFINFO, &info);
551     if (m == 0)
552         return;

553     ifm = mtod(m, struct if_msghdr *);
554     ifm->ifm_index = ifp->if_index;
555     ifm->ifm_flags = ifp->if_flags;
556     ifm->ifm_data = ifp->if_data;    /* structure assignment */
557     ifm->ifm_addrs = 0;

558     route_proto.sp_protocol = 0;
559     raw_input(m, &route_proto, &route_src, &route_dst);
560 }
                                                                    ── rtsock.c
```

Figure 19.27 rt_ifmsg function.

547–548   If there aren't any routing socket listeners, the function returns immediately.

Build message in mbuf chain

549–552   An rt_addrinfo structure is set to 0 and rt_msg1 builds an appropriate message in an mbuf chain. Notice that all socket address pointers in the rt_addrinfo structure are null, so only the fixed-length if_msghdr structure becomes the routing message; there are no addresses.

Finish building message

553–557   The interface's index, flags, and `if_data` structure are copied into the message in the mbuf and the `ifm_addrs` bitmask is set to 0.

Set protocol of message, call `raw_input`

558–559   The protocol of the routing message is set to 0 because this message can apply to all protocol suites. It is a message about an interface, not about some specific destination. `raw_input` delivers the message to the appropriate listeners.

19.11 `rt_newaddrmsg` Function

In Figure 19.13 we saw that `rtinit` calls `rt_newaddrmsg` with a command of RTM_ADD or RTM_DELETE when an interface has an address added or deleted. Figure 19.28 shows the first half of the function.

── rtsock.c

```
569 void
570 rt_newaddrmsg(cmd, ifa, error, rt)
571 int     cmd, error;
572 struct ifaddr *ifa;
573 struct rtentry *rt;
574 {
575     struct rt_addrinfo info;
576     struct sockaddr *sa;
577     int     pass;
578     struct mbuf *m;
579     struct ifnet *ifp = ifa->ifa_ifp;

580     if (route_cb.any_count == 0)
581         return;

582     for (pass = 1; pass < 3; pass++) {
583         bzero((caddr_t) & info, sizeof(info));
584         if ((cmd == RTM_ADD && pass == 1) ||
585             (cmd == RTM_DELETE && pass == 2)) {
586             struct ifa_msghdr *ifam;
587             int     ncmd = cmd == RTM_ADD ? RTM_NEWADDR : RTM_DELADDR;

588             ifaaddr = sa = ifa->ifa_addr;
589             ifpaddr = ifp->if_addrlist->ifa_addr;
590             netmask = ifa->ifa_netmask;
591             brdaddr = ifa->ifa_dstaddr;
592             if ((m = rt_msg1(ncmd, &info)) == NULL)
593                 continue;
594             ifam = mtod(m, struct ifa_msghdr *);
595             ifam->ifam_index = ifp->if_index;
596             ifam->ifam_metric = ifa->ifa_metric;
597             ifam->ifam_flags = ifa->ifa_flags;
598             ifam->ifam_addrs = info.rti_addrs;
599         }
```

── rtsock.c

Figure 19.28   `rt_newaddrmsg` function: first half: create `ifa_msghdr` message.

580–581   If there aren't any routing socket listeners, the function returns immediately.

Generate two routing messages

582   The `for` loop iterates twice because two messages are generated. If the command is RTM_ADD, the first message is of type RTM_NEWADDR and the second message is of type RTM_ADD. If the command is RTM_DELETE, the first message is of type RTM_DELETE and the second message is of type RTM_DELADDR. The RTM_NEWADDR and RTM_DELADDR messages are built from an `ifa_msghdr` structure, while the RTM_ADD and RTM_DELETE messages are built from an `rt_msghdr` structure. The function generates two messages because one message provides information about the interface and the other about the addresses.

583   An `rt_addrinfo` structure is set to 0.

Generate message with up to four addresses

588–591   Pointers to four socket address structures containing information about the interface address that has been added or deleted are stored in the `rti_info` array. Recall from Figure 19.19 that `ifaaddr`, `ifpaddr`, `netmask`, and `brdaddr` reference elements in the `rti_info` array in `info`. `rt_msg1` builds the appropriate message in an mbuf chain. Notice that `sa` is set to point to the `ifa_addr` structure, and we'll see at the end of the function that the family of this socket address structure becomes the protocol of the routing message.

Remaining members of the `ifa_msghdr` structure are filled in with the interface's index, metric, and flags, along with the bitmask set by `rt_msg1`.

Figure 19.29 shows the second half of `rt_newaddrmsg`, which creates an `rt_msghdr` message with information about the routing table entry that was added or deleted.

Build message

600–609   Pointers to three socket address structures are stored in the `rti_info` array: the `rt_mask`, `rt_key`, and `rt_gateway` structures. `sa` is set to point to the destination address, and its family becomes the protocol of the routing message. `rt_msg1` builds the appropriate message in an mbuf chain.

Additional fields in the `rt_msghdr` structure are filled in, including the bitmask set by `rt_msg1`.

Set protocol of message, call **raw_input**

616–619   The protocol of the routing message is set and `raw_input` passes the message to the appropriate listeners. The function returns after two iterations through the loop.

```
                                                                              ─── rtsock.c
600          if ((cmd == RTM_ADD && pass == 2) ||
601              (cmd == RTM_DELETE && pass == 1)) {
602              struct rt_msghdr *rtm;

603              if (rt == 0)
604                  continue;
605              netmask = rt_mask(rt);
606              dst = sa = rt_key(rt);
607              gate = rt->rt_gateway;
608              if ((m = rt_msg1(cmd, &info)) == NULL)
609                  continue;
610              rtm = mtod(m, struct rt_msghdr *);
611              rtm->rtm_index = ifp->if_index;
612              rtm->rtm_flags |= rt->rt_flags;
613              rtm->rtm_errno = error;
614              rtm->rtm_addrs = info.rti_addrs;
615          }
616          route_proto.sp_protocol = sa ? sa->sa_family : 0;
617          raw_input(m, &route_proto, &route_src, &route_dst);
618      }
619  }
                                                                              ─── rtsock.c
```

Figure 19.29   rt_newaddrmsg function: second half, create rt_msghdr message.

19.12 `rt_msg1` Function

The functions described in the previous three sections each called `rt_msg1` to build the appropriate routing message. In Figure 19.25 we showed the mbuf chain that was built by `rt_msg1` from the `rt_msghdr` and `rt_addrinfo` structures in Figure 19.22. Figure 19.30 shows the function.

Get mbuf and determine fixed size of message

399–422   An mbuf with a packet header is obtained and the length of the fixed-size message is stored in `len`. Two of the message types in Figure 18.9 use an `ifa_msghdr` structure, one uses an `if_msghdr` structure, and the remaining nine use an `rt_msghdr` structure.

Verify structure fits in mbuf

423–424   The size of the fixed-length structure must fit entirely within the data portion of the packet header mbuf, because the mbuf pointer is cast to a structure pointer using `mtod` and the structure is then referenced through the pointer. The largest of the three structures is `if_msghdr`, which at 84 bytes is less than MHLEN (100).

Initialize mbuf packet header and zero structure

425–428   The two fields in the packet header are initialized and the structure in the mbuf is set to 0.

```
                                                              ─ rtsock.c
399 static struct mbuf *
400 rt_msg1(type, rtinfo)
401 int     type;
402 struct rt_addrinfo *rtinfo;
403 {
404     struct rt_msghdr *rtm;
405     struct mbuf *m;
406     int     i;
407     struct sockaddr *sa;
408     int     len, dlen;

409     m = m_gethdr(M_DONTWAIT, MT_DATA);
410     if (m == 0)
411         return (m);
412     switch (type) {

413     case RTM_DELADDR:
414     case RTM_NEWADDR:
415         len = sizeof(struct ifa_msghdr);
416         break;

417     case RTM_IFINFO:
418         len = sizeof(struct if_msghdr);
419         break;

420     default:
421         len = sizeof(struct rt_msghdr);
422     }
423     if (len > MHLEN)
424         panic("rt_msg1");
425     m->m_pkthdr.len = m->m_len = len;
426     m->m_pkthdr.rcvif = 0;
427     rtm = mtod(m, struct rt_msghdr *);
428     bzero((caddr_t) rtm, len);

429     for (i = 0; i < RTAX_MAX; i++) {
430         if ((sa = rtinfo->rti_info[i]) == NULL)
431             continue;
432         rtinfo->rti_addrs |= (1 << i);
433         dlen = ROUNDUP(sa->sa_len);
434         m_copyback(m, len, dlen, (caddr_t) sa);
435         len += dlen;
436     }
437     if (m->m_pkthdr.len != len) {
438         m_freem(m);
439         return (NULL);
440     }
441     rtm->rtm_msglen = len;
442     rtm->rtm_version = RTM_VERSION;
443     rtm->rtm_type = type;
444     return (m);
445 }
                                                              ─ rtsock.c
```

Figure 19.30 rt_msg1 function: obtain and initialize mbuf.

Copy socket address structures into mbuf chain

429–436   The caller passes a pointer to an `rt_addrinfo` structure. The socket address structures corresponding to all the nonnull pointers in the `rti_info` are copied into the mbuf by `m_copyback`. The value 1 is left shifted by the `RTAX_xxx` index to generate the corresponding `RTA_xxx` bitmask (Figure 19.19), and each individual bitmask is logically ORed into the `rti_addrs` member, which the caller can store on return into the corresponding member of the message structure. The `ROUNDUP` macro rounds the size of each socket address structure up to the next multiple of 4 bytes.

437–440   If, when the loop terminates, the length in the mbuf packet header does not equal `len`, the function `m_copyback` wasn't able to obtain a required mbuf.

Store length, version, and type

441–445   The length, version, and message type are stored in the first three members of the message structure. Again, all three *xxx_msghdr* structures start with the same three members, so this code works with all three structures even though the pointer `rtm` is a pointer to an `rt_msghdr` structure.

19.13 `rt_msg2` Function

`rt_msg1` constructs a routing message in an mbuf chain, and the three functions that called it then called `raw_input` to append the mbuf chain to one or more socket's receive buffer. `rt_msg2` is different—it builds a routing message in a memory buffer, not an mbuf chain, and has as an argument a pointer to a `walkarg` structure that is used when `rt_msg2` is called by the two functions that handle the `sysctl` system call for the routing domain. `rt_msg2` is called in two different scenarios:

1. from `route_output` to process the `RTM_GET` command, and

2. from `sysctl_dumpentry` and `sysctl_iflist` to process a `sysctl` system call.

Before looking at `rt_msg2`, Figure 19.31 shows the `walkarg` structure that is used in scenario 2. We go through all these members as we encounter them.

```
                                                                      ─── rtsock.c
41 struct walkarg {
42     int      w_op;           /* NET_RT_xxx */
43     int      w_arg;          /* RTF_xxx for FLAGS, if_index for IFLIST */
44     int      w_given;        /* size of process' buffer */
45     int      w_needed;       /* #bytes actually needed (at end) */
46     int      w_tmemsize;     /* size of buffer pointed to by w_tmem */
47     caddr_t  w_where;        /* ptr to process' buffer (maybe null) */
48     caddr_t  w_tmem;         /* ptr to our malloc'ed buffer */
49 };
                                                                      ─── rtsock.c
```

Figure 19.31   `walkarg` structure: used with the `sysctl` system call in the routing domain.

Figure 19.32 shows the first half of the `rt_msg2` function. This portion is similar to the first half of `rt_msg1`.

```
                                                                      ─── rtsock.c
446 static int
447 rt_msg2(type, rtinfo, cp, w)
448 int      type;
449 struct rt_addrinfo *rtinfo;
450 caddr_t cp;
451 struct walkarg *w;
452 {
453     int     i;
454     int     len, dlen, second_time = 0;
455     caddr_t cp0;

456     rtinfo->rti_addrs = 0;
457 again:
458     switch (type) {

459     case RTM_DELADDR:
460     case RTM_NEWADDR:
461         len = sizeof(struct ifa_msghdr);
462         break;

463     case RTM_IFINFO:
464         len = sizeof(struct if_msghdr);
465         break;

466     default:
467         len = sizeof(struct rt_msghdr);
468     }
469     if (cp0 = cp)
470         cp += len;
471     for (i = 0; i < RTAX_MAX; i++) {
472         struct sockaddr *sa;

473         if ((sa = rtinfo->rti_info[i]) == 0)
474             continue;
475         rtinfo->rti_addrs |= (1 << i);
476         dlen = ROUNDUP(sa->sa_len);
477         if (cp) {
478             bcopy((caddr_t) sa, cp, (unsigned) dlen);
479             cp += dlen;
480         }
481         len += dlen;
482     }
                                                                      ─── rtsock.c
```

Figure 19.32   rt_msg2 function: copy socket address structures.

446–455   Since this function stores the resulting message in a memory buffer, the caller specifies the start of that buffer in the cp argument. It is the caller's responsibility to ensure that the buffer is large enough for the message that is generated. To help the caller determine this size, if the cp argument is null, rt_msg2 doesn't store anything but processes the input and returns the total number of bytes required to hold the result. We'll see that route_output uses this feature and calls this function twice: first to determine the size and then to store the result, after allocating a buffer of the correct size. When rt_msg2 is called by route_output, the final argument is null. This final argument is nonnull when called as part of the sysctl system call processing.

Determine size of structure

458–470   The size of the fixed-length message structure is set based on the message type. If the `cp` pointer is nonnull, it is incremented by this size.

Copy socket address structures

471–482   The `for` loop goes through the `rti_info` array, and for each element that is a non-null pointer it sets the appropriate bit in the `rti_addrs` bitmask, copies the socket address structure (if `cp` is nonnull), and updates the length.

Figure 19.33 shows the second half of `rt_msg2`, most of which handles the optional `walkarg` structure.

```
                                                                     ──── rtsock.c
483     if (cp == 0 && w != NULL && !second_time) {
484         struct walkarg *rw = w;

485         rw->w_needed += len;
486         if (rw->w_needed <= 0 && rw->w_where) {
487             if (rw->w_tmemsize < len) {
488                 if (rw->w_tmem)
489                     free(rw->w_tmem, M_RTABLE);
490                 if (rw->w_tmem = (caddr_t)
491                     malloc(len, M_RTABLE, M_NOWAIT))
492                     rw->w_tmemsize = len;
493             }
494             if (rw->w_tmem) {
495                 cp = rw->w_tmem;
496                 second_time = 1;
497                 goto again;
498             } else
499                 rw->w_where = 0;
500         }
501     }
502     if (cp) {
503         struct rt_msghdr *rtm = (struct rt_msghdr *) cp0;

504         rtm->rtm_version = RTM_VERSION;
505         rtm->rtm_type = type;
506         rtm->rtm_msglen = len;
507     }
508     return (len);
509 }
                                                                     ──── rtsock.c
```

Figure 19.33   `rt_msg2` function: handle optional `walkarg` argument.

483–484   This `if` statement is true only when a pointer to a `walkarg` structure was passed and this is the first loop through the function. The variable `second_time` was initialized to 0 but can be set to 1 within this `if` statement, and a jump made back to the label `again` in Figure 19.32. The test for `cp` being a null pointer is superfluous since whenever the `w` pointer is nonnull, the `cp` pointer is null, and vice versa.

Check if data to be stored

485–486   `w_needed` is incremented by the size of the message. This variable is initialized to 0 minus the size of the user's buffer to the `sysctl` function. For example, if the buffer size is 500 bytes, w_needed is initialized to −500. As long as it remains negative, there is room in the buffer. w_where is a pointer to the buffer in the calling process. It is null if the process doesn't want the result—the process just wants sysctl to return the size of the result, so the process can allocate a buffer and call sysctl again. rt_msg2 doesn't copy the data back to the process—that is up to the caller—but if the w_where pointer is null, there's no need for rt_msg2 to malloc a buffer to hold the result and loop back through the function again, storing the result in this buffer. There are really five different scenarios that this function handles, summarized in Figure 19.34.

called from	cp	w	w.w_where	second_time	Description
route_output	null	null			wants return length
	nonnull	null			wants result
sysctl_rtable	null	nonnull	null	0	process wants return length
	null	nonnull	nonnull	0	first time around to calculate length
	nonnull	nonnull	nonnull	1	second time around to store result

Figure 19.34　Summary of different scenarios for rt_msg2.

Allocate buffer first time or if message length increases

487–493　　　w_tmemsize is the size of the buffer pointed to by w_tmem. It is initialized to 0 by sysctl_rtable, so the first time rt_msg2 is called for a given sysctl request, the buffer must be allocated. Also, if the size of the result increases, the existing buffer must be released and a new (larger) buffer allocated.

Go around again and store result

494–499　　　If w_tmem is nonnull, a buffer already exists or one was just allocated. cp is set to point to this buffer, second_time is set to 1, and a jump is made to again. The if statement at the beginning of this figure won't be true during this second pass, since second_time is now 1. If w_tmem is null, the call to malloc failed, so the pointer to the buffer in the process is set to null, preventing anything from being returned.

Store length, version, and type

502–509　　　If cp is nonnull, the first three elements of the message header are stored. The function returns the length of the message.

19.14 sysctl_rtable Function

This function handles the sysctl system call on a routing socket. It is called by net_sysctl as shown in Figure 18.11.

Before going through the source code, Figure 19.35 shows the typical use of this system call with respect to the routing table. This example is from the arp program.

The first three elements in the mib array cause the kernel to call sysctl_rtable to process the remaining elements.

```
int      mib[6];
size_t   needed;
char     *buf, *lim, *next;
struct rt_msghdr  *rtm;

mib[0] = CTL_NET;
mib[1] = PF_ROUTE;
mib[2] = 0;
mib[3] = AF_INET;        /* address family; can be 0 */
mib[4] = NET_RT_FLAGS;   /* operation */
mib[5] = RTF_LLINFO;     /* flags; can be 0 */

if (sysctl(mib, 6, NULL, &needed, NULL, 0) < 0)
    quit("sysctl error, estimate");

if ( (buf = malloc(needed)) == NULL)
    quit("malloc");

if (sysctl(mib, 6, buf, &needed, NULL, 0) < 0)
    quit("sysctl error, retrieval");

lim = buf + needed;
for (next = buf; next < lim; next += rtm->rtm_msglen) {
    rtm = (struct rt_msghdr *)next;
    ...  /* do whatever */
}
```

Figure 19.35 Example of sysctl with routing table.

mib[4] specifies the operation. Three operations are supported.

1. NET_RT_DUMP: return the routing table corresponding to the address family
   specified by mib[3]. If the address family is 0, all routing tables are returned.

   An RTM_GET routing message is returned for each routing table entry containing two, three, or four socket address structures per message: those addresses
   pointed to by rt_key, rt_gateway, rt_netmask, and rt_genmask. The
   final two pointers might be null.

2. NET_RT_FLAGS: the same as the previous command except mib[5] specifies an
   RTF_*xxx* flag (Figure 18.25), and only entries with this flag set are returned.

3. NET_RT_IFLIST: return information on all the configured interfaces. If the
   mib[5] value is nonzero it specifies an interface index and only the interface
   with the corresponding if_index is returned. Otherwise all interfaces on the
   ifnet linked list are returned.

   For each interface one RTM_IFINFO message is returned, with information
   about the interface itself, followed by one RTM_NEWADDR message for each
   ifaddr structure on the interface's if_addrlist linked list. If the mib[3]
   value is nonzero, RTM_NEWADDR messages are returned for only the addresses

with an address family that matches the `mib[3]` value. Otherwise `mib[3]` is 0 and information on all addresses is returned.

> This operation is intended to replace the `SIOCGIFCONF` `ioctl` (Figure 4.26).

One problem with this system call is that the amount of information returned can vary, depending on the number of routing table entries or the number of interfaces. Therefore the first call to `sysctl` typically specifies a null pointer as the third argument, which means: don't return any data, just return the number of bytes of return information. As we see in Figure 19.35, the process then calls `malloc`, followed by `sysctl` to fetch the information. This second call to `sysctl` again returns the number of bytes through the fourth argument (which might have changed since the previous call), and this value provides the pointer `lim` that points just beyond the final byte of data that was returned. The process then steps through the routing messages in the buffer, using the `rtm_msglen` member to step to the next message.

Figure 19.36 shows the values for these six `mib` variables that various Net/3 programs specify to access the routing table and interface list.

mib[]	arp	route	netstat	routed	gated	rwhod
0	CTL_NET	CTL_NET	CTL_NET	CTL_NET	CTL_NET	CTL_NET
1	PF_ROUTE	PF_ROUTE	PF_ROUTE	PF_ROUTE	PF_ROUTE	PF_ROUTE
2	0	0	0	0	0	0
3	AF_INET	0	0	AF_INET	0	AF_INET
4	NET_RT_FLAGS	NET_RT_DUMP	NET_RT_DUMP	NET_RT_IFLIST	NET_RT_IFLIST	NET_RT_IFLIST
5	RTF_LLINFO	0	0	0	0	0

Figure 19.36 Examples of programs that call `sysctl` to obtain routing table and interface list.

The first three programs fetch entries from the routing table and the last three fetch the interface list. The `routed` program supports only the Internet routing protocols, so it specifies a `mib[3]` value of `AF_INET`, while `gated` supports other protocols, so its value for `mib[3]` is 0.

Figure 19.37 shows the organization of the three `sysctl_xxx` functions that we cover in the following sections.

Figure 19.38 shows the `sysctl_rtable` function.

Validate arguments

705–719   The `new` argument is used when the process is calling `sysctl` to set the value of a variable, which isn't supported with the routing tables. Therefore this argument must be a null pointer.

720–721   `namelen` must be 3 because at this point in the processing of the system call, three elements in the `name` array remain: `name[0]`, the address family (what the process specifies as `mib[3]`); `name[1]`, the operation (`mib[4]`); and `name[2]`, the flags (`mib[5]`).

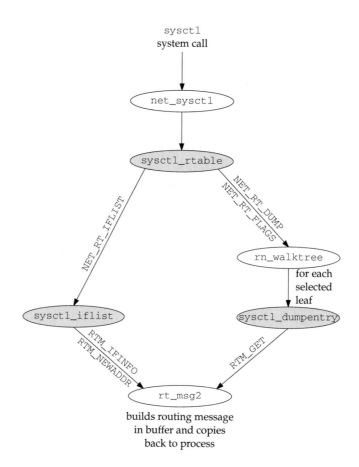

Figure 19.37 Functions that support the `sysctl` system call for routing sockets.

```
                                                                    ─── rtsock.c
705 int
706 sysctl_rtable(name, namelen, where, given, new, newlen)
707 int     *name;
708 int      namelen;
709 caddr_t where;
710 size_t *given;
711 caddr_t *new;
712 size_t  newlen;
713 {
714     struct radix_node_head *rnh;
715     int     i, s, error = EINVAL;
716     u_char  af;
717     struct walkarg w;

718     if (new)
719         return (EPERM);
```

```
720      if (namelen != 3)
721          return (EINVAL);
722      af = name[0];
723      Bzero(&w, sizeof(w));
724      w.w_where = where;
725      w.w_given = *given;
726      w.w_needed = 0 - w.w_given;
727      w.w_op = name[1];
728      w.w_arg = name[2];

729      s = splnet();
730      switch (w.w_op) {

731      case NET_RT_DUMP:
732      case NET_RT_FLAGS:
733          for (i = 1; i <= AF_MAX; i++)
734              if ((rnh = rt_tables[i]) && (af == 0 || af == i) &&
735                  (error = rnh->rnh_walktree(rnh,
736                                          sysctl_dumpentry, &w)))
737                      break;
738          break;

739      case NET_RT_IFLIST:
740          error = sysctl_iflist(af, &w);
741      }
742      splx(s);
743      if (w.w_tmem)
744          free(w.w_tmem, M_RTABLE);
745      w.w_needed += w.w_given;
746      if (where) {
747          *given = w.w_where - where;
748          if (*given < w.w_needed)
749              return (ENOMEM);
750      } else {
751          *given = (11 * w.w_needed) / 10;
752      }
753      return (error);
754  }
```
                                                                              rtsock.c

Figure 19.38   `sysctl_rtable` function: process `sysctl` system call requests.

Initialize `walkarg` structure

723–728   A `walkarg` structure (Figure 19.31) is set to 0 and the following members are initialized: w_where is the address in the calling process of the buffer for the results (this can be a null pointer, as we mentioned); w_given is the size of the buffer in bytes (this is meaningless on input if w_where is a null pointer, but it must be set on return to the amount of data that would have been returned); w_needed is set to the negative of the buffer size; w_op is the operation (the NET_RT_*xxx* value); and w_arg is the flags value.

Dump routing table

731–738   The NET_RT_DUMP and NET_RT_FLAGS operations are handled the same way: a loop is made through all the routing tables (the rt_tables array), and if the routing table is in use and either the address family argument was 0 or the address family argument matches the family of this routing table, the rnh_walktree function is called to process the entire routing table. In Figure 18.17 we show that this function is normally rn_walktree. The second argument to this function is the address of another function that is called for each leaf of the routing tree (sysctl_dumpentry). The third argument is just a pointer to anything that rn_walktree passes to the sysctl_dumpentry function. This argument is a pointer to the walkarg structure that contains all the information about this sysctl call.

Return interface list

739–740   The NET_RT_IFLIST operation calls the function sysctl_iflist, which goes through all the ifnet structures.

Release buffer

743–744   If a buffer was allocated by rt_msg2 to contain a routing message, it is now released.

Update w_needed

745   The size of each message was added to w_needed by rt_msg2. Since this variable was initialized to the negative of w_given, its value can now be expressed as

    w_needed = 0 - w_given + totalbytes

where totalbytes is the sum of all the message lengths added by rt_msg2. By adding the value of w_given back into w_needed, we get

    w_needed = 0 - w_given + totalbytes + w_given
             = totalbytes

the total number of bytes. Since the two values of w_given in this equation end up canceling each other, when the process specifies w_where as a null pointer it need not initialize the value of w_given. Indeed, we see in Figure 19.35 that the variable needed was not initialized.

Return actual size of message

746–749   If where is nonnull, the number of bytes stored in the buffer is returned through the given pointer. If this value is less than the size of the buffer specified by the process, an error is returned because the return information has been truncated.

Return estimated size of message

750–752   When the where pointer is null, the process just wants the total number of bytes returned. A 10% fudge factor is added to the size, in case the size of the desired tables increases between this call to sysctl and the next.

19.15 sysctl_dumpentry Function

In the previous section we described how this function is called by rn_walktree, which in turn is called by sysctl_rtable. Figure 19.39 shows the function.

```
                                                                    —————— rtsock.c
623  int
624  sysctl_dumpentry(rn, w)
625  struct radix_node *rn;
626  struct walkarg *w;
627  {
628      struct rtentry *rt = (struct rtentry *) rn;
629      int      error = 0, size;
630      struct rt_addrinfo info;

631      if (w->w_op == NET_RT_FLAGS && !(rt->rt_flags & w->w_arg))
632          return 0;
633      bzero((caddr_t) & info, sizeof(info));
634      dst = rt_key(rt);
635      gate = rt->rt_gateway;
636      netmask = rt_mask(rt);
637      genmask = rt->rt_genmask;
638      size = rt_msg2(RTM_GET, &info, 0, w);
639      if (w->w_where && w->w_tmem) {
640          struct rt_msghdr *rtm = (struct rt_msghdr *) w->w_tmem;

641          rtm->rtm_flags = rt->rt_flags;
642          rtm->rtm_use = rt->rt_use;
643          rtm->rtm_rmx = rt->rt_rmx;
644          rtm->rtm_index = rt->rt_ifp->if_index;
645          rtm->rtm_errno = rtm->rtm_pid = rtm->rtm_seq = 0;
646          rtm->rtm_addrs = info.rti_addrs;
647          if (error = copyout((caddr_t) rtm, w->w_where, size))
648              w->w_where = NULL;
649          else
650              w->w_where += size;
651      }
652      return (error);
653  }
                                                                    —————— rtsock.c
```

Figure 19.39 sysctl_dumpentry function: process one routing table entry.

623–630   Each time this function is called, its first argument points to a radix_node structure, which is also a pointer to a rtentry structure. The second argument points to the walkarg structure that was initialized by sysctl_rtable.

Check flags of routing table entry

631–632   If the process specified a flag value (mib[5]), this entry is skipped if the rt_flags member doesn't have the desired flag set. We see in Figure 19.36 that the arp program uses this to select only those entries with the RTF_LLINFO flag set, since these are the entries of interest to ARP.

Form routing message

633–638   The following four pointers in the rti_info array are copied from the routing table entry: dst, gate, netmask, and genmask. The first two are always nonnull, but the other two can be null. rt_msg2 forms an RTM_GET message.

Copy message back to process

639–651   If the process wants the message returned and a buffer was allocated by `rt_msg2`, the remainder of the routing message is formed in the buffer pointed to by `w_tmem` and `copyout` copies the message back to the process. If the copy was successful, `w_where` is incremented by the number of bytes copied.

19.16 `sysctl_iflist` Function

This function, shown in Figure 19.40, is called directly by `sysctl_rtable` to return the interface list to the process.

————————————————————————————————————— *rtsock.c*

```
654 int
655 sysctl_iflist(af, w)
656 int      af;
657 struct walkarg *w;
658 {
659     struct ifnet *ifp;
660     struct ifaddr *ifa;
661     struct rt_addrinfo info;
662     int     len, error = 0;

663     bzero((caddr_t) & info, sizeof(info));
664     for (ifp = ifnet; ifp; ifp = ifp->if_next) {
665         if (w->w_arg && w->w_arg != ifp->if_index)
666             continue;
667         ifa = ifp->if_addrlist;
668         ifpaddr = ifa->ifa_addr;
669         len = rt_msg2(RTM_IFINFO, &info, (caddr_t) 0, w);
670         ifpaddr = 0;
671         if (w->w_where && w->w_tmem) {
672             struct if_msghdr *ifm;

673             ifm = (struct if_msghdr *) w->w_tmem;
674             ifm->ifm_index = ifp->if_index;
675             ifm->ifm_flags = ifp->if_flags;
676             ifm->ifm_data = ifp->if_data;
677             ifm->ifm_addrs = info.rti_addrs;
678             if (error = copyout((caddr_t) ifm, w->w_where, len))
679                 return (error);
680             w->w_where += len;
681         }
682         while (ifa = ifa->ifa_next) {
683             if (af && af != ifa->ifa_addr->sa_family)
684                 continue;
685             ifaaddr = ifa->ifa_addr;
686             netmask = ifa->ifa_netmask;
687             brdaddr = ifa->ifa_dstaddr;
688             len = rt_msg2(RTM_NEWADDR, &info, 0, w);
689             if (w->w_where && w->w_tmem) {
690                 struct ifa_msghdr *ifam;
```

```
691                        ifam = (struct ifa_msghdr *) w->w_tmem;
692                        ifam->ifam_index = ifa->ifa_ifp->if_index;
693                        ifam->ifam_flags = ifa->ifa_flags;
694                        ifam->ifam_metric = ifa->ifa_metric;
695                        ifam->ifam_addrs = info.rti_addrs;
696                        if (error = copyout(w->w_tmem, w->w_where, len))
697                            return (error);
698                        w->w_where += len;
699                    }
700                }
701            ifaaddr = netmask = brdaddr = 0;
702        }
703        return (0);
704 }
```

—————————————————————————————————— rtsock.c

Figure 19.40   `sysctl_iflist` function: return list of interfaces and their addresses.

This function is a `for` loop that iterates through each interface starting with the one pointed to by `ifnet`. Then a `while` loop proceeds through the linked list of `ifaddr` structures for each interface. An `RTM_IFINFO` routing message is generated for each interface and an `RTM_NEWADDR` message for each address.

Check interface index

654–666   The process can specify a nonzero flags argument (`mib[5]` in Figure 19.36) to select only the interface with a matching `if_index` value.

Build routing message

667–670   The only socket address structure returned with the `RTM_IFINFO` message is `ifpaddr`. The message is built by `rt_msg2`. The pointer `ifpaddr` in the `info` structure is then set to 0, since the same `info` structure is used for generating the subsequent `RTM_NEWADDR` messages.

Copy message back to process

671–681   If the process wants the message returned, the remainder of the `if_msghdr` structure is filled in, `copyout` copies the buffer to the process, and `w_where` is incremented.

Iterate through address structures, check address family

682–684   Each `ifaddr` structure for the interface is processed and the process can specify a nonzero address family (`mib[3]` in Figure 19.36) to select only the interface addresses of the given family.

Build routing message

685–688   Up to three socket address structures are returned in each `RTM_NEWADDR` message: `ifaaddr`, `netmask`, and `brdaddr`. The message is built by `rt_msg2`.

Copy message back to process

689–699   If the process wants the message returned, the remainder of the `ifa_msghdr` structure is filled in, `copyout` copies the buffer to the process, and `w_where` is incremented.

701   These three pointers in the `info` array are set to 0, since the same array is used for the next interface message.

19.17 Summary

Routing messages all have the same format—a fixed-length structure followed by a variable number of socket address structures. There are three different types of messages, each corresponding to a different fixed-length structure, and the first three elements of each structure identify the length, version, and type of message. A bitmask in each structure identifies which socket address structures follow the fixed-length structure.

These messages are passed between a process and the kernel in two different ways. Messages can be passed in either direction, one message per read or write, across a routing socket. This allows a superuser process complete read and write access to the kernel's routing tables. This is how routing daemons such as routed and gated implement their desired routing policy.

Alternatively any process can read the contents of the kernel's routing tables using the sysctl system call. This does not involve a routing socket and does not require special privileges. The entire result, normally consisting of many routing messages, is returned as part of the system call. Since the process does not know the size of the result, a method is provided for the system call to return this size without returning the actual result.

Exercises

19.1   What is the difference in the RTF_DYNAMIC and RTF_MODIFIED flags? Can both be set for a given routing table entry?

19.2   What happens when the default route is entered with a command of the form

```
bsdi $ route add default -cloning -genmask 255.255.255.255 sun
```

19.3   Estimate the space required by sysctl to dump a routing table that contains 15 ARP entries and 20 routes.

20

Routing Sockets

20.1 Introduction

A process sends and receives the routing messages described in the previous chapter by using a socket in the *routing domain*. The socket system call is issued specifying a family of PF_ROUTE and a socket type of SOCK_RAW.

The process can then send five routing messages to the kernel:

1. RTM_ADD: add a new route.
2. RTM_DELETE: delete an existing route.
3. RTM_GET: fetch all the information about a route.
4. RTM_CHANGE: change the gateway, interface, or metrics of an existing route.
5. RTM_LOCK: specify which metrics the kernel should not modify.

Additionally, the process can receive any of the other seven types of routing messages that are generated by the kernel when some event, such as interface down, redirect received, etc., occurs.

This chapter looks at the routing domain, the routing control blocks that are created for each routing socket, the function that handles messages from a process (route_output), the function that sends routing messages to one or more processes (raw_input), and the various functions that support all the socket operations on a routing socket.

20.2 `routedomain` **and** `protosw` **Structures**

Before describing the routing socket functions, we need to discuss additional details about the routing domain; the `SOCK_RAW` protocol supported in the routing domain; and routing control blocks, one of which is associated with each routing socket.

Figure 20.1 lists the `domain` structure for the `PF_ROUTE` domain, named `routedomain`.

Member	Value	Description
dom_family	PF_ROUTE	protocol family for domain
dom_name	route	name
dom_init	route_init	domain initialization, Figure 18.30
dom_externalize	0	not used in routing domain
dom_dispose	0	not used in routing domain
dom_protosw	routesw	protocol switch structure, Figure 20.2
dom_protoswNPROTOSW		pointer past end of protocol switch structure
dom_next		filled in by domaininit, Figure 7.15
dom_rtattach	0	not used in routing domain
dom_rtoffset	0	not used in routing domain
dom_maxrtkey	0	not used in routing domain

Figure 20.1 `routedomain` structure.

Unlike the Internet domain, which supports multiple protocols (TCP, UDP, ICMP, etc.), only one protocol (of type `SOCK_RAW`) is supported in the routing domain. Figure 20.2 lists the protocol switch entry for the `PF_ROUTE` domain.

Member	routesw[0]	Description
pr_type	SOCK_RAW	raw socket
pr_domain	&routedomain	part of the routing domain
pr_protocol	0	
pr_flags	PR_ATOMIC|PR_ADDR	socket layer flags, not used by protocol processing
pr_input	raw_input	this entry not used; raw_input called directly
pr_output	route_output	called for PRU_SEND requests
pr_ctlinput	raw_ctlinput	control input function
pr_ctloutput	0	not used
pr_usrreq	route_usrreq	respond to communication requests from a process
pr_init	raw_init	initialization
pr_fasttimo	0	not used
pr_slowtimo	0	not used
pr_drain	0	not used
pr_sysctl	sysctl_rtable	for sysctl(8) system call

Figure 20.2 The routing protocol `protosw` structure.

20.3 Routing Control Blocks

Each time a routing socket is created with a call of the form

```
socket(PF_ROUTE, SOCK_RAW, protocol);
```

the corresponding PRU_ATTACH request to the protocol's user-request function (route_usrreq) allocates a routing control block and links it to the socket structure. The *protocol* can restrict the messages sent to the process on this socket to one particular family. If a *protocol* of AF_INET is specified, for example, only routing messages containing Internet addresses will be sent to the process. A *protocol* of 0 causes all routing messages from the kernel to be sent on the socket.

> Recall that we call these structures *routing control blocks*, not *raw control blocks*, to avoid confusion with the raw IP control blocks in Chapter 32.

Figure 20.3 shows the definition of the rawcb structure.

```
                                                                    ─ raw_cb.h
39 struct rawcb {
40      struct rawcb *rcb_next;      /* doubly linked list */
41      struct rawcb *rcb_prev;
42      struct socket *rcb_socket;   /* back pointer to socket */
43      struct sockaddr *rcb_faddr;  /* destination address */
44      struct sockaddr *rcb_laddr;  /* socket's address */
45      struct sockproto rcb_proto;  /* protocol family, protocol */
46 };

47 #define sotorawcb(so)          ((struct rawcb *)(so)->so_pcb)
                                                                    ─ raw_cb.h
```

Figure 20.3 rawcb structure.

Additionally, a global of the same name, rawcb, is allocated as the head of the doubly linked list. Figure 20.4 shows the arrangement.

39–47   We showed the sockproto structure in Figure 19.26. Its sp_family member is set to PF_ROUTE and its sp_protocol member is set to the third argument to the socket system call. The rcb_faddr member is permanently set to point to route_src, which we described with Figure 19.26. rcb_laddr is always a null pointer.

20.4 raw_init Function

The raw_init function, shown in Figure 20.5, is the protocol initialization function in the protosw structure in Figure 20.2. We described the entire initialization of the routing domain with Figure 18.29.

38–42   The function initializes the doubly linked list of routing control blocks by setting the next and previous pointers of the head structure to point to itself.

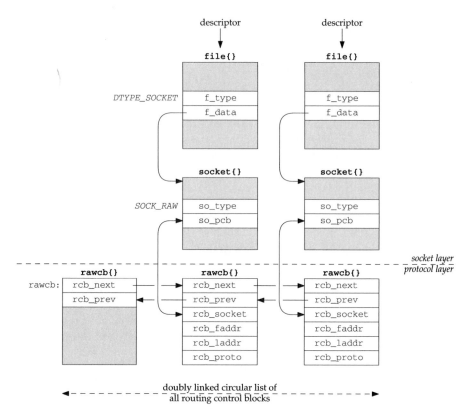

Figure 20.4   Relationship of raw protocol control blocks to other data structures.

```
                                                              ─── raw_usrreq.c
38 void
39 raw_init()
40 {

41        rawcb.rcb_next = rawcb.rcb_prev = &rawcb;
42 }
                                                              ─── raw_usrreq.c
```

Figure 20.5   `raw_init` function: initialize doubly linked list of routing control blocks.

20.5   `route_output` **Function**

As we showed in Figure 18.11, `route_output` is called when the PRU_SEND request is
issued to the protocol's user-request function, which is the result of a write operation by
a process to a routing socket. In Figure 18.9 we indicated that five different types of
routing messages are accepted by the kernel from a process.

Since this function is invoked as a result of a write by a process, the data from the
process (the routing message to process) is in an mbuf chain from `sosend`. Figure 20.6

shows an overview of the processing steps, assuming the process sends an RTM_ADD command, specifying three addresses: the destination, its gateway, and a network mask (hence this is a network route, not a host route).

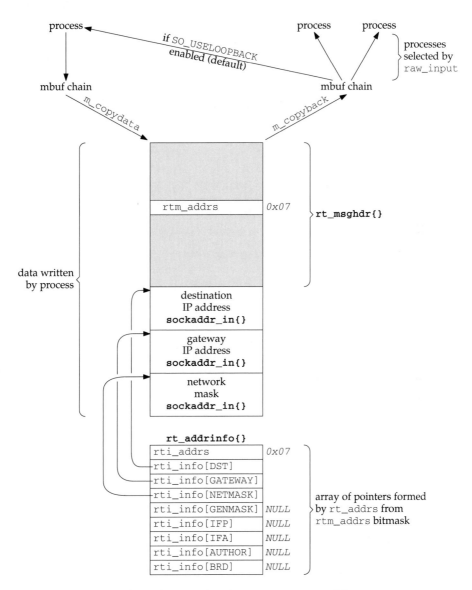

Figure 20.6 Example processing of an RTM_ADD command from a process.

There are numerous points to note in this figure, most of which we'll cover as we proceed through the source code for route_output. Also note that, to save space, we omit the RTAX_ prefix for each array index in the rt_addrinfo structure.

- The process specifies which socket address structures follow the fixed-length `rt_msghdr` structure by setting the bitmask `rtm_addrs`. We show a bitmask of `0x07`, which corresponds to a destination address, a gateway address, and a network mask (Figure 19.19). The `RTM_ADD` command requires the first two; the third is optional. Another optional address, the `genmask` specifies the mask to be used for generating cloned routes.

- The `write` system call (the `sosend` function) copies the buffer from the process into an mbuf chain in the kernel.

- `m_copydata` copies the mbuf chain into a buffer that `route_output` obtains using `malloc`. It is easier to access all the information in the structure and the socket address structures that follow when stored in a single contiguous buffer than it is when stored in an mbuf chain.

- The function `rt_xaddrs` is called by `route_output` to take the bitmask and build the `rt_addrinfo` structure that points into the buffer. The code in `route_output` references these structures using the names shown in the fifth column in Figure 19.19. The bitmask is also copied into the `rti_addrs` member.

- `route_output` normally modifies the `rt_msghdr` structure. If an error occurs, the corresponding `errno` value is returned in `rtm_errno` (for example, `EEXIST` if the route already exists); otherwise the flag `RTF_DONE` is logically ORed into the `rtm_flags` supplied by the process.

- The `rt_msghdr` structure and the addresses that follow become input to 0 or more processes that are reading from a routing socket. The buffer is first converted back into an mbuf chain by `m_copyback`. `raw_input` goes through all the routing PCBs and passes a copy to the appropriate processes. We also show that a process with a routing socket receives a copy of each message it writes to that socket unless it disables the `SO_USELOOPBACK` socket option.

> To avoid receiving a copy of their own routing messages, some programs, such as `route`, call `shutdown` with a second argument of 0 to prevent any data from being received on the routing socket.

We examine the source code for `route_output` in seven parts. Figure 20.7 shows an overview of the function.

```
int
route_output()
{
    R_Malloc() to allocate buffer;
    m_copydata() to copy from mbuf chain into buffer;
    rt_xaddrs() to build rt_addrinfo{};

    switch (message type) {
    case RTM_ADD:
        rtrequest(RTM_ADD);
        rt_setmetrics();
        break;
```

```
    case RTM_DELETE:
        rtrequest(RTM_DELETE);
        break;

    case RTM_GET:
    case RTM_CHANGE:
    case RTM_LOCK:
        rtalloc1();

        switch (message type) {
        case RTM_GET:
            rt_msg2(RTM_GET);
            break;

        case RTM_CHANGE:
            change appropriate fields;
            /* fall through */

        case RTM_LOCK:
            set rmx_locks;
            break;
        }
        break;
    }

    set rtm_error if error, else set RTF_DONE flag;

    m_copyback() to copy from buffer into mbuf chain;

    raw_input();      /* mbuf chain to appropriate processes */
}
```

Figure 20.7   Summary of `route_output` processing steps.

The first part of `route_output` is shown in Figure 20.8.

Check mbuf for validity

113–136   The mbuf chain is checked for validity: its length must be at least the size of an `rt_msghdr` structure. The first longword is fetched from the data portion of the mbuf, which contains the `rtm_msglen` value.

Allocate buffer

137–142   A buffer is allocated to hold the entire message and `m_copydata` copies the message from the mbuf chain into the buffer.

Check version number

143–146   The version of the message is checked. In the future, should a new version of the routing messages be introduced, this member could be used to provide support for older versions.

147–149   The process ID is copied into `rtm_pid` and the bitmask supplied by the process is copied into `info.rti_addrs`, a structure local to this function. The function `rt_xaddrs` (shown in the next section) fills in the eight socket address pointers in the `info` structure to point into the buffer now containing the message.

```
                                                                                    rtsock.c
113 int
114 route_output(m, so)
115 struct mbuf *m;
116 struct socket *so;
117 {
118     struct rt_msghdr *rtm = 0;
119     struct rtentry *rt = 0;
120     struct rtentry *saved_nrt = 0;
121     struct rt_addrinfo info;
122     int     len, error = 0;
123     struct ifnet *ifp = 0;
124     struct ifaddr *ifa = 0;

125 #define senderr(e) { error = e; goto flush;}
126     if (m == 0 || ((m->m_len < sizeof(long)) &&
127                         (m = m_pullup(m, sizeof(long))) == 0))
128             return (ENOBUFS);
129     if ((m->m_flags & M_PKTHDR) == 0)
130         panic("route_output");
131     len = m->m_pkthdr.len;
132     if (len < sizeof(*rtm) ||
133         len != mtod(m, struct rt_msghdr *)->rtm_msglen) {
134         dst = 0;
135         senderr(EINVAL);
136     }
137     R_Malloc(rtm, struct rt_msghdr *, len);
138     if (rtm == 0) {
139         dst = 0;
140         senderr(ENOBUFS);
141     }
142     m_copydata(m, 0, len, (caddr_t) rtm);
143     if (rtm->rtm_version != RTM_VERSION) {
144         dst = 0;
145         senderr(EPROTONOSUPPORT);
146     }
147     rtm->rtm_pid = curproc->p_pid;

148     info.rti_addrs = rtm->rtm_addrs;
149     rt_xaddrs((caddr_t) (rtm + 1), len + (caddr_t) rtm, &info);

150     if (dst == 0)
151         senderr(EINVAL);

152     if (genmask) {
153         struct radix_node *t;
154         t = rn_addmask((caddr_t) genmask, 1, 2);
155         if (t && Bcmp(genmask, t->rn_key, *(u_char *) genmask) == 0)
156             genmask = (struct sockaddr *) (t->rn_key);
157         else
158             senderr(ENOBUFS);
159     }
                                                                                    rtsock.c
```

Figure 20.8 route_output function: initial processing, copy message from mbuf chain.

Destination address required

150–151   A destination address is a required address for all commands. If the
info.rti_info[RTAX_DST] element is a null pointer, EINVAL is returned. Remember that dst refers to this array element (Figure 19.19).

Handle optional genmask

152–159   A genmask is optional and is used as the network mask for routes created when the
RTF_CLONING flag is set (Figure 19.8). rn_addmask adds the mask to the tree of
masks, first searching for an existing entry for the mask and then referencing that entry
if found. If the mask is found or added to the mask tree, an additional check is made
that the entry in the mask tree really equals the genmask value, and, if so, the genmask
pointer is replaced with a pointer to the mask in the mask tree.

Figure 20.9 shows the next part of route_output, which handles the RTM_ADD
and RTM_DELETE commands.

```
                                                                    ── rtsock.c
160        switch (rtm->rtm_type) {

161        case RTM_ADD:
162            if (gate == 0)
163                senderr(EINVAL);
164            error = rtrequest(RTM_ADD, dst, gate, netmask,
165                              rtm->rtm_flags, &saved_nrt);
166            if (error == 0 && saved_nrt) {
167                rt_setmetrics(rtm->rtm_inits,
168                              &rtm->rtm_rmx, &saved_nrt->rt_rmx);
169                saved_nrt->rt_refcnt--;
170                saved_nrt->rt_genmask = genmask;
171            }
172            break;

173        case RTM_DELETE:
174            error = rtrequest(RTM_DELETE, dst, gate, netmask,
175                              rtm->rtm_flags, (struct rtentry **) 0);
176            break;
                                                                    ── rtsock.c
```

Figure 20.9 route_output function: process RTM_ADD and RTM_DELETE commands.

162–163   An RTM_ADD command requires the process to specify a gateway.

164–165   rtrequest processes the request. The netmask pointer can be null if the route
being entered is a host route. If all is OK, the pointer to the new routing table entry is
returned through saved_nrt.

166–172   The rt_metrics structure is copied from the caller's buffer into the routing table
entry. The reference count is decremented and the genmask pointer is stored (possibly
a null pointer).

173–176   Processing the RTM_DELETE command is simple because all the work is done by
rtrequest. Since the final argument is a null pointer, rtrequest calls rtfree if the
reference count is 0, deleting the entry from the routing table (Figure 19.7).

The next part of the processing is shown in Figure 20.10, which handles the common code for the RTM_GET, RTM_CHANGE, and RTM_LOCK commands.

```
                                                                        rtsock.c
177    case RTM_GET:
178    case RTM_CHANGE:
179    case RTM_LOCK:
180        rt = rtalloc1(dst, 0);
181        if (rt == 0)
182            senderr(ESRCH);
183        if (rtm->rtm_type != RTM_GET) {       /* XXX: too grotty */
184            struct radix_node *rn;
185            extern struct radix_node_head *mask_rnhead;

186            if (Bcmp(dst, rt_key(rt), dst->sa_len) != 0)
187                senderr(ESRCH);
188            if (netmask && (rn = rn_search(netmask,
189                                     mask_rnhead->rnh_treetop)))
190                netmask = (struct sockaddr *) rn->rn_key;
191            for (rn = rt->rt_nodes; rn; rn = rn->rn_dupedkey)
192                if (netmask == (struct sockaddr *) rn->rn_mask)
193                    break;
194            if (rn == 0)
195                senderr(ETOOMANYREFS);
196            rt = (struct rtentry *) rn;
197        }
                                                                        rtsock.c
```

Figure 20.10   route_output function: common processing for RTM_GET, RTM_CHANGE, and RTM_LOCK.

Locate existing entry

177–182   Since all three commands reference an existing entry, rtalloc1 locates the entry. If the entry isn't found, ESRCH is returned.

Do not allow network match

183–187   For the RTM_CHANGE and RTM_LOCK commands, a network match is inadequate: an exact match with the routing table key is required. Therefore, if the dst argument doesn't equal the routing table key, the match was a network match and ESRCH is returned.

Use network mask to find correct entry

188–193   Even with an exact match, if there are duplicate keys, each with a different network mask, the correct entry must still be located. If a netmask argument was supplied, it is looked up in the mask table (mask_rnhead). If found, the netmask pointer is replaced with the pointer to the mask in the mask tree. Each leaf node in the duplicate key list is examined, looking for an entry with an rn_mask pointer that equals netmask. This test compares the pointers, not the structures that they point to. This works because all masks appear in the mask tree, and only one copy of each unique mask is stored in this tree. In the common case, keys are not duplicated, so the for loop iterates once. If a host entry is being modified, a mask must not be specified and then both netmask and rn_mask are null pointers (which are equal). But if an entry that has an associated mask is being modified, that mask must be specified as the netmask argument.

194–195   If the for loop terminates without finding a matching network mask, ETOOMANYREFS is returned.

> The comment XXX is because this function must go to all this work to find the desired entry. All these details should be hidden in another function similar to rtalloc1 that detects a network match and handles a mask argument.

The next part of this function, shown in Figure 20.11, continues processing the RTM_GET command. This command is unique among the commands supported by route_output in that it can return more data than it was passed. For example, only a single socket address structure is required as input, the destination, but at least two are returned: the destination and its gateway. With regard to Figure 20.6, this means the buffer allocated for m_copydata to copy into might need to be increased in size.

```
                                                                        rtsock.c
198        switch (rtm->rtm_type) {

199        case RTM_GET:
200            dst = rt_key(rt);
201            gate = rt->rt_gateway;
202            netmask = rt_mask(rt);
203            genmask = rt->rt_genmask;
204            if (rtm->rtm_addrs & (RTA_IFP | RTA_IFA)) {
205                if (ifp = rt->rt_ifp) {
206                    ifpaddr = ifp->if_addrlist->ifa_addr;
207                    ifaaddr = rt->rt_ifa->ifa_addr;
208                    rtm->rtm_index = ifp->if_index;
209                } else {
210                    ifpaddr = 0;
211                    ifaaddr = 0;
212                }
213            }
214            len = rt_msg2(RTM_GET, &info, (caddr_t) 0,
215                            (struct walkarg *) 0);
216            if (len > rtm->rtm_msglen) {
217                struct rt_msghdr *new_rtm;
218                R_Malloc(new_rtm, struct rt_msghdr *, len);
219                if (new_rtm == 0)
220                    senderr(ENOBUFS);
221                Bcopy(rtm, new_rtm, rtm->rtm_msglen);
222                Free(rtm);
223                rtm = new_rtm;
224            }
225            (void) rt_msg2(RTM_GET, &info, (caddr_t) rtm,
226                            (struct walkarg *) 0);
227            rtm->rtm_flags = rt->rt_flags;
228            rtm->rtm_rmx = rt->rt_rmx;
229            rtm->rtm_addrs = info.rti_addrs;
230            break;
                                                                        rtsock.c
```

Figure 20.11   route_output function: RTM_GET processing.

Return destination, gateway, and masks

198–203   Four pointers are stored in the `rti_info` array: `dst`, `gate`, `netmask`, and `genmask`. The latter two might be null pointers. These pointers in the `info` structure point to the socket address structures that will be returned to the process.

Return interface information

204–213   The process can set the masks `RTA_IFP` and `RTA_IFA` in the `rtm_flags` bitmask. If either or both are set, the process wants to receive the contents of both the `ifaddr` structures pointed to by this routing table entry: the link-level address of the interface (pointed to by `rt_ifp->if_addrlist`) and the protocol address for this entry (pointed to by `rt_ifa->ifa_addr`). The interface index is also returned.

Construct reply

214–224   `rt_msg2` is called with a null third pointer to calculate the length of the routing message corresponding to `RTM_GET` and the addresses pointed to by the `info` structure. If the length of the result message exceeds the length of the input message, then a new buffer is allocated, the input message is copied into the new buffer, the old buffer is released, and `rtm` is set to point to the new buffer.

225–230   `rt_msg2` is called again, this time with a nonnull third pointer, which builds the result message in the buffer. The final three members in the `rt_msghdr` structure are then filled in.

Figure 20.12 shows the processing of the `RTM_CHANGE` and `RTM_LOCK` commands.

Change gateway

231–233   If a `gate` address was passed by the process, `rt_setgate` is called to change the gateway for the entry.

Locate new interface

234–244   The new gateway (if changed) can also require new `rt_ifp` and `rt_ifa` pointers. The process can specify these new values by passing either an `ifpaddr` socket address structure or an `ifaddr` socket address structure. The former is tried first, and then the latter. If neither is passed by the process, the `rt_ifp` and `rt_ifa` pointers are left alone.

Check if interface changed

245–256   If an interface was located (`ifa` is nonnull), then the existing `rt_ifa` pointer for the route is compared to the new value. If it has changed, new values for `rt_ifp` and `rt_ifa` are stored in the routing table entry. Before doing this the interface request function (if defined) is called with a command of `RTM_DELETE`. The delete is required because the link-layer information from one type of network to another can be quite different, say changing a route from an X.25 network to an Ethernet, and the output routines must be notified.

Update metrics

257–258   The metrics in the routing table entry are updated by `rt_setmetrics`.

```
                                                                      ——— rtsock.c
231          case RTM_CHANGE:
232              if (gate && rt_setgate(rt, rt_key(rt), gate))
233                  senderr(EDQUOT);
234              /* new gateway could require new ifaddr, ifp; flags may also be
235                  different; ifp may be specified by ll sockaddr when protocol
236      .          address is ambiguous */
237              if (ifpaddr && (ifa = ifa_ifwithnet(ifpaddr)) &&
238                  (ifp = ifa->ifa_ifp))
239                  ifa = ifaof_ifpforaddr(ifaaddr ? ifaaddr : gate,
240                                                  ifp);
241              else if ((ifaaddr && (ifa = ifa_ifwithaddr(ifaaddr))) ||
242      .          (ifa = ifa_ifwithroute(rt->rt_flags,
243                                          rt_key(rt), gate)))
244                  ifp = ifa->ifa_ifp;
245              if (ifa) {
246                  struct ifaddr *oifa = rt->rt_ifa;
247                  if (oifa != ifa) {
248                      if (oifa && oifa->ifa_rtrequest)
249                          oifa->ifa_rtrequest(RTM_DELETE,
250                                              rt, gate);
251                      IFAFREE(rt->rt_ifa);
252                      rt->rt_ifa = ifa;
253                      ifa->ifa_refcnt++;
254                      rt->rt_ifp = ifp;
255                  }
256              }
257              rt_setmetrics(rtm->rtm_inits, &rtm->rtm_rmx,
258                          &rt->rt_rmx);
259              if (rt->rt_ifa && rt->rt_ifa->ifa_rtrequest)
260                  rt->rt_ifa->ifa_rtrequest(RTM_ADD, rt, gate);
261              if (genmask)
262                  rt->rt_genmask = genmask;
263              /*
264               * Fall into
265               */
266          case RTM_LOCK:
267              rt->rt_rmx.rmx_locks &= ~(rtm->rtm_inits);
268              rt->rt_rmx.rmx_locks |=
269                  (rtm->rtm_inits & rtm->rtm_rmx.rmx_locks);
270              break;
271          }
272          break;
273      default:
274          senderr(EOPNOTSUPP);
275      }
                                                                      ——— rtsock.c
```

Figure 20.12   route_output function: RTM_CHANGE and RTM_LOCK processing.

Call interface request function

259–260   If an interface request function is defined, it is called with a command of RTM_ADD.

Store clone generation mask

261–262   If the process specifies the `genmask` argument, the pointer to the mask that was obtained in Figure 20.8 is saved in `rt_genmask`.

Update bitmask of locked metrics

266–270   The `RTM_LOCK` command updates the bitmask stored in `rt_rmx.rmx_locks`. Figure 20.13 shows the values of the different bits in this bitmask, one value per metric.

Constant	Value	Description
RTV_MTU	0x01	initialize or lock `rmx_mtu`
RTV_HOPCOUNT	0x02	initialize or lock `rmx_hopcount`
RTV_EXPIRE	0x04	initialize or lock `rmx_expire`
RTV_RPIPE	0x08	initialize or lock `rmx_recvpipe`
RTV_SPIPE	0x10	initialize or lock `rmx_sendpipe`
RTV_SSTHRESH	0x20	initialize or lock `rmx_ssthresh`
RTV_RTT	0x40	initialize or lock `rmx_rtt`
RTV_RTTVAR	0x80	initialize or lock `rmx_rttvar`

Figure 20.13   Constants to initialize or lock metrics.

The `rmx_locks` member of the `rt_metrics` structure in the routing table entry is the bitmask telling the kernel which metrics to leave alone. That is, those metrics specified by `rmx_locks` won't be updated by the kernel. The only use of these metrics by the kernel is with TCP, as noted with Figure 27.3. The `rmx_pksent` metric cannot be locked or initialized, but it turns out this member is never even referenced or updated by the kernel.

The `rtm_inits` value in the message from the process specifies the bitmask of which metrics were just initialized by `rt_setmetrics`. The `rtm_rmx.rmx_locks` value in the message specifies the bitmask of which metrics should now be locked. The value of `rt_rmx.rmx_locks` is the bitmask in the routing table of which metrics are currently locked. First, any bits to be initialized (`rtm_inits`) are unlocked. Any bits that are both initialized (`rtm_inits`) and locked (`rtm_rmx.rmx_locks`) are locked.

273–275   This `default` is for the `switch` at the beginning of Figure 20.9 and catches any of the routing commands other than the five that are supported in messages from a process.

The final part of `route_output`, shown in Figure 20.14, sends the reply to `raw_input`.

```
276    flush:                                                          ─── rtsock.c
277       if (rtm) {
278           if (error)
279               rtm->rtm_errno = error;
280           else
281               rtm->rtm_flags |= RTF_DONE;
282       }
283       if (rt)
284           rtfree(rt);
285       {
286           struct rawcb *rp = 0;
287           /*
288            * Check to see if we don't want our own messages.
289            */
290           if ((so->so_options & SO_USELOOPBACK) == 0) {
291               if (route_cb.any_count <= 1) {
292                   if (rtm)
293                       Free(rtm);
294                   m_freem(m);
295                   return (error);
296               }
297               /* There is another listener, so construct message */
298               rp = sotorawcb(so);
299           }
300           if (rtm) {
301               m_copyback(m, 0, rtm->rtm_msglen, (caddr_t) rtm);
302               Free(rtm);
303           }
304           if (rp)
305               rp->rcb_proto.sp_family = 0;      /* Avoid us */
306           if (dst)
307               route_proto.sp_protocol = dst->sa_family;
308           raw_input(m, &route_proto, &route_src, &route_dst);
309           if (rp)
310               rp->rcb_proto.sp_family = PF_ROUTE;
311       }
312       return (error);
313  }
```
─── rtsock.c

Figure 20.14 route_output function: pass results to raw_input.

Return error or OK

276–282   flush is the label jumped to by the senderr macro defined at the beginning of the function. If an error occurred it is returned in the rtm_errno member; otherwise the RTF_DONE flag is set.

Release held route

283–284   If a route is being held, it is released. The call to rtalloc1 at the beginning of Figure 20.10 holds the route, if found.

No process to receive message

285–296   The SO_USELOOPBACK socket option is true by default and specifies that the sending process is to receive a copy of each routing message that it writes to a routing socket. (If the sender doesn't receive a copy, it can't receive any of the information returned by RTM_GET.) If that option is not set, and the total count of routing sockets is less than or equal to 1, there are no other processes to receive the message and the sender doesn't want a copy. The buffer and mbuf chain are both released and the function returns.

Other listeners but no loopback copy

297–299   There is at least one other listener but the sending process does not want a copy. The pointer rp, which defaults to null, is set to point to the routing control block for the sender and is also used as a flag that the sender doesn't want a copy.

Convert buffer into mbuf chain

300–303   The buffer is converted back into an mbuf chain (Figure 20.6) and the buffer released.

Avoid loopback copy

304–305   If rp is set, some other process might want the message but the sender does not want a copy. The sp_family member of the sender's routing control block is temporarily set to 0, but the sp_family of the message (the route_proto structure, shown with Figure 19.26) has a family of PF_ROUTE. This trick prevents raw_input from passing a copy of the result to the sending process because raw_input does not pass a copy to any socket with an sp_family of 0.

Set address family of routing message

306–308   If dst is a nonnull pointer, the address family of that socket address structure becomes the protocol of the routing message. With the Internet protocols this value would be PF_INET. A copy is passed to the appropriate listeners by raw_input.

309–313   If the sp_family member in the calling process was temporarily set to 0, it is reset to PF_ROUTE, its normal value.

20.6   `rt_xaddrs` Function

The rt_xaddrs function is called only once from route_output (Figure 20.8) after the routing message from the process has been copied from the mbuf chain into a buffer and after the bitmask from the process (rtm_addrs) has been copied into the rti_info member of an rt_addrinfo structure. The purpose of rt_xaddrs is to take this bitmask and set the pointers in the rti_info array to point to the corresponding address in the buffer. Figure 20.15 shows the function.

—— *rtsock.c*

```
330 #define ROUNDUP(a) \
331     ((a) > 0 ? (1 + (((a) - 1) | (sizeof(long) - 1))) : sizeof(long))
332 #define ADVANCE(x, n) (x += ROUNDUP((n)->sa_len))
```

```
333 static void
334 rt_xaddrs(cp, cplim, rtinfo)
335 caddr_t cp, cplim;
336 struct rt_addrinfo *rtinfo;
337 {
338     struct sockaddr *sa;
339     int     i;
340     bzero(rtinfo->rti_info, sizeof(rtinfo->rti_info));
341     for (i = 0; (i < RTAX_MAX) && (cp < cplim); i++) {
342         if ((rtinfo->rti_addrs & (1 << i)) == 0)
343             continue;
344         rtinfo->rti_info[i] = sa = (struct sockaddr *) cp;
345         ADVANCE(cp, sa);
346     }
347 }
```
                                                                  ──────── *rtsock.c*

Figure 20.15   rt_xaddrs function: fill rti_into array with pointers.

330–340   The array of pointers is set to 0 so all the pointers to address structures not appearing in the bitmask will be null.

341–347   Each of the 8 (RTAX_MAX) possible bits in the bitmask is tested and, if set, a pointer is stored in the rti_info array to the corresponding socket address structure. The ADVANCE macro takes the sa_len field of the socket address structure, rounds it up to the next multiple of 4 bytes, and increments the pointer cp accordingly.

20.7   rt_setmetrics **Function**

This function was called twice from route_output: when a new route was added and when an existing route was changed. The rtm_inits member in the routing message from the process specifies which of the metrics the process wants to initialize from the rtm_rmx array. The bit values in the bitmask are shown in Figure 20.13.

Notice that both rtm_addrs and rtm_inits are bitmasks in the message from the process, the former specifying the socket address structures that follow, and the latter specifying which metrics are to be initialized. Socket address structures whose bits don't appear in rtm_addrs don't even appear in the routing message, to save space. But the entire rt_metrics array always appears in the fixed-length rt_msghdr structure—elements in the array whose bits are not set in rtm_inits are ignored.

Figure 20.16 shows the rt_setmetrics function.

314–318   The which argument is always the rtm_inits member of the routing message from the process. in points to the rt_metrics structure from the process, and out points to the rt_metrics structure in the routing table entry that is being created or modified.

319–329   Each of the 8 bits in the bitmask is tested and if set, the corresponding metric is copied. Notice that when a new routing table entry is being created with the RTM_ADD command, route_output calls rtrequest, which sets the entire routing table entry to 0 (Figure 19.9). Hence, any metrics not specified by the process in the routing message default to 0.

```
                                                                            ── rtsock.c
314 void
315 rt_setmetrics(which, in, out)
316 u_long  which;
317 struct rt_metrics *in, *out;
318 {
319 #define metric(f, e) if (which & (f)) out->e = in->e;
320     metric(RTV_RPIPE, rmx_recvpipe);
321     metric(RTV_SPIPE, rmx_sendpipe);
322     metric(RTV_SSTHRESH, rmx_ssthresh);
323     metric(RTV_RTT, rmx_rtt);
324     metric(RTV_RTTVAR, rmx_rttvar);
325     metric(RTV_HOPCOUNT, rmx_hopcount);
326     metric(RTV_MTU, rmx_mtu);
327     metric(RTV_EXPIRE, rmx_expire);
328 #undef metric
329 }
                                                                            ── rtsock.c
```

Figure 20.16   rt_setmetrics function: set elements of the rt_metrics structure.

20.8   `raw_input` **Function**

All routing messages destined for a process—those that originate from within the kernel and those that originate from a process—are given to raw_input, which selects the processes to receive the message. Figure 18.11 summarizes the four functions that call raw_input.

When a routing socket is created, the family is always PF_ROUTE and the protocol, the third argument to socket, can be 0, which means the process wants to receive all routing messages, or a value such as AF_INET, which restricts the socket to messages containing addresses of that specific protocol family. A routing control block is created for each routing socket (Section 20.3) and these two values are stored in the sp_family and sp_protocol members of the rcb_proto structure.

Figure 20.17 shows the raw_input function.

```
                                                                         ── raw_usrreq.c
51 void
52 raw_input(m0, proto, src, dst)
53 struct mbuf *m0;
54 struct sockproto *proto;
55 struct sockaddr *src, *dst;
56 {
57     struct rawcb *rp;
58     struct mbuf *m = m0;
59     int     sockets = 0;
60     struct socket *last;
```

```
 61     last = 0;
 62     for (rp = rawcb.rcb_next; rp != &rawcb; rp = rp->rcb_next) {
 63         if (rp->rcb_proto.sp_family != proto->sp_family)
 64             continue;
 65         if (rp->rcb_proto.sp_protocol &&
 66             rp->rcb_proto.sp_protocol != proto->sp_protocol)
 67             continue;
 68         /*
 69          * We assume the lower level routines have
 70          * placed the address in a canonical format
 71          * suitable for a structure comparison.
 72          *
 73          * Note that if the lengths are not the same
 74          * the comparison will fail at the first byte.
 75          */
 76 #define equal(a1, a2) \
 77    (bcmp((caddr_t)(a1), (caddr_t)(a2), a1->sa_len) == 0)
 78         if (rp->rcb_laddr && !equal(rp->rcb_laddr, dst))
 79             continue;
 80         if (rp->rcb_faddr && !equal(rp->rcb_faddr, src))
 81             continue;
 82         if (last) {
 83             struct mbuf *n;
 84             if (n = m_copy(m, 0, (int) M_COPYALL)) {
 85                 if (sbappendaddr(&last->so_rcv, src,
 86                                 n, (struct mbuf *) 0) == 0)
 87                     /* should notify about lost packet */
 88                     m_freem(n);
 89                 else {
 90                     sorwakeup(last);
 91                     sockets++;
 92                 }
 93             }
 94         }
 95         last = rp->rcb_socket;
 96     }
 97     if (last) {
 98         if (sbappendaddr(&last->so_rcv, src,
 99                         m, (struct mbuf *) 0) == 0)
100             m_freem(m);
101         else {
102             sorwakeup(last);
103             sockets++;
104         }
105     } else
106         m_freem(m);
107 }
```
                                                                    raw_usrreq.c

Figure 20.17 raw_input function: pass routing messages to 0 or more processes.

51–61   In all four calls to `raw_input` that we've seen, the `proto`, `src`, and `dst` arguments are pointers to the three globals `route_proto`, `route_src`, and `route_dst`, which are declared and initialized as shown with Figure 19.26.

Compare address family and protocol

62–67   The `for` loop goes through every routing control block checking for a match. The family in the control block (normally `PF_ROUTE`) must match the family in the `sockproto` structure or the control block is skipped. Next, if the protocol in the control block (the third argument to `socket`) is nonzero, it must match the family in the `sockproto` structure, or the message is skipped. Hence a process that creates a routing socket with a protocol of 0 receives all routing messages.

Compare local and foreign addresses

68–81   These two tests compare the local address in the control block and the foreign address in the control block, if specified. Currently the process is unable to set the `rcb_laddr` or `rcb_faddr` members of the control block. Normally a process would set the former with `bind` and the latter with `connect`, but that is not possible with routing sockets in Net/3. Instead, we'll see that `route_usrreq` permanently connects the socket to the `route_src` socket address structure, which is OK since that is always the `src` argument to this function.

Append message to socket receive buffer

82–107   If `last` is nonnull, it points to the most recently seen `socket` structure that should receive this message. If this variable is nonnull, a copy of the message is appended to that socket's receive buffer by `m_copy` and `sbappendaddr`, and any processes waiting on this receive buffer are awakened. Then `last` is set to point to this socket that just matched the previous tests. The use of `last` is to avoid calling `m_copy` (an expensive operation) if only one process is to receive the message.

   If *N* processes are to receive the message, the first $N - 1$ receive a copy and the final one receives the message itself.

   The variable `sockets` that is incremented within this function is not used. Since it is incremented only when a message is passed to a process, if it is 0 at the end of the function it indicates that no process received the message (but the value isn't stored anywhere).

20.9 `route_usrreq` Function

   `route_usrreq` is the routing protocol's user-request function. It is called for a variety of operations. Figure 20.18 shows the function.

```
                                                              ─── rtsock.c
64 int
65 route_usrreq(so, req, m, nam, control)
66 struct socket *so;
67 int      req;
68 struct mbuf *m, *nam, *control;
69 {
```

```
70      int     error = 0;
71      struct rawcb *rp = sotorawcb(so);
72      int     s;

73      if (req == PRU_ATTACH) {
74          MALLOC(rp, struct rawcb *, sizeof(*rp), M_PCB, M_WAITOK);
75          if (so->so_pcb = (caddr_t) rp)
76              bzero(so->so_pcb, sizeof(*rp));
77      }
78      if (req == PRU_DETACH && rp) {
79          int     af = rp->rcb_proto.sp_protocol;
80          if (af == AF_INET)
81              route_cb.ip_count--;
82          else if (af == AF_NS)
83              route_cb.ns_count--;
84          else if (af == AF_ISO)
85              route_cb.iso_count--;
86          route_cb.any_count--;
87      }
88      s = splnet();
89      error = raw_usrreq(so, req, m, nam, control);
90      rp = sotorawcb(so);
91      if (req == PRU_ATTACH && rp) {
92          int     af = rp->rcb_proto.sp_protocol;
93          if (error) {
94              free((caddr_t) rp, M_PCB);
95              splx(s);
96              return (error);
97          }
98          if (af == AF_INET)
99              route_cb.ip_count++;
100         else if (af == AF_NS)
101             route_cb.ns_count++;
102         else if (af == AF_ISO)
103             route_cb.iso_count++;
104         route_cb.any_count++;

105         rp->rcb_faddr = &route_src;
106         soisconnected(so);
107         so->so_options |= SO_USELOOPBACK;
108     }
109     splx(s);
110     return (error);
111 }
```
—— *rtsock.c*

Figure 20.18   route_usrreq function: process PRU_*xxx* requests.

PRU_ATTACH: allocate control block

64–77   The PRU_ATTACH request is issued when the process calls socket. Memory is allocated for a routing control block. The pointer returned by MALLOC is stored in the
so_pcb member of the socket structure, and if the memory was allocated, the rawcb
structure is set to 0.

PRU_DETACH: decrement counters

78–87   The close system call issues the PRU_DETACH request. If the socket structure points to a protocol control block, two of the counters in the route_cb structure are decremented: one is the any_count and one is based on the protocol.

Process request

88–90   The function raw_usrreq is called to process the PRU_*xxx* request further.

Increment counters

91–104   If the request is PRU_ATTACH and the socket points to a routing control block, a check is made for an error from raw_usrreq. Two of the counters in the route_cb structure are then incremented: one is the any_count and one is based on the protocol.

Connect socket

105–106   The foreign address in the routing control block is set to route_src. This permanently connects the new socket to receive routing messages from the PF_ROUTE family.

Enable SO_USELOOPBACK by default

107–111   The SO_USELOOPBACK socket option is enabled. This is a socket option that defaults to being enabled—all others default to being disabled.

20.10 raw_usrreq Function

raw_usrreq performs most of the processing for the user request in the routing domain. It was called by route_usrreq in the previous section. The reason the user-request processing is divided between these two functions is that other protocols (e.g., the OSI CLNP) call raw_usrreq but not route_usrreq. raw_usrreq is not intended to be the pr_usrreq function for a protocol. Instead it is a common subroutine called by the various pr_usrreq functions.

Figure 20.19 shows the beginning and end of the raw_usrreq function. The body of the switch is discussed in separate figures following this figure.

PRU_CONTROL requests invalid

119–129   The PRU_CONTROL request is from the ioctl system call and is not supported in the routing domain.

Control information invalid

130–133   If control information was passed by the process (using the sendmsg system call) an error is returned, since the routing domain doesn't use this optional information.

Socket must have a control block

134–137   If the socket structure doesn't point to a routing control block, an error is returned. If a new socket is being created, it is the caller's responsibility (i.e., route_usrreq) to allocate this control block and store the pointer in the so_pcb member before calling this function.

262–269   The default for this switch catches two requests that are not handled by case statements: PRU_BIND and PRU_CONNECT. The code for these two requests is present but commented out in Net/3. Therefore issuing the bind or connect system calls on a

raw_usrreq.c

```
119 int
120 raw_usrreq(so, req, m, nam, control)
121 struct socket *so;
122 int     req;
123 struct mbuf *m, *nam, *control;
124 {
125     struct rawcb *rp = sotorawcb(so);
126     int     error = 0;
127     int     len;

128     if (req == PRU_CONTROL)
129         return (EOPNOTSUPP);
130     if (control && control->m_len) {
131         error = EOPNOTSUPP;
132         goto release;
133     }
134     if (rp == 0) {
135         error = EINVAL;
136         goto release;
137     }
138     switch (req) {


                                    /* switch cases */


262     default:
263         panic("raw_usrreq");
264     }
265   release:
266     if (m != NULL)
267         m_freem(m);
268     return (error);
269 }
```

raw_usrreq.c

Figure 20.19 Body of raw_usrreq function.

routing socket causes a kernel panic. This is a bug. Fortunately it requires a superuser
process to create this type of socket.

We now discuss the individual case statements. Figure 20.20 shows the processing
for the PRU_ATTACH and PRU_DETACH requests.

139–148   The PRU_ATTACH request is a result of the socket system call. A routing socket
must be created by a superuser process.

149–150   The function raw_attach (Figure 20.24) links the control block into the doubly
linked list. The nam argument is the third argument to socket and gets stored in the
control block.

151–159   The PRU_DETACH is issued by the close system call. The test of a null rp pointer
is superfluous, since the test was already done before the switch statement.

160–161   raw_detach (Figure 20.25) removes the control block from the doubly linked list.

raw_usrreq.c

```
139            /*
140             * Allocate a raw control block and fill in the
141             * necessary info to allow packets to be routed to
142             * the appropriate raw interface routine.
143             */
144       case PRU_ATTACH:
145           if ((so->so_state & SS_PRIV) == 0) {
146               error = EACCES;
147               break;
148           }
149           error = raw_attach(so, (int) nam);
150           break;

151            /*
152             * Destroy state just before socket deallocation.
153             * Flush data or not depending on the options.
154             */
155       case PRU_DETACH:
156           if (rp == 0) {
157               error = ENOTCONN;
158               break;
159           }
160           raw_detach(rp);
161           break;
```

raw_usrreq.c

Figure 20.20 `raw_usrreq` function: `PRU_ATTACH` and `PRU_DETACH` requests.

Figure 20.21 shows the processing of the `PRU_CONNECT2`, `PRU_DISCONNECT`, and `PRU_SHUTDOWN` requests.

raw_usrreq.c

```
186       case PRU_CONNECT2:
187           error = EOPNOTSUPP;
188           goto release;

189       case PRU_DISCONNECT:
190           if (rp->rcb_faddr == 0) {
191               error = ENOTCONN;
192               break;
193           }
194           raw_disconnect(rp);
195           soisdisconnected(so);
196           break;

197            /*
198             * Mark the connection as being incapable of further input.
199             */
200       case PRU_SHUTDOWN:
201           socantsendmore(so);
202           break;
```

raw_usrreq.c

Figure 20.21 `raw_usrreq` function: `PRU_CONNECT2`, `PRU_DISCONNECT`, and `PRU_SHUTDOWN` requests.

186–188   The `PRU_CONNECT2` request is from the `socketpair` system call and is not supported in the routing domain.

189–196   Since a routing socket is always connected (Figure 20.18), the `PRU_DISCONNECT` request is issued by `close` before the `PRU_DETACH` request. The socket must already be connected to a foreign address, which is always true for a routing socket. `raw_disconnect` and `soisdisconnected` complete the processing.

197–202   The `PRU_SHUTDOWN` request is from the `shutdown` system call when the argument specifies that no more writes will be performed on the socket. `socantsendmore` disables further writes.

The most common request for a routing socket, `PRU_SEND`, and the `PRU_ABORT` and `PRU_SENSE` requests are shown in Figure 20.22.

raw_usrreq.c
```
203          /*
204           * Ship a packet out.  The appropriate raw output
205           * routine handles any massaging necessary.
206           */
207      case PRU_SEND:
208          if (nam) {
209              if (rp->rcb_faddr) {
210                  error = EISCONN;
211                  break;
212              }
213              rp->rcb_faddr = mtod(nam, struct sockaddr *);
214          } else if (rp->rcb_faddr == 0) {
215              error = ENOTCONN;
216              break;
217          }
218          error = (*so->so_proto->pr_output) (m, so);
219          m = NULL;
220          if (nam)
221              rp->rcb_faddr = 0;
222          break;

223      case PRU_ABORT:
224          raw_disconnect(rp);
225          sofree(so);
226          soisdisconnected(so);
227          break;

228      case PRU_SENSE:
229          /*
230           * stat: don't bother with a blocksize.
231           */
232          return (0);
```
raw_usrreq.c

Figure 20.22 `raw_usrreq` function: `PRU_SEND`, `PRU_ABORT`, and `PRU_SENSE` requests.

203–217   The `PRU_SEND` request is issued by `sosend` when the process writes to the socket. If a `nam` argument is specified, that is, the process specified a destination address using either `sendto` or `sendmsg`, an error is returned because `route_usrreq` always sets `rcb_faddr` for a routing socket.

218–222   The message in the mbuf chain pointed to by m is passed to the protocol's
pr_output function, which is route_output.

223–227   If a PRU_ABORT request is issued, the control block is disconnected, the socket is
released, and the socket is disconnected.

228–232   The PRU_SENSE request is issued by the fstat system call. The function returns
OK.

Figure 20.23 shows the remaining PRU_*xxx* requests.

```
                                                             ─── raw_usrreq.c
233        /*
234         * Not supported.
235         */
236    case PRU_RCVOOB:
237    case PRU_RCVD:
238        return (EOPNOTSUPP);

239    case PRU_LISTEN:
240    case PRU_ACCEPT:
241    case PRU_SENDOOB:
242        error = EOPNOTSUPP;
243        break;

244    case PRU_SOCKADDR:
245        if (rp->rcb_laddr == 0) {
246            error = EINVAL;
247            break;
248        }
249        len = rp->rcb_laddr->sa_len;
250        bcopy((caddr_t) rp->rcb_laddr, mtod(nam, caddr_t), (unsigned) len);
251        nam->m_len = len;
252        break;

253    case PRU_PEERADDR:
254        if (rp->rcb_faddr == 0) {
255            error = ENOTCONN;
256            break;
257        }
258        len = rp->rcb_faddr->sa_len;
259        bcopy((caddr_t) rp->rcb_faddr, mtod(nam, caddr_t), (unsigned) len);
260        nam->m_len = len;
261        break;
                                                             ─── raw_usrreq.c
```

Figure 20.23   raw_usrreq function: final part.

233–243   These five requests are not supported.

244–261   The PRU_SOCKADDR and PRU_PEERADDR requests are from the getsockname and
getpeername system calls respectively. The former always returns an error, since the
bind system call, which sets the local address, is not supported in the routing domain.
The latter always returns the contents of the socket address structure route_src,
which was set by route_usrreq as the foreign address.

20.11 `raw_attach`, `raw_detach`, and `raw_disconnect` **Functions**

The `raw_attach` function, shown in Figure 20.24, was called by `raw_input` to finish processing the PRU_ATTACH request.

─── *raw_cb.c*
```
49 int
50 raw_attach(so, proto)
51 struct socket *so;
52 int       proto;
53 {
54     struct rawcb *rp = sotorawcb(so);
55     int       error;

56     /*
57      * It is assumed that raw_attach is called
58      * after space has been allocated for the
59      * rawcb.
60      */
61     if (rp == 0)
62         return (ENOBUFS);
63     if (error = soreserve(so, raw_sendspace, raw_recvspace))
64         return (error);
65     rp->rcb_socket = so;
66     rp->rcb_proto.sp_family = so->so_proto->pr_domain->dom_family;
67     rp->rcb_proto.sp_protocol = proto;
68     insque(rp, &rawcb);
69     return (0);
70 }
```
─── *raw_cb.c*

Figure 20.24   `raw_attach` function.

49–64   The caller must have already allocated the raw protocol control block. `soreserve` sets the high-water marks for the send and receive buffers to 8192. This should be more than adequate for the routing messages.

65–67   A pointer to the `socket` structure is stored in the protocol control block along with the `dom_family` (which is PF_ROUTE from Figure 20.1 for the routing domain) and the `proto` argument (which is the third argument to `socket`).

68–70   `insque` adds the control block to the front of the doubly linked list headed by the global `rawcb`.

The `raw_detach` function, shown in Figure 20.25, was called by `raw_input` to finish processing the PRU_DETACH request.

75–84   The `so_pcb` pointer in the `socket` structure is set to null and the socket is released. The control block is removed from the doubly linked list by `remque` and the memory used for the control block is released by `free`.

The `raw_disconnect` function, shown in Figure 20.26, was called by `raw_input` to process the PRU_DISCONNECT and PRU_ABORT requests.

88–94   If the socket does not reference a descriptor, `raw_detach` releases the socket and control block.

```
                                                                                     raw_cb.c
75 void
76 raw_detach(rp)
77 struct rawcb *rp;
78 {
79     struct socket *so = rp->rcb_socket;

80     so->so_pcb = 0;
81     sofree(so);
82     remque(rp);
83     free((caddr_t) (rp), M_PCB);
84 }
                                                                                     raw_cb.c
```

Figure 20.25   raw_detach function.

```
                                                                                     raw_cb.c
88 void
89 raw_disconnect(rp)
90 struct rawcb *rp;
91 {
92     if (rp->rcb_socket->so_state & SS_NOFDREF)
93         raw_detach(rp);
94 }
                                                                                     raw_cb.c
```

Figure 20.26   raw_disconnect function.

20.12 Summary

A routing socket is a raw socket in the PF_ROUTE domain. Routing sockets can be created only by a superuser process. If a nonprivileged process wants to read the routing information contained in the kernel, the sysctl system call supported by the routing domain can be used (we described this in the previous chapter).

This chapter was our first encounter with the protocol control blocks (PCBs) that are normally associated with each socket. In the routing domain a special rawcb contains information about the routing socket: the local and foreign addresses, the address family, and the protocol. We'll see in Chapter 22 that the larger Internet protocol control block (inpcb) is used with UDP, TCP, and raw IP sockets. The concepts are the same, however: the socket structure is used by the socket layer, and the PCB, a rawcb or an inpcb, is used by the protocol layer. The socket structure points to the PCB and vice versa.

The route_output function handles the five routing requests that can be issued by a process. raw_input delivers a routing message to one or more routing sockets, depending on the protocol and address family. The various PRU_xxx requests for a routing socket are handled by raw_usrreq and route_usrreq. In later chapters we'll encounter additional xxx_usrreq functions, one per protocol (UDP, TCP, and raw IP), each consisting of a switch statement to handle each request.

Exercises

20.1   List two ways a process can receive the return value from `route_output` when the process writes a message to a routing socket. Which method is more reliable?

20.2   What happens when a process specifies a nonzero *protocol* argument to the `socket` system call, since the `pr_protocol` member of the `routesw` structure is 0?

20.3   Routes in the routing table (other than ARP entries) never time out. Implement a timeout on routes.

21

ARP: Address Resolution Protocol

21.1 Introduction

ARP, the Address Resolution Protocol, handles the translation of 32-bit IP addresses into the corresponding hardware address. For an Ethernet, the hardware addresses are 48-bit Ethernet addresses. In this chapter we only consider mapping IP addresses into 48-bit Ethernet addresses, although ARP is more general and can work with other types of data links. ARP is specified in RFC 826 [Plummer 1982].

When a host has an IP datagram to send to another host on a locally attached Ethernet, the local host first looks up the destination host in the *ARP cache*, a table that maps a 32-bit IP address into its corresponding 48-bit Ethernet address. If the entry is found for the destination, the corresponding Ethernet address is copied into the Ethernet header and the datagram is added to the appropriate interface's output queue. If the entry is not found, the ARP functions hold onto the IP datagram, broadcast an ARP request asking the destination host for its Ethernet address, and, when a reply is received, send the datagram to its destination.

This simple overview handles the common case, but there are many details that we describe in this chapter as we examine the Net/3 implementation of ARP. Chapter 4 of Volume 1 contains additional ARP examples.

21.2 ARP and the Routing Table

The Net/3 implementation of ARP is tied to the routing table, which is why we postponed discussing ARP until we had described the structure of the Net/3 routing tables. Figure 21.1 shows an example that we use in this chapter when describing ARP.

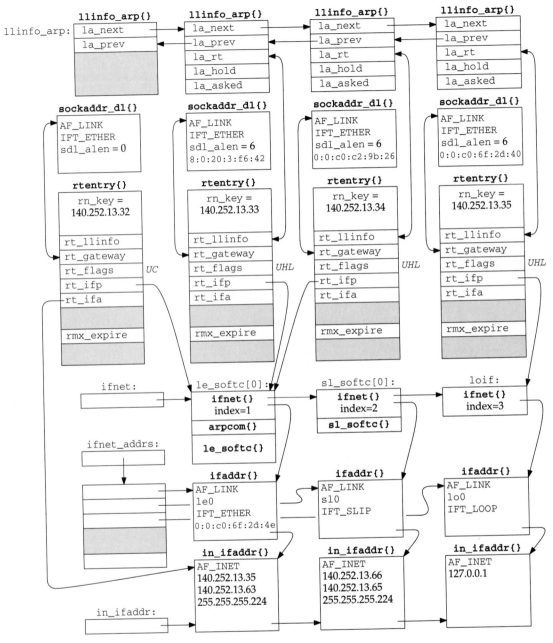

Figure 21.1 Relationship of ARP to routing table and interface structures.

The entire figure corresponds to the example network used throughout the text (Figure 1.17). It shows the ARP entries on the system `bsdi`. The `ifnet`, `ifaddr`, and `in_ifaddr` structures are simplified from Figures 3.32 and 6.5. We have removed some of the details from these three structures, which were covered in Chapters 3 and 6.

For example, we don't show the two `sockaddr_dl` structures that appear after each `ifaddr` structure—instead we summarize the information contained in these two structures. Similarly, we summarize the information contained in the three `in_ifaddr` structures.

We briefly summarize some relevant points from this figure, the details of which we cover as we proceed through the chapter.

1. A doubly linked list of `llinfo_arp` structures contains a minimal amount of information for each hardware address known by ARP. The global `llinfo_arp` is the head of this list. Not shown in this figure is that the `la_prev` pointer of the first entry points to the last entry, and the `la_next` pointer of the last entry points to the first entry. This linked list is processed by the ARP timer function every 5 minutes.

2. For each IP address with a known hardware address, a routing table entry exists (an `rtentry` structure). The `llinfo_arp` structure points to the corresponding `rtentry` structure, and vice versa, using the `la_rt` and `rt_llinfo` pointers. The three routing table entries in this figure with an associated `llinfo_arp` structure are for the hosts sun (140.252.13.33), svr4 (140.252.13.34), and bsdi itself (140.252.13.35). These three are also shown in Figure 18.2.

3. We show a fourth routing table entry on the left, without an `llinfo_arp` structure, which is the entry for the network route to the local Ethernet (140.252.13.32). We show its `rt_flags` with the C bit on, since this entry is cloned to form the other three routing table entries. This entry is created by the call to `rtinit` when the IP address is assigned to the interface by `in_ifinit` (Figure 6.19). The other three entries are host entries (the H flag) and are generated by ARP (the L flag) when a datagram is sent to that IP address.

4. The `rt_gateway` member of the `rtentry` structure points to a `sockaddr_dl` structure. This data-link socket address structure contains the hardware address if the `sdl_alen` member equals 6.

5. The `rt_ifp` member of the routing table entry points to the `ifnet` structure of the outgoing interface. Notice that the two routing table entries in the middle, for other hosts on the local Ethernet, both point to `le_softc[0]`, but the routing table entry on the right, for the host bsdi itself, points to the loopback structure. Since `rt_ifp.if_output` (Figure 8.25) points to the output routine, packets sent to the local IP address are routed to the loopback interface.

6. Each routing table entry also points to the corresponding `in_ifaddr` structure. (Actually the `rt_ifa` member points to an `ifaddr` structure, but recall from Figure 6.8 that the first member of an `in_ifaddr` structure is an `ifaddr` structure.) We show only one of these pointers in the figure, although all four point to the same structure. Remember that a single interface, say `le0`, can have multiple IP addresses, each with its own `in_ifaddr` structure, which is why the `rt_ifa` pointer is required in addition to the `rt_ifp` pointer.

7. The `la_hold` member is a pointer to an mbuf chain. An ARP request is broadcast because a datagram is sent to that IP address. While the kernel awaits the ARP reply it holds onto the mbuf chain for the datagram by storing its address in `la_hold`. When the ARP reply is received, the mbuf chain pointed to by `la_hold` is sent.

8. Finally, we show the variable `rmx_expire`, which is in the `rt_metrics` structure within the routing table entry. This value is the timer associated with each ARP entry. Some time after an ARP entry has been created (normally 20 minutes) the ARP entry is deleted.

> Even though major routing table changes took place with 4.3BSD Reno, the ARP cache was left alone with 4.3BSD Reno and Net/2. 4.4BSD, however, removed the stand-alone ARP cache and moved the ARP information into the routing table.
>
> The ARP table in Net/2 was an array of structures composed of the following members: an IP address, an Ethernet address, a timer, flags, and a pointer to an mbuf (similar to the `la_hold` member in Figure 21.1). We see with Net/3 that the same information is now spread throughout multiple structures, all of which are linked.

21.3 Code Introduction

There are nine ARP functions in a single C file and definitions in two headers, as shown in Figure 21.2.

File	Description
`net/if_arp.h`	`arphdr` structure definition
`netinet/if_ether.h`	various structure and constant definitions
`netinet/if_ether.c`	ARP functions

Figure 21.2   Files discussed in this chapter.

Figure 21.3 shows the relationship of the ARP functions to other kernel functions. In this figure we also show the relationship between the ARP functions and some of the routing functions from Chapter 19. We describe all these relationships as we proceed through the chapter.

Global Variables

Ten global variables are introduced in this chapter, which are shown in Figure 21.4.

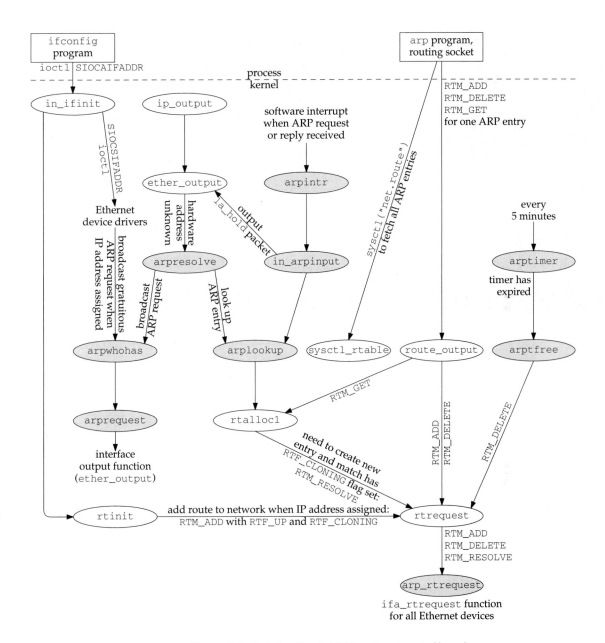

Figure 21.3   Relationship of ARP functions to rest of kernel.

Variable	Datatype	Description
llinfo_arp	struct llinfo_arp	head of `llinfo_arp` doubly linked list (Figure 21.1)
arpintrq	struct ifqueue	ARP input queue from Ethernet device drivers (Figure 4.9)
arpt_prune	int	#seconds between checking ARP list (5 × 60)
arpt_keep	int	#seconds ARP entry valid once resolved (20 × 60)
arpt_down	int	#seconds between ARP flooding algorithm (20)
arp_inuse	int	#ARP entries currently in use
arp_allocated	int	#ARP entries ever allocated
arp_maxtries	int	max #tries for an IP address before pausing (5)
arpinit_done	int	initialization-performed flag
useloopback	int	use loopback for local host (default true)

Figure 21.4   Global variables introduced in this chapter.

Statistics

The only statistics maintained by ARP are the two globals `arp_inuse` and `arp_allocated`, from Figure 21.4. The former counts the number of ARP entries currently in use and the latter counts the total number of ARP entries allocated since the system was initialized. Neither counter is output by the `netstat` program, but they can be examined with a debugger.

The entire ARP cache can be listed using the `arp -a` command, which uses the `sysctl` system call with the arguments shown in Figure 19.36. Figure 21.5 shows the output from this command, for the entries shown in Figure 18.2.

```
bsdi $ arp -a
sun.tuc.noao.edu (140.252.13.33) at 8:0:20:3:f6:42
svr4.tuc.noao.edu (140.252.13.34) at 0:0:c0:c2:9b:26
bsdi.tuc.noao.edu (140.252.13.35) at 0:0:c0:6f:2d:40 permanent
ALL-SYSTEMS.MCAST.NET (224.0.0.1) at (incomplete)
```

Figure 21.5   arp -a output corresponding to Figure 18.2.

Since the multicast group 224.0.0.1 has the L flag set in Figure 18.2, and since the `arp` program looks for entries with the `RTF_LLINFO` flag set, the multicast groups are output by the program. Later in this chapter we'll see why this entry is marked as "incomplete" and why the entry above it is "permanent."

SNMP Variables

As described in Section 25.8 of Volume 1, the original SNMP MIB defined an address translation group that was the system's ARP cache. MIB-II deprecated this group and instead each network protocol group (i.e., IP) contains its own address translation tables. Notice that the change in Net/2 to Net/3 from a stand-alone ARP table to an integration of the ARP information within the IP routing table parallels this SNMP change.

Figure 21.6 shows the IP address translation table from MIB-II, named
`ipNetToMediaTable`. The values returned by SNMP for this table are taken from the
routing table entry and its corresponding `ifnet` structure.

IP address translation table, index = < *ipNetToMediaIfIndex* >.< *ipNetToMediaNetAddress* >		
Name	Member	Description

`ipNetToMediaIfIndex`
`ipNetToMediaPhysAddress`
`ipNetToMediaNetAddress`
`ipNetToMediaType`
	`if_index`
	`rt_gateway`
	`rt_key`
	`rt_flags`
		corresponding interface: `ifIndex`
		physical address
		IP address
		type of mapping: 1 = other, 2 = invalidated,
		3 = dynamic, 4 = static (see text)

Figure 21.6 IP address translation table: `ipNetToMediaTable`.

If the routing table entry has an expiration time of 0 it is considered permanent and
hence "static." Otherwise the entry is considered "dynamic."

21.4 ARP Structures

Figure 21.7 shows the format of an ARP packet when transmitted on an Ethernet.

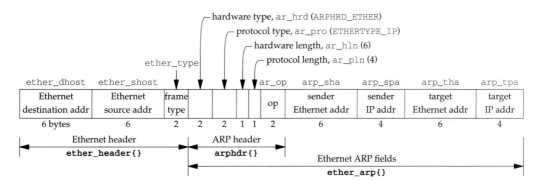

Figure 21.7 Format of an ARP request or reply when used on an Ethernet.

The `ether_header` structure (Figure 4.10) defines the 14-byte Ethernet header; the
`arphdr` structure defines the next five fields, which are common to ARP requests and
ARP replies on any type of media; and the `ether_arp` structure combines the `arphdr`
structure with the sender and target addresses when ARP is used on an Ethernet.

Figure 21.8 shows the definition of the `arphdr` structure. Figure 21.7 shows the
values of the first four fields in this structure when ARP is mapping IP addresses to
Ethernet addresses.

Figure 21.9 shows the combination of the `arphdr` structure with the fields used
with IP addresses and Ethernet addresses, forming the `ether_arp` structure. Notice
that ARP uses the terms *hardware* to describe the 48-bit Ethernet address, and *protocol* to
describe the 32-bit IP address.

—— *if_arp.h*
```
45 struct arphdr {
46     u_short ar_hrd;            /* format of hardware address */
47     u_short ar_pro;            /* format of protocol address */
48     u_char  ar_hln;            /* length of hardware address */
49     u_char  ar_pln;            /* length of protocol address */
50     u_short ar_op;             /* ARP/RARP operation, Figure 21.15 */
51 };
```
—— *if_arp.h*

Figure 21.8   `arphdr` structure: common ARP request/reply header.

—— *if_ether.h*
```
79 struct ether_arp {
80     struct arphdr ea_hdr;      /* fixed-size header */
81     u_char  arp_sha[6];        /* sender hardware address */
82     u_char  arp_spa[4];        /* sender protocol address */
83     u_char  arp_tha[6];        /* target hardware address */
84     u_char  arp_tpa[4];        /* target protocol address */
85 };

86 #define arp_hrd ea_hdr.ar_hrd
87 #define arp_pro ea_hdr.ar_pro
88 #define arp_hln ea_hdr.ar_hln
89 #define arp_pln ea_hdr.ar_pln
90 #define arp_op  ea_hdr.ar_op
```
—— *if_ether.h*

Figure 21.9   `ether_arp` structure.

One `llinfo_arp` structure, shown in Figure 21.10, exists for each ARP entry.
Additionally, one of these structures is allocated as a global of the same name and used
as the head of the linked list of all these structures. We often refer to this list as the *ARP
cache*, since it is the only data structure in Figure 21.1 that has a one-to-one correspon-
dence with the ARP entries.

—— *if_ether.h*
```
103 struct llinfo_arp {
104     struct llinfo_arp *la_next;
105     struct llinfo_arp *la_prev;
106     struct rtentry *la_rt;
107     struct mbuf *la_hold;      /* last packet until resolved/timeout */
108     long    la_asked;          /* #times we've queried for this addr */
109 };

110 #define la_timer la_rt->rt_rmx.rmx_expire   /* deletion time in seconds */
```
—— *if_ether.h*

Figure 21.10   `llinfo_arp` structure.

With Net/2 and earlier systems it was easy to identify the structure called the *ARP cache*, since
a single structure contained everything for each ARP entry. Since Net/3 stores the ARP information among multiple structures, no single structure can be called the *ARP cache*. Nevertheless, having the concept of an ARP cache, which is the collection of information describing a
single ARP entry, simplifies the discussion.

104–106   The first two entries form the doubly linked list, which is updated by the `insque` and `remque` functions. `la_rt` points to the associated routing table entry, and the `rt_llinfo` member of the routing table entry points to this structure.

107   When ARP receives an IP datagram to send to another host but the destination's hardware address is not in the ARP cache, an ARP request must be sent and the ARP reply received before the datagram can be sent. While waiting for the reply the mbuf pointer to the datagram is saved in `la_hold`. When the ARP reply is received, the packet pointed to by `la_hold` (if any) is sent.

108–109   `la_asked` counts how many consecutive times an ARP request has been sent to this IP address without receiving a reply. We'll see in Figure 21.24 that when this counter reaches a limit, that host is considered down and another ARP request won't be sent for a while.

110   This definition uses the `rmx_expire` member of the `rt_metrics` structure in the routing table entry as the ARP timer. When the value is 0, the ARP entry is considered permanent. When nonzero, the value is the number of seconds since the Unix Epoch when the entry expires.

21.5   `arpwhohas` Function

The `arpwhohas` function is normally called by `arpresolve` to broadcast an ARP request. It is also called by each Ethernet device driver to issue a *gratuitous ARP* request when the IP address is assigned to the interface (the `SIOCSIFADDR ioctl` in Figure 6.28). Section 4.7 of Volume 1 describes gratuitous ARP—it detects if another host on the Ethernet is using the same IP address and also allows other hosts with ARP entries for this host to update their ARP entry if this host has changed its Ethernet address. `arpwhohas` simply calls `arprequest`, shown in the next section, with the correct arguments.

```
                                                                  ─── if_ether.c
196 void
197 arpwhohas(ac, addr)
198 struct arpcom *ac;
199 struct in_addr *addr;
200 {
201     arprequest(ac, &ac->ac_ipaddr.s_addr, &addr->s_addr, ac->ac_enaddr);
202 }
                                                                  ─── if_ether.c
```

Figure 21.11   `arpwhohas` function: broadcast an ARP request.

196–202   The `arpcom` structure (Figure 3.26) is common to all Ethernet devices and is part of the `le_softc` structure, for example (Figure 3.20). The `ac_ipaddr` member is a copy of the interface's IP address, which is set by the driver when the `SIOCSIFADDR ioctl` is executed (Figure 6.28). `ac_enaddr` is the Ethernet address of the device.

The second argument to this function, `addr`, is the IP address for which the ARP request is being issued: the target IP address. In the case of a gratuitous ARP request, `addr` equals `ac_ipaddr`, so the second and third arguments to `arprequest` are the same, which means the sender IP address will equal the target IP address in the gratuitous ARP request.

21.6 `arprequest` Function

The `arprequest` function is called by `arpwhohas` to broadcast an ARP request. It builds an ARP request packet and passes it to the interface's output function.

Before looking at the source code, let's examine the data structures built by the function. To send the ARP request the interface output function for the Ethernet device (`ether_output`) is called. One argument to `ether_output` is an mbuf containing the data to send: everything that follows the Ethernet type field in Figure 21.7. Another argument is a socket address structure containing the destination address. Normally this destination address is an IP address (e.g., when `ip_output` calls `ether_output` in Figure 21.3). For the special case of an ARP request, the `sa_family` member of the socket address structure is set to `AF_UNSPEC`, which tells `ether_output` that it contains a filled-in Ethernet header, including the destination Ethernet address. This prevents `ether_output` from calling `arpresolve`, which would cause an infinite loop. We don't show this loop in Figure 21.3, but the "interface output function" below `arprequest` is `ether_output`. If `ether_output` were to call `arpresolve` again, the infinite loop would occur.

Figure 21.12 shows the mbuf and the socket address structure built by this function. We also show the two pointers `eh` and `ea`, which are used in the function.

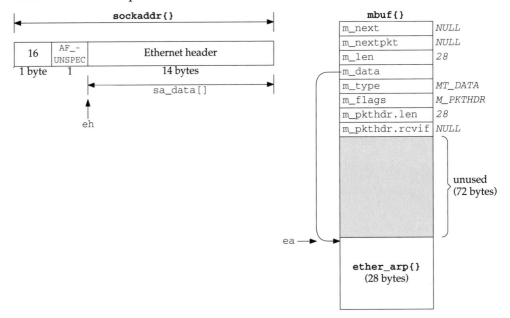

Figure 21.12   `sockaddr` and mbuf built by `arprequest`.

Figure 21.13 shows the `arprequest` function.

```
                                                                  ─── if_ether.c
209  static void
210  arprequest(ac, sip, tip, enaddr)
211  struct arpcom *ac;
212  u_long *sip, *tip;
213  u_char *enaddr;
214  {
215      struct mbuf *m;
216      struct ether_header *eh;
217      struct ether_arp *ea;
218      struct sockaddr sa;

219      if ((m = m_gethdr(M_DONTWAIT, MT_DATA)) == NULL)
220          return;
221      m->m_len = sizeof(*ea);
222      m->m_pkthdr.len = sizeof(*ea);
223      MH_ALIGN(m, sizeof(*ea));

224      ea = mtod(m, struct ether_arp *);
225      eh = (struct ether_header *) sa.sa_data;
226      bzero((caddr_t) ea, sizeof(*ea));

227      bcopy((caddr_t) etherbroadcastaddr, (caddr_t) eh->ether_dhost,
228              sizeof(eh->ether_dhost));
229      eh->ether_type = ETHERTYPE_ARP;      /* if_output() will swap */

230      ea->arp_hrd = htons(ARPHRD_ETHER);
231      ea->arp_pro = htons(ETHERTYPE_IP);
232      ea->arp_hln = sizeof(ea->arp_sha);  /* hardware address length */
233      ea->arp_pln = sizeof(ea->arp_spa);  /* protocol address length */
234      ea->arp_op = htons(ARPOP_REQUEST);
235      bcopy((caddr_t) enaddr, (caddr_t) ea->arp_sha, sizeof(ea->arp_sha));
236      bcopy((caddr_t) sip, (caddr_t) ea->arp_spa, sizeof(ea->arp_spa));
237      bcopy((caddr_t) tip, (caddr_t) ea->arp_tpa, sizeof(ea->arp_tpa));

238      sa.sa_family = AF_UNSPEC;
239      sa.sa_len = sizeof(sa);

240      (*ac->ac_if.if_output) (&ac->ac_if, m, &sa, (struct rtentry *) 0);
241  }
                                                                  ─── if_ether.c
```

Figure 21.13 arprequest function: build an ARP request packet and send it.

Allocate and initialize mbuf

209–223   A packet header mbuf is allocated and the two length fields are set. MH_ALIGN allows room for a 28-byte ether_arp structure at the end of the mbuf, and sets the m_data pointer accordingly. The reason for moving this structure to the end of the mbuf is to allow ether_output to prepend the 14-byte Ethernet header in the same mbuf.

Initialize pointers

224–226   The two pointers `ea` and `eh` are set and the `ether_arp` structure is set to 0. The only purpose of the call to `bzero` is to set the target hardware address to 0, because the other eight fields in this structure are explicitly set to their respective value.

Fill in Ethernet header

227–229   The destination Ethernet address is set to the Ethernet broadcast address and the Ethernet type field is set to `ETHERTYPE_ARP`. Note the comment that this 2-byte field will be converted from host byte order to network byte order by the interface output function. This function also fills in the Ethernet source address field. Figure 21.14 shows the different values for the Ethernet type field.

Constant	Value	Description
ETHERTYPE_IP	0x0800	IP frames
ETHERTYPE_ARP	0x0806	ARP frames
ETHERTYPE_REVARP	0x8035	reverse ARP (RARP) frames
ETHERTYPE_IPTRAILERS	0x1000	trailer encapsulation (deprecated)

Figure 21.14   Ethernet type fields.

RARP maps an Ethernet address to an IP address and is used when a diskless system bootstraps. RARP is normally not part of the kernel's implementation of TCP/IP, so it is not covered in this text. Chapter 5 of Volume 1 describes RARP.

Fill in ARP fields

230–237   All fields in the `ether_arp` structure are filled in, except the target hardware address, which is what the ARP request is looking for. The constant `ARPHRD_ETHER`, which has a value of 1, specifies the format of the hardware addresses as 6-byte Ethernet addresses. To identify the protocol addresses as 4-byte IP addresses, `arp_pro` is set to the Ethernet type field for IP from Figure 21.14. Figure 21.15 shows the various ARP operation codes. We encounter the first two in this chapter. The last two are used with RARP.

Constant	Value	Description
ARPOP_REQUEST	1	ARP request to resolve protocol address
ARPOP_REPLY	2	reply to ARP request
ARPOP_REVREQUEST	3	RARP request to resolve hardware address
ARPOP_REVREPLY	4	reply to RARP request

Figure 21.15   ARP operation codes.

Fill in `sockaddr` and call interface output function

238–241   The `sa_family` member of the socket address structure is set to `AF_UNSPEC` and the `sa_len` member is set to 16. The interface output function is called, which we said is `ether_output`.

21.7 `arpintr` **Function**

In Figure 4.13 we saw that when `ether_input` receives an Ethernet frame with a type
field of `ETHERTYPE_ARP`, it schedules a software interrupt of priority `NETISR_ARP` and
appends the frame to ARP's input queue: `arpintrq`. When the kernel processes the
software interrupt, the function `arpintr`, shown in Figure 21.16, is called.

```
                                                                            —— if_ether.c
319 void
320 arpintr()
321 {
322     struct mbuf *m;
323     struct arphdr *ar;
324     int     s;

325     while (arpintrq.ifq_head) {
326         s = splimp();
327         IF_DEQUEUE(&arpintrq, m);
328         splx(s);
329         if (m == 0 || (m->m_flags & M_PKTHDR) == 0)
330             panic("arpintr");

331         if (m->m_len >= sizeof(struct arphdr) &&
332             (ar = mtod(m, struct arphdr *)) &&
333             ntohs(ar->ar_hrd) == ARPHRD_ETHER &&
334             m->m_len >= sizeof(struct arphdr) + 2*ar->ar_hln + 2*ar->ar_pln)

335                 switch (ntohs(ar->ar_pro)) {
336                 case ETHERTYPE_IP:
337                 case ETHERTYPE_IPTRAILERS:
338                     in_arpinput(m);
339                     continue;
340                 }

341         m_freem(m);
342     }
343 }
                                                                            —— if_ether.c
```

Figure 21.16 `arpintr` function: process Ethernet frames containing ARP requests or replies.

319–343   The `while` loop processes one frame at a time, as long as there are frames on the
queue. The frame is processed if the hardware type specifies Ethernet addresses, and if
the size of the frame is greater than or equal to the size of an `arphdr` structure plus the
sizes of two hardware addresses and two protocol addresses. If the type of protocol
addresses is either `ETHERTYPE_IP` or `ETHERTYPE_IPTRAILERS`, the `in_arpinput`
function, shown in the next section, is called. Otherwise the frame is discarded.

Notice the order of the tests within the `if` statement. The length is checked twice.
First, if the length is at least the size of an `arphdr` structure, then the fields in that structure can be examined. The length is checked again, using the two length fields in the
`arphdr` structure.

21.8 `in_arpinput` **Function**

This function is called by `arpintr` to process each received ARP request or ARP reply. While ARP is conceptually simple, numerous rules add complexity to the implementation. The following two scenarios are typical:

1. If a request is received for one of the host's IP addresses, a reply is sent. This is the normal case of some other host on the Ethernet wanting to send this host a packet. Also, since we're about to receive a packet from that other host, and we'll probably send a reply, an ARP entry is created for that host (if one doesn't already exist) because we have its IP address and hardware address. This optimization avoids another ARP exchange when the packet is received from the other host.

2. If a reply is received in response to a request sent by this host, the corresponding ARP entry is now complete (the hardware address is known). The other host's hardware address is stored in the `sockaddr_dl` structure and any queued packet for that host can now be sent. Again, this is the normal case.

ARP requests are normally broadcast so each host sees *all* ARP requests on the Ethernet, even those requests for which it is not the target. Recall from `arprequest` that when a request is sent, it contains the *sender's* IP address and hardware address. This allows the following tests also to occur.

3. If some other host sends a request or reply with a sender IP address that equals this host's IP address, one of the two hosts is misconfigured. Net/3 detects this error and logs a message for the administrator. (We say "request or reply" here because `in_arpinput` doesn't examine the operation type. But ARP replies are normally unicast, in which case only the target host of the reply receives the reply.)

4. If this host receives a request or reply from some other host for which an ARP entry already exists, and if the other host's hardware address has changed, the hardware address in the ARP entry is updated accordingly. This can happen if the other host is shut down and then rebooted with a different Ethernet interface (hence a different hardware address) before its ARP entry times out. The use of this technique, along with the other host sending a gratuitous ARP request when it reboots, prevents this host from being unable to communicate with the other host after the reboot because of an ARP entry that is no longer valid.

5. This host can be configured as a *proxy ARP server*. This means it responds to ARP requests for some other host, supplying the other host's hardware address in the reply. The host whose hardware address is supplied in the proxy ARP reply must be one that is able to forward IP datagrams to the host that is the target of the ARP request. Section 4.6 of Volume 1 discusses proxy ARP.

   A Net/3 system can be configured as a proxy ARP server. These ARP entries are added with the `arp` command, specifying the IP address, hardware address, and the keyword pub. We'll see the support for this in Figure 21.20 and we describe it in Section 21.12.

We examine in_arpinput in four parts. Figure 21.17 shows the first part.

```
                                                                ── if_ether.c
358 static void
359 in_arpinput(m)
360 struct mbuf *m;
361 {
362     struct ether_arp *ea;
363     struct arpcom *ac = (struct arpcom *) m->m_pkthdr.rcvif;
364     struct ether_header *eh;
365     struct llinfo_arp *la = 0;
366     struct rtentry *rt;
367     struct in_ifaddr *ia, *maybe_ia = 0;
368     struct sockaddr_dl *sdl;
369     struct sockaddr sa;
370     struct in_addr isaddr, itaddr, myaddr;
371     int     op;

372     ea = mtod(m, struct ether_arp *);
373     op = ntohs(ea->arp_op);
374     bcopy((caddr_t) ea->arp_spa, (caddr_t) & isaddr, sizeof(isaddr));
375     bcopy((caddr_t) ea->arp_tpa, (caddr_t) & itaddr, sizeof(itaddr));

376     for (ia = in_ifaddr; ia; ia = ia->ia_next)
377         if (ia->ia_ifp == &ac->ac_if) {
378             maybe_ia = ia;
379             if ((itaddr.s_addr == ia->ia_addr.sin_addr.s_addr) ||
380                 (isaddr.s_addr == ia->ia_addr.sin_addr.s_addr))
381                 break;
382         }
383     if (maybe_ia == 0)
384         goto out;
385     myaddr = ia ? ia->ia_addr.sin_addr : maybe_ia->ia_addr.sin_addr;
                                                                ── if_ether.c
```

Figure 21.17 in_arpinput function: look for matching interface.

358–375   The length of the ether_arp structure was verified by the caller, so ea is set to point to the received packet. The ARP operation (request or reply) is copied into op but it isn't examined until later in the function. The sender's IP address and target IP address are copied into isaddr and itaddr.

Look for matching interface and IP address

376–382   The linked list of Internet addresses for the host is scanned (the list of in_ifaddr structures, Figure 6.5). Remember that a given interface can have multiple IP addresses. Since the received packet contains a pointer (in the mbuf packet header) to the receiving interface's ifnet structure, the only IP addresses considered in the for loop are those associated with the receiving interface. If either the target IP address or the sender's IP address matches one of the IP addresses for the receiving interface, the break terminates the loop.

383–384   If the loop terminates with the variable `maybe_ia` equal to 0, the entire list of configured IP addresses was searched and not one was associated with the received interface. The function jumps to `out` (Figure 21.19), where the mbuf is discarded and the function returns. This should only happen if an ARP request is received on an interface that has been initialized but has not been assigned an IP address.

385   If the `for` loop terminates having located a receiving interface (`maybe_ia` is nonnull) but none of its IP addresses matched the sender or target IP address, `myaddr` is set to the final IP address assigned to the interface. Otherwise (the normal case) `myaddr` contains the local IP address that matched either the sender or target IP address.

Figure 21.18 shows the next part of the `in_arpinput` function, which performs some validation of the packet.

```
                                                                    ── if_ether.c
386     if (!bcmp((caddr_t) ea->arp_sha, (caddr_t) ac->ac_enaddr,
387             sizeof(ea->arp_sha)))
388         goto out;                   /* it's from me, ignore it. */
389     if (!bcmp((caddr_t) ea->arp_sha, (caddr_t) etherbroadcastaddr,
390             sizeof(ea->arp_sha))) {
391         log(LOG_ERR,
392             "arp: ether address is broadcast for IP address %x!\n",
393             ntohl(isaddr.s_addr));
394         goto out;
395     }
396     if (isaddr.s_addr == myaddr.s_addr) {
397         log(LOG_ERR,
398             "duplicate IP address %x!! sent from ethernet address: %s\n",
399             ntohl(isaddr.s_addr), ether_sprintf(ea->arp_sha));
400         itaddr = myaddr;
401         goto reply;
402     }
                                                                    ── if_ether.c
```

Figure 21.18 `in_arpinput` function: validate received packet.

Validate sender's hardware address

386–388   If the sender's hardware address equals the hardware address of the interface, the host received a copy of its own request, which is ignored.

389–395   If the sender's hardware address is the Ethernet broadcast address, this is an error. The error is logged and the packet is discarded.

Check sender's IP address

396–402   If the sender's IP address equals `myaddr`, then the sender is using the same IP address as this host. This is also an error—probably a configuration error by the system administrator on either this host or the sending host. The error is logged and the function jumps to `reply` (Figure 21.19), after setting the target IP address to `myaddr` (the duplicate address). Notice that this ARP packet could have been destined for some other host on the Ethernet—it need not have been sent to this host. Nevertheless, if this form of IP address spoofing is detected, the error is logged and a reply generated.

Figure 21.19 shows the next part of `in_arpinput`.

—————————————————————————————————————— *if_ether.c*
```
403     la = arplookup(isaddr.s_addr, itaddr.s_addr == myaddr.s_addr, 0);
404     if (la && (rt = la->la_rt) && (sdl = SDL(rt->rt_gateway))) {
405         if (sdl->sdl_alen &&
406             bcmp((caddr_t) ea->arp_sha, LLADDR(sdl), sdl->sdl_alen))
407             log(LOG_INFO, "arp info overwritten for %x by %s\n",
408                   isaddr.s_addr, ether_sprintf(ea->arp_sha));
409         bcopy((caddr_t) ea->arp_sha, LLADDR(sdl),
410               sdl->sdl_alen = sizeof(ea->arp_sha));
411         if (rt->rt_expire)
412             rt->rt_expire = time.tv_sec + arpt_keep;
413         rt->rt_flags &= ~RTF_REJECT;
414         la->la_asked = 0;
415         if (la->la_hold) {
416             (*ac->ac_if.if_output) (&ac->ac_if, la->la_hold,
417                                     rt_key(rt), rt);
418             la->la_hold = 0;
419         }
420     }

421 reply:
422     if (op != ARPOP_REQUEST) {
423       out:
424         m_freem(m);
425         return;
426     }
```
—————————————————————————————————————— *if_ether.c*

Figure 21.19 in_arpinput function: create a new ARP entry or update existing entry.

Search routing table for match with sender's IP address

403   arplookup searches the ARP cache for the sender's IP address (isaddr). The second argument is 1 if the target IP address equals myaddr (meaning create a new entry if an entry doesn't exist), or 0 otherwise (do not create a new entry). An entry is always created for the sender if this host is the target; otherwise the host is processing a broadcast intended for some other target, so it just looks for an existing entry for the sender. As mentioned earlier, this means that if a host receives an ARP request for itself from another host, an ARP entry is created for that other host on the assumption that, since that host is about to send us a packet, we'll probably send a reply.

The third argument is 0, which means do not look for a proxy ARP entry (described later). The return value is a pointer to an llinfo_arp structure, or a null pointer if an entry is not found or created.

Update existing entry or fill in new entry

404   The code associated with the if statement is executed only if the following three conditions are all true:

  1. an ARP entry was found or a new ARP entry was successfully created (la is nonnull),

  2. the ARP entry points to a routing table entry (rt), and

3. the `rt_gateway` field of the routing table entry points to a `sockaddr_dl` structure.

The first condition is false for every broadcast ARP request not directed to this host, from some other host whose IP address is not currently in the routing table.

Check if sender's hardware addresses changed

405–408   If the link-level address length (`sdl_alen`) is nonzero (meaning that an existing entry is being referenced and not a new entry that was just created), the link-level address is compared to the sender's hardware address. If they are different, the sender's Ethernet address has changed. This can happen if the sending host is shut down, its Ethernet interface card replaced, and it reboots before the ARP entry times out. While not common, this is a possibility that must be handled. An informational message is logged and the code continues, which will update the hardware address with its new value.

> The sender's IP address in the log message should be converted to host byte order. This is a bug.

Record sender's hardware address

409–410   The sender's hardware address is copied into the `sockaddr_dl` structure pointed to by the `rt_gateway` member of the routing table entry. The link-level address length (`sdl_alen`) in the `sockaddr_dl` structure is also set to 6. This assignment of the length field is required if this is a newly created entry (Exercise 21.3).

Update newly resolved ARP entry

411–412   When the sender's hardware address is resolved, the following steps occur. If the expiration time is nonzero, it is reset to 20 minutes (`arpt_keep`) in the future. This test exists because the `arp` command can create permanent entries: entries that never time out. These entries are marked with an expiration time of 0. We'll also see in Figure 21.24 that when an ARP request is sent (i.e., for a nonpermanent ARP entry) the expiration time is set to the current time, which is nonzero.

413–414   The `RTF_REJECT` flag is cleared and the `la_asked` counter is set to 0. We'll see that these last two steps are used in `arpresolve` to avoid ARP flooding.

415–420   If ARP is holding onto an mbuf awaiting ARP resolution of that host's hardware address (the `la_hold` pointer), the mbuf is passed to the interface output function. (We show this in Figure 21.3.) Since this mbuf was being held by ARP, the destination address must be on a local Ethernet so the interface output function is `ether_output`. This function again calls `arpresolve`, but the hardware address was just filled in, allowing the mbuf to be queued on the actual device's output queue.

Finished with ARP reply packets

421–426   If the ARP operation is not a request, the received packet is discarded and the function returns.

The remainder of the function, shown in Figure 21.20, generates a reply to an ARP request. A reply is generated in only two instances:

1. this host is the target of a request for its hardware address, or

2. this host receives a request for another host's hardware address for which this host has been configured to act as an ARP proxy server.

At this point in the function, an ARP request has been received, but since ARP requests are normally broadcast, the request could be for any system on the Ethernet.

```
                                                                        ─── if_ether.c
427     if (itaddr.s_addr == myaddr.s_addr) {
428         /* I am the target */
429         bcopy((caddr_t) ea->arp_sha, (caddr_t) ea->arp_tha,
430             sizeof(ea->arp_sha));
431         bcopy((caddr_t) ac->ac_enaddr, (caddr_t) ea->arp_sha,
432             sizeof(ea->arp_sha));
433     } else {
434         la = arplookup(itaddr.s_addr, 0, SIN_PROXY);
435         if (la == NULL)
436             goto out;
437         rt = la->la_rt;
438         bcopy((caddr_t) ea->arp_sha, (caddr_t) ea->arp_tha,
439             sizeof(ea->arp_sha));
440         sdl = SDL(rt->rt_gateway);
441         bcopy(LLADDR(sdl), (caddr_t) ea->arp_sha, sizeof(ea->arp_sha));
442     }

443     bcopy((caddr_t) ea->arp_spa, (caddr_t) ea->arp_tpa, sizeof(ea->arp_spa));
444     bcopy((caddr_t) & itaddr, (caddr_t) ea->arp_spa, sizeof(ea->arp_spa));
445     ea->arp_op = htons(ARPOP_REPLY);
446     ea->arp_pro = htons(ETHERTYPE_IP);   /* let's be sure! */
447     eh = (struct ether_header *) sa.sa_data;
448     bcopy((caddr_t) ea->arp_tha, (caddr_t) eh->ether_dhost,
449         sizeof(eh->ether_dhost));
450     eh->ether_type = ETHERTYPE_ARP;
451     sa.sa_family = AF_UNSPEC;
452     sa.sa_len = sizeof(sa);
453     (*ac->ac_if.if_output) (&ac->ac_if, m, &sa, (struct rtentry *) 0);
454     return;
455 }
                                                                        ─── if_ether.c
```

Figure 21.20 in_arpinput function: form ARP reply and send it.

This host is the target

427–432   If the target IP address equals myaddr, this host is the target of the request. The source hardware address is copied into the target hardware address (i.e., whoever sent it becomes the target) and the Ethernet address of the interface is copied from the arpcom structure into the source hardware address. The remainder of the ARP reply is constructed after the else clause.

Check if this host is a proxy server for target

433–436   Even if this host is not the target, this host can be configured to be a proxy server for the specified target. arplookup is called again with the create flag set to 0 (the second argument) and the third argument set to SIN_PROXY. This finds an entry in the routing table only if that entry's SIN_PROXY flag is set. If an entry is not found (the typical case where this host receives a copy of some other ARP request on the Ethernet), the code at out discards the mbuf and returns.

Form proxy reply

437–442   To handle a proxy ARP request, the sender's hardware address becomes the target hardware address and the Ethernet address from the ARP entry is copied into the sender hardware address field. This value from the ARP entry can be the Ethernet address of any host on the Ethernet capable of sending IP datagrams to the target IP address. Normally the host providing the proxy ARP service supplies its own Ethernet address, but that's not required. Proxy entries are created by the system administrator using the arp command, with the keyword pub, specifying the target IP address (which becomes the key of the routing table entry) and an Ethernet address to return in the ARP reply.

Complete construction of ARP reply packet

443–444   The remainder of the function completes the construction of the ARP reply. The sender and target hardware addresses have been filled in. The sender and target IP addresses are now swapped. The target IP address is contained in itaddr, which might have been changed if another host was found using this host's IP address (Figure 21.18).

445–446   The ARP operation is set to ARPOP_REPLY and the type of protocol address is set to ETHERTYPE_IP. The comment "let's be sure!" is because arpintr also calls this function when the type of protocol address is ETHERTYPE_IPTRAILERS, but the use of trailer encapsulation is no longer supported.

Fill in sockaddr with Ethernet header

447–452   A sockaddr structure is filled in with the 14-byte Ethernet header, as shown in Figure 21.12. The target hardware address also becomes the Ethernet destination address.

453–455   The ARP reply is passed to the interface's output routine and the function returns.

21.9   ARP Timer Functions

ARP entries are normally dynamic—they are created when needed and time out automatically. It is also possible for the system administrator to create permanent entries (i.e., no timeout), and the proxy entries we discussed in the previous section are always permanent. Recall from Figure 21.1 and the #define at the end of Figure 21.10 that the rmx_expire member of the routing metrics structure is used by ARP as a timer.

arptimer Function

This function, shown in Figure 21.21, is called every 5 minutes. It goes through all the ARP entries to see if any have expired.

```
                                                                  ─── if_ether.c
74 static void
75 arptimer(ignored_arg)
76 void    *ignored_arg;
77 {
78     int      s = splnet();
79     struct llinfo_arp *la = llinfo_arp.la_next;

80     timeout(arptimer, (caddr_t) 0, arpt_prune * hz);
81     while (la != &llinfo_arp) {
82         struct rtentry *rt = la->la_rt;
83         la = la->la_next;
84         if (rt->rt_expire && rt->rt_expire <= time.tv_sec)
85             arptfree(la->la_prev);   /* timer has expired, clear */
86     }
87     splx(s);
88 }
                                                                  ─── if_ether.c
```

Figure 21.21   arptimer function: check all ARP timers every 5 minutes.

Set next timeout

80   We'll see that the arp_rtrequest function causes arptimer to be called the first time, and from that point arptimer causes itself to be called 5 minutes (arpt_prune) in the future.

Check all ARP entries

81–86   Each entry in the linked list is processed. If the timer is nonzero (it is not a permanent entry) and if the timer has expired, arptfree releases the entry. If rt_expire is nonzero, it contains a count of the number of seconds since the Unix Epoch when the entry expires.

arptfree Function

This function, shown in Figure 21.22, is called by arptimer to delete a single entry from the linked list of llinfo_arp entries.

Invalidate (don't delete) entries in use

467–473   If the routing table reference count is greater than 0 and the rt_gateway member points to a sockaddr_dl structure, arptfree takes the following steps:

1. the link-layer address length is set to 0,

2. the la_asked counter is reset to 0, and

3. the RTF_REJECT flag is cleared.

The function then returns. Since the reference count is nonzero, the routing table entry is not deleted. But setting sdl_alen to 0 invalidates the entry, so the next time the entry is used, an ARP request will be generated.

```
                                                                     ── if_ether.c
459 static void
460 arptfree(la)
461 struct llinfo_arp *la;
462 {
463     struct rtentry *rt = la->la_rt;
464     struct sockaddr_dl *sdl;
465     if (rt == 0)
466         panic("arptfree");
467     if (rt->rt_refcnt > 0 && (sdl = SDL(rt->rt_gateway)) &&
468         sdl->sdl_family == AF_LINK) {
469         sdl->sdl_alen = 0;
470         la->la_asked = 0;
471         rt->rt_flags &= ~RTF_REJECT;
472         return;
473     }
474     rtrequest(RTM_DELETE, rt_key(rt), (struct sockaddr *) 0, rt_mask(rt),
475             0, (struct rtentry **) 0);
476 }
                                                                     ── if_ether.c
```

Figure 21.22   arptfree function: delete or invalidate an ARP entry.

Delete unreferenced entries

474–475   rtrequest deletes the routing table entry, and we'll see in Section 21.13 that it calls arp_rtrequest. This latter function frees any mbuf chain held by the ARP entry (the la_hold pointer) and deletes the corresponding llinfo_arp entry.

21.10 arpresolve Function

We saw in Figure 4.16 that ether_output calls arpresolve to obtain the Ethernet address for an IP address. arpresolve returns 1 if the destination Ethernet address is known, allowing ether_output to queue the IP datagram on the interface's output queue. A return value of 0 means arpresolve does not know the Ethernet address. The datagram is "held" by arpresolve (using the la_hold member of the llinfo_arp structure) and an ARP request is sent. If and when an ARP reply is received, in_arpinput completes the ARP entry and sends the held datagram.

arpresolve must also avoid *ARP flooding*, that is, it must not repeatedly send ARP requests at a high rate when an ARP reply is not received. This can happen when several datagrams are sent to the same unresolved IP address before an ARP reply is received, or when a datagram destined for an unresolved address is fragmented, since each fragment is sent to ether_output as a separate packet. Section 11.9 of Volume 1 contains an example of ARP flooding caused by fragmentation, and discusses the associated problems. Figure 21.23 shows the first half of arpresolve.

252–261   dst is a pointer to a sockaddr_in containing the destination IP address and desten is an array of 6 bytes that is filled in with the corresponding Ethernet address, if known.

if_ether.c

```
252 int
253 arpresolve(ac, rt, m, dst, desten)
254 struct arpcom *ac;
255 struct rtentry *rt;
256 struct mbuf *m;
257 struct sockaddr *dst;
258 u_char *desten;
259 {
260     struct llinfo_arp *la;
261     struct sockaddr_dl *sdl;

262     if (m->m_flags & M_BCAST) { /* broadcast */
263         bcopy((caddr_t) etherbroadcastaddr, (caddr_t) desten,
264                 sizeof(etherbroadcastaddr));
265         return (1);
266     }
267     if (m->m_flags & M_MCAST) { /* multicast */
268         ETHER_MAP_IP_MULTICAST(&SIN(dst)->sin_addr, desten);
269         return (1);
270     }
271     if (rt)
272         la = (struct llinfo_arp *) rt->rt_llinfo;
273     else {
274         if (la = arplookup(SIN(dst)->sin_addr.s_addr, 1, 0))
275             rt = la->la_rt;
276     }
277     if (la == 0 || rt == 0) {
278         log(LOG_DEBUG, "arpresolve: can't allocate llinfo");
279         m_freem(m);
280         return (0);
281     }
```

if_ether.c

Figure 21.23   arpresolve function: find ARP entry if required.

Handle broadcast and multicast destinations

262–270   If the M_BCAST flag of the mbuf is set, the destination is filled in with the Ethernet broadcast address and the function returns 1. If the M_MCAST flag is set, the ETHER_MAP_IP_MULTICAST macro (Figure 12.6) converts the class D address into the corresponding Ethernet address.

Get pointer to llinfo_arp structure

271–276   The destination address is a unicast address. If a pointer to a routing table entry is passed by the caller, la is set to the corresponding llinfo_arp structure. Otherwise arplookup searches the routing table for the specified IP address. The second argument is 1, telling arplookup to create the entry if it doesn't already exist; the third argument is 0, which means don't look for a proxy ARP entry.

277–281   If either rt or la are null pointers, one of the allocations failed, since arplookup should have created an entry if one didn't exist. An error message is logged, the packet released, and the function returns 0.

Figure 21.24 contains the last half of `arpresolve`. It checks whether the ARP entry is still valid, and, if not, sends an ARP request.

```
                                                                    ─── if_ether.c
282        sdl = SDL(rt->rt_gateway);
283        /*
284         * Check the address family and length is valid, the address
285         * is resolved; otherwise, try to resolve.
286         */
287        if ((rt->rt_expire == 0 || rt->rt_expire > time.tv_sec) &&
288            sdl->sdl_family == AF_LINK && sdl->sdl_alen != 0) {
289            bcopy(LLADDR(sdl), desten, sdl->sdl_alen);
290            return 1;
291        }
292        /*
293         * There is an arptab entry, but no ethernet address
294         * response yet.  Replace the held mbuf with this
295         * latest one.
296         */
297        if (la->la_hold)
298            m_freem(la->la_hold);
299        la->la_hold = m;

300        if (rt->rt_expire) {
301            rt->rt_flags &= ~RTF_REJECT;
302            if (la->la_asked == 0 || rt->rt_expire != time.tv_sec) {
303                rt->rt_expire = time.tv_sec;
304                if (la->la_asked++ < arp_maxtries)
305                    arpwhohas(ac, &(SIN(dst)->sin_addr));
306                else {
307                    rt->rt_flags |= RTF_REJECT;
308                    rt->rt_expire += arpt_down;
309                    la->la_asked = 0;
310                }
311            }
312        }
313        return (0);
314 }
                                                                    ─── if_ether.c
```

Figure 21.24 `arpresolve` function: check if ARP entry valid, send ARP request if not.

Check ARP entry for validity

282–291   Even though an ARP entry is located, it must be checked for validity. The entry is valid if the following conditions are all true:

1. the entry is permanent (the expiration time is 0) or the expiration time is greater than the current time, and

2. the family of the socket address structure pointed to by `rt_gateway` is AF_LINK, and

3. the link-level address length (`sdl_alen`) is nonzero.

Recall that `arptfree` invalidated an ARP entry that was still referenced by setting `sdl_alen` to 0. If the entry is valid, the Ethernet address contained in the `sockaddr_dl` is copied into `desten` and the function returns 1.

Hold only most recent IP datagram

292–299   At this point an ARP entry exists but it does not contain a valid Ethernet address. An ARP request must be sent. First the pointer to the mbuf chain is saved in `la_hold`, after releasing any mbuf chain that was already pointed to by `la_hold`. This means that if multiple IP datagrams are sent quickly to a given destination, and an ARP entry does not already exist for the destination, during the time it takes to send an ARP request and receive a reply only the *last* datagram is held, and all prior ones are discarded. An example that generates this condition is NFS. If NFS sends an 8500-byte IP datagram that is fragmented into six IP fragments, and if all six fragments are sent by `ip_output` to `ether_output` in the time it takes to send an ARP request and receive a reply, the first five fragments are discarded and only the final fragment is sent when the reply is received. This in turn causes an NFS timeout, and a retransmission of all six fragments.

Send ARP request but avoid ARP flooding

300–314   RFC 1122 requires ARP to avoid sending ARP requests to a given destination at a high rate when a reply is not received. The technique used by Net/3 to avoid ARP flooding is as follows.

- Net/3 never sends more than one ARP request in any given second to a destination.

- If a reply is not received after five ARP requests (i.e., after about 5 seconds), the `RTF_REJECT` flag in the routing table is set and the expiration time is set for 20 seconds in the future. This causes `ether_output` to refuse to send IP datagrams to this destination for 20 seconds, returning EHOSTDOWN or EHOSTUNREACH instead (Figure 4.15).

- After the 20-second pause in ARP requests, `arpresolve` will send ARP requests to that destination again.

If the expiration time is nonzero (i.e., this is not a permanent entry) the `RTF_REJECT` flag is cleared, in case it had been set earlier to avoid flooding. The counter `la_asked` counts the number of consecutive times an ARP request has been sent to this destination. If the counter is 0 or if the expiration time does not equal the current time (looking only at the seconds portion of the current time), an ARP request might be sent. This comparison avoids sending more than one ARP request during any second. The expiration time is then set to the current time in seconds (i.e., the microseconds portion, `time.tv_usec` is ignored).

The counter is compared to the limit of 5 (`arp_maxtries`) and then incremented. If the value was less than 5, `arpwhohas` sends the request. If the request equals 5, however, ARP has reached its limit: the `RTF_REJECT` flag is set, the expiration time is set to 20 seconds in the future, and the counter `la_asked` is reset to 0.

Figure 21.25 shows an example to explain further the algorithm used by
arpresolve and ether_output to avoid ARP flooding.

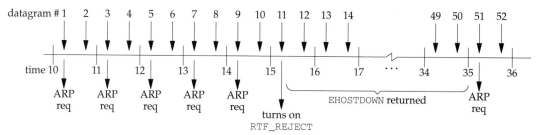

Figure 21.25   Algorithm used to avoid ARP flooding.

We show 26 seconds of time, labeled 10 through 36. We assume a process is sending an
IP datagram every one-half second, causing two datagrams to be sent every second.
The datagrams are numbered 1 through 52. We also assume that the destination host is
down, so there are no replies to the ARP requests. The following actions take place:

- We assume la_asked is 0 when datagram 1 is written by the process. la_hold
  is set to point to datagram 1, rt_expire is set to the current time (10),
  la_asked becomes 1, and an ARP request is sent. The function returns 0.

- When datagram 2 is written by the process, datagram 1 is discarded and
  la_hold is set to point to datagram 2. Since rt_expire equals the current
  time (10), nothing else happens (an ARP request is not sent) and the function
  returns 0.

- When datagram 3 is written, datagram 2 is discarded and la_hold is set to
  point to datagram 3. The current time (11) does not equal rt_expire (10), so
  rt_expire is set to 11. la_asked is less than 5, so la_asked becomes 2 and
  an ARP request is sent.

- When datagram 4 is written, datagram 3 is discarded and la_hold is set to
  point to datagram 4. Since rt_expire equals the current time (11), nothing else
  happens and the function returns 0.

- Similar actions occur for datagrams 5 through 10. After datagram 9 causes an
  ARP request to be sent, la_asked is 5.

- When datagram 11 is written, datagram 10 is discarded and la_hold is set to
  point to datagram 11. The current time (15) does not equal rt_expire (14), so
  rt_expire is set to 15. la_asked is no longer less than 5, so the ARP flooding
  avoidance algorithm takes place: RTF_REJECT flag is set, rt_expire is set to
  35 (20 seconds in the future), and la_asked is reset to 0. The function returns 0.

- When datagram 12 is written, ether_output notices that the RTF_REJECT flag
  is set and that the current time is less than rt_expire (35) causing EHOSTDOWN
  to be returned to the sender (normally ip_output).

- The EHOSTDOWN error is returned for datagrams 13 through 50.

- When datagram 51 is written, even though the RTF_REJECT flag is set ether_output does not return the error because the current time (35) is no longer less than rt_expire (35). arpresolve is called and the entire process starts over again: five ARP requests are sent in 5 seconds, followed by a 20-second pause. This continues until the sending process gives up or the destination host responds to an ARP request.

21.11 arplookup Function

arplookup calls the routing function rtalloc1 to look up an ARP entry in the Internet routing table. We've seen three calls to arplookup:

1. from in_arpinput to look up and possibly create an entry corresponding to the source IP address of a received ARP packet,

2. from in_arpinput to see if a proxy ARP entry exists for the destination IP address of a received ARP request, and

3. from arpresolve to look up or create an entry corresponding to the destination IP address of a datagram that is about to be sent.

If arplookup succeeds, a pointer is returned to the corresponding llinfo_arp structure; otherwise a null pointer is returned.

arplookup has three arguments. The first is the IP address to search for, the second is a flag that is true if a new entry should be created if the entry is not found, and the third is a flag that is true if a proxy ARP entry should be searched for and possibly created.

Proxy ARP entries are handled by defining a different form of the Internet socket address structure, a sockaddr_inarp structure, shown in Figure 21.26 This structure is used only by ARP.

―― *if_ether.h*
```
111 struct sockaddr_inarp {
112     u_char  sin_len;          /* sizeof(struct sockaddr_inarp) = 16 */
113     u_char  sin_family;       /* AF_INET */
114     u_short sin_port;
115     struct in_addr sin_addr;   /* IP address */
116     struct in_addr sin_srcaddr; /* not used */
117     u_short sin_tos;           /* not used */
118     u_short sin_other;         /* 0 or SIN_PROXY */
119 };
```
―― *if_ether.h*

Figure 21.26   sockaddr_inarp structure.

111–119   The first 8 bytes are the same as a sockaddr_in structure and the sin_family is also set to AF_INET. The final 8 bytes, however, are different: the sin_srcaddr, sin_tos, and sin_other members. Of these three, only the final one is used, being set to SIN_PROXY (1) if the entry is a proxy entry.

Figure 21.27 shows the `arplookup` function.

```
                                                                    ——— if_ether.c
480 static struct llinfo_arp *
481 arplookup(addr, create, proxy)
482 u_long  addr;
483 int     create, proxy;
484 {
485     struct rtentry *rt;
486     static struct sockaddr_inarp sin =
487     {sizeof(sin), AF_INET};

488     sin.sin_addr.s_addr = addr;
489     sin.sin_other = proxy ? SIN_PROXY : 0;
490     rt = rtalloc1((struct sockaddr *) &sin, create);
491     if (rt == 0)
492         return (0);
493     rt->rt_refcnt--;
494     if ((rt->rt_flags & RTF_GATEWAY) || (rt->rt_flags & RTF_LLINFO) == 0 ||
495         rt->rt_gateway->sa_family != AF_LINK) {
496         if (create)
497             log(LOG_DEBUG, "arptnew failed on %x\n", ntohl(addr));
498         return (0);
499     }
500     return ((struct llinfo_arp *) rt->rt_llinfo);
501 }
                                                                    ——— if_ether.c
```

Figure 21.27 `arplookup` function: look up an ARP entry in the routing table.

Initialize `sockaddr_inarp` to look up

480–489   The `sin_addr` member is set to the IP address that is being looked up. The `sin_other` member is set to `SIN_PROXY` if the `proxy` argument is nonzero, or 0 otherwise.

Look up entry in routing table

490–492   `rtalloc1` looks up the IP address in the Internet routing table, creating a new entry if the `create` argument is nonzero. If the entry is not found, the function returns 0 (a null pointer).

Decrement routing table reference count

493   If the entry is found, the reference count for the routing table entry is decremented. This is because ARP is not considered to "hold onto" a routing table entry like the transport layers, so the increment of `rt_refcnt` that was done by the routing table lookup is undone here by ARP.

494–499   If the `RTF_GATEWAY` flag is set, or the `RTF_LLINFO` flag is not set, or the address family of the socket address structure pointed to by `rt_gateway` is not `AF_LINK`, something is wrong and a null pointer is returned. If the entry was created this way, a log message is created.

> The log message with the function name `arptnew` refers to the older Net/2 function that created ARP entries.

If `rtalloc1` creates a new entry because the matching entry had the `RTF_CLONING` flag set, the function `arp_rtrequest` (which we describe in Section 21.13) is also called by `rtrequest`.

21.12 Proxy ARP

Net/3 supports proxy ARP, as we saw in the previous section. Two different types of proxy ARP entries can be added to the routing table. Both are added with the `arp` command, specifying the `pub` option. Adding a proxy ARP entry always causes a gratuitous ARP request to be issued by `arp_rtrequest` (Figure 21.28) because the `RTF_ANNOUNCE` flag is set when the entry is created.

The first type of proxy ARP entry allows an IP address for a host on an attached network to be entered into the ARP cache. Any Ethernet address can be assigned to the entry. These entries are added to the routing table with an explicit mask of `0xffffffff`. The purpose of this mask is to allow the call to `rtalloc1` in Figure 21.27 to match this entry, even if the `SIN_PROXY` flag is set in the socket address structure of the search key. This in turn allows the call to `arplookup` from Figure 21.20 to match this entry when a search is made for the target address with the `SIN_PROXY` flag set.

This type of entry can be used if a host H1 that doesn't implement ARP is on an attached network. The host with the proxy entry answers all ARP requests for H1's hardware address, supplying the Ethernet address that was specified when the proxy entry was created (i.e., the Ethernet address of H1). These entries are output with the notation "published" by the `arp -a` command.

The second type of proxy ARP entry is for a host for which a routing table entry already exists. The kernel creates another routing table entry for the destination, with this new entry containing the link-layer information (i.e., the Ethernet address). The `SIN_PROXY` flag is set in the `sin_other` member of the `sockaddr_inarp` structure (Figure 21.26) in the new routing table entry. Recall that routing table searches compare 12 bytes of the Internet socket address structure (Figure 18.39). This use of the `SIN_PROXY` flag is the only time the final 8 bytes of the structure are nonzero. When `arplookup` specifies the `SIN_PROXY` value in the `sin_other` member of the structure passed to `rtalloc1`, the only entries in the routing table that will match are ones that also have the `SIN_PROXY` flag set.

This type of entry normally specifies the Ethernet address of the host acting as the proxy server. If the proxy entry was created for a host HD, the sequence of steps is as follows.

1. The proxy server receives a broadcast ARP request for HD's hardware address from some other host HS. The host HS thinks HD is on the local network.

2. The proxy server responds, supplying its own Ethernet address.

3. HS sends the datagram with a destination IP address of HD to the proxy server's Ethernet address.

4. The proxy server receives the datagram for HD and forwards it, using the nor-
    mal routing table entry for HD.

This type of entry was used on the router `netb` in the example in Section 4.6 of
Volume 1. These entries are output by the `arp -a` command with the notation "published (proxy only)."

21.13 `arp_rtrequest` Function

Figure 21.3 provides an overview of the relationship between the ARP functions and the
routing functions. We've encountered two calls to the routing table functions from the
ARP functions.

1. `arplookup` calls `rtalloc1` to look up an ARP entry and possibly create a new
    entry if a match isn't found.

    If a matching entry is found in the routing table and the `RTF_CLONING` flag is
    not set (i.e., it is a matching entry for the destination host), the pointer to the
    matching entry is returned. But if the `RTF_CLONING` bit is set, `rtalloc1` calls
    `rtrequest` with a command of `RTM_RESOLVE`. This is how the entries for
    140.252.13.33 and 140.252.13.34 in Figure 18.2 were created—they were cloned
    from the entry for 140.252.13.32.

2. `arptfree` calls `rtrequest` with a command of `RTM_DELETE` to delete an
    entry from the routing table that corresponds to an ARP entry.

Additionally, the `arp` command manipulates the ARP cache by sending and receiving
routing messages on a routing socket. The `arp` command issues routing messages with
commands of `RTM_ADD`, `RTM_DELETE`, and `RTM_GET`. The first two commands cause
`rtrequest` to be called and the third causes `rtalloc1` to be called.

Finally, when an Ethernet device driver has an IP address assigned to the interface,
`rtinit` adds a route to the network. This causes `rtrequest` to be called with a command of `RTM_ADD` and with the flags of `RTF_UP` and `RTF_CLONING`. This is how the
entry for 140.252.13.32 in Figure 18.2 was created.

As described in Chapter 19, each `ifaddr` structure can contain a pointer to a function (the `ifa_rtrequest` member) that is automatically called when a routing table
entry is added or deleted for that interface. We saw in Figure 6.17 that `in_ifinit` sets
this pointer to the function `arp_rtrequest` for all Ethernet devices. Therefore, whenever the routing functions are called to add or delete a routing table entry for ARP,
`arp_rtrequest` is also called. The purpose of this function is to do whatever type of
initialization or cleanup is required above and beyond what the generic routing table
functions perform. For example, this is where a new `llinfo_arp` structure is allocated
and initialized whenever a new ARP entry is created. In a similar way, the
`llinfo_arp` structure is deleted by this function after the generic routing routines
have completed processing an `RTM_DELETE` command.

Figure 21.28 shows the first part of the `arp_rtrequest` function.

─── *if_ether.c*
```
92 void
93 arp_rtrequest(req, rt, sa)
94 int     req;
95 struct rtentry *rt;
96 struct sockaddr *sa;
97 {
98     struct sockaddr *gate = rt->rt_gateway;
99     struct llinfo_arp *la = (struct llinfo_arp *) rt->rt_llinfo;
100    static struct sockaddr_dl null_sdl =
101    {sizeof(null_sdl), AF_LINK};

102    if (!arpinit_done) {
103        arpinit_done = 1;
104        timeout(arptimer, (caddr_t) 0, hz);
105    }
106    if (rt->rt_flags & RTF_GATEWAY)
107        return;
108    switch (req) {

109    case RTM_ADD:
110        /*
111         * XXX: If this is a manually added route to interface
112         * such as older version of routed or gated might provide,
113         * restore cloning bit.
114         */
115        if ((rt->rt_flags & RTF_HOST) == 0 &&
116            SIN(rt_mask(rt))->sin_addr.s_addr != 0xffffffff)
117            rt->rt_flags |= RTF_CLONING;
118        if (rt->rt_flags & RTF_CLONING) {
119            /*
120             * Case 1: This route should come from a route to iface.
121             */
122            rt_setgate(rt, rt_key(rt),
123                        (struct sockaddr *) &null_sdl);
124            gate = rt->rt_gateway;
125            SDL(gate)->sdl_type = rt->rt_ifp->if_type;
126            SDL(gate)->sdl_index = rt->rt_ifp->if_index;
127            rt->rt_expire = time.tv_sec;
128            break;
129        }
130        /* Announce a new entry if requested. */
131        if (rt->rt_flags & RTF_ANNOUNCE)
132            arprequest((struct arpcom *) rt->rt_ifp,
133                        &SIN(rt_key(rt))->sin_addr.s_addr,
134                        &SIN(rt_key(rt))->sin_addr.s_addr,
135                        (u_char *) LLADDR(SDL(gate)));
136        /* FALLTHROUGH */
```
─── *if_ether.c*

Figure 21.28 `arp_rtrequest` function: RTM_ADD command.

Initialize ARP timeout function

92–105   The first time `arp_rtrequest` is called (when the first Ethernet interface is assigned an IP address during system initialization), the `timeout` function schedules the function `arptimer` to be called in 1 second. This starts the ARP timer code running every 5 minutes, since `arptimer` always calls `timeout`.

Ignore indirect routes

106–107   If the `RTF_GATEWAY` flag is set, the function returns. This flag indicates an indirect routing table entry and all ARP entries are direct routes.

108   The remainder of the function is a `switch` with three cases: `RTM_ADD`, `RTM_RESOLVE`, and `RTM_DELETE`. (The latter two are shown in figures that follow.)

RTM_ADD command

109   The first `case` for `RTM_ADD` is invoked by either the `arp` command manually creating an ARP entry or by an Ethernet interface being assigned an IP address by `rtinit` (Figure 21.3).

Backward compatibility

110–117   If the `RTF_HOST` flag is cleared, this routing table entry has an associated mask (i.e., it is a network route, not a host route). If that mask is not all one bits, then the entry is really a route to an interface, so the `RTF_CLONING` flag is set. As the comment indicates, this is for backward compatibility with older versions of some routing daemons. Also, the command

```
route add -net 224.0.0.0 -interface bsdi
```

that is in the file `/etc/netstart` creates the entry for this network shown in Figure 18.2 that has the `RTF_CLONING` flag set.

Initialize entry for network route to interface

118–126   If the `RTF_CLONING` flag is set (which `in_ifinit` sets for all Ethernet interfaces), this entry is probably being added by `rtinit`. `rt_setgate` allocates space for a `sockaddr_dl` structure, which is pointed to by the `rt_gateway` member. This data-link socket address structure is the one associated with the routing table entry for 140.252.13.32 in Figure 21.1. The `sdl_len` and `sdl_family` members are initialized from the `static` definition of `null_sdl` at the beginning of the function, and the `sdl_type` (probably `IFT_ETHER`) and `sdl_index` members are copied from the interface's `ifnet` structure. This structure never contains an Ethernet address and the `sdl_alen` member remains 0.

127–128   Finally, the expiration time is set to the current time, which is simply the time the entry was created, and the `break` causes the function to return. For entries created at system initialization, their `rmx_expire` value is the time at which the system was bootstrapped. Notice in Figure 21.1 that this routing table entry does not have an associated `llinfo_arp` structure, so it is never processed by `arptimer`. Nevertheless this `sockaddr_dl` structure is used: since it is the `rt_gateway` structure for the entry that is cloned for host-specific entries on this Ethernet, it is copied by `rtrequest` when the newly cloned entries are created with the `RTM_RESOLVE` command. Also, the `netstat` program prints the `sdl_index` value as `link#n`, as we see in Figure 18.2.

Send gratuitous ARP request

130–135   If the RTF_ANNOUNCE flag is set, this entry is being created by the arp command with the pub option. This option has two ramifications: (1) the SIN_PROXY flag will be set in the sin_other member of the sockaddr_inarp structure, and (2) the RTF_ANNOUNCE flag will be set. Since the RTF_ANNOUNCE flag is set, arprequest broadcasts a gratuitous ARP request. Notice that the second and third arguments are the same, which causes the sender IP address to equal the target IP address in the ARP request.

136   The code falls through to the case for the RTM_RESOLVE command.

Figure 21.29 shows the next part of the arp_rtrequest function, which handles the RTM_RESOLVE command. This command is issued when rtalloc1 matches an entry with the RTF_CLONING flag set and its second argument is nonzero (the create argument to arplookup). A new llinfo_arp structure must be allocated and initialized.

Verify sockaddr_dl structure

137–144   The family and length of the sockaddr_dl structure pointed to by the rt_gateway pointer are verified. The interface type (probably IFT_ETHER) and index are then copied into the new sockaddr_dl structure.

Handle route changes

145–146   Normally the routing table entry is new and does not point to an llinfo_arp structure. If the la pointer is nonnull, however, arp_rtrequest was called when a route changed for an existing routing table entry. Since the llinfo_arp structure is already allocated, the break causes the function to return.

Initialize llinfo_arp structure

147–158   An llinfo_arp structure is allocated and its pointer is stored in the rt_llinfo pointer of the routing table entry. The two statistics arp_inuse and arp_allocated are incremented and the llinfo_arp structure is set to 0. This sets la_hold to a null pointer and la_asked to 0.

159–161   The rt pointer is stored in the llinfo_arp structure and the RTF_LLINFO flag is set. In Figure 18.2 we see that the three routing table entries created by ARP, 140.252.13.33, 140.252.13.34, and 140.252.13.35, all have the L flag enabled, as does the entry for 224.0.0.1. Recall that the arp program looks only for entries with this flag (Figure 19.36). Finally the new structure is added to the front of the linked list of llinfo_arp structures by insque.

The ARP entry has been created: rtrequest creates the routing table entry (often cloning a network-specific entry for the Ethernet) and arp_rtrequest allocates and initializes an llinfo_arp structure. All that remains is for an ARP request to be broadcast so that an ARP reply can fill in the host's Ethernet address. In the common sequence of events, arp_rtrequest is called because arpresolve called arplookup (the intermediate sequence of function calls can be followed in Figure 21.3). When control returns to arpresolve, it broadcasts the ARP request.

—— *if_ether.c*

```
137    case RTM_RESOLVE:
138        if (gate->sa_family != AF_LINK ||
139            gate->sa_len < sizeof(null_sdl)) {
140            log(LOG_DEBUG, "arp_rtrequest: bad gateway value");
141            break;
142        }
143        SDL(gate)->sdl_type = rt->rt_ifp->if_type;
144        SDL(gate)->sdl_index = rt->rt_ifp->if_index;
145        if (la != 0)
146            break;                  /* This happens on a route change */
147        /*
148         * Case 2:  This route may come from cloning, or a manual route
149         * add with a LL address.
150         */
151        R_Malloc(la, struct llinfo_arp *, sizeof(*la));
152        rt->rt_llinfo = (caddr_t) la;
153        if (la == 0) {
154            log(LOG_DEBUG, "arp_rtrequest: malloc failed\n");
155            break;
156        }
157        arp_inuse++, arp_allocated++;
158        Bzero(la, sizeof(*la));

159        la->la_rt = rt;
160        rt->rt_flags |= RTF_LLINFO;
161        insque(la, &llinfo_arp);

162        if (SIN(rt_key(rt))->sin_addr.s_addr ==
163            (IA_SIN(rt->rt_ifa))->sin_addr.s_addr) {
164            /*
165             * This test used to be
166             *  if (loif.if_flags & IFF_UP)
167             * It allowed local traffic to be forced
168             * through the hardware by configuring the loopback down.
169             * However, it causes problems during network configuration
170             * for boards that can't receive packets they send.
171             * It is now necessary to clear "useloopback" and remove
172             * the route to force traffic out to the hardware.
173             */
174            rt->rt_expire = 0;
175            Bcopy(((struct arpcom *) rt->rt_ifp)->ac_enaddr,
176                  LLADDR(SDL(gate)), SDL(gate)->sdl_alen = 6);
177            if (useloopback)
178                rt->rt_ifp = &loif;

179        }
180        break;
```

—— *if_ether.c*

Figure 21.29 `arp_rtrequest` function: RTM_RESOLVE command.

Handle local host specially

162–173   This portion of code is a special test that is new with 4.4BSD (although the comment is left over from earlier releases). It creates the rightmost routing table entry in Figure 21.1 with a key consisting of the local host's IP address (140.252.13.35). The `if` test checks whether the routing table key equals the IP address of the interface. If so, the entry that was just created (probably as a clone of the interface entry) refers to the local host.

Make entry permanent and set Ethernet address

174–176   The expiration time is set to 0, making the entry permanent—it will never time out. The Ethernet address is copied from the `arpcom` structure of the interface into the `sockaddr_dl` structure pointed to by the `rt_gateway` member.

Set interface pointer to loopback interface

177–178   If the global `useloopback` is nonzero (it defaults to 1), the interface pointer in the routing table entry is changed to point to the loopback interface. This means that any datagrams sent to the host's own IP address are sent to the loopback interface instead. Prior to 4.4BSD, the route from the host's own IP address to the loopback interface was established using a command of the form

```
route add 140.252.13.35 127.0.0.1
```

in the `/etc/netstart` file. Although this still works with 4.4BSD, it is unnecessary because the code we just looked at creates an equivalent route automatically, the first time an IP datagram is sent to the host's own IP address. Also realize that this piece of code is executed only once per interface. Once the routing table entry and the permanent ARP entry are created, they don't expire, so another `RTM_RESOLVE` for this IP address won't occur.

The final part of `arp_rtrequest`, shown in Figure 21.30, handles the `RTM_DELETE` request. From Figure 21.3 we see that this command can be generated from the `arp` command, to delete an entry manually, and from the `arptfree` function, when an ARP entry times out.

―― *if_ether.c*
```
181     case RTM_DELETE:
182         if (la == 0)
183             break;
184         arp_inuse--;
185         remque(la);
186         rt->rt_llinfo = 0;
187         rt->rt_flags &= ~RTF_LLINFO;
188         if (la->la_hold)
189             m_freem(la->la_hold);
190         Free((caddr_t) la);
191     }
192 }
```
―― *if_ether.c*

Figure 21.30 `arp_rtrequest` function: `RTM_DELETE` command.

Verify `la` pointer

182–183   The `la` pointer should always be nonnull (that is, the routing table entry should always point to an `llinfo_arp` structure); otherwise the `break` causes the function to return.

Delete `llinfo_arp` structure

184–190   The `arp_inuse` statistic is decremented and the `llinfo_arp` structure is removed from the doubly linked list by `remque`. The `rt_llinfo` pointer is set to 0 and the `RTF_LLINFO` flag is cleared. If an mbuf is held by the ARP entry (i.e., an ARP request is outstanding), that mbuf is released. Finally the `llinfo_arp` structure is released.

Notice that the `switch` statement does not provide a `default` case and does not provide a `case` for the `RTM_GET` command. This is because the `RTM_GET` command issued by the `arp` program is handled entirely by the `route_output` function, and `rtrequest` is not called. Also, the call to `rtalloc1` that we show in Figure 21.3, which is caused by an `RTM_GET` command, specifies a second argument of 0; therefore `rtalloc1` does not call `rtrequest` in this case.

21.14 ARP and Multicasting

If an IP datagram is destined for a multicast group, `ip_output` checks whether the process has assigned a specific interface to the socket (Figure 12.40), and if so, the datagram is sent out that interface. Otherwise, `ip_output` selects the outgoing interface using the normal IP routing table (Figure 8.24). Therefore, on a system with more than one multicast-capable interface, the IP routing table specifies the default interface for each multicast group.

We saw in Figure 18.2 that an entry was created in our routing table for the 224.0.0.0 network and since that entry has its "clone" flag set, all multicast groups starting with 224 had the associated interface (`le0`) as its default. Additional routing table entries can be created for the other multicast groups (the ones beginning with 225–239), or specific entries can be created for particular multicast groups to assign an explicit default. For example, a routing table entry could be created for 224.0.1.1 (the network time protocol) with an interface that differs from the interface for 224.0.0.0. If an entry for a multicast group does not exist in the routing table, and the process doesn't specify an interface with the `IP_MULTICAST_IF` socket option, the default interface for the group becomes the interface associated with the "default" route in the table. In Figure 18.2 the entry for 224.0.0.0 isn't really needed, since both it and the default route use the interface `le0`.

Once the interface is selected, if the interface is an Ethernet, `arpresolve` is called to convert the multicast group address into its corresponding Ethernet address. In Figure 21.23 this was done by invoking the macro `ETHER_MAP_IP_MULTICAST`. Since this simple macro logically ORs the low-order 23 bits of the multicast group with a constant (Figure 12.6), an ARP request–reply is not required and the mapping does not need to go into the ARP cache. The macro is just invoked each time the conversion is required.

Multicast group addresses appear in the Net/3 ARP cache if the multicast group is cloned from another entry, as we saw in Figure 21.5. This is because these entries have the `RTF_LLINFO` flag set. These are not true ARP entries because they do not require an ARP request–reply, and they do not have an associated link-layer address, since the mapping is done when needed by the `ETHER_MAP_IP_MULTICAST` macro.

The timeout of the ARP entries for these multicast group addresses is different from normal ARP entries. When a routing table entry is created for a multicast group, such as the entry for 224.0.0.1 in Figure 18.2, `rtrequest` copies the `rt_metrics` structure from the entry being cloned (Figure 19.9). We mentioned with Figure 21.28 that the network entry has an `rmx_expire` value of the time the `RTM_ADD` command was executed, normally the time the system was initialized. The new entry for 224.0.0.1 has this same expiration time.

This means the ARP entry for a multicast group such as 224.0.0.1 expires the next time `arptimer` executes, because its expiration time is always in the past. The entry is created again the next time it is looked up in the routing table.

21.15 Summary

ARP provides the dynamic mapping between IP addresses and hardware addresses. This chapter has examined an implementation of ARP that maps IP addresses to Ethernet addresses.

The Net/3 implementation is a major change from previous BSD releases. The ARP information is now stored in various structures: the routing table, a data-link socket address structure, and an `llinfo_arp` structure. Figure 21.1 shows the relationships between all the structures.

Sending an ARP request is simple: the appropriate fields are filled in and the request is sent as a broadcast. Processing a received request is more complicated because each host receives *all* broadcast ARP requests. Besides responding to requests for one of the host's IP addresses, `in_arpinput` also checks that some other host isn't using the host's IP address. Since all ARP requests contain the sender's IP and hardware addresses, any host on the Ethernet can use this information to update an existing ARP entry for the sender.

ARP flooding can be a problem on a LAN and Net/3 is the first BSD release to handle this. A maximum of one ARP request per second is sent to any given destination, and after five consecutive requests without a reply, a 20-second pause occurs before another ARP request is sent to that destination.

Exercises

21.1   What assumption is made in the assignment of the local variable `ac` in Figure 21.17?

21.2   If we ping the broadcast address of the local Ethernet and then execute `arp -a`, we see that this causes the ARP cache to be filled with entries for almost every other host on the local Ethernet. Why?

21.3   Follow through the code and explain why the assignment of 6 to `sdl_alen` is required in Figure 21.19.

21.4 With the separate ARP table in Net/2, independent of the routing table, each time `arpresolve` was called, a search was made of the ARP table. Compare this to the Net/3 approach. Which is more efficient?

21.5 The ARP code in Net/2 explicitly set a timeout of 3 minutes for an incomplete entry in the ARP cache, that is, for an entry that is awaiting an ARP reply. We've never explicitly said how Net/3 handles this timeout. When does Net/3 time out an incomplete ARP entry?

21.6 What changes in the avoidance of ARP flooding when a Net/3 system is acting as a router and the packets that cause the flooding are from some other host?

21.7 What are the values of the four `rmx_expire` variables shown in Figure 21.1? Where in the code are the values set?

21.8 What change would be required to the code in this chapter to cause an ARP entry to be created for every host that broadcasts an ARP request?

21.9 To verify the example in Figure 21.25 the authors ran the `sock` program from Appendix C of Volume 1, writing a UDP datagram every 500 ms to a nonexistent host on the local Ethernet. (The `-p` option of the program was modified to allow millisecond waits.) But only 10 UDP datagrams were sent without an error, instead of the 11 shown in Figure 21.25, before the first `EHOSTDOWN` error was returned. Why?

21.10 Modify ARP to hold onto *all* packets for a destination, awaiting an ARP reply, instead of just the most recent one. What are the implications of this change? Should there be a limit, as there is for each interface's output queue? Are any changes required to the data structures?

22

Protocol Control Blocks

22.1 Introduction

Protocol control blocks (PCBs) are used at the protocol layer to hold the various pieces of information required for each UDP or TCP socket. The Internet protocols maintain *Internet protocol control blocks* and *TCP control blocks*. Since UDP is connectionless, everything it needs for an end point is found in the Internet PCB; there are no UDP control blocks.

The Internet PCB contains the information common to all UDP and TCP end points: foreign and local IP addresses, foreign and local port numbers, IP header prototype, IP options to use for this end point, and a pointer to the routing table entry for the destination of this end point. The TCP control block contains all of the state information that TCP maintains for each connection: sequence numbers in both directions, window sizes, retransmission timers, and the like.

In this chapter we describe the Internet PCBs used in Net/3, saving TCP's control blocks until we describe TCP in detail. We examine the numerous functions that operate on Internet PCBs, since we'll encounter them when we describe UDP and TCP. Most of the functions begin with the six characters in_pcb.

Figure 22.1 summarizes the protocol control blocks that we describe and their relationship to the file and socket structures. There are numerous points to consider in this figure.

- When a socket is created by either socket or accept, the socket layer creates a file structure and a socket structure. The file type is DTYPE_SOCKET and the socket type is SOCK_DGRAM for UDP end points or SOCK_STREAM for TCP end points.

713

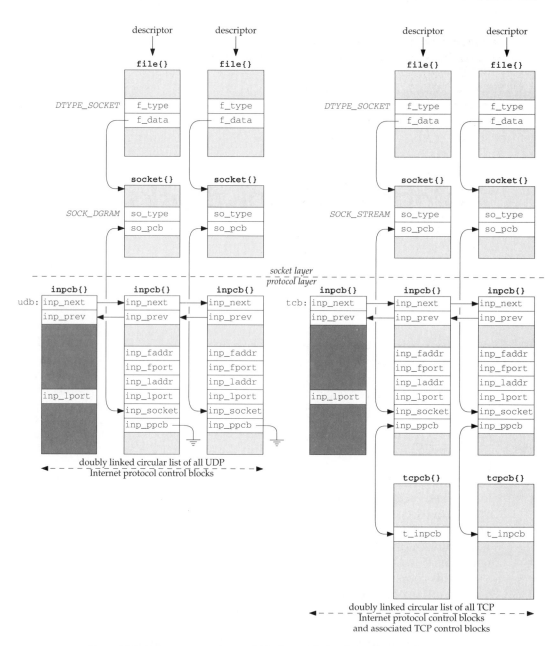

Figure 22.1   Internet protocol control blocks and their relationship to other structures.

- The protocol layer is then called. UDP creates an Internet PCB (an `inpcb` structure) and links it to the `socket` structure: the `so_pcb` member points to the `inpcb` structure and the `inp_socket` member points to the `socket` structure.

- TCP does the same and also creates its own control block (a `tcpcb` structure) and links it to the `inpcb` using the `inp_ppcb` and `t_inpcb` pointers. In the two UDP `inpcbs` the `inp_ppcb` member is a null pointer, since UDP does not maintain its own control block.

- The four other members of the `inpcb` structure that we show, `inp_faddr` through `inp_lport`, form the socket pair for this end point: the foreign IP address and port number along with the local IP address and port number.

- Both UDP and TCP maintain a doubly linked list of all their Internet PCBs, using the `inp_next` and `inp_prev` pointers. They allocate a global `inpcb` structure as the head of their list (named `udb` and `tcb`) and only use three members in the structure: the next and previous pointers, and the local port number. This latter member contains the next ephemeral port number to use for this protocol.

The Internet PCB is a transport layer data structure. It is used by TCP, UDP, and raw IP, but not by IP, ICMP, or IGMP.

We haven't described raw IP yet, but it too uses Internet PCBs. Unlike TCP and UDP, raw IP does not use the port number members in the PCB, and raw IP uses only two of the functions that we describe in this chapter: `in_pcballoc` to allocate a PCB, and `in_pcbdetach` to release a PCB. We return to raw IP in Chapter 32.

22.2 Code Introduction

All the PCB functions are in a single C file and a single header contains the definitions, as shown in Figure 22.2.

File	Description
`netinet/in_pcb.h`	`inpcb` structure definition
`netinet/in_pcb.c`	PCB functions

Figure 22.2 Files discussed in this chapter.

Global Variables

One global variable is introduced in this chapter, which is shown in Figure 22.3.

Variable	Datatype	Description
`zeroin_addr`	`struct in_addr`	32-bit IP address of all zero bits

Figure 22.3 Global variable introduced in this chapter.

Statistics

Internet PCBs and TCP PCBs are both allocated by the kernel's `malloc` function with a type of `M_PCB`. This is just one of the approximately 60 different types of memory allocated by the kernel. Mbufs, for example, are allocated with a type of M_BUF, and socket structures are allocated with a type of M_SOCKET.

Since the kernel can keep counters of the different types of memory buffers that are allocated, various statistics on the number of PCBs can be maintained. The command vmstat -m shows the kernel's memory allocation statistics and the netstat -m command shows the mbuf allocation statistics.

22.3   `inpcb` **Structure**

Figure 22.4 shows the definition of the inpcb structure. It is not a big structure, and occupies only 84 bytes.

```
                                                                  ── in_pcb.h
42 struct inpcb {
43     struct inpcb *inp_next, *inp_prev;   /* doubly linked list */
44     struct inpcb *inp_head;      /* pointer back to chain of inpcb's for
45                                     this protocol */
46     struct in_addr inp_faddr;    /* foreign IP address */
47     u_short inp_fport;           /* foreign port# */
48     struct in_addr inp_laddr;    /* local IP address */
49     u_short inp_lport;           /* local port# */
50     struct socket *inp_socket;   /* back pointer to socket */
51     caddr_t inp_ppcb;            /* pointer to per-protocol PCB */
52     struct route inp_route;      /* placeholder for routing entry */
53     int     inp_flags;           /* generic IP/datagram flags */
54     struct ip inp_ip;            /* header prototype; should have more */
55     struct mbuf *inp_options;    /* IP options */
56     struct ip_moptions *inp_moptions;   /* IP multicast options */
57 };
                                                                  ── in_pcb.h
```

Figure 22.4   inpcb structure.

43–45   inp_next and inp_prev form the doubly linked list of all PCBs for UDP and TCP. Additionally, each PCB has a pointer to the head of the protocol's linked list (inp_head). For PCBs on the UDP list, inp_head always points to udb (Figure 22.1); for PCBs on the TCP list, this pointer always points to tcb.

46–49   The next four members, inp_faddr, inp_fport, inp_laddr, and inp_lport, contain the socket pair for this IP end point: the foreign IP address and port number and the local IP address and port number. These four values are maintained in the PCB in network byte order, not host byte order.

> The Internet PCB is used by both transport layers, TCP and UDP. While it makes sense to store the local and foreign IP addresses in this structure, the port numbers really don't belong here. The definition of a port number and its size are specified by each transport layer and could differ between different transport layers. This problem was identified in [Partridge 1987], where 8-bit port numbers were used in version 1 of RDP, which required reimplementing several standard kernel routines to use 8-bit port numbers. Version 2 of RDP [Partridge and Hinden 1990] uses 16-bit port numbers. The port numbers really belong in a transport-specific control block, such as TCP's tcpcb. A new UDP-specific PCB would then be required. While doable, this would complicate some of the routines we'll examine shortly.

50–51   inp_socket is a pointer to the socket structure for this PCB and inp_ppcb is a pointer to an optional transport-specific control block for this PCB. We saw in Figure 22.1 that the inp_ppcb pointer is used with TCP to point to the corresponding tcpcb, but is not used by UDP. The link between the socket and inpcb is two way because sometimes the kernel starts at the socket layer and needs to find the corresponding Internet PCB (e.g., user output), and sometimes the kernel starts at the PCB and needs to locate the corresponding socket structure (e.g., processing a received IP datagram).

52   If IP has a route to the foreign address, it is stored in the inp_route entry. We'll see that when an ICMP redirect message is received, all Internet PCBs are scanned and all those with a foreign IP address that matches the redirected IP address have their inp_route entry marked as invalid. This forces IP to find a new route to the foreign address the next time the PCB is used for output.

53   Various flags are stored in the inp_flags member. Figure 22.5 lists the individual flags.

inp_flags	Description
INP_HDRINCL	process supplies entire IP header (raw socket only)
INP_RECVOPTS	receive incoming IP options as control information (UDP only, not implemented)
INP_RECVRETOPTS	receive IP options for reply as control information (UDP only, not implemented)
INP_RECVDSTADDR	receive IP destination address as control information (UDP only)
INP_CONTROLOPTS	INP_RECVOPTS | INP_RECVRETOPTS | INP_RECVDSTADDR

Figure 22.5 inp_flags values.

54   A copy of an IP header is maintained in the PCB but only two members are used, the TOS and TTL. The TOS is initialized to 0 (normal service) and the TTL is initialized by the transport layer. We'll see that TCP and UDP both default the TTL to 64. A process can change these defaults using the IP_TOS or IP_TTL socket options, and the new value is recorded in the inpcb.inp_ip structure. This structure is then used by TCP and UDP as the prototype IP header when sending IP datagrams.

55–56   A process can set the IP options for outgoing datagrams with the IP_OPTIONS socket option. A copy of the caller's options are stored in an mbuf by the function ip_pcbopts and a pointer to that mbuf is stored in the inp_options member. Each time TCP or UDP calls the ip_output function, a pointer to these IP options is passed for IP to insert into the outgoing IP datagram. Similarly, a pointer to a copy of the user's IP multicast options is maintained in the inp_moptions member.

22.4 in_pcballoc and in_pcbdetach Functions

An Internet PCB is allocated by TCP, UDP, and raw IP when a socket is created. A PRU_ATTACH request is issued by the socket system call. In the case of UDP, we'll see in Figure 23.33 that the resulting call is

```
       struct socket   *so;
       int  error;

       error = in_pcballoc(so, &udb);
```

Figure 22.6 shows the in_pcballoc function.

in_pcb.c

```
36 int
37 in_pcballoc(so, head)
38 struct socket *so;
39 struct inpcb *head;
40 {
41     struct inpcb *inp;

42     MALLOC(inp, struct inpcb *, sizeof(*inp), M_PCB, M_WAITOK);
43     if (inp == NULL)
44         return (ENOBUFS);
45     bzero((caddr_t) inp, sizeof(*inp));

46     inp->inp_head = head;
47     inp->inp_socket = so;
48     insque(inp, head);
49     so->so_pcb = (caddr_t) inp;
50     return (0);
51 }
```

in_pcb.c

Figure 22.6   in_pcballoc function: allocate an Internet PCB.

Allocate PCB and initialize to zero

36–45   in_pcballoc calls the kernel's memory allocator using the macro MALLOC. Since these PCBs are always allocated as the result of a system call, it is OK to wait for one.

> Net/2 and earlier Berkeley releases stored both Internet PCBs and TCP PCBs in mbufs. Their sizes were 80 and 108 bytes, respectively. With the Net/3 release, the sizes went to 84 and 140 bytes, so TCP control blocks no longer fit into an mbuf. Net/3 uses the kernel's memory allocator instead of mbufs for both types of control blocks.

> Careful readers may note that the example in Figure 2.6 shows 17 mbufs allocated for PCBs, yet we just said that Net/3 no longer uses mbufs for Internet PCBs or TCP PCBs. Net/3 does, however, use mbufs for Unix domain PCBs, and that is what this counter refers to. The mbuf statistics output by netstat are for all mbufs in the kernel across all protocol suites, not just the Internet protocols.

bzero sets the PCB to 0. This is important because the IP addresses and port numbers in the PCB must be initialized to 0.

Link structures together

46–49   The inp_head member points to the head of the protocol's PCB list (either udb or tcb), the inp_socket member points to the socket structure, the new PCB is added to the protocol's doubly linked list (insque), and the socket structure points to the PCB. The insque function puts the new PCB at the head of the protocol's list.

An Internet PCB is deallocated when a `PRU_DETACH` request is issued. This happens when the socket is closed. The function `in_pcbdetach`, shown in Figure 22.7, is eventually called.

```
                                                                  —— in_pcb.c
252 int
253 in_pcbdetach(inp)
254 struct inpcb *inp;
255 {
256     struct socket *so = inp->inp_socket;

257     so->so_pcb = 0;
258     sofree(so);
259     if (inp->inp_options)
260         (void) m_free(inp->inp_options);
261     if (inp->inp_route.ro_rt)
262         rtfree(inp->inp_route.ro_rt);
263     ip_freemoptions(inp->inp_moptions);
264     remque(inp);
265     FREE(inp, M_PCB);
266 }
                                                                  —— in_pcb.c
```

Figure 22.7 `in_pcbdetach` function: deallocate an Internet PCB.

252–263   The PCB pointer in the `socket` structure is set to 0 and that structure is released by `sofree`. If an mbuf with IP options was allocated for this PCB, it is released by `m_free`. If a route is held by this PCB, it is released by `rtfree`. Any multicast options are also released by `ip_freemoptions`.

264–265   The PCB is removed from the protocol's doubly linked list by `remque` and the memory used by the PCB is returned to the kernel.

22.5 Binding, Connecting, and Demultiplexing

Before examining the kernel functions that bind sockets, connect sockets, and demultiplex incoming datagrams, we describe the rules imposed by the kernel on these actions.

Binding of Local IP Address and Port Number

Figure 22.8 shows the six different combinations of a local IP address and local port number that a process can specify in a call to `bind`.

The first three lines are typical for servers—they bind a specific port, termed the server's *well-known port*, whose value is known by the client. The last three lines are typical for clients—they don't care what the local port, termed an *ephemeral port*, is, as long as it is unique on the client host.

Most servers and most clients specify the wildcard IP address in the call to `bind`. This is indicated in Figure 22.8 by the notation * on lines 3 and 6.

Local IP address	Local port	Description
unicast or broadcast	nonzero	one local interface, specific port
multicast	nonzero	one local multicast group, specific port
*	nonzero	any local interface or multicast group, specific port
unicast or broadcast	0	one local interface, kernel chooses port
multicast	0	one multicast group, kernel chooses port
*	0	any local interface, kernel chooses port

Figure 22.8   Combination of local IP address and local port number for `bind`.

If a server binds a specific IP address to a socket (i.e., not the wildcard address), then only IP datagrams arriving with that specific IP address as the destination IP address—be it unicast, broadcast, or multicast—are delivered to the process. Naturally, when the process binds a specific unicast or broadcast IP address to a socket, the kernel verifies that the IP address corresponds to a local interface.

It is rare, though possible, for a client to bind a specific IP address (lines 4 and 5 in Figure 22.8). Normally a client binds the wildcard IP address (the final line in Figure 22.8), which lets the kernel choose the outgoing interface based on the route chosen to reach the server.

What we don't show in Figure 22.8 is what happens if the client tries to bind a local port that is already in use with another socket. By default a process cannot bind a port number if that port is already in use. The error `EADDRINUSE` (address already in use) is returned if this occurs. The definition of *in use* is simply whether a PCB exists with that port as its local port. This notion of "in use" is relative to a given protocol: TCP or UDP, since TCP port numbers are independent of UDP port numbers.

Net/3 allows a process to change this default behavior by specifying one of following two socket options:

SO_REUSEADDR   Allows the process to bind a port number that is already in use, but the IP address being bound (including the wildcard) must not already be bound to that same port.

For example, if an attached interface has the IP address 140.252.1.29 then one socket can be bound to 140.252.1.29, port 5555; another socket can be bound to 127.0.0.1, port 5555; and another socket can be bound to the wildcard IP address, port 5555. The call to `bind` for the second and third cases must be preceded by a call to `setsockopt`, setting the SO_REUSEADDR option.

SO_REUSEPORT   Allows a process to reuse both the IP address and port number, but *each* binding of the IP address and port number, including the first, must specify this socket option. With SO_REUSEADDR, the first binding of the port number need not specify the socket option.

For example, if an attached interface has the IP address 140.252.1.29 and a socket is bound to 140.252.1.29, port 6666 specifying the

SO_REUSEPORT socket option, then another socket can also specify
this same socket option and bind 140.252.1.29, port 6666.

Later in this section we describe what happens in this final example when an IP datagram arrives with a destination address of 140.252.1.29 and a destination port of 6666,
since two sockets are bound to that end point.

> The SO_REUSEPORT option is new with Net/3 and was introduced with the support for multi-
> casting in 4.4BSD. Before this release it was never possible for two sockets to be bound to the
> same IP address and same port number.
>
> Unfortunately the SO_REUSEPORT option was not part of the original Stanford multicast
> sources and is therefore not widely supported. Other systems that support multicasting, such
> as Solaris 2.x, let a process specify SO_REUSEADDR to specify that it is OK to bind multiple
> sockets to the same IP address and same port number.

Connecting a UDP Socket

We normally associate the connect system call with TCP clients, but it is also possible
for a UDP client or a UDP server to call connect and specify the foreign IP address and
foreign port number for the socket. This restricts the socket to exchanging UDP datagrams with that one particular peer.
    There is a side effect when a UDP socket is connected: the local IP address, if not
already specified by a call to bind, is automatically set by connect. It is set to the local
interface address chosen by IP routing to reach the specified peer.
    Figure 22.9 shows the three different states of a UDP socket along with the pseudo-
code of the function calls to end up in that state.

Local socket	Foreign socket	Description
localIP.lport	*foreignIP.fport*	restricted to one peer: socket(), bind(*, *lport*), connect(*foreignIP, fport*) socket(), bind(*localIP, lport*), connect(*foreignIP, fport*)
localIP.lport	*.*	restricted to datagrams arriving on one local interface: *localIP* socket(), bind(*localIP, lport*)
.lport	*.*	receives all datagrams sent to *lport*: socket(), bind(*, *lport*)

Figure 22.9   Specification of local and foreign IP addresses and port numbers for UDP sockets.

The first of the three states is called a *connected UDP socket* and the next two states are
called *unconnected UDP sockets*. The difference between the two unconnected sockets is
that the first has a fully specified local address and the second has a wildcarded local IP
address.

Demultiplexing of Received IP Datagrams by TCP

Figure 22.10 shows the state of three Telnet server sockets on the host sun. The first two
sockets are in the LISTEN state, waiting for incoming connection requests, and the third

is connected to a client at port 1500 on the host with an IP address of 140.252.1.11. The first listening socket will handle connection requests that arrive on the 140.252.1.29 interface and the second listening socket will handle all other interfaces (since its local IP address is the wildcard).

Local address	Local port	Foreign address	Foreign port	TCP state
140.252.1.29	23	*	*	LISTEN
*	23	*	*	LISTEN
140.252.1.29	23	140.252.1.11	1500	ESTABLISHED

Figure 22.10   Three TCP sockets with a local port of 23.

We show both of the listening sockets with unspecified foreign IP addresses and port numbers because the sockets API doesn't allow a TCP server to restrict either of these values. A TCP server must `accept` the client's connection and is then told of the client's IP address and port number after the connection establishment is complete (i.e., when TCP's three-way handshake is complete). Only then can the server close the connection if it doesn't like the client's IP address and port number. This isn't a required TCP feature, it is just the way the sockets API has always worked.

When TCP receives a segment with a destination port of 23 it searches through its list of Internet PCBs looking for a match by calling `in_pcblookup`. When we examine this function shortly we'll see that it has a preference for the smallest number of *wildcard matches*. To determine the number of wildcard matches we consider only the local and foreign IP addresses. We do not consider the foreign port number. The local port number must match, or we don't even consider the PCB. The number of wildcard matches can be 0, 1 (local IP address or foreign IP address), or 2 (both local and foreign IP addresses).

For example, assume the incoming segment is from 140.252.1.11, port 1500, destined for 140.252.1.29, port 23. Figure 22.11 shows the number of wildcard matches for the three sockets from Figure 22.10.

Local address	Local port	Foreign address	Foreign port	TCP state	#wildcard matches
140.252.1.29	23	*	*	LISTEN	1
*	23	*	*	LISTEN	2
140.252.1.29	23	140.252.1.11	1500	ESTABLISHED	0

Figure 22.11   Incoming segment from {140.252.1.11, 1500} to {140.252.1.29, 23}.

The first socket matches these four values, but with one wildcard match (the foreign IP address). The second socket also matches the incoming segment, but with two wildcard matches (the local and foreign IP addresses). The third socket is a complete match with no wildcards. Net/3 uses the third socket, the one with the smallest number of wildcard matches.

Continuing this example, assume the incoming segment is from 140.252.1.11, port 1501, destined for 140.252.1.29, port 23. Figure 22.12 shows the number of wildcard matches.

Local address	Local port	Foreign address	Foreign port	TCP state	#wildcard matches
140.252.1.29	23	*	*	LISTEN	1
*	23	*	*	LISTEN	2
140.252.1.29	23	140.252.1.11	1500	ESTABLISHED	

Figure 22.12   Incoming segment from {140.252.1.11, 1501} to {140.252.1.29, 23}.

The first socket matches with one wildcard match; the second socket matches with two wildcard matches; and the third socket doesn't match at all, since the foreign port numbers are unequal. (The foreign port numbers are compared only if the foreign IP address in the PCB is not a wildcard.) The first socket is chosen.

In these two examples we never said what type of TCP segment arrived: we assume that the segment in Figure 22.11 contains data or an acknowledgment for an established connection since it is delivered to an established socket. We also assume that the segment in Figure 22.12 is an incoming connection request (a SYN) since it is delivered to a listening socket. But the demultiplexing code in `in_pcblookup` doesn't care. If the TCP segment is the wrong type for the socket that it is delivered to, we'll see later how TCP handles this. For now the important fact is that the demultiplexing code only compares the source and destination socket pair from the IP datagram against the values in the PCB.

Demultiplexing of Received IP Datagrams by UDP

The delivery of UDP datagrams is more complicated than the TCP example we just examined, since UDP datagrams can be sent to a broadcast or multicast address. Since Net/3 (and most systems with multicast support) allow multiple sockets to have identical local IP addresses and ports, how are multiple recipients handled? The Net/3 rules are:

1. An incoming UDP datagram destined for either a broadcast IP address or a multicast IP address is delivered to *all* matching sockets. There is no concept of a "best" match here (i.e., the one with the smallest number of wildcard matches).

2. An incoming UDP datagram destined for a unicast IP address is delivered only to *one* matching socket, the one with the smallest number of wildcard matches. If there are multiple sockets with the same "smallest" number of wildcard matches, which socket receives the incoming datagram is implementation-dependent.

Figure 22.13 shows four UDP sockets that we'll use for some examples. Having four UDP sockets with the same local port number requires using either SO_REUSEADDR or SO_REUSEPORT. The first two sockets have been connected to a foreign IP address and port number, and the last two are unconnected.

Local address	Local port	Foreign address	Foreign port	Comment
140.252.1.29	577	140.252.1.11	1500	connected, local IP = unicast
140.252.13.63	577	140.252.13.35	1500	connected, local IP = broadcast
140.252.13.63	577	*	*	unconnected, local IP = broadcast
*	577	*	*	unconnected, local IP = wildcard

Figure 22.13   Four UDP sockets with a local port of 577.

Consider an incoming UDP datagram destined for 140.252.13.63 (the broadcast address on the 140.252.13 subnet), port 577, from 140.252.13.34, port 1500. Figure 22.14 shows that it is delivered to the third and fourth sockets.

Local address	Local port	Foreign address	Foreign port	Delivered?
140.252.1.29	577	140.252.1.11	1500	no, local and foreign IP mismatch
140.252.13.63	577	140.252.13.35	1500	no, foreign IP mismatch
140.252.13.63	577	*	*	yes
*	577	*	*	yes

Figure 22.14   Received datagram from {140.252.13.34, 1500} to {140.252.13.63, 577}.

The broadcast datagram is not delivered to the first socket because the local IP address doesn't match the destination IP address and the foreign IP address doesn't match the source IP address. It isn't delivered to the second socket because the foreign IP address doesn't match the source IP address.

As the next example, consider an incoming UDP datagram destined for 140.252.1.29 (a unicast address), port 577, from 140.252.1.11, port 1500. Figure 22.15 shows to which sockets the datagram is delivered.

Local address	Local port	Foreign address	Foreign port	Delivered?
140.252.1.29	577	140.252.1.11	1500	yes, 0 wildcard matches
140.252.13.63	577	140.252.13.35	1500	no, local and foreign IP mismatch
140.252.13.63	577	*	*	no, local IP mismatch
*	577	*	*	no, 2 wildcard matches

Figure 22.15   Received datagram from {140.252.1.11, 1500} to {140.252.1.29, 577}.

The datagram matches the first socket with no wildcard matches and also matches the fourth socket with two wildcard matches. It is delivered to the first socket, the best match.

22.6 `in_pcblookup` Function

The function `in_pcblookup` serves four different purposes.

1. When either TCP or UDP receives an IP datagram, `in_pcblookup` scans the protocol's list of Internet PCBs looking for a matching PCB to receive the

datagram. This is transport layer demultiplexing of a received datagram.

2. When a process executes the `bind` system call, to assign a local IP address and local port number to a socket, in_pcbbind is called by the protocol to verify that the requested local address pair is not already in use.

3. When a process executes the `bind` system call, requesting an ephemeral port be assigned to its socket, the kernel picks an ephemeral port and calls in_pcbbind to check if the port is in use. If it is in use, the next ephemeral port number is tried, and so on, until an unused port is located.

4. When a process executes the `connect` system call, either explicitly or implicitly, in_pcbbind verifies that the requested socket pair is unique. (An implicit call to `connect` happens when a UDP datagram is sent on an unconnected socket. We'll see this scenario in Chapter 23.)

In cases 2, 3, and 4 in_pcbbind calls in_pcblookup. Two options confuse the logic of the function. First, a process can specify either the SO_REUSEADDR or SO_REUSEPORT socket option to say that a duplicate local address is OK.

Second, sometimes a wildcard match is OK (e.g., an incoming UDP datagram can match a PCB that has a wildcard for its local IP address, meaning that the socket will accept UDP datagrams that arrive on any local interface), while other times a wildcard match is forbidden (e.g., when connecting to a foreign IP address and port number).

> In the original Stanford IP multicast code appears the comment that "The logic of in_pcblookup is rather opaque and there is not a single comment, . . ." The adjective *opaque* is an understatement.
>
> The publicly available IP multicast code available for BSD/386, which is derived from the port to 4.4BSD done by Craig Leres, fixed the overloaded semantics of this function by using in_pcblookup only for case 1 above. Cases 2 and 4 are handled by a new function named in_pcbconflict, and case 3 is handled by a new function named in_uniqueport. Dividing the original functionality into separate functions is much clearer, but in the Net/3 release, which we're describing in this text, the logic is still combined into the single function in_pcblookup.

Figure 22.16 shows the in_pcblookup function.

The function starts at the head of the protocol's PCB list and potentially goes through every PCB on the list. The variable `match` remembers the pointer to the entry with the best match so far, and `matchwild` remembers the number of wildcards in that match. The latter is initialized to 3, which is a value greater than the maximum number of wildcard matches that can be encountered. (Any value greater than 2 would work.) Each time around the loop, the variable `wildcard` starts at 0 and counts the number of wildcard matches for each PCB.

Compare local port number

416–417   The first comparison is the local port number. If the PCB's local port doesn't match the `lport` argument, the PCB is ignored.

in_pcb.c

```
405 struct inpcb *
406 in_pcblookup(head, faddr, fport_arg, laddr, lport_arg, flags)
407 struct inpcb *head;
408 struct in_addr faddr, laddr;
409 u_int    fport_arg, lport_arg;
410 int      flags;
411 {
412     struct inpcb *inp, *match = 0;
413     int     matchwild = 3, wildcard;
414     u_short fport = fport_arg, lport = lport_arg;

415     for (inp = head->inp_next; inp != head; inp = inp->inp_next) {
416         if (inp->inp_lport != lport)
417             continue;              /* ignore if local ports are unequal */

418         wildcard = 0;

419         if (inp->inp_laddr.s_addr != INADDR_ANY) {
420             if (laddr.s_addr == INADDR_ANY)
421                 wildcard++;
422             else if (inp->inp_laddr.s_addr != laddr.s_addr)
423                 continue;
424         } else {
425             if (laddr.s_addr != INADDR_ANY)
426                 wildcard++;
427         }

428         if (inp->inp_faddr.s_addr != INADDR_ANY) {
429             if (faddr.s_addr == INADDR_ANY)
430                 wildcard++;
431             else if (inp->inp_faddr.s_addr != faddr.s_addr ||
432                     inp->inp_fport != fport)
433                 continue;
434         } else {
435             if (faddr.s_addr != INADDR_ANY)
436                 wildcard++;
437         }

438         if (wildcard && (flags & INPLOOKUP_WILDCARD) == 0)
439             continue;              /* wildcard match not allowed */

440         if (wildcard < matchwild) {
441             match = inp;
442             matchwild = wildcard;
443             if (matchwild == 0)
444                 break;             /* exact match, all done */
445         }
446     }
447     return (match);
448 }
```

in_pcb.c

Figure 22.16   in_pcblookup function: search all the PCBs for a match.

Compare local address

419–427   in_pcblookup compares the local address in the PCB with the laddr argument. If one is a wildcard and the other is not a wildcard, the wildcard counter is incremented. If both are not wildcards, then they must be the same, or this PCB is ignored. If both are wildcards, nothing changes: they can't be compared and the wildcard counter isn't incremented. Figure 22.17 summarizes the four different conditions.

PCB local IP	laddr argument	Description
not *	*	wildcard++
not *	not *	compare IP addresses, skip PCB if not equal
*	*	can't compare
*	not *	wildcard++

Figure 22.17   Four scenarios for the local IP address comparison done by in_pcblookup.

Compare foreign address and foreign port number

428–437   These lines perform the same test that we just described, but using the foreign addresses instead of the local addresses. Also, if both foreign addresses are not wildcards then not only must the two IP addresses be equal, but the two foreign ports must also be equal. Figure 22.18 summarizes the foreign IP comparisons.

PCB foreign IP	faddr argument	Description
not *	*	wildcard++
not *	not *	compare IP addresses and ports, skip PCB if not equal
*	*	can't compare
*	not *	wildcard++

Figure 22.18   Four scenarios for the foreign IP address comparison done by in_pcblookup.

The additional comparison of the foreign port numbers can be performed for the second line of Figure 22.18 because it is not possible to have a PCB with a nonwildcard foreign address and a foreign port number of 0. This restriction is enforced by connect, which we'll see shortly requires a nonwildcard foreign IP address and a nonzero foreign port. It is possible, however, and common, to have a wildcard local address with a nonzero local port. We saw this in Figures 22.10 and 22.13.

Check if wildcard match allowed

438–439   The flags argument can be set to INPLOOKUP_WILDCARD, which means a match containing wildcards is OK. If a match is found containing wildcards (wildcard is nonzero) and this flag was not specified by the caller, this PCB is ignored. When TCP and UDP call this function to demultiplex an incoming datagram, INPLOOKUP_WILDCARD is always set, since a wildcard match is OK. (Recall our examples using Figures 22.10 and 22.13.) But when this function is called as part of the connect system call, in order to verify that a socket pair is not already in use, the flags argument is set to 0.

Remember best match, return if exact match found

440–447   These statements remember the best match found so far. Again, the best match is considered the one with the fewest number of wildcard matches. If a match is found with one or two wildcards, that match is remembered and the loop continues. But if an exact match is found (`wildcard` is 0), the loop terminates, and a pointer to the PCB with that exact match is returned.

Example—Demultiplexing of Received TCP Segment

Figure 22.19 is from the TCP example we discussed with Figure 22.11. Assume `in_pcblookup` is demultiplexing a received datagram from 140.252.1.11, port 1500, destined for 140.252.1.29, port 23. Also assume that the order of the PCBs is the order of the rows in the figure. `laddr` is the destination IP address, `lport` is the destination TCP port, `faddr` is the source IP address, and `fport` is the source TCP port.

PCB values				wildcard
Local address	Local port	Foreign address	Foreign port	
140.252.1.29	23	*	*	1
*	23	*	*	2
140.252.1.29	23	140.252.1.11	1500	0

Figure 22.19   `laddr` = 140.252.1.29, `lport` = 23, `faddr` = 140.252.1.11, `fport` = 1500.

When the first row is compared to the incoming segment, `wildcard` is 1 (the foreign IP address), `flags` is set to `INPLOOKUP_WILDCARD`, so `match` is set to point to this PCB and `matchwild` is set to 1. The loop continues since an exact match has not been found yet. The next time around the loop, `wildcard` is 2 (the local and foreign IP addresses) and since this is greater than `matchwild`, the entry is not remembered, and the loop continues. The next time around the loop, `wildcard` is 0, which is less than `matchwild` (1), so this entry is remembered in `match`. The loop also terminates since an exact match has been found and the pointer to this PCB is returned to the caller.

If `in_pcblookup` were used by TCP and UDP only to demultiplex incoming datagrams, it could be simplified. First, there's no need to check whether the `faddr` or `laddr` arguments are wildcards, since these are the source and destination IP addresses from the received datagram. Also the `flags` argument could be removed, along with its corresponding test, since wildcard matches are always OK.

This section has covered the mechanics of the `in_pcblookup` function. We'll return to this function and discuss its meaning after seeing how it is called from the `in_pcbbind` and `in_pcbconnect` functions.

22.7   `in_pcbbind` Function

The next function, `in_pcbbind`, binds a local address and port number to a socket. It is called from five functions:

1. from `bind` for a TCP socket (normally to bind a server's well-known port);

2. from `bind` for a UDP socket (either to bind a server's well-known port or to bind an ephemeral port to a client's socket);

3. from `connect` for a TCP socket, if the socket has not yet been bound to a nonzero port (this is typical for TCP clients);

4. from `listen` for a TCP socket, if the socket has not yet been bound to a nonzero port (this is rare, since `listen` is called by a TCP server, which normally binds a well-known port, not an ephemeral port); and

5. from `in_pcbconnect` (Section 22.8), if the local IP address and local port number have not been set (typical for a call to `connect` for a UDP socket or for each call to `sendto` for an unconnected UDP socket).

In cases 3, 4, and 5, an ephemeral port number is bound to the socket and the local IP address is not changed (in case it is already set).

We call cases 1 and 2 *explicit binds* and cases 3, 4, and 5 *implicit binds*. We also note that although it is normal in case 2 for a server to bind a well-known port, servers invoked using remote procedure calls (RPC) often bind ephemeral ports and then register their ephemeral port with another program that maintains a mapping between the server's RPC program number and its ephemeral port (e.g., the Sun port mapper described in Section 29.4 of Volume 1).

We'll show the `in_pcbbind` function in three sections. Figure 22.20 is the first section.

```
52 int                                                                          ─── in_pcb.c
53 in_pcbbind(inp, nam)
54 struct inpcb *inp;
55 struct mbuf *nam;
56 {
57     struct socket *so = inp->inp_socket;
58     struct inpcb *head = inp->inp_head;
59     struct sockaddr_in *sin;
60     struct proc *p = curproc;    /* XXX */
61     u_short lport = 0;
62     int     wild = 0, reuseport = (so->so_options & SO_REUSEPORT);
63     int     error;

64     if (in_ifaddr == 0)
65         return (EADDRNOTAVAIL);
66     if (inp->inp_lport || inp->inp_laddr.s_addr != INADDR_ANY)
67         return (EINVAL);

68     if ((so->so_options & (SO_REUSEADDR | SO_REUSEPORT)) == 0 &&
69         ((so->so_proto->pr_flags & PR_CONNREQUIRED) == 0 ||
70         (so->so_options & SO_ACCEPTCONN) == 0))
71         wild = INPLOOKUP_WILDCARD;
```
                                                                                ─── in_pcb.c

Figure 22.20 `in_pcbbind` function: bind a local address and port number.

64–67   The first two tests verify that at least one interface has been assigned an IP address and that the socket is not already bound. You can't bind a socket twice.

68–71   This `if` statement is confusing. The net result sets the variable `wild` to `INPLOOKUP_WILDCARD` if neither `SO_REUSEADDR` or `SO_REUSEPORT` are set.

The second test is true for UDP sockets since `PR_CONNREQUIRED` is false for connectionless sockets and true for connection-oriented sockets.

The third test is where the confusion lies [Torek 1992]. The socket flag `SO_ACCEPTCONN` is set only by the `listen` system call (Section 15.9), which is valid only for a connection-oriented server. In the normal scenario, a TCP server calls `socket`, `bind`, and then `listen`. Therefore, when `in_pcbbind` is called by `bind`, this socket flag is cleared. Even if the process calls `socket` and then `listen`, without calling `bind`, TCP's `PRU_LISTEN` request calls `in_pcbbind` to assign an ephemeral port to the socket *before* the socket layer sets the `SO_ACCEPTCONN` flag. This means the third test in the `if` statement, testing whether `SO_ACCEPTCONN` is not set, is always true. The `if` statement is therefore equivalent to

```
if ((so->so_options & (SO_REUSEADDR|SO_REUSEPORT)) == 0 &&
    ((so->so_proto->pr_flags & PR_CONNREQUIRED) == 0 || 1)
        wild = INPLOOKUP_WILDCARD;
```

Since anything logically ORed with 1 is always true, this is equivalent to

```
if ((so->so_options & (SO_REUSEADDR|SO_REUSEPORT)) == 0)
        wild = INPLOOKUP_WILDCARD;
```

which is simpler to understand: if either of the REUSE socket options is set, `wild` is left as 0. If neither of the REUSE socket options are set, `wild` is set to `INPLOOKUP_WILDCARD`. In other words, when `in_pcblookup` is called later in the function, a wildcard match is allowed only if *neither* of the REUSE socket options are on.

The next section of the `in_pcbbind`, shown in Figure 22.22, function processes the optional `nam` argument.

72–75   The `nam` argument is a nonnull pointer only when the process calls `bind` explicitly. For an implicit bind (a side effect of `connect`, `listen`, or `in_pcbconnect`, cases 3, 4, and 5 from the beginning of this section), `nam` is a null pointer. When the argument is specified, it is an mbuf containing a `sockaddr_in` structure. Figure 22.21 shows the four cases for the nonnull `nam` argument.

nam argument:		PCB member gets set to:		Comment
localIP	*lport*	inp_laddr	inp_lport	
not *	0	*localIP*	ephemeral port	*localIP* must be local interface
not *	nonzero	*localIP*	*lport*	subject to in_pcblookup
*	0	*	ephemeral port	
*	nonzero	*	*lport*	subject to in_pcblookup

Figure 22.21   Four cases for nam argument to `in_pcbbind`.

76–83   The test for the correct address family is commented out, yet the identical test in the `in_pcbconnect` function (Figure 22.25) is performed. We expect either both to be in or both to be out.

--- *in_pcb.c*

```
 72     if (nam) {
 73         sin = mtod(nam, struct sockaddr_in *);
 74         if (nam->m_len != sizeof(*sin))
 75             return (EINVAL);
 76 #ifdef notdef
 77         /*
 78          * We should check the family, but old programs
 79          * incorrectly fail to initialize it.
 80          */
 81         if (sin->sin_family != AF_INET)
 82             return (EAFNOSUPPORT);
 83 #endif
 84         lport = sin->sin_port;    /* might be 0 */
 85         if (IN_MULTICAST(ntohl(sin->sin_addr.s_addr))) {
 86             /*
 87              * Treat SO_REUSEADDR as SO_REUSEPORT for multicast;
 88              * allow complete duplication of binding if
 89              * SO_REUSEPORT is set, or if SO_REUSEADDR is set
 90              * and a multicast address is bound on both
 91              * new and duplicated sockets.
 92              */
 93             if (so->so_options & SO_REUSEADDR)
 94                 reuseport = SO_REUSEADDR | SO_REUSEPORT;
 95         } else if (sin->sin_addr.s_addr != INADDR_ANY) {
 96             sin->sin_port = 0;    /* yech... */
 97             if (ifa_ifwithaddr((struct sockaddr *) sin) == 0)
 98                 return (EADDRNOTAVAIL);
 99         }
100         if (lport) {
101             struct inpcb *t;
102             /* GROSS */
103             if (ntohs(lport) < IPPORT_RESERVED &&
104                 (error = suser(p->p_ucred, &p->p_acflag)))
105                 return (error);
106             t = in_pcblookup(head, zeroin_addr, 0,
107                              sin->sin_addr, lport, wild);
108             if (t && (reuseport & t->inp_socket->so_options) == 0)
109                 return (EADDRINUSE);
110         }
111         inp->inp_laddr = sin->sin_addr;      /* might be wildcard */
112     }
```
--- *in_pcb.c*

Figure 22.22   in_pcbbind function: process optional nam argument.

85–94   Net/3 tests whether the IP address being bound is a multicast group. If so, the
SO_REUSEADDR option is considered identical to SO_REUSEPORT.

95–99   Otherwise, if the local address being bound by the caller is not the wildcard,
ifa_ifwithaddr verifies that the address corresponds to a local interface.

> The comment "yech" is probably because the port number in the socket address structure
> must be 0 because ifa_ifwithaddr does a binary comparison of the entire structure, not just
> a comparison of the IP addresses.

This is one of the few instances where the process *must* zero the socket address structure before issuing the system call. If `bind` is called and the final 8 bytes of the socket address structure (`sin_zero[8]`) are nonzero, `ifa_ifwithaddr` will not find the requested interface, and `in_pcbbind` will return an error.

100–105   The next `if` statement is executed when the caller is binding a nonzero port, that is, the process wants to bind one particular port number (the second and fourth scenarios from Figure 22.21). If the requested port is less than 1024 (`IPPORT_RESERVED`) the process must have superuser privilege. This is not part of the Internet protocols, but a Berkeley convention. A port number less than 1024 is called a *reserved port* and is used, for example, by the `rcmd` function [Stevens 1990], which in turn is used by the `rlogin` and `rsh` client programs as part of their authentication with their servers.

106–109   The function `in_pcblookup` (Figure 22.16) is then called to check whether a PCB already exists with the same local IP address and local port number. The second argument is the wildcard IP address (the foreign IP address) and the third argument is a port number of 0 (the foreign port). The wildcard value for the second argument causes `in_pcblookup` to ignore the foreign IP address and foreign port in the PCB—only the local IP address and local port are compared to `sin->sin_addr` and `lport`, respectively. We mentioned earlier that `wild` is set to `INPLOOKUP_WILDCARD` only if neither of the `REUSE` socket options are set.

111   The caller's value for the local IP address is stored in the PCB. This can be the wildcard address, if that's the value specified by the caller. In this case the local IP address is chosen by the kernel, but not until the socket is connected at some later time. This is because the local IP address is determined by IP routing, based on foreign IP address.

The final section of `in_pcbbind` handles the assignment of an ephemeral port when the caller explicitly binds a port of 0, or when the `nam` argument is a null pointer (an implicit bind).

```
                                                                         in_pcb.c
113      if (lport == 0)
114          do {
115              if (head->inp_lport++ < IPPORT_RESERVED ||
116                  head->inp_lport > IPPORT_USERRESERVED)
117                  head->inp_lport = IPPORT_RESERVED;
118              lport = htons(head->inp_lport);
119          } while (in_pcblookup(head,
120                                zeroin_addr, 0, inp->inp_laddr, lport, wild));
121      inp->inp_lport = lport;
122      return (0);
123 }
                                                                         in_pcb.c
```

Figure 22.23   `in_pcbbind` function: choose an ephemeral port.

113–122   The next ephemeral port number to use for this protocol (TCP or UDP) is maintained in the `head` of the protocol's PCB list: `tcb` or `udb`. Other than the `inp_next` and `inp_back` pointers in the protocol's `head` PCB, the only other element of the `inpcb` structure that is used is the local port number. Confusingly, this local port number is maintained in host byte order in the `head` PCB, but in network byte order in all the other PCBs on the list! The ephemeral port numbers start at 1024

(IPPORT_RESERVED) and get incremented by 1 until port 5000 is used
(IPPORT_USERRESERVED), then cycle back to 1024. The loop is executed until
in_pcbbind does not find a match.

SO_REUSEADDR Examples

Let's look at some common examples to see the interaction of in_pcbbind with
in_pcblookup and the two REUSE socket options.

1. A TCP or UDP server normally starts by calling socket and bind. Assume a TCP
    server that calls bind, specifying the wildcard IP address and its nonzero well-
    known port, say 23 (the Telnet server). Also assume that the server is not already
    running and that the process does not set the SO_REUSEADDR socket option.

    in_pcbbind calls in_pcblookup with INPLOOKUP_WILDCARD as the final argu-
    ment. The loop in in_pcblookup won't find a matching PCB, assuming no other
    process is using the server's well-known TCP port, causing a null pointer to be
    returned. This is OK and in_pcbbind returns 0.

2. Assume the same scenario as above, but with the server already running when
    someone tries to start the server a second time.

    When in_pcblookup is called it finds the PCB with a local socket of {*, 23}. Since
    the wildcard counter is 0, in_pcblookup returns the pointer to this entry. Since
    reuseport is 0, in_pcbbind returns EADDRINUSE.

3. Assume the same scenario as the previous example, but when the attempt is made
    to start the server a second time, the SO_REUSEADDR socket option is specified.

    Since this socket option is specified, in_pcbbind calls in_pcblookup with a final
    argument of 0. But the PCB with a local socket of {*, 23} is still matched and
    returned because wildcard is 0, since in_pcblookup cannot compare the two
    wildcard addresses (Figure 22.17). in_pcbbind again returns EADDRINUSE, pre-
    venting us from starting two instances of the server with identical local sockets,
    regardless of whether we specify SO_REUSEADDR or not.

4. Assume that a Telnet server is already running with a local socket of {*, 23} and we
    try to start another with a local socket of {140.252.13.35, 23}.

    Assuming SO_REUSEADDR is not specified, in_pcblookup is called with a final
    argument of INPLOOKUP_WILDCARD. When it compares the PCB containing *.23,
    the counter wildcard is set to 1. Since a wildcard match is allowed, this match is
    remembered as the best match and a pointer to it is returned after all the TCP PCBs
    are scanned. in_pcbbind returns EADDRINUSE.

5. This example is the same as the previous one, but we specify the SO_REUSEADDR
    socket option for the second server that tries to bind the local socket {140.252.13.35,
    23}.

    The final argument to in_pcblookup is now 0, since the socket option is specified.
    When the PCB with the local socket {*, 23} is compared, the wildcard counter is 1,

but since the final `flags` argument is 0, this entry is skipped and is not remembered as a match. After comparing all the TCP PCBs, the function returns a null pointer and `in_pcbbind` returns 0.

6. Assume the first Telnet server is started with a local socket of {140.252.13.35, 23} when we try to start a second server with a local socket of {*, 23}. This is the same as the previous example, except we're starting the servers in reverse order this time.

    The first server is started without a problem, assuming no other socket has already bound port 23. When we start the second server, the final argument to `in_pcblookup` is `INPLOOKUP_WILDCARD`, assuming the `SO_REUSEADDR` socket option is not specified. When the PCB with the local socket of {140.252.13.35, 23} is compared, the `wildcard` counter is set to 1 and this entry is remembered. After all the TCP PCBs are compared, the pointer to this entry is returned, causing `in_pcbbind` to return `EADDRINUSE`.

7. What if we start two instances of a server, both with a nonwildcard local IP address? Assume we start the first Telnet server with a local socket of {140.252.13.35, 23} and then try to start a second with a local socket of {127.0.0.1, 23}, without specifying `SO_REUSEADDR`.

    When the second server calls `in_pcbbind`, it calls `in_pcblookup` with a final argument of `INPLOOKUP_WILDCARD`. When the PCB with the local socket of {140.252.13.35, 23} is compared, it is skipped because the local IP addresses are not equal. `in_pcblookup` returns a null pointer, and `in_pcbbind` returns 0.

    From this example we see that the `SO_REUSEADDR` socket option has no effect on nonwildcard IP addresses. Indeed the test on the flags value `INPLOOKUP_WILDCARD` in `in_pcblookup` is made only when `wildcard` is greater than 0, that is, when either the PCB entry has a wildcard IP address or the IP address being bound is the wildcard.

8. As a final example, assume we try to start two instances of the same server, both with the same nonwildcard local IP address, say 127.0.0.1.

    When the second server is started, `in_pcblookup` always returns a pointer to the matching PCB with the same local socket. This happens regardless of the `SO_REUSEADDR` socket option, because the `wildcard` counter is always 0 for this comparison. Since `in_pcblookup` returns a nonnull pointer, `in_pcbbind` returns `EADDRINUSE`.

From these examples we can state the rules about the binding of local IP addresses and the `SO_REUSEADDR` socket option. These rules are shown in Figure 22.24. We assume that *localIP1* and *localIP2* are two different unicast or broadcast IP addresses valid on the local host, and that *localmcastIP* is a multicast group. We also assume that the process is trying to bind the same nonzero port number that is already bound to the existing PCB.

We need to differentiate between a unicast or broadcast address and a multicast address, because we saw that `in_pcbbind` considers `SO_REUSEADDR` to be the same as `SO_REUSEPORT` for a multicast address.

Existing PCB	Try to bind	SO_REUSEADDR off	SO_REUSEADDR on	Description
localIP1	localIP1	error	error	one server per IP address and port
localIP1	localIP2	OK	OK	one server for each local interface
localIP1	*	error	OK	one server for one interface, other server for remaining interfaces
*	localIP1	error	OK	one server for one interface, other server for remaining interfaces
*	*	error	error	can't duplicate local sockets (same as first example)
localmcastIP	localmcastIP	error	OK	multiple multicast recipients

Figure 22.24 Effect of SO_REUSEADDR socket option on binding of local IP address.

SO_REUSEPORT Socket Option

The handling of SO_REUSEPORT in Net/3 changes the logic of in_pcbbind to allow duplicate local sockets as long as both sockets specify SO_REUSEPORT. In other words, all the servers must agree to share the same local port.

22.8 in_pcbconnect Function

The function in_pcbconnect specifies the foreign IP address and foreign port number for a socket. It is called from four functions:

1. from connect for a TCP socket (required for a TCP client);

2. from connect for a UDP socket (optional for a UDP client, rare for a UDP server);

3. from sendto when a datagram is output on an unconnected UDP socket (common); and

4. from tcp_input when a connection request (a SYN segment) arrives on a TCP socket that is in the LISTEN state (standard for a TCP server).

In all four cases it is common, though not required, for the local IP address and local port be unspecified when in_pcbconnect is called. Therefore one function of in_pcbconnect is to assign the local values when they are unspecified.

We'll discuss the in_pcbconnect function in four sections. Figure 22.25 shows the first section.

―― in_pcb.c
```
130 int
131 in_pcbconnect(inp, nam)
132 struct inpcb *inp;
133 struct mbuf *nam;
134 {
135     struct in_ifaddr *ia;
136     struct sockaddr_in *ifaddr;
137     struct sockaddr_in *sin = mtod(nam, struct sockaddr_in *);
```

```
138        if (nam->m_len != sizeof(*sin))
139            return (EINVAL);
140        if (sin->sin_family != AF_INET)
141            return (EAFNOSUPPORT);
142        if (sin->sin_port == 0)
143            return (EADDRNOTAVAIL);
144        if (in_ifaddr) {
145            /*
146             * If the destination address is INADDR_ANY,
147             * use the primary local address.
148             * If the supplied address is INADDR_BROADCAST,
149             * and the primary interface supports broadcast,
150             * choose the broadcast address for that interface.
151             */
152 #define satosin(sa)     ((struct sockaddr_in *)(sa))
153 #define sintosa(sin)    ((struct sockaddr *)(sin))
154 #define ifatoia(ifa)    ((struct in_ifaddr *)(ifa))
155            if (sin->sin_addr.s_addr == INADDR_ANY)
156                sin->sin_addr = IA_SIN(in_ifaddr)->sin_addr;
157            else if (sin->sin_addr.s_addr == (u_long) INADDR_BROADCAST &&
158                    (in_ifaddr->ia_ifp->if_flags & IFF_BROADCAST))
159                sin->sin_addr = satosin(&in_ifaddr->ia_broadaddr)->sin_addr;
160        }
```
—— *in_pcb.c*

Figure 22.25   `in_pcbconnect` function: verify arguments, check foreign IP address.

Validate argument

130–143   The `nam` argument points to an mbuf containing a `sockaddr_in` structure with the foreign IP address and port number. These lines validate the argument and verify that the caller is not trying to connect to a port number of 0.

Handle connection to 0.0.0.0 and 255.255.255.255 specially

144–160   The test of the global `in_ifaddr` verifies that an IP interface has been configured. If the foreign IP address is 0.0.0.0 (`INADDR_ANY`), then 0.0.0.0 is replaced with the IP address of the primary IP interface. This means the calling process is connecting to a peer on this host. If the foreign IP address is 255.255.255.255 (`INADDR_BROADCAST`) and the primary interface supports broadcasting, then 255.255.255.255 is replaced with the broadcast address of the primary interface. This allows a UDP application to broadcast on the primary interface without having to figure out its IP address—it can simply send datagrams to 255.255.255.255, and the kernel converts this to the appropriate IP address for the interface.

The next section of code, Figure 22.26, handles the case of an unspecified local address. This is the common scenario for TCP and UDP clients, cases 1, 2, and 3 from the list at the beginning of this section.

```
                                                                        in_pcb.c
161     if (inp->inp_laddr.s_addr == INADDR_ANY) {
162         struct route *ro;

163         ia = (struct in_ifaddr *) 0;
164         /*
165          * If route is known or can be allocated now,
166          * our src addr is taken from the i/f, else punt.
167          */
168         ro = &inp->inp_route;
169         if (ro->ro_rt &&
170             (satosin(&ro->ro_dst)->sin_addr.s_addr !=
171              sin->sin_addr.s_addr ||
172              inp->inp_socket->so_options & SO_DONTROUTE)) {
173             RTFREE(ro->ro_rt);
174             ro->ro_rt = (struct rtentry *) 0;
175         }
176         if ((inp->inp_socket->so_options & SO_DONTROUTE) == 0 &&      /* XXX */
177             (ro->ro_rt == (struct rtentry *) 0 ||
178              ro->ro_rt->rt_ifp == (struct ifnet *) 0)) {
179             /* No route yet, so try to acquire one */
180             ro->ro_dst.sa_family = AF_INET;
181             ro->ro_dst.sa_len = sizeof(struct sockaddr_in);
182             ((struct sockaddr_in *) &ro->ro_dst)->sin_addr =
183                 sin->sin_addr;
184             rtalloc(ro);
185         }
186         /*
187          * If we found a route, use the address
188          * corresponding to the outgoing interface
189          * unless it is the loopback (in case a route
190          * to our address on another net goes to loopback).
191          */
192         if (ro->ro_rt && !(ro->ro_rt->rt_ifp->if_flags & IFF_LOOPBACK))
193             ia = ifatoia(ro->ro_rt->rt_ifa);
194         if (ia == 0) {
195             u_short fport = sin->sin_port;

196             sin->sin_port = 0;
197             ia = ifatoia(ifa_ifwithdstaddr(sintosa(sin)));
198             if (ia == 0)
199                 ia = ifatoia(ifa_ifwithnet(sintosa(sin)));
200             sin->sin_port = fport;
201             if (ia == 0)
202                 ia = in_ifaddr;
203             if (ia == 0)
204                 return (EADDRNOTAVAIL);
205         }
                                                                        in_pcb.c
```

Figure 22.26   in_pcbconnect function: local IP address not yet specified.

Release route if no longer valid

164–175   If a route is held by the PCB but the destination of that route differs from the foreign address being connected to, or the SO_DONTROUTE socket option is set, that route is released.

To understand why a PCB may have an associated route, consider case 3 from the list at the beginning of this section: in_pcbconnect is called *every time* a UDP datagram is sent on an unconnected socket. Each time a process calls sendto, the UDP output function calls in_pcbconnect, ip_output, and in_pcbdisconnect. If all the datagrams sent on the socket go to the same destination IP address, then the first time through in_pcbconnect the route is allocated and it can be used from that point on. But since a UDP application can send datagrams to a different IP address with each call to sendto, the destination address must be compared to the saved route and the route released when the destination changes. This same test is done in ip_output, which seems to be redundant.

The SO_DONTROUTE socket option tells the kernel to bypass the normal routing decisions and send the IP datagram to the locally attached interface whose IP network address matches the network portion of the destination address.

Acquire route

176–185   If the SO_DONTROUTE socket option is not set, and a route to the destination is not held by the PCB, try to acquire one by calling rtalloc.

Determine outgoing interface

186–205   The goal in this section of code is to have ia point to an interface address structure (in_ifaddr, Section 6.5), which contains the IP address of the interface. If the PCB holds a route that is still valid, or if rtalloc found a route, and the route is not to the loopback interface, the corresponding interface is used. Otherwise ifa_withdstaddr and ifa_withnet are called to check if the foreign IP address is on the other end of a point-to-point link or on an attached network. Both of these functions require that the port number in the socket address structure be 0, so it is saved in fport across the calls. If this fails, the primary IP address is used (in_ifaddr), and if no interfaces are configured (in_ifaddr is zero), an error is returned.

Figure 22.27 shows the next section of in_pcbconnect, which handles a destination address that is a multicast address.

206–223   If the destination address is a multicast address and the process has specified the outgoing interface to use for multicast packets (using the IP_MULTICAST_IF socket option), then the IP address of that interface is used as the local address. A search is made of all IP interfaces for the one matching the interface that was specified with the socket option. An error is returned if that interface is no longer up.

224–225   The code that started at the beginning of Figure 22.26 to handle the case of a wildcard local address is complete. The pointer to the sockaddr_in structure for the local interface ia is saved in ifaddr.

The final section of in_pcblookup is shown in Figure 22.28.

in_pcb.c
```
206          /*
207           * If the destination address is multicast and an outgoing
208           * interface has been set as a multicast option, use the
209           * address of that interface as our source address.
210           */
211          if (IN_MULTICAST(ntohl(sin->sin_addr.s_addr)) &&
212              inp->inp_moptions != NULL) {
213              struct ip_moptions *imo;
214              struct ifnet *ifp;

215              imo = inp->inp_moptions;
216              if (imo->imo_multicast_ifp != NULL) {
217                  ifp = imo->imo_multicast_ifp;
218                  for (ia = in_ifaddr; ia; ia = ia->ia_next)
219                      if (ia->ia_ifp == ifp)
220                          break;
221                  if (ia == 0)
222                      return (EADDRNOTAVAIL);
223              }
224          }
225          ifaddr = (struct sockaddr_in *) &ia->ia_addr;
226      }
```
in_pcb.c

Figure 22.27 in_pcbconnect function: destination address is a multicast address.

in_pcb.c
```
227      if (in_pcblookup(inp->inp_head,
228                       sin->sin_addr,
229                       sin->sin_port,
230              inp->inp_laddr.s_addr ? inp->inp_laddr : ifaddr->sin_addr,
231                       inp->inp_lport,
232                       0))
233          return (EADDRINUSE);

234      if (inp->inp_laddr.s_addr == INADDR_ANY) {
235          if (inp->inp_lport == 0)
236              (void) in_pcbbind(inp, (struct mbuf *) 0);
237          inp->inp_laddr = ifaddr->sin_addr;
238      }
239      inp->inp_faddr = sin->sin_addr;
240      inp->inp_fport = sin->sin_port;
241      return (0);
242  }
```
in_pcb.c

Figure 22.28 in_pcbconnect function: verify that socket pair is unique.

Verify that socket pair is unique

227–233   in_pcblookup verifies that the socket pair is unique. The foreign address and foreign port are the values specified as arguments to in_pcbconnect. The local address is either the value that was already bound to the socket or the value in ifaddr that was calculated in the code we just described. The local port can be 0, which is typical for a TCP client, and we'll see that later in this section of code an ephemeral port is chosen for the local port.

This test prevents two TCP connections to the same foreign address and foreign port from the same local address and local port. For example, if we establish a TCP connection with the echo server on the host sun and then try to establish another connection to the same server from the same local port (8888, specified with the -b option), the call to in_pcblookup returns a match, causing connect to return the error EADDRINUSE. (We use the sock program from Appendix C of Volume 1.)

```
bsdi $ sock -b 8888 sun echo &        start first one in the background
bsdi $ sock -A -b 8888 sun echo       then try again
connect() error: Address already in use
```

We specify the -A option to set the SO_REUSEADDR socket option, which lets the bind succeed, but the connect cannot succeed. This is a contrived example, as we explicitly bound the same local port (8888) to both sockets. In the normal scenario of two different clients from the host bsdi to the echo server on the host sun, the local port will be 0 when the second client calls in_pcblookup from Figure 22.28.

This test also prevents two UDP sockets from being connected to the same foreign address from the same local port. This test does not prevent two UDP sockets from alternately sending datagrams to the same foreign address from the same local port, as long as neither calls connect, since a UDP socket is only temporarily connected to a peer for the duration of a sendto system call.

Implicit bind and assignment of ephemeral port

234–238   If the local address is still wildcarded for the socket, it is set to the value saved in ifaddr. This is an implicit bind: cases 3, 4, and 5 from the beginning of Section 22.7. First a check is made as to whether the local port has been bound yet, and if not, in_pcbbind binds an ephemeral port to the socket. The order of the call to in_pcbbind and the assignment to inp_laddr is important, since in_pcbbind fails if the local address is not the wildcard address.

Store foreign address and foreign port in PCB

239–240   The final step of this function sets the foreign IP address and foreign port number in the PCB. We are guaranteed, on successful return from this function, that both socket pairs in the PCB—the local and foreign—are filled in with specific values.

IP Source Address Versus Outgoing Interface Address

There is a subtle difference between the source address in the IP datagram versus the IP address of the interface used to send the datagram.

The PCB member inp_laddr is used by TCP and UDP as the source address of the IP datagram. It can be set by the process to the IP address of *any* configured interface by bind. (The call to ifa_ifwithaddr in in_pcbbind verifies the local address desired by the application.) in_pcbconnect assigns the local address only if it is a wildcard, and when this happens the local address is based on the outgoing interface (since the destination address is known).

The outgoing interface, however, is also determined by `ip_output` based on the destination IP address. On a multihomed host it is possible for the source address to be a local interface that is not the outgoing interface, when the process explicitly binds a local address that differs from the outgoing interface. This is allowed because Net/3 chooses the weak end system model (Section 8.4).

22.9 `in_pcbdisconnect` Function

A UDP socket is disconnected by `in_pcbdisconnect`. This removes the foreign association by setting the foreign IP address to all 0s (`INADDR_ANY`) and foreign port number to 0.

This is done after a datagram has been sent on an unconnected UDP socket and when `connect` is called on a connected UDP socket. In the first case the sequence of steps when the process calls `sendto` is: UDP calls `in_pcbconnect` to connect the socket temporarily to the destination, `udp_output` sends the datagram, and then `in_pcbdisconnect` removes the temporary connection.

`in_pcbdisconnect` is not called when a socket is closed since `in_pcbdetach` handles the release of the PCB. A disconnect is required only when the PCB needs to be reused for a different foreign address or port number.

Figure 22.29 shows the function `in_pcbdisconnect`.

```
                                                                      ─── in_pcb.c
243 int
244 in_pcbdisconnect(inp)
245 struct inpcb *inp;
246 {
247     inp->inp_faddr.s_addr = INADDR_ANY;
248     inp->inp_fport = 0;
249     if (inp->inp_socket->so_state & SS_NOFDREF)
250         in_pcbdetach(inp);
251 }
                                                                      ─── in_pcb.c
```

Figure 22.29 `in_pcbdisconnect` function: disconnect from foreign address and port number.

If there is no longer a file table reference for this PCB (`SS_NOFDREF` is set) then `in_pcbdetach` (Figure 22.7) releases the PCB.

22.10 `in_setsockaddr` and `in_setpeeraddr` Functions

The `getsockname` system call returns the local protocol address of a socket (e.g., the IP address and port number for an Internet socket) and the `getpeername` system call returns the foreign protocol address. Both system calls end up issuing a `PRU_SOCKADDR` request or a `PRU_PEERADDR` request. The protocol then calls either `in_setsockaddr` or `in_setpeeraddr`. We show the first of these in Figure 22.30.

in_pcb.c
```
267 int
268 in_setsockaddr(inp, nam)
269 struct inpcb *inp;
270 struct mbuf *nam;
271 {
272     struct sockaddr_in *sin;

273     nam->m_len = sizeof(*sin);
274     sin = mtod(nam, struct sockaddr_in *);
275     bzero((caddr_t) sin, sizeof(*sin));
276     sin->sin_family = AF_INET;
277     sin->sin_len = sizeof(*sin);
278     sin->sin_port = inp->inp_lport;
279     sin->sin_addr = inp->inp_laddr;
280 }
```
in_pcb.c

Figure 22.30   in_setsockaddr function: return local address and port number.

The argument nam is a pointer to an mbuf that will hold the result: a sockaddr_in structure that the system call copies back to the process. The code fills in the socket address structure and copies the IP address and port number from the Internet PCB into the sin_addr and sin_port members.

Figure 22.31 shows the in_setpeeraddr function. It is nearly identical to Figure 22.30, but copies the foreign IP address and port number from the PCB.

in_pcb.c
```
281 int
282 in_setpeeraddr(inp, nam)
283 struct inpcb *inp;
284 struct mbuf *nam;
285 {
286     struct sockaddr_in *sin;

287     nam->m_len = sizeof(*sin);
288     sin = mtod(nam, struct sockaddr_in *);
289     bzero((caddr_t) sin, sizeof(*sin));
290     sin->sin_family = AF_INET;
291     sin->sin_len = sizeof(*sin);
292     sin->sin_port = inp->inp_fport;
293     sin->sin_addr = inp->inp_faddr;
294 }
```
in_pcb.c

Figure 22.31   in_setpeeraddr function: return foreign address and port number.

22.11 in_pcbnotify, in_rtchange, and in_losing Functions

The function in_pcbnotify is called when an ICMP error is received, in order to notify the appropriate process of the error. The "appropriate process" is found by searching all the PCBs for one of the protocols (TCP or UDP) and comparing the local and foreign IP addresses and port numbers with the values returned in the ICMP error. For example, when an ICMP source quench error is received in response to a TCP segment that some router discarded, TCP must locate the PCB for the connection that caused the error and slow down the transmission on that connection.

Before showing the function we must review how it is called. Figure 22.32 summarizes the functions called to process an ICMP error. The two shaded ellipses are the functions described in this section.

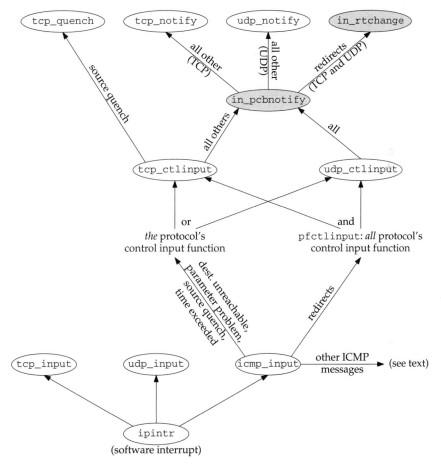

Figure 22.32 Summary of processing of ICMP errors.

When an ICMP message is received, `icmp_input` is called. Five of the ICMP messages are classified as errors (Figures 11.1 and 11.2):

- destination unreachable,
- parameter problem,
- redirect,
- source quench, and
- time exceeded.

Redirects are handled differently from the other four errors. All other ICMP messages (the queries) are handled as described in Chapter 11.

Each protocol defines its control input function, the `pr_ctlinput` entry in the `protosw` structure (Section 7.4). The ones for TCP and UDP are named `tcp_ctlinput` and `udp_ctlinput`, and we'll show their code in later chapters. Since the ICMP error that is received contains the IP header of the datagram that caused the error, the protocol that caused the error (TCP or UDP) is known. Four of the five ICMP errors cause that protocol's control input function to be called. Redirects are handled differently: the function `pfctlinput` is called, and it in turn calls the control input functions for *all* the protocols in the family (Internet). TCP and UDP are the only protocols in the Internet family with control input functions.

Redirects are handled specially because they affect *all* IP datagrams going to that destination, not just the one that caused the redirect. On the other hand, the other four errors need only be processed by the protocol that caused the error.

The final points we need to make about Figure 22.32 are that TCP handles source quenches differently from the other errors, and redirects are handled specially by `in_pcbnotify`: the function `in_rtchange` is called, regardless of the protocol that caused the error.

Figure 22.33 shows the `in_pcbnotify` function. When it is called by TCP, the first argument is the address of `tcb` and the final argument is the address of the function `tcp_notify`. For UDP, these two arguments are the address of `udb` and the address of the function `udp_notify`.

Verify arguments

306–324   The `cmd` argument and the address family of the destination are verified. The foreign address is checked to ensure it is not 0.0.0.0.

Handle redirects specially

325–338   If the error is a redirect it is handled specially. (The error `PRC_HOSTDEAD` is an old error that was generated by the IMPs. Current systems should never see this error—it is a historical artifact.) The foreign port, local port, and local address are all set to 0 so that the `for` loop that follows won't compare them. For a redirect we want that loop to select the PCBs to receive notification based only on the foreign IP address, because that is the IP address for which our host received a redirect. Also, the function that is called for a redirect is `in_rtchange` (Figure 22.34) instead of the `notify` argument specified by the caller.

339   The global array `inetctlerrmap` maps one of the protocol-independent error codes (the PRC_*xxx* values from Figure 11.19) into its corresponding Unix `errno` value (the final column in Figure 11.1).

```
306 int                                                                ─────── in_pcb.c
307 in_pcbnotify(head, dst, fport_arg, laddr, lport_arg, cmd, notify)
308 struct inpcb *head;
309 struct sockaddr *dst;
310 u_int    fport_arg, lport_arg;
311 struct in_addr laddr;
312 int      cmd;
313 void     (*notify) (struct inpcb *, int);
314 {
315     extern u_char inetctlerrmap[];
316     struct inpcb *inp, *oinp;
317     struct in_addr faddr;
318     u_short fport = fport_arg, lport = lport_arg;
319     int     errno;

320     if ((unsigned) cmd > PRC_NCMDS || dst->sa_family != AF_INET)
321         return;
322     faddr = ((struct sockaddr_in *) dst)->sin_addr;
323     if (faddr.s_addr == INADDR_ANY)
324         return;

325     /*
326      * Redirects go to all references to the destination,
327      * and use in_rtchange to invalidate the route cache.
328      * Dead host indications: notify all references to the destination.
329      * Otherwise, if we have knowledge of the local port and address,
330      * deliver only to that socket.
331      */
332     if (PRC_IS_REDIRECT(cmd) || cmd == PRC_HOSTDEAD) {
333         fport = 0;
334         lport = 0;
335         laddr.s_addr = 0;
336         if (cmd != PRC_HOSTDEAD)
337             notify = in_rtchange;
338     }
339     errno = inetctlerrmap[cmd];
340     for (inp = head->inp_next; inp != head;) {
341         if (inp->inp_faddr.s_addr != faddr.s_addr ||
342             inp->inp_socket == 0 ||
343             (lport && inp->inp_lport != lport) ||
344             (laddr.s_addr && inp->inp_laddr.s_addr != laddr.s_addr) ||
345             (fport && inp->inp_fport != fport)) {
346             inp = inp->inp_next;
347             continue;               /* skip this PCB */
348         }
349         oinp = inp;
350         inp = inp->inp_next;
351         if (notify)
352             (*notify) (oinp, errno);
353     }
354 }
                                                                       ─────── in_pcb.c
```

Figure 22.33 in_pcbnotify function: pass error notification to processes.

Call notify function for selected PCBs

340–353   This loop selects the PCBs to be notified. Multiple PCBs can be notified—the loop keeps going even after a match is located. The first `if` statement combines five tests, and if any one of the five is true, the PCB is skipped: (1) if the foreign addresses are unequal, (2) if the PCB does not have a corresponding `socket` structure, (3) if the local ports are unequal, (4) if the local addresses are unequal, or (5) if the foreign ports are unequal. The foreign addresses *must* match, while the other three foreign and local elements are compared only if the corresponding argument is nonzero. When a match is found, the `notify` function is called.

`in_rtchange` Function

We saw that `in_pcbnotify` calls the function `in_rtchange` when the ICMP error is a redirect. This function is called for all PCBs with a foreign address that matches the IP address that has been redirected. Figure 22.34 shows the `in_rtchange` function.

```
                                                                    ── in_pcb.c
391 void
392 in_rtchange(inp, errno)
393 struct inpcb *inp;
394 int      errno;
395 {
396     if (inp->inp_route.ro_rt) {
397         rtfree(inp->inp_route.ro_rt);
398         inp->inp_route.ro_rt = 0;
399         /*
400          * A new route can be allocated the next time
401          * output is attempted.
402          */
403     }
404 }
                                                                    ── in_pcb.c
```

Figure 22.34   `in_rtchange` function: invalidate route.

If the PCB holds a route, that route is released by `rtfree`, and the PCB member is marked as empty. We don't try to update the route at this time, using the new router address returned in the redirect. The new route will be allocated by `ip_output` when this PCB is used next, based on the kernel's routing table, which is updated by the redirect, before `pfctlinput` is called.

Redirects and Raw Sockets

Let's examine the interaction of redirects, raw sockets, and the cached route in the PCB. If we run the Ping program, which uses a raw socket, and an ICMP redirect error is received for the IP address being pinged, Ping continues using the original route, not the redirected route. We can see this as follows.

We ping the host `svr4` on the 140.252.13 network from the host `gemini` on the 140.252.1 network. The default router for `gemini` is `gateway`, but the packets should be sent to the router `netb` instead. Figure 22.35 shows the arrangement.

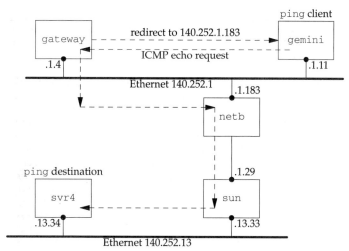

Figure 22.35   Example of ICMP redirect.

We expect `gateway` to send a redirect when it receives the first ICMP echo request.

```
gemini $ ping -sv svr4
PING 140.252.13.34: 56 data bytes
ICMP Host redirect from gateway 140.252.1.4
  to netb (140.252.1.183) for svr4 (140.252.13.34)
64 bytes from svr4 (140.252.13.34): icmp_seq=0. time=572. ms
ICMP Host redirect from gateway 140.252.1.4
  to netb (140.252.1.183) for svr4 (140.252.13.34)
64 bytes from svr4 (140.252.13.34): icmp_seq=1. time=392. ms
```

The `-s` option causes an ICMP echo request to be sent once a second, and the `-v` option prints every received ICMP message (instead of only the ICMP echo replies).

Every ICMP echo request elicits a redirect, but the raw socket used by ping never notices the redirect to change the route that it is using. The route that is first calculated and stored in the PCB, causing the IP datagrams to be sent to the router `gateway` (140.252.1.4), should be updated so that the datagrams are sent to the router `netb` (140.252.1.183) instead. We see that the ICMP redirects are received by the kernel on `gemini`, but they appear to be ignored.

If we terminate the program and start it again, we never see a redirect:

```
gemini $ ping -sv svr4
PING 140.252.13.34: 56 data bytes
64 bytes from svr4 (140.252.13.34): icmp_seq=0. time=388. ms
64 bytes from svr4 (140.252.13.34): icmp_seq=1. time=363. ms
```

The reason for this anomaly is that the raw IP socket code (Chapter 32) does not have a control input function. Only TCP and UDP have a control input function. When the redirect error is received, ICMP updates the kernel's routing table accordingly, and `pfctlinput` is called (Figure 22.32). But since there is no control input function for the raw IP protocol, the cached route in the PCB associated with Ping's raw socket is never released. When we start the Ping program a second time, however, the route that is allocated is based on the kernel's updated routing table, and we never see the redirects.

ICMP Errors and UDP Sockets

One confusing part of the sockets API is that ICMP errors received on a UDP socket are not passed to the application unless the application has issued a `connect` on the socket, restricting the foreign IP address and port number for the socket. We now see where this limitation is enforced by `in_pcbnotify`.

Consider an ICMP port unreachable, probably the most common ICMP error on a UDP socket. The foreign IP address and the foreign port number in the `dst` argument to `in_pcbnotify` are the IP address and port number that caused the ICMP error. But if the process has not issued a `connect` on the socket, the `inp_faddr` and `inp_fport` members of the PCB are both 0, preventing `in_pcbnotify` from ever calling the `notify` function for this socket. The `for` loop in Figure 22.33 will skip every UDP PCB.

This limitation arises for two reasons. First, if the sending process has an unconnected UDP socket, the only nonzero element in the socket pair is the local port. (This assumes the process did not call `bind`.) This is the only value available to `in_pcbnotify` to demultiplex the incoming ICMP error and pass it to the correct process. Although unlikely, there could be multiple processes bound to the same local port, making it ambiguous which process should receive the error. There's also the possibility that the process that sent the datagram that caused the ICMP error has terminated, with another process then starting and using the same local port. This is also unlikely since ephemeral ports are assigned in sequential order from 1024 to 5000 and reused only after cycling around (Figure 22.23).

The second reason for this limitation is because the error notification from the kernel to the process—an `errno` value—is inadequate. Consider a process that calls `sendto` on an unconnected UDP socket three times in a row, sending a UDP datagram to three different destinations, and then waits for the replies with `recvfrom`. If one of the datagrams generates an ICMP port unreachable error, and if the kernel were to return the corresponding error (`ECONNREFUSED`) to the `recvfrom` that the process issued, the `errno` value doesn't tell the process which of the three datagrams caused the error. The kernel has all the information required in the ICMP error, but the sockets API doesn't provide a way to return this to the process.

Therefore the design decision was made that if a process wants to be notified of these ICMP errors on a UDP socket, that socket must be connected to a single peer. If the error `ECONNREFUSED` is returned on that connected socket, there's no question which peer generated the error.

There is still a remote possibility of an ICMP error being delivered to the wrong process. One process sends the UDP datagram that elicits the ICMP error, but it terminates before the error is received. Another process then starts up before the error is received, binds the same local port, and connects to the same foreign address and foreign port, causing this new process to receive the error. There's no way to prevent this from occurring, given UDP's lack of memory. We'll see that TCP handles this with its TIME_WAIT state.

In our preceding example, one way for the application to get around this limitation is to use three connected UDP sockets instead of one unconnected socket, and call select to determine when any one of the three has a received datagram or an error to be read.

> Here we have a scenario where the kernel has the information but the API (sockets) is inadequate. With most implementations of Unix System V and the other popular API (TLI), the reverse is true: the TLI function t_rcvuderr can return the peer's IP address, port number, and an error value, but most SVR4 streams implementations of TCP/IP don't provide a way for ICMP to pass the error to an unconnected UDP end point.

> In an ideal world, in_pcbnotify delivers the ICMP error to all UDP sockets that match, even if the only nonwildcard match is the local port. The error returned to the process would include the destination IP address and destination UDP port that caused the error, allowing the process to determine if the error corresponds to a datagram sent by the process.

in_losing Function

The final function dealing with PCBs is in_losing, shown in Figure 22.36. It is called by TCP when its retransmission timer has expired four or more times in a row for a given connection (Figure 25.26).

```
                                                                    — in_pcb.c
361 int
362 in_losing(inp)
363 struct inpcb *inp;
364 {
365     struct rtentry *rt;
366     struct rt_addrinfo info;

367     if ((rt = inp->inp_route.ro_rt)) {
368         inp->inp_route.ro_rt = 0;
369         bzero((caddr_t) & info, sizeof(info));
370         info.rti_info[RTAX_DST] =
371             (struct sockaddr *) &inp->inp_route.ro_dst;
372         info.rti_info[RTAX_GATEWAY] = rt->rt_gateway;
373         info.rti_info[RTAX_NETMASK] = rt_mask(rt);
374         rt_missmsg(RTM_LOSING, &info, rt->rt_flags, 0);

375         if (rt->rt_flags & RTF_DYNAMIC)
376             (void) rtrequest(RTM_DELETE, rt_key(rt),
377                             rt->rt_gateway, rt_mask(rt), rt->rt_flags,
378                             (struct rtentry **) 0);
379         else
380             /*
381              * A new route can be allocated
382              * the next time output is attempted.
383              */
384             rtfree(rt);
385     }
386 }
                                                                    — in_pcb.c
```

Figure 22.36 in_losing function: invalidate cached route information.

Generate routing message

361–374   If the PCB holds a route, that route is discarded. An rt_addrinfo structure is filled in with information about the cached route that appears to be failing. The function rt_missmsg is then called to generate a message from the routing socket of type RTM_LOSING, indicating a problem with the route.

Delete or release route

375–384   If the cached route was generated by a redirect (RTF_DYNAMIC is set), the route is deleted by calling rtrequest with a request of RTM_DELETE. Otherwise the cached route is released, causing the next output on the socket to allocate another route to the destination—hopefully a better route.

22.12 Implementation Refinements

Undoubtedly the most time-consuming algorithm we've encountered in this chapter is the linear searching of the PCBs done by in_pcblookup. At the beginning of Section 22.6 we noted four instances when this function is called. We can ignore the calls to bind and connect, as they occur much less frequently than the calls to in_pcblookup from TCP and UDP, to demultiplex *every* received IP datagram.

In later chapters we'll see that TCP and UDP both try to help this linear search by maintaining a pointer to the last PCB that the protocol referenced: a one-entry cache. If the local address, local port, foreign address, and foreign port in the cached PCB match the values in the received datagram, the protocol doesn't even call in_pcblookup. If the protocol's data fits the packet train model [Jain and Routhier 1986], this simple cache works well. But if the data does not fit this model and, for example, looks like data entry into an on-line transaction processing system, the one-entry cache performs poorly [McKenney and Dove 1992].

One proposal for a better PCB arrangement is to move a PCB to the front of the PCB list when the PCB is referenced. ([McKenney and Dove 1992] attribute this idea to Jon Crowcroft; [Partridge and Pink 1993] attribute it to Gary Delp.) This movement of the PCB is easy to do since it is a doubly linked list and a pointer to the head of the list is the first argument to in_pcblookup.

[McKenney and Dove 1992] compare the original Net/1 implementation (no cache), an enhanced one-entry send–receive cache, the move-to-the-front heuristic, and their own algorithm that uses hash chains. They show that maintaining a linear list of PCBs on hash chains provides an order of magnitude improvement over the other algorithms. The only cost for the hash chains is the memory required for the hash chain headers and the computation of the hash function. They also consider adding the move-to-the-front heuristic to their hash-chain algorithm and conclude that it is easier simply to add more hash chains.

Another comparison of the BSD linear search to a hash table search is in [Hutchinson and Peterson 1991]. They show that the time required to demultiplex an incoming UDP datagram is constant as the number of sockets increases for a hash table, but with a linear search the time increases as the number of sockets increases.

22.13 Summary

An Internet PCB is associated with every Internet socket: TCP, UDP, and raw IP. It contains information common to all Internet sockets: local and foreign IP addresses, pointer to a route structure, and so on. All the PCBs for a given protocol are placed on a doubly linked list maintained by that protocol.

In this chapter we've looked at numerous functions that manipulate the PCBs, and three in detail.

1. `in_pcblookup` is called by TCP and UDP to demultiplex every received datagram. It chooses which socket receives the datagram, taking into account wildcard matches.

    This function is also called by `in_pcbbind` to verify that the local address and local process are unique, and by `in_pcbconnect` to verify that the combination of a local address, local process, foreign address, and foreign process are unique.

2. `in_pcbbind` explicitly or implicitly binds a local address and local port to a socket. An explicit bind occurs when the process calls `bind`, and an implicit bind occurs when a TCP client calls `connect` without calling `bind`, or when a UDP process calls `sendto` or `connect` without calling `bind`.

3. `in_pcbconnect` sets the foreign address and foreign process. If the local address has not been set by the process, a route to the foreign address is calculated and the resulting local interface becomes the local address. If the local port has not been set by the process, `in_pcbbind` chooses an ephemeral port for the socket.

Figure 22.37 summarizes the common scenarios for various TCP and UDP applications and the values stored in the PCB for the local address and port and the foreign address and port. We have not yet covered all the actions shown in Figure 22.37 for TCP and UDP processes, but will examine the code in later chapters.

Application	local address: inp_laddr	local port: inp_lport	foreign address: inp_faddr	foreign port: inp_fport
TCP client: connect (*foreignIP, fport*)	in_pcbconnect calls rtalloc to allocate route to *foreignIP*. Local address is local interface.	in_pcbconnect calls in_pcbbind to choose ephemeral port.	*foreignIP*	*fport*
TCP client: bind (*localIP, lport*) connect (*foreignIP, fport*)	*localIP*	*lport*	*foreignIP*	*fport*
TCP client: bind (*, *lport*) connect (*foreignIP, fport*)	in_pcbconnect calls rtalloc to allocate route to *foreignIP*. Local address is local interface.	*lport*	*foreignIP*	*fport*
TCP client: bind (*localIP*, 0) connect (*foreignIP, fport*)	*localIP*	in_pcbbind chooses ephemeral port.	*foreignIP*	*fport*
TCP server: bind (*localIP, lport*) listen() accept()	*localIP*	*lport*	Source address from IP header.	Source port from TCP header.
TCP server: bind (*, *lport*) listen() accept()	Destination address from IP header.	*lport*	Source address from IP header.	Source port from TCP header.
UDP client: sendto (*foreignIP, fport*)	in_pcbconnect calls rtalloc to allocate route to *foreignIP*. Local address is local interface. Reset to 0.0.0.0 after datagram sent.	in_pcbconnect calls in_pcbbind to choose ephemeral port. Not changed on subsequent calls to sendto.	*foreignIP*. Reset to 0.0.0.0 after datagram sent.	*fport*. Reset to 0 after datagram sent.
UDP client: connect (*foreignIP, fport*) write()	in_pcbconnect calls rtalloc to allocate route to *foreignIP*. Local address is local interface. Not changed on subsequent calls to write.	in_pcbconnect calls in_pcbbind to choose ephemeral port. Not changed on subsequent calls to write.	*foreignIP*	*fport*

Figure 22.37   Summary of in_pcbbind and in_pcbconnect.

Exercises

22.1 What happens in Figure 22.23 when the process asks for an ephemeral port and every ephemeral port is in use?

22.2 In Figure 22.10 we showed two Telnet servers with listening sockets: one with a specific local IP address and one with the wildcard for its local IP address. Does your system's Telnet daemon allow you to specify the local IP address, and if so, how?

22.3 Assume a socket is bound to the local socket {140.252.1.29, 8888}, and this is the only socket using local port 8888. (1) Go through the steps performed by `in_pcbbind` when another socket is bound to {140.252.13.33, 8888}, without any socket options. (2) Go through the steps performed when another socket is bound to the wildcard IP address, port 8888, without any socket options. (3) Go through the steps performed when another socket is bound to the wildcard IP address, port 8888, with the `SO_REUSEADDR` socket option.

22.4 What is the first ephemeral port number allocated by UDP?

22.5 When a process calls `bind`, which elements in the `sockaddr_in` structure must be filled in?

22.6 What happens if a process tries to `bind` a local broadcast address? What happens if a process tries to `bind` the limited broadcast address (255.255.255.255)?

23

UDP: User Datagram Protocol

23.1 Introduction

The User Datagram Protocol, or UDP, is a simple, datagram-oriented, transport-layer protocol: each output operation by a process produces exactly one UDP datagram, which causes one IP datagram to be sent.

A process accesses UDP by creating a socket of type `SOCK_DGRAM` in the Internet domain. By default the socket is termed *unconnected*. Each time the process sends a datagram it must specify the destination IP address and port number. Each time a datagram is received for the socket, the process can receive the source IP address and port number from the datagram.

We mentioned in Section 22.5 that a UDP socket can also be *connected* to one particular IP address and port number. This causes all datagrams written to the socket to go to that destination, and only datagrams arriving from that IP address and port number are passed to the process.

This chapter examines the implementation of UDP.

23.2 Code Introduction

There are nine UDP functions in a single C file and various UDP definitions in two headers, as shown in Figure 23.1.

Figure 23.2 shows the relationship of the six main UDP functions to other kernel functions. The shaded ellipses are the six functions that we cover in this chapter. We also cover three additional UDP functions that are called by some of these six functions.

File	Description
netinet/udp.h netinet/udp_var.h	udphdr structure definition other UDP definitions
netinet/udp_usrreq.c	UDP functions

Figure 23.1   Files discussed in this chapter.

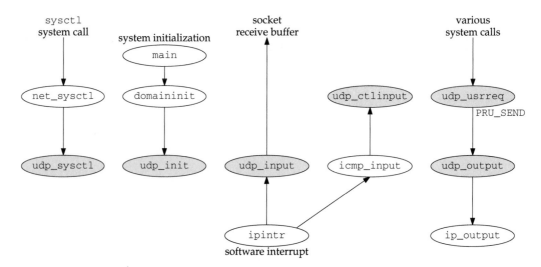

Figure 23.2   Relationship of UDP functions to rest of kernel.

Global Variables

Seven global variables are introduced in this chapter, which are shown in Figure 23.3.

Variable	Datatype	Description
udb udp_last_inpcb	struct inpcb struct inpcb *	head of the UDP PCB list pointer to PCB for last received datagram: one-behind cache
udpcksum udp_in udpstat	int struct sockaddr_in struct udpstat	flag for calculating and verifying UDP checksum holds sender's IP address and port on input UDP statistics (Figure 23.4)
udp_recvspace udp_sendspace	u_long u_long	default size of socket receive buffer, 41,600 bytes default size of socket send buffer, 9216 bytes

Figure 23.3   Global variables introduced in this chapter.

Statistics

Various UDP statistics are maintained in the global structure `udpstat`, described in Figure 23.4. We'll see where these counters are incremented as we proceed through the code.

`udpstat` member	Description	Used by SNMP
`udps_badlen`	#received datagrams with data length larger than packet	•
`udps_badsum`	#received datagrams with checksum error	•
`udps_fullsock`	#received datagrams not delivered because input socket full	
`udps_hdrops`	#received datagrams with packet shorter than header	•
`udps_ipackets`	total #received datagrams	•
`udps_noport`	#received datagrams with no process on destination port	•
`udps_noportbcast`	#received broadcast/multicast datagrams with no process on dest. port	•
`udps_opackets`	total #output datagrams	•
`udpps_pcbcachemiss`	#received input datagrams missing pcb cache	

Figure 23.4   UDP statistics maintained in the `udpstat` structure.

Figure 23.5 shows some sample output of these statistics, from the `netstat -s` command.

`netstat -s` output	`udpstat` member
18,575,142 datagrams received	`udps_ipackets`
0 with incomplete header	`udps_hdrops`
18 with bad data length field	`udps_badlen`
58 with bad checksum	`udps_badsum`
84,079 dropped due to no socket	`udps_noport`
446 broadcast/multicast datagrams dropped due to no socket	`udps_noportbcast`
5,356 dropped due to full socket buffers	`udps_fullsock`
18,485,185 delivered	(see text)
18,676,277 datagrams output	`udps_opackets`

Figure 23.5   Sample UDP statistics.

The number of UDP datagrams delivered (the second from last line of output) is the number of datagrams received (`udps_ipackets`) minus the six variables that precede it in Figure 23.5.

SNMP Variables

Figure 23.6 shows the four simple SNMP variables in the UDP group and which counters from the `udpstat` structure implement that variable.

Figure 23.7 shows the UDP listener table, named `udpTable`. The values returned by SNMP for this table are taken from a UDP PCB, not the `udpstat` structure.

SNMP variable	udpstat member	Description
udpInDatagrams	udps_ipackets	#received datagrams delivered to processes
udpInErrors	udps_hdrops + udps_badsum + udps_badlen	#undeliverable UDP datagrams for reasons other than no application at destination port (e.g., UDP checksum error)
udpNoPorts	udps_noport + udps_noportbcast	#received datagrams for which no application process was at the destination port
udpOutDatagrams	udps_opackets	#datagrams sent

Figure 23.6   Simple SNMP variables in udp group.

UDP listener table, index = < *udpLocalAddress* >.< *udpLocalPort* >		
SNMP variable	PCB variable	Description
udpLocalAddress	inp_laddr	local IP address for this listener
udpLocalPort	inp_lport	local port number for this listener

Figure 23.7   Variables in UDP listener table: udpTable.

23.3 UDP `protosw` Structure

Figure 23.8 lists the protocol switch entry for UDP.

Member	inetsw[1]	Description
pr_type	*SOCK_DGRAM*	UDP provides datagram packet services
pr_domain	*&inetdomain*	UDP is part of the Internet domain
pr_protocol	*IPPROTO_UDP (17)*	appears in the ip_p field of the IP header
pr_flags	*PR_ATOMIC|PR_ADDR*	socket layer flags, not used by protocol processing
pr_input	*udp_input*	receives messages from IP layer
pr_output	*0*	not used by UDP
pr_ctlinput	*udp_ctlinput*	control input function for ICMP errors
pr_ctloutput	*ip_ctloutput*	respond to administrative requests from a process
pr_usrreq	*udp_usrreq*	respond to communication requests from a process
pr_init	*udp_init*	initialization for UDP
pr_fasttimo	*0*	not used by UDP
pr_slowtimo	*0*	not used by UDP
pr_drain	*0*	not used by UDP
pr_sysctl	*udp_sysctl*	for sysctl(8) system call

Figure 23.8   The UDP protosw structure.

We describe the five functions that begin with udp_ in this chapter. We also cover a sixth function, udp_output, which is not in the protocol switch entry but is called by udp_usrreq when a UDP datagram is output.

23.4 UDP Header

The UDP header is defined as a `udphdr` structure. Figure 23.9 shows the C structure and Figure 23.10 shows a picture of the UDP header.

── udp.h
```
39 struct udphdr {
40     u_short uh_sport;           /* source port */
41     u_short uh_dport;           /* destination port */
42     short   uh_ulen;            /* udp length */
43     u_short uh_sum;             /* udp checksum */
44 };
```
── udp.h

Figure 23.9 `udphdr` structure.

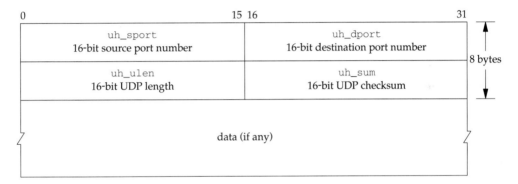

Figure 23.10 UDP header and optional data.

In the source code the UDP header is normally referenced as an IP header immediately followed by a UDP header. This is how `udp_input` processes received IP datagrams, and how `udp_output` builds outgoing IP datagrams. This combined IP/UDP header is a `udpiphdr` structure, shown in Figure 23.11.

── udp_var.h
```
38 struct udpiphdr {
39     struct ipovly ui_i;         /* overlaid ip structure */
40     struct udphdr ui_u;         /* udp header */
41 };
42 #define ui_next     ui_i.ih_next
43 #define ui_prev     ui_i.ih_prev
44 #define ui_x1       ui_i.ih_x1
45 #define ui_pr       ui_i.ih_pr
46 #define ui_len      ui_i.ih_len
47 #define ui_src      ui_i.ih_src
48 #define ui_dst      ui_i.ih_dst
49 #define ui_sport    ui_u.uh_sport
50 #define ui_dport    ui_u.uh_dport
51 #define ui_ulen     ui_u.uh_ulen
52 #define ui_sum      ui_u.uh_sum
```
── udp_var.h

Figure 23.11 `udpiphdr` structure: combined IP/UDP header.

The 20-byte IP header is defined as an `ipovly` structure, shown in Figure 23.12.

```
                                                                              ip_var.h
38 struct ipovly {
39     caddr_t ih_next, ih_prev;    /* for protocol sequence q's */
40     u_char  ih_x1;               /* (unused) */
41     u_char  ih_pr;               /* protocol */
42     short   ih_len;              /* protocol length */
43     struct in_addr ih_src;       /* source internet address */
44     struct in_addr ih_dst;       /* destination internet address */
45 };
                                                                              ip_var.h
```

Figure 23.12 `ipovly` structure.

Unfortunately this structure is not a real IP header, as shown in Figure 8.8. The size is the same (20 bytes) but the fields are different. We'll return to this discrepancy when we discuss the calculation of the UDP checksum in Section 23.6.

23.5 `udp_init` Function

The `domaininit` function calls UDP's initialization function (`udp_init`, Figure 23.13) at system initialization time.

```
                                                                           udp_usrreq.c
50 void
51 udp_init()
52 {
53     udb.inp_next = udb.inp_prev = &udb;
54 }
                                                                           udp_usrreq.c
```

Figure 23.13 `udp_init` function.

The only action performed by this function is to set the next and previous pointers in the head PCB (`udb`) to point to itself. This is an empty doubly linked list.

The remainder of the `udb` PCB is initialized to 0, although the only other field used in this head PCB is `inp_lport`, the next UDP ephemeral port number to allocate. In the solution for Exercise 22.4 we mention that because this local port number is initialized to 0, the first ephemeral port number will be 1024.

23.6 `udp_output` Function

UDP output occurs when the application calls one of the five write functions: `send`, `sendto`, `sendmsg`, `write`, or `writev`. If the socket is connected, any of the five functions can be called, although a destination address cannot be specified with `sendto` or `sendmsg`. If the socket is unconnected, only `sendto` and `sendmsg` can be called, and a destination address must be specified. Figure 23.14 summarizes how these five write functions end up with `udp_output` being called, which in turn calls `ip_output`.

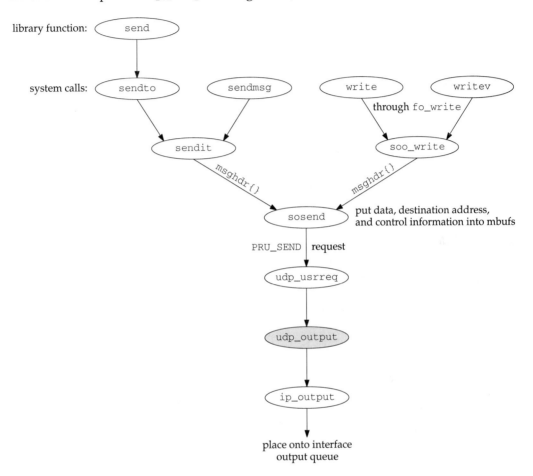

Figure 23.14   How the five write functions end up calling `udp_output`.

All five functions end up calling `sosend`, passing a pointer to a `msghdr` structure as an argument. The data to output is packaged into an mbuf chain and an optional destination address and optional control information are also put into mbufs by `sosend`. A `PRU_SEND` request is issued.

UDP calls the function `udp_output`, which we show the first half of in Figure 23.15. The four arguments are `inp`, a pointer to the socket Internet PCB; `m`, a pointer to the mbuf chain for output; `addr`, an optional pointer to an mbuf with the destination address packaged as a `sockaddr_in` structure; and `control`, an optional pointer to an mbuf with control information from `sendmsg`.

—— udp_usrreq.c
```
333 int
334 udp_output(inp, m, addr, control)
335 struct inpcb *inp;
336 struct mbuf *m;
337 struct mbuf *addr, *control;
338 {
339     struct udpiphdr *ui;
340     int     len = m->m_pkthdr.len;
341     struct in_addr laddr;
342     int     s, error = 0;

343     if (control)
344         m_freem(control);        /* XXX */

345     if (addr) {
346         laddr = inp->inp_laddr;
347         if (inp->inp_faddr.s_addr != INADDR_ANY) {
348             error = EISCONN;
349             goto release;
350         }
351         /*
352          * Must block input while temporarily connected.
353          */
354         s = splnet();
355         error = in_pcbconnect(inp, addr);
356         if (error) {
357             splx(s);
358             goto release;
359         }
360     } else {
361         if (inp->inp_faddr.s_addr == INADDR_ANY) {
362             error = ENOTCONN;
363             goto release;
364         }
365     }
366     /*
367      * Calculate data length and get an mbuf for UDP and IP headers.
368      */
369     M_PREPEND(m, sizeof(struct udpiphdr), M_DONTWAIT);
370     if (m == 0) {
371         error = ENOBUFS;
372         goto release;
373     }

                    /* remainder of function shown in Figure 23.20 */

409 release:
410     m_freem(m);
411     return (error);
412 }
```
—— udp_usrreq.c

Figure 23.15 udp_output function: temporarily connect an unconnected socket.

Discard optional control information

333–344   Any optional control information is discarded by m_freem, without generating an error. UDP output does not use control information for any purpose.

> The comment XXX is because the control information is ignored without generating an error. Other protocols, such as the routing domain and TCP, generate an error if the process passes control information.

Temporarily connect an unconnected socket

345–359   If the caller specifies a destination address for the UDP datagram (addr is nonnull), the socket is temporarily connected to that destination address by in_pcbconnect. The socket will be disconnected at the end of this function. Before doing this connect, a check is made as to whether the socket is already connected, and, if so, the error EISCONN is returned. This is why a sendto that specifies a destination address on a connected socket returns an error.

Before the socket is temporarily connected, IP input processing is stopped by splnet. This is done because the temporary connect changes the foreign address, foreign port, and possibly the local address in the socket's PCB. If a received UDP datagram were processed while this PCB was temporarily connected, that datagram could be delivered to the wrong process. Setting the processor priority to splnet only stops a software interrupt from causing the IP input routine to be executed (Figure 1.12), it does not prevent the interface layer from accepting incoming packets and placing them onto IP's input queue.

> [Partridge and Pink 1993] note that this operation of temporarily connecting the socket is expensive and consumes nearly one-third of the cost of each UDP transmission.

The local address from the PCB is saved in laddr before temporarily connecting, because if it is the wildcard address it will be changed by in_pcbconnect when it calls in_pcbbind.

The same rules apply to the destination address that would apply if the process called connect, since in_pcbconnect is called for both cases.

360–364   If the process doesn't specify a destination address, and the socket is not connected, ENOTCONN is returned.

Prepend IP and UDP headers

366–373   M_PREPEND allocates room for the IP and UDP headers in front of the data. Figure 1.8 showed one scenario, assuming there is not room in the first mbuf on the chain for the 28 bytes of header. Exercise 23.1 details the other possible scenarios. The flag M_DONTWAIT is specified because if the socket is temporarily connected, IP processing is blocked, and M_PREPEND should not block.

> Earlier Berkeley releases incorrectly specified M_WAIT here.

Prepending IP/UDP Headers and Mbuf Clusters

There is a subtle interaction between the M_PREPEND macro and mbuf clusters. If the user data is placed into a cluster by sosend, then 56 bytes (max_hdr from Figure 7.17) are left unused at the beginning of the cluster, allowing room for the Ethernet, IP, and UDP headers. This is to prevent M_PREPEND from allocating another mbuf just to hold these headers. M_PREPEND calls M_LEADINGSPACE to calculate how much space is available at the beginning of the mbuf:

```
#define M_LEADINGSPACE(m) \
    ((m)->m_flags & M_EXT ? /* (m)->m_data - (m)->m_ext.ext_buf */ 0 : \
        (m)->m_flags & M_PKTHDR ? (m)->m_data - (m)->m_pktdat : \
        (m)->m_data - (m)->m_dat)
```

The code that correctly calculates the amount of room at the front of a cluster is commented out, and the macro always returns 0 if the data is in a cluster. This means that when the user data is in a cluster, M_PREPEND always allocates a new mbuf for the protocol headers instead of using the room allocated for this purpose by sosend.

> The reason for commenting out the correct code in M_LEADINGSPACE is that the cluster might be shared (Section 2.9), and, if it is shared, using the space before the user's data in the cluster could wipe out someone else's data.

> With UDP data, clusters are not shared, since udp_output does not save a copy of the data. TCP, however, saves a copy of the data in its send buffer (waiting for the data to be acknowledged), and if the data is in a cluster, it is shared. But tcp_output doesn't call M_LEADINGSPACE, because sosend leaves room for only 56 bytes at the beginning of the cluster for datagram protocols. tcp_output always calls MGETHDR instead, to allocate an mbuf for the protocol headers.

UDP Checksum Calculation and Pseudo-Header

Before showing the last half of udp_output we describe how UDP fills in some of the fields in the IP/UDP headers, calculates the UDP checksum, and passes the IP/UDP headers and the data to IP for output. The way this is done with the ipovly structure is tricky.

Figure 23.16 shows the 28-byte IP/UDP headers that are built by udp_output in the first mbuf in the chain pointed to by m. The unshaded fields are filled in by udp_output and the shaded fields are filled in by ip_output. This figure shows the format of the headers as they appear on the wire.

The UDP checksum is calculated over three areas: (1) a 12-byte pseudo-header containing fields from the IP header, (2) the 8-byte UDP header, and (3) the UDP data. Figure 23.17 shows the 12 bytes of pseudo-header used for the checksum computation, along with the UDP header. The UDP header used for the checksum calculation is identical to the UDP header that appears on the wire (Figure 23.16).

The following three facts are used in computing the UDP checksum. (1) The third 32-bit word in the pseudo-header (Figure 23.17) looks similar to the third 32-bit word in the IP header (Figure 23.16): two 8-bit values and a 16-bit value. (2) The order of the three 32-bit values in the pseudo-header is irrelevant. Actually, the computation of the Internet checksum does not depend on the order of the 16-bit values that are used (Section 8.7). (3) Including additional 32-bit words of 0 in the checksum computation has no effect.

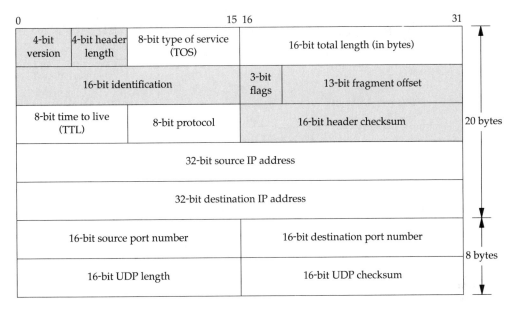

Figure 23.16 IP/UDP headers: unshaded fields filled in by UDP; shaded fields filled in by IP.

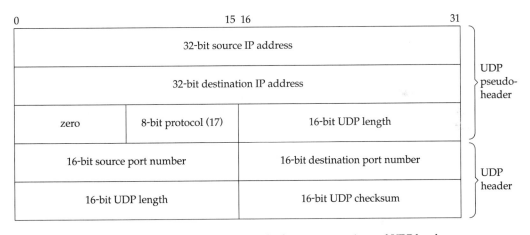

Figure 23.17 Pseudo-header used for checksum computation and UDP header.

udp_output takes advantage of these three facts and fills in the fields in the udpiphdr structure (Figure 23.11), which we depict in Figure 23.18. This structure is contained in the first mbuf in the chain pointed to by the argument m.

The last three 32-bit words in the 20-byte IP header (the five members ui_x1, ui_pr, ui_len, ui_src, and ui_dst) are used as the pseudo-header for the checksum computation. The first two 32-bit words in the IP header (ui_next and ui_prev) are also used in the checksum computation, but they're initialized to 0, and don't affect the checksum.

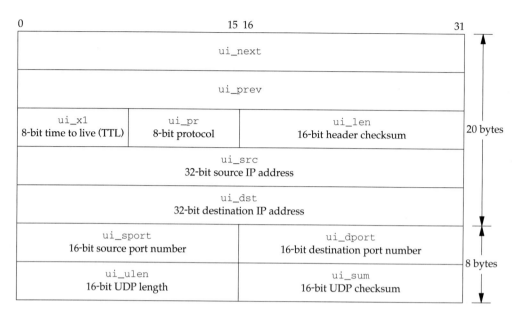

Figure 23.18   `udpiphdr` structure used by `udp_output`.

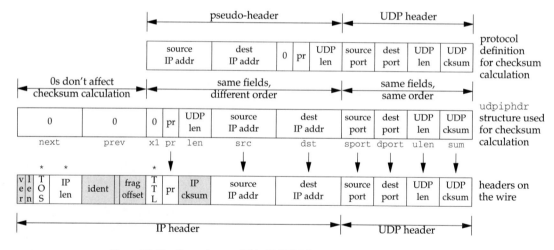

Figure 23.19   Operations to fill in IP/UDP headers and calculate UDP checksum.

Figure 23.19 summarizes the operations we've described.

1. The top picture shown in Figure 23.19 is the protocol definition of the pseudo-
    header, which corresponds to Figure 23.17.

2. The middle picture is the `udpiphdr` structure that is used in the source code, which corresponds to Figure 23.11. (To make the figure readable, the prefix `ui_` has been left off all the members.) This is the structure built by `udp_output` in the first mbuf and then used to calculate the UDP checksum.

3. The bottom picture shows the IP/UDP headers that appear on the wire, which corresponds to Figure 23.16. The seven fields with an arrow above are filled in by `udp_output` before the checksum computation. The three fields with an asterisk above are filled in by `udp_output` after the checksum computation. The remaining six shaded fields are filled in by `ip_output`.

Figure 23.20 shows the last half of the `udp_output` function.

—— udp_usrreq.c
```
374     /*
375      * Fill in mbuf with extended UDP header
376      * and addresses and length put into network format.
377      */
378     ui = mtod(m, struct udpiphdr *);
379     ui->ui_next = ui->ui_prev = 0;
380     ui->ui_x1 = 0;
381     ui->ui_pr = IPPROTO_UDP;
382     ui->ui_len = htons((u_short) len + sizeof(struct udphdr));
383     ui->ui_src = inp->inp_laddr;
384     ui->ui_dst = inp->inp_faddr;
385     ui->ui_sport = inp->inp_lport;
386     ui->ui_dport = inp->inp_fport;
387     ui->ui_ulen = ui->ui_len;

388     /*
389      * Stuff checksum and output datagram.
390      */
391     ui->ui_sum = 0;
392     if (udpcksum) {
393         if ((ui->ui_sum = in_cksum(m, sizeof(struct udpiphdr) + len)) == 0)
394                     ui->ui_sum = 0xffff;
395     }
396     ((struct ip *) ui)->ip_len = sizeof(struct udpiphdr) + len;
397     ((struct ip *) ui)->ip_ttl = inp->inp_ip.ip_ttl;      /* XXX */
398     ((struct ip *) ui)->ip_tos = inp->inp_ip.ip_tos;      /* XXX */
399     udpstat.udps_opackets++;
400     error = ip_output(m, inp->inp_options, &inp->inp_route,
401             inp->inp_socket->so_options & (SO_DONTROUTE | SO_BROADCAST),
402                     inp->inp_moptions);

403     if (addr) {
404         in_pcbdisconnect(inp);
405         inp->inp_laddr = laddr;
406         splx(s);
407     }
408     return (error);
```
—— udp_usrreq.c

Figure 23.20   `udp_output` function: fill in headers, calculate checksum, pass to IP.

Prepare pseudo-header for checksum computation

374–387   All the members in the udpiphdr structure (Figure 23.18) are set to their respective values. The local and foreign sockets from the PCB are already in network byte order, but the UDP length must be converted to network byte order. The UDP length is the number of bytes of data (len, which can be 0) plus the size of the UDP header (8). The UDP length field appears twice in the UDP checksum calculation: ui_len and ui_ulen. One of them is redundant.

Calculate checksum

388–395   The checksum is calculated by first setting it to 0 and then calling in_cksum. If UDP checksums are disabled (a bad idea—see Section 11.3 of Volume 1), 0 is sent as the checksum. If the calculated checksum is 0, 16 one bits are stored in the header instead of 0. (In one's complement arithmetic, all one bits and all zero bits are both considered 0.) This allows the receiver to distinguish between a UDP packet without a checksum (the checksum field is 0) versus a UDP packet with a checksum whose value is 0 (the checksum is 16 one bits).

> The variable udpcksum (Figure 23.3) normally defaults to 1, enabling UDP checksums. The kernel can be compiled for 4.2BSD compatibility, which initializes udpcksum to 0.

Fill in UDP length, TTL, and TOS

396–398   The pointer ui is cast to a pointer to a standard IP header (ip), and three fields in the IP header are set by UDP. The IP length field is set to the amount of data in the UDP datagram, plus 28, the size of the IP/UDP headers. Notice that this field in the IP header is stored in host byte order, not network byte order like the rest of the multibyte fields in the header. ip_output converts it to network byte order before transmission.

The TTL and TOS fields in the IP header are then set from the values in the socket's PCB. These values are defaulted by UDP when the socket is created, but can be changed by the process using setsockopt. Since these three fields—IP length, TTL, and TOS—are not part of the pseudo-header and not used in the UDP checksum computation, they must be set after the checksum is calculated but before ip_output is called.

Send datagram

400–402   ip_output sends the datagram. The second argument, inp_options, are IP options the process can set using setsockopt. These IP options are placed into the IP header by ip_output. The third argument is a pointer to the cached route in the PCB, and the fourth argument is the socket options. The only socket options that are passed to ip_output are SO_DONTROUTE (bypass the routing tables) and SO_BROADCAST (allow broadcasting). The final argument is a pointer to the multicast options for this socket.

Disconnect temporarily connected socket

403–407   If the socket was temporarily connected, in_pcbdisconnect disconnects the socket, the local IP address is restored in the PCB, and the interrupt level is restored to its saved value.

23.7   `udp_input` **Function**

UDP output is driven by a process calling one of the five write functions. The functions shown in Figure 23.14 are all called directly as part of the system call. UDP input, on the other hand, occurs when IP input receives an IP datagram on its input queue whose protocol field specifies UDP. IP calls the function `udp_input` through the `pr_input` function in the protocol switch table (Figure 8.15). Since IP input is at the software interrupt level, `udp_input` also executes at this level. The goal of `udp_input` is to place the UDP datagram onto the appropriate socket's buffer and wake up any process blocked for input on that socket.

We'll divide our discussion of the `udp_input` function into three sections:

1. the general validation that UDP performs on the received datagram,

2. processing UDP datagrams destined for a unicast address: locating the appropriate PCB and placing the datagram onto the socket's buffer, and

3. processing UDP datagrams destined for a broadcast or multicast address: the datagram may be delivered to multiple sockets.

This last step is new with the support of multicasting in Net/3, but consumes almost one-third of the code.

General Validation of Received UDP Datagram

Figure 23.21 shows the first section of UDP input.

55–65   The two arguments to `udp_input` are `m`, a pointer to an mbuf chain containing the IP datagram, and `iphlen`, the length of the IP header (including possible IP options).

Discard IP options

67–76   If IP options are present they are discarded by `ip_stripoptions`. As the comments indicate, UDP should save a copy of the IP options and make them available to the receiving process through the `IP_RECVOPTS` socket option, but this isn't implemented yet.

77–88   If the length of the first mbuf on the mbuf chain is less than 28 bytes (the size of the IP header plus the UDP header), `m_pullup` rearranges the mbuf chain so that at least 28 bytes are stored contiguously in the first mbuf.

```
55  void
56  udp_input(m, iphlen)
57  struct mbuf *m;
58  int     iphlen;
59  {
60      struct ip *ip;
61      struct udphdr *uh;
62      struct inpcb *inp;
63      struct mbuf *opts = 0;
64      int     len;
65      struct ip save_ip;

66      udpstat.udps_ipackets++;

67      /*
68       * Strip IP options, if any; should skip this,
69       * make available to user, and use on returned packets,
70       * but we don't yet have a way to check the checksum
71       * with options still present.
72       */
73      if (iphlen > sizeof(struct ip)) {
74          ip_stripoptions(m, (struct mbuf *) 0);
75          iphlen = sizeof(struct ip);
76      }
77      /*
78       * Get IP and UDP header together in first mbuf.
79       */
80      ip = mtod(m, struct ip *);
81      if (m->m_len < iphlen + sizeof(struct udphdr)) {
82          if ((m = m_pullup(m, iphlen + sizeof(struct udphdr))) == 0) {
83              udpstat.udps_hdrops++;
84              return;
85          }
86          ip = mtod(m, struct ip *);
87      }
88      uh = (struct udphdr *) ((caddr_t) ip + iphlen);

89      /*
90       * Make mbuf data length reflect UDP length.
91       * If not enough data to reflect UDP length, drop.
92       */
93      len = ntohs((u_short) uh->uh_ulen);
94      if (ip->ip_len != len) {
95          if (len > ip->ip_len) {
96              udpstat.udps_badlen++;
97              goto bad;
98          }
99          m_adj(m, len - ip->ip_len);
100         /* ip->ip_len = len; */
101     }
102     /*
103      * Save a copy of the IP header in case we want to restore
104      * it for sending an ICMP error message in response.
105      */
106     save_ip = *ip;
```

```
107       /*
108        * Checksum extended UDP header and data.
109        */
110       if (udpcksum && uh->uh_sum) {
111           ((struct ipovly *) ip)->ih_next = 0;
112           ((struct ipovly *) ip)->ih_prev = 0;
113           ((struct ipovly *) ip)->ih_x1 = 0;
114           ((struct ipovly *) ip)->ih_len = uh->uh_ulen;
115           if (uh->uh_sum = in_cksum(m, len + sizeof(struct ip))) {
116               udpstat.udps_badsum++;
117               m_freem(m);
118               return;
119           }
120       }
```
                                                                    ——— udp_usrreq.c

Figure 23.21   udp_input function: general validation of received UDP datagram.

Verify UDP length

89–101   There are two lengths associated with a UDP datagram: the length field in the IP
header (ip_len) and the length field in the UDP header (uh_ulen). Recall that
ipintr subtracted the length of the IP header from ip_len before calling udp_input
(Figure 10.11). The two lengths are compared and there are three possibilities:

1. ip_len equals uh_ulen. This is the common case.

2. ip_len is greater than uh_ulen. The IP datagram is too big, as shown in Figure 23.22.

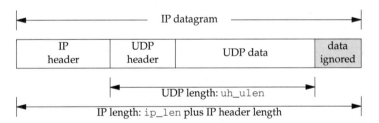

Figure 23.22   UDP length too small.

The code believes the smaller of the two lengths (the UDP header length) and
m_adj removes the excess bytes of data from the end of the datagram. In the
code the second argument to m_adj is negative, which we said in Figure 2.20
trims data from the end of the mbuf chain. It is possible in this scenario that the
UDP length field has been corrupted. If so, the datagram will probably be discarded shortly, assuming the sender calculated the UDP checksum, that this
checksum detects the error, and that the receiver verifies the checksum. The IP
length field should be correct since it was verified by IP against the amount of
data received from the interface, and the IP length field is covered by the
mandatory IP header checksum.

3. `ip_len` is less than `uh_ulen`. The IP datagram is smaller than possible, given the length in the UDP header. Figure 23.23 shows this case.

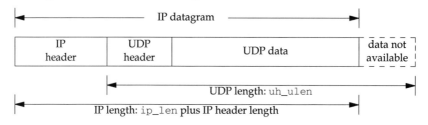

Figure 23.23   UDP length too big.

Something is wrong and the datagram is discarded. There is no other choice here: if the UDP length field has been corrupted, it can't be detected with the UDP checksum. The correct UDP length is needed to calculate the checksum.

> As we've said, the UDP length is redundant. In Chapter 28 we'll see that TCP does not have a length field in its header—it uses the IP length field, minus the lengths of the IP and TCP headers, to determine the amount of data in the datagram. Why does the UDP length field exist? Possibly to add a small amount of error checking, since UDP checksums are optional.

Save copy of IP header and verify UDP checksum

102–106   `udp_input` saves a copy of the IP header before verifying the checksum, because the checksum computation wipes out some of the fields in the original IP header.

110   The checksum is verified only if UDP checksums are enabled for the kernel (`udpcksum`), and if the sender calculated a UDP checksum (the received checksum is nonzero).

> This test is incorrect. If the sender calculated a checksum, it should be verified, regardless of whether outgoing checksums are calculated or not. The variable `udpcksum` should only specify whether outgoing checksums are calculated. Unfortunately many vendors have copied this incorrect test, although many vendors today finally ship their kernels with UDP checksums enabled by default.

111–120   Before calculating the checksum, the IP header is referenced as an `ipovly` structure (Figure 23.18) and the fields are initialized as described in the previous section when the UDP checksum is calculated by `udp_output`.

At this point special code is executed if the datagram is destined for a broadcast or multicast IP address. We defer this code until later in the section.

Demultiplexing Unicast Datagrams

Assuming the datagram is destined for a unicast address, Figure 23.24 shows the code that is executed.

—— udp_usrreq.c

```
                    /* demultiplex broadcast & multicast datagrams (Figure 23.26) */

206     /*
207      * Locate pcb for unicast datagram.
208      */
209     inp = udp_last_inpcb;
210     if (inp->inp_lport != uh->uh_dport ||
211         inp->inp_fport != uh->uh_sport ||
212         inp->inp_faddr.s_addr != ip->ip_src.s_addr ||
213         inp->inp_laddr.s_addr != ip->ip_dst.s_addr) {

214         inp = in_pcblookup(&udb, ip->ip_src, uh->uh_sport,
215                             ip->ip_dst, uh->uh_dport, INPLOOKUP_WILDCARD);
216         if (inp)
217             udp_last_inpcb = inp;
218         udpstat.udpps_pcbcachemiss++;
219     }
220     if (inp == 0) {
221         udpstat.udps_noport++;
222         if (m->m_flags & (M_BCAST | M_MCAST)) {
223             udpstat.udps_noportbcast++;
224             goto bad;
225         }
226         *ip = save_ip;
227         ip->ip_len += iphlen;
228         icmp_error(m, ICMP_UNREACH, ICMP_UNREACH_PORT, 0, 0);
229         return;
230     }
```

—— udp_usrreq.c

Figure 23.24   udp_input function: demultiplex unicast datagram.

Check one-behind cache

206–209   UDP maintains a pointer to the last Internet PCB for which it received a datagram, udp_last_inpcb. Before calling in_pcblookup, which might have to search many PCBs on the UDP list, the foreign and local addresses and ports of that last PCB are compared against the received datagram. This is called a *one-behind cache* [Partridge and Pink 1993], and it is based on the assumption that the next datagram received has a high probability of being destined for the same socket as the last received datagram [Mogul 1991]. This cache was introduced with the 4.3BSD Tahoe release.

210–213   The order of the four comparisons between the cached PCB and the received datagram is intentional. If the PCBs don't match, the comparisons should stop as soon as possible. The highest probability is that the destination port numbers are different—this is therefore the first test. The lowest probability of a mismatch is between the local addresses, especially on a host with just one interface, so this is the last test.

Unfortunately this one-behind cache, as coded, is practically useless [Partridge and Pink 1993]. The most common type of UDP server binds only its well-known port, leaving its local address, foreign address, and foreign port wildcarded. The most common type of UDP client does not connect its UDP socket; it specifies the destination address for each datagram using `sendto`. Therefore most of the time the three values in the PCB `inp_laddr`, `inp_faddr`, and `inp_fport` are wildcards. In the cache comparison the four values in the received datagram are never wildcards, meaning the cache entry will compare equal with the received datagram only when the PCB has all four local and foreign values specified to nonwildcard values. This happens only for a connected UDP socket.

> On the system `bsdi`, the counter `udpps_pcbcachemiss` was 41,253 and the counter `udps_ipackets` was 42,485. This is less than a 3% cache hit rate.

> The `netstat -s` command prints most of the fields in the `udpstat` structure (Figure 23.5). Unfortunately the Net/3 version, and most vendor's versions, never print `udpps_pcbcachemiss`. If you want to see the value, use a debugger to examine the variable in the running kernel.

Search all UDP PCBs

214–218   Assuming the comparison with the cached PCB fails, `in_pcblookup` searches for a match. The `INPLOOKUP_WILDCARD` flag is specified, allowing a wildcard match. If a match is found, the pointer to the PCB is saved in `udp_last_inpcb`, which we said is a cache of the last received UDP datagram's PCB.

Generate ICMP port unreachable error

220–230   If a matching PCB is not found, UDP normally generates an ICMP port unreachable error. First the `m_flags` for the received mbuf chain is checked to see if the datagram was sent to a link-level broadcast or multicast destination address. It is possible to receive an IP datagram with a unicast IP address that was sent to a broadcast or multicast link-level address, but an ICMP port unreachable error must not be generated. If it is OK to generate the ICMP error, the IP header is restored to its received value (`save_ip`) and the IP length is also set back to its original value.

> This check for a link-level broadcast or multicast address is redundant. `icmp_error` also performs this check. The only advantage in this redundant check is to maintain the counter `udps_noportbcast` in addition to the counter `udps_noport`.

> The addition of `iphlen` back into `ip_len` is a bug. `icmp_error` will also do this, causing the IP length field in the IP header returned in the ICMP error to be 20 bytes too large. You can tell if a system has this bug by adding a few lines of code to the Traceroute program (Chapter 8 of Volume 1) to print this field in the ICMP port unreachable that is returned when the destination host is finally reached.

Figure 23.25 is the next section of processing for a unicast datagram, delivering the datagram to the socket corresponding to the destination PCB.

——— udp_usrreq.c
```
231      /*
232       * Construct sockaddr format source address.
233       * Stuff source address and datagram in user buffer.
234       */
235      udp_in.sin_port = uh->uh_sport;
236      udp_in.sin_addr = ip->ip_src;

237      if (inp->inp_flags & INP_CONTROLOPTS) {
238          struct mbuf **mp = &opts;

239          if (inp->inp_flags & INP_RECVDSTADDR) {
240              *mp = udp_saveopt((caddr_t) & ip->ip_dst,
241                               sizeof(struct in_addr), IP_RECVDSTADDR);
242              if (*mp)
243                  mp = &(*mp)->m_next;
244          }
245 #ifdef notyet
246          /* IP options were tossed above */
247          if (inp->inp_flags & INP_RECVOPTS) {
248              *mp = udp_saveopt((caddr_t) opts_deleted_above,
249                               sizeof(struct in_addr), IP_RECVOPTS);
250              if (*mp)
251                  mp = &(*mp)->m_next;
252          }
253          /* ip_srcroute doesn't do what we want here, need to fix */
254          if (inp->inp_flags & INP_RECVRETOPTS) {
255              *mp = udp_saveopt((caddr_t) ip_srcroute(),
256                               sizeof(struct in_addr), IP_RECVRETOPTS);
257              if (*mp)
258                  mp = &(*mp)->m_next;
259          }
260 #endif
261      }
262      iphlen += sizeof(struct udphdr);
263      m->m_len -= iphlen;
264      m->m_pkthdr.len -= iphlen;
265      m->m_data += iphlen;
266      if (sbappendaddr(&inp->inp_socket->so_rcv, (struct sockaddr *) &udp_in,
267                      m, opts) == 0) {
268          udpstat.udps_fullsock++;
269          goto bad;
270      }
271      sorwakeup(inp->inp_socket);
272      return;

273  bad:
274      m_freem(m);
275      if (opts)
276          m_freem(opts);
277 }
```
——— udp_usrreq.c

Figure 23.25 udp_input function: deliver unicast datagram to socket.

Return source IP address and source port

231–236   The source IP address and source port number from the received IP datagram are stored in the global `sockaddr_in` structure `udp_in`. This structure is passed as an argument to `sbappendaddr` later in the function.

Using a global to hold the IP address and port number is OK because `udp_input` is single threaded. When this function is called by `ipintr` it processes the received datagram completely before returning. Also, `sbappendaddr` copies the socket address structure from the global into an mbuf.

IP_RECVDSTADDR socket option

237–244   The constant `INP_CONTROLOPTS` is the combination of the three socket options that the process can set to cause control information to be returned through the `recvmsg` system call for a UDP socket (Figure 22.5). The `IP_RECVDSTADDR` socket option returns the destination IP address from the received UDP datagram as control information. The function `udp_saveopt` allocates an mbuf of type `MT_CONTROL` and stores the 4-byte destination IP address in the mbuf. We show this function in Section 23.8.

> This socket option appeared with 4.3BSD Reno and was intended for applications such as TFTP, the Trivial File Transfer Protocol, that should not respond to client requests that are sent to a broadcast address. Unfortunately, even if the receiving application uses this option, it is nontrivial to determine if the destination IP address is a broadcast address or not (Exercise 23.6).

> When the multicasting changes were added in 4.4BSD, this code was left in only for datagrams destined for a unicast address. We'll see in Figure 23.26 that this option is not implemented for datagrams sent to a broadcast of multicast address. This defeats the purpose of the option!

Unimplemented socket options

245–260   This code is commented out because it doesn't work. The intent of the `IP_RECVOPTS` socket option is to return the IP options from the received datagram as control information, and the intent of `IP_RECVRETOPTS` socket option is to return source route information. The manipulation of the `mp` variable by all three `IP_RECV` socket options is to build a linked list of up to three mbufs that are then placed onto the socket's buffer by `sbappendaddr`. The code shown in Figure 23.25 only returns one option as control information, so the `m_next` pointer of that mbuf is always a null pointer.

Append data to socket's receive queue

262–272   At this point the received datagram (the mbuf chain pointed to by `m`), is ready to be placed onto the socket's receive queue along with a socket address structure representing the sender's IP address and port (`udp_in`), and optional control information (the destination IP address, the mbuf pointed to by `opts`). This is done by `sbappendaddr`. Before calling this function, however, the pointer and lengths of the first mbuf on the chain are adjusted to ignore the IP and UDP headers. Before returning, `sorwakeup` is called for the receiving socket to wake up any processes asleep on the socket's receive queue.

Error return

273–276   If an error is encountered during UDP input processing, `udp_input` jumps to the label `bad`. The mbuf chain containing the datagram is released, along with the mbuf chain containing any control information (if present).

Demultiplexing Multicast and Broadcast Datagrams

We now return to the portion of `udp_input` that handles datagrams sent to a broadcast or multicast IP address. The code is shown in Figure 23.26.

121–138   As the comments indicate, these datagrams are delivered to *all* sockets that match, not just a single socket. The inadequacy of the UDP interface that is mentioned refers to the inability of a process to receive asynchronous errors on a UDP socket (notably ICMP port unreachables) unless the socket is connected. We described this in Section 22.11.

139–145   The source IP address and port number are saved in the global `sockaddr_in` structure `udp_in`, which is passed to `sbappendaddr`. The mbuf chain's length and data pointer are updated to ignore the IP and UDP headers.

146–164   The large `for` loop scans each UDP PCB to find all matching PCBs. `in_pcblookup` is not called for this demultiplexing because it returns only one PCB, whereas the broadcast or multicast datagram may be delivered to more than one PCB.

If the local port in the PCB doesn't match the destination port from the received datagram, the entry is ignored. If the local address in the PCB is not the wildcard, it is compared to the destination IP address and the entry is skipped if they're not equal. If the foreign address in the PCB is not a wildcard, it is compared to the source IP address and if they match, the foreign port must also match the source port. This last test assumes that if the socket is connected to a foreign IP address it must also be connected to a foreign port, and vice versa. This is the same logic we saw in `in_pcblookup`.

165–177   If this is not the first match found (`last` is nonnull), a copy of the datagram is placed onto the receive queue for the previous match. Since `sbappendaddr` releases the mbuf chain when it is done, a copy is first made by `m_copy`. Any processes waiting for this data are awakened by `sorwakeup`. A pointer to this matching `socket` structure is saved in `last`.

This use of the variable `last` avoids calling `m_copy` (an expensive operation since an entire mbuf chain is copied) unless there are multiple recipients for a given datagram. In the common case of a single recipient, the `for` loop just sets `last` to the single matching PCB, and when the loop terminates, `sbappendaddr` places the mbuf chain onto the socket's receive queue—a copy is not made.

178–188   If this matching socket doesn't have either the `SO_REUSEPORT` or the `SO_REUSEADDR` socket option set, then there's no need to check for additional matches and the loop is terminated. The datagram is placed onto the single socket's receive queue in the call to `sbappendaddr` outside the loop.

189–197   If `last` is null at the end of the loop, no matches were found. An ICMP error is not generated because the datagram was sent to a broadcast or multicast IP address.

```
121     if (IN_MULTICAST(ntohl(ip->ip_dst.s_addr)) ||
122         in_broadcast(ip->ip_dst, m->m_pkthdr.rcvif)) {
123         struct socket *last;
124         /*
125          * Deliver a multicast or broadcast datagram to *all* sockets
126          * for which the local and remote addresses and ports match
127          * those of the incoming datagram.  This allows more than
128          * one process to receive multi/broadcasts on the same port.
129          * (This really ought to be done for unicast datagrams as
130          * well, but that would cause problems with existing
131          * applications that open both address-specific sockets and
132          * a wildcard socket listening to the same port -- they would
133          * end up receiving duplicates of every unicast datagram.
134          * Those applications open the multiple sockets to overcome an
135          * inadequacy of the UDP socket interface, but for backwards
136          * compatibility we avoid the problem here rather than
137          * fixing the interface.  Maybe 4.5BSD will remedy this?)
138          */

139         /*
140          * Construct sockaddr format source address.
141          */
142         udp_in.sin_port = uh->uh_sport;
143         udp_in.sin_addr = ip->ip_src;
144         m->m_len -= sizeof(struct udpiphdr);
145         m->m_data += sizeof(struct udpiphdr);
146         /*
147          * Locate pcb(s) for datagram.
148          * (Algorithm copied from raw_intr().)
149          */
150         last = NULL;
151         for (inp = udb.inp_next; inp != &udb; inp = inp->inp_next) {
152             if (inp->inp_lport != uh->uh_dport)
153                 continue;
154             if (inp->inp_laddr.s_addr != INADDR_ANY) {
155                 if (inp->inp_laddr.s_addr !=
156                     ip->ip_dst.s_addr)
157                     continue;
158             }
159             if (inp->inp_faddr.s_addr != INADDR_ANY) {
160                 if (inp->inp_faddr.s_addr !=
161                     ip->ip_src.s_addr ||
162                     inp->inp_fport != uh->uh_sport)
163                     continue;
164             }
165             if (last != NULL) {
166                 struct mbuf *n;

167                 if ((n = m_copy(m, 0, M_COPYALL)) != NULL) {
168                     if (sbappendaddr(&last->so_rcv,
169                                 (struct sockaddr *) &udp_in,
170                                 n, (struct mbuf *) 0) == 0) {
171                         m_freem(n);
172                         udpstat.udps_fullsock++;
```

```
173                         } else
174                             sorwakeup(last);
175                     }
176                 }
177                 last = inp->inp_socket;
178                 /*
179                  * Don't look for additional matches if this one does
180                  * not have either the SO_REUSEPORT or SO_REUSEADDR
181                  * socket options set.  This heuristic avoids searching
182                  * through all pcbs in the common case of a non-shared
183                  * port.  It assumes that an application will never
184                  * clear these options after setting them.
185                  */
186                 if ((last->so_options & (SO_REUSEPORT | SO_REUSEADDR) == 0))
187                     break;
188             }
189         if (last == NULL) {
190             /*
191              * No matching pcb found; discard datagram.
192              * (No need to send an ICMP Port Unreachable
193              * for a broadcast or multicast datgram.)
194              */
195             udpstat.udps_noportbcast++;
196             goto bad;
197         }
198         if (sbappendaddr(&last->so_rcv, (struct sockaddr *) &udp_in,
199                     m, (struct mbuf *) 0) == 0) {
200             udpstat.udps_fullsock++;
201             goto bad;
202         }
203         sorwakeup(last);
204         return;
205     }
```
udp_usrreq.c

Figure 23.26   udp_input function: demultiplexing of broadcast and multicast datagrams.

198-204   The final matching entry (which could be the only matching entry) has the original datagram (m) placed onto its receive queue. After sorwakeup is called, udp_input returns, since the processing the broadcast or multicast datagram is complete.

The remainder of the function (shown previously in Figure 23.24) handles unicast datagrams.

Connected UDP Sockets and Multihomed Hosts

There is a subtle problem when using a connected UDP socket to exchange datagrams with a process on a multihomed host. Datagrams from the peer may arrive with a different source IP address and will not be delivered to the connected socket.
Consider the example shown in Figure 23.27.

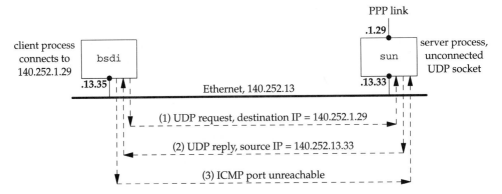

Figure 23.27 Example of connected UDP socket sending datagram to a multihomed host.

Three steps take place.

1. The client on `bsdi` creates a UDP socket and connects it to 140.252.1.29, the PPP interface on `sun`, not the Ethernet interface. A datagram is sent on the socket to the server.

   The server on `sun` receives the datagram and accepts it, even though it arrives on an interface that differs from the destination IP address. (`sun` is acting as a router, so whether it implements the weak end system model or the strong end system model doesn't matter.) The datagram is delivered to the server, which is waiting for client requests on an unconnected UDP socket.

2. The server sends a reply, but since the reply is being sent on an unconnected UDP socket, the source IP address for the reply is chosen by the kernel based on the outgoing interface (140.252.13.33). The destination IP address in the request is not used as the source address for the reply.

   When the reply is received by `bsdi` it is not delivered to the client's connected UDP socket since the IP addresses don't match.

3. `bsdi` generates an ICMP port unreachable error since the reply can't be demultiplexed. (This assumes that there is not another process on `bsdi` eligible to receive the datagram.)

The problem in this example is that the server does not use the destination IP address from the request as the source IP address of the reply. If it did, the problem wouldn't exist, but this solution is nontrivial—see Exercise 23.10. We'll see in Figure 28.16 that a TCP server uses the destination IP address from the client as the source IP address from the server, if the server has not explicitly bound a local IP address to its socket.

23.8 udp_saveopt **Function**

If a process specifies the IP_RECVDSTADDR socket option, to receive the destination IP address from the received datagram udp_saveopt is called by udp_input:

```
*mp = udp_saveopt((caddr_t) &ip->ip_dst, sizeof(struct in_addr),
                  IP_RECVDSTADDR);
```

Figure 23.28 shows this function.

```
                                                            ─────── udp_usrreq.c
278 /*
279  * Create a "control" mbuf containing the specified data
280  * with the specified type for presentation with a datagram.
281  */
282 struct mbuf *
283 udp_saveopt(p, size, type)
284 caddr_t p;
285 int     size;
286 int     type;
287 {
288     struct cmsghdr *cp;
289     struct mbuf *m;

290     if ((m = m_get(M_DONTWAIT, MT_CONTROL)) == NULL)
291         return ((struct mbuf *) NULL);
292     cp = (struct cmsghdr *) mtod(m, struct cmsghdr *);
293     bcopy(p, CMSG_DATA(cp), size);
294     size += sizeof(*cp);
295     m->m_len = size;
296     cp->cmsg_len = size;
297     cp->cmsg_level = IPPROTO_IP;
298     cp->cmsg_type = type;
299     return (m);
300 }
                                                            ─────── udp_usrreq.c
```

Figure 23.28 udp_saveopt function: create mbuf with control information.

278–289   The arguments are p, a pointer to the information to be stored in the mbuf (the destination IP address from the received datagram); size, its size in bytes (4 in this example, the size of an IP address); and type, the type of control information (IP_RECVDSTADDR).

290–299   An mbuf is allocated, and since the code is executing at the software interrupt layer, M_DONTWAIT is specified. The pointer cp points to the data portion of the mbuf, and it is cast into a pointer to a cmsghdr structure (Figure 16.14). The IP address is copied from the IP header into the data portion of the cmsghdr structure by bcopy. The length of the mbuf is then set (to 16 in this example), followed by the remainder of the cmsghdr structure. Figure 23.29 shows the final state of the mbuf.

The cmsg_len field contains the length of the cmsghdr structure (12) plus the size of the cmsg_data field (4 for this example). If the application calls recvmsg to receive the control information, it must go through the cmsghdr structure to determine the type and length of the cmsg_data field.

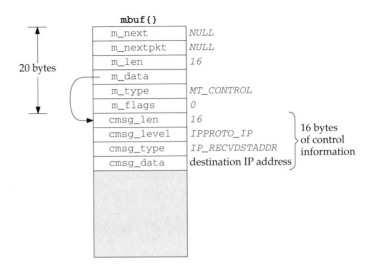

Figure 23.29   Mbuf containing destination address from received datagram as control information.

23.9   udp_ctlinput **Function**

When icmp_input receives an ICMP error (destination unreachable, parameter problem, redirect, source quench, and time exceeded) the corresponding protocol's pr_ctlinput function is called:

```
if (ctlfunc = inetsw[ ip_protox[icp->icmp_ip.ip_p] ].pr_ctlinput)
    (*ctlfunc)(code, (struct sockaddr *)&icmpsrc, &icp->icmp_ip);
```

For UDP, Figure 22.32 showed that the function udp_ctlinput is called. We show this function in Figure 23.30.

314–322   The arguments are cmd, one of the PRC_*xxx* constants from Figure 11.19; sa, a pointer to a sockaddr_in structure containing the source IP address from the ICMP message; and ip, a pointer to the IP header that caused the error. For the destination unreachable, parameter problem, source quench, and time exceeded errors, the pointer ip points to the IP header that caused the error. But when udp_ctlinput is called by pfctlinput for redirects (Figure 22.32), sa points to a sockaddr_in structure containing the destination address that should be redirected, and ip is a null pointer. There is no loss of information in this final case, since we saw in Section 22.11 that a redirect is applied to all TCP and UDP sockets connected to the destination address. The nonnull third argument is needed, however, for other errors, such as a port unreachable, since the protocol header following the IP header contains the unreachable port.

323–325   If the error is not a redirect, and either the PRC_*xxx* value is too large or there is no error code in the global array inetctlerrmap, the ICMP error is ignored. To understand this test we need to review what happens to a received ICMP message.

1. icmp_input converts the ICMP type and code into a PRC_*xxx* error code.

2. The PRC_*xxx* error code is passed to the protocol's control-input function.

udp_usrreq.c

```
314 void
315 udp_ctlinput(cmd, sa, ip)
316 int     cmd;
317 struct sockaddr *sa;
318 struct ip *ip;
319 {
320     struct udphdr *uh;
321     extern struct in_addr zeroin_addr;
322     extern u_char inetctlerrmap[];

323     if (!PRC_IS_REDIRECT(cmd) &&
324         ((unsigned) cmd >= PRC_NCMDS || inetctlerrmap[cmd] == 0))
325         return;
326     if (ip) {
327         uh = (struct udphdr *) ((caddr_t) ip + (ip->ip_hl << 2));
328         in_pcbnotify(&udb, sa, uh->uh_dport, ip->ip_src, uh->uh_sport,
329                     cmd, udp_notify);
330     } else
331         in_pcbnotify(&udb, sa, 0, zeroin_addr, 0, cmd, udp_notify);
332 }
```

udp_usrreq.c

Figure 23.30 udp_ctlinput function: process received ICMP errors.

3. The Internet protocols (TCP and UDP) map the PRC_*xxx* error code into one of the Unix errno values using inetctlerrmap, and this value is returned to the process.

Figures 11.1 and 11.2 summarize this processing of ICMP messages.

Returning to Figure 23.30, we can see what happens to an ICMP source quench that arrives in response to a UDP datagram. icmp_input converts the ICMP message into the error PRC_QUENCH and udp_ctlinput is called. But since the errno column for this ICMP error is blank in Figure 11.2, the error is ignored.

326–331   The function in_pcbnotify notifies the appropriate PCBs of the ICMP error. If the third argument to udp_ctlinput is nonnull, the source and destination UDP ports from the datagram that caused the error are passed to in_pcbnotify along with the source IP address.

udp_notify **Function**

The final argument to in_pcbnotify is a pointer to a function that in_pcbnotify calls for each PCB that is to receive the error. The function for UDP is udp_notify and we show it in Figure 23.31.

301–313   The errno value, the second argument to this function, is stored in the socket's so_error variable. By setting this socket variable, the socket becomes readable and writable if the process calls select. Any processes waiting to receive or send on the socket are then awakened to receive the error.

udp_usrreq.c

```
305 static void
306 udp_notify(inp, errno)
307 struct inpcb *inp;
308 int      errno;
309 {
310     inp->inp_socket->so_error = errno;
311     sorwakeup(inp->inp_socket);
312     sowwakeup(inp->inp_socket);
313 }
```

udp_usrreq.c

Figure 23.31 udp_notify function: notify process of an asynchronous error.

23.10 udp_usrreq Function

The protocol's user-request function is called for a variety of operations. We saw in Figure 23.14 that a call to any one of the five write functions on a UDP socket ends up calling UDP's user-request function with a request of PRU_SEND.

Figure 23.32 shows the beginning and end of udp_usrreq. The body of the switch is discussed in separate figures following this figure. The function arguments are described in Figure 15.17.

udp_usrreq.c

```
417 int
418 udp_usrreq(so, req, m, addr, control)
419 struct socket *so;
420 int      req;
421 struct mbuf *m, *addr, *control;
422 {
423     struct inpcb *inp = sotoinpcb(so);
424     int      error = 0;
425     int      s;

426     if (req == PRU_CONTROL)
427         return (in_control(so, (int) m, (caddr_t) addr,
428                             (struct ifnet *) control));
429     if (inp == NULL && req != PRU_ATTACH) {
430         error = EINVAL;
431         goto release;
432     }
433     /*
434      * Note: need to block udp_input while changing
435      * the udp pcb queue and/or pcb addresses.
436      */
437     switch (req) {

                            /* switch cases */
```

```
522    default:
523        panic("udp_usrreq");
524    }

525    release:
526    if (control) {
527        printf("udp control data unexpectedly retained\n");
528        m_freem(control);
529    }
530    if (m)
531        m_freem(m);
532    return (error);
533    }
```
                                                                    —— *udp_usrreq.c*

Figure 23.32 Body of udp_usrreq function.

417–428   The PRU_CONTROL request is from the ioctl system call. The function in_control processes the request completely.

429–432   The socket pointer was converted to the PCB pointer when inp was declared at the beginning of the function. The only time a null PCB pointer is allowed is when a new socket is being created (PRU_ATTACH).

433–436   The comment indicates that whenever entries are being added to or deleted from UDP's PCB list, the code must be protected by splnet. This is done because udp_usrreq is called as part of a system call, and it doesn't want to be interrupted by UDP input (called by IP input, which is called as a software interrupt) while it is modifying the doubly linked list of PCBs. UDP input is also blocked while modifying the local or foreign addresses or ports in a PCB, to prevent a received UDP datagram from being delivered incorrectly by in_pcblookup.

We now discuss the individual case statements. The PRU_ATTACH request, shown in Figure 23.33, is from the socket system call.

438–447   If the socket structure already points to a PCB, EINVAL is returned. in_pcballoc allocates a new PCB, adds it to the front of UDP's PCB list, and links the socket structure and the PCB to each other.

448–450   soreserve reserves buffer space for a receive buffer and a send buffer for the socket. As noted in Figure 16.7, soreserve just enforces system limits; the buffer space is not actually allocated. The default values for the send and receive buffer sizes are 9216 bytes (udp_sendspace) and 41,600 bytes (udp_recvspace). The former allows for a maximum UDP datagram size of 9200 bytes (to hold 8 Kbytes of data in an NFS packet), plus the 16-byte sockaddr_in structure for the destination address. The latter allows for 40 1024-byte datagrams to be queued at one time for the socket. The process can change these defaults by calling setsockopt.

451–452   There are two fields in the prototype IP header in the PCB that the process can change by calling setsockopt: the TTL and the TOS. The TTL defaults to 64 (ip_defttl) and the TOS defaults to 0 (normal service), since the PCB is initialized to 0 by in_pcballoc.

```
                                                                          udp_usrreq.c
438    case PRU_ATTACH:
439        if (inp != NULL) {
440            error = EINVAL;
441            break;
442        }
443        s = splnet();
444        error = in_pcballoc(so, &udb);
445        splx(s);
446        if (error)
447            break;
448        error = soreserve(so, udp_sendspace, udp_recvspace);
449        if (error)
450            break;
451        ((struct inpcb *) so->so_pcb)->inp_ip.ip_ttl = ip_defttl;
452        break;

453    case PRU_DETACH:
454        udp_detach(inp);
455        break;
                                                                          udp_usrreq.c
```

Figure 23.33   udp_usrreq function: PRU_ATTACH and PRU_DETACH requests.

453–455   The close system call issues the PRU_DETACH request. The function
udp_detach, shown in Figure 23.34, is called. This function is also called later in this
section for the PRU_ABORT request.

```
                                                                          udp_usrreq.c
534 static void
535 udp_detach(inp)
536 struct inpcb *inp;
537 {
538     int     s = splnet();

539     if (inp == udp_last_inpcb)
540         udp_last_inpcb = &udb;
541     in_pcbdetach(inp);
542     splx(s);
543 }
                                                                          udp_usrreq.c
```

Figure 23.34   udp_detach function: delete a UDP PCB.

If the last-received PCB pointer (the one-behind cache) points to the PCB being
detached, the cache pointer is set to the head of the UDP list (udb). The function
in_pcbdetach removes the PCB from UDP's list and releases the PCB.

Returning to udp_usrreq, a PRU_BIND request is the result of the bind system
call and a PRU_LISTEN request is the result of the listen system call. Both are shown
in Figure 23.35.
456–460   All the work for a PRU_BIND request is done by in_pcbbind.
461–463   The PRU_LISTEN request is invalid for a connectionless protocol—it is used only
by connection-oriented protocols.

udp_usrreq.c
```
456        case PRU_BIND:
457            s = splnet();
458            error = in_pcbbind(inp, addr);
459            splx(s);
460            break;

461        case PRU_LISTEN:
462            error = EOPNOTSUPP;
463            break;
```
udp_usrreq.c

Figure 23.35 udp_usrreq function: PRU_BIND and PRU_LISTEN requests.

We mentioned earlier that a UDP application, either a client or server (normally a client), can call connect. This fixes the foreign IP address and port number that this socket can send to or receive from. Figure 23.36 shows the PRU_CONNECT, PRU_CONNECT2, and PRU_ACCEPT requests.

udp_usrreq.c
```
464        case PRU_CONNECT:
465            if (inp->inp_faddr.s_addr != INADDR_ANY) {
466                error = EISCONN;
467                break;
468            }
469            s = splnet();
470            error = in_pcbconnect(inp, addr);
471            splx(s);
472            if (error == 0)
473                soisconnected(so);
474            break;

475        case PRU_CONNECT2:
476            error = EOPNOTSUPP;
477            break;

478        case PRU_ACCEPT:
479            error = EOPNOTSUPP;
480            break;
```
udp_usrreq.c

Figure 23.36 udp_usrreq function: PRU_CONNECT, PRU_CONNECT2, and PRU_ACCEPT requests.

464–474   If the socket is already connected, EISCONN is returned. The socket should never be connected at this point, because a call to connect on an already-connected UDP socket generates a PRU_DISCONNECT request before this PRU_CONNECT request. Otherwise in_pcbconnect does all the work. If no errors are encountered, soisconnected marks the socket structure as being connected.

475–477   The socketpair system call issues the PRU_CONNECT2 request, which is defined only for the Unix domain protocols.

478–480   The PRU_ACCEPT request is from the accept system call, which is defined only for connection-oriented protocols.

The PRU_DISCONNECT request can occur in two cases for a UDP socket:

1. When a connected UDP socket is closed, PRU_DISCONNECT is called before PRU_DETACH.
2. When a connect is issued on an already-connected UDP socket, soconnect issues the PRU_DISCONNECT request before the PRU_CONNECT request.

Figure 23.37 shows the PRU_DISCONNECT request.

```
                                                                  ─── udp_usrreq.c
481        case PRU_DISCONNECT:
482            if (inp->inp_faddr.s_addr == INADDR_ANY) {
483                error = ENOTCONN;
484                break;
485            }
486            s = splnet();
487            in_pcbdisconnect(inp);
488            inp->inp_laddr.s_addr = INADDR_ANY;
489            splx(s);
490            so->so_state &= ~SS_ISCONNECTED;     /* XXX */
491            break;
                                                                  ─── udp_usrreq.c
```

Figure 23.37 udp_usrreq function: PRU_DISCONNECT request.

If the socket is not already connected, ENOTCONN is returned. Otherwise in_pcbdisconnect sets the foreign IP address to 0.0.0.0 and the foreign port to 0. The local address is also set to 0.0.0.0, since this PCB variable could have been set by connect.

A call to shutdown specifying that the process has finished sending data generates the PRU_SHUTDOWN request, although it is rare for a process to issue this system call for a UDP socket. Figure 23.38 shows the PRU_SHUTDOWN, PRU_SEND, and PRU_ABORT requests.

```
                                                                  ─── udp_usrreq.c
492        case PRU_SHUTDOWN:
493            socantsendmore(so);
494            break;

495        case PRU_SEND:
496            return (udp_output(inp, m, addr, control));

497        case PRU_ABORT:
498            soisdisconnected(so);
499            udp_detach(inp);
500            break;
                                                                  ─── udp_usrreq.c
```

Figure 23.38 udp_usrreq function: PRU_SHUTDOWN, PRU_SEND, and PRU_ABORT requests.

492–494   socantsendmore sets the socket's flags to prevent any future output.

495–496   In Figure 23.14 we showed how the five write functions ended up calling `udp_usrreq` with a `PRU_SEND` request. `udp_output` sends the datagram. `udp_usrreq` returns, to avoid falling through to the label `release` (Figure 23.32), since the mbuf chain containing the data (`m`) must not be released yet. IP output appends this mbuf chain to the appropriate interface output queue, and the device driver will release the mbuf when the data has been transmitted.

    The only buffering of UDP output within the kernel is on the interface's output queue. If there is room in the socket's send buffer for the datagram and destination address, `sosend` calls `udp_usrreq`, which we see calls `udp_output`. We saw in Figure 23.20 that `ip_output` is then called, which calls `ether_output` for an Ethernet, placing the datagram onto the interface's output queue (if there is room). If the process calls `sendto` faster than the interface can transmit the datagrams, `ether_output` can return `ENOBUFS`, which is returned to the process.

497–500   A `PRU_ABORT` request should never be generated for a UDP socket, but if it is, the socket is disconnected and the PCB detached.

    The `PRU_SOCKADDR` and `PRU_PEERADDR` requests are from the `getsockname` and `getpeername` system calls, respectively. These two requests, and the `PRU_SENSE` request, are shown in Figure 23.39.

---
                                                                 udp_usrreq.c

```
501       case PRU_SOCKADDR:
502           in_setsockaddr(inp, addr);
503           break;

504       case PRU_PEERADDR:
505           in_setpeeraddr(inp, addr);
506           break;

507       case PRU_SENSE:
508           /*
509            * fstat: don't bother with a blocksize.
510            */
511           return (0);
```
                                                                 udp_usrreq.c

---

Figure 23.39 `udp_usrreq` function: `PRU_SOCKADDR`, `PRU_PEERADDR`, and `PRU_SENSE` requests.

501–506   The functions `in_setsockaddr` and `in_setpeeraddr` fetch the information from the PCB, storing the result in the `addr` argument.

507–511   The `fstat` system call generates the `PRU_SENSE` request. The function returns OK, but doesn't return any other information. We'll see later that TCP returns the size of the send buffer as the `st_blksize` element of the `stat` structure.

    The remaining seven PRU_*xxx* requests, shown in Figure 23.40, are not supported for a UDP socket.

```
                                                                   ── udp_usrreq.c
512     case PRU_SENDOOB:
513     case PRU_FASTTIMO:
514     case PRU_SLOWTIMO:
515     case PRU_PROTORCV:
516     case PRU_PROTOSEND:
517         error = EOPNOTSUPP;
518         break;

519     case PRU_RCVD:
520     case PRU_RCVOOB:
521         return (EOPNOTSUPP);    /* do not free mbuf's */
                                                                   ── udp_usrreq.c
```

Figure 23.40 udp_usrreq function: unsupported requests.

There is a slight difference in how the last two are handled because PRU_RCVD
doesn't pass a pointer to an mbuf as an argument (m is a null pointer) and PRU_RCVOOB
passes a pointer to an mbuf for the protocol to fill in. In both cases the error is immediately returned, without breaking out of the switch and releasing the mbuf chain. With
PRU_RCVOOB the caller releases the mbuf that it allocated.

23.11 udp_sysctl Function

The sysctl function for UDP supports only a single option, the UDP checksum flag.
The system administrator can enable or disable UDP checksums using the sysctl(8)
program. Figure 23.41 shows the udp_sysctl function. This function calls
sysctl_int to fetch or set the value of the integer udpcksum.

```
                                                                   ── udp_usrreq.c
547 udp_sysctl(name, namelen, oldp, oldlenp, newp, newlen)
548 int     *name;
549 u_int   namelen;
550 void    *oldp;
551 size_t  *oldlenp;
552 void    *newp;
553 size_t  newlen;
554 {
555     /* All sysctl names at this level are terminal. */
556     if (namelen != 1)
557         return (ENOTDIR);

558     switch (name[0]) {
559     case UDPCTL_CHECKSUM:
560         return (sysctl_int(oldp, oldlenp, newp, newlen, &udpcksum));
561     default:
562         return (ENOPROTOOPT);
563     }
564     /* NOTREACHED */
565 }
                                                                   ── udp_usrreq.c
```

Figure 23.41 udp_sysctl function.

23.12 Implementation Refinements

UDP PCB Cache

In Section 22.12 we talked about some general features of PCB searching and how the code we've seen uses a linear search of the protocol's PCB list. We now tie this together with the one-behind cache used by UDP in Figure 23.24.

The problem with the one-behind cache occurs when the cached PCB contains wild-card values (for either the local address, foreign address, or foreign port): the cached value never matches any received datagram. One solution tested in [Partridge and Pink 1993] is to modify the cache to not compare wildcarded values. That is, instead of comparing the foreign address in the PCB with the source address in the datagram, compare these two values only if the foreign address in the PCB is not a wildcard.

There's a subtle problem with this approach [Partridge and Pink 1993]. Assume there are two sockets bound to local port 555. One has the remaining three elements wildcarded, while the other has connected to the foreign address 128.1.2.3 and the foreign port 1600. If we cache the first PCB and a datagram arrives from 128.1.2.3, port 1600, we can't ignore comparing the foreign addresses just because the cached value has a wildcarded foreign address. This is called *cache hiding*. The cached PCB has hidden another PCB that is a better match in this example.

To get around cache hiding requires more work when a new entry is added to or deleted from the cache. Those PCBs that hide other PCBs cannot be cached. This is not a problem, however, because the normal scenario is to have one socket per local port. The example we just gave with two sockets bound to local port 555, while possible (especially on a multihomed host), is rare.

The next enhancement tested in [Partridge and Pink 1993] is to also remember the PCB of the last datagram sent. This is motivated by [Mogul 1991], who shows that half of all datagrams received are replies to the last datagram that was sent. Cache hiding is a problem here also, so PCBs that would hide other PCBs are not cached.

The results of these two caches shown in [Partridge and Pink 1993] on a general-purpose system measured for around 100,000 received UDP datagrams show a 57% hit rate for the last-received PCB cache and a 30% hit rate for the last-sent PCB cache. The amount of CPU time spent in `udp_input` is more than halved, compared to the version with no caching.

These two caches still depend on a certain amount of locality: that with a high probability the UDP datagram that just arrived is either from the same peer as the last UDP datagram received or from the peer to whom the last datagram was sent. The latter is typical for request–response applications that send a datagram and wait for a reply. [McKenney and Dove 1992] show that some applications, such as data entry into an on-line transaction processing (OLTP) system, don't yield the high cache hit rates that [Partridge and Pink 1993] observed. As we mentioned in Section 22.12, placing the PCBs onto hash chains provided an order of magnitude improvement over the last-received and last-sent caches for a system with thousands of OLTP connections.

UDP Checksum

The next area for improving the implementation is to combine the copying of data between the process and the kernel with the calculation of the checksum. In Net/3, each byte of data is processed twice during an output operation: once when copied from the process into an mbuf (the function `uiomove`, which is called by `sosend`), and again when the UDP checksum is calculated (by the function `in_cksum`, which is called by `udp_output`). This happens on input as well as output.

[Partridge and Pink 1993] modified the UDP output processing from what we showed in Figure 23.14 so that a UDP-specific function named `udp_sosend` is called instead of `sosend`. This new function calculates the checksum of the UDP header and the pseudo-header in-line (instead of calling the general-purpose function `in_cksum`) and then copies the data from the process into an mbuf chain using a special function named `in_uiomove` (instead of the general-purpose `uiomove`). This new function copies the data *and* updates the checksum. The amount of time spent copying the data and calculating the checksum is reduced with this technique by about 40 to 45%.

On the receive side the scenario is different. UDP calculates the checksum of the UDP header and the pseudo-header, removes the UDP header, and queues the data for the appropriate socket. When the application reads the data, a special version of `soreceive` (called `udp_soreceive`) completes the calculation of the checksum while copying the data into the user's buffer. If the checksum is in error, however, the error is not detected until the entire datagram has been copied into the user's buffer. In the normal case of a blocking socket, `udp_soreceive` just waits for the next datagram to arrive. But if the socket is nonblocking, the error EWOULDBLOCK must be returned if another datagram is not ready to be passed to the process. This implies two changes in the socket interface for a nonblocking read from a UDP socket:

1. The `select` function can indicate that a nonblocking UDP socket is readable, yet the error EWOULDBLOCK is unexpectedly returned by one of the read functions if the checksum fails.

2. Since a checksum error is detected after the datagram has been copied into the user's buffer, the application's buffer is changed even though no data is returned by the read.

Even with a blocking socket, if the datagram with the checksum error contains 100 bytes of data and the next datagram without an error contains 40 bytes of data, `recvfrom` returns a length of 40, but the 60 bytes that follow in the user's buffer have also been modified.

[Partridge and Pink 1993] compare the timings for a copy versus a copy-with-checksum for six different computers. They show that the checksum is calculated for free during the copy operation on many architectures. This occurs when memory access speeds and CPU processing speeds are mismatched, as is true for many current RISC processors.

23.13 Summary

UDP is a simple, connectionless protocol, which is why we cover it before looking at TCP. UDP output is simple: IP and UDP headers are prepended to the user's data, as much of the header is filled in as possible, and the result is passed to `ip_output`. The only complication is calculating the UDP checksum, which involves prepending a pseudo-header just for the checksum computation. We'll encounter a similar pseudo-header for the calculation of the TCP checksum in Chapter 26.

When `udp_input` receives a datagram, it first performs a general validation (the length and checksum); the processing then differs depending on whether the destination IP address is a unicast address or a broadcast or multicast address. A unicast datagram is delivered to at most one process, but a broadcast or multicast datagram can be delivered to multiple processes. A one-behind cache is maintained for unicast datagrams, which maintains a pointer to the last Internet PCB for which a UDP datagram was received. We saw, however, that because of the prevalence of wildcard addressing with UDP applications, this cache is practically useless.

The `udp_ctlinput` function is called to handle received ICMP messages, and the `udp_usrreq` function handles the PRU_*xxx* requests from the socket layer.

Exercises

23.1   List the five types of mbuf chains that `udp_output` passes to `ip_output`. (*Hint*: look at `sosend`.)

23.2   What happens to the answer for the previous exercise when the process specifies IP options for the outgoing datagram?

23.3   Does a UDP client need to call `bind`? Why or why not?

23.4   What happens to the processor priority level in `udp_output` if the socket is unconnected and the call to `M_PREPEND` in Figure 23.15 fails?

23.5   `udp_output` does not check for a destination port of 0. Is it possible to send a UDP datagram with a destination port of 0?

23.6   Assuming the `IP_RECVDSTADDR` socket option worked when a datagram was sent to a broadcast address, how can you then determine if this address is a broadcast address?

23.7   Who releases the mbuf that `udp_saveopt` (Figure 23.28) allocates?

23.8   How can a process disconnect a connected UDP socket? That is, the process calls `connect` and exchanges datagrams with that peer, and then the process wants to disconnect the socket, allowing it to call `sendto` and send a datagram to some other host.

23.9   In our discussion of Figure 22.25 we noted that a UDP application that calls `connect` with a foreign IP address of 255.255.255.255 actually sends datagrams out the primary interface with a destination IP address corresponding to the broadcast address of that interface. What happens if a UDP application uses an unconnected socket instead, calling `sendto` with a destination address of 255.255.255.255?

23.10 After discussing the problem with Figure 23.27, we mentioned that this problem would not exist if the server used the destination IP address from the request as the source IP address of the reply. Explain how the server could do this.

23.11 Implement changes to allow a process to perform path MTU discovery using UDP: the process must be able to set the "don't fragment" bit in the resulting IP datagram and be told if the corresponding ICMP destination unreachable error is received.

23.12 Does the variable udp_in need to be global?

23.13 Modify udp_input to save the IP options and make them available to the receiver with the IP_RECVOPTS socket option.

23.14 Fix the one-behind cache in Figure 23.24.

23.15 Fix udp_input to implement the IP_RECVOPTS and IP_RETOPTS socket options.

23.16 Fix udp_input so that the IP_RECVDSTADDR socket option works for datagrams sent to a broadcast or multicast address.

24

TCP: Transmission Control Protocol

24.1 Introduction

The Transmission Control Protocol, or TCP, provides a connection-oriented, reliable, byte-stream service between the two end points of an application. This is completely different from UDP's connectionless, unreliable, datagram service.

The implementation of UDP presented in Chapter 23 comprised 9 functions and about 800 lines of C code. The TCP implementation we're about to describe comprises 28 functions and almost 4,500 lines of C code. Therefore we divide the presentation of TCP into multiple chapters.

These chapters are not an introduction to TCP. We assume the reader is familiar with the operation of TCP from Chapters 17–24 of Volume 1.

24.2 Code Introduction

The TCP functions appear in six C files and numerous TCP definitions are in seven headers, as shown in Figure 24.1.

Figure 24.2 shows the relationship of the various TCP functions to other kernel functions. The shaded ellipses are the nine main TCP functions that we cover. Eight of these functions appear in the TCP `protosw` structure (Figure 24.8) and the ninth is `tcp_output`.

File	Description
netinet/tcp.h	tcphdr structure definition
netinet/tcp_debug.h	tcp_debug structure definition
netinet/tcp_fsm.h	definitions for TCP's finite state machine
netinet/tcp_seq.h	macros for comparing TCP sequence numbers
netinet/tcp_timer.h	definitions for TCP timers
netinet/tcp_var.h	tcpcb (control block) and tcpstat (statistics) structure definitions
netinet/tcpip.h	TCP plus IP header definition
netinet/tcp_debug.c	support for SO_DEBUG socket debugging (Section 27.10)
netinet/tcp_input.c	tcp_input and ancillary functions (Chapters 28 and 29)
netinet/tcp_output.c	tcp_output and ancillary functions (Chapter 26)
netinet/tcp_subr.c	miscellaneous TCP subroutines (Chapter 27)
netinet/tcp_timer.c	TCP timer handling (Chapter 25)
netinet/tcp_usrreq.c	PRU_xxx request handling (Chapter 30)

Figure 24.1   Files discussed in the TCP chapters.

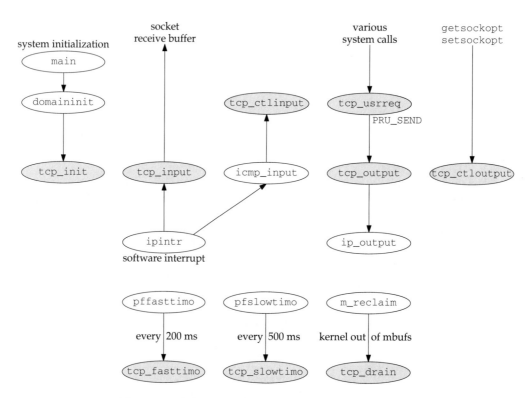

Figure 24.2   Relationship of TCP functions to rest of the kernel.

Global Variables

Figure 24.3 shows the global variables we encounter throughout the TCP functions.

Variable	Datatype	Description
tcb	struct inpcb	head of the TCP Internet PCB list
tcp_last_inpcb	struct inpcb *	pointer to PCB for last received segment: one-behind cache
tcpstat	struct tcpstat	TCP statistics (Figure 24.4)
tcp_outflags	u_char	array of output flags, indexed by connection state (Figure 24.16)
tcp_recvspace	u_long	default size of socket receive buffer (8192 bytes)
tcp_sendspace	u_long	default size of socket send buffer (8192 bytes)
tcp_iss	tcp_seq	initial send sequence number (ISS)
tcprexmtthresh	int	number of duplicate ACKs to trigger fast retransmit (3)
tcp_mssdflt	int	default MSS (512 bytes)
tcp_rttdflt	int	default RTT if no data (3 seconds)
tcp_do_rfc1323	int	if true (default), request window scale and timestamp options
tcp_now	u_long	500 ms counter for RFC 1323 timestamps
tcp_keepidle	int	keepalive: idle time before first probe (2 hours)
tcp_keepintvl	int	keepalive: interval between probes when no response (75 sec) (also used as timeout for connect)
tcp_maxidle	int	keepalive: time after probing before giving up (10 min)

Figure 24.3 Global variables introduced in the following chapters.

Statistics

Various TCP statistics are maintained in the global structure tcpstat, described in Figure 24.4. We'll see where these counters are incremented as we proceed through the code.

Figure 24.5 shows some sample output of these statistics, from the netstat -s command. These statistics were collected after the host had been up for 30 days. Since some counters come in pairs—one counts the number of packets and the other the number of bytes—we abbreviate these in the figure. For example, the two counters for the second line of the table are tcps_sndpack and tcps_sndbyte.

> The counter for tcps_sndbyte should be 3,722,884,824, not –22,194,928 bytes. This is an average of about 405 bytes per segment, which makes sense. Similarly, the counter for tcps_rcvackbyte should be 3,738,811,552, not –21,264,360 bytes (for an average of about 565 bytes per segment). These numbers are incorrectly printed as negative numbers because the printf calls in the netstat program use %d (signed decimal) instead of %lu (long integer, unsigned decimal). All the counters are unsigned long integers, and these two counters are near the maximum value of an unsigned 32-bit long integer ($2^{32} - 1 = 4,294,967,295$).

tcpstat member	Description	Used by SNMP
tcps_accepts	#SYNs received in LISTEN state	•
tcps_closed	#connections closed (includes drops)	
tcps_connattempt	#connections initiated (calls to connect)	•
tcps_conndrops	#embryonic connections dropped (before SYN received)	•
tcps_connects	#connections established actively or passively	
tcps_delack	#delayed ACKs sent	
tcps_drops	#connections dropped (after SYN received)	•
tcps_keepdrops	#connections dropped in keepalive (established or awaiting SYN)	
tcps_keepprobe	#keepalive probes sent	
tcps_keeptimeo	#times keepalive timer or connection-establishment timer expire	
tcps_pawsdrop	#segments dropped due to PAWS	
tcps_pcbcachemiss	#times PCB cache comparison fails	
tcps_persisttimeo	#times persist timer expires	
tcps_predack	#times header prediction correct for ACKs	
tcps_preddat	#times header prediction correct for data packets	
tcps_rcvackbyte	#bytes ACKed by received ACKs	
tcps_rcvackpack	#received ACK packets	
tcps_rcvacktoomuch	#received ACKs for unsent data	
tcps_rcvafterclose	#packets received after connection closed	
tcps_rcvbadoff	#packets received with invalid header length	•
tcps_rcvbadsum	#packets received with checksum errors	•
tcps_rcvbyte	#bytes received in sequence	
tcps_rcvbyteafterwin	#bytes received beyond advertised window	
tcps_rcvdupack	#duplicate ACKs received	
tcps_rcvdupbyte	#bytes received in completely duplicate packets	
tcps_rcvduppack	#packets received with completely duplicate bytes	
tcps_rcvoobyte	#out-of-order bytes received	
tcps_rcvoopack	#out-of-order packets received	
tcps_rcvpack	#packets received in sequence	
tcps_rcvpackafterwin	#packets with some data beyond advertised window	
tcps_rcvpartdupbyte	#duplicate bytes in part-duplicate packets	
tcps_rcvpartduppack	#packets with some duplicate data	
tcps_rcvshort	#packets received too short	•
tcps_rcvtotal	total #packets received	•
tcps_rcvwinprobe	#window probe packets received	
tcps_rcvwinupd	#received window update packets	
tcps_rexmttimeo	#retransmit timeouts	
tcps_rttupdated	#times RTT estimators updated	
tcps_segstimed	#segments for which TCP tried to measure RTT	
tcps_sndacks	#ACK-only packets sent (data length = 0)	
tcps_sndbyte	#data bytes sent	
tcps_sndctrl	#control (SYN, FIN, RST) packets sent (data length = 0)	
tcps_sndpack	#data packets sent (data length > 0)	
tcps_sndprobe	#window probes sent (1 byte of data forced by persist timer)	
tcps_sndrexmitbyte	#data bytes retransmitted	•
tcps_sndrexmitpack	#data packets retransmitted	•
tcps_sndtotal	total #packets sent	•
tcps_sndurg	#packets sent with URG-only (data length = 0)	
tcps_sndwinup	#window update-only packets sent (data length = 0)	
tcps_timeoutdrop	#connections dropped in retransmission timeout	

Figure 24.4   TCP statistics maintained in the tcpstat structure.

`netstat -s` output	`tcpstat` members
10,655,999 packets sent	`tcps_sndtotal`
9,177,823 data packets (-22,194,928 bytes)	`tcps_snd{pack,byte}`
257,295 data packets (81,075,086 bytes) retransmitted	`tcps_sndrexmit{pack,byte}`
862,900 ack-only packets (531,285 delayed)	`tcps_sndacks,tcps_delack`
229 URG-only packets	`tcps_sndurg`
3,453 window probe packets	`tcps_sndprobe`
74,925 window update packets	`tcps_sndwinup`
279,387 control packets	`tcps_sndctrl`
8,801,953 packets received	`tcps_rcvtotal`
6,617,079 acks (for -21,264,360 bytes)	`tcps_rcvack{pack,byte}`
235,311 duplicate acks	`tcps_rcvdupack`
0 acks for unsent data	`tcps_rcvacktoomuch`
4,670,615 packets (324,965,351 bytes) rcvd in-sequence	`tcps_rcv{pack,byte}`
46,953 completely duplicate packets (1,549,785 bytes)	`tcps_rcvdup{pack,byte}`
22 old duplicate packets	`tcps_pawsdrop`
3,442 packets with some dup. data (54,483 bytes duped)	`tcps_rcvpartdup{pack,byte}`
77,114 out-of-order packets (13,938,456 bytes)	`tcps_rcvoo{pack,byte}`
1,892 packets (1,755 bytes) of data after window	`tcps_rcv{pack,byte}afterwin`
1,755 window probes	`tcps_rcvwinprobe`
175,476 window update packets	`tcps_rcvwindup`
1,017 packets received after close	`tcps_rcvafterclose`
60,370 discarded for bad checksums	`tcps_rcvbadsum`
279 discarded for bad header offset fields	`tcps_rcvbadoff`
0 discarded because packet too short	`tcps_rcvshort`
144,020 connection requests	`tcps_connattempt`
92,595 connection accepts	`tcps_accepts`
126,820 connections established (including accepts)	`tcps_connects`
237,743 connections closed (including 1,061 drops)	`tcps_closed,tcps_drops`
110,016 embryonic connections dropped	`tcps_conndrops`
6,363,546 segments updated rtt (of 6,444,667 attempts)	`tcps_{rttupdated,segstimed}`
114,797 retransmit timeouts	`tcps_rexmttimeo`
86 connection dropped by rexmit timeout	`tcps_timeoutdrop`
1,173 persist timeouts	`tcps_persisttimeo`
16,419 keepalive timeouts	`tcps_keeptimeo`
6,899 keepalive probes sent	`tcps_keepprobe`
3,219 connections dropped by keepalive	`tcps_keepdrops`
733,130 correct ACK header predictions	`tcps_predack`
1,266,889 correct data packet header predictions	`tcps_preddat`
1,851,557 cache misses	`tcps_pcbcachemiss`

Figure 24.5   Sample TCP statistics.

SNMP Variables

Figure 24.6 shows the 14 simple SNMP variables in the TCP group and the counters from the `tcpstat` structure implementing that variable. The constant values shown for the first four entries are fixed by the Net/3 implementation. The counter `tcpCurrEstab` is computed as the number of Internet PCBs on the TCP PCB list.

Figure 24.7 shows `tcpTable`, the TCP listener table.

SNMP variable	`tcpstat` members or constant	Description
`tcpRtoAlgorithm`	4	algorithm used to calculate retransmission timeout value: 1 = none of the following, 2 = a constant RTO, 3 = MIL–STD–1778 Appendix B, 4 = Van Jacobson's algorithm.
`tcpRtoMin`	1000	minimum retransmission timeout value, in milliseconds
`tcpRtoMax`	64000	maximum retransmission timeout value, in milliseconds
`tcpMaxConn`	-1	maximum #TCP connections (-1 if dynamic)
`tcpActiveOpens`	`tcps_connattempt`	#transitions from CLOSED to SYN_SENT states
`tcpPassiveOpens`	`tcps_accepts`	#transitions from LISTEN to SYN_RCVD states
`tcpAttemptFails`	`tcps_conndrops`	#transitions from SYN_SENT or SYN_RCVD to CLOSED, plus #transitions from SYN_RCVD to LISTEN
`tcpEstabResets`	`tcps_drops`	#transitions from ESTABLISHED or CLOSE_WAIT states to CLOSED
`tcpCurrEstab`	(see text)	#connections currently in ESTABLISHED or CLOSE_WAIT states
`tcpInSegs`	`tcps_rcvtotal`	total #segments received
`tcpOutSegs`	`tcps_sndtotal - tcps_sndrexmitpack`	total #segments sent, excluding those containing only retransmitted bytes
`tcpRetransSegs`	`tcps_sndrexmitpack`	total #retransmitted segments
`tcpInErrs`	`tcps_rcvbadsum + tcps_rcvbadoff + tcps_rcvshort`	total #segments received with an error
`tcpOutRsts`	(not implemented)	total #segments sent with RST flag set

Figure 24.6   Simple SNMP variables in `tcp` group.

index = < *tcpConnLocalAddress* >.< *tcpConnLocalPort* >.< *tcpConnRemAddress* >.< *tcpConnRemPort* >		
SNMP variable	PCB variable	Description
`tcpConnState`	`t_state`	state of connection: 1 = CLOSED, 2 = LISTEN, 3 = SYN_SENT, 4 = SYN_RCVD, 5 = ESTABLISHED, 6 = FIN_WAIT_1, 7 = FIN_WAIT_2, 8 = CLOSE_WAIT, 9 = LAST_ACK, 10 = CLOSING, 11 = TIME_WAIT, 12 = delete TCP control block.
`tcpConnLocalAddress`	`inp_laddr`	local IP address
`tcpConnLocalPort`	`inp_lport`	local port number
`tcpConnRemAddress`	`inp_faddr`	foreign IP address
`tcpConnRemPort`	`inp_fport`	foreign port number

Figure 24.7   Variables in TCP listener table: `tcpTable`.

The first PCB variable (`t_state`) is from the TCP control block (Figure 24.13) and the remaining four are from the Internet PCB (Figure 22.4).

24.3 TCP `protosw` Structure

Figure 24.8 lists the TCP `protosw` structure, the protocol switch entry for TCP.

Member	inetsw[2]	Description
pr_type	*SOCK_STREAM*	TCP provides a byte-stream service
pr_domain	*&inetdomain*	TCP is part of the Internet domain
pr_protocol	*IPPROTO_TCP (6)*	appears in the ip_p field of the IP header
pr_flags	*PR_CONNREQUIRED|PR_WANTRCVD*	socket layer flags, not used by protocol processing
pr_input	*tcp_input*	receives messages from IP layer
pr_output	*0*	not used by TCP
pr_ctlinput	*tcp_ctlinput*	control input function for ICMP errors
pr_ctloutput	*tcp_ctloutput*	respond to administrative requests from a process
pr_usrreq	*tcp_usrreq*	respond to communication requests from a process
pr_init	*tcp_init*	initialization for TCP
pr_fasttimo	*tcp_fasttimo*	fast timeout function, called every 200 ms
pr_slowtimo	*tcp_slowtimo*	slow timeout function, called every 500 ms
pr_drain	*tcp_drain*	called when kernel runs out of mbufs
pr_sysctl	*0*	not used by TCP

Figure 24.8 The TCP `protosw` structure.

24.4 TCP Header

The TCP header is defined as a `tcphdr` structure. Figure 24.9 shows the C structure and Figure 24.10 shows a picture of the TCP header.

```
                                                                    tcp.h
40 struct tcphdr {
41     u_short th_sport;            /* source port */
42     u_short th_dport;            /* destination port */
43     tcp_seq th_seq;             /* sequence number */
44     tcp_seq th_ack;             /* acknowledgement number */
45 #if BYTE_ORDER == LITTLE_ENDIAN
46     u_char  th_x2:4,             /* (unused) */
47             th_off:4;            /* data offset */
48 #endif
49 #if BYTE_ORDER == BIG_ENDIAN
50     u_char  th_off:4,            /* data offset */
51             th_x2:4;             /* (unused) */
52 #endif
53     u_char  th_flags;            /* ACK, FIN, PUSH, RST, SYN, URG */
54     u_short th_win;              /* advertised window */
55     u_short th_sum;              /* checksum */
56     u_short th_urp;              /* urgent offset */
57 };
                                                                    tcp.h
```

Figure 24.9 `tcphdr` structure.

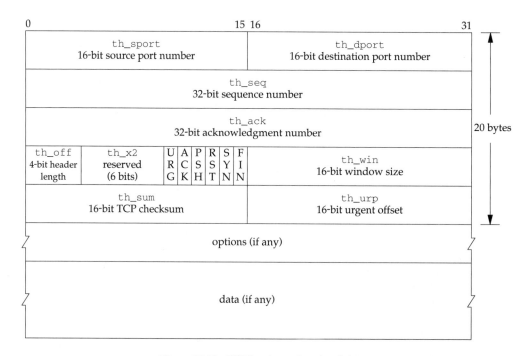

Figure 24.10   TCP header and optional data.

Most RFCs, most books (including Volume 1), and the code we'll examine call th_urp the *urgent pointer*. A better term is the *urgent offset*, since this field is a 16-bit unsigned offset that must be added to the sequence number field (th_seq) to give the 32-bit sequence number of the *last* byte of urgent data. (There is a continuing debate over whether this sequence number points to the last byte of urgent data or to the byte that follows. This is immaterial for the present discussion.) We'll see in Figure 24.13 that TCP correctly calls the 32-bit sequence number of the last byte of urgent data snd_up the *send urgent pointer*. But using the term *pointer* for the 16-bit offset in the TCP header is misleading. In Exercise 26.6 we'll reiterate the distinction between the urgent pointer and the urgent offset.

The 4-bit header length, the 6 reserved bits that follow, and the 6 flag bits are defined in C as two 4-bit bit-fields, followed by 8 bits of flags. To handle the difference in the order of these 4-bit fields within an 8-bit byte, the code contains an #ifdef based on the byte order of the system.

Also notice that we call the 4-bit th_off the *header length*, while the C code calls it the *data offset*. Both are correct since it is the length of the TCP header, including options, in 32-bit words, which is the offset of the first byte of data.

The th_flags member contains 6 flag bits, accessed using the names in Figure 24.11.

In Net/3 the TCP header is normally referenced as an IP header immediately followed by a TCP header. This is how tcp_input processes received IP datagrams and how tcp_output builds outgoing IP datagrams. This combined IP/TCP header is a tcpiphdr structure, shown in Figure 24.12.

th_flags	Description
TH_ACK	the acknowledgment number (th_ack) is valid
TH_FIN	the sender is finished sending data
TH_PUSH	receiver should pass the data to application without delay
TH_RST	reset the connection
TH_SYN	synchronize sequence numbers (establish connection)
TH_URG	the urgent offset (th_urp) is valid

Figure 24.11 th_flags values.

─── *tcpip.h*
```
38 struct tcpiphdr {
39     struct ipovly ti_i;        /* overlaid ip structure */
40     struct tcphdr ti_t;        /* tcp header */
41 };

42 #define ti_next     ti_i.ih_next
43 #define ti_prev     ti_i.ih_prev
44 #define ti_x1       ti_i.ih_x1
45 #define ti_pr       ti_i.ih_pr
46 #define ti_len      ti_i.ih_len
47 #define ti_src      ti_i.ih_src
48 #define ti_dst      ti_i.ih_dst
49 #define ti_sport    ti_t.th_sport
50 #define ti_dport    ti_t.th_dport
51 #define ti_seq      ti_t.th_seq
52 #define ti_ack      ti_t.th_ack
53 #define ti_x2       ti_t.th_x2
54 #define ti_off      ti_t.th_off
55 #define ti_flags    ti_t.th_flags
56 #define ti_win      ti_t.th_win
57 #define ti_sum      ti_t.th_sum
58 #define ti_urp      ti_t.th_urp
```
─── *tcpip.h*

Figure 24.12 tcpiphdr structure: combined IP/TCP header.

38–58   The 20-byte IP header is defined as an ipovly structure, which we showed earlier in Figure 23.12. As we discussed with Figure 23.19, this structure is not a real IP header, although the lengths are the same (20 bytes).

24.5 TCP Control Block

In Figure 22.1 we showed that TCP maintains its own control block, a tcpcb structure, in addition to the standard Internet PCB. In contrast, UDP has everything it needs in the Internet PCB—it doesn't need its own control block.

The TCP control block is a large structure, occupying 140 bytes. As shown in Figure 22.1 there is a one-to-one relationship between the Internet PCB and the TCP control block, and each points to the other. Figure 24.13 shows the definition of the TCP control block.

── tcp_var.h
```
41 struct tcpcb {
42     struct tcpiphdr *seg_next;   /* reassembly queue of received segments */
43     struct tcpiphdr *seg_prev;   /* reassembly queue of received segments */
44     short   t_state;             /* connection state (Figure 24.16) */
45     short   t_timer[TCPT_NTIMERS];  /* tcp timers (Chapter 25) */
46     short   t_rxtshift;          /* log(2) of rexmt exp. backoff */
47     short   t_rxtcur;            /* current retransmission timeout (#ticks) */
48     short   t_dupacks;           /* #consecutive duplicate ACKs received */
49     u_short t_maxseg;            /* maximum segment size to send */
50     char    t_force;             /* 1 if forcing out a byte (persist/OOB) */
51     u_short t_flags;             /* (Figure 24.14) */
52     struct tcpiphdr *t_template;    /* skeletal packet for transmit */
53     struct inpcb *t_inpcb;       /* back pointer to internet PCB */
54 /*
55  * The following fields are used as in the protocol specification.
56  * See RFC783, Dec. 1981, page 21.
57  */
58 /* send sequence variables */
59     tcp_seq snd_una;             /* send unacknowledged */
60     tcp_seq snd_nxt;             /* send next */
61     tcp_seq snd_up;              /* send urgent pointer */
62     tcp_seq snd_wl1;             /* window update seg seq number */
63     tcp_seq snd_wl2;             /* window update seg ack number */
64     tcp_seq iss;                 /* initial send sequence number */
65     u_long  snd_wnd;             /* send window */
66 /* receive sequence variables */
67     u_long  rcv_wnd;             /* receive window */
68     tcp_seq rcv_nxt;             /* receive next */
69     tcp_seq rcv_up;              /* receive urgent pointer */
70     tcp_seq irs;                 /* initial receive sequence number */
71 /*
72  * Additional variables for this implementation.
73  */
74 /* receive variables */
75     tcp_seq rcv_adv;             /* advertised window by other end */
76 /* retransmit variables */
77     tcp_seq snd_max;             /* highest sequence number sent;
78                                   * used to recognize retransmits */
79 /* congestion control (slow start, source quench, retransmit after loss) */
80     u_long  snd_cwnd;            /* congestion-controlled window */
81     u_long  snd_ssthresh;        /* snd_cwnd size threshhold for slow start
82                                   * exponential to linear switch */
83 /*
84  * transmit timing stuff.  See below for scale of srtt and rttvar.
85  * "Variance" is actually smoothed difference.
86  */
87     short   t_idle;              /* inactivity time */
88     short   t_rtt;               /* round-trip time */
89     tcp_seq t_rtseq;             /* sequence number being timed */
90     short   t_srtt;              /* smoothed round-trip time */
91     short   t_rttvar;            /* variance in round-trip time */
92     u_short t_rttmin;            /* minimum rtt allowed */
93     u_long  max_sndwnd;          /* largest window peer has offered */
```

```
 94 /* out-of-band data */
 95     char    t_oobflags;          /* TCPOOB_HAVEDATA, TCPOOB_HADDATA */
 96     char    t_iobc;              /* input character, if not SO_OOBINLINE */
 97     short   t_softerror;         /* possible error not yet reported */
 98 /* RFC 1323 variables */
 99     u_char  snd_scale;           /* scaling for send window (0-14) */
100     u_char  rcv_scale;           /* scaling for receive window (0-14) */
101     u_char  request_r_scale;     /* our pending window scale */
102     u_char  requested_s_scale;   /* peer's pending window scale */
103     u_long  ts_recent;           /* timestamp echo data */
104     u_long  ts_recent_age;       /* when last updated */
105     tcp_seq last_ack_sent;       /* sequence number of last ack field */
106 };
107 #define intotcpcb(ip)    ((struct tcpcb *)(ip)->inp_ppcb)
108 #define sototcpcb(so)    (intotcpcb(sotoinpcb(so)))
```
——— *tcp_var.h*

Figure 24.13 `tcpcb` structure: TCP control block.

We'll save the discussion of these variables until we encounter them in the code. Figure 24.14 shows the values for the `t_flags` member.

t_flags	Description
TF_ACKNOW	send ACK immediately
TF_DELACK	send ACK, but try to delay it
TF_NODELAY	don't delay packets to coalesce (disable Nagle algorithm)
TF_NOOPT	don't use TCP options (never set)
TF_SENTFIN	have sent FIN
TF_RCVD_SCALE	set when other side sends window scale option in SYN
TF_RCVD_TSTMP	set when other side sends timestamp option in SYN
TF_REQ_SCALE	have/will request window scale option in SYN
TF_REQ_TSTMP	have/will request timestamp option in SYN

Figure 24.14 `t_flags` values.

24.6 TCP State Transition Diagram

Many of TCP's actions, in response to different types of segments arriving on a connection, can be summarized in a state transition diagram, shown in Figure 24.15. We also duplicate this diagram on one of the front end papers, for easy reference while reading the TCP chapters.

These state transitions define the TCP finite state machine. Although the transition from LISTEN to SYN_SENT is allowed by TCP, there is no way to do this using the sockets API (i.e., a `connect` is not allowed after a `listen`).

The `t_state` member of the control block holds the current state of a connection, with the values shown in Figure 24.16.

This figure also shows the `tcp_outflags` array, which contains the outgoing flags for `tcp_output` to use when the connection is in that state.

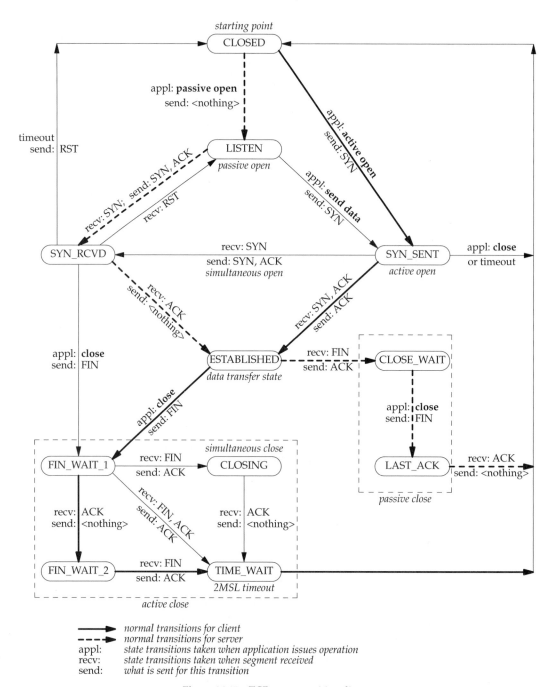

Figure 24.15   TCP state transition diagram.

`t_state`	value	Description	`tcp_outflags[]`
`TCPS_CLOSED`	0	closed	`TH_RST | TH_ACK`
`TCPS_LISTEN`	1	listening for connection (passive open)	`0`
`TCPS_SYN_SENT`	2	have sent SYN (active open)	`TH_SYN`
`TCPS_SYN_RECEIVED`	3	have sent and received SYN; awaiting ACK	`TH_SYN | TH_ACK`
`TCPS_ESTABLISHED`	4	established (data transfer)	`TH_ACK`
`TCPS_CLOSE_WAIT`	5	received FIN, waiting for application close	`TH_ACK`
`TCPS_FIN_WAIT_1`	6	have closed, sent FIN; awaiting ACK and FIN	`TH_FIN | TH_ACK`
`TCPS_CLOSING`	7	simultaneous close; awaiting ACK	`TH_FIN | TH_ACK`
`TCPS_LAST_ACK`	8	received FIN have closed; awaiting ACK	`TH_FIN | TH_ACK`
`TCPS_FIN_WAIT_2`	9	have closed; awaiting FIN	`TH_ACK`
`TCPS_TIME_WAIT`	10	2MSL wait state after active close	`TH_ACK`

Figure 24.16 `t_state` values.

Figure 24.16 also shows the numerical values of these constants since the code uses their numerical relationships. For example, the following two macros are defined:

```
#define  TCPS_HAVERCVDSYN(s)  ((s) >= TCPS_SYN_RECEIVED)
#define  TCPS_HAVERCVDFIN(s)  ((s) >= TCPS_TIME_WAIT)
```

Similarly, we'll see that `tcp_notify` handles ICMP errors differently when the connection is not yet established, that is, when `t_state` is less than `TCPS_ESTABLISHED`.

> The name `TCPS_HAVERCVDSYN` is correct, but the name `TCPS_HAVERCVDFIN` is misleading. A FIN has also been received in the CLOSE_WAIT, CLOSING, and LAST_ACK states. We encounter this macro in Chapter 29.

Half-Close

When a process calls `shutdown` with a second argument of 1, it is called a *half-close*. TCP sends a FIN but allows the process to continue receiving on the socket. (Section 18.5 of Volume 1 contains examples of TCP's half-close.)

For example, even though we label the ESTABLISHED state "data transfer," if the process does a half-close, moving the connection to the FIN_WAIT_1 and then the FIN_WAIT_2 states, data can continue to be received by the process in these two states.

24.7 TCP Sequence Numbers

Every byte of data exchanged across a TCP connection, along with the SYN and FIN flags, is assigned a 32-bit *sequence number*. The sequence number field in the TCP header (Figure 24.10) contains the sequence number of the first byte of data in the segment. The *acknowledgment number* field in the TCP header contains the next sequence number that the sender of the ACK expects to receive, which acknowledges all data bytes through the acknowledgment number minus 1. In other words, the acknowledgment number is the *next* sequence number expected by the sender of the ACK. The acknowledgment number is valid only if the ACK flag is set in the header. We'll see that TCP always sets the ACK flag except for the first SYN sent by an active open (the SYN_SENT state; see `tcp_outflags[2]` in Figure 24.16) and in some RST segments.

Since a TCP connection is *full-duplex*, each end must maintain a set of sequence numbers for both directions of data flow. In the TCP control block (Figure 24.13) there are 13 sequence numbers: eight for the send direction (the *send sequence space*) and five for the receive direction (the *receive sequence space*).

Figure 24.17 shows the relationship of four of the variables in the send sequence space: snd_wnd, snd_una, snd_nxt, and snd_max. In this example we number the bytes 1 through 11.

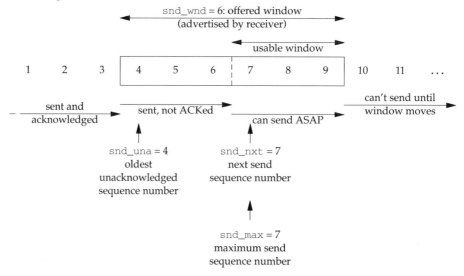

Figure 24.17   Example of send sequence space.

An *acceptable ACK* is one for which the following inequality holds:

    snd_una < acknowledgment field <= snd_max

In Figure 24.17 an acceptable ACK has an acknowledgment field of 5, 6, or 7. An acknowledgment field less than or equal to snd_una is a duplicate ACK—it acknowledges data that has already been ACKed, or else snd_una would not have incremented past those bytes.

We encounter the following test a few times in `tcp_output`, which is true if a segment is being retransmitted:

    snd_nxt < snd_max

Figure 24.18 shows the other end of the connection in Figure 24.17: the receive sequence space, assuming the segment containing sequence numbers 4, 5, and 6 has not been received yet. We show the three variables rcv_nxt, rcv_wnd, and rcv_adv.

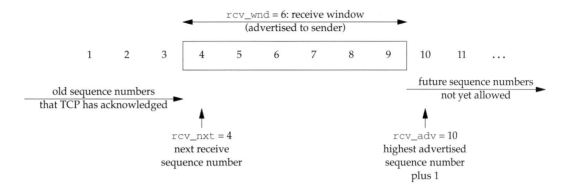

Figure 24.18 Example of receive sequence space.

The receiver considers a received segment valid if it contains data within the window, that is, if either of the following two inequalities is true:

```
rcv_nxt <= beginning sequence number of segment < rcv_nxt + rcv_wnd
```

```
rcv_nxt <= ending sequence number of segment < rcv_nxt + rcv_wnd
```

The beginning sequence number of a segment is just the sequence number field in the TCP header, `ti_seq`. The ending sequence number is the sequence number field plus the number of bytes of TCP data, minus 1.

For example, Figure 24.19 could represent the TCP segment containing the 3 bytes with sequence numbers 4, 5, and 6 in Figure 24.17.

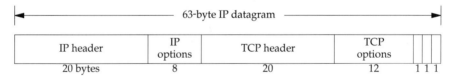

Figure 24.19 TCP segment transmitted as an IP datagram.

We assume that there are 8 bytes of IP options and 12 bytes of TCP options. Figure 24.20 shows the values of the relevant variables.

Variable	Value	Description
`ip_hl`	7	length of IP header + options in 32-bit words (= 28 bytes)
`ip_len`	63	length of IP datagram in bytes $(20 + 8 + 20 + 12 + 3)$
`ti_off`	8	length of TCP header + options in 32-bit words (= 32 bytes)
`ti_seq`	4	sequence number of first byte of data
`ti_len`	3	#bytes of TCP data: $\texttt{ip\_len} - (\texttt{ip\_hl} \times 4) - (\texttt{ti\_off} \times 4)$
	6	sequence number of last byte of data: $\texttt{ti\_seq} + \texttt{ti\_len} - 1$

Figure 24.20 Values of variables corresponding to Figure 24.19.

`ti_len` is not a field that is transmitted in the TCP header. Instead, it is computed as shown in Figure 24.20 and stored in the overlaid IP structure (Figure 24.12) once the received header fields have been checksummed and verified. The last value in this figure is not stored in the header, but is computed from the other values when needed.

Modular Arithmetic with Sequence Numbers

A problem that TCP must deal with is that the sequence numbers are from a finite 32-bit number space: 0 through 4,294,967,295. If more than 2^{32} bytes of data are exchanged across a TCP connection, the sequence numbers will be reused. Sequence numbers wrap around from 4,294,967,295 to 0.

Even if less than 2^{32} bytes of data are exchanged, wrap around is still a problem because the sequence numbers for a connection don't necessarily start at 0. The initial sequence number for each direction of data flow across a connection can start anywhere between 0 and 4,294,967,295. This complicates the comparison of sequence numbers. For example, sequence number 1 is "greater than" 4,294,967,295, as we discuss below.

TCP sequence numbers are defined as `unsigned longs` in `tcp.h`:

```
typedef  u_long  tcp_seq;
```

The four macros shown in Figure 24.21 compare sequence numbers.

―― *tcp_seq.h*
```
40 #define SEQ_LT(a,b)    ((int)((a)-(b)) < 0)
41 #define SEQ_LEQ(a,b)   ((int)((a)-(b)) <= 0)
42 #define SEQ_GT(a,b)    ((int)((a)-(b)) > 0)
43 #define SEQ_GEQ(a,b)   ((int)((a)-(b)) >= 0)
```
―― *tcp_seq.h*

Figure 24.21   Macros for TCP sequence number comparison.

Example—Sequence Number Comparisons

Let's look at an example to see how TCP's sequence numbers operate. Assume 3-bit sequence numbers, 0 through 7. Figure 24.22 shows these eight sequence numbers, their 3-bit binary representation, and their two's complement representation. (To form the two's complement take the binary number, convert each 0 to a 1 and vice versa, then add 1.) We show the two's complement because to form $a - b$ we just add a to the two's complement of b.

The final three columns of this table are 0 minus x, 1 minus x, and 2 minus x. In these final three columns, if the value is considered to be a *signed* integer (notice the cast to `int` in all four macros in Figure 24.21), the value is less than 0 (the `SEQ_LT` macro) if the high-order bit is 1, and the value is greater than 0 (the `SEQ_GT` macro) if the high-order bit is 0 and the value is not 0. We show horizontal lines in these final three columns to distinguish between the four negative and the four nonnegative values.

If we look at the fourth column of Figure 24.22, (labeled "0 − x"), we see that 0 (i.e., x), is less than 1, 2, 3, and 4 (the high-order bit of the result is 1), and 0 is greater than 5, 6, and 7 (the high-order bit is 0 and the result is not 0). We show this relationship pictorially in Figure 24.23.

x	binary	two's complement	0 − x	1 − x	2 − x
0	000	000	000	001	010
1	001	111	111	000	001
2	010	110	110	111	000
3	011	101	101	110	111
4	100	100	100	101	110
5	101	011	011	100	101
6	110	010	010	011	100
7	111	001	001	010	011

Figure 24.22   Example using 3-bit sequence numbers.

Figure 24.23   TCP sequence number comparisons for 3-bit sequence numbers.

Figure 24.24 shows a similar figure using the fifth row of the table (1 − x).

Figure 24.24   TCP sequence number comparisons for 3-bit sequence numbers.

Figure 24.25 is another representation of the two previous figures, using circles to reiterate the wrap around of sequence numbers.

Figure 24.25   Another way to visualize Figures 24.23 and 24.24.

With regard to TCP, these sequence number comparisons determine whether a given sequence number is in the future or in the past (a retransmission). For example, using Figure 24.24, if TCP is expecting sequence number 1 and sequence number 6 arrives, since 6 is less than 1 using the sequence number arithmetic we showed, the data byte is considered a retransmission of a previously received data byte and is discarded. But if sequence number 5 is received, since it is greater than 1 it is considered a future data byte and is saved by TCP, awaiting the arrival of the missing bytes 2, 3, and 4 (assuming byte 5 is within the receive window).

Figure 24.26 is an expansion of the left circle in Figure 24.25, using TCP's 32-bit sequence numbers instead of 3-bit sequence numbers.

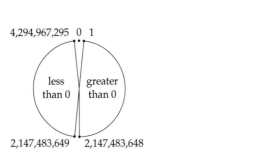 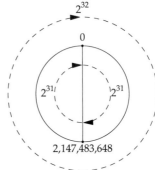

Figure 24.26   Comparisons against 0, using 32-bit sequence numbers.

The right circle in Figure 24.26 is to reiterate that one-half of the 32-bit sequence space uses 2^{31} numbers.

24.8 `tcp_init` Function

The `domaininit` function calls TCP's initialization function, `tcp_init` (Figure 24.27), at system initialization time.

```
                                                                    tcp_subr.c
43 void
44 tcp_init()
45 {
46     tcp_iss = 1;                    /* wrong */
47     tcb.inp_next = tcb.inp_prev = &tcb;

48     if (max_protohdr < sizeof(struct tcpiphdr))
49             max_protohdr = sizeof(struct tcpiphdr);
50     if (max_linkhdr + sizeof(struct tcpiphdr) > MHLEN)
51             panic("tcp_init");
52 }
                                                                    tcp_subr.c
```

Figure 24.27   `tcp_init` function.

Set initial send sequence number (ISS)

46   The initial send sequence number (ISS), `tcp_iss`, is initialized to 1. As the comment indicates, this is wrong. We discuss the implications behind this choice shortly, when we describe TCP's *quiet time*. Compare this to the initialization of the IP identifier in Figure 7.23, which used the time-of-day clock.

Initialize linked list of TCP Internet PCBs

47   The next and previous pointers in the head PCB (tcb) point to itself. This is an empty doubly linked list. The remainder of the tcb PCB is initialized to 0 (all un-initialized globals are set to 0), although the only other field used in this head PCB is inp_lport, the next TCP ephemeral port number to allocate. The first ephemeral port used by TCP will be 1024, for the reasons described in the solution for Exercise 22.4.

Calculate maximum protocol header length

48–51   If the maximum protocol header encountered so far is less than 40 bytes, max_protohdr is set to 40 (the size of the combined IP and TCP headers, without any options). This variable is described in Figure 7.17. If the sum of max_linkhdr (normally 16) and 40 is greater than the amount of data that fits into an mbuf with a packet header (100 bytes, MHLEN from Figure 2.7), the kernel panics (Exercise 24.2).

MSL and Quiet Time Concept

TCP requires any host that crashes without retaining any knowledge of the last sequence numbers used on active connections to refrain from sending any TCP segments for one MSL (2 minutes, the quiet time) on reboot. Few TCPs, if any, retain this knowledge over a crash or operator shutdown.

MSL is the *maximum segment lifetime*. Each implementation chooses a value for the MSL. It is the maximum amount of time any segment can exist in the network before being discarded. A connection that is actively closed remains in the CLOSE_WAIT state (Figure 24.15) for twice the MSL.

> RFC 793 [Postel 1981c] recommends an MSL of 2 minutes, but Net/3 uses an MSL of 30 seconds (the constant TCPTV_MSL in Figure 25.3).

The problem occurs if packets are delayed somewhere in the network (RFC 793 calls these *wandering duplicates*). Assume a Net/3 system starts up, initializes tcp_iss to 1 (as in Figure 24.27) and then crashes just after the sequence numbers wrap. We'll see in Section 25.5 that TCP increments tcp_iss by 128,000 every second, causing the wrap around of the ISS to occur about 9.3 hours after rebooting. Also, tcp_iss is incremented by 64,000 each time a connect is issued, which can cause the wrap around to occur earlier than 9.3 hours. The following scenario is one example of how an old segment can incorrectly be delivered to a connection:

1. A client and server have an established connection. The client's port number is 1024. The client sends a data segment with a starting sequence number of 2. This data segment gets trapped in a routing loop somewhere between the two end points and is not delivered to the server. This data segment becomes a wandering duplicate.

2. The client retransmits the data segment starting with sequence number 2, which is delivered to the server.

3. The client closes the connection.

4. The client host crashes.

5. The client host reboots about 40 seconds after crashing, causing TCP to initialize `tcp_iss` to 1 again.

6. Another connection is immediately established by the same client to the same server, using the same socket pair: the client uses 1024 again, and the server uses its well-known port. The client's SYN uses sequence number 1. This new connection using the same socket pair is called a new *incarnation* of the old connection.

7. The wandering duplicate from step 1 is delivered to the server, and it thinks this datagram belongs to the new connection, when it is really from the old connection.

Figure 24.28 is a time line of this sequence of steps.

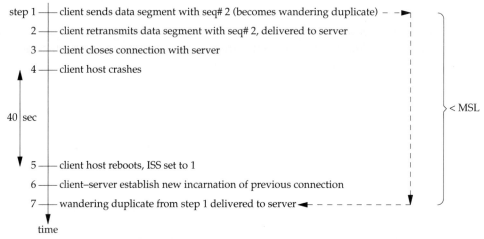

Figure 24.28   Example of old segment delivered to new incarnation of a connection.

This problem exists even if the rebooting TCP were to use an algorithm based on its time-of-day clock to choose the ISS on rebooting: regardless of the ISS for the previous incarnation of a connection, because of sequence number wrap it is possible for the ISS after rebooting to nearly equal the sequence number in use before the reboot.

Besides saving the sequence number of all established connections, the only other way around this problem is for the rebooting TCP to be quiet (i.e., not send any TCP segments) for MSL seconds after crashing. Few TCPs do this, however, since it takes most hosts longer than MSL seconds just to reboot.

24.9   Summary

This chapter is an introduction to the TCP source code in the six chapters that follow. TCP maintains its own control block for each connection, containing all the variable and state information for the connection.

A state transition diagram is defined for TCP that shows under what conditions TCP moves from one state to another and what segments get sent by TCP for each transition. This diagram shows how connections are established and terminated. We'll refer to this state transition diagram frequently in our description of TCP.

Every byte exchanged across a TCP connection has an associated sequence number, and TCP maintains numerous sequence numbers in the connection control block: some for sending and some for receiving (since TCP is full-duplex). Since these sequence numbers are from a finite 32-bit sequence space, they wrap around from the maximum value back to 0. We explained how the sequence numbers are compared to each other using less-than and greater-than tests, which we'll encounter repeatedly in the TCP code.

Finally, we looked at one of the simplest of the TCP functions, `tcp_init`, which initializes TCP's linked list of Internet PCBs. We also discussed TCP's choice of an initial send sequence number, which is used when actively opening a connection.

Exercises

24.1   What is the average number of bytes transmitted and received per connection from the statistics in Figure 24.5?

24.2   Is the kernel panic in `tcp_init` reasonable?

24.3   Execute `netstat -a` to see how many TCP end points your system currently has active.

25

TCP Timers

25.1 Introduction

We start our detailed description of the TCP source code by looking at the various TCP timers. We encounter these timers throughout most of the TCP functions.

TCP maintains seven timers for *each* connection. They are briefly described here, in the approximate order of their occurrence during the lifetime of a connection.

1. A *connection-establishment* timer starts when a SYN is sent to establish a new connection. If a response is not received within 75 seconds, the connection establishment is aborted.

2. A *retransmission* timer is set when TCP sends data. If the data is not acknowledged by the other end when this timer expires, TCP retransmits the data. The value of this timer (i.e., the amount of time TCP waits for an acknowledgment) is calculated dynamically, based on the round-trip time measured by TCP for this connection, and based on the number of times this data segment has been retransmitted. The retransmission timer is bounded by TCP to be between 1 and 64 seconds.

3. A *delayed ACK* timer is set when TCP receives data that must be acknowledged, but need not be acknowledged immediately. Instead, TCP waits up to 200 ms before sending the ACK. If, during this 200-ms time period, TCP has data to send on this connection, the pending acknowledgment is sent along with the data (called *piggybacking*).

4. A *persist* timer is set when the other end of a connection advertises a window of 0, stopping TCP from sending data. Since window advertisements from the other end are not sent reliably (that is, ACKs are not acknowledged, only data is acknowledged), there's a chance that a future window update, allowing TCP to send some data, can be lost. Therefore, if TCP has data to send and the other end advertises a window of 0, the persist timer is set and when it expires, 1 byte of data is sent to see if the window has opened. Like the retransmission timer, the persist timer value is calculated dynamically, based on the round-trip time. The value of this is bounded by TCP to be between 5 and 60 seconds.

5. A *keepalive* timer can be set by the process using the SO_KEEPALIVE socket option. If the connection is idle for 2 hours, the keepalive timer expires and a special segment is sent to the other end, forcing it to respond. If the expected response is received, TCP knows that the other host is still up, and TCP won't probe it again until the connection is idle for another 2 hours. Other responses to the keepalive probe tell TCP that the other host has crashed and rebooted. If no response is received to a fixed number of keepalive probes, TCP assumes that the other end has crashed, although it can't distinguish between the other end being down (i.e., it crashed and has not yet rebooted) and a temporary lack of connectivity to the other end (i.e., an intermediate router or phone line is down).

6. A *FIN_WAIT_2* timer. When a connection moves from the FIN_WAIT_1 state to the FIN_WAIT_2 state (Figure 24.15) *and* the connection cannot receive any more data (implying the process called close, instead of taking advantage of TCP's half-close with shutdown), this timer is set to 10 minutes. When this timer expires it is reset to 75 seconds, and when it expires the second time the connection is dropped. The purpose of this timer is to avoid leaving a connection in the FIN_WAIT_2 state forever, if the other end never sends a FIN. (We don't show this timeout in Figure 24.15.)

7. A *TIME_WAIT* timer, often called the *2MSL* timer. The term *2MSL* means twice the MSL, the maximum segment lifetime defined in Section 24.8. It is set when a connection enters the TIME_WAIT state (Figure 24.15), that is, when the connection is actively closed. Section 18.6 of Volume 1 describes the reasoning for the 2MSL wait state in detail. The timer is set to 1 minute (Net/3 uses an MSL of 30 seconds) when the connection enters the TIME_WAIT state and when it expires, the TCP control block and Internet PCB are deleted, allowing that socket pair to be reused.

TCP has two timer functions: one is called every 200 ms (the fast timer) and the other every 500 ms (the slow timer). The delayed ACK timer is different from the other six: when the delayed ACK timer is set for a connection it means that a delayed ACK must be sent the next time the 200-ms timer expires (i.e., the elapsed time is between 0 and 200 ms). The other six timers are decremented every 500 ms, and only when the counter reaches 0 does the corresponding action take place.

25.2 Code Introduction

The delayed ACK timer is enabled for a connection when the TF_DELACK flag (Figure 24.14) is set in the TCP control block. The array t_timer in the TCP control block contains four (TCPT_NTIMERS) counters used to implement the other six timers. The indexes into this array are shown in Figure 25.1. We describe briefly how the six timers (other than the delayed ACK timer) are implemented by these four counters.

Constant	Value	Description
TCPT_REXMT	0	retransmission timer
TCPT_PERSIST	1	persist timer
TCPT_KEEP	2	keepalive timer *or* connection-establishment timer
TCPT_2MSL	3	2MSL timer *or* FIN_WAIT_2 timer

Figure 25.1 Indexes into the t_timer array.

Each entry in the t_timer array contains the number of 500-ms clock ticks until the timer expires, with 0 meaning that the timer is not set. Since each timer is a short, if 16 bits hold a short, the maximum timer value is 16,383.5 seconds, or about 4.5 hours.

Notice in Figure 25.1 that four "timer counters" implement six TCP "timers," because some of the timers are mutually exclusive. We'll distinguish between the counters and the timers. The TCPT_KEEP counter implements both the keepalive timer and the connection-establishment timer, since the two timers are never used at the same time for a connection. Similarly, the 2MSL timer and the FIN_WAIT_2 timer are implemented using the TCPT_2MSL counter, since a connection is only in one state at a time. The first section of Figure 25.2 summarizes the implementation of the seven TCP timers. The second and third sections of the table show how four of the seven timers are initialized using three global variables from Figure 24.3 and two constants from Figure 25.3. Notice that two of the three globals are used with multiple timers. We've already said that the delayed ACK timer is tied to TCP's 200-ms timer, and we describe how the other two timers are set later in this chapter.

	conn. estab.	rexmit	delayed ACK	persist	keep-alive	FIN_-WAIT_2	2MSL
t_timer[TCPT_REXMT]		•					
t_timer[TCPT_PERSIST]				•			
t_timer[TCPT_KEEP]	•				•		
t_timer[TCPT_2MSL]						•	•
t_flags & TF_DELACK			•				
tcp_keepidle (2 hr)					•		
tcp_keepintvl (75 sec)					•	•	
tcp_maxidle (10 min)					•	•	
2 * TCPTV_MSL (60 sec)							•
TCPTV_KEEP_INIT (75 sec)	•						

Figure 25.2 Implementation of the seven TCP timers.

Figure 25.3 shows the fundamental timer values for the Net/3 implementation.

Constant	#500-ms clock ticks	#sec	Description
TCPTV_MSL	60	30	MSL, maximum segment lifetime
TCPTV_MIN	2	1	minimum value of retransmission timer
TCPTV_REXMTMAX	128	64	maximum value of retransmission timer
TCPTV_PERSMIN	10	5	minimum value of persist timer
TCPTV_PERSMAX	120	60	maximum value of persist timer
TCPTV_KEEP_INIT	150	75	connection-establishment timer value
TCPTV_KEEP_IDLE	14400	7200	idle time for connection before first probe (2 hours)
TCPTV_KEEPINTVL	150	75	time between probes when no response
TCPTV_SRTTBASE	0		special value to denote no measurements yet for connection
TCPTV_SRTTDFLT	6	3	default RTT when no measurements yet for connection

Figure 25.3 Fundamental timer values for the implementation.

Figure 25.4 shows other timer constants that we'll encounter.

Constant	Value	Description
TCP_LINGERTIME	120	maximum #seconds for SO_LINGER socket option
TCP_MAXRXTSHIFT	12	maximum #retransmissions waiting for an ACK
TCPTV_KEEPCNT	8	maximum #keepalive probes when no response received

Figure 25.4 Timer constants.

The TCPT_RANGESET macro, shown in Figure 25.5, sets a timer to a given value, making certain the value is between the specified minimum and maximum.

tcp_timer.h
```
102 #define TCPT_RANGESET(tv, value, tvmin, tvmax) { \
103     (tv) = (value); \
104     if ((tv) < (tvmin)) \
105         (tv) = (tvmin); \
106     else if ((tv) > (tvmax)) \
107         (tv) = (tvmax); \
108 }
```
tcp_timer.h

Figure 25.5 TCPT_RANGESET macro.

We see in Figure 25.3 that the retransmission timer and the persist timer have upper and lower bounds, since their values are calculated dynamically, based on the measured round-trip time. The other timers are set to constant values.

There is one additional timer that we allude to in Figure 25.4 but don't discuss in this chapter: the linger timer for a socket, set by the SO_LINGER socket option. This is a socket-level timer used by the close system call (Section 15.15). We will see in Figure 30.12 that when a socket is closed, TCP checks whether this socket option is set and whether the linger time is 0. If so, the connection is aborted with an RST instead of TCP's normal close.

25.3 `tcp_canceltimers` Function

The function `tcp_canceltimers`, shown in Figure 25.6, is called by `tcp_input` when the TIME_WAIT state is entered. All four timer counters are set to 0, which turns off the retransmission, persist, keepalive, and FIN_WAIT_2 timers, before `tcp_input` sets the 2MSL timer.

```
                                                                      —— tcp_timer.c
107 void
108 tcp_canceltimers(tp)
109 struct tcpcb *tp;
110 {
111     int     i;

112     for (i = 0; i < TCPT_NTIMERS; i++)
113         tp->t_timer[i] = 0;
114 }
                                                                      —— tcp_timer.c
```

Figure 25.6 `tcp_canceltimers` function.

25.4 `tcp_fasttimo` Function

The function `tcp_fasttimo`, shown in Figure 25.7, is called by `pr_fasttimo` every 200 ms. It handles only the delayed ACK timer.

```
                                                                      —— tcp_timer.c
41 void
42 tcp_fasttimo()
43 {
44     struct inpcb *inp;
45     struct tcpcb *tp;
46     int     s = splnet();

47     inp = tcb.inp_next;
48     if (inp)
49         for (; inp != &tcb; inp = inp->inp_next)
50             if ((tp = (struct tcpcb *) inp->inp_ppcb) &&
51                 (tp->t_flags & TF_DELACK)) {
52                 tp->t_flags &= ~TF_DELACK;
53                 tp->t_flags |= TF_ACKNOW;
54                 tcpstat.tcps_delack++;
55                 (void) tcp_output(tp);
56             }
57     splx(s);
58 }
                                                                      —— tcp_timer.c
```

Figure 25.7 `tcp_fasttimo` function, which is called every 200 ms.

Each Internet PCB on the TCP list that has a corresponding TCP control block is checked. If the TF_DELACK flag is set, it is cleared and the TF_ACKNOW flag is set instead. `tcp_output` is called, and since the TF_ACKNOW flag is set, an ACK is sent.

How can TCP have an Internet PCB on its PCB list that doesn't have a TCP control block (the test at line 50)? When a socket is created (the `PRU_ATTACH` request, in response to the `socket` system call) we'll see in Figure 30.11 that the creation of the Internet PCB is done first, followed by the creation of the TCP control block. Between these two operations a high-priority clock interrupt can occur (Figure 1.13), which calls `tcp_fasttimo`.

25.5   `tcp_slowtimo` Function

The function `tcp_slowtimo`, shown in Figure 25.8, is called by `pr_slowtimo` every 500 ms. It handles the other six TCP timers: connection establishment, retransmission, persist, keepalive, FIN_WAIT_2, and 2MSL.

71   `tcp_maxidle` is initialized to 10 minutes. This is the maximum amount of time TCP will send keepalive probes to another host, waiting for a response from that host. This variable is also used with the FIN_WAIT_2 timer, as we describe in Section 25.6. This initialization statement could be moved to `tcp_init`, since it only needs to be evaluated when the system is initialized (see Exercise 25.2).

Check each timer counter in all TCP control blocks

72–89   Each Internet PCB on the TCP list that has a corresponding TCP control block is checked. Each of the four timer counters for each connection is tested, and if nonzero, the counter is decremented. When the timer reaches 0, a `PRU_SLOWTIMO` request is issued. We'll see that this request calls the function `tcp_timers`, which we describe later in this chapter.

The fourth argument to `tcp_usrreq` is a pointer to an mbuf. But this argument is actually used for different purposes when the mbuf pointer is not required. Here we see the index `i` is passed, telling the request which timer has expired. The funny-looking cast of `i` to an mbuf pointer is to avoid a compile-time error.

Check if TCP control block has been deleted

90–93   Before examining the timers for a control block, a pointer to the next Internet PCB is saved in `ipnxt`. Each time the `PRU_SLOWTIMO` request returns, `tcp_slowtimo` checks whether the next PCB in the TCP list still points to the PCB that's being processed. If not, it means the control block has been deleted—perhaps the 2MSL timer expired or the retransmission timer expired and TCP is giving up on this connection—causing a jump to `tpgone`, skipping the remaining timers for this control block, and moving on to the next PCB.

Count idle time

94   `t_idle` is incremented for the control block. This counts the number of 500-ms clock ticks since the last segment was received on this connection. It is set to 0 by `tcp_input` when a segment is received on the connection and used for three purposes: (1) by the keepalive algorithm to send a probe after the connection is idle for 2 hours, (2) to drop a connection in the FIN_WAIT_2 state that is idle for 10 minutes and 75 seconds, and (3) by `tcp_output` to return to the slow start algorithm after the connection has been idle for a while.

tcp_timer.c

```
64 void
65 tcp_slowtimo()
66 {
67     struct inpcb *ip, *ipnxt;
68     struct tcpcb *tp;
69     int     s = splnet();
70     int     i;

71     tcp_maxidle = TCPTV_KEEPCNT * tcp_keepintvl;
72     /*
73      * Search through tcb's and update active timers.
74      */
75     ip = tcb.inp_next;
76     if (ip == 0) {
77         splx(s);
78         return;
79     }
80     for (; ip != &tcb; ip = ipnxt) {
81         ipnxt = ip->inp_next;
82         tp = intotcpcb(ip);
83         if (tp == 0)
84             continue;
85         for (i = 0; i < TCPT_NTIMERS; i++) {
86             if (tp->t_timer[i] && --tp->t_timer[i] == 0) {
87                 (void) tcp_usrreq(tp->t_inpcb->inp_socket,
88                                 PRU_SLOWTIMO, (struct mbuf *) 0,
89                                 (struct mbuf *) i, (struct mbuf *) 0);
90                 if (ipnxt->inp_prev != ip)
91                     goto tpgone;
92             }
93         }
94         tp->t_idle++;
95         if (tp->t_rtt)
96             tp->t_rtt++;
97     tpgone:
98         ;
99     }
100    tcp_iss += TCP_ISSINCR / PR_SLOWHZ;      /* increment iss */
101    tcp_now++;                     /* for timestamps */
102    splx(s);
103 }
```

tcp_timer.c

Figure 25.8 tcp_slowtimo function, which is called every 500 ms.

Increment RTT counter

95–96   If this connection is timing an outstanding segment, t_rtt is nonzero and counts the number of 500-ms clock ticks until that segment is acknowledged. It is initialized to 1 by tcp_output when a segment is transmitted whose RTT should be timed. tcp_slowtimo increments this counter.

Increment initial send sequence number

100   `tcp_iss` was initialized to 1 by `tcp_init`. Every 500 ms it is incremented by 64,000: 128,000 (`TCP_ISSINCR`) divided by 2 (`PR_SLOWHZ`). This is a rate of about once every 8 microseconds, although `tcp_iss` is incremented only twice a second. We'll see that `tcp_iss` is also incremented by 64,000 each time a connection is established, either actively or passively.

> RFC 793 specifies that the initial sequence number should increment roughly every 4 microseconds, or 250,000 times a second. The Net/3 value increments at about one-half this rate.

Increment RFC 1323 timestamp value

101   `tcp_now` is initialized to 0 on bootstrap and incremented every 500 ms. It is used by the timestamp option defined in RFC 1323 [Jacobson, Braden, and Borman 1992], which we describe in Section 26.6.

75–79   Notice that if there are no TCP connections active on the host (`tcb.inp_next` is null), neither `tcp_iss` nor `tcp_now` is incremented. This would occur only when the system is being initialized, since it would be rare to find a Unix system attached to a network without a few TCP servers active.

25.6 `tcp_timers` Function

The function `tcp_timers` is called by TCP's `PRU_SLOWTIMO` request (Figure 30.10):

```
case PRU_SLOWTIMO:
    tp = tcp_timers(tp, (int)nam);
```

when any one of the four TCP timer counters reaches 0 (Figure 25.8).

The structure of the function is a `switch` statement with one `case` per timer, as outlined in Figure 25.9.

```
                                                              ─── tcp_timer.c
120 struct tcpcb *
121 tcp_timers(tp, timer)
122 struct tcpcb *tp;
123 int     timer;
124 {
125     int     rexmt;

126     switch (timer) {


                           /* switch cases */


256     }
257     return (tp);
258 }
                                                              ─── tcp_timer.c
```

Figure 25.9 `tcp_timers` function: general organization.

We now discuss three of the four timer counters (five of TCP's timers), saving the retransmission timer for Section 25.11.

FIN_WAIT_2 and 2MSL Timers

TCP's TCPT_2MSL counter implements two of TCP's timers.

1. FIN_WAIT_2 timer. When tcp_input moves from the FIN_WAIT_1 state to the FIN_WAIT_2 state *and* the socket cannot receive any more data (implying the process called close, instead of taking advantage of TCP's half-close with shutdown), the FIN_WAIT_2 timer is set to 10 minutes (tcp_maxidle). We'll see that this prevents the connection from staying in the FIN_WAIT_2 state forever.

2. 2MSL timer. When TCP enters the TIME_WAIT state, the 2MSL timer is set to 60 seconds (TCPTV_MSL times 2).

Figure 25.10 shows the case for the 2MSL timer—executed when the timer reaches 0.

```
                                                            ─── tcp_timer.c
127          /*
128           * 2 MSL timeout in shutdown went off.  If we're closed but
129           * still waiting for peer to close and connection has been idle
130           * too long, or if 2MSL time is up from TIME_WAIT, delete connection
131           * control block.  Otherwise, check again in a bit.
132           */
133      case TCPT_2MSL:
134          if (tp->t_state != TCPS_TIME_WAIT &&
135              tp->t_idle <= tcp_maxidle)
136              tp->t_timer[TCPT_2MSL] = tcp_keepintvl;
137          else
138              tp = tcp_close(tp);
139          break;
                                                            ─── tcp_timer.c
```

Figure 25.10 tcp_timers function: expiration of 2MSL timer counter.

2MSL timer

127–139   The puzzling logic in the conditional is because the two different uses of the TCPT_2MSL counter are intermixed (Exercise 25.4). Let's first look at the TIME_WAIT state. When the timer expires after 60 seconds, tcp_close is called and the control blocks are released. We have the scenario shown in Figure 25.11. This figure shows the series of function calls that occurs when the 2MSL timer expires. We also see that setting one of the timers for N seconds in the future ($2 \times N$ ticks), causes the timer to expire somewhere between $2 \times N - 1$ and $2 \times N$ ticks in the future, since the time until the first decrement of the counter is between 0 and 500 ms in the future.

FIN_WAIT_2 timer

127–139   If the connection state is not TIME_WAIT, the TCPT_2MSL counter is the FIN_WAIT_2 timer. As soon as the connection has been idle for more than 10 minutes (tcp_maxidle) the connection is closed. But if the connection has been idle for less than or equal to 10 minutes, the FIN_WAIT_2 timer is reset for 75 seconds in the future. Figure 25.12 shows the typical scenario.

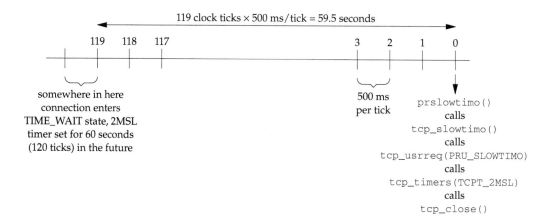

Figure 25.11   Setting and expiration of 2MSL timer in TIME_WAIT state.

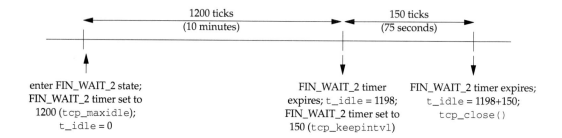

Figure 25.12   FIN_WAIT_2 timer to avoid infinite wait in FIN_WAIT_2 state.

The connection moves from the FIN_WAIT_1 state to the FIN_WAIT_2 state on the receipt of an ACK (Figure 24.15). Receiving this ACK sets t_idle to 0 and the FIN_WAIT_2 timer is set to 1200 (tcp_maxidle). In Figure 25.12 we show the up arrow just to the right of the tick mark starting the 10-minute period, to reiterate that the first decrement of the counter occurs between 0 and 500 ms after the counter is set. After 1199 ticks the timer expires, but since t_idle is incremented *after* the test and decrement of the four counters in Figure 25.8, t_idle is 1198. (We assume the connection is idle for this 10-minute period.) The comparison of 1198 as less than or equal to 1200 is true, so the FIN_WAIT_2 timer is set to 150 (tcp_keepintvl). When the timer expires again in 75 seconds, assuming the connection is still idle, t_idle is now 1348, the test is false, and tcp_close is called.

The reason for the 75-second timeout after the first 10-minute timeout is as follows: a connection in the FIN_WAIT_2 state is not dropped until the connection has been idle for *more than* 10 minutes. There's no reason to test t_idle until at least 10 minutes have expired, but once this time has passed, the value of t_idle is checked every 75 seconds. Since a duplicate segment could be received, say a duplicate of the ACK that moved the connection from the FIN_WAIT_1 state to the FIN_WAIT_2 state, the 10-minute wait is restarted when the segment is received (since `t_idle` will be set to 0).

> Terminating an idle connection after more than 10 minutes in the FIN_WAIT_2 state violates the protocol specification, but this is practical. In the FIN_WAIT_2 state the process has called `close`, all outstanding data on the connection has been sent and acknowledged, the other end has acknowledged the FIN, and TCP is waiting for the process at the other end of the connection to issue its `close`. If the other process never closes its end of the connection, our end can remain in the FIN_WAIT_2 forever. A counter should be maintained for the number of connections terminated for this reason, to see how often this occurs.

Persist Timer

Figure 25.13 shows the `case` for when the persist timer expires.

```
                                                              ─── tcp_timer.c
210            /*
211             * Persistence timer into zero window.
212             * Force a byte to be output, if possible.
213             */
214        case TCPT_PERSIST:
215            tcpstat.tcps_persisttimeo++;
216            tcp_setpersist(tp);
217            tp->t_force = 1;
218            (void) tcp_output(tp);
219            tp->t_force = 0;
220            break;
                                                              ─── tcp_timer.c
```

Figure 25.13 `tcp_timers` function: expiration of persist timer.

Force window probe segment

210–220   When the persist timer expires, there is data to send on the connection but TCP has been stopped by the other end's advertisement of a zero-sized window. `tcp_setpersist` calculates the next value for the persist timer and stores it in the `TCPT_PERSIST` counter. The flag `t_force` is set to 1, forcing `tcp_output` to send 1 byte, even though the window advertised by the other end is 0.

Figure 25.14 shows typical values of the persist timer for a LAN, assuming the retransmission timeout for the connection is 1.5 seconds (see Figure 22.1 of Volume 1).

Figure 25.14   Time line of persist timer when probing a zero window.

Once the value of the persist timer reaches 60 seconds, TCP continues sending window probes every 60 seconds. The reason the first two values are both 5, and not 1.5 and 3, is that the persist timer is lower bounded at 5 seconds. It is also upper bounded at 60 seconds. The multiplication of each value by 2 to give the next value is called an *exponential backoff*, and we describe how it is calculated in Section 25.9.

Connection Establishment and Keepalive Timers

TCP's `TCPT_KEEP` counter implements two timers:

1. When a SYN is sent, the connection-establishment timer is set to 75 seconds (`TCPTV_KEEP_INIT`). This happens when `connect` is called, putting a connection into the SYN_SENT state (active open), or when a connection moves from the LISTEN to the SYN_RCVD state (passive open). If the connection doesn't enter the ESTABLISHED state within 75 seconds, the connection is dropped.

2. When a segment is received on a connection, `tcp_input` resets the keepalive timer for that connection to 2 hours (`tcp_keepidle`), and the `t_idle` counter for the connection is reset to 0. This happens for every TCP connection on the system, whether the keepalive option is enabled for the socket or not. If the keepalive timer expires (2 hours after the last segment was received on the connection), and if the socket option is set, a keepalive probe is sent to the other end. If the timer expires and the socket option is not set, the keepalive timer is just reset for 2 hours in the future.

Figure 25.16 shows the `case` for TCP's `TCPT_KEEP` counter.

Connection-establishment timer expires after 75 seconds

221–228   If the state is less than ESTABLISHED (Figure 24.16), the `TCPT_KEEP` counter is the connection-establishment timer. At the label `dropit`, `tcp_drop` is called to terminate the connection attempt with an error of `ETIMEDOUT`. We'll see that this error is the default error—if, for example, a soft error such as an ICMP host unreachable was received on the connection, the error returned to the process will be changed to `EHOSTUNREACH` instead of the default.

In Figure 30.4 we'll see that when TCP sends a SYN, two timers are initialized: the connection-establishment timer as we just described, with a value of 75 seconds, and the retransmission timer, to cause the SYN to be retransmitted if no response is received. Figure 25.15 shows these two timers.

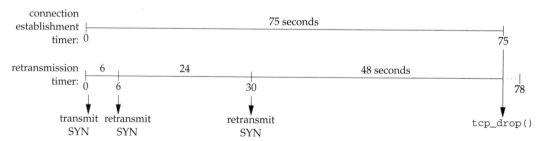

Figure 25.15   Connection-establishment timer and retransmission timer after SYN is sent.

The retransmission timer is initialized to 6 seconds for a new connection (Figure 25.19), and successive values are calculated to be 24 and 48 seconds. We describe how these values are calculated in Section 25.7. The retransmission timer causes the SYN to be

——— *tcp_timer.c*
```
221              /*
222               * Keep-alive timer went off; send something
223               * or drop connection if idle for too long.
224               */
225          case TCPT_KEEP:
226              tcpstat.tcps_keeptimeo++;
227              if (tp->t_state < TCPS_ESTABLISHED)
228                  goto dropit;        /* connection establishment timer */

229              if (tp->t_inpcb->inp_socket->so_options & SO_KEEPALIVE &&
230                  tp->t_state <= TCPS_CLOSE_WAIT) {
231                  if (tp->t_idle >= tcp_keepidle + tcp_maxidle)
232                      goto dropit;
233                  /*
234                   * Send a packet designed to force a response
235                   * if the peer is up and reachable:
236                   * either an ACK if the connection is still alive,
237                   * or an RST if the peer has closed the connection
238                   * due to timeout or reboot.
239                   * Using sequence number tp->snd_una-1
240                   * causes the transmitted zero-length segment
241                   * to lie outside the receive window;
242                   * by the protocol spec, this requires the
243                   * correspondent TCP to respond.
244                   */
245                  tcpstat.tcps_keepprobe++;
246                  tcp_respond(tp, tp->t_template, (struct mbuf *) NULL,
247                          tp->rcv_nxt, tp->snd_una - 1, 0);
248                  tp->t_timer[TCPT_KEEP] = tcp_keepintvl;
249              } else
250                  tp->t_timer[TCPT_KEEP] = tcp_keepidle;
251              break;
252          dropit:
253              tcpstat.tcps_keepdrops++;
254              tp = tcp_drop(tp, ETIMEDOUT);
255              break;
```
——— *tcp_timer.c*

Figure 25.16 tcp_timers function: expiration of keepalive timer.

transmitted a total of three times, at times 0, 6, and 30. At time 75, 3 seconds before the retransmission timer would expire again, the connection-establishment timer expires, and tcp_drop terminates the connection attempt.

Keepalive timer expires after 2 hours of idle time

229–230   This timer expires after 2 hours of idle time on every connection, not just ones with the SO_KEEPALIVE socket option enabled. If the socket option is set, probes are sent only if the connection is in the ESTABLISHED or CLOSE_WAIT states (Figure 24.15). Once the process calls close (the states greater than CLOSE_WAIT), keepalive probes are not sent, even if the connection is idle for 2 hours.

Drop connection when no response

231–232   If the total idle time for the connection is greater than or equal to 2 hours (`tcp_keepidle`) plus 10 minutes (`tcp_maxidle`), the connection is dropped. This means that TCP has sent its limit of nine keepalive probes, 75 seconds apart (`tcp_keepintvl`), with no response. One reason TCP must send multiple keepalive probes before considering the connection dead is that the ACKs sent in response do not contain data and therefore are not reliably transmitted by TCP. An ACK that is a response to a keepalive probe can get lost.

Send a keepalive probe

233–248   If TCP hasn't reached the keepalive limit, `tcp_respond` sends a keepalive packet. The acknowledgment field of the keepalive packet (the fourth argument to `tcp_respond`) contains `rcv_nxt`, the next sequence number expected on the connection. The sequence number field of the keepalive packet (the fifth argument) deliberately contains `snd_una` minus 1, which is the sequence number of a byte of data that the other end has already acknowledged (Figure 24.17). Since this sequence number is outside the window, the other end must respond with an ACK, specifying the next sequence number it expects.

Figure 25.17 summarizes this use of the keepalive timer.

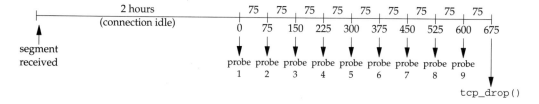

Figure 25.17   Summary of keepalive timer to detect unreachability of other end.

The nine keepalive probes are sent every 75 seconds, starting at time 0, through time 600. At time 675 (11.25 minutes after the 2-hour timer expired) the connection is dropped. Notice that nine keepalive probes are sent, even though the constant TCPTV_KEEPCNT (Figure 25.4) is 8. This is because the variable `t_idle` is incremented in Figure 25.8 *after* the timer is decremented, compared to 0, and possibly handled. When `tcp_input` receives a segment on a connection, it sets the keepalive timer to 14400 (`tcp_keepidle`) and `t_idle` to 0. The next time `tcp_slowtimo` is called, the keepalive timer is decremented to 14399 and `t_idle` is incremented to 1. About 2 hours later, when the keepalive timer is decremented from 1 to 0 and `tcp_timers` is called, the value of `t_idle` will be 14399. We can build the table in Figure 25.18 to see the value of `t_idle` each time `tcp_timers` is called.

The code in Figure 25.16 is waiting for `t_idle` to be greater than or equal to 15600 (`tcp_keepidle + tcp_maxidle`) and that only happens at time 675 in Figure 25.17, after nine keepalive probes have been sent.

probe#	time in Figure 25.17	t_idle
1	0	14399
2	75	14549
3	150	14699
4	225	14849
5	300	14999
6	375	15149
7	450	15299
8	525	15449
9	600	15599
	675	15749

Figure 25.18   The value of t_idle when tcp_timers is called for keepalive processing.

Reset keepalive timer

249–250   If the socket option is not set or the connection state is greater than CLOSE_WAIT, the keepalive timer for this connection is reset to 2 hours (tcp_keepidle).

> Unfortunately the counter tcps_keepdrops (line 253) counts both uses of the TCPT_KEEP counter: the connection-establishment timer and the keepalive timer.

25.7 Retransmission Timer Calculations

The timers that we've described so far in this chapter have fixed times associated with them: 200 ms for the delayed ACK timer, 75 seconds for the connection-establishment timer, 2 hours for the keepalive timer, and so on. The final two timers that we describe, the retransmission timer and the persist timer, have values that depend on the measured RTT for the connection. Before going through the source code that calculates and sets these timers we need to understand how TCP measures the RTT for a connection.

Fundamental to the operation of TCP is setting a retransmission timer when a segment is transmitted and an ACK is required from the other end. If the ACK is not received when the retransmission timer expires, the segment is retransmitted. TCP requires an ACK for data segments but does not require an ACK for a segment without data (i.e., a pure ACK segment). If the calculated retransmission timeout is too small, it can expire prematurely, causing needless retransmissions. If the calculated value is too large, after a segment is lost, additional time is lost before the segment is retransmitted, degrading performance. Complicating this is that the round-trip times between two hosts can vary widely and dynamically over the course of a connection.

TCP in Net/3 calculates the retransmission timeout (*RTO*) by measuring the round-trip time (*nticks*) of data segments and keeping track of the smoothed RTT estimator (*srtt*) and a smoothed mean deviation estimator (*rttvar*). The mean deviation is a good approximation of the standard deviation, but easier to compute since, unlike the standard deviation, the mean deviation does not require square root calculations. [Jacobson 1988b] provides additional details on these RTT measurements, which lead to the following equations:

$$delta = nticks - srtt$$

$$srtt \leftarrow srtt + g \times delta$$

$$rttvar \leftarrow rttvar + h(\,|\,delta\,|\, - rttvar)$$

$$RTO = srtt + 4 \times rttvar$$

delta is the difference between the measured round trip just obtained (*nticks*) and the current smoothed RTT estimator (*srtt*). *g* is the gain applied to the RTT estimator and equals ⅛. *h* is the gain applied to the mean deviation estimator and equals ¼. The two gains and the multiplier 4 in the *RTO* calculation are purposely powers of 2, so they can be calculated using shift operations instead of multiplying or dividing.

> [Jacobson 1988b] specified $2 \times rttvar$ in the calculation of *RTO*, but after further research, [Jacobson 1990d] changed the value to $4 \times rttvar$, which is what appeared in the Net/1 implementation.

We now describe the variables and calculations used to calculate TCP's retransmission timer, as we'll encounter them throughout the TCP code. Figure 25.19 lists the variables in the control block related to the retransmission timer.

tcpcb member	Units	tcp_newtcpcb initial value	#sec	Description
t_srtt	ticks × 8	0		smoothed RTT estimator: $srtt \times 8$
t_rttvar	ticks × 4	24	3	smoothed mean deviation estimator: $rttvar \times 4$
t_rxtcur	ticks	12	6	current retransmission timeout: *RTO*
t_rttmin	ticks	2	1	minimum value for retransmission timeout
t_rxtshift	n.a.	0		index into tcp_backoff[] array (exponential backoff)

Figure 25.19   Control block variables for calculation of retransmission timer.

We show the tcp_backoff array at the end of Section 25.9. The tcp_newtcpcb function sets the initial values for these variables, and we cover it in the next section. The term *shift* in the variable t_rxtshift and its limit TCP_MAXRXTSHIFT is not entirely accurate. The former is not used for bit shifting, but as Figure 25.19 indicates, it is an index into an array.

The confusing part of TCP's timeout calculations is that the two smoothed estimators maintained in the C code (t_srtt and t_rttvar) are fixed-point integers, instead of floating-point values. This is done to avoid floating-point calculations within the kernel, but it complicates the code.

To keep the scaled and unscaled variables distinct, we'll use the italic variables *srtt* and *rttvar* to refer to the unscaled variables in the earlier equations, and t_srtt and t_rttvar to refer to the scaled variables in the TCP control block.

Figure 25.20 shows four constants we encounter, which define the scale factors of 8 for t_srtt and 4 for t_rttvar.

Constant	Value	Description	
TCP_RTT_SCALE	8	multiplier:	$t\_srtt = srtt \times 8$
TCP_RTT_SHIFT	3	shift:	$t\_srtt = srtt << 3$
TCP_RTTVAR_SCALE	4	multiplier:	$t\_rttvar = rttvar \times 4$
TCP_RTTVAR_SHIFT	2	shift:	$t\_rttvar = rttvar << 2$

Figure 25.20 Multipliers and shifts for RTT estimators.

25.8 `tcp_newtcpcb` Function

A new TCP control block is allocated and initialized by `tcp_newtcpcb`, shown in Figure 25.21. This function is called by TCP's PRU_ATTACH request when a new socket is created (Figure 30.2). The caller has previously allocated an Internet PCB for this connection, pointed to by the argument inp. We present this function now because it initializes the TCP timer variables.

tcp_subr.c
```
167 struct tcpcb *
168 tcp_newtcpcb(inp)
169 struct inpcb *inp;
170 {
171     struct tcpcb *tp;

172     tp = malloc(sizeof(*tp), M_PCB, M_NOWAIT);
173     if (tp == NULL)
174         return ((struct tcpcb *) 0);
175     bzero((char *) tp, sizeof(struct tcpcb));
176     tp->seg_next = tp->seg_prev = (struct tcpiphdr *) tp;
177     tp->t_maxseg = tcp_mssdflt;
178     tp->t_flags = tcp_do_rfc1323 ? (TF_REQ_SCALE | TF_REQ_TSTMP) : 0;
179     tp->t_inpcb = inp;
180     /*
181      * Init srtt to TCPTV_SRTTBASE (0), so we can tell that we have no
182      * rtt estimate.  Set rttvar so that srtt + 2 * rttvar gives
183      * reasonable initial retransmit time.
184      */
185     tp->t_srtt = TCPTV_SRTTBASE;
186     tp->t_rttvar = tcp_rttdflt * PR_SLOWHZ << 2;
187     tp->t_rttmin = TCPTV_MIN;
188     TCPT_RANGESET(tp->t_rxtcur,
189                   ((TCPTV_SRTTBASE >> 2) + (TCPTV_SRTTDFLT << 2)) >> 1,
190                   TCPTV_MIN, TCPTV_REXMTMAX);

191     tp->snd_cwnd = TCP_MAXWIN << TCP_MAX_WINSHIFT;
192     tp->snd_ssthresh = TCP_MAXWIN << TCP_MAX_WINSHIFT;

193     inp->inp_ip.ip_ttl = ip_defttl;
194     inp->inp_ppcb = (caddr_t) tp;
195     return (tp);
196 }
```
tcp_subr.c

Figure 25.21 `tcp_newtcpcb` function: create and initialize a new TCP control block.

167–175   The kernel's `malloc` function allocates memory for the control block, and `bzero` sets it to 0.

176   The two variables `seg_next` and `seg_prev` point to the reassembly queue for out-of-order segments received for this connection. We discuss this queue in detail in Section 27.9.

177–179   The maximum segment size to send, `t_maxseg`, defaults to 512 (`tcp_mssdflt`). This value can be changed by the `tcp_mss` function after an MSS option is received from the other end. (TCP also sends an MSS option to the other end when a new connection is established.) The two flags `TF_REQ_SCALE` and `TF_REQ_TSTMP` are set if the system is configured to request window scaling and timestamps as defined in RFC 1323 (the global `tcp_do_rfc1323` from Figure 24.3, which defaults to 1). The `t_inpcb` pointer in the TCP control block is set to point to the Internet PCB passed in by the caller.

180–185   The four variables `t_srtt`, `t_rttvar`, `t_rttmin`, and `t_rxtcur`, described in Figure 25.19, are initialized. First, the smoothed RTT estimator `t_srtt` is set to 0 (`TCPTV_SRTTBASE`), which is a special value that means no RTT measurements have been made yet for this connection. `tcp_xmit_timer` recognizes this special value when the first RTT measurement is made.

186–187   The smoothed mean deviation estimator `t_rttvar` is set to 24: 3 (`tcp_rttdflt`, from Figure 24.3) times 2 (`PR_SLOWHZ`) multiplied by 4 (the left shift of 2 bits). Since this scaled estimator is 4 times the variable *rttvar*, this value equals 6 clock ticks, or 3 seconds. The minimum *RTO*, stored in `t_rttmin`, is 2 ticks (`TCPTV_MIN`).

188–190   The current *RTO* in clock ticks is calculated and stored in `t_rxtcur`. It is bounded by a minimum value of 2 ticks (`TCPTV_MIN`) and a maximum value of 128 ticks (`TCPTV_REXMTMAX`). The value calculated as the second argument to `TCPT_RANGESET` is 12 ticks, or 6 seconds. This is the first *RTO* for the connection.

Understanding these C expressions involving the scaled RTT estimators can be a challenge. It helps to start with the unscaled equation and substitute the scaled variables. The unscaled equation we're solving is

$$RTO = srtt + 2 \times rttvar$$

where we use the multipler of 2 instead of 4 to calculate the first *RTO*.

> The use of the multiplier 2 instead of 4 appears to be a leftover from the original 4.3BSD Tahoe code [Paxson 1994].

Substituting the two scaling relationships

$$t\_srtt = 8 \times srtt$$

$$t\_rttvar = 4 \times rttvar$$

we get

$$RTO = \frac{t\_srtt}{8} + 2 \times \frac{t\_rttvar}{4}$$

$$= \frac{\dfrac{t\_srtt}{4} + t\_rttvar}{2}$$

which is the C code for the second argument to `TCPT_RANGESET`. In this code the variable `t_rttvar` is not used—the constant `TCPTV_SRTTDFLT`, whose value is 6 ticks, is used instead, and it must be multiplied by 4 to have the same scale as `t_rttvar`.

191–192   The congestion window (`snd_cwnd`) and slow start threshold (`snd_ssthresh`) are set to 1,073,725,440 (approximately one gigabyte), which is the largest possible TCP window if the window scale option is in effect. (Slow start and congestion avoidance are described in Section 21.6 of Volume 1.) It is calculated as the maximum value for the window size field in the TCP header (65535, `TCP_MAXWIN`) times 2^{14}, where 14 is the maximum value for the window scale factor (`TCP_MAX_WINSHIFT`). We'll see that when a SYN is sent or received on the connection, `tcp_mss` resets `snd_cwnd` to a single segment.

193–194   The default IP TTL in the Internet PCB is set to 64 (`ip_defttl`) and the PCB is set to point to the new TCP control block.

Not shown in this code is that numerous variables, such as the shift variable `t_rxtshift`, are implicitly initialized to 0 since the control block is initialized by `bzero`.

25.9   `tcp_setpersist` Function

The next function we look at that uses TCP's retransmission timeout calculations is `tcp_setpersist`. In Figure 25.13 we saw this function called when the persist timer expired. This timer is set when TCP has data to send on a connection, but the other end is advertising a window of 0. This function, shown in Figure 25.22, calculates and stores the next value for the timer.

```
                                                                  ─── tcp_output.c
493 void
494 tcp_setpersist(tp)
495 struct tcpcb *tp;
496 {
497     t = ((tp->t_srtt >> 2) + tp->t_rttvar) >> 1;

498     if (tp->t_timer[TCPT_REXMT])
499         panic("tcp_output REXMT");
500     /*
501      * Start/restart persistance timer.
502      */
503     TCPT_RANGESET(tp->t_timer[TCPT_PERSIST],
504                 t * tcp_backoff[tp->t_rxtshift],
505                 TCPTV_PERSMIN, TCPTV_PERSMAX);
506     if (tp->t_rxtshift < TCP_MAXRXTSHIFT)
507         tp->t_rxtshift++;
508 }
                                                                  ─── tcp_output.c
```

Figure 25.22   `tcp_setpersist` function: calculate and store a new value for the persist timer.

Check retransmission timer not enabled

493–499   A check is made that the retransmission timer is not enabled when the persist timer is about to be set, since the two timers are mutually exclusive: if data is being sent, the

other side must be advertising a nonzero window, but the persist timer is being set only
if the advertised window is 0.

Calculate RTO

500–505 The variable `t` is set to the *RTO* value that was calculated at the beginning of the
function. The equation being solved is

$$RTO = srtt + 2 \times rttvar$$

which is identical to the formula used at the end of the previous section. With substitu-
tion we get

$$RTO = \frac{\dfrac{t\_srtt}{4} + t\_rttvar}{2}$$

which is the value computed for the variable `t`.

Apply exponential backoff

506–507 An *exponential backoff* is also applied to the *RTO*. This is done by multiplying the
RTO by a value from the `tcp_backoff` array:

```
int  tcp_backoff[TCP_MAXRXTSHIFT + 1] =
    { 1, 2, 4, 8, 16, 32, 64, 64, 64, 64, 64, 64, 64 };
```

When `tcp_output` initially sets the persist timer for a connection, the code is

```
tp->t_rxtshift = 0;
tcp_setpersist(tp);
```

so the first time `tcp_setpersist` is called, `t_rxtshift` is 0. Since the value of
`tcp_backoff[0]` is 1, `t` is used as the persist timeout. The `TCPT_RANGESET` macro
bounds this value between 5 and 60 seconds. `t_rxtshift` is incremented by 1 until it
reaches a maximum of 12 (`TCP_MAXRXTSHIFT`), since `tcp_backoff[12]` is the final
entry in the array.

25.10 `tcp_xmit_timer` Function

The next function we look at, `tcp_xmit_timer`, is called each time an RTT measurement is collected, to update the smoothed RTT estimator (*srtt*) and the smoothed mean
deviation estimator (*rttvar*).

The argument `rtt` is the RTT measurement to be applied. It is the value *nticks* + 1,
using the notation from Section 25.7. It can be from one of two sources:

1. If the timestamp option is present in a received segment, the measured RTT is
   the current time (`tcp_now`) minus the timestamp value. We'll examine the
   timestamp option in Section 26.6, but for now all we need to know is that
   `tcp_now` is incremented every 500 ms (Figure 25.8). When a data segment is
   sent, `tcp_now` is sent as the timestamp, and the other end echoes this timestamp in the acknowledgment it sends back.

2. If timestamps are not in use and a data segment is being timed, we saw in Figure 25.8 that the counter `t_rtt` is incremented every 500 ms for the connection. We also mentioned in Section 25.5 that this counter is initialized to 1, so when the acknowledgment is received the counter is the measured RTT (in ticks) plus 1.

Typical code in `tcp_input` that calls `tcp_xmit_timer` is

```
if (ts_present)
    tcp_xmit_timer(tp, tcp_now - ts_ecr + 1);

else if (tp->t_rtt && SEQ_GT(ti->ti_ack, tp->t_rtseq))
    tcp_xmit_timer(tp, tp->t_rtt);
```

If a timestamp was present in the segment (`ts_present`), the RTT estimators are updated using the current time (`tcp_now`) minus the echoed timestamp (`ts_ecr`) plus 1. (We describe the reason for adding 1 below.)

If a timestamp is not present, the RTT estimators are updated only if the received segment acknowledges a data segment that was being timed. There is only one RTT counter per TCP control block (`t_rtt`), so only one outstanding data segment can be timed per connection. The starting sequence number of that segment is stored in `t_rtseq` when the segment is transmitted, to tell when an acknowledgment is received that covers that sequence number. If the received acknowledgment number (`ti_ack`) is greater than the starting sequence number of the segment being timed (`t_rtseq`), the RTT estimators are updated using `t_rtt` as the measured RTT.

> Before RFC 1323 timestamps were supported, TCP measured the RTT only by counting clock ticks in `t_rtt`. But this variable is also used as a flag that specifies whether a segment is being timed (Figure 25.8): if `t_rtt` is greater than 0, then `tcp_slowtimo` adds 1 to it every 500 ms. Hence when `t_rtt` is nonzero, it is the number of ticks plus 1. We'll see shortly that `tcp_xmit_timer` always decrements its second argument by 1 to account for this offset. Therefore when timestamps are being used, 1 is added to the second argument to account for the decrement by 1 in `tcp_xmit_timer`.

The greater-than test of the sequence numbers is because ACKs are cumulative: if TCP sends and times a segment with sequence numbers 1–1024 (`t_rtseq` equals 1), then immediately sends (but can't time) a segment with sequence numbers 1025–2048, and then receives an ACK with `ti_ack` equal to 2049, this is an ACK for sequence numbers 1–2048 and the ACK acknowledges the first segment being timed as well as the second (untimed) segment. Notice that when RFC 1323 timestamps are in use there is no comparison of sequence numbers. If the other end sends a timestamp option, it chooses the echo reply value (`ts_ecr`) to allow TCP to calculate the RTT.

Figure 25.23 shows the first part of the function that updates the estimators.

Update smoothed estimators

1310–1325   Recall that `tcp_newtcpcb` initialized the smoothed RTT estimator (`t_srtt`) to 0, indicating that no measurements have been made for this connection. `delta` is the difference between the measured RTT and the current value of the smoothed RTT estimator, in unscaled ticks. `t_srtt` is divided by 8 to convert from scaled to unscaled ticks.

```
                                                                            ──── tcp_input.c
1310 void
1311 tcp_xmit_timer(tp, rtt)
1312 struct tcpcb *tp;
1313 short    rtt;
1314 {
1315     short    delta;

1316     tcpstat.tcps_rttupdated++;
1317     if (tp->t_srtt != 0) {
1318         /*
1319          * srtt is stored as fixed point with 3 bits after the
1320          * binary point (i.e., scaled by 8).  The following magic
1321          * is equivalent to the smoothing algorithm in rfc793 with
1322          * an alpha of .875 (srtt = rtt/8 + srtt*7/8 in fixed
1323          * point).  Adjust rtt to origin 0.
1324          */
1325         delta = rtt - 1 - (tp->t_srtt >> TCP_RTT_SHIFT);
1326         if ((tp->t_srtt += delta) <= 0)
1327             tp->t_srtt = 1;
1328         /*
1329          * We accumulate a smoothed rtt variance (actually, a
1330          * smoothed mean difference), then set the retransmit
1331          * timer to smoothed rtt + 4 times the smoothed variance.
1332          * rttvar is stored as fixed point with 2 bits after the
1333          * binary point (scaled by 4).  The following is
1334          * equivalent to rfc793 smoothing with an alpha of .75
1335          * (rttvar = rttvar*3/4 + |delta| / 4).  This replaces
1336          * rfc793's wired-in beta.
1337          */
1338         if (delta < 0)
1339             delta = -delta;
1340         delta -= (tp->t_rttvar >> TCP_RTTVAR_SHIFT);
1341         if ((tp->t_rttvar += delta) <= 0)
1342             tp->t_rttvar = 1;
1343     } else {
1344         /*
1345          * No rtt measurement yet - use the unsmoothed rtt.
1346          * Set the variance to half the rtt (so our first
1347          * retransmit happens at 3*rtt).
1348          */
1349         tp->t_srtt = rtt << TCP_RTT_SHIFT;
1350         tp->t_rttvar = rtt << (TCP_RTTVAR_SHIFT - 1);
1351     }
                                                                            ──── tcp_input.c
```

Figure 25.23 `tcp_xmit_timer` function: apply new RTT measurement to smoothed estimators.

1326–1327   The smoothed RTT estimator is updated using the equation

$$srtt \leftarrow srtt + g \times delta$$

Since the gain g is ⅛, this equation is

$$8 \times srtt \leftarrow 8 \times srtt + delta$$

which is

$$\texttt{t\_srtt} \leftarrow \texttt{t\_srtt} + delta$$

1328–1342   The mean deviation estimator is updated using the equation

$$rttvar \leftarrow rttvar + h(\,|\,delta\,|\, - rttvar)$$

Substituting ¼ for h and the scaled variable $\texttt{t\_rttvar}$ for $4 \times rttvar$, we get

$$\frac{\texttt{t\_rttvar}}{4} \leftarrow \frac{\texttt{t\_rttvar}}{4} + \frac{|\,delta\,| - \dfrac{\texttt{t\_rttvar}}{4}}{4}$$

which is

$$\texttt{t\_rttvar} \leftarrow \texttt{t\_rttvar} + |\,delta\,| - \frac{\texttt{t\_rttvar}}{4}$$

This final equation corresponds to the C code.

Initialize smoothed estimators on first RTT measurement

1343–1350   If this is the first RTT measured for this connection, the smoothed RTT estimator is initialized to the measured RTT. These calculations use the value of the argument $\texttt{rtt}$, which we said is the measured RTT plus 1 ($nticks + 1$), whereas the earlier calculation of $\texttt{delta}$ subtracted 1 from $\texttt{rtt}$.

$$srtt = nticks + 1$$

or

$$\frac{\texttt{t\_srtt}}{8} = nticks + 1$$

which is

$$\texttt{t\_srtt} = (nticks + 1) \times 8$$

The smoothed mean deviation is set to one-half of the measured RTT:

$$rttvar = \frac{srtt}{2}$$

which is

$$\frac{\texttt{t\_rttvar}}{4} = \frac{nticks + 1}{2}$$

or

$$\texttt{t\_rttvar} = (nticks + 1) \times 2$$

The comment in the code states that this initial setting for the smoothed mean deviation yields an initial RTO of $3 \times srtt$. Since the RTO is calculated as

$$RTO = srtt + 4 \times rttvar$$

substituting for *rttvar* gives us

$$RTO = srtt + 4 \times \frac{srtt}{2}$$

which is indeed

$$RTO = 3 \times srtt$$

Figure 25.24 shows the final part of the `tcp_xmit_timer` function.

─── *tcp_input.c*
```
1352        tp->t_rtt = 0;
1353        tp->t_rxtshift = 0;
1354        /*
1355         * the retransmit should happen at rtt + 4 * rttvar.
1356         * Because of the way we do the smoothing, srtt and rttvar
1357         * will each average +1/2 tick of bias.  When we compute
1358         * the retransmit timer, we want 1/2 tick of rounding and
1359         * 1 extra tick because of +-1/2 tick uncertainty in the
1360         * firing of the timer.  The bias will give us exactly the
1361         * 1.5 tick we need.  But, because the bias is
1362         * statistical, we have to test that we don't drop below
1363         * the minimum feasible timer (which is 2 ticks).
1364         */
1365        TCPT_RANGESET(tp->t_rxtcur, TCP_REXMTVAL(tp),
1366                     tp->t_rttmin, TCPTV_REXMTMAX);
1367        /*
1368         * We received an ack for a packet that wasn't retransmitted;
1369         * it is probably safe to discard any error indications we've
1370         * received recently.  This isn't quite right, but close enough
1371         * for now (a route might have failed after we sent a segment,
1372         * and the return path might not be symmetrical).
1373         */
1374        tp->t_softerror = 0;
1375 }
```
─── *tcp_input.c*

Figure 25.24 `tcp_xmit_timer` function: final part.

1352–1353   The RTT counter (`t_rtt`) and the retransmission shift count (`t_rxtshift`) are both reset to 0 in preparation for timing and transmission of the next segment.

1354–1366   The next *RTO* to use for the connection (`t_rxtcur`) is calculated using the macro

```
#define  TCP_REXMTVAL(tp) \
         (((tp)->t_srtt >> TCP_RTT_SHIFT) + (tp)->t_rttvar)
```

This is the now-familiar equation

$$RTO = srtt + 4 \times rttvar$$

using the scaled variables updated by `tcp_xmit_timer`. Substituting these scaled variables for *srtt* and *rttvar*, we have

$$RTO = \frac{t\_srtt}{8} + 4 \times \frac{t\_rttvar}{4}$$

$$= \frac{\texttt{t\_srtt}}{8} + \texttt{t\_rttvar}$$

which corresponds to the macro. The calculated value for the *RTO* is bounded by the minimum *RTO* for this connection (`t_rttmin`, which `t_newtcpcb` set to 2 ticks), and 128 ticks (`TCPTV_REXMTMAX`).

Clear soft error variable

1367–1374   Since `tcp_xmit_timer` is called only when an acknowledgment is received for a data segment that was sent, if a soft error was recorded for this connection (`t_softerror`), that error is discarded. We describe soft errors in more detail in the next section.

25.11 Retransmission Timeout: `tcp_timers` Function

We now return to the `tcp_timers` function and cover the final `case` that we didn't present in Section 25.6: the one that handles the expiration of the retransmission timer. This code is executed when a data segment that was transmitted has not been acknowledged by the other end within the *RTO*.

Figure 25.25 summarizes the actions caused by the retransmission timer. We assume that the first timeout calculated by `tcp_output` is 1.5 seconds, which is typical for a LAN (see Figure 21.1 of Volume 1).

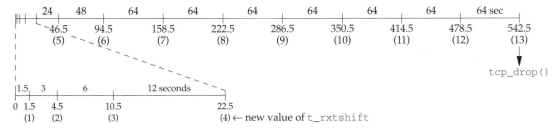

Figure 25.25   Summary of retransmission timer when sending data.

The x-axis is labeled with the time in seconds: 0, 1.5, 4.5, and so on. Below each of these numbers we show the value of `t_rxtshift` that is used in the code we're about to examine. Only after 12 retransmissions and a total of 542.5 seconds (just over 9 minutes) does TCP give up and drop the connection.

> RFC 793 recommended that an open of a new connection, active or passive, allow a parameter specifying the total timeout period for data sent by TCP. This is the total amount of time TCP will try to send a given segment before giving up and terminating the connection. The recommended default was 5 minutes.
>
> RFC 1122 requires that an application must be able to specify a parameter for a connection giving either the total number of retransmissions or the total timeout value for data sent by TCP. This parameter can be specified as "infinity," meaning TCP never gives up, allowing, perhaps, an interactive user the choice of when to give up.

We'll see in the code described shortly that Net/3 does not give the application any of this control: a fixed number of retransmissions (12) always occurs before TCP gives up, and the total timeout before giving up depends on the RTT.

The first half of the retransmission timeout case is shown in Figure 25.26.

```
                                                                    ─── tcp_timer.c
140         /*
141          * Retransmission timer went off.  Message has not
142          * been acked within retransmit interval.  Back off
143          * to a longer retransmit interval and retransmit one segment.
144          */
145     case TCPT_REXMT:
146         if (++tp->t_rxtshift > TCP_MAXRXTSHIFT) {
147             tp->t_rxtshift = TCP_MAXRXTSHIFT;
148             tcpstat.tcps_timeoutdrop++;
149             tp = tcp_drop(tp, tp->t_softerror ?
150                         tp->t_softerror : ETIMEDOUT);
151             break;
152         }
153         tcpstat.tcps_rexmttimeo++;
154         rexmt = TCP_REXMTVAL(tp) * tcp_backoff[tp->t_rxtshift];
155         TCPT_RANGESET(tp->t_rxtcur, rexmt,
156                     tp->t_rttmin, TCPTV_REXMTMAX);
157         tp->t_timer[TCPT_REXMT] = tp->t_rxtcur;
158         /*
159          * If losing, let the lower level know and try for
160          * a better route.  Also, if we backed off this far,
161          * our srtt estimate is probably bogus.  Clobber it
162          * so we'll take the next rtt measurement as our srtt;
163          * move the current srtt into rttvar to keep the current
164          * retransmit times until then.
165          */
166         if (tp->t_rxtshift > TCP_MAXRXTSHIFT / 4) {
167             in_losing(tp->t_inpcb);
168             tp->t_rttvar += (tp->t_srtt >> TCP_RTT_SHIFT);
169             tp->t_srtt = 0;
170         }
171         tp->snd_nxt = tp->snd_una;
172         /*
173          * If timing a segment in this window, stop the timer.
174          */
175         tp->t_rtt = 0;
                                                                    ─── tcp_timer.c
```

Figure 25.26 `tcp_timers` function: expiration of retransmission timer, first half.

Increment shift count

146   The retransmission shift count ($t\_rxtshift$) is incremented, and if the value exceeds 12 (TCP_MAXRXTSHIFT) it is time to drop the connection. This new value of $t\_rxtshift$ is what we show in Figure 25.25. Notice the difference between this dropping of a connection because an acknowledgment is not received from the other end in response to data sent by TCP, and the keepalive timer, which drops a connection after a

long period of inactivity and no response from the other end. Both report the error
ETIMEDOUT to the process, unless a soft error is received for the connection.

Drop connection

147–152   A *soft error* is one that doesn't cause TCP to terminate an established connection or
an attempt to establish a connection, but the soft error is recorded in case TCP gives up
later. For example, if TCP retransmits a SYN segment to establish a connection, receiving nothing in response, the error returned to the process will be ETIMEDOUT. But if
during the retransmissions an ICMP host unreachable is received for the connection,
that is considered a soft error and stored in t_softerror by tcp_notify. If TCP
finally gives up the retransmissions, the error returned to the process will be
EHOSTUNREACH instead of ETIMEDOUT, providing more information to the process. If
TCP receives an RST on the connection in response to the SYN, that's considered a *hard
error* and the connection is terminated immediately with an error of ECONNREFUSED
(Figure 28.18).

Calculate new RTO

153–157   The next *RTO* is calculated using the TCP_REXMTVAL macro, applying an exponential backoff. In this code, t_rxtshift will be 1 the first time a given segment is
retransmitted, so the *RTO* will be twice the value calculated by TCP_REXMTVAL. This
value is stored in t_rxtcur and as the retransmission timer for the connection,
t_timer[TCPT_REXMT]. The value stored in t_rxtcur is used in tcp_input when
the retransmission timer is restarted (Figures 28.12 and 29.6).

Ask IP to find a new route

158–167   If this segment has been retransmitted four or more times, in_losing releases the
cached route (if there is one), so when the segment is retransmitted by tcp_output (at
the end of this case statement in Figure 25.27) a new, and hopefully better, route will be
chosen. In Figure 25.25 in_losing is called each time the retransmission timer
expires, starting with the retransmission at time 22.5.

Clear estimators

168–170   The smoothed RTT estimator (t_srtt) is set to 0, which is what t_newtcpcb did.
This forces tcp_xmit_timer to use the next measured RTT as the smoothed RTT estimator. This is done because the retransmitted segment has been sent four or more
times, implying that TCP's smoothed RTT estimator is probably way off. But if the
retransmission timer expires again, at the beginning of this case statement the *RTO* is
calculated by TCP_REXMTVAL. That calculation should generate the same value as it
did for this retransmission (which will then be exponentially backed off), even though
t_srtt is set to 0. (The retransmission at time 42.464 in Figure 25.28 is an example of
what's happening here.)

To accomplish this the value of t_rttvar is changed as follows. The next time the
RTO is calculated, the equation

$$RTO = \frac{t\_srtt}{8} + t\_rttvar$$

is evaluated. Since t_srtt will be 0, if t_rttvar is increased by t_srtt divided by

8, *RTO* will have the same value. If the retransmission timer expires again for this segment (e.g., times 84.064 through 217.184 in Figure 25.28), when this code is executed again t_srtt will be 0, so t_rttvar won't change.

Force retransmission of oldest unacknowledged data

171   The next send sequence number (snd_nxt) is set to the oldest unacknowledged sequence number (snd_una). Recall from Figure 24.17 that snd_nxt can be greater than snd_una. By moving snd_nxt back, the retransmission will be the oldest segment that hasn't been acknowledged.

Karn's algorithm

172–175   The RTT counter, t_rtt, is set to 0, in case the last segment transmitted was being timed. Karn's algorithm says that even if an ACK of that segment is received, since the segment is about to be retransmitted, any timing of the segment is worthless since the ACK could be for the first transmission or for the retransmission. The algorithm is described in [Karn and Partridge 1987] and in Section 21.3 of Volume 1. Therefore the only segments that are timed using the t_rtt counter and used to update the RTT estimators are those that are not retransmitted. We'll see in Figure 29.6 that the use of RFC 1323 timestamps overrides Karn's algorithm.

Slow Start and Congestion Avoidance

The second half of this case is shown in Figure 25.27. It performs slow start and congestion avoidance and retransmits the oldest unacknowledged segment.

Since a retransmission timeout has occurred, this is a strong indication of congestion in the network. TCP's *congestion avoidance algorithm* comes into play, and when a segment is eventually acknowledged by the other end, TCP's *slow start* algorithm will continue the data transmission on the connection at a slower rate. Sections 20.6 and 21.6 of Volume 1 describe the two algorithms in detail.

176–205   win is set to one-half of the current window size (the minimum of the receiver's advertised window, snd_wnd, and the sender's congestion window, snd_cwnd) in segments, not bytes (hence the division by t_maxseg). Its minimum value is two segments. This records one-half of the window size when the congestion occurred, assuming one cause of the congestion is our sending segments too rapidly into the network. This becomes the slow start threshold, t_ssthresh (which is stored in bytes, hence the multiplication by t_maxseg). The congestion window, snd_cwnd, is set to one segment, which forces slow start.

> This code is enclosed in braces because it was added between the 4.3BSD and Net/1 releases and required its own local variable (win).

206   The counter of consecutive duplicate ACKs, t_dupacks (which is used by the fast retransmit algorithm in Section 29.4), is set to 0. We'll see how this counter is used with TCP's fast retransmit and fast recovery algorithms in Chapter 29.

208   tcp_output resends a segment containing the oldest unacknowledged sequence number. This is the retransmission caused by the retransmission timer expiring.

```
                                                             ── tcp_timer.c
176          /*
177           * Close the congestion window down to one segment
178           * (we'll open it by one segment for each ack we get).
179           * Since we probably have a window's worth of unacked
180           * data accumulated, this "slow start" keeps us from
181           * dumping all that data as back-to-back packets (which
182           * might overwhelm an intermediate gateway).
183           *
184           * There are two phases to the opening: Initially we
185           * open by one mss on each ack.  This makes the window
186           * size increase exponentially with time.  If the
187           * window is larger than the path can handle, this
188           * exponential growth results in dropped packet(s)
189           * almost immediately.  To get more time between
190           * drops but still "push" the network to take advantage
191           * of improving conditions, we switch from exponential
192           * to linear window opening at some threshhold size.
193           * For a threshhold, we use half the current window
194           * size, truncated to a multiple of the mss.
195           *
196           * (the minimum cwnd that will give us exponential
197           * growth is 2 mss.  We don't allow the threshhold
198           * to go below this.)
199           */
200          {
201              u_int   win = min(tp->snd_wnd, tp->snd_cwnd) / 2 / tp->t_maxseg;
202              if (win < 2)
203                  win = 2;
204              tp->snd_cwnd = tp->t_maxseg;
205              tp->snd_ssthresh = win * tp->t_maxseg;
206              tp->t_dupacks = 0;
207          }
208          (void) tcp_output(tp);
209          break;
                                                             ── tcp_timer.c
```

Figure 25.27   `tcp_timers` function: expiration of retransmission timer, second half.

Accuracy

How accurate are these estimators that TCP maintains? At first they appear too coarse, since the RTTs are measured in multiples of 500 ms. The mean and mean deviation are maintained with additional accuracy (factors of 8 and 4 respectively), but LANs have RTTs on the order of milliseconds, and a transcontinental RTT is around 60 ms. What these estimators provide is a solid upper bound on the RTT so that the retransmission timeout can be set without worrying that the timeout is too small, causing unnecessary and wasteful retransmissions.

[Brakmo, O'Malley, and Peterson 1994] describe a TCP implementation that provides higher-resolution RTT measurements. This is done by recording the system clock (which has a much higher resolution than 500 ms) when a segment is transmitted and reading the system clock when the ACK is received, calculating a higher-resolution RTT.

The timestamp option provided by Net/3 (Section 26.6) can provide higher-resolution RTTs, but Net/3 sets the resolution of these timestamps to 500 ms.

25.12 An RTT Example

We now go through an actual example to see how the calculations are performed. We transfer 12288 bytes from the host bsdi to vangogh.cs.berkeley.edu. During the transfer we purposely bring down the PPP link being used and then bring it back up, to see how timeouts and retransmissions are handled. To transfer the data we use our sock program (described in Appendix C of Volume 1) with the -D option, to enable the SO_DEBUG socket option (Section 27.10). After the transfer is complete we examine the debug records left in the kernel's circular buffer using the trpt(8) program and print the desired timer variables from the TCP control block.

Figure 25.28 shows the calculations that occur at the various times. We use the notation $M:N$ to mean that sequence numbers M through and including $N-1$ are sent. Each segment in this example contains 512 bytes. The notation "ack M" means that the acknowledgment field of the ACK is M. The column labeled "actual delta (ms)" shows the time difference between the RTT timer going on and going off. The column labeled "rtt (arg.)" shows the second argument to the tcp_xmit_timer function: the number of clock ticks plus 1 between the RTT timer going on and going off.

The function tcp_newtcpcb initializes t_srtt, t_rttvar, and t_rxtcur to the values shown at time 0.0.

The first segment timed is the initial SYN. When its ACK is received 365 ms later, tcp_xmit_timer is called with an rtt argument of 2. Since this is the first RTT measurement (t_srtt is 0), the else clause in Figure 25.23 calculates the first values of the smoothed estimators.

The data segment containing bytes 1 through 512 is the next segment timed, and the RTT variables are updated at time 1.259 when its ACK is received.

The next three segments show how ACKs are cumulative. The timer is started at time 1.260 when bytes 513 through 1024 are sent. Another segment is sent with bytes 1025 through 1536, and the ACK received at time 2.206 acknowledges both data segments. The RTT estimators are then updated, since the ACK covers the starting sequence number being timed (513).

The segment with bytes 1537 through 2048 is transmitted at time 2.206 and the timer is started. Just that segment is acknowledged at time 3.132, and the estimators updated.

The data segment at time 3.132 is timed and the retransmission timer is set to 5 ticks (the current value of t_rxtcur). Somewhere around this time the PPP link between the routers sun and netb is taken down and then brought back up, a procedure that takes a few minutes. When the retransmission timer expires at time 6.064, the code in Figure 25.26 is executed to update the RTT variables. t_rxtshift is incremented from 0 to 1 and t_rxtcur is set to 10 ticks (the exponential backoff). A segment starting with the oldest unacknowledged sequence number (snd_una, which is 3073) is retransmitted. After 5 seconds the timer expires again, t_rxtshift is incremented to 2, and the retransmission timer is set to 20 ticks.

xmit time	send	recv	RTT timer	actual delta (ms)	rtt arg.	t_srtt (ticks × 8)	t_rttvar (ticks × 4)	t_rxtcur (ticks)	t_rxtshift
0.0	SYN		on			0	24	12	
0.365		SYN,ACK	off	365	2	16	4	6	
0.365	ACK								
0.415	1:513		on						
1.259		ack 513	off	844	2	15	4	5	
1.260	513:1025		on						
1.261	1025:1537								
2.206		ack 1537	off	946	3	16	4	6	
2.206	1537:2049		on						
2.207	2049:2561								
2.209	2561:3073								
3.132		ack 2049	off	926	3	16	3	5	
3.132	3073:3585		on						
3.133	3585:4097								
3.736		ack 2561							
3.736	4097:4609								
3.737	4609:5121								
3.739		ack 3073							
3.739	5121:5633								
3.740	5633:6145								
6.064	3073:3585		off			16	3	10	1
11.264	3073:3585		off			16	3	20	2
21.664	3073:3585		off			16	3	40	3
42.464	3073:3585		off			0	5	80	4
84.064	3073:3585		off			0	5	128	5
150.624	3073:3585		off			0	5	128	6
217.184	3073:3585		off			0	5	128	7
217.944		ack 6145							
217.944	6145:6657		on						
217.945	6657:7169								
218.834		ack 6657	off	890	3	24	6	9	
218.834	7169:7681		on						
218.836	7681:8193								
219.209		ack 7169							
219.209	8193:8705								
219.760		ack 7681	off	926	2	22	7	9	
219.760	8705:9217		on						
220.103		ack 8705							
220.103	9217:9729								
220.105	9729:10241								
220.106	10241:10753								
220.821		ack 9217	off	1061	3	22	6	8	
220.821	10753:11265		on						
221.310		ack 9729							
221.310	11265:11777								
221.312		ack 10241							
221.312	11777:12289								
221.674		ack 10753							
221.955		ack 11265	off	1134	3	22	5	7	

Figure 25.28   Values of RTT variables and estimators during example.

When the retransmission timer expires at time 42.464, `t_srtt` is set to 0 and `t_rttvar` is set to 5. As we mentioned in our discussion of Figure 25.26, this leaves the calculation of `t_rxtcur` the same (so the next calculation yields 160), but by setting `t_srtt` to 0, the next time the RTT estimators are updated (at time 218.834), the measured RTT becomes the smoothed RTT, as if the connection were starting fresh.

The rest of the data transfer continues, and the estimators are updated a few more times.

25.13 Summary

The two functions `tcp_fasttimo` and `tcp_slowtimo` are called by the kernel every 200 ms and every 500 ms, respectively. These two functions drive TCP's per-connection timer maintenance.

TCP maintains the following seven timers for each connection:

- a connection-establishment timer,
- a retransmission timer,
- a delayed ACK timer,
- a persist timer,
- a keepalive timer,
- a FIN_WAIT_2 timer, and
- a 2MSL timer.

The delayed ACK timer is different from the other six, since when it is set it means a delayed ACK must be sent the next time TCP's 200-ms timer expires. The other six timers are counters that are decremented by 1 every time TCP's 500-ms timer expires. When any one of the counters reaches 0, the appropriate action is taken: drop the connection, retransmit a segment, send a keepalive probe, and so on, as described in this chapter. Since some of the timers are mutually exclusive, the six timers are really implemented using four counters, which complicates the code.

This chapter also introduced the recommended way to calculate values for the retransmission timer. TCP maintains two smoothed estimators for a connection: the round-trip time and the mean deviation of the RTT. Although the algorithms are simple and elegant, these estimators are maintained as scaled fixed-point numbers (to provide adequate precision without using floating-point code within the kernel), which complicates the code.

Exercises

25.1 How efficient is TCP's fast timeout function? (*Hint*: Look at the number of delayed ACKs in Figure 24.5.) Suggest alternative implementations.

25.2 Why do you think the initialization of `tcp_maxidle` is in the `tcp_slowtimo` function instead of the `tcp_init` function?

25.3 `tcp_slowtimo` increments `t_idle`, which we said counts the clock ticks since a segment was last received on the connection. Should TCP also count the idle time since a segment was last sent on a connection?

25.4 Rewrite the code in Figure 25.10 to separate the logic for the two different uses of the `TCPT_2MSL` counter.

25.5 75 seconds after the connection in Figure 25.12 enters the FIN_WAIT_2 state a duplicate ACK is received on the connection. What happens?

25.6 A connection has been idle for 1 hour when the application sets the `SO_KEEPALIVE` option. Will the first keepalive probe be sent 1 or 2 hours in the future?

25.7 Why is `tcp_rttdflt` a global variable and not a constant?

25.8 Rewrite the code related to Exercise 25.6 to implement the alternate behavior.

26

TCP Output

26.1 Introduction

The function `tcp_output` is called whenever a segment needs to be sent on a connection. There are numerous calls to this function from other TCP functions:

- `tcp_usrreq` calls it for various requests: `PRU_CONNECT` to send the initial SYN, `PRU_SHUTDOWN` to send a FIN, `PRU_RCVD` in case a window update can be sent after the process has read some data from the socket receive buffer, `PRU_SEND` to send data, and `PRU_SENDOOB` to send out-of-band data.

- `tcp_fasttimo` calls it to send a delayed ACK.

- `tcp_timers` calls it to retransmit a segment when the retransmission timer expires.

- `tcp_timers` calls it to send a persist probe when the persist timer expires.

- `tcp_drop` calls it to send an RST.

- `tcp_disconnect` calls it to send a FIN.

- `tcp_input` calls it when output is required or when an immediate ACK should be sent.

- `tcp_input` calls it when a pure ACK is processed by the header prediction code and there is more data to send. (A *pure ACK* is a segment without data that just acknowledges data.)

- `tcp_input` calls it when the third consecutive duplicate ACK is received, to send a single segment (the fast retransmit algorithm).

tcp_output first determines whether a segment should be sent or not. TCP output is controlled by numerous factors other than data being ready to send to the other end of the connection. For example, the other end might be advertising a window of size 0 that stops TCP from sending anything, the Nagle algorithm prevents TCP from sending lots of small segments, and slow start and congestion avoidance limit the amount of data TCP can send on a connection. Conversely, some functions set flags just to force tcp_output to send a segment, such as the TF_ACKNOW flag that means an ACK should be sent immediately and not delayed. If tcp_output decides not to send a segment, the data (if any) is left in the socket's send buffer for a later call to this function.

26.2 tcp_output Overview

tcp_output is a large function, so we'll discuss it in 14 parts. Figure 26.1 shows the outline of the function.

Is an ACK expected from the other end?

61　　idle is true if the maximum sequence number sent (snd_max) equals the oldest unacknowledged sequence number (snd_una), that is, if an ACK is not expected from the other end. In Figure 24.17 idle would be 0, since an ACK is expected for sequence numbers 4–6, which have been sent but not yet acknowledged.

Go back to slow start

62–68　　If an ACK is not expected from the other end and a segment has not been received from the other end in one RTO, the congestion window is set to one segment (t_maxseg bytes). This forces slow start to occur for this connection the next time a segment is sent. When a significant pause occurs in the data transmission ("significant" being more than the RTT), the network conditions can change from what was previously measured on the connection. Net/3 assumes the worst and returns to slow start.

Send more than one segment

69–70　　When send is jumped to, a single segment is sent by calling ip_output. But if tcp_output determines that more than one segment can be sent, sendalot is set to 1, and the function tries to send another segment. Therefore, one call to tcp_output can result in multiple segments being sent.

26.3 Determine if a Segment Should be Sent

Sometimes tcp_output is called but a segment is not generated. For example, the PRU_RCVD request is generated when the socket layer removes data from the socket's receive buffer, passing the data to a process. It is possible that the process removed enough data that TCP should send a segment to the other end with a new window advertisement, but this is just a possibility, not a certainty. The first half of tcp_output determines if there is a reason to send a segment to the other end. If not, the function returns without sending a segment.

── *tcp_output.c*

```
43 int
44 tcp_output(tp)
45 struct tcpcb *tp;
46 {
47     struct socket *so = tp->t_inpcb->inp_socket;
48     long    len, win;
49     int     off, flags, error;
50     struct mbuf *m;
51     struct tcpiphdr *ti;
52     u_char  opt[MAX_TCPOPTLEN];
53     unsigned optlen, hdrlen;
54     int     idle, sendalot;

55     /*
56      * Determine length of data that should be transmitted
57      * and flags that will be used.
58      * If there are some data or critical controls (SYN, RST)
59      * to send, then transmit; otherwise, investigate further.
60      */
61     idle = (tp->snd_max == tp->snd_una);
62     if (idle && tp->t_idle >= tp->t_rxtcur)
63         /*
64          * We have been idle for "a while" and no acks are
65          * expected to clock out any data we send --
66          * slow start to get ack "clock" running again.
67          */
68         tp->snd_cwnd = tp->t_maxseg;

69 again:
70     sendalot = 0;   /* set nonzero if more than one segment to output */
```

```
                    /* look for a reason to send a segment;  */
                    /* goto send if a segment should be sent */
```

```
218    /*
219     * No reason to send a segment, just return.
220     */
221    return (0);

222 send:
```

```
                    /* form output segment, call ip_output() */
```

```
489    if (sendalot)
490        goto again;
491    return (0);
492 }
```
── *tcp_output.c*

Figure 26.1 tcp_output function: overview.

Figure 26.2 shows the first of the tests to determine whether a segment should be sent.

```
                                                                ──── tcp_output.c
71      off = tp->snd_nxt - tp->snd_una;
72      win = min(tp->snd_wnd, tp->snd_cwnd);

73      flags = tcp_outflags[tp->t_state];
74      /*
75       * If in persist timeout with window of 0, send 1 byte.
76       * Otherwise, if window is small but nonzero
77       * and timer expired, we will send what we can
78       * and go to transmit state.
79       */
80      if (tp->t_force) {
81          if (win == 0) {
82              /*
83               * If we still have some data to send, then
84               * clear the FIN bit.  Usually this would
85               * happen below when it realizes that we
86               * aren't sending all the data.  However,
87               * if we have exactly 1 byte of unsent data,
88               * then it won't clear the FIN bit below,
89               * and if we are in persist state, we wind
90               * up sending the packet without recording
91               * that we sent the FIN bit.
92               *
93               * We can't just blindly clear the FIN bit,
94               * because if we don't have any more data
95               * to send then the probe will be the FIN
96               * itself.
97               */
98              if (off < so->so_snd.sb_cc)
99                  flags &= ~TH_FIN;
100             win = 1;
101         } else {
102             tp->t_timer[TCPT_PERSIST] = 0;
103             tp->t_rxtshift = 0;
104         }
105     }
                                                                ──── tcp_output.c
```

Figure 26.2 `tcp_output` function: data is being forced out.

71–72   `off` is the offset in bytes from the beginning of the send buffer of the first data byte to send. The first `off` bytes in the send buffer, starting with `snd_una`, have already been sent and are waiting to be ACKed.

`win` is the minimum of the window advertised by the receiver (`snd_wnd`) and the congestion window (`snd_cwnd`).

73   The `tcp_outflags` array was shown in Figure 24.16. The value of this array that is fetched and stored in `flags` depends on the current state of the connection. `flags` contains the combination of the `TH_ACK`, `TH_FIN`, `TH_RST`, and `TH_SYN` flag bits to send to the other end. The other two flag bits, `TH_PUSH` and `TH_URG`, will be logically ORed into `flags` if necessary before the segment is sent.

74–105   The flag `t_force` is set nonzero when the persist timer expires or when out-of-band data is being sent. These two conditions invoke `tcp_output` as follows:

```
tp->t_force = 1;
error = tcp_output(tp);
tp->t_force = 0;
```

This forces TCP to send a segment when it normally wouldn't send anything.

If `win` is 0, the connection is in the persist state (since `t_force` is nonzero). The FIN flag is cleared if there is more data in the socket's send buffer. `win` must be set to 1 byte to force out a single byte.

If `win` is nonzero, out-of-band data is being sent, so the persist timer is cleared and the exponential backoff index, `t_rxtshift`, is set to 0.

Figure 26.3 shows the next part of `tcp_output`, which calculates how much data to send.

─── *tcp_output.c*
```
106    len = min(so->so_snd.sb_cc, win) - off;
107    if (len < 0) {
108        /*
109         * If FIN has been sent but not acked,
110         * but we haven't been called to retransmit,
111         * len will be -1.  Otherwise, window shrank
112         * after we sent into it.  If window shrank to 0,
113         * cancel pending retransmit and pull snd_nxt
114         * back to (closed) window.  We will enter persist
115         * state below.  If the window didn't close completely,
116         * just wait for an ACK.
117         */
118        len = 0;
119        if (win == 0) {
120            tp->t_timer[TCPT_REXMT] = 0;
121            tp->snd_nxt = tp->snd_una;
122        }
123    }
124    if (len > tp->t_maxseg) {
125        len = tp->t_maxseg;
126        sendalot = 1;
127    }
128    if (SEQ_LT(tp->snd_nxt + len, tp->snd_una + so->so_snd.sb_cc))
129        flags &= ~TH_FIN;

130    win = sbspace(&so->so_rcv);
```
─── *tcp_output.c*

Figure 26.3   `tcp_output` function: calculate how much data to send.

Calculate amount of data to send

106   `len` is the minimum of the number of bytes in the send buffer and `win` (which is the minimum of the receiver's advertised window and the congestion window, perhaps 1 byte if output is being forced). `off` is subtracted because that many bytes at the beginning of the send buffer have already been sent and are awaiting acknowledgment.

Check for window shrink

107–117   One way for `len` to be less than 0 occurs if the receiver *shrinks* the window, that is, the receiver moves the right edge of the window to the left. The following example demonstrates how this can happen. First the receiver advertises a window of 6 bytes and TCP transmits a segment with bytes 4, 5, and 6. TCP immediately transmits another segment with bytes 7, 8, and 9. Figure 26.4 shows the status of our end after the two segments are sent.

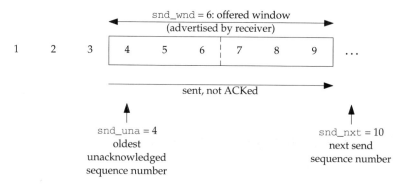

Figure 26.4   Send buffer after bytes 4 through 9 are sent.

Then an ACK is received with an acknowledgment field of 7 (acknowledging all data up through and including byte 6) but with a window of 1. The receiver has shrunk the window, as shown in Figure 26.5.

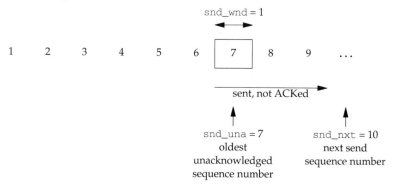

Figure 26.5   Send buffer after receiving acknowledgment of bytes 4 through 6.

Performing the calculations in Figures 26.2 and 26.3, after the window is shrunk, we have

```
off = snd_nxt - snd_una = 10 - 7 = 3
win = 1
len = min(so_snd.sb_cc, win) - off = min(3, 1) - 3 = -2
```

assuming the send buffer contains only bytes 7, 8, and 9.

Both RFC 793 and RFC 1122 strongly discourage shrinking the window. Nevertheless, implementations must be prepared for this. Handling scenarios such as this comes under the *Robustness Principle*, first mentioned in RFC 791: "Be liberal in what you accept, and conservative in what you send."

Another way for `len` to be less than 0 occurs if the FIN has been sent but not acknowledged and not retransmitted. (See Exercise 26.2.) We show this in Figure 26.6.

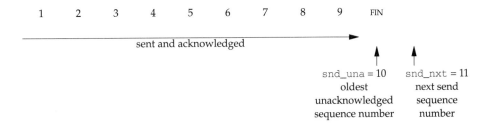

Figure 26.6 Bytes 1 through 9 have been sent and acknowledged, and then connection is closed.

This figure continues Figure 26.4, assuming the final segment with bytes 7, 8, and 9 is acknowledged, which sets `snd_una` to 10. The process then closes the connection, causing the FIN to be sent. We'll see later in this chapter that when the FIN is sent, `snd_nxt` is incremented by 1 (since the FIN takes a sequence number), which in this example sets `snd_nxt` to 11. The sequence number of the FIN is 10. Performing the calculations in Figures 26.2 and 26.3, we have

```
off = snd_nxt - snd_una = 11 - 10 = 1
win = 6
len = min(so_snd.sb_cc, win) - off = min(0, 6) - 1 = -1
```

We assume that the receiver advertises a window of 6, which makes no difference, since the number of bytes in the send buffer (0) is less than this.

Enter persist state

118–122   `len` is set to 0. If the advertised window is 0, any pending retransmission is canceled by setting the retransmission timer to 0. `snd_nxt` is also pulled to the left of the window by setting it to the value of `snd_una`. The connection will enter the persist state later in this function, and when the receiver finally opens its window, TCP starts retransmitting from the left of the window.

Send one segment at a time

124–127   If the amount of data to send exceeds one segment, `len` is set to a single segment and the `sendalot` flag is set to 1. As shown in Figure 26.1, this causes another loop through `tcp_output` after the segment is sent.

Turn off FIN flag if send buffer not emptied

128–129   If the send buffer is not being emptied by this output operation, the FIN flag must be cleared (in case it is set in `flags`). Figure 26.7 shows an example of this.

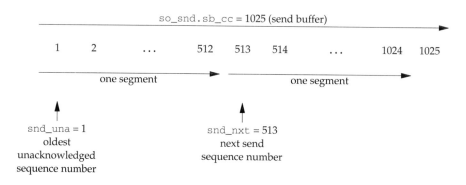

Figure 26.7   Example of send buffer not being emptied when FIN is set.

In this example the first 512-byte segment has already been sent (and is waiting to be acknowledged) and TCP is about to send the next 512-byte segment (bytes 512–1024). There is still 1 byte left in the send buffer (byte 1025) and the process closes the connection. `len` equals 512 (one segment), and the C expression becomes

```
SEQ_LT(1025, 1026)
```

which is true, so the FIN flag is cleared. If the FIN flag were mistakenly left on, TCP couldn't send byte 1025 to the receiver.

Calculate window advertisement

130   `win` is set to the amount of space available in the receive buffer, which becomes TCP's window advertisement to the other end. Be aware that this is the second use of this variable in this function. Earlier it contained the maximum amount of data TCP could send, but for the remainder of this function it contains the receive window advertised by this end of the connection.

The silly window syndrome (called *SWS* and described in Section 22.3 of Volume 1) occurs when small amounts of data, instead of full-sized segments, are exchanged across a connection. It can be caused by a receiver who advertises small windows and by a sender who transmits small segments. Correct avoidance of the silly window syndrome must be performed by both the sender and the receiver. Figure 26.8 shows silly window avoidance by the sender.

Sender silly window avoidance

142–143   If a full-sized segment can be sent, it is sent.

144–146   If an ACK is not expected (`idle` is true), or if the Nagle algorithm is disabled (`TF_NODELAY` is true) *and* TCP is emptying the send buffer, the data is sent. The Nagle algorithm (Section 19.4 of Volume 1) prevents TCP from sending less than a full-sized segment when an ACK is expected for the connection. It can be disabled using the `TCP_NODELAY` socket option. For a normal interactive connection (e.g., Telnet or Rlogin), if there is unacknowledged data, this `if` statement is false, since the Nagle algorithm is enabled by default .

147–148   If output is being forced by either the persist timer or sending out-of-band data, some data is sent.

```
                                                                   ─ tcp_output.c
131        /*
132         * Sender silly window avoidance.  If connection is idle
133         * and can send all data, a maximum segment,
134         * at least a maximum default-sized segment do it,
135         * or are forced, do it; otherwise don't bother.
136         * If peer's buffer is tiny, then send
137         * when window is at least half open.
138         * If retransmitting (possibly after persist timer forced us
139         * to send into a small window), then must resend.
140         */
141        if (len) {
142            if (len == tp->t_maxseg)
143                goto send;
144            if ((idle || tp->t_flags & TF_NODELAY) &&
145                len + off >= so->so_snd.sb_cc)
146                goto send;
147            if (tp->t_force)
148                goto send;
149            if (len >= tp->max_sndwnd / 2)
150                goto send;
151            if (SEQ_LT(tp->snd_nxt, tp->snd_max))
152                goto send;
153        }
                                                                   ─ tcp_output.c
```

Figure 26.8 `tcp_output` function: sender silly window avoidance.

149–150   If the receiver's window is at least half open, data is sent. This is to deal with peers that always advertise tiny windows, perhaps smaller than the segment size. The variable `max_sndwnd` is calculated by `tcp_input` as the largest window advertisement ever advertised by the other end. It is an attempt to guess the size of the other end's receive buffer and assumes the other end never reduces the size of its receive buffer.

151–152   If the retransmission timer expired, then a segment must be sent. `snd_max` is the highest sequence number that has been transmitted. We saw in Figure 25.26 that when the retransmission timer expires, `snd_nxt` is set to `snd_una`, that is, `snd_nxt` is moved to the left edge of the window, making it less than `snd_max`.

The next portion of `tcp_output`, shown in Figure 26.9, determines if TCP must send a segment just to advertise a new window to the other end. This is called a *window update*.

154–168   The expression

```
min(win, (long)TCP_MAXWIN << tp->rcv_scale)
```

is the smaller of the amount of available space in the socket's receive buffer (`win`) and the maximum size of the window allowed for this connection. This is the maximum window TCP can currently advertise to the other end. The expression

```
(tp->rcv_adv - tp->rcv_nxt)
```

is the number of bytes remaining in the last window advertisement that TCP sent to the other end. Subtracting this from the maximum window yields `adv`, the number of

```
                                                                        ──── tcp_output.c
154     /*
155      * Compare available window to amount of window
156      * known to peer (as advertised window less
157      * next expected input).  If the difference is at least two
158      * max size segments, or at least 50% of the maximum possible
159      * window, then want to send a window update to peer.
160      */
161     if (win > 0) {
162         /*
163          * "adv" is the amount we can increase the window,
164          * taking into account that we are limited by
165          * TCP_MAXWIN << tp->rcv_scale.
166          */
167         long    adv = min(win, (long) TCP_MAXWIN << tp->rcv_scale) -
168             (tp->rcv_adv - tp->rcv_nxt);
169         if (adv >= (long) (2 * tp->t_maxseg))
170             goto send;
171         if (2 * adv >= (long) so->so_rcv.sb_hiwat)
172             goto send;
173     }
                                                                        ──── tcp_output.c
```

Figure 26.9 `tcp_output` function: check if a window update should be sent.

bytes by which the window has opened. `rcv_nxt` is incremented by `tcp_input` when data is received in sequence, and `rcv_adv` is incremented by `tcp_output` in Figure 26.32 when the edge of the advertised window moves to the right.

Consider Figure 24.18 and assume that a segment with bytes 4, 5, and 6 is received and that these three bytes are passed to the process. Figure 26.10 shows the state of the receive space at this point in `tcp_output`.

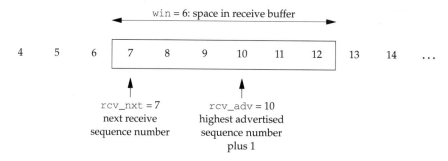

Figure 26.10 Transition from Figure 24.18 after bytes 4, 5, and 6 are received.

The value of `adv` is 3, since there are 3 more bytes of the receive space (bytes 10, 11, and 12) for the other end to fill.

169–170   If the window has opened by two or more segments, a window update is sent. When data is received as full-sized segments, this code causes every other received segment to be acknowledged: TCP's ACK-every-other-segment property. (We show an example of this shortly.)

171–172   If the window has opened by at least 50% of the maximum possible window (the socket's receive buffer high-water mark), a window update is sent.

The next part of `tcp_output`, shown in Figure 26.11, checks whether various flags require TCP to send a segment.

```
                                                                  ─── tcp_output.c
174     /*
175      * Send if we owe peer an ACK.
176      */
177     if (tp->t_flags & TF_ACKNOW)
178         goto send;
179     if (flags & (TH_SYN | TH_RST))
180         goto send;
181     if (SEQ_GT(tp->snd_up, tp->snd_una))
182         goto send;
183     /*
184      * If our state indicates that FIN should be sent
185      * and we have not yet done so, or we're retransmitting the FIN,
186      * then we need to send.
187      */
188     if (flags & TH_FIN &&
189         ((tp->t_flags & TF_SENTFIN) == 0 || tp->snd_nxt == tp->snd_una))
190         goto send;
                                                                  ─── tcp_output.c
```

Figure 26.11   `tcp_output` function: should a segment should be sent?

174–178   If an immediate ACK is required, a segment is sent. The `TF_ACKNOW` flag is set by various functions: when the 200-ms delayed ACK timer expires, when a segment is received out of order (for the fast retransmit algorithm), when a SYN is received during the three-way handshake, when a persist probe is received, and when a FIN is received.

179–180   If `flags` specifies that a SYN or RST should be sent, a segment is sent.

181–182   If the urgent pointer, `snd_up`, is beyond the start of the send buffer, a segment is sent. The urgent pointer is set by the `PRU_SENDOOB` request (Figure 30.9).

183–190   If `flags` specifies that a FIN should be sent, a segment is sent only if the FIN has not already been sent, or if the FIN is being retransmitted. The flag `TF_SENTFIN` is set later in this function when the FIN is sent.

At this point in `tcp_output` there is no need to send a segment. Figure 26.12 shows the final piece of code before `tcp_output` returns.

191–217   If there is data in the send buffer to send (`so_snd.sb_cc` is nonzero) and both the retransmission timer and the persist timer are off, turn the persist timer on. This scenario happens when the window advertised by the other end is too small to receive a full-sized segment, and there is no other reason to send a segment.

218–221   `tcp_output` returns, since there is no reason to send a segment.

```
                                                                          ── tcp_output.c
191     /*
192      * TCP window updates are not reliable, rather a polling protocol
193      * using 'persist' packets is used to ensure receipt of window
194      * updates.  The three 'states' for the output side are:
195      *  idle            not doing retransmits or persists
196      *  persisting         to move a small or zero window
197      *  (re)transmitting   and thereby not persisting
198      *
199      * tp->t_timer[TCPT_PERSIST]
200      *      is set when we are in persist state.
201      * tp->t_force
202      *      is set when we are called to send a persist packet.
203      * tp->t_timer[TCPT_REXMT]
204      *      is set when we are retransmitting
205      * The output side is idle when both timers are zero.
206      *
207      * If send window is too small, there is data to transmit, and no
208      * retransmit or persist is pending, then go to persist state.
209      * If nothing happens soon, send when timer expires:
210      * if window is nonzero, transmit what we can,
211      * otherwise force out a byte.
212      */
213     if (so->so_snd.sb_cc && tp->t_timer[TCPT_REXMT] == 0 &&
214         tp->t_timer[TCPT_PERSIST] == 0) {
215         tp->t_rxtshift = 0;
216         tcp_setpersist(tp);
217     }
218     /*
219      * No reason to send a segment, just return.
220      */
221     return (0);
                                                                          ── tcp_output.c
```

Figure 26.12   `tcp_output` function: enter persist state.

Example

A process writes 100 bytes, followed by a write of 50 bytes, on an idle connection. Assume a segment size of 512 bytes. When the first write occurs, the code in Figure 26.8 (lines 144–146) sends a segment with 100 bytes of data since the connection is idle and TCP is emptying the send buffer.

When 50-byte write occurs, the code in Figure 26.8 does not send a segment: the amount of data is not a full-sized segment, the connection is not idle (assume TCP is awaiting the ACK for the 100 bytes that it just sent), the Nagle algorithm is enabled by default, t_force is not set, and assuming a typical receive window of 4096, 50 is not greater than or equal to 2048. These 50 bytes remain in the send buffer, probably until the ACK for the 100 bytes is received. This ACK will probably be delayed by the other end, causing more delay in sending the final 50 bytes.

This example shows the timing delays that can occur when sending less than full-sized segments with the Nagle algorithm enabled. See also Exercise 26.12.

Example

This example demonstrates the ACK-every-other-segment property of TCP. Assume a connection is established with a segment size of 1024 bytes and a receive buffer size of 4096. There is no data to send—TCP is just receiving.

A window of 4096 is advertised in the ACK of the SYN, and Figure 26.13 shows the two variables `rcv_nxt` and `rcv_adv`. The receive buffer is empty.

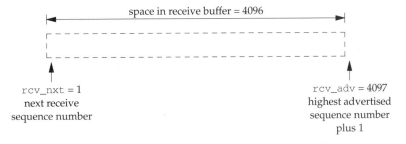

Figure 26.13   Receiver advertising a window of 4096.

The other end sends a segment with bytes 1–1024. `tcp_input` processes the segment, sets the delayed-ACK flag for the connection, and appends the 1024 bytes of data to the socket's receiver buffer (Figure 28.13). `rcv_nxt` is updated as shown in Figure 26.14.

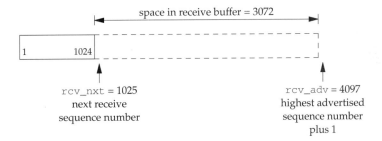

Figure 26.14   Transition from Figure 26.13 after bytes 1–1024 received.

The process reads the 1024 bytes in its socket receive buffer. We'll see in Figure 30.6 that the resulting PRU_RCVD request causes `tcp_output` to be called, because a window update might need to be sent after the process reads data from the receive buffer. When `tcp_output` is called, the two variables still have the values shown in Figure 26.14 and the only difference is that the amount of space in the receive buffer has increased to 4096 since the process has read the first 1024 bytes. The calculations in Figure 26.9 are performed:

```
adv = min(4096, 65535) - (4097 - 1025)
    = 1024
```

TCP_MAXWIN is 65535 and we assume a receive window scale shift of 0. Since the window has increased by less than two segments (2048), nothing is sent. But the delayed-ACK flag is still set, so if the 200-ms timer expires, an ACK will be sent.

When TCP receives the next segment with bytes 1025–2048, tcp_input processes the segment, sets the delayed-ACK flag for the connection (which was already on), and appends the 1024 bytes of data to the socket's receiver buffer. rcv_nxt is updated as shown in Figure 26.15.

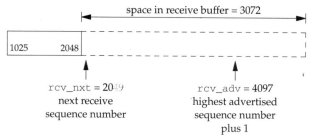

Figure 26.15   Transition from Figure 26.14 after bytes 1025–2048 received.

The process reads bytes 1025–2048 and tcp_output is called. The two variables still have the values shown in Figure 26.15, although the space in the receive buffer increases to 4096 when the process reads the 1024 bytes of data. The calculations in Figure 26.9 are performed:

```
adv = min(4096, 65535) - (4097 - 2049)
    = 2048
```

This value is now greater than or equal to two segments, so a segment is sent with an acknowledgment field of 2049 and an advertised window of 4096. This is a window update. The receiver is willing to receive bytes 2049 through 6145. We'll see later in this function that when this segment is sent, the value of rcv_adv also gets updated to 6145.

This example shows that when receiving data faster than the 200-ms delayed ACK timer, an ACK is sent when the receive window changes by more than two segments due to the process reading the data. If data is received for the connection but the process is not reading the data from the socket's receive buffer, the ACK-every-other-segment property won't occur. Instead the sender will only see the delayed ACKs, each advertising a smaller window, until the receive buffer is filled and the window goes to 0.

26.4   TCP Options

The TCP header can contain options. We digress to discuss these options since the next piece of tcp_output decides which options to send and constructs the options in the outgoing segment. Figure 26.16 shows the format of the options supported by Net/3.

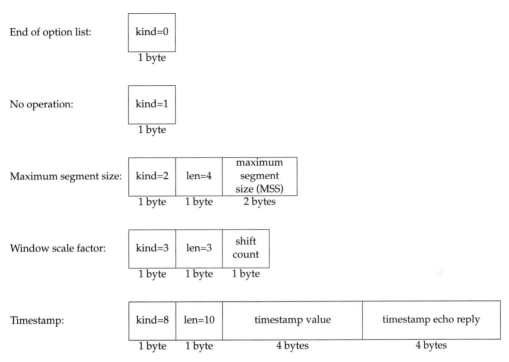

Figure 26.16   TCP options supported by Net/3.

Every option begins with a 1-byte *kind* that specifies the type of option. The first two options (with *kind*s of 0 and 1) are single-byte options. The other three are multibyte options with a *len* byte that follows the *kind* byte. The length is the total length, including the *kind* and *len* bytes.

The multibyte integers—the MSS and the two timestamp values—are stored in network byte order.

The final two options, window scale and timestamp, are new and therefore not supported by many systems. To provide interoperability with these older systems, the following rules apply.

1. TCP can send one of these options (or both) with the initial SYN segment corresponding to an active open (that is, a SYN without an ACK). Net/3 does this for both options if the global `tcp_do_rfc1323` is nonzero (it defaults to 1). This is done in `tcp_newtcpcb`.

2. The option is enabled only if the SYN reply from the other end also includes the desired option. This is handled in Figures 28.20 and 29.2.

3. If TCP performs a passive open and receives a SYN specifying the option, the response (the SYN plus ACK) must contain the option if TCP wants to enable the option. This is done in Figure 26.23.

Since a system must ignore options that it doesn't understand, the newer options are enabled by both ends only if both ends understand the option and both ends want the option enabled.

The processing of the MSS option is covered in Section 27.5. The next two sections summarize the Net/3 handling of the two newer options: window scale and timestamp.

> Other options have been proposed. *kind*s of 4, 5, 6, and 7, called the selective-ACK and echo options, are defined in RFC 1072 [Jacobson and Braden 1988]. We don't show them in Figure 26.16 because the echo options were replaced with the timestamp option, and selective ACKs, as currently defined, are still under discussion and were not included in RFC 1323. Also, the T/TCP proposal for TCP transactions (RFC 1644 [Braden 1994], and Section 24.7 of Volume 1) specifies three options with *kind*s of 11, 12, and 13.

26.5 Window Scale Option

The window scale option, defined in RFC 1323, avoids the limitation of a 16-bit window size field in the TCP header (Figure 24.10). Larger windows are required for what are called *long fat pipes*, networks with either a high bandwidth or a long delay (i.e., a long RTT). Section 24.3 of Volume 1 gives examples of current networks that require larger windows to obtain maximum TCP throughput.

The 1-byte shift count in Figure 26.16 is between 0 (no scaling performed) and 14. This maximum value of 14 provides a maximum window of 1,073,725,440 bytes (65535×2^{14}). Internally Net/3 maintains window sizes as 32-bit values, not 16-bit values.

The window scale option can only appear in a SYN segment; therefore the scale factor is fixed in each direction when the connection is established.

The two variables `snd_scale` and `rcv_scale` in the TCP control block specify the shift count for the send window and the receive window, respectively. Both default to 0 for no scaling. Every 16-bit advertised window received from the other end is left shifted by `snd_scale` bits to obtain the real 32-bit advertised window size (Figure 28.6). Every time TCP sends a window advertisement to the other end, the internal 32-bit window size is right shifted by `rcv_scale` bits to give the value that is placed into the TCP header (Figure 26.29).

When TCP sends a SYN, either actively or passively, it chooses the value of `rcv_scale` to request, based on the size of the socket's receive buffer (Figures 28.7 and 30.4).

26.6 Timestamp Option

The timestamp option is also defined in RFC 1323 and lets the sender place a timestamp in every segment. The receiver sends the timestamp back in the acknowledgment, allowing the sender to calculate the RTT for each received ACK. Figure 26.17 summarizes the timestamp option and the variables involved.

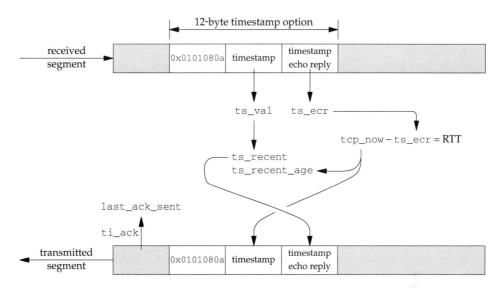

Figure 26.17   Summary of variables used with timestamp option.

The global variable `tcp_now` is the timestamp clock. It is initialized to 0 when the kernel is initialized and incremented by 1 every 500 ms (Figure 25.8). Three variables are maintained in the TCP control block for the timestamp option:

- `ts_recent` is a copy of the most-recent valid timestamp from the other end. (We describe shortly what makes a timestamp "valid.")

- `ts_recent_age` is the value of `tcp_now` when `ts_recent` was last copied from a received segment.

- `last_ack_sent` is the value of the acknowledgment field (`ti_ack`) the last time a segment was sent (Figure 26.32). This is normally equal to `rcv_nxt`, the next expected sequence number, unless ACKs are delayed.

The two variables `ts_val` and `ts_ecr` are local variables in the function `tcp_input` that contain the two values from the timestamp option.

- `ts_val` is the timestamp sent by the other end with its data.

- `ts_ecr` is the timestamp from the segment that is being acknowledged by the received segment.

In an outgoing segment, the first 4 bytes of the timestamp option are set to `0x0101080a`. This is the recommended value from Appendix A of RFC 1323. The 2 bytes of 1 are NOPs from Figure 26.16, followed by a *kind* of 8 and a *len* of 10, which identify the timestamp option. By placing two NOPs in front of the option, the two 32-bit timestamps in the option and the data that follows are aligned on 32-bit boundaries. Also, we show the received timestamp option in Figure 26.17 with the recommended 12-byte format (which Net/3 always generates), but the code that processes received options (Figure 28.10) does not require this format. The 10-byte format shown in Figure 26.16, without two preceding NOPs, is handled fine on input (but see Exercise 28.4).

The RTT of a transmitted segment and its ACK is calculated as `tcp_now` minus `ts_ecr`. The units are 500-ms clock ticks, since that is the units of the Net/3 timestamps.

The presence of the timestamp option also allows TCP to perform PAWS: protection against wrapped sequence numbers. We describe this algorithm in Section 28.7. The variable `ts_recent_age` is used with PAWS.

`tcp_output` builds a timestamp option in an outgoing segment by copying `tcp_now` into the timestamp and `ts_recent` into the echo reply (Figure 26.24). This is done for every segment when the option is in use, unless the RST flag is set.

Which Timestamp to Echo, RFC 1323 Algorithm

The test for a valid timestamp determines whether the value in `ts_recent` is updated, and since this value is always sent as the timestamp echo reply, the test for validity determines which timestamp gets echoed back to the other end. RFC 1323 specified the following test:

```
ti_seq <= last_ack_sent < ti_seq + ti_len
```

which is implemented in C as shown in Figure 26.18.

```
if (ts_present && SEQ_LEQ(ti->ti_seq, tp->last_ack_sent) &&
    SEQ_LT(tp->last_ack_sent, ti->ti_seq + ti->ti_len)) {
    tp->ts_recent_age = tcp_now;
    tp->ts_recent = ts_val;
}
```

Figure 26.18   Typical code to determine if received timestamp is valid.

The variable `ts_present` is true if a timestamp option was received in the segment. We encounter this code twice in `tcp_input`: Figure 28.11 does the test in the header prediction code, and Figure 28.35 does the test in the normal input processing.

To see what this test is doing, Figure 26.19 shows show five different scenarios, corresponding to five different segments received on a connection. In each scenario `ti_len` is 3.

The left edge of the receive window begins with sequence number 4. In scenario 1 the segment contains completely duplicate data. The `SEQ_LEQ` test in Figure 28.11 is true, but the `SEQ_LT` test fails. For scenarios 2, 3, and 4, both the `SEQ_LEQ` and `SEQ_LT` tests are true because the left edge of the window is advanced by any one of these three segments, even though scenario 2 contains two duplicate bytes of data, and scenario 3 contains one duplicate byte of data. Scenario 5 fails the `SEQ_LEQ` test, because it doesn't advance the left edge of the window. This segment is one in the future that's not the next expected, implying that a previous segment was lost or reordered.

Unfortunately this test to determine whether to update `ts_recent` is flawed [Braden 1993]. Consider the following example.

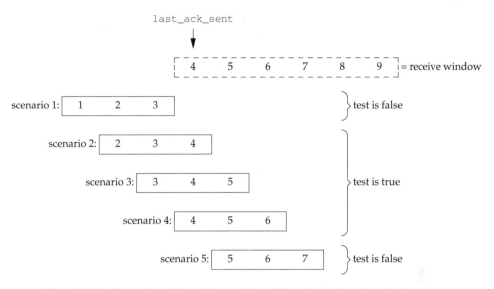

Figure 26.19 Example receive window and five different scenarios of received segment.

1. In Figure 26.19 a segment that we don't show arrives with bytes 1, 2, and 3. The timestamp in this segment is saved in `ts_recent` because `last_ack_sent` is 1. An ACK is sent with an acknowledgment field of 4, and `last_ack_sent` is set to 4 (the value of `rcv_nxt`). We have the receive window shown in Figure 26.19.

2. This ACK is lost.

3. The other end times out and retransmits the segment with bytes 1, 2, and 3. This segment arrives and is the one labeled "scenario 1" in Figure 26.19. Since the `SEQ_LT` test in Figure 26.18 fails, `ts_recent` is not updated with the value from the retransmitted segment.

4. A duplicate ACK is sent with an acknowledgment field of 4, but the timestamp echo reply is `ts_recent`, the value copied from the segment in step 1. But when the receiver calculates the RTT using this value, it will (incorrectly) take into account the original transmission, the lost ACK, the timeout, the retransmission, and the duplicate ACK.

For correct RTT estimation by the other end, the timestamp value from the retransmission should be returned in the duplicate ACK.

The tests in Figure 26.18 also fail to update `ts_recent` if the length of the received segment is 0, since the left edge of the window is not moved. This incorrect test can also lead to problems with long-lived (greater than 24 days, the PAWS limit described in Section 28.7), unidirectional connections (all the data flow is in one direction so the sender of the data always sends the same ACKs).

Which Timestamp to Echo, Corrected Algorithm

The algorithm we'll encounter in the Net/3 sources is from Figure 26.18. The correct algorithm given in [Braden 1993] replaces Figure 26.18 with the one in Figure 26.20.

```
if (ts_present && TSTMP_GEQ(ts_val, tp->ts_recent) &&
    SEQ_LEQ(ti->ti_seq, tp->last_ack_sent)) {
```

Figure 26.20   Correct code to determine if received timestamp is valid.

This doesn't test whether the left edge of the window moves or not, it just verifies that the new timestamp (`ts_val`) is greater than or equal to the previous timestamp (`ts_recent`), and that the starting sequence number of the received segment is not greater than the left edge of the window. Scenario 5 in Figure 26.19 would fail this new test since it is out of order.

The macro `TSTMP_GEQ` is identical to `SEQ_GEQ` in Figure 24.21. It is used with timestamps, since timestamps are 32-bit unsigned values that wrap around just like sequence numbers.

Timestamps and Delayed ACKs

It is constructive to see how timestamps and RTT calculations are affected by delayed ACKs. Recall from Figure 26.17 that the value saved by TCP in `ts_recent` becomes the echoed timestamp in segments that are sent, which are used by the other end in calculating its RTT. When ACKs are delayed, the delay time should be taken into account by the side that sees the delays, or else it might retransmit too quickly. In the example that follows we only consider the code in Figure 26.20, but the incorrect code in Figure 26.18 also handles delayed ACKs correctly.

Consider the receive sequence space in Figure 26.21 when the received segment contains bytes 4 and 5.

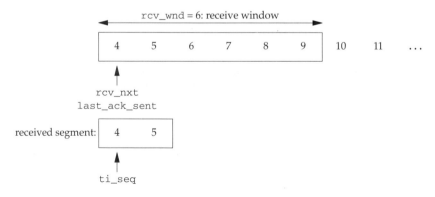

Figure 26.21   Receive sequence space when segment with bytes 4 and 5 arrives.

Since `ti_seq` is less than or equal to `last_ack_sent`, `ts_recent` is copied from the segment. `rcv_nxt` is also increased by 2.

Assume that the ACK for these 2 bytes is delayed, and before that delayed ACK is sent, the next in-order segment arrives. This is shown in Figure 26.22.

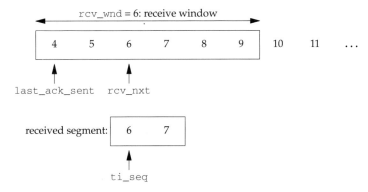

Figure 26.22   Receive sequence space when segment with bytes 6 and 7 arrives.

This time `ti_seq` is greater than `last_ack_sent`, so `ts_recent` is not updated. This is intentional. Assuming TCP now sends an ACK for sequence numbers 4–7, the other end's RTT will take into account the delayed ACK, since the echoed timestamp (Figure 26.24) is the one from the segment with sequence numbers 4 and 5. These figures also demonstrate that `rcv_nxt` equals `last_ack_sent` except when ACKs are delayed.

26.7 Send a Segment

The last half of `tcp_output` sends the segment—it fills in all the fields in the TCP header and passes the segment to IP for output.

Figure 26.23 shows the first part, which sends the MSS and window scale options with a SYN segment.

223–234   The TCP options are built in the array `opt`, and the integer `optlen` keeps a count of the number of bytes accumulated (since multiple options can be sent at once). If the SYN flag bit is set, `snd_nxt` is set to the initial send sequence number (`iss`). If TCP is performing an active open, `iss` is set by the `PRU_CONNECT` request when the TCP control block is created. If this is a passive open, `tcp_input` creates the TCP control block and sets `iss`. In both cases, `iss` is set from the global `tcp_iss`.

235   The flag `TF_NOOPT` is checked, but this flag is never enabled and there is no way to turn it on. Hence, the MSS option is always sent with a SYN segment.

> In the Net/1 version of `tcp_newtcpcb`, the comment "send options!" appeared on the line that initialized `t_flags` to 0. The `TF_NOOPT` flag is probably a historical artifact from a pre-Net/1 system that had problems interoperating with other hosts when it sent the MSS option, so the default was to not send the option.

```
——————————————————————————————————————————— tcp_output.c
222    send:
223      /*
224       * Before ESTABLISHED, force sending of initial options
225       * unless TCP set not to do any options.
226       * NOTE: we assume that the IP/TCP header plus TCP options
227       * always fit in a single mbuf, leaving room for a maximum
228       * link header, i.e.
229       *   max_linkhdr + sizeof (struct tcpiphdr) + optlen <= MHLEN
230       */
231      optlen = 0;
232      hdrlen = sizeof(struct tcpiphdr);
233      if (flags & TH_SYN) {
234          tp->snd_nxt = tp->iss;
235          if ((tp->t_flags & TF_NOOPT) == 0) {
236              u_short mss;

237              opt[0] = TCPOPT_MAXSEG;
238              opt[1] = 4;
239              mss = htons((u_short) tcp_mss(tp, 0));
240              bcopy((caddr_t) & mss, (caddr_t) (opt + 2), sizeof(mss));
241              optlen = 4;

242              if ((tp->t_flags & TF_REQ_SCALE) &&
243                  ((flags & TH_ACK) == 0 ||
244                  (tp->t_flags & TF_RCVD_SCALE))) {
245                  *((u_long *) (opt + optlen)) = htonl(TCPOPT_NOP << 24 |
246                                                    TCPOPT_WINDOW << 16 |
247                                                    TCPOLEN_WINDOW << 8 |
248                                                    tp->request_r_scale);
249                  optlen += 4;
250              }
251          }
252      }
——————————————————————————————————————————— tcp_output.c
```

Figure 26.23   `tcp_output` function: send options with first SYN segment.

Build MSS option

236–241   `opt[0]` is set to 2 (`TCPOPT_MAXSEG`) and `opt[1]` is set to 4, the length of the MSS
option in bytes. The function `tcp_mss` calculates the MSS to announce to the other
end; we cover this function in Section 27.5. The 16-bit MSS is stored in `opt[2]` and
`opt[3]` by `bcopy` (Exercise 26.5). Notice that Net/3 always sends an MSS announcement with the SYN for a connection.

Should window scale option be sent?

242–244   If TCP is to request the window scale option, this option is sent only if this is an
active open (`TH_ACK` is not set) or if this is a passive open and the window scale option
was received in the SYN from the other end. Recall that `t_flags` was set to
`TF_REQ_SCALE|TF_REQ_TSTMP` when the TCP control block was created in Figure 25.21, if the global variable `tcp_do_rfc1323` was nonzero (its default value).

Build window scale option

245–249   Since the window scale option occupies 3 bytes (Figure 26.16), a 1-byte NOP is stored before the option, forcing the option length to be 4 bytes. This causes the data in the segment that follows the options to be aligned on a 4-byte boundary. If this is an active open, `request_r_scale` is calculated by the `PRU_CONNECT` request. If this is a passive open, the window scale factor is calculated by `tcp_input` when the SYN is received.

RFC 1323 specifies that if TCP is prepared to scale windows it should send this option even if its own shift count is 0. This is because the option serves two purposes: to notify the other end that it supports the option, and to announce its shift count. Even though TCP may calculate its own shift count as 0, the other end might want to use a different value.

The next part of `tcp_output` is shown in Figure 26.24. It finishes building the options in the outgoing segment.

```
                                                                  tcp_output.c
253     /*
254      * Send a timestamp and echo-reply if this is a SYN and our side
255      * wants to use timestamps (TF_REQ_TSTMP is set) or both our side
256      * and our peer have sent timestamps in our SYN's.
257      */
258     if ((tp->t_flags & (TF_REQ_TSTMP | TF_NOOPT)) == TF_REQ_TSTMP &&
259         (flags & TH_RST) == 0 &&
260         ((flags & (TH_SYN | TH_ACK)) == TH_SYN ||
261          (tp->t_flags & TF_RCVD_TSTMP))) {
262         u_long *lp = (u_long *) (opt + optlen);

263         /* Form timestamp option as shown in appendix A of RFC 1323. */
264         *lp++ = htonl(TCPOPT_TSTAMP_HDR);
265         *lp++ = htonl(tcp_now);
266         *lp = htonl(tp->ts_recent);
267         optlen += TCPOLEN_TSTAMP_APPA;
268     }
269     hdrlen += optlen;

270     /*
271      * Adjust data length if insertion of options will
272      * bump the packet length beyond the t_maxseg length.
273      */
274     if (len > tp->t_maxseg - optlen) {
275         len = tp->t_maxseg - optlen;
276         sendalot = 1;
277     }
                                                                  tcp_output.c
```

Figure 26.24 `tcp_output` function: finish sending options.

Should timestamp option be sent?

253–261   If the following three conditions are all true, a timestamp option is sent: (1) TCP is configured to request the timestamp option, (2) the segment being formed does not contain the RST flag, and (3) either this is an active open (i.e., `flags` specifies the SYN flag

but not the ACK flag) or TCP has received a timestamp from the other end
(TF_RCVD_TSTMP). Unlike the MSS and window scale options, a timestamp option can
be sent with every segment once both ends agree to use the option.

Build timestamp option

263–267   The timestamp option (Section 26.6) consists of 12 bytes (TCPOLEN_TSTAMP_APPA).
The first 4 bytes are 0x0101080a (the constant TCPOPT_TSTAMP_HDR), as described
with Figure 26.17. The timestamp value is taken from tcp_now (the number of 500-ms
clock ticks since the system was initialized), and the timestamp echo reply is taken from
ts_recent, which is set by tcp_input.

Check if options have overflowed segment

270–277   The size of the TCP header is incremented by the number of option bytes (optlen).
If the amount of data to send (len) exceeds the MSS minus the size of the options
(optlen), the data length is decreased accordingly and the sendalot flag is set, to
force another loop through this function after this segment is sent (Figure 26.1).

The MSS and window scale options only appear in SYN segments, which Net/3
always sends without data, so this adjustment of the data length doesn't apply. When
the timestamp option is in use, however, it appears in all segments. This reduces the
amount of data in each full-sized data segment from the announced MSS to the
announced MSS minus 12 bytes.

The next part of tcp_output, shown in Figure 26.25, updates some statistics and
allocates an mbuf for the IP and TCP headers. This code is executed when the segment
being output contains some data (len is greater than 0).

Update statistics

284–292   If t_force is nonzero and TCP is sending a single byte of data, this is a window
probe. If snd_nxt is less than snd_max, this is a retransmission. Otherwise, this is
normal data transmission.

Allocate an mbuf for IP and TCP headers

293–297   An mbuf with a packet header is allocated by MGETHDR. This is for the IP and TCP
headers, and possibly the data (if there's room). Although tcp_output is often called
as part of a system call (e.g., write) it is also called at the software interrupt level by
tcp_input, and as part of the timer processing. Therefore M_DONTWAIT is specified.
If an error is returned, a jump is made to the label out. This label is near the end of the
function, in Figure 26.32.

Copy data into mbuf

298–308   If the amount of data is less than 44 bytes (100 – 40 – 16, assuming no TCP options),
the data is copied directly from the socket send buffer into the new packet header mbuf
by m_copydata. Otherwise m_copy creates a new mbuf chain with the data from the
socket send buffer and this chain is linked to the new packet header mbuf. Recall our
description of m_copy in Section 2.9, where we showed that if the data is in a cluster,
m_copy just references that cluster and doesn't make a copy of the data.

tcp_output.c
```
278     /*
279      * Grab a header mbuf, attaching a copy of data to
280      * be transmitted, and initialize the header from
281      * the template for sends on this connection.
282      */
283     if (len) {
284         if (tp->t_force && len == 1)
285             tcpstat.tcps_sndprobe++;
286         else if (SEQ_LT(tp->snd_nxt, tp->snd_max)) {
287             tcpstat.tcps_sndrexmitpack++;
288             tcpstat.tcps_sndrexmitbyte += len;
289         } else {
290             tcpstat.tcps_sndpack++;
291             tcpstat.tcps_sndbyte += len;
292         }
293         MGETHDR(m, M_DONTWAIT, MT_HEADER);
294         if (m == NULL) {
295             error = ENOBUFS;
296             goto out;
297         }
298         m->m_data += max_linkhdr;
299         m->m_len = hdrlen;
300         if (len <= MHLEN - hdrlen - max_linkhdr) {
301             m_copydata(so->so_snd.sb_mb, off, (int) len,
302                        mtod(m, caddr_t) + hdrlen);
303             m->m_len += len;
304         } else {
305             m->m_next = m_copy(so->so_snd.sb_mb, off, (int) len);
306             if (m->m_next == 0)
307                 len = 0;
308         }
309         /*
310          * If we're sending everything we've got, set PUSH.
311          * (This will keep happy those implementations that
312          * give data to the user only when a buffer fills or
313          * a PUSH comes in.)
314          */
315         if (off + len == so->so_snd.sb_cc)
316             flags |= TH_PUSH;
```
tcp_output.c

Figure 26.25 `tcp_output` function: update statistics, allocate mbuf for IP and TCP headers.

Set PSH flag

309–316   If TCP is sending everything it has from the send buffer, the PSH flag is set. As the comment indicates, this is intended for receiving systems that only pass received data to an application when the PSH flag is received or when a buffer fills. We'll see in `tcp_input` that Net/3 never holds data in a socket receive buffer waiting for a received PSH flag.

The next part of `tcp_output`, shown in Figure 26.26, starts with the code that is executed when `len` equals 0: there is no data in the segment TCP is sending.

```
                                                                    ─── tcp_output.c
317        } else {                          /* len == 0 */
318            if (tp->t_flags & TF_ACKNOW)
319                tcpstat.tcps_sndacks++;
320            else if (flags & (TH_SYN | TH_FIN | TH_RST))
321                tcpstat.tcps_sndctrl++;
322            else if (SEQ_GT(tp->snd_up, tp->snd_una))
323                tcpstat.tcps_sndurg++;
324            else
325                tcpstat.tcps_sndwinup++;

326            MGETHDR(m, M_DONTWAIT, MT_HEADER);
327            if (m == NULL) {
328                error = ENOBUFS;
329                goto out;
330            }
331            m->m_data += max_linkhdr;
332            m->m_len = hdrlen;
333        }
334        m->m_pkthdr.rcvif = (struct ifnet *) 0;
335        ti = mtod(m, struct tcpiphdr *);
336        if (tp->t_template == 0)
337            panic("tcp_output");
338        bcopy((caddr_t) tp->t_template, (caddr_t) ti, sizeof(struct tcpiphdr));
                                                                    ─── tcp_output.c
```

Figure 26.26   `tcp_output` function: update statistics and allocate mbuf for IP and TCP headers.

Update statistics

318–325   Various statistics are updated: `TF_ACKNOW` and a length of 0 means this is an ACK-only segment. If any one of the flags SYN, FIN, or RST is set, this is a control segment. If the urgent pointer exceeds `snd_una`, the segment is being sent to notify the other end of the urgent pointer. If none of these conditions are true, this segment is a window update.

Get mbuf for IP and TCP headers

326–335   An mbuf with a packet header is allocated to contain the IP and TCP headers.

Copy IP and TCP header templates into mbuf

336–338   The template of the IP and TCP headers is copied from `t_template` into the mbuf by `bcopy`. This template was created by `tcp_template`.

Figure 26.27 shows the next part of `tcp_output`, which fills in some remaining fields in the TCP header.

Decrement `snd_nxt` if FIN is being retransmitted

339–346   If TCP has already transmitted the FIN, the send sequence space appears as shown in Figure 26.28.

tcp_output.c

```
339     /*
340      * Fill in fields, remembering maximum advertised
341      * window for use in delaying messages about window sizes.
342      * If resending a FIN, be sure not to use a new sequence number.
343      */
344     if (flags & TH_FIN && tp->t_flags & TF_SENTFIN &&
345         tp->snd_nxt == tp->snd_max)
346         tp->snd_nxt--;
347     /*
348      * If we are doing retransmissions, then snd_nxt will
349      * not reflect the first unsent octet.  For ACK only
350      * packets, we do not want the sequence number of the
351      * retransmitted packet, we want the sequence number
352      * of the next unsent octet.  So, if there is no data
353      * (and no SYN or FIN), use snd_max instead of snd_nxt
354      * when filling in ti_seq.  But if we are in persist
355      * state, snd_max might reflect one byte beyond the
356      * right edge of the window, so use snd_nxt in that
357      * case, since we know we aren't doing a retransmission.
358      * (retransmit and persist are mutually exclusive...)
359      */
360     if (len || (flags & (TH_SYN | TH_FIN)) || tp->t_timer[TCPT_PERSIST])
361         ti->ti_seq = htonl(tp->snd_nxt);
362     else
363         ti->ti_seq = htonl(tp->snd_max);

364     ti->ti_ack = htonl(tp->rcv_nxt);

365     if (optlen) {
366         bcopy((caddr_t) opt, (caddr_t) (ti + 1), optlen);
367         ti->ti_off = (sizeof(struct tcphdr) + optlen) >> 2;
368     }
369     ti->ti_flags = flags;
```

tcp_output.c

Figure 26.27 `tcp_output` function: set `ti_seq`, `ti_ack`, and `ti_flags`.

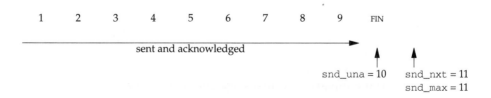

Figure 26.28 Send sequence space after FIN has been transmitted.

Therefore, if the FIN flag is set, and if the `TF_SENTFIN` flag is set, and if `snd_nxt` equals `snd_max`, TCP knows the FIN is being retransmitted. We'll see shortly (Figure 26.31) that when a FIN is sent, `snd_nxt` is incremented 1 one (since the FIN occupies a sequence number), so this piece of code decrements `snd_nxt` by 1.

Set sequence number field of segment

347–363   The sequence number field of the segment is normally set to snd_nxt, but is set to snd_max if (1) there is no data to send (len equals 0), (2) neither the SYN flag nor the FIN flag is set, and (3) the persist timer is not set.

Set acknowledgment field of segment

364   The acknowledgment field of the segment is always set to rcv_nxt, the next expected receive sequence number.

Set header length if options present

365–368   If TCP options are present (optlen is greater than 0), the options are copied into the TCP header and the 4-bit header length in the TCP header (th_off in Figure 24.10) is set to the fixed size of the TCP header (20 bytes) plus the length of the options, divided by 4. This field is the number of 32-bit words in the TCP header, including options.

369   The flags field in the TCP header is set from the variable flags.

The next part of code, shown in Figure 26.29, fills in more fields in the TCP header and calculates the TCP checksum.

Don't advertise less than one full-sized segment

370–375   Avoidance of the silly window syndrome is performed, this time in calculating the window size that is advertised to the other end (ti_win). Recall that win was set at the end of Figure 26.3 to the amount of space in the socket's receive buffer. If win is less than one-fourth of the receive buffer size (so_rcv.sb_hiwat) and less than one full-sized segment, the advertised window will be 0. This is subject to the later test that prevents the window from shrinking. In other words, when the amount of available space reaches either one-fourth of the receive buffer size or one full-sized segment, the available space will be advertised.

Observe upper limit for advertised window on this connection

376–377   If win is larger than the maximum value for this connection, reduce it to its maximum value.

Do not shrink window

378–379   Recall from Figure 26.10 that rcv_adv minus rcv_nxt is the amount of space still available to the sender that was previously advertised. If win is less than this value, win is set to this value, because we must not shrink the window. This can happen when the available space is less than one full-sized segment (hence win was set to 0 at the beginning of this figure), but there is room in the receive buffer for some data. Figure 22.3 of Volume 1 shows an example of this scenario.

Set urgent offset

381–383   If the urgent pointer (snd_up) is greater than snd_nxt, TCP is in urgent mode. The urgent offset in the TCP header is set to the 16-bit offset of the urgent pointer from the starting sequence number of the segment, and the URG flag bit is set. TCP sends the urgent offset and the URG flag regardless of whether the referenced byte of urgent data is contained in this segment or not.

tcp_output.c
```
370        /*
371         * Calculate receive window.  Don't shrink window,
372         * but avoid silly window syndrome.
373         */
374        if (win < (long) (so->so_rcv.sb_hiwat / 4) && win < (long) tp->t_maxseg)
375            win = 0;
376        if (win > (long) TCP_MAXWIN << tp->rcv_scale)
377            win = (long) TCP_MAXWIN << tp->rcv_scale;
378        if (win < (long) (tp->rcv_adv - tp->rcv_nxt))
379            win = (long) (tp->rcv_adv - tp->rcv_nxt);
380        ti->ti_win = htons((u_short) (win >> tp->rcv_scale));
381        if (SEQ_GT(tp->snd_up, tp->snd_nxt)) {
382            ti->ti_urp = htons((u_short) (tp->snd_up - tp->snd_nxt));
383            ti->ti_flags |= TH_URG;
384        } else
385            /*
386             * If no urgent pointer to send, then we pull
387             * the urgent pointer to the left edge of the send window
388             * so that it doesn't drift into the send window on sequence
389             * number wraparound.
390             */
391            tp->snd_up = tp->snd_una;   /* drag it along */
392        /*
393         * Put TCP length in extended header, and then
394         * checksum extended header and data.
395         */
396        if (len + optlen)
397            ti->ti_len = htons((u_short) (sizeof(struct tcphdr) +
398                                          optlen + len));
399        ti->ti_sum = in_cksum(m, (int) (hdrlen + len));
```
tcp_output.c

Figure 26.29   `tcp_output` function: fill in more TCP header fields and calculate checksum.

Figure 26.30 shows an example of how the urgent offset is calculated, assuming the process executes

```
send(fd, buf, 3, MSG_OOB);
```

and the send buffer is empty when this call to send takes place. This shows that Berkeley-derived systems consider the urgent pointer to point to the first byte of data *after* the out-of-band byte. Recall our discussion after Figure 24.10 where we distinguished between the 32-bit *urgent pointer* in the data stream (`snd_up`), and the 16-bit *urgent offset* in the TCP header (`ti_urp`).

> There is a subtle bug here. The bug occurs when the send buffer is larger than 65535, regardless of whether the window scale option is in use or not. If the send buffer is greater than 65535 and is nearly full, and the process sends out-of-band data, the offset of the urgent pointer from `snd_nxt` can exceed 65535. But the urgent pointer is a 16-bit unsigned value, and if the calculated value exceeds 65535, the 16 high-order bits are discarded, delivering a bogus urgent pointer to the other end. See Exercise 26.6 for a solution.

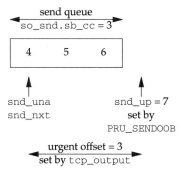

Figure 26.30   Example of urgent pointer and urgent offset calculation.

384–391   If TCP is not in urgent mode, the urgent pointer is moved to the left edge of the window (snd_una).

392–399   The TCP length is stored in the pseudo-header and the TCP checksum is calculated. All the fields in the TCP header have been filled in, and when the IP and TCP header template were copied from t_template (Figure 26.26), the fields in the IP header that are used as the pseudo-header were initialized (as shown in Figure 23.19 for the UDP checksum calculation).

The next part of tcp_output, shown in Figure 26.31, updates the sequence number if the SYN or FIN flags are set and initializes the retransmission timer.

Remember starting sequence number

400–405   If TCP is not in the persist state, the starting sequence number is saved in startseq. This is used later in Figure 26.31 if the segment is timed.

Increment snd_nxt

406–417   Since both the SYN and FIN flags take a sequence number, snd_nxt is incremented if either is set. TCP also remembers that the FIN has been sent, by setting the flag TF_SENTFIN. snd_nxt is then incremented by the number of bytes of data (len), which can be 0.

Update snd_max

418–419   If the new value of snd_nxt is larger than snd_max, this is not a retransmission. The new value of snd_max is stored.

420–428   If a segment is not currently being timed for this connection (t_rtt equals 0), the timer is started (t_rtt is set to 1) and the starting sequence number of the segment being timed is saved in t_rtseq. This sequence number is used by tcp_input to determine when the segment being timed is acknowledged, to update the RTT estimators. The sample code we discussed in Section 25.10 looked like

```
if (tp->t_rtt && SEQ_GT(ti->ti_ack, tp->t_rtseq))
    tcp_xmit_timer(tp, tp->t_rtt);
```

tcp_output.c

```
400     /*
401      * In transmit state, time the transmission and arrange for
402      * the retransmit.  In persist state, just set snd_max.
403      */
404     if (tp->t_force == 0 || tp->t_timer[TCPT_PERSIST] == 0) {
405         tcp_seq startseq = tp->snd_nxt;

406         /*
407          * Advance snd_nxt over sequence space of this segment.
408          */
409         if (flags & (TH_SYN | TH_FIN)) {
410             if (flags & TH_SYN)
411                 tp->snd_nxt++;
412             if (flags & TH_FIN) {
413                 tp->snd_nxt++;
414                 tp->t_flags |= TF_SENTFIN;
415             }
416         }
417         tp->snd_nxt += len;
418         if (SEQ_GT(tp->snd_nxt, tp->snd_max)) {
419             tp->snd_max = tp->snd_nxt;
420             /*
421              * Time this transmission if not a retransmission and
422              * not currently timing anything.
423              */
424             if (tp->t_rtt == 0) {
425                 tp->t_rtt = 1;
426                 tp->t_rtseq = startseq;
427                 tcpstat.tcps_segstimed++;
428             }
429         }
430         /*
431          * Set retransmit timer if not currently set,
432          * and not doing an ack or a keepalive probe.
433          * Initial value for retransmit timer is smoothed
434          * round-trip time + 2 * round-trip time variance.
435          * Initialize  counter which is used for backoff
436          * of retransmit time.
437          */
438         if (tp->t_timer[TCPT_REXMT] == 0 &&
439             tp->snd_nxt != tp->snd_una) {
440             tp->t_timer[TCPT_REXMT] = tp->t_rxtcur;
441             if (tp->t_timer[TCPT_PERSIST]) {
442                 tp->t_timer[TCPT_PERSIST] = 0;
443                 tp->t_rxtshift = 0;
444             }
445         }
446     } else if (SEQ_GT(tp->snd_nxt + len, tp->snd_max))
447         tp->snd_max = tp->snd_nxt + len;
```

tcp_output.c

Figure 26.31 tcp_output function: update sequence number, initialize retransmit timer.

Set retransmission timer

430–440   If the retransmission timer is not currently set, and if this segment contains data, the retransmission timer is set to `t_rxtcur`. Recall that `t_rxtcur` is set by `tcp_xmit_timer`, when an RTT measurement is made. This is an ACK-only segment if `snd_nxt` equals `snd_una` (since `len` was added to `snd_nxt` earlier in this figure), and the retransmission timer is set only for segments containing data.

441–444   If the persist timer is enabled, it is disabled. Either the retransmission timer or the persist timer can be enabled at any time for a given connection, but not both.

Persist state

446–447   The connection is in the persist state since `t_force` is nonzero and the persist timer is enabled. (This `else` clause is associated with the `if` at the beginning of the figure.) `snd_max` is updated, if necessary. In the persist state, `len` will be one.

The final part of `tcp_output`, shown in Figure 26.32 completes the formation of the outgoing segment and calls `ip_output` to send the datagram.

Add trace record for socket debugging

448–452   If the `SO_DEBUG` socket option is enabled, `tcp_trace` adds a record to TCP's circular trace buffer. We describe this function in Section 27.10.

Set IP length, TTL, and TOS

453–462   The final three fields in the IP header that must be set by the transport layer are stored: IP length, TTL, and TOS. These three fields are marked with an asterisk at the bottom of Figure 23.19.

> The comments XXX are because the latter two fields normally remain constant for a connection and should be stored in the header template, instead of being assigned explicitly each time a segment is sent. But these two fields cannot be stored in the IP header until after the TCP checksum is calculated.

Pass datagram to IP

463–464   `ip_output` sends the datagram containing the TCP segment. The socket options are logically ANDed with `SO_DONTROUTE`, which means that the only socket option passed to `ip_output` is `SO_DONTROUTE`. The only other socket option examined by `ip_output` is `SO_BROADCAST`, so this logical AND turns off the `SO_BROADCAST` bit, if set. This means that a process cannot issue a `connect` to a broadcast address, even if it sets the `SO_BROADCAST` socket option.

467–470   The error ENOBUFS is returned if the interface queue is full or if IP needs to obtain an mbuf and can't. The function `tcp_quench` puts the connection into slow start, by setting the congestion window to one full-sized segment. Notice that `tcp_output` still returns 0 (OK) in this case, instead of the error, even though the datagram was discarded. This differs from `udp_output` (Figure 23.20), which returned the error. The difference is that UDP is unreliable, so the ENOBUFS error return is the only indication to the process that the datagram was discarded. TCP, however, will time out (if the segment contains data) and retransmit the datagram, and it is hoped that there will be space on the interface output queue or more available mbufs. If the TCP segment

```
                                                                    ─── tcp_output.c
448     /*
449      * Trace.
450      */
451     if (so->so_options & SO_DEBUG)
452         tcp_trace(TA_OUTPUT, tp->t_state, tp, ti, 0);

453     /*
454      * Fill in IP length and desired time to live and
455      * send to IP level.  There should be a better way
456      * to handle ttl and tos; we could keep them in
457      * the template, but need a way to checksum without them.
458      */
459     m->m_pkthdr.len = hdrlen + len;
460     ((struct ip *) ti)->ip_len = m->m_pkthdr.len;
461     ((struct ip *) ti)->ip_ttl = tp->t_inpcb->inp_ip.ip_ttl;    /* XXX */
462     ((struct ip *) ti)->ip_tos = tp->t_inpcb->inp_ip.ip_tos;    /* XXX */
463     error = ip_output(m, tp->t_inpcb->inp_options, &tp->t_inpcb->inp_route,
464                       so->so_options & SO_DONTROUTE, 0);
465     if (error) {
466       out:
467         if (error == ENOBUFS) {
468             tcp_quench(tp->t_inpcb, 0);
469             return (0);
470         }
471         if ((error == EHOSTUNREACH || error == ENETDOWN)
472             && TCPS_HAVERCVDSYN(tp->t_state)) {
473             tp->t_softerror = error;
474             return (0);
475         }
476         return (error);
477     }
478     tcpstat.tcps_sndtotal++;

479     /*
480      * Data sent (as far as we can tell).
481      * If this advertises a larger window than any other segment,
482      * then remember the size of the advertised window.
483      * Any pending ACK has now been sent.
484      */
485     if (win > 0 && SEQ_GT(tp->rcv_nxt + win, tp->rcv_adv))
486         tp->rcv_adv = tp->rcv_nxt + win;
487     tp->last_ack_sent = tp->rcv_nxt;
488     tp->t_flags &= ~(TF_ACKNOW | TF_DELACK);

489     if (sendalot)
490         goto again;
491     return (0);
492 }
                                                                    ─── tcp_output.c
```

Figure 26.32 tcp_output function: call ip_output to send segment.

doesn't contain data, the other end will time out when the ACK isn't received and will retransmit the data whose ACK was discarded.

471–475   If a route can't be located for the destination, and if the connection has received a SYN, the error is recorded as a soft error for the connection.

When `tcp_output` is called by `tcp_usrreq` as part of a system call by a process (Chapter 30, the `PRU_CONNECT`, `PRU_SEND`, `PRU_SENDOOB`, and `PRU_SHUTDOWN` requests), the process receives the return value from `tcp_output`. Other functions that call `tcp_output`, such as `tcp_input` and the fast and slow timeout functions, ignore the return value (because these functions don't return an error to a process).

Update `rcv_adv` and `last_ack_sent`

479–486   If the highest sequence number advertised in this segment (`rcv_nxt` plus `win`) is larger than `rcv_adv`, the new value is saved. Recall that `rcv_adv` was used in Figure 26.9 to determine how much the window had opened since the last segment that was sent, and in Figure 26.29 to make certain TCP was not shrinking the window.

487   The value of the acknowledgment field in the segment is saved in `last_ack_sent`. This variable is used by `tcp_input` with the timestamp option (Section 26.6).

488   Any pending ACK has been sent, so the `TF_ACKNOW` and `TF_DELACK` flags are cleared.

More data to send?

489–490   If the `sendalot` flag is set, a jump is made back to the label `again` (Figure 26.1). This occurs if the send buffer contains more than one full-sized segment that can be sent (Figure 26.3), or if a full-sized segment was being sent and TCP options were included that reduced the amount of data in the segment (Figure 26.24).

26.8 `tcp_template` Function

The function `tcp_newtcpcb` (from the previous chapter) is called when the socket is created, to allocate and partially initialize the TCP control block. When the first segment is sent or received on the socket (an active open is performed, the `PRU_CONNECT` request, or a SYN arrives for a listening socket), `tcp_template` creates a template of the IP and TCP headers for the connection. This minimizes the amount of work required by `tcp_output` when a segment is sent on the connection.

Figure 26.33 shows the `tcp_template` function.

Allocate mbuf

59–72   The template of the IP and TCP headers is formed in an mbuf, and a pointer to the mbuf is stored in the `t_template` member of the TCP control block. Since this function can be called at the software interrupt level, from `tcp_input`, the `M_DONTWAIT` flag is specified.

Initialize header fields

73–88   All the fields in the IP and TCP headers are set to 0 except as follows: `ti_pr` is set to the IP protocol value for TCP (6); `ti_len` is set to 20, the default length of the TCP

——————————————————————————————————— *tcp_subr.c*

```
59 struct tcpiphdr *
60 tcp_template(tp)
61 struct tcpcb *tp;
62 {
63     struct inpcb *inp = tp->t_inpcb;
64     struct mbuf *m;
65     struct tcpiphdr *n;

66     if ((n = tp->t_template) == 0) {
67         m = m_get(M_DONTWAIT, MT_HEADER);
68         if (m == NULL)
69             return (0);
70         m->m_len = sizeof(struct tcpiphdr);
71         n = mtod(m, struct tcpiphdr *);
72     }
73     n->ti_next = n->ti_prev = 0;
74     n->ti_x1 = 0;
75     n->ti_pr = IPPROTO_TCP;
76     n->ti_len = htons(sizeof(struct tcpiphdr) - sizeof(struct ip));
77     n->ti_src = inp->inp_laddr;
78     n->ti_dst = inp->inp_faddr;
79     n->ti_sport = inp->inp_lport;
80     n->ti_dport = inp->inp_fport;
81     n->ti_seq = 0;
82     n->ti_ack = 0;
83     n->ti_x2 = 0;
84     n->ti_off = 5;                      /* 5 32-bit words = 20 bytes */
85     n->ti_flags = 0;
86     n->ti_win = 0;
87     n->ti_sum = 0;
88     n->ti_urp = 0;
89     return (n);
90 }
```

——————————————————————————————————— *tcp_subr.c*

Figure 26.33 `tcp_template` function: create template of IP and TCP headers.

header; and `ti_off` is set to 5, the number of 32-bit words in the 20-byte TCP header. Also the source and destination IP addresses and TCP port numbers are copied from the Internet PCB into the TCP header template.

Pseudo-header for TCP checksum computation

73–88   The initialization of many of the fields in the combined IP and TCP header simplifies the computation of the TCP checksum, using the same pseudo-header technique as discussed for UDP in Section 23.6. Examining the `udpiphdr` structure in Figure 23.19 shows why `tcp_template` initializes fields such as `ti_next` and `ti_prev` to 0.

26.9 `tcp_respond` Function

The function `tcp_respond` is a special-purpose function that also calls `ip_output` to send IP datagrams. `tcp_respond` is called in two cases:

1. by `tcp_input` to generate an RST segment, with or without an ACK, and

2. by `tcp_timers` to send a keepalive probe.

Instead of going through all the logic of `tcp_output` for these two cases, the special-purpose function `tcp_respond` is called. We also note that the function `tcp_drop` that we cover in the next chapter also generates RST segments by calling `tcp_output`. Not all RST segments are generated by `tcp_respond`.

Figure 26.34 shows the first half of `tcp_respond`.

```
                                                                           tcp_subr.c
104 void
105 tcp_respond(tp, ti, m, ack, seq, flags)
106 struct tcpcb *tp;
107 struct tcpiphdr *ti;
108 struct mbuf *m;
109 tcp_seq ack, seq;
110 int      flags;
111 {
112     int      tlen;
113     int      win = 0;
114     struct route *ro = 0;

115     if (tp) {
116         win = sbspace(&tp->t_inpcb->inp_socket->so_rcv);
117         ro = &tp->t_inpcb->inp_route;
118     }
119     if (m == 0) {                   /* generate keepalive probe */
120         m = m_gethdr(M_DONTWAIT, MT_HEADER);
121         if (m == NULL)
122             return;
123         tlen = 0;                   /* no data is sent */
124         m->m_data += max_linkhdr;
125         *mtod(m, struct tcpiphdr *) = *ti;
126         ti = mtod(m, struct tcpiphdr *);
127         flags = TH_ACK;

128     } else {                        /* generate RST segment */
129         m_freem(m->m_next);
130         m->m_next = 0;
131         m->m_data = (caddr_t) ti;
132         m->m_len = sizeof(struct tcpiphdr);
133         tlen = 0;
134 #define xchg(a,b,type) { type t; t=a; a=b; b=t; }
135         xchg(ti->ti_dst.s_addr, ti->ti_src.s_addr, u_long);
136         xchg(ti->ti_dport, ti->ti_sport, u_short);
137 #undef xchg
138     }
                                                                           tcp_subr.c
```

Figure 26.34   `tcp_respond` function: first half.

104–110   Figure 26.35 shows the different arguments to `tcp_respond` for the three cases in which it is called.

	Arguments					
	tp	ti	m	ack	seq	flags
generate RST without ACK	tp	ti	m	0	ti_ack	TH_RST
generate RST with ACK	tp	ti	m	ti_seq + ti_len	0	TH_RST | TH_ACK
generate keepalive	tp	t_template	NULL	rcv_nxt	snd_una	0

Figure 26.35 Arguments to `tcp_respond`.

`tp` is a pointer to the TCP control block (possibly a null pointer); `ti` is a pointer to an IP/TCP header template; `m` is a pointer to the mbuf containing the segment causing the RST to be generated; and the last three arguments are the acknowledgment field, sequence number field, and flags field of the segment being generated.

113–118　　It is possible for `tcp_input` to generate an RST when a segment is received that does not have an associated TCP control block. This happens, for example, when a segment is received that doesn't reference an existing connection (e.g., a SYN for a port without an associated listening server). In this case `tp` is null and the initial values for `win` and `ro` are used. If `tp` is not null, the amount of space in the receive buffer will be sent as the advertised window, and the pointer to the cached route is saved in `ro` for the call to `ip_output`.

Send keepalive probe when keepalive timer expires

119–127　　The argument `m` is a pointer to the mbuf chain for the received segment. But a keepalive probe is sent in response to the keepalive timer expiring, not in response to a received TCP segment. Therefore `m` is null and `m_gethdr` allocates a packet header mbuf to contain the IP and TCP headers. `tlen`, the length of the TCP data, is set to 0, since the keepalive probe doesn't contain any data.

> Some older implementations based on 4.2BSD do not respond to these keepalive probes unless the segment contains data. Net/3 can be configured to send 1 garbage byte of data in the probe to elicit the response by defining the name `TCP_COMPAT_42` when the kernel is compiled. This assigns 1, instead of 0, to `tlen`. The garbage byte causes no harm, because it is not the expected byte (it is a byte that the receiver has previously received and acknowledged), so it is thrown away by the receiver.

The assignment of `*ti` copies the TCP header template structure pointed to by `ti` into the data portion of the mbuf. The pointer `ti` is then set to point to the header template in the mbuf.

Send RST segment in response to received segment

128–138　　An RST segment is being sent by `tcp_input` in response to a received segment. The mbuf containing the input segment is reused for the response. All the mbufs on the chain are released by `m_free` except the first mbuf (the packet header), since the segment generated by `tcp_respond` consists of only an IP header and a TCP header. The source and destination IP address and port numbers are swapped in the IP and TCP header.

Figure 26.36 shows the final half of `tcp_respond`.

```
                                                                            tcp_subr.c
139     ti->ti_len = htons((u_short) (sizeof(struct tcphdr) + tlen));
140     tlen += sizeof(struct tcpiphdr);
141     m->m_len = tlen;
142     m->m_pkthdr.len = tlen;
143     m->m_pkthdr.rcvif = (struct ifnet *) 0;
144     ti->ti_next = ti->ti_prev = 0;
145     ti->ti_x1 = 0;
146     ti->ti_seq = htonl(seq);
147     ti->ti_ack = htonl(ack);
148     ti->ti_x2 = 0;
149     ti->ti_off = sizeof(struct tcphdr) >> 2;
150     ti->ti_flags = flags;
151     if (tp)
152         ti->ti_win = htons((u_short) (win >> tp->rcv_scale));
153     else
154         ti->ti_win = htons((u_short) win);
155     ti->ti_urp = 0;
156     ti->ti_sum = 0;
157     ti->ti_sum = in_cksum(m, tlen);
158     ((struct ip *) ti)->ip_len = tlen;
159     ((struct ip *) ti)->ip_ttl = ip_defttl;
160     (void) ip_output(m, NULL, ro, 0, NULL);
161 }
                                                                            tcp_subr.c
```

Figure 26.36   `tcp_respond` function: second half.

139–157   The fields in the IP and TCP headers must be initialized for the TCP checksum computation. These statements are similar to the way `tcp_template` initializes the `t_template` field. The sequence number and acknowledgment fields are passed by the caller as arguments. Finally `ip_output` sends the datagram.

26.10 Summary

This chapter has looked at the general-purpose function that generates most TCP segments (`tcp_output`) and the special-purpose function that generates RST segments and keepalive probes (`tcp_respond`).

Many factors determine whether TCP can send a segment or not: the flags in the segment, the window advertised by the other end, the amount of data ready to send, whether unacknowledged data already exists for the connection, and so on. Therefore the logic of `tcp_output` determines whether a segment can be sent (the first half of the function), and if so, what values to set all the TCP header fields to (the last half of the function). If a segment is sent, the TCP control block variables for the send sequence space must be updated.

One segment at a time is generated by `tcp_output`, and at the end of the function a check is made of whether more data can still be sent. If so, the function loops around and tries to send another segment. This looping continues until there is no more data to send, or until some other condition (e.g., the receiver's advertised window) stops the transmission.

A TCP segment can also contain options. The options supported by Net/3 specify the maximum segment size, a window scale factor, and a pair of timestamps. The first two can only appear with SYN segments, while the timestamp option (if supported by both ends) normally appears in every segment. Since the window scale and timestamp options are newer and optional, if the first end to send a SYN wants to use the option, it sends the option with its SYN and uses the option only if the other end's SYN also contains the option.

Exercises

26.1 Slow start is resumed in Figure 26.1 when there is a pause in the *sending* of data, yet the amount of idle time is calculated as the amount of time since the last segment was *received* on the connection. Why doesn't TCP calculate the idle time as the amount of time since the last segment was *sent* on the connection?

26.2 With Figure 26.6 we said that `len` is less than 0 if the FIN has been sent but not acknowledged and not retransmitted. What happens if the FIN is retransmitted?

26.3 Net/3 always sends the window scale and timestamp options with an active open. Why does the global variable `tcp_do_rfc1323` exist?

26.4 In Figure 25.28, which did not use the timestamp option, the RTT estimators are updated eight times. If the timestamp option had been used in this example, how many times would the RTT estimators have been updated?

26.5 In Figure 26.23 `bcopy` is called to store the received MSS in the variable `mss`. Why not cast the pointer to `opt[2]` into a pointer to an unsigned short and perform an assignment?

26.6 After Figure 26.29 we described a bug in the code, which can cause a bogus urgent offset to be sent. Propose a solution. (*Hint*: What is the largest amount of TCP data that can be sent in a segment?)

26.7 With Figure 26.32 we mentioned that an error of `ENOBUFS` is not returned to the process because (1) if the discarded segment contained data, the retransmission timer will expire and the data will be retransmitted, or (2) if the discarded segment was an ACK-only segment, the other end will retransmit its data when it doesn't receive the ACK. What if the discarded segment contains an RST?

26.8 Explain the settings of the PSH flag in Figure 20.3 of Volume 1.

26.9 Why does Figure 26.36 use the value of `ip_defttl` for the TTL, while Figure 26.32 uses the value in the PCB?

26.10 Describe what happens with the mbuf allocated in Figure 26.25 when IP options are specified by the process for the TCP connection. Implement a better solution.

26.11 `tcp_output` is a long function (about 500 lines, including comments), which can appear to be inefficient. But lots of the code handles special cases. Assume the function is called with a full-sized segment ready to be sent, and no special cases: no IP options and no special flags such as SYN, FIN, or URG. About how many lines of C code are actually executed? How many functions are called before the segment is passed to `ip_output`?

26.12 In the example at the end of Section 26.3 in which the application did a write of 100 bytes followed by a write of 50 bytes, would anything change if the application called `writev` once for both buffers, instead of calling `write` twice? Does anything change with `writev` if the two buffer lengths are 200 and 300, instead of 100 and 50?

26.13 The timestamp that is sent in the timestamp option is taken from the global `tcp_now`, which is incremented every 500 ms. Modify TCP to use a higher resolution timestamp value.

27

TCP Functions

27.1 Introduction

This chapter presents numerous TCP functions that we need to cover before discussing TCP input in the next two chapters:

- `tcp_drain` is the protocol's drain function, called when the kernel is out of mbufs. It does nothing.

- `tcp_drop` aborts a connection by sending an RST.

- `tcp_close` performs the normal TCP connection termination: send a FIN and wait for the four-way exchange to complete. Section 18.2 of Volume 1 talks about the four packets that are exchanged when a connection is closed.

- `tcp_mss` processes a received MSS option and calculates the MSS to announce when TCP sends an MSS option of its own.

- `tcp_ctlinput` is called when an ICMP error is received in response to a TCP segment, and it calls `tcp_notify` to process the ICMP error. `tcp_quench` is a special case function that handles ICMP source quench errors.

- The `TCP_REASS` macro and the `tcp_reass` function manipulate segments on TCP's reassembly queue for a given connection. This queue handles the receipt of out-of-order segments, some of which might overlap.

- `tcp_trace` adds records to the kernel's circular debug buffer for TCP (the `SO_DEBUG` socket option) that can be printed with the `trpt(8)` program.

27.2 `tcp_drain` Function

The simplest of all the TCP functions is `tcp_drain`. It is the protocol's `pr_drain` function, called by `m_reclaim` when the kernel runs out of mbufs. We saw in Figure 10.32 that `ip_drain` discards all the fragments on its reassembly queue, and UDP doesn't define a drain function. Although TCP holds onto mbufs—segments that have arrived out of order, but within the receive window for the socket—the Net/3 implementation of TCP does not discard these pending mbufs if the kernel runs out of space. Instead, `tcp_drain` does nothing, on the assumption that a received (but out-of-order) TCP segment is "more important" than an IP fragment.

27.3 `tcp_drop` Function

`tcp_drop` is called from numerous places to drop a connection by sending an RST and to report an error to the process. This differs from closing a connection (the `tcp_disconnect` function), which sends a FIN to the other end and follows the connection termination steps in the state transition diagram.

Figure 27.1 shows the seven places where `tcp_drop` is called and the `errno` argument.

Function	errno	Description
tcp_input	ENOBUFS	SYN arrives on listening socket, but kernel out of mbufs for t_template.
tcp_input	ECONNREFUSED	RST received in response to SYN.
tcp_input	ECONNRESET	RST received on existing connection.
tcp_timers	ETIMEDOUT	Retransmission timer has expired 13 times in a row with no ACK from other end (Figure 25.25).
tcp_timers	ETIMEDOUT	Connection-establishment timer has expired (Figure 25.15), or keepalive timer has expired with no response to nine consecutive probes (Figure 25.17)
tcp_usrreq	ECONNABORTED	PRU_ABORT request.
tcp_usrreq	0	Socket closed and SO_LINGER socket option set with linger time of 0.

Figure 27.1 Calls to `tcp_drop` and `errno` argument.

Figure 27.2 shows the `tcp_drop` function.

202–213   If TCP has received a SYN, the connection is synchronized and an RST must be sent to the other end. This is done by setting the state to CLOSED and calling `tcp_output`. In Figure 24.16 the value of `tcp_outflags` for the CLOSED state includes the RST flag.

214–216   If the error is ETIMEDOUT but a soft error was received on the connection (e.g., EHOSTUNREACH), the soft error becomes the socket error, instead of the less specific ETIMEDOUT.

217   `tcp_close` finishes closing the socket.

tcp_subr.c

```
202 struct tcpcb *
203 tcp_drop(tp, errno)
204 struct tcpcb *tp;
205 int      errno;
206 {
207     struct socket *so = tp->t_inpcb->inp_socket;

208     if (TCPS_HAVERCVDSYN(tp->t_state)) {
209         tp->t_state = TCPS_CLOSED;
210         (void) tcp_output(tp);
211         tcpstat.tcps_drops++;
212     } else
213         tcpstat.tcps_conndrops++;
214     if (errno == ETIMEDOUT && tp->t_softerror)
215         errno = tp->t_softerror;
216     so->so_error = errno;
217     return (tcp_close(tp));
218 }
```

tcp_subr.c

Figure 27.2 tcp_drop function.

27.4 tcp_close **Function**

tcp_close is normally called by tcp_input when the process has done a passive close and the ACK is received in the LAST_ACK state, and by tcp_timers when the 2MSL timer expires and the socket moves from the TIME_WAIT to CLOSED state. It is also called in other states, possibly after an error has occurred, as we saw in the previous section. It releases the memory occupied by the connection (the IP and TCP header template, the TCP control block, the Internet PCB, and any out-of-order segments remaining on the connection's reassembly queue) and updates the route characteristics.

We describe this function in three parts, the first two dealing with the route characteristics and the final part showing the release of resources.

Route Characteristics

Nine variables are maintained in the rt_metrics structure (Figure 18.26), six of which are used by TCP. Eight of these can be examined and changed with the route(8) command (the ninth, rmx_pksent is never used): these variables are shown in Figure 27.3.

Additionally, the -lock modifier can be used with the route command to set the corresponding RTV_*xxx* bit in the rmx_locks member (Figure 20.13). Setting the RTV_*xxx* bit tells the kernel not to update that metric.

When a TCP socket is closed, tcp_close updates three of the routing metrics—the smoothed RTT estimator, the smoothed mean deviation estimator, and the slow start threshold—but only if enough data was transferred on the connection to yield meaningful statistics and the variable is not locked.

Figure 27.4 shows the first part of tcp_close.

rt_metrics member	saved by tcp_close?	used by tcp_mss?	route(8) modifier
rmx_expire			-expire
rmx_hopcount			-hopcount
rmx_mtu		•	-mtu
rmx_recvpipe		•	-recvpipe
rmx_rtt	•	•	-rtt
rmx_rttvar	•	•	-rttvar
rmx_sendpipe		•	-sendpipe
rmx_ssthresh	•	•	-ssthresh

Figure 27.3   Members of the rt_metrics structure used by TCP.

Check if enough data sent to update statistics

234–248   The default send buffer size is 8192 bytes (sb_hiwat), so the first test is whether 131,072 bytes (16 full buffers) have been transferred across the connection. The initial send sequence number is compared to the maximum sequence number sent on the connection. Additionally, the socket must have a cached route and that route cannot be the default route. (See Exercise 19.2.)

> Notice there is a small chance for an error in the first test, because of sequence number wrap, if the amount of data transferred is within $N \times 2^{32}$ and $N \times 2^{32} + 131072$, for any N greater than 1. But few connections (today) transfer 4 gigabytes of data.

> Despite the prevalence of default routes in the Internet, this information is still useful to maintain in the routing table. If a host continually exchanges data with another host (or network), even if a default route can be used, a host-specific or network-specific route can be entered into the routing table with the route command just to maintain this information across connections. (See Exercise 19.2.) This information is lost when the system is rebooted.

250   The administrator can lock any of the variables from Figure 27.3, preventing them from being updated by the kernel, so before modifying each variable this lock must be checked.

Update RTT

251–264   t_srtt is stored as ticks × 8 (Figure 25.19) and rmx_rtt is stored as microseconds. So t_srtt is multiplied by 1,000,000 (RTM_RTTUNIT) and then divided by 2 (ticks/second) times 8. If a value for rmx_rtt already exists, the new value is one-half the old value plus one-half the new value. Otherwise the new value is stored in rmx_rtt.

Update mean deviation

265–273   The same algorithm is applied to the mean deviation estimator. It too is stored as microseconds, requiring a conversion from the t_rttvar units of ticks × 4.

```
                                                                    —— tcp_subr.c
225 struct tcpcb *
226 tcp_close(tp)
227 struct tcpcb *tp;
228 {
229     struct tcpiphdr *t;
230     struct inpcb *inp = tp->t_inpcb;
231     struct socket *so = inp->inp_socket;
232     struct mbuf *m;
233     struct rtentry *rt;

234     /*
235      * If we sent enough data to get some meaningful characteristics,
236      * save them in the routing entry.  'Enough' is arbitrarily
237      * defined as the sendpipesize (default 8K) * 16.  This would
238      * give us 16 rtt samples assuming we only get one sample per
239      * window (the usual case on a long haul net).  16 samples is
240      * enough for the srtt filter to converge to within 5% of the correct
241      * value; fewer samples and we could save a very bogus rtt.
242      *
243      * Don't update the default route's characteristics and don't
244      * update anything that the user "locked".
245      */
246     if (SEQ_LT(tp->iss + so->so_snd.sb_hiwat * 16, tp->snd_max) &&
247         (rt = inp->inp_route.ro_rt) &&
248         ((struct sockaddr_in *) rt_key(rt))->sin_addr.s_addr != INADDR_ANY) {
249         u_long  i;

250         if ((rt->rt_rmx.rmx_locks & RTV_RTT) == 0) {
251             i = tp->t_srtt *
252                 (RTM_RTTUNIT / (PR_SLOWHZ * TCP_RTT_SCALE));
253             if (rt->rt_rmx.rmx_rtt && i)
254                 /*
255                  * filter this update to half the old & half
256                  * the new values, converting scale.
257                  * See route.h and tcp_var.h for a
258                  * description of the scaling constants.
259                  */
260                 rt->rt_rmx.rmx_rtt =
261                     (rt->rt_rmx.rmx_rtt + i) / 2;
262             else
263                 rt->rt_rmx.rmx_rtt = i;
264         }
265         if ((rt->rt_rmx.rmx_locks & RTV_RTTVAR) == 0) {
266             i = tp->t_rttvar *
267                 (RTM_RTTUNIT / (PR_SLOWHZ * TCP_RTTVAR_SCALE));
268             if (rt->rt_rmx.rmx_rttvar && i)
269                 rt->rt_rmx.rmx_rttvar =
270                     (rt->rt_rmx.rmx_rttvar + i) / 2;
271             else
272                 rt->rt_rmx.rmx_rttvar = i;
273         }
                                                                    —— tcp_subr.c
```

Figure 27.4 tcp_close function: update RTT and mean deviation.

Figure 27.5 shows the next part of `tcp_close`, which updates the slow start threshold for the route.

── tcp_subr.c
```
274        /*
275         * update the pipelimit (ssthresh) if it has been updated
276         * already or if a pipesize was specified & the threshhold
277         * got below half the pipesize.  I.e., wait for bad news
278         * before we start updating, then update on both good
279         * and bad news.
280         */
281        if ((rt->rt_rmx.rmx_locks & RTV_SSTHRESH) == 0 &&
282            (i = tp->snd_ssthresh) && rt->rt_rmx.rmx_ssthresh ||
283            i < (rt->rt_rmx.rmx_sendpipe / 2)) {
284            /*
285             * convert the limit from user data bytes to
286             * packets then to packet data bytes.
287             */
288            i = (i + tp->t_maxseg / 2) / tp->t_maxseg;
289            if (i < 2)
290                i = 2;
291            i *= (u_long) (tp->t_maxseg + sizeof(struct tcpiphdr));
292            if (rt->rt_rmx.rmx_ssthresh)
293                rt->rt_rmx.rmx_ssthresh =
294                    (rt->rt_rmx.rmx_ssthresh + i) / 2;
295            else
296                rt->rt_rmx.rmx_ssthresh = i;
297        }
298    }
```
── tcp_subr.c

Figure 27.5 `tcp_close` function: update slow start threshold.

274–283   The slow start threshold is updated only if (1) it has been updated already (`rmx_ssthresh` is nonzero) or (2) `rmx_sendpipe` is specified by the administrator and the new value of `snd_ssthresh` is less than one-half the value of `rmx_sendpipe`. As the comment in the code indicates, TCP does not update the value of `rmx_ssthresh` until it is forced to because of packet loss; from that point on it considers itself free to adjust the value either up or down.

284–290   The variable `snd_ssthresh` is maintained in bytes. The first conversion divides this variable by the MSS (`t_maxseg`), yielding the number of segments. The addition of one-half `t_maxseg` rounds the integer result. The lower bound on this result is two segments.

291–297   The size of the IP and TCP headers (40) is added to the MSS and multipled by the number of segments. This value updates `rmx_ssthresh`, using the same filtering as in Figure 27.4 (one-half the old plus one-half the new).

Resource Release

The final part of `tcp_close`, shown in Figure 27.6, releases the memory resources held by the socket.

tcp_subr.c

```
299     /* free the reassembly queue, if any */
300     t = tp->seg_next;
301     while (t != (struct tcpiphdr *) tp) {
302         t = (struct tcpiphdr *) t->ti_next;
303         m = REASS_MBUF((struct tcpiphdr *) t->ti_prev);
304         remque(t->ti_prev);
305         m_freem(m);
306     }
307     if (tp->t_template)
308         (void) m_free(dtom(tp->t_template));
309     free(tp, M_PCB);
310     inp->inp_ppcb = 0;
311     soisdisconnected(so);
312     /* clobber input pcb cache if we're closing the cached connection */
313     if (inp == tcp_last_inpcb)
314         tcp_last_inpcb = &tcb;
315     in_pcbdetach(inp);
316     tcpstat.tcps_closed++;
317     return ((struct tcpcb *) 0);
318 }
```

tcp_subr.c

Figure 27.6 tcp_close function: release connection resources.

Release any mbufs on reassembly queue

299–306   If any segments are left on the connection's reassembly queue, they are discarded. This queue is for segments that arrive out of order but within the receive window. They are held in a reassembly queue until the required "earlier" segments are received, at which time they are reassembled and passed to the application in the correct order. We discuss this in more detail in Section 27.9.

Release header template and TCP control block

307–311   The template of the IP and TCP headers is released by m_free and the TCP control block is released by free. soisdisconnected marks the socket as disconnected.

Release PCB

312–318   If the Internet PCB for this socket is the one currently cached by TCP, the cache is marked as empty by setting tcp_last_inpcb to the head of TCP's PCB list. The PCB is then detached, which releases the memory used by the PCB.

27.5 tcp_mss Function

The tcp_mss function is called from two other functions:

1. from tcp_output, when a SYN segment is being sent, to include an MSS option, and

2. from tcp_input, when an MSS option is received in a SYN segment.

The `tcp_mss` function checks for a cached route to the destination and calculates the MSS to use for this connection.

Figure 27.7 shows the first part of `tcp_mss`, which acquires a route to the destination if one is not already held by the PCB.

```
                                                                    ─── tcp_input.c
1391 int
1392 tcp_mss(tp, offer)
1393 struct tcpcb *tp;
1394 u_int   offer;
1395 {
1396     struct route *ro;
1397     struct rtentry *rt;
1398     struct ifnet *ifp;
1399     int     rtt, mss;
1400     u_long  bufsize;
1401     struct inpcb *inp;
1402     struct socket *so;
1403     extern int tcp_mssdflt;

1404     inp = tp->t_inpcb;
1405     ro = &inp->inp_route;

1406     if ((rt = ro->ro_rt) == (struct rtentry *) 0) {
1407         /* No route yet, so try to acquire one */
1408         if (inp->inp_faddr.s_addr != INADDR_ANY) {
1409             ro->ro_dst.sa_family = AF_INET;
1410             ro->ro_dst.sa_len = sizeof(ro->ro_dst);
1411             ((struct sockaddr_in *) &ro->ro_dst)->sin_addr =
1412                 inp->inp_faddr;
1413             rtalloc(ro);
1414         }
1415         if ((rt = ro->ro_rt) == (struct rtentry *) 0)
1416             return (tcp_mssdflt);
1417     }
1418     ifp = rt->rt_ifp;
1419     so = inp->inp_socket;
                                                                    ─── tcp_input.c
```

Figure 27.7 `tcp_mss` function: acquire a route if one is not held by the PCB.

Acquire a route if necessary

1391–1417   If the socket does not have a cached route, `rtalloc` acquires one. The interface pointer associated with the outgoing route is saved in `ifp`. Knowing the outgoing interface is important, since its associated MTU can affect the MSS announced by TCP. If a route is not acquired, the default of 512 (`tcp_mssdflt`) is returned immediately.

The next part of `tcp_mss`, shown in Figure 27.8, checks whether the route has metrics associated with it; if so, the variables `t_rttmin`, `t_srtt`, and `t_rttvar` can be initialized from the metrics.

——— *tcp_input.c*
```
1420    /*
1421     * While we're here, check if there's an initial rtt
1422     * or rttvar.  Convert from the route-table units
1423     * to scaled multiples of the slow timeout timer.
1424     */
1425    if (tp->t_srtt == 0 && (rtt = rt->rt_rmx.rmx_rtt)) {
1426        /*
1427         * XXX the lock bit for RTT indicates that the value
1428         * is also a minimum value; this is subject to time.
1429         */
1430        if (rt->rt_rmx.rmx_locks & RTV_RTT)
1431            tp->t_rttmin = rtt / (RTM_RTTUNIT / PR_SLOWHZ);
1432        tp->t_srtt = rtt / (RTM_RTTUNIT / (PR_SLOWHZ * TCP_RTT_SCALE));

1433        if (rt->rt_rmx.rmx_rttvar)
1434            tp->t_rttvar = rt->rt_rmx.rmx_rttvar /
1435                (RTM_RTTUNIT / (PR_SLOWHZ * TCP_RTTVAR_SCALE));
1436        else
1437            /* default variation is +- 1 rtt */
1438            tp->t_rttvar =
1439                tp->t_srtt * TCP_RTTVAR_SCALE / TCP_RTT_SCALE;

1440        TCPT_RANGESET(tp->t_rxtcur,
1441                ((tp->t_srtt >> 2) + tp->t_rttvar) >> 1,
1442                tp->t_rttmin, TCPTV_REXMTMAX);
1443    }
```
——— *tcp_input.c*

Figure 27.8 tcp_mss function: check if the route has an associated RTT metric.

Initialize smoothed RTT estimator

1420–1432   If there are no RTT measurements yet for the connection (t_srtt is 0) and rmx_rtt is nonzero, the latter initializes the smoothed RTT estimator t_srtt. If the RTV_RTT bit in the routing metric lock flag is set, it indicates that rmx_rtt should also be used to initialize the minimum RTT for this connection (t_rttmin). We saw that tcp_newtcpcb initializes t_rttmin to 2 ticks.

rmx_rtt (in units of microseconds) is converted to t_srtt (in units of ticks × 8). This is the reverse of the conversion done in Figure 27.4. Notice that t_rttmin is set to one-eighth the value of t_srtt, since the former is not divided by the scale factor TCP_RTT_SCALE.

Initialize smoothed mean deviation estimator

1433–1439   If the stored value of rmx_rttvar is nonzero, it is converted from units of microseconds into ticks × 4 and stored in t_rttvar. But if the value is 0, t_rttvar is set to t_rtt, that is, the variation is set to the mean. This defaults the variation to ± 1 RTT. Since the units of the former are ticks × 4 and the units of the latter are ticks × 8, the value of t_srtt is converted accordingly.

Calculate initial RTO

1440–1442   The current *RTO* is calculated and stored in `t_rxtcur`, using the unscaled equation

$$RTO = srtt + 2 \times rttvar$$

A multipler of 2, instead of 4, is used to calculate the first *RTO*. This is the same equation that was used in Figure 25.21. Substituting the scaling relationships we get

$$RTO = \frac{t\_srtt}{8} + 2 \times \frac{t\_rttvar}{4}$$

$$= \frac{\dfrac{t\_srtt}{4} + t\_rttvar}{2}$$

which is the second argument to `TCPT_RANGESET`.

The next part of `tcp_mss`, shown in Figure 27.9, calculates the MSS.

```
                                                                         ─── tcp_input.c
1444      /*
1445       * if there's an mtu associated with the route, use it
1446       */
1447      if (rt->rt_rmx.rmx_mtu)
1448          mss = rt->rt_rmx.rmx_mtu - sizeof(struct tcpiphdr);
1449      else {
1450          mss = ifp->if_mtu - sizeof(struct tcpiphdr);
1451 #if (MCLBYTES & (MCLBYTES - 1)) == 0
1452          if (mss > MCLBYTES)
1453              mss &= ~(MCLBYTES - 1);
1454 #else
1455          if (mss > MCLBYTES)
1456              mss = mss / MCLBYTES * MCLBYTES;
1457 #endif
1458          if (!in_localaddr(inp->inp_faddr))
1459              mss = min(mss, tcp_mssdflt);
1460      }
                                                                         ─── tcp_input.c
```

Figure 27.9 `tcp_mss` function: calculate MSS.

Use MSS from routing table MTU

1444–1450   If the MTU is set in the routing table, `mss` is set to that value. Otherwise `mss` starts at the value of the outgoing interface MTU minus 40 (the default size of the IP and TCP headers). For an Ethernet, `mss` would start at 1460.

Round MSS down to multiple of MCLBYTES

1451–1457   The goal of these lines of code is to reduce the value of `mss` to the next-lower multiple of the mbuf cluster size, if `mss` exceeds `MCLBYTES`. If the value of `MCLBYTES` (typically 1024 or 2048) logically ANDed with the value minus 1 equals 0, then `MCLBYTES` is a power of 2. For example, 1024 (`0x400`) logically ANDed with 1023 (`0x3ff`) is 0.

The value of mss is reduced to the next-lower multiple of MCLBYTES by clearing the appropriate number of low-order bits: if the cluster size is 1024, logically ANDing mss with the one's complement of 1023 (0xfffffc00) clears the low-order 10 bits. For an Ethernet, this reduces mss from 1460 to 1024. If the cluster size is 2048, logically ANDing mss with the one's complement of 2047 (0xffff8000) clears the low-order 11 bits. For a token ring with an MTU of 4464, this reduces the value of mss from 4424 to 4096. If MCLBYTES is not a power of 2, the rounding down to the next-lower multiple of MCLBYTES is done with an integer division followed by a multiplication.

Check if destination local or nonlocal

1458–1459   If the foreign IP address is not local (in_localaddr returns 0), and if mss is greater than 512 (tcp_mssdflt), it is set to 512.

> Whether an IP address is "local" or not depends on the value of the global subnetsarelocal, which is initialized from the symbol SUBNETSARELOCAL when the kernel is compiled. The default value is 1, meaning that an IP address with the same network ID as one of the host's interfaces is considered local. If the value is 0, an IP address must have the same network ID and the same subnet ID as one of the host's interfaces to be considered local.

> This minimization for nonlocal hosts is an attempt to avoid fragmentation across wide-area networks. It is a historical artifact from the ARPANET when the MTU across most WAN links was 1006. As discussed in Section 11.7 of Volume 1, most WANs today support an MTU of 1500 or greater. See also the discussion of the path MTU discovery feature (RFC 1191 [Mogul and Deering 1990]), in Section 24.2 of Volume 1. Net/3 does not support path MTU discovery.

The final part of tcp_mss is shown in Figure 27.10.

Other end's MSS is upper bound

1461–1472   The argument offer is nonzero when this function is called from tcp_input, and its value is the MSS advertised by the other end. If the value of mss is greater than the value advertised by the other end, it is set to the value of offer. For example, if the function calculates an mss of 1024 but the advertised value from the other end is 512, mss must be set to 512. Conversely, if mss is calculated as 536 (say the outgoing MTU is 576) and the other end advertises an MSS of 1460, TCP will use 536. TCP can always use a value less than the advertised MSS, but it can't exceed the advertised value. The argument offer is 0 when this function is called by tcp_output to send an MSS option. The value of mss is also lower-bounded by 32.

1473–1483   If the value of mss has decreased from the default set by tcp_newtcpcb in the variable t_maxseg (512), or if TCP is processing a received MSS option (offer is nonzero), the following steps occur. First, if the value of rmx_sendpipe has been stored for the route, its value will be used as the send buffer high-water mark (Figure 16.4). If the buffer size is less than mss, the smaller value is used. This should never happen unless the application explicitly sets the send buffer size to a small value, or the administrator sets rmx_sendpipe to a small value, since the high-water mark of the send buffer defaults to 8192, larger than most values for the MSS.

—— *tcp_input.c*

```
1461      /*
1462       * The current mss, t_maxseg, was initialized to the default value
1463       * of 512 (tcp_mssdflt) by tcp_newtcpcb().
1464       * If we compute a smaller value, reduce the current mss.
1465       * If we compute a larger value, return it for use in sending
1466       * a max seg size option, but don't store it for use
1467       * unless we received an offer at least that large from peer.
1468       * However, do not accept offers under 32 bytes.
1469       */
1470      if (offer)
1471          mss = min(mss, offer);
1472      mss = max(mss, 32);              /* sanity */
1473      if (mss < tp->t_maxseg || offer != 0) {
1474          /*
1475           * If there's a pipesize, change the socket buffer
1476           * to that size.  Make the socket buffers an integral
1477           * number of mss units; if the mss is larger than
1478           * the socket buffer, decrease the mss.
1479           */
1480          if ((bufsize = rt->rt_rmx.rmx_sendpipe) == 0)
1481              bufsize = so->so_snd.sb_hiwat;
1482          if (bufsize < mss)
1483              mss = bufsize;
1484          else {
1485              bufsize = roundup(bufsize, mss);
1486              if (bufsize > sb_max)
1487                  bufsize = sb_max;
1488              (void) sbreserve(&so->so_snd, bufsize);
1489          }
1490          tp->t_maxseg = mss;

1491          if ((bufsize = rt->rt_rmx.rmx_recvpipe) == 0)
1492              bufsize = so->so_rcv.sb_hiwat;
1493          if (bufsize > mss) {
1494              bufsize = roundup(bufsize, mss);
1495              if (bufsize > sb_max)
1496                  bufsize = sb_max;
1497              (void) sbreserve(&so->so_rcv, bufsize);
1498          }
1499      }
1500      tp->snd_cwnd = mss;
1501      if (rt->rt_rmx.rmx_ssthresh) {
1502          /*
1503           * There's some sort of gateway or interface
1504           * buffer limit on the path.  Use this to set
1505           * the slow start threshhold, but set the
1506           * threshold to no less than 2*mss.
1507           */
1508          tp->snd_ssthresh = max(2 * mss, rt->rt_rmx.rmx_ssthresh);
1509      }
1510      return (mss);
1511 }
```

—— *tcp_input.c*

Figure 27.10 `tcp_mss` function: complete processing.

Round buffer sizes to multiple of MSS

1484–1489   The send buffer size is rounded up to the next integral multiple of the MSS, bounded by the value of sb_max (262,144 on Net/3, which is 256×1024). The socket's high-water mark is set by sbreserve. For example, the default high-water mark is 8192, but for a local TCP connection on an Ethernet with a cluster size of 2048 (i.e., an MSS of 1460) this code increases the high-water mark to 8760 (which is 6×1460). But for a nonlocal connection with an MSS of 512, the high-water mark is left at 8192.

1490   The value of t_maxseg is set, either because it decreased from the default (512) or because an MSS option was received from the other end.

1491–1499   The same logic just applied to the send buffer is also applied to the receive buffer.

Initialize congestion window and slow start threshold

1500–1509   The value of the congestion window, snd_cwnd, is set to one segment. If the rmx_ssthresh value in the routing table is nonzero, the slow start threshold (snd_ssthresh) is set to that value, but the value must not be less than two segments.

1510   The value of mss is returned by the function. tcp_input ignores this value in Figure 28.10 (since it received an MSS from the other end), but tcp_output sends this value as the announced MSS in Figure 26.23.

Example

Let's go through an example of a TCP connection establishment and the operation of tcp_mss, since it can be called twice: once when the SYN is sent and once when a SYN is received with an MSS option.

1.   The socket is created and tcp_newtcpcb sets t_maxseg to 512.

2.   The process calls connect, and tcp_output calls tcp_mss with an offer argument of 0, to include an MSS option with the SYN. Assuming a local destination, an Ethernet LAN, and an mbuf cluster size of 2048, mss is set to 1460 by the code in Figure 27.9. Since offer is 0, Figure 27.10 leaves the value as 1460 and this is the function's return value. The buffer sizes aren't modified, since 1460 is larger than the default (512) and a value hasn't been received from the other end yet. tcp_output sends an MSS option announcing a value of 1460.

3.   The other end replies with its SYN, announcing an MSS of 1024. tcp_input calls tcp_mss with an offer argument of 1024. The logic in Figure 27.9 still yields a value of 1460 for mss, but the call to min at the beginning of Figure 27.10 reduces this to 1024. Since the value of offer is nonzero, the buffer sizes are rounded up to the next integral multiple of 1024 (i.e., they're left at 8192). t_maxseg is set to 1024.

> It might appear that the logic of tcp_mss is flawed: TCP announces an MSS of 1460 but receives an MSS of 1024 from the other end. While TCP is restricted to sending 1024-byte segments, the other end is free to send 1460-byte segments. We might think that the send buffer should be a multiple of 1024, but the receive buffer should be a multiple of 1460. Yet the code in Figure 27.10 sets both buffer sizes based on the *received* MSS. The reasoning is that even if TCP announces an MSS of 1460, since it receives an MSS of 1024 from the other end, the other end probably won't send 1460-byte segments, but will restrict itself to 1024-byte segments.

27.6 `tcp_ctlinput` Function

Recall from Figure 22.32 that `tcp_ctlinput` processes five types of ICMP errors: destination unreachable, parameter problem, source quench, time exceeded, and redirects. All redirects are passed to both TCP and UDP. For the other four errors, `tcp_ctlinput` is called only if a TCP segment caused the error.

`tcp_ctlinput` is shown in Figure 27.11. It is similar to `udp_ctlinput`, shown in Figure 23.30.

```
                                                                        ─── tcp_subr.c
355 void
356 tcp_ctlinput(cmd, sa, ip)
357 int     cmd;
358 struct sockaddr *sa;
359 struct ip *ip;
360 {
361     struct tcphdr *th;
362     extern struct in_addr zeroin_addr;
363     extern u_char inetctlerrmap[];
364     void    (*notify) (struct inpcb *, int) = tcp_notify;

365     if (cmd == PRC_QUENCH)
366         notify = tcp_quench;
367     else if (!PRC_IS_REDIRECT(cmd) &&
368             ((unsigned) cmd > PRC_NCMDS || inetctlerrmap[cmd] == 0))
369         return;
370     if (ip) {
371         th = (struct tcphdr *) ((caddr_t) ip + (ip->ip_hl << 2));
372         in_pcbnotify(&tcb, sa, th->th_dport, ip->ip_src, th->th_sport,
373                 cmd, notify);
374     } else
375         in_pcbnotify(&tcb, sa, 0, zeroin_addr, 0, cmd, notify);
376 }
                                                                        ─── tcp_subr.c
```

Figure 27.11 `tcp_ctlinput` function.

365–366   The only difference in the logic from `udp_ctlinput` is how an ICMP source quench error is handled. UDP ignores these errors since the `PRC_QUENCH` entry of `inetctlerrmap` is 0. TCP explicitly checks for this error, changing the `notify` function from its default of `tcp_notify` to `tcp_quench`.

27.7 `tcp_notify` Function

`tcp_notify` is called by `tcp_ctlinput` to handle destination unreachable, parameter problem, time exceeded, and redirect errors. This function is more complicated than its UDP counterpart, since TCP must intelligently handle soft errors for an established connection. Figure 27.12 shows the `tcp_notify` function.

```
                                                                      ─── tcp_subr.c
328 void
329 tcp_notify(inp, error)
330 struct inpcb *inp;
331 int       error;
332 {
333     struct tcpcb *tp = (struct tcpcb *) inp->inp_ppcb;
334     struct socket *so = inp->inp_socket;

335     /*
336      * Ignore some errors if we are hooked up.
337      * If connection hasn't completed, has retransmitted several times,
338      * and receives a second error, give up now.  This is better
339      * than waiting a long time to establish a connection that
340      * can never complete.
341      */
342     if (tp->t_state == TCPS_ESTABLISHED &&
343         (error == EHOSTUNREACH || error == ENETUNREACH ||
344          error == EHOSTDOWN)) {
345         return;
346     } else if (tp->t_state < TCPS_ESTABLISHED && tp->t_rxtshift > 3 &&
347               tp->t_softerror)
348         so->so_error = error;
349     else
350         tp->t_softerror = error;
351     wakeup((caddr_t) & so->so_timeo);
352     sorwakeup(so);
353     sowwakeup(so);
354 }
                                                                      ─── tcp_subr.c
```

Figure 27.12 `tcp_notify` function.

328–345   If the connection is ESTABLISHED, the errors EHOSTUNREACH, ENETUNREACH, and
EHOSTDOWN are ignored.

> This handling of these three errors is new with 4.4BSD. Net/2 and earlier releases recorded
> these errors in the connection's soft error variable ($t\_softerror$), and the error was reported
> to the process should the connection eventually fail. Recall that tcp_xmit_timer resets this
> variable to 0 when an ACK is received for a segment that hasn't been retransmitted.

346–353   If the connection is not yet established, TCP has retransmitted the current segment
four or more times, and an error has already been recorded in t_softerror, the current error is recorded in the socket's so_error variable. By setting this socket variable,
the socket becomes readable and writable if the process calls select. Otherwise the
current error is just saved in t_softerror. We saw that tcp_drop sets the socket
error to this saved value if the connection is subsequently dropped because of a timeout. Any processes waiting to receive or send on the socket are then awakened to
receive the error.

27.8 `tcp_quench` Function

`tcp_quench`, which is shown in Figure 27.13, is called by `tcp_ctlinput` when a source quench is received for the connection, and by `tcp_output` (Figure 26.32) when `ip_output` returns ENOBUFS.

―― *tcp_subr.c*
```
381 void
382 tcp_quench(inp, errno)
383 struct inpcb *inp;
384 int     errno;
385 {
386     struct tcpcb *tp = intotcpcb(inp);

387     if (tp)
388         tp->snd_cwnd = tp->t_maxseg;
389 }
```
―― *tcp_subr.c*

Figure 27.13   `tcp_quench` function.

The congestion window is set to one segment, causing slow start to take over. The slow start threshold is not changed (as it is when `tcp_timers` handles a retransmission timeout), so the window will open up exponentially until `snd_ssthresh` is reached, or congestion occurs.

27.9 `TCP_REASS` Macro and `tcp_reass` Function

TCP segments can arrive out of order, and it is TCP's responsibility to place the misordered segments into the correct order for presentation to the process. For example, if a receiver advertises a window of 4096 with byte number 0 as the next expected byte, and receives a segment with bytes 0–1023 (an in-order segment) followed by a segment with bytes 2048–3071, this second segment is out of order. TCP does not discard the out-of-order segment if it is within the receive window. Instead it places the segment on the reassembly list for the connection, waiting for the missing segment to arrive (with bytes 1024–2047), at which time it can acknowledge bytes 1024–3071 and pass these 2048 bytes to the process. In this section we examine the code that manipulates the TCP reassembly queue, before discussing `tcp_input` in the next two chapters.

If we assume that a single mbuf contains the IP header, TCP header, and 4 bytes of TCP data (recall the left half of Figure 2.14) we would have the arrangement shown in Figure 27.14. We also assume the data bytes are sequence numbers 7, 8, 9, and 10.

The `ipovly` and `tcphdr` structures form the `tcpiphdr` structure, which we showed in Figure 24.12. We showed a picture of the `tcphdr` structure in Figure 24.10. In Figure 27.14 we show only the variables used in the reassembly: `ti_next`, `ti_prev`, `ti_len`, `ti_sport`, `ti_dport`, and `ti_seq`. The first two are pointers that form a doubly linked list of all the out-of-order segments for a given connection. The head of this list is the TCP control block for the connection: the `seg_next` and `seg_prev` members, which are the first two members of the structure. The `ti_next` and `ti_prev`

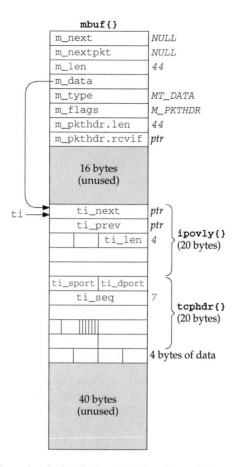

Figure 27.14 Example mbuf with IP and TCP headers and 4 bytes of data.

pointers overlay the first 8 bytes of the IP header, which aren't needed once the datagram reaches TCP. `ti_len` is the length of the TCP data, and is calculated and stored by TCP before verifying the TCP checksum.

TCP_REASS **Macro**

When data is received by `tcp_input`, the macro `TCP_REASS`, shown in Figure 27.15, is invoked to place the data onto the connection's reassembly queue. This macro is called from only one place: see Figure 29.22.

54–63   `tp` is a pointer to the TCP control block for the connection and `ti` is a pointer to the `tcpiphdr` structure for the received segment. If the following three conditions are all true:

1. this segment is in-order (the sequence number `ti_seq` equals the next expected sequence number for the connection, `rcv_nxt`), and

```
                                                                        ─ tcp_input.c
53  #define TCP_REASS(tp, ti, m, so, flags) { \
54      if ((ti)->ti_seq == (tp)->rcv_nxt && \
55          (tp)->seg_next == (struct tcpiphdr *)(tp) && \
56          (tp)->t_state == TCPS_ESTABLISHED) { \
57          tp->t_flags |= TF_DELACK; \
58          (tp)->rcv_nxt += (ti)->ti_len; \
59          flags = (ti)->ti_flags & TH_FIN; \
60          tcpstat.tcps_rcvpack++; \
61          tcpstat.tcps_rcvbyte += (ti)->ti_len; \
62          sbappend(&(so)->so_rcv, (m)); \
63          sorwakeup(so); \
64      } else { \
65          (flags) = tcp_reass((tp), (ti), (m)); \
66          tp->t_flags |= TF_ACKNOW; \
67      } \
68  }
                                                                        ─ tcp_input.c
```

Figure 27.15 TCP_REASS macro: add data to reassembly queue for connection.

2. the reassembly queue for the connection is empty (`seg_next` points to itself, not some mbuf), and

3. the connection is ESTABLISHED,

the following steps take place: a delayed ACK is scheduled, `rcv_nxt` is updated with the amount of data in the segment, the `flags` argument is set to `TH_FIN` if the FIN flag is set in the TCP header of the segment, two statistics are updated, the data is appended to the socket's receive buffer, and any receiving processes waiting for the socket are awakened.

The reason all three conditions must be true is that, first, if the data is out of order, it must be placed onto the connection's reassembly queue and the "preceding" segments must be received before anything can be passed to the process. Second, even if the data is in order, if there is out-of-order data already on the reassembly queue, there's a chance that the new segment might fill a hole, allowing the received segment and one or more segments on the queue to all be passed to the process. Third, it is OK for data to arrive with a SYN segment that establishes a connection, but that data cannot be passed to the process until the connection is ESTABLISHED—any such data is just added to the reassembly queue when it arrives.

64–67   If these three conditions are not all true, the `TCP_REASS` macro calls the function `tcp_reass` to add the segment to the reassembly queue. Since the segment is either out of order, or the segment might fill a hole from previously received out-of-order segments, an immediate ACK is scheduled. One important feature of TCP is that a receiver should generate an immediate ACK when an out-of-order segment is received. This aids the *fast retransmit* algorithm (Section 29.4).

Before looking at the code for the `tcp_reass` function, we need to explain what's done with the two port numbers in the TCP header in Figure 27.14, `ti_sport` and ti_dport. Once the TCP control block is located and tcp_reass is called, these two port numbers are no longer needed. Therefore, when a TCP segment is placed on a reassembly queue, the address of the corresponding mbuf is stored over these two port numbers. In Figure 27.14 this isn't needed, because the IP and TCP headers are in the data portion of the mbuf, so the dtom macro works. But recalling our discussion of m_pullup in Section 2.6, if the IP and TCP headers are in a cluster (as in Figure 2.16, which is the normal case for a full-sized TCP segment), the dtom macro doesn't work. We mentioned in that section that TCP stores its own back pointer from the TCP header to the mbuf, and that back pointer is stored over the two TCP port numbers.

Figure 27.16 shows an example of this technique with two out-of-order segments for a connection, each segment stored in an mbuf cluster. The head of the doubly linked list of out-of-order segments is the seg_next member of the control block for this connection. To simplify the figure we don't show the seg_prev pointer and the ti_next pointer of the last segment on the list.

The next expected sequence number is 1 (rcv_nxt) but we assume that segment was lost. The next two segments have been received, containing bytes 1461–4380, but they are out of order. The segments were placed into clusters by m_devget, as shown in Figure 2.16.

The first 32 bits of the TCP header contain a back pointer to the corresponding mbuf. This back pointer is used in the tcp_reass function, shown next.

tcp_reass Function

Figure 27.17 shows the first part of the tcp_reass function. The arguments are: tp, a pointer to the TCP control block for the received segment; ti, a pointer to the IP and TCP headers of the received segment; and m, a pointer to the mbuf chain for the received segment. As mentioned earlier, ti can point into the data area of the mbuf pointed to by m, or ti can point into a cluster.

69–83   We'll see that tcp_input calls tcp_reass with a null ti pointer when a SYN is acknowledged (Figures 28.20 and 29.2). This means the connection is now established, and any data that might have arrived with the SYN (which tcp_reass had to queue earlier) can now be passed to the application. Data that arrives with a SYN cannot be passed to the process until the connection is established. The label present is in Figure 27.23.

84–90   Go through the list of segments for this connection, starting at seg_next, to find the first one with a sequence number that is greater than the received sequence number (ti_seq). Note that the if statement is the entire body of the for loop.

Figure 27.18 shows an example with two out-of-order segments already on the queue when a new segment arrives. We show the pointer q pointing to the next segment on the list, the one with bytes 10–15. In this figure we also show the two pointers ti_next and ti_prev, the starting sequence number (ti_seq), the length (ti_len), and the sequence numbers of the data bytes. With the small segments we show, each segment is probably in a single mbuf, as in Figure 27.14.

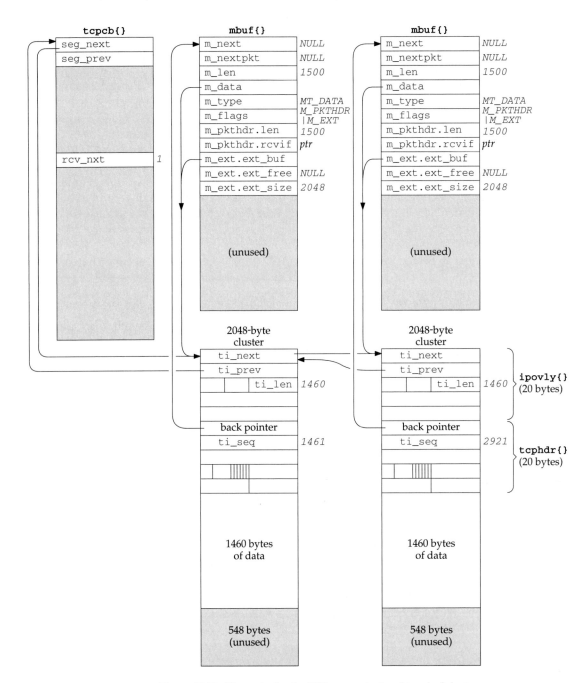

Figure 27.16   Two out-of-order TCP segments stored in mbuf clusters.

tcp_input.c

```
69 int
70 tcp_reass(tp, ti, m)
71 struct tcpcb *tp;
72 struct tcpiphdr *ti;
73 struct mbuf *m;
74 {
75     struct tcpiphdr *q;
76     struct socket *so = tp->t_inpcb->inp_socket;
77     int      flags;

78     /*
79      * Call with ti==0 after become established to
80      * force pre-ESTABLISHED data up to user socket.
81      */
82     if (ti == 0)
83         goto present;

84     /*
85      * Find a segment that begins after this one does.
86      */
87     for (q = tp->seg_next; q != (struct tcpiphdr *) tp;
88          q = (struct tcpiphdr *) q->ti_next)
89         if (SEQ_GT(q->ti_seq, ti->ti_seq))
90             break;
```

tcp_input.c

Figure 27.17   `tcp_reass` function: first part.

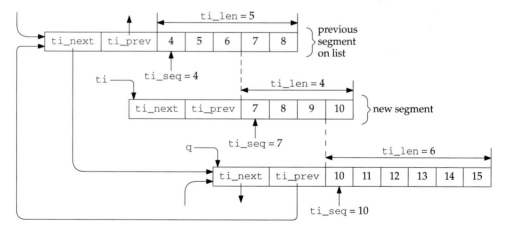

Figure 27.18   Example of TCP reassembly queue with overlapping segments.

The next part of `tcp_reass` is shown in Figure 27.19.

```
                                                                   tcp_input.c
91      /*
92       * If there is a preceding segment, it may provide some of
93       * our data already.  If so, drop the data from the incoming
94       * segment.  If it provides all of our data, drop us.
95       */
96      if ((struct tcpiphdr *) q->ti_prev != (struct tcpiphdr *) tp) {
97          int     i;
98          q = (struct tcpiphdr *) q->ti_prev;
99          /* conversion to int (in i) handles seq wraparound */
100         i = q->ti_seq + q->ti_len - ti->ti_seq;
101         if (i > 0) {
102             if (i >= ti->ti_len) {
103                 tcpstat.tcps_rcvduppack++;
104                 tcpstat.tcps_rcvdupbyte += ti->ti_len;
105                 m_freem(m);
106                 return (0);
107             }
108             m_adj(m, i);
109             ti->ti_len -= i;
110             ti->ti_seq += i;
111         }
112         q = (struct tcpiphdr *) (q->ti_next);
113     }
114     tcpstat.tcps_rcvoopack++;
115     tcpstat.tcps_rcvoobyte += ti->ti_len;
116     REASS_MBUF(ti) = m;              /* XXX */
                                                                   tcp_input.c
```

Figure 27.19 `tcp_reass` function: second part.

91–107   If there is a segment before the one pointed to by `q`, that segment may overlap the new segment. The pointer `q` is moved to the previous segment on the list (the one with bytes 4–8 in Figure 27.18) and the number of bytes of overlap is calculated and stored in `i`:

```
i = q->ti_seq + q->ti_len - ti->ti_seq;
  = 4 + 5 - 7
  = 2
```

If `i` is greater than 0, there is overlap, as we have in our example. If the number of bytes of overlap in the previous segment on the list (`i`) is greater than or equal to the size of the new segment, then all the data bytes in the new segment are already contained in the previous segment on the list. In this case the duplicate segment is discarded.

108–112   If there is only partial overlap (as there is in Figure 27.18), `m_adj` discards `i` bytes of data from the beginning of the new segment. The sequence number and length of the new segment are updated accordingly. `q` is moved to the next segment on the list. Figure 27.20 shows our example at this point.

116   The address of the mbuf `m` is stored in the TCP header, over the source and destination TCP ports. We mentioned earlier in this section that this provides a back pointer

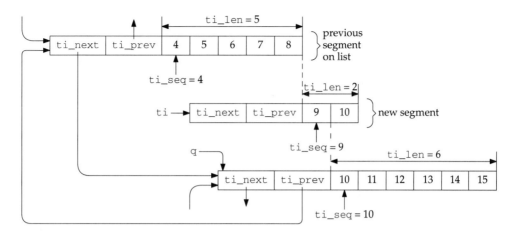

Figure 27.20 Update of Figure 27.18 after bytes 7 and 8 have been removed from new segment.

from the TCP header to the mbuf, in case the TCP header is stored in a cluster, meaning that the macro dtom won't work. The macro REASS_MBUF is

```
#define  REASS_MBUF(ti)   (*(struct mbuf **)&((ti)->ti_t))
```

ti_t is the tcphdr structure (Figure 24.12) and the first two members of the structure are the two 16-bit port numbers. The comment XXX in Figure 27.19 is because this hack assumes that a pointer fits in the 32 bits occupied by the two port numbers.

The third part of tcp_reass is shown in Figure 27.21. It removes any overlap from the next segment in the queue.

117–135   If there is another segment on the list, the number of bytes of overlap between the new segment and that segment is calculated in i. In our example we have

```
i = 9 + 2 - 10
  = 1
```

since byte number 10 overlaps the two segments.

Depending on the value of i, one of three conditions exists:

1. If i is less than or equal to 0, there is no overlap.
2. If i is less than the number of bytes in the next segment (q->ti_len), there is partial overlap and m_adj removes the first i bytes from the next segment on the list.
3. If i is greater than or equal to the number of bytes in the next segment, there is complete overlap and that next segment on the list is deleted.

136–139   The new segment is inserted into the reassembly list for this connection by insque. Figure 27.22 shows the state of our example at this point.

—— *tcp_input.c*
```
117      /*
118       * While we overlap succeeding segments trim them or,
119       * if they are completely covered, dequeue them.
120       */
121      while (q != (struct tcpiphdr *) tp) {
122          int     i = (ti->ti_seq + ti->ti_len) - q->ti_seq;
123          if (i <= 0)
124              break;
125          if (i < q->ti_len) {
126              q->ti_seq += i;
127              q->ti_len -= i;
128              m_adj(REASS_MBUF(q), i);
129              break;
130          }
131          q = (struct tcpiphdr *) q->ti_next;
132          m = REASS_MBUF((struct tcpiphdr *) q->ti_prev);
133          remque(q->ti_prev);
134          m_freem(m);
135      }

136      /*
137       * Stick new segment in its place.
138       */
139      insque(ti, q->ti_prev);
```
—— *tcp_input.c*

Figure 27.21   `tcp_reass` function: third part.

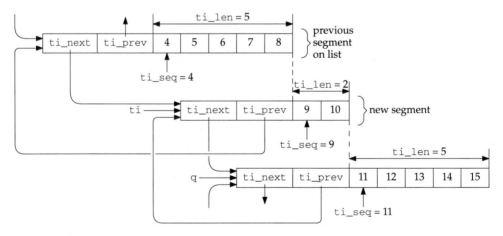

Figure 27.22   Update of Figure 27.20 after removal of all overlapping bytes.

Figure 27.23 shows the final part of `tcp_reass`. It passes the data to the process, if possible.

```
                                                                 ── tcp_input.c
140   present:
141     /*
142      * Present data to user, advancing rcv_nxt through
143      * completed sequence space.
144      */
145     if (TCPS_HAVERCVDSYN(tp->t_state) == 0)
146         return (0);
147     ti = tp->seg_next;
148     if (ti == (struct tcpiphdr *) tp || ti->ti_seq != tp->rcv_nxt)
149         return (0);
150     if (tp->t_state == TCPS_SYN_RECEIVED && ti->ti_len)
151         return (0);
152     do {
153         tp->rcv_nxt += ti->ti_len;
154         flags = ti->ti_flags & TH_FIN;
155         remque(ti);
156         m = REASS_MBUF(ti);
157         ti = (struct tcpiphdr *) ti->ti_next;
158         if (so->so_state & SS_CANTRCVMORE)
159             m_freem(m);
160         else
161             sbappend(&so->so_rcv, m);
162     } while (ti != (struct tcpiphdr *) tp && ti->ti_seq == tp->rcv_nxt);
163     sorwakeup(so);
164     return (flags);
165 }
                                                                 ── tcp_input.c
```

Figure 27.23 `tcp_reass` function: fourth part.

145–146   If the connection has not received a SYN (i.e., it is in the LISTEN or SYN_SENT state), data cannot be passed to the process and the function returns. When this function is called by TCP_REASS, the return value of 0 is stored in the `flags` argument to the macro. This can have the side effect of clearing the FIN flag. We'll see that this side effect is a possibility when TCP_REASS is invoked in Figure 29.22, and the received segment contains a SYN, FIN, and data (not a typical segment, but valid).

147–149   `ti` starts at the first segment on the list. If the list is empty, or if the starting sequence number of the first segment on the list (`ti->ti_seq`) does not equal the next receive sequence number (`rcv_nxt`), the function returns a value of 0. If the second condition is true, there is still a hole in the received data starting with the next expected sequence number. For instance, in our example (Figure 27.22), if the segment with bytes 4–8 is the first on the list but `rcv_nxt` equals 2, bytes 2 and 3 are still missing, so bytes 4–15 cannot be passed to the process. The return of 0 turns off the FIN flag (if set), because one or more data segments are still missing, so a received FIN cannot be processed yet.

150–151   If the state is SYN_RCVD and the length of the segment is nonzero, the function returns a value of 0. If both of these conditions are true, the socket is a listening socket that has received in-order data with the SYN. The data is left on the connection's queue, waiting for the three-way handshake to complete.

152-164   This loop starts with the first segment on the list (which is known to be in order) and appends it to the socket's receive buffer. `rcv_nxt` is incremented by the number of bytes in the segment. The loop stops when the list is empty or when the sequence number of the next segment on the list is out of order (i.e., there is a hole in the sequence space). When the loop terminates, the `flags` variable (which becomes the return value of the function) is 0 or `TH_FIN`, depending on whether the final segment placed in the socket's receive buffer has the FIN flag set or not.

After all the mbufs have been placed onto the socket's receive buffer, `sorwakeup` wakes any process waiting for data to be received on the socket.

27.10 `tcp_trace` Function

In `tcp_output`, before sending a segment to IP for output, we saw the following call to `tcp_trace` in Figure 26.32:

```
if (so->so_options & SO_DEBUG)
    tcp_trace(TA_OUTPUT, tp->t_state, tp, ti, 0);
```

This call adds a record to a circular buffer in the kernel that can be examined with the `trpt(8)` program. Additionally, if the kernel is compiled with `TCPDEBUG` defined, and if the variable `tcpconsdebug` is nonzero, information is output on the system console.

> Any process can set the `SO_DEBUG` socket option for a TCP socket, causing the information to be stored in the kernel's circular buffer. But `trpt` must read the kernel memory (`/dev/kmem`) to fetch this information, and this often requires special privileges.
>
> The `SO_DEBUG` socket option can be set for any type of socket (e.g., UDP or raw IP), but TCP is the only protocol that looks at the option.

The information saved by the kernel is a `tcp_debug` structure, shown in Figure 27.24.

```
                                                                    ─ tcp_debug.h
35 struct tcp_debug {
36     n_time   td_time;          /* iptime(): ms since midnight, UTC */
37     short    td_act;           /* TA_xxx value (Figure 27.25) */
38     short    td_ostate;        /* old state */
39     caddr_t  td_tcb;           /* addr of TCP connection block */
40     struct tcpiphdr td_ti;     /* IP and TCP headers */
41     short    td_req;           /* PRU_xxx value for TA_USER */
42     struct tcpcb td_cb;        /* TCP connection block */
43 };

53 #define TCP_NDEBUG 100
54 struct tcp_debug tcp_debug[TCP_NDEBUG];
55 int      tcp_debx;
                                                                    ─ tcp_debug.h
```

Figure 27.24   `tcp_debug` structure.

35-43   This is a large structure (196 bytes), since it contains two other structures: the `tcpiphdr` structure with the IP and TCP headers; and the `tcpcb` structure, the entire TCP control block. Since the entire TCP control block is saved, any variable in the control block can be printed by `trpt`. Also, if `trpt` doesn't print the variable we're interested in, we can modify the source code (it is available with the Net/3 release) to print whatever information we would like from the control block. The RTT variables in Figure 25.28 were obtained using this technique.

53–55   We also show the declaration of the array `tcp_debug`, which is used as the circular buffer. The index into the array (`tcp_debx`) is initialized to 0. This array occupies almost 20,000 bytes.

There are only four calls to `tcp_trace` in the kernel. Each call stores a different value in the `td_act` member of the structure, as shown in Figure 27.25.

td_act	Description	Reference
TA_DROP	from `tcp_input`, when input segment is dropped	Figure 29.27
TA_INPUT	after input processing complete, before call to `tcp_output`	Figure 29.26
TA_OUTPUT	before calling `ip_output` to send segment	Figure 26.32
TA_USER	from `tcp_usrreq`, after processing PRU_*xxx* request	Figure 30.1

Figure 27.25 `td_act` values and corresponding call to `tcp_trace`.

Figure 27.27 shows the main body of the `tcp_trace` function. We omit the code that outputs directly to the console.

48–133   `ostate` is the old state of the connection, when the function was called. By saving this value and the new state of the connection (which is in the control block) we can see the state transition that occurred. In Figure 27.25, TA_OUTPUT doesn't change the state of the connection, but the other three calls can change the state.

Sample Output

Figure 27.26 shows the first four lines of `tcpdump` output corresponding to the three-way handshake and the first data segment from the example in Section 25.12. (Appendix A of Volume 1 provides additional details on the `tcpdump` output format.)

```
1   0.0                     bsdi.1025 > vangogh.discard: S 20288001:20288001(0)
                                                         win 4096 <mss 512>

2   0.362719 (0.3627)       vangogh.discard > bsdi.1025: S 3202722817:3202722817(0)
                                                         ack 20288002 win 8192
                                                         <mss 512>

3   0.364316 (0.0016)       bsdi.1025 > vangogh.discard: . ack 1 win 4096

4   0.415859 (0.0515)       bsdi.1025 > vangogh.discard: . 1:513(512) ack 1 win 4096
```

Figure 27.26 `tcpdump` output from example in Figure 25.28.

Figure 27.28 shows the corresponding output from `trpt`.

> This output contains a few changes from the normal `trpt` output. The 32-bit decimal sequence numbers are printed as unsigned values (`trpt` incorrectly prints them as signed numbers). Some values printed by `trpt` in hexadecimal have been output in decimal. The values from `t_rtt` through `t_rxtcur` were added to `trpt` by the authors, for Figure 25.28.

```
                                                                    ─── tcp_debug.c
48 void
49 tcp_trace(act, ostate, tp, ti, req)
50 short   act, ostate;
51 struct tcpcb *tp;
52 struct tcpiphdr *ti;
53 int     req;
54 {
55     tcp_seq seq, ack;
56     int     len, flags;
57     struct tcp_debug *td = &tcp_debug[tcp_debx++];

58     if (tcp_debx == TCP_NDEBUG)
59         tcp_debx = 0;              /* circle back to start */

60     td->td_time = iptime();
61     td->td_act = act;
62     td->td_ostate = ostate;
63     td->td_tcb = (caddr_t) tp;
64     if (tp)
65         td->td_cb = *tp;           /* structure assignment */
66     else
67         bzero((caddr_t) & td->td_cb, sizeof(*tp));
68     if (ti)
69         td->td_ti = *ti;           /* structure assignment */
70     else
71         bzero((caddr_t) & td->td_ti, sizeof(*ti));
72     td->td_req = req;

73 #ifdef TCPDEBUG
74     if (tcpconsdebug == 0)
75         return;
```

```
                       /* output information on console */
```

```
132 #endif
133 }
                                                                    ─── tcp_debug.c
```

Figure 27.27   tcp_trace function: save information in kernel's circular buffer.

At time 953738 the SYN is sent. Notice that only the lower 6 digits of the millisecond time are output—it would take 8 digits to represent 1 minute before midnight. The ending sequence number that is output is wrong (20288005). Four bytes are sent with the SYN, but these are the MSS option, not data. The retransmit timer is 6 seconds (REXMT) and the keepalive timer is 75 seconds (KEEP). These timer values are in 500-ms ticks. The value of 1 for t_rtt means this segment is being timed for an RTT measurement.

This SYN segment is sent in response to the process calling connect. One millisecond later the trace record for this system call is added to the kernel's buffer. Even though the call to connect generates the SYN segment, since the call to tcp_trace

```
953738 SYN_SENT: output 20288001:20288005(4) @0 (win=4096)
         <SYN> -> SYN_SENT
         rcv_nxt 0, rcv_wnd 0
         snd_una 20288001, snd_nxt 20288002, snd_max 20288002
         snd_wl1 0, snd_wl2 0, snd_wnd 0
         REXMT=12 (t_rxtshift=0), KEEP=150
         t_rtt=1, t_srtt=0, t_rttvar=24, t_rxtcur=12

953739 CLOSED: user CONNECT -> SYN_SENT
         rcv_nxt 0, rcv_wnd 0
         snd_una 20288001, snd_nxt 20288002, snd_max 20288002
         snd_wl1 0, snd_wl2 0, snd_wnd 0
         REXMT=12 (t_rxtshift=0), KEEP=150
         t_rtt=1, t_srtt=0, t_rttvar=24, t_rxtcur=12

954103 SYN_SENT: input 3202722817:3202722817(0) @20288002 (win=8192)
         <SYN,ACK> -> ESTABLISHED
         rcv_nxt 3202722818, rcv_wnd 4096
         snd_una 20288002, snd_nxt 20288002, snd_max 20288002
         snd_wl1 3202722818, snd_wl2 20288002, snd_wnd 8192
         KEEP=14400
         t_rtt=0, t_srtt=16, t_rttvar=4, t_rxtcur=6

954103 ESTABLISHED: output 20288002:20288002(0) @3202722818 (win=4096)
         <ACK> -> ESTABLISHED
         rcv_nxt 3202722818, rcv_wnd 4096
         snd_una 20288002, snd_nxt 20288002, snd_max 20288002
         snd_wl1 3202722818, snd_wl2 20288002, snd_wnd 8192
         KEEP=14400
         t_rtt=0, t_srtt=16, t_rttvar=4, t_rxtcur=6

954153 ESTABLISHED: output 20288002:20288514(512) @3202722818 (win=4096)
         <ACK> -> ESTABLISHED
         rcv_nxt 3202722818, rcv_wnd 4096
         snd_una 20288002, snd_nxt 20288514, snd_max 20288514
         snd_wl1 3202722818, snd_wl2 20288002, snd_wnd 8192
         REXMT=6 (t_rxtshift=0), KEEP=14400
         t_rtt=1, t_srtt=16, t_rttvar=4, t_rxtcur=6
```

Figure 27.28   trpt output from example in Figure 25.28.

appears after processing the PRU_CONNECT request, the two trace records appear backward in the buffer. Also, when the process called connect, the connection state was CLOSED, and it changes to SYN_SENT. Nothing else changes from the first trace record to this one.

The third trace record, at time 954103, occurs 365 ms after the first. (tcpdump shows a 362.7 ms difference.) This is how the values in the column "actual delta (ms)" in Figure 25.28 were computed. The connection state changes from SYN_SENT to ESTABLISHED when the segment with a SYN and an ACK is received. The RTT estimators are updated because the segment being timed was acknowledged.

The fourth trace record is the third segment of the three-way handshake: the ACK of the other end's SYN. Since this segment contains no data, it is not timed (rtt is 0).

After the ACK has been sent at time 954103, the `connect` system call returns to the process, which then calls `write` to send data. This generates TCP output, shown in trace record 5 at time 954153, 50 ms after the three-way handshake is complete. 512 bytes of data are sent, starting with sequence number 20288002. The retransmission timer is set to 3 seconds and the segment is timed.

This output is caused by an application `write`. Although we don't show any more trace records, the next four are from `PRU_SEND` requests. The first `PRU_SEND` request generates the output of the first 512-byte segment that we show, but the other three do not cause output, since the connection has just started and is in slow start. Four trace records are generated because the system used for this example uses a TCP send buffer of 4096 and a cluster size of 1024. Once the send buffer is full, the process is put to sleep.

27.11 Summary

This chapter has covered a wide range of TCP functions that we'll encounter in the following chapters.

TCP connections can be aborted by sending an RST or they can be closed down gracefully, by sending a FIN and waiting for the four-way exchange of segments to complete.

Eight variables are stored in each routing table entry, three of which are updated when a connection is closed and six of which can be used later when a new connection is established. This lets the kernel keep track of certain variables, such as the RTT estimators and the slow start threshold, between successive connections to the same destination. The system administrator can also set and lock some of these variables, such as the MTU, receive pipe size, and send pipe size, that affect TCP connections to that destination.

TCP is tolerant of received ICMP errors—none cause Net/3 to terminate an established connection. This handling of ICMP errors by Net/3 differs from earlier Berkeley releases.

Received TCP segments can arrive out of order and can contain duplicate data, and TCP must handle these anomalies. We saw that a reassembly queue is maintained for each connection, and this holds the out-of-order segments along with segments that arrive before they can be passed to the application.

Finally we looked at the type of information saved by the kernel when the `SO_DEBUG` socket option is enabled for a TCP socket. This trace information can be a useful diagnostic tool in addition to programs such as `tcpdump`.

Exercises

27.1   Why is the `errno` value 0 for the last row in Figure 27.1?

27.2   What is the maximum value that can be stored in `rmx_rtt`?

27.3   To save the route information in Figure 27.3 for a given host, we enter a route into the routing table by hand for this destination. We then run the FTP client to send data to this host, making certain we send enough data, as described with Figure 27.4. But after terminating the FTP client we look at the routing table, and all the values for this host are still 0. What's happening?

28

TCP Input

28.1 Introduction

TCP input processing is the largest piece of code that we examine in this text. The function `tcp_input` is about 1100 lines of code. The processing of incoming segments is not complicated, just long and detailed. Many implementations, including the one in Net/3, closely follow the input event processing steps in RFC 793, which spell out in detail how to respond to the various input segments, based on the current state of the connection.

The `tcp_input` function is called by `ipintr` (through the `pr_input` function in the protocol switch table) when a datagram is received with a protocol field of TCP. `tcp_input` executes at the software interrupt level.

The function is so long that we divide its discussion into two chapters. Figure 28.1 outlines the processing steps in `tcp_input`. This chapter discusses the steps through RST processing, and the next chapter starts with ACK processing.

The first few steps are typical: validate the input segment (checksum, length, etc.) and locate the PCB for this connection. Given the length of the remainder of the function, however, an attempt is made to bypass all this logic with an algorithm called *header prediction* (Section 28.4). This algorithm is based on the assumption that segments are not typically lost or reordered, hence for a given connection TCP can often guess what the next received segment will be. If the header prediction algorithm works, notice that the function returns. This is the fast path through `tcp_input`.

The slow path through the function ends up at the label `dodata`, which tests a few flags and calls `tcp_output` if a segment should be sent in response to the received segment.

```
void
tcp_input()
{
    checksum TCP header and data;
findpcb:
    locate PCB for segment;
    if (not found)
        goto dropwithreset;

    reset idle time to 0 and keepalive timer to 2 hours;

    process options if not LISTEN state;

    if (packet matched by header prediction) {
        completely process received segment;
        return;
    }

    switch (tp->t_state) {
    case TCPS_LISTEN:
        if SYN flag set, accept new connection request;
        goto trimthenstep6;

    case TCPS_SYN_SENT:
        if ACK of our SYN, connection completed;
trimthenstep6:
        trim any data not within window;
        goto step6;
    }

    process RFC 1323 timestamp;

    check if some data bytes are within the receive window;

    trim data segment to fit within window;

    if (RST flag set) {
        process depending on state;
        goto drop;
    }                                   /* Chapter 28 finishes here */

    if (ACK flag set) {        /* Chapter 29 starts here */
        if (SYN_RCVD state)
            passive open or simultaneous open complete;
        if (duplicate ACK)
            fast recovery algorithm;
        update RTT estimators if segment timed;
        open congestion window;
        remove ACKed data from send buffer;
        change state if in FIN_WAIT_1, CLOSING, or LAST_ACK state;
    }

step6:
    update window information;

    process URG flag;
```

```
dodata:
    process data in segment, add to reassembly queue;

    if (FIN flag is set)
        process depending on state;

    if (SO_DEBUG socket option)
        tcp_trace(TA_INPUT);

    if (need output || ACK now)
        tcp_output();
    return;

dropafterack:
    tcp_output() to generate ACK;
    return;

dropwithreset:
    tcp_respond() to generate RST;
    return;

drop:
    if (SO_DEBUG socket option)
        tcp_trace(TA_DROP);
    return;
}
```

Figure 28.1 Summary of TCP input processing steps.

There are also three labels at the end of the function that are jumped to when errors occur: `dropafterack`, `dropwithreset`, and `drop`. The term *drop* means to drop the segment being processed, not drop the connection, but when an RST is sent by `dropwithreset` it normally causes the connection to be dropped.

The only other branching in the function occurs when a valid SYN is received in either the LISTEN or SYN_SENT states, at the `switch` following header prediction. When the code at `trimthenstep6` finishes, it jumps to `step6`, which continues the normal flow.

28.2 Preliminary Processing

Figure 28.2 shows the declarations and the initial processing of the received TCP segment.

Get IP and TCP headers in first mbuf

170–204   The argument `iphlen` is the length of the IP header, including possible IP options. If the length is greater than 20 bytes, options are present, and `ip_stripoptions` discards the options. TCP ignores all IP options other than a source route, which is saved specially by IP (Section 9.6) and fetched later by TCP in Figure 28.7. If the number of bytes in the first mbuf in the chain is less than the size of the combined IP/TCP header (40 bytes), `m_pullup` moves the first 40 bytes into the first mbuf.

```
                                                                    ───── tcp_input.c
170 void
171 tcp_input(m, iphlen)
172 struct mbuf *m;
173 int     iphlen;
174 {
175     struct tcpiphdr *ti;
176     struct inpcb *inp;
177     caddr_t optp = NULL;
178     int     optlen;
179     int     len, tlen, off;
180     struct tcpcb *tp = 0;
181     int     tiflags;
182     struct socket *so;
183     int     todrop, acked, ourfinisacked, needoutput = 0;
184     short   ostate;
185     struct in_addr laddr;
186     int     dropsocket = 0;
187     int     iss = 0;
188     u_long  tiwin, ts_val, ts_ecr;
189     int     ts_present = 0;

190     tcpstat.tcps_rcvtotal++;
191     /*
192      * Get IP and TCP header together in first mbuf.
193      * Note: IP leaves IP header in first mbuf.
194      */
195     ti = mtod(m, struct tcpiphdr *);
196     if (iphlen > sizeof(struct ip))
197             ip_stripoptions(m, (struct mbuf *) 0);
198     if (m->m_len < sizeof(struct tcpiphdr)) {
199         if ((m = m_pullup(m, sizeof(struct tcpiphdr))) == 0) {
200             tcpstat.tcps_rcvshort++;
201             return;
202         }
203         ti = mtod(m, struct tcpiphdr *);
204     }
                                                                    ───── tcp_input.c
```

Figure 28.2 tcp_input function: declarations and preliminary processing.

The next piece of code, shown in Figure 28.3, verifies the TCP checksum and offset field.

Verify TCP checksum

205–217   tlen is the TCP length, the number of bytes following the IP header. Recall that IP has already subtracted the IP header length from ip_len. The variable len is then set to the length of the IP datagram, the number of bytes to be checksummed, including the pseudo-header. The fields in the pseudo-header are set, as required for the checksum calculation, as shown in Figure 23.19.

Verify TCP offset field

218–228   The TCP offset field, ti_off, is the number of 32-bit words in the TCP header, including any TCP options. It is multiplied by 4 (to become the byte offset of the first

```
                                                              ── tcp_input.c
205    /*
206     * Checksum extended TCP header and data.
207     */
208    tlen = ((struct ip *) ti)->ip_len;
209    len = sizeof(struct ip) + tlen;
210    ti->ti_next = ti->ti_prev = 0;
211    ti->ti_x1 = 0;
212    ti->ti_len = (u_short) tlen;
213    HTONS(ti->ti_len);
214    if (ti->ti_sum = in_cksum(m, len)) {
215        tcpstat.tcps_rcvbadsum++;
216        goto drop;
217    }
218    /*
219     * Check that TCP offset makes sense,
220     * pull out TCP options and adjust length.      XXX
221     */
222    off = ti->ti_off << 2;
223    if (off < sizeof(struct tcphdr) || off > tlen) {
224        tcpstat.tcps_rcvbadoff++;
225        goto drop;
226    }
227    tlen -= off;
228    ti->ti_len = tlen;
                                                              ── tcp_input.c
```

Figure 28.3 `tcp_input` function: verify TCP checksum and offset field.

data byte in the TCP segment) and checked for sanity. It must be greater than or equal to the size of the standard TCP header (20) and less than or equal to the TCP length.

The byte offset of the first data byte is subtracted from the TCP length, leaving `tlen` with the number of bytes of data in the segment (possibly 0). This value is stored back into the TCP header, in the variable `ti_len`, and will be used throughout the function.

Figure 28.4 shows the next part of processing: handling of certain TCP options.

Get headers plus option into first mbuf

230–236   If the byte offset of the first data byte is greater than 20, TCP options are present. `m_pullup` is called, if necessary, to place the standard IP header, standard TCP header, and any TCP options in the first mbuf in the chain. Since the maximum size of these three pieces is 80 bytes (20 + 20 + 40), they all fit into the first packet header mbuf on the chain.

> Since the only way `m_pullup` can fail here is when fewer than 20 plus `off` bytes are in the IP datagram, and since the TCP checksum has already been verified, we expect this call to `m_pullup` never to fail. Unfortunately the counter `tcps_rcvshort` is also shared by the call to `m_pullup` in Figure 28.2, so looking at the counter doesn't tell us which call failed. Nevertheless, Figure 24.5 shows that after receiving almost 9 million TCP segments, this counter is 0.

```
                                                                        ── tcp_input.c
229    if (off > sizeof(struct tcphdr)) {
230        if (m->m_len < sizeof(struct ip) + off) {
231            if ((m = m_pullup(m, sizeof(struct ip) + off)) == 0) {
232                tcpstat.tcps_rcvshort++;
233                return;
234            }
235            ti = mtod(m, struct tcpiphdr *);
236        }
237        optlen = off - sizeof(struct tcphdr);
238        optp = mtod(m, caddr_t) + sizeof(struct tcpiphdr);
239        /*
240         * Do quick retrieval of timestamp options ("options
241         * prediction?").  If timestamp is the only option and it's
242         * formatted as recommended in RFC 1323 Appendix A, we
243         * quickly get the values now and not bother calling
244         * tcp_dooptions(), etc.
245         */
246        if ((optlen == TCPOLEN_TSTAMP_APPA ||
247             (optlen > TCPOLEN_TSTAMP_APPA &&
248              optp[TCPOLEN_TSTAMP_APPA] == TCPOPT_EOL)) &&
249            *(u_long *) optp == htonl(TCPOPT_TSTAMP_HDR) &&
250            (ti->ti_flags & TH_SYN) == 0) {
251            ts_present = 1;
252            ts_val = ntohl(*(u_long *) (optp + 4));
253            ts_ecr = ntohl(*(u_long *) (optp + 8));
254            optp = NULL;            /* we've parsed the options */
255        }
256    }
                                                                        ── tcp_input.c
```

Figure 28.4   `tcp_input` function: handle certain TCP options.

Process timestamp option quickly

237–255   `optlen` is the number of bytes of options, and `optp` is a pointer to the first option byte. If the following three conditions are all true, only the timestamp option is present and it is in the desired format:

1. (a) The TCP option length equals 12 (`TCPOLEN_TSTAMP_APPA`), or (b) the TCP option length is greater than 12 and `optp[12]` equals the end-of-option byte.

2. The first 4 bytes of options equals `0x0101080a` (`TCPOPT_TSTAMP_HDR`, which we described in Section 26.6).

3. The SYN flag is not set (i.e., this segment is for an established connection, hence if a timestamp option is present, we know both sides have agreed to use the option).

If all three conditions are true, `ts_present` is set to 1; the two timestamp values are fetched and stored in `ts_val` and `ts_ecr`; and `optp` is set to null, since all the options have been parsed. The benefit in recognizing the timestamp option this way is to avoid calling the general option processing function `tcp_dooptions` later in the code. The general option processing function is OK for the other options that appear only with the

SYN segment that creates a connection (the MSS and window scale options), but when the timestamp option is being used, it will appear with almost every segment on an established connection, so the faster it can be recognized, the better.

The next piece of code, shown in Figure 28.5, locates the Internet PCB for the segment.

```
                                                                    ── tcp_input.c
257     tiflags = ti->ti_flags;

258     /*
259      * Convert TCP protocol specific fields to host format.
260      */
261     NTOHL(ti->ti_seq);
262     NTOHL(ti->ti_ack);
263     NTOHS(ti->ti_win);
264     NTOHS(ti->ti_urp);

265     /*
266      * Locate pcb for segment.
267      */
268 findpcb:
269     inp = tcp_last_inpcb;
270     if (inp->inp_lport != ti->ti_dport ||
271         inp->inp_fport != ti->ti_sport ||
272         inp->inp_faddr.s_addr != ti->ti_src.s_addr ||
273         inp->inp_laddr.s_addr != ti->ti_dst.s_addr) {
274         inp = in_pcblookup(&tcb, ti->ti_src, ti->ti_sport,
275                         ti->ti_dst, ti->ti_dport, INPLOOKUP_WILDCARD);
276         if (inp)
277             tcp_last_inpcb = inp;
278         ++tcpstat.tcps_pcbcachemiss;
279     }
                                                                    ── tcp_input.c
```

Figure 28.5 `tcp_input` function: locate Internet PCB for segment.

Save input flags and convert fields to host byte order

257–264 The received flags (SYN, FIN, etc.) are saved in the local variable `tiflags`, since they are referenced throughout the code. Two 16-bit values and the two 32-bit values in the TCP header are converted from network byte order to host byte order. The two 16-bit port numbers are left in network byte order, since the port numbers in the Internet PCB are in that order.

Locate Internet PCB

265–279 TCP maintains a one-behind cache (`tcp_last_inpcb`) containing the address of the PCB for the last received TCP segment. This is the same technique used by UDP. The comparison of the four elements in the socket pair is in the same order as done by `udp_input`. If the cache entry does not match, `in_pcblookup` is called, and the cache is set to the new PCB entry.

TCP does not have the same problem that we encountered with UDP: wildcard entries in the cache causing a high miss rate. The only time a TCP socket has a wildcard entry is for a server listening for connection requests. Once a connection is made, all

four entries in the socket pair contain nonwildcard values. In Figure 24.5 we see a cache
hit rate of almost 80%.

Figure 28.6 shows the next piece of code.

```
                                                                        tcp_input.c
280     /*
281      * If the state is CLOSED (i.e., TCB does not exist) then
282      * all data in the incoming segment is discarded.
283      * If the TCB exists but is in CLOSED state, it is embryonic,
284      * but should either do a listen or a connect soon.
285      */
286     if (inp == 0)
287         goto dropwithreset;
288     tp = intotcpcb(inp);
289     if (tp == 0)
290         goto dropwithreset;
291     if (tp->t_state == TCPS_CLOSED)
292         goto drop;

293     /* Unscale the window into a 32-bit value. */
294     if ((tiflags & TH_SYN) == 0)
295         tiwin = ti->ti_win << tp->snd_scale;
296     else
297         tiwin = ti->ti_win;
                                                                        tcp_input.c
```

Figure 28.6 `tcp_input` function: check if segment should be dropped.

Drop segment and generate RST

280–287   If the PCB was not found, the input segment is dropped and an RST is sent as a
reply. This is how TCP handles SYNs that arrive for a server that doesn't exist, for
example. Recall that UDP sends an ICMP port unreachable in this case.

288–290   If the PCB exists but a corresponding TCP control block does not exist, the socket is
probably being closed (`tcp_close` releases the TCP control block first, and then
releases the PCB), so the input segment is dropped and an RST is sent as a reply.

Silently drop segment

291–292   If the TCP control block exists, but the connection state is CLOSED, the socket has
been created and a local address and local port may have been assigned, but neither
`connect` nor `listen` has been called. The segment is dropped but nothing is sent as a
reply. This scenario can happen if a client catches a server between the server's call to
`bind` and `listen`. By silently dropping the segment and not replying with an RST, the
client's connection request should time out, causing the client to retransmit the SYN.

Unscale advertised window

293–297   If window scaling is to take place for this connection, both ends must specify their
send scale factor using the window scale option when the connection is established. If
the segment contains a SYN, the window scale factor has not been established yet, so
`tiwin` is copied from the value in the TCP header. Otherwise the 16-bit value in the
header is left shifted by the send scale factor into a 32-bit value.

The next piece of code, shown in Figure 28.7, does some preliminary processing if the socket debug option is enabled or if the socket is listening for incoming connection requests.

```
                                                                      ───── tcp_input.c
298         so = inp->inp_socket;
299         if (so->so_options & (SO_DEBUG | SO_ACCEPTCONN)) {
300             if (so->so_options & SO_DEBUG) {
301                 ostate = tp->t_state;
302                 tcp_saveti = *ti;
303             }
304             if (so->so_options & SO_ACCEPTCONN) {
305                 so = sonewconn(so, 0);
306                 if (so == 0)
307                     goto drop;
308                 /*
309                  * This is ugly, but ....
310                  *
311                  * Mark socket as temporary until we're
312                  * committed to keeping it.  The code at
313                  * 'drop' and 'dropwithreset' check the
314                  * flag dropsocket to see if the temporary
315                  * socket created here should be discarded.
316                  * We mark the socket as discardable until
317                  * we're committed to it below in TCPS_LISTEN.
318                  */
319                 dropsocket++;
320                 inp = (struct inpcb *) so->so_pcb;
321                 inp->inp_laddr = ti->ti_dst;
322                 inp->inp_lport = ti->ti_dport;
323 #if BSD>=43
324                 inp->inp_options = ip_srcroute();
325 #endif
326                 tp = intotcpcb(inp);
327                 tp->t_state = TCPS_LISTEN;

328                 /* Compute proper scaling value from buffer space */
329                 while (tp->request_r_scale < TCP_MAX_WINSHIFT &&
330                         TCP_MAXWIN << tp->request_r_scale < so->so_rcv.sb_hiwat)
331                     tp->request_r_scale++;
332             }
333         }
                                                                      ───── tcp_input.c
```

Figure 28.7   `tcp_input` function: handle debug option and listening sockets.

Save connection state and IP/TCP headers if socket debug option enabled

300–303   If the `SO_DEBUG` socket option is enabled the current connection state is saved (`ostate`) as well as the IP and TCP headers (`tcp_saveti`). These become arguments to `tcp_trace` when it is called at the end of the function (Figure 29.26).

Create new socket if segment arrives for listening socket

304–319   When a segment arrives for a listening socket (`SO_ACCEPTCONN` is enabled by `listen`), a new socket is created by `sonewconn`. This issues the protocol's

PRU_ATTACH request (Figure 30.2), which allocates an Internet PCB and a TCP control block. But more processing is needed before TCP commits to accept the connection request (such as the fundamental question of whether the segment contains a SYN or not), so the flag dropsocket is set, to cause the code at the labels drop and dropwithreset to discard the new socket if an error is encountered. If the received segment is OK, dropsocket is set back to 0 in Figure 28.17.

320–326   inp and tp point to the new socket that has been created. The local address and local port are copied from the destination address and destination port of the IP and TCP headers. If the input datagram contained a source route, it was saved by save_rte. TCP calls ip_srcroute to fetch that source route, saving a pointer to the mbuf containing the source route option in inp_options. This option is passed to ip_output by tcp_output, and the reverse route is used for datagrams sent on this connection.

327   The state of the new socket is set to LISTEN. If the received segment contains a SYN, the code in Figure 28.16 completes the connection request.

Compute window scale factor

328–331   The window scale factor that will be requested is calculated from the size of the receive buffer. 65535 (TCP_MAXWIN) is left shifted until the result exceeds the size of the receive buffer, or until the maximum window scale factor is encountered (14, TCP_MAX_WINSHIFT). Notice that the requested window scale factor is chosen based on the size of the listening socket's receive buffer. This means the process must set the SO_RCVBUF socket option before listening for incoming connection requests or it inherits the default value in tcp_recvspace.

> The maximum scale factor is 14, and 65535×2^{14} is 1,073,725,440. This is far greater than the maximum size of the receive buffer (262,144 in Net/3), so the loop should always terminate with a scale factor much less than 14. See Exercises 28.1 and 28.2.

Figure 28.8 shows the next part of TCP input processing.

```
                                                            ─── tcp_input.c
334     /*
335      * Segment received on connection.
336      * Reset idle time and keepalive timer.
337      */
338     tp->t_idle = 0;
339     tp->t_timer[TCPT_KEEP] = tcp_keepidle;

340     /*
341      * Process options if not in LISTEN state,
342      * else do it below (after getting remote address).
343      */
344     if (optp && tp->t_state != TCPS_LISTEN)
345         tcp_dooptions(tp, optp, optlen, ti,
346                       &ts_present, &ts_val, &ts_ecr);
                                                            ─── tcp_input.c
```

Figure 28.8 tcp_input function: reset idle time and keepalive timer, process options.

Reset idle time and keepalive timer

334–339   t_idle is set to 0 since a segment has been received on the connection. The keep-alive timer is also reset to 2 hours.

Process TCP options if not in LISTEN state

340–346   If options are present in the TCP header, and if the connection state is not LISTEN, tcp_dooptions processes the options. Recall that if only a timestamp option appears for an established connection, and that option is in the format recommended by Appendix A of RFC 1323, it was already processed in Figure 28.4 and optp was set to a null pointer. If the socket is in the LISTEN state, tcp_dooptions is called in Figure 28.17 after the peer's address has been recorded in the PCB, because processing the MSS option requires knowledge of the route that will be used to this peer.

28.3 tcp_dooptions Function

This function processes the five TCP options supported by Net/3 (Section 26.4): the EOL, NOP, MSS, window scale, and timestamp options. Figure 28.9 shows the first part of this function.

```
                                                              ─── tcp_input.c
1213 void
1214 tcp_dooptions(tp, cp, cnt, ti, ts_present, ts_val, ts_ecr)
1215 struct tcpcb *tp;
1216 u_char *cp;
1217 int      cnt;
1218 struct tcpiphdr *ti;
1219 int     *ts_present;
1220 u_long *ts_val, *ts_ecr;
1221 {
1222     u_short mss;
1223     int     opt, optlen;

1224     for (; cnt > 0; cnt -= optlen, cp += optlen) {
1225         opt = cp[0];
1226         if (opt == TCPOPT_EOL)
1227             break;
1228         if (opt == TCPOPT_NOP)
1229             optlen = 1;
1230         else {
1231             optlen = cp[1];
1232             if (optlen <= 0)
1233                 break;
1234         }
1235         switch (opt) {

1236         default:
1237             continue;
                                                              ─── tcp_input.c
```

Figure 28.9 tcp_dooptions function: handle EOL and NOP options.

Fetch option type and length

1213–1229   The options are scanned and an EOL (end-of-options) terminates the processing, causing the function to return. The length of a NOP is set to 1, since this option is not followed by a length byte (Figure 26.16). The NOP will be ignored via the `default` in the `switch` statement.

1230–1234   All other options have a length byte that is stored in `optlen`.

Any new options that are not understood by this implementation of TCP are also ignored. This occurs because:

1. Any new options defined in the future will have an option length (NOP and EOL are the only two without a length), and the `for` loop skips `optlen` bytes each time around the loop.

2. The `default` in the `switch` statement ignores unknown options.

The final part of `tcp_dooptions`, shown in Figure 28.10, handles the MSS, window scale, and timestamp options.

MSS option

1238–1246   If the length is not 4 (`TCPOLEN_MAXSEG`), or the segment does not have the SYN flag set, the option is ignored. Otherwise the 2 MSS bytes are copied into a local variable, converted to host byte order, and processed by `tcp_mss`. This has the side effect of setting the variable `t_maxseg` in the control block, the maximum number of bytes that can be sent in a segment to the other end.

Window scale option

1247–1254   If the length is not 3 (`TCPOLEN_WINDOW`), or the segment does not have the SYN flag set, the option is ignored. Net/3 remembers that it received a window scale request, and the scale factor is saved in `requested_s_scale`. Since only 1 byte is referenced by `cp[2]`, there can't be alignment problems. When the ESTABLISHED state is entered, if both ends requested window scaling, it is enabled.

Timestamp option

1255–1273   If the length is not 10 (`TCPOLEN_TIMESTAMP`), the segment is ignored. Otherwise the flag pointed to by `ts_present` is set to 1, and the two timestamps are saved in the variables pointed to by `ts_val` and `ts_ecr`. If the received segment contains the SYN flag, Net/3 remembers that a timestamp request was received. `ts_recent` is set to the received timestamp and `ts_recent_age` is set to `tcp_now`, the counter of the number of 500-ms clock ticks since the system was initialized.

28.4 Header Prediction

We now continue with the code in `tcp_input`, from where we left off in Figure 28.8.

Header prediction was put into the 4.3BSD Reno release by Van Jacobson. The only description of the algorithm, other than the source code we're about to examine, is in [Jacobson 1990b], which is a copy of three slides showing the code.

tcp_input.c

```
1238          case TCPOPT_MAXSEG:
1239              if (optlen != TCPOLEN_MAXSEG)
1240                  continue;
1241              if (!(ti->ti_flags & TH_SYN))
1242                  continue;
1243              bcopy((char *) cp + 2, (char *) &mss, sizeof(mss));
1244              NTOHS(mss);
1245              (void) tcp_mss(tp, mss);    /* sets t_maxseg */
1246              break;

1247          case TCPOPT_WINDOW:
1248              if (optlen != TCPOLEN_WINDOW)
1249                  continue;
1250              if (!(ti->ti_flags & TH_SYN))
1251                  continue;
1252              tp->t_flags |= TF_RCVD_SCALE;
1253              tp->requested_s_scale = min(cp[2], TCP_MAX_WINSHIFT);
1254              break;

1255          case TCPOPT_TIMESTAMP:
1256              if (optlen != TCPOLEN_TIMESTAMP)
1257                  continue;
1258              *ts_present = 1;
1259              bcopy((char *) cp + 2, (char *) ts_val, sizeof(*ts_val));
1260              NTOHL(*ts_val);
1261              bcopy((char *) cp + 6, (char *) ts_ecr, sizeof(*ts_ecr));
1262              NTOHL(*ts_ecr);

1263              /*
1264               * A timestamp received in a SYN makes
1265               * it ok to send timestamp requests and replies.
1266               */
1267              if (ti->ti_flags & TH_SYN) {
1268                  tp->t_flags |= TF_RCVD_TSTMP;
1269                  tp->ts_recent = *ts_val;
1270                  tp->ts_recent_age = tcp_now;
1271              }
1272              break;
1273          }
1274      }
1275 }
```

tcp_input.c

Figure 28.10   `tcp_dooptions` function: process MSS, window scale, and timestamp options.

Header prediction helps unidirectional data transfer by handling the two common cases.

1. If TCP is sending data, the next expected segment for this connection is an ACK for outstanding data.

2. If TCP is receiving data, the next expected segment for this connection is the next in-sequence data segment.

In both cases a small set of tests determines if the next expected segment has been received, and if so, it is handled in-line, faster than the general processing that follows later in this chapter and the next.

> [Partridge 1993] shows an even faster version of TCP header prediction from a research implementation developed by Van Jacobson.

Figure 28.11 shows the first part of header prediction.

```
                                                              ──────── tcp_input.c
347     /*
348      * Header prediction: check for the two common cases
349      * of a uni-directional data xfer.  If the packet has
350      * no control flags, is in-sequence, the window didn't
351      * change and we're not retransmitting, it's a
352      * candidate.  If the length is zero and the ack moved
353      * forward, we're the sender side of the xfer.  Just
354      * free the data acked & wake any higher-level process
355      * that was blocked waiting for space.  If the length
356      * is non-zero and the ack didn't move, we're the
357      * receiver side.  If we're getting packets in order
358      * (the reassembly queue is empty), add the data to
359      * the socket buffer and note that we need a delayed ack.
360      */
361     if (tp->t_state == TCPS_ESTABLISHED &&
362         (tiflags & (TH_SYN | TH_FIN | TH_RST | TH_URG | TH_ACK)) == TH_ACK &&
363          (!ts_present || TSTMP_GEQ(ts_val, tp->ts_recent)) &&
364          ti->ti_seq == tp->rcv_nxt &&
365          tiwin && tiwin == tp->snd_wnd &&
366          tp->snd_nxt == tp->snd_max) {

367          /*
368           * If last ACK falls within this segment's sequence numbers,
369           *  record the timestamp.
370           */
371          if (ts_present && SEQ_LEQ(ti->ti_seq, tp->last_ack_sent) &&
372              SEQ_LT(tp->last_ack_sent, ti->ti_seq + ti->ti_len)) {
373              tp->ts_recent_age = tcp_now;
374              tp->ts_recent = ts_val;
375          }
                                                              ──────── tcp_input.c
```

Figure 28.11 `tcp_input` function: header prediction, first part.

Check if segment is the next expected

347–366   The following six conditions must *all* be true for the segment to be the next expected data segment or the next expected ACK:

1. The connection state must be ESTABLISHED.

2. The following four control flags must not be on: SYN, FIN, RST, or URG. The ACK flag must be on. In other words, of the six TCP control flags, the ACK flag must be set, the four just listed must be cleared, and it doesn't matter whether

PSH is set or cleared. (Normally in the ESTABLISHED state the ACK flag is always on unless the RST flag is on.)

3. If the segment contains a timestamp option, the timestamp value from the other end (`ts_val`) must be greater than or equal to the previous timestamp received for this connection (`ts_recent`). This is basically the PAWS test, which we describe in detail in Section 28.7. If `ts_val` is less than `ts_recent`, this segment is out of order because it was sent before the most previous segment received on this connection. Since the other end always sends its timestamp clock (the global variable `tcp_now` in Net/3) as its timestamp value, the received timestamps of in-order segments always form a monotonic increasing sequence.

   The timestamp need not increase with every in-order segment. Indeed, on a Net/3 system that increments the timestamp clock (`tcp_now`) every 500 ms, multiple segments are often sent on a connection before that clock is incremented. Think of the timestamp and sequence number as forming a 64-bit value, with the sequence number in the low-order 32 bits and the timestamp in the high-order 32 bits. This 64-bit value always increases by at least 1 for every in-order segment (taking into account the modulo arithmetic).

4. The starting sequence number of the segment (`ti_seq`) must equal the next expected receive sequence number (`rcv_nxt`). If this test is false, then the received segment is either a retransmission or a segment beyond the one expected.

5. The window advertised by the segment (`tiwin`) must be nonzero, and must equal the current send window (`snd_wnd`). This means the window has not changed.

6. The next sequence number to send (`snd_nxt`) must equal the highest sequence number sent (`snd_max`). This means the last segment sent by TCP was not a retransmission.

Update `ts_recent` from received timestamp

367–375   If a timestamp option is present and if its value passes the test described with Figure 26.18, the received timestamp (`ts_val`) is saved in `ts_recent`. Also, the current time (`tcp_now`) is recorded in `ts_recent_age`.

> Recall our discussion with Figure 26.18 on how this test for a valid timestamp is flawed, and the correct test presented in Figure 26.20. In this header prediction code the TSTMP_GEQ test in Figure 26.20 is redundant, since it was already done as step 3 of the `if` test at the beginning of Figure 28.11.

The next part of the header prediction code, shown in Figure 28.12, is for the sender of unidirectional data: process an ACK for outstanding data.

Test for pure ACK

376–379   If the following four conditions are all true, this segment is a pure ACK.

tcp_input.c

```
376            if (ti->ti_len == 0) {
377                if (SEQ_GT(ti->ti_ack, tp->snd_una) &&
378                    SEQ_LEQ(ti->ti_ack, tp->snd_max) &&
379                    tp->snd_cwnd >= tp->snd_wnd) {
380                    /*
381                     * this is a pure ack for outstanding data.
382                     */
383                    ++tcpstat.tcps_predack;
384                    if (ts_present)
385                        tcp_xmit_timer(tp, tcp_now - ts_ecr + 1);
386                    else if (tp->t_rtt &&
387                            SEQ_GT(ti->ti_ack, tp->t_rtseq))
388                        tcp_xmit_timer(tp, tp->t_rtt);

389                    acked = ti->ti_ack - tp->snd_una;
390                    tcpstat.tcps_rcvackpack++;
391                    tcpstat.tcps_rcvackbyte += acked;
392                    sbdrop(&so->so_snd, acked);
393                    tp->snd_una = ti->ti_ack;
394                    m_freem(m);

395                    /*
396                     * If all outstanding data is acked, stop
397                     * retransmit timer, otherwise restart timer
398                     * using current (possibly backed-off) value.
399                     * If process is waiting for space,
400                     * wakeup/selwakeup/signal.  If data
401                     * is ready to send, let tcp_output
402                     * decide between more output or persist.
403                     */
404                    if (tp->snd_una == tp->snd_max)
405                        tp->t_timer[TCPT_REXMT] = 0;
406                    else if (tp->t_timer[TCPT_PERSIST] == 0)
407                        tp->t_timer[TCPT_REXMT] = tp->t_rxtcur;

408                    if (so->so_snd.sb_flags & SB_NOTIFY)
409                        sowwakeup(so);
410                    if (so->so_snd.sb_cc)
411                        (void) tcp_output(tp);
412                    return;
413                }
```

tcp_input.c

Figure 28.12 `tcp_input` function: header prediction, sender processing.

1. The segment contains no data (`ti_len` is 0).

2. The acknowledgment field in the segment (`ti_ack`) is greater than the largest unacknowledged sequence number (`snd_una`). Since this test is "greater than" and not "greater than or equal to," it is true only if some positive amount of data is acknowledged by the ACK.

3. The acknowledgment field in the segment (`ti_ack`) is less than or equal to the maximum sequence number sent (`snd_max`).

4. The congestion window (`snd_cwnd`) is greater than or equal to the current send window (`snd_wnd`). This test is true only if the window is fully open, that is, the connection is not in the middle of slow start or congestion avoidance.

Update RTT estimators

384–388   If the segment contains a timestamp option, or if a segment was being timed and the acknowledgment field is greater than the starting sequence number being timed, `tcp_xmit_timer` updates the RTT estimators.

Delete acknowledged bytes from send buffer

389–394   `acked` is the number of bytes acknowledged by the segment. `sbdrop` deletes those bytes from the send buffer. The largest unacknowledged sequence number (`snd_una`) is set to the acknowledgment field and the received mbuf chain is released. (Since the length is 0, there should be just a single mbuf containing the headers.)

Stop retransmit timer

395–407   If the received segment acknowledges all outstanding data (`snd_una` equals `snd_max`), the retransmission timer is turned off. Otherwise, if the persist timer is off, the retransmit timer is restarted using `t_rxtcur` as the timeout.

Recall that when `tcp_output` sends a segment, it sets the retransmit timer only if the timer is not currently enabled. If two segments are sent one right after the other, the timer is set when the first is sent, but not touched when the second is sent. But if an ACK is received only for the first segment, the retransmit timer must be restarted, in case the second was lost.

Awaken waiting processes

408–409   If a process must be awakened when the send buffer is modified, `sowwakeup` is called. From Figure 16.5, `SB_NOTIFY` is true if a process is waiting for space in the buffer, if a process is `select`ing on the buffer, or if a process wants the `SIGIO` signal for this socket.

Generate more output

410–411   If there is data in the send buffer, `tcp_output` is called because the sender's window has moved to the right. `snd_una` was just incremented and `snd_wnd` did not change, so in Figure 24.17 the entire window has shifted to the right.

The next part of header prediction, shown in Figure 28.13, is the receiver processing when the segment is the next in-sequence data segment.

Test for next in-sequence data segment

414–416   If the following four conditions are all true, this segment is the next expected data segment for the connection, and there is room in the socket buffer for the data.

1. The amount of data in the segment (`ti_len`) is greater than 0. This is the `else` portion of the `if` at the beginning of Figure 28.12.

2. The acknowledgment field (`ti_ack`) equals the largest unacknowledged sequence number. This means no data is acknowledged by this segment.

tcp_input.c
```
414              } else if (ti->ti_ack == tp->snd_una &&
415                          tp->seg_next == (struct tcpiphdr *) tp &&
416                          ti->ti_len <= sbspace(&so->so_rcv)) {
417                  /*
418                   * this is a pure, in-sequence data packet
419                   * with nothing on the reassembly queue and
420                   * we have enough buffer space to take it.
421                   */
422                  ++tcpstat.tcps_preddat;
423                  tp->rcv_nxt += ti->ti_len;
424                  tcpstat.tcps_rcvpack++;
425                  tcpstat.tcps_rcvbyte += ti->ti_len;
426                  /*
427                   * Drop TCP, IP headers and TCP options then add data
428                   * to socket buffer.
429                   */
430                  m->m_data += sizeof(struct tcpiphdr) + off - sizeof(struct tcphdr);
431                  m->m_len -= sizeof(struct tcpiphdr) + off - sizeof(struct tcphdr);
432                  sbappend(&so->so_rcv, m);
433                  sorwakeup(so);
434                  tp->t_flags |= TF_DELACK;
435                  return;
436              }
437          }
```
tcp_input.c

Figure 28.13   `tcp_input` function: header prediction, receiver processing.

3. The reassembly list of out-of-order segments for the connection is empty (`seg_next` equals `tp`).

4. There is room in the receive buffer for the data in the segment.

Complete processing of received data

423–435   The next expected receive sequence number (`rcv_nxt`) is incremented by the number of bytes of data. The IP header, TCP header, and any TCP options are dropped from the mbuf, and the mbuf chain is appended to the socket's receive buffer. The receiving process is awakened by `sorwakeup`. Notice that this code avoids calling the `TCP_REASS` macro, since the tests performed by that macro have already been performed by the header prediction tests. The delayed-ACK flag is set and the input processing is complete.

Statistics

How useful is header prediction? A few simple unidirectional transfers were run across a LAN (between `bsdi` and `svr4`, in both directions) and across a WAN (between `vangogh.cs.berkeley.edu` and `ftp.uu.net` in both directions). The `netstat` output (Figure 24.5) shows the two header prediction counters.

On the LAN, with no packet loss but a few duplicate ACKs, header prediction worked between 97 and 100% of the time. Across the WAN, however, the header prediction percentages dropped slightly to between 83 and 99%.

Realize that header prediction works on a per-connection basis, regardless how much additional TCP traffic is being received by the host, while the PCB cache works on a per-host basis. Even though lots of TCP traffic can cause PCB cache misses, if packets are not lost on a given connection, header prediction still works on that connection.

28.5 TCP Input: Slow Path Processing

We continue with the code that's executed if header prediction fails, the slow path through `tcp_input`. Figure 28.14 shows the next piece of code, which prepares the received segment for input processing.

```
                                                           ———— tcp_input.c
438     /*
439      * Drop TCP, IP headers and TCP options.
440      */
441     m->m_data += sizeof(struct tcpiphdr) + off - sizeof(struct tcphdr);
442     m->m_len -= sizeof(struct tcpiphdr) + off - sizeof(struct tcphdr);

443     /*
444      * Calculate amount of space in receive window,
445      * and then do TCP input processing.
446      * Receive window is amount of space in rcv queue,
447      * but not less than advertised window.
448      */
449     {
450         int     win;

451         win = sbspace(&so->so_rcv);
452         if (win < 0)
453             win = 0;
454         tp->rcv_wnd = max(win, (int) (tp->rcv_adv - tp->rcv_nxt));
455     }
                                                           ———— tcp_input.c
```

Figure 28.14 `tcp_input` function: drop IP and TCP headers.

Drop IP and TCP headers, including TCP options

438–442   The data pointer and length of the first mbuf in the chain are updated to skip over the IP header, TCP header, and any TCP options. Since `off` is the number of bytes in the TCP header, including options, the size of the normal TCP header (20) must be subtracted from the expression.

Calculate receive window

443–455   `win` is set to the number of bytes available in the socket's receive buffer. `rcv_adv` minus `rcv_nxt` is the current advertised window. The receive window is the maximum of these two values. The `max` is taken to ensure that the value is not less than the currently advertised window. Also, if the process has taken data out of the socket receive buffer since the window was last advertised, `win` could exceed the advertised window, so TCP accepts up to `win` bytes of data (even though the other end should not be sending more than the advertised window).

This value is calculated now, since the code later in this function must determine how much of the received data (if any) fits within the advertised window. Any received data outside the advertised window is dropped: data to the left of the window is duplicate data that has already been received and acknowledged, and data to the right should not be sent by the other end.

28.6 Initiation of Passive Open, Completion of Active Open

If the state is LISTEN or SYN_SENT, the code shown in this section is executed. The expected segment in these two states is a SYN, and we'll see that any other received segment is dropped.

Initiation of Passive Open

Figure 28.15 shows the processing when the connection is in the LISTEN state. In this code the variables `tp` and `inp` refer to the *new* socket that was created in Figure 28.7, not the server's listening socket.

```
                                                                              —— tcp_input.c
456      switch (tp->t_state) {

457          /*
458           * If the state is LISTEN then ignore segment if it contains an RST.
459           * If the segment contains an ACK then it is bad and send an RST.
460           * If it does not contain a SYN then it is not interesting; drop it.
461           * Don't bother responding if the destination was a broadcast.
462           * Otherwise initialize tp->rcv_nxt, and tp->irs, select an initial
463           * tp->iss, and send a segment:
464           *     <SEQ=ISS><ACK=RCV_NXT><CTL=SYN,ACK>
465           * Also initialize tp->snd_nxt to tp->iss+1 and tp->snd_una to tp->iss.
466           * Fill in remote peer address fields if not previously specified.
467           * Enter SYN_RECEIVED state, and process any other fields of this
468           * segment in this state.
469           */
470          case TCPS_LISTEN:{
471                  struct mbuf *am;
472                  struct sockaddr_in *sin;

473                  if (tiflags & TH_RST)
474                      goto drop;
475                  if (tiflags & TH_ACK)
476                      goto dropwithreset;
477                  if ((tiflags & TH_SYN) == 0)
478                      goto drop;
                                                                              —— tcp_input.c
```

Figure 28.15 `tcp_input` function: check if SYN received for listening socket.

Drop if RST, ACK, or no SYN

473–478   If the received segment contains the RST flag, it is dropped. If it contains an ACK, it is dropped and an RST is sent as the reply. (The initial SYN to open a connection is one of the few segments that does not contain an ACK.) If the SYN flag is not set, the segment is dropped. The remaining code for this `case` handles the reception of a SYN for a connection in the LISTEN state. The new state will be SYN_RCVD.

Figure 28.16 shows the next piece of code for this `case`.

```
                                                                    tcp_input.c
479         /*
480          * RFC1122 4.2.3.10, p. 104: discard bcast/mcast SYN
481          * in_broadcast() should never return true on a received
482          * packet with M_BCAST not set.
483          */
484         if (m->m_flags & (M_BCAST | M_MCAST) ||
485             IN_MULTICAST(ti->ti_dst.s_addr))
486             goto drop;

487         am = m_get(M_DONTWAIT, MT_SONAME);  /* XXX */
488         if (am == NULL)
489             goto drop;
490         am->m_len = sizeof(struct sockaddr_in);
491         sin = mtod(am, struct sockaddr_in *);
492         sin->sin_family = AF_INET;
493         sin->sin_len = sizeof(*sin);
494         sin->sin_addr = ti->ti_src;
495         sin->sin_port = ti->ti_sport;
496         bzero((caddr_t) sin->sin_zero, sizeof(sin->sin_zero));

497         laddr = inp->inp_laddr;
498         if (inp->inp_laddr.s_addr == INADDR_ANY)
499             inp->inp_laddr = ti->ti_dst;
500         if (in_pcbconnect(inp, am)) {
501             inp->inp_laddr = laddr;
502             (void) m_free(am);
503             goto drop;
504         }
505         (void) m_free(am);
                                                                    tcp_input.c
```

Figure 28.16 `tcp_input` function: process SYN for listening socket.

Drop if broadcast or multicast

479–486   If the packet was sent to a broadcast or multicast address, it is dropped. TCP is defined only for unicast applications. Recall that the `M_BCAST` and `M_MCAST` flags were set by `ether_input`, based on the destination hardware address of the frame. The `IN_MULTICAST` macro tests whether the IP address is a class D address.

> The comment reference to `in_broadcast` is because the Net/1 code (which did not support multicasting) called that function here, to check whether the destination IP address was a broadcast address. The setting of the `M_BCAST` and `M_MCAST` flags by `ether_input`, based on the destination hardware address, was introduced with Net/2.

This Net/3 code tests only whether the destination hardware address is a broadcast address, and does not call `in_broadcast` to test whether the destination IP address is a broadcast address, on the assumption that a packet should never be received with a destination IP address that is a broadcast address unless the packet was sent to the hardware broadcast address. This assumption is made to avoid calling `in_broadcast`. Nevertheless, if a Net/3 system receives a SYN destined for a broadcast IP address but a unicast hardware address, that segment will be processed by the code in Figure 28.16.

The destination address argument to `IN_MULTICAST` needs to be converted to host byte order.

Get mbuf for client's IP address and port

487–496   An mbuf is allocated to hold a `sockaddr_in` structure, and the structure is filled in with the client's IP address and port number. The IP address is copied from the source address in the IP header and the port number is copied from the source port number in the TCP header. This structure is used shortly to connect the server's PCB to the client, and then the mbuf is released.

> The XXX comment is probably because of the cost associated with obtaining an mbuf just for the call to `in_pcbconnect` that follows. But this is the slow processing path for TCP input. Figure 24.5 shows that less than 2% of all received segments execute this code.

Set local address in PCB

497–499   `laddr` is the local address bound to the socket. If the server bound the wildcard address to the socket (the normal scenario), the destination address from the IP header becomes the local address in the PCB. Note that the destination address from the IP header is used, regardless of which local interface the datagram was received on.

> Notice that `laddr` cannot be the wildcard address, because in Figure 28.7 it is explicitly set to the destination IP address from the received datagram.

Connect PCB to peer

500–505   `in_pcbconnect` connects the server's PCB to the client. This fills in the foreign address and foreign process in the PCB. The mbuf is then released.

The next piece of code, shown in Figure 28.17 completes the processing for this case.

Allocate and initialize IP and TCP header template

506–511   A template of the IP and TCP headers is created by `tcp_template`. The call to `sonewconn` in Figure 28.7 allocated the PCB and TCP control block for the new connection, but not the header template.

Process any TCP options

512–514   If TCP options are present, they are processed by `tcp_dooptions`. The call to this function in Figure 28.8 was done only if the connection was not in the LISTEN state. This function is called now for a listening socket, after the foreign address is set in the PCB, since the foreign address is used by the `tcp_mss` function: to get a route to the peer, and to check if the peer is "local" or "foreign" (with regard to the peer's network ID and subnet ID, used to select the MSS).

tcp_input.c
```
506                  tp->t_template = tcp_template(tp);
507                  if (tp->t_template == 0) {
508                      tp = tcp_drop(tp, ENOBUFS);
509                      dropsocket = 0; /* socket is already gone */
510                      goto drop;
511                  }
512                  if (optp)
513                      tcp_dooptions(tp, optp, optlen, ti,
514                                  &ts_present, &ts_val, &ts_ecr);
515                  if (iss)
516                      tp->iss = iss;
517                  else
518                      tp->iss = tcp_iss;
519                  tcp_iss += TCP_ISSINCR / 2;
520                  tp->irs = ti->ti_seq;
521                  tcp_sendseqinit(tp);
522                  tcp_rcvseqinit(tp);
523                  tp->t_flags |= TF_ACKNOW;
524                  tp->t_state = TCPS_SYN_RECEIVED;
525                  tp->t_timer[TCPT_KEEP] = TCPTV_KEEP_INIT;
526                  dropsocket = 0;      /* committed to socket */
527                  tcpstat.tcps_accepts++;
528                  goto trimthenstep6;
529              }
```
tcp_input.c

Figure 28.17 `tcp_input` function: complete processing of SYN received in LISTEN state.

Initialize ISS

515–519   The initial send sequence number is normally copied from the global `tcp_iss`, which is then incremented by 64,000 (`TCP_ISSINCR` divided by 2). If the local variable `iss` is nonzero, however, its value is used instead of `tcp_iss` to initialize the send sequence number for the connection.

The local `iss` variable is used for the following scenario.

- A server is started on port 27 on the host with an IP address of 128.1.2.3.

- A client on host 192.3.4.5 establishes a connection with this server. The client's ephemeral port is 3000. The socket pair on the server is {128.1.2.3, 27, 192.3.4.5, 3000}.

- The server actively closes the connection, putting this socket pair into the TIME_WAIT state. While the connection is in this state, the last receive sequence number is remembered in the TCP control block. Assume its value is 100,000.

- Before this connection leaves the TIME_WAIT state, a new SYN is received from the same port on the same client host (192.3.4.5, port 3000), which locates the PCB corresponding to the connection in the TIME_WAIT state, not the PCB for the listening server. Assume the sequence number of this new SYN is 200,000.

- Since this connection does not correspond to a listening socket in the LISTEN state, the code we just looked at is not executed. Instead, the code in Figure 28.29 is executed, and we'll see that it contains the following logic: if the sequence number of the new SYN (200,000) is greater than the last sequence number received from this client (100,000), then (1) the local variable iss is set to 100,000 plus 128,000, (2) the connection in the TIME_WAIT state is completely closed (its PCB and TCP control block are deleted), and (3) a jump is made to findpcb (Figure 28.5).

- This time the server's listening PCB will be located (assuming the listening server is still running), causing the code in this section to be executed. The local variable iss (now 228,000) is used in Figure 28.17 to initialize tcp_iss for the new connection.

This logic, which is allowed by RFC 1122, lets the same client and server reuse the same socket pair as long as the server does the active close. This also explains why the global variable tcp_iss is incremented by 64,000 each time any process issues a connect (Figure 30.4): to ensure that if a single client reopens the same connection with the same server repeatedly, a larger ISS is used each time, even if no data was transferred on the previous connection, and even if the 500-ms timer (which increments tcp_iss) has not expired since the last connection.

Initialize sequence number variables in control block

520–522   In Figure 28.17, the initial receive sequence number (irs) is copied from the sequence number in the SYN segment. The following two macros initialize the appropriate variables in the TCP control block:

```
#define  tcp_rcvseqinit(tp) \
    (tp)->rcv_adv = (tp)->rcv_nxt = (tp)->irs + 1

#define  tcp_sendseqinit(tp) \
    (tp)->snd_una = (tp)->snd_nxt = (tp)->snd_max = (tp)->snd_up = \
        (tp)->iss
```

The addition of 1 in the first macro is because the SYN occupies a sequence number.

ACK the SYN and change state

523–525   The TF_ACKNOW flag is set since the ACK of a SYN is not delayed. The connection state becomes SYN_RCVD, and the connection-establishment timer is set to 75 seconds (TCPTV_KEEP_INIT). Since the TF_ACKNOW flag is set, at the bottom of this function tcp_output will be called. Looking at Figure 24.16 we see that tcp_outflags will cause a segment with the SYN and ACK flags to be sent.

526–528   TCP is now committed to the new socket created in Figure 28.7, so the dropsocket flag is cleared. The code at trimthenstep6 is jumped to, to complete processing of the SYN segment. Remember that a SYN segment can contain data, although the data cannot be passed to the application until the connection enters the ESTABLISHED state.

Completion of Active Open

Figure 28.18 shows the first part of processing when the connection is in the SYN_SENT state. TCP is expecting to receive a SYN.

tcp_input.c
```
530             /*
531              * If the state is SYN_SENT:
532              *   if seg contains an ACK, but not for our SYN, drop the input.
533              *   if seg contains an RST, then drop the connection.
534              *   if seg does not contain SYN, then drop it.
535              * Otherwise this is an acceptable SYN segment
536              *   initialize tp->rcv_nxt and tp->irs
537              *   if seg contains ack then advance tp->snd_una
538              *   if SYN has been acked change to ESTABLISHED else SYN_RCVD state
539              *   arrange for segment to be acked (eventually)
540              *   continue processing rest of data/controls, beginning with URG
541              */
542         case TCPS_SYN_SENT:
543             if ((tiflags & TH_ACK) &&
544                 (SEQ_LEQ(ti->ti_ack, tp->iss) ||
545                  SEQ_GT(ti->ti_ack, tp->snd_max)))
546                 goto dropwithreset;
547             if (tiflags & TH_RST) {
548                 if (tiflags & TH_ACK)
549                     tp = tcp_drop(tp, ECONNREFUSED);
550                 goto drop;
551             }
552             if ((tiflags & TH_SYN) == 0)
553                 goto drop;
```
tcp_input.c

Figure 28.18 `tcp_input` function: check if SYN in response to active open.

Verify received ACK

530–546   When TCP sends a SYN in response to an active open by a process, we'll see in Figure 30.4 that the connection's `iss` is copied from the global `tcp_iss` and the macro `tcp_sendseqinit` (shown at the end of the previous section) is executed. Assuming the ISS is 365, Figure 28.19 shows the send sequence variables after the SYN is sent by `tcp_output`.

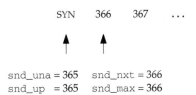

Figure 28.19 Send variables after SYN is sent with sequence number 365.

`tcp_sendseqinit` sets all four of these variables to 365, then Figure 26.31 increments two of them to 366 when the SYN segment is output. Therefore, if the received segment in Figure 28.18 contains an ACK, and if the acknowledgment field is less than or equal to `iss` (365) or greater than `snd_max` (366), the ACK is invalid, causing the segment to be dropped and an RST sent in reply. Notice that the received segment for a connection in the SYN_SENT state need not contain an ACK. It can contain only a SYN, which is called a *simultaneous open* (Figure 24.15), and is described shortly.

Process and drop RST segment

547–551   If the received segment contains an RST, it is dropped. But the ACK flag was checked first because receipt of an acceptable ACK (which was just verified) *and* an RST in response to a SYN is how the other end tells TCP that its connection request was refused. Normally this is caused by the server process not being started on the other host. In this case `tcp_drop` sets the socket's `so_error` variable, causing an error to be returned to the process that called `connect`.

Verify SYN flag set

552–553   If the SYN flag is not set in the received segment, it is dropped.

The remainder of this `case` handles the receipt of a SYN (with an optional ACK) in response to TCP's SYN. The next part of `tcp_input`, shown in Figure 28.20, continues processing the SYN.

Process ACK

554–558   If the received segment contains an ACK, `snd_una` is set to the acknowledgment field. In Figure 28.19, `snd_una` becomes 366, since 366 is the only acceptable value for the acknowledgment field. If `snd_nxt` is less than `snd_una` (which shouldn't happen, given Figure 28.19), `snd_nxt` is set to `snd_una`.

Turn off retransmission timer

559   The retransmission timer is turned off.

> This is a bug. This timer should be turned off only if the ACK flag is set, since the receipt of a SYN without an ACK is a simultaneous open, and doesn't mean the other end received TCP's SYN.

Initialize receive sequence numbers

560–562   The initial receive sequence number is copied from the sequence number of the received segment. The `tcp_rcvseqinit` macro (shown at the end of the previous section) initializes `rcv_adv` and `rcv_nxt` to the receive sequence number, plus 1. The `TF_ACKNOW` flag is set, causing `tcp_output` to be called at the bottom of this function. The segment it sends will contain `rcv_nxt` as the acknowledgment field (Figure 26.27), which acknowledges the SYN just received.

563–564   If the received segment contains an ACK, and if `snd_una` is greater than the ISS for the connection, the active open is complete, and the connection is established.

> This second test appears superfluous. At the beginning of Figure 28.20 snd_una was set to the received acknowledgment field if the ACK flag was on. Also the if following the case

tcp_input.c

```
554          if (tiflags & TH_ACK) {
555              tp->snd_una = ti->ti_ack;
556              if (SEQ_LT(tp->snd_nxt, tp->snd_una))
557                  tp->snd_nxt = tp->snd_una;
558          }
559          tp->t_timer[TCPT_REXMT] = 0;
560          tp->irs = ti->ti_seq;
561          tcp_rcvseqinit(tp);
562          tp->t_flags |= TF_ACKNOW;
563          if (tiflags & TH_ACK && SEQ_GT(tp->snd_una, tp->iss)) {
564              tcpstat.tcps_connects++;
565              soisconnected(so);
566              tp->t_state = TCPS_ESTABLISHED;
567              /* Do window scaling on this connection? */
568              if ((tp->t_flags & (TF_RCVD_SCALE | TF_REQ_SCALE)) ==
569                  (TF_RCVD_SCALE | TF_REQ_SCALE)) {
570                  tp->snd_scale = tp->requested_s_scale;
571                  tp->rcv_scale = tp->request_r_scale;
572              }
573              (void) tcp_reass(tp, (struct tcpiphdr *) 0,
574                          (struct mbuf *) 0);
575              /*
576               * if we didn't have to retransmit the SYN,
577               * use its rtt as our initial srtt & rtt var.
578               */
579              if (tp->t_rtt)
580                  tcp_xmit_timer(tp, tp->t_rtt);
581          } else
582              tp->t_state = TCPS_SYN_RECEIVED;
```

tcp_input.c

Figure 28.20 `tcp_input` function: process received SYN in response to an active open.

statement in Figure 28.18 verified that the received acknowledgment field is greater than the ISS. So at this point in the code, if the ACK flag is set, we're already guaranteed that `snd_una` is greater than the ISS.

Connection is established

565–566   `soisconnected` sets the socket state to connected, and the state of the TCP connection is set to ESTABLISHED.

Check for window scale option

567–572   If TCP sent the window scale option in its SYN and the received SYN also contains the option, the option is enabled and the two variables `snd_scale` and `rcv_scale` are set. Since the TCP control block is initialized to 0 by `tcp_newtcpcb`, these two variables correctly default to 0 if the window scale option is not used.

Pass any queued data to process

573–574   Since data can arrive for a connection before the connection is established, any such data is now placed in the receive buffer by calling `tcp_reass` with a null pointer as the second argument.

This test is unnecessary. In this piece of code, TCP has just received the SYN with an ACK that moves it from the SYN_SENT state to the ESTABLISHED state. If data appears with this received SYN segment, it isn't processed until the label `dodata` near the end of the function. If TCP just received a SYN without an ACK (a simultaneous open) but with some data, that data is handled later (Figure 29.2) when the ACK is received that moves the connection from the SYN_RCVD state to the ESTABLISHED state.

Although it is valid for data to accompany a SYN, and Net/3 handles this type of received segment correctly, Net/3 never generates such a segment.

Update RTT estimators

575–580   If the SYN that is ACKed was being timed, `tcp_xmit_timer` initializes the RTT estimators based on the measured RTT for the SYN.

TCP ignores a received timestamp option here, and checks only the `t_rtt` counter. TCP sends a timestamp in a SYN generated by an active open (Figure 26.24) and if the other end agrees to the option, the other end should echo the received timestamp in its SYN. (Net/3 echoes the received timestamp in a SYN in Figure 28.10.) This would allow TCP to use the received timestamp here, instead of `t_rtt`, but since both have the same precision (500 ms) there's no advantage in using the timestamp value. The real advantage in using the timestamp option, instead of the `t_rtt` counter, is with large pipes, when lots of segments are in flight at once, providing more RTT timings and (it is hoped) better estimators.

Simultaneous open

581–582   When TCP receives a SYN without an ACK in the SYN_SENT state, it is a simultaneous open and the connection moves to the SYN_RCVD state.

The next piece of code, shown in Figure 28.21, handles any data received with the SYN. The label `trimthenstep6` is also jumped to at the end of Figure 28.17.

```
                                                                    ─── tcp_input.c
583          trimthenstep6:
584              /*
585               * Advance ti->ti_seq to correspond to first data byte.
586               * If data, trim to stay within window,
587               * dropping FIN if necessary.
588               */
589              ti->ti_seq++;
590              if (ti->ti_len > tp->rcv_wnd) {
591                  todrop = ti->ti_len - tp->rcv_wnd;
592                  m_adj(m, -todrop);
593                  ti->ti_len = tp->rcv_wnd;
594                  tiflags &= ~TH_FIN;
595                  tcpstat.tcps_rcvpackafterwin++;
596                  tcpstat.tcps_rcvbyteafterwin += todrop;
597              }
598              tp->snd_wl1 = ti->ti_seq - 1;
599              tp->rcv_up = ti->ti_seq;
600              goto step6;
601          }
                                                                    ─── tcp_input.c
```

Figure 28.21   `tcp_input` function: common processing for receipt of SYN.

584–589   The sequence number of the segment is incremented by 1 to account for the SYN. If there is any data in the segment, $\texttt{ti\_seq}$ now contains the starting sequence number of the first byte of data.

Drop any received data that follows receive window

590–597 $\texttt{ti\_len}$ is the number of data bytes in the segment. If it is greater than the receive window, the excess data ($\texttt{ti\_len}$ minus $\texttt{rcv\_wnd}$) is dropped by $\texttt{m\_adj}$. The negative argument to this function causes the data to be trimmed from the end of the mbuf chain (Figure 2.20). $\texttt{ti\_len}$ is updated to be the new amount of data in the mbuf chain and in case the FIN flag was set, it is cleared. This is because the FIN would follow the final data byte, which was just discarded because it was outside the receive window.

> If too much data is received with a SYN, and if the SYN is in response to an active open, the other end received TCP's SYN, which contained a window advertisement. This means the other end ignored the advertised window and is exhibiting unsocial behavior. But if too much data accompanies a SYN performing an active open, the other end has not received a window advertisement, so it has to guess how much data can accompany its SYN.

Force update of window variables

598–599 $\texttt{snd\_wl1}$ is set the received sequence number minus 1. We'll see in Figure 29.15 that this causes the three window update variables, $\texttt{snd\_wnd}$, $\texttt{snd\_wl1}$, and $\texttt{snd\_wl2}$, to be updated. The receive urgent pointer ($\texttt{rcv\_up}$) is set to the received sequence number. A jump is made to $\texttt{step6}$, which refers to a step in RFC 793, and we cover this in Figure 29.15.

28.7 PAWS: Protection Against Wrapped Sequence Numbers

The next part of $\texttt{tcp\_input}$, shown in Figure 28.22, provides protection against wrapped sequence numbers: the PAWS algorithm from RFC 1323. Also recall our discussion of the timestamp option in Section 26.6.

Basic PAWS test

602–613 $\texttt{ts\_present}$ was set by $\texttt{tcp\_dooptions}$ if a timestamp option was present. If the following three conditions are all true, the segment is dropped:

1. the RST flag is not set (Exercise 28.8),

2. TCP has received a valid timestamp from this peer ($\texttt{ts\_recent}$ is nonzero), and

3. the received timestamp in this segment ($\texttt{ts\_val}$) is less than the previously received timestamp from this peer.

PAWS is built on the premise that the 32-bit timestamp values wrap around at a much lower frequency than the 32-bit sequence numbers, on a high-speed connection. Exercise 28.6 shows that even at the highest possible timestamp counter frequency (incrementing by 1 bit every millisecond), the sign bit of the timestamp wraps around only every 24 days. On a high-speed network such as a gigabit network, the sequence

```
                                                                        ─── tcp_input.c
602     /*
603      * States other than LISTEN or SYN_SENT.
604      * First check timestamp, if present.
605      * Then check that at least some bytes of segment are within
606      * receive window.  If segment begins before rcv_nxt,
607      * drop leading data (and SYN); if nothing left, just ack.
608      *
609      * RFC 1323 PAWS: If we have a timestamp reply on this segment
610      * and it's less than ts_recent, drop it.
611      */
612     if (ts_present && (tiflags & TH_RST) == 0 && tp->ts_recent &&
613         TSTMP_LT(ts_val, tp->ts_recent)) {

614         /* Check to see if ts_recent is over 24 days old.  */
615         if ((int) (tcp_now - tp->ts_recent_age) > TCP_PAWS_IDLE) {
616             /*
617              * Invalidate ts_recent.  If this segment updates
618              * ts_recent, the age will be reset later and ts_recent
619              * will get a valid value.  If it does not, setting
620              * ts_recent to zero will at least satisfy the
621              * requirement that zero be placed in the timestamp
622              * echo reply when ts_recent isn't valid.  The
623              * age isn't reset until we get a valid ts_recent
624              * because we don't want out-of-order segments to be
625              * dropped when ts_recent is old.
626              */
627             tp->ts_recent = 0;
628         } else {
629             tcpstat.tcps_rcvduppack++;
630             tcpstat.tcps_rcvdupbyte += ti->ti_len;
631             tcpstat.tcps_pawsdrop++;
632             goto dropafterack;
633         }
634     }
```
                                                                        ─── tcp_input.c

Figure 28.22   tcp_input function: process timestamp option.

number can wrap in 17 seconds (Section 24.3 of Volume 1). Therefore, if the received timestamp value is less than the most recent one from this peer, this segment is old and must be discarded (subject to the outdated timestamp test that follows). The packet might be discarded later in the input processing because the sequence number is "old," but PAWS is intended for high-speed connections where the sequence numbers can wrap quickly.

Notice that the PAWS algorithm is symmetric: it not only discards duplicate data segments but also discards duplicate ACKs. All received segments are subject to PAWS. Recall that the header prediction code also applied the PAWS test (Figure 28.11).

Check for outdated timestamp

614–627   There is a small possibility that the reason the PAWS test fails is because the connection has been idle for a long time. The received segment is not a duplicate; it is just that because the connection has been idle for so long, the peer's timestamp value has wrapped around when compared to the most recent timestamp from that peer.

Whenever `ts_recent` is copied from the timestamp in a received segment, `ts_recent_age` records the current time (`tcp_now`). If the time at which `ts_recent` was saved is more than 24 days ago, it is set to 0 to invalidate it. The constant `TCP_PAWS_IDLE` is defined to be $(24 \times 24 \times 60 \times 60 \times 2)$, the final 2 being the number of ticks per second. The received segment is not dropped in this case, since the problem is not a duplicated segment, but an outdated timestamp. See also Exercises 28.6 and 28.7.

Figure 28.23 shows an example of an outdated timestamp. The system on the left is a non-Net/3 system that increments its timestamp clock at the highest frequency allowed by RFC 1323: once every millisecond. The system on the right is a Net/3 system.

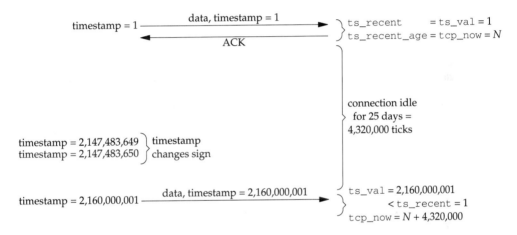

Figure 28.23   Example of outdated timestamp.

When the data segment arrives with a timestamp of 1, that value is saved in `ts_recent` and `ts_recent_age` is set to the current time (`tcp_now`), as shown in Figures 28.11 and 28.35. The connection is then idle for 25 days, during which time `tcp_now` will increase by 4,320,000 $(25 \times 24 \times 60 \times 60 \times 2)$. During these 25 days the other end's timestamp clock will increase by 2,160,000,000 $(25 \times 24 \times 60 \times 60 \times 1000)$. During this interval the timestamp "changes sign" with regard to the value 1, that is, 2,147,483,649 is greater than 1, but 2,147,483,650 is less than 1 (recall Figure 24.26). Therefore, when the data segment is received with a timestamp of 2,160,000,001, this value is less than `ts_recent` (1), when compared using the `TSTMP_LT` macro, so the PAWS test fails. But since `tcp_now` minus `ts_recent_age` is greater than 24 days, the reason for the failure is that the connection has been idle for more than 24 days, and the segment is accepted.

Drop duplicate segment

628–633   The segment is determined to be a duplicate based on the PAWS algorithm, and the timestamp is not outdated. It is dropped, after being acknowledged (since all duplicate segments are acknowledged).

Figure 24.5 shows a much smaller value for `tcps_pawsdrop` (22) than for
`tcps_rcvduppack` (46,953). This is probably because fewer systems support the timestamp
option today, causing most duplicate packets to be discarded by later tests in TCP's input processing instead of by PAWS.

28.8 Trim Segment so Data is Within Window

This section trims the received segment so that it contains only data that is within the
advertised window:

- duplicate data at the beginning of the received segment is discarded, and
- data that is beyond the end of the window is discarded from the end of the segment.

What remains is new data within the window. The code shown in Figure 28.24 checks if
there is any duplicate data at the beginning of the segment.

```
                                                                            tcp_input.c
635        todrop = tp->rcv_nxt - ti->ti_seq;
636        if (todrop > 0) {
637            if (tiflags & TH_SYN) {
638                tiflags &= ~TH_SYN;
639                ti->ti_seq++;
640                if (ti->ti_urp > 1)
641                    ti->ti_urp--;
642                else
643                    tiflags &= ~TH_URG;
644                todrop--;
645            }
                                                                            tcp_input.c
```

Figure 28.24   `tcp_input` function: check for duplicate data at beginning of segment.

Check if any duplicate data at front of segment

635–636   If the starting sequence number of the received segment (`ti_seq`) is less than the
next receive sequence number expected (`rcv_nxt`), data at the beginning of the segment is old and `todrop` will be greater than 0. These data bytes have already been
acknowledged and passed to the application (Figure 24.18).

Remove duplicate SYN

637–645   If the SYN flag is set, it refers to the first sequence number in the segment, which is
known to be old. The SYN flag is cleared and the starting sequence number of the segment is incremented by 1 to skip over the duplicate SYN. Furthermore, if the urgent offset in the received segment (`ti_urp`) is greater than 1, it must be decremented by 1,
since the urgent offset is relative to the starting sequence number, which was just incremented. If the urgent offset is 0 or 1, it is left alone, but in case it was 1, the URG flag is
cleared. Finally `todrop` is decremented by 1 (since the SYN occupies a sequence number).

The handling of duplicate data at the front of the segment continues in Figure 28.25.

tcp_input.c

```
646          if (todrop >= ti->ti_len) {
647              tcpstat.tcps_rcvduppack++;
648              tcpstat.tcps_rcvdupbyte += ti->ti_len;
649              /*
650               * If segment is just one to the left of the window,
651               * check two special cases:
652               * 1. Don't toss RST in response to 4.2-style keepalive.
653               * 2. If the only thing to drop is a FIN, we can drop
654               *    it, but check the ACK or we will get into FIN
655               *    wars if our FINs crossed (both CLOSING).
656               * In either case, send ACK to resynchronize,
657               * but keep on processing for RST or ACK.
658               */
659              if ((tiflags & TH_FIN && todrop == ti->ti_len + 1)
660                      ) {
661                  todrop = ti->ti_len;
662                  tiflags &= ~TH_FIN;
663                  tp->t_flags |= TF_ACKNOW;
664              } else {
665                  /*
666                   * Handle the case when a bound socket connects
667                   * to itself. Allow packets with a SYN and
668                   * an ACK to continue with the processing.
669                   */
670                  if (todrop != 0 || (tiflags & TH_ACK) == 0)
671                      goto dropafterack;
672              }
673          } else {
674              tcpstat.tcps_rcvpartduppack++;
675              tcpstat.tcps_rcvpartdupbyte += todrop;
676          }
677          m_adj(m, todrop);
678          ti->ti_seq += todrop;
679          ti->ti_len -= todrop;
680          if (ti->ti_urp > todrop)
681              ti->ti_urp -= todrop;
682          else {
683              tiflags &= ~TH_URG;
684              ti->ti_urp = 0;
685          }
686      }
```

tcp_input.c

Figure 28.25 `tcp_input` function: handle completely duplicate segment.

Check for entire duplicate packet

646–648   If the amount of duplicate data at the front of the segment is greater than or equal to the size of the segment, the entire segment is a duplicate.

Check for duplicate FIN

649–663   The next check is whether the FIN is duplicated. Figure 28.26 shows an example of this.

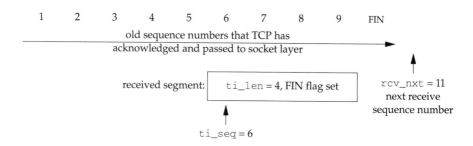

Figure 28.26   Example of duplicate packet with FIN flag set.

In this example `todrop` equals 5, which is greater than or equal to `ti_len` (4). Since the FIN flag is set and `todrop` equals `ti_len` plus 1, `todrop` is set to 4, the FIN flag is cleared, and the `TF_ACKNOW` flag is set, forcing an immediate ACK to be sent at the end of this function. This example also works for other segments if `ti_seq` plus `ti_len` equals 10.

> The code contains the comment regarding 4.2BSD keepalives. This code (another test within the `if` statement) is omitted.

Generate duplicate ACK

664–672   If `todrop` is nonzero (the completely duplicate segment contains data) or the ACK flag is not set, the segment is dropped and an ACK is generated by `dropafterack`. This normally occurs when the other end did not receive our ACK, causing the other end to retransmit the segment. TCP generates another ACK.

Handle simultaneous open or self-connect

664–672   This code also handles either a simultaneous open or a socket that connects to itself. We go over both of these scenarios in the next section. If `todrop` equals 0 (there is no data in the completely duplicate segment) and the ACK flag is set, processing is allowed to continue.

> This `if` statement is new with 4.4BSD. Earlier Berkeley-derived systems just had a jump to `dropafterack`. These systems could not handle either a simultaneous open or a socket connecting to itself.
>
> Nevertheless, the piece of code in this figure still has bugs, which we describe at the end of this section.

Update statistics for partial duplicate segments

673–676   This `else` clause is executed when `todrop` is less than the segment length: only part of the segment contains duplicate bytes.

Remove duplicate data and update urgent offset

677–685   The duplicate bytes are removed from the front of the mbuf chain by `m_adj` and the starting sequence number and length adjusted appropriately. If the urgent offset points to data still in the mbuf, it is also adjusted. Otherwise the urgent offset is set to 0 and the URG flag is cleared.

The next part of input processing, shown in Figure 28.27, handles data that arrives after the process has terminated.

————————————————————————————————— tcp_input.c
```
687    /*
688     * If new data is received on a connection after the
689     * user processes are gone, then RST the other end.
690     */
691    if ((so->so_state & SS_NOFDREF) &&
692        tp->t_state > TCPS_CLOSE_WAIT && ti->ti_len) {
693        tp = tcp_close(tp);
694        tcpstat.tcps_rcvafterclose++;
695        goto dropwithreset;
696    }
```
————————————————————————————————— tcp_input.c

Figure 28.27   `tcp_input` function: handle data that arrives after the process terminates.

687–696   If the socket has no descriptor referencing it, the process has closed the connection (the state is any one of the five with a value greater than CLOSE_WAIT in Figure 24.16), and there is data in the received segment, the connection is closed. The segment is then dropped and an RST is output.

Because of TCP's half-close, if a process terminates unexpectedly (perhaps it is terminated by a signal), when the kernel closes all open descriptors as part of process termination, a FIN is output by TCP. The connection moves into the FIN_WAIT_1 state. But the receipt of the FIN by the other end doesn't tell TCP whether this end performed a half-close or a full-close. If the other end assumes a half-close, and sends more data, it will receive an RST from the code in Figure 28.27.

The next piece of code, shown in Figure 28.29, removes any data from the end of the received segment that is beyond the right edge of the advertised window.

Calculate number of bytes beyond right edge of window

697–703   `todrop` contains the number of bytes of data beyond the right edge of the window. For example, in Figure 28.28, `todrop` would be $(6 + 5)$ minus $(4 + 6)$, or 1.

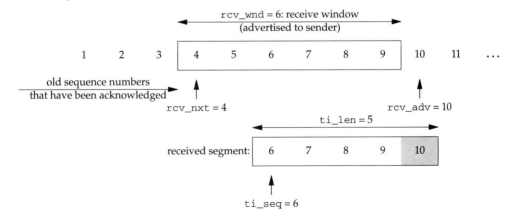

Figure 28.28   Example of received segment with data beyond right edge of window.

```
                                                                 ───────── tcp_input.c
697        /*
698         * If segment ends after window, drop trailing data
699         * (and PUSH and FIN); if nothing left, just ACK.
700         */
701        todrop = (ti->ti_seq + ti->ti_len) - (tp->rcv_nxt + tp->rcv_wnd);
702        if (todrop > 0) {
703            tcpstat.tcps_rcvpackafterwin++;
704            if (todrop >= ti->ti_len) {
705                tcpstat.tcps_rcvbyteafterwin += ti->ti_len;
706                /*
707                 * If a new connection request is received
708                 * while in TIME_WAIT, drop the old connection
709                 * and start over if the sequence numbers
710                 * are above the previous ones.
711                 */
712                if (tiflags & TH_SYN &&
713                    tp->t_state == TCPS_TIME_WAIT &&
714                    SEQ_GT(ti->ti_seq, tp->rcv_nxt)) {
715                    iss = tp->rcv_nxt + TCP_ISSINCR;
716                    tp = tcp_close(tp);
717                    goto findpcb;
718                }
719                /*
720                 * If window is closed can only take segments at
721                 * window edge, and have to drop data and PUSH from
722                 * incoming segments.  Continue processing, but
723                 * remember to ack.  Otherwise, drop segment
724                 * and ack.
725                 */
726                if (tp->rcv_wnd == 0 && ti->ti_seq == tp->rcv_nxt) {
727                    tp->t_flags |= TF_ACKNOW;
728                    tcpstat.tcps_rcvwinprobe++;
729                } else
730                    goto dropafterack;
731            } else
732                tcpstat.tcps_rcvbyteafterwin += todrop;
733            m_adj(m, -todrop);
734            ti->ti_len -= todrop;
735            tiflags &= ~(TH_PUSH | TH_FIN);
736        }
                                                                 ───────── tcp_input.c
```

Figure 28.29 `tcp_input` function: remove data beyond right edge of window.

Check for new incarnation of a connection in the TIME_WAIT state

704–718   If `todrop` is greater than or equal to the length of the segment, the entire segment
will be dropped. If the following three conditions are all true:

1. the SYN flag is set, and

2. the connection is in the TIME_WAIT state, and

3. the new starting sequence number is greater than the final sequence number for the connection,

this is a request for a new incarnation of a connection that was recently terminated and is currently in the TIME_WAIT state. This is allowed by RFC 1122, but the ISS for the new connection must be greater than the last sequence number used (`rcv_nxt`). TCP adds 128,000 (`TCP_ISSINCR`), which becomes the ISS when the code in Figure 28.17 is executed. The PCB and TCP control block for the connection in the TIME_WAIT state is discarded by `tcp_close`. A jump is made to `findpcb` (Figure 28.5) to locate the PCB for the listening server, assuming it is still running. The code in Figure 28.7 is then executed, creating a new socket for the new connection, and finally the code in Figures 28.16 and 28.17 will complete the new connection request.

Check for probe of closed window

719–728   If the receive window is closed (`rcv_wnd` equals 0) and the received segment starts at the left edge of the window (`rcv_nxt`), then the other end is probing TCP's closed window. An immediate ACK is sent as the reply, even though the ACK may still advertise a window of 0. Processing of the received segment also continues for this case.

Drop other segments that are completely outside window

729–730   The entire segment lies outside the window and it is not a window probe, so the segment is discarded and an ACK is sent as the reply. This ACK will contain the expected sequence number.

Handle segments that contain some valid data

731–735   The data to the right of the window is discarded from the mbuf chain by `m_adj` and `ti_len` is updated. In the case of a probe into a closed window, this discards all the data in the mbuf chain and sets `ti_len` to 0. Finally the FIN and PSH flags are cleared.

When to Drop an ACK

The code in Figure 28.25 has a bug that causes a jump to `dropafterack` in several cases when the code should fall through for further processing of the segment [Carlson 1993; Lanciani 1993]. In an actual scenario, when both ends of a connection had a hole in the data on the reassembly queue and both ends enter the persist state, the connection becomes deadlocked as both ends throw away perfectly good ACKs.

The fix is to simplify the code at the beginning of Figure 28.25. Instead of jumping to `dropafterack`, a completely duplicate segment causes the FIN flag to be turned off and an immediate ACK to be generated at the end of the function. Lines 646–676 in Figure 28.25 are replaced with the code shown in Figure 28.30. This code also corrects another bug present in the original code (Exercise 28.9).

```
if (todrop > ti->ti_len ||
    todrop == ti->ti_len && (tiflags & TH_FIN) == 0) {

    /*
     * Any valid FIN must be to the left of the window.
     * At this point the FIN must be a duplicate or
     * out of sequence; drop it.
     */
    tiflags &= ~TH_FIN;

    /*
     * Send an ACK to resynchronize and drop any data.
     * But keep on processing for RST or ACK.
     */
    tp->t_flags |= TF_ACKNOW;
    todrop = ti->ti_len;
    tcpstat.tcps_rcvdupbyte += todrop;
    tcpstat.tcps_rcvduppack++;

} else {
    tcpstat.tcps_rcvpartduppack++;
    tcpstat.tcps_rcvpartdupbyte += todrop;
}
```

Figure 28.30   Correction for lines 646–676 of Figure 28.25.

28.9 Self-Connects and Simultaneous Opens

It is instructive to look at the steps involved in a socket connecting to itself to see how the one-line fix to Figure 28.25 that was added to 4.4BSD allows this. This same fix allowed simultaneous opens to work, which wasn't handled correctly prior to 4.4BSD.

A process creates a socket and connects it to itself using the system calls: socket, bind a local port (say 3000), and then connect to this same port and some local IP address. If the connect succeeds, the socket is connected to itself: anything written to the socket can be read back from the socket. This is similar to a full-duplex pipe, but with a single descriptor instead of two descriptors. Although this is of limited use within a process, we'll see that the state transitions are the same as they are for a simultaneous open. If your system doesn't allow a socket to connect to itself, it probably doesn't handle simultaneous opens correctly either, and the latter are required by RFC 1122. Some people are surprised that a self-connect even works, given that a single Internet PCB and a single TCP control block are used. But TCP is a full-duplex, symmetric protocol and it maintains separate variables for each direction of data flow.

Figure 28.31 shows the send sequence space when the process calls connect. A SYN segment is sent and the state becomes SYN_SENT.

The SYN is received and processed in Figures 28.18 and 28.20, but since the SYN does not contain an ACK the resulting state is SYN_RCVD. According to the state transition diagram (Figure 24.15), this looks like a simultaneous open. Figure 28.32 shows the receive sequence space.

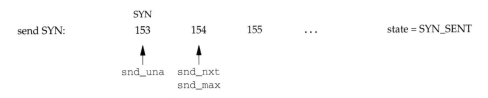

Figure 28.31 Send sequence space when SYN is sent for self-connect.

Figure 28.32 Receive sequence space after received SYN is processed.

Figure 28.20 sets the `TF_ACKNOW` flag and the segment generated by `tcp_output` will contain a SYN and an ACK (the `tcp_outflags` value in Figure 24.16). The sequence number of the SYN is 153 and the acknowledgment number is 154.

Nothing changes in the send sequence space from Figure 28.20, except the state is now SYN_SENT. Figure 28.33 shows the receive sequence space when the segment with the SYN and ACK is received.

Figure 28.33 Receive sequence space when segment with SYN and ACK received.

Since the connection state is SYN_RCVD, the segment is not processed by the active open or passive open code that we saw earlier in this chapter. It must be processed by the SYN_RCVD code that we'll examine in Figure 29.2. But it is first processed by Figure 28.24, and it looks like a duplicate SYN:

```
todrop = rcv_nxt - ti_seq
       = 154 - 153
       = 1
```

Since the SYN flag is set, the flag is cleared, `ti_seq` becomes 154, and `todrop` becomes 0. But the test at the beginning of Figure 28.25 is true, because `todrop` equals the length of the segment (0). The segment is counted as a duplicate packet and the code with the comment "Handle the case when a bound socket connects to itself" is executed. Earlier releases jumped to `dropafterack`, which skipped the necessary code to handle the SYN_RCVD state, preventing the connection from ever being established. Instead, Net/3 continues processing the received segment if `todrop` equals 0 and the

ACK flag is set, both of which are true in this example. This allows the SYN_RCVD processing to happen later in the function, which moves the connection to the ESTAB-LISHED state.

It is also interesting to look at the sequence of function calls in this self-connect. This is shown in Figure 28.34.

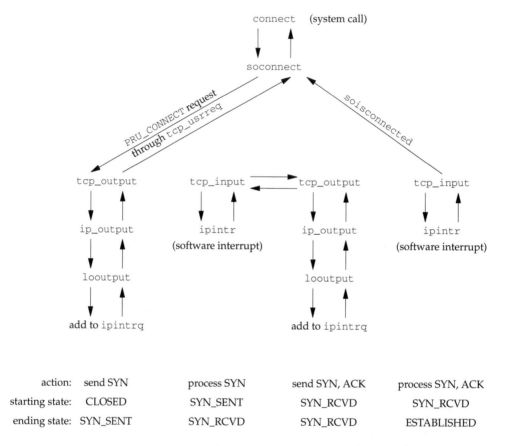

Figure 28.34   Sequence of function calls for self-connect.

The order of the operations goes from the left to the right. The steps that we show begin with the process calling `connect`. This issues the PRU_CONNECT request, which sends a SYN down the protocol stack. Since the segment is destined for the host's own IP address it is routed to the loopback interface, which adds the segment to `ipintrq` and generates a software interrupt.

The software interrupt causes `ipintr` to execute, which calls `tcp_input`. This function calls `tcp_output`, causing a SYN segment with an ACK to be sent down the protocol stack. It is again added to `ipintrq` by the loopback interface, and a software interrupt is generated. When this interrupt is processed by `ipintr`, the function `tcp_input` is called, and it moves the connection to the ESTABLISHED state.

28.10 Record Timestamp

The next part of `tcp_input`, shown in Figure 28.35, handles a received timestamp option.

```
                                                                  ──────── tcp_input.c
737     /*
738      * If last ACK falls within this segment's sequence numbers,
739      * record its timestamp.
740      */
741     if (ts_present && SEQ_LEQ(ti->ti_seq, tp->last_ack_sent) &&
742         SEQ_LT(tp->last_ack_sent, ti->ti_seq + ti->ti_len +
743                 ((tiflags & (TH_SYN | TH_FIN)) != 0))) {
744         tp->ts_recent_age = tcp_now;
745         tp->ts_recent = ts_val;
746     }
                                                                  ──────── tcp_input.c
```

Figure 28.35 `tcp_input` function: record timestamp.

737–746   If the received segment contains a timestamp, the timestamp value is saved in `ts_recent`. We discussed in Section 26.6 how this code used by Net/3 is flawed. The expression

        ((tiflags & (TH_SYN|TH_FIN)) != 0)

is 0 if neither of the two flags is set, or 1 if either is set. This effectively adds 1 to `ti_len` if either flag is set.

28.11 RST Processing

Figure 28.36 shows the `switch` statement to handle the RST flag, which depends on the connection state.

SYN_RCVD state

759–761   The socket's error code is set to `ECONNREFUSED`, and a jump is made a few lines forward to close the socket.

This state can be entered from two directions. Normally it is entered from the LISTEN state, after a SYN has been received. TCP replied with a SYN and an ACK but received an RST in reply. Perhaps the other end sent its SYN and then terminated before the reply arrived, causing it to send an RST. In this case the socket referred to by `so` is the new socket created by `sonewconn` in Figure 28.7. Since `dropsocket` will still be true, the socket is discarded at the label `drop`. The listening descriptor isn't affected at all. This is why we show the state transition from SYN_RCVD back to LISTEN in Figure 24.15.

This state can also be entered by a simultaneous open, after a process has called `connect`. In this case the socket error is returned to the process.

```
                                                                              tcp_input.c
747     /*
748      * If the RST bit is set examine the state:
749      *    SYN_RECEIVED state:
750      *  If passive open, return to LISTEN state.
751      *  If active open, inform user that connection was refused.
752      *    ESTABLISHED, FIN_WAIT_1, FIN_WAIT2, CLOSE_WAIT states:
753      *  Inform user that connection was reset, and close tcb.
754      *    CLOSING, LAST_ACK, TIME_WAIT states
755      * Close the tcb.
756      */
757     if (tiflags & TH_RST)
758         switch (tp->t_state) {

759         case TCPS_SYN_RECEIVED:
760             so->so_error = ECONNREFUSED;
761             goto close;

762         case TCPS_ESTABLISHED:
763         case TCPS_FIN_WAIT_1:
764         case TCPS_FIN_WAIT_2:
765         case TCPS_CLOSE_WAIT:
766             so->so_error = ECONNRESET;
767           close:
768             tp->t_state = TCPS_CLOSED;
769             tcpstat.tcps_drops++;
770             tp = tcp_close(tp);
771             goto drop;

772         case TCPS_CLOSING:
773         case TCPS_LAST_ACK:
774         case TCPS_TIME_WAIT:
775             tp = tcp_close(tp);
776             goto drop;
777         }
                                                                              tcp_input.c
```

Figure 28.36   `tcp_input` function: process RST flag.

Other states

762–777   The receipt of an RST in the ESTABLISHED, FIN_WAIT_1, FIN_WAIT_2, or CLOSE_WAIT states returns the error `ECONNRESET`. In the CLOSING, LAST_ACK, and TIME_WAIT state an error is not generated, since the process has closed the socket.

> Allowing an RST to terminate a connection in the TIME_WAIT state circumvents the reason this state exists. RFC 1337 [Braden 1992] discusses this and other forms of "TIME_WAIT assassination hazards" and recommends *not* letting an RST prematurely terminate the TIME_WAIT state. See Exercise 28.10 for an example.

The next piece of code, shown in Figure 28.37, checks for erroneous SYNs and verifies that an ACK is present.

```
                                                                    ── tcp_input.c
778    /*
779     * If a SYN is in the window, then this is an
780     * error and we send an RST and drop the connection.
781     */
782    if (tiflags & TH_SYN) {
783        tp = tcp_drop(tp, ECONNRESET);
784        goto dropwithreset;
785    }
786    /*
787     * If the ACK bit is off we drop the segment and return.
788     */
789    if ((tiflags & TH_ACK) == 0)
790        goto drop;
                                                                    ── tcp_input.c
```

Figure 28.37 `tcp_input` function: handle SYN-full and ACK-less segments.

778–785   If the SYN flag is still set, this is an error and the connection is dropped with the error ECONNRESET.

786–790   If the ACK flag is not set, the segment is dropped. The remainder of this function, which we continue in the next chapter, assumes the ACK flag is set.

28.12 Summary

This chapter has started our detailed look at TCP input. It continues in the next chapter.

The code in this chapter verifies the segment's checksum, processes any TCP options, handles SYNs that initiate or complete connection requests, trims excess data from the beginning or end of the segment, and processes the RST flag.

Header prediction is a successful attempt to handle common cases with the minimum amount of processing. Although the general processing steps that we've covered handle all possible cases (which they must), many segments are well behaved and the processing steps can be minimized.

Exercises

28.1   Given that the maximum size of a socket buffer is 262,144 in Net/3, what are the possible window scale shift factors calculated by Figure 28.7?

28.2   Given that the maximum size of a socket buffer is 262,144 in Net/3, what is the maximum throughput possible with a round-trip time of 60 ms? (*Hint*: See Figure 24.5 in Volume 1 and solve for the bandwidth.)

28.3   Why are the two timestamp values fetched using `bcopy` in Figure 28.10?

28.4   We mentioned in Section 26.6 that TCP correctly handles timestamp options in a format other than the one recommended in Appendix A of RFC 1323. While this is true, what is the penalty for not following the recommended format?

28.5   The PRU_ATTACH request allocates the PCB and the TCP control block, but doesn't call tcp_template to allocate the header template. Instead we saw in Figure 28.17 that the header template is allocated when the SYN arrives. Why doesn't the PRU_ATTACH request allocate this template?

28.6   Read RFC 1323 to determine why the limit of 24 days was chosen in Figure 28.22.

28.7   The comparison of tcp_now minus ts_recent_age to TCP_PAWS_IDLE in Figure 28.22 is also subject to sign bit wrap around, if the connection is idle for a period much longer than 24 days. With the 500-ms timestamp clock used by Net/3, when does this become a problem?

28.8   Read RFC 1323 to find out why RST segments are exempt from the PAWS test in Figure 28.22.

28.9   A client sends a SYN and the server responds with a SYN/ACK. The client moves to the ESTABLISHED state and responds with an ACK, but this ACK is lost. The server resends its SYN/ACK. Describe the processing steps when the client receives this duplicate SYN/ACK.

28.10   A client and server have an established connection and the server performs the active close. The connection terminates normally and the socket pair goes into the TIME_WAIT state on the server. Before this 2MSL wait expires on the server, the same client (i.e., the same socket pair on the client) sends a SYN to the server's socket pair but with a sequence number that is less than the ending sequence number from the previous incarnation of this connection. Describe what happens.

29

TCP Input (Continued)

29.1 Introduction

This chapter continues the discussion of TCP input processing, picking up where the previous chapter left off. Recall that the final test in Figure 28.37 was that either the ACK flag was set or, if not, the segment was dropped.

The ACK flag is handled, the window information is updated, the URG flag is processed, and any data in the segment is processed. Finally the FIN flag is processed and `tcp_output` is called, if required.

29.2 ACK Processing Overview

We begin this chapter with ACK processing, a summary of which is shown in Figure 29.1. The SYN_RCVD state is handled specially, followed by common processing for all remaining states. (Remember that a received ACK in either the LISTEN or SYN_SENT state was discussed in the previous chapter.) This is followed by special processing for the three states in which a received ACK causes a state transition, and for the TIME_WAIT state, in which the receipt of an ACK causes the 2MSL timer to be restarted.

29.3 Completion of Passive Opens and Simultaneous Opens

The first part of the ACK processing, shown in Figure 29.2, handles the SYN_RCVD state. As mentioned in the previous chapter, this handles the completion of a passive open (the common case) and also handles simultaneous opens and self-connects (the infrequent case).

```
    switch (tp->t_state) {

    case TCPS_SYN_RECEIVED:
        complete processing of passive open and process
            simultaneous open or self-connect;
        /* fall into ... */

    case TCPS_ESTABLISHED:
    case TCPS_FIN_WAIT_1:
    case TCPS_FIN_WAIT_2:
    case TCPS_CLOSE_WAIT:
    case TCPS_CLOSING:
    case TCPS_LAST_ACK:
    case TCPS_TIME_WAIT:
        process duplicate ACK;
        update RTT estimators;
        if all outstanding data ACKed, turn off retransmission timer;
        remove ACKed data from socket send buffer;

        switch (tp->t_state) {

        case TCPS_FIN_WAIT_1:
            if (FIN is ACKed) {
                move to FIN_WAIT_2 state;
                start FIN_WAIT_2 timer;
            }
            break;

        case TCPS_CLOSING:
            if (FIN is ACKed) {
                move to TIME_WAIT state;
                start TIME_WAIT timer;
            }
            break;

        case TCPS_LAST_ACK:
            if (FIN is ACKed)
                move to CLOSED state;
            break;

        case TCPS_TIME_WAIT:
            restart TIME_WAIT timer;
            goto dropafterack;
        }
    }
```

Figure 29.1   Summary of ACK processing.

Verify received ACK

801–806   For the ACK to acknowledge the SYN that was sent, it must be greater than
snd_una (which is set to the ISS for the connection, the sequence number of the SYN,
by tcp_sendseqinit) and less than or equal to snd_max. If so, the socket is marked
as connected and the state becomes ESTABLISHED.

```
                                                            ─────── tcp_input.c
791     /*
792      * Ack processing.
793      */
794     switch (tp->t_state) {

795         /*
796          * In SYN_RECEIVED state if the ack ACKs our SYN then enter
797          * ESTABLISHED state and continue processing, otherwise
798          * send an RST.
799          */
800     case TCPS_SYN_RECEIVED:
801         if (SEQ_GT(tp->snd_una, ti->ti_ack) ||
802             SEQ_GT(ti->ti_ack, tp->snd_max))
803             goto dropwithreset;
804         tcpstat.tcps_connects++;
805         soisconnected(so);
806         tp->t_state = TCPS_ESTABLISHED;
807         /* Do window scaling? */
808         if ((tp->t_flags & (TF_RCVD_SCALE | TF_REQ_SCALE)) ==
809             (TF_RCVD_SCALE | TF_REQ_SCALE)) {
810             tp->snd_scale = tp->requested_s_scale;
811             tp->rcv_scale = tp->request_r_scale;
812         }
813         (void) tcp_reass(tp, (struct tcpiphdr *) 0, (struct mbuf *) 0);
814         tp->snd_wl1 = ti->ti_seq - 1;
815         /* fall into ... */
                                                            ─────── tcp_input.c
```

Figure 29.2 `tcp_input` function: received ACK in SYN_RCVD state.

Since `soisconnected` wakes up the process that performed the passive open (normally a server), we see that this doesn't occur until the last of the three segments in the three-way handshake has been received. If the server is blocked in a call to `accept`, that call now returns; if the server is blocked in a call to `select` waiting for the listening descriptor to become readable, it is now readable.

Check for window scale option

807–812   If TCP sent a window scale option and received one, the send and receive scale factors are saved in the TCP control block. Otherwise the default values of `snd_scale` and `rcv_scale` in the TCP control block are 0 (no scaling).

Pass queued data to process

813   Any data queued for the connection can now be passed to the process. This is done by `tcp_reass` with a null pointer as the second argument. This data would have arrived with the SYN that moved the connection into the SYN_RCVD state.

814   `snd_wl1` is set to the received sequence number minus 1. We'll see in Figure 29.15 that this causes the three window update variables to be updated.

29.4   Fast Retransmit and Fast Recovery Algorithms

The next part of ACK processing, shown in Figure 29.3, handles duplicate ACKs and determines if TCP's fast retransmit and fast recovery algorithms [Jacobson 1990c] should come into play. The two algorithms are separate but are normally implemented together [Floyd 1994].

- The *fast retransmit* algorithm occurs when TCP deduces from a small number (normally 3) of consecutive duplicate ACKs that a segment has been lost and deduces the starting sequence number of the missing segment. The missing segment is retransmitted. The algorithm is mentioned in Section 4.2.2.21 of RFC 1122, which states that TCP may generate an immediate ACK when an out-of-order segment is received. We saw that Net/3 generates the immediate duplicate ACKs in Figure 27.15. This algorithm first appeared in the 4.3BSD Tahoe release and the subsequent Net/1 release. In these two implementations, after the missing segment was retransmitted, the slow start phase was entered.

- The *fast recovery* algorithm says that after the fast retransmit algorithm (that is, after the missing segment has been retransmitted), congestion avoidance but not slow start is performed. This is an improvement that allows higher throughput under moderate congestion, especially for large windows. This algorithm appeared in the 4.3BSD Reno release and the subsequent Net/2 release.

Net/3 implements both fast retransmit and fast recovery, as we describe shortly.

In the discussion of Figure 24.17 we noted that an acceptable ACK must be in the range

```
snd_una < acknowledgment field <= snd_max
```

This first test of the acknowledgment field compares it only to `snd_una`. The comparison against `snd_max` is in Figure 29.5. The reason for separating the tests is so that the following five tests can be applied to the received segment:

1. If the acknowledgment field is less than or equal to `snd_una`, and
2. the length of the received segment is 0, and
3. the advertised window (`tiwin`) has not changed, and
4. TCP has outstanding data that has not been acknowledged (the retransmission timer is nonzero), and
5. the received segment contains the biggest ACK TCP has seen (the acknowledgment field equals `snd_una`),

then this segment is a completely duplicate ACK. (Tests 1, 2, and 3 are in Figure 29.3; tests 4 and 5 are at the beginning of Figure 29.4.)

TCP counts the number of these duplicate ACKs that are received in a row (in the variable `t_dupacks`), and when the number reaches a threshold of 3 (`tcprexmtthresh`), the lost segment is retransmitted. This is the *fast retransmit* algorithm described in Section 21.7 of Volume 1. It works in conjunction with the code we

```
                                                                    ──── tcp_input.c
816          /*
817           * In ESTABLISHED state: drop duplicate ACKs; ACK out-of-range
818           * ACKs.  If the ack is in the range
819           *   tp->snd_una < ti->ti_ack <= tp->snd_max
820           * then advance tp->snd_una to ti->ti_ack and drop
821           * data from the retransmission queue.  If this ACK reflects
822           * more up-to-date window information we update our window information.
823           */
824      case TCPS_ESTABLISHED:
825      case TCPS_FIN_WAIT_1:
826      case TCPS_FIN_WAIT_2:
827      case TCPS_CLOSE_WAIT:
828      case TCPS_CLOSING:
829      case TCPS_LAST_ACK:
830      case TCPS_TIME_WAIT:

831          if (SEQ_LEQ(ti->ti_ack, tp->snd_una)) {
832              if (ti->ti_len == 0 && tiwin == tp->snd_wnd) {
833                  tcpstat.tcps_rcvdupack++;
834                  /*
835                   * If we have outstanding data (other than
836                   * a window probe), this is a completely
837                   * duplicate ack (ie, window info didn't
838                   * change), the ack is the biggest we've
839                   * seen and we've seen exactly our rexmt
840                   * threshold of them, assume a packet
841                   * has been dropped and retransmit it.
842                   * Kludge snd_nxt & the congestion
843                   * window so we send only this one
844                   * packet.
845                   *
846                   * We know we're losing at the current
847                   * window size so do congestion avoidance
848                   * (set ssthresh to half the current window
849                   * and pull our congestion window back to
850                   * the new ssthresh).
851                   *
852                   * Dup acks mean that packets have left the
853                   * network (they're now cached at the receiver)
854                   * so bump cwnd by the amount in the receiver
855                   * to keep a constant cwnd packets in the
856                   * network.
857                   */
                                                                    ──── tcp_input.c
```

Figure 29.3 tcp_input function: check for completely duplicate ACK.

saw in Figure 27.15: when TCP receives an out-of-order segment, it is required to generate an immediate duplicate ACK, telling the other end that a segment might have been lost and telling it the value of the next expected sequence number. The goal of the fast retransmit algorithm is for TCP to retransmit immediately what appears to be the missing segment, instead of waiting for the retransmission timer to expire. Figure 21.7 of Volume 1 gives a detailed example of how this algorithm works.

The receipt of a duplicate ACK also tells TCP that a packet has "left the network," because the other end had to receive an out-of-order segment to send the duplicate ACK. The *fast recovery* algorithm says that after some number of consecutive duplicate ACKs have been received, TCP should perform congestion avoidance (i.e., slow down) but need not wait for the pipe to empty between the two connection end points (slow start). The expression "a packet has left the network" means a packet has been received by the other end and has been added to the out-of-order queue for the connection. The packet is not still in transit somewhere between the two end points.

If only the first three tests shown earlier are true, the ACK is still a duplicate and is counted by the statistic `tcps_rcvdupack`, but the counter of the number of consecutive duplicate ACKs for this connection (`t_dupacks`) is reset to 0. If only the first test is true, the counter `t_dupacks` is reset to 0.

The remainder of the fast recovery algorithm is shown in Figure 29.4. When all five tests are true, the fast recovery algorithm processes the segment depending on the number of these consecutive duplicate ACKs that have been received.

1. `t_dupacks` equals 3 (`tcprexmtthresh`). Congestion avoidance is performed and the missing segment is retransmitted.

2. `t_dupacks` exceeds 3. Increase the congestion window and perform normal TCP output.

3. `t_dupacks` is less than 3. Do nothing.

Number of consecutive duplicate ACKs reaches threshold of 3

861–868   When `t_dupacks` reaches 3 (`tcprexmtthresh`), the value of `snd_nxt` is saved in `onxt` and the slow start threshold (`ssthresh`) is set to one-half the current congestion window, with a minimum value of two segments. This is what was done with the slow start threshold when the retransmission timer expired in Figure 25.27, but we'll see later in this piece of code that the fast recovery algorithm does not set the congestion window to one segment, as was done with the timeout.

Turn off retransmission timer

869–870   The retransmission timer is turned off and, in case a segment is currently being timed, `t_rtt` is set to 0.

Retransmit missing segment

871–873   `snd_nxt` is set to the starting sequence number of the segment that appears to have been lost (the acknowledgment field of the duplicate ACK) and the congestion window is set to one segment. This causes `tcp_output` to send only the missing segment. (This is shown by segment 63 in Figure 21.7 of Volume 1.)

Set congestion window

874–875   The congestion window is set to the slow start threshold plus the number of segments that the other end has cached. By *cached* we mean the number of out-of-order segments that the other end has received and generated duplicate ACKs for. These cannot be passed to the process at the other end until the missing segment (which was just

```
                                                        ─── tcp_input.c
858                 if (tp->t_timer[TCPT_REXMT] == 0 ||
859                     ti->ti_ack != tp->snd_una)
860                     tp->t_dupacks = 0;
861                 else if (++tp->t_dupacks == tcprexmtthresh) {
862                     tcp_seq onxt = tp->snd_nxt;
863                     u_int win =
864                         min(tp->snd_wnd, tp->snd_cwnd) / 2 /
865                             tp->t_maxseg;

866                     if (win < 2)
867                         win = 2;
868                     tp->snd_ssthresh = win * tp->t_maxseg;
869                     tp->t_timer[TCPT_REXMT] = 0;
870                     tp->t_rtt = 0;
871                     tp->snd_nxt = ti->ti_ack;
872                     tp->snd_cwnd = tp->t_maxseg;
873                     (void) tcp_output(tp);
874                     tp->snd_cwnd = tp->snd_ssthresh +
875                         tp->t_maxseg * tp->t_dupacks;
876                     if (SEQ_GT(onxt, tp->snd_nxt))
877                         tp->snd_nxt = onxt;
878                     goto drop;
879                 } else if (tp->t_dupacks > tcprexmtthresh) {
880                     tp->snd_cwnd += tp->t_maxseg;
881                     (void) tcp_output(tp);
882                     goto drop;
883                 }
884             } else
885                 tp->t_dupacks = 0;
886             break;                   /* beyond ACK processing (to step 6) */
887         }
                                                        ─── tcp_input.c
```

Figure 29.4 `tcp_input` function: duplicate ACK processing.

sent) is received. Figures 21.10 and 21.11 in Volume 1 show what happens with the congestion window and slow start threshold when the fast recovery algorithm is in effect.

Set `snd_nxt`

876–878   The value of the next sequence number to send is set to the maximum of its previous value (`onxt`) and its current value. Its current value was modified by `tcp_output` when the segment was retransmitted. Normally this causes `snd_nxt` to be set back to its previous value, which means that only the missing segment is retransmitted, and that future calls to `tcp_output` carry on with the next segment in sequence.

Number of consecutive duplicate ACKs exceeds threshold of 3

879–883   The missing segment was retransmitted when `t_dupacks` equaled 3, so the receipt of each additional duplicate ACK means that another packet has left the network. The congestion window is incremented by one segment. `tcp_output` sends the next segment in sequence, and the duplicate ACK is dropped. (This is shown by segments 67, 69, and 71 in Figure 21.7 of Volume 1.)

884–885   This statement is executed when the received segment contains a duplicate ACK, but either the length is nonzero or the advertised window changed. Only the first of the five tests described earlier is true. The counter of consecutive duplicate ACKs is set to 0.

Skip remainder of ACK processing

886   This `break` is executed in three cases: (1) only the first of the five tests described earlier is true, or (2) only the first three of the five tests is true, or (3) the ACK is a duplicate, but the number of consecutive duplicates is less than the threshold of 3. For any of these cases the ACK is still a duplicate and the `break` goes to the end of the `switch` that started in Figure 29.2, which continues processing at the label `step6`.

To understand the purpose in this aggressive window manipulation, consider the following example. Assume the window is eight segments, and segments 1 through 8 are sent. Segment 1 is lost, but the remainder arrive OK and are acknowledged. After the ACKs for segments 2, 3, and 4 arrive, the missing segment (1) is retransmitted. TCP would like the subsequent ACKs for 5 through 8 to allow some of the segments starting with 9 to be sent, to keep the pipe full. But the window is 8, which prevents segments 9 and above from being sent. Therefore, the congestion window is temporarily inflated by one segment each time another duplicate ACK is received, since the receipt of the duplicate ACK tells TCP that another segment has left the pipe at the other end. When the acknowledgment of segment 1 is finally received, the next figure reduces the congestion window back to the slow start threshold. This increase in the congestion window as the duplicate ACKs arrive, and its subsequent decrease when the fresh ACK arrives, can be seen visually in Figure 21.10 of Volume 1.

29.5 ACK Processing

The ACK processing continues with Figure 29.5.

```
                                                                ── tcp_input.c
888        /*
889         * If the congestion window was inflated to account
890         * for the other side's cached packets, retract it.
891         */
892        if (tp->t_dupacks > tcprexmtthresh &&
893            tp->snd_cwnd > tp->snd_ssthresh)
894            tp->snd_cwnd = tp->snd_ssthresh;
895        tp->t_dupacks = 0;

896        if (SEQ_GT(ti->ti_ack, tp->snd_max)) {
897            tcpstat.tcps_rcvacktoomuch++;
898            goto dropafterack;
899        }
900        acked = ti->ti_ack - tp->snd_una;
901        tcpstat.tcps_rcvackpack++;
902        tcpstat.tcps_rcvackbyte += acked;
                                                                ── tcp_input.c
```

Figure 29.5 `tcp_input` function: ACK processing continued.

Adjust congestion window

888–895   If the number of consecutive duplicate ACKs exceeds the threshold of 3, this is the first nonduplicate ACK after a string of four or more duplicate ACKs. The fast recovery algorithm is complete. Since the congestion window was incremented by one segment for every consecutive duplicate after the third, if it now exceeds the slow start threshold, it is set back to the slow start threshold. The counter of consecutive duplicate ACKs is set to 0.

Check for out-of-range ACK

896–899   Recall the definition of an acceptable ACK,

     snd_una < acknowledgment field <= snd_max

If the acknowledgment field is greater than snd_max, the other end is acknowledging data that TCP hasn't even sent yet! This probably occurs on a high-speed connection when the sequence numbers wrap and a missing ACK reappears later. As we can see in Figure 24.5, this rarely happens (since today's networks aren't fast enough).

Calculate number of bytes acknowledged

900–902   At this point TCP knows that it has an acceptable ACK. acked is the number of bytes acknowledged.

    The next part of ACK processing, shown in Figure 29.6, deals with RTT measurements and the retransmission timer.

Update RTT estimators

903–915   If either (1) a timestamp option was present, or (2) a segment was being timed and the acknowledgment number is greater than the starting sequence number of the segment being timed, tcp_xmit_timer updates the RTT estimators. Notice that the second argument to this function when timestamps are used is the current time (tcp_now) minus the timestamp echo reply (ts_ecr) plus 1 (since the function subtracts 1).

    Delayed ACKs are the reason for the greater-than test of the sequence numbers. For example, if TCP sends and times a segment with bytes 1–1024, followed by a segment with bytes 1025–2048, if an ACK of 2049 is returned, this test will consider whether 2049 is greater than 1 (the starting sequence number of the segment being timed), and since this is true, the RTT estimators are updated.

Check if all outstanding data has been acknowledged

916–924   If the acknowledgment field of the received segment (ti_ack) equals the maximum sequence number that TCP has sent (snd_max), all outstanding data has been acknowledged. The retransmission timer is turned off and the needoutput flag is set to 1. This flag forces a call to tcp_output at the end of this function. Since there is no more data waiting to be acknowledged, TCP may have more data to send that it has not been able to send earlier because the data was beyond the right edge of the window. Now that a new ACK has been received, the window will probably move to the right (snd_una is updated in Figure 29.8), which could allow more data to be sent.

```
                                                              ── tcp_input.c
903        /*
904         * If we have a timestamp reply, update smoothed
905         * round-trip time.  If no timestamp is present but
906         * transmit timer is running and timed sequence
907         * number was acked, update smoothed round-trip time.
908         * Since we now have an rtt measurement, cancel the
909         * timer backoff (cf., Phil Karn's retransmit alg.).
910         * Recompute the initial retransmit timer.
911         */
912        if (ts_present)
913            tcp_xmit_timer(tp, tcp_now - ts_ecr + 1);
914        else if (tp->t_rtt && SEQ_GT(ti->ti_ack, tp->t_rtseq))
915            tcp_xmit_timer(tp, tp->t_rtt);

916        /*
917         * If all outstanding data is acked, stop retransmit
918         * timer and remember to restart (more output or persist).
919         * If there is more data to be acked, restart retransmit
920         * timer, using current (possibly backed-off) value.
921         */
922        if (ti->ti_ack == tp->snd_max) {
923            tp->t_timer[TCPT_REXMT] = 0;
924            needoutput = 1;
925        } else if (tp->t_timer[TCPT_PERSIST] == 0)
926            tp->t_timer[TCPT_REXMT] = tp->t_rxtcur;
                                                              ── tcp_input.c
```

Figure 29.6   `tcp_input` function: RTT measurements and retransmission timer.

Unacknowledged data outstanding

925–926   Since there is additional data that has been sent but not acknowledged, if the persist timer is not on, the retransmission timer is restarted using the current value of `t_rxtcur`.

Karn's Algorithm and Timestamps

Notice that timestamps overrule the portion of Karn's algorithm (Section 21.3 of Volume 1) that says: when a timeout and retransmission occurs, the RTT estimators cannot be updated when the acknowledgment for the retransmitted data is received (the *retransmission ambiguity problem*). In Figure 25.26 we saw that `t_rtt` was set to 0 when a retransmission took place, because of Karn's algorithm. If timestamps are not present and it is a retransmission, the code in Figure 29.6 does not update the RTT estimators because `t_rtt` will be 0 from the retransmission. But if a timestamp is present, `t_rtt` isn't examined, allowing the RTT estimators to be updated using the received timestamp echo reply. With RFC 1323 timestamps the ambiguity is gone since the `ts_ecr` value was copied by the other end from the segment being acknowledged. The other half of Karn's algorithm, specifying that an exponential backoff must be used with retransmissions, still holds, of course.

Figure 29.7 shows the next part of ACK processing, updating the congestion window.

```
                                                            ─── tcp_input.c
927         /*
928          * When new data is acked, open the congestion window.
929          * If the window gives us less than ssthresh packets
930          * in flight, open exponentially (maxseg per packet).
931          * Otherwise open linearly: maxseg per window
932          * (maxseg^2 / cwnd per packet), plus a constant
933          * fraction of a packet (maxseg/8) to help larger windows
934          * open quickly enough.
935          */
936         {
937             u_int    cw = tp->snd_cwnd;
938             u_int    incr = tp->t_maxseg;

939             if (cw > tp->snd_ssthresh)
940                 incr = incr * incr / cw + incr / 8;
941             tp->snd_cwnd = min(cw + incr, TCP_MAXWIN << tp->snd_scale);
942         }
                                                            ─── tcp_input.c
```

Figure 29.7 `tcp_input` function: open congestion window in response to ACKs.

Update congestion window

927–942   One of the rules of slow start and congestion avoidance is that a received ACK increases the congestion window. By default the congestion window is increased by one segment for each received ACK (slow start). But if the current congestion window is greater than the slow start threshold, it is increased by 1 divided by the congestion window, plus a constant fraction of a segment. The term

```
incr * incr / cw
```

is

```
t_maxseg * t_maxseg / snd_cwnd
```

which is 1 divided by the congestion window, taking into account that `snd_cwnd` is maintained in bytes, not segments. The constant fraction is the segment size divided by 8. The congestion window is then limited by the maximum value of the send window for this connection. Example calculations of this algorithm are in Section 21.8 of Volume 1.

> Adding in the constant fraction (the segment size divided by 8) is wrong [Floyd 1994]. But it has been in the BSD sources since 4.3BSD Reno and is still in 4.4BSD and Net/3. It should be removed.

The next part of `tcp_input`, shown in Figure 29.8, removes the acknowledged data from the send buffer.

```
                                                                       ─ tcp_input.c
943            if (acked > so->so_snd.sb_cc) {
944                    tp->snd_wnd -= so->so_snd.sb_cc;
945                    sbdrop(&so->so_snd, (int) so->so_snd.sb_cc);
946                    ourfinisacked = 1;
947            } else {
948                    sbdrop(&so->so_snd, acked);
949                    tp->snd_wnd -= acked;
950                    ourfinisacked = 0;
951            }
952            if (so->so_snd.sb_flags & SB_NOTIFY)
953                    sowwakeup(so);
954            tp->snd_una = ti->ti_ack;
955            if (SEQ_LT(tp->snd_nxt, tp->snd_una))
956                    tp->snd_nxt = tp->snd_una;
                                                                       ─ tcp_input.c
```

Figure 29.8   `tcp_input` function: remove acknowledged data from send buffer.

Remove acknowledged bytes from the send buffer

943–946   If the number of bytes acknowledged *exceeds* the number of bytes on the send buffer, `snd_wnd` is decremented by the number of bytes in the send buffer and TCP knows that its FIN has been ACKed. That number of bytes is then removed from the send buffer by `sbdrop`. This method for detecting the ACK of a FIN works only because the FIN occupies 1 byte in the sequence number space.

947–951   Otherwise the number of bytes acknowledged is less than or equal to the number of bytes in the send buffer, so `ourfinisacked` is set to 0, and `acked` bytes of data are dropped from the send buffer.

Wakeup processes waiting on send buffer

951–956   `sowwakeup` awakens any processes waiting on the send buffer. `snd_una` is updated to contain the oldest unacknowledged sequence number. If this new value of `snd_una` exceeds `snd_nxt`, the latter is updated, since the intervening bytes have been acknowledged.

Figure 29.9 shows how `snd_nxt` can end up with a sequence number that is less than `snd_una`. Assume two segments are transmitted, the first with bytes 1–512 and the second with bytes 513–1024.

Figure 29.9   Two segments sent on a connection.

The retransmission timer then expires before an acknowledgment is returned. The code in Figure 25.26 sets `snd_nxt` back to `snd_una`, slow start is entered, `tcp_output` is called, and one segment containing bytes 1–512 is retransmitted. `tcp_output` increases `snd_nxt` to 513, and we have the scenario shown in Figure 29.10.

Figure 29.10 Continuation of Figure 29.9 after retransmission timer expires.

At this point an ACK of 1025 arrives (either the two original segments or the ACK was delayed somewhere in the network). The ACK is valid since it is less than or equal to `snd_max`, but `snd_nxt` will be less than the updated value of `snd_una`.

The general ACK processing is now complete, and the `switch` shown in Figure 29.11 handles four special cases.

```
                                                                      ── tcp_input.c
957          switch (tp->t_state) {

958              /*
959               * In FIN_WAIT_1 state in addition to the processing
960               * for the ESTABLISHED state if our FIN is now acknowledged
961               * then enter FIN_WAIT_2.
962               */
963          case TCPS_FIN_WAIT_1:
964              if (ourfinisacked) {
965                  /*
966                   * If we can't receive any more
967                   * data, then closing user can proceed.
968                   * Starting the timer is contrary to the
969                   * specification, but if we don't get a FIN
970                   * we'll hang forever.
971                   */
972                  if (so->so_state & SS_CANTRCVMORE) {
973                      soisdisconnected(so);
974                      tp->t_timer[TCPT_2MSL] = tcp_maxidle;
975                  }
976                  tp->t_state = TCPS_FIN_WAIT_2;
977              }
978              break;
                                                                      ── tcp_input.c
```

Figure 29.11 `tcp_input` function: receipt of ACK in FIN_WAIT_1 state.

Receipt of ACK in FIN_WAIT_1 state

958–971   In this state the process has closed the connection and TCP has sent the FIN. But other ACKs can be received for data segments sent before the FIN. Therefore the connection moves into the FIN_WAIT_2 state only when the FIN has been acknowledged. The flag `ourfinisacked` is set in Figure 29.8; this depends on whether the number of bytes ACKed exceeds the amount of data in the send buffer or not.

Set FIN_WAIT_2 timer

972–975   We also described in Section 25.6 how Net/3 sets a FIN_WAIT_2 timer to prevent an infinite wait in the FIN_WAIT_2 state. This timer is set only if the process completely closed the connection (i.e., the `close` system call or its kernel equivalent if the process was terminated by a signal), and not if the process performed a half-close (i.e., the FIN was sent but the process can still receive data on the connection).

Figure 29.12 shows the receipt of an ACK in the CLOSING state.

```
                                                                     ──── tcp_input.c
979                     /*
980                      * In CLOSING state in addition to the processing for
981                      * the ESTABLISHED state if the ACK acknowledges our FIN
982                      * then enter the TIME-WAIT state, otherwise ignore
983                      * the segment.
984                      */
985             case TCPS_CLOSING:
986                 if (ourfinisacked) {
987                     tp->t_state = TCPS_TIME_WAIT;
988                     tcp_canceltimers(tp);
989                     tp->t_timer[TCPT_2MSL] = 2 * TCPTV_MSL;
990                     soisdisconnected(so);
991                 }
992                 break;
                                                                     ──── tcp_input.c
```

Figure 29.12   `tcp_input` function: receipt of ACK in CLOSING state.

Receipt of ACK in CLOSING state

979–992   If the ACK is for the FIN (and not for some previous data segment), the connection moves into the TIME_WAIT state. Any pending timers are cleared (such as a pending retransmission timer), and the TIME_WAIT timer is started with a value of twice the MSL.

The processing of an ACK in the LAST_ACK state is shown in Figure 29.13.

```
                                                                     ──── tcp_input.c
993                      /*
994                       * In LAST_ACK, we may still be waiting for data to drain
995                       * and/or to be acked, as well as for the ack of our FIN.
996                       * If our FIN is now acknowledged, delete the TCB,
997                       * enter the closed state, and return.
998                       */
999              case TCPS_LAST_ACK:
1000                 if (ourfinisacked) {
1001                     tp = tcp_close(tp);
1002                     goto drop;
1003                 }
1004                 break;
                                                                     ──── tcp_input.c
```

Figure 29.13   `tcp_input` function: receipt of ACK in LAST_ACK state.

Receipt of ACK in LAST_ACK state

993–1004   If the FIN is ACKed, the new state is CLOSED. This state transition is handled by `tcp_close`, which also releases the Internet PCB and TCP control block.

Figure 29.14 shows the processing of an ACK in the TIME_WAIT state.

```
                                                                  tcp_input.c
1005                    /*
1006                     * In TIME_WAIT state the only thing that should arrive
1007                     * is a retransmission of the remote FIN.  Acknowledge
1008                     * it and restart the finack timer.
1009                     */
1010            case TCPS_TIME_WAIT:
1011                    tp->t_timer[TCPT_2MSL] = 2 * TCPTV_MSL;
1012                    goto dropafterack;
1013            }
1014      }
                                                                  tcp_input.c
```

Figure 29.14   `tcp_input` function: receipt of ACK in TIME_WAIT state.

Receipt of ACK in TIME_WAIT state

1005–1014   In this state both ends have sent a FIN and both FINs have been acknowledged. If TCP's ACK of the remote FIN was lost, however, the other end will retransmit the FIN (with an ACK). TCP drops the segment and resends the ACK. Additionally, the TIME_WAIT timer must be restarted with a value of twice the MSL.

29.6   Update Window Information

There are two variables in the TCP control block that we haven't described yet: `snd_wl1` and `snd_wl2`.

- `snd_wl1` records the sequence number of the last segment used to update the send window (`snd_wnd`).

- `snd_wl2` records the acknowledgment number of the last segment used to update the send window.

Our only encounter with these variables so far was when a connection was established (active, passive, or simultaneous open) and `snd_wl1` was set to `ti_seq` minus 1. We said this was to guarantee a window update, which we'll see in the following code.

The send window (`snd_wnd`) is updated from the advertised window in the received segment (`tiwin`) if any one of the following three conditions is true:

1. The segment contains new data. Since `snd_wl1` contains the starting sequence number of the last segment that was used to update the send window, if

    ```
    snd_wl1 < ti_seq
    ```

    this condition is true.

2. The segment does not contain new data (snd_wl1 equals `ti_seq`), but the segment acknowledges new data. The latter condition is true if

   ```
   snd_wl2 < ti_ack
   ```

   since `snd_wl2` records the acknowledgment number of the last segment that updated the send window.

3. The segment does not contain new data, and the segment does not acknowledge new data, but the advertised window is larger than the current send window.

The purpose of these tests is to prevent an old segment from affecting the send window, since the send window is not an absolute sequence number, but is an offset from `snd_una`.

Figure 29.15 shows the code that implements the update of the send window.

```
                                                                        ─── tcp_input.c
1015    step6:
1016        /*
1017         * Update window information.
1018         * Don't look at window if no ACK: TAC's send garbage on first SYN.
1019         */
1020        if ((tiflags & TH_ACK) &&
1021            (SEQ_LT(tp->snd_wl1, ti->ti_seq) || tp->snd_wl1 == ti->ti_seq &&
1022             (SEQ_LT(tp->snd_wl2, ti->ti_ack) ||
1023              tp->snd_wl2 == ti->ti_ack && tiwin > tp->snd_wnd))) {

1024            /* keep track of pure window updates */
1025            if (ti->ti_len == 0 &&
1026                tp->snd_wl2 == ti->ti_ack && tiwin > tp->snd_wnd)
1027                tcpstat.tcps_rcvwinupd++;

1028            tp->snd_wnd = tiwin;
1029            tp->snd_wl1 = ti->ti_seq;
1030            tp->snd_wl2 = ti->ti_ack;
1031            if (tp->snd_wnd > tp->max_sndwnd)
1032                tp->max_sndwnd = tp->snd_wnd;
1033            needoutput = 1;
1034        }
                                                                        ─── tcp_input.c
```

Figure 29.15 `tcp_input` function: update window information.

Check if send window should be updated

1015–1023   This `if` test verifies that the ACK flag is set along with any one of the three previously stated conditions. Recall that a jump was made to `step6` after the receipt of a SYN in either the LISTEN or SYN_SENT state, and in the LISTEN state the SYN does not contain an ACK.

> The term *TAC* referred to in the comment is a "terminal access controller." These were Telnet clients on the ARPANET.

1024–1027   If the received segment is a pure window update (the length is 0 and the ACK does not acknowledge new data, but the advertised window is larger), the statistic `tcps_rcvwinupd` is incremented.

Update variables

1028–1033   The send window is updated and new values of `snd_wl1` and `snd_wl2` are recorded. Additionally, if this advertised window is the largest one TCP has received from this peer, the new value is recorded in `max_sndwnd`. This is an attempt to guess the size of the other end's receive buffer, and it is used in Figure 26.8. `needoutput` is set to 1 since the new value of `snd_wnd` might enable a segment to be sent.

29.7 Urgent Mode Processing

The next part of TCP input processing handles segments with the URG flag set.

—————————————————————————————————————— tcp_input.c
```
1035     /*
1036      * Process segments with URG.
1037      */
1038     if ((tiflags & TH_URG) && ti->ti_urp &&
1039         TCPS_HAVERCVDFIN(tp->t_state) == 0) {
1040         /*
1041          * This is a kludge, but if we receive and accept
1042          * random urgent pointers, we'll crash in
1043          * soreceive.  It's hard to imagine someone
1044          * actually wanting to send this much urgent data.
1045          */
1046         if (ti->ti_urp + so->so_rcv.sb_cc > sb_max) {
1047             ti->ti_urp = 0;      /* XXX */
1048             tiflags &= ~TH_URG; /* XXX */
1049             goto dodata;         /* XXX */
1050         }
```
—————————————————————————————————————— tcp_input.c

Figure 29.16 `tcp_input` function: urgent mode processing.

Check if URG flag should be processed

1035–1039   These segments must have the URG flag set, a nonzero urgent offset (`ti_urp`), and the connection must not have received a FIN. The macro `TCPS_HAVERCVDFIN` is true only for the TIME_WAIT state, so the URG is processed in any other state. This is contrary to a comment appearing later in the code stating that the URG flag is ignored in the CLOSE_WAIT, CLOSING, LAST_ACK, or TIME_WAIT states.

Ignore bogus urgent offsets

1040–1050   If the urgent offset plus the number of bytes already in the receive buffer exceeds the maximum size of a socket buffer, the urgent notification is ignored. The urgent offset is set to 0, the URG flag is cleared, and the rest of the urgent mode processing is skipped.

The next piece of code, shown in Figure 29.17, processes the urgent pointer.

```
                                                              ──── tcp_input.c
1051            /*
1052             * If this segment advances the known urgent pointer,
1053             * then mark the data stream.  This should not happen
1054             * in CLOSE_WAIT, CLOSING, LAST_ACK or TIME_WAIT states since
1055             * a FIN has been received from the remote side.
1056             * In these states we ignore the URG.
1057             *
1058             * According to RFC961 (Assigned Protocols),
1059             * the urgent pointer points to the last octet
1060             * of urgent data.  We continue, however,
1061             * to consider it to indicate the first octet
1062             * of data past the urgent section as the original
1063             * spec states (in one of two places).
1064             */
1065            if (SEQ_GT(ti->ti_seq + ti->ti_urp, tp->rcv_up)) {
1066                tp->rcv_up = ti->ti_seq + ti->ti_urp;
1067                so->so_oobmark = so->so_rcv.sb_cc +
1068                    (tp->rcv_up - tp->rcv_nxt) - 1;
1069                if (so->so_oobmark == 0)
1070                    so->so_state |= SS_RCVATMARK;
1071                sohasoutofband(so);
1072                tp->t_oobflags &= ~(TCPOOB_HAVEDATA | TCPOOB_HADDATA);
1073            }
1074            /*
1075             * Remove out-of-band data so doesn't get presented to user.
1076             * This can happen independent of advancing the URG pointer,
1077             * but if two URG's are pending at once, some out-of-band
1078             * data may creep in... ick.
1079             */
1080            if (ti->ti_urp <= ti->ti_len
1081 #ifdef SO_OOBINLINE
1082                && (so->so_options & SO_OOBINLINE) == 0
1083 #endif
1084                )
1085                tcp_pulloutofband(so, ti, m);
1086        } else {
1087            /*
1088             * If no out-of-band data is expected, pull receive
1089             * urgent pointer along with the receive window.
1090             */
1091            if (SEQ_GT(tp->rcv_nxt, tp->rcv_up))
1092                tp->rcv_up = tp->rcv_nxt;
1093        }
                                                              ──── tcp_input.c
```

Figure 29.17   `tcp_input` function: processing of received urgent pointer.

1051–1065   If the starting sequence number of the received segment plus the urgent offset exceeds the current receive urgent pointer, a new urgent pointer has been received. For example, when the 3-byte segment that was sent in Figure 26.30 arrives at the receiver, we have the scenario shown in Figure 29.18.

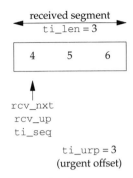

Figure 29.18 Receiver side when segment from Figure 26.30 arrives.

Normally the receive urgent pointer (`rcv_up`) equals `rcv_nxt`. In this example, since the `if` test is true (4 plus 3 is greater than 4), the new value of `rcv_up` is calculated as 7.

Calculate receive urgent pointer

1066–1070   The out-of-band mark in the socket's receive buffer is calculated, taking into account any data bytes already in the receive buffer (`so_rcv.sb_cc`). In our example, assuming there is no data already in the receive buffer, `so_oobmark` is set to 2: that is, the byte with the sequence number 6 is considered the out-of-band byte. If this out-of-band mark is 0, the socket is currently at the out-of-band mark. This happens if the `send` system call that sends the out-of-band byte specifies a length of 1, and if the receive buffer is empty when this segment arrives at the other end. This reiterates that Berkeley-derived systems consider the urgent pointer to point to the first byte of data *after* the out-of-band byte.

Notify process of TCP's urgent mode

1071–1072   `sohasoutofband` notifies the process that out-of-band data has arrived for the socket. The two flags `TCPOOB_HAVEDATA` and `TCPOOB_HADDATA` are cleared. These two flags are used with the `PRU_RCVOOB` request in Figure 30.8.

Pull out-of-band byte out of normal data stream

1074–1085   If the urgent offset is less than or equal to the number of bytes in the received segment, the out-of-band byte is contained in the segment. With TCP's urgent mode it is possible for the urgent offset to point to a data byte that has not yet been received. If the `SO_OOBINLINE` constant is defined (which it always is for Net/3), and if the corresponding socket option is not enabled, the receiving process wants the out-of-band byte pulled out of the normal stream of data and placed into the variable `t_iobc`. This is done by `tcp_pulloutofband`, which we cover in the next section.

Notice that the receiving process is notified that the sender has entered urgent mode, regardless of whether the byte pointed to by the urgent pointer is readable or not. This is a feature of TCP's urgent mode.

Adjust receive urgent pointer if not urgent mode

1086–1093   When the receiver is not processing an urgent pointer, if `rcv_nxt` is greater than the receive urgent pointer, `rcv_up` is moved to the right and set equal to `rcv_nxt`. This keeps the receive urgent pointer at the left edge of the receive window so that the comparison using SEQ_GT at the beginning of Figure 29.17 will work correctly when an URG flag is received.

> If the solution to Exercise 26.6 is implemented, corresponding changes will have to go into Figures 29.16 and 29.17 also.

29.8 `tcp_pulloutofband` Function

This function is called from Figure 29.17 when

1. urgent mode notification arrives in a received segment, and
2. the out-of-band byte is contained within the segment (i.e., the urgent pointer points into the received segment), and
3. the SO_OOBINLINE socket option is not enabled for this socket.

This function removes the out-of-band byte from the normal stream of data (i.e., the mbuf chain containing the received segment) and places it into the t_iobc variable in the TCP control block for the connection. The process reads this variable using the MSG_OOB flag with the recv system call: the PRU_RCVOOB request in Figure 30.8. Figure 29.19 shows the function.

```
                                                                    ──────── tcp_input.c
1282 void
1283 tcp_pulloutofband(so, ti, m)
1284 struct socket *so;
1285 struct tcpiphdr *ti;
1286 struct mbuf *m;
1287 {
1288     int     cnt = ti->ti_urp - 1;
1289     while (cnt >= 0) {
1290         if (m->m_len > cnt) {
1291             char    *cp = mtod(m, caddr_t) + cnt;
1292             struct tcpcb *tp = sototcpcb(so);

1293             tp->t_iobc = *cp;
1294             tp->t_oobflags |= TCPOOB_HAVEDATA;
1295             bcopy(cp + 1, cp, (unsigned) (m->m_len - cnt - 1));
1296             m->m_len--;
1297             return;
1298         }
1299         cnt -= m->m_len;
1300         m = m->m_next;
1301         if (m == 0)
1302             break;
1303     }
1304     panic("tcp_pulloutofband");
1305 }
                                                                    ──────── tcp_input.c
```

Figure 29.19 `tcp_pulloutofband` function: place out-of-band byte into `t_iobc`.

1282–1289   Consider the example in Figure 29.20. The urgent offset is 3, therefore the urgent pointer is 7, and the sequence number of the out-of-band byte is 6. There are 5 bytes in the received segment, all contained in a single mbuf.

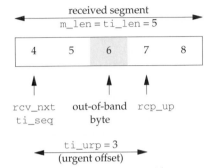

Figure 29.20   Received segment with an out-of-band byte.

The variable `cnt` is 2 and since `m_len` (which is 5) is greater than 2, the true portion of the `if` statement is executed.

1290–1298   `cp` points to the shaded byte with a sequence number of 6. This is placed into the variable `t_iobc`, which contains the out-of-band byte. The `TCPOOB_HAVEDATA` flag is set and `bcopy` moves the next 2 bytes (with sequence numbers 7 and 8) left 1 byte, giving the arrangement shown in Figure 29.21.

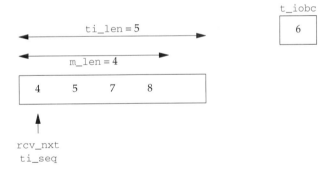

Figure 29.21   Result from Figure 29.20 after removal of out-of-band byte.

Remember that the numbers 7 and 8 specify the sequence numbers of the data bytes, not the contents of the data bytes. The length of the mbuf is decremented from 5 to 4 but `ti_len` is left as 5, for sequencing of the segment into the socket's receive buffer. Both the `TCP_REASS` macro and the `tcp_reass` function (which are called in the next section) increment `rcv_nxt` by `ti_len`, which in this example must be 5, because the next expected receive sequence number is 9. Also notice in this function that the length field in the packet header (`m_pkthdr.len`) in the first mbuf is not decremented by 1. This is because that length field is not used by `sbappend`, which appends the data to the socket's receive buffer.

Skip to next mbuf in chain

1299–1302   The out-of-band byte is not contained in this mbuf, so `cnt` is decremented by the number of bytes in the mbuf and the next mbuf in the chain is processed. Since this function is called only when the urgent offset points into the received segment, if there is not another mbuf on the chain, the `break` causes the call to `panic`.

29.9 Processing of Received Data

`tcp_input` continues by taking the received data (if any) and either appending it to the socket's receive buffer (if it is the next expected segment) or placing it onto the socket's out-of-order queue. Figure 29.22 shows the code that performs this task.

```
                                                                    ─ tcp_input.c
1094    dodata:                            /* XXX */
1095        /*
1096         * Process the segment text, merging it into the TCP sequencing queue,
1097         * and arranging for acknowledgment of receipt if necessary.
1098         * This process logically involves adjusting tp->rcv_wnd as data
1099         * is presented to the user (this happens in tcp_usrreq.c,
1100         * case PRU_RCVD).  If a FIN has already been received on this
1101         * connection then we just ignore the text.
1102         */
1103        if ((ti->ti_len || (tiflags & TH_FIN)) &&
1104            TCPS_HAVERCVDFIN(tp->t_state) == 0) {
1105            TCP_REASS(tp, ti, m, so, tiflags);
1106            /*
1107             * Note the amount of data that peer has sent into
1108             * our window, in order to estimate the sender's
1109             * buffer size.
1110             */
1111            len = so->so_rcv.sb_hiwat - (tp->rcv_adv - tp->rcv_nxt);
1112        } else {
1113            m_freem(m);
1114            tiflags &= ~TH_FIN;
1115        }
                                                                    ─ tcp_input.c
```

Figure 29.22 `tcp_input` function: merge received data into sequencing queue for socket.

1094–1105   Segment data is processed if

1. the length of the received data is greater than 0 or the FIN flag is set, and
2. a FIN has not yet been received for the connection.

The macro `TCP_REASS` processes the data. If the data is in sequence (i.e., the next expected data for this connection), the delayed-ACK flag is set, `rcv_nxt` is incremented, and the data is appended to the socket's receive buffer. If the data is out of order, the macro calls `tcp_reass` to add the data to the connection's reassembly queue (which might fill a hole and cause already-queued data to be appended to the socket's receive buffer).

Recall that the final argument to the macro (`tiflags`) can be modified. Specifically, if the data is out of order, `tcp_reass` sets `tiflags` to 0, clearing the FIN flag (if it was set). That's why the `if` statement is true if the FIN flag is set even if there is no data in the segment.

Consider the following example. A connection is established and the sender immediately transmits three segments: one with bytes 1–1024, another with bytes 1025–2048, and another with the FIN flag but no data. The first segment is lost, so when the second arrives (bytes 1025–2048) the receiver places it onto the out-of-order list and generates an immediate ACK. When the third segment with the FIN flag is received, the code in Figure 29.22 is executed. Even though the data length is 0, since the FIN flag is set, `TCP_REASS` is invoked, which calls `tcp_reass`. Since `ti_seq` (2049, the sequence number of the FIN) does not equal `rcv_nxt` (1), `tcp_reass` returns 0 (Figure 27.23), which in the `TCP_REASS` macro sets `tiflags` to 0. This clears the FIN flag, preventing the code that follows (Section 29.10) from processing the FIN flag.

Guess size of other end's send buffer

1106–1111   The calculation of `len` is attempt to guess the size of the other end's send buffer. Consider the following example. A socket has a receive buffer size of 8192 (the Net/3 default), so TCP advertises a window of 8192 in its SYN. The first segment with bytes 1–1024 is then received. Figure 29.23 shows the state of the receive space after `TCP_REASS` has incremented `rcv_nxt` to account for the received segment.

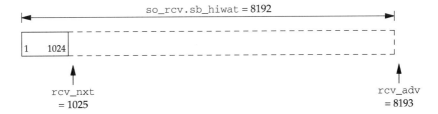

Figure 29.23   Receipt of bytes 1–1024 into a 8192-byte receive window.

The calculation of `len` yields 1024. The value of `len` will increase as the other end sends more data into the receive window, but it will never exceed the size of the other end's send buffer. Recall that the variable `max_sndwnd`, calculated in Figure 29.15, is an attempt to guess the size of the other end's receive buffer.

> This variable `len` is never used! It is left over code from Net/1 when the variable `max_rcvd` was stored in the TCP control block after the calculation of `len`:
>
>   if (len > tp->max_rcvd)
>   tp->max_rcvd = len;
>
> But even in Net/1 the variable `max_rcvd` was never used.

1112–1115   If the length is 0 and the FIN flag is not set, or if a FIN has already been received for the connection, the received mbuf chain is discarded and the FIN flag is cleared.

29.10 FIN Processing

The next step in `tcp_input`, shown in Figure 29.24, handles the FIN flag.

```
                                                                  ─── tcp_input.c
1116      /*
1117       * If FIN is received ACK the FIN and let the user know
1118       * that the connection is closing.
1119       */
1120      if (tiflags & TH_FIN) {
1121          if (TCPS_HAVERCVDFIN(tp->t_state) == 0) {
1122              socantrcvmore(so);
1123              tp->t_flags |= TF_ACKNOW;
1124              tp->rcv_nxt++;
1125          }
1126          switch (tp->t_state) {

1127          /*
1128           * In SYN_RECEIVED and ESTABLISHED states
1129           * enter the CLOSE_WAIT state.
1130           */
1131          case TCPS_SYN_RECEIVED:
1132          case TCPS_ESTABLISHED:
1133              tp->t_state = TCPS_CLOSE_WAIT;
1134              break;
                                                                  ─── tcp_input.c
```

Figure 29.24   `tcp_input` function: FIN processing, first half.

Process first FIN received on connection

1116–1125   If the FIN flag is set and this is the first FIN received for this connection, `socantrcvmore` marks the socket as write-only, `TF_ACKNOW` is set to acknowledge the FIN immediately (i.e., it is not delayed), and `rcv_nxt` steps over the FIN in the sequence space.

1126   The remainder of FIN processing is handled by a `switch` that depends on the connection state. Notice that the FIN is not processed in the CLOSED, LISTEN, or SYN_SENT states, since in these three states a SYN has not been received to synchronize the received sequence number, making it impossible to validate the sequence number of the FIN. A FIN is also ignored in the CLOSING, CLOSE_WAIT, and LAST_ACK states, because in these three states the FIN is a duplicate.

SYN_RCVD or ESTABLISHED states

1127–1134   From either the ESTABLISHED or SYN_RCVD states, the CLOSE_WAIT state is entered.

> The receipt of a FIN in the SYN_RCVD state is unusual, but legal. It is not shown in Figure 24.15. It means a socket is in the LISTEN state when a segment containing a SYN and a FIN is received. Alternatively, a SYN is received for a listening socket, moving the connection to the SYN_RCVD state but before the ACK is received a FIN is received. (We know the segment does not contain a valid ACK, because if it did the code in Figure 29.2 would have moved the connection to the ESTABLISHED state.)

The next part of FIN processing is shown in Figure 29.25

tcp_input.c
```
1135                    /*
1136                     * If still in FIN_WAIT_1 state FIN has not been acked so
1137                     * enter the CLOSING state.
1138                     */
1139            case TCPS_FIN_WAIT_1:
1140                    tp->t_state = TCPS_CLOSING;
1141                    break;

1142                    /*
1143                     * In FIN_WAIT_2 state enter the TIME_WAIT state,
1144                     * starting the time-wait timer, turning off the other
1145                     * standard timers.
1146                     */
1147            case TCPS_FIN_WAIT_2:
1148                    tp->t_state = TCPS_TIME_WAIT;
1149                    tcp_canceltimers(tp);
1150                    tp->t_timer[TCPT_2MSL] = 2 * TCPTV_MSL;
1151                    soisdisconnected(so);
1152                    break;

1153                    /*
1154                     * In TIME_WAIT state restart the 2 MSL time_wait timer.
1155                     */
1156            case TCPS_TIME_WAIT:
1157                    tp->t_timer[TCPT_2MSL] = 2 * TCPTV_MSL;
1158                    break;
1159            }
1160    }
```
tcp_input.c

Figure 29.25   `tcp_input` function: FIN processing, second half.

FIN_WAIT_1 state

1135–1141   Since ACK processing is already complete for this segment, if the connection is in the FIN_WAIT_1 state when the FIN is processed, it means a simultaneous close is taking place—the two FINs from each end have passed in the network. The connection enters the CLOSING state.

FIN_WAIT_2 state

1142–1148   The receipt of the FIN moves the connection into the TIME_WAIT state. When a segment containing a FIN and an ACK is received in the FIN_WAIT_1 state (the typical scenario), although Figure 24.15 shows the transition directly from the FIN_WAIT_1 state to the TIME_WAIT state, the ACK is processed in Figure 29.11, moving the connection to the FIN_WAIT_2 state. The FIN processing here moves the connection into the TIME_WAIT state. Because the ACK is processed before the FIN, the FIN_WAIT_2 state is always passed through, albeit momentarily.

Start TIME_WAIT timer

1149–1152   Any pending TCP timer is turned off and the TIME_WAIT timer is started with a value of twice the MSL. (If the received segment contained a FIN and an ACK, Figure 29.11 started the FIN_WAIT_2 timer.) The socket is disconnected.

TIME_WAIT state

1153–1159   If a FIN arrives in the TIME_WAIT state, it is a duplicate, and similar to Figure 29.14, the TIME_WAIT timer is restarted with a value of twice the MSL.

29.11 Final Processing

The final part of the slow path through `tcp_input` along with the label `dropafterack` is shown in Figure 29.26.

```
                                                                    ── tcp_input.c
1161     if (so->so_options & SO_DEBUG)
1162         tcp_trace(TA_INPUT, ostate, tp, &tcp_saveti, 0);
1163     /*
1164      * Return any desired output.
1165      */
1166     if (needoutput || (tp->t_flags & TF_ACKNOW))
1167         (void) tcp_output(tp);
1168     return;

1169   dropafterack:
1170     /*
1171      * Generate an ACK dropping incoming segment if it occupies
1172      * sequence space, where the ACK reflects our state.
1173      */
1174     if (tiflags & TH_RST)
1175         goto drop;
1176     m_freem(m);
1177     tp->t_flags |= TF_ACKNOW;
1178     (void) tcp_output(tp);
1179     return;
                                                                    ── tcp_input.c
```

Figure 29.26   `tcp_input` function: final processing.

SO_DEBUG socket option

1161–1162   If the `SO_DEBUG` socket option is enabled, `tcp_trace` appends the trace record to the kernel's circular buffer. Remember that the code in Figure 28.7 saved both the original connection state and the IP and TCP headers, since these values may have changed in this function.

Call `tcp_output`

1163–1168   If either the `needoutput` flag was set (Figures 29.6 and 29.15) or if an immediate ACK is required, `tcp_output` is called.

`dropafterack`

1169–1179   An ACK is generated only if the RST flag was not set. (A segment with an RST is never ACKed.) The mbuf chain containing the received segment is released, and `tcp_output` generates an immediate ACK.

Figure 29.27 completes the `tcp_input` function.

tcp_input.c

```
1180    dropwithreset:
1181        /*
1182         * Generate an RST, dropping incoming segment.
1183         * Make ACK acceptable to originator of segment.
1184         * Don't bother to respond if destination was broadcast/multicast.
1185         */
1186        if ((tiflags & TH_RST) || m->m_flags & (M_BCAST | M_MCAST) ||
1187            IN_MULTICAST(ti->ti_dst.s_addr))
1188            goto drop;
1189        if (tiflags & TH_ACK)
1190            tcp_respond(tp, ti, m, (tcp_seq) 0, ti->ti_ack, TH_RST);
1191        else {
1192            if (tiflags & TH_SYN)
1193                ti->ti_len++;
1194            tcp_respond(tp, ti, m, ti->ti_seq + ti->ti_len, (tcp_seq) 0,
1195                        TH_RST | TH_ACK);
1196        }
1197        /* destroy temporarily created socket */
1198        if (dropsocket)
1199            (void) soabort(so);
1200        return;

1201    drop:
1202        /*
1203         * Drop space held by incoming segment and return.
1204         */
1205        if (tp && (tp->t_inpcb->inp_socket->so_options & SO_DEBUG))
1206            tcp_trace(TA_DROP, ostate, tp, &tcp_saveti, 0);
1207        m_freem(m);
1208        /* destroy temporarily created socket */
1209        if (dropsocket)
1210            (void) soabort(so);
1211        return;
1212 }
```

tcp_input.c

Figure 29.27 `tcp_input` function: final processing.

dropwithreset

1180–1188   An RST is generated unless the received segment also contained an RST, or the received segment was sent as a broadcast or multicast. An RST is never generated in response to an RST, since this could lead to RST storms (a continual exchange of RST segments between two end points).

> This code contains the same error that we noted in Figure 28.16: it does not check whether the destination address of the received segment was a broadcast address.

> Similarly, the destination address argument to `IN_MULTICAST` needs to be converted to host byte order.

Sequence number and acknowledgment number of RST segment

1189–1196   The values of the sequence number field, the acknowledgment field, and the ACK flag of the RST segment depend on whether the received segment contained an ACK.

Figure 29.28 summarizes these fields in the RST segment that is generated.

received segment	RST segment generated		
	seq#	ack. field	flags
contains ACK	received ack. field	0	`TH_RST`
ACK-less	0	received seq# field	`TH_RST	TH_ACK`

Figure 29.28   Values of fields in RST segment generated.

Realize that the ACK flag is normally set in all segments except when an initial SYN is sent (Figure 24.16). The fourth argument to `tcp_respond` is the acknowledgment field, and the fifth argument is the sequence number.

Rejecting connections

1192–1193   If the SYN flag is set, `ti_len` must be incremented by 1, causing the acknowledgment field of the RST to be 1 greater than the received sequence number of the SYN. This code is executed when a SYN arrives for a nonexistent server. When the Internet PCB is not found in Figure 28.6, a jump is made to `dropwithreset`. But for the received RST to be acceptable to the other end, the acknowledgment field must ACK the SYN (Figure 28.18). Figure 18.14 of Volume 1 contains an example of this type of RST segment.

Finally note that `tcp_respond` builds the RST in the first mbuf of the received chain and releases any remaining mbufs in the chain. When that mbuf finally makes its way to the device driver, it will be discarded.

Destroy temporarily created socket

1197–1199   If a temporary socket was created in Figure 28.7 for a listening server, but the code in Figure 28.16 found the received segment to contain an error, `dropsocket` will be 1. If so, that socket is now destroyed.

Drop (without ACK or RST)

1201–1206   `tcp_trace` is called when a segment is dropped without generating an ACK or an RST. If the `SO_DEBUG` flag is set and an ACK is generated, `tcp_output` generates a trace record. If the `SO_DEBUG` flag is set and an RST is generated, a trace record is not generated for the RST.

1207–1211   The mbuf chain containing the received segment is released and the temporary socket is destroyed if `dropsocket` is nonzero.

29.12 Implementation Refinements

The refinements to speed up TCP processing are similar to the ones described for UDP (Section 23.12). Multiple passes over the data should be avoided and the checksum computation should be combined with a copy. [Dalton et al. 1993] describe these modifications.

The linear search of the TCP PCBs is also a bottleneck when the number of connections increases. [McKenney and Dove 1992] address this problem by replacing the linear search with hash tables.

[Partridge 1993] describes a research implementation being developed by Van Jacobson that greatly reduces the TCP input processing. The received packet is processed by IP (about 25 instructions on a RISC system), then by a demultiplexer to locate the PCB (about 10 instructions), and then by TCP (about 30 instructions). These 30 instructions perform header prediction and calculate the pseudo-header checksum. If the segment passes the header prediction test, contains data, and the process is waiting for the data, the data is copied into the process buffer and the remainder of the TCP checksum is calculated and verified (a one-pass copy and checksum). If the TCP header prediction fails, the slow path through the TCP input processing occurs.

29.13 Header Compression

We now describe TCP *header compression*. Although header compression is not part of TCP input, we needed to cover TCP thoroughly before describing header compression. Header compression is described in detail in RFC 1144 [Jacobson 1990a]. It was designed by Van Jacobson and is sometimes called *VJ header compression*. Our purpose in this section is not to go through the header compression source code (a well-commented version of which is presented in RFC 1144, and which is approximately the same size as `tcp_output`), but to provide an overview of the algorithm. Be sure to distinguish between header prediction (Section 28.4) and header compression.

Introduction

Most implementations of SLIP and PPP support header compression. Although header compression could, in theory, be used with any data link, it is intended for slow-speed serial links. Header compression works with TCP segments only—it does nothing with other IP datagrams (e.g., ICMP, IGMP, UDP, etc.). Header compression reduces the size of the combined IP/TCP header from its normal 40 bytes to as few as 3 bytes. This reduces the size of a typical TCP segment from an interactive application such as Rlogin or Telnet from 41 bytes to 4 bytes—a big saving on a slow-speed serial link.

Each end of the serial link maintains two connection state tables, one for datagrams sent and one for datagrams received. Each table allows a maximum of 256 entries, but typically there are 16 entries in this table, allowing up to 16 different TCP connections to be compressed at any time. Each entry contains an 8-bit connection ID (hence the limit of 256), some flags, and the complete uncompressed IP/TCP header from the most recent datagram. The 96-bit socket pair that uniquely identifies each connection—the source and destination IP addresses and source and destination TCP ports—are contained in this uncompressed header. Figure 29.29 shows an example of these tables.

Since a TCP connection is full duplex, header compression can be applied in both directions. Each end must implement both compression and decompression. A connection appears in both tables, as shown in Figure 29.29. In this example, the entry with a connection ID of 1 in the top two tables has a source IP address of 128.1.2.3, source TCP port of 1500, destination IP address of 192.3.4.5, and a destination TCP port of 25. The entry with a connection ID of 2 in the bottom two tables is for the other direction of the same connection.

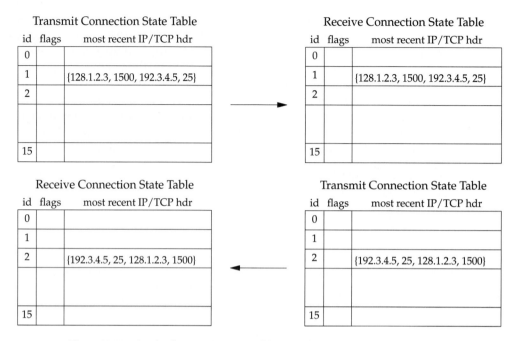

Figure 29.29   A pair of connection state tables at each end of a link (e.g., SLIP link).

We show these tables as arrays, but the source code defines each entry as a structure, and a connection table is a circular linked list of these structures. The most recently used structure is stored at the head of the list.

By saving the most recent uncompressed header at each end, only the *differences* in various header fields from the previous datagram to the current datagram are transmitted across the link (along with a special first byte indicating which fields follow). Since some header fields don't change at all from one datagram to the next, and other header fields change by small amounts, this differential coding provides the savings. Header compression works with the IP and TCP headers only—the data contents of the TCP segment are not modified.

Figure 29.30 shows the steps involved at the sending side when it has an IP datagram to send across a link using header compression.

Three different types of datagrams are sent and must be recognized at the receiver:

1. Type `IP` is specified with the high-order 4 bits of the first byte equal to 4. This is the normal IP version number in the IP header (Figure 8.8). The normal, uncompressed datagram is transmitted across the link.

2. Type `COMPRESSED_TCP` is specified by setting the high-order bit of the first byte. This looks like an IP version between 8 and 15 (i.e., the remaining 7 bits of this byte are used by the compression algorithm). The compressed header and uncompressed data are transmitted across the link, as we describe later in this section.

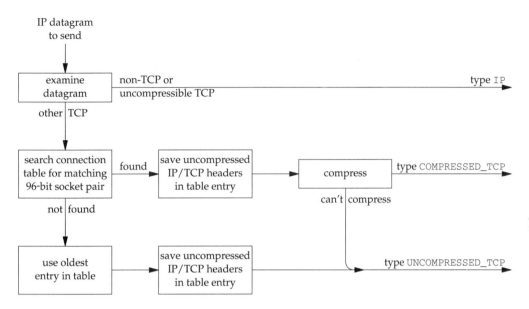

Figure 29.30   Steps involved in header compression at sender side.

3. Type `UNCOMPRESSED_TCP` is specified with the high-order 4 bits of the first byte equal to 7. The normal, uncompressed datagram is transmitted across the link, but the IP protocol field (which equals 6 for TCP), is replaced with the connection ID. This identifies the connection state table entry for the receiver.

The receiver can identify the datagram type by examining its first byte. The code that does this was shown in Figure 5.13. In Figure 5.16 the sender calls `sl_compress_tcp` to check if a TCP segment is compressible, and the return value of this function is logically ORed into the first byte of the datagram.

Figure 29.31 shows an illustration of the first byte that is sent across the link.

first byte transmitted across link	4-bit version				4-bit header length				
	0	1	0	0	–	–	–	–	IP
	0	1	1	1	–	–	–	–	UNCOMPRESSED_TCP
	1	C	I	P	S	A	W	U	COMPRESSED_TCP

Figure 29.31   First byte transmitted across link.

The 4 bits shown as "`-`" comprise the normal IP header length field. The 7 bits shown as `C`, `I`, `P`, `S`, `A`, `W`, and `U` indicate which optional fields follow. We describe these fields shortly.

Figure 29.32 shows the complete IP datagram for the various datagrams that are sent.

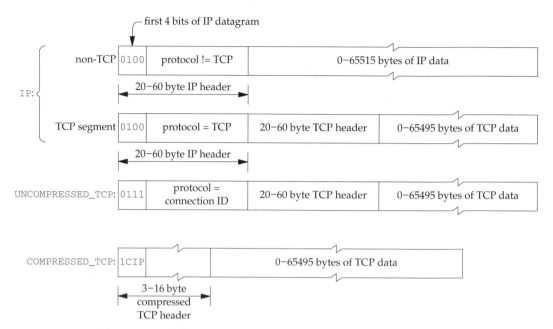

Figure 29.32   Different types of IP datagrams possible with header compression.

We show two datagrams with a type of IP: one that is not a TCP segment (e.g., a proto-col of UDP, ICMP, or IGMP), and one that is a TCP segment. This is to illustrate the differences between the TCP segment sent as type IP and the TCP segment sent as type UNCOMPRESSED_TCP: the first 4 bits are different as is the protocol field in the IP header.

Datagrams are not candidates for header compression if the protocol is not TCP, or if the protocol is TCP but any one of the following conditions is true.

- The datagram is an IP fragment: either the fragment offset is nonzero or the more-fragments bit is set.
- Any one of the SYN, FIN, or RST flags is set.
- The ACK flag is not set.

If any one of these three conditions is true, the datagram is sent as type IP.

Furthermore, even if the datagram is a TCP segment that looks compressible, it is possible to abort the compression and send the datagram as type UNCOMPRESSED_TCP if certain fields have changed between the current datagram and the last datagram sent for this connection. These are fields that normally do not change for a given connection, so the compression scheme was not designed to encode their differences from one datagram to the next. The TOS field and the don't fragment bit are examples. Also, when the differences in some fields are greater than 65535, the compression algorithm fails and the datagram is sent uncompressed.

Compression of Header Fields

We now describe how the fields in the IP and TCP headers, shown in Figure 29.33, are compressed. The shaded fields normally don't change during a connection.

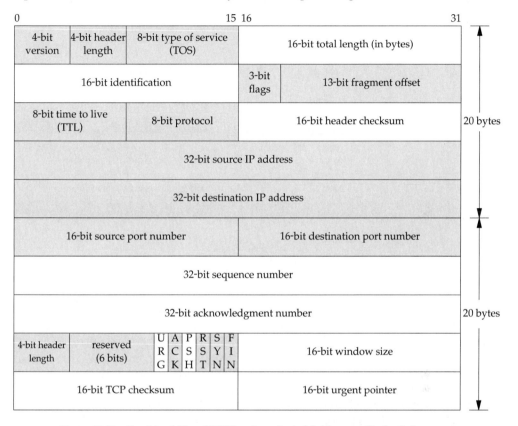

Figure 29.33   Combined IP and TCP headers: shaded fields normally don't change.

If any of the shaded fields have changed from the previous segment on this connection to the current segment, the segment is sent uncompressed. We don't show IP options or TCP options in this figure, but if either are present and have changed from the previous segment, the segment is sent uncompressed (Exercise 29.7).

If the algorithm transmitted only the nonshaded fields when the shaded fields do not change from the previous segment, about a 50% savings would result. VJ header compression does even better than this, by knowing which fields in the IP and TCP headers *normally* don't change. Figure 29.34 shows the format of the compressed IP/TCP header.

The smallest compressed header consists of 3 bytes: the first byte (the flag bits) followed by the 16-bit TCP checksum. For protection against possible link errors, the TCP checksum is always transmitted without any change. (SLIP provides no link-layer checksum, although PPP does provide one.)

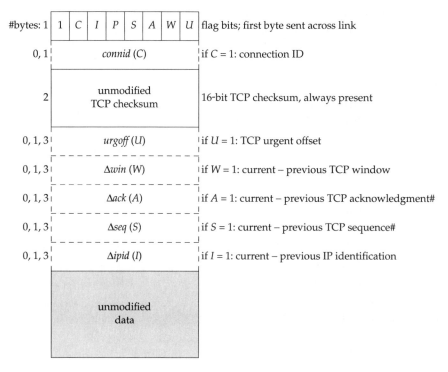

Figure 29.34   Format of compressed IP/TCP header.

The other six fields, *connid*, *urgoff*, Δ*win*, Δ*ack*, Δ*seq*, and Δ*ipid*, are optional. We show the number of bytes used to encode all the fields to the left of the field in Figure 29.34. The largest compressed header appears to be 19 bytes, but we'll see shortly that the 4 bits *SAWU* can never be set at the same time in a compressed header, so the largest size is actually 16 bytes.

Six of the 7 bits in the first byte specify which of the six optional fields are present. The high-order bit of the first byte is always set to 1. This identifies the datagram type as COMPRESSED_TCP. Figure 29.35 summarizes the 7 bits, which we now describe.

Flag bit	Description	Structure member	Meaning if flag = 0	Meaning if flag = 1
C	connection ID		same connection ID as last	*connid* = connection ID
I	IP identification	ip_id	ip_id has increased by 1	Δ*ipid* = current – previous
P	TCP push flag		PSH flag off	PSH flag on
S	TCP sequence#	th_seq	same th_seq as last	Δ*seq* = current – previous
A	TCP acknowledgment#	th_ack	same th_ack as last	Δ*ack* = current – previous
W	TCP window	th_win	same th_win as last	Δ*win* = current – previous
U	TCP urgent offset	th_urg	URG flag not set	*urgoff* = urgent offset

Figure 29.35   The 7 bits in the compressed header.

C   If this bit is 0, this segment has the same connection ID as the previous compressed or uncompressed segment. If this flag is 1, *connid* is the connection ID, a value between 0 and 255.

I   If this bit is 0, the IP identification field has increased by 1 (the typical case). If this bit is 1, $\Delta ipid$ is the current value of `ip_id` minus its previous value.

P   This bit is a copy of the PSH flag from the TCP segment. Since the PSH flag doesn't follow any established pattern, it must be explicitly specified for each segment.

S   If this bit is 0, the TCP sequence number has not changed. If this bit is 1, Δseq is the current value of `th_seq` minus its previous value.

A   If this bit is 0, the TCP acknowledgment number has not changed (the typical case). If this bit is 1, Δack is the current value of `th_ack` minus its previous value.

W   If this bit is 0, the TCP window has not changed (the typical case). If this bit is 1, Δwin is the current value of `th_win` minus its previous value.

U   If this bit is 0, the URG flag in the segment is not set and the urgent offset has not changed from its previous value (the typical case). If this bit is 1, *urgoff* is the current value of `th_urg` and the URG flag is set. If the urgent offset changes without the URG flag being set, the segment is sent uncompressed. (This often occurs in the first segment following urgent data.)

The differences are encoded as the current value minus the previous value, because most of these differences will be small positive numbers (with Δwin being an exception) given the way these fields normally change.

We note that five of the optional fields in Figure 29.34 are encoded in 0, 1, or 3 bytes.

0 bytes: If the corresponding flag is not set, nothing is encoded for the field.

1 byte: If the value to send is between 1 and 255, a single byte encodes the value.

3 bytes: If the value to send is either 0 or between 256 and 65535, 3 bytes encode the value: the first byte is 0, followed by the 2-byte value. This always works for the three 16-bit values, *urgoff*, Δwin, and $\Delta ipid$; but if the difference to encode for the two 32-bit values, Δack and Δseq, is less than 0 or greater than 65535, the segment is sent uncompressed.

If we compare the nonshaded fields in Figure 29.33 with the possible fields in Figure 29.34 we notice that some fields are never transmitted.

*   The IP total length field is not transmitted since most link layers provide the length of a received message to the receiver.

*   Since the only field in the IP header that is being transmitted is the identification field, the IP checksum is also omitted. This is a hop-by-hop checksum that protects only the IP header across any given link.

Special Cases

Two common cases are detected and transmitted as special combinations of the 4 low-order bits: *SAWU*. Since urgent data is rare, if the URG flag in the segment is set and both the sequence number and window also change (implying that the 4 low-order bits would be 1011 or 1111), the segment is sent uncompressed. Therefore if the 4 low-order bits are sent as 1011 (called **SA*) or 1111 (called **S*), the following two special cases apply:

*SA   The sequence number and acknowledgment number both increase by the amount of data in the last segment, the window and urgent offset don't change, and the URG flag is not set. This special case avoids encoding both Δseq and Δack.

This case occurs frequently for both directions of echoed terminal traffic. Figures 19.3 and 19.4 of Volume 1 give examples of this type of data flow across an Rlogin connection.

*S   The sequence number changes by the amount of data in the last segment, the acknowledgment number, window, and urgent offset don't change, and the URG flag is not set. This special case avoids encoding Δseq.

This case occurs frequently for the sending side of a unidirectional data transfer (e.g., FTP). Figures 20.1, 20.2, and 20.3 of Volume 1 give examples of this type of data transfer. This case also occurs for the sender of nonechoed terminal traffic (e.g., commands that are not echoed by a full-screen editor).

Examples

Two simple examples were run across the SLIP link between the systems `bsdi` and `slip` in Figure 1.17. This SLIP link uses header compression in both directions. The `tcpdump` program described in Appendix A of Volume 1 was also run on the host `bsdi` to save a copy of all the frames. This program has an option that outputs the compressed header, showing all the fields in Figure 29.34.

Two traces were obtained: a short portion of an Rlogin connection and a file transfer from `bsdi` to `slip` using FTP. Figure 29.36 shows a summary of the different frame types for both connections.

The two entries of 75 verify our claim that this special case often occurs for both directions of echoed terminal traffic. The entry of 325 verifies our claim that this special case occurs frequently for the sending side of a unidirectional data transfer.

The 10 frames of type `IP` for the FTP example correspond to four segments with the SYN flag set and six segments with the FIN flag set. FTP uses two connections: one for the interactive commands and one for the file transfer.

The `UNCOMPRESSED_TCP` frame types normally correspond to the first segment following connection establishment, the one that establishes the connection ID. An additional few are seen in these examples when the type of service is set (the Net/3 Rlogin and FTP clients and servers all set the TOS field *after* the connection is established).

frame type	Rlogin		FTP	
	input	output	input	output
IP	1	1	5	5
UNCOMPRESSED_TCP	3	2	2	3
COMPRESSED_TCP				
SA special case	75	75	0	0
S special case	25	1	1	325
nonspecial	9	93	337	13
Total	113	172	345	346

Figure 29.36   Counts of different frame types for Rlogin and FTP connections.

#bytes	Rlogin		FTP	
	input	output	input	output
3	102	44	2	250
4		94		78
5	7	12	5	2
6		6	325	5
7		13	2	1
8				1
9			4	1
Total	109	169	338	338

Figure 29.37   Distribution of compressed-header sizes.

Figure 29.37 shows the distribution of the compressed-header sizes. The average size of the compressed header for the final four columns in Figure 29.37 is 3.1, 4.1, 6.0, and 3.3 bytes, a significant savings compared to the uncompressed 40-byte headers, especially for the interactive connection.

Almost all of the 325 6-byte headers in the FTP input column contain only a Δack of 256, which being greater than 255 is encoded in 3 bytes. The SLIP MTU is 296, so TCP uses an MSS of 256. Almost all of the 250 3-byte headers in the FTP output column contain the *S* special case (sequence number change only) with a change of 256 bytes. But since this change refers to the amount of data in the previous segment, nothing is transmitted other than the flag byte and the TCP checksum. The 78 4-byte headers in the FTP output column are this same special case, but with a change in the IP identification field also (Exercise 29.8).

Configuration

Header compression must be enabled on a given SLIP or PPP link. With a SLIP link there are normally two flags that can be set when the interface is configured: enable header compression and autoenable header compression. These two flags are set using the `link0` and `link2` flags to the `ifconfig` command, respectively. Normally a client (the dialin host) decides whether to use header compression or not. The server (the host or terminal server to which the client dials in) specifies the autoenable flag only. If header compression is enabled by the client, its TCP will send a datagram of type `UNCOMPRESSED_TCP` to specify the connection ID. When the server sees this packet it enables header compression (since it was in the autoenable mode). If the server never sees this type of packet, it never enables header compression for this line.

PPP allows the negotiation of options between the two ends of the link when the link is established. One of the options that can be negotiated is whether to use header compression or not.

29.14 Summary

This chapter completes our detailed look at TCP input processing. We started with the processing of an ACK in the SYN_RCVD state, which completes a passive open, a simultaneous open, or a self-connect.

The fast retransmit algorithm lets TCP detect a dropped segment after receiving a specified number of consecutive duplicate ACKs and retransmit the segment before the retransmission timer expires. Net/3 combines the fast retransmit algorithm with the fast recovery algorithm, which tries to keep the data flowing from the sender to the receiver, albeit at a slower rate, using congestion avoidance but not slow start.

ACK processing then discards the acknowledged data from the socket's send buffer and handles a few TCP states specially, when the receipt of an ACK changes the connection state.

The URG flag is processed, if set, and TCP's urgent mode is mapped into the socket abstraction of out-of-band data. This is complicated because the process can receive the out-of-band byte inline or in a special out-of-band buffer, and TCP can receive urgent notification before the data byte referenced by the urgent pointer has been received.

TCP input processing completes by calling TCP_REASS to merge the received data into either the socket's receive buffer or the socket's out-of-order queue, processing the FIN flag, and calling `tcp_output` if a segment must be generated in response to the received segment.

TCP header compression is a technique used on SLIP and PPP links to reduce the size of the IP and TCP headers from the normal 40 bytes to around 3–6 bytes (typically). This is done by recognizing that most fields in these headers don't change from one segment to the next on a given connection, and the fields that do change often change by a small amount. This allows a flag byte to be sent indicating which fields have changed, and the changes are encoded as differences from the previous segment.

Exercises

29.1 A client connects to a server and no segments are lost. Which process, the client or server, completes its open of the connection first?

29.2 A Net/3 system receives a SYN for a listening socket and the SYN segment also contains 50 bytes of data. What happens?

29.3 Continue the previous exercise assuming that the client does not retransmit the 50 bytes of data; instead the client responds with a segment that acknowledges the server's SYN/ACK and contains a FIN. What happens?

29.4 A Net/3 client performs a passive open to a listening server. The server's response to the client's SYN is a segment with the expected SYN/ACK, but the segment also contains 50 bytes of data and the FIN flag. List the processing steps for the client's TCP.

29.5 Figure 18.19 in Volume 1 and Figure 14 in RFC 793 both show four segments exchanged during a simultaneous close. But if we trace a simultaneous close between two Net/3 systems, or if we watch the close sequence following a self-connect on a Net/3 system, we see six segments, not four. The extra two segments are a retransmission of the FIN by each end when the other's FIN is received. Where is the bug and what is the fix?

29.6 Page 72 of RFC 793 says that when data in the send buffer is acknowledged by the other end "Users should receive positive acknowledgments for buffers which have been sent and fully acknowledged (i.e., send buffer should be returned with 'ok' response)." Does Net/3 provide this notification?

29.7 What effect do the options defined in RFC 1323 have on TCP header compression?

29.8 What effect does the Net/3 assignment of the IP identification field have on TCP header compression?

30

TCP User Requests

30.1 Introduction

This chapter looks at the TCP user-request function `tcp_usrreq`, which is called as the protocol's `pr_usrreq` function to handle many of the system calls that reference a TCP socket. We also look at `tcp_ctloutput`, which is called when the process calls `setsockopt` for a TCP socket.

30.2 `tcp_usrreq` Function

TCP's user-request function is called for a variety of operations. Figure 30.1 shows the beginning and end of `tcp_usrreq`. The body of the `switch` is shown in following figures. The function arguments, some of which differ depending on the request, are described in Figure 15.17.

`in_control` processes `ioctl` requests

45–58   The `PRU_CONTROL` request is from the `ioctl` system call. The function `in_control` processes the request completely.

Control information is invalid

59–64   A call to `sendmsg` specifying control information is invalid for a TCP socket. If this happens, the mbufs are released and `EINVAL` is returned.

65–66   This remainder of the function executes at `splnet`. This is overly conservative locking to avoid sprinkling the individual `case` statements with calls to `splnet` when the calls are really necessary. As we mentioned with Figure 23.15, setting the processor priority to `splnet` only stops a software interrupt from causing the IP input routine to

```
———————————————————————————————————————————————————— tcp_usrreq.c
45 int
46 tcp_usrreq(so, req, m, nam, control)
47 struct socket *so;
48 int     req;
49 struct mbuf *m, *nam, *control;
50 {
51     struct inpcb *inp;
52     struct tcpcb *tp;
53     int     s;
54     int     error = 0;
55     int     ostate;

56     if (req == PRU_CONTROL)
57         return (in_control(so, (int) m, (caddr_t) nam,
58                             (struct ifnet *) control));
59     if (control && control->m_len) {
60         m_freem(control);
61         if (m)
62             m_freem(m);
63         return (EINVAL);
64     }
65     s = splnet();
66     inp = sotoinpcb(so);
67     /*
68      * When a TCP is attached to a socket, then there will be
69      * a (struct inpcb) pointed at by the socket, and this
70      * structure will point at a subsidary (struct tcpcb).
71      */
72     if (inp == 0 && req != PRU_ATTACH) {
73         splx(s);
74         return (EINVAL);        /* XXX */
75     }
76     if (inp) {
77         tp = intotcpcb(inp);
78         /* WHAT IF TP IS 0? */
79         ostate = tp->t_state;
80     } else
81         ostate = 0;

82     switch (req) {


                                /* switch cases */


276 default:
277     panic("tcp_usrreq");
278 }
279 if (tp && (so->so_options & SO_DEBUG))
280     tcp_trace(TA_USER, ostate, tp, (struct tcpiphdr *) 0, req);
281 splx(s);
282 return (error);
283 }
———————————————————————————————————————————————————— tcp_usrreq.c
```

Figure 30.1   Body of `tcp_usrreq` function.

be executed (which could call `tcp_input`). It does not prevent the interface layer from accepting incoming packets and placing them onto IP's input queue.

The pointer to the Internet PCB is obtained from the `socket` structure pointer. The only time the resulting PCB pointer is allowed to be a null pointer is when the `PRU_ATTACH` request is issued, which occurs in response to the `socket` system call.

67–81   If `inp` is nonnull, the current connection state is saved in `ostate` for the call to `tcp_trace` at the end of the function.

We now discuss the individual `case` statements. The `PRU_ATTACH` request, shown in Figure 30.2, is issued by the `socket` system call and by `sonewconn` when a connection request arrives for a listening socket (Figure 28.7).

```
                                                                    ── tcp_usrreq.c
 83        /*
 84         * TCP attaches to socket via PRU_ATTACH, reserving space,
 85         * and an internet control block.
 86         */
 87    case PRU_ATTACH:
 88        if (inp) {
 89            error = EISCONN;
 90            break;
 91        }
 92        error = tcp_attach(so);
 93        if (error)
 94            break;
 95        if ((so->so_options & SO_LINGER) && so->so_linger == 0)
 96            so->so_linger = TCP_LINGERTIME;
 97        tp = sototcpcb(so);
 98        break;

 99        /*
100         * PRU_DETACH detaches the TCP protocol from the socket.
101         * If the protocol state is non-embryonic, then can't
102         * do this directly: have to initiate a PRU_DISCONNECT,
103         * which may finish later; embryonic TCB's can just
104         * be discarded here.
105         */
106    case PRU_DETACH:
107        if (tp->t_state > TCPS_LISTEN)
108            tp = tcp_disconnect(tp);
109        else
110            tp = tcp_close(tp);
111        break;
                                                                    ── tcp_usrreq.c
```

Figure 30.2 `tcp_usrreq` function: `PRU_ATTACH` and `PRU_DETACH` requests.

`PRU_ATTACH` request

83–94   If the socket structure already points to a PCB, `EISCONN` is returned. `tcp_attach` completes the processing: it allocates and initializes the Internet PCB and the TCP control block.

95–96   If the `SO_LINGER` socket option is set, and the linger time is 0, it is set to 120 (`TCP_LINGERTIME`).

How can a socket option be set before the PRU_ATTACH request is issued? It is impossible to set a socket option before calling socket, but sonewconn also issues the PRU_ATTACH request. The PRU_ATTACH request is issued after sonewconn copies the so_options from the listening socket to the newly created socket. This code prevents a newly accepted connection from inheriting a linger time of 0 from the listening socket.

There is a bug here. The constant TCP_LINGERTIME is initialized to 120 in the header tcp_timer.h with the comment "linger at most 2 minutes." But the so_linger value becomes the final argument to the kernel's tsleep function (called from soclose), which becomes the final argument to the kernel's timeout function and is in clock ticks, not seconds. If the system's clock-tick frequency (hz) is 100, this value for the linger time is 1.2 seconds, not 2 minutes.

97   tp is now set to the pointer to the socket's TCP control block. This is required at the end, in case the SO_DEBUG socket option is set.

PRU_DETACH request

99–111   The close system call issues the PRU_DETACH request if the PRU_DISCONNECT request fails. If the connection has not been completed (the connection state is less than ESTABLISHED), nothing needs to be sent to the other end. But if the connection has been established, tcp_disconnect initiates TCP's connection-close sequence (e.g., any pending data is sent, followed by a FIN).

The test for the state being greater than LISTEN is incorrect, because if the state is SYN_SENT or SYN_RCVD, both of which are greater than LISTEN, tcp_disconnect just calls tcp_close. This case could be simplified by just calling tcp_disconnect.

Figure 30.3 shows the processing for the bind and listen system calls.

```
                                                                    ── tcp_usrreq.c
112            /*
113             * Give the socket an address.
114             */
115        case PRU_BIND:
116            error = in_pcbbind(inp, nam);
117            if (error)
118                break;
119            break;

120            /*
121             * Prepare to accept connections.
122             */
123        case PRU_LISTEN:
124            if (inp->inp_lport == 0)
125                error = in_pcbbind(inp, (struct mbuf *) 0);
126            if (error == 0)
127                tp->t_state = TCPS_LISTEN;
128            break;
                                                                    ── tcp_usrreq.c
```

Figure 30.3 tcp_usrreq function: PRU_BIND and PRU_LISTEN requests.

112–119   All the work for a PRU_BIND request is done by in_pcbbind.

120–128   For the PRU_LISTEN request, if the socket has not been bound with a local port, in_pcbbind assigns one automatically. This is rare, since most servers explicitly bind their well-known port, although RPC (remote procedure call) servers typically bind an ephemeral port and then register the port with the *Port Mapper*. (Section 29.4 of Volume 1 describes the Port Mapper.) The connection state is set to LISTEN. This is the main purpose of listen: to set the socket's state so that incoming connections are accepted (i.e., a passive open).

Figure 30.4 shows the processing for the connect system call: an active open normally initiated by a client.

```
                                                                        ────── tcp_usrreq.c
129        /*
130         * Initiate connection to peer.
131         * Create a template for use in transmissions on this connection.
132         * Enter SYN_SENT state, and mark socket as connecting.
133         * Start keepalive timer, and seed output sequence space.
134         * Send initial segment on connection.
135         */
136    case PRU_CONNECT:
137        if (inp->inp_lport == 0) {
138            error = in_pcbbind(inp, (struct mbuf *) 0);
139            if (error)
140                break;
141        }
142        error = in_pcbconnect(inp, nam);
143        if (error)
144            break;

145        tp->t_template = tcp_template(tp);
146        if (tp->t_template == 0) {
147            in_pcbdisconnect(inp);
148            error = ENOBUFS;
149            break;
150        }
151        /* Compute window scaling to request.   */
152        while (tp->request_r_scale < TCP_MAX_WINSHIFT &&
153                (TCP_MAXWIN << tp->request_r_scale) < so->so_rcv.sb_hiwat)
154            tp->request_r_scale++;
155        soisconnecting(so);
156        tcpstat.tcps_connattempt++;
157        tp->t_state = TCPS_SYN_SENT;
158        tp->t_timer[TCPT_KEEP] = TCPTV_KEEP_INIT;

159        tp->iss = tcp_iss;
160        tcp_iss += TCP_ISSINCR / 2;
161        tcp_sendseqinit(tp);

162        error = tcp_output(tp);
163        break;
                                                                        ────── tcp_usrreq.c
```

Figure 30.4 tcp_usrreq function: PRU_CONNECT request.

Assign ephemeral port

129–141   If the socket has not been bound with a local port, `in_pcbbind` assigns one automatically. This is typical for clients, which normally don't care about the value of the local port.

Connect PCB

142–144   `in_pcbconnect` acquires a route to the destination, determines the outgoing interface, and verifies that the socket pair is unique.

Initialize IP and TCP headers

145–150   `tcp_template` allocates an mbuf for a copy of the IP and TCP headers, and it initializes both headers with as much information as possible. The only way for this function to fail is for the kernel to run out of mbufs.

Calculate window scale factor

151–154   The window scale value for the receive buffer is calculated: 65535 (`TCP_MAXWIN`) is left shifted until the value is greater than or equal to the size of the receive buffer (`so_rcv.sb_hiwat`). The resulting shift count (between 0 and 14) is the scale factor that will be sent in the SYN. (We saw identical code in Figure 28.7 that was executed for a passive open.) Since the window scale option is sent in the SYN resulting from a `connect`, the process must set the `SO_RCVBUF` socket option before calling `connect`, or the default buffer size is used (`tcp_recvspace` from Figure 24.3).

Set socket and connection state

155–158   `soisconnecting` sets the appropriate bits in the socket's state variable, and the state of the TCP connection is set to SYN_SENT. This causes the call to `tcp_output` that follows to send the SYN (see the `tcp_outflags` value in Figure 24.16). The connection-establishment timer is initialized to 75 seconds. `tcp_output` will also set the retransmission timer for the SYN, as shown in Figure 25.15.

Initialize sequence numbers

159–161   The initial send sequence number is copied from the global `tcp_iss`. This global is then incremented by 64,000 (`TCP_ISSINCR` divided by 2). We saw this same handling of `tcp_iss` when the ISS was initialized after a listening server received a SYN (Figure 28.17). The send sequence numbers are then initialized by `tcp_sendseqinit`.

Send initial SYN

162   `tcp_output` sends the initial SYN to initiate the connection. A local error (for example, out of mbufs or no route to destination) is returned by `tcp_output`, which becomes the return value from `tcp_usrreq`, which is returned to the process.

Figure 30.5 shows the processing for the `PRU_CONNECT2`, `PRU_DISCONNECT`, and `PRU_ACCEPT` requests.

164–169   The `PRU_CONNECT2` request, a result of the `socketpair` system call, is invalid for the TCP protocol.

170–183   The `close` system call issues the `PRU_DISCONNECT` request. If the connection has been established, a FIN must be sent and the normal TCP close sequence followed. This is done by `tcp_disconnect`.

```
                                                                ─── tcp_usrreq.c
164        /*
165         * Create a TCP connection between two sockets.
166         */
167    case PRU_CONNECT2:
168        error = EOPNOTSUPP;
169        break;

170        /*
171         * Initiate disconnect from peer.
172         * If connection never passed embryonic stage, just drop;
173         * else if don't need to let data drain, then can just drop anyway,
174         * else have to begin TCP shutdown process: mark socket disconnecting,
175         * drain unread data, state switch to reflect user close, and
176         * send segment (e.g. FIN) to peer.  Socket will be really disconnected
177         * when peer sends FIN and acks ours.
178         *
179         * SHOULD IMPLEMENT LATER PRU_CONNECT VIA REALLOC TCPCB.
180         */
181    case PRU_DISCONNECT:
182        tp = tcp_disconnect(tp);
183        break;

184        /*
185         * Accept a connection.  Essentially all the work is
186         * done at higher levels; just return the address
187         * of the peer, storing through addr.
188         */
189    case PRU_ACCEPT:
190        in_setpeeraddr(inp, nam);
191        break;
                                                                ─── tcp_usrreq.c
```

Figure 30.5 tcp_usrreq function: PRU_CONNECT2, PRU_DISCONNECT, and PRU_ACCEPT requests.

The comment beginning with "SHOULD IMPLEMENT" refers to the fact that a socket that encounters an error cannot be reused. For example, if a client issues a connect and receives an error, it cannot issue another connect on the same socket. Instead, the socket with the error must be closed, a new socket created with socket, and the connect issued on the new socket.

184–191   All the work associated with the accept system call is done by the socket layer and the protocol layer. The PRU_ACCEPT request just returns the IP address and port number of the peer to the process.

The PRU_SHUTDOWN, PRU_RCVD, and PRU_SEND requests are processed in Figure 30.6.

PRU_SHUTDOWN **request**

192–200   This request is issued by soshutdown when the process calls shutdown to prevent any further output. socantsendmore sets the socket's flags to prevent any future output. tcp_usrclosed sets the connection state according to Figure 24.15. tcp_output attempts to send the FIN, but if there is still pending data to send to the other end, that data is sent before the FIN is sent.

```
                                                                              ── tcp_usrreq.c
192          /*
193           * Mark the connection as being incapable of further output.
194           */
195      case PRU_SHUTDOWN:
196          socantsendmore(so);
197          tp = tcp_usrclosed(tp);
198          if (tp)
199              error = tcp_output(tp);
200          break;

201          /*
202           * After a receive, possibly send window update to peer.
203           */
204      case PRU_RCVD:
205          (void) tcp_output(tp);
206          break;

207          /*
208           * Do a send by putting data in output queue and updating urgent
209           * marker if URG set.  Possibly send more data.
210           */
211      case PRU_SEND:
212          sbappend(&so->so_snd, m);
213          error = tcp_output(tp);
214          break;
                                                                              ── tcp_usrreq.c
```

Figure 30.6   `tcp_usrreq` function: PRU_SHUTDOWN, PRU_RCVD, and PRU_SEND requests.

PRU_RCVD **request**

201–206   This request is issued by `soreceive` after the process has read data from the
socket's receive buffer. TCP needs to know about this since the receive buffer may now
have enough room to allow the advertised window to increase. `tcp_output` will
determine whether a window update segment should be sent.

PRU_SEND **request**

207–214   In Figure 23.14 we showed how the five write functions ended up issuing this
request. `sbappend` adds the data to the socket's send buffer (where it must wait until
acknowledged by the other end), and `tcp_output` sends a segment, if possible.

Figure 30.7 shows the processing of the PRU_ABORT and PRU_SENSE requests.

PRU_ABORT **request**

215–220   A PRU_ABORT request is issued for a TCP socket by `soclose` if the socket is a listening socket (e.g., a server) and if there are pending connections for the server that
have already initiated or completed the three-way handshake, but have not been
`accept`ed by the server yet. `tcp_drop` sends an RST if the connection is synchronized.

```
                                                                    ── tcp_usrreq.c
215            /*
216             * Abort the TCP.
217             */
218        case PRU_ABORT:
219            tp = tcp_drop(tp, ECONNABORTED);
220            break;

221        case PRU_SENSE:
222            ((struct stat *) m)->st_blksize = so->so_snd.sb_hiwat;
223            (void) splx(s);
224            return (0);
                                                                    ── tcp_usrreq.c
```

Figure 30.7 tcp_usrreq function: PRU_ABORT and PRU_SENSE requests.

PRU_SENSE request

221–224   The fstat system call generates the PRU_SENSE request. TCP returns the size of
the send buffer as the st_blksize element of the stat structure.

Figure 30.8 shows the PRU_RCVOOB request, issued by soreceive when the process issues a read system call specifying the MSG_OOB flag to read out-of-band data.

```
                                                                    ── tcp_usrreq.c
225        case PRU_RCVOOB:
226            if ((so->so_oobmark == 0 &&
227                (so->so_state & SS_RCVATMARK) == 0) ||
228                so->so_options & SO_OOBINLINE ||
229                tp->t_oobflags & TCPOOB_HADDATA) {
230                error = EINVAL;
231                break;
232            }
233            if ((tp->t_oobflags & TCPOOB_HAVEDATA) == 0) {
234                error = EWOULDBLOCK;
235                break;
236            }
237            m->m_len = 1;
238            *mtod(m, caddr_t) = tp->t_iobc;
239            if (((int) nam & MSG_PEEK) == 0)
240                tp->t_oobflags ^= (TCPOOB_HAVEDATA | TCPOOB_HADDATA);
241            break;
                                                                    ── tcp_usrreq.c
```

Figure 30.8 tcp_usrreq function: PRU_RCVOOB request.

Verify that reading out-of-band data is appropriate

225–232   It is an error for the process to try to read out-of-band data if any one of the following three conditions is true:

1. if the socket's out-of-band mark is 0 (so_oobmark) and the socket is not at the
    mark (the SS_RCVATMARK flag is not set), or

2. if the `SO_OOBINLINE` socket option is set, or

3. if the `TCPOOB_HADDATA` flag is set for the connection (i.e., the connection did have an out-of-band byte, but it has already been read).

The error `EINVAL` is returned if any one of these is true.

Check that out-of-band byte has arrived

233–236   If none of the three conditions above is true, but the `TCPOOB_HAVEDATA` flag is false, this indicates that TCP has received an urgent mode notification from the other end, but the byte whose sequence number is 1 less than the urgent pointer has not been received yet (Figure 29.17). The error `EWOULDBLOCK` is returned. It is possible for TCP to send an urgent notification with an urgent offset referencing a byte that the sender has not been able to send yet. Figure 26.7 of Volume 1 shows an example of this scenario, which often happens if the sender's data transmission has been stopped by a zero-window advertisement.

Return out-of-band byte

237–238   The single byte of out-of-band data that was stored in `t_iobc` by `tcp_pulloutofband` is returned to the process.

Flip flags

239–241   If the process is actually reading the out-of-band byte (as compared to peeking at it with the `MSG_PEEK` flag), this exclusive OR turns the HAVE flag off and the HAD flag on. We are guaranteed at this point in the `case` statement that the HAVE flag is set and the HAD flag is cleared. The purpose of the HAD flag is to prevent the process from trying to read the out-of-band byte more than once. Once the HAD flag is set, it is not cleared until a new urgent pointer is received from the other end (Figure 29.17).

> The reason for this hard-to-understand exclusive OR, instead of the simpler
>
> ```
> tp->t_oobflags = TCPOOB_HADDATA;
> ```
>
> is to allow additional bits in `t_oobflags` to be used. Net/3, however, only uses the 2 bits that we've described.

The `PRU_SENDOOB` request, shown in Figure 30.9, is issued by `sosend` when the process writes data and specifies the `MSG_OOB` flag.

Check for room and append to send buffer

242–247   The process is allowed to exceed the size of the send buffer by up to 512 bytes when sending out-of-band data. The socket layer is more permissive, allowing out-of-band data to exceed the size of the send buffer by 1024 bytes (Figure 16.24). `sbappend` adds the data to the end of the send buffer.

Calculate urgent pointer

248–257   The urgent pointer (`snd_up`) points to the byte following the final byte from the write request. We showed this in Figure 26.30, assuming the process writes 3 bytes of data with the `MSG_OOB` flag set and that the send buffer was empty. Realize that if the

```
                                                                      ── tcp_usrreq.c
242        case PRU_SENDOOB:
243            if (sbspace(&so->so_snd) < -512) {
244                m_freem(m);
245                error = ENOBUFS;
246                break;
247            }
248            /*
249             * According to RFC961 (Assigned Protocols),
250             * the urgent pointer points to the last octet
251             * of urgent data.  We continue, however,
252             * to consider it to indicate the first octet
253             * of data past the urgent section.
254             * Otherwise, snd_up should be one lower.
255             */
256            sbappend(&so->so_snd, m);
257            tp->snd_up = tp->snd_una + so->so_snd.sb_cc;

258            tp->t_force = 1;
259            error = tcp_output(tp);
260            tp->t_force = 0;

261            break;
                                                                      ── tcp_usrreq.c
```

Figure 30.9 tcp_usrreq function: PRU_SENDOOB request.

process writes more than 1 byte of data with the MSG_OOB flag set, only the final byte is considered the out-of-band byte when the data is received by a Berkeley-derived system.

Force TCP output

258–261   t_force is set to 1 and tcp_output is called. This causes a segment to be sent with the URG flag set and with a nonzero urgent offset, even if no data can be sent because of a zero-window advertisement. Figure 26.7 of Volume 1 shows the transmission of an urgent segment into a closed window.

The final three requests are shown in Figure 30.10.

262–267   The getsockname and getpeername system calls issue the PRU_SOCKADDR and PRU_PEERADDR requests, respectively. The functions in_setsockaddr and in_setpeeraddr fetch the information from the PCB, storing the result in the addr argument.

268–275   The PRU_SLOWTIMO request is issued by the tcp_slowtimo function. As the comment indicates, the only reason tcp_slowtimo doesn't call tcp_timers directly is to allow the timer expiration to be traced by the call to tcp_trace at the end of the function (Figure 30.1). For the trace record to show which one of the four TCP timer counters expired, tcp_slowtimo passes the index into the t_timer array (Figure 25.1) as the nam argument, and this is left shifted 8 bits and logically ORed into the request value (req). The trpt program knows about this hack and handles it accordingly.

```
262        case PRU_SOCKADDR:                                                  ── tcp_usrreq.c
263            in_setsockaddr(inp, nam);
264            break;

265        case PRU_PEERADDR:
266            in_setpeeraddr(inp, nam);
267            break;

268        /*
269         * TCP slow timer went off; going through this
270         * routine for tracing's sake.
271         */
272        case PRU_SLOWTIMO:
273            tp = tcp_timers(tp, (int) nam);
274            req |= (int) nam << 8;   /* for debug's sake */
275            break;
                                                                               ── tcp_usrreq.c
```

Figure 30.10   tcp_usrreq function: PRU_SOCKADDR, PRU_PEERADDR, and PRU_SLOWTIMO requests.

30.3 `tcp_attach` Function

The `tcp_attach` function is called by `tcp_usrreq` to process the PRU_ATTACH request (i.e., when the `socket` system call is issued or when a new connection request arrives for a listening socket). Figure 30.11 shows the code.

Allocate space for send buffer and receive buffer

361–372   If space has not been allocated for the socket's send and receive buffers, `sbreserve` sets them both to 8192, the default values of the global variables `tcp_sendspace` and `tcp_recvspace` (Figure 24.3).

> Whether these defaults are adequate depends on the MSS for each direction of the connection, which depends on the MTU. For example, [Comer and Lin 1994] show that anomalous behavior occurs if the send buffer is less than three times the MSS, which drastically reduces performance. Some implementations have much higher defaults, such as 61,444 bytes, realizing the effect these defaults have on performance, especially with higher MTUs (e.g., FDDI and ATM).

Allocate Internet PCB and TCP control block

373–377   `in_pcballoc` allocates an Internet PCB and `tcp_newtcpcb` allocates a TCP control block and links it to the PCB.

378–384   The code with the comment XXX is executed if the call to `malloc` in `tcp_newtcpcb` fails. Remember that the PRU_ATTACH request is issued as a result of the `socket` system call, and when a connection request arrives for a listening socket (`sonewconn`). In the latter case the socket flag SS_NOFDREF is set. If this flag is left on, the call to `sofree` by `in_pcbdetach` releases the `socket` structure. As we saw in `tcp_input`, this structure should not be released until that function is done with the received segment (the `dropsocket` flag in Figure 29.27). Therefore the current value of the SS_NOFDREF flag is saved in the variable `nofd` when `in_pcbdetach` is called, and reset before `tcp_attach` returns.

385–386   The TCP connection state is initialized to CLOSED.

```
                                                           ———— tcp_usrreq.c
361 int
362 tcp_attach(so)
363 struct socket *so;
364 {
365     struct tcpcb *tp;
366     struct inpcb *inp;
367     int     error;

368     if (so->so_snd.sb_hiwat == 0 || so->so_rcv.sb_hiwat == 0) {
369         error = soreserve(so, tcp_sendspace, tcp_recvspace);
370         if (error)
371             return (error);
372     }
373     error = in_pcballoc(so, &tcb);
374     if (error)
375         return (error);
376     inp = sotoinpcb(so);
377     tp = tcp_newtcpcb(inp);
378     if (tp == 0) {
379         int     nofd = so->so_state & SS_NOFDREF;    /* XXX */

380         so->so_state &= ~SS_NOFDREF;    /* don't free the socket yet */
381         in_pcbdetach(inp);
382         so->so_state |= nofd;
383         return (ENOBUFS);
384     }
385     tp->t_state = TCPS_CLOSED;
386     return (0);
387 }
                                                           ———— tcp_usrreq.c
```

Figure 30.11 tcp_attach function: create a new TCP socket.

30.4 tcp_disconnect Function

tcp_disconnect, shown in Figure 30.12, initiates a TCP disconnect.

Connection not yet synchronized

396–402   If the socket is not yet in the ESTABLISHED state (i.e., LISTEN, SYN_SENT, or SYN_RCVD), tcp_close just releases the PCB and the TCP control block. Nothing needs to be sent to the other end since the connection has not been synchronized.

Hard disconnect

403–404   If the connection is synchronized, the SO_LINGER socket option is set, and the linger time (so_linger) is set to 0, the connection is dropped by tcp_drop. This sets the connection state to CLOSED, sends an RST to the other end, and releases the PCB and TCP control block. The connection does not pass through the TIME_WAIT state. The call to close that caused the PRU_DISCONNECT request will discard any data still in the send or receive buffers.

If the SO_LINGER socket option has been set with a nonzero linger time, it is handled by soclose.

——— *tcp_usrreq.c*
```
396 struct tcpcb *
397 tcp_disconnect(tp)
398 struct tcpcb *tp;
399 {
400     struct socket *so = tp->t_inpcb->inp_socket;

401     if (tp->t_state < TCPS_ESTABLISHED)
402         tp = tcp_close(tp);
403     else if ((so->so_options & SO_LINGER) && so->so_linger == 0)
404         tp = tcp_drop(tp, 0);
405     else {
406         soisdisconnecting(so);
407         sbflush(&so->so_rcv);
408         tp = tcp_usrclosed(tp);
409         if (tp)
410             (void) tcp_output(tp);
411     }
412     return (tp);
413 }
```
——— *tcp_usrreq.c*

Figure 30.12 `tcp_disconnect` function: initiate TCP disconnect.

Graceful disconnect

405–406　　This code is executed when the connection has been synchronized but the
SO_LINGER option either was not set or was set with a nonzero linger time. TCP's normal connection termination steps must be followed. `soisdisconnecting` sets the
socket's state.

Discard pending receive data

407　　　Any pending data in the receive buffer is discarded by `sbflush`, since the process
has closed the socket. The send buffer is left alone, however, and `tcp_output` will try
to send what remains. We say "try" because there's no guarantee that the data still to be
sent will be transmitted successfully. The other end might crash before it receives and
acknowledges the data, or even if the TCP module at the other end receives and
acknowledges the data, the system might crash before the application at the other end
reads the data. Since the local process has closed the socket, if TCP gives up trying to
send what remains in the send buffer (because its retransmission timer finally expires),
there is no way to notify the process of the error.

Change connection state

408–410　　`tcp_usrclosed` moves the connection into the next state, based on the current
state. This normally moves the connection to the FIN_WAIT_1 state, since the connection is typically closed from the ESTABLISHED state. We'll see that `tcp_usrclosed`
always returns the current control block pointer (`tp`), since the state must be synchronized to get to this point in the code, so `tcp_output` is always called to send a segment. If the connection moves from the ESTABLISHED to the FIN_WAIT_1 state, this
causes a FIN to be sent.

30.5 `tcp_usrclosed` **Function**

This function, shown in Figure 30.13, is called from `tcp_disconnect` and when the `PRU_SHUTDOWN` request is processed.

```
                                                                          ── tcp_usrreq.c
424 struct tcpcb *
425 tcp_usrclosed(tp)
426 struct tcpcb *tp;
427 {

428     switch (tp->t_state) {

429     case TCPS_CLOSED:
430     case TCPS_LISTEN:
431     case TCPS_SYN_SENT:
432         tp->t_state = TCPS_CLOSED;
433         tp = tcp_close(tp);
434         break;

435     case TCPS_SYN_RECEIVED:
436     case TCPS_ESTABLISHED:
437         tp->t_state = TCPS_FIN_WAIT_1;
438         break;

439     case TCPS_CLOSE_WAIT:
440         tp->t_state = TCPS_LAST_ACK;
441         break;
442     }
443     if (tp && tp->t_state >= TCPS_FIN_WAIT_2)
444         soisdisconnected(tp->t_inpcb->inp_socket);
445     return (tp);
446 }
                                                                          ── tcp_usrreq.c
```

Figure 30.13 `tcp_usrclosed` function: move connection to next state, based on process close.

Simple close when SYN not received

429–434   If a SYN has not been received on the connection, a FIN need not be sent. The new state is CLOSED and `tcp_close` releases the Internet PCB and the TCP control block.

Move to FIN_WAIT_1 state

435–438   In the SYN_RCVD and ESTABLISHED states, the new state is FIN_WAIT_1, which causes the next call to `tcp_output` to send a FIN (the `tcp_outflags` value in Figure 24.16).

Move to LAST_ACK state

439–441   In the CLOSE_WAIT state, the close moves the connection into the LAST_ACK state. The next call to `tcp_output` will cause a FIN to be sent.

443–444   If the connection state is either FIN_WAIT_2 or TIME_WAIT, `soisdisconnected` marks the socket state appropriately.

30.6 `tcp_ctloutput` **Function**

The `tcp_ctloutput` function is called by the `getsockopt` and `setsockopt` system calls when the descriptor argument refers to a TCP socket and when the level is not SOL_SOCKET. Figure 30.14 shows the two socket options supported by TCP.

optname	Variable	Access	Description
TCP_NODELAY	t_flags	read, write	Nagle algorithm (Figure 26.8)
TCP_MAXSEG	t_maxseg	read, write	maximum segment size TCP will send

Figure 30.14 Socket options supported by TCP.

Figure 30.15 shows the first part of the function.

```
                                                                    ── tcp_usrreq.c
284 int
285 tcp_ctloutput(op, so, level, optname, mp)
286 int      op;
287 struct socket *so;
288 int      level, optname;
289 struct mbuf **mp;
290 {
291     int      error = 0, s;
292     struct inpcb *inp;
293     struct tcpcb *tp;
294     struct mbuf *m;
295     int      i;

296     s = splnet();
297     inp = sotoinpcb(so);
298     if (inp == NULL) {
299         splx(s);
300         if (op == PRCO_SETOPT && *mp)
301             (void) m_free(*mp);
302         return (ECONNRESET);
303     }
304     if (level != IPPROTO_TCP) {
305         error = ip_ctloutput(op, so, level, optname, mp);
306         splx(s);
307         return (error);
308     }
309     tp = intotcpcb(inp);
                                                                    ── tcp_usrreq.c
```

Figure 30.15 `tcp_ctloutput` function: first part.

296–303   The processor priority is set to `splnet` while the function executes, and `inp` points to the Internet PCB for the socket. If `inp` is null, the mbuf is released if the operation was to set a socket option, and an error is returned.

304–308   If the *level* (the second argument to the `getsockopt` and `setsockopt` system calls) is not `IPPROTO_TCP`, the command is for some other protocol (i.e., IP). For example, it is possible to create a TCP socket and set the IP source routing socket option. In

309

this example IP processes the socket option, not TCP. `ip_ctloutput` handles the command.

The command is for TCP, so `tp` is set to the TCP control block.

The remainder of the function is a `switch` with two cases: one for `PRCO_SETOPT` (shown in Figure 30.16) and one for `PRCO_GETOPT` (shown in Figure 30.17).

———————————————————————————————— tcp_usrreq.c
```
310     switch (op) {

311     case PRCO_SETOPT:
312         m = *mp;
313         switch (optname) {

314         case TCP_NODELAY:
315             if (m == NULL || m->m_len < sizeof(int))
316                     error = EINVAL;
317             else if (*mtod(m, int *))
318                     tp->t_flags |= TF_NODELAY;
319             else
320                 tp->t_flags &= ~TF_NODELAY;
321             break;

322         case TCP_MAXSEG:
323             if (m && (i = *mtod(m, int *)) > 0 && i <= tp->t_maxseg)
324                     tp->t_maxseg = i;
325             else
326                 error = EINVAL;
327             break;

328         default:
329             error = ENOPROTOOPT;
330             break;
331         }
332         if (m)
333             (void) m_free(m);
334         break;
```
———————————————————————————————— tcp_usrreq.c

Figure 30.16 `tcp_ctloutput` function: set a socket option.

315–316   `m` is an mbuf containing the fourth argument to `setsockopt`. For both of the TCP options the mbuf must contain an integer value. If either the mbuf pointer is null, or the amount of data in the mbuf is less than the size of an integer, an error is returned.

TCP_NODELAY option

317–321   If the integer value is nonzero, the `TF_NODELAY` flag is set. This disables the Nagle algorithm in Figure 26.8. If the integer value is 0, the Nagle algorithm is enabled (the default) and the `TF_NODELAY` flag is cleared.

TCP_MAXSEG option

322–327   A process can only decrease the MSS. When a TCP socket is created, `tcp_newtcpcb` initializes `t_maxseg` to its default of 512. When a SYN is received from the other end with an MSS option, `tcp_input` calls `tcp_mss`, and `t_maxseg` can be set as high as the outgoing interface MTU (minus 40 bytes for the default IP and TCP headers), which is 1460 for an Ethernet. Therefore, after a call to socket but before a connection is established, a process can only decrease the MSS from its default of 512. After a connection is established, the process can decrease the MSS from whatever value was selected by tcp_mss.

> 4.4BSD was the first Berkeley release to allow the MSS to be set with a socket option. Prior releases only allowed a getsockopt for the MSS.

Release mbuf

332–333   The mbuf chain is released.

Figure 30.17 shows the processing for the PRCO_GETOPT command.

```
                                                                    ── tcp_usrreq.c
335     case PRCO_GETOPT:
336         *mp = m = m_get(M_WAIT, MT_SOOPTS);
337         m->m_len = sizeof(int);

338         switch (optname) {
339         case TCP_NODELAY:
340             *mtod(m, int *) = tp->t_flags & TF_NODELAY;
341             break;
342         case TCP_MAXSEG:
343             *mtod(m, int *) = tp->t_maxseg;
344             break;
345         default:
346             error = ENOPROTOOPT;
347             break;
348         }
349         break;
350     }
351     splx(s);
352     return (error);
353 }
                                                                    ── tcp_usrreq.c
```

Figure 30.17 tcp_ctloutput function: get a socket option.

335–337   Both TCP socket options return an integer to the process, so m_get obtains an mbuf and its length is set to the size of an integer.

339–341   TCP_NODELAY returns the current status of the TF_NODELAY flag: 0 if the flag is not set (the Nagle algorithm is enabled) or TF_NODELAY if the flag is set.

342–344   The TCP_MAXSEG option returns the current value of t_maxseg. As we said in our discussion of the PRCO_SETOPT command, the value returned depends whether the socket has been connected yet.

30.7 Summary

The `tcp_usrreq` function is straightforward because most of the required processing is done by other functions. The PRU_*xxx* requests form the glue between the protocol-independent system calls and the TCP protocol processing.

The `tcp_ctloutput` function is also simple because only two socket options are supported by TCP: enable or disable the Nagle algorithm, and set or fetch the maximum segment size.

Exercises

30.1 Now that we've covered all of TCP, list the processing steps and the TCP state transitions when a client goes through the normal steps of `socket`, `connect`, `write` (a request to the server), `read` (a reply from the server), and `close`. Do the same exercise for the server end.

30.2 If a process sets the `SO_LINGER` socket option with a linger time of 0 and then calls `close`, we showed how `tcp_disconnect` is called, which causes an RST to be sent. What happens if a process sets this socket option with a linger time of 0 but is then killed by a signal instead of calling `close`? Is the RST segment still sent?

30.3 The description for `TCP_LINGERTIME` in Figure 25.4 is the "maximum #seconds for `SO_LINGER` socket option." Given the code in Figure 30.2, is this description correct?

30.4 A Net/3 client calls `socket` and `connect` to actively open a connection to a server. The server is reached through the client's default router. A total of 1,129 segments are sent by the client host to the server. Assuming the route to the destination does not change, how many routing table lookups are done on the client host for this connection? Explain.

30.5 Obtain the `sock` program described in Appendix C of Volume 1. Run it as a sink server with a pause before reading (`-P`) and a large receive buffer. Then run the same program on another system as a source client. Watch the data with `tcpdump`. Verify that TCP's ACK-every-other-segment does not occur and that the only ACKs seen from the server are delayed ACKs.

30.6 Modify the `SO_KEEPALIVE` socket option so that the parameters can be configured on a per-connection basis.

30.7 Read RFC 1122 to determine why it recommends that an implementation should allow an RST to carry data. Modify the Net/3 code to implement this.

31

BPF: BSD Packet Filter

31.1 Introduction

The BSD Packet Filter (BPF) is a software device that "taps" network interfaces. A process accesses a BPF device by opening /dev/bpf0, /dev/bpf1, and so on. Each BPF device can be opened only by one process at a time.

> Since each BPF device allocates 8192 bytes of buffer space, the system administrator typically limits the number of BPF devices. If open returns EBUSY, the device is in use, and a process tries the next device until the open succeeds.

The device is configured with several ioctl commands that associate the device with a network interface and install filters to receive incoming packets selectively. Packets are received by reading from the device, and packets are queued on the network interface by writing to the device.

> We will use the term *packet* even though *frame* is more accurate, since BPF works at the data-link layer and includes the link-layer headers in the frames it sends and receives.

BPF works only with network interfaces that been modified to support BPF. In Chapter 3 we saw that the Ethernet, SLIP, and loopback drivers call bpfattach. This call configures the interface for access through the BPF devices. In this section we show how the BPF device driver is organized and how packets move between the driver and the network interfaces.

BPF is normally used as a diagnostic tool to examine the traffic on a locally attached network. The tcpdump program is the best example of such a tool and is described in Appendix A of Volume 1. Normally the user is interested in packets between a given set of machines, or for a particular protocol, or even for a particular TCP connection. A BPF device can be configured with a filter that discards or accepts incoming packets according to a filter specification. Filters are specified as instructions to a pseudo-machine. The details of BPF filters are not discussed in this text. For more information about filters, see bpf(4) and [McCanne and Jacobson 1993].

31.2 Code Introduction

The code for the portion of the BPF device driver that we describe resides in the two headers and one C file listed in Figure 31.1.

File	Description
net/bpf.h	BPF constants
net/bpfdesc.h	BPF structures
net/bpf.c	BPF device support

Figure 31.1   Files discussed in this chapter.

Global Variables

The global variables introduced in this chapter are shown in Figure 31.2.

Variable	Datatype	Description
bpf_iflist	struct bpf_if *	linked list of BPF-capable interfaces
bpf_dtab	struct bpf_d []	array of BPF descriptor structures
bpf_bufsize	int	default size of BPF buffers

Figure 31.2   Global variables introduced in this chapter.

Statistics

Figure 31.3 shows the two statistics collected in the bpf_d structure for every active BPF device.

bpf_d member	Description
bd_rcount	#packets received from network interface
bd_dcount	#packets dropped because of insufficient buffer space

Figure 31.3   Statistics collected in this chapter.

The remainder of this chapter is divided into four sections:

- BPF interface structures,
- BPF device descriptors,
- BPF input processing, and
- BPF output processing.

31.3 bpf_if **Structure**

BPF keeps a list of the network interfaces that support BPF. Each interface is described by a bpf_if structure, and the global pointer bpf_iflist points to the first structure in the list. Figure 31.4 shows a BPF interface structure.

```
───────────────────────────────────────────────────────────── bpfdesc.h
67  struct bpf_if {
68      struct bpf_if *bif_next;      /* list of all interfaces */
69      struct bpf_d *bif_dlist;      /* descriptor list */
70      struct bpf_if **bif_driverp;    /* pointer into softc */
71      u_int   bif_dlt;              /* link layer type */
72      u_int   bif_hdrlen;          /* length of header (with padding) */
73      struct ifnet *bif_ifp;       /* correspoding interface */
74  };
───────────────────────────────────────────────────────────── bpfdesc.h
```

Figure 31.4 bpf_if structure.

67–69   bif_next points to the next BPF interface structure in the list. bif_dlist points to a list of BPF devices that have been opened and configured to tap this interface.

70   bif_driverp points to a bpf_if pointer stored in the ifnet structure of the tapped interface. When the interface is *not* tapped, *bif_driverp is null. When a BPF device is configured to tap an interface, *bif_driverp is changed to point back to the bpf_if structure and tells the interface to begin passing packets to BPF.

71   The type of interface is saved in bif_dlt. The values for our example interfaces are shown in Figure 31.5.

bif_dlt	Description
DLT_EN10MB	10Mb Ethernet interface
DLT_SLIP	SLIP interface
DLT_NULL	loopback interface

Figure 31.5 bif_dlt values.

72–74   Each packet accepted by BPF has a BPF header prepended to it. bif_hdrlen is the size of the header. Finally, bif_ifp points to the ifnet structure for the associated interface.

Figure 31.6 shows the bpf_hdr structure that is prepended to every incoming packet.

```
───────────────────────────────────────────────────────────── bpf.h
122  struct bpf_hdr {
123      struct timeval bh_tstamp;    /* time stamp */
124      u_long  bh_caplen;           /* length of captured portion */
125      u_long  bh_datalen;          /* original length of packet */
126      u_short bh_hdrlen;           /* length of bpf header (this struct plus
127                                      alignment padding) */
128  };
───────────────────────────────────────────────────────────── bpf.h
```

Figure 31.6 bpf_hdr structure.

122–128   bh_tstamp records the time the packet was captured. bh_caplen is the number of bytes saved by BPF, and bh_datalen is the number of bytes in the original packet. bh_headlen is the size of the bpf_hdr structure plus any padding. This value should match bif_hdrlen for the receiving interface and is used by processes to interpret the packets read from the BPF device.

Figure 31.7 shows how bpf_if structures are connected to the ifnet structures for each of our three sample interfaces (le_softc[0], sl_softc[0], and loif).

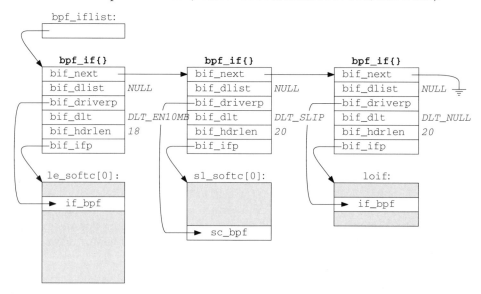

Figure 31.7 bpf_if and ifnet structures.

Notice that bif_driverp points to the if_bpf and sc_bpf pointers in the network interfaces and *not* to the interface structures.

> The SLIP device uses sc_bpf, instead of the if_bpf member. One reason might be that the SLIP BPF code was written before the if_bpf member was added to the ifnet structure. The ifnet structure in Net/2 does not include a if_bpf member.

The link-type and header-length members are initialized for all three interfaces according to the information passed by each driver in the call to bpfattach.

In Chapter 3 we saw that bpfattach was called by the Ethernet, SLIP, and loop-back drivers. The linked list of BPF interface structures is built as each device driver calls bpfattach during initialization. The function is shown in Figure 31.8.

1053–1063   bpfattach is called by each device driver that supports BPF. The first argument is the pointer saved in bif_driverp (described with Figure 31.4). The second argument points to the ifnet structure of the interface. The third argument identifies the data-link type, and the fourth argument identifies the size of link-layer header passed with the packet. A new bpf_if structure is allocated for the interface.

bpf.c

```
1053 void
1054 bpfattach(driverp, ifp, dlt, hdrlen)
1055 caddr_t *driverp;
1056 struct ifnet *ifp;
1057 u_int   dlt, hdrlen;
1058 {
1059     struct bpf_if *bp;
1060     int     i;
1061     bp = (struct bpf_if *) malloc(sizeof(*bp), M_DEVBUF, M_DONTWAIT);
1062     if (bp == 0)
1063         panic("bpfattach");

1064     bp->bif_dlist = 0;
1065     bp->bif_driverp = (struct bpf_if **) driverp;
1066     bp->bif_ifp = ifp;
1067     bp->bif_dlt = dlt;

1068     bp->bif_next = bpf_iflist;
1069     bpf_iflist = bp;

1070     *bp->bif_driverp = 0;

1071     /*
1072      * Compute the length of the bpf header.  This is not necessarily
1073      * equal to SIZEOF_BPF_HDR because we want to insert spacing such
1074      * that the network layer header begins on a longword boundary (for
1075      * performance reasons and to alleviate alignment restrictions).
1076      */
1077     bp->bif_hdrlen = BPF_WORDALIGN(hdrlen + SIZEOF_BPF_HDR) - hdrlen;

1078     /*
1079      * Mark all the descriptors free if this hasn't been done.
1080      */
1081     if (!D_ISFREE(&bpf_dtab[0]))
1082         for (i = 0; i < NBPFILTER; ++i)
1083             D_MARKFREE(&bpf_dtab[i]);

1084     printf("bpf: %s%d attached\n", ifp->if_name, ifp->if_unit);
1085 }
```

bpf.c

Figure 31.8 bpfattach function.

Initialize bpf_if structure

1064–1070   The bpf_if structure is initialized from the arguments and inserted into the front of the BPF interface list, bpf_iflist.

Compute BPF header size

1071–1077   bif_hdrlen is set to force the *network-layer* header (e.g., the IP header) to start on a longword boundary. This improves performance and avoids unnecessary alignment restrictions for the BPF filter. Figure 31.9 shows the overall organization of the captured BPF packet for each of our three sample interfaces.

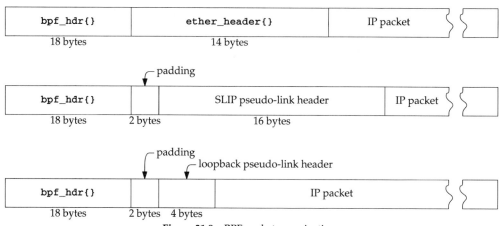

Figure 31.9   BPF packet organization.

The `ether_header` structure was described with Figure 4.10, the SLIP pseudo-link header was described with Figure 5.14, and the loopback pseudo-link header was described with Figure 5.28.

Notice that the SLIP and loopback packets require 2 bytes of padding to force the IP header to appear on a 4-byte boundary.

Initialize `bpf_dtab` table

1078–1083   This code initializes the BPF descriptor table, which is described with Figure 31.10. The initialization occurs the first time `bpfattach` is called and is skipped thereafter.

Print console message

1084–1085   A short message is printed to the console to announce that the interface has been configured for use by BPF.

31.4   `bpf_d` Structure

To begin tapping an interface, a process opens a BPF device and issues `ioctl` commands to select the interface, the read buffer size, and timeouts, and to specify a BPF filter. Each BPF device has an associated `bpf_d` structure, shown in Figure 31.10.

45–46   `bpf_d` structures are placed on a linked list when more than one BPF device is attached to the same network interface. `bd_next` points to the next structure in the list.

Packet buffers

47–52   Each `bpf_d` structure has two packet buffers associated with it. Incoming packets are always stored in the buffer attached to `bd_sbuf` (the store buffer). The other buffer is either attached to `bd_fbuf` (the free buffer), which means it is empty, or to `bd_hbuf` (the hold buffer), which means it contains packets that are being read by a process. `bd_slen` and `bd_hlen` record the number of bytes saved in the store and hold buffer respectively.

bpfdesc.h
```
45 struct bpf_d {
46      struct bpf_d *bd_next;      /* Linked list of descriptors */
47      caddr_t bd_sbuf;           /* store slot */
48      caddr_t bd_hbuf;           /* hold slot */
49      caddr_t bd_fbuf;           /* free slot */
50      int     bd_slen;           /* current length of store buffer */
51      int     bd_hlen;           /* current length of hold buffer */

52      int     bd_bufsize;        /* absolute length of buffers */

53      struct bpf_if *bd_bif;     /* interface descriptor */
54      u_long  bd_rtout;          /* Read timeout in 'ticks' */
55      struct bpf_insn *bd_filter; /* filter code */
56      u_long  bd_rcount;         /* number of packets received */
57      u_long  bd_dcount;         /* number of packets dropped */

58      u_char  bd_promisc;        /* true if listening promiscuously */
59      u_char  bd_state;          /* idle, waiting, or timed out */
60      u_char  bd_immediate;      /* true to return on packet arrival */
61      u_char  bd_pad;            /* explicit alignment */
62      struct selinfo bd_sel;     /* bsd select info */
63 };
```
bpfdesc.h

Figure 31.10   bpf_d structure.

When the store buffer becomes full, it is attached to bd_hbuf and the free buffer is attached to bd_sbuf. When the hold buffer is emptied, it is attached to bd_fbuf. The macro ROTATE_BUFFERS attaches the store buffer to bd_hbuf, attaches the free buffer to bd_sbuf, and clears bd_fbuf. It is called when the store buffer becomes full, or when the process doesn't want to wait for more packets.

bd_bufsize records the size of the two buffers associated with the device. It defaults to 4096 (BPF_BUFSIZE) bytes. The default value can be changed by patching the kernel, or bd_bufsize can be changed for a particular BPF device with the BIOCSBLEN ioctl command. The BIOCGBLEN command returns the current value of bd_bufsize, which can never exceed 32768 (BPF_MAXBUFSIZE) bytes. There is also a minimum size of 32 (BPF_MINBUFSIZE) bytes.

53–57   bd_bif points to the bpf_if structure associated with the BPF device. The BIOCSETIF command specifies the device. bd_rtout is the number of clock ticks to delay while waiting for packets to appear. bd_filter points to the BPF filter code for this device. Two statistics, which are available to a process through the BIOCGSTATS command, are kept in bd_rcount and bd_dcount.

58–63   bd_promisc is set with the BIOCPROMISC command and causes the interface to operate in promiscuous mode. bd_state is unused. bd_immediate is set with the BIOCIMMEDIATE command and causes the driver to return each packet as it is received instead of waiting for the hold buffer to fill. bd_pad pads the bpf_d structure to a longword boundary, and bd_sel holds the selinfo structure for the select system call. We don't describe the use of select with a BPF device, but select itself is described in Section 16.13.

bpfopen Function

When open is called for a BPF device, the call is routed to bpfopen (Figure 31.11) for processing.

—— *bpf.c*
```
256 int
257 bpfopen(dev, flag)
258 dev_t   dev;
259 int     flag;
260 {
261     struct bpf_d *d;

262     if (minor(dev) >= NBPFILTER)
263         return (ENXIO);
264     /*
265      * Each minor can be opened by only one process.  If the requested
266      * minor is in use, return EBUSY.
267      */
268     d = &bpf_dtab[minor(dev)];
269     if (!D_ISFREE(d))
270         return (EBUSY);

271     /* Mark "free" and do most initialization. */
272     bzero((char *) d, sizeof(*d));
273     d->bd_bufsize = bpf_bufsize;

274     return (0);
275 }
```
—— *bpf.c*

Figure 31.11   bpfopen function.

256–263   The number of BPF devices is limited at compile time to NBPFILTER. The minor device number specifies the device and ENXIO is returned if it is too large. This happens when the system administrator creates more /dev/bpf*x* entries than the value NBPFILTER.

Allocate bpf_d structure

264–275   Only one process is allowed access to a BPF device at a time. If the bpf_d structure is already active, EBUSY is returned. Programs such as tcpdump try the next device when this error is returned. If the device is available, the entry in the bpf_dtab table specified by the minor device number is cleared and the size of the packet buffers is set to the default value.

bpfioctl Function

Once the device is opened, it is configured with ioctl commands. Figure 31.12 summarizes the ioctl commands used with BPF devices. Figure 31.13 shows the bpfioctl function. Only the code for BIOCSETF and BIOCSETIF is shown. We have omitted the ioctl commands that are not discussed in this text.

Command	Third argument	Function	Description
FIONREAD	u_int	bpfioctl	return #bytes in hold buffer and store buffers.
BIOCGBLEN	u_int	bpfioctl	return size of packet buffers
BIOCSBLEN	u_int	bpfioctl	set size of packet buffers
BIOCSETF	struct bpf_program	bpf_setf	install BPF program
BIOCFLUSH		reset_d	discard pending packets
BIOCPROMISC		ifpromisc	enable promiscuous mode
BIOCGDLT	u_int	bpfioctl	return bif_dlt
BIOCGETIF	struct ifreq	bpf_ifname	return name of attached interface
BIOCSETIF	struct ifreq	bpf_setif	attach network interface to device
BIOCSRTIMEOUT	struct timeval	bpfioctl	set read timeout value
BIOCGRTIMEOUT	struct timeval	bpfioctl	return read timeout value
BIOCGSTATS	struct bpf_stat	bpfioctl	return BPF statistics
BIOCIMMEDIATE	u_int	bpfioctl	enable immediate mode
BIOCVERSION	struct bpf_version	bpfioctl	return BPF version information

Figure 31.12 BPF ioctl commands.

── *bpf.c*
```
501 int
502 bpfioctl(dev, cmd, addr, flag)
503 dev_t   dev;
504 int     cmd;
505 caddr_t addr;
506 int     flag;
507 {
508     struct bpf_d *d = &bpf_dtab[minor(dev)];
509     int    s, error = 0;
510     switch (cmd) {
511         /*
512          * Set link layer read filter.
513          */
514     case BIOCSETF:
515         error = bpf_setf(d, (struct bpf_program *) addr);
516         break;

517         /*
518          * Set interface.
519          */
520     case BIOCSETIF:
521         error = bpf_setif(d, (struct ifreq *) addr);
522         break;

                    /* other ioctl commands from Figure 31.12 */

668     default:
669         error = EINVAL;
670         break;
671     }
672     return (error);
673 }
```
── *bpf.c*

Figure 31.13 bpfioctl function.

501–509   As with bpfopen, the minor device number selects the bpf_d structure from the
bpf_dtab table. The command is processed by the cases within the switch. We show
two commands, BIOCSETF and BIOCSETIF, as well as the default case.

510–522   The bpf_setf function installs the filter passed in addr, and bpf_setif attaches
the named interface to the bpf_d structure. We don't show the implementation of
bpf_setf in this text.

668–673   If the command is not recognized, EINVAL is returned.

Figure 31.14 shows the bpf_d structure after bpf_setif has attached it to the
LANCE interface in our example system.

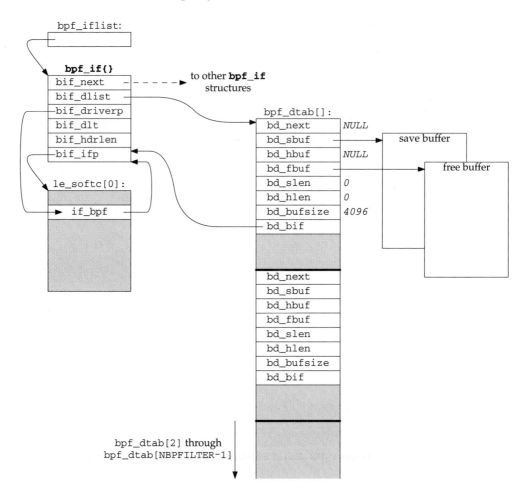

Figure 31.14   BPF device attached to the Ethernet interface.

In the figure, bif_dlist points to bpf_dtab[0], the first and only descriptor in
the descriptor list for the Ethernet interface. In bpf_dtab[0], the bd_sbuf and
bd_hbuf members point to the store and hold buffers. Each buffer is 4096

(bd_bufsize) bytes long. bd_bif points back to the bpf_if structure for the interface.

if_bpf in the ifnet structure (le_softc[0]) also points back to the bpf_if structure. As shown in Figures 4.19 and 4.11, when if_bpf is nonnull, the driver begins passing packets to the BPF device by calling bpf_tap.

Figure 31.15 shows the same structures after a second BPF device is opened and attached to the same Ethernet network interface as in Figure 31.10.

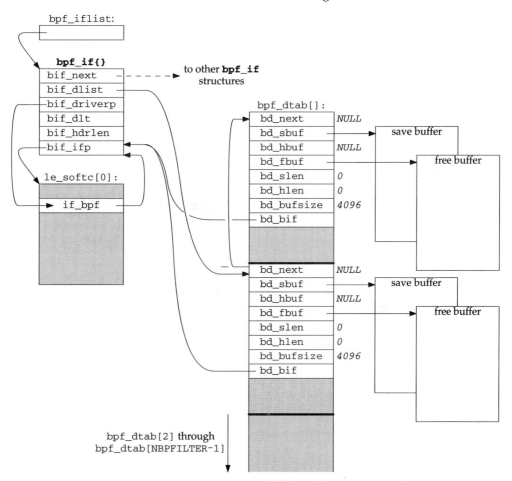

Figure 31.15   Two BPF devices attached to the Ethernet interface.

When the second BPF device is opened, a new bpf_d structure is allocated from the bpf_dtab table , in this case, bpf_dtab[1]. The second BPF device is also attached to the Ethernet interface, so bif_dlist points to bpf_dtab[1], and bpf_dtab[1].bd_next points to bpf_dtab[0], which is the first BPF descriptor attached to the Ethernet interface. Separate store and hold buffers are allocated and attached to the new descriptor structure.

bpf_setif **Function**

The bpf_setif function, which associates the BPF descriptor with a network interface, is shown in Figure 31.16.

―― *bpf.c*
```
721 static int
722 bpf_setif(d, ifr)
723 struct bpf_d *d;
724 struct ifreq *ifr;
725 {
726     struct bpf_if *bp;
727     char    *cp;
728     int     unit, s, error;

729     /*
730      * Separate string into name part and unit number.  Put a null
731      * byte at the end of the name part, and compute the number.
732      * If the a unit number is unspecified, the default is 0,
733      * as initialized above.  XXX This should be common code.
734      */
735     unit = 0;
736     cp = ifr->ifr_name;
737     cp[sizeof(ifr->ifr_name) - 1] = '\0';
738     while (*cp++) {
739         if (*cp >= '0' && *cp <= '9') {
740             unit = *cp - '0';
741             *cp++ = '\0';
742             while (*cp)
743                 unit = 10 * unit + *cp++ - '0';
744             break;
745         }
746     }
747     /*
748      * Look through attached interfaces for the named one.
749      */
750     for (bp = bpf_iflist; bp != 0; bp = bp->bif_next) {
751         struct ifnet *ifp = bp->bif_ifp;

752         if (ifp == 0 || unit != ifp->if_unit
753             || strcmp(ifp->if_name, ifr->ifr_name) != 0)
754             continue;
755         /*
756          * We found the requested interface.
757          * If it's not up, return an error.
758          * Allocate the packet buffers if we need to.
759          * If we're already attached to requested interface,
760          * just flush the buffer.
761          */
762         if ((ifp->if_flags & IFF_UP) == 0)
763             return (ENETDOWN);
```

```
764          if (d->bd_sbuf == 0) {
765              error = bpf_allocbufs(d);
766              if (error != 0)
767                  return (error);
768          }
769          s = splimp();
770          if (bp != d->bd_bif) {
771              if (d->bd_bif)
772                  /*
773                   * Detach if attached to something else.
774                   */
775                  bpf_detachd(d);
776              bpf_attachd(d, bp);
777          }
778          reset_d(d);
779          splx(s);
780          return (0);
781      }
782      /* Not found. */
783      return (ENXIO);
784  }
```
── *bpf.c*

Figure 31.16 bpf_setif function.

721–746　　The first part of bpf_setif separates the text portion of the name in the ifreq structure (Figure 4.23) from the numeric portion. The numeric portion is saved in unit. For example, if the first 4 bytes of ifr_name start is "sl1\0", after this code executes they are "sl\0\0" and unit is 1.

Locate matching ifnet structure

747–754　　The for loop searches the interfaces that support BPF (the ones in bpf_iflist) for the one specified in the ifreq structure.

755–768　　If the matching interface is not up ENETDOWN is returned. If the interface is up, bpf_allocate attaches the free and store buffers to the bpf_d structure, if they have not already been allocated.

Attach bpf_d structure

769–777　　If no interface is attached to the BPF device, or if a different interface from the one specified in the ifreq structure is attached, bpf_detachd discards the previous interface (if any), and bpf_attachd attaches the new interface to the device.

778–784　　reset_d resets the packet buffers, discarding any pending packets in the process. The function returns 0 to indicate success or returns ENXIO if the interface was not located.

bpf_attachd Function

The bpf_attachd function shown in Figure 31.17 associates a BPF descriptor structure with a BPF device and with a network interface.

—— bpf.c
```
189 static void
190 bpf_attachd(d, bp)
191 struct bpf_d *d;
192 struct bpf_if *bp;
193 {
194     /*
195      * Point d at bp, and add d to the interface's list of listeners.
196      * Finally, point the driver's bpf cookie at the interface so
197      * it will divert packets to bpf.
198      */
199     d->bd_bif = bp;
200     d->bd_next = bp->bif_dlist;
201     bp->bif_dlist = d;

202     *bp->bif_driverp = bp;
203 }
```
—— bpf.c

Figure 31.17   bpf_attachd function.

189–203   First, bd_bif is set to point to the BPF interface structure for the network device. Next, the bpf_d structure is inserted into the front of the list of bpf_d structures associated with the device. Finally, the BPF pointer within the network interface is changed to point to the BPF structure, which causes the interface to begin passing packets to the BPF device.

31.5   BPF Input

Once the BPF device is opened and configured, a process uses the read system call to receive packets from the interface. The BPF tap collects *copies* of the incoming packets so BPF does not interfere with normal network processing. Incoming packets are collected in the store and hold buffers associated with each BPF device.

bpf_tap Function

We described the call to bpf_tap by the LANCE device driver with Figure 4.11 and use this call to describe the bpf_tap. The call (from Figure 4.11) is:

```
bpf_tap(le->sc_if.if_bpf, buf, len + sizeof(struct ether_header));
```

The bpf_tap function is shown in Figure 31.18.

869–882   The first argument is a pointer to the bpf_if structure, which is set by bpfattach. The second argument is a pointer to the incoming packet, including the Ethernet header. The third argument is the number of bytes contained in the buffer, in this case, the size of the Ethernet header (14 bytes) plus the size of the data portion of the Ethernet frame.

bpf.c
```
869 void
870 bpf_tap(arg, pkt, pktlen)
871 caddr_t arg;
872 u_char *pkt;
873 u_int   pktlen;
874 {
875     struct bpf_if *bp;
876     struct bpf_d *d;
877     u_int   slen;
878     /*
879      * Note that the ipl does not have to be raised at this point.
880      * The only problem that could arise here is that if two different
881      * interfaces shared any data.  This is not the case.
882      */
883     bp = (struct bpf_if *) arg;
884     for (d = bp->bif_dlist; d != 0; d = d->bd_next) {
885         ++d->bd_rcount;
886         slen = bpf_filter(d->bd_filter, pkt, pktlen, pktlen);
887         if (slen != 0)
888             catchpacket(d, pkt, pktlen, slen, bcopy);
889     }
890 }
```
bpf.c

Figure 31.18 bpf_tap function.

Pass packet to one or more BPF devices

883–890   The for loop traverses the list of BPF devices attached to the interface. For each
device, the packet is passed to bpf_filter. If the filter accepts the packet, it returns
the number of bytes to capture and catchpacket saves a copy of the packet. If the filter rejects the packet, slen is 0 and the loop continues. When the loop completes,
bpf_tap returns. This mechanism enables each BPF device to have a separate filter
when multiple BPF devices are associated with the same network interface.

The loopback driver calls bpf_mtap to pass packets to BPF. This function is similar
to bpf_tap but copies the packet from an mbuf chain instead of from a contiguous area
of memory. This function is not described in this text.

catchpacket **Function**

In Figure 31.18 we saw that catchpacket is called when the filter accepts the packet.
The function is shown in Figure 31.19.

946–955   The arguments to catchpacket are: d, a pointer to the BPF device structure; pkt a
generic pointer to the incoming packet; pktlen the length of the packet as it was
received; snaplen the number of bytes to save from the packet; and cpfn a pointer to a
function that will copy the packet from pkt to a contiguous area of memory. When the
packet is already in a contiguous area of memory, cpfn is bcopy. When the packet is
stored in an mbuf (i.e., pkt points to the first mbuf in a chain such as with the loopback
driver), cpfn is bpf_mcopy.

―――――――――――――――――――――――――――――――――――――― *bpf.c*

```
946 static void
947 catchpacket(d, pkt, pktlen, snaplen, cpfn)
948 struct bpf_d *d;
949 u_char *pkt;
950 u_int   pktlen, snaplen;
951 void    (*cpfn) (const void *, void *, u_int);
952 {
953     struct bpf_hdr *hp;
954     int     totlen, curlen;
955     int     hdrlen = d->bd_bif->bif_hdrlen;
956     /*
957      * Figure out how many bytes to move.  If the packet is
958      * greater or equal to the snapshot length, transfer that
959      * much.  Otherwise, transfer the whole packet (unless
960      * we hit the buffer size limit).
961      */
962     totlen = hdrlen + min(snaplen, pktlen);
963     if (totlen > d->bd_bufsize)
964         totlen = d->bd_bufsize;

965     /*
966      * Round up the end of the previous packet to the next longword.
967      */
968     curlen = BPF_WORDALIGN(d->bd_slen);
969     if (curlen + totlen > d->bd_bufsize) {
970         /*
971          * This packet will overflow the storage buffer.
972          * Rotate the buffers if we can, then wakeup any
973          * pending reads.
974          */
975         if (d->bd_fbuf == 0) {
976             /*
977              * We haven't completed the previous read yet,
978              * so drop the packet.
979              */
980             ++d->bd_dcount;
981             return;
982         }
983         ROTATE_BUFFERS(d);
984         bpf_wakeup(d);
985         curlen = 0;
986     } else if (d->bd_immediate)
987         /*
988          * Immediate mode is set.  A packet arrived so any
989          * reads should be woken up.
990          */
991         bpf_wakeup(d);
992     /*
993      * Append the bpf header.
994      */
995     hp = (struct bpf_hdr *) (d->bd_sbuf + curlen);
996     microtime(&hp->bh_tstamp);
997     hp->bh_datalen = pktlen;
998     hp->bh_hdrlen = hdrlen;
```

```
999     /*
1000     * Copy the packet data into the store buffer and update its length.
1001     */
1002    (*cpfn) (pkt, (u_char *) hp + hdrlen, (hp->bh_caplen = totlen - hdrlen));
1003    d->bd_slen = curlen + totlen;
1004 }
```
── *bpf.c*

Figure 31.19 `catchpacket` function.

956–964   In addition to the link-layer header and the packet, `catchpacket` appends a `bpf_hdr` to every packet. The number of bytes to save from the packet is the smaller of `snaplen` and `pktlen`. The resulting packet and `bpf_hdr` must fit within the packet buffers (`bd_bufsize` bytes).

Will the packet fit?

965–985   `curlen` is the number of bytes already in the store buffer plus enough bytes to align the next packet on a longword boundary. If the incoming packet doesn't fit in the remaining buffer space, the store buffer is full. If a free buffer is not available (i.e., a process is still reading data from the hold buffer), the incoming packet is discarded. If a free buffer is available, it is rotated into place by `ROTATE_BUFFERS` and any process waiting for incoming data is awakened by `bpf_wakeup`.

Immediate mode processing

986–991   If the device is operating in immediate mode, any waiting processes are awakened to process the incoming packet—there is no buffering of packets in the kernel.

Append BPF header

992–1004   The current time (`microtime`), the packet length, and the header length are saved in a `bpf_hdr`. The function pointed to by `cpfn` is called to copy the packet into the store buffer and the length of the store buffer is updated. Since `bpf_tap` is called directly from `leread` even before the packet is transferred from a device buffer to an mbuf chain, the receive timestamp is close to the actual reception time.

`bpfread` Function

The kernel routes a `read` on a BPF device to `bpfread`. BPF supports a timed read through the `BIOCSRTIMEOUT` command. This "feature" is easily emulated by the more general `select` system call, but `tcpdump`, for example, uses `BIOCSRTIMEOUT` and not `select`. The process must provide a read buffer that matches the size of the hold buffer for the device. The `BIOCGBLEN` command returns the size of the buffer. Normally, a read returns when the store buffer becomes full. The kernel rotates the store buffer to the hold buffer, which is copied to the buffer provided with the `read` system call while the BPF device continues collecting incoming packets in the store buffer. `bpfread` is shown in Figure 31.20.

```
344 int
345 bpfread(dev, uio)
346 dev_t   dev;
347 struct uio *uio;
348 {
349     struct bpf_d *d = &bpf_dtab[minor(dev)];
350     int     error;
351     int     s;

352     /*
353      * Restrict application to use a buffer the same size as
354      * as kernel buffers.
355      */
356     if (uio->uio_resid != d->bd_bufsize)
357         return (EINVAL);

358     s = splimp();
359     /*
360      * If the hold buffer is empty, then do a timed sleep, which
361      * ends when the timeout expires or when enough packets
362      * have arrived to fill the store buffer.
363      */
364     while (d->bd_hbuf == 0) {
365         if (d->bd_immediate && d->bd_slen != 0) {
366             /*
367              * A packet(s) either arrived since the previous
368              * read or arrived while we were asleep.
369              * Rotate the buffers and return what's here.
370              */
371             ROTATE_BUFFERS(d);
372             break;
373         }
374         error = tsleep((caddr_t) d, PRINET | PCATCH, "bpf", d->bd_rtout);
375         if (error == EINTR || error == ERESTART) {
376             splx(s);
377             return (error);
378         }
379         if (error == EWOULDBLOCK) {
380             /*
381              * On a timeout, return what's in the buffer,
382              * which may be nothing.  If there is something
383              * in the store buffer, we can rotate the buffers.
384              */
385             if (d->bd_hbuf)
386                 /*
387                  * We filled up the buffer in between
388                  * getting the timeout and arriving
389                  * here, so we don't need to rotate.
390                  */
391                 break;
```

bpf.c

```
392                 if (d->bd_slen == 0) {
393                     splx(s);
394                     return (0);
395                 }
396                 ROTATE_BUFFERS(d);
397                 break;
398             }
399         }
400         /*
401          * At this point, we know we have something in the hold slot.
402          */
403         splx(s);

404         /*
405          * Move data from hold buffer into user space.
406          * We know the entire buffer is transferred since
407          * we checked above that the read buffer is bpf_bufsize bytes.
408          */
409         error = uiomove(d->bd_hbuf, d->bd_hlen, UIO_READ, uio);

410         s = splimp();
411         d->bd_fbuf = d->bd_hbuf;
412         d->bd_hbuf = 0;
413         d->bd_hlen = 0;
414         splx(s);

415         return (error);
416 }
```
——— *bpf.c*

Figure 31.20   `bpfread` function.

344–357   The minor device number selects the BPF device from the `bpf_dtab` table. If the read buffer doesn't match the size of the BPF device buffers, `EINVAL` is returned.

Wait for data

358–364   Since multiple processes may be reading from the same BPF device, the `while` loop forces the read to continue when some other process gets to the data first. If there is data in the hold buffer, the loop is skipped. This is different from two processes tapping the same network interface through two different BPF devices (Exercise 31.2).

Immediate mode

365–373   If the device is in immediate mode and there is some data in the store buffer, the buffers are rotated and the `while` loop terminates.

No packets available

374–384   If the device is not in the immediate mode, or there is no data in the store buffer, the process sleeps until a signal arrives, the read timer expires, or data arrives in the hold buffer. If a signal arrives, `EINTR` or `ERESTART` is returned.

> Remember that a process never sees the `ERESTART` error because the error is handled by the `syscall` function and never returned to a process.

Check hold buffer

385–391   If the timer expired and data is in the hold buffer, the loop terminates.

Check store buffer

392–399   If the timer expired and there is no data in the store buffer, the read returns 0. The process must handle this case when using a timed read. If the timer expired and there is data in the store buffer, it is rotated to the hold buffer and the loop terminates.

If `tsleep` returns without an error and data is present, the `while` loop test is false and the loop terminates.

Packets are available

400–416   At this point, there is data in the hold buffer. `uiomove` moves `bd_hlen` bytes of data from the hold buffer to the process. After the move, the hold buffer is moved to the free buffer, and the buffer counts are cleared before the function returns. The comment before `uiomove` indicates that `uiomove` will always be able to copy `bd_hlen` bytes into the process because the read buffer was checked to ensure it can hold the maximum number of bytes, `bd_bufsize`.

31.6   BPF Output

Finally, we describe how to add packets to the network interface output queues with BPF. An entire data-link frame must be constructed by the process. For Ethernet this includes the source and destination hardware addresses and the frame type (Figure 4.8). The kernel will not modify the frame before putting it on the interface's output queue.

`bpfwrite` Function

The frame is passed to the BPF device with the `write` system call, which the kernel routes to `bpfwrite`, shown in Figure 31.21.

Check device number

437–449   The minor device number selects the BPF device, which must be attached to a network interface. If it isn't, `ENXIO` is returned.

Copy data into mbuf chain

450–457   If the write specified 0 bytes, 0 is returned immediately. `bpf_movein` copies the data from the process into an mbuf chain. Based on the interface type passed from `bif_dlt`, it computes the length of the packet excluding the link-layer header and returns the value in `datlen`. It also returns an initialized `sockaddr` structure in `dst`. For Ethernet, the type of this address structure will be `AF_UNSPEC`, indicating that the mbuf chain contains the data-link header for the outgoing frame. If the packet is larger than the MTU of the interface, `EMSGSIZE` is returned.

Queue packet

458–465   The resulting mbuf chain is passed to the network interface using the `if_output` function specified in the `ifnet` structure. For Ethernet, `if_output` is `ether_output`.

```
                                                                            ——— bpf.c
437 int
438 bpfwrite(dev, uio)
439 dev_t   dev;
440 struct uio *uio;
441 {
442     struct bpf_d *d = &bpf_dtab[minor(dev)];
443     struct ifnet *ifp;
444     struct mbuf *m;
445     int     error, s;
446     static struct sockaddr dst;
447     int     datlen;

448     if (d->bd_bif == 0)
449         return (ENXIO);

450     ifp = d->bd_bif->bif_ifp;

451     if (uio->uio_resid == 0)
452         return (0);

453     error = bpf_movein(uio, (int) d->bd_bif->bif_dlt, &m, &dst, &datlen);
454     if (error)
455         return (error);

456     if (datlen > ifp->if_mtu)
457         return (EMSGSIZE);

458     s = splnet();
459     error = (*ifp->if_output) (ifp, m, &dst, (struct rtentry *) 0);
460     splx(s);
461     /*
462      * The driver frees the mbuf.
463      */
464     return (error);
465 }
                                                                            ——— bpf.c
```

Figure 31.21 `bpfwrite` function.

31.7 Summary

In this chapter we showed how BPF devices are configured, how incoming frames are passed to BPF devices, and how outgoing frames can be transmitted on a BPF device.

We showed that a single network interface can have multiple BPF taps, each with a separate filter. The store and hold buffers minimize the number of read system calls required to process incoming frames.

We focused only on the major features of BPF in this chapter. For a more detailed description of the filtering code and the other features of the BPF device, the interested reader should examine the source code and the Net/3 manual pages.

Exercises

31.1   Why is it OK to call `bpf_wakeup` in `catchpacket` before the packet is stored in the BPF buffers?

31.2   With Figure 31.20, we noted that two processes may be waiting for data from the same BPF device. With Figure 31.11, we noted that only one process at a time can open a particular BPF device. How can both of these statements be true?

31.3   What happens if the device named in the `BIOCSETIF` command does not support BPF?

32

Raw IP

32.1 Introduction

A process accesses the raw IP layer by creating a socket of type SOCK_RAW in the Internet domain. There are three uses for raw sockets:

1. Raw sockets allow a process to send and receive ICMP and IGMP messages.

    The Ping program uses this type of socket to send ICMP echo requests and to receive ICMP echo replies.

    Some routing daemons use this feature to track ICMP redirects that are processed by the kernel. We saw in Section 19.7 that Net/3 generates an RTM_REDIRECT message on a routing socket when a redirect is processed, obviating the need for this use of raw sockets.

    This feature is also used to implement protocols based on ICMP, such as router advertisement and router solicitation (Section 9.6 of Volume 1), which use ICMP but are better implemented as user processes than within the kernel.

    The multicast routing daemon uses a raw IGMP socket to send and receive IGMP messages.

2. Raw sockets let a process build its own IP headers. The Traceroute program uses this feature to build its own UDP datagrams, including the IP and UDP headers.

3. Raw sockets let a process read and write IP datagrams with an IP protocol type that the kernel doesn't support.

   The `gated` program uses this to support three routing protocols that are built directly on IP: EGP, HELLO, and OSPF.

   This type of raw socket can also be used to experiment with new transport layers on top of IP, instead of adding support to the kernel. It is usually much easier to debug code within a user process than it is within the kernel.

This chapter examines the implementation of raw IP sockets.

32.2 Code Introduction

There are five raw IP functions in a single C file, shown in Figure 32.1.

File	Description
netinet/raw_ip.c	raw IP functions

Figure 32.1   File discussed in this chapter.

Figure 32.2 shows the relationship of the five raw IP functions to other kernel functions.

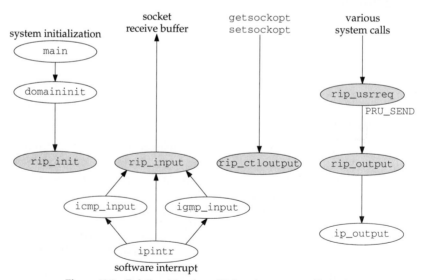

Figure 32.2   Relationship of raw IP functions to rest of kernel.

The shaded ellipses are the five functions that we cover in this chapter. Be aware that the "rip" prefix used within the raw IP functions stands for "raw IP" and not the "Routing Information Protocol," whose common acronym is RIP.

Global Variables

Four global variables are introduced in this chapter, which are shown in Figure 32.3.

Variable	Datatype	Description
`rawinpcb`	`struct inpcb`	head of the raw IP Internet PCB list
`ripsrc`	`struct sockaddr_in`	contains sender's IP address on input
`rip_recvspace`	`u_long`	default size of socket receive buffer, 8192 bytes
`rip_sendspace`	`u_long`	default size of socket send buffer, 8192 bytes

Figure 32.3   Global variables introduced in this chapter.

Statistics

Raw IP maintains two of the counters in the `ipstat` structure (Figure 8.4). We describe these in Figure 32.4.

`ipstat` member	Description	Used by SNMP
`ips_noproto`	#packets with an unknown or unsupported protocol	•
`ips_rawout`	total #raw ip packets generated	

Figure 32.4   Raw IP statistics maintained in the `ipstat` structure.

The use of the `ips_noproto` counter with SNMP is shown in Figure 8.6. Figure 8.5 shows some sample output of these two counters.

32.3   Raw IP `protosw` Structure

Unlike all other protocols, raw IP is accessed through multiple entries in the `inetsw` array. There are four entries in this structure with a socket type of SOCK_RAW, each with a different protocol value:

- `IPPROTO_ICMP` (protocol value of 1),
- `IPPROTO_IGMP` (protocol value of 2),
- `IPPROTO_RAW` (protocol value of 255), and
- raw wildcard entry (protocol value of 0).

The first two entries for ICMP and IGMP were described earlier (Figures 11.12 and 13.9). The difference in these four entries can be summarized as follows:

- If the process creates a raw socket (SOCK_RAW) with a nonzero protocol value (the third argument to `socket`), and if that value matches IPPROTO_ICMP, IPPROTO_IGMP, or IPPROTO_RAW, then the corresponding `protosw` entry is used.

- If the process creates a raw socket with a nonzero protocol value that is not known to the kernel, the wildcard entry with a protocol of 0 is matched by `pffindproto`. This allows a process to handle any IP protocol that is not known to the kernel, without making kernel modifications.

We saw in Section 7.8 that all entries in the `ip_protox` array that are unknown are set to point to the entry for `IPPROTO_RAW`, whose protocol switch entry we show in Figure 32.5.

Member	inetsw[3]	Description
pr_type	SOCK_RAW	raw socket
pr_domain	&inetdomain	raw IP is part of the Internet domain
pr_protocol	IPPROTO_RAW (255)	appears in the ip_p field of the IP header
pr_flags	PR_ATOMIC|PR_ADDR	socket layer flags, not used by protocol processing
pr_input	rip_input	receives messages from IP layer
pr_output	0	not used by raw IP
pr_ctlinput	0	not used by raw IP
pr_ctloutput	rip_ctloutput	respond to administrative requests from a process
pr_usrreq	rip_usrreq	respond to communication requests from a process
pr_init	0	not used by raw IP
pr_fasttimo	0	not used by raw IP
pr_slowtimo	0	not used by raw IP
pr_drain	0	not used by raw IP
pr_sysctl	0	not used by raw IP

Figure 32.5   The raw IP `protosw` structure.

We describe the three functions that begin with `rip_` in this chapter. We also cover the function `rip_output`, which is not in the protocol switch entry but is called by `rip_usrreq` when a raw IP datagram is output.

The fifth raw IP function, `rip_init`, is contained only in the wildcard entry. The initialization function must be called only once, so it could appear in either the `IPPROTO_RAW` entry or in the wildcard entry.

What Figure 32.5 doesn't show, however, is that other protocols (ICMP and IGMP) also reference some of the raw IP functions in their `protosw` entries. Figure 32.6 compares the relevant fields in the `protosw` entries for the four `SOCK_RAW` protocols. To highlight the differences, values in these rows are in a bolder font when they differ.

protosw	SOCK_RAW protocol type			
entry	IPPROTO_ICMP (1)	IPPROTO_IGMP (2)	IPPROTO_RAW (255)	wildcard (0)
pr_input	*icmp_input*	*igmp_input*	*rip_input*	*rip_input*
pr_output	rip_output	rip_output	rip_output	rip_output
pr_ctloutput	rip_ctloutput	rip_ctloutput	rip_ctloutput	rip_ctloutput
pr_usrreq	rip_usrreq	rip_usrreq	rip_usrreq	rip_usrreq
pr_init	0	*igmp_init*	0	*rip_init*
pr_sysctl	*icmp_sysctl*	0	0	0
pr_fasttimo	0	*igmp_fasttimo*	0	0

Figure 32.6   Comparison of protocol switch values for raw sockets.

The implementation of raw sockets has changed with the different BSD releases. The entry with a protocol of IPPROTO_RAW has always been used as the wildcard entry in the ip_protox table for unknown IP protocols. The entry with a protocol of 0 has always been the default entry, to allow processes to read and write IP datagrams with a protocol that the kernel doesn't support.

Usage of the IPPROTO_RAW entry by a process started when Traceroute was developed by Van Jacobson, because Traceroute was the first process that needed to write its own IP headers (to change the TTL field). The kernel patches to 4.3BSD and Net/1 to support Traceroute included a change to rip_output so that if the protocol was IPPROTO_RAW, it was assumed the process had passed a complete IP datagram, including the IP header. This was changed with Net/2 when the IP_HDRINCL socket option was introduced, removing this overloading of the IPPROTO_RAW protocol and allowing a process to send its own IP header with the wildcard entry.

32.4 rip_init Function

The domaininit function calls the raw IP initialization function rip_init (Figure 32.7) at system initialization time.

――― *raw_ip.c*
```
47 void
48 rip_init()
49 {
50     rawinpcb.inp_next = rawinpcb.inp_prev = &rawinpcb;
51 }
```
――― *raw_ip.c*

Figure 32.7 rip_init function.

The only action performed by this function is to set the next and previous pointers in the head PCB (rawinpcb) to point to itself. This is an empty doubly linked list.

Whenever a socket of type SOCK_RAW is created by the socket system call, we'll see that the raw IP PRU_ATTACH function creates an Internet PCB and puts it onto the rawinpcb list.

32.5 rip_input Function

Since all entries in the ip_protox array for unknown protocols are set to point to the entry for IPPROTO_RAW (Section 7.8), and since the pr_input function for this protocol is rip_input (Figure 32.6), this function is called for all IP datagrams that have a protocol value that the kernel doesn't recognize. But from Figure 32.2 we see that both ICMP and IGMP also call rip_input. This happens under the following conditions:

- icmp_input calls rip_input for all unknown ICMP message types and for all ICMP messages that are not reflected.
- igmp_input calls rip_input for all IGMP packets.

One reason for calling `rip_input` in these two cases is to allow a process with a raw socket to handle new ICMP and IGMP messages that might not be supported by the kernel.

Figure 32.8 shows the `rip_input` function.

```
                                                                    ——— raw_ip.c
59 void
60 rip_input(m)
61 struct mbuf *m;
62 {
63     struct ip *ip = mtod(m, struct ip *);
64     struct inpcb *inp;
65     struct socket *last = 0;

66     ripsrc.sin_addr = ip->ip_src;
67     for (inp = rawinpcb.inp_next; inp != &rawinpcb; inp = inp->inp_next) {
68         if (inp->inp_ip.ip_p && inp->inp_ip.ip_p != ip->ip_p)
69             continue;
70         if (inp->inp_laddr.s_addr &&
71             inp->inp_laddr.s_addr == ip->ip_dst.s_addr)
72             continue;
73         if (inp->inp_faddr.s_addr &&
74             inp->inp_faddr.s_addr == ip->ip_src.s_addr)
75             continue;
76         if (last) {
77             struct mbuf *n;
78             if (n = m_copy(m, 0, (int) M_COPYALL)) {
79                 if (sbappendaddr(&last->so_rcv, &ripsrc,
80                                 n, (struct mbuf *) 0) == 0)
81                     /* should notify about lost packet */
82                     m_freem(n);
83                 else
84                     sorwakeup(last);
85             }
86         }
87         last = inp->inp_socket;
88     }
89     if (last) {
90         if (sbappendaddr(&last->so_rcv, &ripsrc,
91                         m, (struct mbuf *) 0) == 0)
92             m_freem(m);
93         else
94             sorwakeup(last);
95     } else {
96         m_freem(m);
97         ipstat.ips_noproto++;
98         ipstat.ips_delivered--;
99     }
100 }
                                                                    ——— raw_ip.c
```

Figure 32.8   `rip_input` function.

Save source IP address

59–66   The source address from the IP datagram is put into the global variable `ripsrc`, which becomes an argument to `sbappendaddr` whenever a matching PCB is found. Unlike UDP, there is no concept of a port number with raw IP, so the `sin_port` field in the `sockaddr_in` structure is always 0.

Search all raw IP PCBs for one or more matching entries

67–88   Raw IP handles its list of PCBs differently from UDP and TCP. We saw that these two protocols maintain a pointer to the PCB for the most recently received datagram (a one-behind cache) and call the generic function `in_pcblookup` to search for a single "best" match when the received datagram does not equal the cache entry. Raw IP has completely different criteria for a matching PCB, so it searches the PCB list itself. `in_pcblookup` cannot be used because a raw IP datagram can be delivered to multiple sockets, so every PCB on the raw PCB list must be scanned. This is similar to UDP's handling of a received datagram destined for a broadcast or multicast address (Figure 23.26).

Compare protocols

68–69   If the protocol field in the PCB is nonzero, and if it doesn't match the protocol field in the IP header, the PCB is ignored. This implies that a raw socket with a protocol value of 0 (the third argument to `socket`) can match any received raw IP datagram.

Compare local and foreign IP addresses

70–75   If the local address in the PCB is nonzero, and if it doesn't match the destination IP address in the IP header, the PCB is ignored. If the foreign address in the PCB is nonzero, and if it doesn't match the source IP address in the IP header, the PCB is ignored.

These three tests imply that a process can create a raw socket with a protocol of 0, not bind a local address, and not connect to a foreign address, and the process receives *all* datagrams processed by `rip_input`.

> Lines 71 and 74 both contain the same bug: the test for equality should be a test for inequality.

Pass copy of received datagram to processes

76–94   `sbappendaddr` passes a copy of the received datagram to the process. The use of the variable `last` is similar to what we saw in Figure 23.26: since `sbappendaddr` releases the mbuf after placing it onto the appropriate queue, if more than one process receives a copy of the datagram, `rip_input` must make a copy by calling `m_copy`. But if only one process receives the datagram, there's no need to make a copy.

Undeliverable datagram

95–99   If no matching sockets are found for the datagram, the mbuf is released, `ips_noproto` is incremented, and `ips_delivered` is decremented. This latter counter was incremented by IP just before calling the `rip_input` (Figure 8.15). It must be decremented so that the two SNMP counters, `ipInDiscards` and `ipInDelivers` (Figure 8.6) are correct, since the datagram was not really delivered to a transport layer.

At the beginning of this section we mentioned that `icmp_input` calls `rip_input` for unknown message types and for messages that are not reflected. This means that the receipt of an ICMP host unreachable causes `ips_noproto` to be incremented if there are no raw listeners whose PCB is matched by `rip_input`. That's one reason this counter has such a large value in Figure 8.5. The description of this counter as being "unknown or unsupported protocols" is not entirely accurate.

Net/3 does not generate an ICMP destination unreachable message with code 2 (protocol unreachable) when an IP datagram is received with a protocol field that is not handled by either the kernel or some process through a raw socket. RFC 1122 says an implementation should generate this ICMP error. (See Exercise 32.4.)

32.6 `rip_output` Function

We saw in Figure 32.6 that `rip_output` is called for output for raw sockets by ICMP, IGMP, and raw IP. Output occurs when the application calls one of the five write functions: `send`, `sendto`, `sendmsg`, `write`, or `writev`. If the socket is connected, any of the five functions can be called, although a destination address cannot be specified with `sendto` or `sendmsg`. If the socket is unconnected, only `sendto` and `sendmsg` can be called, and a destination address must be specified.

The function `rip_output` is shown in Figure 32.9.

Kernel fills in IP header

119–128   If the `IP_HDRINCL` socket option is not defined, `M_PREPEND` allocates room for an IP header, and fields in the IP header are filled in. The fields that are not filled in here are left for `ip_output` to initialize (Figure 8.22). The protocol field is set to the value stored in the PCB, which we'll see in Figure 32.10 is the third argument to the `socket` system call.

The TOS is set to 0 and the TTL to 255. These values are always used for a raw socket when the kernel fills in the header. This differs from UDP and TCP where the process had the capability of setting the `IP_TTL` and `IP_TOS` socket options.

129   Any IP options set by the process with the `IP_OPTIONS` socket options are passed to `ip_output` through the `opts` variable.

Caller fills in IP header: `IP_HDRINCL` socket option

130–133   If the `IP_HDRINCL` socket option is set, the caller supplies a completed IP header at the front of the datagram. The only modification made to this IP header is to set the ID field if the value supplied by the process is 0. The ID field of an IP datagram can be 0. The assignment of the ID field here by `rip_output` is just a convention that allows the process to set it to 0, asking the kernel to assign an ID value based on the kernel's current `ip_id` variable.

134–136   The `opts` variable is set to a null pointer, which ignores any IP options the process may have set with the `IP_OPTIONS` socket option. The convention here is that if the caller builds its own IP header, that header includes any IP options the caller might want. The `flags` variable must also include the `IP_RAWOUTPUT` flag, telling `ip_output` to leave the header alone.

```
                                                                ——— raw_ip.c
105 int
106 rip_output(m, so, dst)
107 struct mbuf *m;
108 struct socket *so;
109 u_long  dst;
110 {
111     struct ip *ip;
112     struct inpcb *inp = sotoinpcb(so);
113     struct mbuf *opts;
114     int     flags = (so->so_options & SO_DONTROUTE) | IP_ALLOWBROADCAST;

115     /*
116      * If the user handed us a complete IP packet, use it.
117      * Otherwise, allocate an mbuf for a header and fill it in.
118      */
119     if ((inp->inp_flags & INP_HDRINCL) == 0) {
120         M_PREPEND(m, sizeof(struct ip), M_WAIT);
121         ip = mtod(m, struct ip *);
122         ip->ip_tos = 0;
123         ip->ip_off = 0;
124         ip->ip_p = inp->inp_ip.ip_p;
125         ip->ip_len = m->m_pkthdr.len;
126         ip->ip_src = inp->inp_laddr;
127         ip->ip_dst.s_addr = dst;
128         ip->ip_ttl = MAXTTL;
129         opts = inp->inp_options;
130     } else {
131         ip = mtod(m, struct ip *);
132         if (ip->ip_id == 0)
133             ip->ip_id = htons(ip_id++);
134         opts = NULL;
135         /* XXX prevent ip_output from overwriting header fields */
136         flags |= IP_RAWOUTPUT;
137         ipstat.ips_rawout++;
138     }
139     return (ip_output(m, opts, &inp->inp_route, flags, inp->inp_moptions));
140 }
```
                                                                ——— raw_ip.c

Figure 32.9 rip_output function.

137   The counter ips_rawout is incremented. Running Traceroute causes this variable
to be incremented by 1 for each datagram sent by Traceroute.

> The operation of rip_output has changed over time. When the IP_HDRINCL socket option
> is used in Net/3, the only change made to the IP header by rip_output is to set the ID field,
> if the process sets it to 0. The Net/3 ip_output function does nothing to the IP header fields
> because the IP_RAWOUTPUT flag is set. Net/2, however, always set certain fields in the IP
> header, even if the IP_HDRINCL socket option was set: the IP version was set to 4, the frag-
> ment offset was set to 0, and the more-fragments flag was cleared.

32.7   `rip_usrreq` Function

The protocol's user-request function is called for a variety of operations. As with the
UDP and TCP user-request functions, `rip_usrreq` is a large `switch` statement, with
one `case` for each `PRU_xxx` request.

The `PRU_ATTACH` request, shown in Figure 32.10, is from the `socket` system call.

```
                                                                              ─── raw_ip.c
194 int
195 rip_usrreq(so, req, m, nam, control)
196 struct socket *so;
197 int      req;
198 struct mbuf *m, *nam, *control;
199 {
200     int      error = 0;
201     struct inpcb *inp = sotoinpcb(so);
202     extern struct socket *ip_mrouter;
203     switch (req) {

204     case PRU_ATTACH:
205         if (inp)
206             panic("rip_attach");
207         if ((so->so_state & SS_PRIV) == 0) {
208             error = EACCES;
209             break;
210         }
211         if ((error = soreserve(so, rip_sendspace, rip_recvspace)) ||
212             (error = in_pcballoc(so, &rawinpcb)))
213             break;
214         inp = (struct inpcb *) so->so_pcb;
215         inp->inp_ip.ip_p = (int) nam;
216         break;
                                                                              ─── raw_ip.c
```

Figure 32.10   `rip_usrreq` function: `PRU_ATTACH` request.

194–206   Since the `socket` function creates a new `socket` structure each time it is called,
that structure cannot point to an Internet PCB.

Verify superuser

207–210   Only the superuser can create a raw socket. This is to prevent random users from
writing their own IP datagrams to the network.

Create Internet PCB and reserve buffer space

211–215   Space is reserved for input and output queues, and `in_pcballoc` allocates a new
Internet PCB. The PCB is added to the raw IP PCB list (`rawinpcb`). The PCB is linked
to the `socket` structure. The `nam` argument to `rip_usrreq` is the third argument to
the `socket` system call: the protocol. It is stored in the PCB since it is used by
`rip_input` to demultiplex received datagrams, and its value is placed into the protocol
field of outgoing datagrams by `rip_output` (if `IP_HDRINCL` is not set).

A raw IP socket can be connected to a foreign IP address similar to a UDP socket
being connected to a foreign IP address. This fixes the foreign IP address from which
the raw socket receives datagrams, as we saw in `rip_input`. Since raw IP is a

connectionless protocol like UDP, a `PRU_DISCONNECT` request can occur in two cases:

1. When a connected raw socket is closed, `PRU_DISCONNECT` is called before `PRU_DETACH`.

2. When a `connect` is issued on an already-connected raw socket, `soconnect` issues the `PRU_DISCONNECT` request before the `PRU_CONNECT` request.

Figure 32.11 shows the `PRU_DISCONNECT`, `PRU_ABORT`, and `PRU_DETACH` requests.

—————————————————————————————————————— raw_ip.c

```
217        case PRU_DISCONNECT:
218            if ((so->so_state & SS_ISCONNECTED) == 0) {
219                error = ENOTCONN;
220                break;
221            }
222            /* FALLTHROUGH */

223        case PRU_ABORT:
224            soisdisconnected(so);
225            /* FALLTHROUGH */

226        case PRU_DETACH:
227            if (inp == 0)
228                panic("rip_detach");
229            if (so == ip_mrouter)
230                ip_mrouter_done();
231            in_pcbdetach(inp);
232            break;
```
—————————————————————————————————————— raw_ip.c

Figure 32.11 `rip_usrreq` function: `PRU_DISCONNECT`, `PRU_ABORT`, and `PRU_DETACH` requests.

217–222   The socket must already be connected to disconnect or else an error is returned.

223–225   A `PRU_ABORT` abort should never be issued for a raw IP socket, but this `case` also handles the fall through from `PRU_DISCONNECT`. The socket is marked as disconnected.

226–230   The `close` system call issues the `PRU_DETACH` request, and this `case` also handles the fall through from the `PRU_DISCONNECT` request. If the `socket` structure is the one used for multicast routing (`ip_mrouter`), multicast routing is disabled by calling `ip_mrouter_done`. Normally the `mrouted(8)` daemon issues the `DVMRP_DONE` socket option to disable multicast routing, so this check handles the case of the router daemon terminating (i.e., crashing) without issuing the socket option.

231   The Internet PCB is released by `in_pcbdetach`, which also removes the PCB from the list of raw IP PCBs (`rawinpcb`).

A raw IP socket can be bound to a local IP address with the `PRU_BIND` request, shown in Figure 32.12. We saw in `rip_input` that the socket will receive only datagrams sent to this IP address.

233–250   The process fills in a `sockaddr_in` structure with the local IP address. The following three conditions must all be true, or else the error `EADDRNOTAVAIL` is returned:

```
                                                                              ———— raw_ip.c
233    case PRU_BIND:
234        {
235            struct sockaddr_in *addr = mtod(nam, struct sockaddr_in *);
236            if (nam->m_len != sizeof(*addr)) {
237                error = EINVAL;
238                break;
239            }
240            if ((ifnet == 0) ||
241                ((addr->sin_family != AF_INET) &&
242                 (addr->sin_family != AF_IMPLINK)) ||
243                (addr->sin_addr.s_addr &&
244                 ifa_ifwithaddr((struct sockaddr *) addr) == 0)) {
245                error = EADDRNOTAVAIL;
246                break;
247            }
248            inp->inp_laddr = addr->sin_addr;
249            break;
250        }
                                                                              ———— raw_ip.c
```

Figure 32.12 `rip_usrreq` function: PRU_BIND request.

1. at least one interface must be configured,

2. the address family must be AF_INET (or AF_IMPLINK, a historical artifact), and

3. if the IP address being bound is not 0.0.0.0, it must correspond to a local interface. For the call to `ifa_ifwithaddr` to succeed, the port number in the caller's `sockaddr_in` must be 0.

The local IP address is stored in the PCB.

A process can also connect a raw IP socket to a particular foreign IP address. We saw in `rip_input` that this restricts the process so that it receives only IP datagrams with a source IP address equal to the connected IP address. A process has the option of calling `bind`, `connect`, both, or neither, depending on the type of filtering it wants `rip_input` to place on received datagrams. Figure 32.13 shows the PRU_CONNECT request.

251–270   If the caller's `sockaddr_in` is initialized correctly and at least one IP interface is configured, the specified foreign IP address is stored in the PCB. Notice that this process differs from the connection of a UDP socket to a foreign address. In the UDP case, `in_pcbconnect` acquires a route to the foreign address and also stores the outgoing interface as the local address (Figure 22.9). With raw IP, only the foreign IP address is stored in the PCB, and unless the process also calls `bind`, only the foreign address is compared by `rip_input`.

```raw_ip.c
251        case PRU_CONNECT:
252            {
253                struct sockaddr_in *addr = mtod(nam, struct sockaddr_in *);

254                if (nam->m_len != sizeof(*addr)) {
255                    error = EINVAL;
256                    break;
257                }
258                if (ifnet == 0) {
259                    error = EADDRNOTAVAIL;
260                    break;
261                }
262                if ((addr->sin_family != AF_INET) &&
263                    (addr->sin_family != AF_IMPLINK)) {
264                    error = EAFNOSUPPORT;
265                    break;
266                }
267                inp->inp_faddr = addr->sin_addr;
268                soisconnected(so);
269                break;
270            }
```
raw_ip.c

Figure 32.13 `rip_usrreq` function: PRU_CONNECT request.

A call to `shutdown` specifying that the process has finished sending data generates the PRU_SHUTDOWN request, although it is rare for a process to issue this system call for a raw IP socket. Figure 32.14 shows the PRU_CONNECT2 and PRU_SHUTDOWN requests.

```raw_ip.c
271        case PRU_CONNECT2:
272            error = EOPNOTSUPP;
273            break;

274            /*
275             * Mark the connection as being incapable of further input.
276             */
277        case PRU_SHUTDOWN:
278            socantsendmore(so);
279            break;
```
raw_ip.c

Figure 32.14 `rip_usrreq` function: PRU_CONNECT2 and PRU_SHUTDOWN requests.

271–273   The PRU_CONNECT2 request is not supported for a raw IP socket.

274–279   `socantsendmore` sets the socket's flags to prevent any future output.

In Figure 23.14 we showed how the five write functions call the protocol's `pr_usrreq` function with a `PRU_SEND` request. We show this request in Figure 32.15.

```
                                                                    ─── raw_ip.c
280        /*
281         * Ship a packet out.  The appropriate raw output
282         * routine handles any massaging necessary.
283         */
284    case PRU_SEND:
285        {
286            u_long   dst;

287            if (so->so_state & SS_ISCONNECTED) {
288                if (nam) {
289                    error = EISCONN;
290                    break;
291                }
292                dst = inp->inp_faddr.s_addr;
293            } else {
294                if (nam == NULL) {
295                    error = ENOTCONN;
296                    break;
297                }
298                dst = mtod(nam, struct sockaddr_in *)->sin_addr.s_addr;
299            }
300            error = rip_output(m, so, dst);
301            m = NULL;
302            break;
303        }
                                                                    ─── raw_ip.c
```

Figure 32.15   `rip_usrreq` function: `PRU_SEND` request.

280–303   If the socket state is connected, the caller cannot specify a destination address (the `nam` argument). Likewise, if the state is unconnected, a destination address is required. If all is OK, in either state, `dst` is set to the destination IP address. `rip_output` sends the datagram. The mbuf pointer `m` is set to a null pointer, to prevent it from being released at the end of the function. This is because the interface output routine will release the mbuf after it has been output. (Remember that `rip_output` passes the mbuf chain to `ip_output`, who appends it to the interface's output queue.)

The final part of `rip_usrreq` is shown in Figure 32.16. The `PRU_SENSE` request, generated by the `fstat` system call, returns nothing. The `PRU_SOCKADDR` and `PRU_PEERADDR` requests are from the `getsockname` and `getpeername` system calls, respectively. The remaining requests are not supported.

319–324   The functions `in_setsockaddr` and `in_setpeeraddr` fetch the information from the PCB, storing the result in the `nam` argument.

raw_ip.c

```
304      case PRU_SENSE:
305          /*
306           * fstat: don't bother with a blocksize.
307           */
308          return (0);

309          /*
310           * Not supported.
311           */
312      case PRU_RCVOOB:
313      case PRU_RCVD:
314      case PRU_LISTEN:
315      case PRU_ACCEPT:
316      case PRU_SENDOOB:
317          error = EOPNOTSUPP;
318          break;

319      case PRU_SOCKADDR:
320          in_setsockaddr(inp, nam);
321          break;

322      case PRU_PEERADDR:
323          in_setpeeraddr(inp, nam);
324          break;

325      default:
326          panic("rip_usrreq");
327      }
328      if (m != NULL)
329          m_freem(m);
330      return (error);
331  }
```

raw_ip.c

Figure 32.16   `rip_usrreq` function: remaining requests.

32.8   `rip_ctloutput` **Function**

The `setsockopt` and `getsockopt` system calls invoke the `rip_ctloutput` function. Only one IP socket option is handled here, along with eight socket options related to multicast routing.

Figure 32.17 shows the first part of the `rip_ctloutput` function.

144–172   The size of the mbuf that contains either the new value of the option or will hold the current value of the option must be at least as large as an integer. For the `setsockopt` system call, the flag is set if the integer value in the mbuf is nonzero, or cleared otherwise. For the `getsockopt` system call, the value returned in the mbuf is either 0 or the nonzero value of the flag. The function returns, to avoid the processing at the end of the `switch` statement for other IP options.

```
                                                                      raw_ip.c
144  int
145  rip_ctloutput(op, so, level, optname, m)
146  int      op;
147  struct socket *so;
148  int      level, optname;
149  struct mbuf **m;
150  {
151      struct inpcb *inp = sotoinpcb(so);
152      int      error;

153      if (level != IPPROTO_IP)
154          return (EINVAL);

155      switch (optname) {

156      case IP_HDRINCL:
157          if (op == PRCO_SETOPT || op == PRCO_GETOPT) {
158              if (m == 0 || *m == 0 || (*m)->m_len < sizeof(int))
159                      return (EINVAL);
160              if (op == PRCO_SETOPT) {
161                  if (*mtod(*m, int *))
162                              inp->inp_flags |= INP_HDRINCL;
163                  else
164                      inp->inp_flags &= ~INP_HDRINCL;
165                  (void) m_free(*m);
166              } else {
167                  (*m)->m_len = sizeof(int);
168                  *mtod(*m, int *) = inp->inp_flags & INP_HDRINCL;
169              }
170              return (0);
171          }
172          break;
                                                                      raw_ip.c
```

Figure 32.17   rip_usrreq function: process IP_HDRINCL socket option.

```
                                                                      raw_ip.c
173      case DVMRP_INIT:
174      case DVMRP_DONE:
175      case DVMRP_ADD_VIF:
176      case DVMRP_DEL_VIF:
177      case DVMRP_ADD_LGRP:
178      case DVMRP_DEL_LGRP:
179      case DVMRP_ADD_MRT:
180      case DVMRP_DEL_MRT:


                              /* shown in Figure 14.9 */


188      }
189      return (ip_ctloutput(op, so, level, optname, m));
190  }
                                                                      raw_ip.c
```

Figure 32.18   rip_usrreq function: process multicast routing socket option.

Figure 32.18 shows the last portion of the `rip_ctloutput` function. It handles eight multicast routing socket options.

173–188   These eight socket options are valid only for the `setsockopt` system call. They are processed by the `ip_mrouter_cmd` function as discussed with Figure 14.9.

189   Any other IP socket options, such as `IP_OPTIONS` to set the IP options, are processed by `ip_ctloutput`.

32.9 Summary

Raw sockets provide three capabilities for an IP host.

1.   They are used to send and receive ICMP and IGMP messages.
2.   They allow a process to build its own IP headers.
3.   They allow additional IP-based protocols to be supported in a user process.

We saw that raw IP output is simple—it just fills in a few fields in the IP header—but it allows a process to supply its own IP header. This allows diagnostic programs to create any type of IP datagram.

Raw IP input provides three types of filtering for incoming IP datagrams. The process chooses to receive datagrams based on (1) the protocol field, (2) the source IP address (set by `connect`), and (3) the destination IP address (set by `bind`). The process chooses which combination of these three filters (if any) to apply.

Exercises

32.1   Assume the `IP_HDRINCL` socket option is not set. What value will `rip_output` place into the IP header protocol field (`ip_p`) when the third argument to `socket` is 0? What value will `rip_output` place into this field when the third argument to `socket` is `IPPROTO_RAW` (255)?

32.2   A process creates a raw socket with a protocol value of `IPPROTO_RAW` (255). What type of IP datagrams will the process receive on this socket?

32.3   A process creates a raw socket with a protocol value of 0. What type of IP datagrams will the process receive on this socket?

32.4   Modify `rip_input` to send an ICMP destination unreachable with code 2 (protocol unreachable) when appropriate. Be careful not to generate the error for received ICMP and IGMP packets for which `rip_input` is called.

32.5   If a process wants to write its own IP datagrams with its own IP header, what are the differences in using a raw IP socket with the `IP_HDRINCL` option, and using BPF (Chapter 31)?

32.6   When would a process read from a raw IP socket, and when would it read from BPF?

Epilogue

"We have come a long way. Nine chapters stuffed with code is a lot to negotiate. If you didn't assimilate all of it the first time through, don't worry—you weren't really expected to. Even the best of code takes time to absorb, and you seldom grasp all the implications until you try to use and modify the program. Much of what you learn about programming comes only from working with the code: reading, revising and rereading."

From the Epilogue of *Software Tools* [Kernighan and Plauger 1976].

"In fact, this RFC will argue that modularity is one of the chief villains in attempting to obtain good performance, so that the designer is faced with a delicate and inevitable tradeoff between good structure and good performance."

From RFC 817 [Clark 1982].

This text has provided a long and detailed examination of a significant piece of a real operating system. Versions of the code presented in the text are shipped as part of the Unix kernel with most flavors of Unix today, along with many non-Unix systems.

The code that we've examined is not perfect and it is not the only way to write a TCP/IP protocol stack. It has been modified, enhanced, tweaked, and maligned over the past 15 years by many people. Large portions of the code that we've presented weren't even written at the U. C. Berkeley Computer Systems Research Group: the multicasting code was written by Steve Deering, the long fat pipe support was added by Thomas Skibo, portions of the TCP code were written by Van Jacobson, and so on. The code contains `goto`s (221 to be exact), many large functions (e.g., `tcp_input` and `tcp_output`), and numerous examples of questionable coding style. (We tried to note these items when discussing the code.) Nevertheless, the code is unquestionably "industrial strength" and continues to be the base upon which new features are added and the standard upon which other implementations are measured.

The Berkeley networking code was designed on VAXes when a VAX-11/780 with 4 megabytes of memory was a big system. For that reason some of the design features (e.g., mbufs) emphasized memory savings over higher performance. This would change if the code were rewritten from scratch today.

There has been a strong push over the last few years toward higher performance of networking software, as the underlying networks become faster (e.g., FDDI and ATM) and as high-bandwidth applications become more prevalent (e.g., voice and video). Whenever designing networking software within the kernel of an operating system, clarity normally gives way to speed [Clark 1982]. This will continue in any real-world implementation.

The research implementation of the Internet protocols described in [Partridge 1993] and [Jacobson 1993] is a move toward much higher performance. [Jacobson 1993] reports the code is 10 to 100 times faster than the implementation described in this book. Mbufs, software interrupts, and much of the protocol layering evident in BSD systems are gone. If widely released, this implementation could become the standard that others are measured against in the future.

In July 1994 the successor to IP version 4, IP version 6 (IPv6), was announced. It uses 128-bit (16-byte) addresses. Many changes will take place with the IP and ICMP protocols, but the transport layers, UDP and TCP, will remain virtually the same. (There is talk of a TCPng, the next generation of TCP, but the authors think just upgrading IP will provide enough of a challenge for the hundreds of vendors and millions of users across the world to put off any changes to TCP.) It will take a year or two for vendor-supported implementations to appear, and many years after that for end users to migrate their hosts and routers to IPv6. Research implementations of IPv6 based on the code in this text should appear in early 1995.

To continue your understanding of the Berkeley networking code, the best course of action at this point is to obtain the source code, and modify it. The source code is easily obtainable (Appendix B) and numerous exercises throughout the text suggest modifications.

Appendix A

Solutions to Selected Exercises

Chapter 1

1.2 SLIP drivers execute at `spltty` (Figure 1.13), which must be a priority lower than or equal to `splimp` and must be a priority higher than `splnet`. Therefore the SLIP drivers are blocked from interrupting.

Chapter 2

2.1 The `M_EXT` flag is a property of the mbuf itself, not a property of the packet described by the mbuf.

2.2 The caller asks for more than 100 (`MHLEN`) contiguous bytes.

2.3 This is infeasible since clusters can be pointed to by multiple mbufs (Section 2.9). Also, there is no room in a cluster for a back pointer (Exercise 2.4).

2.4 In the macros `MCLALLOC` and `MCLFREE` in `<sys/mbuf.h>` we see that the reference count is an array named `mclrefcnt`. This array is allocated when the kernel is initialized in the file `machdep.c`.

Chapter 3

3.3 A large interactive queue would defeat the purpose of the queue by delaying new interactive traffic behind the existing interactive data.

3.4 Since the `sl_softc` structures are all declared as global variables, they are initialized to 0 when the kernel starts.

3.5

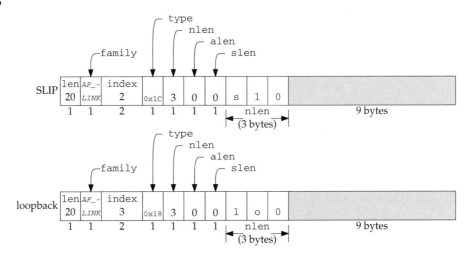

Chapter 4

4.1 `leread` must examine the packet to decide if it needs to be discarded after it is passed to BPF. Since a BPF tap can enable promiscuous mode on the interface, packets may be addressed to some other system on the Ethernet and must be discarded after BPF has processed them.

When the interface is not tapped, the tests must be done in `ether_input`.

4.2 If the tests were reversed, the broadcast flag would never be set.

If the second `if` wasn't preceded by an `else`, every broadcast packet would also have the multicast flag set.

Chapter 5

5.1 The loopback interface does not need an input function because all its packets are received directly from `looutput`, which performs the "input" functions.

5.2 The stack allocation is faster than dynamic memory allocation. Performance is important for BPF processing, since the code is executed for each incoming packet.

5.5 The first character that overflows the buffer is discarded, `SC_ERROR` is set, and `slinput` resets the cluster pointers to begin collecting characters at the start of the buffer. Because `SC_ERROR` is set, `slinput` discards the frame when it receives the SLIP END character.

5.6 IP discards the packet when the checksum is found to be invalid or when it notices that the length in the IP header does not match the physical packet size.

5.7   Since `ifp` points to the first member of a `le_softc` structure,

```
sc = (struct le_softc *)ifp;
```

initializes `sc` correctly.

5.8   This is very hard to do. Some routers may send ICMP source quench messages when they begin discarding packets but Net/3 discards these messages for UDP sockets (Figure 23.30). An application would have to begin using the same techniques used by TCP: estimation of the available bandwidth and delay on roundtrip times for acknowledged datagrams.

Chapter 6

6.1   Before IP subnetting (RFC 950 [Mogul and Postel 1985]), the network and host portions of IP addresses always appeared on byte boundaries. The definition of an `in_addr` structure was

```
struct in_addr {
        union {
                struct { u_char s_b1, s_b2, s_b3, s_b4; } S_un_b;
                struct { u_short s_w1, s_w2; } S_un_w;
                u_long S_addr;
        } S_un;
#define s_addr   S_un.S_addr           /* should be used for all code */
#define s_host   S_un.S_un_b.s_b2      /* OBSOLETE: host on imp */
#define s_net    S_un.S_un_b.s_b1      /* OBSOLETE: network */
#define s_imp    S_un.S_un_w.s_w2      /* OBSOLETE: imp */
#define s_impno  S_un.S_un_b.s_b4      /* OBSOLETE: imp # */
#define s_lh     S_un.S_un_b.s_b3      /* OBSOLETE: logical host */
};
```

The Internet address could be accessed as 8-bit bytes, 16-bit words, or a single 32-bit address. The macros s_host, s_net, s_imp, and so on have names that correspond to the physical structure of early TCP/IP networks.

The use of subnetting and supernetting makes the byte and word divisions obsolete.

6.2   A pointer to the structure labeled `sl_softc[0]` is returned.

6.3   The interface output functions, such as `ether_output`, have a pointer only to the `ifnet` structure for the interface, and not to an `ifaddr` structure. Using the IP address in the `arpcom` structure (which is the last IP address assigned to the interface) avoids having to select an address from the `ifaddr` address list.

6.4   Only a superuser process can create a raw IP socket. By using a UDP socket, any process can examine the interface configurations but the kernel can still require superuser privileges to modify the interface addresses.

6.5   Three functions loop through a netmask 1 byte at a time. These are `ifa_ifwithnet`, `ifaof_ifpforaddr`, and `rt_maskedcopy`. A shorter mask improves the performance of these functions.

6.6   The Telnet connection is established with the remote system. Net/2 systems shouldn't forward these packets, and other systems should never accept loopback packets that arrive on any interface other than the loopback interface.

Chapter 7

7.1   The following call returns a pointer to `inetsw[6]`:

```
pffindproto(PF_INET, 0, SOCK_RAW);
```

Chapter 8

8.1   Probably not. The system could not respond to any broadcasts since it would have no source address to use in the reply.

8.4   Since the packet has been damaged, there is no way of knowing if the addresses in the header are correct or not.

8.5   If an application selects a source address that differs from the address of the selected outgoing interface, redirects from the selected next-hop router fail. The next-hop router sees a source address different from that of the subnetwork on which it was transmitted and does not send a redirect message. This is a consequence of implementing the weak end system model and is noted in RFC 1122.

8.6   The new host thinks the broadcast packet is the address of some other host in the unsubnetted network and trys to send it back out on the network. The network interface begins broadcasting ARP requests for the broadcast address, which are never answered.

8.7   The decrement of the TTL is done after the comparison for less than or equal to 1 to avoid the potential error of decrementing a received TTL of 0 to become 255.

8.8   If two routers each consider the other the best next-hop for a packet, a routing loop exists. Until the loop is removed, the original packet bounces between the two routers and each one sends an ICMP redirect back to the source host if that host is on the same network as the routers. Loops may exist when the routing tables are temporarily inconsistent during a routing update.

The TTL of the original packet eventually reaches 0 and the packet is discarded. This is one of the primary reasons why the TTL field exists.

8.9   The four Ethernet broadcast addresses would not be checked because they do not belong to the receiving interface. The limited-broadcast addresses would be checked. This implies that a system on a SLIP link can communicate with the system on the other end without knowing the other system's address by utilizing the limited-broadcast address.

8.10 ICMP error messages are generated only for the initial fragment of a datagram, which always has an offset of 0. The host and network forms for 0 are the same, so no conversion is necessary.

Chapter 9

9.1 RFC 1122 says that the behavior is implementation dependent when conflicting options appear in a packet. Net/3 processes the first source route option correctly, but since this updates `ip_dst` in the packet header, the second source route processing will be incorrect.

9.2 The host within the network can be used as a relay to access other hosts within the network. To communicate with an otherwise-blocked host, the source host need only construct packets with a loose route to the relay host and then to the final destination host. The router does not drop the packets because the destination address is the relay host, which will process the route and forward the packet to the final destination host. The destination host reverses the route and uses the relay host to return packets.

9.3 The same principle from the previous exercise applies. We pick a relay router that can communicate with the source and destination hosts and construct source routes to pass through the relay and to the destination. The relay router must be on the same network as the destination host so that a default route is not required for communication.

This technique can be extended to allow two hosts to communicate even if they do not have routes to each other, as long as they can find willing relay hosts.

9.4 If the source route is the only IP option, the NOP option causes all the IP addresses to be on a 4-byte boundary in the IP header. This can optimize memory references to these addresses on many architectures. This alignment technique also works when multiple options are present if each option is padded with NOPs to a 4-byte boundary.

9.5 A nonstandard time value cannot be confused with a standard value since the largest standard time value is 86,399,999 ($24 \times 60 \times 60 \times 1000 - 1$) and this value can be represented in 28 bits, which avoids any conflict with the high-order bit since time values are 32 bits long.

9.6 The source route option code may change `ip_dst` in the packet during processing. The destination is saved so that the timestamp processing code uses the original destination.

Chapter 10

10.2 After reassembly, only the options from the initial fragment are available to the transport protocols.

10.3 The fragment is read into a cluster since the data length (216 + 20) is greater than 208 (Figure 2.16).

`m_pullup` in Figure 10.11 moves the first 40 bytes into a separate mbuf as in Figure 2.18.

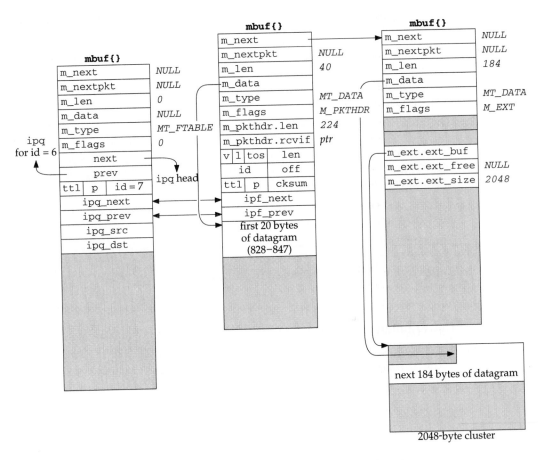

10.5   The average number of received fragments per datagram is

$$\frac{72,786 - 349}{16,557} = 4.4$$

The average number of fragments created for an outgoing datagram is

$$\frac{796,084}{260,484} = 3.1$$

10.6   In Figure 10.11 the packet is initially processed as a fragment. The reserved bit is discarded when ip_off is left shifted. The resulting packet is processed as a fragment or as a complete datagram, depending on the values of the MF and offset bits.

Chapter 11

11.1   The outgoing reply uses the source address of the interface on which the request was received. Hosts are not required to recognize 0.0.0.0 as a valid broadcast address, so the request may be ignored. The recommended broadcast address is 255.255.255.255.

11.2 Assume that a host sends link-level broadcasts packets with the IP source address of another host and the packet contains errors such as an improperly formed option. Every host receives and detects the error because of the link-level broadcast and because options are processed before a final destination check. Many hosts that detect the error try to send an ICMP message back to the IP source of the packet even though the original packet was sent as a link-level broadcast. The unfortunate host will begin receiving many bogus ICMP error messages. This is one reason why ICMP errors must not be sent in response to link-level broadcasts.

11.3 In the first case, such a redirect message can fool the host into sending packets to an arbitrary host on an alternate subnetwork. This host may be masquerading as a router but recording the traffic it receives instead. RFC 1009 requires that routers only generate redirect messages for other routers on the same subnet. Even if the host ignores these messages to redirect packets to a new subnetwork, a host on the same subnetwork can fool the host. The second case guards against this by requiring that the host only accept the redirect advice from the original router that it had (erroneously) selected to receive the traffic. Presumably this incorrect router was a default router specified by an administrator.

11.4 By passing the message to `rip_input`, a process-level daemon could respond and old systems that relied on this behavior could continue to be supported.

11.5 ICMP errors are sent only for the initial fragment of an IP datagram. Since the offset value of an initial fragment is always 0, the byte ordering of the field is unimportant.

11.6 If the ICMP request was received on an interface that was not yet configured with an IP address, `ia` would be null and no reply could be generated.

11.7 Net/3 reflects the data along with the timestamp reply.

11.10 The high-order bit is reserved and must be 0. If it is sent, `icmp_error` will discard the packet.

11.11 The return value is discarded because `icmp_send` does not return an error, but more significantly, errors generated during ICMP processing are discarded to avoid generating an endless series of error messages.

Chapter 12

12.1 On an Ethernet, the IP broadcast address 255.255.255.255 translates to the Ethernet broadcast address `ff:ff:ff:ff:ff:ff` and is received by *every* Ethernet interface on the network. Systems that aren't running IP software must actively receive and discard each of these broadcast packets.

A packet sent to the IP all-hosts multicast group 224.0.0.1 translates to the Ethernet multicast address `01:00:5e:00:00:01` and is received only by systems that have explicitly instructed their interfaces to receive IP multicast datagrams. Systems that aren't running IP or that aren't level-2 compliant never receive these datagrams, as they are discarded by the Ethernet interface hardware itself.

12.2   One alternative would be to specify interfaces by their text name as with the `ifreq` structure and the `ioctl` commands for accessing interface information. `ip_setmoptions` and `ip_getmoptions` would have to call `ifunit` instead of `INADDR_TO_IFP` to locate the pointer to the interface's `ifnet` structure.

12.3   The high-order 4 bits of a multicast group are always 1110, so only 5 significant bits are discarded by the mapping function.

12.4   The entire `ip_moptions` structure must fit within an mbuf, which limits the size of the structure to 108 bytes (remember the 20-byte mbuf header). `IP_MAX_MEMBERSHIPS` can be larger but must be less than or equal to 25. $(4 + 1 + 1 + 2 + (4 \times 25) = 108)$

12.5   The datagram is duplicated and two copies appear on the IP input queue. A multicast application must be prepared to discard duplicate datagrams.

12.6

12.8   The process could create a second socket and request another `IP_MAX_MEMBERSHIPS` through the second socket.

12.9   Define a new mbuf flag `M_LOCAL` for the `m_flags` member of the mbuf header. The flag can be set on loopback packets by `ip_output` instead of computing the checksum. `ipintr` can skip the checksum verification if the flag is on. SunOS 5.X has an option to do this (`ip_local_cksum`, page 531, Volume 1).

12.10   There are $2^{23} - 1$ (8,388,607) unique Ethernet IP multicast addresses. Remember that IP group 224.0.0.0 is reserved.

12.11   This assumption is correct since `in_addmulti` rejects all add requests if the interface does not have an `ioctl` function, and this implies that `in_delmulti` is never called if `if_ioctl` is null.

12.12   The mbuf is never released. It appears that `ip_getmoptions` contains a memory leak. `ip_getmoptions` is called from `ip_ctloutput`, which allows a call such as:

```
ip_getmoptions(IP_ADD_MEMBERSHIP, 0, mp)
```

which exercises the bug in `ip_getmoptions`.

Chapter 13

13.1   Responding to an IGMP query from the loopback interface is unnecessary since the local host is the only system on the loopback network and it already knows its membership status.

13.2   `max_linkhdr + sizeof(struct ip) + IGMP_MINLEN` $= 16 + 20 + 8 = 44 < 100$

13.3   The primary reason for the random delay in reporting memberships is to minimize (ideally to 1) the number of reports that appear on a multicast network. A point-to-point network consists only of two interfaces, so the delay is not necessary to minimize the response to the query. One interface (presumably a multicast router) generates the query, and the other interface responds.

There is another reason not to flood the interface's output queue with all the membership reports. The output queue may have a packet or byte limit that could be exceeded by many IGMP membership reports. For example, in the SLIP driver, if the output queue is full or the device is too busy, the entire queue of pending packets is discarded (Figure 5.17).

Chapter 14

14.1   Five. One each for networks A through E.

14.2   `grplst_member` is called only by `ip_mforward`, but `ip_mforward` can be called by `ipintr` during protocol processing, or by `ip_output`, which can be called indirectly from the socket layer. The cache is a shared data structure that must be protected while it is being updated. The membership list itself is protected by `splx` calls in `add_lgrp` and `del_lgrp`, where it is modified.

14.3   The `SIOCDELMULTI` command affects only the Ethernet multicast list for the interface. The IP multicast group list remains unchanged, so the interface remains a member of the group. The interface continues accepting multicast datagrams for any groups that are still on the IP group membership list for the interface. Specifically, when `ether_delmulti` returns `ENETRESET` to `leioctl`, the function `lereset` is called to reconfigure the interface (Figure 12.31).

14.4   Only one virtual interface is considered to be the parent interface for a multicast spanning tree. If the packet is accepted on the tunnel, then the physical interface cannot be the parent and `ip_mforward` discards the packet.

Chapter 15

15.1   The socket could be shared across a fork or passed to a process through a Unix domain socket ([Stevens 1990]).

15.2   The `sa_len` member of the structure is larger than the size of the buffer after `accept` returns. This is usually not a problem with the fixed-length Internet address, but it can be when using variable-length addresses supported by the OSI protocols, for example.

15.4 The call to `soqremque` is only made when `so_qlen` is not equal to 0. If `soqremque` returns a null pointer there must be an error in the socket queueing code so the kernel panics.

15.5 The copy is made so that `bzero` can clear the structure while it is locked and so that `dom_dispose` and `sbrelease` can be called after `splx`. This minimizes the amount of time the CPU is kept at `splimp` and therefore the amount of time that network interrupts are blocked.

15.6 The `sbspace` macro will return 0. As a result, the `sbappendaddr` and `sbappendcontrol` functions (used by UDP) will refuse to queue additional packets. TCP uses `sbappend`, which assumes that the caller has checked for space first. TCP calls `sbappend` even when `sbspace` returns 0. The data placed in the receive queue is not available to a process because the `SS_CANTRCVMORE` flag prevents the read system calls from returning any data.

Chapter 16

16.1 When the value is assigned to `uio_resid` in the `uio` structure it becomes a large negative number. `sosend` rejects the message with `EINVAL`.

> Net/2 did *not* check for a negative value. This problem is described by the comment at the start of `sosend` (Figure 16.23).

16.2 No. The only time the cluster is ever filled with less than `MCLBYTES` is at the end of a message when less than `MCLBYTES` remain. `resid` is 0 at this time and the loop is terminated by the `break` on line 394 before reaching the test for `space > 0`.

16.5 The process blocks until the buffer is unlocked. In this case the lock exists only while another process is examining the buffer or passing data to the protocol layer, and not when a process must wait for space in the buffer, which may take an indefinite amount of time.

16.6 If the send buffer contained many mbufs, each of which contained only a few bytes of data, `sb_cc` may be well below the limit specified by `sb_hiwat` while a large amount of memory would be allocated for the mbufs. If the kernel didn't limit the number of mbufs attached to each buffer, a process could easily create a memory shortage.

16.7 `recvit` is called from `recvfrom` and `recvmsg`. Only `recvmsg` handles control information. The entire `msghdr` structure, including the length of the control message, is copied back to the process by `recvmsg`. For address information, `recvmsg` sets the `namelenp` argument to null because it expects the length in `msg_namelen`. When `recvfrom` calls `recvit`, the `namelenp` is nonnull because it expects the length in `*namelenp`.

16.8 `MSG_EOR` is cleared by `soreceive` so that it is not inadvertently returned by `soreceive` before an `M_EOR` mbuf is processed.

16.9   There would be a race condition while `select` examined the descriptors. If a selectable event occurred after `selscan` examined the descriptor but before `select` called `tsleep`, it would not be detected and the process would sleep until another selectable event occurred.

Chapter 17

17.1   This simplifies the code that copies data between the kernel and the process. `copyin` and `copyout` can be used for a single mbuf, but `uiomove` is needed to handle multiple mbufs.

17.2   The code works correctly because the first member of a `linger` structure is the expected integer flag.

Chapter 18

18.1   Write eight rows, one for each possible combination of the bits from the search key, the routing table key, and the routing table mask.

row	1 search key	2 table key	3 table mask	1 & 3	2 == 4?	1 ^ 2	6 & 3
1	0	0	0	0	yes	0	0=yes
2	0	0	1	0	yes	0	0=yes
3	0	1	0	0	no	1	0=yes
4	0	1	1	0	no	1	1=no
5	1	0	0	0	yes	1	0=yes
6	1	0	1	1	no	1	1=no
7	1	1	0	0	no	0	0=yes
8	1	1	1	1	yes	0	0=yes

The column "2 == 4?" should equal the final column "6 & 3." On first glance they are not the same, but we can ignore rows 3 and 7 because in these two rows the routing table bit is 1 while the same bit in the routing table mask is 0. When the routing table is built the key is logically ANDed with the mask, guaranteeing that for every bit of 0 in the mask, the corresponding bit in the key is also 0.

Another way to look at the exclusive OR and logical AND in Figure 18.40 is that the exclusive OR becomes 1 only if the the search key bit differs from the bit in the routing table key. The logical AND then ignores any differences that correspond to a bit that's 0 in the mask. If the result is still nonzero, the search key does not match the routing table key.

18.2   The size of an `rtentry` structure is 120 bytes, which includes the two `radix_node` structures. Each entry also requires two `sockaddr_in` structures (Figure 18.28), for 152 bytes per routing table entry. The total is about 3 megabytes.

18.3   Since `rn_b` is a short integer, assuming 16 bits for a short imposes a limit of 32767 bits per key (4095 bytes).

Chapter 19

19.1   The RTF_DYNAMIC flag is set in Figure 19.15 when the route is created by a redirect, and the RTF_MODIFIED flag is set when the gateway field of an existing route is modified by a redirect. If a route is created by a redirect and then later modified by another redirect, both flags will be set.

19.2   A host route is created for each host accessed through the default route. TCP can then maintain and update routing metrics for each individual host (Figure 27.3).

19.3   Each rt_msghdr structure requires 76 bytes. Two sockaddr_in structures are present for a host route (destination and gateway) giving a message size of 108 bytes. The message size for each ARP entry is 112 bytes: one sockaddr_in and one sockaddr_dl. The total size is then $(15 \times 112 + 20 \times 108)$ or 3840 bytes. A network route (instead of a host route) requires an additional 8 bytes for the network mask (116 bytes for the message instead of 108), so if the 20 routes are all network routes, the total size is 4000 bytes.

Chapter 20

20.1   The return value is returned in the rtm_errno member of the message (Figure 20.14) and also as the return value from write (Figure 20.22). The latter is more reliable since the former may run into mbuf starvation, causing the reply message to be discarded (Figure 20.17).

20.2   For a SOCK_RAW socket, the pffindproto function (Figure 7.20) returns the entry with a protocol of 0 (the wildcard) if an exact match isn't found.

Chapter 21

21.1   It is assumed that the ifnet structure is at the beginning of the arpcom structure, which it is (Figure 3.20).

21.2   Sending the ICMP echo request does not require ARP, since the destination address is the broadcast address. But the ICMP echo replies are normally unicast, so each sender uses ARP to determine the destination Ethernet address. When the local host receives each ARP request, in_arpinput replies and creates an entry for the other host.

21.3   When a new ARP entry is created, the rt_gateway value, a sockaddr_dl structure in this case, is copied from the entry being cloned by rtrequest in Figure 19.8. In Figure 21.1 we see that the sdl_alen member of this entry is 0.

21.4   With Net/3, if the caller of arpresolve supplies a pointer to a routing table entry, arplookup is not called, and the corresponding Ethernet address is available through the rt_gateway pointer (assuming it hasn't expired). This avoids any type of lookup in the common case. In Chapter 22 we'll see that TCP and UDP store a pointer to their routing table entry in their protocol control block, avoiding a search of the routing table in the case of TCP (where the destination IP address never changes for a connection) and in the case of UDP when the destination doesn't change.

21.5 The timeout of an incomplete ARP entry occurs between 0 and 5 minutes after the entry is created. `arpresolve` sets `rt_expire` to the current time when the ARP request is sent. The next time `arptimer` runs, if that entry is not resolved, it is deleted (assuming its reference count is 0).

21.6 `ether_output` returns `EHOSTUNREACH` instead of `EHOSTDOWN`, causing an ICMP host unreachable error to be sent to the sending host by `ip_forward`.

21.7 The value for 140.252.13.32 is set in Figure 21.28 to the current time when the entry is created. It never changes.

The values for 140.252.13.33 and 140.252.13.34 are copied from the entry for 140.252.13.32 when these two entries are cloned by `rtrequest`. They are then set to the time at which an ARP request is sent by `arpresolve`, and finally set by `in_arpinput` to the time at which an ARP reply is received, plus 20 minutes.

The value for 140.252.13.35 is also copied from the entry for 140.252.13.32 when the entry is cloned, but then set to 0 by the code at the end of Figure 21.29.

21.8 Change the call to `arplookup` at the beginning of Figure 21.19 to always specify a second argument of 1 (the create flag).

21.9 The first datagram was sent *after* the halfway mark to the next second. Therefore both the first and second datagrams caused ARP requests to be sent, about 500 ms apart, since the kernel's `time.tv_sec` variable had different values when these two datagrams were sent.

21.10 Each packet to send is an mbuf chain. The `m_nextpkt` pointer in the first mbuf in each chain could be used to form a list of mbufs awaiting transmission.

Chapter 22

22.1 An infinite loop occurs, waiting for a port to become available. This assumes the process is allowed to open enough descriptors to tie up all ephemeral ports.

22.2 Few, if any, servers support this option. [Cheswick and Bellovin 1994] mention how this would be nice for implementing firewall systems.

22.4 The `udb` structure is initialized to 0 so `udb.inp_lport` starts at 0. The first time through `in_pcbbind` it is incremented to 1, which is less than 1024, so it is set to 1024.

22.5 Normally the caller sets the address family (`sa_family`) to `AF_INET`, but we saw in Figure 22.20 that the test for this is commented out. The caller can set the length member (`sa_len`), but we saw in Figure 15.20 that the function `sockargs` always sets this to the third argument to `bind`, which for a `sockaddr_in` structure is specified as 16, normally using C's `sizeof` operator.

The local IP address (`sin_addr`) can be specified as a wildcard address or as a local IP address. The local port number (`sin_port`), can be either 0 (telling the kernel to choose an ephemeral port) or nonzero if the process wants a particular port. Normally a TCP or UDP server specifies a wildcard IP address and a nonzero port, and a UDP client often specifies a wildcard IP address and a port number of 0.

22.6   A process is allowed to `bind` a local broadcast address, because the call to `ifa_ifwithaddr` in Figure 22.22 succeeds. That address is used as the source address for IP datagrams sent on the socket. As noted in Section C.2, this behavior is not allowed by RFC 1122.

An attempt to `bind` 255.255.255.255, however, fails, since that address is not acceptable to `ifa_ifwithaddr`.

Chapter 23

23.1   `sosend` places the user data into a single mbuf if the size is less than or equal to 100 bytes; into two mbufs if the size is less than or equal to 207 bytes; or into one or more mbufs, each with a cluster, otherwise. Furthermore, `sosend` calls `MH_ALIGN` if the size is less than 100 bytes, which, it is hoped, will allow room at the beginning of the mbuf for the protocol headers. Since `udp_output` calls `M_PREPEND`, the following five scenarios are possible: (1) If the size of the user data is less than or equal to 72 bytes, a single mbuf contains the IP header, UDP header, and data. (2) If the size is between 73 and 100 bytes, one mbuf is allocated by `sosend` for the data and another is allocated by `M_PREPEND` for the IP and UDP headers. (3) If the size is between 101 and 207 bytes, two mbufs are allocated by `sosend` for the data and another by `M_PREPEND` for the IP and UDP headers. (4) If the size is between 208 and `MCLBYTES`, one mbuf with a cluster is allocated by `sosend` for the data and another by `M_PREPEND` for the IP and UDP headers. (5) Beyond this size, `sosend` allocates as many mbufs with clusters as necessary to hold the data (up to 64 for a maximum data size of 65507 bytes with 1024-byte clusters), and one mbuf is allocated by `M_PREPEND` for the IP and UDP headers.

23.2   IP options are passed to `ip_output`, which calls `ip_insertoptions` to insert the options into the outgoing IP datagram. This function in turn allocates a new mbuf to hold the IP header including options if the first mbuf in the chain points to a cluster (which never happens with UDP output) or if there is not enough room at the beginning of the first mbuf in the chain for the options. In scenario 1 from the previous solution, the size of the options determines whether another mbuf is allocated by `ip_insertoptions`: if the size of the user data is less than $100 - 28 - optlen$, (where *optlen* is the number of bytes of IP options), there is room in the mbuf for the IP header with options, the UDP header, and the data.

In scenarios 2, 3, 4, and 5, the first mbuf in the chain is always allocated by `M_PREPEND` just for the IP and UDP headers. `M_PREPEND` calls `m_prepend`, which calls MH_ALIGN, moving the 28 bytes of headers to the end of the mbuf, hence there is always room for the maximum of 40 bytes of IP options in this first mbuf in the chain.

23.3   No. The function in_pcbconnect is called, either when the application calls connect or when the first datagram is sent on an unconnected UDP socket. Since the local address is a wildcard and the local port is 0, in_pcbconnect sets the local port to an ephemeral port (by calling in_pcbbind) and sets the local address based on the route to the destination.

23.4   The processor priority level is left at splnet; it is not restored to the saved value. This is a bug.

23.5   No. in_pcbconnect will not allow a connection to port 0. Even if the process doesn't call connect directly, an implicit connect is performed, so in_pcbconnect is called regardless.

23.6   The application must call ioctl with the SIOCGIFCONF command to return information on all configured IP interfaces. The destination address in the received UDP datagram must then be compared against all the IP addresses and broadcast addresses in the list returned by ioctl. (As an alternative to ioctl, the sysctl system call described in Section 19.14 can also be used to obtain the information on all the configured interfaces.)

23.7   recvit releases the mbuf with the control information.

23.8   To disconnect a connected UDP socket, call connect with an invalid address, such as 0.0.0.0, and a port of 0. Since the socket is already connected, soconnect calls sodisconnect, which calls udp_usrreq with a PRU_DISCONNECT request. This sets the foreign address to 0.0.0.0 and the foreign port to 0, allowing a subsequent call to sendto that specifies a destination address to succeed. Specifying the invalid address causes the PRU_CONNECT request from sodisconnect to fail. We don't want the connect to succeed, we just want the PRU_DISCONNECT request executed and this back door through connect is the only way to execute this request, since the sockets API doesn't provide a disconnect function.

The manual page for connect(2) usually contains the following note that hints at this: "Datagram sockets may dissolve the association by connecting to an invalid address, such as a null address." What this note fails to mention is that the call to connect for the invalid address is expected to return an error. The term *null address* is also vague: it means the IP address 0.0.0.0, not a null pointer for the second argument to bind.

23.9   Since an unconnected UDP socket is temporarily connected to the foreign IP address by in_pcbconnect, the scenario is the same as if the process calls connect: the datagram is sent out the primary interface with a destination IP address corresponding to the broadcast address of that interface.

23.10 The server must set the IP_RECVDSTADDR socket option and use recvmsg to obtain the destination IP address from the client's request. For this address to be the source IP address of the reply requires that this IP address be bound to the socket. Since you cannot `bind` a socket more than once, the server must create a brand new socket for each reply.

23.11 Notice in `ip_output` (Figure 8.22) that IP does not modify the DF bit supplied by the caller. A new socket option could be defined to cause `udp_output` to set the DF bit before passing datagrams to IP.

23.12 No. It is used only in the `udp_input` function and should be local to that function.

Chapter 24

24.1 The total number of ESTABLISHED connections is 126,820. Dividing this into the total number of bytes transmitted and received yields an average of about 30,000 bytes in each direction.

24.2 In `tcp_output`, the mbuf obtained for the IP and TCP headers also contains room for the link-layer headers (`max_linkhdr`). The IP and TCP header prototype is copied into the mbuf using `bcopy`, which won't work if the 40-byte header were split between two mbufs. Although the 40-byte headers must fit into one mbuf, the link-layer header need not. But a performance penalty would occur later (`ether_output`) because a separate mbuf would be required for the link-layer header.

24.3 On the author's system `bsdi`, the count was 16, 15 of which were standard system daemons (Telnet, Rlogin, FTP, etc.). On `vangogh.cs.berkeley.edu`, a medium-sized multiuser system with around 20 users, the count was 60. On a large multiuser system (`world.std.com`) with around 150 users, the count was 417 TCP end points and 809 UDP end points.

Chapter 25

25.1 In Figure 24.5 there were 531,285 delayed ACKs over 2,592,000 seconds (30 days). This is an average of about one delayed ACK every 5 seconds, or one delayed ACK every 25 times `tcp_fasttimo` is called. This means 96% of the time (24 times out of every 25) *every* TCP control block is checked for the delayed-ACK flag, when not one is set. On the large multiuser system in the solution to Exercise 24.3, this involves looking at over 400 control blocks, 5 times a second.

One alternative implementation would be to set a global flag when a delayed ACK is needed and only go through the list of control blocks when the flag is set. Alternatively, another list could be maintained that contains only the control blocks that require a delayed ACK. See, for example, the variable `igmp_timers_are_running` in Figure 13.14.

25.2 This allows the variable `tcp_keepintvl` to be patched in the running kernel, which then changes the value of `tcp_maxidle` the next time `tcp_slowtimo` is called.

25.3 `t_idle` actually counts the time since a segment was last received or transmitted. This is because TCP output must be acknowledged by the other end and the receipt of the ACK clears `t_idle`, as does the receipt of a data segment (Figure 28.8).

25.4 Here is one way to rewrite the code:

```
case TCPT_2MSL:
    if (tp->t_state == TCPS_TIME_WAIT)
        tp = tcp_close(tp);
    else {
        if (tp->t_idle <= tcp_maxidle)
            tp->t_timer[TCPT_2MSL] = tcp_keepintvl;
        else
            tp = tcp_close(tp);
    }
    break;
```

25.5 When the duplicate ACK is received, `t_idle` is 150, but it is reset to 0. When the FIN_WAIT_2 timer expires, `t_idle` will be 1048 (1198 − 150), so the timer is set to 150 ticks. When the timer expires the next time, `t_idle` will be 1198, so the timer is set to 150 ticks. When the timer expires the next time, `t_idle` will be 1198 + 150, so the connection is closed. The duplicate ACK extends the time until the connection is closed.

25.6 The first keepalive probe will be sent 1 hour in the future. When the process sets the option, nothing happens other than setting the `SO_KEEPALIVE` option in the `socket` structure. When the timer expires 1 hour in the future, since the option is enabled, the code in Figure 25.16 sends the first probe.

25.7 The value of `tcp_rttdflt` initializes the RTT estimators for every TCP connection. A site can change the default of 3, if desired, by patching the global variable. If the value were a `#define` constant, it could be changed only by recompiling the kernel.

Chapter 26

26.1 The counter `t_idle` is always running for a connection, whereas TCP does not measure the amount of time since the last segment was sent on a connection.

26.2 In Figure 25.26 `snd_nxt` is set to `snd_una`, giving a value of 0 for `len`.

26.3 If you're running a Net/3 system and encounter a peer that can't handle either of these two newer options (i.e., that peer refuses to establish the connection, even though a host is required to ignore options it doesn't understand), this global can be patched in the kernel to disable one or both of these options.

26.4 The timestamp option would have updated the RTT estimators each time an ACK was received for new data: 16 times, twice the number of times without the option. The value calculated when the ACK of 6145 was received at time 217.944, however, would have been bogus—either the data segment with bytes

5633 through 6144 that was sent at time 3.740, or the received ACK of 6145, was delayed somewhere for about 200 seconds.

26.5   There is no guarantee that the 2-byte MSS value is correctly aligned for such a memory reference.

26.6   (This solution is from Dave Borman.) The maximum amount of TCP data in a segment is 65495 bytes, which is 65535 minus the minimum IP and TCP headers (40). Hence there are 39 values of the urgent offset that make no sense: 65496 through and including 65535. Whenever the sender has a 32-bit urgent offset that exceeds 65495, 65535 is sent as the urgent offset instead, and the URG flag is set. This puts the receiver into urgent mode and tells the receiver that the urgent offset points to data that has not been sent yet. The special value of 65535 continues to be sent as the urgent offset (with the URG flag set) until the urgent offset is less than or equal to 65495, at which point the real urgent offset is sent.

26.7   We've mentioned that data segments are transmitted reliably (i.e., the retransmission timer is set) but ACKs are not. RST segments are not transmitted reliably either. RST segments are generated when a bogus segment arrives (either a segment that is wrong for a connection, or a segment for a nonexistent connection). If the RST segment is discarded by `ip_output`, when the other end retransmits the segment that caused the RST to be generated, another RST will be generated.

26.8   The application does eight writes of 1024 bytes. The first four times `sosend` is called, `tcp_output` is called, and a segment is sent. Since these four segments each contain the final bytes of data in the send buffer, the PSH flag is set for each segment (Figure 26.25). The send buffer is also full, so the next write by the process puts the process to sleep in `sosend`. When the ACK is returned with an advertised window of 0, the 4096 bytes of data in the send buffer have been acknowledged and are discarded, and the process wakes up and continues filling the send buffer with the next four writes. But nothing can be sent until a nonzero window is advertised by the receiver. When this happens, the next four segments are sent, but only the final segment contains the PSH flag, since the first three segments do not empty the send buffer.

26.9   The `tp` argument to `tcp_respond` can be a null pointer if the segment being sent does not correspond to a connection. The code should check the value of `tp` and use the default only if the pointer is null.

26.10 `tcp_output` always allocates an mbuf just to contain the IP and TCP headers, by calling MGETHDR in Figures 26.25 and 26.26. This code allocates room at the front of the new mbuf only for the link-layer header (`max_linkhdr`). If IP options are in use and the size of the options exceeds `max_linkhdr`, another mbuf is allocated by `ip_insertoptions`. If the size of the IP options is less than or equal to `max_linkhdr`, then even though `ip_insertoptions` will use the space at the beginning of the mbuf, this will cause `ether_output` to allocate another mbuf for the link-layer header (assuming Ethernet output).

To try to avoid the extra mbuf, Figures 26.25 and 26.26 could call MH_ALIGN if the segment will contain IP options.

26.11 About 80 lines of C code, assuming RFC 1323 timestamps are in use and the segment is timed.

The macro MGETHDR invokes the macro MALLOC, which might call the function malloc. The function m_copy is also called, but a full-sized segment will be in a cluster, so the mbuf is not copied, a reference is made to the cluster. The call to MGET by m_copy might call malloc. The function bcopy copies the header template and in_cksum calculates the TCP checksum.

26.12 Nothing changes with writev because of the logic in sosend. Since the total size of the data (150) is less than MINCLSIZE (208), one mbuf is allocated for the first 100 bytes, and since the protocol is not atomic, the PRU_SEND request is issued. Another mbuf is allocated for the next 50 bytes, and another PRU_SEND is issued. TCP still generates two segments. (writev only generates a single "record," that is, a single PRU_SEND request, for PR_ATOMIC protocols such as UDP.)

With two buffers of length 200 and 300 the total size now exceeds MINCLSIZE. An mbuf cluster is allocated and only one PRU_SEND is issued. One 500-byte segment is generated by TCP.

Chapter 27

27.1 The first six rows of the table are asynchronous errors that are generated by the receipt of a segment or the expiration of a timer. By storing the nonzero error code in so_error, the process receives the error on the next read or write. The call from tcp_disconnect, however, occurs when the process calls close, or when the descriptor is closed automatically on process termination. In either case of the descriptor being closed, the process won't issue a read or write call to fetch the error. Also, since the process had to set the socket option explicitly to force the RST, returning an error provides no useful information to the process.

27.2 Assuming a 32-bit u_long, the maximum value is just under 4298 seconds (1.2 hours).

27.3 The statistics in the routing table are updated by tcp_close and it is called only when the connection enters the CLOSED state. Since the sending of data to the other end is terminated by the FTP client (it does the active close), the local end point enters the TIME_WAIT state. The routing table statistics won't be updated until twice the MSL has elapsed.

Chapter 28

28.1 0, 1, 2, and 3.

28.2 34.9 Mbits/sec. For higher speeds, larger buffers are required on both ends.

28.3 In the general case, tcp_dooptions doesn't know whether the two timestamp values are aligned on 32-bit boundaries or not. The special code in Figure 28.4,

however, knows that the values are on 32-bit boundaries, and avoids calling
`bcopy`.

28.4   The "options prediction" code in Figure 28.4 handles only the recommended format, so systems that send other than the recommended format cause the slower
processing of `tcp_dooptions` to occur for every received segment.

28.5   If `tcp_template` were called every time a socket were created, instead of every
time a connection is established, each listening server on a system would have
one allocated, which it would never use.

28.6   The timestamp clock frequency should be between 1 bit/ms and 1 bit/sec.
(Net/3 uses 2 bits/sec.) With the highest frequency of 1 bit/ms, a 32-bit timestamp wraps its sign bit in $2^{31}/(24 \times 60 \times 60 \times 1000)$ days, which is 24.8 days.

28.7   With a frequency of 1 bit per 500 ms, a 32-bit timestamp wraps its sign bit in
$2^{31}/(24 \times 60 \times 60 \times 2)$ days, which is 12,427 days, or about 34 years, longer than
the uptime of current computer systems.

28.8   The cleanup function of an RST should take precedence over timestamps, and it
is recommended that RSTs not carry timestamps (which is enforced by
`tcp_input` in Figure 26.24).

28.9   Since the client is in the ESTABLISHED state, processing ends up in Figure 28.24.
`todrop` is 1 because `rcv_nxt` was incremented over the SYN when it was first
received. The SYN flag is cleared (since it is a duplicate), `ti_seq` is incremented, and `todrop` is decremented to 0. The `if` statement at the top of Figure 28.25 is executed since `todrop` and `ti_len` are both 0. The next `if`
statement is skipped, and processing continues with the call to `m_adj`. But
`tcp_output` is not called in the continuation of `tcp_input` in the next chapter,
therefore the client does not respond to the duplicate SYN/ACK. The server will
time out and resend the SYN/ACK (recall the timer set in Figure 28.17 when a
passive socket receives a SYN), which will also be ignored. This is another bug
in the code in Figure 28.25 and this one is also fixed with the code shown in Figure 28.30.

28.10   The client's SYN arrives at the server and is delivered to the socket in the
TIME_WAIT state. The code in Figure 28.24 turns off the SYN flag and the code
in Figure 28.25 jumps to `dropafterack`, dropping the segment but generating
an ACK with an acknowledgment field of `rcv_nxt` (Figure 26.27). This is called
a *resynchronization ACK* because its purpose is to tell the other end what sequence
number it expects. When this ACK is received at the client (which is in the
SYN_SENT state), its acknowledgment field is not the expected value (Figure 28.18), causing an RST to be sent. The sequence number of the RST is the
acknowledgment field from the resynchronization ACK, and the ACK flag of the
RST segment is off (Figure 29.28). When the server receives the RST, its
TIME_WAIT state is prematurely terminated and the socket is closed on the
server's host (Figure 28.36). The client times out after 6 seconds and retransmits
its SYN. Assuming a listening server process is running on the server host, the
new connection is established. Because of this form of TIME_WAIT

assassination, a new connection is established not only when a SYN arrives with a higher sequence number (as checked for in Figure 28.29), but also when a SYN with a lower sequence number arrives.

Chapter 29

29.1   Assume a 2-second RTT. The server has a passive open pending and the client issues its active open at time 0. The server receives the SYN at time 1 and responds with its own SYN and an ACK of the client's SYN. The client receives this segment at time 2, and the code in Figure 28.20 completes the active open with the call to `soisconnected` (waking up the client process) and an ACK will be sent back to the server. The server receives the ACK at time 3, and the code in Figure 29.2 completes the server's passive open, returning control to the server process. In general, the client process receives control about one-half RTT before the server.

29.2   Assume the sequence number of the SYN is 1000 and the 50 bytes of data are numbered 1001–1050. When the SYN is processed by `tcp_input`, first the `case` starting in Figure 28.15 is executed, which sets `rcv_nxt` to 1001, and then a jump is made to `step6`. Figure 29.22 calls `tcp_reass` and the data is placed onto the socket's reassembly queue. But the data cannot be appended to the socket's receive buffer yet (Figure 27.23) so `rcv_nxt` is left at 1001. When `tcp_output` is called to generate the immediate ACK, `rcv_nxt` (1001) is sent as the acknowledgment field. In summary, the SYN is acknowledged, but not the 50 bytes of data. Since the client will retransmit the 50 bytes of data, there is no advantage in sending data with a SYN generated by an active open.

29.3   The server's socket is in the SYN_RCVD state when the client's ACK/FIN arrives, so `tcp_input` ends up processing the ACK in Figure 29.2. The connection moves to the ESTABLISHED state and `tcp_reass` appends the already-queued data to the socket's receive buffer. `rcv_nxt` is incremented to 1051. `tcp_input` continues and the FIN is handled in Figure 29.24 where the `TF_ACKNOW` flag is set and `rcv_nxt` becomes 1052. `socantrcvmore` sets the socket's state so that after the server reads the 50 bytes of data, the server will receive an end-of-file. The server's socket also moves to the CLOSE_WAIT state. `tcp_output` will be called to ACK the client's FIN (since `rcv_nxt` equals 1052). Assuming the server process closes its socket when it reads the end-of-file, the server will then send a FIN for the client to ACK.

In this example six segments requiring three round trips are required to pass the 50 bytes from the client to server. To reduce the number of segments requires the TCP extensions for transactions [Braden 1994].

29.4   The client's socket is in the SYN_SENT state when the server's response is received. Figure 28.20 processes the segment and moves the connection to the ESTABLISHED state. A jump is made to `step6` and the data is processed in Figure 29.22. `TCP_REASS` appends the data to the socket's receive buffer and `rcv_nxt` is incremented to acknowledge the data. The FIN is then processed in Figure 29.24, incrementing `rcv_nxt` again and moving the connection to the CLOSE_WAIT state. When `tcp_output` is called, the acknowledgment field ACKs the SYN, the 50 bytes of data, and the FIN. The client process then reads the 50 bytes of data, followed by the end-of-file, and then probably closes its socket. This moves the connection to the LAST_ACK state and causes a FIN to be sent by the client, which the server should acknowledge.

29.5   The bug is in the entry `tcp_outflags[TCPS_CLOSING]` shown in Figure 24.16. It specifies the `TH_FIN` flag, whereas the state transition diagram (Figure 24.15) doesn't specify that the FIN should be retransmitted. To fix this, remove `TH_FIN` from the `tcp_outflags` entry for this state. The bug is relatively harmless—it just causes two extra segments to be exchanged—and a simultaneous close or a close following a self-connect is rare.

29.6   No. An OK return from a write system call only means the data has been copied into the socket buffer. Net/3 does not notify the process when that data is acknowledged by the other end. An application-level acknowledgment is required to obtain this information.

29.7   RFC 1323 timestamps defeat header compression because whenever the timestamps change, the TCP options change, and the segment is sent uncompressed. The window scale option has no effect because the value in the TCP header is still a 16-bit value.

29.8   IP assigns the ID field from a global variable that is incremented each time *any* IP datagram is sent. This increases the probability that two consecutive TCP segments sent on the same connection will have ID values that differ by more than 1. A difference other than 1 causes the Δ*ipid* field in Figure 29.34 to be transmitted, increasing the size of the compressed header. A better scheme would be for TCP to maintain its own counter for assigning IDs.

Chapter 30

30.2   Yes, the RST is still sent. Part of process termination is the closing of all open descriptors. The same function (`soclose`) is eventually called, regardless of whether the process explicitly closes the socket descriptor or implicitly closes it (by terminating first).

30.3   No. The only use of this constant is when a listening socket sets the SO_LINGER socket option with a linger time of 0. Normally this causes an RST to be sent when the connection is closed (Figure 30.12), but Figure 30.2 changes this value of 0 to 120 (clock ticks) for a listening socket that receives a connection request.

30.4   Two if this is the first use of the default route; otherwise one. When the socket is created the Internet PCB is set to 0 by `in_pcballoc`. This sets the `route` structure in the PCB to 0. When the first segment is sent (the SYN), `tcp_output` calls `ip_output`. Since the `ro_rt` pointer is null, `ro_dst` is filled in with the destination address of the IP datagram and `rtalloc` is called. The pointer to the default route is saved in the `ro_rt` member of the `route` structure within the PCB for this connection. When `ether_output` is called by `ip_output`, it checks whether the `rt_gwroute` member of the routing table entry is null, and, if so, `rtalloc1` is called. Assuming the route doesn't change, each time `tcp_output` is called for this connection, the cached `ro_rt` pointer is used, avoiding any additional routing table lookups.

Chapter 31

31.1   Because `catchpacket` will always run to completion before any sleeping processes are awakened by the `bpf_wakeup` call.

31.2   A process that opens a BPF device may call `fork` resulting in multiple processes with access to the same BPF device.

31.3   Only supported devices are on the BPF interface list (`bpf_iflist`), so `bpf_setif` returns `ENXIO` when the interface is not found.

Chapter 32

32.1   0 in the first example, and 255 in the second. Both of these values are reserved in RFC 1700 [Reynolds and Postel 1994] and should not appear in datagrams. This means, for example, that a socket created with a protocol of `IPPROTO_RAW` should always have the `IP_HDRINCL` socket option set, and datagrams written to the socket should have a valid protocol value.

32.2   Since the IP protocol value of 255 is reserved, datagrams should never appear on the wire with this protocol value. Since this is a nonzero protocol value, the first of the three tests in `rip_input` will ignore every received datagram that does not have this protocol value. Therefore the process should not receive any datagrams on the socket.

32.3   Even though this protocol value is reserved and datagrams should never appear on the wire with this value, the first of the three tests in `rip_input` allows datagrams with any protocol value to be received by sockets of this type. The only input filtering that occurs for this type of raw socket is based on the source and destination IP addresses, if the process calls either `connect` or `bind`, or both.

32.4   Since the array `ip_protox` array (Figure 7.22) contains information about which protocol the kernel supports, the ICMP error should be generated only when there are no raw listeners for the protocol and the pointer `inetsw[ip_protox[ip->ip_p]].pr_input` equals `rip_input`.

32.5   In both cases the process must build its own IP header, in addition to whatever follows the IP header (UDP datagram, TCP segment, or whatever). With a raw IP socket, output is normally done using `sendto` specifying the destination address as an Internet socket address structure containing an IP address. `ip_output` is called and normal IP routing is done based on the destination IP address.

BPF requires the process to supply a complete data-link header, such as an Ethernet header. Output is normally done by calling `write`, since a destination address cannot be specified. The packet is passed directly to the interface output function, bypassing `ip_output` (Figure 31.20). The process selects the outgoing interface using the `BIOCSETIF` `ioctl` (Figure 31.16). Since IP routing is not performed, the destination of the packet is limited to another system on an attached network (unless the process duplicates the IP routing function and sends the packet to a router on an attached network, for the router to forward based on the destination IP address).

32.6 A raw IP socket receives only IP datagrams destined for an IP protocol that the kernel does not process itself. A process cannot receive TCP segments or UDP datagrams on a raw socket, for example.

BPF can receive *all* frames received on a specified interface, regardless of whether they are IP datagrams or not. The `BIOCPROMISC` `ioctl` can put the interface into a promiscuous mode, to receive datagrams that are not even destined for this host.

Appendix B

Source Code Availability

URLs: Uniform Resource Locators

This text uses URLs to specify the location and method of access of resources on the Internet. For example, the common "anonymous FTP" technique is designated as

```
ftp://ftp.cdrom.com/pub/bsd-sources/4.4BSD-Lite.tar.gz
```

This specifies anonymous FTP to the host `ftp.cdrom.com`. The filename is `4.4BSD-Lite.tar.gz` in the directory `pub/bsd-sources`. The suffix `.tar` implies the standard Unix `tar`(1) format, and the additional `.gz` suffix implies that the file has been compressed with the GNU `gzip`(1) program.

4.4BSD-Lite

There are numerous ways to obtain the 4.4BSD-Lite release. The entire 4.4BSD-Lite release is available from Walnut Creek CD-ROM as

```
ftp://ftp.cdrom.com/pub/bsd-sources/4.4BSD-Lite.tar.gz
```

You can also obtain this release on CD-ROM. Contact 1 800 786 9907 or +1 510 674 0783.

O'Reilly & Associates publishes the entire set of 4.4BSD manuals along with the 4.4BSD-Lite release on CD-ROM. Contact 1 800 889 8969 or +1 707 829 0515.

Operating Systems that Run the 4.4BSD-Lite Networking Software

The 4.4BSD-Lite release is *not* a complete operating system. To experiment with the networking software described in this text you need an operating system that is built from the 4.4BSD-Lite release or an environment that supports the 4.4BSD-Lite networking code.

The operating system used by the authors is commercially available from Berkeley Software Design, Inc. Contact 1 800 ITS BSD8, +1 719 260 8114, or `info@bsdi.com` for additional information.

There are also freely available operating systems built on 4.4BSD-Lite. These are known by the names NetBSD, 386BSD, and FreeBSD. Additional information is available from Walnut Creek CD-ROM (`ftp.cdrom.com`) or on the various `comp.os.386bsd` Usenet newsgroups.

RFCs

All RFCs are available at no charge through electronic mail or by using anonymous FTP across the Internet. Sending electronic mail as shown here:

```
To: rfc-info@ISI.EDU
Subject: getting rfcs

help: ways_to_get_rfcs
```

returns a detailed listing of various ways to obtain the RFCs using either email or anonymous FTP.

Remember that the starting place is to obtain the current index and look up the RFC that you want in the index. This entry tells you if that RFC has been made obsolete or updated by a newer RFC.

GNU Software

The GNU Indent program was used to format all the source code presented in the text, and the GNU Gzip program is often used on the Internet to compress files. These programs are available as

```
ftp://prep.ai.mit.edu/pub/gnu/indent-1.9.1.tar.gz
ftp://prep.ai.mit.edu/pub/gnu/gzip-1.2.2.tar
```

The numbers in the filenames will change as newer versions are released. There are also versions of the Gzip program for other operating systems, such as MS-DOS.

There are many sites around the world that also provide the GNU archives, and the FTP greeting on `prep.ai.mit.edu` displays their names.

PPP Software

There are several freely available implementations of PPP. Part 5 of the `comp.protocols.ppp` FAQ is a good place to start:

```
http://cs.uni-bonn.de/ppp/part5.html
```

`mrouted` **Software**

Current releases of the `mrouted` software as well as other multicast applications can be found at the Xerox Palo Alto Research Center:

```
ftp://parcftp.xerox.com/pub/net-research/
```

ISODE Software

An SNMP agent implementation compatible with Net/3 is part of the ISODE software package. For more information, start with the ISODE Consortium's World Wide Web page at

```
http://www.isode.com/
```

Appendix C

RFC 1122 Compliance

This appendix summarizes the compliance of the Net/3 implementation with RFC 1122 [Braden 1989a]. This RFC summarizes these requirements in four categories

- link layer
- internet layer
- UDP
- TCP

We have chosen to present these requirements in the same breakdown and order as the chapters of this text.

C.1 Link-Layer Requirements

This section summarizes the link-layer requirements from Section 2.5 of RFC 1122 and the compliance of the Net/3 code that we've examined to those requirements.

- *May* support trailer encapsulation.
  Partially: Net/3 does not send IP datagrams with trailer encapsulation but some Net/3 device drivers may be able to receive such datagrams. We have omitted all the trailer encapsulation code in this text. Interested readers are referred to RFC 893 and Section 11.8 of [Leffler et al. 1989] for additional details.

- *Must* not send trailers by default without negotiation.
  Not applicable: Net/2 would negotiate the use of trailers but Net/3 ignores requests to send trailers and does not request trailers itself.

- *Must* be able to send and receive RFC 894 Ethernet encapsulation.
  Yes: Net/3 supports RFC 894 Ethernet encapsulation.

- *Should* be able to receive RFC 1042 (IEEE 802) encapsulation.
  No: Net/3 processes packets received with 802.3 encapsulation but only for use with OSI protocols. IP packets that arrive with 802.3 encapsulation are discarded by `ether_input` (Figure 4.13).

- *May* send RFC 1042 encapsulation, in which case there must be a software configuration switch to select the encapsulation method and RFC 894 must be the default.
  No: Net/3 does not send IP packets in RFC 1042 encapsulation.

- *Must* report link-layer broadcasts to the IP layer.
  Yes: The link layer reports link-layer broadcasts by setting the `M_BCAST` flag (or the `M_MCAST` flag for multicasts) in the mbuf packet header.

- *Must* pass the IP TOS value to the link layer.
  Yes: The TOS value is not passed explicitly, but is part of the IP header available to the link layer.

C.2   IP Requirements

This section summarizes the IP requirements from Section 3.5 of RFC 1122 and the compliance of the Net/3 code that we've examined to those requirements.

- *Must* implement IP and ICMP.
  Yes: `inetsw[0]` implements the IP protocol and `inetsw[4]` implements ICMP.

- *Must* handle remote multihoming in application layer.
  Yes: The kernel is unaware of communication to remote multihomed hosts and neither hinders nor supports such communication by an application.

- *May* support local multihoming.
  Yes: Net/3 supports multiple IP interfaces with the `ifnet` list and multiple addresses per IP interface with the `ifaddr` list for each `ifnet` structure.

- *Must* meet router specifications if forwarding datagrams.
  Partially: See Chapter 18 for a discussion of the router requirements.

- *Must* provide configuration switch for embedded router functionality. The switch must default to host operation.
  Yes: The `ipforwarding` variable defaults to false and controls the IP packet forwarding mechanism in Net/3.

- *Must not* enable routing based on number of interfaces.
  Yes: The `if_attach` function does not modify `ipforwarding` according to the number of interfaces configured at system initialization time.

- *Should* log discarded datagrams, including the contents of the datagram, and record the event in a statistics counter.
  Partially: Net/3 does not provide a mechanism for logging the contents of discarded datagrams but maintains a variety of statistics counters.

- *Must* silently discard datagrams that arrive with an IP version other than 4.
  Yes: `ipintr` implements this requirement.

- *Must* verify IP checksum and silently discard an invalid datagram.
  Yes: `ipintr` calls `in_cksum` and implements this requirement.

- *Must* support subnet addressing (RFC 950).
  Yes: Every IP address has an associated subnet mask in the `in_ifaddr` structure.

- *Must* transmit packets with host's own IP address as the source address.
  Partially: When the transport layer sends an IP datagram with all-0 bits as the source address, IP inserts the IP address of the outgoing interface in its place. A process can bind one of the local IP broadcast addresses to the local socket, and IP will transmit it as an invalid source address.

- *Must* silently discard datagrams not destined for the host.
  Yes: If the system is not configured as a router, `ipintr` discards datagrams that arrive with a bad destination address (i.e., an unrecognized unicast, broadcast, or multicast address).

- *Must* silently discard datagrams with bad source address (nonunicast address).
  No: `ipintr` does not examine the source address of incoming datagrams before delivering the datagram to the transport protocols.

- *Must* support reassembly.
  Yes: `ip_reass` implements reassembly.

- *May* retain same ID field in identical datagrams.
  No: `ip_output` assigns a new ID to every outgoing datagram and does not allow the ID to be specified by the transport protocols. See Chapter 32.

- *Must* allow the transport layer to set TOS.
  Yes: `ip_output` accepts any TOS value set in the IP header by the transport protocols. The transport layer must default TOS to all 0s. The TOS value for a particular datagram or connection may be set by the application through the `IP_TOS` socket option.

- *Must* pass received TOS up to transport layer.
  Yes: Net/3 preserves the TOS field during input processing. The entire IP header is made available to the transport layer when IP calls the `pr_input` function for the receiving protocol. Unfortunately, the UDP and TCP transport layers ignore it.

- *Should not* use RFC 795 [Postel 1981d] link-layer mappings for TOS.
  Yes: Net/3 does not use these mappings.

- *Must not* send packet with TTL of 0.
  Partially: The IP layer (`ip_output`) in Net/3 does not check this requirement and relies on the transport layers not to construct an IP header with a TTL of 0. UDP, TCP, ICMP, and IGMP all select a nonzero TTL default value. The default value can be overridden by the `IP_TTL` option.

- *Must not* discard received packets with a TTL less than 2.
  Yes: If the system is the final destination of the packet, `ipintr` accepts it regardless of the TTL value. The TTL is examined only when the packet is being forwarded.

- *Must* allow transport layer to set TTL.
  Yes: The transport layer must set TTL before calling `ip_output`.

- *Must* enable configuration of a fixed TTL.
  Yes: The default TTL is specified by the global integer `ip_defttl`, which defaults to 64 (`IPDEFTTL`). Both UDP and TCP use this value unless the `IP_TTL` socket option has specified a different value for a particular socket. `ip_defttl` can be modified through the `IPCTL_DEFTTL` name for `sysctl`.

Multihoming

- *Should* select, as the source address for a reply, the specific address received as the destination address of the request.
  Yes: Responses generated by the kernel (ICMP reply messages) include the correct source address (Section C.5). Responses generated by the transport protocols are described in their respective chapters.

- *Must* allow application to choose local IP address.
  Yes: An application can bind a socket to a specific local IP address (Section 15.8).

- *May* silently discard datagrams addressed to an interface other than the one on which it is received.
  No: Net/3 implements the weak end system model and `ipintr` accepts such packets.

- *May* require packets to exit the system through the interface with an IP address that corresponds to the source address of the packet. This requirement pertains only to packets that are not source routed.

No: Net/3 allows packets to exit the system through any interface—another weak end system characteristic.

Broadcast

- *Must* not select an IP broadcast address as a source address.
  Partially: If an application explicitly selects a source address, the IP layer does not override the selection. Otherwise, IP selects as a source address the specific IP address associated with the outgoing interface.

- *Should* accept an all-0s or all-1s broadcast address.
  Yes: `ipintr` accepts packets sent to either address.

- *May* support a configurable option to send all 0s or all 1s as the broadcast address on an interface. If provided, the configurable broadcast address *must* default to all 1s.
  No: A process must explicitly send to either the all-0s (`INADDR_ANY`) or all-1s broadcast address (`INADDR_BROADCAST`). There is no configurable default.

- *Must* recognize all broadcast address formats.
  Yes: `ipintr` recognizes the limited (all-1s and all-0s) and the network-directed and subnet-directed broadcast addresses.

- *Must* use an IP broadcast or IP multicast destination address in a link-layer broadcast.
  Yes: `ip_output` enables the link-layer multicast or broadcast flags only when the destination is an IP multicast or broadcast address.

- *Should* silently discard link-layer broadcasts when the packet does not specify an IP broadcast address as its destination.
  No: There is no explicit test for the `M_BCAST` or `M_MCAST` flags on incoming packets in Net/3, but `ip_forward` will discard these packets before forwarding them.

- *Should* use limited broadcast address for connected networks.
  Partially: The decision to use the limited broadcast address (versus a subnet-directed or network-directed broadcast) is left to the application level by Net/3.

IP Interface

- *Must* allow transport layer to use all IP mechanisms (e.g., IP options, TTL, TOS).
  Yes: All the IP mechanisms are available to the transport layer in Net/3.

- *Must* pass interface identification up to transport layer.
  Yes: The `m_pkthdr.rcvif` member of each mbuf containing an incoming packet points to the `ifnet` structure of the interface that received the packet.

- *Must* pass all IP options to transport layer.
  Yes: The entire IP header, including options, is present in the packet passed to the `pr_input` function of the receiving transport protocol by `ipintr`.

- *Must* allow transport layer to send ICMP port unreachable and any of the ICMP query messages.
  Yes: The transport layer may send any ICMP error messages by calling `icmp_error` or may format and send any type of IP datagram by calling the `ip_output` function.

- *Must* pass the following ICMP messages to the transport layer: destination unreachable, source quench, echo reply, timestamp reply, and time exceeded.
  Yes: These messages are distributed by ICMP to other transport protocols or to any waiting processes using the raw IP socket mechanism.

- *Must* include contents of ICMP message (IP header plus the data bytes present) in ICMP message passed to the transport layer.
  Yes: `icmp_input` passes the portion of the original IP packet contained within the ICMP message to the transport layers.

- *Should* be able to leap tall buildings at a single bound.
  No: The next version of IP may meet this requirement.

C.3   IP Options Requirements

This section summarizes the IP option processing requirements from Section 3.5 of RFC 1122 and the compliance of the Net/3 code that we've examined to those requirements.

- *Must* allow transport layer to send IP options.
  Yes: The second argument to `ip_output` is a list of IP options to include in the outgoing IP datagram.

- *Must* pass all IP options received to higher layer.
  Yes: The IP header and options are passed to the `pr_input` function of the receiving transport protocol.

- *Must* silently ignore unknown options.
  Yes: The `default` case in `ip_dooptions` skips over unknown options.

- *May* support the security option.
  No: Net/3 does not support the IP security option.

- *Should not* send the stream identifier option and *must ignore* it in received datagrams.
  Yes: Net/3 does not support the stream identifier option and ignores it on incoming datagrams.

- *May* support the record route option.
  Yes: Net/3 supports the record route option.

- *May* support the timestamp option.
  Partially: Net/3 supports the timestamp option but does not implement it exactly as specified. The originating host does not insert a timestamp when required but the destination host records a timestamp before passing the datagram to the transport layer. The timestamp value follows the rules regarding standard values as specified in Section 3.2.2.8 of RFC 1122 for the ICMP timestamp message.

- *Must* support originating a source route and *must* be able to act as the final destination of a source route.
  Yes: A source route may be included in the options passed to `ip_output,` and `ip_dooptions` correctly terminates a source route and saves it for use in constructing return routes.

- *Must* pass a datagram with completed source route up to the transport layer.
  Yes: The source route option is passed up with any other options that may have appeared in the datagram.

- *Must* build correct (nonredundant) return route.
  No: Net/3 blindly reverses the source route and does not check or correct for a route that was built incorrectly with a redundant hop for the original source host.

- *Must* not send multiple source route options in one header.
  No: The IP layer in Net/3 does not prohibit a transport protocol from constructing and sending multiple source route options in a single datagram.

Source Route Forwarding

- *May* support packet forwarding with the source route option.
  Yes: Net/3 supports the source route options. `ip_dooptions` does all the work.

- *Must* obey corresponding router rules while processing source routes.
  Yes: Net/3 follows the router rules whether or not the packet contains a source route.

- *Must* update TTL according to gateway rules.
  Yes: `ip_forward` implements this requirement.

- *Must* generate ICMP error codes 4 and 5 (fragmentation required and source route failed).
  Yes: `ip_output` is able to generate a fragmentation required message, and `ip_dooptions` is able to generate the source route failed message.

- *Must* allow the IP source address of a source routed packet to not be an IP address of the forwarding host.
  Yes: `ip_output` transmits such packets.

  > RFC 1122 lists this as a *may* requirement because the addresses *may* be different, which *must* be allowed.

- *Must* update timestamp and record route options.
  Yes: `ip_dooptions` processes these options for source routed packets.

- *Must* support a configurable switch for *nonlocal source routing*. The switch *must* default to off.
  No: Net/3 always allows nonlocal source routing and does not provide a switch to disable this function. Nonlocal source routing is routing packets between two different interfaces instead of receiving and sending the packet on the same interface.

- *Must* satisfy gateway access rules for nonlocal source routing.
  Yes: Net/3 follows the forwarding rules for nonlocal source routing.

- *Should* send an ICMP destination unreachable error (source route failed) if a source routed packet cannot be forwarded (except for ICMP error messages).
  Yes: `ip_dooptions` sends the ICMP destination unreachable error. `icmp_error` discards it if the original datagram was an ICMP error message.

C.4   IP Fragmentation and Reassembly Requirements

This section summarizes the IP fragmentation and reassembly requirements from Section 3.5 of RFC 1122 and the compliance of the Net/3 code that we've examined to those requirements.

- *Must* be able to reassemble incoming datagrams of at least 576 bytes.
  Yes: `ip_reass` supports reassembly of datagrams of indefinite size.

- *Should* support a configurable or indefinite maximum size for incoming datagrams.
  Yes: Net/3 supports an indefinite maximum size for incoming datagrams.

- *Must* provide a mechanism for the transport layer to learn the maximum datagram size to receive.
  Not applicable: Net/3 has an indefinite limit based on available memory.

- *Must* send ICMP time exceeded error on reassembly timeout.
  No: Net/3 does not send an ICMP time exceeded error. See Figure 10.30 and Exercise 10.1.

- *Should* support a fixed reassembly timeout value. The remaining TTL value in a received IP fragment *should not* be used as a reassembly timeout value.
  Yes: Net/3 uses a compile-time value of 30 seconds (`IPFRAGTTL` is 60 slow-timeout intervals, which equals 30 seconds).

- *Must* provide the MMS_S (maximum message size to send) to higher layers.
  Partially: TCP derives the MMS_S from the MTU found in the route entry for the destination or from the MTU of the outgoing interface. A UDP application does not have access to this information.

- *May* support local fragmentation of outgoing packets.
  Yes: `ip_output` fragments an outgoing packet if it is too large for the selected interface.

- *Must* not allow transport layer to send a message larger than MMS_S if local fragmentation is not supported.
  Not applicable: This is a transport-level requirement that does not apply to Net/3 since local fragmentation is supported.

- *Should not* send messages larger than 576 bytes to a remote destination in the absence of other information regarding the path MTU to the destination.
  Partially: Net/3 TCP defaults to a segment size of 552 (512 data bytes + 40 header bytes). Net/3 UDP applications cannot determine if a destination is local or remote and so they often restrict their messages to 540 bytes (512 + 20 + 8). There is no kernel mechanism that prohibits sending larger messages.

- *May* support an all-subnets-MTU configuration flag.
  Yes: The global integer `subnetsarelocal` defaults to true. TCP uses this flag to select a larger segment size (the size of the outgoing interface's MTU) instead of the default segment size for destinations on a subnet of the local network.

C.5   ICMP Requirements

This section summarizes the ICMP requirements from Section 3.5 of RFC 1122 and the compliance of the Net/3 code that we've examined to those requirements.

- *Must* silently discard ICMP messages with unknown type.
  Partially: `icmp_input` ignores these messages and passes them to `rip_input`, which delivers the message to any waiting processes or silently discards the message if no process is prepared to receive the message.

- *May* include more than 8 bytes of the original datagram.
  No: The `icmp_error` function returns only a maximum of 8 bytes of the original datagram in the ICMP error message, Exercise 11.9.

- *Must* return the header and data unchanged from the received datagram.
  Partially: Net/3 converts the ID, offset, and length fields of an IP packet from network byte order to host byte order in `ipintr`. This facilitates processing the packet, but Net/3 neglects to return the offset and length fields to network byte order before including the header in an ICMP error message. If the system operates with the same byte ordering as the network, this error is harmless. If it operates with a different ordering, the IP header contained within the ICMP error message has incorrect offset and length values.

  > The authors found that an Intel implementation of SVR4 and AIX 3.2 (Net/2 based) both return the length byte-swapped. Implementations other than Net/2 or Net/3 that were tried (Cisco, NetBlazer, VM, and Solaris 2.3) did not have this bug.

  > Another error occurs when an ICMP port unreachable error is sent from the UDP code: the header length of the received datagram is changed incorrectly (Section 23.7). The authors found this error in Net/2 and Net/3 implementations. Net/1, however, did not have the bug.

- *Must* demultiplex received ICMP error message to transport protocol.
  Yes: `icmp_error` uses the protocol field from the original header to select the appropriate transport protocol to respond to the error.

- *Should* send ICMP error messages with a TOS field of 0.
  Yes: All ICMP error messages are constructed with a TOS of 0 by `icmp_error`.

- *Must not* send an ICMP error message caused by a previous ICMP error message.
  Partially: `icmp_error` sends an error for an ICMP redirect message, which Section 3.2.2 of RFC 1122 classifies as an ICMP error message.

- *Must not* send an ICMP error message caused by an IP broadcast or IP multicast datagram.
  No: `icmp_error` does not check for this case.

  > The `icmp_error` function from the original Deering multicast code for BSD checks for this case.

- *Must not* send an ICMP error message caused by a link-layer broadcast.
  Yes: `icmp_error` discards ICMP messages in response to packets that arrived as link-layer broadcasts or multicasts.

- *Must not* send an ICMP error message caused by a noninitial fragment.
  Yes: `icmp_error` discards errors generated in this case.

- *Must not* send an ICMP error message caused by a datagram with nonunique source address.

Yes: `icmp_reflect` checks for experimental and multicast addresses. `ip_output` discards messages sent from a broadcast address.

- *Must* return ICMP error messages when not prohibited.
  Partially: In general, Net/3 sends appropriate ICMP error messages. It fails to send an ICMP reassembly timeout message at the appropriate time (Exercise 10.1).

- *Should* generate ICMP destination unreachable (protocol and port).
  Partially: Datagrams for unsupported protocols are delivered to `rip_input` where they are silently discarded if there are no processes registered to accept the datagrams. UDP generates an ICMP port unreachable error.

- *Must* pass ICMP destination unreachable to higher layer.
  Yes: `icmp_input` passes the message to the `pr_ctlinput` function defined for the protocol (`udp_ctlinput` and `tcp_ctlinput` for UDP and TCP, respectively).

- *Should* respond to destination unreachable error.
  See Sections 23.9 and 27.6.

- *Must* interpret destination unreachable as only a hint, as it may indicate a transient condition.
  See Sections 23.9 and 27.6.

- *Must not* send an ICMP redirect when configured as a host.
  Yes: `ip_forward`, the only function that detects and sends redirects, is not called unless the system is configured as a router.

- *Must* update route cache when an ICMP redirect is received.
  Yes: `ipintr` calls `rtredirect` to process the message.

- *Must* handle both host and network redirects. Furthermore, network redirects must be treated as host redirects.
  Yes: `ipintr` calls `rtredirect` for both types of messages.

- *Should* discard illegal redirects.
  Yes: `rtredirect` discards illegal redirects (Section 19.7).

- *May* send source quench if memory is unavailable.
  Yes: `ip_forward` sends a source quench if `ip_output` returns ENOBUFS. This occurs when there is a shortage of mbufs or when an interface output queue is full.

- *Must* pass source quench to higher layer.
  Yes: `icmp_input` passes source quench errors to the transport layers.

- *Should* respond to source quench in higher layer.
  See Sections 23.9 and 27.6 for UDP and TCP processing. Neither ICMP nor IGMP

accept ICMP error messages (they don't define a `pr_ctlinput` function), in which case they are discarded by IP.

- *Must* pass time exceeded error to transport layer.
  Yes: `icmp_input` passes this message to the transport layers.

- *Should* send parameter problem errors.
  Yes: `ip_dooptions` complains about incorrectly formed options.

- *Must* pass parameter problem errors to transport layer.
  Yes: `icmp_input` passes parameter problem errors to the transport layer.

- *May* report parameter problem errors to process.
  See Sections 23.9 and 27.6 for UDP and TCP processing. Neither ICMP nor IGMP accept ICMP error messages.

- *Must* support an echo server and *should* support an echo client.
  Yes: `icmp_input` implements the echo server and the `ping` program implements the echo client using a raw IP socket.

- *May* discard echo requests to a broadcast address.
  No: The reply is sent by `icmp_reflect`.

- *May* discard echo request to multicast address.
  No: Net/3 responds to multicast echo requests. Both `icmp_reflect` and `ip_output` permit multicast destination addresses.

- *Must* use specific destination address as echo reply source.
  Yes: `icmp_reflect` converts a broadcast or multicast destination to the specific address of the receiving interface and uses the result as the source address for the echo reply.

- *Must* return echo request data in echo reply.
  Yes: The data portion of the echo request is not altered by `icmp_reflect`.

- *Must* pass echo reply to higher layer.
  Yes: ICMP echo replies are passed to `rip_input` for receipt by registered processes.

- *Must* reflect record route and timestamp options in ICMP echo request message.
  Yes: `icmp_reflect` includes the record route and timestamp options in the echo reply message.

- *Must* reverse and reflect source route option.
  Yes: `icmp_reflect` retrieves the reversed source route with `ip_srcroute` and includes it in the outgoing echo reply.

- *Should not* support the ICMP information request or reply.
  Partially: The kernel does not generate or respond to either message, but a process may send or receive the messages through the raw IP mechanism.

- *May* implement the ICMP timestamp request and timestamp reply messages.
  Yes: `icmp_input` implements the timestamp server functionality. The timestamp client may be implemented through the raw IP mechanism.

- *Must* minimize timestamp delay variability (if implementing the timestamp messages).
  Partially: The receive timestamp is applied after the message is taken off the IP input queue and the transmit timestamp is applied before the message is placed in the interface output queue.

- *May* silently discard broadcast timestamp request.
  No: `icmp_input` responds to broadcast timestamp requests.

- *May* silently discard multicast timestamp requests.
  No: `icmp_input` responds to broadcast timestamp requests.

- *Must* use specific destination address as timestamp reply source address.
  Yes: `icmp_reflect` converts a broadcast or multicast destination to the specific address of the receiving interface and uses the result as the source address for the timestamp reply.

- *Should* reflect record route and timestamp options in an ICMP timestamp request.
  Yes: `icmp_reflect` includes the record route and timestamp options in the timestamp reply message.

- *Must* reverse and reflect source route option in ICMP timestamp request.
  Yes: `icmp_reflect` retrieves the reversed source route with `ip_srcroute` and includes it in the outgoing timestamp reply.

- *Must* pass timestamp reply to higher layer.
  Yes: ICMP timestamp replies are passed to `rip_input` for receipt by registered processes.

- *Must* obey rules for standard timestamp value.
  Yes: `icmp_input` calls `iptime`, which returns a standard time value.

- *Must* provide a configurable method for selecting the address mask selection method for an interface.
  No: Net/3 supports only static configuration of address masks through the `ifconfig` program.

- *Must* support static configuration of address mask.
  Yes: This is accomplished indirectly by specifying static information when the `ifconfig` program configures an interface during system initialization, typically in the `/etc/netstart` start-up script.

- *May* get address mask dynamically during system initialization.
  No: Net/3 does not support the use of BOOTP or DHCP to acquire address mask information.

- *May* get address with an ICMP address mask request and reply messages.
  No: Net/3 does not support the use ICMP messages to acquire address mask information.

- *Must* retransmit address mask request if no reply.
  Not Applicable: Not required since this method is not implemented by Net/3.

- *Should* assume default mask if no reply is received.
  Not Applicable: Not required since this method is not implemented by Net/3.

- *Must* update address mask from first reply only.
  Not Applicable: Not required since this method is not implemented by Net/3.

- *Should* perform reasonableness check on any installed address mask.
  No: Net/3 performs no reasonableness check on address masks.

- *Must not* send unauthorized address mask reply messages and *must* be explicitly configured to be agent.
  Yes: `icmp_input` only responds to address mask requests if `icmpmaskrepl` is nonzero (it defaults to 0).

- *Should* support an associated address mask authority flag with each static address mask configuration.
  No: Net/3 consults a global authority flag (`icmpmaskrepl`) to determine if it should send address mask replies for *any* interface.

- *Must* broadcast address mask reply when initialized.
  No: Net/3 does not broadcast an address mask reply when an interface is configured.

C.6   Multicasting Requirements

This section summarizes the IP multicast requirements from Section 3.5 of RFC 1122 and the compliance of the Net/3 code that we've examined to those requirements.

- *Should* support local IP multicasting (RFC 1112).
  Yes: Net/3 supports IP multicasting.

- *Should* join the all-hosts group at start-up.
  Yes: `in_ifinit` joins the all-hosts group while initializing an interface.

- *Should* provide a mechanism for higher layers to discover an interface's IP multicast capability.
  Yes: The `IFF_MULTICAST` flag in the interface's `ifnet` structure is available directly to kernel code and by the `SIOCGIFFLAGS` command for processes.

C.7   IGMP Requirements

This section summarizes the IGMP requirements from Section 3.5 of RFC 1122 and the compliance of the Net/3 code that we've examined to those requirements.

- *May* support IGMP (RFC 1112).
  Yes: Net/3 supports IGMP.

C.8   Routing Requirements

This section summarizes the routing requirements from Section 3.5 of RFC 1122 and the compliance of the Net/3 code that we've examined to those requirements. Be aware that the requirements of this RFC apply to a host and not necessarily the kernel implementation. Some items are not explicitly handled by the kernel routing functions in Net/3, but they are expected to be provided by a routing daemon such as `routed` or `gated`.

- *Must* use address mask in determining whether a datagram's destination is on a connected network.
  Yes: When an interface for a connected network such as an Ethernet is configured, its address mask is specified (or a default is chosen based on the class of IP address) and stored in the routing table entry. This mask is used by `rn_match` when it checks a leaf for a network match.

- *Must* operate correctly in a minimal environment when there are no routers (all networks are directly connected).
  Yes: The system administrator must not configure a default route in this case.

- *Must* keep a "route cache" of mappings to next-hop routers.
  Yes: The routing table is the cache.

- *Should* treat a received network redirect the same as a host redirect.
  Yes, as described in Section 19.7.

- *Must* use a default router when no entry exists for the destination in the routing table.
  Yes, if a default route has been entered into the routing table.

- *Must* support multiple default routers.
  Multiple defaults are not supported by the kernel. Instead, this should be provided by a routing daemon.

- *May* implement a table of static routes.
  Yes: These can be created at system initialization time with the `route` command.

- *May* include a flag with each static route specifying whether or not the route can be overridden by a redirect.
  No.

- *May* allow the routing table key to be a complete host address and not just a network address.
  Yes: Host routes take priority over a network route to the same network.

- *Should* include the TOS in the routing table entry.
  No: There is a TOS field in the `sockaddr_inarp` that we describe in Chapter 21, but it is not currently used.

- *Must* be able to detect the failure of a next-hop router that appears as the gateway field in the routing table and be able to choose an alternate next-hop router.
  Negative advice, the `RTM_LOSING` message generated by `in_losing`, is passed to any processes reading from a routing socket, which allows the process (e.g., a routing daemon) to handle this event.

- *Should not* assume that a route is good forever.
  Yes: There are no timeouts on routing table entries in the kernel other than those created by ARP. Again, the standard Unix routing daemons time out routes and replace them with alternatives when possible.

- *Must not* ping routers continuously (ICMP echo request).
  Yes: The Net/3 kernel does not do this. The routing daemons don't generate ICMP echo requests either.

- *Must* use pinging of a router only when traffic is being sent to that router.
  The Net/3 kernel never generates pings to a next-hop router.

- *Should* allow higher and lower layers to give positive and negative advice.
  Partially: The only information passed by other layers to the Net/3 routing functions

is by `in_losing`, which is called only from TCP. The only action performed by the routing layer is to generate the `RTM_LOSING` message.

- *Must* switch to another default router when the existing default fails.
  Yes, although the Net/3 kernel does not do this, it is supported by the routing daemons.

- *Must* allow the following information to be configured manually in the routing table: IP address, network mask, list of defaults.
  Yes, but only one default is supported in the kernel.

C.9   ARP Requirements

This section summarizes the ARP requirements from Section 2.5 of RFC 1122 and the compliance of the Net/3 code that we've examined to those requirements.

- *Must* provide a mechanism to flush out-of-date ARP entries. If this mechanism involves a timeout, it *should* be configurable.
  Yes and yes: `arptimer` provides this mechanism. The timeout is configurable (the `arpt_prune` and `arpt_keep` globals) but the only ways to change their values are to recompile the kernel or modify the kernel with a debugger.
- *Must* include a mechanism to prevent ARP flooding.
  Yes, as we described with Figure 21.24.
- *Should* save (rather than discard) at least one (the latest) packet of each set of packets destined to the same unresolved IP address, and transmit the saved packet when the address has been resolved.
  Yes: This is the purpose of the `la_hold` member of the `llinfo_arp` structure.

C.10   UDP Requirements

This section summarizes the UDP requirements from Section 4.1.5 of RFC 1122 and the compliance of the Net/3 code that we've examined to those requirements.

- *Should* send ICMP port unreachable.
  Yes: `udp_input` does this.
- *Must* pass received IP options to application.
  No: The code to do this is commented out in `udp_input`. This means that a process that receives a UDP datagram with a source route option cannot send a reply using the reversed route.
- *Must* allow application to specify IP options to send.
  Yes: The `IP_OPTIONS` socket option does this. The options are saved in the PCB and placed into the outgoing IP datagram by `ip_output`.

- *Must* pass IP options down to IP layer.
  Yes: As mentioned above, IP places the options into the IP datagram.

- *Must* pass received ICMP messages to application.
  Yes: We must look at the exact wording from the RFC: "A UDP-based application that wants to receive ICMP error messages is responsible for maintaining the state necessary to demultiplex these messages when they arrive; for example, the application may keep a pending receive operation for this purpose." The state required by Berkeley-derived systems is that the socket be connected to the foreign address and port. As the comments at the beginning of Figure 23.26 indicate, some applications create both a connected and an unconnected socket for a given foreign port, using the connected socket to receive asynchronous errors.

- *Must* be able to generate and verify UDP checksum.
  Yes: This is done by udp_input, based on the global integer udpcksum.

- *Must* silently discard datagrams with bad checksum.
  Yes: This is done only if udpcksum is nonzero. As we mentioned earlier, this variable controls both the sending of checksums and the verification of received checksums. If this variable is 0, the kernel does not verify a received nonzero checksum.

- *May* allow sending application to specify whether outgoing checksum is calculated, but *must* default to on.
  No: The application has no control over UDP checksums. Regarding the default, UDP checksums are generated unless the kernel is compiled with 4.2BSD compatibility defined, or unless the administrator has disabled UDP checksums using sysctl(8).

- *May* allow receiving application to specify whether received UDP datagrams without a checksum (i.e., the received checksum is 0) are discarded or passed to the application.
  No: Received datagrams with a checksum field of 0 are passed to the receiving process.

- *Must* pass destination IP address to application.
  Yes: The application must call recvmsg and specify the IP_RECVDSTADDR socket option. Also recall our discussion following Figure 23.25 noting that 4.4BSD broke this option when the destination address is a multicast or broadcast address.

- *Must* allow application to specify local IP address to be used when sending a UDP datagram.
  Yes: The application can call bind to set the local IP address. Recall our discussion at the end of Section 22.8 about the difference between the source IP address and the IP address of the outgoing interface. Net/3 does not allow the application to choose the outgoing interface—that is done by ip_output, based on the route to the destination IP address.

- *Must* allow application to specify wildcard local IP address.
  Yes: If the IP address INADDR_ANY is specified in the call to bind, the local IP address is chosen by in_pcbconnect, based on the route to the destination.

- *Should* allow application to learn of the local address that was chosen.
  Yes: The application must call `connect`. When a datagram is sent on an unconnected socket with a wildcard local address, `ip_output` chooses the outgoing interface, which also becomes the source address. The `inp_laddr` member of the PCB,
  however, is restored to the wildcard address at the end of `udp_output` before
  `sendto` returns. Therefore, `getsockname` cannot return the value. But the application can `connect` a UDP socket to the destination, causing `in_pcbconnect` to
  determine the local interface and store the address in the PCB. The application can
  then call `getsockname` to fetch the IP address of the local interface.

- *Must* silently discard a received UDP datagram with an invalid source IP address
  (broadcast or multicast).
  No: A received UDP datagram with an invalid source address is delivered to a
  socket, if a socket is bound to the destination port.

- *Must* send a valid IP source address.
  Yes: If the local IP address is set by `bind`, it checks the validity of the address. If the
  local IP address is wildcarded, `ip_output` chooses the local address.

- *Must* provide the full IP interface from Section 3.4 of RFC 1122.
  Refer to Section C.2.

- *Must* allow application to specify TTL, TOS, and IP options for output datagrams.
  Yes: The application can use the `IP_TTL`, `IP_TOS`, and `IP_OPTIONS` socket
  options.

- *May* pass received TOS to application.
  No: There is no way for the application to receive this value from the IP header.
  Notice that a `getsockopt` of `IP_TOS` returns the value used in outgoing datagrams, not the value from a received datagram. The received `ip_tos` value is available to `udp_input`, but is discarded along with the entire IP header.

C.11 TCP Requirements

This section summarizes the TCP requirements from Section 4.2.5 of RFC 1122 and the
compliance of the Net/3 code that we've examined to those requirements.

PSH Flag

- *May* aggregate data sent by the user without the PSH flag.
  Yes and no: Net/3 does not give the process a way to specify the PSH flag with a
  write operation, but Net/3 does aggregate data sent by the user in separate write
  operations.

- *May* queue data received without the PSH flag.
  No: The absence or presence of a PSH flag in a received datagram makes no difference. Received data is placed onto the socket's received queue when it is processed.

- Sender *should* collapse successive PSH flags when it packetizes data.
  No.
- *May* implement PSH flag on write calls.
  No: This is not part of the sockets API.
- Since the PSH flag is not part of the write calls, *must not* buffer data indefinitely and *must* set the PSH flag in the last buffered segment.
  Yes: This is the method used by Berkeley-derived implementations.
- *May* pass received PSH flag to application.
  No: This is not part of the sockets API.
- *Should* send maximum-sized segment whenever possible, to improve performance.
  Yes.

Window

- *Must* treat window size as an unsigned number. *Should* treat window size as 32-bit value.
  Yes: All the window sizes in Figure 24.13 are `unsigned longs`, which is also required by the window scale option of RFC 1323.
- Receiver *must not* shrink the window (move the right edge to the left).
  Yes, in Figure 26.29.
- Sender *must* be robust against window shrinking.
  Yes, in Figure 29.15.
- *May* keep offered receive window closed indefinitely.
  Yes.
- Sender *must* probe a zero window.
  Yes, this is the purpose of the persist timer.
- *Should* send first zero-window probe when the window has been closed for the RTO.
  No: Net/3 sets a lower bound for the persist timer of 5 seconds, which is normally greater than the RTO.
- *Should* exponentially increase the interval between successive probes.
  Yes, as shown in Figure 25.14.
- *Must* allow peer's window to stay closed indefinitely.
  Yes, TCP never gives up probing a closed window.
- Sender *must not* timeout a connection just because the other end keeps advertising a zero window.
  Yes.

Urgent Data

- *Must* have urgent pointer point to last byte of urgent data.
  No: Berkeley-derived implementations continue to interpret the urgent pointer as pointing just beyond the last byte of urgent data.

- *Must* support a sequence of urgent data of any length.
  Yes, with the bug fix discussed in Exercise 26.6.

- *Must* inform the receiving process (1) when TCP receives an urgent pointer and there was no previously pending urgent data, or (2) when the urgent pointer advances in the data stream.
  Yes, in Figure 29.17.

- *Must* be a way for the process to determine how much urgent data remains, or at least whether more urgent data remains to be read.
  Yes, this is the purpose of the out-of-band mark, the `SIOCATMARK` ioctl.

TCP Options

- *Must* be able to receive TCP options in any segment.
  Yes.

- *Must* ignore any options not supported.
  Yes, in Section 28.3.

- *Must* cope with an illegal option length.
  Yes, in Section 28.3.

- *Must* implement both sending and receiving the MSS option.
  Yes, a received MSS option is handled in Figure 28.10, and Figure 26.23 always sends an MSS option with a SYN.

- *Should* send an MSS option in every SYN when its receive MSS differs from 536, and *may* send it always.
  Yes, as mentioned earlier, an MSS option is always sent by Net/3 with a SYN.

- If an MSS option is not received with a SYN, *must* assume a default MSS of 536.
  No: The default MSS is 512, not 536.

  > This is probably a historical artifact because VAXes had a physical page size of 512 bytes and trailer protocols working only with data that is a multiple of 512.

- *Must* calculate the "effective send MSS."
  Yes, in Section 27.5.

TCP Checksums

- *Must* generate a TCP checksum in outgoing segments and *must* verify received checksums.
  Yes, TCP checksums are always calculated and verified.

Initial Sequence Number Selection

- *Must* use the specified clock-driven selection from RFC 793.
  No: RFC 793 specifies a clock that changes by 125,000 every half-second, whereas

the Net/3 ISN (the global variable `tcp_iss`) is incremented by 64,000 every half-second, about one-half the specified rate.

Opening Connections

- *Must* support simultaneous open attempts.
  Yes, although Berkeley-derived systems prior to 4.4BSD did not support this, as described in Section 28.9.

- *Must* keep track of whether it reached the SYN_RCVD state from the LISTEN or SYN_SENT states.
  Yes, same result, different technique. The purpose of this requirement is to allow a passive open that receives an RST to return to the LISTEN state (as shown in Figure 24.15), but force an active open that ends up in SYN_RCVD and then receives an RST to be aborted. This is described following Figure 28.36.

- A passive open *must not* affect previously created connections.
  Yes.

- *Must* allow a listening socket with a given local port at the same time that another socket with the same local port is in the SYN_SENT or SYN_RCVD state.
  Yes: The stated purpose of this requirement is to allow a given application to accept multiple connection attempts at about the same time. This is done in Berkeley-derived implementations by cloning new connections from the socket in the LISTEN state when the incoming SYN arrives.

- *Must* ask IP to select a local IP address to be used as the source IP address when the source IP address is not specified by the process performing an active open on a multihomed host.
  Yes, done by `in_pcbconnect`.

- *Must* continue to use the same source IP address for all segments sent on a connection.
  Yes: Once `in_pcbconnect` selects the source address, it doesn't change.

- *Must not* allow an active open for a broadcast or multicast foreign address.
  Yes and no: TCP will not send segments to a broadcast address because the call to `ip_output` in Figure 26.32 does not specify the SO_BROADCAST option. Net/3, however, allows connection attempts to multicast addresses.

- *Must* ignore incoming SYNs with an invalid source address.
  Yes: The code in Figure 28.16 checks for these invalid source addresses.

Closing Connections

- *Should* allow an RST to contain data.
  No: The RST processing in Figure 28.36 ends up jumping to `drop`, which skips the processing of any segment data in Figure 29.22.

- *Must* inform process whether other end closed the connection normally (e.g., sent a FIN) or aborted the connection with an RST.

Yes: The read system calls return 0 (end-of-file) when the FIN is processed, but −1 with an error of `ECONNRESET` when an RST is received.

- *May* implement a half-close.
  Yes: The process calls `shutdown` with a second argument of 1 to send a FIN. The process can still read from the connection.

- If the process completely closes a connection (i.e., not a half-close) and received data is still pending in TCP, or if new data arrives after the close, TCP *should* send an RST to indicate data was lost.
  No and yes: If a process calls `close` and unread data is in the socket's receive buffer, an RST is not sent. But if data arrives after a socket is closed, an RST is returned to the sender.

- *Must* linger in TIME_WAIT state for twice the MSL.
  Yes, although the Net/3 MSL of 30 seconds is much smaller than the RFC 793 recommended value of 2 minutes.

- *May* accept a new SYN from a peer to reopen a connection directly from the TIME_WAIT state.
  Yes, as shown in Figure 28.29.

Retransmissions

- *Must* implement Van Jacobson's slow start and congestion avoidance.
  Yes.

- *May* reuse the same IP identifier field when a retransmission is identical to the original packet.
  No: The IP identifier is assigned by `ip_output` from the global variable `ip_id`, which increments each time an IP datagram is sent. It is not assigned by TCP.

- *Must* implement Jacobson's algorithm for calculating the RTO and Karn's algorithm for selecting the RTT measurements.
  Yes, but realize that when RFC 1323 timestamps are present, the retransmission ambiguity problem is gone, obviating half of Karn's algorithm, as we discussed with Figure 29.6.

- *Must* include an exponential backoff for successive RTO values.
  Yes, as described with Figure 25.22.

- Retransmission of SYN segments *should* use the same algorithm as data segments.
  Yes, as shown in Figure 25.15.

- *Should* initialize estimation parameters to calculate an initial RTO of 3 seconds.
  No: The initial value of `t_rxtcur` calculated by `tcp_newtcpcb` is 6 seconds. This is also seen in Figure 25.15.

- *Should* have a lower bound on the RTO measured in fractions of a second and an upper bound of twice the MSL.
  No: The lower bound is 1 second and the upper bound is 64 seconds (Figure 25.3).

Generating ACKs

- *Should* queue out-of-order segments.
  Yes, done by `tcp_reass`.

- *Must* process all queued segments before sending any ACKs.
  Yes, but only for in-order segments. `ipintr` calls `tcp_input` for each queued datagram that is a TCP segment. For in-order segments, `tcp_input` schedules a delayed ACK and returns to `ipintr`. If there are additional TCP segments on IP's input queue, `tcp_input` is called by `ipintr` for each one. Only when `ipintr` finds no more IP datagrams on its input queue and returns can `tcp_fasttimo` be called to generate a delayed ACK. This ACK will contain the highest acknowledgment number in all the segments processed by `tcp_input`.

  The problem is with out-of-order segments: `tcp_input` calls `tcp_output` itself, before returning to `ipintr`, to generate the ACK for the out-of-order segment. If there are additional segments on IP's input queue that would have made the out-of-order segment be in order, they are processed after the immediate ACK is sent.

- *May* generate an immediate ACK for an out-of-order segment.
  Yes, this is needed for the fast retransmit and fast recovery algorithms (Section 29.4).

- *Should* implement delayed ACKs and the delay *must* be less than 0.5 seconds.
  Yes: The `TF_DELACK` flag is checked by the `tcp_fasttimo` function every 200 ms.

- *Should* send an ACK for at least every second segment.
  Yes, the code in Figure 26.9 generates an ACK for every second segment. We also discussed that this happens only if the process receiving the data reads the data as it arrives, since the calls to `tcp_output` that cause every other segment to be acknowledged are driven by the `PRU_RCVD` request.

- *Must* include silly window syndrome avoidance in the receiver.
  Yes, as seen in Figure 26.29.

Sending Data

- The TTL value for TCP segments *must* be configurable.
  Yes: The TTL is initialized to 64 (`IPDEFTTL`) by `tcp_newtcpcb`, but can then be changed by a process using the `IP_TTL` socket option.

- *Must* include sender silly window syndrome avoidance.
  Yes, in Figure 26.8.

- *Should* implement the Nagle algorithm.
  Yes, in Figure 26.8.

- *Must* allow a process to disable the Nagle algorithm on a given connection.
  Yes, with the `TCP_NODELAY` socket option.

Connection Failures

- *Must* pass negative advice to IP when the number of retransmissions for a given segment exceeds some value R1.
  Yes: The value of R1 is 4, and in Figure 25.26, when the number of retransmissions exceeds 4, in_losing is called.
- *Must* close a connection when the number of retransmissions for a given segment exceeds some value R2.
  Yes: The value of R2 is 12 (Figure 25.26).
- *Must* allow process to set the value of R2.
  No: The value 12 is hardcoded in Figure 25.26.
- *Should* inform the process when R1 is reached and before R2 is reached.
  No.
- *Should* default R1 to at least 3 retransmissions and R2 to at least 100 seconds.
  Yes: R1 is 4 retransmissions, and with a minimum RTO of 1 second, the tcp_backoff array (Section 25.9) guarantees a minimum value of R2 of over 500 seconds.
- *Must* handle SYN retransmissions in the same general way as data retransmissions.
  Yes, but R1 is normally not reached for the retransmission of a SYN (Figure 25.15).
- *Must* set R2 to at least 3 minutes for a SYN.
  No: R2 for a SYN is limited to 75 seconds by the connection-establishment timer (Figure 25.15).

Keepalive Packets

- *May* provide keepalives.
  Yes, they are provided.
- *Must* allow process to turn keepalives on or off, and *must* default to off.
  Yes: Default is off and process must turn them on with the SO_KEEPALIVE socket option.
- *Must* send keepalives only when connection is idle for a given period.
  Yes.
- *Must* allow the keepalive interval to be configurable and *must* default to no less than 2 hours.
  No and yes: The idle time before sending keepalive probes is not easily configurable, but it defaults to 2 hours. If the default idle time is changed (by changing the global variable tcp_keepidle), it affects all users of the keepalive option on the host—it cannot be configured on a per-connection basis as many users would like.
- *Must not* interpret the failure to respond to any given probe as a dead connection.
  Yes: Nine probes are sent before the connection is considered dead.

IP Options

- *Must* ignore received IP options it doesn't understand.
  Yes: This is done by the IP layer.

- *May* support the timestamp and record route options in received segments.
  No: Net/3 only reflects these options for ICMP packets that are reflected back to the sender (`icmp_reflect`). `tcp_input` discards any received IP options by calling `ip_stripoptions` in Figure 28.2.

- *Must* allow process to specify a source route when a connection is actively opened, and this route must take precedence over a source route received for this connection.
  Yes: The source route is specified with the `IP_OPTIONS` socket option. `tcp_input` never looks at a received source route when the connection is actively opened.

- *Must* save a received source route in a connection that is passively opened and use the return route for all segments sent on this connection. If a different source route arrives in a later segment, the later route *should* override the earlier one.
  Yes and no: Figure 28.7 calls `ip_srcroute`, but only when the SYN arrives for a listening socket. If a different source route arrives later, it is not used.

Receiving ICMP Messages from IP

- Receipt of an ICMP source quench *should* trigger slow start.
  Yes: The function `tcp_quench` is called by `tcp_ctlinput`.

- Receipt of a network unreachable, host unreachable, or source route failed *must not* cause TCP to abort the connection and the process *should* be informed.
  Yes and no: As described following Figure 27.12, Net/3 now completely ignores host unreachable and network unreachable errors for an established connection.

- Receipt of a protocol unreachable, port unreachable, or fragmentation required and DF bit set *should* abort an existing connection.
  No: `tcp_notify` records these ICMP errors in `t_softerror`, which is reported to the process if the connection is eventually dropped.

- *Should* handle time exceeded and parameter problem errors the same as required previously for network and host unreachable.
  Yes: ICMP parameter problem errors are just recorded in `t_softerror` by `tcp_notify`. ICMP time exceeded errors are ignored by `tcp_ctlinput`. Neither type of ICMP error causes the connection to be aborted.

Application Programming Interface

- *Must* be a method for reporting soft errors to the process, normally in an asynchronous fashion.
  No: Soft errors are returned to the process if the connection is aborted.

- *Must* allow process to specify TOS for segments sent on a connection. *Should* let application change this during a connection's lifetime.
  Yes to both, with the `IP_TOS` socket option.

- *May* pass most recently received TOS to process.
  No: There is no way to do this with the sockets API. Calling `getsockopt` for `IP_TOS` returns only the current value being sent; it does not return the most recently received value.

- *May* implement a "flush" call.
  No: TCP sends the data from the process as quickly as it can.

- *Must* allow process to specify local IP address before either an active open or a passive open.
  Yes: This is done by calling `bind` before either `connect` or `accept`.

Bibliography

All the RFCs are available at no charge through electronic mail or by using anonymous FTP across the Internet as described in Appendix B.

Whenever the authors were able to locate an electronic copy of papers and reports referenced in this bibliography, its URL (Uniform Resource Locator, Appendix B) is included.

Almquist, P. 1992. "Type of Service in the Internet Protocol Suite," RFC 1349, 28 pages (July).

Almquist, P., and Kastenholz, F. J. 1994. "Towards Requirements for IP Routers," RFC 1716, 186 pages (Nov.).

> This RFC is an intermediate step to replace RFC 1009 [Braden and Postel 1987].

Auerbach, K. 1994. "Max IP Packet Length and MTU," Message-ID <karl.3.000A4DD7 @cavebear.com>, Usenet, comp.protocols.tcp-ip Newsgroup (July).

Boggs, D. R. 1982. "Internet Broadcasting," Xerox PARC CSL-83-3, Stanford University, Palo Alto, Calif. (Jan.).

Braden, R. T., ed. 1989a. "Requirements for Internet Hosts—Communication Layers," RFC 1122, 116 pages (Oct.).

> The first half of the Host Requirements RFC. This half covers the link layer, IP, TCP, and UDP.

Braden, R. T., ed. 1989b. "Requirements for Internet Hosts—Application and Support," RFC 1123, 98 pages (Oct.).

> The second half of the Host Requirements RFC. This half covers Telnet, FTP, TFTP, SMTP, and the DNS.

Braden, R. T. 1989c. "Perspective on the Host Requirements RFCs," RFC 1127, 20 pages (Oct.).

> An informal summary of the discussions and conclusions of the IETF working group that developed the Host Requirements RFC.

Braden, R. T. 1992. "TIME-WAIT Assassination Hazards in TCP," RFC 1337, 11 pages (May).

> Shows how the receipt of an RST while in the TIME_WAIT state can lead to problems.

Braden, R. T. 1993. "TCP Extensions for High Performance: An Update," Internet Draft, 10 pages (June).

> This is an update to RFC 1323 [Jacobson, Braden, and Borman 1992].
>
> `http://www.noao.edu/~rstevens/tcplw-extensions.txt`

Braden, R. T. 1994. "T/TCP—TCP Extensions for Transactions, Functional Specification," RFC 1644, 38 pages (July).

Braden, R. T., Borman, D. A., and Partridge, C. 1988. "Computing the Internet Checksum," RFC 1071, 24 pages (Sept.).

> Provides techniques and algorithms for calculating the checksum used by IP, ICMP, IGMP, UDP, and TCP.

Braden, R. T., and Postel, J. B. 1987. "Requirements for Internet Gateways," RFC 1009, 55 pages (June).

> The equivalent of the Host Requirements RFC for routers. This RFC is being replaced by RFC 1716 [Almquist and Kastenholz 1994].

Brakmo, L. S., O'Malley, S. W., and Peterson, L. L. 1994. "TCP Vegas: New Techniques for Congestion Detection and Avoidance," *Computer Communication Review*, vol. 24, no. 4, pp. 24–35 (Oct.).

> Describes modifications to the 4.3BSD Reno TCP implementation to improve throughput and reduce retransmissions.
>
> `ftp://ftp.cs.arizona.edu/xkernel/Papers/vegas.ps`

Carlson, J. 1993. "Re: Bug in Many Versions of TCP," Message-ID <1993Jul12.130854.26176 @xylogics.com>, Usenet, comp.protocols.tcp-ip Newsgroup (July).

Casner, S., *Frequently Asked Questions (FAQ) on the Multicast Backbone (MBONE)*, 1993.

> `ftp://ftp.isi.edu/mbone/faq.txt`

Cheswick, W. R., and Bellovin, S. M. 1994. *Firewalls and Internet Security: Repelling the Wily Hacker.* Addison-Wesley, Reading, Mass.

> Describes how to set up and administer a firewall gateway and the security issues involved.

Clark, D. D. 1982. "Modularity and Efficiency in Protocol Implementation," RFC 817, 26 pages (July).

Comer, D. E., and Lin, J. C. 1994. "TCP Buffering and Performance Over an ATM Network," Purdue Technical Report CSD-TR 94-026, Purdue University, West Lafayette, Ind. (Mar.).

> `ftp://gwen.cs.purdue.edu/pub/lin/TCP.atm.ps.Z`

Comer, D. E., and Stevens, D. L. 1993. *Internetworking with TCP/IP: Vol. III: Client–Server Programming and Applications, BSD Socket Version.* Prentice-Hall, Englewood Cliffs, N.J.

Croft, W., and Gilmore, J. 1985. "Bootstrap Protocol (BOOTP)," RFC 951, 12 pages (Sept.).

Crowcroft, J., Wakeman, I., Wang, Z., and Sirovica, D. 1992. "Is Layering Harmful?," *IEEE Network*, vol. 6, no. 1, pp. 20–24 (Jan.).

> The seven missing figures from this paper appear in the next issue, vol. 6, no. 2 (March).

Dalton, C., Watson, G., Banks, D., Calamvokis, C., Edwards, A., and Lumley, J. 1993. "Afterburner," *IEEE Network*, vol. 7, no. 4, pp. 36–43 (July).

> Describes how to speed up TCP by reducing the number of data copies performed, and a special-purpose interface card that supports this design.

Deering, S. E. 1989. "Host Extensions for IP Multicasting," RFC 1112, 17 pages (Aug.).

> The specification of IP multicasting and IGMP.

Deering, S. E., ed. 1991a. "ICMP Router Discovery Messages," RFC 1256, 19 pages (Sept.).

Deering, S. E. 1991b. "Multicast Routing in a Datagram Internetwork," STAN-CS-92-1415, Stanford University, Palo Alto, Calif. (Dec.).

> ftp://gregorio.stanford.edu/vmtp-ip/sdthesis.part1.ps.Z

Deering, S. E., and Cheriton, D. P. 1990. "Multicast Routing in Datagram Internetworks and Extended LANs," *ACM Transactions on Computer Systems*, vol. 8, no. 2, pp. 85–110 (May).

> Proposes extensions to common routing techniques to support multicasting.

Deering, S., Estrin, D., Farinacci, D., Jacobson, V., Liu, C., and Wei, L. 1994. "An Architecture for Wide-Area Multicast Routing," *Computer Communication Review*, vol. 24, no. 4, pp. 126–135 (Oct.).

Droms, R. 1993. "Dynamic Host Configuration Protocol," RFC 1541, 39 pages (Oct.).

Finlayson, R., Mann, T., Mogul, J. C., and Theimer, M. 1984. "A Reverse Address Resolution Protocol," RFC 903, 4 pages (June).

Floyd, S. 1994. Private Communication.

Forgie, J. 1979. "ST—A Proposed Internet Stream Protocol," IEN 119, MIT Lincoln Laboratory (Sept.).

Fuller, V., Li, T., Yu, J. Y., and Varadhan, K. 1993. "Classless Inter-Domain Routing (CIDR): An Address Assignment and Aggregation Strategy," RFC 1519, 24 pages (Sept.).

Hornig, C. 1984. "Standard for the Transmission of IP Datagrams over Ethernet Networks," RFC 894, 3 pages (Apr.).

Hutchinson, N. C., and Peterson, L. L. 1991. "The x-Kernel: An Architecture for Implementing Network Protocols," *IEEE Transactions on Software Engineering*, vol. 17, no. 1, pp. 64–76 (Jan.).

> ftp://ftp.cs.arizona.edu/xkernel/Papers/architecture.ps

Itano, W. M., and Ramsey, N. F. 1993. "Accurate Measurement of Time," *Scientific American*, vol. 269, p. 56 (July).

> Overview of historical and current methods for accurate timekeeping. Includes a short discussion of international time scales including International Atomic Time (TAI) and Coordinated Universal Time (UTC).

Jacobson, V. 1988a. "Some Interim Notes on the BSD Network Speedup," Message-ID <8807200426.AA01221@helios.ee.lbl.gov>, Usenet, comp.protocols.tcp-ip Newsgroup (July).

Jacobson, V. 1988b. "Congestion Avoidance and Control," *Computer Communication Review*, vol. 18, no. 4, pp. 314–329 (Aug.).

> A classic paper describing the slow start and congestion avoidance algorithms for TCP.
>
> ftp://ftp.ee.lbl.gov/papers/congavoid.ps.Z

Jacobson, V. 1990a. "Compressing TCP/IP Headers for Low-Speed Serial Links," RFC 1144, 43 pages (Feb.).

> Describes CSLIP, a version of SLIP with the TCP and IP headers compressed.

Jacobson, V. 1990b. "4BSD TCP Header Prediction," *Computer Communication Review*, vol. 20, no. 2, pp. 13–15 (Apr.).

Jacobson, V. 1990c. "Modified TCP Congestion Avoidance Algorithm," April 30, 1990, end2end-interest mailing list (Apr.).

> Describes the fast retransmit and fast recovery algorithms.
>
> `ftp://ftp.isi.edu/end2end/end2end-interest-1990.mail`

Jacobson, V. 1990d. "Berkeley TCP Evolution from 4.3-Tahoe to 4.3-Reno," *Proceedings of the Eighteenth Internet Engineering Task Force*, p. 365 (Sept.), University of British Columbia, Vancouver, B.C.

Jacobson, V. 1993. "Some Design Issues for High-Speed Networks," *Networkshop '93* (Nov.), Melbourne, Australia.

> A set of 21 overheads.
>
> `ftp://ftp.ee.lbl.gov/talks/vj-nws93-1.ps.Z`

Jacobson, V., and Braden, R. T. 1988. "TCP Extensions for Long-Delay Paths," RFC 1072, 16 pages (Oct.).

> Describes the selective acknowledgment option for TCP, which was removed from the later RFC 1323, and the echo options, which were replaced with the timestamp option in RFC 1323.

Jacobson, V., Braden, R. T., and Borman, D. A. 1992. "TCP Extensions for High Performance," RFC 1323, 37 pages (May).

> Describes the window scale option, the timestamp option, and the PAWS algorithm, along with the reasons these modifications are needed. [Braden 1993] updates this RFC.

Jain, R., and Routhier, S. A. 1986. "Packet Trains: Measurements and a New Model for Computer Network Traffic," *IEEE Journal on Selected Areas in Communications*, vol. 4, pp. 1162–1167.

Karels, M. J., and McKusick, M. K. 1986. "Network Performance and Management with 4.3BSD and IP/TCP," *Proceedings of the 1986 Summer USENIX Conference*, pp. 182–188, Atlanta, Ga.

> Describes the changes made from 4.2BSD to 4.3BSD with regard to TCP/IP.

Karn, P., and Partridge, C. 1987. "Improving Round-Trip Time Estimates in Reliable Transport Protocols," *Computer Communication Review*, vol. 17, no. 5, pp. 2–7 (Aug.).

> Details of Karn's algorithm to handle the retransmission timeout for segments that have been retransmitted.
>
> `ftp://sics.se/users/craig/karn-partridge.ps`

Kay, J., and Pasquale, J. 1993. "The Importance of Non-Data Touching Processing Overheads in TCP/IP," *Computer Communication Review*, vol. 23, no. 4, pp. 259–268 (Sept.).

Kent, C. A., and Mogul, J. C. 1987. "Fragmentation Considered Harmful," *Computer Communication Review*, vol. 17, no. 5, pp. 390–401 (Aug.).

Kernighan, B. W., and Plauger, P. J. 1976. *Software Tools*. Addison-Wesley, Reading, Mass.

Krol, E. 1994. *The Whole Internet, Second Edition*. O'Reilly & Associates, Sebastopol, Calif.

> An introduction into the Internet, common Internet applications, and various resources available on the Internet.

Krol, E., and Hoffman, E. 1993. "FYI on 'What is the Internet?'," RFC 1462, 11 pages (May).

Lanciani, D. 1993. "Re: Bug in Many Versions of TCP," Message-ID <1993Jul10.015938.15951 @burrhus.harvard.edu>, Usenet, comp.protocols.tcp-ip Newsgroup (July).

Leffler, S. J., McKusick, M. K., Karels, M. J., and Quarterman, J. S. 1989. *The Design and Implementation of the 4.3BSD UNIX Operating System.* Addison-Wesley, Reading, Mass.

> An entire book on the 4.3BSD Unix system. This book describes the Tahoe release of 4.3BSD.

Lynch, D. C. 1993. "Historical Perspective," in *Internet System Handbook,* eds. D. C. Lynch and M. T. Rose, pp. 3–14. Addison-Wesley, Reading, Mass.

> A historical overview of the Internet and its precursor, the ARPANET.

Mallory, T., and Kullberg, A. 1990. "Incremental Updating of the Internet Checksum," RFC 1141, 2 pages (Jan.).

> This RFC is updated by RFC 1624 [Rijsinghani 1994].

Mano, M. M. 1993. *Computer System Architecture, Third Edition.* Prentice-Hall, Englewood Cliffs, N.J.

McCanne, S., and Jacobson, V. 1993. "The BSD Packet Filter: A New Architecture for User-Level Packet Capture," *Proceedings of the 1993 Winter USENIX Conference,* pp. 259–269, San Diego, Calif.

> A detailed description of the BSD Packet Filter (BPF) and comparisons with Sun's Network Interface Tap (NIT).
>
> `ftp://ftp.ee.lbl.gov/papers/bpf-usenix93.ps.Z`

McCloghrie, K., and Farinacci, D. 1994a. "Internet Group Management Protocol MIB," Internet Draft, 12 pages (Jul.).

McCloghrie, K., and Farinacci, D. 1994b. "IP Multicast Routing MIB," Internet Draft, 15 pages (Jul.).

McCloghrie, K., and Rose, M. T. 1991. "Management Information Base for Network Management of TCP/IP-based Internets: MIB-II," RFC 1213 (Mar.).

McGregor, G. 1992. "PPP Internet Protocol Control Protocol (IPCP)," RFC 1332, 12 pages (May).

McKenney, P. E., and Dove, K. F. 1992. "Efficient Demultiplexing of Incoming TCP Packets," *Computer Communication Review,* vol. 22, no. 4, pp. 269–279 (Oct.).

Mogul, J. C. 1991. "Network Locality at the Scale of Processes," *Computer Communication Review,* vol. 21, no. 4, pp. 273–284 (Sept.).

Mogul, J. C. 1993. "IP Network Performance," in *Internet System Handbook,* eds. D. C. Lynch and M. T. Rose, pp. 575–675. Addison-Wesley, Reading, Mass.

> Covers numerous topics in the Internet protocols that are candidates for tuning to obtain optimal performance.

Mogul, J. C., and Deering, S. E. 1990. "Path MTU Discovery," RFC 1191, 19 pages (Apr.).

Mogul, J. C., and Postel, J. B. 1985. "Internet Standard Subnetting Procedure," RFC 950, 18 pages (Aug.).

Moy, J. 1994. "Multicast Extensions to OSPF," RFC 1584, 102 pages (Mar.).

Olivier, G. 1994. "What is the Diameter of the Internet?," Message-ID <1994Jan22.094832 @mines.u-nancy.fr>, Usenet, comp.unix.wizards Newsgroup (Jan.).

Partridge, C. 1987. "Implementing the Reliable Data Protocol (RDP)," *Proceedings of the 1987 Summer USENIX Conference,* pp. 367–379, Phoenix, Ariz.

Partridge, C. 1993. "Jacobson on TCP in 30 Instructions," Message-ID <1993Sep8.213239.28992 @sics.se>, Usenet, comp.protocols.tcp-ip Newsgroup (Sept.).

> Describes a research implementation of TCP/IP being developed by Van Jacobson that reduces TCP receive packet processing down to 30 instructions on a RISC system.
> `http://www.kohala.com/~rstevens/vanj.93sep07.txt`

Partridge, C., and Hinden, R. 1990. "Version 2 of the Reliable Data Protocol (RDP)," RFC 1151, 4 pages (Apr.).

Partridge, C., Mendez, T., and Milliken, W. 1993. "Host Anycasting Service," RFC 1546, 9 pages (Nov.).

Partridge, C., and Pink, S. 1993. "A Faster UDP," *IEEE/ACM Transactions on Networking*, vol. 1, no. 4, pp. 429–440 (Aug.).

> Describes implementation improvements to the Berkeley sources to speed up UDP performance about 30%.

Paxson, V. 1994. Private Communication.

Perlman, R. 1992. *Interconnections: Bridges and Routers*. Addison-Wesley, Reading, Mass.

Piscitello, D. M., and Chapin, A. L. 1993. *Open Systems Networking: TCP/IP and OSI*. Addison-Wesley, Reading, Mass.

Plummer, D. C. 1982. "An Ethernet Address Resolution Protocol," RFC 826, 10 pages (Nov.).

Postel, J. B., ed. 1981a. "Internet Protocol," RFC 791, 45 pages (Sept.).

Postel, J. B. 1981b. "Internet Control Message Protocol," RFC 792, 21 pages (Sept.).

Postel, J. B., ed. 1981c. "Transmission Control Protocol," RFC 793, 85 pages (Sept.).

Postel, J. B. 1981d. "Service Mappings," RFC 795, 4 pages (Sept.).

Postel, J. B., and Reynolds, J. K. 1988. "Standard for the Transmission of IP Datagrams over IEEE 802 Networks," RFC 1042, 15 pages (Apr.).

Rago, S. A. 1993. *UNIX System V Network Programming*. Addison-Wesley, Reading, Mass.

Reynolds, J. K., and Postel, J. B. 1994. "Assigned Numbers," RFC 1700, 230 pages (Oct.).

Rijsinghani, A. 1994. "Computation of the Internet Checksum via Incremental Update," RFC 1624, 6 pages (May).

> An update to RFC 1141 [Mallory and Kullberg 1990].

Romkey, J. L. 1988. "A Nonstandard for Transmission of IP Datagrams Over Serial Lines: SLIP," RFC 1055, 6 pages (June).

Rose, M. T. 1990. *The Open Book: A Practical Perspective on OSI*. Prentice-Hall, Englewood Cliffs, N.J.

Salus, P. H. 1994. *A Quarter Century of Unix*. Addison-Wesley, Reading, Mass.

Sedgewick, R. 1990. *Algorithms in C*. Addison-Wesley, Reading, Mass.

Simpson, W. A. 1993. "The Point-to-Point Protocol (PPP)," RFC 1548, 53 pages (Dec.).

Sklower, K. 1991. "A Tree-Based Packet Routing Table for Berkeley Unix," *Proceedings of the 1991 Winter USENIX Conference*, pp. 93–99, Dallas, Tex.

Stallings, W. 1987. *Handbook of Computer-Communications Standards, Volume 2: Local Network Standards.* Macmillan, New York.

Stallings, W. 1993. *Networking Standards: A Guide to OSI, ISDN, LAN, and MAN Standards.* Addison-Wesley, Reading, Mass.

Stevens, W. R. 1990. *UNIX Network Programming.* Prentice-Hall, Englewood Cliffs, N.J.

Stevens, W. R. 1992. *Advanced Programming in the UNIX Environment.* Addison-Wesley, Reading, Mass.

Stevens, W. R. 1994. *TCP/IP Illustrated, Volume 1: The Protocols.* Addison-Wesley, Reading, Mass.
> The first volume in this series, which provides a complete introduction to the Internet protocols.

Tanenbaum, A. S. 1989. *Computer Networks, Second Edition.* Prentice-Hall, Englewood Cliffs, N.J.

Topolcic, C. 1990. "Experimental Stream Protocol, Version 2 (SY-II)," RFC 1190, 148 pages (Oct.).

Torek, C. 1992. "Re: A Problem in Bind System Call," Message-ID <27240@dog.ee.lbl.gov>, Usenet, comp.unix.internals Newsgroup (Nov.).

Waitzman, D., Partridge, C., and Deering, S. E. 1988. "Distance Vector Multicast Routing Protocol," RFC 1075, 24 pages (Nov.).

Index

Rather than provide a separate glossary (with most of the entries being acronyms), this index also serves as a glossary for all the acronyms used in the book. The primary entry for the acronym appears under the acronym name. For example, all references to the Address Resolution Protocol appear under ARP. The entry under the compound term "Address Resolution Protocol" refers back to the main entry under ARP.

The two end papers at the back of the book contain a list of all the functions and macros presented or described in the text, along with the starting page number of the source code. Similarly one front end paper contains a list of all the structures presented in the text. These end papers should be the starting point to locate the definition of a function or structure.

The various functions, constants, variables, and the like that appear in this index refer to their appearance in the text. We have not attempted to index all these names when they appear in source code files that are included in the text. The definitive answer to a question such as "where are all the references to the constant IP_RECVOPTS" can only be obtained by obtaining the Net/3 source code (Appendix B) and using a tool such as grep.

The entries in this index for RFCs refer only to the reference for that RFC in the Bibliography. This is to help locate an RFC if you encounter a reference to it by number within the text.